7th Workshop on Statistical Machine Translation 2012

(WMT 2012)

Montreal, Quebec, Canada
7 – 8 June 2012

ISBN: 978-1-62276-592-8

Printed from e-media with permission by:

Curran Associates, Inc.
57 Morehouse Lane
Red Hook, NY 12571

CURRAN ASSOCIATES INC.
proceedings.com

Some format issues inherent in the e-media version may also appear in this print version.

Printed by Curran Associates, Inc. (2012)

Association for Computational Linguistics
209 N. Eighth Street
Stroudsburg, Pennsylvania 18360

Phone: 1-570-476-8006
Fax: 1-570-476-0860

acl@aclweb.org

Additional copies of this publication are available from:

Curran Associates, Inc.
57 Morehouse Lane
Red Hook, NY 12571 USA
Phone: 845-758-0400
Fax: 845-758-2634
Email: curran@proceedings.com
Web: www.proceedings.com

Introduction

The NAACL 2012 Workshop on Statistical Machine Translation (WMT-2012) took place on Thursday and Friday, June 7–8, 2012 in Montreal, Canada, immediately following the Conference of the North-American Chapter of the Association for Computational Linguistics - Human Language Technologies (NAACL HLT).

This is the seventh time this workshop has been held. The first time it was held at HLT-NAACL 2006 in New York City, USA. In the following years the Workshop on Statistical Machine Translation was held at ACL 2007 in Prague, Czech Republic, ACL 2008, Columbus, Ohio, USA, EACL 2009 in Athens, Greece, ACL 2010 in Uppsala, Sweden, and EMNLP 2011 in Edinburgh, Scotland.

The focus of our workshop was to use parallel corpora for machine translation. Recent experimentation has shown that the performance of SMT systems varies greatly with the source language. In this workshop we encouraged researchers to investigate ways to improve the performance of SMT systems for diverse languages, including morphologically more complex languages, languages with partial free word order, and low-resource languages.

Prior to the workshop, in addition to soliciting relevant papers for review and possible presentation, we conducted three shared tasks: a translation task, a quality estimation task, and a task to test automatic evaluation metrics. The results of the shared tasks were announced at the workshop, and these proceedings also include an overview paper for the shared tasks that summarizes the results, as well as provides information about the data used and any procedures that were followed in conducting or scoring the task. In addition, there are short papers from each participating team that describe their underlying system in greater detail.

Like in previous years, we have received a far larger number of submission than we could accept for presentation. This year we have received 45 full paper submissions and 39 shared task submissions. In total WMT-2012 featured 20 full paper oral presentations and 39 shared task poster presentations.

The invited talk was given by Salim Roukos (IBM Research, USA), entitled "Deployment of Statistical Machine Translation for the IBM Enterprise".

We would like to thank the members of the Program Committee for their timely reviews. We also would like to thank the participants of the shared task and all the other volunteers who helped with the evaluations.

Chris Callison-Burch, Philipp Koehn, Christof Monz, Matt Post, Radu Soricut, and Lucia Specia

Co-Organizers

WMT 5-year Retrospective Best Paper Award

Last year we created a WMT 5-year Retrospective Best Paper Award. This year we selected the best paper from 2007's Workshop on Statistical Machine Translation, which was collocated with ACL in Prague. The goals of this retrospective award are to recognize high-quality work that has stood the test of time, and to highlight the excellent work that appears at WMT.

The WMT12 program committee voted on the best paper from a list of eight nominated papers. Six of these were nominated by high citation counts, which we defined as having 10 or more citations in the ACL anthology network (excluding self-citations), and more than 30 citations on Google Scholar. We also opened the nomination process to the committee, which yielded two further nomination for papers that did not reach the citation threshold but were deemed to be excellent.

The program committee decided to award the WMT 5-year Retrospective Best Paper Award to:

Alon Lavie and Abhaya Agarwal. 2007. *METEOR: An Automatic Metric for MT Evaluation with High Levels of Correlation with Human Judgments*. In Proceedings of the Workshop on Statistical Machine Translation. Pages 228-231.

Like last year's best paper award winner, Lavie and Agarwal's publication was a short paper describing the authors' submission to one of the WMT shared tasks. WMT07 introduced a new shared task to evaluate the quality of automatic metrics for machine translation quality by comparing the metrics' rankings to human rankings of MT systems. In the shared task, METEOR demonstrated higher correlation than BLEU (the de facto standard) across a variety of human evaluation measures, including adequacy and fluency, ranking the translations of whole sentences, and ranking the translation of smaller constituents within sentences.

The program committee members who selected Lavie and Agarwal's paper pointed out that METEOR is the only metric that has managed to compete with BLEU for attention in the MT world without a major funder backing the metric. They pointed out that TER and HTER have also become prominent, but it is not clear whether that would have happened without backing from DARPA. Furthermore, METEOR has contributed substantially to improving the assessment of the quality of MT systems by showing the importance of word similarity beyond surface form.

In many ways this paper represents the ideals of the WMT workshops. It introduced a novel approach to the automatic evaluation of machine translation and demonstrated the metric's value empirically by comparing it to other state-of-the-art metrics on a public data set.

Congratulations to Alon Lavie and Abhaya Agarwal for their excellent work!

Organizers:

Chris Callison-Burch (Johns Hopkins University)
Philipp Koehn (University of Edinburgh)
Christof Monz (University of Amsterdam)
Matt Post (Johns Hopkins University)
Radu Soricut (SDL Language Weaver)
Lucia Specia (University of Sheffield)

Invited Talk:

Salim Roukos (IBM Research)

Program Committee:

Steve Abney (University of Michigan)
Lars Ahrenberg (Linköping University)
Necip Fazil Ayan (SRI International)
Oliver Bender (RWTH Aachen)
Nicola Bertoldi (FBK)
Alexandra Birch (University of Edinburgh)
Arianna Bisazza (FBK)
Graeme Blackwood (IBM)
Ondrej Bojar (Charles University)
Antal van Den Bosch (Radboud University Nijmegen)
Chris Brockett (Microsoft)
Hailong Cao (NICT)
Michael Carl (Saarland University)
Marine Carpuat (Columbia University)
Francisco Casacuberta (University of Valencia)
Daniel Cer (Stanford University)
Mauro Cettolo (FBK)
Boxing Chen (National Research Council Canada)
Colin Cherry (National Research Council Canada)
David Chiang (ISI)
Michael Denkowski (Carnegie Mellon University)
Markus Dreyer (SDL Language Weaver)
Kevin Duh (NAIST)
Chris Dyer (CMU)

Yang Feng (Sheffield University)
Andrew Finch (NICT)
Jose Fonollosa (University of Catalonia)
George Foster (National Research Council Canada)
Alex Fraser (University of Stuttgart)
Michel Galley (Microsoft)
Niyu Ge (IBM)
Josef van Genabith (Dublin City University)
Ulrich Germann (University of Toronto)
Daniel Gildea (University of Rochester)
Kevin Gimpel (CMU)
Cyril Goutte (National Research Council Canada)
Barry Haddow (University of Edinburgh)
Keith Hall (Google)
Greg Hanneman (Carnegie Mellon University)
Christian Hardmeier (Uppsala University)
Xiadong He (Microsoft)
Yifan He (Dublin City University)
Kenneth Heafield (Carnegie Mellon University)
John Henderson (MITRE)
Silja Hildebrand (Carnegie Mellon University)
Hieu Hoang (University of Edinburgh)
Young-Sook Hwang (SK Telecom)
Gonzalo Iglesias (University of Cambridge)
Pierre Isabelle (National Research Council Canada)
Abe Ittycheriah (IBM)
Howard Johnson (National Research Council Canada)
Doug Jones (Lincoln Labs)
Damianos Karakos (Johns Hopkins University)
Maxim Khalilov (TAUS)
Kevin Knight (ISI)
Greg Kondrak (University of Alberta)
Roland Kuhn (National Research Council Canada)
Shankar Kumar (Google)
Philippe Langlais (University of Montreal)
Gregor Leusch (SAIC)
Zhifei Li (Google)
Qun Liu (Chinese Academy of Sciences)
Shujie Liu (Harbin Institute of Technology)
Zhanyi Liu (Harbin Institute of Technology)
Klaus Macherey (Google)
Wolfgang Macherey (Google)

Daniel Marcu (ISI)
Jose Marino (University of Catalonia)
Lambert Mathias (JHU)
Spyros Matsoukas (Raytheon BBN Technologies)
Arne Mauser (RWTH Aachen)
Yashar Mehdad (FBK)
Arul Menezes (Microsoft)
Shachar Mirkin (Xerox)
Bob Moore (Google)
Dragos Munteanu (SDL Language Weaver)
Markos Mylonakis (Xerox)
Preslav Nakov (Qatar Computing Research Institute)
Steve de Neefe (SDL Language Weaver)
Vassilina Nikoulina (Xerox)
Kemal Oflazer (CMU)
Sergio Penkale (Dublin City University)
Kay Peterson (NIST)
Daniele Pighin (University of Catalonia)
Maja Popovic (DFKI)
Chris Quirk (Microsoft)
Stefan Riezler (University of Heidelberg)
Marta Ruiz Costa-Jussa (University of Catalonia)
Felipe Sanchez-Martinez (University of Alicante)
Anoop Sarkar (Simon Fraser University)
Jean Senellart (Systran)
Wade Shen (Lincoln Labs)
Joerg Tiedemann (Uppsala University)
Christoph Tillmann (IBM)
Roy Tromble (Google)
Dan Tufis (Romanian Academy)
Jakob Uszkoreit (Google)
Masao Utiyama (NICT)
David Vilar (RWTH Aachen)
Martin Volk (University of Zurich)
Clare Voss (Army Research Labs)
Haifeng Wang (Baidu)
Taro Watanabe (NICT)
Ralph Weischedel (Raytheon BBN Technologies)
Hua Wu (Baidu)
Ning Xi (Nanjing University)
Peng Xu (Google)
Francois Yvon (LIMSI)

Daniel Zeman (Charles University)
Richard Zens (Google)
Bing Zhang (Raytheon BBN Technologies)
Hao Zhang (Google)
Joy Zhang (CMU)

Table of Contents

Conference Program

Thursday, June 7, 2012

9:00–9:10 Opening Remarks: Future Funding and Research Survey Wiki

Session 1: Shared Tasks and their Evaluation

9:10–9:30 *Putting Human Assessments of Machine Translation Systems in Order*
Adam Lopez

9:30–10:30 *Findings of the 2012 Workshop on Statistical Machine Translation*
Chris Callison-Burch, Philipp Koehn, Christof Monz, Matt Post, Radu Soricut and Lucia Specia

10:30–11:00 Coffee

Session 2: Shared Quality Estimation and Metrics Tasks

11:00–12:40 Poster Session: Evaluation Metrics

Semantic Textual Similarity for MT evaluation
Julio Castillo and Paula Estrella

Improving AMBER, an MT Evaluation Metric
Boxing Chen, Roland Kuhn and George Foster

TerrorCat: a Translation Error Categorization-based MT Quality Metric
Mark Fishel, Rico Sennrich, Maja Popović and Ondřej Bojar

Class error rates for evaluation of machine translation output
Maja Popovic

SPEDE: Probabilistic Edit Distance Metrics for MT Evaluation
Mengqiu Wang and Christopher Manning

11:00–12:40 Poster Session: Quality Estimation Task

Quality estimation for Machine Translation output using linguistic analysis and decoding features
Eleftherios Avramidis

Thursday, June 7, 2012 (continued)

Black Box Features for the WMT 2012 Quality Estimation Shared Task
Christian Buck

Linguistic Features for Quality Estimation
Mariano Felice and Lucia Specia

PRHLT Submission to the WMT12 Quality Estimation Task
Jesús González-Rubio, Alberto Sanchís and Francisco Casacuberta

Tree Kernels for Machine Translation Quality Estimation
Christian Hardmeier, Joakim Nivre and Jörg Tiedemann

LORIA System for the WMT12 Quality Estimation Shared Task
David Langlois, Sylvain Raybaud and Kamel Smaïli

Quality Estimation: an experimental study using unsupervised similarity measures
Erwan Moreau and Carl Vogel

The UPC Submission to the WMT 2012 Shared Task on Quality Estimation
Daniele Pighin, Meritxell González and Lluís Màrquez

Morpheme- and POS-based IBM1 and language model scores for translation quality estimation
Maja Popovic

DCU-Symantec Submission for the WMT 2012 Quality Estimation Task
Raphael Rubino, Jennifer Foster, Joachim Wagner, Johann Roturier, Rasul Samad Zadeh Kaljahi and Fred Hollowood

The SDL Language Weaver Systems in the WMT12 Quality Estimation Shared Task
Radu Soricut, Nguyen Bach and Ziyuan Wang

Regression with Phrase Indicators for Estimating MT Quality
Chunyang Wu and Hai Zhao

12:40–14:00 Lunch

Thursday, June 7, 2012 (continued)

Session 3: Invited Talk

14:00–15:30 Salim Roukas: Deployment of SMT for the IBM Enterprise

15:30–16:00 Coffee

Session 4: Confidence Estimation and System Combination

16:00–16:20 *Non-Linear Models for Confidence Estimation*
Yong Zhuang, Guillaume Wisniewski and François Yvon

16:20–16:40 *Combining Quality Prediction and System Selection for Improved Automatic Translation Output*
Radu Soricut and Sushant Narsale

16:40–17:00 *Match without a Referee: Evaluating MT Adequacy without Reference Translations*
Yashar Mehdad, Matteo Negri and Marcello Federico

17:00–17:20 *Comparing human perceptions of post-editing effort with post-editing operations*
Maarit Koponen

17:20–17:40 *Review of Hypothesis Alignment Algorithms for MT System Combination via Confusion Network Decoding*
Antti-Veikko Rosti, Xiaodong He, Damianos Karakos, Gregor Leusch, Yuan Cao, Markus Freitag, Spyros Matsoukas, Hermann Ney, Jason Smith and Bing Zhang

Friday, June 8, 2012

Session 5: Reordering, Syntax and Semantics

9:00–9:20 *On Hierarchical Re-ordering and Permutation Parsing for Phrase-based Decoding*
Colin Cherry, Robert C. Moore and Chris Quirk

9:20–9:40 *CCG Syntactic Reordering Models for Phrase-based Machine Translation*
Dennis Nolan Mehay and Christopher Hardie Brew

9:40–10:00 *Using Categorial Grammar to Label Translation Rules*
Jonathan Weese, Chris Callison-Burch and Adam Lopez

Friday, June 8, 2012 (continued)

10:20–10:20 *Using Syntactic Head Information in Hierarchical Phrase-Based Translation*
Junhui Li, Zhaopeng Tu, Guodong Zhou and Josef van Genabith

10:20–10:40 *Fully Automatic Semantic MT Evaluation*
Chi-kiu Lo, Anand Karthik Tumuluru and Dekai Wu

10:40–11:00 Coffee

Session 6: Translation Task

11:00–12:40 Poster Session: Translation Task

Probes in a Taxonomy of Factored Phrase-Based Models
Ondřej Bojar, Bushra Jawaid and Amir Kamran

The CMU-Avenue French-English Translation System
Michael Denkowski, Greg Hanneman and Alon Lavie

Formemes in English-Czech Deep Syntactic MT
Ondřej Dušek, Zdeněk Žabokrtský, Martin Popel, Martin Majliš, Michal Novák and David Mareček

The TALP-UPC phrase-based translation systems for WMT12: Morphology simplification and domain adaptation
Lluis Formiga, Carlos A. Henríquez Q., Adolfo Hernández, José B. Mariño, Enric Monte and José A. R. Fonollosa

Joshua 4.0: Packing, PRO, and Paraphrases
Juri Ganitkevitch, Yuan Cao, Jonathan Weese, Matt Post and Chris Callison-Burch

Syntax-aware Phrase-based Statistical Machine Translation: System Description
Ulrich Germann

QCRI at WMT12: Experiments in Spanish-English and German-English Machine Translation of News Text
Francisco Guzman, Preslav Nakov, Ahmed Thabet and Stephan Vogel

The RWTH Aachen Machine Translation System for WMT 2012
Matthias Huck, Stephan Peitz, Markus Freitag, Malte Nuhn and Hermann Ney

Friday, June 8, 2012 (continued)

Friday, June 8, 2012 (continued)

	GHKM Rule Extraction and Scope-3 Parsing in Moses Philip Williams and Philipp Koehn
	Data Issues of the Multilingual Translation Matrix Daniel Zeman
12:40–14:00	Lunch
	Session 7: Corpus Creation and Adaptation
14:00–14:20	*Constructing Parallel Corpora for Six Indian Languages via Crowdsourcing* Matt Post, Chris Callison-Burch and Miles Osborne
14:20–14:40	*Twitter Translation using Translation-Based Cross-Lingual Retrieval* Laura Jehl, Felix Hieber and Stefan Riezler
14:40–15:00	*Analysing the Effect of Out-of-Domain Data on SMT Systems* Barry Haddow and Philipp Koehn
15:00–15:20	*Evaluating the Learning Curve of Domain Adaptive Statistical Machine Translation Systems* Nicola Bertoldi, Mauro Cettolo, Marcello Federico and Christian Buck
15:20–15:40	*The Trouble with SMT Consistency* Marine Carpuat and Michel Simard
15:40–16:00	Coffee

Session 8: Phrase Model Training and Optimization

Putting Human Assessments of Machine Translation Systems in Order

Adam Lopez
Human Language Technology Center of Excellence
Johns Hopkins University

Abstract

Human assessment is often considered the gold standard in evaluation of translation systems. But in order for the evaluation to be meaningful, the rankings obtained from human assessment must be consistent and repeatable. Recent analysis by Bojar et al. (2011) raised several concerns about the rankings derived from human assessments of English-Czech translation systems in the 2010 Workshop on Machine Translation. We extend their analysis to *all* of the ranking tasks from 2010 and 2011, and show through an extension of their reasoning that the ranking is naturally cast as an instance of finding the minimum feedback arc set in a tournament, a well-known NP-complete problem. All instances of this problem in the workshop data are efficiently solvable, but in some cases the rankings it produces are surprisingly different from the ones previously published. This leads to strong caveats and recommendations for both producers and consumers of these rankings.

1 Introduction

The value of machine translation depends on its utility to human users, either directly through their use of it, or indirectly through downstream tasks such as cross-lingual information extraction or retrieval. It is therefore essential to assess machine translation systems according to this utility, but there is a widespread perception that direct human assessment is costly, unreproducible, and difficult to interpret. Automatic metrics that predict human utility have therefore attracted substantial attention since they are at least cheap and reproducible given identical data conditions, though they are frequently and correctly criticized for low interpretability and correlation with true utility. Their use (and abuse) remains contentious.

The organizers of the annual Workshop on Machine Translation (WMT) have taken a strong stance in this debate, asserting the primacy of human evaluation. Every annual report of their findings since 2007 has included a variant of the following statement:

> *It is our contention that automatic measures are an imperfect substitute for human assessment of translation quality. Therefore, we define the manual evaluation to be primary, and use the human judgments to validate automatic metrics.* (Callison-Burch et al., 2011)

The workshop's human evaluation component has been gradually refined over several years, and as a consequence it has produced a fantastic collection of publicly available data consisting primarily of *pairwise judgements* of translation systems made by human assessors across a wide variety of languages and tasks. Despite superb effort in the collection of these assessments, less attention has been focused on the final product derived from them: a *totally-ordered ranking* of translation systems participating in each task. Many of the official workshop results depend crucially on this ranking, including the evaluation of both machine translation systems and automatic metrics. Considering the enormous costs and consequences of the ranking, it is important to ask: is the method of constructing it accurate? The number of possible rankings is combinatorially large—with at least ten systems (accounting for more than half the cases we analyzed) there are over three million possible rankings, and with at least twenty (occurring a few times), there are over 10^{18} possible rankings. Exceptional care is therefore required in producing the rankings.

Bojar et al. (2011) observed a number of discrepancies in the ranking of English-Czech systems from the 2010 workshop, making these questions ever more pressing. We extend their analysis in several ways.

1. We show, through a logical extension of their reasoning about flaws in the evaluation, that the final ranking can be naturally cast as an instance of the *minimal feedback arc set* problem, a well-known NP-Hard problem.

2. We analyze 25 tasks that were evaluated using pairwise assessments from human annotators in 2010 and 2011.

3. We produce new rankings for each of the tasks, which are in some cases surprisingly different from the published rankings.

4. We identify a new set of concerns about sources of error and uncertainty in the data.

2 Human Assessment as Pairwise Ranking

The workshop has conducted a variety of different manual evaluation tasks over the last several years, but its mainstay has been the *relative ranking* task. Assessors are presented with a source sentence followed by up to five translations, and are asked to rank the translations from best to worst, with ties allowed. Since it is usually infeasible to collect individual judgements for all sentences for all pairs of systems on each task, consecutive sequences of three sentences were randomly sampled from the test data, with each sentence in each sequence presented to the same annotator. Some samples were presented multiple times to the same assessor or to multiple assessors in order to measure intra- and inter-annotator agreement rates. Since there are often more than five systems participating in the campaign, the candidate translations are likewise sampled from a pool consisting of the machine translations *and a human reference translation*, which is included for quality control purposes. It is important to note that the algorithm used to compute the published final rankings included *all* of this data, including comparisons against the reference and the redundant assessments used to compute inter-annotator agreement.

JHU	1	JHU≺BBN-COMBO
BBN-COMBO	2	JHU≺RWTH
RWTH	3	JHU≺RWTH-COMBO
RWTH-COMBO	3	JHU≺CMU
CMU	4	BBN-COMBO≺RWTH
		BBN-COMBO≺RWTH-COMBO
		BBN-COMBO≺CMU
		RWTH≡RWTH-COMBO
		RWTH≺CMU
		RWTH-COMBO≺CMU

Figure 1: Example human relative ranking of five systems (left) and the inferred pairwise rankings (right) on a single sentence from the WMT 2010 German-English campaign.

The raw data obtained from this process is a large set of assessments. Each assessment consists of a list of up to five systems (including the reference), and a partial or total ordering of the list. The relative ranking of each pair of systems contained in the list is then taken to be their pairwise ranking. Hence a single assessment of five systems yields ten implicit pairwise rankings, as illustrated in Figure 1.

3 From Pairwise to Total Ranking

Given these pairwise rankings, the question now becomes: how do we decide on a total ordering of the systems? In the WMT evaluation, this total ordering has two critical functions: it is published as the official ranking of the participating systems; and it is used as the ground truth against which automatic evaluation metrics are graded, using Spearman's rank correlation coefficient (without ties) as the measure of accuracy. Choosing a total order is non-trivial: there are $N!$ possible orderings of N systems. Even with relatively small N of the workshop, this number can grow extremely large (over 10^{25} in the worst case of 25 systems).

The method used to generate the published rankings is simple. For each system A among the set S of ranked systems (which includes the reference), compute the number of times that A is ranked better than or equivalent to *any* system $B \in S$, and then divide by the total number of comparisons involving A, yielding the following statistic for system A, which we call WMT-OFFICAL.

$$score(A) = \frac{\sum_{B \in S} count(A \preceq B)}{\sum_{B \in S, \diamond \in \{\prec, \equiv, \succ\}}, count(A \diamond B)} \quad (1)$$

The systems are ranked according to this statistic, with higher scores resulting in a better rank.

Bojar et al. (2011) raise many concerns about this method for ranking the systems. While we refer the reader to their paper for a detailed analysis, we focus on two issues here:

- Since ties are rewarded, systems may be unduly rewarded for merely being similar to others, rather than clearly better. This is of particular concern since there is often a cohort of very similar systems in the pool, such as those based on very similar techniques.
- Since the reference is overwhelmingly favored by the assessors, those systems that are more frequently compared against the reference in the random sample will be unfairly penalized.

These observations suggest that the statistic should be changed to reward only outright wins in pairwise comparisons, and to lessen the number of comparisons to the reference. While they do not recommend a specific sampling rate for comparisons against the reference, the logical conclusion of their reasoning is that it should not be sampled at all. This yields the following statistic similar to one reported in the appendices of the WMT proceedings, which we call HEURISTIC 2.

$$score(A) = \frac{\sum_{B \in S-ref} count(A \prec B)}{\sum_{B \in S-ref, \diamond \in \{\prec, \equiv, \succ\}}, count(A \diamond B)} \quad (2)$$

However, the analysis by Bojar et al. (2011) goes further and suggests disregarding the effect of ties altogether by removing them from the denominator. This yields their final recommended statistic, which we call BOJAR.

$$score(A) = \frac{\sum_{B \in S-ref} count(A \prec B)}{\sum_{B \in S-ref, \diamond \in \{\prec, \succ\}}, count(A \diamond B)} \quad (3)$$

Superficially, this appears to be an improvement. However, we observe in the rankings that two anonymized commercial systems, denoted ONLINEA and ONLINEB, consistently appear at or near the top of the rankings in all tasks. It is natural to wonder: even if we leave out the reference from comparisons, couldn't a system still be penalized simply by being compared against ONLINEA and ONLINEB more frequently than its competitors? On the other hand, couldn't a system be rewarded simply by being compared against a bad system more frequently than its competitors?

There are many possible decisions that we could make, each leading to a different ranking. However, there is a more fundamental problem: each of these heuristic scores is based on statistics aggregated over completely incomparable sets of data. Any total ordering of the systems must make a decision between every pair of systems. When that ranking is computed using scores computed with any of Equations 1 through 3, we aggregate over completely different sets of sentences, rates of comparison with other systems, and even annotators! Deriving statistical conclusions from such comparisons is at best suspect. If we want to rank A and B relative to each other, it would be more reliable to aggregate over the *same* set of sentences, *same* rates of comparison, and the *same* annotators. Fortunately, we have this data in abundance: it is the collection of pairwise judgements that we started with.

4 Pairwise Ranking as a Tournament

The human assessments are a classic example of a *tournament*. A tournament is a graph of N vertices with exactly $\binom{N}{2}$ directed edges—one between each pair of vertices. The edge connecting each pair of vertices A and B points to whichever vertex which is *worse* in an observed pairwise comparison between them. Tournaments are a natural representation of many ranking problems, including search results, transferable voting systems, and ranking of sports teams.[1]

Consider the simple weighted tournament depicted in Figure 2. This tournament is acyclic, which means that we can obtain a total ordering of the ver-

[1]The original motivating application was modeling the pecking order of chickens (Landau, 1951).

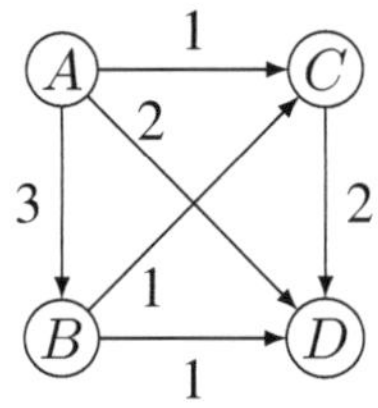

Consistent ranking: $A \prec B \prec C \prec D$

Ranking according to Eq. 1: $A \prec C \prec B \prec D$

Figure 2: A weighted tournament and two different rankings of its vertices.

tices that is consistent with all of the pairwise rankings simply by sorting the vertices topologically. We start by choosing the vertex with no incoming edges (i.e. the one that wins in all pairwise comparisons), place it at the top of the ranking, and remove it along with all of its outgoing edges from the graph. We then repeat the procedure with the remaining vertices in the graph, placing the next vertex behind the first one, and so on. The result is a ranking that preserves all of the pairwise rankings in the original graph.

This example also highlights a problem in Equation 1. Imagine an idealized case in which the consistent ranking of the vertices in Figure 2 is their true ranking, and furthermore that this ranking is unambiguous: that is, no matter how many times we sample the comparison A with B, the result is always that $A \prec B$, and likewise for all vertices. If the weights in this example represented the number of random samples for each system, then Equation 1 will give the inaccurate ranking shown, since it produces a score of $\frac{2}{5}$ for B and $\frac{2}{4}$ for C.

Tournaments can contain cycles, and as we will show this is often the case in the WMT data. When this happens, a reasonable solution is to minimize the discrepancy between the ranking and the observed data. We can do this by *reversing* a set of edges in the graph such that (1) the resulting graph is acyclic, and (2) the summed weights of the reversed edges is minimized. A set of edges satisfying these constraints is called the *minimum feedback arc set* (Figure 3).

The feedback arc set problem on general graphs

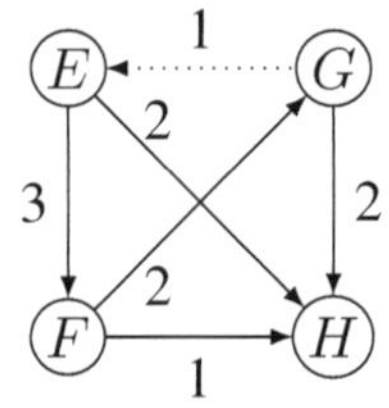

Figure 3: A tournament with a cycle on vertices E, F, and G. The dotted edge is the only element of a minimum feedback arc set: reversing it produces an acyclic graph.

Algorithm 1 Minimum feedback arc set solver

Input: Graph $\mathcal{G} = (V, E)$, weights $w : E \rightarrow \mathbb{R}^+$
Initialize all costs to ∞
Let $cost(\emptyset) \leftarrow 0$
Add $\emptyset$ to agenda $\mathcal{A}$
repeat
  Let $\hat{R} \leftarrow \text{argmin}_{R \in \mathcal{A}}\, cost(R)$
  Remove $\hat{R}$ from $\mathcal{A}$ ▷ $\hat{R}$ is a partial ranking
  Let $U \leftarrow V \backslash \hat{R}$ ▷ set of unranked vertices
  for each vertex $v \in U$ **do**
    Add $\hat{R} \cup v$ to agenda
    Let $c \leftarrow \sum_{v' \in U : \langle v', v \rangle \in E} w(\langle v', v \rangle)$
    Let $d \leftarrow cost(\hat{R}) + c$
    Let $cost(\hat{R} \cup \{v\}) \leftarrow \min(cost(\hat{R} \cup \{v\}), d)$
until $\text{argmin}_{R \in \mathcal{A}}\, cost(h) = V$

is one of the 21 classic problems shown to be NP-complete by Karp (1972).[2] Finding the minimum feedback arc set in a tournament was shown to be NP-hard by Alon (2006) and Charbit et al. (2007). However, the specific instances exhibited in the workshop data tend to have only a few cycles, so a relatively straightforward algorithm (formalized above for completeness) solves them exactly without much difficulty. The basic idea is to construct a dynamic program over the possible rankings. Each item in the dynamic program represents a ranking of some subset of the vertices. An item is extended by choosing one of the unranked vertices and appending it to the hypothesis, adding to its cost the weights of all edges from the other unranked vertices to the newly appended vertex (the

[2]Karp proved NP-completeness of the decision problem that asks whether there is a feedback arc set of size k; NP-hardness of the minimization problem follows.

Task name	#sys	#pairs	Task name	#sys	#pairs
2010 Czech-English	12	5375	2011 English-French individual	17	9086
2010 English-Czech	17	13538	2011 English-German syscomb	4	4374
2010 English-French	19	7962	2011 English-German individual	22	12996
2010 English-German	18	13694	2011 English-Spanish syscomb	4	5930
2010 English-Spanish	16	5174	2011 English-Spanish individual	15	11130
2010 French-English	24	8294	2011 French-English syscomb	6	3000
2010 German-English	25	10424	2011 French-English individual	18	6986
2010 Spanish-English	14	11307	2011 German-English syscomb	8	3844
2011 Czech-English syscomb	4	2602	2011 German-English individual	20	9079
2011 Czech-English individual	8	4922	2011 Spanish-English syscomb	6	4156
2011 English-Czech syscomb	2	2686	2011 Spanish-English individual	15	5652
2011 English-Czech individual	10	17875	2011 Urdu-English tunable metrics	8	6257
2011 English-French syscomb	2	880			

Table 1: The set of tasks we analyzed, including the number of participating systems (*excluding* the reference, #sys), and the number of implicit pairwise judgements collected (*including* the reference, #pairs).

edges to be reversed). This hypothesis space should be familiar to most machine translation researchers since it closely resembles the search space defined by a phrase-based translation model (Koehn, 2004). We use Dijkstra's algorithm (1959) to explore it efficiently; the complete algorithm is simply a generalization of the simple algorithm for acyclic tournaments described above.

5 Experiments and Analysis

We experimented with 25 relative ranking tasks produced by WMT 2010 (Callison-Burch et al., 2010) and WMT 2011 (Callison-Burch et al., 2011); the full set is shown in Table 1. For each task we considered four possible methods of ranking the data: sorting by any of Equation 1 through 3, and sorting consistent with reversal of a minimum feedback arc set (MFAS). To weight the edges for the latter approach, we simply used the difference in number of assessments preferring one system over the other; that is, an edge from A to B is weighted $count(A \prec B) - count(A \succ B)$. If this quantity is negative, there is instead an edge from B to A. The purpose of this simple weighting is to ensure a solution that minimizes the number of disagreements with all available evidence, counting each pairwise comparison as equal.[3]

WMT-OFFICIAL (Eq 1)	MFAS	BOJAR (Eq 3)
ONLINE-B	CU-MARECEK	ONLINE-B
CU-BOJAR	ONLINE-B	CU-BOJAR
CU-MARECEK	CU-BOJAR	CU-MARECEK
CU-TAMCHYNA	CU-TAMCHYNA	CU-TAMCHYNA
UEDIN	CU-POPEL	CU-POPEL
CU-POPEL	UEDIN	UEDIN
COMMERCIAL2	COMMERCIAL1	COMMERCIAL2
COMMERCIAL1	COMMERCIAL2	COMMERCIAL1
JHU	JHU	JHU
CU-ZEMAN	CU-ZEMAN	CU-ZEMAN
38	0	69

Table 2: Different rankings of the 2011 Czech-English task. Only the MFAS ranking is acyclic with respect to pairwise judgements. The final row indicates the weight of the voilated edges.

An MFAS solution written in Python took only a few minutes to produce rankings for all 25 tasks on a 2.13 GHz Intel Core 2 Duo processor, demonstrating that it is completely feasible despite being theoretically intractible. One value of computing this solution is that it enables us to answer several questions,

[3]This is not necessarily the best choice of weighting. For instance, (Bojar et al., 2011) observe that human assessments of shorter sentences tend to be more consistent with each other, so perhaps they should be weighted more highly. Unfortunately, it is not clear how to evaluate alternative weighting schemes, since there is no ground truth for such meta-evaluations.

ONLINEB	LIUM ≺ ONLINEB	1	RWTH-COMBO
RWTH-COMBO	UPV-COMBO ≺ CAMBRIDGE	6	CMU-HYPOSEL-COMBO
CMU-HYPOSEL-COMBO	JHU ≺ CAMBRIDGE	1	DCU-COMBO
CAMBRIDGE	LIMSI ≺ UEDIN	1	ONLINEB
LIUM	LIMSI ≺ CMU-HYPOSEL-COMBO	1	LIUM
DCU-COMBO	LIUM-COMBO ≺ CAMBRIDGE	1	CMU-HEAFIELD-COMBO
CMU-HEAFIELD-COMBO	LIUM-COMBO ≺ NRC	3	UPV-COMBO
UPV-COMBO	RALI ≺ UEDIN	1	NRC
NRC	RALI ≺ UPV-COMBO	4	CAMBRIDGE
UEDIN	RALI ≺ JHU	1	UEDIN
JHU	RALI ≺ LIUM	3	JHU-COMBO
LIMSI	LIG ≺ UEDIN	6	LIMSI
JHU-COMBO	BBN-COMBO ≺ NRC	3	RALI
LIUM-COMBO	BBN-COMBO ≺ UEDIN	5	LIUM-COMBO
RALI	BBN-COMBO ≺ UPV-COMBO	5	BBN-COMBO
LIG	BBN-COMBO ≺ JHU	4	JHU
BBN-COMBO	RWTH ≺ UPV-COMBO	3	RWTH
RWTH	CMU-STATXFER ≺ JHU	1	LIG
CMU-STATXFER	CMU-STATXFER ≺ LIG	1	ONLINEA
ONLINEA	ONLINEA ≺ RWTH	1	CMU-STATXFER
HUICONG	ONLINEA ≺ JHU	2	HUICONG
DFKI	HUICONG ≺ LIG	3	DFKI
CU-ZEMAN	DFKI ≺ RWTH	3	GENEVA
GENEVA	DFKI ≺ CMU-STATXFER	1	CU-ZEMAN

Table 3: 2010 French-English reranking with MFAS solver. The left column shows the optimal ranking, while the center shows the pairwise rankings that are violated by this ranking, along with their edge weights. The right column shows the ranking under WMT-OFFICIAL (Eq. 1), originally published as two separate tables.

both about the pairwise data itself, and the proposed heuristic ranking of Bojar et al. (2011).

5.1 Cycles in the Pairwise Rankings

Our first experiment checks for cycles in the tournaments. Only nine were acyclic, including all eight of the system combination tasks, each of which contained only a handful of systems. The most interesting, however, is the 2011 English-Czech individual task. This task is notable because the heuristic rankings *do not* produce a ranking that is consistent with all of the pairwise judgements, even though one exists. The three rankings are illustrated side-by-side in Table 2. One obvious problem is that neither heuristic score correctly identifies CU-MARECEK as the best system, even though it wins pairwise comparisons against all other systems (the WMT 2011 proceedings do identify it as a winner, despite not placing it in the highest rank).

On the other hand, the most difficult task to disentangle is the 2010 French-English task (Table 3), which included 25 systems (individual and system combinations were evaluated as a group for this task, despite being reported in separate tables in official results). Its optimal ranking with MFAS still violates 61 pairwise ranking samples — there is simply no sensible way to put these systems into a total order. On the other hand, the heuristic rankings based on Equations 1 through 3 violate even more comparisons: 107, 108, and 118, respectively. Once again we see a curious result in the top of the heuristic rankings, with system ONLINEB falling several spots below the top position in the heurstic ranking, despite losing out only to LIUM by one vote.

Our major concern, however, is that over half of the tasks included cycles of one form or another in the tournaments. This represents a strong inconsistency in the data.

5.2 Evaluation of Heuristic Scores

Taking the analysis above further, we find that the total number of violations of pairwise preferences across all tasks stands at 396 for the MFAS solution, and at 1140, 1215, 979 for Equations 1 through 3. This empirically validates the suggestion by Bojar et al. (2011) to remove ties from both the numerator and denominator of the heuristic measure. On the other hand, despite the intuitive arguments in its favor, the empirical evidence does not strongly favor any of the heuristic measures, all of which are substantially worse than the MFAS solution.

In fact, HEURISTIC 2 (Eq. 2) fails quite spectacularly in one case: on the ranking of the systems produced by the tunable metrics task of WMT 2011 (Figure 4). Apart from producing a ranking very inconsistent with the pairwise judgements, it achieves a Spearman's rank correlation coefficent of 0.43 with the MFAS solution. By comparison, WMT-OFFICIAL (Eq. 1) produces the best ranking, with a correlation of 0.93 with the MFAS solution. The two heuristic measures obtain an even lower correlation of 0.19 with each other. This difference in the two rankings was noted in the WMT 2011 report; however comparison with the MFAS ranker suggests that the published rankings according to the official metric are about as accurate as those based on other heuristic metrics.

MFAS Ranking	HEURISTIC 2 Ranking
CMU-BLEU	CU-SEMPOS-BLEU
CMU-BLEU-SINGLE	NUS-TESLA-F
CU-SEMPOS-BLEU	CMU-BLEU
RWTH-CDER	CMU-BLEU-SINGLE
CMU-METEOR	STANFORD-DCP
STANFORD-DCP	CMU-METEOR
NUS-TESLA-F	RWTH-CDER
SHEFFIELD-ROSE	SHEFFIELD-ROSE

Table 4: Rankings of the WMT 2011 tunable metrics task. MFAS finds a near-optimal solution, violating only six judgements with reversals of CMU-METEOR $\prec$ CMU-BLEU and STANFORD-DCP $\prec$ CMU-BLEU-SINGLE. In contrast, the HEURISTIC2 (Eq. 2) solution violates 103 pairwise judgements.

6 Discussion

Unfortunately, reliably ranking translation systems based on human assessments appears to be a difficult task, and it is unclear that WMT has succeeded yet. Some results presented here, such as the complete inability to obtain a sensible ordering on the 2010 French-English task—or to produce an acyclic tournament on more than half the tasks—indicate that further work is needed, and we feel that the published results of the human assessment should be regarded with a healthy skepticism. There are many potential sources of uncertainty in the data:

- It is quite rare that one system is uniformly better than another. Rather, one system will tend to perform better in aggregate across many sentences. The number of sentences on which this improvement can be reliably observed will vary greatly. In many cases, it may be less than the number of samples.
- Individual assessors may be biased or malicious.
- The reliability of pairwise judgements varies with sentence length, as noted by Bojar et al. (2011).
- The pairwise judgements are not made directly, but inferred from a larger relative ranking.
- The pairwise judgements are not independent, since each sample consists of consecutive sentences from the same document. It is likely that some systems are systematically better or worse on particular documents.
- The pairwise judgements are not independent, since many of the assessments are intentionally repeated to assess intra- and inter-annotator agreement.
- Many of the systems will covary, since they are often based on the same underlying techniques and software.

How much does any one or all of these factors affect the final ranking? The technique described above does not even attempt to address this question. Indeed, modeling this kind of data still appears to be unsolved: a recent paper by Wauthier and Jordan (2011) on modeling latent annotator bias presents one of the first attempts at solving just *one* of the above problems, let alone all of them.

Simple hypothesis testing of the type reported in the workshop results is simply inadequate to tease apart the many interacting effects in this type of data and may lead to many unjustified conclusions. The tables in the Appendix of Callison-Burch et al. (2011) report p-values of up to 1%, computed for every pairwise comparison in the dataset. However, there are over two thousand comparisons in this appendix, so even at an error rate of 1% we would expect more than twenty to be wrong. Making matters worse, many of the p-values are in fact much than higher than 1%. It is quite reasonable to assume that hundreds of the pairwise rankings inferred from these tables are incorrect, or at least meaningless. Methods for multiple hypothesis testing (Benjamini and Hochberg, 1995) should be explored.

In short, there is much work to be done. This paper has raised more questions than it answered, but we offer several recommendations.

- We recommend *against* using the metric proposed by Bojar et al. (2011). While their analysis is very insightful, their proposed heuristic metric is not substantially better than the metric used in the official rankings. If anything, an MFAS-based ranking should be preferred since it can minimize discrepancies with the pairwise rankings, but as we have discussed, we believe this is far from a complete solution.

- Reconsider the use of total ordering, especially for the evaluation of automatic metrics. As demonstrated in this paper, there are many possible ways to generate a total ordering, and the choice of one may be arbitrary. In some cases there may not be enough evidence to support a total ordering, or the evidence is contradictory, and committing to one may be a source of substantial noise in the gold standard for evaluating automatic metrics.

- Consider a pilot study to clearly identify which sources of uncertainty in the data affect the rankings and devise methods to account for it, which may involve redesigning the data collection protocol. The current approach is designed to collect data for a variety of different goals, including intra- and inter-annotator agreement, pairwise coverage, and maximum throughput. However, some of goals are at cross-purposes in that they make it more difficult to make reliable statistical inferences about any one aspect of the data. Additional care should be taken to minimize dependencies between the samples used to produce the final ranking.

- Encourage further detailed analysis of the existing datasets, perhaps through a shared task. The data that has been amassed so far through WMT is the best available resource for making progress on solving the difficult problem of producing reliable and *repeatable* human rankings of machine translation systems. However, this problem is not solved yet, and it will require sustained effort to make that progress.

Acknowledgements

Thanks to Ondřej Bojar, Philipp Koehn, and Martin Popel for very helpful discussion related to this work, the anonymous reviewers for detailed and helpful comments, and Chris Callison-Burch for encouraging this investigation and for many explanations and additional data from the workshop.

References

N. Alon. 2006. Ranking tournaments. *SIAM Journal on Discrete Mathematics*, 20(1):137–142.

Y. Benjamini and Y. Hochberg. 1995. Controlling the false discovery rate: a practical and powerful approach to multiple testing. *Journal of the Royal Statistical Society*, 57:289–300.

O. Bojar, M. Ercegovčević, M. Popel, and O. F. Zaidan. 2011. A grain of salt for the WMT manual evaluation. In *Proc. of WMT*.

C. Callison-Burch, P. Koehn, C. Monz, K. Peterson, M. Przybocki, and O. Zaidan. 2010. Findings of the 2010 joint workshop on statistical machine translation and metrics for machine translation. In *Proc. of WMT*.

C. Callison-Burch, P. Koehn, C. Monz, and O. F. Zaidan. 2011. Findings of the 2011 workshop on statistical machine translation. In *Proc. of WMT*.

P. Charbit, S. Thomass, and A. Yeo. 2007. The minimum feedback arc set problem is NP-hard for tournaments. *Combinatorics, Probability and Computing*, 16.

E. W. Dijkstra. 1959. A note on two problems in connexion with graphs. *Numerische Mathematik*, 1:269–271.

R. M. Karp. 1972. Reducibility among combinatorial problems. In *Symposium on the Complexity of Computer Computations*.

P. Koehn. 2004. Pharaoh: a beam search decoder for phrase-based statistical machine translation models. In *Proc. of AMTA*.

H. G. Landau. 1951. On dominance relations and the structure of animal societies: I effect of inherent characteristics. *Bulletin of Mathematical Biology*, 13(1):1–19.

F. L. Wauthier and M. I. Jordan. 2011. Bayesian bias mitigation for crowdsourcing. In *Proc. of NIPS*.

Findings of the 2012 Workshop on Statistical Machine Translation

Chris Callison-Burch
Johns Hopkins University

Philipp Koehn
University of Edinburgh

Christof Monz
University of Amsterdam

Matt Post
Johns Hopkins University

Radu Soricut
SDL Language Weaver

Lucia Specia
University of Sheffield

Abstract

This paper presents the results of the WMT12 shared tasks, which included a translation task, a task for machine translation evaluation metrics, and a task for run-time estimation of machine translation quality. We conducted a large-scale manual evaluation of 103 machine translation systems submitted by 34 teams. We used the ranking of these systems to measure how strongly automatic metrics correlate with human judgments of translation quality for 12 evaluation metrics. We introduced a new quality estimation task this year, and evaluated submissions from 11 teams.

1 Introduction

This paper presents the results of the shared tasks of the Workshop on statistical Machine Translation (WMT), which was held at NAACL 2012. This workshop builds on six previous WMT workshops (Koehn and Monz, 2006; Callison-Burch et al., 2007; Callison-Burch et al., 2008; Callison-Burch et al., 2009; Callison-Burch et al., 2010; Callison-Burch et al., 2011). In the past, the workshops have featured a number of shared tasks: a translation task between English and other languages, a task for automatic evaluation metrics to predict human judgments of translation quality, and a system combination task to get better translation quality by combining the outputs of multiple translation systems. This year we discontinued the system combination task, and introduced a new task in its place:

- **Quality estimation task** – Structured prediction tasks like MT are difficult, but the difficulty is not uniform across all input types. It would thus be useful to have some measure of confidence in the quality of the output, which has potential usefulness in a range of settings, such as deciding whether output needs human post-editing or selecting the best translation from outputs from a number of systems. This shared task focused on sentence-level estimation, and challenged participants to rate the quality of sentences produced by a standard Moses translation system on an English-Spanish news corpus in one of two tasks: *ranking* and *scoring*. Predictions were scored against a blind test set manually annotated with relevant quality judgments.

The primary objectives of WMT are to evaluate the state of the art in machine translation, to disseminate common test sets and public training data with published performance numbers, and to refine evaluation methodologies for machine translation. As with previous workshops, all of the data, translations, and collected human judgments are publicly available.[1] We hope these datasets form a valuable resource for research into statistical machine translation, system combination, and automatic evaluation or automatic prediction of translation quality.

2 Overview of the Shared Translation Task

The recurring task of the workshop examines translation between English and four other languages: German, Spanish, French, and Czech. We created a

[1] `http://statmt.org/wmt12/results.html`

test set for each language pair by translating newspaper articles. We additionally provided training data and two baseline systems.

2.1 Test data

The test data for this year's task was created by hiring people to translate news articles that were drawn from a variety of sources from November 15, 2011. A total of 99 articles were selected, in roughly equal amounts from a variety of Czech, English, French, German, and Spanish news sites:[2]

Czech: Blesk (1), CTK (1), E15 (1), deník (4), iDNES.cz (3), iHNed.cz (3), Ukacko (2), Zheny (1)

French: Canoe (3), Croix (3), Le Devoir (3), Les Echos (3), Equipe (2), Le Figaro (3), Liberation (3)

Spanish: ABC.es (4), Milenio (4), Noroeste (4), Nacion (3), El Pais (3), El Periodico (3), Prensa Libre (3), El Universal (4)

English: CNN (3), Fox News (2), Los Angeles Times (3), New York Times (3), Newsweek (1), Time (3), Washington Post (3)

German: Berliner Kurier (1), FAZ (3), Giessener Allgemeine (2), Morgenpost (3), Spiegel (3), Welt (3)

The translations were created by the professional translation agency CEET.[3] All of the translations were done directly, and not via an intermediate language.

Although the translations were done professionally, we observed a number of errors. These errors ranged from minor typographical mistakes (*I was terrible...* instead of *It was terrible...*) to more serious errors of incorrect verb choices and nonsensical constructions. An example of the latter is the French sentence (translated from German):

> *Il a gratté une planche de béton, perdit des pièces du véhicule.*
> *(He scraped against a concrete crash barrier and lost parts of the car.)*

Here, the French verb *gratter* is incorrect, and the phrase *planche de béton* does not make any sense.

We did not quantify errors, but collected a number of examples during the course of the manual evaluation. These errors were present in the data available to all the systems and therefore did not bias the results, but we suggest that next year a manual review of the professionally-collected translations be taken prior to releasing the data in order to correct mistakes and provide feedback to the translation agency.

2.2 Training data

As in past years we provided parallel corpora to train translation models, monolingual corpora to train language models, and development sets to tune system parameters. Some statistics about the training materials are given in Figure 1.

2.3 Submitted systems

We received submissions from 34 groups across 18 institutions. The participants are listed in Table 1. We also included two commercial off-the-shelf MT systems, three online statistical MT systems, and three online rule-based MT systems. Not all systems supported all language pairs. We note that the eight companies that developed these systems did not submit entries themselves, but were instead gathered by translating the test data via their interfaces (web or PC).[4] They are therefore anonymized in this paper. The data used to construct these systems is not subject to the same constraints as the shared task participants. It is possible that part of the reference translations that were taken from online news sites could have been included in the systems' models, for instance. We therefore categorize all commercial systems as unconstrained when evaluating the results.

3 Human Evaluation

As with past workshops, we placed greater emphasis on the human evaluation than on the automatic evaluation metric scores. It is our contention that automatic measures are an imperfect substitute for human assessment of translation quality. Therefore, we define the manual evaluation to be primary, and

[2]For more details see the XML test files. The `docid` tag gives the source and the date for each document in the test set, and the `origlang` tag indicates the original source language.

[3]`http://www.ceet.eu/`

[4]We would like to thank Ondřej Bojar for harvesting the commercial entries, Christian Federmann for the statistical MT entries, and Hervé Saint-Amand for the rule-based MT entries.

Europarl Training Corpus

	Spanish ↔ English		French ↔ English		German ↔ English		Czech ↔ English	
Sentences	1,965,734		2,007,723		1,920,209		646,605	
Words	56,895,229	54,420,026	60,125,563	55,642,101	50,486,398	53,008,851	14,946,399	17,376,433
Distinct words	176,258	117,481	140,915	118,404	381,583	115,966	172,461	63,039

News Commentary Training Corpus

	Spanish ↔ English		French ↔ English		German ↔ English		Czech ↔ English	
Sentences	157,302		137,097		158,840		136,151	
Words	4,449,786	3,903,339	3,915,218	3,403,043	3,950,394	3,856,795	2,938,308	3,264,812
Distinct words	78,383	57,711	63,805	53,978	130,026	57,464	136,392	52,488

United Nations Training Corpus

	Spanish ↔ English		French ↔ English	
Sentences	11,196,913		12,886,831	
Words	318,788,686	365,127,098	411,916,781	360,341,450
Distinct words	593,567	581,339	565,553	666,077

10^9 Word Parallel Corpus

	French ↔ English	
Sentences	22,520,400	
Words	811,203,407	668,412,817
Distinct words	2,738,882	2,861,836

CzEng Training Corpus

	Czech ↔ English	
Sentences	14,833,358	
Words	200,658,857	228,040,794
Distinct words	1,389,803	920,824

Europarl Language Model Data

	English	Spanish	French	German	Czech
Sentence	2,218,201	2,123,835	2,190,579	2,176,537	668,595
Words	59,848,044	60,476,282	63,439,791	53,534,167	14,946,399
Distinct words	123,059	181,837	145,496	394,781	172,461

News Language Model Data

	English	Spanish	French	German	Czech
Sentence	51,827,706	8,627,438	16,708,622	30,663,107	18,931,106
Words	1,249,883,955	247,722,726	410,581,568	576,833,910	315,167,472
Distinct words	2,265,254	926,999	1,267,582	3,336,078	2,304,933

News Test Set

	English	Spanish	French	German	Czech
Sentences	3003				
Words	73,785	78,965	81,478	73,433	65,501
Distinct words	9,881	12,137	11,441	14,252	17,149

Figure 1: Statistics for the training and test sets used in the translation task. The number of words and the number of distinct words (case-insensitive) is based on the provided tokenizer.

ID	Participant
CMU	Carnegie Mellon University (Denkowski et al., 2012)
CU-BOJAR	Charles University - Bojar (Bojar et al., 2012)
CU-DEPFIX	Charles University - DEPFIX (Rosa et al., 2012)
CU-POOR-COMB	Charles University - Bojar (Bojar et al., 2012)
CU-TAMCH	Charles University - Tamchyna (Tamchyna et al., 2012)
CU-TECTOMT	Charles University - TectoMT (Dušek et al., 2012)
DFKI-BERLIN	German Research Center for Artificial Intelligence (Vilar, 2012)
DFKI-HUNSICKER	German Research Center for Artificial Intelligence - Hunsicker (Hunsicker et al., 2012)
GTH-UPM	Technical University of Madrid (López-Ludeña et al., 2012)
ITS-LATL	Language Technology Laboratory @ University of Geneva (Wehrli et al., 2009)
JHU	Johns Hopkins University (Ganitkevitch et al., 2012)
KIT	Karlsruhe Institute of Technology (Niehues et al., 2012)
LIMSI	LIMSI (Le et al., 2012)
LIUM	University of Le Mans (Servan et al., 2012)
PROMT	ProMT (Molchanov, 2012)
QCRI	Qatar Computing Research Institute (Guzman et al., 2012)
QUAERO	The QUAERO Project (Markus et al., 2012)
RWTH	RWTH Aachen (Huck et al., 2012)
SFU	Simon Fraser University (Razmara et al., 2012)
UEDIN-WILLIAMS	University of Edinburgh - Williams (Williams and Koehn, 2012)
UEDIN	University of Edinburgh (Koehn and Haddow, 2012)
UG	University of Toronto (Germann, 2012)
UK	Charles University - Zeman (Zeman, 2012)
UPC	Technical University of Catalonia (Formiga et al., 2012)
COMMERCIAL-[1,2]	Two commercial machine translation systems
ONLINE-[A,B,C]	Three online statistical machine translation systems
RBMT-[1,3,4]	Three rule-based statistical machine translation systems

Table 1: Participants in the shared translation task. Not all teams participated in all language pairs. The translations from the commercial, online, and rule-based systems were crawled by us, not submitted by the respective companies, and are therefore anonymized. Anonymized identifiers were chosen so as to correspond with the WMT11 systems.

Language Pair	Num Systems	Label Count	Labels per System
Czech-English	6	6,470	1,078.3
English-Czech	13	11,540	887.6
German-English	16	7,135	445.9
English-German	15	8,760	584.0
Spanish-English	12	5,705	475.4
English-Spanish	11	7,375	670.4
French-English	15	6,975	465.0
English-French	15	7,735	515.6
Overall	**103**	**61,695**	**598**

Table 2: A summary of the WMT12 ranking task, showing the number of systems and number of labels (rankings) collected for each of the language translation tasks.

use the human judgments to validate automatic metrics.

Manual evaluation is time consuming, and it requires a large effort to conduct on the scale of our workshop. We distributed the workload across a number of people, beginning with shared-task participants and interested volunteers. This year, we also opened up the evaluation to non-expert annotators hired on Amazon Mechanical Turk (Callison-Burch, 2009). To ensure that the Turkers provided high quality annotations, we used controls constructed from the machine translation ranking tasks from prior years. Control items were selected such that there was high agreement across the system developers who completed that item. In all, there were 229 people who participated in the manual evaluation, with 91 workers putting in more than an hour's worth of effort, and 21 putting in more than four hours. After filtering Turker rankings against the controls to discard Turkers who fell below a threshold level of agreement on the control questions, there was a collective total of 336 hours of usable labor. This is similar to the total of 361 hours of labor collected for WMT11.

We asked annotators to evaluate system outputs by ranking translated sentences relative to each other. This was our official determinant of translation quality. The total number of judgments collected for each of the language pairs is given in Table 2.

3.1 Ranking translations of sentences

Ranking translations relative to each other is a reasonably intuitive task. We therefore kept the instructions simple:

> *You are shown a source sentence followed by several candidate translations.*
> *Your task is to rank the translations from best to worst (ties are allowed).*

Each screen for this task involved judging translations of three consecutive source segments. For each source segment, the annotator was shown the outputs of five submissions, and asked to rank them. We refer to each of these as *ranking tasks* or sometimes *blocks*.

Every language task had more than five participating systems — up to a maximum of 16 for the German-English task. Rather than attempting to get a complete ordering over the systems in each ranking task, we instead relied on random selection and a reasonably large sample size to make the comparisons fair.

We use the collected rank labels to assign each system a score that reflects how highly that system was usually ranked by the annotators. The score for some system A reflects how frequently it was judged to be better than other systems. Specifically, each block in which A appears includes four implicit pairwise comparisons (against the other presented systems). A is rewarded once for each of the four comparisons in which A wins, and its score is the number of such winning pairwise comparisons, divided by the total number of non-tying pairwise comparisons involving A.

This scoring metric is different from that used in prior years in two ways. First, the score previously included ties between system rankings. In that case, the score for A reflected how often A was rated as better than *or equal to* other systems, and was normalized by all comparisons involving A. However, this approach unfairly rewards systems that are similar (and likely to be ranked as tied). This is problematic since many of the systems use variations of the same underlying decoder (Bojar et al., 2011).

A second difference is that this year we no longer include comparisons against reference translations. In the past, reference translations were included among the systems to be ranked as controls, and the pairwise comparisons were used in determining the best system. However, workers have a very clear preference for reference translations, so including them unduly penalized systems that, through (un)luck of the draw, were pitted against the references more often. These changes are part of a broader discussion of the best way to produce the system ranking, which we discuss at length in Section 4.

The system scores are reported in Section 3.3. Appendix A provides detailed tables that contain pairwise head-to-head comparisons between pairs of systems.

3.2 Inter- and Intra-annotator agreement in the ranking task

Each year we calculate the inter- and intra-annotator agreement for the human evaluation, since a reasonable degree of agreement must exist to support our process as a valid evaluation setup. To ensure we had enough data to measure agreement, we occasionally showed annotators items that were repeated from previously completed items. These repeated items were drawn from ones completed by the same annotator and from different annotators.

We measured pairwise agreement among annotators using Cohen's kappa coefficient (κ) (Cohen, 1960), which is defined as

$$\kappa = \frac{P(A) - P(E)}{1 - P(E)}$$

where $P(A)$ is the proportion of times that the annotators agree, and $P(E)$ is the proportion of time that they would agree by chance. Note that κ is basically a normalized version of $P(A)$, one which takes into account how meaningful it is for annotators to agree with each other, by incorporating $P(E)$. Note also that κ has a value of at most 1 (and could possibly be negative), with higher rates of agreement resulting in higher κ.

We calculate $P(A)$ by examining all pairs of systems which had been judged by two or more judges, and calculating the proportion of time that they agreed that $A > B$, $A = B$, or $A < B$. In other words, $P(A)$ is the empirical, observed rate at which annotators agree, in the context of pairwise comparisons. $P(A)$ is computed similarly for *intra*-annotator agreement (i.e. self-consistency), but over pairwise comparisons that were annotated more than once by a *single* annotator.

As for $P(E)$, it should capture the probability that two annotators would agree randomly. Therefore:

$$P(E) = P(\text{A>B})^2 + P(\text{A=B})^2 + P(\text{A<B})^2$$

Note that each of the three probabilities in $P(E)$'s definition are squared to reflect the fact that we are considering the chance that *two* annotators would agree by chance. Each of these probabilities is computed empirically, by observing how often annotators actually rank two systems as being tied. We note here that this empirical computation is a departure from previous years' analyses, where we had assumed that the three categories are equally likely (yielding $P(E) = \frac{1}{9} + \frac{1}{9} + \frac{1}{9} = \frac{1}{3}$). We believe that this is a more principled approach, which faithfully reflects the motivation of accounting for $P(E)$ in the first place.

Table 3 gives κ values for inter-annotator and intra-annotator agreement. These give an indication of how often different judges agree, and how often single judges are consistent for repeated judgments, respectively. The exact interpretation of the kappa coefficient is difficult, but according to Landis and Koch (1977), $0 - 0.2$ is slight, $0.2 - 0.4$ is fair, $0.4 - 0.6$ is moderate, $0.6 - 0.8$ is substantial, and $0.8 - 1.0$ is almost perfect. Based on these interpretations, the agreement for sentence-level ranking is fair for inter-annotator and moderate for intra-annotator agreement. Consistent with previous years, intra-annotator agreement is higher than inter-annotator agreement, except for English–Czech.

An important difference from last year is that the evaluations were not constrained only to workshop participants, but were made available to all Turkers. The workshop participants were trusted to complete the tasks in good faith, and we have multiple years of data establishing general levels of inter- and intra-annotator agreement. Their HITs were unpaid, and access was limited with the use of a qualification. The Turkers completed paid tasks, and we used controls to filter out fraudulent and unconscientious workers.

	INTER-ANNOTATOR AGREEMENT			INTRA-ANNOTATOR AGREEMENT		
LANGUAGE PAIRS	$P(A)$	$P(E)$	κ	$P(A)$	$P(E)$	κ
Czech-English	0.567	0.405	0.272	0.660	0.405	0.428
English-Czech	0.576	0.383	0.312	0.566	0.383	0.296
German-English	0.595	0.401	0.323	0.733	0.401	0.554
English-German	0.598	0.394	0.336	0.732	0.394	0.557
Spanish-English	0.540	0.408	0.222	0.792	0.408	0.648
English-Spanish	0.504	0.398	0.176	0.566	0.398	0.279
French-English	0.568	0.406	0.272	0.719	0.406	0.526
English-French	0.519	0.388	0.214	0.634	0.388	0.401
WMT12	0.568	0.396	0.284	0.671	0.396	0.455
WMT11	0.601	0.362	0.375	0.722	0.362	0.564

Table 3: Inter- and intra-annotator agreement rates for the WMT12 manual evaluation. For comparison, the WMT11 rows contain the results from the European languages individual systems task (Callison-Burch et al. (2011), Table 7).

Agreement rates vary widely across languages. For inter-annotator agreements, the range is 0.176 to 0.336, while intra-annotator agreement ranges from 0.279 to 0.648. We note in particular the low agreement rates among judgments in the English-Spanish task, which is reflected in the relative lack of statistical significance Table 4. The agreement rates for this year were somewhat lower than last year.

3.3 Results of the Translation Task

We used the results of the manual evaluation to analyze the translation quality of the different systems that were submitted to the workshop. In our analysis, we aimed to address the following questions:

- Which systems produced the best translation quality for each language pair?
- Which of the systems that used only the provided training materials produced the best translation quality?

Table 4 shows the system ranking for each of the translation tasks. For each language pair, we define a system as 'winning' if no other system was found statistically significantly better (using the Sign Test, at $p \leq 0.10$). In some cases, multiple systems are listed as winners, either due to a large number of participants or a low number of judgments per system pair, both of which are factors that make it difficult to achieve statistical significance.

As in prior years, unconstrained online systems A and B are among the best for many tasks, with a few notable exceptions. CU-DEPFIX, which post-processes the output of ONLINE-B, was judged as the best system for English-Czech. For the French-English and English-French tasks, constrained systems came out on top, with LIMSI appearing both times. Consistent with prior years, the rule-based systems performed very well on the English-German task. A rule-based system also had a good showing for English-Spanish, but not really anywhere else. Among the systems competing in all tasks, no single system consistently appeared among the top entrants. Participants that competed in all tasks tended to fair worse, with the exception of UEDIN. Additionally, KIT appeared in four tasks and was a constrained winner each time.

4 Methods for Overall Ranking

Last year one of the long papers published at WMT criticized our method for compiling the overall ranking for systems in the translation task (Bojar et al., 2011). This year another paper shows some additional potential inconsistencies in the rankings (Lopez, 2012). In this section we delve into a detailed analysis of a variety of methods that use the human evaluation to create an overall ranking of systems.

In the human evaluation, we collect ranking judgments for output from five systems at a time. We interpret them as $10 \cdot \binom{5\times 4}{2}$ pairwise judgments over systems and use these to analyze how each system faired compared against each of the others. Not all

Czech-English
3,603–3,718 comparisons/system

System	C?	>others
ONLINE-B •	N	0.65
UEDIN ⋆	Y	0.60
CU-BOJAR	Y	0.53
ONLINE-A	N	0.53
UK	Y	0.37
JHU	Y	0.32

Spanish-English
1,527–1,775 comparisons/system

System	C?	>others
ONLINE-A •	N	0.62
ONLINE-B •	N	0.61
QCRI ⋆	Y	0.60
UEDIN •⋆	Y	0.58
UPC	Y	0.57
GTH-UPM	Y	0.52
RBMT-3	N	0.51
JHU	Y	0.48
RBMT-4	N	0.46
RBMT-1	N	0.42
ONLINE-C	N	0.42
UK	Y	0.19

French-English
1,437–1,701 comparisons/system

System	C?	>others
LIMSI •⋆	Y	0.63
KIT •⋆	Y	0.61
ONLINE-A •	N	0.59
CMU •⋆	Y	0.57
ONLINE-B •	N	0.57
UEDIN	Y	0.55
LIUM	Y	0.52
RWTH	Y	0.52
RBMT-1	N	0.46
RBMT-3	N	0.46
UK	Y	0.44
SFU	Y	0.44
RBMT-4	N	0.43
JHU	Y	0.41
ONLINE-C	N	0.32

English-Czech
2,652–3,146 comparisons/system

System	C?	>others
CU-DEPFIX •	N	0.66
ONLINE-B	N	0.63
UEDIN ⋆	Y	0.56
CU-TAMCH	N	0.56
CU-BOJAR ⋆	Y	0.54
CU-TECTOMT ⋆	Y	0.53
ONLINE-A	N	0.53
COMMERCIAL-1	N	0.48
COMMERCIAL-2	N	0.46
CU-POOR-COMB	Y	0.44
UK	Y	0.44
SFU	Y	0.36
JHU	Y	0.32

English-Spanish
2,013–2,294 comparisons/system

System	C?	>others
ONLINE-B •	N	0.65
RBMT-3	N	0.58
ONLINE-A •	N	0.56
PROMT	N	0.55
UPC ⋆	Y	0.52
UEDIN ⋆	Y	0.52
RBMT-4	N	0.46
RBMT-1	N	0.45
ONLINE-C	N	0.43
UK	Y	0.41
JHU	Y	0.36

English-French
1,410–1,697 comparisons/system

System	C?	>others
LIMSI •⋆	Y	0.66
RWTH	Y	0.62
ONLINE-B	N	0.60
KIT •⋆	Y	0.59
LIUM	Y	0.55
UEDIN	Y	0.53
RBMT-3	N	0.52
ONLINE-A	N	0.51
PROMT	N	0.51
RBMT-1	N	0.48
JHU	Y	0.44
UK	Y	0.40
RBMT-4	N	0.39
ONLINE-C	N	0.39
ITS-LATL	N	0.36

German-English
1,386–1,567 comparisons/system

System	C?	>others
ONLINE-A •	N	0.65
ONLINE-B •	N	0.65
QUAERO	Y	0.61
RBMT-3	N	0.60
UEDIN ⋆	Y	0.60
RWTH ⋆	Y	0.56
KIT ⋆	Y	0.55
LIMSI	Y	0.54
QCRI	Y	0.52
RBMT-1	N	0.51
RBMT-4	N	0.50
ONLINE-C	N	0.43
DFKI-BERLIN	Y	0.40
UK	Y	0.37
JHU	Y	0.34
UG	Y	0.17

English-German
1,777–2,160 comparisons/system

System	C?	>others
ONLINE-B •	N	0.64
RBMT-3	N	0.63
RBMT-4 •	N	0.58
RBMT-1	N	0.56
LIMSI ⋆	Y	0.55
ONLINE-A	N	0.54
UEDIN-WILLIAMS ⋆	Y	0.51
KIT ⋆	Y	0.50
DFKI-HUNSICKER	N	0.48
UEDIN ⋆	Y	0.47
RWTH ⋆	Y	0.47
ONLINE-C	N	0.47
UK	Y	0.45
JHU	Y	0.43
DFKI-BERLIN	Y	0.25

C? indicates whether system is constrained (unhighlighted rows): trained only using supplied training data, standard monolingual linguistic tools, and, optionally, LDC's English Gigaword.
• indicates a **win**: no other system is statistically significantly better at p-level ≤ 0.10 in pairwise comparison.
⋆ indicates a ***constrained* win**: no other *constrained* system is statistically better.

Table 4: Official results for the WMT12 translation task. Systems are ordered by their > others score, reflecting how often their translations won in pairwise comparisons. For detailed head-to-head comparisons, see Appendix A.

pairwise comparisons detect statistical significantly superior quality of either system, and we note this accordingly.

It is desirable to additionally produce an overall ranking. In the past evaluation campaigns, we used two different methods to obtain such a ranking, and this year we use yet another one. In this section, we discuss each of these overall ranking methods and a few more.

4.1 Rank Ranges

In the first human evaluation, we use fluency and adequacy judgments on a scale from 1 to 5 (Koehn and Monz, 2006). We normalized the scores on a per-sentence basis, thus converting them to a relative ranking in a 5-system comparison. We listed systems by the average of these scores over all sentences, in which they were judged.

We did not report ranks, but rank ranges. To give an example: if a system scored neither *statistically significantly* better nor *statistically significantly* worse than 3 other systems, we assign it the rank range 1–4. The given evidence is not sufficient to rank it exactly, but it does rank somewhere in the top 4.

In subsequent years, we did not continue the reporting of rank ranges (although they can be obtained by examining the pairwise comparison tables), but we continued to report systems as *winners* whenever there was not *statistically significantly* outperformed by any other system.

4.2 Ratio of Wins and Ties

In the following years (Callison-Burch et al., 2007; Callison-Burch et al., 2008; Callison-Burch et al., 2009; Callison-Burch et al., 2010; Callison-Burch et al., 2011), we abandoned the idea of using fluency and adequacy judgments, since they showed to be less reliable than simple ranking of system translations. We also started to interpret the 5-system comparison as a set of pairwise comparisons.

Systems were then ranked by the ratio of how often they were ranked better or equal to any of the other systems.

Given a set J of sentence-level judgments (s_1, s_2, c) where $s_1 \in S$ and $s_2 \in S$ are two systems and

$$c = \begin{cases} \textit{win} & \text{if } s_1 \text{ better than } s_2 \\ \textit{tie} & \text{if } s_1 \text{ equal to } s_2 \\ \textit{loss} & \text{if } s_1 \text{ worse than } s_2 \end{cases} \quad (1)$$

then we can count the total number of wins and ties of a system s as

$$\begin{aligned} \text{win}(s) = & \ |\{(s_1, s_2, c) \in J : s = s_1, c = \textit{win}\}| + \\ & \ |\{(s_1, s_2, c) \in J : s = s_2, c = \textit{loss}\}| \\ \text{loss}(s) = & \ |\{(s_1, s_2, c) \in J : s = s_1, c = \textit{loss}\}| + \\ & \ |\{(s_1, s_2, c) \in J : s = s_2, c = \textit{win}\}| \\ \text{tie}(s) = & \ |\{(s_1, s_2, c) \in J : s = s_1, c = \textit{tie}\}| + \\ & \ |\{(s_1, s_2, c) \in J : s = s_2, c = \textit{tie}\}| \end{aligned} \quad (2)$$

and rank systems by the ratio

$$\text{score}(s) = \frac{\text{win}(s) + \text{tie}(s)}{\text{win}(s) + \text{loss}(s) + \text{tie}(s)} \quad (3)$$

This ratio was used for the official rankings over the last five years.

4.3 Ratio of Wins (Ignoring Ties)

Bojar et al. (2011) present a persuasive argument that our ranking scheme is biased towards systems that are similar to many other systems. Given that most of the systems are based on phrase-based models trained on the same training data, this is indeed a valid concern.

They suggest ignoring ties, and using as ranking score instead the following ratio:

$$\text{score}(s) = \frac{\text{win}(s)}{\text{win}(s) + \text{loss}(s)} \quad (4)$$

This ratio is used for the official ranking this year.

4.4 Minimizing Pairwise Ranking Violations

Lopez (2012, *in this volume)* argues against using aggregate statistics over a set of very diverse judgments. Instead, a ranking that has the least number of pairwise ranking violations is said to be preferred.

If we define the number of pairwise wins as

$$\begin{aligned} \text{win}(s_1, s_2) = & \ |\{(s_1, s_2, c) \in J : c = \textit{win}\}| + \\ & \ |\{(s_2, s_1, c) \in J : c = \textit{loss}\}| \end{aligned} \quad (5)$$

then we define a count function for pairwise order violations as

$$\text{score}(s_1, s_2) = \max(0, \text{win}(s_2, s_1) - \text{win}(s_1, s_2)) \tag{6}$$

Given a bijective ranking function $R(s) \rightarrow i$ with the codomain of consecutive integers starting at 1, the total number of pairwise ranking violations is defined as

$$\text{score}(R) = \sum_{R(s_i)<R(s_j)} \text{score}(s_i, s_j) \tag{7}$$

Finding the optimal ranking R that minimizes this score is not trivial, but given the number of systems involved in this evaluation campaign, it is quite manageable.

4.5 Most Probable Ranking

We now introduce a variant to Lopez's ranking method. We motivate it first.

Consider the following scenario:

$$\begin{array}{ll} \text{win}(A, B) = 20 & \text{win}(B, A) = 0 \\ \text{win}(B, C) = 40 & \text{win}(C, B) = 20 \\ \text{win}(C, A) = 60 & \text{win}(A, C) = 40 \end{array}$$

Since this constitutes a circle, there are three rankings with the minimum number of 20 violation (ABC, BCA, CAB).

However, we may want to take the ratio of wins and losses for each pairwise ranking into account. Using maximum likelihood estimation, we can define the probability that system s_1 is better than system s_2 on a randomly drawn sentence as

$$p(s_1 > s_2) = \frac{\text{win}(s_1, s_2)}{\text{win}(s_1, s_2) + \text{win}(s_2, s_1)} \tag{8}$$

We can then go on to define[5] the probability of a ranking of three systems as:

$$p(s_1 > s_2 > s_3) = p(s_1 > s_2)p(s_1 > s_3)p(s_2 > s_3) \tag{9}$$

This function scores the three rankings in the example above as follows:

$$\begin{array}{lll} p(A > B > C) = & \frac{20}{20}\frac{40}{100}\frac{40}{60} & = 0.27 \\ p(B > C > A) = & \frac{40}{60}\frac{0}{20}\frac{60}{100} & = 0 \\ p(C > A > B) = & \frac{60}{100}\frac{20}{60}\frac{20}{20} & = 0.20 \end{array}$$

One disadvantage of this and the previous ranking method is that they do not take advantage of all available evidence. Consider the example:

$$\begin{array}{ll} \text{win}(A, B) = 100 & \text{win}(B, A) = 0 \\ \text{win}(A, C) = 60 & \text{win}(C, A) = 40 \\ \text{win}(B, C) = 50 & \text{win}(C, B) = 50 \end{array}$$

Here, system A is clearly ahead, but how about B and C? They are tied in their pairwise comparison. So, both ABC and ACB have no pairwise ranking violations and their most probable ranking score, as defined above, is the same.

B is clearly worse than A, but C has a fighting chance, and this should be reflected in the ranking. The following two overall ranking methods overcome this problem.

4.6 Monte Carlo Playoffs

The sports world is accustomed to the problem of finding a ranking of sports teams, but being only able to have pairwise competitions (think basketball or football). One strategy is to stage playoffs.

Let's say there are 4 systems: A, B, C, and D. As in well-known play-off fashion, they are first seeded. In our case, this happens randomly, say, 1:A, 2:B, 3:C, 4:D (for simplicity's sake).

First round: A plays against D, B plays against C. How do they play? We randomly select a sentence on which they were compared (no ties). If A is better according to human judgment than D, then A wins.

Let's say, A wins against D, and B loses against C. This leads us to the final A against C and the 3rd place game D against B, in which, say, A and D win. The resulting final ranking is ACDB.

We repeat this a million times with a different random seeding every time, and compute the average rank, which is then used for overall ranking.

[5]**Sketch of derivation**:

$$\begin{array}{rcl} p(s_1 > s_2 > s_3) = & p(s_1 \text{ first})p(s_2 \text{ second}|s_1 \text{ first}) \\ & \textit{(chain rule)} \\ p(s_1 \text{ first}) = & p(s_1 > s_2 \text{ and } s_1 > s_3) \\ = & p(s_1 > s_2)p(s_1 > s_3) \\ & \textit{(independence assumption)} \\ p(s_2 \text{ sec.}|s_1 \text{ first}) = & p(s_2 \text{ second}) \\ & \textit{(independence assumption)} \\ = & p(s_2 > s_3) \end{array}$$

	Bojar	Lopez	Most Probable	MC Playoffs	Expected Wins
1	0.641: ONLINE-B	RBMT-4	RBMT-4	6.16: ONLINE-B	0.640 (1-2): ONLINE-B
2	0.627: RBMT-3	ONLINE-B	ONLINE-B	6.39: RBMT-3	0.622 (1-2): RBMT-3
3	0.577: RBMT-4	RBMT-3	RBMT-3	6.98: RBMT-4	0.578 (3-5): RBMT-4
4	0.557: RBMT-1	RBMT-1	RBMT-1	7.32: RBMT-1	0.553 (3-6): RBMT-1
5	0.547: LIMSI	ONLINE-A	ONLINE-A	7.46: LIMSI	0.543 (3-7): LIMSI
6	0.537: ONLINE-A	UEDIN-WILLIAMS	LIMSI	7.57: ONLINE-A	0.534 (4-8): ONLINE-A
7	0.509: UEDIN-WILLIAMS	LIMSI	UEDIN-WILLIAMS	7.87: UEDIN-WILLIAMS	0.511 (5-9): UEDIN-WILLIAMS
8	0.503: KIT	KIT	KIT	7.98: KIT	0.503 (6-11): KIT
9	0.476: DFKI-HUNSICKER	DFKI-HUNSICKER	DFKI-HUNSICKER	8.32: UEDIN	0.477 (7-13): UEDIN
10	0.475: UEDIN	ONLINE-C	ONLINE-C	8.38: DFKI-HUNSICKER	0.472 (8-13): DFKI-HUNSICKER
11	0.470: RWTH	UEDIN	UEDIN	8.41: ONLINE-C	0.470 (8-13): ONLINE-C
12	0.470: ONLINE-C	UK	UK	8.44: RWTH	0.468 (8-13): RWTH
13	0.448: UK	RWTH	RWTH	8.72: UK	0.447 (10-14): UK
14	0.435: JHU	JHU	JHU	8.87: JHU	0.434 (12-14): JHU
15	0.249: DFKI-BERLIN	DFKI-BERLIN	DFKI-BERLIN	11.15: DFKI-BERLIN	0.249 (15): DFKI-BERLIN

Table 5: Overall ranking with different methods (English–German)

4.7 Expected Wins

In European national football competitions, each team plays against each other team, and at the end the number of wins decides the rankings.[6] We can simulate this type of tournament as well with Monte Carlo methods. However, in the limit, each team will be on average ranked based on its expected number of wins in the competition. We can compute the expected number of wins straightforward as

$$score(s_i) = \frac{1}{|S|-1} \sum_{j,j \neq i} p(s_i > s_j) \qquad (10)$$

Note that this is very similar to Bojar's method of ranking systems, with one additional and important twist. We can rewrite Equation 4, the variant that ignores ties, as:

$$\text{score}(s_i) = \frac{\text{win}(s_i)}{\text{win}(s_i)+\text{loss}(s_i)} \qquad (11)$$

$$= \frac{\sum_{j,j\neq i} \text{win}(s_i,s_j)}{\sum_{j,j\neq i} \text{win}(s_i,s_j)+\text{loss}(s_i,s_j)} \qquad (12)$$

This section's Equation 10 can be rewritten as:

$$\text{score}(s_i) = \frac{1}{|S|} \sum_{j,j\neq i} \frac{\text{win}(s_i,s_j)}{\text{win}(s_i,s_j)+\text{loss}(s_i,s_j)} \qquad (13)$$

The difference is that the new overall ranking method normalizes the win ratios per pairwise ranking. And this makes sense, since it overcomes one problem with our traditional and Bojar's ranking method.

Previously, some systems were put at an disadvantage, if they are compared more frequently against good systems than against bad systems. This could happen, if participants were not allowed to rank their own systems (a constraint we enforced in the past, but no longer). This was noticed by judges a few years ago, when we had instant reporting of rankings during the evaluation period. If you have one of the best systems and carry out a lot of human judgments, then competitors' systems will creep up higher, since they are not compared against your own (very good) system anymore, but more frequently against bad systems.

4.8 Comparison

Table 5 shows the different rankings for English–German, a rather typical example. The table displays the ranking of the systems according to five different methods, alongside with system scores according to the ranking method: the win ratio (Bojar), the average rank (MC Playoffs), and the expected win ratio (Expected Wins). For the latter, we performed bootstrap resampling and computed rank ranges that lie in a 95% confidence interval. You can find the tables for the other language pairs in the annex.

The win-based methods (Bojar, MC Playoffs, Expected Wins) give very similar rankings — exhibiting mostly just the occasional pairwise flip or for

[6]They actually play twice against each other, to balance out home field advantage, which is not a concern here.

many language pairs the ranking is identical. The same is true for the two methods based on pairwise rankings (Lopez, Most Probable). However, the two types of ranking lead to significantly different outcomes.

For instance, the win-based methods are pretty sure that ONLINE-B and RBMT-3 are the two top performers. Bootstrap resampling of rankings according to Expected Wins ranking draws a clear line between them and the rest. However, Lopez's method ranks RBMT-4 first. Why? In direct comparison of the three systems, RBMT-4 beats statistically insignificantly ONLINE-B 45% wins against 42% wins and essentially ties with RBMT-3 41% wins against 41% wins (ONLINE-B beats RBMT-3 49%–35%, $p \leq 0.01$).

We use Bojar's method as our official method for ranking in Table 4 and as the human judgments that we used when calculating how well automatic evaluation metrics correlate with human judgments.

4.9 Number of Judgments Needed

In general, there are not enough judgments to rank systems unambiguously. How many judgments do we need?

We may extrapolate this number from the number of judgments we have. Figure 2 provides some hints. The outlier is Czech–English, for which only 6 systems were submitted and we can separate them almost completely even at p-level 0.01. For all the other language pairs, we can only draw for around 40% of the pairwise comparisons conclusions with that level of statistical significance.

Since the plots also contains the ratio of significant conclusions when sub-sampling the number of judgments, we obtain curves with a clear upward slope. For English–Czech, for which we were able to collect much more judgments, we can draw over 60% significant conclusions. The curve for this language pair does not look much different than the other languages, suggesting that doubling the number of judgments should allow similar levels for them as well.

5 Metrics Task

In addition to allowing us to analyze the translation quality of different systems, the data gathered during

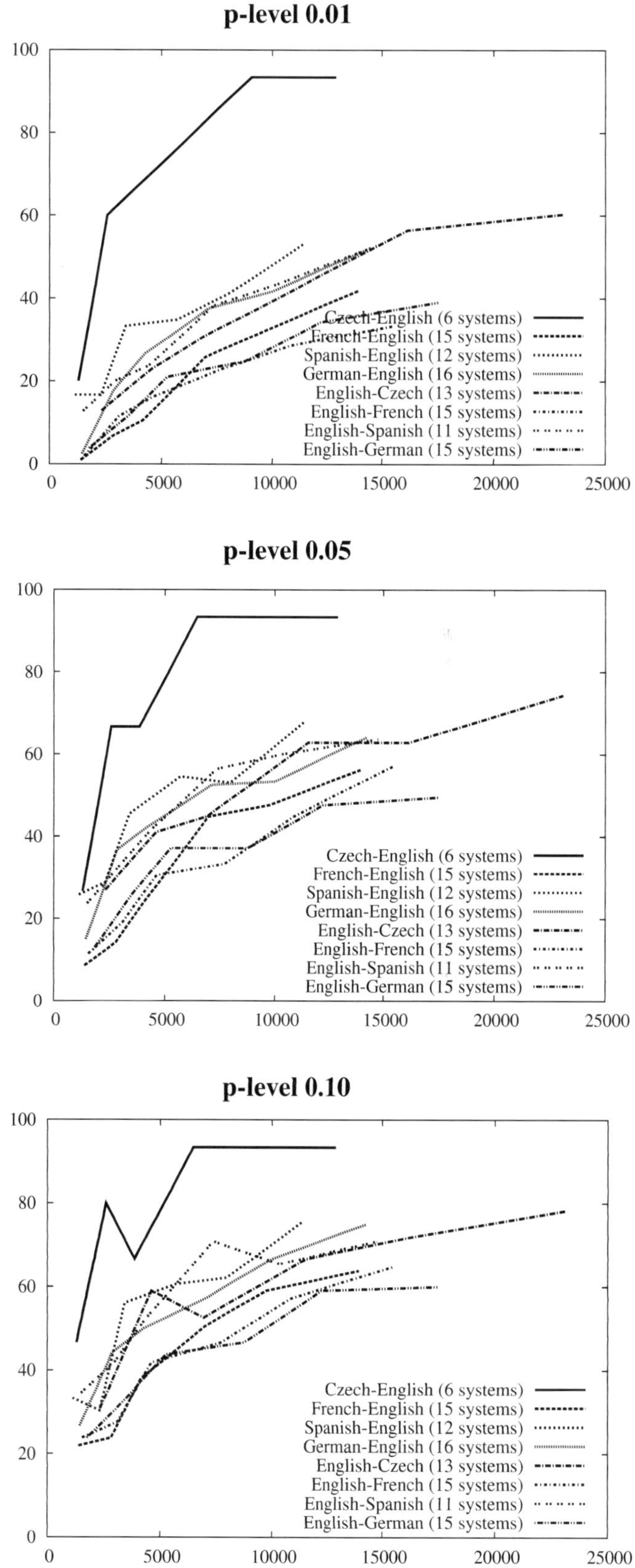

Figure 2: Ratio of statistically significant pairwise comparisons at different p-levels, based on number of pairwise judgments collected.

Metric IDs	Participant
AMBER	National Research Council Canada (Chen et al., 2012)
METEOR	CMU (Denkowski and Lavie, 2011)
SAGAN-STS	FaMAF, UNC, Argentina (Castillo and Estrella, 2012)
SEMPOS	Charles University (Macháček and Bojar, 2011)
SIMBLEU	University of Sheffield (Song and Cohn, 2011)
SPEDE	Stanford University (Wang and Manning, 2012)
TERRORCAT	University of Zurich, DFKI, Charles U (Fishel et al., 2012)
BLOCKERRCATS, ENXERRCATS, WORDBLOCKERRCATS, XENERRCATS, POSF	DFKI (Popovic, 2012)

Table 6: Participants in the metrics task.

the manual evaluation is useful for validating automatic evaluation metrics. Table 6 lists the participants in this task, along with their metrics.

A total of 12 metrics and their variants were submitted to the metrics task by 8 research groups. We provided BLEU and TER scores as baselines. We asked metrics developers to score the outputs of the machine translation systems and system combinations at the system-level and at the segment-level. The system-level metrics scores are given in the Appendix in Tables 29–36. The main goal of the metrics shared task is not to score the systems, but instead to validate the use of automatic metrics by measuring how strongly they correlate with human judgments. We used the human judgments collected during the manual evaluation for the translation task and the system combination task to calculate how well metrics correlate at system-level and at the segment-level.

5.1 System-Level Metric Analysis

We measured the correlation of the automatic metrics with the human judgments of translation quality at the system-level using Spearman's rank correlation coefficient ρ. We converted the raw scores assigned to each system into ranks. We assigned a human ranking to the systems based on the percent of time that their translations were judged to be better than the translations of any other system in the manual evaluation (Equation 4).

When there are no ties, ρ can be calculated using the simplified equation:

$$\rho = 1 - \frac{6 \sum d_i^2}{n(n^2-1)}$$

	CS-EN - 6 SYSTEMS	DE-EN - 16 SYSTEMS	ES-EN - 12 SYSTEMS	FR-EN - 15 SYSTEMS	AVERAGE
System-level correlation for translations into English					
SEMPOS	**.94**	**.92**	.94	.80	**.90**
AMBER	.83	.79	**.97**	.85	.86
METEOR	.66	.89	.95	.84	.83
TERRORCAT	.71	.76	**.97**	**.88**	.83
SIMPBLEU	.89	.70	.89	.82	.82
TER	-.89	-.62	-.92	-.82	.81
BLEU	.89	.67	.87	.81	.81
POSF	.66	.66	.87	.83	.75
BLOCKERRCATS	-.64	-.75	-.88	-.74	.75
WORDBLOCKEC	-.66	-.67	-.85	-.77	.74
XENERRCATS	-.66	-.64	-.87	-.77	.74
SAGAN-STS	.66	n/a	.91	n/a	n/a

Table 7: System-level Spearman's rho correlation of the automatic evaluation metrics with the human judgments for translation into English, ordered by average absolute value.

	EN-CZ - 10 SYSTEMS	EN-DE - 22 SYSTEMS	EN-ES - 15 SYSTEMS	EN-FR - 17 SYSTEMS	AVERAGE
System-level correlation for translations out of English					
SIMPBLEU	**.83**	.46	.42	**.94**	**.66**
BLOCKERRCATS	-.65	-.53	-.47	-.93	.64
ENXERRCATS	-.74	-.38	-.47	-.93	.63
POSF	.80	**.54**	.37	.69	.60
WORDBLOCKEC	-.71	-.37	-.47	-.81	.59
TERRORCAT	.65	.48	**.58**	.53	.56
AMBER	.71	.25	.50	.75	.55
TER	-.69	-.41	-.45	-.66	.55
METEOR	.73	.18	.45	.82	.54
BLEU	.80	.22	.40	.71	.53
SEMPOS	.52	n/a	n/a	n/a	n/a

Table 8: System-level Spearman's rho correlation of the automatic evaluation metrics with the human judgments for translation out of English, ordered by average absolute value.

where d_i is the difference between the rank for system$_i$ and n is the number of systems. The possible values of ρ range between 1 (where all systems are ranked in the same order) and -1 (where the systems are ranked in the reverse order). Thus an automatic evaluation metric with a higher absolute value for ρ is making predictions that are more similar to the human judgments than an automatic evaluation metric with a lower absolute ρ.

The system-level correlations are shown in Table 7 for translations into English, and Table 8 out of English, sorted by average correlation across the language pairs. The highest correlation for each language pair and the highest overall average are bolded. Once again this year, many of the metrics had stronger correlation with human judgments than BLEU. The metrics that had the strongest correlation this year were SEMPOS for the into English direction and SIMPBLEU for the out of English direction.

5.2 Segment-Level Metric Analysis

We measured the metrics' segment-level scores with the human rankings using Kendall's tau rank corre-

	FR-EN (11594 PAIRS)	DE-EN (11934 PAIRS)	ES-EN (9796 PAIRS)	CS-EN (11021 PAIRS)	AVERAGE
Segment-level correlation for translations into English					
SPEDE07-PP	**.26**	**.28**	**.26**	**.21**	**.25**
METEOR	.25	.27	.25	**.21**	**.25**
AMBER	.24	.25	.23	.19	.23
SIMPBLEU	.19	.17	.19	.13	.17
TERRORCAT	.18	.19	.18	.19	.19
XENERRCATS	.17	.18	.18	.13	.17
POSF	.16	.18	.15	.12	.15
WORDBLOCKEC	.15	.16	.17	.13	.15
BLOCKERRCATS	.07	.08	.08	.06	.07
SAGAN-STS	n/a	n/a	.21	.20	n/a

Table 9: Segment-level Kendall's tau correlation of the automatic evaluation metrics with the human judgments for translation into English, ordered by average correlation.

	EN-FR (11562 PAIRS)	EN-DE (14553 PAIRS)	EN-ES (11834 PAIRS)	EN-CS (18805 PAIRS)	AVERAGE
Segment-level correlation for translations out of English					
METEOR	**.26**	.18	.21	.16	**.20**
AMBER	.23	.17	**.22**	.15	.19
TERRORCAT	.18	**.19**	.18	**.18**	.18
SIMPBLEU	.2	.13	.18	.10	.15
ENXERRCATS	.20	.11	.17	.09	.14
POSF	.15	.13	.15	.13	.14
WORDBLOCKEC	.19	.1	.17	.1	.14
BLOCKERRCATS	.13	.04	.12	.01	.08

Table 10: Segment-level Kendall's tau correlation of the automatic evaluation metrics with the human judgments for translation out of English, ordered by average correlation.

lation coefficient. We calculated Kendall's tau as:

$$\tau = \frac{\text{num concordant pairs - num discordant pairs}}{\text{total pairs}}$$

where a concordant pair is a pair of two translations of the same segment in which the ranks calculated from the same human ranking task and from the corresponding metric scores agree; in a discordant pair, they disagree. In order to account for accuracy- vs. error-based metrics correctly, counts of concordant vs. discordant pairs were calculated specific to these two metric types. The possible values of τ range between 1 (where all pairs are concordant) and -1 (where all pairs are discordant). Thus an automatic evaluation metric with a higher value for τ is making predictions that are more similar to the human judgments than an automatic evaluation metric with a lower τ.

We did not include cases where the human ranking was tied for two systems. As the metrics produce absolute scores, compared to five relative ranks in the human assessment, it would be potentially unfair to the metric to count a slightly different metric score as discordant with a tie in the relative human rankings. A tie in automatic metric rank for two translations was counted as discordant with two corresponding non-tied human judgments.

The correlations are shown in Table 9 for translations into English, and Table 10 out of English, sorted by average correlation across the four language pairs. The highest correlation for each language pair and the highest overall average are bolded. For the into English direction SPEDE and METEOR tied for the highest segment-level correlation. METEOR performed the best for the out of English direction, with AMBER doing admirably well in both the into- and the out-of-English directions.

6 Quality Estimation task

Quality estimation aims to provide a quality indicator for machine translated sentences at various granularity levels. It differs from MT evaluation, because quality estimation techniques do not rely on reference translations. Instead, quality estimation is generally addressed using machine learning techniques to predict quality scores. Potential applications of quality estimation include:

- Deciding whether a given translation is good enough for publishing as is
- Informing readers of the target language only whether or not they can rely on a translation
- Filtering out sentences that are not good enough even for post-editing by professional translators
- Selecting the best translation among options from multiple systems.

This shared-task provides a first common ground for development and comparison of quality estimation systems, focusing on sentence-level estimation. It provides training and test datasets, along with evaluation metrics and a baseline system. The goals of this shared task are:

- To identify new and effective quality indicators (features)
- To identify alternative machine learning techniques for the problem
- To test the suitability of the proposed evaluation metrics for quality estimation systems
- To establish the state of the art performance in the field
- To contrast the performance of regression and ranking techniques.

The task provides datasets for a single language pair, text domain and MT system: English-Spanish news texts produced by a phrase-based SMT system (Moses) trained on Europarl and News Commentaries corpora provided in the WMT10 translation task. As training data, translations were manually annotated for quality in terms of post-editing effort (1-5 scores) and were provided together with their source sentences, reference translations, and post-edited translations (Section 6.1). The shared-task consisted on automatically producing quality-estimations for a blind test-set, where English source sentences and their MT-translations were used as inputs. Hidden (and subsequently publicly-released) manual effort-annotations of those translations (obtained in the same fashion as for the training data) were used as reference labels to evaluate the performance of the participating systems (Section 6.1). Participants also had full access to the translation engine-related resources (Section 6.1) and could use any additional external resources. We have also provided a software package to extract baseline quality estimation features (Section 6.3).

Participants could submit up to two systems for two variations of the task: **ranking**, where participants submit a ranking of translations (no ties allowed), without necessarily giving any explicit scores for translations, and **scoring**, where participants submit a score for each sentence (in the [1,5] range). Each of these subtasks is evaluated using specific metrics (Section 6.2).

6.1 Datasets and resources

Training data

The training data used was selected from data available from previous WMT shared-tasks for machine-translation: a subset of the WMT10 English-Spanish test set, and a subset of the WMT09 English-Spanish test set, for a total of 1832 sentences.

The training data consists of the following resources:

- English source sentences
- Spanish machine-translation outputs, created using the SMT Moses engine
- Effort scores, created by using three professional post-editors using guidelines describing Post-Editing (PE) effort from highest effort (score 1) to lowest effort (score 5)
- Post-Editing output, created by a pool of professional post-editors starting from the source sentences and the Moses translations; these PE outputs were created before the effort scores were elicited, and were shown to the PE-effort judges to facilitate their effort estimates
- Spanish translation outputs, created as part of the WMT machine-translation shared-task as reference translations for the English source sentences (independent of any MT output).

The guidelines used by the PE-effort judges to assign scores 1-5 for each of the ⟨source, MT-output, PE-output⟩ triplets are the following:

[1] The MT output is incomprehensible, with little or no information transferred accurately. It cannot be edited, needs to be translated from scratch.

[2] About 50-70% of the MT output needs to be edited. It requires a significant editing effort in order to reach publishable level.

[3] About 25-50% of the MT output needs to be edited. It contains different errors and mistranslations that need to be corrected.

[4] About 10-25% of the MT output needs to be edited. It is generally clear and intelligible.

[5] The MT output is perfectly clear and intelligible. It is not necessarily a perfect translation, but requires little or no editing.

Providing reliable effort estimates turned out to be a difficult task for the PE-effort judges, even in the current set-up (with post edited outputs available for consultation). To eliminate some of the noise from these judgments, we performed an intermediate cleaning step, in which we eliminated the sentences for which the difference between the maximum score and the minimum score assigned between the three judges was > 1. We started the data-creation process from a total of 2000 sentences for the training set, and the final 1832 sentences we selected as training data were the ones that passed through this intermediate cleaning step.

Besides score disagreement, we noticed another trend on the human judgements of PE-effort. Some judges tend to give more moderate scores (in the middle of available range), while others like to commit also to scores that are more in the extremes of the available range. Since the quality estimation task would be negatively influenced by having most of the scores in the middle of the range, we have chosen to compute the final effort scores as an weighted average between the three PE-effort scores, with more weight given to the judges with higher standard deviation from their own mean score. We have used weights 3, 2, and 1 for the three PE-effort judges according to this criterion. There is an additional advantage resulting from this weighted average score: instead of obtaining average numbers only at values x.0, x.33, and x.66 (for unweighted average)[7], the weighted averages are spread more evenly in the range $[1, 5]$.

A few variations of the training data were provided, including version with cases restored and a version detokenized. In addition, engine-internal information from Moses such as phrase and word alignments, detailed model scores, etc. (parameter *-trace*), n-best lists and stack information from the search graph as a word graph (parameter *-output-word-graph*) as produced by the Moses engine were provided.

The rationale behind releasing this engine-internal data was to make it possible for this shared-task to address quality estimation using a glass-box approach, that is, making use of information from the internal workings of the MT engine.

Test data

The test data was a subset of the WMT12 English-Spanish test set, consisting of 442 sentences. The test data consists of the following files:

- English source sentences
- Spanish machine-translation outputs, created using the same SMT Moses engine used to create the training data
- Effort scores, created by using three professional post-editors[8] using guidelines describing PE effort from highest effort (score 1) to lowest effort (score 5)

The first two files were the input for the quality-estimation shared-task participating systems. Since the Moses engine used to create the MT outputs was the same as the one used for generating the training data, the engine-internal resources are the same as the ones we released as part of the training data package.

The effort scores were released after the participants submitted their shared-task submission, and were solely used to evaluate the submissions according to the established metrics. The guidelines used by the PE-effort judges to assign 1-5 scores were the same as the ones used for creating the training data. We have used the same criteria to ensure the consistency of the human judgments. The initial set of candidates consisted of 604 sentences, of which only 442 met this criteria. The final scores used as gold-values have been obtained using the same weighted-average scheme as for the training data.

Resources

In addition to the training and test materials, we made several additional resources that were used for the baseline QE system and/or the SMT system that produced the training and test datasets:

- The SMT training corpus: source and target sides of the corpus used to train the Moses engine. These are a concatenation of the Europarl and the news-commentary data sets from WMT10 that were tokenized, cleaned (removing sentences longer than 80 tokens) and truecased.
- Two Language models: 5-gram LM generated from the interpolation of the two target corpora after tokenization and truecasing (used by Moses) and a trigram LM generated from the two source corpora and filtered to remove singletons (used by the baseline QE system). We also provided unigram, bigram and trigram counts (used in the baseline QE system).
- An IBM Model 1 table that generated by Giza++ using the SMT training corpora.
- A word-alignment file as produced by the *grow-diag-final* heuristic in Moses for the SMT training set.
- A phrase table with word alignment information generated from the parallel corpora.
- The Moses configuration file used for decoding.

[7]These three values are the only ones possible given the cleaning step we perform prior to averaging the scores, which ensures that the difference between the maximum score and the minimum score is at most 1.

[8]The same post-editors that were used to create the training data were used to create the test data.

6.2 Evaluation metrics

Ranking metrics

For the ranking task, we defined a novel metric that provides some advantages over a more traditional ranking metrics like Spearman correlation. Our metric, called DeltaAvg, assumes that the reference test set has a number associated with each entry that represents its extrinsic value. For instance, using the effort scale we described in Section 6.1, we associate a value between 1 and 5 with each sentence, representing the quality of that sentence. Given these values, our metric does not need an explicit reference ranking, the way the Spearman ranking correlation does.[9] The goal of the DeltaAvg metric is to measure how valuable a proposed ranking (which we call a *hypothesis* ranking) is according to the extrinsic values associated with the test entries.

We first define a parameterized version of this metric, called DeltaAvg$[n]$. The following notations are used: for a given entry sentence s, $V(s)$ represents the function that associates an extrinsic value to that entry; we extend this notation to a set S, with $V(S)$ representing the average of all $V(s), s \in S$. Intuitively, $V(S)$ is a quantitative measure of the "quality" of the set S, as induced by the extrinsic values associated with the entries in S. For a set of ranked entries S and a parameter n, we denote by S_1 the first quantile of set S (the highest-ranked entries), S_2 the second quantile, and so on, for n quantiles of equal sizes.[10] We also use the notation $S_{i,j} = \bigcup_{k=i}^{j} S_k$. Using these notations, we define:

$$\text{DeltaAvg}_V[n] = \frac{\sum_{k=1}^{n-1} V(S_{1,k})}{n-1} - V(S) \quad (14)$$

When the valuation function V is clear from the context, we write DeltaAvg$[n]$ for DeltaAvg$_V[n]$. The parameter n represents the number of quantiles we want to split the set S into. For instance, $n = 2$ gives DeltaAvg[2] = $V(S_1) - V(S)$, hence it measures the difference between the quality of the top quantile (top half) S_1 and the overall quality (represented by $V(S)$). For $n = 3$, DeltaAvg[3] = $(V(S_1)+V(S_{1,2})/2-V(S) = ((V(S_1)-V(S))+(V(S_{1,2} - V(S)))/2$, hence it measures an average difference across two cases: between the quality of the top quantile (top third) and the overall quality, and between the quality of the top two quantiles ($S_1 \cup S_2$, top two-thirds) and the overall quality. In general, DeltaAvg$[n]$ measures an average difference in quality across $n-1$ cases, with each case measuring the impact in quality of adding an additional quantile, from top to bottom. Finally, we define:

$$\text{DeltaAvg}_V = \frac{\sum_{n=2}^{N} \text{DeltaAvg}_V[n]}{N-1} \quad (15)$$

where $N = |S|/2$. As before, we write DeltaAvg for DeltaAvg$_V$ when the valuation function V is clear from the context. The DeltaAvg metric is an average across all DeltaAvg$[n]$ values, for those n values for which the resulting quantiles have at least 2 entries (no singleton quantiles). The DeltaAvg metric has some important properties that are desired for a ranking metric (see Section 6.4 for the results of the shared-task that substantiate these claims):

- it is non-parametric (i.e., it does not depend on setting particular parameters)
- it is automatic and deterministic (and therefore consistent)
- it measures the quality of a hypothesis ranking from an extrinsic perspective (as offered by function V)
- its values are interpretable: for a given set of ranked entries, a value DeltaAvg of 0.5 means that, on average, the difference in quality between the top-ranked quantiles and the overall quality is 0.5
- it has a high correlation with the Spearman rank correlation coefficient, which makes it as useful as the Spearman correlation, with the added advantage of its values being extrinsically interpretable.

[9] A reference ranking can be implicitly induced according to these values; if, as in our case, higher values mean better sentences, then the reference ranking is defined such that higher-scored sentences rank higher than lower-scored sentences.

[10] If the size $|S|$ is not divisible by n, then the last quantile S_n is assumed to contain the rest of the entries.

In the rest of this paper, we present results for DeltaAvg using as valuation function V the Post-Editing effort scores, as defined in Section 6.1.

We also report the results of the ranking task using the more-traditional Spearman correlation.

Scoring metrics

For the scoring task, we use two metrics that have been traditionally used for measuring performance for regression tasks: Mean Absolute Error (MAE) as a primary metric, and Root of Mean Squared Error (RMSE) as a secondary metric. For a given test set S with entries $s_i, 1 \leq i \leq |S|$, we denote by $H(s_i)$ the proposed score for entry s_i (hypothesis), and by $V(s_i)$ the reference value for entry s_i (gold-standard value). We formally define our metrics as follows:

$$\text{MAE} = \frac{\sum_{i=1}^{N} |H(s_i) - V(s_i)|}{N} \quad (16)$$

$$\text{RMSE} = \sqrt{\frac{\sum_{i=1}^{N} (H(s_i) - V(s_i))^2}{N}} \quad (17)$$

where $N = |S|$. Both these metrics are non-parametric, automatic and deterministic (and therefore consistent), and extrinsically interpretable. For instance, a MAE value of 0.5 means that, on average, the absolute difference between the hypothesized score and the reference score value is 0.5. The interpretation of RMSE is similar, with the difference that RMSE penalizes larger errors more (via the square function).

6.3 Participants

Eleven teams (listed in Table 11) submitted one or more systems to the shared task, with most teams submitting for both ranking and scoring subtasks. Each team was allowed up to two submissions (for each subtask). In the descriptions below participation in the ranking is denoted (R) and scoring is denoted (S).

Baseline system (R, S): the baseline system used the feature extraction software (also provided to all participants). It analyzed the source and translation files and the SMT training corpus to extract the following 17 system-independent features that were found to be relevant in previous work (Specia et al., 2009):

- number of tokens in the source and target sentences
- average source token length
- average number of occurrences of the target word within the target sentence
- number of punctuation marks in source and target sentences
- LM probability of source and target sentences using language models described in Section 6.1
- average number of translations per source word in the sentence: as given by IBM 1 model thresholded so that $P(t|s) > 0.2$, and so that $P(t|s) > 0.01$ weighted by the inverse frequency of each word in the source side of the SMT training corpus
- percentage of unigrams, bigrams and trigrams in frequency quartiles 1 (lower frequency words) and 4 (higher frequency words) in the source side of the SMT training corpus
- percentage of unigrams in the source sentence seen in the source side of the SMT training corpus

These features are used to train a Support Vector Machine (SVM) regression algorithm using a radial basis function kernel with the LIBSVM package (Chang and Lin, 2011). The γ, ϵ and C parameters were optimized using a grid-search and 5-fold cross validation on the training set. We note that although the system is referred to as a "baseline", it is in fact a strong system. Although it is simple it has proved to be robust across a range of language pairs, MT systems, and text domains. It is a simpler variant of the system used in (Specia, 2011). The rationale behind having such a strong baseline was to push systems to exploit alternative sources of information and combination / learning approaches.

SDLLW (R, S): Both systems use 3 sets of features: the 17 baseline features, 8 system-dependent features from the decoder logs of Moses, and 20 features developed internally. Some of these features made use of additional data and/or resources, such as a secondary

ID	Participating team
PRHLT-UPV	Universitat Politecnica de Valencia, Spain (González-Rubio et al., 2012)
UU	Uppsala University, Sweden (Hardmeier et al., 2012)
SDLLW	SDL Language Weaver, USA (Soricut et al., 2012)
Loria	LORIA Institute, France (Langlois et al., 2012)
UPC	Universitat Politecnica de Catalunya, Spain (Pighin et al., 2012)
DFKI	DFKI, Germany (Avramidis, 2012)
WLV-SHEF	University of Wolverhampton & University of Sheffield, UK (Felice and Specia, 2012)
SJTU	Shanghai Jiao Tong University, China (Wu and Zhao, 2012)
DCU-SYMC	Dublin City University, Ireland & Symantec, Ireland (Rubino et al., 2012)
UEdin	University of Edinburgh, UK (Buck, 2012)
TCD	Trinity College Dublin, Ireland (Moreau and Vogel, 2012)

Table 11: Participants in the WMT12 Quality Evaluation shared task.

MT system that was used as pseudo-reference for the hypothesis, and POS taggers for both languages. Feature-selection algorithms were used to select subsets of features that directly optimize the metrics used in the task. System "SDLLW_M5PbestAvgDelta" uses a resulting 15-feature set optimized towards the AvgDelta metric. It employs an M5P model to learn a decision-tree with only two linear equations. System "SDLLW_SVM" uses a 20-feature set and an SVM epsilon regression model with radial basis function kernel with parameters C, gamma, and epsilon tuned on a development set (305 training instances). The model was trained with 10-fold cross validation and the tuning process was restarted several times using different starting points and step sizes to avoid overfitting. The final model was selected based on its performance on the development set and the number of support vectors.

UU (R, S): System "UU_best" uses the 17 baseline features, plus 82 features from Hardmeier (2011) (with some redundancy and some overlap with baseline features), and constituency trees over input sentences generated by the Stanford parser and dependency trees over both input and output sentences generated by the MaltParser. System "UU_bltk" uses only the 17 baseline features plus constituency and dependency trees as above. The machine learning component in both cases is SVM regression (SVMlight software). For the ranking task, the ranking induced by the regression output is used. The system uses polynomial kernels of degree 2 (UU_best) and 3 (UU_bltk) as well as two different types of tree kernels for constituency and dependency trees, respectively. The SVM margin/error trade-off, the mixture proportion between tree kernels and polynomial kernels and the degree of the polynomial kernels were optimised using grid search with 5-fold cross-validation over the training set.

TCD (R, S): "TCD_M5P-resources-only" uses only the baseline features, while "TCD_M5P-all" uses the baseline and additional features. A number of metrics (used as features in TCD_M5P-all) were proposed which work in the following way: given a sentence to evaluate (source sentence for complexity or target sentence for fluency), it is compared against some reference data using similarity measures (various metrics which compare distributions of n-grams). The training data was used as reference, along with the Google n-grams dataset. Several learning methods were tested using Weka on the training data (10-fold cross-validation). The system submission uses the M5P (regression with decision trees) algorithm which performed best. Contrary to what had been observed on the training data using cross-validation, "TCD_M5P-resources-only" performs better than "TCD_M5P-all" on the test data.

PRHLT-UPV (R, S): The system addresses the task using a regression algorithm with 475 features, including the 17 the baseline features. Most of the features are defined as word scores. Among them, the features obtained form a smoothed naive Bayes classifier have shown to be particularly interesting. Different methods to combine word-level scores into sentence-level features were investigated. For model building, SVM regression was used. Given the large number of features, the training data provided as part of the task was insufficient yielding unstable systems with not so good performance. Different feature selection methods were implemented to determine a subset of relevant features. The final submission used these relevant features to train an SVM system whose parameters were optimized with respect to the final evaluation metrics.

UEDIN (R, S): The system uses the baseline features along with some additional features: binary features for named entities in source using Stanford NER Tagger; binary indicators for occurrence of quotes or parenthetical segments, words in upper case and numbers; geometric mean of target word probabilities and probability of worst scoring word under a Discriminative Word Lexicon Model; Sparse Neural Network directly mapping from source to target (using the vector space model) with source and target side either filtered to relevant words or hashed to reduce dimensionality; number of times at least a 3-gram is seen normalized by sentence length; and Levenshtein distance of either source or translation to closest entry of the SMT training corpus on word or character level. An ensemble of neural networks optimized for RMSE was used for prediction (scoring) and ranking. The contribution of new features was tested by adding them to the baseline features using 5-fold cross-validation. Most features did not result in any improvement over the baseline. The final submission was a combination of all feature sets that showed improvement.

SJTU (R, S): The task is treated as a regression problem using the epsilon-SVM method. All features are extracted from the official data, involving no external NLP tools/resources. Most of them come from the phrase table, decoding data and SMT training data. The focus is on special word relations and special phrase patterns, thus several feature templates on this topic are extracted. Since the training data is not large enough to assign weights to all features, methods for estimating common strings or sequences of words are used. The training data is divided in $3/4$ for training and $1/4$ for development to filter ineffective features. Besides the baseline features, the final submission contains 18 feature templates and about 4 million features in total.

WLV-SHEF (R, S): The systems integrates novel linguistic features from the source and target texts in an attempt to overcome the limitations of existing shallow features for quality estimation. These linguistically-informed features include part-of-speech information, phrase constituency, subject-verb agreement and target lexicon analysis, which are extracted using parsers, corpora and auxiliary resources. Systems are built using epsilon-SVM regression with parameters optimised using 5-fold cross-validation on the training set and two different feature sets: "WLV-SHEF_BL" uses the 17 baseline features plus 70 linguistically inspired features, while "WLV-SHEF_FS" uses a larger set of 70 linguistic plus 77 shallow features (including the baseline). Although results indicate that the models fall slightly below the baseline, further analysis shows that linguistic information is indeed informative and complementary to shallow indicators.

DFKI (R, S): "DFKI_morphPOSibm1LM" (R) is a simple linear interpolation of POS 6-gram language model scores, morpheme 6-gram language model scores, IBM 1 scores (both "direct" and "inverse") for POS 4-grams and for morphemes. The parallel News corpora from WMT10 is used as extra data to train the language model and the IBM 1 model. "DFKI_cfs-plsreg" and "DFKI_grcfs-mars" (S) use a collection of 264 features generated containing the baseline features and additional resources. Numerous methods of feature selection were tested using 10-fold cross validation on the training data, reducing these to 23 feature sets. Several regression and (discretized) classification algorithms were employed to train prediction models. The best-performing models included features derived from PCFG parsing, language quality checking and LM scoring, of both source and target, besides features from the SMT search graph and a few baseline features. "DFKI_cfs-plsreg" uses a Best First correlation-based feature selection technique, trained with Partial Least Squares Regression, while "DFKI_grcfs-mars" uses a Greedy Stepwise correlation-based feature selection technique, trained with multivariate adaptive regression splines.

DCU-SYMC (R, S): Systems are based on a classification approach using a set of features that includes the baseline features. The manually assigned quality scores provided for each MT output in the training set were rounded in order to apply classification algorithms on a limited set of classes (integer values from 1 to 5). Three classifiers were combined by averaging the predicted classes: SVM using sequential minimal optimization and RBF kernel (parameters optimized by grid search), Naive Bayes and Random Forest. "DCU-SYMC_constrained" is based on a set of 70 features derived only from the data provided for the task. These include a set of features which attempt to model translation adequacy using a bilingual topic model built using Latent Dirichlet Allocation. "DCU-SYMC_unconstrained" is based on 308 features including the constrained ones and others extracted using external tools: grammaticality features extracted from the source segments using the TreeTagger part-of-speech tagger, an English precision grammar, the XLE parser and the Brown re-ranking parser and features based on part-of-speech tag counts extracted from the MT output using a Spanish TreeTagger model.

Loria (S): Several numerical or boolean features are computed from the source and target sentences and used to train an SVM regression algorithm with linear ("Loria_SVMlinear") and radial basis function ("Loria_SVMrbf") as kernel. For the radial basis function, a grid search is performed to optimise the parameter γ. The official submission use the baseline features and a number of features proposed in previous work (Raybaud et al., 2011), amounting to 66 features. A feature selection algorithm is used in order to remove non-informative features. No additional data other than that provided for the shared task is considered. The training data is split into a training part (1000 sentences) and a development part (832 sentences) to learn the regression model and optimise the parameters of the regression and for feature selection.

UPC (R, S): The systems use several features on top of the baseline features. These are mostly based on different language models estimated on reference and automatic Spanish translations of the news-v7 corpus. The automatic translations are generated by the system used for the shared task. N-gram LMs are estimated on word forms, POS tags, stop words interleaved by POS tags, stop-word patterns, plus variants in which the POS tags are replaced with the stem or root of each target word. The POS tags on the target side are obtained by projecting source side annotations via automatic alignments. The resulting features are: the perplexity of each additional language model, according to the two translations, and the ratio between the two perplexities. Additionally, features that estimate the likelihood of the projection of dependency parses on the two translations are encoded. For learning, linear SVM regression is used. Optimization was done via 5-fold cross-validation on a development data. Features are encoded by means of their z-scores, i.e. how many standard deviations the observed value is above or below the mean. A variant of the system, "UPC-2" uses an option of SVMLight that removes inconsistent points from the training set and retrains the model until convergence.

6.4 Results

Here we give the official results for the ranking and scoring subtasks followed by a discussion that highlights the main findings of the task.

Ranking subtask

Table 12 gives the results for the ranking subtask. The table is sorted from best to worse using the DeltaAvg metric scores (Equation 15) as primary key and the Spearman correlation scores as secondary key.

The winning submissions for the ranking subtask are SDLLW's M5PbestDeltaAvg and SVM entries, which have DeltaAvg scores of 0.63 and 0.61, respectively. The difference with respect to all the other submissions is statistically significant at $p = 0.05$, using pairwise bootstrap resampling (Koehn, 2004). The state-of-the-art baseline system has a DeltaAvg score of 0.55 (Spearman rank correlation of 0.58). Five other submissions have performances that are not different from the baseline at a statistically-significant level ($p = 0.05$), as shown by the gray area in the middle of Table 12. Three submissions scored higher than the baseline system at $p = 0.05$ (systems above the middle gray area), which indicates that this shared-task succeeded in pushing the state-of-the-art performance to new levels. The range of performance for the submissions in the ranking task varies from a DeltaAvg of 0.65 down to a DeltaAvg of 0.15 (with Spearman values varying from 0.64 down to 0.19).

In addition to the performance of the official submission, we report here results obtained by various oracle methods. The oracle methods make use of various metrics that are associated in a oracle manner to the test input: the gold-label Effort metric for "Oracle Effort", the HTER metric computed against the post-edited translations as reference for "Oracle HTER", and the BLEU metric computed against the same post-edited translations as reference for "Oracle (H)BLEU".[11] The "Oracle Effort" DeltaAvg score of 0.95 gives an upperbound in terms of DeltaAvg for the test set used in this evaluation. It basically indicates that, for this set, the difference in PE effort between the top-quality quantiles and the overall quality is 0.95 on average. We would like to emphasize here that the DeltaAvg metric does not have any a-priori range for its values. The upperbound, for instance, is test-dependent, and therefore an "Oracle Effort" score is useful for understanding the performance level of real system-submissions. The "Oracle HTER" DeltaAvg score of 0.77 is a more realistic upperbound for the current set. Since the HTER metric is considered a good approximation for the effort required in post-editing, ranking the test set based on the HTER scores (from lowest HTER to highest HTER) provides a good oracle comparison point. The oracle based on (H)BLEU gives a lower DeltaAvg score, which can be interpreted to mean that the BLEU metric provides a lower correlation to post-editing effort compared to HTER. We also note here that there is room for improvement between the highest-scoring submission (at DeltaAvg 0.63) and the "Oracle HTER" DeltaAvg score of 0.77. We are not sure if this difference can be bridged completely, but having measured a quantitative difference between the current best-performance and a realistic upperbound is an important achievement of this shared-task.

Scoring subtask

The results for the scoring task are presented in Table 13, sorted from best to worse by using the MAE metric scores (Equation 16) as primary key and the RMSE metric scores (Equation 17) as secondary key.

The winning submission is SDLLW's M5PbestDeltaAvg, with an MAE of 0.61 and an RMSE of 0.75 (the difference with respect to all the other submissions is statistically significant at $p = 0.05$, using pairwise bootstrap resampling (Koehn, 2004)). The strong, state-of-the-art quality-estimation baseline system is measured to have an MAE of 0.69 and RMSE of 0.82, with six other submissions having performances that are not different from the baseline at a statistically-significant level ($p = 0.05$), as shown by the gray area in the middle of Table 13). Five submissions scored higher than the baseline system at $p = 0.05$ (systems above the middle gray area), which indicates that this shared-task also succeeded in pushing the state-of-the-art performance to new

[11] We use the (H)BLEU notation to underscore the use of Post-Edited translations as reference, as opposed to using references that are not the product of a Post-Editing process, as for the traditional BLEU metric.

System ID	DeltaAvg	Spearman Corr
• SDLLW_M5PbestDeltaAvg	0.63	0.64
• SDLLW_SVM	0.61	0.60
UU_bltk	0.58	0.61
UU_best	0.56	0.62
TCD_M5P-resources-only*	0.56	0.56
Baseline (17FFs SVM)	0.55	0.58
PRHLT-UPV	0.55	0.55
UEdin	0.54	0.58
SJTU	0.53	0.53
WLV-SHEF_FS	0.51	0.52
WLV-SHEF_BL	0.50	0.49
DFKI_morphPOSibm1LM	0.46	0.46
DCU-SYMC_unconstrained	0.44	0.41
DCU-SYMC_constrained	0.43	0.41
TCD_M5P-all*	0.42	0.41
UPC_1	0.22	0.26
UPC_2	0.15	0.19
Oracle Effort	0.95	1.00
Oracle HTER	0.77	0.70
Oracle (H)BLEU	0.71	0.62

Table 12: Official results for the ranking subtask of the WMT12 Quality Evaluation shared-task. The winning submissions are indicated by a • (the difference with respect to other systems is statistically significant with $p = 0.05$). The systems in the gray area are not significantly different from the baseline system. Entries with * represent submissions for which a bug-fix was applied after the submission deadline.

System ID	MAE	RMSE
• SDLLW_M5PbestDeltaAvg	0.61	0.75
UU_best	0.64	0.79
SDLLW_SVM	0.64	0.78
UU_bltk	0.64	0.79
Loria_SVMlinear	0.68	0.82
UEdin	0.68	0.82
TCD_M5P-resources-only*	0.68	0.82
Baseline (17FFs SVM)	0.69	0.82
Loria_SVMrbf	0.69	0.83
SJTU	0.69	0.83
WLV-SHEF_FS	0.69	0.85
PRHLT-UPV	0.70	0.85
WLV-SHEF_BL	0.72	0.86
DCU-SYMC_unconstrained	0.75	0.97
DFKI_grcfs-mars	0.82	0.98
DFKI_cfs-plsreg	0.82	0.99
UPC_1	0.84	1.01
DCU-SYMC_constrained	0.86	1.12
UPC_2	0.87	1.04
TCD_M5P-all	2.09	2.32
Oracle Effort	0.00	0.00
Oracle HTER (linear mapping into [1.5-5.0])	0.56	0.73
Oracle (H)BLEU (linear mapping into [1.5-5.0])	0.61	0.84

Table 13: Official results for the scoring subtask of the WMT12 Quality Evaluation shared-task. The winning submission is indicated by a • (the difference with respect to the other submissions is statistically significant at $p = 0.05$). The systems in the gray area are not different from the baseline system at a statistically significant level ($p = 0.05$). Entries with * represent submissions for which a bug-fix was applied after the submission deadline.

levels in terms of absolute scoring. The range of performance for the submissions in the scoring task varies from an MAE of 0.61 up to an MAE of 0.87 (the outlier MAE of 2.09 is reportedly due to bugs).

We also calculate scoring Oracles using the methods used for the ranking Oracles. The difference is that the HTER and (H)BLEU oracles need a way of mapping their scores (which are usually in the $[0, 100]$ range) into the $[1, 5]$ range. For the comparison here, we did the mapping by excluding the 5% top and bottom outlier scores, and then linearly mapping the remaining range into the $[1.5, 5]$ range. The "Oracle Effort" scores are not very indicative in this case. However, the "Oracle HTER" MAE score of 0.56 is a somewhat realistic lowerbound for the current set (although the score could be decreased by a smarter mapping from the HTER range to the Effort range). We argue that since the HTER metric is considered a good approximation for the effort required in post-editing, effort-like scores derived from the HTER score provide a good way to compute oracle scores in a deterministic manner. Note that again the oracle based on (H)BLEU gives a worse MAE score at 0.61, which support the interpretation that the (H)BLEU metric provides a lower correlation to post-editing effort compared to (H)TER. Overall, we consider the MAE values for these HTER and (H)BLEU-based oracles to indicate high error margins. Most notably the performance of the best system gets the same MAE score as the (H)BLEU oracle, at 0.61 MAE. We take this to mean that the scoring task is more difficult compared to the ranking task, since even oracle-based solutions get high error scores.

6.5 Discussion

When looking back at the goals that we identified for this shared-task, most of them have been successfully accomplished. In addition, we have achieved additional ones that were not explicitly stated from the beginning. In this section, we discuss the accomplishments of this shared-task in more detail, starting from the defined goals and beyond.

Identify new and effective quality indicators The vast majority of the participating systems use external resources in addition to those provided for the task, such as parsers, part-of-speech taggers, named entity recognizers, etc. This has resulted in a wide variety of features being used. Many of the novel features have tried to exploit linguistically-oriented features. While some systems did not achieve improvements over the baseline while exploiting such features, others have (the "UU" submissions, for instance, exploiting both constituency and dependency trees).

Another significant set of features that has been previously overlooked is the feature set of the MT decoder. Considering statistical engines, these features are immediately available for quality prediction from the internal trace of the MT decoder (in a glass-box prediction scenario), and its contribution is significant. These features, which reflect the "confidence" of the SMT system on the translations it produces, have been shown to be complementary to other, system-independent (black-box) features. For example, the "SDLLW" submissions incorporate these features, and their feature selection strategy consistently favored this feature set. The power of this set of features alone is enough to yield (when used with an M5P model) outputs that would have been placed 4th in the ranking task and 5th in the scoring task, a remarkable achievement. Another interesting feature used by the "SDLLW" submissions rely on pseudo-references, i.e., translations produced by other MT systems for the same input sentence.

Identify alternative machine learning techniques Although SVM regression was used to compute the baseline performance, the baseline "system" provided for the task consisted solely of a software to extract features, as opposed to a model built using the regression algorithm. The rationale behind this decision was to encourage participants to experiment with alternative methods for combining different quality indicators. This was achieved to a large extent.

The best-performing machine learning techniques were found to be the M5P Regression Trees and the SVM Regression (SVR) models. The merit of the M5P Regression Trees is that it provides compact models that are less prone to overfitting. In contrast, the SVR models can easily overfit given the small amount of training data available and the large numbers of features commonly used. Indeed, many of the submissions that fell below the baseline performance can blame overfitting for (part of) their sub-optimal performance. However, SVR models can achieve high performance through the use of tuning and feature selection techniques to avoid overfitting. Structured learning techniques were successfully used by the "UU" submissions – the second best performing team – to represent parse trees. This seems an interesting direction to encode other sorts of linguistic information about source and translation texts. Other interesting learning techniques have been tried, such as Neural Networks, Partial Least Squares Regression, or multivariate adaptive regression splines, but their performance does not suggest they are strong candidates for learning highly-performing quality-estimation models.

Test the suitability of evaluation metrics for quality estimation DeltaAvg, our proposed metric for measuring ranking performance, proved suitable for scoring the ranking subtask. Its high correlation with the Spearman ranking metric, coupled with its extrinsic interpretability, makes it a preferred choice for future measurements. It is also versatile, in the sense that the its valuation function V can change to reflect different extrinsic measures of quality.

Establish the state of the art performance The results on both the ranking and the scoring subtasks established new state of the art levels on the test set used in this shared task. In addition to these levels, the oracle performance numbers also help understand the current performance level, and how much of a gap in performance there still exists. Additional data points regarding quality estimation performance are needed to establish how stable this measure of the performance gap is.

Contrast the performance of regression and ranking techniques Most of the submissions in the ranking task used the results provided by a regression solution (submitted for the scoring task) to infer the rankings. Also, optimizing for ranking performance via a regression solution seems to result in regression models that perform very well, as in the case of the top-ranked submission.

6.6 Quality Estimation Conclusions

There appear to be significant differences between considering the quality estimation task as a ranking problem versus a scoring problem. The ranking-based approach appears to be somewhat simpler and more easily amenable to automatic solutions, and at the same time provides immediate benefits when integrated into larger applications (see, for instance, the post-editing application described in Specia (2011)). The scoring-based approach is more difficult, as the high error rate even of oracle-based solutions indicates. It is also well-known from human evaluations of MT outputs that human judges also have a difficult time agreeing on absolute-number judgements to translations.

Our experience in creating the current datasets confirms that, even with highly-trained professionals, it is difficult to arrive at consistent judgements. We plan to have future investigations on how to achieve more consistent ways of generating absolute-number scores that reflect the quality of automated translations.

7 Summary

As in previous incarnations of this workshop we carried out an extensive manual and automatic evaluation of machine translation performance, and we used the human judgements that we collected to validate automatic metrics of translation quality. This year was also the debut of a new quality estimation task, which tries to predict the effort involved in having post editors correct MT output. The quality estimation task differs from the metrics task in that it does not involve reference translations.

As in previous years, all data sets generated by this workshop, including the human judgments, system translations and automatic scores, are publicly available for other researchers to analyze.[12]

Acknowledgments

This work was supported in parts by the EuroMatrixPlus project funded by the European Commission (7th Framework Programme), the GALE program of the US Defense Advanced Research Projects Agency, Contract No. HR0011-06-C-0022,

[12]http://statmt.org/wmt12/results.html

the US National Science Foundation under grant IIS-0713448, and the CoSyne project FP7-ICT-4-248531 funded by the European Commission. The views and findings are the authors' alone. Thanks for Adam Lopez for discussions about alternative ways of ranking the overall system scores. The Quality Estimation shared task organizers thank Wilker Aziz for his help with the SMT models and resources, and Mariano Felice for his help with the system for the extraction of baseline features.

References

Eleftherios Avramidis. 2012. Quality estimation for machine translation output using linguistic analysis and decoding features. In *Proceedings of the Seventh Workshop on Statistical Machine Translation*, Montreal, Canada, June. Association for Computational Linguistics.

Ondřej Bojar, Miloš Ercegovčević, Martin Popel, and Omar Zaidan. 2011. A grain of salt for the wmt manual evaluation. In *Proceedings of the Sixth Workshop on Statistical Machine Translation*, pages 1–11, Edinburgh, Scotland, July. Association for Computational Linguistics.

Ondrej Bojar, Bushra Jawaid, and Amir Kamran. 2012. Probes in a taxonomy of factored phrase-based models. In *Proceedings of the Seventh Workshop on Statistical Machine Translation*, Montreal, Canada, June. Association for Computational Linguistics.

Christian Buck. 2012. Black box features for the WMT 2012 quality estimation shared task. In *Proceedings of the Seventh Workshop on Statistical Machine Translation*, Montreal, Canada, June. Association for Computational Linguistics.

Chris Callison-Burch, Cameron Fordyce, Philipp Koehn, Christof Monz, and Josh Schroeder. 2007. (Meta-) evaluation of machine translation. In *Proceedings of the Second Workshop on Statistical Machine Translation (WMT07)*, Prague, Czech Republic.

Chris Callison-Burch, Cameron Fordyce, Philipp Koehn, Christof Monz, and Josh Schroeder. 2008. Further meta-evaluation of machine translation. In *Proceedings of the Third Workshop on Statistical Machine Translation (WMT08)*, Colmbus, Ohio.

Chris Callison-Burch, Philipp Koehn, Christof Monz, and Josh Schroeder. 2009. Findings of the 2009 workshop on statistical machine translation. In *Proceedings of the Fourth Workshop on Statistical Machine Translation (WMT09)*, Athens, Greece.

Chris Callison-Burch, Philipp Koehn, Christof Monz, Kay Peterson, Mark Przybocki, and Omar F. Zaidan. 2010. Findings of the 2010 joint workshop on statistical machine translation and metrics for machine translation. In *Proceedings of the Fourth Workshop on Statistical Machine Translation (WMT10)*, Uppsala, Sweden.

Chris Callison-Burch, Philipp Koehn, Christof Monz, and Omar Zaidan. 2011. Findings of the 2011 workshop on statistical machine translation. In *Proceedings of the Sixth Workshop on Statistical Machine Translation*, pages 22–64, Edinburgh, Scotland, July.

Chris Callison-Burch. 2009. Fast, cheap, and creative: Evaluating translation quality using Amazon's Mechanical Turk. In *Proceedings of the 2009 Conference on Empirical Methods in Natural Language Processing (EMNLP-2009)*, Singapore.

Julio Castillo and Paula Estrella. 2012. Semantic textual similarity for MT evaluation. In *Proceedings of the Seventh Workshop on Statistical Machine Translation*, Montreal, Canada, June. Association for Computational Linguistics.

Chih-Chung Chang and Chih-Jen Lin. 2011. LIBSVM: A library for support vector machines. *ACM Transactions on Intelligent Systems and Technology*, 2:27:1–27:27. Software available at `http://www.csie.ntu.edu.tw/~cjlin/libsvm`.

Boxing Chen, Roland Kuhn, and George Foster. 2012. Improving amber, an MT evaluation metric. In *Proceedings of the Seventh Workshop on Statistical Machine Translation*, Montreal, Canada, June. Association for Computational Linguistics.

Jacob Cohen. 1960. A coefficient of agreement for nominal scales. *Educational and Psychological Measurment*, 20(1):37–46.

Michael Denkowski and Alon Lavie. 2011. Meteor 1.3: Automatic metric for reliable optimization and evaluation of machine translation systems. In *Proceedings of the Sixth Workshop on Statistical Machine Translation*.

Michael Denkowski, Greg Hanneman, and Alon Lavie. 2012. The CMU-avenue French-English translation system. In *Proceedings of the Seventh Workshop on Statistical Machine Translation*, Montreal, Canada, June. Association for Computational Linguistics.

Ondřej Dušek, Zdeněk Žabokrtský, Martin Popel, Martin Majliš, Michal Novák, and David Mareček. 2012. Formemes in English-Czech deep syntactic mt. In *Proceedings of the Seventh Workshop on Statistical Machine Translation*, Montreal, Canada, June. Association for Computational Linguistics.

Mariano Felice and Lucia Specia. 2012. Linguistic features for quality estimation. In *Proceedings of the Seventh Workshop on Statistical Machine Translation*, Montreal, Canada, June. Association for Computational Linguistics.

Mark Fishel, Rico Sennrich, Maja Popović, and Ondřej Bojar. 2012. TerrorCat: a translation error categorization-based MT quality metric. In *Proceedings of the Seventh Workshop on Statistical Machine Translation*, Montreal, Canada, June. Association for Computational Linguistics.

Lluis Formiga, Carlos A. Henríquez Q., Adolfo Hernández, José B. Mariño, Enric Monte, and José A. R. Fonollosa. 2012. The TALP-UPC phrase-based translation systems for WMT12: Morphology simplification and domain adaptation. In *Proceedings of the Seventh Workshop on Statistical Machine Translation*, Montreal, Canada, June. Association for Computational Linguistics.

Juri Ganitkevitch, Yuan Cao, Jonathan Weese, Matt Post, and Chris Callison-Burch. 2012. Joshua 4.0: Packing, PRO, and paraphrases. In *Proceedings of the Seventh Workshop on Statistical Machine Translation*, Montreal, Canada, June. Association for Computational Linguistics.

Ulrich Germann. 2012. Syntax-aware phrase-based statistical machine translation: System description. In *Proceedings of the Seventh Workshop on Statistical Machine Translation*, Montreal, Canada, June. Association for Computational Linguistics.

Jesús González-Rubio, Alberto Sanchís, and Francisco Casacuberta. 2012. PRHLT submission to the WMT12 quality estimation task. In *Proceedings of the Seventh Workshop on Statistical Machine Translation*, Montreal, Canada, June. Association for Computational Linguistics.

Francisco Guzman, Preslav Nakov, Ahmed Thabet, and Stephan Vogel. 2012. QCRI at WMT12: Experiments in Spanish-English and German-English machine translation of news text. In *Proceedings of the Seventh Workshop on Statistical Machine Translation*, Montreal, Canada, June. Association for Computational Linguistics.

Christian Hardmeier, Joakim Nivre, and Jörg Tiedemann. 2012. Tree kernels for machine translation quality estimation. In *Proceedings of the Seventh Workshop on Statistical Machine Translation*, Montreal, Canada, June. Association for Computational Linguistics.

Christian Hardmeier. 2011. Improving machine translation quality prediction with syntactic tree kernels. In *Proceedings of the 15th conference of the European Association for Machine Translation*, pages 233–240, Leuven, Belgium.

Matthias Huck, Stephan Peitz, Markus Freitag, Malte Nuhn, and Hermann Ney. 2012. The RWTH aachen machine translation system for WMT 2012. In *Proceedings of the Seventh Workshop on Statistical Machine Translation*, Montreal, Canada, June. Association for Computational Linguistics.

Sabine Hunsicker, Chen Yu, and Christian Federmann. 2012. Machine learning for hybrid machine translation. In *Proceedings of the Seventh Workshop on Statistical Machine Translation*, Montreal, Canada, June. Association for Computational Linguistics.

Philipp Koehn and Barry Haddow. 2012. Towards effective use of training data in statistical machine translation. In *Proceedings of the Seventh Workshop on Statistical Machine Translation*, Montreal, Canada, June. Association for Computational Linguistics.

Philipp Koehn and Christof Monz. 2006. Manual and automatic evaluation of machine translation between European languages. In *Proceedings of NAACL 2006 Workshop on Statistical Machine Translation*, New York, New York.

Philipp Koehn. 2004. Statistical Significance Tests for Machine Translation Evaluation. In *Proceedings of the Empirical Methods in Natural Language Processing Conference*.

J. Richard Landis and Gary G. Koch. 1977. The measurement of observer agreement for categorical data. *Biometrics*, 33:159–174.

David Langlois, Sylvain Raybaud, and Kamel Smaïli. 2012. LORIA system for the WMT12 quality estimation shared task. In *Proceedings of the Seventh Workshop on Statistical Machine Translation*, Montreal, Canada, June. Association for Computational Linguistics.

Hai-Son Le, Thomas Lavergne, Alexandre Allauzen, Marianna Apidianaki, Li Gong, Aurélien Max, Artem Sokolov, Guillaume Wisniewski, and François Yvon. 2012. LIMSI @ WMT12. In *Proceedings of the Seventh Workshop on Statistical Machine Translation*, Montreal, Canada, June. Association for Computational Linguistics.

Verónica López-Ludeña, Rubén San-Segundo, and Juan M. Montero. 2012. UPM system for WMT 2012. In *Proceedings of the Seventh Workshop on Statistical Machine Translation*, Montreal, Canada, June. Association for Computational Linguistics.

Adam Lopez. 2012. Putting human assessments of machine translation systems in order. In *Proceedings of the Seventh Workshop on Statistical Machine Translation*, Montreal, Canada, June. Association for Computational Linguistics.

Matouš Macháček and Ondej Bojar. 2011. Approximating a deep-syntactic metric for mt evaluation and tuning. In *Proceedings of the Sixth Workshop on Statistical Machine Translation*, pages 373–379, Edinburgh, Scotland, July. Association for Computational Linguistics.

Freitag Markus, Peitz Stephan, Huck Matthias, Ney Hermann, Niehues Jan, Herrmann Teresa, Waibel Alex,

Hai-son Le, Lavergne Thomas, Allauzen Alexandre, Buschbeck Bianka, Crego Joseph Maria, and Senellart Jean. 2012. Joint WMT 2012 submission of the QUAERO project. In *Proceedings of the Seventh Workshop on Statistical Machine Translation*, Montreal, Canada, June. Association for Computational Linguistics.

Alexander Molchanov. 2012. PROMT deephybrid system for WMT12 shared translation task. In *Proceedings of the Seventh Workshop on Statistical Machine Translation*, Montreal, Canada, June. Association for Computational Linguistics.

Erwan Moreau and Carl Vogel. 2012. Quality estimation: an experimental study using unsupervised similarity measures. In *Proceedings of the Seventh Workshop on Statistical Machine Translation*, Montreal, Canada, June. Association for Computational Linguistics.

Jan Niehues, Yuqi Zhang, Mohammed Mediani, Teresa Herrmann, Eunah Cho, and Alex Waibel. 2012. The karlsruhe institute of technology translation systems for the WMT 2012. In *Proceedings of the Seventh Workshop on Statistical Machine Translation*, Montreal, Canada, June. Association for Computational Linguistics.

Daniele Pighin, Meritxell González, and Lluís Màrquez. 2012. The upc submission to the WMT 2012 shared task on quality estimation. In *Proceedings of the Seventh Workshop on Statistical Machine Translation*, Montreal, Canada, June. Association for Computational Linguistics.

Maja Popovic. 2012. Class error rates for evaluation of machine translation output. In *Proceedings of the Seventh Workshop on Statistical Machine Translation*, Montreal, Canada, June. Association for Computational Linguistics.

Sylvain Raybaud, David Langlois, and Kamel Smaïli. 2011. "This sentence is wrong." Detecting errors in machine-translated sentences. *Machine Translation*, 25(1):1–34.

Majid Razmara, Baskaran Sankaran, Ann Clifton, and Anoop Sarkar. 2012. Kriya - the SFU system for translation task at WMT-12. In *Proceedings of the Seventh Workshop on Statistical Machine Translation*, Montreal, Canada, June. Association for Computational Linguistics.

Rudolf Rosa, David Mareček, and Ondřej Dušek. 2012. DEPFIX: A system for automatic correction of czech MT outputs. In *Proceedings of the Seventh Workshop on Statistical Machine Translation*, Montreal, Canada, June. Association for Computational Linguistics.

Raphael Rubino, Jennifer Foster, Joachim Wagner, Johann Roturier, Rasul Samad Zadeh Kaljahi, and Fred Hollowood. 2012. DCU-Symantec submission for the WMT 2012 quality estimation task. In *Proceedings of the Seventh Workshop on Statistical Machine Translation*, Montreal, Canada, June. Association for Computational Linguistics.

Christophe Servan, Patrik Lambert, Anthony Rousseau, Holger Schwenk, and Loïc Barrault. 2012. LIUM's smt machine translation systems for WMT 2012. In *Proceedings of the Seventh Workshop on Statistical Machine Translation*, Montreal, Canada, June. Association for Computational Linguistics.

Xingyi Song and Trevor Cohn. 2011. Regression and ranking based optimisation for sentence level MT evaluation. In *Proceedings of the Sixth Workshop on Statistical Machine Translation*.

Radu Soricut, Nguyen Bach, and Ziyuan Wang. 2012. The SDL Language Weaver systems in the WMT12 quality estimation shared task. In *Proceedings of the Seventh Workshop on Statistical Machine Translation*, Montreal, Canada, June. Association for Computational Linguistics.

Lucia Specia, Marco Turchi, Nicola Cancedda, Marc Dymetman, and Nello Cristianini. 2009. Estimating the Sentence-Level Quality of Machine Translation Systems. In *Proceedings of the 13th Conference of the European Association for Machine Translation*, pages 28–37, Barcelona.

Lucia Specia. 2011. Exploiting Objective Annotations for Measuring Translation Post-editing Effort. In *Proceedings of the 15th Conference of the European Association for Machine Translation*, pages 73–80, Leuven.

Aleš Tamchyna, Petra Galuščáková, Amir Kamran, Miloš Stanojević, and Ondřej Bojar. 2012. Selecting data for English-to-Czech machine translation. In *Proceedings of the Seventh Workshop on Statistical Machine Translation*, Montreal, Canada, June. Association for Computational Linguistics.

David Vilar. 2012. DFKI's smt system for WMT 2012. In *Proceedings of the Seventh Workshop on Statistical Machine Translation*, Montreal, Canada, June. Association for Computational Linguistics.

Mengqiu Wang and Christopher Manning. 2012. SPEDE: Probabilistic edit distance metrics for MT evaluation. In *Proceedings of the Seventh Workshop on Statistical Machine Translation*, Montreal, Canada, June. Association for Computational Linguistics.

Eric Wehrli, Luka Nerima, and Yves Scherrer. 2009. Deep linguistic multilingual translation and bilingual dictionaries. In *Proceedings of the Fourth Workshop on Statistical Machine Translation*, pages 90–94.

Philip Williams and Philipp Koehn. 2012. GHKM rule extraction and scope-3 parsing in Moses. In *Proceedings of the Seventh Workshop on Statistical Machine*

Translation, Montreal, Canada, June. Association for Computational Linguistics.

Chunyang Wu and Hai Zhao. 2012. Regression with phrase indicators for estimating MT quality. In *Proceedings of the Seventh Workshop on Statistical Machine Translation*, Montreal, Canada, June. Association for Computational Linguistics.

Daniel Zeman. 2012. Data issues of the multilingual translation matrix. In *Proceedings of the Seventh Workshop on Statistical Machine Translation*, Montreal, Canada, June. Association for Computational Linguistics.

	CU-BOJAR	JHU	ONLINE-A	ONLINE-B	UEDIN	UK
CU-BOJAR	–	.29⋆	.43	**.53**⋆	**.47**⋆	.31⋆
JHU	**.59**⋆	–	**.59**⋆	**.67**⋆	**.65**⋆	**.44**⋆
ONLINE-A	**.44**	.28⋆	–	**.52**⋆	**.46**⋆	.32⋆
ONLINE-B	.36⋆	.23⋆	.34⋆	–	.38⋆	.25⋆
UEDIN	.36⋆	.23⋆	.36⋆	**.48**⋆	–	.27⋆
UK	**.56**⋆	.33⋆	**.56**⋆	**.63**⋆	**.60**⋆	–
> others	0.53	0.32	0.53	**0.65**	0.60	0.37

Table 14: Head to head comparison for Czech-English systems

A Pairwise System Comparisons by Human Judges

Tables 14–21 show pairwise comparisons between systems for each language pair. The numbers in each of the tables' cells indicate the percentage of times that the system in that column was judged to be better than the system in that row. Bolding indicates the winner of the two systems. The difference between 100 and the sum of the complementary cells is the percent of time that the two systems were judged to be equal.

Because there were so many systems and data conditions the significance of each pairwise comparison needs to be quantified. We applied the Sign Test to measure which comparisons indicate genuine differences (rather than differences that are attributable to chance). In the following tables ⋆ indicates statistical significance at $p \leq 0.10$, † indicates statistical significance at $p \leq 0.05$, and ‡ indicates statistical significance at $p \leq 0.01$, according to the Sign Test.

Each table contains a final row showing how often a system was ranked to be > than the others. As suggested by Bojar et al. (2011) present, this is calculated ignoring ties as:

$$\text{score}(s) = \frac{\text{win}(s)}{\text{win}(s) + \text{loss}(s)} \tag{18}$$

B Automatic Scores

Tables 29–36 give the automatic scores for each of the systems.

	COMMERCIAL2	CU-BOJAR	CU-DEPFIX	CU-POOR-COMB	CU-TAMCH	CU-TECTOMT	JHU	ONLINE-A	ONLINE-B	COMMERCIAL1	SFU	UEDIN	UK
COMMERCIAL2	–	**.48⋆**	**.56⋆**	**.43**	**.49†**	**.50⋆**	.32⋆	**.49†**	**.54⋆**	.36	.38‡	**.50†**	.42
CU-BOJAR	.33⋆	–	**.49†**	.29†	**.26**	.39	.26⋆	.40	**.51⋆**	.37‡	.27⋆	**.43**	.33⋆
CU-DEPFIX	.28⋆	.36†	–	.26⋆	.30⋆	.32⋆	.18⋆	.31⋆	.13⋆	.33⋆	.21⋆	.31⋆	.25⋆
CU-POOR-COMB	.42	**.40†**	**.59⋆**	–	**.41⋆**	**.51⋆**	.34⋆	**.49†**	**.57⋆**	**.45**	.33†	**.47⋆**	.42
CU-TAMCH	.38†	.24	**.51⋆**	.27⋆	–	.39	.22⋆	.42	**.47†**	.38†	.28⋆	**.39**	.28⋆
CU-TECTOMT	.32⋆	**.42**	**.49⋆**	.33⋆	**.47**	–	.24⋆	.42	**.46†**	.36†	.33⋆	**.46**	.40
JHU	**.54⋆**	**.59⋆**	**.69⋆**	**.50⋆**	**.62⋆**	**.60⋆**	–	**.59⋆**	**.61⋆**	**.52⋆**	**.44**	**.62⋆**	**.48⋆**
ONLINE-A	.36†	**.41**	**.51⋆**	.36†	**.43**	**.43**	.24⋆	–	**.51⋆**	.40	.26⋆	**.45**	.32⋆
ONLINE-B	.32⋆	.34⋆	**.24⋆**	.28⋆	.35†	.35†	.22⋆	.33⋆	–	.31⋆	.23⋆	.33⋆	.22⋆
COMMERCIAL1	**.41**	**.48‡**	**.55⋆**	.41	**.50†**	**.49†**	.36⋆	**.46**	**.54⋆**	–	.30⋆	**.48**	.41
SFU	**.47‡**	**.56⋆**	**.64⋆**	**.47†**	**.55⋆**	**.52⋆**	.36	**.53⋆**	**.64⋆**	**.56⋆**	–	**.58⋆**	**.48†**
UEDIN	.36†	.36	**.50⋆**	.29⋆	.38	.43	.24⋆	.37	**.48⋆**	.40	.25⋆	–	.30⋆
UK	**.43**	**.47⋆**	**.59⋆**	**.43**	**.52⋆**	**.44**	.26⋆	**.50⋆**	**.59⋆**	**.47**	.35†	**.52⋆**	–
> others	0.46	0.54	**0.66**	0.44	0.56	0.53	0.32	0.53	0.63	0.48	0.36	0.56	0.44

Table 15: Head to head comparison for English-Czech systems

	ITS-LATL	JHU	KIT	LIMSI	LIUM	ONLINE-A	ONLINE-B	RBMT-4	RBMT-3	ONLINE-C	RBMT-1	PROMT	RWTH	UEDIN	UK
ITS-LATL	–	**.49‡**	**.54⋆**	**.55⋆**	**.53⋆**	**.59⋆**	**.58⋆**	**.38**	**.47†**	.32	**.45†**	**.47⋆**	**.62⋆**	**.53⋆**	**.48**
JHU	.35‡	–	**.47⋆**	**.55⋆**	**.42**	**.45**	**.55⋆**	.36	**.49‡**	.37	**.46**	**.46‡**	**.47⋆**	**.46†**	.29
KIT	.25⋆	.25⋆	–	**.37**	.29‡	.28‡	**.39**	.27⋆	.35	.30†	.32†	.33	**.36**	.24†	.22⋆
LIMSI	.23⋆	.23⋆	.34	–	.26	.21⋆	.29‡	.25⋆	.29†	.19⋆	.19⋆	.32†	.22†	.29	.16⋆
LIUM	.25⋆	.36	**.42‡**	**.34**	–	.27†	**.46‡**	.21⋆	.40	.25⋆	.37	.34	**.35**	.29	.30‡
ONLINE-A	.22⋆	.33	**.40‡**	**.45⋆**	**.42†**	–	**.44†**	.26⋆	**.43**	.33†	.38	.33	**.47⋆**	**.35**	.30‡
ONLINE-B	.20⋆	.22⋆	.33	**.43‡**	.32‡	.29†	–	.27⋆	.36	.26⋆	.33	.34	**.39**	.29‡	.24⋆
RBMT-4	.37	**.47**	**.56⋆**	**.60⋆**	**.60⋆**	**.55⋆**	**.52⋆**	–	**.41**	.36	**.39**	**.40**	**.58⋆**	**.51†**	**.42**
RBMT-3	.30†	.35‡	**.43**	**.45†**	.40	.39	**.37**	.34	–	.27⋆	.29	**.23**	**.55⋆**	**.42**	.34†
ONLINE-C	**.36**	**.46**	**.46†**	**.55⋆**	**.49⋆**	**.50†**	**.58⋆**	**.38**	**.48⋆**	–	**.45‡**	**.43**	**.62⋆**	**.45**	.39
RBMT-1	.28†	.36	**.49†**	**.58⋆**	**.40**	**.42**	**.44**	.35	**.38**	.31‡	–	**.41**	**.45**	**.37**	.30†
PROMT	.20⋆	.34‡	**.41**	**.50†**	**.46**	**.40**	**.40**	.34	.22	.33	.32	–	**.48†**	**.41**	.27⋆
RWTH	.22⋆	.28⋆	.34	**.37†**	.31	.28⋆	.32	.27⋆	.26⋆	.22⋆	.34	.31†	–	.29	.17⋆
UEDIN	.28⋆	.29†	**.40†**	**.39**	**.34**	.35	**.42‡**	.31†	.39	.34	.36	.34	**.34**	–	.27⋆
UK	.37	**.36**	**.53⋆**	**.53⋆**	**.44‡**	**.43‡**	**.48⋆**	.38	**.52†**	.39	**.44†**	**.46⋆**	**.52⋆**	**.46⋆**	–
> others	0.36	0.44	0.59	**0.66**	0.55	0.51	0.6	0.39	0.52	0.39	0.48	0.51	0.62	0.53	0.4

Table 16: Head to head comparison for English-French systems

	DFKI-BERLIN	DFKI-HUNSICKER	JHU	KIT	LIMSI	ONLINE-A	ONLINE-B	RBMT-4	RBMT-3	ONLINE-C	RBMT-1	RWTH	UEDIN-WILLIAMS	UEDIN	UK
DFKI-BERLIN	–	**.62⋆**	**.58⋆**	**.64⋆**	**.71⋆**	**.68⋆**	**.80⋆**	**.68⋆**	**.71⋆**	**.58⋆**	**.65⋆**	**.62⋆**	**.64⋆**	**.61⋆**	**.60⋆**
DFKI-HUNSICKER	.28⋆	–	.42	**.48**	**.51‡**	**.47**	**.52†**	**.49⋆**	**.57⋆**	.38	**.53⋆**	.39	.39	.41	.39
JHU	.24⋆	**.45**	–	**.43†**	**.43**	**.47‡**	**.62⋆**	**.56⋆**	**.60⋆**	**.46**	**.47‡**	**.46†**	**.47†**	.39	**.42**
KIT	.22⋆	.41	.27†	–	**.39**	**.45**	**.60⋆**	**.54⋆**	**.58⋆**	.37	**.47**	.33	**.43**	**.39**	.26⋆
LIMSI	.15⋆	.37‡	.34	.36	–	**.47**	**.49‡**	.43	**.43**	.35	**.48**	.36	**.37**	.32	.31⋆
ONLINE-A	.20⋆	.37	.35‡	.41	.39	–	**.45†**	.42	**.51†**	.38	**.49**	.42	.40	.37	.36‡
ONLINE-B	.15⋆	.35†	.26⋆	.27⋆	.35‡	.30†	–	**.45**	.35‡	.29⋆	.41	.30⋆	.34⋆	.30⋆	.18⋆
RBMT-4	.25⋆	.22⋆	.31⋆	.31⋆	**.45**	**.45**	.42	–	.41	.38	.40	.44	.35†	.36†	.36†
RBMT-3	.18⋆	.27⋆	.24⋆	.28⋆	.38	.36†	**.49‡**	.41	–	.33⋆	.26⋆	.29⋆	.28⋆	.31⋆	.34†
ONLINE-C	.27⋆	**.47**	.35	**.49**	**.46**	**.44**	**.63⋆**	**.48**	**.55⋆**	–	**.49†**	.40	**.43**	.43	**.46**
RBMT-1	.19⋆	.30⋆	.33‡	.41	.41	.39	**.45**	**.45**	**.50⋆**	.32†	–	.34†	.40	.39	.39
RWTH	.20⋆	**.43**	.30†	**.45**	**.45**	**.44**	**.58⋆**	**.50**	**.58⋆**	**.43**	**.53†**	–	**.41**	**.40**	**.41**
UEDIN-WILLIAMS	.20⋆	**.46**	.30†	.36	.36	**.45**	**.54⋆**	**.52†**	**.54⋆**	.41	**.46**	.38	–	.32	.30†
UEDIN	.20⋆	**.45**	**.40**	.38	**.43**	**.48**	**.56⋆**	**.56†**	**.53⋆**	**.47**	**.48**	.29	**.39**	–	.35
UK	.25⋆	**.49**	.40	**.45⋆**	**.51⋆**	**.49‡**	**.64⋆**	**.51†**	**.52†**	.44	**.47**	.34	**.48†**	**.40**	–
> others	0.25	0.48	0.43	0.50	0.55	0.54	**0.64**	0.58	0.63	0.47	0.56	0.47	0.51	0.47	0.45

Table 17: Head to head comparison for English-German systems

	JHU	ONLINE-A	ONLINE-B	RBMT-4	RBMT-3	ONLINE-C	RBMT-1	PROMT	UEDIN	UK	UPC
JHU	–	**.52⋆**	**.59⋆**	**.50⋆**	**.58⋆**	**.48⋆**	**.49‡**	**.56⋆**	**.48⋆**	**.44†**	**.52⋆**
ONLINE-A	.27⋆	–	**.45**	.34⋆	**.44**	.31⋆	.31⋆	**.44**	.37	.28⋆	.37
ONLINE-B	.21⋆	.37	–	.28⋆	.35‡	.25⋆	.28⋆	.31⋆	.30⋆	.23⋆	.31⋆
RBMT-4	.35⋆	**.52⋆**	**.56⋆**	–	**.49†**	.39	**.40**	**.46†**	**.45**	.38‡	**.45**
RBMT-3	.26⋆	.39	**.46‡**	.34†	–	.32⋆	.28⋆	.24	.34†	.32⋆	.37
ONLINE-C	.33⋆	**.54⋆**	**.61⋆**	**.40**	**.47⋆**	–	**.43**	**.50⋆**	**.50⋆**	**.42**	**.48**
RBMT-1	.39‡	**.51⋆**	**.61⋆**	.39	**.49⋆**	.34	–	**.47†**	**.50†**	.39	**.46**
PROMT	.28⋆	.41	**.51⋆**	.33†	**.29**	.33⋆	.34†	–	.42	.32⋆	.40
UEDIN	.25⋆	**.41**	**.48⋆**	.38	**.47†**	.30⋆	.35†	**.43**	–	.28⋆	**.39**
UK	.31†	**.52⋆**	**.57⋆**	**.48‡**	**.53⋆**	.42	**.44**	**.52⋆**	**.42⋆**	–	**.50⋆**
UPC	.24⋆	**.40**	**.53⋆**	.40	**.43**	.39	.39	**.46**	.36	.28⋆	–
> others	0.36	0.56	**0.65**	0.46	0.58	0.43	0.45	0.55	0.52	0.41	0.52

Table 18: Head to head comparison for English-Spanish systems

	CMU	JHU	KIT	LIMSI	LIUM	ONLINE-A	ONLINE-B	RBMT-4	RBMT-3	ONLINE-C	RBMT-1	RWTH	SFU	UEDIN	UK
CMU	–	.34‡	.32	**.46**	.35	.41	.39	.30⋆	.36	.29⋆	.35†	.32	.28⋆	**.45**	.33‡
JHU	**.50‡**	–	**.63⋆**	**.55⋆**	**.53⋆**	**.63⋆**	**.57⋆**	**.43**	.42	.31⋆	**.46**	**.52‡**	**.43**	**.53†**	**.43**
KIT	**.40**	.21⋆	–	.36	.30	.35	**.44**	.33⋆	.33†	.23⋆	.31⋆	.25⋆	.28⋆	.23⋆	.30†
LIMSI	.35	.26⋆	**.37**	–	.31⋆	.35	.40	.29⋆	.32†	.23⋆	.33†	.29⋆	.28⋆	.29	.23⋆
LIUM	**.47**	.25⋆	**.43**	**.53⋆**	–	**.44**	**.42**	.36	.43	.28⋆	.38	.38	.32‡	.40	.42
ONLINE-A	**.45**	.22⋆	**.41**	**.47**	.40	–	**.41**	.30⋆	.25⋆	.28⋆	.23⋆	.40	.27⋆	.40	.25⋆
ONLINE-B	**.45**	.32⋆	.38	**.42**	.41	.39	–	.34†	.39	.30⋆	.33⋆	.30⋆	.34†	**.44**	.32†
RBMT-4	**.56⋆**	.40	**.54⋆**	**.61⋆**	**.48**	**.54⋆**	**.54†**	–	**.43**	.31†	**.48†**	**.45**	**.42**	**.52†**	**.46**
RBMT-3	**.50**	**.46**	**.53†**	**.53†**	**.46**	**.54⋆**	**.47**	.33	–	.28⋆	.40	**.53‡**	**.52**	**.50**	**.48**
ONLINE-C	**.59⋆**	**.57⋆**	**.72⋆**	**.66⋆**	**.59⋆**	**.60⋆**	**.61⋆**	**.45†**	**.54⋆**	–	**.58⋆**	**.65⋆**	**.53†**	**.66⋆**	**.58⋆**
RBMT-1	**.54†**	.43	**.58⋆**	**.54†**	**.48**	**.62⋆**	**.55⋆**	.31†	**.44**	.20⋆	–	**.47**	.41	**.56†**	.38
RWTH	**.39**	.35‡	**.50⋆**	**.52⋆**	**.43**	**.50**	**.55⋆**	.42	.37‡	.23⋆	.40	–	.34†	.36	.29⋆
SFU	**.57⋆**	.38	**.55⋆**	**.54⋆**	**.48‡**	**.55⋆**	**.51†**	.42	.38	.35†	**.45**	**.50†**	–	.41	**.46**
UEDIN	.37	.32†	**.42⋆**	**.42**	.40	**.43**	.40	.34†	.40	.24⋆	.36†	**.39**	.41	–	.29⋆
UK	**.50‡**	.40	**.48†**	**.59⋆**	**.44**	**.58⋆**	**.50†**	.42	.41	.35⋆	**.49**	**.53⋆**	.35	**.51⋆**	–
> others	0.57	0.41	0.61	**0.63**	0.52	0.59	0.57	0.43	0.46	0.32	0.46	0.52	0.44	0.55	0.44

Table 19: Head to head comparison for French-English systems

	DFKI-BERLIN	JHU	KIT	LIMSI	ONLINE-A	ONLINE-B	RBMT-4	RBMT-3	ONLINE-C	RBMT-1	QCRI	QUAERO	RWTH	UEDIN	UG	UK
DFKI-BERLIN	–	.38	**.49**	**.52†**	**.57⋆**	**.65⋆**	**.55†**	**.62⋆**	**.50**	**.49**	**.51†**	**.66⋆**	**.53⋆**	**.61⋆**	.17⋆	.37
JHU	**.45**	–	**.60⋆**	**.66⋆**	**.66⋆**	**.69⋆**	**.57⋆**	**.60⋆**	**.52**	**.62⋆**	**.58⋆**	**.67⋆**	**.59⋆**	**.62⋆**	.21⋆	**.37**
KIT	.36	.16⋆	–	**.47**	**.60⋆**	**.50**	.41	**.50**	.31⋆	.39	.32	**.36**	.32	**.39**	.15⋆	.26⋆
LIMSI	.30†	.14⋆	.35	–	**.49‡**	**.57⋆**	**.49**	**.54**	.34†	.33†	**.43**	.31	**.44**	**.49†**	.14⋆	.30†
ONLINE-A	.32⋆	.20⋆	.22⋆	.32‡	–	**.39**	.30⋆	.44	.20⋆	.30⋆	.37	.35‡	.32‡	.31†	.16⋆	.29⋆
ONLINE-B	.25⋆	.21⋆	.38	.29⋆	.38	–	.27⋆	.39	.31⋆	.37	.30†	.43	.34	.33†	.12⋆	.24⋆
RBMT-4	.33†	.33⋆	**.49**	.44	**.57⋆**	**.63⋆**	–	**.46**	.26⋆	.40	**.53‡**	**.51†**	**.56‡**	**.48**	.21⋆	.32⋆
RBMT-3	.26⋆	.30⋆	.39	.40	**.45**	**.45**	.32	–	.35	.36	.34‡	**.48**	.33⋆	.41	.13⋆	.23⋆
ONLINE-C	.36	.37	**.58⋆**	**.54†**	**.70⋆**	**.62⋆**	**.57⋆**	**.50**	–	**.53†**	**.48**	**.57⋆**	**.55‡**	**.58⋆**	.14⋆	**.45**
RBMT-1	.41	.32⋆	**.48**	**.55†**	**.64⋆**	**.52**	**.42**	**.47**	.34†	–	**.51**	**.49**	**.48**	**.45**	.15⋆	.25⋆
QCRI	.31†	.26⋆	**.43**	.37	**.48**	**.51†**	.36‡	**.52‡**	.43	.38	–	**.48⋆**	**.48†**	**.45‡**	.14⋆	.23⋆
QUAERO	.18⋆	.19⋆	.29	**.33**	**.51‡**	.43	.33†	.42	.31⋆	.37	.23⋆	–	.34	**.48†**	.09⋆	.16⋆
RWTH	.29⋆	.25⋆	**.38**	.34	**.51‡**	**.48**	.37‡	**.58⋆**	.38‡	.40	.29†	**.39**	–	**.44**	.20⋆	.24⋆
UEDIN	.24⋆	.20⋆	.38	.30†	**.55†**	**.52†**	.42	**.44**	.35⋆	.37	.29‡	.32†	.38	–	.08⋆	.22⋆
UG	**.68⋆**	**.61⋆**	**.72⋆**	**.76⋆**	**.76⋆**	**.82⋆**	**.72⋆**	**.80⋆**	**.70⋆**	**.76⋆**	**.73⋆**	**.76⋆**	**.73⋆**	**.84⋆**	–	**.57⋆**
UK	**.43**	.37	**.48⋆**	**.48†**	**.54⋆**	**.62⋆**	**.57⋆**	**.64⋆**	.44	**.59⋆**	**.49⋆**	**.58⋆**	**.51⋆**	**.56⋆**	.20⋆	–
> others	0.40	0.34	0.55	0.54	**0.65**	**0.65**	0.50	0.60	0.43	0.51	0.52	0.61	0.56	0.6	0.17	0.37

Table 20: Head to head comparison for German-English systems

	GTH-UPM	JHU	ONLINE-A	ONLINE-B	RBMT-4	RBMT-3	ONLINE-C	RBMT-1	QCRI	UEDIN	UK	UPC
GTH-UPM	–	**.41**	**.50**†	**.52**†	.38	**.46**	.32⋆	.35⋆	**.44**†	**.46**	.17⋆	.41
JHU	.37	–	**.54**⋆	**.56**⋆	.44	**.48**	.39	.39	**.47**†	**.50**⋆	.15⋆	**.47**†
ONLINE-A	.34†	.31⋆	–	.43	.28⋆	.38‡	.29⋆	.29⋆	.40	.39	.16⋆	.41
ONLINE-B	.36†	.30⋆	**.44**	–	.34⋆	.38	.30⋆	.32⋆	.37‡	.38	.18⋆	.41
RBMT-4	**.50**	**.45**	**.61**⋆	**.57**⋆	–	**.46**	.41	.40	**.53**†	**.57**⋆	.21⋆	**.56**†
RBMT-3	.42	.40	**.53**‡	**.51**	.36	–	.36‡	.31⋆	**.60**⋆	**.54**†	.14⋆	**.54**†
ONLINE-C	**.54**⋆	**.48**	**.58**⋆	**.62**⋆	**.49**	**.50**‡	–	.40	**.58**⋆	**.59**⋆	.23⋆	**.55**⋆
RBMT-1	**.56**⋆	**.50**	**.59**⋆	**.57**⋆	.40	**.53**⋆	**.41**	–	**.57**⋆	**.59**⋆	.23⋆	**.58**⋆
QCRI	.28†	.31†	**.45**	**.50**‡	.38†	.32⋆	.29⋆	.34⋆	–	.31	.12⋆	.33‡
UEDIN	.39	.27⋆	**.49**	**.49**	.33⋆	.38†	.31⋆	.31⋆	**.34**	–	.15⋆	**.38**
UK	**.74**⋆	**.71**⋆	**.81**⋆	**.76**⋆	**.73**⋆	**.76**⋆	**.69**⋆	**.66**⋆	**.76**⋆	**.75**⋆	–	**.77**⋆
UPC	**.42**	.32†	**.49**	**.49**	.38†	.36†	.33⋆	.35⋆	**.44**‡	.36	.14⋆	–
> others	0.52	0.48	**0.62**	0.61	0.46	0.51	0.42	0.42	0.60	0.58	0.19	0.57

Table 21: Head to head comparison for Spanish-English systems

	Bojar	Lopez	Most Probable	MC Playoffs	Expected Wins
1	0.643: ONLINE-B	ONLINE-B	ONLINE-B	2.88: ONLINE-B	0.642 (1): ONLINE-B
2	0.606: UEDIN	UEDIN	UEDIN	3.07: UEDIN	0.603 (2): UEDIN
3	0.530: ONLINE-A	CU-BOJAR	CU-BOJAR	3.40: CU-BOJAR	0.528 (3-4): ONLINE-A
4	0.530: CU-BOJAR	ONLINE-A	ONLINE-A	3.40: ONLINE-A	0.528 (3-4): CU-BOJAR
5	0.375: UK	UK	UK	4.01: UK	0.379 (5): UK
6	0.318: JHU	JHU	JHU	4.24: JHU	0.320 (6): JHU

Table 22: Overall ranking with different methods (Czech–English)

	Bojar	Lopez	Most Probable	MC Playoffs	Expected Wins
1	0.646: ONLINE-A	ONLINE-B	ONLINE-B	6.35: ONLINE-A	0.647 (1-3): ONLINE-A
2	0.645: ONLINE-B	ONLINE-A	ONLINE-A	6.44: ONLINE-B	0.642 (1-3): ONLINE-B
3	0.612: QUAERO	UEDIN	UEDIN	6.94: QUAERO	0.609 (2-5): QUAERO
4	0.599: RBMT-3	QUAERO	QUAERO	7.04: RBMT-3	0.600 (2-6): RBMT-3
5	0.597: UEDIN	RBMT-3	RBMT-3	7.16: UEDIN	0.593 (3-6): UEDIN
6	0.558: RWTH	KIT	KIT	7.76: RWTH	0.551 (5-9): RWTH
7	0.545: LIMSI	RWTH	RWTH	7.83: KIT	0.547 (5-10): KIT
8	0.544: KIT	QCRI	QCRI	7.85: LIMSI	0.545 (6-10): LIMSI
9	0.524: QCRI	RBMT-4	RBMT-4	8.20: QCRI	0.521 (7-11): QCRI
10	0.505: RBMT-1	LIMSI	LIMSI	8.40: RBMT-4	0.506 (8-11): RBMT-1
11	0.502: RBMT-4	RBMT-1	RBMT-1	8.42: RBMT-1	0.506 (8-11): RBMT-4
12	0.434: ONLINE-C	ONLINE-C	ONLINE-C	9.43: ONLINE-C	0.434 (12-13): ONLINE-C
13	0.402: DFKI-BERLIN	DFKI-BERLIN	DFKI-BERLIN	9.86: DFKI-BERLIN	0.405 (12-14): DFKI-BERLIN
14	0.374: UK	UK	UK	10.25: UK	0.377 (13-15): UK
15	0.337: JHU	JHU	JHU	10.81: JHU	0.338 (14-15): JHU
16	0.179: UG	UG	UG	13.26: UG	0.180 (16): UG

Table 23: Overall ranking with different methods (German–English)

	Bojar	Lopez	Most Probable	MC Playoffs	Expected Wins
1	0.630: LIMSI	LIMSI	LIMSI	6.33: LIMSI	0.626 (1-3): LIMSI
2	0.613: KIT	CMU	CMU	6.55: KIT	0.610 (1-4): KIT
3	0.593: ONLINE-A	ONLINE-B	ONLINE-B	6.80: ONLINE-A	0.592 (1-5): ONLINE-A
4	0.573: CMU	KIT	KIT	7.06: CMU	0.571 (2-6): CMU
5	0.569: ONLINE-B	ONLINE-A	ONLINE-A	7.12: ONLINE-B	0.567 (3-7): ONLINE-B
6	0.546: UEDIN	LIUM	LIUM	7.51: UEDIN	0.538 (5-8): UEDIN
7	0.523: LIUM	RWTH	RWTH	7.73: LIUM	0.522 (5-8): LIUM
8	0.515: RWTH	UEDIN	UEDIN	7.88: RWTH	0.510 (6-9): RWTH
9	0.459: RBMT-1	RBMT-1	RBMT-1	8.51: RBMT-1	0.463 (8-12): RBMT-1
10	0.457: RBMT-3	UK	UK	8.56: RBMT-3	0.458 (9-13): RBMT-3
11	0.444: UK	SFU	SFU	8.75: SFU	0.444 (9-14): SFU
12	0.444: SFU	RBMT-3	RBMT-3	8.78: UK	0.441 (9-14): UK
13	0.429: RBMT-4	RBMT-4	RBMT-4	8.92: RBMT-4	0.430 (10-14): RBMT-4
14	0.412: JHU	JHU	JHU	9.19: JHU	0.409 (12-14): JHU
15	0.321: ONLINE-C	ONLINE-C	ONLINE-C	10.31: ONLINE-C	0.319 (15): ONLINE-C

Table 24: Overall ranking with different methods (French–English)

	Bojar	Lopez	Most Probable	MC Playoffs	Expected Wins
1	0.617: ONLINE-A	ONLINE-A	ONLINE-A	5.38: ONLINE-A	0.617 (1-4): ONLINE-A
2	0.612: ONLINE-B	ONLINE-B	ONLINE-B	5.43: ONLINE-B	0.611 (1-4): ONLINE-B
3	0.603: QCRI	QCRI	QCRI	5.56: QCRI	0.600 (1-4): QCRI
4	0.585: UEDIN	UPC	UPC	5.75: UEDIN	0.581 (2-5): UEDIN
5	0.565: UPC	UEDIN	UEDIN	5.89: UPC	0.567 (3-6): UPC
6	0.528: GTH-UPM	RBMT-3	RBMT-3	6.29: GTH-UPM	0.526 (5-7): GTH-UPM
7	0.512: RBMT-3	JHU	JHU	6.37: RBMT-3	0.518 (6-8): RBMT-3
8	0.477: JHU	GTH-UPM	GTH-UPM	6.73: JHU	0.480 (7-9): JHU
9	0.461: RBMT-4	RBMT-4	RBMT-4	6.92: RBMT-4	0.460 (8-10): RBMT-4
10	0.423: RBMT-1	ONLINE-C	ONLINE-C	7.19: RBMT-1	0.429 (9-11): RBMT-1
11	0.420: ONLINE-C	RBMT-1	RBMT-1	7.24: ONLINE-C	0.423 (9-11): ONLINE-C
12	0.189: UK	UK	UK	9.25: UK	0.188 (12): UK

Table 25: Overall ranking with different methods (Spanish–English)

	Bojar	Lopez	Most Probable	MC Playoffs	Expected Wins
1	0.662: CU-DEPFIX	CU-DEPFIX	CU-DEPFIX	5.25: CU-DEPFIX	0.660 (1): CU-DEPFIX
2	0.628: ONLINE-B	ONLINE-B	ONLINE-B	5.78: ONLINE-B	0.616 (2): ONLINE-B
3	0.557: UEDIN	UEDIN	UEDIN	6.42: UEDIN	0.557 (3-6): UEDIN
4	0.555: CU-TAMCH	CU-TAMCH	CU-TAMCH	6.45: CU-TAMCH	0.555 (3-6): CU-TAMCH
5	0.543: CU-BOJAR	CU-BOJAR	CU-BOJAR	6.58: CU-BOJAR	0.541 (3-7): CU-BOJAR
6	0.531: CU-TECTOMT	CU-TECTOMT	CU-TECTOMT	6.69: CU-TECTOMT	0.532 (4-7): CU-TECTOMT
7	0.528: ONLINE-A	ONLINE-A	ONLINE-A	6.72: ONLINE-A	0.529 (4-7): ONLINE-A
8	0.478: COMMERCIAL1	COMMERCIAL2	COMMERCIAL2	7.27: COMMERCIAL1	0.477 (8-10): COMMERCIAL1
9	0.459: COMMERCIAL2	COMMERCIAL1	COMMERCIAL1	7.46: COMMERCIAL2	0.459 (8-11): COMMERCIAL2
10	0.442: CU-POOR-COMB	CU-POOR-COMB	CU-POOR-COMB	7.61: CU-POOR-COMB	0.443 (9-11): CU-POOR-COMB
11	0.437: UK	UK	UK	7.65: UK	0.440 (9-11): UK
12	0.360: SFU	SFU	SFU	8.40: SFU	0.362 (12): SFU
13	0.326: JHU	JHU	JHU	8.72: JHU	0.328 (13): JHU

Table 26: Overall ranking with different methods (English–Czech)

	Bojar	Lopez	Most Probable	MC Playoffs	Expected Wins
1	0.655: LIMSI	LIMSI	LIMSI	5.98: LIMSI	0.651 (1-2): LIMSI
2	0.615: RWTH	RWTH	RWTH	6.57: RWTH	0.609 (2-4): RWTH
3	0.595: ONLINE-B	ONLINE-B	ONLINE-B	6.84: ONLINE-B	0.589 (2-5): ONLINE-B
4	0.590: KIT	KIT	KIT	6.86: KIT	0.587 (2-5): KIT
5	0.554: LIUM	LIUM	LIUM	7.36: LIUM	0.550 (4-8): LIUM
6	0.534: UEDIN	UEDIN	UEDIN	7.67: UEDIN	0.526 (5-9): UEDIN
7	0.516: RBMT-3	RBMT-3	RBMT-3	7.85: RBMT-3	0.514 (5-10): RBMT-3
8	0.513: ONLINE-A	ONLINE-A	ONLINE-A	7.92: PROMT	0.507 (6-10): ONLINE-A
9	0.506: PROMT	PROMT	PROMT	7.92: ONLINE-A	0.507 (6-10): PROMT
10	0.483: RBMT-1	RBMT-1	RBMT-1	8.23: RBMT-1	0.483 (8-11): RBMT-1
11	0.436: JHU	JHU	JHU	8.85: JHU	0.436 (10-12): JHU
12	0.396: UK	UK	RBMT-4	9.34: RBMT-4	0.397 (11-15): RBMT-4
13	0.394: ONLINE-C	RBMT-4	ITS-LATL	9.38: ONLINE-C	0.393 (12-15): ONLINE-C
14	0.394: RBMT-4	ITS-LATL	ONLINE-C	9.41: UK	0.391 (12-15): UK
15	0.360: ITS-LATL	ONLINE-C	UK	9.81: ITS-LATL	0.360 (13-15): ITS-LATL

Table 27: Overall ranking with different methods (English–French)

	Bojar	Lopez	Most Probable	MC Playoffs	Expected Wins
1	0.648: ONLINE-B	ONLINE-B	ONLINE-B	4.70: ONLINE-B	0.646 (1): ONLINE-B
2	0.579: RBMT-3	RBMT-3	RBMT-3	5.35: RBMT-3	0.577 (2-4): RBMT-3
3	0.561: ONLINE-A	PROMT	PROMT	5.49: ONLINE-A	0.561 (2-5): ONLINE-A
4	0.545: PROMT	ONLINE-A	ONLINE-A	5.66: PROMT	0.542 (3-6): PROMT
5	0.526: UEDIN	UPC	UPC	5.78: UEDIN	0.528 (4-6): UEDIN
6	0.524: UPC	UEDIN	UEDIN	5.81: UPC	0.525 (4-6): UPC
7	0.463: RBMT-4	RBMT-1	RBMT-1	6.33: RBMT-4	0.464 (7-9): RBMT-4
8	0.452: RBMT-1	RBMT-4	RBMT-4	6.42: RBMT-1	0.452 (7-9): RBMT-1
9	0.430: ONLINE-C	UK	ONLINE-C	6.57: ONLINE-C	0.434 (8-10): ONLINE-C
10	0.412: UK	ONLINE-C	UK	6.73: UK	0.415 (9-10): UK
11	0.357: JHU	JHU	JHU	7.17: JHU	0.357 (11): JHU

Table 28: Overall ranking with different methods (English–Spanish)

	AMBER	BLEU-4-CLOSEST-CASED	BLOCKERRCATS	METEOR	POSF	SAGAN-STS	SEMPOS	SIMPBLEU	TER	TERRORCAT	WORDBLOCKERRCATS	XENERRCATS
Czech-English News Task												
CU-BOJAR	0.17	0.2	39	0.31	44	0.66	0.50	0.21	0.65	0.2	50	639
JHU	0.16	0.18	41	0.28	41	0.63	0.47	0.19	0.65	0.10	53	692
ONLINE-A	0.18	0.21	40	0.31	43	0.68	0.51	0.21	0.62	0.22	50	648
ONLINE-B	0.18	0.23	40	0.30	42	0.67	0.53	0.23	0.59	0.20	52	660
UEDIN	0.18	0.22	39	0.32	45	0.69	0.53	0.23	0.60	0.25	49	627
UK	0.16	0.18	41	0.29	41	0.63	0.49	0.19	0.67	0.17	53	682

Table 29: Automatic evaluation metric scores for systems in the WMT12 Czech-English News Task

	AMBER	BLEU-4-CLOSEST-CASED	BLOCKERRCATS	METEOR	POSF	SEMPOS	SIMPBLEU	TER	TERRORCAT	WORDBLOCKERRCATS	XENERRCATS
German-English News Task											
DFKI-BERLIN	0.17	0.21	40	0.3	43	0.46	0.18	0.61	0.25	50	653
JHU	0.17	0.2	41	0.29	42	0.42	0.21	0.61	0.20	52	672
KIT	0.18	0.23	39	0.31	45	0.46	0.23	0.58	0.28	49	630
LIMSI	0.18	0.23	39	0.31	45	0.48	0.23	0.6	0.30	49	628
ONLINE-A	0.18	0.21	40	0.32	44	0.50	0.22	0.6	0.27	50	645
ONLINE-B	0.19	0.24	39	0.31	44	0.53	0.24	0.59	0.29	50	636
RBMT-4	0.16	0.16	41	0.29	42	0.44	0.18	0.68	0.24	53	690
RBMT-3	0.16	0.17	40	0.3	42	0.47	0.19	0.66	0.29	52	677
ONLINE-C	0.15	0.14	42	0.28	40	0.43	0.17	0.70	0.26	54	711
RBMT-1	0.15	0.15	43	0.29	40	0.45	0.17	0.69	0.24	54	711
QCRI	0.18	0.23	40	0.31	44	0.46	0.23	0.59	0.26	50	639
QUAERO	0.19	0.24	38	0.32	46	0.49	0.24	0.57	0.3	48	613
RWTH	0.18	0.23	39	0.31	45	0.48	0.24	0.58	0.27	49	626
UEDIN	0.18	0.23	39	0.31	46	0.51	0.23	0.59	0.32	49	630
UG	0.11	0.11	45	0.24	35	0.38	0.14	0.77	0.10	59	768
UK	0.16	0.18	42	0.29	40	0.42	0.2	0.65	0.27	53	683

Table 30: Automatic evaluation metric scores for systems in the WMT12 German-English News Task

	AMBER	BLEU-4-CLOSEST-CASED	BLOCKERRCATS	METEOR	POSF	SEMPOS	SIMPBLEU	TER	TERRORCAT	WORDBLOCKERRCATS	XENERRCATS
					French-English News Task						
CMU	0.20	0.29	36	0.34	51	0.54	0.29	0.52	0.25	44	561
JHU	0.19	0.26	37	0.33	47	0.50	0.26	0.54	0.20	46	596
KIT	0.21	0.30	35	0.34	51	0.54	0.3	0.51	0.25	43	551
LIMSI	0.21	0.30	35	0.34	52	0.55	0.3	0.51	0.25	43	546
LIUM	0.20	0.29	36	0.34	50	0.54	0.29	0.52	0.24	44	558
ONLINE-A	0.2	0.27	37	0.34	48	0.52	0.27	0.53	0.24	45	584
ONLINE-B	0.20	0.30	36	0.33	48	0.55	0.29	0.51	0.22	46	582
RBMT-4	0.18	0.20	38	0.32	45	0.49	0.21	0.64	0.15	48	622
RBMT-3	0.18	0.21	39	0.31	46	0.49	0.22	0.61	0.15	48	637
ONLINE-C	0.18	0.19	38	0.31	45	0.45	0.21	0.64	0.10	48	633
RBMT-1	0.18	0.21	39	0.32	47	0.5	0.22	0.62	0.15	48	626
RWTH	0.20	0.29	36	0.34	50	0.53	0.28	0.53	0.20	44	563
SFU	0.2	0.25	37	0.33	48	0.51	0.26	0.54	0.17	46	596
UEDIN	0.20	0.30	35	0.34	51	0.54	0.3	0.51	0.25	43	549
UK	0.19	0.25	38	0.33	47	0.52	0.25	0.57	0.17	47	602

Table 31: Automatic evaluation metric scores for systems in the WMT12 French-English News Task

	AMBER	BLEU-4-CLOSEST-CASED	BLOCKERRCATS	METEOR	POSF	SAGAN-STS	SEMPOS	SIMPBLEU	TER	TERRORCAT	WORDBLOCKERRCATS	XENERRCATS
					Spanish-English News Task							
GTH-UPM	0.21	0.29	35	0.35	51	0.7	0.55	0.29	0.51	0.31	43	565
JHU	0.21	0.29	35	0.35	51	0.7	0.56	0.29	0.51	0.31	43	560
ONLINE-A	0.22	0.31	34	0.36	52	0.72	0.58	0.31	0.49	0.36	42	535
ONLINE-B	0.22	0.38	33	0.36	53	0.70	0.60	0.35	0.45	0.35	41	523
RBMT-4	0.19	0.23	36	0.33	49	0.69	0.54	0.24	0.60	0.29	45	591
RBMT-3	0.19	0.23	36	0.33	49	0.69	0.54	0.23	0.60	0.29	45	590
ONLINE-C	0.19	0.22	37	0.33	47	0.68	0.5	0.23	0.61	0.24	46	598
RBMT-1	0.18	0.22	38	0.33	48	0.67	0.52	0.23	0.62	0.23	47	607
QCRI	0.22	0.33	33	0.36	54	0.71	0.6	0.32	0.49	0.32	40	523
UEDIN	0.22	0.33	33	0.36	54	0.71	0.59	0.32	0.48	0.32	40	519
UK	0.18	0.22	37	0.30	44	0.6	0.48	0.23	0.60	0.10	48	634
UPC	0.22	0.32	34	0.36	54	0.71	0.57	0.31	0.49	0.33	41	531

Table 32: Automatic evaluation metric scores for systems in the WMT12 Spanish-English News Task

	AMBER	BLEU-4-CLOSEST-CASED	BLOCKERRCATS	ENXERRCATS	METEOR	POSF	SEMPOS	SIMPBLEU	TER	TERRORCAT	WORDBLOCKERRCATS
English-Czech News Task											
COMMERCIAL-2	0.01	0.08	47	693	0.17	23	0.38	0.1	0.76	0.17	61
CU-BOJAR	0.17	0.13	45	644	0.21	28	0.4	0.13	0.69	0.26	57
CU-DEPFIX	0.19	0.16	44	623	0.22	28	0.45	0.15	0.66	0.30	55
CU-POOR-COMB	0.14	0.12	48	710	0.19	27	0.35	0.12	0.67	0.23	60
CU-TAMCH	0.17	0.13	45	647	0.21	28	0.38	0.13	0.69	0.29	57
CU-TECTOMT	0.16	0.12	48	690	0.19	26	0.36	0.12	0.68	0.22	60
JHU	0.16	0.1	47	691	0.2	23	0.39	0.11	0.69	0.10	60
ONLINE-A	0.17	0.13	n/a	n/a	0.21	n/a	0.42	0.13	0.67	0.25	n/a
ONLINE-B	0.19	0.16	44	623	0.21	28	0.45	0.15	0.66	0.30	55
COMMERCIAL-1	0.11	0.09	48	692	0.18	22	0.38	0.10	0.74	0.21	61
SFU	0.15	0.11	47	674	0.19	23	0.39	0.11	0.71	0.21	60
UEDIN	0.18	0.15	45	639	0.21	27	0.41	0.14	0.66	0.40	56
UK	0.15	0.11	47	669	0.19	25	0.39	0.12	0.71	0.35	59

Table 33: Automatic evaluation metric scores for systems in the WMT12 English-Czech News Task

	AMBER	BLEU-4-CLOSEST-CASED	BLOCKERRCATS	ENXERRCATS	METEOR	POSF	SIMPBLEU	TER	TERRORCAT	WORDBLOCKERRCATS
English-German News Task										
DFKI-BERLIN	0.18	0.14	46	628	0.35	41	0.13	0.69	0.10	57
DFKI-HUNSICKER	0.18	0.14	45	621	0.35	42	0.15	0.69	0.17	57
JHU	0.2	0.15	45	618	0.37	42	0.16	0.68	0.17	56
KIT	0.20	0.17	45	606	0.38	43	0.17	0.66	0.14	55
LIMSI	0.2	0.17	45	615	0.37	43	0.17	0.65	0.15	56
ONLINE-A	0.20	0.16	45	617	0.38	43	0.17	0.65	0.36	55
ONLINE-B	0.22	0.18	43	589	0.38	42	0.18	0.64	0.35	55
RBMT-4	0.18	0.14	45	623	0.35	42	0.15	0.69	0.35	57
RBMT-3	0.19	0.15	44	608	0.36	44	0.16	0.68	0.37	56
ONLINE-C	0.16	0.11	47	655	0.32	39	0.13	0.74	0.37	60
RBMT-1	0.17	0.13	47	643	0.34	42	0.15	0.70	0.36	58
RWTH	0.2	0.16	44	609	0.37	43	0.16	0.67	0.25	56
UEDIN-WILLIAMS	0.19	0.16	45	628	0.37	43	0.17	0.66	0.33	57
UEDIN	0.20	0.16	45	611	0.37	43	0.17	0.66	0.29	55
UK	0.18	0.14	46	632	0.36	40	0.15	0.71	0.27	58

Table 34: Automatic evaluation metric scores for systems in the WMT12 English-German News Task

	AMBER	BLEU-4-CLOSEST-CASED	BLOCKERRCATS	ENXERRCATS	METEOR	POSF	SIMPBLEU	TER	TERRORCAT	WORDBLOCKERRCATS
English-French News Task										
ITS-LATL	0.24	0.21	41	548	0.45	48	0.21	0.61	0.15	50
JHU	0.26	0.25	38	511	0.49	51	0.25	0.57	0.15	47
KIT	0.28	0.28	36	480	0.52	55	0.28	0.54	0.22	44
LIMSI	0.28	0.29	36	472	0.52	55	0.28	0.54	0.22	44
LIUM	0.28	0.28	37	480	0.51	54	0.28	0.55	0.20	45
ONLINE-A	0.26	0.25	39	512	0.5	52	0.26	0.57	0.17	47
ONLINE-B	0.24	0.21	36	473	0.48	45	0.26	0.77	0.10	49
RBMT-4	0.24	0.21	40	539	0.46	48	0.22	0.60	0.10	49
RBMT-3	0.26	0.24	39	511	0.48	52	0.24	0.58	0.14	47
ONLINE-C	0.23	0.2	41	550	0.45	50	0.21	0.62	0.10	50
RBMT-1	0.25	0.22	40	531	0.47	51	0.23	0.6	0.13	49
PROMT	0.26	0.24	38	502	0.49	52	0.25	0.58	0.18	46
RWTH	0.28	0.29	36	478	0.52	54	0.28	0.54	0.22	44
UEDIN	0.28	0.28	36	479	0.52	54	0.28	0.55	0.27	45
UK	0.25	0.23	39	523	0.48	51	0.24	0.6	0.17	48

Table 35: Automatic evaluation metric scores for systems in the WMT12 English-French News Task

	AMBER	BLEU-4-CLOSEST-CASED	BLOCKERRCATS	ENXERRCATS	METEOR	POSF	SIMPBLEU	TER	TERRORCAT	WORDBLOCKERRCATS
English-Spanish News Task										
JHU	0.29	0.29	37	494	0.54	52	0.29	0.51	0.14	45
ONLINE-A	0.31	0.31	36	475	0.56	54	0.31	0.48	0.2	43
ONLINE-B	0.33	0.36	34	431	0.57	54	0.34	0.48	0.25	42
RBMT-4	0.27	0.24	39	528	0.5	50	0.25	0.55	0.14	48
RBMT-3	0.28	0.26	39	510	0.51	51	0.26	0.54	0.13	46
ONLINE-C	0.26	0.24	40	532	0.5	49	0.25	0.55	0.10	48
RBMT-1	0.26	0.23	40	534	0.50	49	0.25	0.57	0.13	49
PROMT	0.29	0.27	38	497	0.52	52	0.28	0.53	0.18	45
UEDIN	0.31	0.32	35	466	0.56	55	0.32	0.49	0.19	42
UK	0.29	0.28	38	510	0.54	51	0.28	0.52	0.17	46
UPC	0.31	0.32	36	476	0.56	54	0.31	0.49	0.19	43

Table 36: Automatic evaluation metric scores for systems in the WMT12 English-Spanish News Task

Semantic Textual Similarity for MT evaluation

Julio Castillo[†‡] **Paula Estrella**[‡]
[‡]FaMAF, UNC, Argentina
[†‡]UTN-FRC, Argentina
jotacastillo@gmail.com
pestrella@famaf.unc.edu.ar

Abstract

This paper describes the system used for our participation in the WMT12 Machine Translation evaluation shared task.
We also present a new approach to Machine Translation evaluation based on the recently defined task Semantic Textual Similarity. This problem is addressed using a textual entailment engine entirely based on WordNet semantic features.
We described results for the Spanish-English, Czech-English and German-English language pairs according to our submission on the Eight Workshop on Statistical Machine Translation. Our first experiments reports a competitive score to system level.

1 Introduction

The evaluation of Machine Translation (MT) has become as important as MT itself over the last few years. This is evidenced by the fact that there are now specific forums to present and test new metrics, such as the Workshop for Statistical MT (WMT) or the NIST MetricsMatr. Every year a vast number of MT metrics are created, the majority being automatic, and seeking to find an efficient, low labor-intensive and reliable evaluation method as an alternative to human-based evaluation.

Automatic metrics employ different evaluation strategies: classical MT automatic metrics, such as BLEU (Papineni et al., 2002), NIST (Doddington. 2002), WER (Tillmann et al., 1997), PER (Nießen et al., 2000) are language-independent based on n-gram matching (considering or not the ordering of words in a sentence); other use some kind of language-specific knowledge, for example METEOR (Banerjee et al., 2005), which uses WordNet to match synonyms if exact matchings do not occur, and METEOR-NEXT (Denkowski et al., 2010) that, in addition to METEOR's features, incorporates paraphrases; and more sophisticated metrics use deeper linguistic information, as for example the DCU-LFG metric (Yifan et al., 2010).

However, relatively few attempts have been made to use semantic information for MT evaluation. Moreover, only one work has been published about using semantic equivalence (known as Textual Entailment) of texts for MT evaluation. In this work we propose an improved metric, based on TE features, that indicates to what extent a candidate sentence is equivalent to a reference.

The paper is organized as follows: Section 2 describes the relevant work done on semantic oriented MT evaluation, Section 3 describes the architecture of the system to compute our metric, then Section 4 relates TE and semantic textual similarity to MT, and Section 5 presents some results obtained with our TE-based metric; and finally Section 6 summarize some conclusions and future work.

2 Related work

Given the vast literature in the field of MT evaluation, in this section we briefly mention a few attempts to evaluate MT based on semantic features, which we deem most recent and important.

2.1 Semantics for MT evaluation

Giménez and Márquez (2007) present a set of metrics operating over shallow semantic structures, which they call linguistic elements, with the idea that a sentence can be seen as a 'bag' of LEs. Possible LEs are word forms, part-of-speech tags, dependency relationships, syntactic phrases, named entities, semantic roles, etc. The metrics calculate the similarity of a candidate to one or more references by calculating the overlap and matches of LEs, and the resulting score is the highest obtained from the individual comparisons to each reference. The shallow-semantic evaluation is performed by computing the matching and overlap of named entities and semantic roles, after automatically annotating the sentences.

Following this work, Giménez and Márquez (2009) propose the family of metrics discourse representation structure (DRS) based on the Discourse Representation Theory of Kamp (1981), where a discourse is represented in structure that is essentially a variation of first-order predicate calculus. These sets of metrics are then used to evaluate poor quality MT, concluding that semantic oriented metrics are more stable at the system level, while at the sentence level their performance decreases (probably due to external factors, for example if a parse tree of the sentence is not available, the metric cannot be computed).

More recently, Lo and Wu (2011) present a new semi-automated metric, MEANT, that assesses translation utility by matching semantic role fillers. Their hypothesis is that a good translation is one that lets a reader get the central information of the sentence. Conceptually, MEANT is defined in terms of f-score, calculated by averaging the translation accuracy for all frames in the MT output across the number of frames in the MT output/reference translations. To determine the translation accuracy for each semantic role filler in the reference and machine translations, they ask humans to indicate if a role filler translation is correct, incorrect or partially correct, hence being a semi-automatic metric. According to Lo and Wu (2011) MEANT can be run using inexpensive untrained monolingual human judges and yet it correlates with human judgments on adequacy as well as other labor-intensive metrics, such as HTER (Snover et al., 2006), which needs to train humans to find the closest right translation.

2.2 Textual Entailment in MT

Textual Entailment (TE) is defined as a generic framework for applied semantic inference, where the core task is to determine whether the meaning of a target textual assertion (hypothesis, H) can be inferred from a given text (T). For example, given the pair (H,T):

H: The Tunisian embassy in Switzerland was attacked
T: Fire bombs were thrown at the Tunisian embassy in Bern
we can conclude that T entails H.

The recently created challenge "Recognising Textual Entailment" (RTE) started in 2005 with goal of providing a binary answer for each pair (H,T), namely whether there is entailment holds or not (Dagan et al., 2006). The RTE challenge has mutated over the years, aiming at accomplishing more accurate and specific solutions; for example, 2008 a three-way decision was proposed (instead of the original binary decision) consisting of "entailment", "contradiction" and "unknown"; in 2009 the organizers proposed a pilot task, the Textual Entailment Search (Bentivogli et al., 2009), consisting in finding all the sentences in a set of documents that entail a given Hypothesis and since 2010 there is a Novelty Detection Task, which means that RTE systems are required to judge whether the information contained in each H is novel with respect to (i.e., not entailed by) the information contained in the corpus.

This task is quite close to the goal of MT and MT evaluation given that a correct translation should be semantically equivalent to its reference, and thus both translations should entail each other.

Despite this close relation, at present there are only two works using TE in MT, namely Mirkin et al. (2009) proposes to handle OOV(Out-of-vocabulary words) terms by generating alternative source sentences for translation but instead of simply using paraphrases they use entailed texts; the other contribution is by Aziz et al. (2010), in which TE features are integrated into standard SMT workflow (i.e. they dynamically generate alternative entailed words to replace OOVs).

More directly related to our work, is that of Padó et al., (2009) that uses TE to evaluate MT. The main idea is to find out if the translation paraphrases (entails) the reference using entailment features. This is implementing by checking for entailment both from the candidate to the reference and from the reference to the candidate; best candidates are thus assumed to be those that both entail and are entailed by the references and worst candidates are assumed to be those that neither entail the references nor are entailed by these references. Padó et al. (2009a) found that entailment-based features extracted from partially ill-formed translations are sufficiently robust to be predictive for translation quality.

Our approach differs from that of Padó et al. (2009) in that we do not have a binary entailment relation; instead we try to state in a scale of 0 – 5 the degree of similarity between a candidate and a reference. This approach has very recently been proposed as a new task of the Semantic Evaluation Exercises 2012, called Semantic Textual Similarity (STS) by Aguirre et al. (2012) and is explained in more detail in Section 4.

3 System architecture

Sagan is a RTE textual entailment system which has taken part of several challenges, including the Textual Analysis Conference 2009 and TAC 2010, and the Semantic Textual Similarity (Castillo and Estrella, 2012) and Cross Lingual Textual Entailment for content synchronization (Castillo and Cardenas, 2012) as part of the *SEM 2012 Task8 (Negri et al., 2012).

The system is based on a machine learning approach for STS. We adapted this system to produce feature vectors for all MT outputs for all language pairs ES-EN, DE-EN, FR-EN and CS-EN. It is worth noting that we work on all pairs into English because the system was run in a monolingual setting to take advantage of all the resources available for EN.

This Semantic Textual Similarity engine utilizes eight WordNet-based similarity measures, as explained in (Castillo, 2011), with the purpose of obtaining the maximum similarity between two concepts. These text-to-text similarity measures are based on the following word-to-word similarity metrics: (Resnik, 1995), (Lin, 1997), (Jiang and Conrath, 1997), (Pirrò and Seco, 2008), (Wu & Palmer, 1994), Path Metric, (Leacock & Chodorow, 1998), and a semantic similarity to sentence level named SemSim (Castillo and Cardenas, 2010).

Additional information about how to produce feature vector and metric to word and sentence level can be found in (Castillo, 2011).

The output of the system as modified for this workshop, is a similarity score between 5 and 0, where 5 means a perfect semantic similarity (applied to MT it means that a candidate is indeed a good translation) and 0 means that there is no semantic similarity between the pair, i.e. in MT terms, the candidate is not a translation.

The architecture of the system is shown in Figure 1.

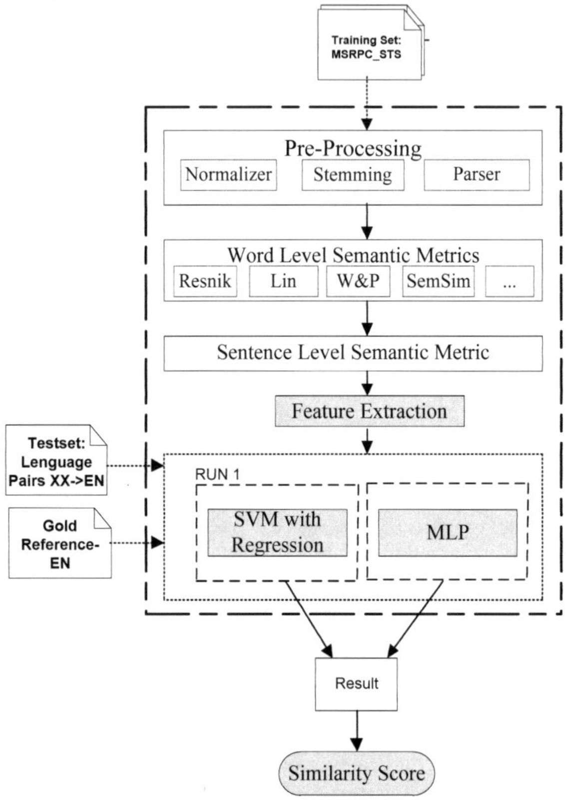

Fig.1. STS system architecture for MT evaluation

The system computes the semantic similarity of two texts (T,H) as a function of the semantic similarity of the constituent words of both phrases. A graph matching algorithm is used to determine the overall similarity between two text fragments.

As a result, a text to text similarity measure is built based on word to word similarity. It is assumed that combining word to word similarity metrics to text level would be a good indicator of text to text similarity.

4 Sagan for MT evaluation

Sagan for MT evaluation is based on a core development to approach the Semantic Textual Similarity task(STS). The pilot task STS was recently defined in Semeval 2012 (Aguirre et al., 2012) and has as main objective measuring the degree of semantic equivalence between two text fragments. STS is related to both Recognizing Textual Entailment (RTE) and Paraphrase Recognition, but has the advantage of being a more suitable model for multiple NLP applications.

As mentioned before, the goal of the RTE task (Bentivogli et al., 2009) is determining whether the meaning of a hypothesis H can be inferred from a text T. Thus, TE is a directional task and we say that T entails H, if a person reading T would infer that H is most likely true. The difference with STS is that STS consists in determining how similar two text fragments are, in a range from 5 (total semantic equivalence) to 0 (no relation). Thus, STS mainly differs from TE and Paraphrasing in that the classification is graded instead of binary. In this manner, STS is filling the gap between TE and Paraphrase.

In view of this, our claim is that the output of MT systems will be more strongly correlated with humans if we have a higher STS score between MT system output and the reference translation.

To apply Sagan to MT evaluation, we first, preprocess the pairs from Microsoft Research Paraphrase Corpus (Dolan and Brockett, 2005) with dates and time normalization, and then optional modules are applied depending on the metric we want to calculate. Second, we compute 8 sentence level semantic features, and, finally, for every segment generated by systems participating at WMT 2012, we determine the semantic similarity score between that output and the given reference translation. The scores are then normalized to a value in the range 0 – 1.

5 Experiments and results

For the WMT 2012 we participated in the Czech-English and Spanish-English evaluation task but we did not have enough time to extensively test our metric on a diverse range of settings (i.e. different corpora and language pairs), given that it was developed for the STS task, which released the data and results only a couple of months ago.

However, we are now running experiments to get a better picture of the metric's ability to rate translation quality. In this section we report results obtained by training the system on the WMT 2011 data and testing on the news test portion, only for the Spanish-English pair. Although the system handles both SVM with regression and MLP classifiers, well known to have good performance on natural language applications, we only submit the results obtained using SVM with regression due to previous experiments that consistently showed higher accuracy using SVM instead of MLP.

At the system level, we calculated the Spearman Rank Correlation Coefficient (ρ) to compare our metric's behavior with respect to the human based metric applied in WMT 2011. The result is ρ = 0.96 indicating a strong positive correlation. Moreover, we successfully reproduce the systems ranking given by humans regarding the best and worst systems.

System Id	Human score	Sagan score
online-B	0.72	0.71
online-A	0.72	0.71
systran	0.66	0.7
koc	0.67	0.69
alacant	0.66	0.69
rbmt-1	0.63	0.69
rbmt-4	0.6	0.69
rbmt-3	0.61	0.69
uedin	0.51	0.68
rbmt-2	0.6	0.68
upm	0.5	0.68
rbmt-5	0.51	0.68
ufal-um	0.47	0.67
cu-zeman	0.16	0.59
hyderabad	0.17	0.58

Table 1. Sagan's score for ES-EN WMT 2011 news test set.

When correlating our metric to other automatic metrics, we find that it better correlates with Meteor-Rank and Adq (Denkowski and Lavie, 2011), Tesla-b (Dahlmaier et al., 2011) and MPF (Popovic, 2011), with a correlation coefficient of 0.96. On the other hand, the worst correlations are found against Tesla-f, F15 (Bicici and Yuret, 2011) and the TER baseline (Snover et al., 2006).

We also performed experiments to segment level with the language pair ES-EN. We used the MSR_STS as training set and the newstest2011 from WMT 2011 as test set. MSR_STS[1] is composed by 750 sentence pairs with a graded semantic relationship ranging from 5 (equivalence) to 0 (no-equivalence).

As result, we obtained a Kendall-tau correlation coefficient of 0.29 to segment-level for translations

[1] http://www.cs.york.ac.uk/semeval-2012/task6/

into English. These preliminary results, although low, shows that STS and Textual Entailment could be used to address the problem of MT evaluation. Clearly, further improvements are needed and we suspect that higher score can be reached using bigger training data. We also remark the necessity of larger corpus of STS providing a graded score among sentences.

At the segment level, we show in Table 2 some examples found by manually inspecting the results.

Example Number	MT output	Texts	Sagan score
2397	Reference	Adelaida, 4 years old, wants a doll or a bicycle, while her sister Isabel, 3 years old, would like a Barbie doll.	0.95
	Online-A	Adelaide, of 4 years, want a doll or a bicycle, while **his** sister Isabel, 3 years, would like a Barbie doll.	
2417	Reference	"I strongly rely on the Charter."	0.18
	Online-A	"Me I based mainly on the letter."	
45	Reference	But there is a snag in that.	0.105
	Alacant	However, there is a fly in the ointment.	
1510	Reference	Unfortunately, even Scarlett Johansson might struggle to raise China's subterranean regard for these city squads.	0.5206
	cu-zeman	**Lamentablemente**, until scarlett johansson should fight to increase the **ínfimo** respect of china for with these **escuadrones** the city.	

Table 2. Sagan's score for some illustrative ES-EN WMT 2011 example pairs showing the score between MT outputs and the reference translation.

The example number 2397 shows a sentence that achieves a high score (0.95) but that has an agreement error (marked in bold), that prevented Sagan from assigning the highest score.

Otherwise, the instance number 2417 has a score of 0.18 showing that Sagan correctly penalizes ill-formed or meaningless sentences. Similarly, the example number 45 has a very low score which quantifies the dissimilarity with the reference translation.

Finally, the last example provided shows that the translation remains words in the original Spanish language (marked in bold).

This manual inspection will be complemented with a deeper study of the correlations at the sentence level.

6 Conclusions and future work

In this paper we introduced a new metric for MT evaluation based on Semantic Textual Similarity computed over textual entailment features. The metric's goal is to provide an indicative score of the extent to which two texts (a candidate translation and a reference) are equivalent. This goal is more complex than classical binary decisions in the field of TE and is a new approach to bring together the knowledge from different areas that a similar ambitions.

While promising results were found at the system level, the metric still needs to be tested on a diversity of settings and at the segment level; this is work in progress and results will be reported in due time.

References

Jesús Giménez and Lluís Márquez. 2007. *Linguistic Features for Automatic Evaluation of Heterogeneous MT Systems*. In Proceedings of the ACL Workshop on Statistical Machine Translation, pages 256–264.

Christoph Tillmann, Stephan Vogel, Hermann Ney, Arkaitz Zubiaga, and Hassan Sawaf. 1997. *Accelerated DP Based Search For Statistical Translation*. In Proceedings of the 5th European Conference on Speech Communication and Technology (EUROSPEECH-97).

Kishore Papineni, Salim Roukos, Todd Ward, and Wei-Jing Zhu. 2002. *BLEU: A Method for Automatic Evaluation of Machine Translation*. In Proceedings of the 40th AnnualMeeting of the Association for Computational Linguistics(ACL-02), pages 311–318.

Sonja Nießen, Franz Josef Och, Gregor Leusch, and Hermann Ney. 2000. *A Evaluation Tool for Machine Translation:Fast Evaluation for MT Research*. In

Proceedings of the 2nd International Conference on Language Resources and Evaluation (LREC-2000).

G. Doddington. 2002. *Automatic Evaluation of Machine Translation Quality using N-gram Co-occurrence Statistics.* In Proceedings of the 2nd International Conference on HLT, pp. 138–145, San Francisco, CA, USA.

Satanjeev Banerjee and Alon Lavie. 2005. *METEOR: An Automatic Metric for MT Evaluation with Improved Correlation with Human Judgments.* In Proceedings of the 43th ACL, pages 65–72.

Michael Denkowski and Alon Lavie. 2010. METEOR-NEXT and the METEOR Paraphrase Tables: Improved Evaluation Support For Five Target Languages. Proceedings of the ACL 2010 Joint Workshop on Statistical Machine Translation and Metrics MATR.

He Yifan, Du Jinhua, Way Andy, and Van Josef . 2010. *The DCU dependency-based metric in WMT-MetricsMATR 2010.* In: WMT 2010 - Joint Fifth Workshop on Statistical Machine Translation and Metrics MATR, ACL, Uppsala, Sweden.

Kamp H. 1981. *A theory of truth and semantic representation.* In Groenendijk, J., Janssen, T., & Stokhof, M. (Eds.), Formal methods in the study of language, No. 135, pp. 277–322. Mathematical Centre, Amsterdam.

Chi-kiu Lo and Dekai Wu. 2011. *MEANT: inexpensive, high-accuracy, semi-automatic metric for evaluating translation utility based on semantic roles.* 49th Annual Meeting of the Association for Computational Linguistic (ACL-2011). Portland, Oregon, US.

Matthew Snover, Bonnie J. Dorr, Richard Schwartz, Linnea Micciulla, and John Makhoul. 2006. *A Study of Translation Edit Rate with Targeted Human Annotation.* In Proceedings of the 7th Conference of the Association for Machine Translation in the Americas (AMTA-06), pages 223–231.

Ido Dagan, Oren Glickman and Bernardo Magnini. 2006. *The PASCAL Recognising Textual Entailment Challenge.* In Quiñonero-Candela, J.; Dagan, I.; Magnini, B.; d'Alché-Buc, F. (Eds.) Machine Learning Challenges. LNCS, Vol. 3944, pp. 177-190.

Shachar Mirkin, Lucia Specia, Nicola Cancedda, Ido Dagan, Marc Dymetman, and Idan Szpektor. 2009. *Source-language entailment modeling for translating unknown terms.* ACL 2009. Vol. 2. Stroudsburg, PA, USA, 791-799.

Wilker Aziz and Marc Dymetmany and Shachar Mirkin and Lucia Specia and Nicola Cancedda and Ido Dagan. 2010. *Learning an Expert from Human Annotations in Statistical Machine Translation: the Case of Out-of-VocabularyWords.* In: Proceedings of the 14th annual meeting of the European Association for Machine Translation (EAMT), Saint-Rapha, France.

Dahlmeier, Daniel and Liu, Chang and Ng, Hwee Tou. 2011.TESLA at WMT 2011: Translation Evaluation and Tunable Metric.In: Proceedings of the Sixth Workshop on Statistical Machine Translation. Association for Computational Linguistics, pages 78-84, Edinburgh, Scotland.

S. Pado, D. Cer, M. Galley, D. Jurafsky and C. Manning. 2009. *Measuring Machine Translation Quality as Semantic Equivalence: A Metric Based on Entailment Features.* Journal of MT 23(2-3), 181-193.

S. Pado, M. Galley, D. Jurafsky and C. Manning. 2009a. *Robust Machine Translation Evaluation with Entailment Features.* Proceedings of ACL 2009.

Eneko Agirre, Daniel Cer, Mona Diab and Aitor Gonzalez-Agirre. 2012. *SemEval-2012 Task 6: A Pilot on Semantic Textual Similarity.* In Proceedings of the 6th International Workshop on Semantic Evaluation (SemEval 2012), in conjunction with the First Joint Conference on Lexical and Computational Semantics (*SEM 2012).

Bentivogli, Luisa, Dagan Ido, Dang Hoa, Giampiccolo, Danilo, Magnini Bernardo.2009.*The Fifth PASCAL RTE Challenge.* In: Proceedings of the TAC.

Castillo Julio. 2011. *A WordNet-based semantic approach to textual entailment and cross-lingual textual entailment.* International Journal of Machine Learning and Cybernetics - Springer, Volume 2, Number 3.

Estrella Paula, Popescu-Belis A. and King M. 2007. *A New Method for the Study of Correlations between MT Evaluation Metrics and Some Surprising Results.* In: Proceedings of TMI-07- 11th Conference on Theoretical and Methodological Issues in Machine Translation -, Skvvde, Sweden.

Castillo Julio and Cardenas Marina. 2010. *Using sentence semantic similarity based onWordNet in recognizing textual entailment.* Iberamia 2010. In LNCS, vol 6433. Springer, Heidelberg, pp 366–375.

Castillo Julio. 2010. *A semantic oriented approach to textual entailment using WordNet-based measures.* MICAI 2010. LNCS, vol 6437. Springer, Heidelberg, pp 44–55.

Castillo Julio. 2010. *Using machine translation systems to expand a corpus in textual entailment.* In: Proceedings of the Icetal 2010. LNCS, vol 6233, pp 97–102.

Resnik P. 1995. *Information content to evaluate semantic similarity in a taxonomy.* In: Proceedings of IJCAI 1995, pp 448–453 907

Lin D. 1997.*An information-theoretic definition of similarity.* In: Proceedings of Conference on Machine Learning, pp 296–304 909

Jiang J, Conrath D.1997. *Semantic similarity based on corpus statistics and lexical taxonomy.* In: Proceedings of theROCLINGX 911

Pirro G., Seco N. 2008. *Design, implementation and evaluation of a new similarity metric combining fea-*

ture and intrinsic information content. In: ODBASE 2008, Springer LNCS.

Wu Z, Palmer M. 1994. *Verb semantics and lexical selection.* In: Proceedings of the 32nd ACL 916.

Leacock C, Chodorow M. 1998. *Combining local context and WordNet similarity for word sense identification.* MIT Press, pp 265–283 919

Hirst G, St-Onge D . 1998. *Lexical chains as representations of context for the detection and correction of malapropisms.* MIT Press, pp 305–332 922

Banerjee S, Pedersen T. 2002. *An adapted lesk algorithm for word sense disambiguation using WordNet.* In: Proceeding of CICLING-02

Castillo Julio and Estrella Paula. 2012. *SAGAN: An approach to Semantic Textual Similarity based on Textual Entailment.* In Proceedings of the 6th International Workshop on Semantic Evaluation (SemEval 2012), in conjunction with the First Joint Conference on Lexical and Computational Semantics (*SEM 2012).

Castillo Julio and Cardenas Marina. 2012. *SAGAN: A Machine Translation Approach for Cross-Lingual Textual Entailment.* In Proceedings of the 6th International Workshop on Semantic Evaluation (SemEval 2012), in conjunction with the First Joint Conference on Lexical and Computational Semantics (*SEM 2012).

Chris Callison-Burch, Philipp Koehn, Christof Monz, Omar Zaidan. 2011.*Findings of the 2011Workshop on Statistical Machine Translation.* WMT 2011.

M. Negri, A. Marchetti, Y. Mehdad, L. Bentivogli, and D. Giampiccolo. 2012. Semeval-2012. *Task 8: Cross-lingual Textual Entailment for Content Synchronization.* In Proceedings of the 6th International Workshop on Semantic Evaluation (SemEval 2012).

William B. Dolan and Chris Brockett.2005. *Automatically Constructing a Corpus of Sentential Paraphrases.* Third International Workshop on Paraphrasing (IWP2005). Asia Federation of Natural Language Processing.

Improving AMBER, an MT Evaluation Metric

Boxing Chen, Roland Kuhn and **George Foster**

National Research Council Canada
283 Alexandre-Taché Boulevard, Gatineau (Québec), Canada J8X 3X7

{Boxing.Chen, Roland.Kuhn, George.Foster}@nrc.ca

Abstract

A recent paper described a new machine translation evaluation metric, AMBER. This paper describes two changes to AMBER. The first one is incorporation of a new ordering penalty; the second one is the use of the downhill simplex algorithm to tune the weights for the components of AMBER. We tested the impact of the two changes, using data from the WMT metrics task. Each of the changes by itself improved the performance of AMBER, and the two together yielded even greater improvement, which in some cases was more than additive. The new version of AMBER clearly outperforms BLEU in terms of correlation with human judgment.

1 Introduction

AMBER is a machine translation evaluation metric first described in (Chen and Kuhn, 2011). It is designed to have the advantages of BLEU (Papineni *et al.*, 2002), such as nearly complete language independence and rapid computability, while attaining even higher correlation with human judgment. According to the paper just cited: "It can be thought of as a weighted combination of dozens of computationally cheap features based on word surface forms for evaluating MT quality". Many recently defined machine translation metrics seek to exploit deeper sources of knowledge than are available to BLEU, such as external lexical and syntactic resources. Unlike these and like BLEU, AMBER relies entirely on matching surface forms in tokens in the hypothesis and reference, thus sacrificing depth of knowledge for simplicity and speed.

In this paper, we describe two improvements to AMBER. The first is a new ordering penalty called "*v*" developed in (Chen *et al.*, 2012). The second remedies a weakness in the 2011 version of AMBER by carrying out automatic, rather than manual, tuning of this metric's free parameters; we now use the simplex algorithm to do the tuning.

2 AMBER

AMBER is the product of a score and a penalty, as in Equation (1); in this, it resembles BLEU. However, both the score part and the penalty part are more sophisticated than in BLEU. The score part (Equation 2) is enriched by incorporating the weighted average of n-gram precisions (*AvgP*), the F-measure derived from the arithmetic averages of precision and recall (*Fmean*), and the arithmetic average of F-measure of precision and recall for each n-gram (*AvgF*). The penalty part is a weighted product of several different penalties (Equation 3). Our original AMBER paper (Chen and Kuhn, 2011) describes the ten penalties used at that time; two of these penalties, the normalized Spearman's correlation penalty and the normalized Kendall's correlation penalty, model word reordering.

$$AMBER = score \times penalty \quad (1)$$

$$score = \theta_1 \times AvgP + \theta_2 \times Fmean + (1 - \theta_1 - \theta_2) \times AvgF \quad (2)$$

$$penalty = \prod_{i=1}^{P} pen_i^{w_i} \quad (3)$$

where θ_1 and θ_2 are weights of each score component; w_i is the weight of each penalty pen_i.

In addition to the more complex score and penalty factors, AMBER differs from BLEU in two other ways:

- Not only fixed n-grams, but three different kinds of flexible n-grams, are used in computing scores and penalties.
- The AMBER score can be computed with different types of text preprocessing, *i.e.* different combinations of several text preprocessing techniques: lowercasing, tokenization, stemming, word splitting, *etc.* 8 types were tried in (Chen and Kuhn, 2011). When using more than one type, the final score is computed as an average over runs, one run per type. In the experiments reported below, we averaged over two types of preprocessing.

3 Improvements to AMBER

3.1 Ordering penalty *v*

We use a simple matching algorithm (Isozaki *et al.*, 2010) to do 1-1 word alignment between the hypothesis and the reference.

After word alignment, represent the reference by a list of normalized positions of those of its words that were aligned with words in the hypothesis, and represent the hypothesis by a list of positions for the corresponding words in the reference. For both lists, unaligned words are ignored. *E.g.*, let P_1 = reference, P_2 = hypothesis:

P_1: $p_1^1 \; p_1^2 \; p_1^3 \; p_1^4 \; \cdots \; p_1^i \; \cdots \; p_1^n$

P_2: $p_2^1 \; p_2^2 \; p_2^3 \; p_2^4 \; \cdots \; p_2^i \; \cdots \; p_2^n$

Suppose we have

Ref: ***in** the **winter** of **2010** , **I visited Paris***
Hyp: ***I visited Paris in 2010** 's **winter***

Then we obtain

P_1: 1 2 3 4 5 6 (the 2nd word "the", 4th word "of" and 6th word "," in the reference are not aligned to any word in the hypothesis. Thus, their positions are not in P_1, so the positions of the matching words "***in winter 2010 I visited Paris***" are normalized to 1 2 3 4 5 6)

P_2: 4 5 6 1 3 2 (the word "*'s*" was unaligned).

The ordering metric *v* is computed from two distance measures. The first is absolute permutation distance:

$$DIST_1(P_1,P_2)=\sum_{i=1}^{n}|p_1^i-p_2^i| \qquad (4)$$

Let
$$v_1=1-\frac{DIST_1(P_1,P_2)}{n(n+1)/2} \qquad (5)$$

v_1 ranges from 0 to 1; a larger value means more similarity between the two permutations. This metric is similar to Spearman's ρ (Spearman, 1904). However, we have found that ρ punishes long-distance reordering too heavily. For instance, v_1 is more tolerant than ρ of the movement of "*recently*" in this example:

Ref: ***Recently , I visited Paris***
Hyp: ***I visited Paris recently***

P_1: 1 2 3 4

P_2: 2 3 4 1

Its $\rho = 1-\frac{6(1+1+1+9)}{4(16-1)} = -0.2$; however, its $v_1 = 1-\frac{1+1+1+3}{4(4+1)/2} = 0.4$.

Inspired by HMM word alignment (Vogel *et al.*, 1996), our second distance measure is based on jump width. This punishes only once a sequence of words that moves a long distance with the internal word order conserved, rather than on every word. In the following, only two groups of words have moved, so the jump width punishment is light:

Ref: *In the winter of 2010, I visited Paris*
Hyp: *I visited Paris in the winter of 2010*

The second distance measure is

$$DIST_2(P_1,P_2)=\sum_{i=1}^{n}|(p_1^i-p_1^{i-1})-(p_2^i-p_2^{i-1})| \qquad (6)$$

where we set $p_1^0=0$ and $p_2^0=0$. Let

$$v_2=1-\frac{DIST_2(P_1,P_2)}{n^2-1} \qquad (7)$$

As with v_1, v_2 is also from 0 to 1, and larger values indicate more similar permutations. The ordering measure v_s is the harmonic mean of v_1 and v_2 (Chen *et al.*, 2012):

$$v_s = 2/(1/v_1+1/v_2) \; . \qquad (8)$$

In (Chen *et al.*, 2012) we found this to be slightly more effective than the geometric mean. v_s in (8) is computed at segment level. We compute document level ordering v_D with a weighted arithmetic mean:

$$v_D = \frac{\sum_{s=1}^{l} v_s \times len_s(R)}{\sum_{s=1}^{l} len_s(R)} \quad (9)$$

where l is the number of segments of the document, and $len(R)$ is the length of the reference after text preprocessing. v_s is the segment-level ordering penalty.

Recall that the penalty part of AMBER is the weighted product of several component penalties. In the original version of AMBER, there were 10 component penalties. In the new version, v is incorporated as an additional, 11th weighted penalty in (3). Thus, the new version of AMBER incorporates three reordering penalties: Spearman's correlation, Kendall's correlation, and v. Note that v is also incorporated in a tuning metric we recently devised (Chen *et al.*, 2012).

3.2 Automatic tuning

In (Chen and Kuhn, 2011), we manually set the 17 free parameters of AMBER (see section 3.2 of that paper). In the experiments reported below, we tuned the 18 free parameters – the original 17 plus the ordering metric v described in the previous section - automatically, using the downhill simplex method of (Nelder and Mead, 1965) as described in (Press *et al.*, 2002). This is a multidimensional optimization technique inspired by geometrical considerations that has shown good performance in a variety of applications.

4 Experiments

The experiments are carried out on WMT metric task data: specifically, the WMT 2008, WMT 2009, WMT 2010, WMT 2011 all-to-English, and English-to-all submissions. The languages "all" ("xx" in Table 1) include French, Spanish, German and Czech. Table 1 summarizes the statistics for these data sets.

Set	Year	Lang.	#system	#sent-pair
Test1	2008	xx-En	43	7,804
Test2	2009	xx-En	45	15,087
Test3	2009	en-Ex	40	14,563
Test4	2010	xx-En	53	15,964
Test5	2010	en-xx	32	18,508
Test6	2011	xx-En	78	16,120
Test7	2011	en-xx	94	23,209

Table 1: Statistics of the WMT dev and test sets.

We used 2008 and 2011 data as dev sets, 2009 and 2010 data as test sets. Spearman's rank correlation coefficient ρ was employed to measure correlation of the metric with system-level human judgments of translation. The human judgment score was based on the "Rank" only, *i.e.*, how often the translations of the system were rated as better than those from other systems (Callison-Burch *et al.*, 2008). Thus, BLEU and the new version of AMBER were evaluated on how well their rankings correlated with the human ones. For the segment level, we followed (Callison-Burch *et al.*, 2010) in using Kendall's rank correlation coefficient τ.

In what follows, "AMBER1" will denote a variant of AMBER as described in (Chen and Kuhn, 2011). Specifically, it is the variant AMBER(1,4) – that is, the variant in which results are averaged over two runs with the following preprocessing:

1. A run with tokenization and lower-casing
2. A run in which tokenization and lower-casing are followed by the word splitting. Each word with more than 4 letters is segmented into two sub-words, with one being the first 4 letters and the other the last 2 letters. If the word has 5 letters, the 4th letter appears twice: *e.g.*, "gangs" becomes "gang" + "gs". If the word has more than 6 letters, the middle part is thrown away.

The second run above requires some explanation. Recall that in AMBER, we wish to avoid use of external resources such as stemmers and morphological analyzers, and we aim at maximal language independence. Here, we are doing a kind of "poor man's morphological analysis". The first four letters of a word are an approximation of its stem, and the last two letters typically carry at least some information about number, gender, case, *etc.* Some information is lost, but on the other hand, when we use the metric for a new language (or at least, a new Indo-European language) we know that it will extract at least some of the information hidden inside morphologically complex words.

The results shown in Tables 2-4 compare the correlation of variants of AMBER with human judgment; Table 5 compares the best version of AMBER (AMBER2) with BLEU. For instance, to calculate segment-level correlations using

Kendall's τ, we carried out 33,071 paired comparisons for out-of-English and 31,051 paired comparisons for into-English. The resulting τ was calculated per system, then averaged for each condition (out-of-English and into-English) to obtain one out-of-English value and one into-English value.

First, we compared the performance of AMBER1 with a version of AMBER1 that includes the new reordering penalty v, at the system and segment levels. The results are shown in Table 2. The greatest impact of v is on "out of English" at the segment level, but none of the results are particularly impressive.

	AMBER1	$+v$	Change
Into-En System	0.860	0.862	0.002 (+0.2%)
Into-En Segment	0.178	0.180	0.002 (+1.1%)
Out-of-En System	0.637	0.637	0 (0%)
Out-of-En Segment	0.167	0.170	0.003 (+1.8%)

Table 2: Correlation with human judgment for AMBER1 *vs.* (AMBER1 including v).

Second, we compared the performance of manually tuned AMBER1 with AMBER1 whose parameters were tuned by the simplex method. The tuning was run four times on the dev set, once for each possible combination of into/out-of English and system/segment level. Table 3 shows the results on the test set. This change had a greater impact, especially on the segment level.

	AMBER1	+Simplex	Change
Into-En System	0.860	0.862	0.002 (+0.2%)
Into-En Segment	0.178	0.184	0.006 (+3.4%)
Out-of-En System	0.637	0.637	0 (0%)
Out-of-En Segment	0.167	0.182	0.015 (+9.0%)

Table 3: Correlation with human judgment for AMBER1 *vs.* simplex-tuned AMBER1.

Then, we compared the performance of AMBER1 with AMBER1 that contains v and that has been tuned by the simplex method. We will denote the new version of AMBER containing both changes "AMBER2". It will be seen from Table 4 that AMBER2 is a major improvement over AMBER1 at the segment level. In the case of "into English" at the segment level, the impact of the two changes seems to have been synergistic: adding together the percentage improvements due to v and simplex from Tables 2 and 3, one would have expected an improvement of 4.5% for both changes together, but the actual improvement was 6.2%. Furthermore, there was no improvement at the system level for "out of English" when either change was tried separately, but there was a small improvement when the two changes were combined.

	AMBER1	AMBER2	Change
Into-En System	0.860	0.870	0.010 (+1.2%)
Into-En Segment	0.178	0.189	0.011 (+6.2%)
Out-of-En System	0.637	0.642	0.005 (+0.8%)
Out-of-En Segment	0.167	0.184	0.017 (+10.2%)

Table 4: Correlation with human judgment for AMBER1 *vs.* AMBER2.

Of course, the most important question is: does the new version of AMBER (AMBER2) perform better than BLEU? Table 5 answers this question (the version of BLEU used here was smoothed BLEU (*mteval-v13a*)). There is a clear advantage for AMBER2 over BLEU at both the system and segment levels, for both "into English" and "out of English".

	BLEU	AMBER2	Change
Into-En System	0.773	0.870	0.097 (+12.5%)
Into-En Segment	0.154	0.189	0.035 (+22.7%)
Out-of-En System	0.574	0.642	0.068 (+11.8%)
Out-of-En Segment	0.149	0.184	0.035 (+23.5%)

Table 5: Correlation with human judgment for BLEU *vs.* AMBER2.

5 Conclusion

We have made two changes to AMBER, a metric described in (Chen and Kuhn, 2011). In our experiments, the new version of AMBER was shown to be an improvement on the original version in terms of correlation with human judgment. Furthermore, it outperformed BLEU by about 12% at the system level and about 23% at the segment level.

A good evaluation metric is not necessarily a good tuning metric, and vice versa. In parallel with our work on AMBER for evaluation, we have also been exploring a machine translation tuning metric called PORT (Chen *et al.*, 2012). AMBER and PORT differ in many details, but they share the same underlying philosophy: to exploit surface similarities between hypothesis and references even more thoroughly than BLEU does, rather than to invoke external resources with richer linguistic knowledge. So far, the results for PORT have been just as encouraging as the ones for AMBER reported here.

Reference

C. Callison-Burch, P. Koehn, C. Monz, K. Peterson, M. Przybocki and O. Zaidan. 2010. Findings of the 2010 Joint Workshop on Statistical Machine Translation and Metrics for Machine Translation. In *Proceedings of WMT*.

C. Callison-Burch, C. Fordyce, P. Koehn, C. Monz and J. Schroeder. 2008. Further Meta-Evaluation of Machine Translation. In *Proceedings of WMT*.

B. Chen, R. Kuhn, and S. Larkin. 2012. PORT: a Precision-Order-Recall MT Evaluation Metric for Tuning. Accepted for publication in *Proceedings of ACL*.

B. Chen and R. Kuhn. 2011. AMBER: a Modified BLEU, Enhanced Ranking Metric. In *Proceedings of the Sixth Workshop on Statistical Machine Translation*, Edinburgh, Scotland.

H. Isozaki, T. Hirao, K. Duh, K. Sudoh, H. Tsukada. 2010. Automatic Evaluation of Translation Quality for Distant Language Pairs. In *Proceedings of EMNLP*.

J. Nelder and R. Mead. 1965. A simplex method for function minimization. *Computer Journal* V. 7, pages 308–313.

K. Papineni, S. Roukos, T. Ward, and W.-J. Zhu. 2002. BLEU: a method for automatic evaluation of machine translation. In *Proceedings of ACL*.

W. Press, S. Teukolsky, W. Vetterling and B. Flannery. 2002. Numerical Recipes in C++. Cambridge University Press, Cambridge, UK.

C. Spearman. 1904. The proof and measurement of association between two things. In *American Journal of Psychology*, V. 15, pages 72–101.

S. Vogel, H. Ney, and C. Tillmann. 1996. HMM based word alignment in statistical translation. In *Proceedings of COLING*.

TerrorCat: a Translation Error Categorization-based MT Quality Metric

Mark Fishel,[γ] **Rico Sennrich,**[γ] **Maja Popović,**[ξ] **Ondřej Bojar**[φ]

[γ] Institute of Computational Linguistics, University of Zurich
{fishel,sennrich}@cl.uzh.ch
[ξ] German Research Center for Artificial Intelligence (DFKI), Berlin
maja.popovic@dfki.de
[φ] Charles University in Prague, Faculty of Mathematics and Physics,
Institute of Formal and Applied Linguistics
bojar@ufal.mff.cuni.cz

Abstract

We present TerrorCat, a submission to the WMT'12 metrics shared task. TerrorCat uses frequencies of automatically obtained translation error categories as base for pairwise comparison of translation hypotheses, which is in turn used to generate a score for every translation. The metric shows high overall correlation with human judgements on the system level and more modest results on the level of individual sentences.

1 The Idea

Recently a couple of methods of automatic translation error analysis have emerged (Zeman et al., 2011; Popović and Ney, 2011). Initial experiments have shown that while agreement with human error analysis is low, these methods show better performance on tasks with a lower granularity, e.g. ranking error categories by frequency (Fishel et al., 2012). In this work we apply translation error analysis to a task with an even lower granularity: ranking translations, one of the shared tasks of WMT'12.

The aim of translation error analysis is to identify the errors that translation systems make and categorize them into different types: e.g. lexical, reordering, punctuation errors, etc. The two tools that we will use – Hjerson and Addicter – both rely on a reference translation. The hypothesis translation that is being analyzed is first aligned to the reference on the word level, and then mistranslated, misplaced, misinflected, missing or superfluous words and other errors are identified.

The main idea of our work is to quantify translation quality based on the frequencies of different error categories. The basic assumption is that different error categories have different importance from the point of view of overall translation quality: for instance, it would be natural to assume that punctuation errors influence translation quality less than missing words or lexical choice errors. Furthermore, an error category can be more important for one output language than the other: for example, word order can influence the meaning in an English sentence more than in a Czech or German one, whereas inflection errors are probably more frequent in the latter two and can thus cause more damage.

In the context of the ranking task, the absolute value of a numeric score has no importance, apart from being greater than, smaller than or equal to the other systems' scores. We therefore start by performing pairwise comparison of the translations – the basic task is to compare two translations and report which one is better. To conform with the WMT submission format we need to generate a numeric score as the output – which is obtained by comparing every possible pair of translations and then using the (normalized) total number of wins per translation as its final score.

The general architecture of the metric is thus this:

- automatic error analysis is applied to the system outputs, yielding the frequencies of every error category for each sentence
- every possible pair of all system outputs is represented as a vector of features, based on the error category frequencies

- a binary classifier takes these feature vectors as input and assigns a win to one of the sentences in every pair (apart from ties)
- the final score of a system equals to the normalized total number of wins per sentence
- the system-level score is averaged out over the individual sentence scores

An illustrative example is given in Figure 1.

We call the result TerrorCat, the translation error categorization-based metric.

2 The Details

In this section we will describe the specifics of the current implementation of the TerrorCat metric: translation error analysis, lemmatization, binary classifier and training data for the binary classifier.

2.1 Translation Error Analysis

Addicter (Zeman et al., 2011) and Hjerson (Popović and Ney, 2011) use different methods for automatic error analysis. Addicter explicitly aligns the hypothesis and reference translations and induces error categories based on the alignment coverage while Hjerson compares words encompassed in the WER (word error rate) and PER (position-independent word error rate) scores to the same end.

Previous evaluation of Addicter shows that hypothesis-reference alignment coverage (in terms of discovered word pairs) directly influences error analysis quality; to increase alignment coverage we used Berkeley aligner (Liang et al., 2006) and trained it on and applied it to the whole set of reference-hypothesis pairs for every language pair.

Both tools use word lemmas for their analysis; we used TreeTagger (Schmid, 1995) for analyzing English, Spanish, German and French and Morče (Spoustová et al., 2007) to analyze Czech. The same tools are used for PoS-tagging in some experiments.

2.2 Binary Classification

Pairwise comparison of sentence pairs is achieved with a binary SVM classifier, trained via sequential minimal optimization (Platt, 1998), implemented in Weka (Hall et al., 2009).

The input feature vectors are composed of frequency differences of every error category; since the maximum (normalized) frequency of any error rate is 1, the feature value range is $[-1, 1]$. To include error analysis from both Addicter and Hjerson their respective features are used side-by-side.

Source: Wir sind Meister!

Translations:

Reference: We are the champions!

HYP-1: Us champions!

HYP-2: The champions we are

HYP-3: We are the champignons!

Error Frequencies:

HYP-1: 1×inflection, 2×missing

HYP-2: 2×order, 1×punctuation

HYP-3: 1×lex.choice

Classifier Output: (or manually created input in the training phase)

HYP-1 < HYP-2

HYP-1 < HYP-3

HYP-2 > HYP-3

Scores:

HYP-1: 0

HYP-2: 1

HYP-3: 0.5

Figure 1: Illustration of TerrorCat's process for a single sentence: translation errors in the hypothesis translations are discovered by comparing them to the reference, error frequencies are extracted, pairwise comparisons are done by the classifier and then converted to scores. The shown translation errors correspond to Hjerson's output.

2.3 Data Extraction

Training data for the SVM classifier is taken from the WMT shared task manual ranking evaluations of previous years (2007–2011), which consist of tuples of 2 to 5 ranked sentences for every language pair. Equal ranks are allowed, and translations of the same sentence by the same pair of systems can be present in several tuples, possibly having conflicting comparison results.

To convert the WMT manual ranking data into the training data for the SVM classifier, we collect all rankings for each pair of translation hypothe-

	2007-2010	2007-2011
fr-en	34 152	46 070
de-en	36 792	53 790
es-en	30 374	41 966
cs-en	19 268	26 418
en-fr	22 734	35 854
en-de	36 076	56 054
en-es	19 352	35 700
en-cs	31 728	52 954

Table 1: Dataset sizes for every language pair, based on manual rankings from WMT shared tasks of previous years: the number of pairs with non-conflicting, non-equivalent ranks.

ses. Pairs with equal ranks are discarded, conflicting ranks for the same pairs are resolved with voting. If the voting is tied, the pair is also discarded.

The kept translation pairs are mirrored (i.e. both directions of every pair are added to the training set as independent entries) to ensure no bias towards the first or second translation in a pair. We will later present analysis of how well that works.

2.4 TerrorCat+You

TerrorCat is distributed via GitHub; information on downloading and using it can be found online.[1] Additionally we are planning to provide more recent evaluations with new datasets, as well as pre-trained models for various languages and language pairs.

3 The Experiments

In the experimental part of our work, we search for the best performing model variant, the aim of which is to evaluate different input features, score calculation strategies and other alternations. The search is done empirically: we evaluate one alternation at a time, and if it successful, it is added to the system before proceeding to test further alternations.

Performance of the models is estimated on a held-out development set, taken from the WMT'11 data; the training data during the optimization phase is composed of ranking data from WMT 2007–2010. In the end we re-trained our system on the whole data set (WMT 2007–2011) and applied it to the unlabeled data from this year's shared task. The resulting dataset sizes are given in Table 1.

All of the resulting scores obtained by different variants of our metric are presented in Tables 2 (for system-level correlations) and 3 (for sentence-level correlations), compared to BLEU and other selected entries in the WMT'11 evaluation shared task. Correlations are computed in the same way as in the WMT evaluations.

3.1 Model Optimization

The following is a brief description of successful modifications to the baseline system.

Weighted Wins

In the baseline model, the score of the winning system in each pairwise comparison is increased by 1. To reduce the impact of low-confidence decisions of the classifier on the final score we tested replacing the constant rewards to the winning system with variable ones, proportional to the classifier's confidence – a measure of which was obtained by fitting a logistic regression model to the SVM output.

As the results show, this leads to minor improvements in sentence-level correlation and more noticeable improvements in system-level correlation (especially English-French and Czech-English). A possible explanation for this difference in performance on different levels is that low classification confidence on the sentence-level does not necessarily affect our ranking for that sentence, but reduces the impact of that sentence on the system-level ranking.

PoS-Split Features

The original model only makes a difference between individual error categories as produced by Hjerson and Addicter. It seems reasonable to assume that errors may be more or less important, depending on the part-of-speech of the words they occur in. We therefore tested using the number of errors per error category per PoS-tag as input features. In other words, unlike the baseline, which relied on counts of missing, misplaced and other erroneous words, this alternation makes a difference between missing nouns/verbs/etc., misplaced nouns, misinflected nouns/adjectives, and so on.

The downside of this approach is that the number of features is multiplied by the size of the PoS tag

[1] `http://terra.cl.uzh.ch/terrorcat.html`

Metric	fr-en	de-en	es-en	cs-en	*-en	en-fr	en-de	en-es	en-cs	en-*
TerrorCat:										
Baseline	0.73	0.74	0.82	0.76	0.76	0.70	0.81	0.69	0.84	0.76
Weighted wins	0.73	0.74	0.82	0.79	0.77	0.75	0.81	0.69	0.84	0.77
PoS-features	0.87	0.76	0.80	0.86	0.82	0.76	**0.86**	0.74	0.87	0.81
GenPoS-features	0.86	0.77	**0.84**	0.88	0.84	0.80	0.85	0.75	**0.90**	0.83
No 2007 data (GenPoS)	**0.89**	**0.80**	0.80	**0.95**	**0.86**	**0.85**	0.84	**0.81**	**0.90**	**0.85**
Other:										
BLEU	0.85	0.48	0.90	0.88	0.78	**0.86**	0.44	0.87	0.65	0.70
mp4ibm1	0.08	0.56	0.12	0.91	0.42	0.61	**0.91**	0.71	**0.76**	**0.75**
MTeRater-Plus	0.93	**0.90**	**0.91**	**0.95**	**0.92**	–	–	–	–	–
AMBER_ti	**0.94**	0.63	0.85	0.88	0.83	0.84	0.54	**0.88**	0.56	0.70
meteor-1.3-rank	0.93	0.71	0.88	0.91	0.86	0.85	0.30	0.74	0.65	0.63

Table 2: System-level Spearman's rank correlation coefficients (ρ) between different variants of TerrorCat and human judgements, based on WMT'11 data. Other metric submissions are shown for comparison. Highest scores per language pair are highlighted in bold separately for TerrorCat variants and for other metrics.

set. Additionally, too specific distinctions can cause data sparsity, especially on the sentence level.

As shown by the results, PoS-tag splitting of the features is successful on the system level, but quite hurtful to the sentence-level correlations. The poor performance on the sentence level can be attributed to the aforementioned data sparsity: the number of different features is higher than the number of words (and hence, the biggest possible number of errors) in the sentences. However, we cannot quite explain, how a sum of these less reliable sentence-level scores leads to more reliable system-level scores.

To somewhat relieve data sparsity we defined subsets of the original PoS tag sets, mostly leaving out morphological information and keeping just the general word types (nouns, verbs, adjectives, etc.). This reduced the number of PoS-tags (and thus, the number of input features) from 2 to 4 times and produced further increase in system-level and a smaller decrease in sentence-level scores, see GenPoS results.

To avoid splitting the metric into different versions for system-level and sentence-level, we gave priority to system-level correlations and adopted the generalized PoS-splitting of the features.

Out-of-Domain Data

The human ranking data from WMT of previous years do not constitute a completely homogeneous dataset. For starters, the test sets are taken from different domains (News/News Commentary/Europarl), whereas the 2012 test set is from the News domain only. Added to this, there might be a difference in the manual data, coming from different organization of the competition – e.g. WMT'07 was the only year when manual scoring of the translations with adequacy/fluency was performed, and ranking had just been introduced into the competition. Therefore we tested whether some subsets of the training data can result in better overall scores.

Interestingly enough, leaving out News Commentary and Europarl test sets caused decreased correlations, although these account for just around 10% of the training data. On the other hand, leaving out the data from WMT'07 led to a significant gain in overall performance.

3.2 Error Meta-Analysis

To better understand why sentence-level correlations are low, we analyzed the core of TerrorCat – its pairwise classifier. Here, we focus on the most successful variant of the metric, which uses general PoS-tags and was trained on the WMT manual rankings from 2008 to 2010. Table 4 presents the confusion matrices of the classifier (one for precision and one for recall), taking into consideration the confidence estimate.

Evaluation is based on the data from 2011; the prediction data was mirrored in the same way as for

Metric	fr-en	de-en	es-en	cs-en	*-en	en-fr	en-de	en-es	en-cs	en-*
TerrorCat:										
Baseline	0.20	0.22	**0.33**	**0.25**	0.25	0.30	0.19	**0.24**	**0.20**	0.23
Weighted wins	0.20	0.23	**0.33**	**0.25**	0.25	**0.31**	**0.20**	**0.24**	**0.20**	**0.24**
PoS-features	0.13	0.18	0.24	0.15	0.18	0.27	0.15	0.15	0.17	0.19
GenPoS-features	0.16	0.24	0.31	0.22	0.23	0.27	0.18	0.22	0.19	0.22
No 2007 data (GenPoS)	**0.21**	**0.30**	**0.33**	0.23	**0.27**	0.29	**0.20**	0.23	**0.20**	0.23
Other:										
mp4ibm1	0.15	0.16	0.18	0.12	0.15	0.21	0.13	0.13	0.06	0.13
MTeRater-Plus	**0.30**	**0.36**	**0.45**	**0.36**	**0.37**	–	–	–	–	–
AMBER_ti	0.24	0.26	0.33	0.27	0.28	**0.32**	**0.22**	**0.31**	**0.21**	**0.27**
meteor-1.3-rank	0.23	0.25	0.38	0.28	0.29	0.31	0.14	0.26	0.19	0.23

Table 3: Sentence-level Kendall's rank correlation coefficients (τ) between different variants of TerrorCat and human judgements, based on WMT'11 data. Other metric submissions are shown for comparison. Highest scores per language pair are highlighted in bold separately for TerrorCat variants and for other metrics.

the training set. Our aim was to measure the bias of the classifier towards first or second translations in a pair (which is obviously an undesired effect). It can be seen that the confusion matrices are completely symmetrical, indicating no position bias of the classifier – even lower-confidence decisions are absolutely consistent.

To make sure that this can be attributed to the mirroring of the training set, we re-trained the classifier on non-mirrored training sets. As a result, 9% of the instances were labelled inconsistently, with the average confidence of such inconsistent decisions being extremely low (2.1%, compared to the overall average of 28.4%). The resulting correlations have slightly dropped as well – all indicating that mirroring the training sets does indeed remove the positional bias and leads to slightly better performance.

Looking at the confusion matrices overall, most decisions fall within the main diagonals (i.e. the cells indicating correct decisions of the classifier). Looking strictly at the classifier's decisions, the recalls and precisions of the non-tied comparison outputs ("$<$" and "$>$") are 57% precision, 69% recall. However, such strict estimates are too pessimistic in our case, since the effect of the classifier's decisions is proportional to the confidence estimate. On the sentence level it means that low-confidence decision errors have less effect on the total score of a system. A definite source of error is the instability of the individual translation errors on the sentence level, an effect both Addicter and Hjerson are known to suffer from (Fishel et al., 2012).

The precision of the classifier predictably drops together with the confidence, and almost half of the misclassifications come from unrecognized equivalent translations – as a result the recall of such pairs of equivalent translations is only 20%. This can be explained by the fact that the binary classifier was trained on instances with just these two labels and with no ties allowed.

On the other hand the classifier's 0-confidence decisions have a high precision (84%) on detecting the equivalent translations; after re-examining the data it turned out that 96% of the 0-confidence decisions were made on input feature vectors containing only zero frequency differences. Such vectors represent pairs of sentences with identical translation error analyses, which are very often simply identical sentences – in which case the classifier cannot (and in fact, should not) make an informed decision of one being better than the other.

4 Related Work

Traditional MT metrics such as BLEU (Papineni et al., 2002) are based on a comparison of the translation hypothesis to one or more human references. TerrorCat still uses a human reference to extract features from the error analysis with Addicter and Hjerson, but at the core, TerrorCat compares hypotheses not to a reference, but to each other.

Manual label	Classifier Output and Confidence: Precision						
	<			< or >	>		
	0.6–1.0	0.3–0.6	0.0–0.3	0.0	0.0–0.3	0.3–0.6	0.6–1.0
<	81%	60%	45%	8%	32%	23%	10%
=	9%	17%	23%	84%	23%	17%	9%
>	10%	23%	32%	8%	45%	60%	81%

Manual label	Classifier Output and Confidence: Recall						
	<			< or >	>		
	0.6–1.0	0.3–0.6	0.0–0.3	0.0	0.0–0.3	0.3–0.6	0.6–1.0
<	23%	18%	28%	1%	20%	7%	3%
=	5%	9%	26%	20%	26%	9%	5%
>	3%	7%	20%	1%	28%	18%	23%

Table 4: The precision and recall confusion matrices of the classifier – judgements on whether one hypothesis is worse than, equivalent to or better than another hypothesis are compared to the classifier's output and confidence.

It is thus most similar to SVM-RANK and Tesla metrics, submissions to the WMT'10 shared metrics task (Callison-Burch et al., 2010) which also used SVMs for ranking translations. However, both metrics used SVMrank (Joachims, 2006) directly for ranking (unlike TerrorCat, which uses a binary classifier for pairwise comparisons). Their features included some of the metric outputs (BLEU, ROUGE, etc.) for SVM-RANK and similarity scores between bags of n-grams for Tesla (Dahlmeier et al., 2011).

5 Conclusions

We introduced the TerrorCat metric, which performs pairwise comparison of translation hypotheses based on frequencies of automatically obtained error categories using a binary classifier, trained on manually ranked data. The comparison outcome is then converted to a numeric score for every sentence or document translation by averaging out the number of wins per translation system.

Our submitted system achieved an average system-level correlation with human judgements in the WMT'11 development set of 0.86 for translation into English and 0.85 for translations from English into other languages. Particularly good performance was achieved on translations from English into Czech (0.90) and back (0.95). Sentence-level scores are more modest: average 0.27 for translation into English and 0.23 for those out of English. The scores remain to be checked against the human judgments from WMT'12.

The introduced TerrorCat metric has certain dependencies. For one thing, in order to apply it to new languages, a training set of manual rankings is required – although this can be viewed as an advantage, since it enables the user to tune the metric to his/her own preference. Additionally, the metric depends on lemmatization and PoS-tagging.

There is a number of directions to explore in the future. For one, both Addicter and Hjerson report MT errors related more to adequacy than fluency, although it was shown last year (Parton et al., 2011) that fluency is an important component in rating translation quality. It is also important to test how well the metric performs if lemmatization and PoS-tagging are not available.

For this year's competition, training data was taken separately for every language pair; it remains to be tested whether combining human judgements with the same target language and different source languages leads to better or worse performance.

To conclude, we have described TerrorCat, one of the submissions to the metrics shared task of WMT'12. TerrorCat is rather demanding to apply on one hand, having more requirements than the common reference-hypothesis translation pair, but at the same time correlates rather well with human judgements on the system level.

References

Chris Callison-Burch, Philipp Koehn, Christof Monz, Kay Peterson, Mark Przybocki, and Omar Zaidan. 2010. Findings of the 2010 joint workshop on statistical machine translation and metrics for machine translation. In *Proceedings of the Joint Fifth Workshop on Statistical Machine Translation and MetricsMATR*, pages 17–53, Uppsala, Sweden.

Daniel Dahlmeier, Chang Liu, and Hwee Tou Ng. 2011. Tesla at wmt 2011: Translation evaluation and tunable metric. In *Proceedings of the Sixth Workshop on Statistical Machine Translation*, pages 78–84, Edinburgh, Scotland.

Mark Fishel, Ondřej Bojar, and Maja Popović. 2012. Terra: a collection of translation error-annotated corpora. In *Proceedings of the 8th LREC*, page in print, Istanbul, Turkey.

Mark Hall, Eibe Frank, Geoffrey Holmes, Bernhard Pfahringer, Peter Reutemann, and Ian H. Witten. 2009. The weka data mining software: An update. *SIGKDD Explorations*, 11.

Thorsten Joachims. 2006. Training linear SVMs in linear time. In *Proceedings of the ACM Conference on Knowledge Discovery and Data Mining (KDD)*, Philadelphia, USA.

Percy Liang, Ben Taskar, and Dan Klein. 2006. Alignment by agreement. In *Proceedings of the HLT-NAACL Conference*, pages 104–111, New York, NY.

Kishore Papineni, Salim Roukos, Todd Ward, and Wei-Jing Zhu. 2002. Bleu: A method for automatic evaluation of machine translation. In *ACL '02: Proceedings of the 40th Annual Meeting on Association for Computational Linguistics*, pages 311–318, Morristown, NJ, USA. Association for Computational Linguistics.

Kristen Parton, Joel Tetreault, Nitin Madnani, and Martin Chodorow. 2011. E-rating machine translation. In *Proceedings of the Sixth Workshop on Statistical Machine Translation*, pages 108–115, Edinburgh, Scotland.

John C. Platt. 1998. Using analytic qp and sparseness to speed training of support vector machines. In *Proceedings of Neural Information Processing Systems 11*, pages 557–564, Denver, CO.

Maja Popović and Hermann Ney. 2011. Towards automatic error analysis of machine translation output. *Computational Linguistics*, 37(4):657–688.

Helmut Schmid. 1995. Improvements in part-of-speech tagging with an application to german. In *Proceedings of the ACL SIGDAT-Workshop*, Dublin, Ireland.

Drahomíra Spoustová, Jan Hajič, Jan Votrubec, Pavel Krbec, and Pavel Květoň. 2007. The best of two worlds: Cooperation of statistical and rule-based taggers for Czech. In *Proceedings of the Workshop on Balto-Slavonic Natural Language Processing, ACL 2007*, pages 67–74, Praha.

Daniel Zeman, Mark Fishel, Jan Berka, and Ondřej Bojar. 2011. Addicter: What is wrong with my translations? *The Prague Bulletin of Mathematical Linguistics*, 96:79–88.

Class error rates for evaluation of machine translation output

Maja Popović
German Research Center for Artificial Intelligence (DFKI)
Language Technology (LT), Berlin, Germany
maja.popovic@dfki.de

Abstract

We investigate the use of error classification results for automatic evaluation of machine translation output. Five basic error classes are taken into account: morphological errors, syntactic (reordering) errors, missing words, extra words and lexical errors. In addition, linear combinations of these categories are investigated. Correlations between the class error rates and human judgments are calculated on the data of the third, fourth, fifth and sixth shared tasks of the Statistical Machine Translation Workshop. Machine translation outputs in five different European languages are used: English, Spanish, French, German and Czech. The results show that the following combinations are the most promising: the sum of all class error rates, the weighted sum optimised for translation into English and the weighted sum optimised for translation from English.

1 Introduction

Recent investigations have shown that it is possible to carry out a reliable automatic error analysis of a given translation output in order to get more information about actual errors and details about particular strengthnesses and weaknesses of a systeml (Popović and Ney, 2011). The obtained results correlate very well with the human error classification results. The question we try to answer is: how the class error rates correlate with the human evaluation (ranking) results? As a first step, we investigate the correlations of five basic class error rates with human rankings. In the next step, linear combinations (sums) of basic class error rates are investigated.

Spearman's rank correlation coefficients on the document (system) level between all the metrics and the human ranking are computed on the English, French, Spanish, German and Czech texts generated by various translation systems in the framework of the third (Callison-Burch et al., 2008), fourth (Callison-Burch et al., 2009), fifth (Callison-Burch et al., 2010) and sixth (Callison-Burch et al., 2011) shared translation tasks.

2 Class error rates

In this work, the method proposed in (Popović and Ney, 2011) is used, i.e. classification of the translation errors into five basic categories based on the Word Error Rate (WER) (Levenshtein, 1966) together with the recall- and precision-based Position-independent Error Rates called Reference PER (RPER) and Hypothesis PER (HPER).

As a result of an error classification, two values are usually of interest: raw error counts for each error class, and error rates for each class, i.e. raw error counts normalised over the total number of running words. Which of the values is preferred depends of the exact task. For example, if only a distribution of error types within a translation output is of interest, the raw error counts are sufficient. On the other hand, if we want to compare different translation outputs, normalised values i.e. error rates are more suitable. Therefore they are appropriate candidates to be used for the evaluation task.

In this work, we explore the error rates calculated on the word level as well as on the block level, where a group of consecutive words labelled with the same error category is called a block. The normalisation in both cases is carried out over the total number of running words. Therefore the block level error rate for a particular error class is always less or equal than the corresponding word level error rate.

2.1 Basic class error rates

The following five basic class error rates are explored:

INFER (**inf**lectional **e**rror **r**ate):
Number of words translated into correct base form but into incorrect full form, normalised over the hypothesis length.

RER (**r**eordering **e**rror **r**ate):
Number of incorrectly positioned words normalised over the hypothesis length.

MISER (**mis**sing word **e**rror **r**ate):
Number of words which should appear in the translation hypothesis but do not, normalised over the reference length.

EXTER (**ext**ra word **e**rror **r**ate):
Number of words which appear in the translation hypothesis but should not, normalised over the hypothesis length.

LEXER (**lex**ical **e**rror **r**ate):
Number of words translated into an incorrect lexical choice in the target language (false disambiguation, unknown/untranslated word, incorrect terminology, etc.) normalised over the hypothesis length.

Table 1 presents an example of word and block level class error rates. Each erroneous word is labelled with the corresponding error category, and the blocks are marked within the parentheses { and }. The error rates on the block level are marked with a letter "b" at the beginning. It should be noted that the used method at its current stage does not enable assigning multiple error tags to one word.

reference:
The famous journalist Gustav Chalupa , born in České Budějovice , also confirms this .
hypothesis containing 14 running words:
The also confirms the famous Austrian journalist Gustav Chalupa , from Budweis Lamborghini .
hypothesis labelled with error classes:
The $\{also_{order}\ confirms_{order}\}$ $\{the_{extra}\}$ $\{famous_{order}\}$ $\{Austrian_{extra}\}$ $\{journalist_{order}\ Gustav_{order}\ Chalupa_{order}\}$, $\{from_{lex}\ Budweis_{lex}\ Lamborghini_{lex}\}$.
class error rates:
word order: RER = 6/14 = 42.8% bRER = 3/14 = 21.4% extra words: EXTER = 2/14 = 14.3% bEXTER = 2/14 = 14.3% lexical errors: LEXER = 3/14 = 21.4% bLEXER = 1/14 = 7.1%

Table 1: Example of word and block level class error rates: the word groups within the parentheses { and } are considered as blocks; all error rates are normalised over the hypothesis length, i.e. 14 running words.

2.2 Combined error rates (sums)

The following linear combinations (sums) of the basic class error rates are investigated:

WΣER (**sum** of **w**ord level **e**rror **r**ates)[1] :
Sum of all basic class error rates on the word level;

BΣER (**sum** of **b**lock level **e**rror **r**ates):
Sum of all basic class error rates on the block level;

WBΣER (**sum** of **w**ord and **b**lock level **e**rror **r**ates):
Arithmetic mean of WΣER and BΣER.

[1]This error rate has already been introduced in (Popović and Ney, 2011) and called ΣER; however, for the sake of clarity, in this work we will call it WΣER, i.e. word level ΣER.

XEnΣER (**X**→**En**glish **sum** of **e**rror **r**ates):
: Linear interpolation of word level and block level class error rates optimised for translation into English;

EnXΣER (**En**glish→**X** **sum** of **e**rror **r**ates):
: Linear interpolation of word level and block level class error rates optimised for translation from English.

For the example sentence shown in Table 1, WΣER = 84.7%, BΣER = 46.2% and WBΣER = 65.4%. XEnΣER and EnXΣER are weighted sums which will be explained in the next section.

The prerequisite for the use of the described metrics is availability of an appropriate morphological analyser for the target language which provides base forms of the words.

3 Experiments on WMT 2008, 2009, 2010 and 2011 test data

3.1 Experimental set-up

The class error rates described in Section 2 were produced for outputs of translations from Spanish, French, German and Czech into English and vice versa using Hjerson (Popović, 2011), an open-source tool for automatic error classification. Spanish, French, German and English base forms were produced using the TreeTagger[2], and the Czech base forms using Morče (Spoustová et al., 2007). In this way, all references and hypotheses were provided with the base forms of the words.

For each error rate, the system level Spearman correlation coefficients ρ with human ranking were calculated for each document. In total, 40 correlation coefficients were obtained for each error rate – twelve English outputs from the WMT 2011, 2010 and 2009 task and eight from the WMT 2008 task, together with twenty outputs in other four target languages. For further analysis, the obtained correlation results were summarised into the following three values:

- *mean*
  average correlation coefficient;

- *rank>*
  percentage of documents where the particular error rate has better correlation than the other error rates;

- *rank≥*
  percentage of documents where the particular error rate has better or equal correlation than the other error rates.

3.2 Comparison of basic class error rates

Our first experiment was to compare correlations for the basic set of class error rates in order to investigate a general behaviour of each class error rate and to see if some of the error categories are particularly (in)convenient for the evaluation task. Since certain differences between English and non-English translation outputs are observed for some error classes, the values described in the previous section were also calculated separately.

Table 2 presents the results of this experiment. The *mean* values over all documents, over the English documents and over the non-English documents are shown.

According to the overall *mean* values, the most promising error categories are lexical and reordering errors. However, the *mean* values for English outputs are significantly different than those for non-English outputs: the best error classes for English are in deed lexical and reordering errors, however for the non-English outputs the inflectional errors and missing words have higher correlations. On the other hand, for the English outputs missing words have even negative correlations, whereas correlations for inflectional errors are relatively low. The extra word class seems to be the least convenient in general, especially for non-English outputs.

Therefore, the *rank≥* values were calculated only separately for English and non-English outputs, and the previous observations were confirmed: for the English outputs lexical and reordering errors are the most relevant, whereas for the non-English outputs all classes except extra words are almost equally important.

Apart from this, it can be noticed that the grouping of words into blocks significantly improves correlation for reordering errors. The reason for this is ambiguity of tagging words as reordering errors.

[2] http://www.ims.uni-stuttgart.de/projekte/corplex/TreeTagger/

error rate	*mean* overall	x→en	en→x	*rank≥* x→en	en→x
INFER	0.398	0.190	*0.595*	46.2	*71.7*
RER	0.360	0.344	0.373	*53.8*	*51.1*
MISER	0.173	-0.101	0.434	26.3	**54.4**
EXTER	0.032	0.212	-0.195	42.7	12.2
LEXER	0.508	**0.669**	0.355	**86.0**	*58.3*
bINFER	0.423	0.211	**0.624**	47.9	**75.6**
bRER	0.508	**0.594**	0.426	**78.3**	**60.0**
bMISER	0.169	-0.121	**0.446**	21.1	*53.9*
bEXTER	-0.031	0.186	-0.238	36.8	10.0
bLEXER	0.515	*0.634*	0.402	*79.5*	**62.8**

Table 2: *mean* and *rank≥* values for each basic word level and block level error rate over all documents, over English documents and over non-English documents.

For example, if the translation reference is "a very good translation", and the obtained hypothesis is "a translation very good" , one possibility is to mark the word "translation" as reordering error, another possibility is to mark the words "very good" as reordering errors, and it is also possible to mark all the words as reordering errors. In such cases, the grouping of consecutive word level errors into blocks is beneficial.

3.3 Comparison of error rate sums

A first step towards combining the basic class error rates was investigation of simple sums, i.e. WΣER, BΣER as well as WBΣER as arithmetic mean of previous two. The overall average correlation coefficients of the sums were shown to be higher than those of the basic class error rates. Further experiments have been carried out taking into account the results described in the previous section. Firstly, extra word class was removed from all sums, however no improvement of correlation coefficients was observed. Then the sums containing only the most promising error categories separately for English and non-English output were investigated, but this also resulted in no improvements. Finally, we introduced weights for each translation direction according to the *rank≥* value for each of the basic class error rates (see Table 2), and this approach was promising. In this way, the specialised sums XENΣER and ENXΣER were introduced.

In Table 3 the results for all five error rate sums are presented. *mean*, *rank>* and *rank≥* values are presented over all translation outputs, over English outputs and over non-English outputs. As already mentioned, the overall correlation coefficients of the sums are higher than those of the basic class error rates. This could be expected, since summing class error rates is oriented towards the overall quality of the translation output whereas the class error rates are giving more information about details.

According to the overall values, the best error rate is combination of all word and block level class error rates, i.e. WBΣER followed by the block sum BΣER, whereas the WΣER and the specialised sums XENΣER and ENXΣER have lower correlations. For the translation into English, this error rate is also very promising, followed by the specialised sum XENΣER. On the other hand, for the translation from English, the most promising error rates are the block sum BΣER and the corresponding specialised sum ENXΣER. Following these observations, we decided to submit WBΣER scores for all translation outputs together with XENΣER and ENXΣER scores, each one for the corresponding translation direction. In addition, we submitted BΣER scores since this error rate also showed rather good results, especially for the translation out of English.

4 Conclusions

The presented results show that the error classification results can be used for evaluation and ranking of machine translation outputs. The most promising way to do it is to sum all word level and block level error rates, i.e. to produce the WBΣER error rate. This error rate has eventually been submitted to the WMT 2012 evaluation task. In addition, the next best metrics have been submitted, i.e. the block level sum BΣER for all translation directions, and the specialised sums XENΣER and ENXΣER each for the corresponding translation outputs.

The experiments described in this work are still at early stage: promising directions for future work are better optimisation of weights[3], further investigation of each language pair and also of each non-English

[3]First steps have already been made in this direction using an SVM classifier, and the resulting evaluation metric has also been submitted to the WMT 2012.

error rate	*mean*			*rank*≥			*rank*>		
	overall	x→en	en→x	overall	x→en	en→x	overall	x→en	en→x
WΣER	0.616	**0.694**	0.541	55.1	50.0	61.2	39.1	48.6	36.2
BΣER	0.629	0.666	0.594	60.3	55.2	**68.8**	46.1	39.5	**52.5**
WBΣER	**0.639**	**0.696**	0.585	**68.0**	**67.1**	63.7	**48.7**	**52.6**	45.0
XENΣER	0.587	**0.692**	0.487	51.9	63.2	41.2	37.8	**52.6**	23.7
ENXΣER	0.599	0.595	**0.602**	50.6	38.1	62.5	39.1	32.9	45.0

Table 3: *mean*, *rank*≥ and *rank*> values for error rate sums compared over all documents, over English documents and over non-English documents.

target language separately, filtering error categories by POS classes, etc.

Acknowledgments

This work has partly been developed within the TARAXÜ project[4] financed by TSB Technologiestiftung Berlin – Zukunftsfonds Berlin, co-financed by the European Union – European fund for regional development. Special thanks to Mark Fishel and Ondřej Bojar.

References

Chris Callison-Burch, Cameron Fordyce, Philipp Koehn, Christof Monz, and Josh Schroeder. 2008. Further Meta-Evaluation of Machine Translation. In *Proceedings of the 3rd ACL 08 Workshop on Statistical Machine Translation (WMT 2008)*, pages 70–106, Columbus, Ohio, June.

Chris Callison-Burch, Philipp Koehn, Christof Monz, and Josh Schroeder. 2009. Findings of the 2009 Workshop on Statistical Machine Translation. In *Proceedings of the Fourth Workshop on Statistical Machine Translation (WMT 2009)*, pages 1–28, Athens, Greece, March.

Chris Callison-Burch, Philipp Koehn, Christof Monz, Kay Peterson, Mark Przybocki, and Omar Zaidan. 2010. Findings of the 2010 Joint Workshop on Statistical Machine Translation and Metrics for Machine Translation. In *Proceedings of the Joint Fifth Workshop on Statistical Machine Translation and Metrics-MATR (WMT 2010)*, pages 17–53, Uppsala, Sweden, July.

Chris Callison-Burch, Philipp Koehn, Christof Monz, and Omar Zaidan. 2011. Findings of the 2011 Workshop on Statistical Machine Translation. In *Proceedings of the Sixth Workshop on Statistical Machine Translation (WMT 2011)*, pages 22–64, Edinburgh, Scotland, July.

Vladimir Iosifovich Levenshtein. 1966. Binary Codes Capable of Correcting Deletions, Insertions and Reversals. *Soviet Physics Doklady*, 10(8):707–710, February.

Maja Popović and Hermann Ney. 2011. Towards Automatic Error Analysis of Machine Translation Output. *Computational Linguistics*, 37(4):657–688, December.

Maja Popović. 2011. Hjerson: An Open Source Tool for Automatic Error Classification of Machine Translation Output. *The Prague Bulletin of Mathematical Linguistics*, (96):59–68, October.

Drahomíra Spoustová, Jan Hajič, Jan Votrubec, Pavel Krbec, and Pavel Květoň. 2007. The best of two worlds: Cooperation of statistical and rule-based taggers for czech. In *Proceedings of the Workshop on Balto-Slavonic Natural Language Processing, ACL 2007*, pages 67–74, Praha.

[4]http://taraxu.dfki.de/

SPEDE: Probabilistic Edit Distance Metrics for MT Evaluation

Mengqiu Wang and **Christopher D. Manning**
Computer Science Department
Stanford University
Stanford, CA 94305 USA
{mengqiu,manning}@cs.stanford.edu

Abstract

This paper describes Stanford University's submission to the Shared Evaluation Task of WMT 2012. Our proposed metric (SPEDE) computes probabilistic edit distance as predictions of translation quality. We learn weighted edit distance in a probabilistic finite state machine (pFSM) model, where state transitions correspond to edit operations. While standard edit distance models cannot capture long-distance word swapping or cross alignments, we rectify these shortcomings using a novel pushdown automaton extension of the pFSM model. Our models are trained in a regression framework, and can easily incorporate a rich set of linguistic features. Evaluated on two different prediction tasks across a diverse set of datasets, our methods achieve state-of-the-art correlation with human judgments.

1 Introduction

We describe the Stanford Probabilistic Edit Distance Evaluation (SPEDE) metric, which makes predictions of translation quality by computing weighted edit distance. We model weighted edit distance in a probabilistic finite state machine (pFSM), where state transitions correspond to edit operations. The weights of the edit operations are then automatically learned in a regression framework. One of the major contributions of this paper is a novel extension of the pFSM model into a probabilistic Pushdown Automaton (pPDA), which enhances traditional edit-distance models with the ability to model phrase shift and word swapping. Furthermore, we give a new log-linear parameterization to the pFSM model, which allows it to easily incorporate rich linguistic features.

We conducted extensive experiments on a diverse set of standard evaluation data sets (NIST OpenMT06, 08; WMT06, 07, 08). Our models achieve or surpass state-of-the-art results on all test sets.

2 Related Work

Research in automatic machine translation (MT) evaluation metrics has been a key driving force behind the recent advances of statistical machine translation (SMT) systems. The early seminal work on automatic MT metrics (e.g., BLEU and NIST) is largely based on n-gram matches (Papineni et al., 2002; Doddington, 2002). Despite their simplicity, these measures have shown good correlation with human judgments, and enabled large-scale evaluations across many different MT systems, without incurring the huge labor cost of human evaluation (Callison-Burch et al. (2009; 2010; 2011), *inter alia*).

Later metrics that move beyond n-grams achieve higher accuracy and improved robustness from resources like WordNet synonyms (Miller et al., 1990), paraphrasing (Zhou et al., 2006; Snover et al., 2009; Denkowski and Lavie, 2010), and syntactic parse structures (Liu et al., 2005; Owczarzak et al., 2008; He et al., 2010). But a common problem in these metrics is they typically resort to ad-hoc tuning methods instead of principled approaches to incorporate linguistic features. Recent models use linear or SVM regression and train them against human judgments to automatic learn feature weights, and have shown state-of-the-art correlation with human judgments (Albrecht and Hwa, 2007a; Albrecht and Hwa, 2007b; Sun et al., 2008; Pado et al., 2009). The drawback, however, is they rely on time-consuming

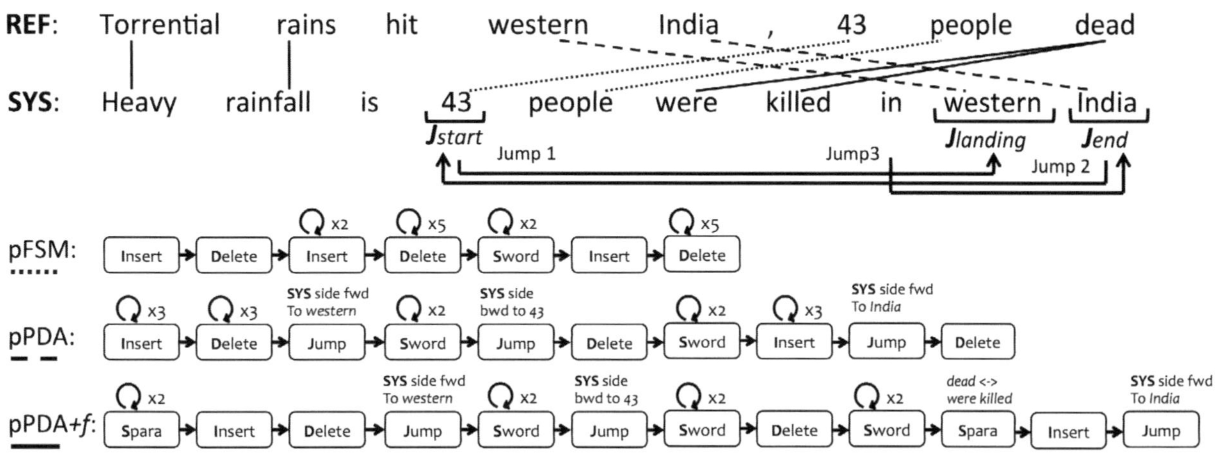

Figure 1: This diagram illustrates an example translation pair in the Chinese-English portion of OpenMT08 data set (Doc:AFP_CMN_20070703.0005, system09, sent 1). The three rows below are the best state transition (edit) sequences that transforms REF to SYS, according to the three proposed models. The corresponding alignments generated by the models (pFSM, pPDA, pPDA+f) are shown with different styled lines, with later models in the order generating strictly more alignments than earlier ones. The gold human evaluation score is 6.5, and model predictions are: pPDA+f 5.5, pPDA 4.3, pFSM 3.1, METEORR 3.2, TERR 2.8.

preprocessing modules to extract linguistic features (e.g., a full end-to-end textual entailment system was needed in Pado et al. (2009)), which severely limits their practical use. Furthermore, these models employ a large number of features (on the order of hundreds), and consequently make the model predictions opaque and hard to analyze.

3 pFSMs for MT Regression

We start off by framing the problem of machine translation evaluation in terms of weighted edit distance calculated using probabilistic finite state machines (pFSMs). A FSM defines a language by accepting a string of input tokens in the language, and rejecting those that are not. A probabilistic FSM defines the probability that a string is in a language, extending on the concept of a FSM. Commonly used models such as HMMs, n-gram models, Markov Chains, probabilistic finite state transducers and PCFGs all fall in the broad family of pFSMs (Knight and Al-Onaizan, 1998; Eisner, 2002; Kumar and Byrne, 2003; Vidal et al., 2005). Unlike all the other applications of FSMs where tokens in the language are words, in our language tokens are edit operations. A string of tokens that our FSM accepts is an edit sequence that transforms a reference translation (denoted as *ref*) into a system translation (*sys*).

Our pFSM has a unique start and stop state, and one state per edit operation (i.e., *Insert*, *Delete*, *Substitution*). The probability of an edit sequence **e** is generated by the model is the product of the state transition probabilities in the pFSM, formally described as:

$$w(\mathbf{e} \mid \mathbf{s}, \mathbf{r}) = \frac{1}{Z} \prod_{i=1}^{|\mathbf{e}|} \exp \theta \cdot \mathbf{f}(e_{i-1}, e_i, \mathbf{s}, \mathbf{r}) \quad (1)$$

We featurize each of the state changes with a log-linear parameterization; **f** is a set of binary feature functions defined over pairs of neighboring states (by the Markov assumption) and the input sentences, and θ are the associated feature weights; r and s are shorthand for *ref* and *sys*; Z is a partition function. In this basic pFSM model, the feature functions are simply identity functions that emit the current state, and the state transition sequence of the previous state and the current state.

The feature weights are then automatically learned by training a global regression model where some translational equivalence judgment score (e.g., human assessment score, or HTER (Snover et al., 2006)) for each *sys* and *ref* translation pair is the regression target ($\hat{y}$). Since the "gold" edit sequence are not given at training or prediction time, we treat the edit sequences as hidden variables and sum over them in our model. We introduce a new regression variable $y \in \mathbb{R}$ which is the log-sum of the unnormalized weights (Eqn. (1)) of all edit sequences, formally expressed as:

$$y = \log \sum_{\mathbf{e}' \subseteq \mathbf{e}^*} \prod_{i=1}^{|\mathbf{e}'|} \exp \theta \cdot \mathbf{f}(e_{i-1}, e_i, \mathbf{s}, \mathbf{r}) \qquad (2)$$

The sum over an exponential number of edit sequences in $\mathbf{e}^*$ is solved efficiently using a forward-backward style dynamic program. Any edit sequence that does not lead to a complete transformation of the translation pair has a probability of zero in our model. Our regression target then seeks to minimize the least squares error with respect to $\hat{y}$, plus a $L2$-norm regularizer term parameterized by λ:

$$\theta^* = \min_{\theta} \{ \sum_{\mathbf{s_i}, \mathbf{r_i}} [\hat{y}_i - (\frac{y}{|\mathbf{s_i}| + |\mathbf{r_i}|} + \alpha)]^2 + \lambda \|\theta\|^2 \} \qquad (3)$$

The $|\mathbf{s_i}| + |\mathbf{r_i}|$ is a length normalization term for the ith training instance, and α is a scaling constant for adjusting to different scoring standards (e.g., 7-point scale vs. 5-point scale), whose value is automatically learned. At test time, $y/(|\mathbf{s}| + |\mathbf{r}|) + \alpha$ is computed as the predicted score.

We replaced the standard substitution edit operation with three new operations: S_{word} for same word substitution, S_{lemma} for same lemma substitution, and S_{punc} for same punctuation substitution. In other words, all but the three matching-based substitutions are disallowed. The start state can transition into any of the edit states with a constant unit cost, and each edit state can transition into any other edit state if and only if the edit operation involved is valid at the current edit position (e.g., the model cannot transition into *Delete* state if it is already at the end of *ref*; similarly it cannot transition into S_{lemma} unless the lemma of the two words under edit in *sys* and *ref* match). When the end of both sentences are reached, the model transitions into the stop state and ends the edit sequence. The first row in Figure 1 starting with pFSM shows a state transition sequence for an example *sys/ref* translation pair. There exists a one-to-one correspondence between substitution edits and word alignments. Therefore this example state transition sequence correctly generates an alignment for the word *43* and *people*.

It is helpful to compare with the TER metric (Snover et al., 2006), which is based on the idea of word error rate measured in edit distance, to better understand the intuition behind our model. There are two major improvements in our model: 1) the edit operations in our model are weighted, as defined by the feature functions and weights; 2) the weights are automatically learned, instead of being uniform or manually set; and 3) we model state transitions, which can be understood as a bigram extension of the unigram edit distance model used in TER. For example, if in our learned model the feature for two consecutive S_{word} states has a positive weight, then our model would favor consecutive same word substitutions, whereas in the TER model the order of the substitution does not matter. The extended TER-plus (Snover et al., 2009) metric addresses the first problem but not the other two.

3.1 pPDA Extension

A shortcoming of edit distance models is that they cannot handle long-distance word swapping — a pervasive phenomenon found in most natural languages. [1] Edit operations in standard edit distance models need to obey strict incremental order in their edit position, in order to admit efficient dynamic programming solutions. The same limitation is shared by our pFSM model, where the Markov assumption is made based on the incremental order of edit positions. Although there is no known solution to the general problem of computing edit distance where long-distance swapping is permitted (Dombb et al., 2010), approximate algorithms do exist. We present a simple but novel extension of the pFSM model to a probabilistic pushdown automaton (pPDA), to capture non-nested word swapping within limited distance, which covers a majority of word swapping in observed in real data (Wu, 2010).

A pPDA, in its simplest form, is a pFSM where each control state is equipped with a stack (Esparza and Kucera, 2005). The addition of stacks for each transition state endows the machine with memory, extending its expressiveness beyond that of context-free formalisms. By construction, at any stage in a normal edit sequence, the pPDA model can "jump"

[1] The edit distance algorithm described in Cormen et al. (2001) can only handle adjacent word swapping (transposition), but not long-distance swapping.

forward within a fixed distance (controlled by a max distance parameter) to a new edit position on either side of the sentence pair, and start a new edit subsequence from there. Assuming the jump was made on the *sys* side, [2] the machine remembers its current edit position in *sys* as J_{start}, and the destination position on *sys* after the jump as $J_{landing}$.

We constrain our model so that the only edit operations that are allowed immediately following a "jump" are from the set of substitution operations (e.g., S_{word}). And after at least one substitution has been made, the device can now "jump" back to J_{start}, remembering the current edit position as J_{end}. Another constraint here is that after the backward "jump", all edit operations are permitted except for *Delete*, which cannot take place until at least one substitution has been made. When the edit sequence advances to position $J_{landing}$, the only operation allowed at that point is another "jump" forward operation to position J_{end}, at which point we also clear all memory about jump positions and reset.

An intuitive explanation is that when pPDA makes the first forward jump, a gap is left in *sys* that has not been edited yet. It remembers where it left off, and comes back to it after some substitutions have been made to complete the edit sequence. The second row in Figure 1 (starting with pPDA) illustrates an edit sequence in a pPDA model that involves three "jump" operations, which are annotated and indexed by number 1-3 in the example. "Jump 1" creates an un-edited gap between word *43* and *western*, after two substitutions, the model makes "jump 2" to go back and edit the gap. The only edit permitted immediately after "jump 2" is deleting the comma in *ref*, since inserting the word *43* in *sys* before any substitution is disallowed. Once the gap is completed, the model resumes at position J_{end} by making "jump 3", and completes the jump sequence.

The "jumps" allowed the model to align words such as *western India*, in addition to the alignments of *43 people* found by the pFSM. In practice, we found that our extension gives a big boost to model performance (*cf.* Section 5.1), with only a modest increase in computation time. [3]

3.2 Parameter Estimation

Since the least squares operator preserves convexity, and the inner log-sum-exponential function is convex, the resulting objective function is also convex. For parameter learning, we used the limited memory quasi-newton method (Liu and Nocedal, 1989) to find the optimal feature weights and scaling constant for the objective. We initialized $\theta = \vec{0}$, $\alpha = 0$, and $\lambda = 5$. We also threw away features occurring fewer than five times in training corpus. Gradient calculation was similar to other pFSM models, such as HMMs, we omitted the details here, for brevity.

4 Rich Linguistic Features

We add new substitution operations beyond those introduced in Section 3, to capture synonyms and paraphrase in the translations. Synonym relations are defined according to WordNet (Miller et al., 1990), and paraphrase matches are given by a lookup table used in TERplus (Snover et al., 2009). To better take advantage of paraphrase information at the multi-word phrase level, we extended our substitution operations to match longer phrases by adding one-to-many and many-to-many bigram block substitutions.

5 Experiments

The goal of our experiments is to test both the accuracy and robustness of the proposed new models. We then show that modeling word swapping and rich linguistics features further improve our results.

To better situate our work among past research and to draw meaningful comparison, we use exactly the same standard evaluation data sets and metrics as Pado et al. (2009), which is currently the state-of-the-art result for regression-based MT evaluation. We consider four widely used MT metrics (BLEU, NIST, METEOR (Banerjee and Lavie, 2005) (v0.7), and TER) as our baselines. Since our models are trained to regress human evaluation scores, to make a direct comparison in the same regression setting, we also train a small linear regression model for each baseline metric in the same way as descried in Pado et al. (2009). These regression models are strictly more powerful than the baseline metrics and show higher robustness and better correlation with human

[2] Recall that we transform *ref* into *sys*, and thus on the *sys* side, we can only insert but not delete. The argument applies equally to the case where the jump was made on the other side.

[3] The length of the longest edit sequence with jumps only increased by $0.5 * max(|\mathbf{s}|, |\mathbf{r}|)$ in the worst case, and by and large swapping is rare in comparison to basic edits.

Data Set		Our Metrics			Baseline Metrics							
train	test	pFSM	pPDA	pPDA+*f*	BLEUR	NISTR	TERR	METR	MTR	RTER	MT+RTER
A+C	U	54.6	55.3	**57.2**	49.9	49.5	50.1	49.1	50.1	54.5	55.6
A+U	C	59.9	63.8	**65.7**	53.9	53.1	50.3	61.1	57.3	58.0	62.7
C+U	A	**61.2**	60.4	59.8	52.5	50.4	54.5	60.1	55.2	59.9	**61.1**
MT08	MT06	**65.2**	63.4	64.5	57.6	55.1	63.8	62.1	62.6	62.2	**65.2**

Table 1: Overall results on OpenMT08 and OpenMT06 evaluation data sets. The R (as in BLEUR) refers to the regression model trained for each baseline metric, same as Pado et al. (2009). The first three rows are round-robin train/test results over three languages on OpenMT08 (A=Arabic, C=Chinese, U=Urdu). The last row are results trained on entire OpenMT08 (A+C+U) and tested on OpenMT06. Numbers in this table are Spearman's rank correlation ρ between human assessment scores and model predictions. The pPDA column describes our pPDA model with jump distance limit 5. METR is shorthand for METEORR. +*f* means the model includes synonyms and paraphrase features (*cf.* Section 4). Best results and scores that are not statistically significantly worse are highlighted in bold in each row.

judgments. [4] We also compare our models with the state-of-the-art linear regression models reported in Pado et al. (2009) that combine features from multiple MT evaluation metrics (MT), as well as rich linguistic features from a textual entailment system (RTE).

In all of our experiments, each reference and system translation sentence pair is tokenized using the PTB (Marcus et al., 1993) tokenization script, and lemmatized by the Porter Stemmer (Porter, 1980). Statistical significance tests are performed using the paired bootstrap resampling method (Koehn, 2004).

We divide our experiments into two sections, based on two different prediction tasks — predicting absolute scores and predicting pairwise preference.

5.1 Exp. 1: Predicting Absolute Scores

The first task is to evaluate a system translation on a seven point Likert scale against a single reference. Higher scores indicate translations that are closer to the meaning intended by the reference. Human ratings in the form of absolute scores are available for standard evaluation data sets such as NIST OpenMT06,08.[5] Since our model makes predictions at the granularity of a whole sentence, we focus on sentence-level evaluation. A metric's goodness is judged by how well it correlates with human judgments, and Spearman's rank correlation (ρ) is reported for all experiments in this section.

We used the NIST OpenMT06 corpus for development purposes, and reserved the NIST OpenMT08 corpus for post-development evaluation. The OpenMT06 data set contains 1,992 English translations of Arabic newswire text from 8 MT systems. For development, we used a 2-fold cross-validation scheme with splits at the first 1,000 and last 992 sentences. The OpenMT08 data set contains English translations of newswire text from three languages (Arabic has 2,769 pairs from 13 MT systems; Chinese has 1,815 pairs from 15; and Urdu has 1,519 pairs, from 7). We followed the same experimental setup as Pado et al. (2009), using a "round robin" training/testing scheme, i.e., we train a model on data from two languages, making predictions for the third. We also show results of models trained on the entire OpenMT08 data set and tested on OpenMT06.

Overall Comparison

Results of our proposed models compared against the baseline models described in Pado et al. (2009) are shown in Table 1. The pFSM and pPDA models do not use any additional information other than words and lemmas, and thus make a fair comparison with the baseline metrics. [6] We can see from the table that pFSM significantly outperforms all baselines on Urdu and Arabic, but trails behind METEORR on Chinese by a small margin (1.2 point in Spearman's ρ). On Chinese data set, the pPDA extension gives results significantly better than the best baseline metrics for Chinese (2.7 better than METEORR). It is also significantly better than pFSM (by

[4] See Pado et al. (2009) for more discussion.

[5] Available from `http://www.nist.gov`.

[6] METEORR actually has an unfair advantage in this comparison, since it uses synonym information from WordNet; TERR on the other hand has a disadvantage because it does not use lemmas. Lemma is added later in the TERplus extension (Snover et al., 2009).

3.9 points), suggesting that modeling word swapping is particularly rewarding for Chinese language. On the other hand, pPDA model does not perform better than the pFSM model on Arabic in MT08 and OpenMT06 (which is also Arabic-to-English). This observation is consistent with findings in earlier work that Chinese-English translations exhibit much more medium and long distance reordering than languages like Arabic (Birch et al., 2009).

Both the pFSM and pPDA models also significantly outperform the MTR linear regression model that combines the outputs of all four baselines, on all three source languages. This demonstrates that our regression model is more robust and accurate than a state-of-the-art system combination linear-regression model. The RTER and MT+RTER linear regression models benefit from the rich linguistic features in the textual entailment system's output. It has access to all the features in pPDA+*f* such as paraphrase and dependency parse relations, and many more (e.g., Norm Bank, part-of-speech, negation, antonyms). However, our pPDA+*f* model rivals the performance of RTER and MT+RTER on Arabic (with no statistically significant difference from RTER), and greatly improve over these two models on Urdu and Chinese. Most noticeably, pPDA+*f* is 7.7 points better than RTER on Chinese.

5.2 Exp. 2: Predicting Pairwise Preferences

To further test our model's robustness, we evaluate it on WMT data sets with a different prediction task in which metrics make pairwise preference judgments between translation systems. The WMT06-08 data sets are much larger in comparison to the OpenMT06 and 08 data. They contain MT outputs of over 40 systems from five different source languages (French, German, Spanish, Czech, and Hungarian). The WMT06, 07 and 08 sets contains 10,159, 5,472 and 6,856 sentence pairs, respectively. We used portions of WMT 06 and 07 data sets [7] that are annotated with absolute scores on a five point scale for training, and the WMT08 data set annotated with pairwise preference for testing.

To generate pairwise preference predictions, we first predict an absolute score for each system translation, then compare the scores between each system pair, and give preference to the higher score. We adopt the sentence-level evaluation metric used in Pado et al. (2009), which measures the consistency (accuracy) of metric predictions with human preferences. The random baseline for this task on WMT08 data set is 39.8%.

Models	WMT06	WMT07	WMT06+07
pPDA+*f*	51.6	**52.4**	52.0
BLEUR	49.7	49.5	49.6
METEORR	51.4	51.4	51.5
NISTR	50.0	50.3	50.2
TERR	50.9	51.0	51.2
MTR	50.8	51.5	51.5
RTER	51.8	50.7	51.9
MT+RTER	**52.3**	51.8	**52.5**

Table 2: Pairwise preference prediction results on WMT08 test set. Each column shows a different training data set. Numbers in this table are model's consistency with human pairwise preference judgments. Best result on each test set is highlighted in bold.

Results are shown in Table 2. Similar to the results on OpenMT experiments, our model consistently outperformed BLEUR, METEORR, NISTR and TERR. Our model also gives better performance than the MTR ensemble model on all three tests; and ties with RTER in two out of the three tests but performs significantly better on the other test. The MT+RTER ensemble model is better on two tests, but worse on the other. But overall the two systems are quite comparable, with less than 0.6% accuracy difference. The results also show that our method is stable across different training sets, with test accuracy differences less than 0.4%.

6 Conclusion

We described the SPEDE metric for sentence level MT evaluation. It is based on probabilistic finite state machines to compute weighted edit distance. Our model admits a rich set of linguistic features, and can be trained to learn feature weights automatically by optimizing a regression objective. A novel pushdown automaton extension was also presented for capturing long-distance word swapping. Our metrics achieve state-of-the-art results on a wide range of standard evaluations, and are much more lightweight than previous regression models.

[7] Available from `http://www.statmt.org`.

Acknowledgements

We gratefully acknowledge the support of Defense Advanced Research Projects Agency (DARPA) Machine Reading Program under Air Force Research Laboratory (AFRL) prime contract no. FA8750-09-C-0181 and the support of the DARPA Broad Operational Language Translation (BOLT) program through IBM. Any opinions, findings, and conclusion or recommendations expressed in this material are those of the author(s) and do not necessarily reflect the view of the DARPA, AFRL, or the US government.

References

J. Albrecht and R. Hwa. 2007a. A re-examination of machine learning approaches for sentence-level MT evaluation. In *Proceedings of ACL*.

J. Albrecht and R. Hwa. 2007b. Regression for sentence-level MT evaluation with pseudo references. In *Proceedings of ACL*.

S. Banerjee and A. Lavie. 2005. Meteor: An automatic metric for MT evaluation with improved correlation with human judgments. In *Proceedings of ACL Workshop on Intrinsic and Extrinsic Evaluation Measures*.

A. Birch, P. Blunsom, and M. Osborne. 2009. A quantitative analysis of reordering phenomena. In *Proceedings of WMT 09*.

C. Callison-Burch, P. Koehn, C. Monz, and J. Schroeder. 2009. Findings of the 2009 Workshop on Statistical Machine Translation. In *Proceedings of the Fourth Workshop on Statistical Machine Translation*.

C. Callison-Burch, P. Koehn, C. Monz, K. Peterson, M. Przybocki, and O. Zaidan. 2010. Findings of the 2010 joint workshop on Statistical Machine Translation and metrics for Machine Translation. In *Proceedings of Joint WMT 10 and MetricsMatr Workshop at ACL*.

C. Callison-Burch, P. Koehn, C. Monz, and O. Zaidan. 2011. Findings of the 2011 workshop on statistical machine translation. In *Proceedings of the Sixth Workshop on Statistical Machine Translation*.

T. H. Cormen, C. E. Leiserson, R. L. Rivest, and C. Stein. 2001. *Introduction to Algorithms, Second Edition*. MIT Press.

M. Denkowski and A. Lavie. 2010. Extending the METEOR machine translation evaluation metric to the phrase level. In *Proceedings of HLT/NAACL*.

G. Doddington. 2002. Automatic evaluation of machine translation quality using n-gram cooccurrence statistics. In *Proceedings of HLT*.

Y. Dombb, O. Lipsky, B. Porat, E. Porat, and A. Tsur. 2010. The approximate swap and mismatch edit distance. *Theoretical Computer Science*, 411(43).

J. Eisner. 2002. Parameter estimation for probabilistic finite-state transducers. In *Proceedings of ACL*.

J. Esparza and A. Kucera. 2005. Quantitative analysis of probabilistic pushdown automata: Expectations and variances. In *Proceedings of the 20th Annual IEEE Symposium on Logic in Computer Science*.

Y. He, J. Du, A. Way, and J. van Genabith. 2010. The DCU dependency-based metric in WMT-MetricsMATR 2010. In *Proceedings of Joint WMT 10 and Metrics-Matr Workshop at ACL*.

K. Knight and Y. Al-Onaizan. 1998. Translation with finite-state devices. In *Proceedings of AMTA*.

P. Koehn. 2004. Statistical significance tests for machine translation evaluation. In *Proceedings of EMNLP*.

S. Kumar and W. Byrne. 2003. A weighted finite state transducer implementation of the alignment template model for statistical machine translation. In *Proceedings of HLT/NAACL*.

D. C. Liu and J. Nocedal. 1989. On the limited memory BFGS method for large scale optimization. *Math. Programming*, 45:503–528.

D. Liu, , and D. Gildea. 2005. Syntactic features for evaluation of machine translation. In *Proceedings of the ACL Workshop on Intrinsic and Extrinsic Evaluation Measures*.

M. P. Marcus, M. A. Marcinkiewicz, and B. Santorini. 1993. Building a large annotated corpus of english: the Penn Treebank. *Computational Linguistics*, 19(2):313–330.

G. A. Miller, R. Beckwith, C. Fellbaum, D. Gross, and K. J. Miller. 1990. WordNet: an on-line lexical database. *International Journal of Lexicography*, 3(4).

F. Och. 2003. Minimum error rate training in statistical machine translation. In *Proceedings of ACL*.

K. Owczarzak, J. van Genabith, and A. Way. 2008. Evaluating machine translation with LFG dependencies. *Machine Translation*, 21(2):95–119.

S. Pado, M. Galley, D. Jurafsky, and C. D. Manning. 2009. Robust machine translation evaluation with entailment features. In *Proceedings of ACL*.

K. Papineni, S. Roukos, T. Ward, and W. Zhu. 2002. BLEU: a method for automatic evaluation of machine translation. In *Proceedings of ACL*.

M.F. Porter. 1980. An algorithm for suffix stripping. *Program*, 14(3):130–137.

M. Snover, B. Dorr, R. Schwartz, L. Micciulla, and J. Makhoul. 2006. A study of translation edit rate with targeted human annotation. In *Proceedings of AMTA*.

M. Snover, , N. Madnani, B. Dorr, and R. Schwartz. 2009. Fluency, adequacy, or HTER? exploring different human judgments with a tunable MT metric. In *Proceedings of WMT09 Workshop*.

S. Sun, Y. Chen, and J. Li. 2008. A re-examination on features in regression based approach to automatic MT evaluation. In *Proceedings of ACL*.

E. Vidal, F. Thollard, C. de la Higuera, F. Casacuberta, and R. C. Carrasco. 2005. Probabilistic finite-state machines part I. *IEEE Transactions on Pattern Analysis and Machine Intelligence*, 27(7):1013–1025.

D. Wu, 2010. *CRC Handbook of Natural Language Processing*, chapter How to Select an Answer String?, pages 367–408. CRC Press.

L. Zhou, C.Y. Lin, and E. Hovy. 2006. Re-evaluating machine translation results with paraphrase support. In *Proceedings of EMNLP*.

Quality Estimation for Machine Translation output using linguistic analysis and decoding features

Eleftherios Avramidis
German Research Center for Artificial Intelligence (DFKI)
Berlin, Germany
eleftherios.avramidis@dfki.de

Abstract

We describe a submission to the WMT12 Quality Estimation task, including an extensive Machine Learning experimentation. Data were augmented with features from linguistic analysis and statistical features from the SMT search graph. Several Feature Selection algorithms were employed. The Quality Estimation problem was addressed both as a regression task and as a discretised classification task, but the latter did not generalise well on the unseen testset. The most successful regression methods had an RMSE of 0.86 and were trained with a feature set given by Correlation-based Feature Selection. Indications that RMSE is not always sufficient for measuring performance were observed.

1 Introduction

As Machine Translation (MT) gradually gains a position into production environments, the need for estimating the quality of its output is increasing. Various use cases refer to it as input assessment for Human Post-editing, as an extension for Hybrid MT or System Combination, or even a method for improving components of existing MT systems.

With the current submission we are trying to address the problem of assigning a quality score to a single MT output per source sentence. Previous work includes regression methods for indicating a binary value of correctness (Quirk, 2001; Blatz et al., 2004; Ueffing and Ney, 2007), human-likeness (Gamon et al., 2005) or continuous scores (Specia et al., 2009). As we also work with continuous scores, we are making an effort to combine previous feature acquisition sources, such as language modelling (Raybaud et al., 2009), language fluency checking (Parton et al., 2011), parsing (Sánchez-Martinez, 2011; Avramidis et al., 2011) and decoding statistics (Specia et al., 2009; Avramidis, 2011). The current submission combines such previous observations in a combinatory experimentation on feature sets, feature selection methods and Machine Learning (ML) algorithms.

The structure of the submission is as follows: The approach is defined and the methods are described in section 2, including features acquisition, feature selection and learning. Section 3 includes information about the experiment setup whereas the results are discussed in Section 4.

2 Methods

2.1 Data and basic approach

This contribution has been built based on the data released for the Quality Estimation task of the Workshop on Machine Translation (WMT) 2012 (Callison-Burch et al., 2012). The organizers provided an English-to-Spanish development set and a test set of 1832 and 422 sentences respectively, derived from WMT09 and WMT10 datasets. For each source sentence of the development set, participants were offered one translation generated by a state-of-the-art phrase-based SMT system. The quality of each SMT translation was assessed by human evaluators, who provided a quality score in the range 1-5. Additionally, statistics and processing information from the execution of the SMT decoding algorithm were given.

The approach presented here is making use of the source sentences, the SMT output and the quality scores in order to follow a typical ML paradigm:

sentence	suggestion
...los líderes de la Unión han descrito como **deducciones político**...	*number agreement*
La articular **y ideológicamente** convencido de asesino de masas...	*transform "y" to "e"*
Right after **hearing** about it, he described it as a "challenge..."	*disambiguate -ing*

Table 1: Sample suggestions generated by rule-based language checking tools, observed in development data

each source and target sentence of the development set are being analyzed to generate a feature vector. One training sample is formed out of the feature vector and the quality score (i.e. as a class value) of each sentence. A ML algorithm is consequently used to train a model given the training samples. The performance of each model is evaluated upon a part of the development set that was kept-out from training.

2.2 Acquiring Features

The features were obtained from two sources: the decoding process and the analysis of the text of the source and the target sentence. The two steps are explained below.

2.2.1 Features from text analysis

The following features were generated with the use of tools for the statistical and/or linguistic analysis of the text. The baseline features included:

- **Tokens count**: Count of tokens in the source and the translated sentence and their ratio, unknown words and also occurrences of the target word within the translated sentence (averaged for all words in the hypothesis - type/token ratio)
- **IBM1-model lookup**: Average number of translations per source word in the sentence, unweighted or weighted by the inverse frequency of each word in the source corpus
- **Language modeling**: Language model probability of the source and translated sentence
- **Corpus lookup**: percentage of unigrams / bigrams / trigrams in quartiles 1 and 4 of frequency (lower and higher frequency words) in a corpus of the source language

Additionally, the following linguistically motivated features were also included:

- **Parsing**: PCFG Parse (Petrov et al., 2006) log-likelihood, size of n-best tree list, confidence for the best parse, average confidence of all parse trees. Ratios of the mentioned target features to the corresponding source features.
- **Shallow grammatical match**: The number of occurences of particular node tags on both the source and the target was counted on the PCFG parses. Additionally, the ratio of the occurences of each tag in the target sentence by the corresponding occurences on the source sentence.
- **Language quality check**: Source and target sentences were subject to automatic rule-based *language quality checking*, providing a wide range of quality suggestions concerning **style**, **grammar** and **terminology**, summed up in an overall quality score. The process employed 786 rules for English and 70 rules for Spanish. We counted the occurences of every rule match in each sentence and the number of characters it affected. Sample rule suggestions can be seen in Table 1.

2.2.2 Features from the decoding process

The organisers provided a verbose output of the decoding process, including probabilistic scores from all steps of the execution of the translation search. We added the scores appearing once per sentence (i.e. referring to the best hypothesis), whereas for the ones being modified over the generation graph, their average (avg), variance (var) and standard deviation (std) was calculated. These features are:

- the log of the phrase translation probability (pC) and the phrase future cost estimate (c)
- the score component vector including the distortion scores ($d_{1...7}$), word penalty, translation scores (e.g. a_1: inverse phrase translation probability, a_2: inverse lexical weighting)

2.3 Feature Selection

Experience has shown difficulties in including hundreds of features into training a statistical model. Several algorithms (such as Naïve Bayes) require statistically-independent features. For others, a search space of hundreds of features may impose increased computational complexity, which is often unsustainable in the time and resources allocated. In these cases we therefore applied several common *Feature Selection* approaches, in order to reduce the available features to an affordable number.

We used the Feature Selection algorithms of *Relieff* (Kononenko, 1994), *Information Gain* and *Gain Ratio* (Kullback and Leibler, 1951), and *Correlation-based Feature Selection* (Hall, 2000). The latter is known for producing feature sets highly correlated with the class, yet uncorrelated with each other; selection was done in two variations, *greedy stepwise* and *best first*.

The data were discretised according to the algorithm requirements and features were scored in a 10-fold cross-validation.

2.4 Machine Learning

We tried to approach the issue with two distinct modelling approaches, *classification* and *regression*.

2.4.1 Classification algorithms

In an effort to interpret Quality Estimation as a classification problem, we expect to build models that are able to assign a discrete value, as a measure of sentence quality. This bears some relation to the way the quality scores were generated; humans were asked to provide an (integer) quality score in the range 1-5. In our case, we try to build classifiers that do the same, but are also able to assign values with smaller intervals. For this purpose, we set up 4 sub-experiments, where the class value in our data was rounded up to intervals of 0.25, 0.5, 0.7 and 1.0 respectively.

In this part of the experiment we used the *Naïve Bayes*, *k-nearest-neighbours* (kNN), *Support Vector Machines* (SVM) and *Tree classification* algorithms. Naïve Bayes' probabilities for our continuous features were estimated with *locally weighted linear regression* (Cleveland, 1979).

2.4.2 Regression algorithms

Regression algorithms produce a model for directly predicting a quality score with continuous values. Experimentation here included *Partial Least Squares Regression* (Stone and Brooks, 1990), *Multivariate Adaptive Regression Splines – MARS* (Friedman, 1991), *Lasso* (Tibshirani, 1994) and *Linear Regression*.

3 Experiment and Results

3.1 Implementation

PCFG parsing features were generated on the output of the Berkeley Parser (Petrov and Klein, 2007), trained over an English and a Spanish treebank (Mariona Taulé and Recasens, 2008). N-gram features have been generated with the SRILM toolkit (Stolcke, 2002). The *Acrolinx IQ*[1] was used to parse the source side, whereas the *Language Tool*[2] was applied on both sides.

The feature selection and learning algorithms were implemented with the Orange (Demšar et al., 2004) and Weka (Hall et al., 2009) toolkits.

3.2 Experiment structure

The methods explained in the previous section provide a wide range of experiment parameters. Consequently, we tried to extensively test all the possible parameter combinations. The development data were separated in two sets, one "training" set and one "keep-out" set, used to test the predictions. In order to give learners better coverage over the data, the development set was split in two ways (70% training - 30% test and 90% training - 10% test), so that all experiments get performed under both settings. The scores of these two were averaged[3].

3.3 Results

The small size of the dataset allowed for fast training and testing of the discrete classification problem, where we could execute 370 experiments. The regression problem was considerably slower, as only 36 experiments concluded in time.

[1] http://www.acrolinx.com (proprietary)

[2] http://languagetool.org (open-source)

[3] Given the disparity of the test sizes, it would have in principle been better to use a weighted average. Though, this would not have lead to significant differences in the results.

			5-fold		avg 70-30%, 90-10% folds			
algorithm	feat. set	discr.	CA	AUC	RMSE	MAE	interval	
Tree	#17, #20	0.25	15.40	54.10	0.84	0.67	1.5	5.0
Tree	#23	0.25	14.60	53.50	0.85	0.68	2.0	5.0
Tree	#12	0.25	13.90	52.00	0.86	0.69	1.8	5.0
Tree	#4	0.25	14.50	53.70	0.86	0.69	2.0	5.0
SVM	#16	0.25	16.00	60.40	0.86	0.69	3.2	3.2
kNN	#22	0.25	12.30	55.50	1.00	0.78	2.0	5.0
Tree	#21	0.50	22.70	54.60	0.87	0.69	2.0	5.0
SVM	#19	0.50	22.40	60.20	0.91	0.73	2.8	5.0
kNN	#12	0.50	20.00	54.70	0.98	0.78	2.2	5.0
Naive	#6	0.50	21.20	59.40	0.99	0.76	1.2	5.0
Tree	#9	0.70	32.70	53.30	0.89	0.71	3.5	4.9
kNN	#12	0.70	28.20	56.10	0.93	0.73	2.5	4.9
SVM	#18	0.70	30.90	55.60	0.97	0.77	3.5	4.2
Tree	#22	1.00	40.30	55.70	0.90	0.71	2.0	5.0
kNN	#22	1.00	40.90	59.10	0.96	0.76	2.5	5.0
Naive	#23	1.00	41.00	65.50	1.02	0.78	1.2	5.0
SVM	#6	1.00	36.60	51.10	1.02	0.84	3.0	4.0

Table 2: Indicative discretised classification results, sorted by best performance and discretisation interval. Classification Accuracy (AC), Area Under Curve (AUC), Root Mean Square Error (RMSE) and Mean Average Error (MAE), Largest Error Percentage (LEP) and Smallest Error Percentage (SEP)

Feature generation resulted (described in Section 2.2) into 266 features, while 90 of them derived from language checking. Feature selection suggested several feature sets containing between 30 and 80 features. We ended up defining 22 feature sets, including the full feature set, the baseline feature set and a couple of manually selected feature sets. Unfortunately, due to size restrictions, not all features can be listed; though, indicative feature sets are listed in Table 5.

The most important results of the **classification approach** can be seen in Table 2 and the results of the **regression approach** in Tables 3 (development set) and 4 (shared task test set).

4 Discussion

4.1 Machine Learning Conclusions

Discrete classifiers (section 2.4.1) do not yield encouraging accuracy, as acceptable levels of accuracies appear only with a discretisation interval of 1.00, which though cannot be accepted due to its high Root Mean Square Error (RMSE). On the development keep-out set, the discretised Tree classifier seemingly outperforms all other methods (including the regression learners), since it yields a RMSE of 0.84, given several different feature vectors. Unfortunately, when applied to the final unknown test data, these classifiers performed obviously bad, providing the same single value for all sentences. We could attribute this to overfitting vs. sparse data and consider how we can handle this better in further work.

Another remarkable observation was the incapability of the RMSE to objectively show the quality of the model, in situations where the predicted values are very close or equal to the average of all real values. A Support Vector Machine with RMSE = 0.86 ranked 3rd among the classifiers, although it "cheated" by producing only the average value: 3.25. This leads to the conclusion that the selection of the best algorithm is not just dictated by the lowest RMSE, but it should consider several other indications such as the standard deviation.

We therefore resort to the **regression learners** (section 2.4.2), whose scores are not worse, having a RMSE of 0.855. We have to notice that the four

		avg. 70-30%, 90-10% folds			
algorithm	f. set	RMSE	MAE	interval	
PLS	**#19**	**0.86**	0.69	**2.5**	**4.3**
Lasso	#19	0.86	0.68	2.7	4.4
Linear	#19	0.86	0.68	2.6	4.5
MARS	#19	0.86	0.68	2.6	4.7
PLS	#18	0.86	0.69	2.7	4.4
Linear	#18	0.86	0.69	2.8	4.4
Lasso	#18	0.86	0.69	2.8	4.4
MARS	**#16**	0.87	0.69	**2.4**	**4.6**
MARS	#18	0.86	0.69	2.4	4.5
MARS	#4	0.86	0.69	3.4	4.5
PLS	#16	0.87	0.70	2.1	4.8
PLS	#4	0.87	0.70	2.1	5.4
Linear	#4	0.88	0.70	2.4	4.8
Linear	#16	0.88	0.70	1.4	4.9
Lasso	#4	0.88	0.70	1.9	5.3
MARS	#2	0.90	0.72	3.0	4.5
Lasso	#16	0.90	0.71	2.7	4.5
Linear	#2	0.90	0.72	3.0	4.0
Lasso	#2	0.90	0.72	3.0	4.0
PLS	#2	0.90	0.73	3.0	3.9
Tree	#21	1.08	0.86	1.5	5.0
Tree	#19	1.19	0.96	1.6	5.0
Tree	#16	1.23	0.98	1.6	5.0
Tree	#18	1.25	0.98	1.4	5.0

Table 3: Regression results. Root Mean Square Error (RMSE) and Mean Average Error (MAE), Largest Error Percentage (LEP) and Smallest Error Percentage (SEP). Bold face indicates submitted sets

regression algorithms have comparable performance given the same features.

The best-performing feature set (#19) which was chosen as the first submission (DFKI_cfs-plsreg) trained with PLS regression, contains features indicated by Correlation-based Feature Selection, run with *bestfirst* on a 10-fold cross-validation. We used the features which were selected on the 100% or 90% of the folds. An equally best-performing feature set (#18) has resulted from exactly the same feature selection execution, but contains only features which were selected in all folds.

The second submission (DFKI_grcfs-mars) was chosen to differentiate both the feature set and the learning method, with respect to a decent interval. Feature set #16 is the result of the Correlation-based Feature Selection, run in a *greedy-stepwise* mode. The regression was trained with MARS.

learner	feat.	name	RMSE	MAE
MARS	#16	grcfs–mars	0.98	0.82
PLS	#19	cfs-plsreg	0.99	0.82

Table 4: Results of the submitted methods on the official testset

The baseline feature set (#2) performed worse. Noticeable was the RMSE of the feature set #4, with features selected based on their *Gain Ratio*, but we did not submit this due to its very narrow interval.

4.2 Feature conclusions

The best performing feature set gives interesting hints on what worked as a best indication of translation quality. We would try to summarize them as follows:

- The language checking of the source sentence detected *complex* or *embedded sentences*, which are often not handled properly by SMT due to their complicated structure.
- The language checking of the target sentence detected several agreement issues.
- Parsing provided of source and target count of verbs, nouns, adjectives and secondary sentences; with the assumption that translations are relatively isomorphic, the loss of a verb or a noun or the inability to properly handle a secondary sentence, would mean a considerably bad translation outcome. The number of parse trees generated for each sentence can be an indication of ambiguity.
- Punctuation (dots, commas) often indicates a complex sentence structure.
- The most useful decoding features were the inverse phrase translation probability (a_1), the inverse lexical weighting (a_2), the phrase probability (pC) and future cost estimate (c) as well as statistics over their incremental values along the search graph.

feature			
set	type	source	target
#19	Baseline	LM, %bi_q_4, punct	LM, punct
	Checker	complex_sent, embedded_sent	pp_v_plural, nom_adj_masc
	Parsing	trees, CC, NP, NN, JJ, comma	trees, S, CC, VB, VP, NN, JJ, dot
	Decoding		avg(a_2), a_1, a_2
#16	Baseline	LM, seen, punct, %uni_q_1, %bi_q_1, %bi_q_4, %tri_q_4	LM, target_occ
	Checker	score: style, spelling, quality; verb: agr, form, obj_inf, close_to_subj; avoid_parenth, complex_sent, these_those_noun, np_num_agr, noun_adj_conf, repeat_subj, wrong_seq, wrong_word, disamb_that, use_rel_pron, use_article, avoid_dangling, repeat_modal, use_complement	double_punct, to_too_confusion, word_repeat, det_nom_sing, pp_v_plural, pp_v_sing, nom_adj_plural, comma_parenth_space, nom_adj_fem, nom_adj_masc, nom_adj_sing, det_nom_fem, del_nom_sing, del_nom_masc, det_nom_plur
	Parsing	trees, S, CC, JJ, comma, VB, NP, NN, VP	trees, S, CC, JJ, NP, VB, NN, VP, dot, PP
	Decoding		avg(pC), avg(a_1), std(pC), var(c), std(lm), avg(a_2), d_2, std(c), a_1, a_2

Table 5: Indicative feature sets for the most successful quality estimation models. Features explained at section 2.2

Acknowledgments

This work has been developed within the TaraXŰ project financed by TSB Technologiestiftung Berlin – Zukunftsfonds Berlin, co-financed by the European Union – European fund for regional development. Many thanks to Lukas Poustka for technical help on feature acquisition, to Melanie Siegel for the proprietary language checking tool, and to the reviewers for the useful comments.

References

Eleftherios Avramidis, Maja Popovic, David Vilar, Aljoscha Burchardt, and Maja Popović. 2011. Evaluate with Confidence Estimation : Machine ranking of translation outputs using grammatical features. *Proceedings of the Sixth Workshop on Statistical Machine Translation*, pages 65–70, July.

Eleftherios Avramidis. 2011. DFKI System Combination with Sentence Ranking at ML4HMT-2011. In *Proceedings of the International Workshop on Using Linguistic Information for Hybrid Machine Translation (LIHMT 2011) and of the Shared Task on Applying Machine Learning Techniques to Optimising the Division of Labour in Hybrid Machine Translation (M. Sha*. Center for Language and Speech Technologies and Applications (TALP), Technical University of Catalonia.

John Blatz, Erin Fitzgerald, George Foster, Simona Gandrabur, Cyril Goutte, Alex Kulesza, Alberto Sanchis, and Nicola Ueffing. 2004. Confidence estimation for machine translation. In *Proceedings of the 20th international conference on Computational Linguistics*, COLING '04, Stroudsburg, PA, USA. Association for Computational Linguistics.

Chris Callison-Burch, Philipp Koehn, Christof Monz, Matt Post, Radu Soricut, and Lucia Specia. 2012. Findings of the 2012 workshop on statistical machine translation. In *Proceedings of the Seventh Workshop on Statistical Machine Translation*, Montreal, Canada, June. Association for Computational Linguistics.

William S Cleveland. 1979. Robust locally weighted regression and smoothing scatterplots. *Journal of the American statistical association*, 74(368):829–836.

Janez Demšar, Blaz Zupan, Gregor Leban, and Tomaz Curk. 2004. Orange: From Experimental Machine Learning to Interactive Data Mining. In *Principles of Data Mining and Knowledge Discovery*, pages 537–539.

Jerome H. Friedman. 1991. Multivariate Adaptive Regression Splines. *The Annals of Statistics*, 19(1):1–67, March.

Michael Gamon, Anthony Aue, and Martine Smets. 2005. Sentence-level MT evaluation without reference translations : Beyond language modeling. *Language*, (2001):103–111.

Mark Hall, Eibe Frank, Geoffrey Holmes, Bernhard Pfahringer, Peter Reutemann, and Ian H Witten.

2009. The WEKA data mining software: an update. *SIGKDD Explorations*, 11(1):10–18.

Mark A Hall. 2000. Correlation-based Feature Selection for Discrete and Numeric Class Machine Learning. In Pat Langley, editor, *Proceedings of 17th International Conference on Machine Learning*, pages 359–366. Morgan Kaufmann Publishers Inc.

Igor Kononenko. 1994. Estimating attributes: analysis and extensions of RELIEF. In *Proceedings of the European conference on machine learning on Machine Learning*, pages 171–182, Secaucus, NJ, USA. Springer-Verlag New York, Inc.

S Kullback and R A Leibler. 1951. On information and sufficiency. *Annals of Mathematical Statistics*, 22:49–86.

M Antònia Martí Mariona Taulé and Marta Recasens. 2008. AnCora: Multilevel Annotated Corpora for Catalan and Spanish. In *Proceedings of the Sixth International Conference on Language Resources and Evaluation (LREC'08)*, Marrakech, Morocco, May. European Language Resources Association (ELRA).

Kristen Parton, Joel Tetreault, Nitin Madnani, and Martin Chodorow. 2011. E-rating Machine Translation. In *Proceedings of the Sixth Workshop on Statistical Machine Translation*, pages 108–115, Edinburgh, Scotland, July. Association for Computational Linguistics.

Slav Petrov and Dan Klein. 2007. Improved inference for unlexicalized parsing. In *In HLT-NAACL 07*.

Slav Petrov, Leon Barrett, Romain Thibaux, and Dan Klein. 2006. Learning Accurate, Compact, and Interpretable Tree Annotation. In *Proceedings of the 21st International Conference on Computational Linguistics and 44th Annual Meeting of the Association for Computational Linguistics*, pages 433–440, Sydney, Australia, July. Association for Computational Linguistics.

Christopher B Quirk. 2001. Training a Sentence-Level Machine Translation Confidence Measure. *Evaluation*, pages 825–828.

Sylvain Raybaud, Caroline Lavecchia, David Langlois, and Kamel Smaïli. 2009. New Confidence Measures for Statistical Machine Translation. *Proceedings of the International Conference on Agents*, pages 394–401.

Felipe Sánchez-Martinez. 2011. Choosing the best machine translation system to translate a sentence by using only source-language information. In Mikel L Forcada, Heidi Depraetere, and Vincent Vandeghinste, editors, *Proceedings of the 15th Annual Conference of the European Associtation for Machine Translation*, number May, pages 97–104, Leuve, Belgium. European Association for Machine Translation.

Lucia Specia, M. Turchi, N. Cancedda, M. Dymetman, and N. Cristianini. 2009. Estimating the Sentence-Level Quality of Machine Translation Systems. In *13th Annual Meeting of the European Association for Machine Translation (EAMT-2009)*, pages pp. 28–35, Barcelona, Spain.

Andreas Stolcke. 2002. SRILM – An Extensible Language Modeling Toolkit. In *Proceedings of the Seventh International Conference on Spoken Language Processing*, pages 901–904. ISCA, September.

M Stone and R J Brooks. 1990. Continuum regression: cross-validated sequentially constructed prediction embracing ordinary least squares, partial least squares and principal components regression. *Journal of the Royal Statistical Society Series B Methodological*, 52(2):237–269.

R Tibshirani. 1994. Regression shrinkage and selection via the lasso.

Nicola Ueffing and Hermann Ney. 2007. Word-Level Confidence Estimation for Machine Translation. *Computational Linguistics*, 33(1):9–40.

Black Box Features for the WMT 2012 Quality Estimation Shared Task

Christian Buck
School of Informatics
University of Edinburgh
Edinburgh, UK, EH8 9AB
christian.buck@ed.ac.uk

Abstract

In this paper we introduce a number of new features for quality estimation in machine translation that were developed for the WMT 2012 quality estimation shared task. We find that very simple features such as indicators of certain characters are able to outperform complex features that aim to model the connection between two languages.

1 Introduction and Task

This paper describes the features and setup used in our submission to the WMT 2012 quality estimation (QE) shared task. Given a machine translation (MT) system and a corpus of its translations which have been rated by humans, the task is to build a predictor that can accurately estimate the quality of further translations. The human ratings range from 1 (incomprehensible) to 5 (perfect translation) and are given as the mean rating of three different judges.

Formally we are presented with a source sentence f_1^J and a translation e_1^I and we need to assign a score $S(f_1^J, e_1^I) \in [1, 5]$ or, in the ranking task, order the source-translation pairs by expected quality.

2 Resources

The organizers have made available a baseline QE system that consists of a number of well established features (Blatz et al., 2004) and serves as a starting point for development. Furthermore the MT system that generated the translations is available along with its training data. Compared to the large training corpus of the MT engine, the QE system is based on a much smaller training set as detailed in Table 1.

	# sentences
europarl-nc	1,714,385
train	1,832
test	422

Table 1: Corpus statistics

3 Features

In the literature (Blatz et al., 2004) a large number of features have been considered for confidence estimation. These can be grouped into four general categories:

1. *Source features* make a statement about the source sentence, assessing the difficulty of translating a particular sentence with the system at hand. Some sentences may be very easy to translate, e.g. short and common phrases, while long and complex sentences are still beyond the system's capabilities.

2. *Translation features* model the connection between source and target. While this is very closely related to the general problem of machine translation, the advantage in confidence estimation is that we can exercise unconstructive criticism, i.e. point out errors without offering a better translation. In addition, there is no need for an efficient search algorithm, thus allowing for more complex models.

3. *Target features* judge the translation of the system without regarding in which way it was produced. They often resemble the language

model used in the noisy channel formulation (Brown et al., 1993) but can also pinpoint more specific issues. In practice, the same features as for the source side can be used; the interpretation however is different.

4. *Engine features* are often referred to as *glass box features* (Specia et al., 2009). They describe the process which produced the translation in question and usually rely on the inner workings of the MT system. Examples include model scores and word posterior probabilities (WPP) (Ueffing et al., 2003).

In this work we focus on the first three categories and ignore the particular system that produced the translations. Such features are commonly referred to as *black box features*. While some glass box features, e.g. word posterior probabilities, have led to promising results in the past, we chose to explore new features potentially applicable to translations from any source, e.g. translations found on the web.

3.1 Binary Indicators

MTranslatability (Bernth and Gdaniec, 2001) gives a notion of the structural complexity of a sentence that relates to the quality of the produced translation. In the literature, several characteristics that may hinder proper translation have been identified, among them poor grammar and misplaced punctuation. As a very simple approximation we implement binary indicators that detect clauses by looking for quotation marks, hyphens, commas, etc. Another binary feature marks numbers and uppercase words.

3.2 Named Entities

Another aspect that might pose a potential problem to MT is the occurrence of words that were only observed a few times or in very particular contexts, as it is often the case for Named Entities. We used the Stanford NER Tagger (Finkel et al., 2005) to detect words that belong to one of four groups: Person, Location, Organization and Misc. Each group is represented by a binary feature.

Counts are given in Table 2. The test set has significantly less support for the *Misc* category, possibly hinting that this data was taken from a different source or document. To avoid the danger of biasing the classifier we decided not to use the *Misc* indicator in our experiments.

	train (src)		test (src)	
	abs	rel	abs	rel
Person	623	34%	141	33%
Location	479	26%	99	23%
Organization	505	28%	110	26%
Misc	428	23%	53	13%

Table 2: Distribution of Named Entities. The counts are based on a binary features, i.e. multiple occurrences are treated as a single one.

3.3 Backoff Behavior

In related work (Raybaud et al., 2011) the backoff behavior of a 3-gram LM was found to be the most powerful feature for word level QE. We compute for each word the longest seen n-gram (up to $n = 4$) and take the average length as a feature. N-grams at the beginning of a sentence are extended with <s> tokens to avoid penalizing short sentences. This is done on both the source and target side.

3.4 Discriminative Word Lexicon

Following the approach of Mauser et al. (2009) we train log-linear binary classifiers that directly model $p(e|f_1^J)$ for each word $e \in e_1^I$:

$$p(e|f_1^J) = \frac{exp\left(\sum_{f \in f_1^J} \lambda_{e,f}\right)}{1 + exp\left(\sum_{f \in f_1^J} \lambda_{e,f}\right)} \quad (1)$$

where $\lambda_{e,f}$ are the trained model weights. Please note that this introduces a global dependence on the source sentence so that every source word may influence the choice of all words in e_1^I as opposed to the local dependencies found in the underlying phrase-based MT system.

Assuming independence among the words in the translated sentence we could compute the probability of the sentence pair as:

$$p(e_1^I|f_1^J) = \prod_{e \in e_1^I} p(e|f_1^J) \cdot \prod_{e \notin e_1^I} \left(1 - p(e|f_1^J)\right). \quad (2)$$

In practice the second part of Equation (2) is too noisy to be useful given the large number of words

source	~~resumption~~ of the session
target	reanudación del período de ~~sesiones~~

Table 3: Example entry of filtered training corpus.

that do not appear in the sentence at hand. We therefore focus on the observed words and use the geometric mean of their individual probabilities:

$$x_{\text{DWL}}(f_1^J, e_1^I) = \left(\prod_{e \in e_1^I} p(e|f_1^J) \right)^{1/I} . \quad (3)$$

We also compute the probability of the lowest scoring word as an additional feature:

$$x_{\text{DWLmin}}(f_1^J, e_1^I) = \min_{e \in e_1^I} p(e|f_1^J). \quad (4)$$

3.5 Neural Networks

We seek to directly predict the words in e_1^I using a neural network. In order to do so, both source and target sentence are encoded as high dimensional vectors in which positive entries mark the occurrence of words. This representation is commonly referred to as the *vector space model* and has been successfully used for information retrieval.

The dimension of the vector representation is determined by the respective sizes of the source and target vocabulary. Without further pre-processing we would need to learn a mapping from a 90k ($|V_f|$) to a 170k ($|V_e|$) dimensional space. Even though our implementation is specifically tailored to exploit the sparsity of the data, such high dimensionality makes training prohibitively expensive.

Two approaches to reduce dimensionality are explored in this work. First, we simply remove all words that never occur in the QE data of 2,254 sentences from the corpus leaving 8,365 input and 9,000 output nodes. This reduces the estimated training time from 11 days to less than 6 hours per iteration[1]. Standard stochastic gradient decent on a three-layer feed-forward network is used.

As shown in Table 3 the filtering can lead to artifacts in which case an erroneous mapping is learned. Moreover the filtering approach does not scale well as the QE corpus and thereby the vocabulary grows.

[1]using a 2.66 GHz Intel Xeon and 2 threads

Our second approach to reduce dimensionality uses the *hashing trick* (Weinberger et al., 2009): a hash function is applied to each word and the sentence is represented by the hashed values which are again transformed using vector space model as above. The dimensionality reduction is due to the fact that there are less possible hash values than words in the vocabulary. To reduce the loss of information due to collisions, several different hash functions are used. The resulting vector representation closely resembles a Bloom Filter (Bloom, 1970).

This approach scales well but introduces two new parameters: the number of hash functions to use and the dimensionality of the resulting space. In our experiments we have used SHA-1 hashes with three different salts of which we used the first 12 bits, thereby mapping the sentences into a 4096-dimensional space.

The results presented in Section 4 based on networks with 500 hidden nodes which were trained for at least 10 iterations. The networks are not trained until convergence due to time constraints; additional training iterations will likely result in better performance. Experiments using 250 or 1000 hidden nodes showed very similar results.

After the models are trained we compare the predicted and the observed target vectors and derive two features: (i) the euclidean distance, denoted as NNdist and HNNdist for the filtered and hashed versions respectively and (ii) the geometric mean of those dimensions where we expect a positive value, denoted as NNprop+ and HNNprob+ in Table 5.

3.6 Edit Distance

Using Levenshtein Distance we computed the distance to the closest entry in the training corpus. The idea is that a sentence that was already seen almost identically would be easier to translate. Likewise, a translation that is very close to an element of the corpus is likely to be a good translation. This was performed for both source and target side and on character as well as on word level giving a total of four (EDIT) scores. The scores are normalized by the length of the respective lines.

source corpus	“	”	"
europarl-nc	37	227	25,637
train	0	0	641
test	78	76	100

Table 4: Counts of different quotation mark characters.

4 Experiments

In this work we focus on the prediction of human assessment of translation quality, i.e. the regression task of the WMT12 QE shared task. Our submission for the ranking task is derived from the order implied by the predicted scores without further re-ranking.

In general our efforts were directed towards feature engineering and not to the machine learning aspects. Therefore, we apply a standard pipeline and use neural networks for regression. All parameter tuning is performed using 5-fold cross validation on the baseline set of 17 features as provided by the organizers.

4.1 Preprocessing and Analysis

To avoid including our own judgment, no more than the first ten lines of the test data were visually inspected in order to ensure that the training and test data was preprocessed in the same manner. Furthermore, the distribution of individual characters was investigated. As shown in Table 4, the test data differs from the training corpus in treatment of quotation marks. Hence, we replaced all typographical quotation marks (“, ”) with the standard double quote symbol (").

Prior to computation of the features described in Subsections 3.3, 3.4 and 3.5 all numbers are replaced with a special `$number` token.

Baseline features are used without further scaling; experiments where all features were scaled to the $[0, 1]$ range showed a drop in accuracy.

While we implemented the training ourselves for the features presented in Subsection 3.5, the open source neural network library FANN[2] is used for all experiments in this section. As the performance of individual classifiers shows a high variance, presumably due to local minima, all experiments are conducted using ensembles on 500 networks trained with random initialization. Their consensus is computed as the average of the individual predictions.

[2]http://leenissen.dk/fann/wp/

Feature (Section)	MAE	RMSE	|PCC|
BACKOFF (3.3)	0.0	0.0	
INDICATORS (3.1)	+0.5	+0.7	
NER (3.2)	+0.5	+0.4	
DWLmin (3.4)	−0.1	−0.1	0.19
DWL (3.4)	0.0	−0.1	0.36
EDIT (3.6) - tgt words	0.0	0.0	0.32
EDIT (3.6) - tgt chars	−0.1	0.0	0.27
EDIT (3.6) - src words	0.0	0.0	0.36
EDIT (3.6) - src chars	+0.2	+0.1	0.37
NNdist (3.5)	0.0	0.0	0.35
NNprob+ (3.5)	+0.1	+0.2	0.35
HNNdist (3.5)	0.0	0.0	0.37
HNNprob+ (3.5)	+0.1	+0.1	0.35

Table 5: Analysis of individual features using 5-fold cross-validation. Positive values indicate improvement over a baseline of MAE 57.7% and RMSE 72.7%; e.g. including the DWL feature actually worsens RMSE from 72.7% to 72.8%.
The last column gives the Pearson correlation coefficient between the feature and the score if the feature is a single column. This information was not used in feature selection as it is not based on cross validation.

4.2 Feature Evaluation

To evaluate the contribution of individual features, each feature is tested in conjunction with all baseline features, using the parameters that were optimized on the baseline set. This slightly favors the baseline features but we still expect that expressive additional features lead to a noticeable performance gain. The results are detailed in Table 5. In addition to the main evaluation metrics, mean average error (MAE) and root mean squared error (RMSE), we report the Pearson correlation coefficient (PCC) as a measure of predictive strength of a single feature. Because features are not used alone this does not directly translate into overall performance. Still, it can be observed that our proposed features show good correlation to the target variable. For comparison, among the baseline features only 2 of 17 reach a PCC of over 0.3.

While the results generally remain inconclusive, some very simple features that indicate difficulties for the translation engine show good performance. In particular binary markers of named entities and and the indicator features introduced in Subsection 3.1 perform well. Further experiments with the latter show their contribution to the systems performance can be attributed to a single feature: the indicator of the genitive case, i.e. occurrences of **'s or s'**.

Testing more combinations of simple and complex features may lead to improvements at the risk of over-fitting on the cross validation setup. As a simple remedy several feature sets were created at random, always combining all baseline features and several new features presented in this paper. Averaging of the individual results of all sets that performed better than the baseline resulted in our submission.

4.3 Results and Discussion

Of all the features detailed only a few lead to a considerable improvement. This is also reflected by our results on the test data which are nearly indistinguishable from the performance of the baseline system. While this is disappointing, our more complex features introduce a number of free parameters and further experimentation will be needed to conclusively assess their usefulness. In particular, features based on neural networks can be further optimized and tested in other settings.

Even though the machine learning aspects of this task are not the focus of this work we are confident that the proposed setup is sound and can be reused in further evaluations.

5 Conclusion

We described a number of new features that can be used to predict human judgment of translation quality. Results suggest pointing out sentences that are hard to translate, e.g. because they are too complex, is a promising approach.

We presented a detailed evaluation of the utility of individual features and a solid baseline setup for further experimentation. The system, based on an ensemble of neural networks, is insensitive to parameter settings and yields competitive results.

Our new features can potentially be applied for a multitude of applications and may deliver insights into the fundamental problems that cause translation errors, thus aiding the progress in MT research.

Acknowledgments

This work was supported by the MateCAT project, which is funded by the EC under the 7th Framework Programme.

References

Arendse Bernth and Claudia Gdaniec. 2001. Mtranslatability. *Machine Translation*, 16(3):175–218, September.

John Blatz, Erin Fitzgerald, George Foster, Simona Gandrabur, Cyril Goutte, Alex Kulesza, Alberto Sanchis, and Nicola Ueffing. 2004. Confidence estimation for machine translation. In *Proceedings of Coling 2004*, pages 315–321, Geneva, Switzerland, August.

Burton H. Bloom. 1970. Space/time trade-offs in hash coding with allowable errors. *Communications of the ACM*, 13(7):422–426, July.

Peter F. Brown, Stephen A. Della Pietra, Vincent J. Della Pietra, and Robert L. Mercer. 1993. The mathematics of statistical machine translation: Parameter estimation. *Computational Linguistics*, 19(2):263–312.

Jenny Rose Finkel, Trond Grenager, and Christopher Manning. 2005. Incorporating non-local information into information extraction systems by gibbs sampling. In *Proceedings of the 43rd Annual Meeting on Association for Computational Linguistics*, ACL 2005, pages 363–370, Stroudsburg, PA, USA.

Arne Mauser, Saša Hasan, and Hermann Ney. 2009. Extending statistical machine translation with discriminative and trigger-based lexicon models. In *Conference on Empirical Methods in Natural Language Processing*, pages 210–217, Singapore, August.

Sylvain Raybaud, David Langlois, and Kamel Smaïli. 2011. "this sentence is wrong." detecting errors in machine-translated sentences. *Machine Translation*, 25(1):1–34, March.

Lucia Specia, Nicola Cancedda, Marc Dymetman, Marco Turchi, and Nello Cristianini. 2009. Estimating the sentence-level quality of machine translation systems. In *Proceedings of the 13th Annual Conference of the European Association for Machine Translation*, EAMT-2009, pages 28–35, Barcelona, Spain, May.

Nicola Ueffing, Klaus Macherey, and Hermann Ney. 2003. Confidence measures for statistical machine translation. In *Machine Translation Summit*, pages 394–401, New Orleans, LA, September.

Kilian Q. Weinberger, Anirban Dasgupta, John Langford, Alexander J. Smola, and Josh Attenberg. 2009. Feature hashing for large scale multitask learning. In *ICML '09: Proceedings of the 26th Annual International Conference on Machine Learning*, ACM International Conference Proceeding Series, pages 1113–1120, Montreal, Quebec, Canada, June.

Linguistic Features for Quality Estimation

Mariano Felice
Research Group in Computational Linguistics
University of Wolverhampton
Stafford Street
Wolverhampton, WV1 1SB, UK
Mariano.Felice@wlv.ac.uk

Lucia Specia
Department of Computer Science
University of Sheffield
Regent Court, 211 Portobello
Sheffield, S1 4DP, UK
L.Specia@dcs.shef.ac.uk

Abstract

This paper describes a study on the contribution of linguistically-informed features to the task of quality estimation for machine translation at sentence level. A standard regression algorithm is used to build models using a combination of linguistic and non-linguistic features extracted from the input text and its machine translation. Experiments with English-Spanish translations show that linguistic features, although informative on their own, are not yet able to outperform shallower features based on statistics from the input text, its translation and additional corpora. However, further analysis suggests that linguistic information is actually useful but needs to be carefully combined with other features in order to produce better results.

1 Introduction

Estimating the quality of automatic translations is becoming a subject of increasing interest within the Machine Translation (MT) community for a number of reasons, such as helping human translators post-editing MT, warning users about non-reliable translations or combining output from multiple MT systems. Different from most classic approaches for measuring the progress of an MT system or comparing MT systems, which assess quality by contrasting system output to reference translations such as BLEU (Papineni et al., 2002), *Quality Estimation* (QE) is a more challenging task, aimed at MT systems in use, and therefore without access to reference translations.

From the findings of previous work on reference-dependent MT evaluation, it is clear that metrics exploiting linguistic information can achieve significantly better correlation with human judgments on quality, particularly at the level of sentences (Giménez and Màrquez, 2010). Intuitively, this should also apply for quality estimation metrics: while evaluation metrics compare linguistic representations of the system output and reference translations (e.g. matching of n-grams of part-of-speech tags or predicate-argument structures), quality estimation metrics would perform the (more complex) comparison og linguistic representations of the input and translation texts. The hypothesis put forward in this paper is therefore that using linguistic information to somehow contrast the input and translation texts can be beneficial for quality estimation.

We test this hypothesis as part of the WMT-12 shared task on quality estimation. The system submitted to this task (WLV-SHEF) integrates linguistic information to a strong baseline system using only shallow statistics from the input and translation texts, with no explicit information from the MT system that produced the translations. A variant also tests the addition of linguistic information to a larger set of shallow features. The quality estimation problem is modelled as a supervised regression task using Support Vector Machines (SVM), which has been shown to achieve good performance in previous work (Specia, 2011). Linguistic features are computed using a number of auxiliary resources such as parsers and monolingual corpora.

The remainder of this paper is organised as follows. Section 2 gives an overview of previous work on quality estimation, Section 3 describes the set of linguistic features proposed in this paper, along with general experimental settings, Section 4 presents our evaluation and Section 5 provides conclusions and a brief discussion of future work.

2 Related Work

Reference-free MT quality assessment was initially approached as a *Confidence Estimation* task, strongly biased towards exploiting data from a Statistical MT (SMT) system and the translation process to model the confidence of the system in the produced translation. Blatz et al. (2004) attempted sentence-level assessment using a set of 91 features (from the SMT system input and translation texts) and automatic annotations such as NIST and WER. Experiments on classification and regression using different machine learning techniques produced not very encouraging results. More successful experiments were later run by Quirk (2004) in a similar setting but using a smaller dataset with human quality judgments.

Specia et al. (2009a) used Partial Least Squares regression to jointly address feature selection and model learning using a similar set of features and datasets annotated with both automatic and human scores. Black-box features (i.e. those extracted from the input and translation texts only) were as discriminative as glass-box features (i.e. those from the MT system). Later work using black-box features only focused on finding an appropriate threshold for discriminating 'good' from 'bad' translations for post-editing purposes (Specia et al., 2009b) and investigating more objective ways of obtaining human annotation, such as post-editing time (Specia, 2011).

Recent approaches have started exploiting linguistic information with promising results. Specia et al. (2011), for instance, used part-of-speech (PoS) tagging, chunking, dependency relations and named entities for English-Arabic quality estimation. Hardmeier (2011) explored the use of constituency and dependency trees for English-Swedish/Spanish quality estimation. Focusing on word-error detection through the estimation of WER, Xiong et al. (2010) used PoS tags of neighbouring words and a link grammar parser to detect words that are not connected to the rest of the sentence. Work by Bach et al. (2011) focused on learning patterns of linguistic information (such as sequences of part-of-speech tags) to predict sub-sentence errors. Finally, Pighin and Màrquez (2011) modelled the expected projections of semantic roles from the input text into the translations.

3 Method

Our work focuses on the use of a wide range of linguistic information for representing different aspects of translation quality to complement shallow, system-independent features that have been proved to perform well in previous work.

3.1 Linguistic features

Non-linguistic features, such as sentence length or n-gram statistics, are limited in their scope since they can only account for very shallow aspects of a translation. They convey no notion of meaning, grammar or content and as a result they could be very biased towards describing only superficial aspects. For this reason, we introduce linguistic features that account for richer aspects of translations and are in closer relation to the way humans make their judgments. All of the proposed features, linguistic or not, are MT-system independent.

The proposal of linguistic features was guided by three main aspects of translation: fidelity, fluency and coherence. The number of features that were eventually extracted was inevitably limited by the availability of suitable tools for the language pair at hand, mainly for Spanish. As a result, many of the features that were initially devised could not be implemented (e.g. grammar checking). A total of 70 linguistic features were extracted, as summarised below, where S and T indicate whether they refer to the source/input or translation texts respectively:

- Sentence 3-gram log-probability and perplexity using a language model (LM) of PoS tags [T]
- Number, percentage and ratio of content words (N, V, ADJ) and function words (DET, PRON, PREP, ADV) [S & T]
- Width and depth of constituency and dependency trees for the input and translation texts and their differences [S & T]

- Percentage of nouns, verbs and pronouns in the sentence and their ratios between [S & T]
- Number and difference in deictic elements in [S & T]
- Number and difference in specific types of named entities (person, organisation, location, other) and the total of named entities [S & T]
- Number and difference in noun, verb and prepositional phrases [S & T]
- Number of "dangling" (i.e. unlinked) determiners [T]
- Number of explicit (pronominal, non-pronominal) and implicit (zero pronoun) subjects [T]
- Number of split contractions in Spanish (i.e. *al=a el, del=de el*) [T]
- Number and percentage of subject-verb disagreement cases [T]
- Number of unknown words estimated using a spell checker [T]

While many of these features attempt to check for general errors (e.g. subject verb disagreement), others are targeted at usual MT errors (e.g. "dangling" determiners, which are commonly introduced by SMT systems and are not linked to any words) or target language peculiarities (e.g. Spanish contractions, zero subjects). In particular, studying deeper aspects such as different types of subjects can provide a good indication of how natural a translation is in Spanish, which is a pro-drop language. Such a distinction is expected to spot unnatural expressions, such as those caused by unnecessary pronoun repetition.[1]

For subject classification, we identified all VPs and categorised them according to their preceding NPs. Thus, explicit subjects were classified as pronominal (PRON+VP) or non-pronominal (NON-PRON-NP+VP) while implicit subjects only included elided (zero) subjects (i.e. a VP not preceded by an NP).

Subject-verb agreement cases were estimated by rules analysing person, number and gender matches in explicit subject cases, considering also internal NP agreement between determiners, nouns, adjectives and pronouns.[2] Deictics, common coherence indicators (Halliday and Hasan, 1976), were checked against manually compiled lists.[3] Unknown words were estimated using the JMySpell[4] spell checker with the publicly available Spanish (es_ES) OpenOffice[5] dictionary. In order to avoid incorrect estimates, all named entities were filtered out before spell-checking.

TreeTagger (Schmid, 1995) was used for PoS tagging of English texts, while Freeling (Padró et al., 2010) was used for PoS tagging in Spanish and for constituency parsing, dependency parsing and named entity recognition in both languages.

In order to compute n-gram statistics over PoS tags, two language models of general and more detailed morphosyntactic PoS were built using the SRILM toolkit (Stolcke, 2002) on the PoS-tagged AnCora corpus (Taulé et al., 2008).

3.2 Shallow features

In a variant of our system, the linguistic features were complemented by a set of 77 non-linguistic features:

- Number and proportion of unique tokens and numbers in the sentence [S & T]
- Sentence length ratios [S & T]
- Number of non-alphabetical tokens and their ratios [S & T]
- Sentence 3-gram perplexity [S & T]

[1] E.g. (1) *The girl beside me was smiling rather brightly. She thought it was an honor that the exchange student should be seated next to her.* → **La niña a mi lado estaba sonriente bastante bien. Ella pensó que era un honor que el intercambio de estudiantes se encuentra próximo a ella.* (superfluous)
(2) *She is thought to have killed herself through suffocation using a plastic bag.* → **Ella se cree que han matado a ella mediante asfixia utilizando una bolsa de plástico.* (confusing)

[2] E.g. **Algunas de estas personas se convertirá en héroes.* (number mismatch), **Barricadas fueron creados en la calle Cortlandt.* (gender mismatch), **Buena mentirosos están cualificados en lectura.* (internal NP gender and number mismatch).

[3] These included common deictic terms compiled from various sources, such as *hoy, allí, tú* (Spanish) or *that, now* or *there* (English).

[4] http://kenai.com/projects/jmyspell

[5] http://www.openoffice.org/

- Type/Token Ratio variations: corrected TTR (Carroll, 1964), Log TTR (Herdan, 1960), Guiraud Index (Guiraud, 1954), Uber Index (Dugast, 1980) and Jarvis TTR (Jarvis, 2002) [S & T]
- Average token frequency from a monolingual corpus [S]
- Mismatches in opening and closing brackets and quotation marks [S & T]
- Differences in brackets, quotation marks, punctuation marks and numbers [S & T]
- Average number of occurrences of all words within the sentence [T]
- Alignment score (IBM-4) and percentage of different types of word alignments by GIZA++ (from the SMT training alignment model provided)

Our basis for comparison is the set of 17 *baseline features*, which are shallow MT system-independent features provided by the WMT-12 QE shared task organizers.

3.3 Building QE models

We created two main feature sets from the features listed above for the WMT-12 QE shared task:

WLV-SHEF_FS: all features, that is, baseline features, shallow features (Section 3.2) and linguistic features (Section 3.1).

WLV-SHEF_BL: baseline features and linguistic features (Section 3.1).

Additionally, we experimented with other variants of these feature sets using 3-fold cross validation on the training set, such as only linguistic features and only non-linguistic features, but these yielded poorer results and are not reported in this paper.

We address the QE problem as a regression task by building SVM models with an epsilon regressor and a radial basis function kernel using the LibSVM toolkit (Chang and Lin, 2011). Values for the cost, epsilon and gamma parameters were optimized using 5-fold cross validation on the training set.

	MAE ↓	RMSE ↓	Pearson ↑
Baseline	**0.69**	**0.82**	**0.562**
WLV-SHEF_FS	**0.69**	0.85	0.514
WLV-SHEF_BL	0.72	0.86	0.490

Table 1: Scoring performance

The training sets distributed for the shared task comprised 1,832 English sentences taken from news texts and their Spanish translations produced by an SMT system, Moses (Koehn et al., 2007), which had been trained on a concatenation of Europarl and news-commentaries data (from WMT-10). Translations were accompanied by a quality score derived from an average of three human judgments of post-editing effort using a 1-5 scale.

The models built for each of these two feature sets were evaluated using the official test set of 422 sentences produced in the same fashion as the training set. Two sub-tasks were considered: (i) **scoring** translations using the 1-5 quality scores, and (ii) **ranking** translations from best to worse. While quality scores were directly predicted by our models, sentence rankings were defined by ordering the translations according to their predicted scores in descending order, with no additional criteria to resolve ties other than the natural ordering given by the sorting algorithm.

4 Results and Evaluation

Table 1 shows the official results of our systems in the **scoring** task in terms of Mean Absolute Error (MAE) and Root Mean Squared Error (RMSE), the metrics used in the shared task, as well as in terms of Pearson correlation.

Results reveal that our models fall slightly below the baseline, although this drop is not statistically significant in any of the cases (paired t-tests for Baseline vs WLV-SHEF_FS and Baseline vs WLV-SHEF_BL yield $p > 0.05$). This may suggest that for this particular dataset the baseline features already cover all relevant aspects of quality on their own, or simply that the representation of the linguistic features is not appropriate for the task. The quality of the resources used to extract the linguistic features may also have been an issue. However, a feature selection method may find a different com-

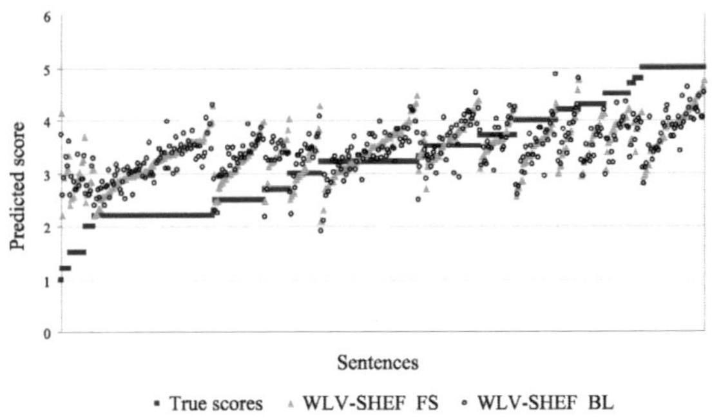

Figure 1: Comparison of true versus predicted scores

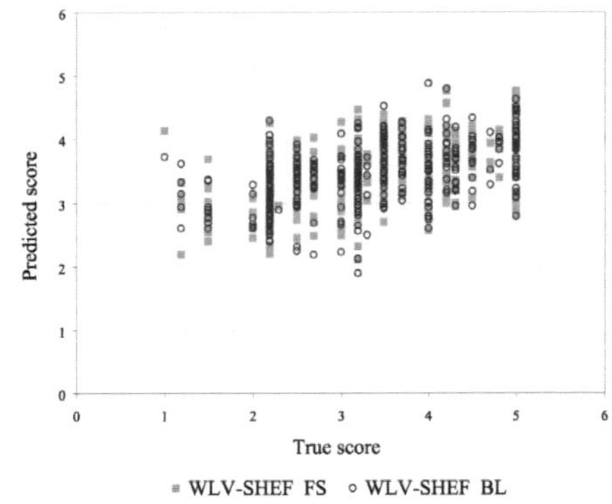

Figure 2: Scatter plot of true versus predicted scores

bination of features that outperforms the baseline, as is later described in this section.

A correlation analysis between our predicted scores and the gold standard (Figure 1) shows some dispersion, especially for the WLV-SHEF_FS set, with lower Pearson coefficients when compared to the baseline. The fluctuation of predicted values for a single score is also very noticeable, spanning more than one score band in some cases. However, if we consider the RMSE achieved by our models, we find that, on average, predictions deviate less than 0.9 absolute points.

A closer look at the score distribution (Figure 2) reveals our models had some difficulty predicting scores in the 1-2 range, possibly affected by the lower proportion of these cases in the training data. In addition, it is interesting to see that the only sentence with a true score of 1 is predicted as a very good translation (with a score greater than 3.5). The reason for this is that the translation has isolated grammatical segments that our features might regard as good but it is actually not faithful to the original.[6] Although the cause for this behaviour can be traced to inaccurate tokenisation, this reveals that our features assess fidelity only superficially and deeper semantically-aware indicators should be explored.

Results for the **ranking** task also fall below the baseline as shown in Table 2, according to the two official metrics: DeltaAvg and Spearman rank correlation coefficient.

4.1 Further analysis

At first glance, the performance of our models seems to indicate that the integration of linguistic information is not beneficial, since both linguistically-informed feature sets lead to poorer performance as compared to the baseline feature set, which contains only shallow, language-independent features. However, there could be many factors affecting performance so further analysis was necessary to assess their contribution.

[6]*I won't give it away.* → **He ganado ' t darle.*

	DeltaAvg ↑	**Spearman** ↑
Baseline	**0.55**	**0.58**
WLV-SHEF_FS	0.51	0.52
WLV-SHEF_BL	0.50	0.49

Table 2: Ranking performance

Our first analysis focuses on the performance of individual features. To this end, we built and tested models using only one feature at a time and repeated the process afterwards using the full WLV-SHEF_FS set without one feature at a time. In Table 3 we report the 5-best and 5-worst performing features. Although purely statistical features lead the rank, linguistic features also appear among the top five (as indicated by Ⓛ), showing that they can be as good as other shallow features. It is interesting to note that a few features appear as the top performing in both columns (e.g. source bigrams in 4th frequency quartile and target LM probability). These constitute the truly top performing features.

Our second analysis studies the optimal subset of features that would yield the best performance on the test set, from which we could draw further conclusions. Since this analysis requires training and testing models using all the possible partitions of the

Rank	One feature	All but one feature
1	*Source bigrams in 4th freq. quartile*	Source average token length
2	Source LM probability	*Source bigrams in 4th freq. quartile*
3	*Target LM probability*	Unknown words in target Ⓛ
4	Number of source bigrams	*Target LM probability*
5	Target PoS LM probability Ⓛ	Difference in constituency tree width Ⓛ
143	Percentage of target S-V agreement Ⓛ	Difference in number of periods
144	Source trigrams in 2nd freq. quartile	Number of source bigrams
145	Target location entities Ⓛ	Target person entities Ⓛ
146	*Source trigrams in 3rd freq. quartile*	Target Corrected TTR
147	Source average translations by inv. freq.	*Source trigrams in 3rd freq. quartile*

Table 3: List of best and worst performing features

full feature set,[7] it is infeasible in practice so we adopted the Sequential Forward Selection method instead (Alpaydin, 2010). Using this method, we start from an empty set and add one feature at a time, keeping in the set only the features that decrease the error until no further improvement is possible. This strategy decreases the number of iterations substantially[8] but it does not guarantee finding a global optimum. Still, a local optimum was acceptable for our purpose. The optimal feature set found by our selection algorithm is shown in Table 4.

Error rates are lower when using this optimal feature set (MAE=0.62 and RMSE=0.76) but the difference is only statistically significant when compared to the baseline with 93% confidence level (paired t-test with $p <= 0.07$). However, this analysis allows us to see how many linguistic features get selected for the optimal feature set.

Out of the total 37 features in the optimal set, 15 are linguistic (40.5%), showing that they are in fact informative when strategically combined with other shallow indicators. This also reveals that feature selection is a key issue for building a quality estimation system that combines linguistic and shallow information. Using a sequential forward selection method, the optimal set is composed of both linguistic and shallow features, reinforcing the idea that they account for different aspects of quality and are not interchangeable but actually complementary.

[7] For 147 features: 2^{147}

[8] For 147 features, worst case is $147 \times (147 + 1)/2 = 10,878$.

5 Conclusions and Future Work

We have explored the use of linguistic information for quality estimation of machine translations. Our approach was not able to outperform a baseline with only shallow features. However, further feature analysis revealed that linguistic features are complementary to shallow features and must be strategically combined in order to be exploited efficiently.

The availability of linguistic tools for processing Spanish is limited, and thus the linguistic features used here only account for a few of the many aspects involved in translation quality. In addition, computing linguistic information is a challenging process for a number of reasons, mainly the fact that translations are often ungrammatical, and thus linguistic processors may return inaccurate results, leading to further errors.

In future work we plan to integrate more global linguistic features such as grammar checkers, along with deeper features such as semantic roles, hybrid n-grams, etc. In addition, we have noticed that representing information for input and translation texts independently seems more appropriate than contrasting input and translation information within the same feature. This representation issue is somehow counter-intuitive and is yet to be investigated.

Acknowledgements

This research was supported by the European Commission, Education & Training, Eramus Mundus: EMMC 2008-0083, Erasmus Mundus Masters in NLP & HLT programme.

Iter.	Feature
1	Source bigrams in 4th frequency quartile
2	Target PoS LM probability Ⓛ
3	Source average token length
4	Guiraud Index of T
5	Unknown words in T Ⓛ
6	Difference in number of VPs between S and T Ⓛ
7	Diff. in constituency trees width of S and T Ⓛ
8	Non-alphabetical tokens in T
9	Ratio of length between S and T
10	Source trigrams in 4th frequency quartile
11	Number of content words in S Ⓛ
12	Source 3-gram perplexity
13	Ratio of PRON percentages in S and T Ⓛ
14	Number of NPs in T Ⓛ
15	Average number of source token translations with $p > 0.05$ weighted by frequency
16	Source 3-gram LM probability
17	Target simple PoS LM probability Ⓛ
18	Difference in dependency trees depth of S and T Ⓛ
19	Number of NPs in S Ⓛ
20	Number of tokens in S
21	Number of content words in T Ⓛ
22	Source unigrams in 3rd frequency quartile
23	Source unigrams in 1st frequency quartile
24	Source unigrams in 2nd frequency quartile
25	Average number of source token translations with $p > 0.01$ weighted by frequency
26	Ratio of non-alpha tokens in S and T
27	Difference of question marks between S and T normalised by T length
28	Percentage of pron subjects in T Ⓛ
29	Percentage of verbs in T Ⓛ
30	Constituency trees width for S Ⓛ
31	Absolute diff. of question marks between S and T
32	Average num. of source token trans. with $p > 0.2$
33	Diff. of person entities between S and T Ⓛ
34	Diff. of periods between S and T norm. by T length
35	Diff. of semicolons between S and T normalised by T length
36	Source 3-gram perplexity without end-of-sentence markers
37	Absolute difference of periods between S and T

Table 4: An optimal set of features for the test set. The number of iteration indicates the order in which features were selected, giving a rough ranking of features by their performance.

References

Ethem Alpaydin. 2010. *Introduction to Machine Learning*. Adaptive Computation and Machine Learning. The MIT Press, Cambridge, MA, 2nd edition.

Nguyen Bach, Fei Huang, and Yaser Al-Onaizan. 2011. Goodness: A method for measuring machine translation confidence. In *Proceedings of the 49th Annual Meeting of the Association for Computational Linguistics: Human Language Technologies*, pages 211–219, Portland, Oregon, USA, June. Association for Computational Linguistics.

John Blatz, Erin Fitzgerald, George Foster, Simona Gandrabur, Cyril Goutte, Alex Kulesza, Alberto Sanchis, and Nicola Ueffing. 2004. Confidence estimation for machine translation. Final Report of Johns Hopkins 2003 Summer Workshop on Speech and Language Engineering, Johns Hopkins University, Baltimore, Maryland, USA, March.

John Bissell Carroll. 1964. *Language and Thought*. Prentice-Hall, Englewood Cliffs, NJ.

Chih-Chung Chang and Chih-Jen Lin. 2011. Libsvm: A library for support vector machines. *ACM Trans. Intell. Syst. Technol.*, 2(3):1–27, May.

Daniel Dugast. 1980. *La statistique lexicale*. Slatkine, Genève.

Jesús Giménez and Lluís Màrquez. 2010. Linguistic measures for automatic machine translation evaluation. *Machine Translation*, 24(3):209–240.

Pierre Guiraud. 1954. *Les Caractères Statistiques du Vocabulaire*. Presses Universitaires de France, Paris.

Michael A. K. Halliday and Ruqaiya Hasan. 1976. *Cohesion in English*. Longman, London.

Christian Hardmeier. 2011. Improving machine translation quality prediction with syntactic tree kernels. In *Proceedings of the 15th conference of the European Association for Machine Translation (EAMT 2011)*, pages 233–240, Leuven, Belgium.

Gustav Herdan. 1960. *Type-token Mathematics: A Textbook of Mathematical Linguistics*. Mouton & Co., The Hague.

Scott Jarvis. 2002. Short texts, best-fitting curves and new measures of lexical diversity. *Language Testing*, 19(1):57–84, January.

Philipp Koehn, Hieu Hoang, Alexandra Birch, Chris Callison-Burch, Marcello Federico, Nicola Bertoldi, Brooke Cowan, Wade Shen, Christine Moran, Richard Zens, Chris Dyer, Ondrej Bojar, Alexandra Constantin, and Evan Herbst. 2007. Moses: Open source toolkit for statistical machine translation. In *Proceedings of the 45th Annual Meeting of the Association for Computational Linguistics Companion Volume Proceedings of the Demo and Poster Sessions*, pages 177–180, Prague, Czech Republic, June. Association for Computational Linguistics.

Llus Padró, Miquel Collado, Samuel Reese, Marina Lloberes, and Irene Castellón. 2010. Freeling 2.1: Five years of open-source language processing tools. In Nicoletta Calzolari (Conference Chair), Khalid Choukri, Bente Maegaard, Joseph Mariani, Jan Odijk, Stelios Piperidis, Mike Rosner, and Daniel Tapias, editors, *Proceedings of the Seventh conference on International Language Resources and Evaluation (LREC'10)*, Valletta, Malta, May. European Language Resources Association (ELRA).

Kishore Papineni, Salim Roukos, Todd Ward, and Wei-Jing Zhu. 2002. Bleu: a method for automatic evaluation of machine translation. In *Proceedings of the 40th Annual Meeting on Association for Computational Linguistics*, pages 311–318.

Daniele Pighin and Lluís Màrquez. 2011. Automatic projection of semantic structures: an application to pairwise translation ranking. In *Fifth Workshop on Syntax, Semantics and Structure in Statistical Translation (SSST-5)*, Portland, Oregon.

Christopher B. Quirk. 2004. Training a sentence-level machine translation confidence metric. In *Proceedings of the International Conference on Language Resources and Evaluation*, volume 4 of *LREC 2004*, pages 825–828, Lisbon, Portugal.

Helmut Schmid. 1995. Improvements in part-of-speech tagging with an application to german. In *In Proceedings of the ACL SIGDAT-Workshop*, pages 47–50, Dublin, Ireland, August.

Lucia Specia, Marco Turchi, Nicola Cancedda, Marc Dymetman, and Nello Cristianini. 2009a. Estimating the sentence-level quality of machine translation systems. In *Proceedings of the 13th Annual Conference of the European Association for Machine Translation (EAMT)*, pages 28–35, Barcelona, Spain, May.

Lucia Specia, Marco Turchi, Zhuoran Wang, John Shawe-Taylor, and Craig Saunders. 2009b. Improving the confidence of machine translation quality estimates. In *Proceedings of the Twelfth Machine Translation Summit (MT Summit XII)*, pages 136–143, Ottawa, Canada, August.

Lucia Specia, Najeh Hajlaoui, Catalina Hallett, and Wilker Aziz. 2011. Predicting machine translation adequacy. In *Machine Translation Summit XIII*, pages 19–23, Xiamen, China, September.

Lucia Specia. 2011. Exploiting objective annotations for measuring translation post-editing effort. In *Proceedings of the 15th Conference of the European Association for Machine Translation*, pages 73–80, Leuven.

Andreas Stolcke. 2002. Srilman extensible language modeling toolkit. In *Proceedings of the 7th International Conference on Spoken Language Processing (ICSLP 2002)*, volume 2, pages 901–904, Denver, USA, November.

Mariona Taulé, M. Antnia Martí, and Marta Recasens. 2008. Ancora: Multilevel annotated corpora for catalan and spanish. In Nicoletta Calzolari (Conference Chair), Khalid Choukri, Bente Maegaard, Joseph Mariani, Jan Odijk, Stelios Piperidis, Mike Rosner, and Daniel Tapias, editors, *Proceedings of the Sixth International Conference on Language Resources and Evaluation (LREC'08)*, Marrakech, Morocco, May. European Language Resources Association (ELRA).

Deyi Xiong, Min Zhang, and Haizhou Li. 2010. Error detection for statistical machine translation using linguistic features. In *Proceedings of the 48th Annual Meeting of the Association for Computational Linguistics*, pages 604–611, Uppsala, Sweden.

PRHLT Submission to the WMT12 Quality Estimation Task

Jesús González Rubio and **Alberto Sanchis** and **Francisco Casacuberta**
D. Sistemas Informáticos y Computación
Universitat Politècnica de València
Camino de vera s/n, 46022, Valencia, Spain
{jegonzalez,josanna,fcn}@dsic.upv.es

Abstract

This is a description of the submissions made by the pattern recognition and human language technology group (PRHLT) of the Universitat Politècnica de València to the quality estimation task of the seventh workshop on statistical machine translation (WMT12). We focus on two different issues: how to effectively combine subsequence-level features into sentence-level features, and how to select the most adequate subset of features. Results showed that an adequate selection of a subset of highly discriminative features can improve efficiency and performance of the quality estimation system.

1 Introduction

Quality estimation (QE) (Ueffing et al., 2003; Blatz et al., 2004; Sanchis et al., 2007; Specia and Farzindar, 2010) is a topic of increasing interest in machine translation (MT). It aims at providing a quality indicator for unseen translations at various granularity levels. Different from MT evaluation, QE do not rely on reference translations and is generally addressed using machine learning techniques to predict quality scores.

Our main focus in this article is in the combination of subsequence features into sentence features, and in the selection of a subset of relevant features to improve performance and efficiency. Section 2 describes the features and the learning algorithm used in the experiments. Section 3 describe two different approaches implemented to select the best-performing subset of features. Section 4 displays the results of the experimentation intended to determine the optimal setup to train our final submission. Finally, section 5 summarizes the submission and discusses the results.

2 Features and Learning Algorithm

2.1 Available Sources of Information

The WMT12 QE task is carried out on English–Spanish news texts produced by a phrase-based MT system. As training data we are given 1832 translations manually annotated for quality in terms of post-editing effort (scores in the range $[1, 5]$), together with their source sentences, decoding information, reference translations, and post-edited translations. Additional training data can be used, as deemed appropriate. Any of these information sources can be used to extract the features, however, test data consists only on source sentence, translation, and search information. Thus, features were extracted from the sources of information available in test data only. Additionally, we compute some extra features from the WMT12 translation task (WMT12TT) training data.

2.2 Features

We extracted a total of 475 features classified into sentence-level and subsequence-level features. We considered subsequences of sizes one to four.

Sentence-level features

- Source and target sentence lengths, and ratio.
- Proportion of dead nodes in the search graph.
- Number of source phrases.
- Number and average size of the translation options under consideration during search.

- Source and target sentence probability and perplexities computed by language models of order one to five.
- Target sentence probability, probability divided by sentence length, and perplexities computed by language models of order one to five. Language models were trained on the 1000-best translations.
- 1000-best average sentence length, 1000-best vocabulary divided by average length, and 1000-best vocabulary divided by source sentence length.
- Percentage of subsequences (sizes one to four) previously unseen in the source training data.

Subsequence-level features

- Frequency of source subsequences in the WMT12TT data.
- IBM Model-1 confidence score for each word in the translation (Ueffing et al., 2003).
- Subsequence confidence scores computed on 1000-best translations as described in (Ueffing et al., 2003; Sanchis et al., 2007). We use four subsequence correctness criteria (Levensthein position, target position, average position, and any position) and three weighting schemes (translation probability, translation rank, and relative frequencies).
- Subsequence confidence scores computed by a smoothed naïve bayes classifier (Sanchis et al., 2007). We computed a confidence score for each correctness criteria (Levensthein, target, average and any). The smoothed classifier was tuned to improve classification error rate on a separate development set (union of news-test sets for years 2008 to 2011).

2.3 Combination of Subsequence-level Features

Since WMT12 focuses on sentence-level QE, subsequence-level features must be combined to obtain sentence-level indicators. We used two different methods to combine subsequence features:

- Average value of subsequence-level scores, as done in (Blatz et al., 2004).
- Percentage of subsequence scores belonging to each frequency quartile[1], as done in (Specia and Farzindar, 2010).

Thus, each subsequence-level feature was represented as five sentence-level features: one average score plus four quartile percentages.

Both methods aim at summarizing the scores of the subsequences in a translations. The average is a rough indicator that measures the "middle" value of the scores while the percentages of subsequences belonging to each quartile are more fine-grained indicators that try to capture how spread out the subsequence scores are.

2.4 Learning Algorithm

We trained our quality estimation model using an implementation of support vector machines (Vapnik, 1995) for regression. Specifically, we used SVM^{light} (Joachims, 2002) for regression with a radial basis function kernel with the parameters C, w and γ optimized. The optimization was performed by cross-validation using ten random subsamples of the training set (1648 samples for training and 184 samples for validation).

3 Feature Selection

One of the principal challenges that we had to confront is the small size of the training data (only 1832 samples) in comparison with the large number of features, 475. This inadequate amount of training data did not allow for an acceptable training of the regression model which yielded instable systems with poor performance. We also verified that many features were highly correlated and were even redundant sometimes. Since the amount of training data is fixed, we tried to improve the robustness of our regression systems by selecting a subset of relevant features.

We implemented two different feature selection techniques: one based on partial component analysis (PCA), and a greedy selection according to the individual performance of each feature.

3.1 PCA Selection (PS)

Principal component analysis (Pearson, 1901) (PCA) is a mathematical procedure that uses an or-

[1]Quartile values were computed on the WMT12TT data.

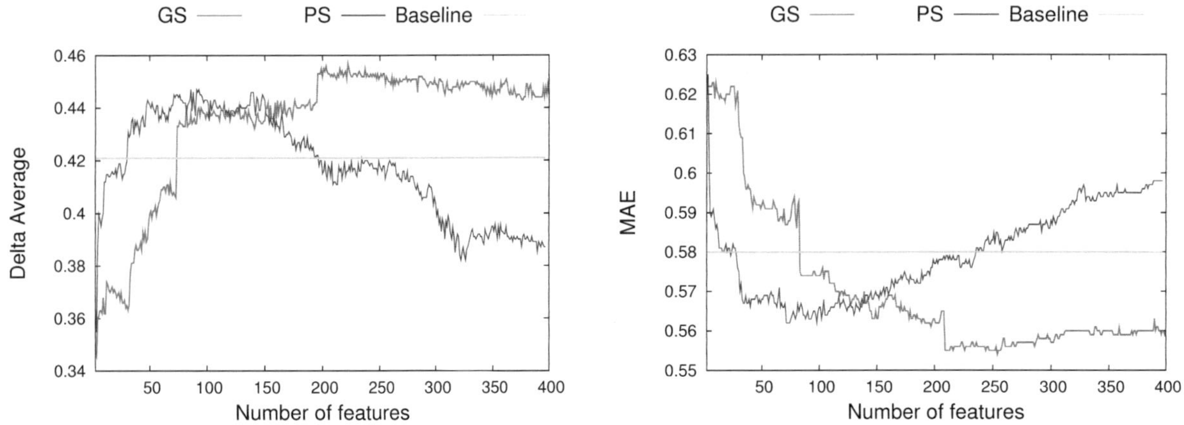

(a) Delta average score (b) Mean Average Error

Figure 1: Delta average score (a) (higher is better) and mean average error (b) (lower is better) as a function of the number of features. Cross-validation results for PCA selection (PS), and greedy selection (GS) methods.

thogonal transformation to convert a set of observations of possibly correlated variables into a set of values of linearly uncorrelated variables called principal components. This transformation is defined in such a way that the first principal component has the largest possible variance (that is, accounts for as much of the variability in the data as possible), and each succeeding component in turn has the highest variance possible under the constraint that it be uncorrelated with the preceding components. Strictly speaking, PCA does not perform a feature selection because the principal components are linear combinations of the individual features.

PCA generates sets of features (the principal components) with almost no correlation. However, it ignores the quality scores to be predicted. Since we want to obtain the best-performing subset of features, there is a mismatch between the selection criterion of PCA and the criterion we are interested in. In other words, although the features generated by PCA contain almost no redundancy, they do not necessarily have to constitute the best-performing subset of features.

3.2 Greedy Performance-driven Selection (GS)

We also implemented a greedy feature selection method which iteratively creates subsets of increasing size with the best-scoring individual features. The score of each feature is given by the performance of a system trained solely on that feature. At a given iteration, we select the K best scoring features and train a regression system with them.

Since we select the features incrementally according to their individual performance, we expect to obtain the subset of features that yield the best performance. However, we do not take into account the correlations that may exist between the different features, thus, the final subset is almost sure to contain a large number of redundant features.

4 Experiments

4.1 Assessment Measures

The organizers propose two variations of the task that will be evaluated separately:

Ranking: Participants are required to submit a ranking of translations. This ranking will used to split the data into n quantiles. The evaluation will be performed in terms of delta average score, the average difference over n between the scores of the top quantiles and the overall score of the corpus. The Spearman correlation will be used as tie-breaking metric.

Scoring: Participants are required to assign a score in the range $[1, 5]$ for each translation. The evaluation will be performed in terms of mean average error (MAE). Root mean squared error (RMSE) will be used as tie-breaking metric.

4.2 Pre-Submission Results

We now describe a number of experiments whose goal is to determine the optimal training setup.

Specifically, we wanted to determine which selection method to use (PCA or greedy) and which features yield a better system. As a preliminary step, we extracted all the features described in section 2. The complete training data consisted on 1832 samples each one with 475 features.

We trained systems using feature sets of increasing size as given by PCA selection (PS) or greedy selection (GS). The parameters of each system were tuned to optimize each of the evaluation measures under consideration. Performance was measured as the average of a ten-fold cross-validation experiment on the training data.

Figure 1 shows the results obtained for the experiments that optimized delta average, and MAE (result optimizing Spearman and RMSE were quite similar). We also display the performance of a system trained on the baseline features. We observed that both selection methods yielded a better performance than the baseline system. PS allowed for a quick improvement in performance as more features are selected, reaching its best results when selecting approximately 80 features. After that, performance rapidly deteriorate. Regarding GS, its improvements in performance were slower in comparison with PS. However, GS finally reached the best scores of the experimentation when selecting $\sim$ 225 features. Specifically, the best performance was reached using the top 222 features for delta average, and using the top 254 features for MAE.

According to these results, our submissions were trained on the best subsets of features as given by the GS method. 222 features were selected according to their delta average score for the ranking task variation, and 254 according to their MAE value for the scoring task variation. Final submissions were trained on the complete training set.

Most of the selected features are sentence-level features calculated from subsequence-based scores. For instance, among the 222 features of the ranking variation of the task, 174 were computed from subsequence scores. Among these 174 features, 129 were calculated from confidence scores computed on 1000-best translations, 29 from confidence scores computed by a smoothed naïve bayes classifier, 11 from the frequencies of the subsequences in the WMT12TT data, and 5 from IBM Model-1 word confidence scores.

Participant ID	Delta average ⇑	MAE ⇓
SDL Language Weaver	0.63	0.61
Uppsala U.	0.58	0.64
LORIA Institute	–	0.68
Trinity College Dublin	0.56	0.68
Baseline	*0.55*	*0.69*
PRHLT	**0.55**	**0.70**
U. Edinburgh	0.54	0.68
Shanghai Jiao Tong U.	0.53	0.69
U. Wolverhampton/Sheffield	0.51	0.69
DFKI	0.46	0.82
Dublin City U.	0.44	0.75
U. Politècnica Catalunya	0.22	0.84

Table 1: Best official evaluation results on each task of the different participating teams. Results for our submissions are displayed in bold. Baseline results in italics.

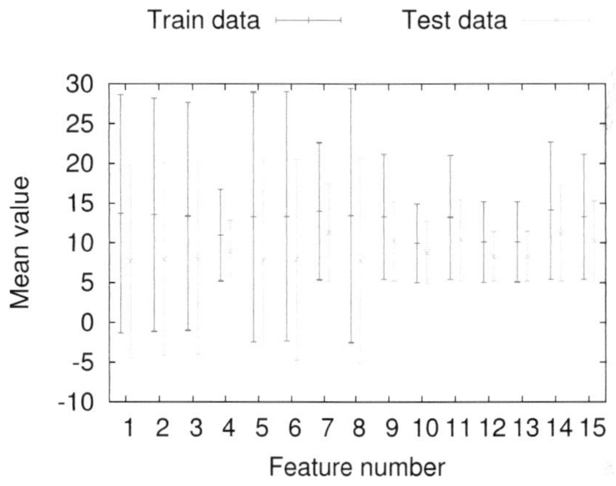

Figure 2: Average value ($\pm$ std. deviation) of the first 15 features used in our final submissions. Feature values follow a similar distribution in the training and test data.

4.3 Official Evaluation Results

After establishing the optimal training setup, we now show the official evaluation results for our submissions. Table 1 shows the performance of the various participants in the ranking (delta average) and scoring (MAE) tasks. Surprisingly our submissions yielded a slightly worse result than the baseline features. However, given the large improvements over the baseline system obtained in the pre-submission experiments, we expected to obtain similar improvements over Baseline in test.

We considered two possible explanations for this counterintuitive result. First, a possibly divergence between the underlying distributions of the training and test data. To investigate this possibility, we studied the distributions of feature values in the training and test data. Figure 2 displays mean±std. deviation for the first 15 features used in our final submissions (similar results are obtained for all the 222 features). We can observe that feature values in training and test data follow a similar distribution, although test values tend to be slightly lower than training values.

A second plausible explanation is the small amount of training data (only 1832 samples). Limited data favors simpler systems that can train its few free parameters more accurately. This is the case of the Baseline system that was trained using only 11 features, in comparison with the 222 features used in our submissions. Since the training and test data seem to have been generated following the same underlying distribution, we hypothesize that the limited training data is the main explanation for the poor test performance of our submissions.

5 Summary and Discussion

We have presented the submissions of the PRHLT group to the WMT12 QE task. The estimation systems were based on support vector machines for regression. Several features were used to train the systems in order to predict human-annotated post-editing effort scores. Our main focus in this article have been the combination of subsequence features into sentence features, and the selection of a subset of relevant features to improve the submitted systems performance.

Results of the experiments showed that PCA selection was able to obtain better performance when selecting a small number of features while GS yielded the best-performing systems but using much more features. Among the selected features, the larger percentage of them were calculated from subsequence features. These facts indicate that the combination of subsequence features yields sentence-level features with a strong individual performance. However, the high number of features selected by GS indicate that these top-scoring features are highly correlated.

Official evaluation results differ from what we expected; baseline system performs better than our submissions while pre-submission experiments yielded just opposite results. After discarding a possibly discrepancy between training and test data distributions, and given that smaller models such as the baseline system can be trained more accurately with limited data, we concluded that the limited training data is the main explanation for the disparity between our training and test results.

A future line of research could be the study of methods that allow to select sets of uncorrelated features, that unlike PCA, also take into account the individual performance of each feature. Specifically, we plan to study a features selection technique based on partial least squares regression.

Acknowledgments

The research leading to these results has received funding from the European Union Seventh Framework Programme (FP7/2007-2013) under grant agreement n° 287576. Work also supported by the EC (FEDER/FSE) and the Spanish MEC under the MIPRCV "Consolider Ingenio 2010" program (CSD2007-00018) and iTrans2 (TIN2009-14511) project and by the Generalitat Valenciana under grant ALMPR (Prometeo/2009/01).

References

John Blatz, Erin Fitzgerald, George Foster, Simona Gandrabur, Cyril Goutte, Alex Kulesza, Alberto Sanchis, and Nicola Ueffing. 2004. Confidence estimation for machine translation. In M. Rollins, editor, *Mental Imagery*. Yale University Press.

Thorsten Joachims. 2002. SVM light.

Karl Pearson. 1901. On lines and planes of closest fit to systems of points in space. *Philosophical Magazine*, 2(11):559–572.

Alberto Sanchis, Alfons Juan, and Enrique Vidal. 2007. Estimation of confidence measures for machine translation. In *In Procedings of the MT Summit XI*. Springer-Verlag.

Lucia Specia and Atefeh Farzindar. 2010. Estimating machine translation post-editing effort with hter. In *AMTA 2010- workshop, Bringing MT to the User: MT Research and the Translation Industry*. The Ninth Conference of the Association for Machine Translation in the Americas, nov.

Nicola Ueffing, Klaus Macherey, and Hermann Ney. 2003. Confidence measures for statistical machine translation. In *In Proceedings of the MT Summit IX*, pages 394–401. Springer-Verlag.

Vladimir N. Vapnik. 1995. *The nature of statistical learning theory*. Springer-Verlag New York, Inc., New York, NY, USA.

Tree Kernels for Machine Translation Quality Estimation

Christian Hardmeier and **Joakim Nivre** and **Jörg Tiedemann**
Uppsala University
Department of Linguistics and Philology
Box 635, 751 26 Uppsala, Sweden
firstname.lastname@lingfil.uu.se

Abstract

This paper describes Uppsala University's submissions to the Quality Estimation (QE) shared task at WMT 2012. We present a QE system based on Support Vector Machine regression, using a number of explicitly defined features extracted from the Machine Translation input, output and models in combination with tree kernels over constituency and dependency parse trees for the input and output sentences. We confirm earlier results suggesting that tree kernels can be a useful tool for QE system construction especially in the early stages of system design.

1 Introduction

The goal of the WMT 2012 Quality Estimation (QE) shared task (Callison-Burch et al., 2012) was to create automatic systems to judge the quality of the translations produced by a Statistical Machine Translation (SMT) system given the input text, the proposed translations and information about the models used by the SMT system. The shared task organisers provided a training set of 1832 sentences drawn from earlier WMT Machine Translation test sets, translated from English to Spanish with a phrase-based SMT system, along with the models used and diagnostic output produced by the SMT system as well as manual translation quality annotations on a 1–5 scale for each sentence. Additionally, a set of 17 baseline features was made available to the participants. Systems were evaluated on a test set of 422 sentences annotated in the same way.

Uppsala University submitted two systems to this shared task. Our systems were fairly successful and achieved results that were outperformed by only one competing group. They improve over the baseline performance in two ways, building on and extending earlier work by Hardmeier (2011), on which the system description in the following sections is partly based: On the one hand, we enhance the set of 17 baseline features provided by the organisers with another 82 explicitly defined features. On the other hand, we use syntactic tree kernels to extract implicit features from constituency and dependency parse trees over the input sentences and the Machine Translation (MT) output. The experimental results confirm the findings of our earlier work, showing tree kernels to be a valuable tool for rapid prototyping of QE systems.

2 Features

Our QE systems used two types of features: On the one hand, we used a set of *explicit features* that were extracted from the data before running the Machine Learning (ML) component. On the other hand, syntactic parse trees of the MT input and output sentences provided *implicit features* that were computed directly by the ML component using tree kernels.

2.1 Explicit features

Both of the QE systems we submitted to the shared task used the complete set of 17 baseline features provided by the workshop organisers. Additionally, the `UU_best` system also contained all the features presented by Hardmeier (2011) with the exception of a few features specific to the film subtitle genre and inapplicable to the text type of the shared task, as well as a small number of features not included in that work. Many of these features were modelled on QE features described by Specia et al. (2009). In particular, the following features were included in addition to the baseline feature set:

- number of words, length ratio (4 features)
- source and target type-token ratios (2 features)
- number of tokens matching particular patterns (3 features each):
  - numbers
  - opening and closing parentheses
  - strong punctuation signs
  - weak punctuation signs
  - ellipsis signs
  - hyphens
  - single and double quotes
  - apostrophe-s tokens
  - short alphabetic tokens (≤ 3 letters)
  - long alphabetic tokens (≥ 4 letters)
- source and target language model (LM) and log-LM scores (4 features)
- LM and log-LM scores normalised by sentence length (4 features)
- number and percentage of out-of-vocabulary words (2 features)
- percentage of source 1-, 2-, 3- and 4-grams occurring in the source part of the training corpus (4 features)
- percentage of source 1-, 2-, 3- and 4-grams in each frequency quartile of the training corpus (16 features)
- a binary feature indicating that the output contains more than three times as many alphabetic tokens as the input (1 feature)
- percentage of unaligned words and words with $1:1$, $1:n$, $n:1$ and $m:n$ alignments (10 features)
- average number of translations per word, unweighted and weighted by word frequency and reciprocal word frequency (3 features)
- translation model entropy for the input words, cumulatively per sentence and averaged per word, computed based on the SMT lexical weight model (2 features).

Whenever applicable, features were computed for both the source and the target language, and additional features were added to represent the squared difference of the source and target language feature values. All feature values were scaled so that their values ranged between 0 and 1 over the training set.

The total number of features of the `UU_best` system amounted to 99. It should be noted, however, that there is considerable redundancy in the feature set and that the 82 features of Hardmeier (2011) overlap with the 17 baseline features to some extent. We did not make any attempt to reduce feature overlap and relied on the learning algorithm for feature selection.

2.2 Parse trees

Both the English input text and the Spanish Machine Translations were annotated with syntactic parse trees from which to derive implicit features. In English, we were able to produce both constituency and dependency parses. In Spanish, we were limited to dependency parses because of the better availability of parsing models. English constituency parses were produced with the Stanford parser (Klein and Manning, 2003) using the model bundled with the parser. For dependency parsing, we used MaltParser (Nivre et al., 2006). POS tagging was done with HunPOS (Halácsy et al., 2007) for English and SVMTool (Giménez and Márquez, 2004) for Spanish, with the models provided by the OPUS project (Tiedemann, 2009). As in previous work (Hardmeier, 2011), we treated the parser as a black box and made no attempt to handle the fact that parsing accuracy may be decreased over malformed SMT output.

To be used with tree kernels, the output of the dependency parser had to be transformed into a single tree structure with a unique label per node and unlabelled edges, similar to a constituency parse tree. We followed Johansson and Moschitti (2010) in using a tree representation which encodes part-of-speech tags, dependency relations and words as sequences of child nodes (see fig. 1).

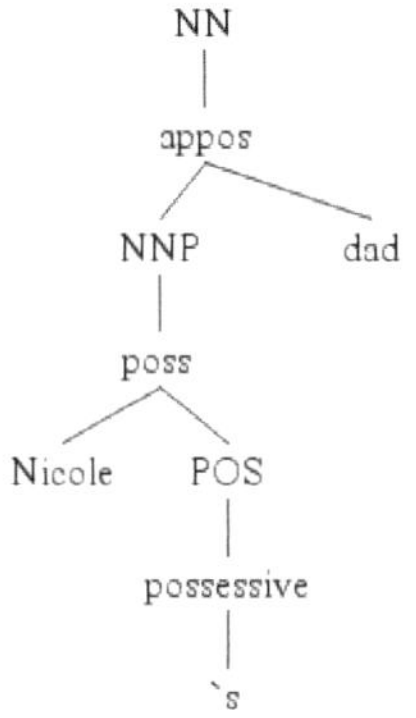

Figure 1: Representation of the dependency tree fragment for the words *Nicole 's dad*

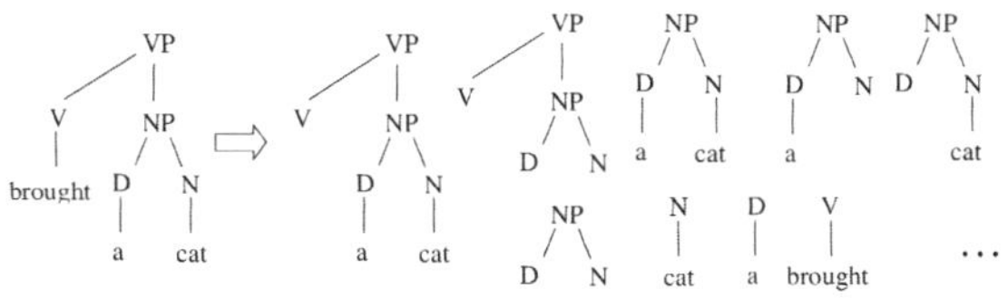

A tree and some of its Subset Tree Fragments

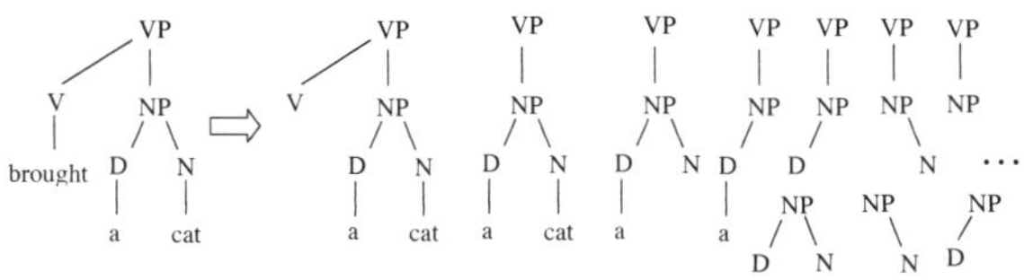

A tree and some of its Partial Tree Fragments

Figure 2: Tree fragments extracted by the Subset Tree Kernel and by the Partial Tree Kernel. Illustrations by Moschitti (2006a).

3 Machine Learning component

3.1 Overview

The QE shared task asked both for an estimate of a 1–5 quality score for each segment in the test set and for a ranking of the sentences according to quality. We decided to treat score estimation as primary and address the task as a regression problem. For the ranking task, we simply submitted the ranking induced by the regression output, breaking ties randomly.

Our system was based on SVM regression as implemented by the SVMlight software (Joachims, 1999) with tree kernel extensions (Moschitti, 2006b). Predicted scores less than 1 were set to 1 and predicted scores greater than 5 were set to 5 as this was known to be the range of valid scores. Our learning algorithm had some free hyperparameters. Three of them were optimised by joint grid search with 5-fold cross-validation over the training set: the SVM training error/margin trade-off (C parameter), one free parameter of the explicit feature kernel and the ratio between explicit feature and tree kernels (see below). All other parameters were left at their default values. Before running it over the test set, the system was retrained on the complete training set using the parameters found with cross-validation.

3.2 Kernels for explicit features

To select a good kernel for our explicit features, we initially followed the advice given by Hsu et al. (2010), using a Gaussian RBF kernel and optimising the SVM C parameter and the γ parameter of the RBF with grid search. While this gave reasonable results, it turned out that slightly better prediction could be achieved by using a polynomial kernel, so we chose to use this kernel for our final submission and used grid search to tune the degree of the polynomial instead. The improvement over the Gaussian kernel was, however, marginal.

3.3 Tree kernels

To exploit parse tree information in our Machine Learning (ML) component, we used tree kernel functions. Tree kernels (Collins and Duffy, 2001) are kernel functions defined over pairs of tree structures. They measure the similarity between two trees by counting the number of common substructures. Implicitly, they define an infinite-dimensional feature space whose dimensions correspond to all possible tree fragments. Features are thus available to cover different kinds of abstract node configurations that can occur in a tree. The important feature dimensions are effectively selected by the SVM training algorithm through the selection and weighting of the support vectors. The intuition behind our use of tree kernels is that they may help us identify constructions that are difficult to translate in the source language, and doubtful syntactic structures in the output language. Note that we do not currently compare parse trees across languages; tree kernels

	Features	T	C	d	Cross-validation Δ	ρ	MAE	RMS	Test set Δ	ρ	MAE	RMS
UU_best	99 explicit + TK	0.05	4	2	0.506	0.566	0.550	0.692	0.56	0.62	0.64	0.79
(a)	99 explicit + TK	0.03	8	3	0.502	0.564	0.552	0.700	0.56	0.61	0.63	0.78
(b)	17 explicit + TK	0.05	4	2	0.462	0.530	0.568	0.714	0.57	0.61	0.65	0.79
UU_bltk	17 explicit + TK	0.03	8	3	0.466	0.534	0.566	0.712	0.58	0.61	0.64	0.79
(c)	99 explicit	0	8	2	0.492	0.560	0.554	0.700	0.56	0.59	0.65	0.80
(d)	17 explicit	0	8	2	0.422	0.466	0.598	0.748	0.52	0.55	0.70	0.83
(e)	TK only	–	4	–	0.364	0.392	0.632	0.782	0.51	0.51	0.70	0.85

T: Tree kernel weight C: Training error/margin trade-off d: Degree of polynomial kernel
Δ: DeltaAvg score ρ: Spearman rank correlation   MAE: Mean Average Error
RMS: Root Mean Square Error   TK: Tree kernels

Table 1: Experimental results

are applied to trees of the same type in the same language only.

We used two different types of tree kernels for the different types of parse trees (see fig. 2). The Subset Tree Kernel (Collins and Duffy, 2001) considers tree fragments consisting of more than one node with the restriction that if one child of a node is included, then all its siblings must be included as well so that the underlying production rule is completely represented. This kind of kernel is well suited for constituency parse trees and was used for the source language constituency parses. For the dependency trees, we used the Partial Tree Kernel (Moschitti, 2006a) instead. It extends the Subset Tree Kernel by permitting also the extraction of tree fragments comprising only part of the children of any given node. Lifting this restriction makes sense for dependency trees since a node and its children do not correspond to a grammatical production in a dependency tree in the same way as they do in a constituency tree (Moschitti, 2006a). It was used for the dependency trees in the source and in the target language.

The explicit feature kernel and the three tree kernels were combined additively, with a single weight parameter to balance the sum of the tree kernels against the explicit feature kernel. This coefficient was optimised together with the other two hyperparameters mentioned above. It turned out that best results could be obtained with a fairly low weight for the tree kernels, but in the cross-validation experiments adding tree kernels did give an improvement over not having them at all.

4 Experimental Results

Results for some of our experiments are shown in table 1. The two systems we submitted to the shared task are marked with their system identifiers. A few other systems are included for comparison and are numbered (a) to (e) for easier reference.

Our system using only the baseline features (d) performs a bit worse than the reference system of the shared task organisers. We use the same learning algorithm, so this seems to indicate that the kernel and the hyperparameters they selected worked slightly better than our choices. Using only tree kernels with no explicit features at all (e) creates a system that works considerably worse under cross-validation, however we note that its performance on the test set is very close to that of system (d).

Adding the 82 additional features of Hardmeier (2011) to the system without tree kernels slightly improves the performance both under cross-validation and on the test set (c). Adding tree kernels has a similar effect, which is a bit less pronounced for the cross-validation setting, but quite comparable on the test set (UU_bltk, b). Finally, combining the full feature set with tree kernels results in an additional gain under cross-validation, but unfortunately the improvement does not carry over to the test set (UU_best, a).

5 Conclusions

In sum, the results confirm the findings made in our earlier work (Hardmeier, 2011). They show that tree kernels can be a valuable tool to boost the initial performance of a Quality Estimation system without spending much effort on feature engineering. Unfortunately, it seems that the gains achieved by tree kernels over simple parse trees and by the additional explicit features used in our systems do not necessarily add up. Nevertheless, comparison with other participating systems shows that either of them is sufficient for state-of-the-art performance.

References

Chris Callison-Burch, Philipp Koehn, Christof Monz, Matt Post, Radu Soricut, and Lucia Specia. 2012. Findings of the 2012 Workshop on Statistical Machine Translation. In *Proceedings of the Seventh Workshop on Statistical Machine Translation*, Montreal, Canada, June. Association for Computational Linguistics.

Michael Collins and Nigel Duffy. 2001. Convolution kernels for natural language. In *Proceedings of NIPS 2001*, pages 625–632.

Jesús Giménez and Lluís Márquez. 2004. SVMTool: A general POS tagger generator based on Support Vector Machines. In *Proceedings of the 4th Conference on International Language Resources and Evaluation (LREC-2004)*, Lisbon.

Péter Halácsy, András Kornai, and Csaba Oravecz. 2007. HunPos – an open source trigram tagger. In *Proceedings of the 45th Annual Meeting of the Association for Computational Linguistics. Companion Volume: Proceedings of the Demo and Poster Sessions*, pages 209–212, Prague, Czech Republic, June. Association for Computational Linguistics.

Christian Hardmeier. 2011. Improving machine translation quality prediction with syntactic tree kernels. In Mikel L. Forcada, Heidi Depraetere, and Vincent Vandeghinste, editors, *Proceedings of the 15th conference of the European Association for Machine Translation (EAMT 2011)*, pages 233–240, Leuven, Belgium.

Chih-Wei Hsu, Chih-Chung Chang, and Chih-Jen Lin. 2010. A practical guide to support vector classification. Technical report, Department of Computer Science, National Taiwan University.

Thorsten Joachims. 1999. Making large-scale SVM learning practical. In B. Schölkopf, C. Burges, and A. Smola, editors, *Advances in Kernel Methods – Support Vector Learning*. MIT Press.

Richard Johansson and Alessandro Moschitti. 2010. Syntactic and semantic structure for opinion expression detection. In *Proceedings of the Fourteenth Conference on Computational Natural Language Learning*, pages 67–76, Uppsala, Sweden, July. Association for Computational Linguistics.

Dan Klein and Christopher D. Manning. 2003. Accurate unlexicalized parsing. In *Proceedings of the 41st Annual Meeting of the Association for Computational Linguistics*, pages 423–430, Sapporo, Japan, July. Association for Computational Linguistics.

Alessandro Moschitti. 2006a. Efficient convolution kernels for dependency and constituent syntactic trees. In *Proceedings of the 17th European Conference on Machine Learning*, Berlin.

Alessandro Moschitti. 2006b. Making tree kernels practical for natural language learning. In *Proceedings of the Eleventh International Conference of the European Association for Computational Linguistics*, Trento.

Joakim Nivre, Johan Hall, and Jens Nilsson. 2006. MaltParser: A language-independent system for data-driven dependency parsing. In *Proceedings of the 5th Conference on International Language Resources and Evaluation (LREC-2006)*, pages 2216–2219, Genoa.

Lucia Specia, Craig Saunders, Marco Turchi, Zhuoran Wang, and John Shawe-Taylor. 2009. Improving the confidence of Machine Translation quality estimates. In *Proceedings of MT Summit XII*, Ottawa.

Jörg Tiedemann. 2009. News from OPUS – a collection of multilingual parallel corpora with tools and interface. In N. Nicolov, K. Bontcheva, G. Angelova, and R. Mitkov, editors, *Recent Advances in Natural Language Processing*, pages 237–248. John Benjamins, Amsterdam.

LORIA System for the WMT12 Quality Estimation Shared Task

Langlois David **Raybaud Sylvain** **Smaïli Kamel**
LORIA, Université de Lorraine
615 rue du Jardin Botanique
54602 Villers les Nancy, France
langlois@loria.fr raybauds@loria.fr smaili@loria.fr

Abstract

In this paper we present the system we submitted to the WMT12 shared task on Quality Estimation. Each translated sentence is given a score between 1 and 5. The score is obtained using several numerical or boolean features calculated according to the source and target sentences. We perform a linear regression of the feature space against scores in the range [1:5]. To this end, we use a Support Vector Machine. We experiment with two kernels: linear and radial basis function. In our submission we use the features from the shared task baseline system and our own features. This leads to 66 features. To deal with this large number of features, we propose an in-house feature selection algorithm. Our results show that a lot of information is already present in baseline features, and that our feature selection algorithm discards features which are linearly correlated.

1 Introduction

Machine translation systems are not reliable enough to be used directly. They can only be used to grasp the general meaning of texts or help human translators. Confidence measures detect erroneous words or sentences. Such information could be useful for users to decide whether or not to post-edit translated sentences (Specia, 2011; Specia et al., 2010) or select documents mostly correctly translated (Soricut and Echihabi, 2010). Moreover, it is possible to use confidence measures to compare outputs from different systems and to recommend the best one (He et al., 2010). One can also imagine that confidence measures at word-level could be also useful for a machine translation system to automatically correct parts of output: for example, a translation system translates the source sentence, then, this output is translated with another translation system (Simard et al., 2007). This last step could be driven by confidence measures.

In previous works (Raybaud et al., 2011; Raybaud et al., 2009a; Raybaud et al., 2009b) we used state-of-the-art features to predict the quality of a translation at sentence- and word-level. Moreover, we proposed our own features based on previous works on cross-lingual triggers (Lavecchia et al., 2008; Latiri et al., 2011). We evaluated our work in terms of Discrimination Error Trade-off, Equal Error Rate and Normalised Mutual Information.

In this article, we compare the features used in the shared task baseline system and our own features. This leads to 66 features which will be detailed in sections 3 and 4. We therefore deal with many features. We used a machine learning approach to perform regression of the feature space against scores given by humans. Machine learning algorithms may not efficiently deal with high dimensional spaces. Moreover, some features may be less discriminant descriptors and then in some cases could add more noise than information. That is why, in this article we propose an in-house feature selection algorithm to remove useless features.

The article is structured as follows. In Section 2, we give an overview of our quality estimation system. Then, in Sections 3 and 4, we describe the features we experimented with. In section 6, we describe the algorithm we propose for feature selection. Then we give the results of several configurations in Section 7.

2 Overview of our quality estimation submission

Each translated sentence is assigned a score between 1 and 5. 5 means that the machine translation output is perfectly clear and intelligible and 1 means that it is incomprehensible. The score is calculated using several numerical or boolean features extracted according to the source and target sentences. We perform a regression of the feature space against $[1 : 5]$.

3 The baseline features

The quality estimation shared task organizers provided a baseline system including several interesting features. Among them, several are yet used in (Raybaud et al., 2011) but we give below a brief review of the whole baseline features set[1]:

- Source and target sentences lengths: there is a correlation between the sizes of source and target sentences.
- Average source token length: this is the average number of letters of the words in the sentence. We guess that this feature can be useful because short words have more chance to be tool words.
- Language model likelihood of source and target sentences: a source sentence with low likelihood is certainly far from training corpus statistics. There is a risk it is badly translated. A target sentence with low likelihood is not suitable in terms of target language.
- Average number of occurrences of the words within the target sentence: too many occurrences of the same word in the target sentence may indicate a bad translation.
- Average number of translations per source word in the sentence: for each word in the source sentence, the feature indicates how many words of the target sentence are indeed translations of this word in the IBM1 table (with probability higher than 0.2).
- Weighted average number of translations per source word in the sentence: this feature is similar to the previous one, but a frequent word is given a low weight in the averaging.
- n-gram frequency based features: the baseline system proposes to group the n-gram frequencies into 4 quartiles. The features indicate how many n-gram (unigram to trigram) in source sentence are in quartiles 1 and 4. These features indicate if the source sentence contains n-grams relevant to the training corpus.
- Punctuation based features: there may exist a correlation between punctuation of source and target sentences. The count of punctuation marks in both sentences may then be useful.

Overall, the baseline system proposes 17 features.

4 The LORIA features

In a previous work (Raybaud et al., 2011), we tested several confidence measures. The Quality Measure Task campaign constitutes a good opportunity for us to compare our approach to others. We give below a brief review of our features (we cite again features which are yet presented in baseline features because sometimes, we use a variant of them):

- lengths: three features are generated, lengths of source and target sentences (already presented in baseline features), and ratio of target over source length
- n-gram based features (Duchateau et al., 2002): each word in the source and target sentences is given its 5-gram probability. Then, the sentence-level score is the average of the scores across all words in the sentence. There are 4 features: one for each language (source and target) and one for each direction (left-to-right and right-to-left 5-gram).
- backoff n-gram based features: in the same way, a score is assigned to a word according to how many times the language model had to back off in order to assign a probability to the sequence (Uhrik and Ward, 1997). Here too, word scores are averaged and we get 4 scores.

[1]Indeed, our system takes into input a set of features, and is able to discard redundant features (see Section 6).

- averaged features: a common property of all n-gram based and backoff based features is that a word can get a low score if it is actually correct but its neighbours are wrong. To compensate for this phenomenon we took into account the average score of the neighbours of the word being considered. More precisely, for every relevant feature $x_.$ defined at word level we also computed:

$$\begin{aligned} x^{left}_.(w_i) &= x_.(w_{i-2}) * x_.(w_{i-1}) * x_.(w_i) \\ x^{centred}_.(w_i) &= x_.(w_{i-1}) * x_.(w_i) * x_.(w_{i+1}) \\ x^{right}_.(w_i) &= x_.(w_{i)} * x_.(w_{i+1}) * x_.(w_{i+2}) \end{aligned}$$

  A sentence level feature is then calculated according to the average of each new "averaged feature".

- intra-lingual features: the intra-lingual score of a word in a sentence is the average of the mutual information between that word and the other words in that sentence. Mutual information is defined by:

$$I(w_1, w_2) = P(w_1, w_2) \times log\left(\frac{P(w_1, w_2)}{P(w_1)P(w_2)}\right) \quad (1)$$

  The intra-lingual score of a sentence is the average of the intra-lingual scores of the words in this sentence. There are two features, one for each language.

- cross-lingual features: the cross-lingual score of a word in a target sentence is the average of the mutual information between that word and the words in the source sentence. The cross-lingual score of a target sentence is the average of its constituents.

- IBM1 features: the score of the target sentence is the average translation probability provided by the IBM1 model.

- basic parser: this produces two scores, a binary flag indicating whether any bracketing inside the target sentence is correct, and one indicating if the sentence ends with an end of sentence symbol (period, colon, semi-colon, question/exclamation/quotation mark, comma, apostrophe, close parenthese)

- out-of-vocabulary: this generates two scores, the number of out-of-vocabulary words in the sentence, and the same one but normalized by the length of the sentence. These scores are used for both sides.

This leads to 49 features. A few ones are equivalent to or are strongly correlated to baseline ones. As we want to be able to integrate several sets of features without prior knowledge, our system is able to discard redundant features (see Section 6).

5 Regression

Our system predicts a score between 1 and 5 for each test sentence. For that, we used the training corpus to perform the linear regression of the input features against scores given by humans. We used SVM algorithm to perform this regression (LibSVM toolkit (Chang and Lin, 2011)). We experimented two kernels: linear, and radial basis function. For the radial basis function, we used grid search to optimise parameters.

6 Feature Selection

We experimented with many features. Some of them may be very poor predictors. Then, these features may disturb the convergence of the training algorithm of SVM. To prevent this drawback, we applied an in-house feature selection algorithm. A feature selection algorithm selects the most relevant features by maximizing a criterion. Feature selection algorithms can be divided into two classes: backward and forward (Guyon and Elisseeff, 2003). Backward algorithms remove useless features from a set. Forward algorithms start with an empty feature set and insert useful features. We implemented a greedy backward elimination algorithm for feature selection. It discards features until a quality criterion stops to decrease. The criterion used is the Mean Average Error (MAE) calculated on the development corpus:

$$MAE(s, r) = \frac{\sum_{i=1}^{n} |s_i - r_i|}{n} \quad (2)$$

where s is the list of scores predicted by the system, r is the list of scores given by experts, n is the size of these lists.

The algorithm is described below:

Algorithm 1: Feature Selection algorithm

```
begin
    Start with a set S of features
    while two features in S are linearly correlated (more than 0.999) do
        discard one of them from S
    Calculate MAE for S
    repeat
        DecreaseMax ← 0
        forall the feature f ∈ S do
            S' ← S \ f
            Calculate newMAE for S'
            if MAE-newMAE > DecreaseMax then
                DecreaseMax ← MAE-newMAE
                fchosen ← f
        if DecreaseMax > 0 then
            S ← S\ fchosen
            MAE ← MAE-DecreaseMax
    until DecreaseMax=0;
```

For calculating the MAE for a feature set, several steps are necessary: performing the regression between the features and the expert scores on the training corpus, using this regression to predict the scores on the development corpus, calculate the MAE between the predicted scores and the expert scores on this development corpus.

7 Results

We used the data provided by the shared task on Quality Estimation[2], without additional corpus. This data is composed of a parallel English-Spanish training corpus. This corpus is made of the concatenation of europarl-v5 and news-commentary10 corpora (from WMT-2010), followed by tokenization, cleaning (sentences with more than 80 tokens removed) and truecasing. It has been used for baseline models provided in the baseline package by the shared task organizers. We used the same training corpus to train additional language models (forward and backward 5-gram with kneyser-ney discounting, obtained with the SRILM toolkit) and triggers required for our features. For feature extraction, we used the files provided by the organizers: 1832 source english sentences, their translations by the baseline translation system, and the score given by humans to these translations. We split these files into a training part (1000 sentences) and a development part (832 sentences). We used the train part to perform the regression between the features and the scores. We used the development corpus to optimise the parameters of the regression and for feature selection. We did not use additional provided information such as phrase alignment, word alignment, word graph, etc.

Table 1 presents our results in terms of MAE and Root Mean Squared Error (RMSE). MAE is described in Formula 2, and RMSE is defined by:

$$RMSE(s,r) = \sqrt{\frac{\sum_{i=1}^{n}(s_i - r_i)^2}{n}} \quad (3)$$

Each line of Table 1 gives the performance for a set of features. BASELINE+LORIA constitutes the union of both features BASELINE (Section 3) and LORIA (Section 4). the 'feature selection' column indicates if feature selection algorithm is applied. We experimented the SVM with two kernels: linear (LIN in Table 1) and radial basis function (RBF in Table 1). As the radial basis function uses parameters, we proposed results with default values (DEF) and with values optimised by grid search on the development corpus (OPT). MAE and RMSE are given for development corpus and for the test corpus. This test corpus (and its reference scores given by humans) is the one released for the shared 2012 task[3]. MAE and RMSE has been computed against the scores given by humans to the translations in this test corpus[4].

The results show that the performance on development corpus are always confirmed by those of the test corpus. The BASELINE features alone achieve already good performance, better than ours. Although the differences are well inside the confidence interval, the fusion of both sets outperforms slightly the BASELINE. The feature selection algorithm allows to gain 0.01 point. The gain is the same for

[2]http://dl.dropbox.com/u/6447503/resources.tbz

[3]https://github.com/lspecia/QualityEstimation/blob/master/test_set.tar.gz

[4]available at https://github.com/lspecia/QualityEstimation/blob/master/test_set.likert

the optimisation of the radial basis function parameters. Surprisingly, the linear kernel, simpler than other kernels, yields the same performance as radial basis function.

In addition to MAE and RMSE results, we studied the linear correlations between features: our objective is to check if BASELINE and LORIA complement each other. We computed the linear correlation between all features (BASELINE+LORIA). This leads to 2145 values. Table 2 shows in line +/- the number of features pairs which correlate with an absolute score higher than thresholds 0.9, 0.8 or 0.7. Among these pairs we give in line + the number of pairs with positive correlation, and in line - the number of pairs with negative correlation. For lines + and -, we give 4 numbers: number of pairs, number of LORIA-LORIA (e.g. the number of correlations between a LORIA feature and another LORIA feature) pairs, number of BASELINE-BASELINE pairs, number of LORIA-BASELINE pairs. We remark that only 6% of the pairs correlates (column 0.7, line +/-) and that the correlations are mostly between LORIA features. This last point is not surprising because there are more LORIA features than BASELINE ones. There are very few correlations between LORIA and BASELINE features. We studied precisely the correlated pairs. There is a strong (more than 0.9) positive correlation between n-gram and backoff based features and their averaged feature versions. Sometimes, there is also a strong correlation between 'forward' and 'backward' features. Source and target sentences lengths linearly correlate (0.98). This is the same case for source and target language model likelihoods. There is also a high correlation between forward and backward 5-gram scores (0.89). There are very few negative correlations between features. As they are not numerous, one can list these pairs with correlation between -1 and -0.7: target sentence length and target language model probability; source sentence length and source language model probability; ratio of OOV words over sentence length in source sentence and percentage of unigrams in the source sentence seen in the SMT training corpus; and number of OOV words in source sentence and percentage of unigrams in the source sentence seen in the SMT training corpus. These correlations are not surprising. First, language model probability is not normalized by the number of tokens: the more tokens, the lower probability. Second, the more OOV in the sentence, the fewer known unigrams.

	≥ 0.9	≥ 0.8	≥ 0.7
+/-	64	103	127
+	56/49/3/4	94/87/3/4	117/105/6/6
-	8/0/4/4	9/0/4/5	10/0/4/6

Table 2: Statistics on the linear correlations between LORIA+BASELINE features

Last, we present the set of features discarded by our feature selection algorithm. We give only this description for the LORIA+BASELINE set, with linear kernel. The algorithm discards 18 LORIA features out of 49 (37%) and 3 BASELINE out of 17 (18%). The features discarded from LORIA are mostly averaged features based on n-gram and backoff. This is consistent with the fact that these features are strongly correlated with n-gram and backoff features. We remark that very few BASELINE features are discarded: lengths of source and target language because these features are yet included in LORIA features, and "average number of translations per source word in the sentence" maybe because the LORIA feature giving the average IBM1 probabilities is more precise. Last, we remark that the target length feature is discarded, and only ratio between target and source length is kept.

8 Conclusion

In this paper, we present our system to evaluate the quality of machine translated sentences. A sentence is given a score between 1 and 5. This score is predicted using a machine learning approach. We use the training data provided by the organizers to perform the regression between numerical features calculated from source and target sentences and scores given by human experts. The features are the baseline ones provided by the organizers and our own features. We proposed a feature selection algorithm to discard useless features. Our results show that baseline features contain already the main part of information for prediction. Concerning our own features, a study of the linear correlations shows that averaged features do not provide new information compared to n-gram and backoff features. This last

			Dev		Test	
Set of features	**feature selection**	**kernel**	**MAE**	**RMSE**	**MAE**	**RMSE**
BASELINE	no	RBF DEF	0.63	0.79	0.69	0.83
LORIA	no	RBF DEF	0.66	0.82	0.73	0.87
BASELINE+LORIA	no	RBF DEF	0.62	0.78	0.69	**0.82**
BASELINE+LORIA	yes	RBF DEF	**0.61**	**0.77**	0.69	0.83
BASELINE+LORIA	no	RBF OPT	0.62	**0.77**	**0.68**	**0.82**
BASELINE+LORIA	no	LIN	0.62	0.78	0.69	0.83
BASELINE+LORIA	yes	LIN	**0.61**	**0.77**	**0.68**	**0.82**

Table 1: Results of the various sets of features in terms of MAE and RMSE

remark is confirmed by our feature selection algorithm. Our feature selection algorithm seems to discard features linearly correlated with others while keeping relevant features for prediction. Last, we remark that the choice of kernel, optimisation of parameters and feature selection have not a strong effect on performance. The main effort may have to be concentrated on features in the future.

References

C.-C. Chang and C.-J. Lin. 2011. LIBSVM: A library for support vector machines. *ACM Transactions on Intelligent Systems and Technology*, 2:27:1–27:27. Software available at http://www.csie.ntu.edu.tw/ cjlin/libsvm.

J. Duchateau, K. Demuynck, and P. Wambacq. 2002. Confidence scoring based on backward language models. In *Proceedings of IEEE International Conference on Acoustics, Speech, and Signal Processing*, volume 1, pages 221–224.

I. Guyon and A. Elisseeff. 2003. An introduction to variable and feature selection. *Journal of Machine Learning Research (Special Issue on Variable and Feature Selection)*, pages 1157–1182.

Y. He, Y. Ma, J. van Genabith, and A. Way. 2010. Bridging SMT and TM with translation recommendation. In *Proceedings of the 48th Annual Meeting of the Association for Computational Linguistics*, pages 622–630.

C. Latiri, K. Smaïli, C. Lavecchia, C. Nasri, and D. Langlois. 2011. Phrase-based machine translation based on text mining and statistical language modeling techniques. In *Proceedings of the 12th International Conference on Intelligent Text Processing and Computational Linguistics*.

C. Lavecchia, K. Smaïli, and D. Langlois. 2008. Discovering phrases in machine translation by simulated annealing. In *Proceedings of the Eleventh Interspeech Conference*.

S. Raybaud, C. Lavecchia, D. Langlois, and K. Smaïli. 2009a. New confidence measures for statistical machine translation. In *Proceedings of the International Conference on Agents and Artificial Intelligence*, pages 61–68.

S. Raybaud, C. Lavecchia, D. Langlois, and K. Smaïli. 2009b. Word- and sentence-level confidence measures for machine translation. In *Proceedings of the 13th Annual Conference of the European Association for Machine Translation*, pages 104–111.

S. Raybaud, D. Langlois, and K. Smaïli. 2011. "This sentence is wrong." Detecting errors in machine-translated sentences. *Machine Translation*, 25(1):1–34.

M. Simard, N. Ueffing, P. Isabelle, and R. Kuhn. 2007. Rule-based translation with statistical phrase-based post-editing. In *Proceedings of the ACL-2007 Workshop on Statistical Machine Translation (WMT-07)*, pages 203–206.

R. Soricut and A. Echihabi. 2010. Trustrank: Inducing trust in automatic translations via ranking. In *Proceedings of the 48th Annual Meeting of the Association for Computational Linguistics*, pages 612–621.

L. Specia, N. Hajlaoui, C. Hallett, and W. Aziz. 2010. Predicting machine translation adequacy. In *Proceedings of the Machine Translation Summit XIII*, pages 612–621.

L. Specia. 2011. Exploiting objective annotations for measuring translation post-editing effort. In *Proceedings of the 15th Conference of the European Association for Machine Translation*, pages 73–80.

C. Uhrik and W. Ward. 1997. Confidence metrics based on n-gram language model backoff behaviors. In *Fifth European Conference on Speech Communication and Technology*, pages 2771–2774.

Quality Estimation: an experimental study using unsupervised similarity measures

Erwan Moreau
CNGL and Computational Linguistics Group
Centre for Computing and Language Studies
School of Computer Science and Statistics
Trinity College Dublin
Dublin 2, Ireland
moreaue@cs.tcd.ie

Carl Vogel
Computational Linguistics Group
Centre for Computing and Language Studies
School of Computer Science and Statistics
Trinity College Dublin
Dublin 2, Ireland
vogel@cs.tcd.ie

Abstract

We present the approach we took for our participation to the WMT12 Quality Estimation Shared Task: our main goal is to achieve reasonably good results without appeal to supervised learning. We have used various similarity measures and also an external resource (Google N-grams). Details of results clarify the interest of such an approach.

1 Introduction

Quality Estimation (or Confidence Estimation) refers here to the task of evaluating the quality of the output produced by a Machine Translation (MT) system. More precisely it consists in evaluating the quality of every individual sentence, in order (for instance) to decide whether a given sentence can be published as it is, should be post-edited, or is so bad that it should be manually re-translated.

To our knowledge, most approaches so far (Specia et al., 2009; Soricut and Echihabi, 2010; He et al., 2010; Specia et al., 2011) use several features combined together using supervised learning in order to predict quality scores. These features belong to two categories: *black box features* which can be extracted given only the input sentence and its translated version, and *glass box features* which rely on various intermediate steps of the internal MT engine (thus require access to this internal data). For the features they studied, Specia et al. (2009) have shown that *black box features* are informative enough and *glass box features* do not significantly contribute to the accuracy of the predicted scores.

In this study, we use only *black box features*, and further, eschew supervised learning except in the broadest sense. Our method requires some reference data, all taken to be equally good exemplars of a positive reference category, against which the experimental sentences are compared automatically. This is the extent of broader-sense supervision. The method does not require a training set of items each annotated by human experts with quality scores (except for the purpose of evaluation of course).

Successful unsupervised learning averts risks of the alternative: supervised learning necessarily makes the predicting system dependent on the annotated training data, i.e. less generic, and requires a costly human evalution stage to obtain a reliable model. Of course, our approach is likely not to perform as well as supervised approaches: here the goal is to find a rather generic robust way to measure quality, not to achieve the best accuracy. Nevertheless, in the context of this Quality Evaluation Shared task (see (Callison-Burch et al., 2012) for a detailed description) we have also used supervised learning as a final stage, in order to submit results which can be compared to other methods (see §4).

We investigate the use of various similarity measures for evaluating the quality of machine translated sentences. These measures compare the sentence to be evaluated against a *reference* text, providing a similarity score result. The reference data is supposed to represent standard (well-formed) language, so that the score is expected to reflect how complex (source side) or how fluent (target side) the given sentence is.

After presenting the similarity measures in section 2, we will show in section 3 how they perform individually on the ranking task; finally we will explain in section 4 how the results that we submitted were obtained using supervised learning.

2 Approach

Our method consists in trying to find the best measure(s) to estimate the quality of machine translated sentences, i.e. the ones which show the highest correlation with the human annotators scores. The measures we have tested work always as follows.

Given a sentence to evaluate (source or target), a score is computed by comparing the sentence against a reference dataset (usually a big set of sentences). This dataset is assumed to represent standard and/or well-formed language.[1] This score represents either the quality (similarity measure) or the faultiness (distance measure) of the sentence. It is not necessarily normalized, and in general cannot be interpreted straightforwardly (for example like the 1 to 5 scale used for this Shared Task, in which every value 1, 2, 3, 4, 5 has a precise meaning). In the context of the Shared task, this means that we focus on the "ranking" evaluation measures provided rather than the "scoring" measures. These scores are rather intended to compare sentences relatively to one another: for instance, they can be used to discard the N% lowest quality sentences from post-editing.

The main interest in such an approach is in avoiding dependence on costly-to-annotate training data—correspondingly costly to obtain and which risk over-tuning the predicting system to the articulated features of the training items. Our method still depends on the dataset used as reference, but this kind of dependency is much less constraining, because the reference dataset can be any text data. To obtain the best possible results, the reference data has to be representative enough of what the evaluated sentences *should* be (if they were of perfect quality), which implies that:

- a high coverage (common words or n-grams) is preferable; this also means that the size of this dataset is important;
- the quality (grammaticality, language register, etc.) must be very good: errors in the reference data will infect the predicted scores.

It is rather easy to use different reference datasets with our approach (as opposed to obtain new human scores and training a new model on this data), since nowadays numerous textual resources are available (at least for the most common languages).

2.1 Similarity measures

All the measures we have used compare (in different ways) the n-grams of the tested sentence against the reference data (represented as a big *bag of n-grams*). There is a variety of parameters for each measure; here are the parameters which are common to all:

Length of n-grams: from unigrams to 6-grams;

Punctuation: with or without punctuation marks;

Case sensitivity: binary;

Sentence boundaries: binary signal of whether special tokens should be added to mark the start and the end of sentences.[2] This permits:

- that there is the same number of n-grams containing a token w, for every w in the sentence;
- to match n-grams starting/ending a sentence only against n-grams which start/end a sentence.

Most configurations of parameters presented in this paper are empirical (i.e. only the parameter settings which performed better during our tests were retained). Below are the main measures explored.[3]

2.1.1 Okapi BM25 similarity (TF-IDF)

Term Frequency-Inverse Document Frequency (TF-IDF) is a widely used similarity measure in Information Retrieval(IR). It has also been shown to perform significantly better than only term frequency in tasks like matching coreferent named entities (see e.g. Cohen et al. (2003)), which is

[1] We use this definition of "reference" in this article. Please notice that this differs from the sense "human translation of a source sentence", which is more common in the MT literature.

[2] With trigrams, "`Hello World !`" (1 trigram) becomes "`# # Hello World ! # #`" (5 trigrams).

[3] One of the measures is not addressed in this paper for IP reasons (this measure obtained good results but was not best).

technically not very different from comparing sentences. The general idea is to compare two documents[4] using their bags of n-grams representations, but weighting the frequency of every n-gram with the IDF weight, which represents "how meaningful" the n-gram is over all documents based on its inverse frequency (because the n-grams which are very common are not very meaningful in general).

There are several variants of TF-IDF comparison measures. The most recent "Okapi BM25" version was shown to perform better in general than the original (more basic) definition (Jones et al., 2000). Moreover, there are different ways to actually combine the vectors together (e.g. L1 or L2 distance). In these experiments we have only used the Cosine distance, with Okapi BM25 weights. The weights are computed as usual (using the number of sentences containing X for any n-gram X), but are based only on the reference data.

2.1.2 Multi-level matching

For a given length N, "simple matching" is defined as follows: for every N-gram in the sentence, the score is incremented if this N-gram appears at least once in the reference data. The score is then relativized to the sentence N-gram length.

"Multi-level matching" (MLM) is similar but with different lengths of n-grams. For (maximum) length N, the algorithm is as follows (for every n-gram): if the n-gram appears in the reference data the score is incremented; otherwise, for all n-grams of length $N-1$ in this n-gram, apply recursively the same method, but apply a penalty factor p ($p < 1$) to the result.[5] This is intended to overcome the binary behaviour of the "simple matching". This way short sentences can always be assigned a score, and more importantly the score is smoothed according to the similarity of shorter n-grams (which is the behaviour one wants to obtain intuitively).

[4]In this case every sentence is compared against the reference data; from an IR viewpoint, one can see the reference data as the request and each sentence as one of the possible documents.

[5]This method is equivalent to computing the "simple matching" for different lengths N of N-grams, and then combine the scores s_N in the following way: if $s_N < s_{N-1}$, then add $p \times (s_{N-1} - s_N)$ to the score, and so on. However this "external" combination of scores can not take into account some of the extensions (e.g. weights).

Two main variants have been tested. The first one consists in using skip-grams.[6] Different sizes and configurations were tested (combining skip-grams and standard sequential n-grams), but none gave better results than using only sequential n-grams. The second variant consists in assigning a more fine-grained value, based on different parameters, instead of always assigning 1 to the score when n-gram occurs in the reference data. An optimal solution is not obvious, so we tried different strategies, as follows.

Firstly, **using the global frequency of the ngram in the reference data**: intuitively, this could be interpreted as "the more an n-gram appears (in the reference data), the more likely it is well-formed". However there are obviously n-grams which appear a lot more than others (especially for short n-grams). This is why we also tried using the logarithm of the frequency, in order to smooth discrepancies.

Secondly, **using the inverse frequency**: this is the opposite idea, thinking that the common n-grams are easy to translate, whereas the rare n-grams are harder. Consequently, the critical parts of the sentence are the rare n-grams: assigning them more weight focuses on these. This works in both cases (if the n-gram is actually translated correctly or not), because the weight assigned to the n-gram is taken into account in the normalization factor.

Finally, **using the Inverse Document Frequency (IDF)**: this is a similar idea as the previous one, except that instead of considering the global frequency the number of sentences containing the n-gram is taken into account. In most cases (and in all cases for long n-grams), this is very similar to the previous option because the cases where an n-gram (at least with $n > 1$) appears several times in the same sentence are not common.

2.2 Resources used as reference data

The reference data against which the sentences are compared is crucial to the success of our approach. As the simplest option, we have used the Europarl data on which the MT model was trained (source/target side for source/target sentences). Separately we tested a very different kind of data, namely the Google Books N-grams (Michel et al.,

[6]The `true-false-true` skip-grams in "`There is no such thing`": `There no`, `is such` and `no thing`.

2011): it is no obstacle that the reference sentences themselves are unavailable, since our measures only need the set of n-grams and possibly their frequency (Google Books N-gram data contains both).

3 Individual measures only

In this section we study how our similarity measures and the baseline features (when used individually) perform on the ranking task. This evaluation can only be done by means of DeltaAvg and Spearman correlation, since the values assigned to sentences are not comparable to quality scores. We have tested numerous combinations of parameters, but show below only the best ones (for every case).

3.1 General observations

Method	Ref. data	DeltaAvg	Spearman
MLM,1-4	Google, eng	0.26	0.22
Baseline feature 1		0.29	0.29
Baseline feature 2		0.29	0.29
MLM,1-3,lf	Google, spa	0.32	0.28
Okapi,3,b	EP, spa	0.33	0.27
Baseline feature 8		0.33	0.32
Okapi,2,b	EP, eng	0.34	0.30
Baseline feature 12		0.34	0.32
Baseline feature 5		0.39	0.39
MLM,1-5,b	EP, spa	0.39	0.39
MLM,1-5,b	EP, eng	0.39	0.40
Baseline feature 4		0.40	0.40

Table 1: Best results by method and by resource on training data. *b* = sentence boundaries ; *lf* = log frequency (Google) ; EP = Europarl.

Table 1 shows the best results that every method achieved on the whole training data with different resources, as well as the results of the best baseline features.[7] Firstly, one can observe that the language model probability (baseline features 4 and 5) performs as good or slightly better than our best measure. Then the best measure is the one which combines different lengths of n-grams (multi-level matching, combining unigrams to 5-grams), followed by baseline feature 12 (percentage of bigrams in quartile 4 of frequency), and then Okapi BM25 applied to bigrams. It is worth noticing that comparing either the source sentence or the target sentence (against the source/target training data) gives very similar results. However, using Google Ngrams as reference data shows a significantly lower correlation. Also using skip-grams or any of our "fined-grained" scoring techniques (see §2.1.2) did not improve the correlation, even if in most cases these were as good as the standard version.

3.2 Detailed analysis: how measures differ

Even when methods yield strongly correlated results, differences can be significant. For example, the correlation between the rankings obtained with the two best methods (baseline 4 and MLM Eng.) is 0.53. The methods do not make the same errors.[8] A method may tend to make a lot of small errors, or on the contrary, very few but big errors.

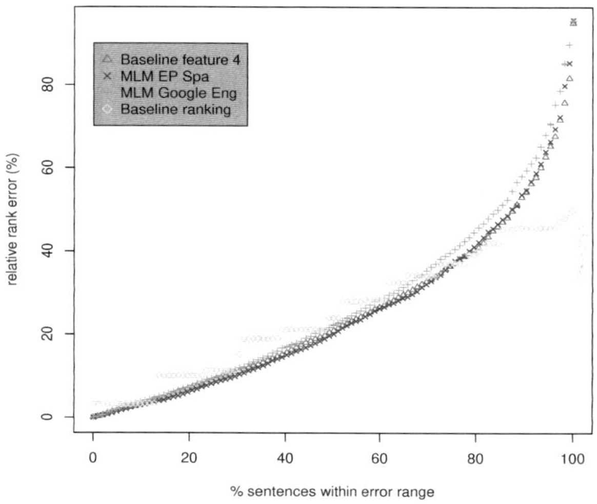

Figure 1: Percentage of best segments within an error range. For every measure, the X axis represents the sentences sorted by the difference between the predicted rank and the actual rank ("rank error"), in such a way that for any (relative) number of sentences x, the y value represents the maximum (relative) rank error for all prior sentences: for instance, 80% of the ranks predicted by these three measures are at most 40% from the actual rank.

Let R and R' be the actual and predicted ranks[9] of sentence, respectively. Compute the difference

[7] Baseline 1,2: length of the source/target sentence; Baseline features 4,5: LM probability of source/target sentence; Baseline feature 8: average number of translations per source word with threshold 0.01, weighted by inverse frequency; Baseline feature 12: percentage of bigrams in quartile 4 of frequency of source words in a corpus of the source language.

[8] This motivates use of supervised learning (but see §1).

[9] It is worth noticing that ties are taken into account here: two

$D = |R - R'|$; then relativize to the total number of sentences (the upper bound for D): $D' = D/N$. D' is the *relative rank error*. On ascending sort by D', the predicted ranks for the first sentences are closest to their actual rank. Taking the relative rank error D'_j for the sentence at position M_j, one knows that all "lower" sentences ($\forall M_i$, $M_i \leq M_j$) are more accurately assigned ($D'_i \leq D'_j$). Thus, if the position is also relativized to the total number sentences: $M'_k = M_k/N$, M'_k is the proportion of sentences for which the predicted rank is at worst $D'_k\%$ from the real rank. Figure 1 shows the percentage of sentences withing a rank error range for three good methods:[10] the error distributions are surprisingly similar. A *baseline ranking* is also represented, which shows the same if all sentences are assigned the same rank (i.e. all sentences are considered of equal quality)[11].

We have also studied effects of some parameters:

- Taking punctuation into account helps a little;
- Ignoring case gives slightly better results;
- Sentences boundaries significantly improve the performance;
- Most of the refinements of the local score (frequency, IDF, etc.) do not perform better than the basic binary approach.

4 Individual measures as features

In this section we explain how we obtained the submitted results using supervised learning.

4.1 Approach

We have tested a wide range of regression algorithms in order to predict the scores, using the Weka[12] toolkit (Hall et al., 2009). All tests were done using the whole training data in a 10 folds cross-validation setting. The main methods were:

- Linear regression
- Pace regression (Wang and Witten, 2002)
- SVM for regression (Shevade et al., 2000) (`SMOreg` in Weka)
- Decision Trees for regression (Quinlan, 1992) (`M5P` in Weka)

We have tested several combinations of features among the features provided as baseline and our measures. The measures were primarily selected on their individual performance (worst measures were discarded). However we also had to take the time constraint into account, because some measures require a fair amount of computing power and/or memory and some were not finished early enough. Finally we have also tested several attributes selection methods before applying the learning method, but they did not achieve a better performance.

4.2 Results

Table 2 shows the best results among the configurations we have tested (expressed using the official evaluation measures, see (Callison-Burch et al., 2012) for details). These results were obtained using the default Weka parameters.In this table, the different features sets are abbreviated as follows:

- **B**: Baseline (17 features);
- **M1**: All measures scores (45 features);
- **M2**: Only scores obtained using the provided resources (33 features);
- **L**: Lengths (of source and target sentence, 2 features).

For every method, the best results were obtained using all possible features (baseline and our measures). The following results can also be observed:

- our measures increase the performance over use of baseline features only (B+M1 vs. B);
- using an external resource (here Google n-grams) with some of our measures increases the performance (B+M1 vs. B+M2);

sentences which are assigned the same score are given the same rank. The ranking sum is preserved by assigning the average rank; for instance if $s_1 > s_2 = s_3 > s_4$ the corresponding ranks are 1, 2.5, 2.5, 4).

[10] Some are not shown, because the curves were too close.

[11] Remark: the plateaus are due to the ties in the *actual* ranks: there is one plateau for each score level. This is not visible on the predicted rankings because it is less likely that an important number of sentences have both the same actual rank and the same predicted rank (whereas they all have the same "predicted" rank in the baseline ranking, by definition).

[12] `www.cs.waikato.ac.nz/ml/weka` – l.v., 04/2012.

Features	Method	DeltaAvg	Spearman	MAE	RMSE
B	SVM	0.398	0.445	0.616	0.761
B	Pace Reg.	0.399	0.458	0.615	0.757
L + M1	SVM	0.401	0.439	0.615	0.764
L + M1	Lin. Reg	0.408	0.441	0.610	0.757
B	Lin. Reg.	0.408	0.461	0.614	0.754
L + M1	M5P	0.409	0.441	0.610	0.757
B + M2	SVM	0.409	0.447	0.605	0.753
B + M2	Pace Reg.	0.417	0.466	0.603	0.744
B + M2	M5P	0.419	0.472	0.601	0.746
L + M1	Pace Reg.	0.426	0.454	0.603	0.751
B + M2	Lin. Reg.	0.428	0.481	0.598	0.740
B	M5P	0.434	0.487	0.586	0.729
B + M1	SVM	0.444	0.489	0.585	0.734
B + M1	Pace Reg.	0.453	0.505	0.584	0.724
B + M1	Lin. Reg.	0.456	0.507	0.583	0.724
B + M1	M5P	0.457	0.508	0.583	0.724

Table 2: Best results on 10-folds cross-validation on the training data (sorted by DeltaAvg score).

- the baseline features contribute positively to the performance (B+M1 vs. L+M1);
- The M5P (Decision trees) method works best in almost all cases (3 out of 4).

Based on these training results, the two systems that we used to submit the test data scores were:

- **TCD-M5P-resources-only**, where scores were predicted from a model trained using M5P on the whole training data, taking only the baseline features (B) into account;
- **TCD-M5P-all**, where scores were predicted from a model trained using M5P on the whole training data, using all features (B+M1).

The **TCD-M5P-resources-only** submission ranked 5th (among 17) in the ranking task, and 5th among 19 (tied with two other systems) in the scoring task (Callison-Burch et al., 2012). Unfortunately the **TCD-M5P-all** submission contained an error.[13] Below are the official results for **TCD-M5P-resources-only** and the corrected results for **TCD-M5P-all** :

[13]In four cases in which Google n-grams formed the reference data, the scores were computed using the wrong language (Spanish instead of English) as the reference. Since this error occured only for the test data (not the training data used to compute the model), it made the predictions totally meaningless.

Submission	DeltaAvg	Spearman	MAE	RMSE
resources-only	0.56	0.58	0.68	0.82
all	0.54	0.54	0.70	0.84

Contrary to previous observations using the training data, these results show a better performance without our measures. We think that this is mainly due to the high variability of the results depending on the data, and that the first experiments are more significant because cross-validation was used.

5 Conclusion

In conclusion, we have shown that the robust approach that we have presented can achieve good results: the best DeltaAvg score reaches 0.40 on the training data, when the best supervised approach is at 0.45. We think that this robust approach complements the more fine-grained approach with supervised learning: the former is useful in the cases where the cost to use the latter is prohibitive.

Additionally, it is interesting to see that using external data (here the Google N-grams) improves the performance (when using supervised learning). As future work, we plan to investigate this question more precisely: when does the external data help? What are the differences between using the training data (used to produce the MT engine) and another dataset? How to select such an external data in order to maximize the performance? In our unsupervised framework, is it possible to combine the score obtained with the external data with the score obtained from the training data? Similarly, can we combine scores obtained by comparing the source side and the target side?

Acknowledgments

This research is supported by Science Foundation Ireland (Grant 07/CE/I1142) as part of the Centre for Next Generation Localisation (www.cngl.ie) funding at Trinity College, University of Dublin.
We thank the organizers who have accepted to apply a bug-fix (wrong numbering of the sentences) in the official results, and for organizing the Shared task.

References

[Callison-Burch et al.2012] Chris Callison-Burch, Philipp Koehn, Christof Monz, Matt Post, Radu

Soricut, and Lucia Specia. 2012. Findings of the 2012 workshop on statistical machine translation. In *Proceedings of the Seventh Workshop on Statistical Machine Translation*, Montreal, Canada, June. Association for Computational Linguistics.

[Cohen et al.2003] W.W. Cohen, P. Ravikumar, and S.E. Fienberg. 2003. A comparison of string distance metrics for name-matching tasks. In *Proceedings of the IJCAI-2003 Workshop on Information Integration on the Web (IIWeb-03)*, pages 73–78.

[Hall et al.2009] M. Hall, E. Frank, G. Holmes, B. Pfahringer, P. Reutemann, and I.H. Witten. 2009. The weka data mining software: an update. *ACM SIGKDD Explorations Newsletter*, 11(1):10–18.

[He et al.2010] Y. He, Y. Ma, J. van Genabith, and A. Way. 2010. Bridging smt and tm with translation recommendation. In *Proceedings of the 48th Annual Meeting of the Association for Computational Linguistics*, pages 622–630. Association for Computational Linguistics.

[Jones et al.2000] Karen Sparck Jones, Steve Walker, and Stephen E. Robertson. 2000. A probabilistic model of information retrieval: development and comparative experiments - parts 1 and 2. *Inf. Process. Manage.*, 36(6):779–840.

[Michel et al.2011] J.B. Michel, Y.K. Shen, A.P. Aiden, A. Veres, M.K. Gray, J.P. Pickett, D. Hoiberg, D. Clancy, P. Norvig, J. Orwant, et al. 2011. Quantitative analysis of culture using millions of digitized books. *science*, 331(6014):176.

[Quinlan1992] J.R. Quinlan. 1992. Learning with continuous classes. In *Proceedings of the 5th Australian joint Conference on Artificial Intelligence*, pages 343–348. Singapore.

[Shevade et al.2000] S.K. Shevade, SS Keerthi, C. Bhattacharyya, and K.R.K. Murthy. 2000. Improvements to the smo algorithm for svm regression. *Neural Networks, IEEE Transactions on*, 11(5):1188–1193.

[Soricut and Echihabi2010] R. Soricut and A. Echihabi. 2010. Trustrank: Inducing trust in automatic translations via ranking. In *Proceedings of the 48th Annual Meeting of the Association for Computational Linguistics*, pages 612–621. Association for Computational Linguistics.

[Specia et al.2009] Lucia Specia, Marco Turchi, Nicola Cancedda, Marc Dymetman, and Nello Cristianini. 2009. Estimating the sentence-level quality of machine translation systems. In *Proceedings of the 13th Conference of the European Association for Machine Translation*, pages 28–35.

[Specia et al.2011] L. Specia, N. Hajlaoui, C. Hallett, and W. Aziz. 2011. Predicting machine translation adequacy. In *Machine Translation Summit XIII*, Xiamen, China.

[Wang and Witten2002] Y. Wang and I.H. Witten. 2002. Modeling for optimal probability prediction. In *Proceedings of the Nineteenth International Conference on Machine Learning*, pages 650–657. Morgan Kaufmann Publishers Inc.

The UPC Submission to the WMT 2012 Shared Task on Quality Estimation

Daniele Pighin Meritxell González Lluís Màrquez
Universitat Politècnica de Catalunya, Barcelona
{pighin,mgonzalez,lluism}@lsi.upc.edu

Abstract

In this paper, we describe the UPC system that participated in the WMT 2012 shared task on Quality Estimation for Machine Translation. Based on the empirical evidence that fluency-related features have a very high correlation with post-editing effort, we present a set of features for the assessment of quality estimation for machine translation designed around different kinds of n-gram language models, plus another set of features that model the quality of dependency parses automatically projected from source sentences to translations. We document the results obtained on the shared task dataset, obtained by combining the features that we designed with the baseline features provided by the task organizers.

1 Introduction

Quality Estimation (QE) for Machine Translations (MT) is the task concerned with the prediction of the quality of automatic translations in the absence of reference translations. The WMT 2012 shared task on QE for MT (Callison-Burch et al., 2012) required participants to score and rank a set of automatic English to Spanish translations output by a state-of-the-art phrase based machine translation system. Task organizers provided a training dataset of $1,832$ source sentences, together with reference, automatic and post-edited translations, as well as human quality assessments for the automatic translations. Post-editing effort, i.e., the amount of editing required to produce an accurate translation, was selected as the quality criterion, with assessments ranging from 1 (extremely bad) to 5 (good as it is). The organizers also provided a set of linguistic resources and processors to extract 17 global indicators of translation quality (*baseline features*) that participants could decide to employ for their models. For the evaluation, these features are used to learn a baseline predictors for participants to compare against. Systems participating in the evaluation are scored based on their ability to correctly rank the 422 test translations (using DeltaAvg and Spearman correlation) and/or to predict the human quality assessment for each translation (using Mean Average Error - MAE and Root Mean Squared Error - RMSE).

Our initial approach to the task consisted of several experiments in which we tried to identify common translation errors and correlate them with quality assessments. However, we soon realized that simple regression models estimated on the baseline features resulted in more consistent predictors of translation quality. For this reason, we eventually decided to focus on the design of a set of global indicators of translation quality to be combined with the strong features already computed by the baseline system.

An analysis of the Pearson correlation of the baseline features (Callison-Burch et al., 2012)[1] with human quality assessments shows that the two strongest individual predictors of post-editing effort are the n-gram language model perplexities estimated on source and target sentences. This evidence suggests that a reasonable approach to im-

[1]Baseline features are also described in `http://www.statmt.org/wmt12/quality-estimation-task.html`.

Feature	Pearson $\|r\|$	Feature	Pearson $\|r\|$
BL/4	0.3618	DEP/C$^+$/Q4/R	0.0749
BL/5	0.3544	BL/13	0.0741
BL/12	0.2823	DEP/C$^-$/Q1/W	0.0726
BL/14	0.2675	DEP/C$^+$/Q4/W	0.0718
BL/2	0.2667	DEP/C$^+$/Q34/R	0.0687
BL/1	0.2620	BL/3	0.0623
BL/8	0.2575	DEP/C$^+$/Q34/W	0.0573
BL/6	0.2143	SEQ/sys-ref/W	0.0495
DEP/C$^-$/S	0.2072	SEQ/sys/W	0.0492
BL/10	0.2033	SEQ/ref-sys/W	0.0390
DEP/C$^-$/Q12/S	0.1858	BL/7	0.0351
BL/17	0.1824	SEQ/sys/SStop	0.0312
BL/16	0.1725	SEQ/sys/RStop	0.0301
DEP/C$^-$/W	0.1584	SEQ/sys-ref/SStop	0.0291
DEP/C$^-$/R	0.1559	SEQ/sys-ref/RStop	0.0289
DEP/C$^-$/Q12/R	0.1447	DEP/Coverage/S	0.0286
DEP/Coverage/W	0.1419	SEQ/ref-sys/S	0.0232
DEP/C$^-$/Q1/S	0.1413	SEQ/ref-sys/R	0.0205
BL/15	0.1368	SEQ/ref-sys/RStop	0.0187
DEP/C$^+$/Q4/S	0.1257	SEQ/sys-ref/R	0.0184
DEP/Coverage/R	0.1239	SEQ/sys/R	0.0177
SEQ/ref-sys/PStop	0.1181	SEQ/ref-sys/Chains	0.0125
SEQ/sys/PStop	0.1173	SEQ/ref-sys/SStop	0.0104
SEQ/sys-ref/PStop	0.1170	SEQ/sys/S	0.0053
DEP/C$^-$/Q12/W	0.1159	SEQ/sys-ref/S	0.0051
DEP/C$^-$/Q1/R	0.1113	SEQ/sys/Chains	0.0032
DEP/C$^+$/Q34/S	0.0933	SEQ/sys-ref/Chains	0.0014
BL/9	0.0889	BL/11	0.0001

Table 1: Pearson correlation (in absolute value) of the baseline (BL) features and the extended feature set (SEQ and DEP) with the quality assessments.

prove the accuracy of the baseline would be to concentrate on the estimation of other n-gram language models, possibly working at different levels of linguistic analysis and combining information coming from the source and the target sentence. On top of that, we add another class of features that capture the quality of grammatical dependencies projected from source to target via automatic alignments, as they could provide clues about translation quality that may not be captured by sequential models.

The novel features that we incorporate are described in full detail in the next section; in Section 3 we describe the experimental setup and the resources that we employ, while in Section 4 we present the results of the evaluation; finally, in Section 5 we draw our conclusions.

2 Extended features set

We extend the set of 17 baseline features with 35 new features:

SEQ: 21 features based on n-gram language models estimated on reference and automatic translations, combining lexical elements of the target sentence and linguistic annotations (POS) automatically projected from the source;

DEP: 18 features that estimate a language model on dependency parse trees automatically projected from source to target via unsupervised alignments.

All the related models are estimated on a corpus of 150K newswire sentences collected from the training/development corpora of previous WMT editions (Callison-Burch et al., 2007; Callison-Burch et al., 2011). We selected this resource because we prefer to estimate the models only on in-domain data. The models for SEQ features are computed based on reference translations (*ref*) and automatic translations generated by the same Moses (Koehn et al., 2007) configuration used by the organizers of this QE task. As features, we encode the perplexity of observed sequences with respect to the two models, or the ratio of these values. For DEP features, we estimate a model that explicitly captures the difference between reference and automatic translations for the same sentence.

2.1 Sequential features (SEQ)

The simplest sequential models that we estimate are 3-gram language models[2] on the following sequences:

W: (Word), the sequence of words as they appear in the target sentence;

R: (Root), the sequence of the roots of the words in the target;

S: (Suffix) the sequence of the suffixes of the words in the target;

As features, for each automatic translation we encode:

- The perplexity of the corresponding sequence according to automatic (*sys*) translations: for

[2]We also considered using longer histories, i.e., 5-grams, but since we could not observe any noticeable difference we finally selected the least over-fitting alternative.

example, *SEQ/sys/R* and *SEQ/sys/W* are the root-sequence and word-sequence perplexities estimated on the corpus of automatic translations;

- The ratio between the perplexities according the two sets of translations: for example, *SEQ/ref-sys/S* is the ratio between the perplexity of suffix-sequences on reference and automatic translations, and *SEQ/sys-ref/S* is its inverse.[3]

We also estimate 3-gram language models on three variants of a sequence in which non-stop words (i.e., all words belonging to an open class) are replaced with either:

RStop: the root of the word;

SStop: the suffix of the word;

PStop: the POS of the aligned source word(s).

This last model (PStop) is the only one that requires source/target pairs in order to be estimated. If the target word is aligned to more than one word, we use the ordered concatenation of the source words POS tags; if the word cannot be aligned, we replace it with the placeholder "*", e.g.: *"el NN de * VBZ JJ en muchos NNS ."*. Also in this case, different features encode the perplexity with respect to automatic translations (e.g., *SEQ/sys/PStop*) or to the ratio between automatic and reference translations (e.g., *SEQ/ref-sys/RStop*).

Finally, a last class of sequences (**Chains**) collapses adjacent stop words into a single token. Content-words or isolated stop-words are not included in the sequence, e.g: *"mediante_la de_los de_la y_de_las y_la a_los"*. Again, we consider the same set of variants, e.g. *SEQ/sys/Chains* or *SEQ/sys-ref/Chains*.

Since there are 7 sequence types and 3 combinations (*sys*, *sys-ref*, *ref-sys*) we end up with 21 new features.

[3]Features extracted solely from reference translations have been considered, but they were dropped during development since we could not observe a noticeable effect on prediction quality.

2.2 Dependency features (DEP)

These features are based on the assumption that by observing how dependency parses are projected from source to target we can gather clues concerning translation quality that cannot be captured by sequential models. The features encode the extent to which the edges of the projected dependency tree are observed in reference-quality translations.

The model for DEP features is estimated on the same set of 150K English sentences and the corresponding reference and automatic translations, based on the following algorithm:

1. Initialize two maps M^+ and M^- to store edge counts;
2. Then, for each source sentence s: parse s with a dependency parser;
3. Align the words of s with the reference and the automatic translations r and a;
4. For each dependency relation $\langle d, s_h, s_m \rangle$ observed in the source, where d is the relation type and s_h and s_m are the head and modifier words, respectively:
   (a) Identify the aligned head/modifier words in r and a, i.e., $\langle r_h, r_m \rangle$ and $\langle a_h, a_m \rangle$;
   (b) If $r_h = a_h$ and $r_m = a_m$, then increment $M^+_{\langle d, a_h, a_m \rangle}$ by one, otherwise increment $M^-_{\langle d, a_h, a_m \rangle}$.

In other terms, M^+ keeps track of how many times a projected dependency is the same in the automatic and in the reference translation, while M^- accounts for the cases in which the two projections differ.

Let T be the set of dependency relations projected on an automatic translation. In the feature space we represent:

Coverage: The ratio of dependency edges found in M^- or M^+ over the total number of projected edges, i.e.

$$\text{Coverage}(T) = \frac{\sum_{D \in T} M^+_D + M^-_D}{|T|} \quad ;$$

C$^+$: The quantity $C^+ = \frac{1}{|T|} \sum_{D \in T} \frac{M^+_D}{M^+_D - M^-_D}$;

C$^-$: The quantity $C^- = \frac{1}{|T|}\sum_{D \in T} \frac{M_D^-}{M_D^+ - M_D^-}$.

Intuitively, high values of C^+ mean that most projected dependencies have been observed in reference translations; conversely, high values of C^- suggest that most of the projected dependencies were only observed in automatic translations.

Similarly to SEQ features, also in this case we actually employ three variants of these features: one in which we use word forms (i.e., *DEP/Coverage/W*, *DEP/*C^+*/W* and *DEP/*C^-*/W*), one in which we look at roots (i.e., *DEP/Coverage/R*, *DEP/*C^+*/R* and *DEP/*C^-*/R*) and one in which we only consider suffixes (i.e., *DEP/Coverage/S*, *DEP/*C^+*/S* and *DEP/*C^-*/S*).

Moreover, we also estimate C^+ in the top (Q4) and top two (Q34) fourths of edge scores, and C^- in the bottom (Q1) and bottom two (Q12) fourths. As an example, the feature *DEP/*C^+*/Q4/R* encodes the value of C^+ within the top fourth of the ranked list of projected dependencies when only considering word roots, while *DEP/*C^-*/W* is the value of $C-$ on the whole edge set estimated using word forms.

3 Experiment setup

To extract the extended feature set we use an alignment model, a POS tagger and a dependency parser. Concerning the former, we trained an unsupervised model with the Berkeley aligner[4], an implementation of the symmetric word-alignment model described by Liang et al. (2006). The model is trained on Europarl and newswire data released as part of WMT 2011 (Callison-Burch et al., 2011) training data. For POS tagging and semantic role annotation we use SVMTool[5] (Jesús Giménez and Lluís Màrquez, 2004) and Swirl[6] (Surdeanu and Turmo, 2005), respectively, with default configurations. To estimate the SEQ and DEP features we use reference and automatic translations of the newswire section of WMT 2011 training data. The automatic translations are generated by the same configuration generating the data for the quality estimation task. The n-gram models are estimated with the SRILM toolkit [7], with order equal to 3 and Kneser-Ney (Kneser and Ney, 1995) smoothing.

Feature set	DeltaAvg	MAE
Baseline	0.4664	0.6346
Extended	**0.4694**	**0.6248**

Table 2: Comparison of the baseline and extended feature set on development data.

As a learning framework we resort to Support Vector Regression (SVR) (Smola and Schölkopf, 2004) and learn a linear separator using the SVM-Light optimizer by Joachims (1999)[8]. We represent feature values by means of their z-scores, i.e., the number of standard deviations that separate a value from the average of the feature distribution. We carry out the system development via 5-fold cross evaluation on the 1,832 development sentences for which we have quality assessments.

4 Evaluation

In Table 1 we show the absolute value of the Pearson correlation of the features used in our model, i.e., the 17 baseline features (BL/*), the 21 sequence (SEQ/*) and the 18 dependency (DEP/*) features, with the human quality assessments. The more correlated features are in the top (left) part of the table. At a first glance, we can see that 9 of the 10 features having highest correlation are already encoded by the baseline. We can also observe that DEP features show a higher correlation than SEQ features. This evidence seems to contradict our initial expectations, but it can be easily ascribed to the limited size of the corpus used to estimate the n-gram models (150K sentences). This point is also confirmed by the fact that the three variants of the *PStop model (based on sequences of target stopwords interleaved by POS tags projected from the source sentence and, hence, on a very small vocabulary) are the three sequential models sporting the highest correlation. Alas, the lack of lexical anchors makes them less useful as predictors of translation quality than BL/4 and BL/5. Another interesting as-

[4] http://code.google.com/p/berkeleyaligner
[5] http://www.lsi.upc.edu/~nlp/SVMTool/
[6] http://www.surdeanu.name/mihai/swirl/
[7] http://www-speech.sri.com/projects/srilm
[8] http://svmlight.joachims.org/

System	DeltaAvg	MAE
Baseline	**0.55**	**0.69**
Official Evaluation	0.22	0.84
Amended Evaluation	0.51	0.71

Table 3: Official and amended evaluation on test data of the extended feature sets.

pect is that DEP/C^- features show higher correlation than DEP/C^+. This is an expected behaviour, as being indicators of possible errors they are intended to have discriminative power with respect to the human assessments. Finally, we can see that more than 50% of the included features, including five baseline features, have negligible (less than 0.1) correlation with the assessments. Even though these features may not have predictive power per se, their combination may be useful to learn more accurate models of quality.[9]

Table 2 shows a comparison of the baseline features against the extended feature set as the average DeltaAvg score and Mean Absolute Error (MAE) on the 10 most accurate development configurations. In both cases, the extended feature set results in slightly more accurate models, even though the improvement is hardly significant.

Table 3 shows the results of the official evaluation. Our submission to the final evaluation (*Official*) was plagued by a bug that affected the values of all the baseline features on the test set. As a consequence, the official performance of the model is extremely poor. The row labeled *Amended* shows the results that we obtained after correcting the problem. As we can see, on both tasks the baseline outperforms our model, even though the difference between the two is only marginal. Ranking-wise, our official submission is last on the ranking task and last-but-one on the quality prediction task. In contrast, the amended model shows very similar accuracy to the baseline, as the majority of the systems that took part in the evaluation.

[9]Our experiments on development data were not significantly affected by the presence or removal of low-correlation features. Given the relatively small feature space, we adopted a conservative strategy and included all the features in the final models.

5 Discussion and conclusions

We have described the system with which we participated in the WMT 2012 shared task on quality estimation. The model incorporates all the baseline features, plus two sets of novel features based on: 1) n-gram language models estimated on mixed sequences of target sentence words and linguistic annotations projected from the source sentence by means of automatic alignments; and 2) the likelihood of the projection of dependency relations from source to target.

On development data we found out that the extended feature set granted only a very marginal improvement with respect to the strong feature set of the baseline. In the official evaluation, our submission was plagued by a bug affecting the generation of baseline features for the test set, and as a result we had an incredibly low performance. After fixing the bug, re-evaluating on the test set confirmed that the extended set of features, at least in the current implementation, does not have the potential to significantly improve over the baseline features. On the contrary, the accuracy of the corrected model is slightly lower than the baseline on both the ranking and the quality estimation task.

During system development it was clear that improving significantly over the results of the baseline features would be very difficult. In our experience, this is especially due to the presence among the baseline features of extremely strong predictors of translation quality such as the perplexity of the automatic translation. We could also observe that the parametrization of the learning algorithm had a much stronger impact on the final accuracy than the inclusion/exclusion of specific features from the model.

We believe that the information that we encode, and in particular dependency parses and stop-word sequences, has the potential to be quite relevant for this task. On the other hand, it may be necessary to estimate the models on much larger datasets in order to compensate for their inherent sparsity. Furthermore, more refined methods may be required in order to incorporate the relevant information in a more determinant way.

Acknowledgments

This research has been partially funded by the Spanish Ministry of Education and Science (OpenMT-2, TIN2009-14675-C03) and the European Community's Seventh Framework Programme (FP7/2007-2013) under grant agreement numbers 247762 (FAUST project, FP7-ICT-2009-4-247762) and 247914 (MOLTO project, FP7-ICT-2009-4-247914).

References

[Callison-Burch et al.2007] Chris Callison-Burch, Philipp Koehn, Cameron Shaw Fordyce, and Christof Monz, editors. 2007. *Proceedings of the Second Workshop on Statistical Machine Translation.* ACL, Prague, Czech Republic.

[Callison-Burch et al.2011] Chris Callison-Burch, Philipp Koehn, Christof Monz, and Omar F. Zaidan, editors. 2011. *Proceedings of the Sixth Workshop on Statistical Machine Translation.* Association for Computational Linguistics, Edinburgh, Scotland, July.

[Callison-Burch et al.2012] Chris Callison-Burch, Philipp Koehn, Christof Monz, Matt Post, Radu Soricut, and Lucia Specia. 2012. Findings of the 2012 workshop on statistical machine translation. In *Proceedings of the Seventh Workshop on Statistical Machine Translation*, Montreal, Canada, June. Association for Computational Linguistics.

[Jesús Giménez and Lluís Màrquez2004] Jesús Giménez and Lluís Màrquez. 2004. SVMTool: A general POS tagger generator based on Support Vector Machines. In *Proceedings of the 4th LREC.*

[Joachims1999] Thorsten Joachims. 1999. Making large-Scale SVM Learning Practical. In B. Schölkopf, C. Burges, and A. Smola, editors, *Advances in Kernel Methods - Support Vector Learning.*

[Kneser and Ney1995] Reinhard Kneser and Hermann Ney. 1995. Improved backing-off for m-gram language modeling. In *In Proceedings of the IEEE International Conference on Acoustics, Speech and Signal Processing*, volume I, pages 181–184, Detroit, Michigan, May.

[Koehn et al.2007] Philipp Koehn, Hieu Hoang, Alexandra Birch, Chris Callison-Burch, Marcello Federico, Nicola Bertoldi, Brooke Cowan, Wade Shen, Christine Moran, Richard Zens, Chris Dyer, Ondrej Bojar, Alexandra Constantin, and Evan Herbst. 2007. Moses: Open source toolkit for statistical machine translation. In *Proceedings of the 45th Annual Meeting of the Association for Computational Linguistics Companion Volume Proceedings of the Demo and Poster Sessions*, pages 177–180, Prague, Czech Republic, June. Association for Computational Linguistics.

[Liang et al.2006] Percy Liang, Benjamin Taskar, and Dan Klein. 2006. Alignment by agreement. In *HLT-NAACL.*

[Smola and Schölkopf2004] Alex J. Smola and Bernhard Schölkopf. 2004. A tutorial on support vector regression. *Statistics and Computing*, 14(3):199–222, August.

[Surdeanu and Turmo2005] Mihai Surdeanu and Jordi Turmo. 2005. Semantic Role Labeling Using Complete Syntactic Analysis. In *Proceedings of the Ninth Conference on Computational Natural Language Learning (CoNLL-2005)*, pages 221–224, Ann Arbor, Michigan, June.

Morpheme- and POS-based IBM1 scores and language model scores for translation quality estimation

Maja Popović
German Research Center for Artificial Intelligence (DFKI)
Language Technology (LT), Berlin, Germany
maja.popovic@dfki.de

Abstract

We present a method we used for the quality estimation shared task of WMT 2012 involving IBM1 and language model scores calculated on morphemes and POS tags. The IBM1 scores calculated on morphemes and POS-4grams of the source sentence and obtained translation output are shown to be competitive with the classic evaluation metrics for ranking of translation systems. Since these scores do not require any reference translations, they can be used as features for the quality estimation task presenting a connection between the source language and the obtained target language. In addition, target language model scores of morphemes and POS tags are investigated as estimates for the obtained target language quality.

1 Introduction

Automatic quality estimation is a topic of increasing interest in machine translation. Different from evaluation task, quality estimation does not rely on any reference translations – it relies only on information about the input source text, obtained target language text, and translation process. Being a new topic, it still does not have well established baselines, datasets or standard evaluation metrics. The usual approach is to use a set of features which are used to train a classifier in order to assign a prediction score to each sentence.

In this work, we propose a set of features based on the morphological and syntactic properties of involved languages thus abstracting away from word surface particularities (such as vocabulary and domain). This approach is shown to be very useful for evaluation task (Popović, 2011; Popović et al., 2011; Callison-Burch et al., 2011). The features investigated in this work are based on the language model (LM) scores and on the IBM1 lexicon scores (Brown et al., 1993).

The inclusion of IBM1 scores in translation systems has shown experimentally to improve translation quality (Och et al., 2003). They also have been used for confidence estimation for machine translation (Blatz et al., 2003). The IBM1 scores calculated on morphemes and POS-4grams are shown to be competitive with the classic evaluation metrics based on comparison with given reference translations (Popović et al., 2011; Callison-Burch et al., 2011). To the best of our knowledge, these scores have not yet been used for translation quality estimation. The LM scores of words and POS tags are used for quality estimation in previous work (Specia et al., 2009), and in our work we investigate the scores calculated on morphemes and POS tags.

At this point, only preliminary experiments have been carried out in order to determine if the proposed features are promising at all. We did not use any classifier, we used the obtained scores to rank the sentences of a given translation output from the best to the worst. The Spearman's rank correlation coefficients between our ranking and the ranking obtained using human scores are then computed on the provided manually annotated data sets.

2 Morpheme- and POS-based features

A number of features for quality estimation have been already investigated in previous work (Specia et al., 2009). In this paper, we investigate two sets of features which do not depend on any aspect of translation process but only on the morphological and syntactic structures of the involved languages: the IBM1 scores and the LM scores calculated on morphemes and POS tags. The IBM1 scores describe the correspondences between the structures of the source and the target language, and the LM scores describe the structure of the target language. In addition to the input source text and translated target language hypothesis, a parallel bilingual corpus for the desired language pair and a monolingual corpus for the desired target language are required in order to learn IBM1 and LM probabilities. Appropriate POS taggers and tools for splitting words into morphemes are necessary for each of the languages. The POS tags cannot be only basic but must have all details (e.g. verb tenses, cases, number, gender, etc.).

2.1 IBM1 scores

The IBM1 model is a bag-of-word translation model which gives the sum of all possible alignment probabilities between the words in the source sentence and the words in the target sentence. Brown et al. (1993) defined the IBM1 probability score for a translation pair f_1^J and e_1^I in the following way:

$$P(f_1^J|e_1^I) = \frac{1}{(I+1)^J} \prod_{j=1}^{J} \sum_{i=0}^{I} p(f_j|e_i) \quad (1)$$

where f_1^J is the source language sentence of length J and e_1^I is the target language sentence of length I.

As it is a conditional probability distribution, we investigated both directions as quality scores. In order to avoid frequent confusions about what is the source and what the target language, we defined our scores in the following way:

- source-to-hypothesis (sh) IBM1 score:

$$\text{IBM1}_{sh} = \frac{1}{(H+1)^S} \prod_{j=1}^{S} \sum_{i=0}^{H} p(s_j|h_i) \quad (2)$$

- hypothesis-to-source (hs) IBM1 score:

$$\text{IBM1}_{hs} = \frac{1}{(S+1)^H} \prod_{i=1}^{H} \sum_{j=0}^{S} p(h_i|s_j) \quad (3)$$

where s_j are the units of the original source language sentence, S is the length of this sentence, h_i are the units of the target language hypothesis, and H is the length of this hypothesis.

The units investigated in this work are morphemes and POS-4grams, thus we have the following four IBM1 scores:

- MIBM1$_{sh}$ and MIBM1$_{hs}$:

  IBM1 scores of word morphemes in each direction;

- P4IBM1$_{sh}$ and P4IBM1$_{hs}$:

  IBM1 scores of POS 4grams in each direction.

2.2 Language model scores

The n-gram language model score is defined as:

$$P(e_1^I) = \prod_{i=1}^{I} p(e_i|e_i...e_{i-n}) \quad (4)$$

where e_i is the current target language word and $e_i...e_{i-n}$ is the history, i.e. the preceeding n words.

In this paper, the two following language model scores are explored:

- MLM6:

  morpheme-6gram language model score;

- PLM6:

  POS-6gram language model score.

3 Experimental set-up

The IBM1 probabilities necessary for the IBM1 scores are learnt using the WMT 2010 News Commentary Spanish-English, French-English and German-English parallel texts. The language models are trained on the corresponding target parts of this corpus using the SRI language model tool (Stolcke, 2002). The POS tags for all languages were produced using the TreeTagger[1], and the morphemes are obtained using the Morfessor tool (Creutz and Lagus, 2005). The tool is corpus-based and language-independent: it takes a text as input and produces a segmentation of the word forms observed in the text. The obtained results are not strictly

[1]http://www.ims.uni-stuttgart.de/projekte/corplex/TreeTagger/

linguistic, however they often resemble a linguistic morpheme segmentation. Once a morpheme segmentation has been learnt from some text, it can be used for segmenting new texts. In our experiments, the splitting are learnt from the training corpus used for the IBM1 lexicon probabilities. The obtained segmentation is then used for splitting the corresponding source texts and hypotheses. Detailed corpus statistics are shown in Table 1.

Using the obtained probabilities, the scores described in Section 2 are calculated for the provided annotated data: the English-Spanish data from WMT 2008 consisting of four translation outputs produced by four different systems (Specia et al., 2010), the French-English and English-Spanish data from WMT 2010 (Specia, 2011), as well as for an additional WMT 2011 German-English and English-German annotated data. The human quality scores for the first two data sets range from 1 to 4, and for the third data set from 1 to 3. The interpretation of human scores is:

1. requires complete retranslation (*bad*)
2. post-editing quicker than retranslation ($edit^{-}$); this class was omitted for the third data set
3. little post-editing needed ($edit^{+}$)
4. fit for purpose (*good*)

As a first step, the arithmetic means and standard deviations are calculated for each feature and each class in order to see if the features are at all possible candidates for quality estimation, i.e. if the values for different classes are distinct.

After that, the main test is carried out: for each of the features, the Spearman correlation coefficient ρ with the human ranking are calculated for each document. In total, 9 correlation coefficients are obtained for each score – four Spanish outputs from the WMT 2008 task, one Spanish and one English output from the WMT 2010 as well as one English and two German outputs from the WMT 2011 task.

The obtained correlation results were then summarised into the following two values:

- *mean*
  a correlation coefficient averaged over all translation outputs;
- *rank>*
  percentage of translation outputs where the particular feature has better correlation than the other investigated features.

4 Results

4.1 Arithmetic means

The preliminary experiments consisted of comparing arithmetic means of scores for each feature and each class. The idea is: if the values are distinct enough, the feature is a potential candidate for quality estimation. In addition, standard deviations were calculated in order to estimate the overlapping.

For most translation outputs, all of our features have distinct arithmetic means for different classes and decent standard deviations, indicating that they are promising for further investigation. On all WMT 2011 outputs annotated with three classes, the distinction is rather clear, as well as for the majority of the four class outputs.

However, on some of the four class translation outputs, the values of the *bad* translation class were unexpected in the following two ways:

- the *bad* class overlaps with the $edit^{-}$ class;
- the *bad* class overlaps with the $edit^{+}$ class.

The first overlapping problem occured on two translation outputs of the 2011 set, and the second one on the both outputs of the 2010 set.

Examples for the PLM6 and P4IBM1$_{sh}$ features are shown in Table 2. First two rows present three class and four class outputs with separated arithmetic means, the first problem is shown in the third row, and the second (and more serious) problem is presented in the last row.

These overlaps have not been investigated further in the framework of this work, however this should be studied deeply (especially the second problem) in order to better understand the underlying phenomena and improve the features.

4.2 Spearman correlation coefficients

As mentioned in the previous section, Spearman rank correlation coefficients are calculated for each translation output and for each feature, and summarised into two values described in Section 3, i.e.

	Spanish	English	French	English	German	English
sentences	97122		83967		100222	
running words	2661344	2338495	2395141	2042085	2475359	2398780
vocabulary:						
words	69620	53527	56295	50082	107278	54270
morphemes	14178	13449	12004	12485	22211	13499
POS tags	69	44	33	44	54	44
POS-4grams	135166	121182	62177	114555	114314	123550

Table 1: Statistics of the corpora for training IBM1 lexicon models and language models.

feature	output / class	*ok*	*edit*$^+$	*edit*$^-$	*bad*
PLM6	de-en	13.5 / 7.3	23.7 / 13.6		33.0 / 19.7
	es-en4	10.9 / 5.0	20.7 / 8.7	34.6 / 16.4	49.0 / 23.7
	es-en3	18.5 / 11.0	30.2 / 15.6	**38.4 / 17.4**	**37.9 / 18.9**
	fr-en	15.2 / 8.8	**26.2 / 13.7**	34.5 / 18.4	**21.7 / 11.3**
P4IBM1$_{sh}$	de-en	50.5 / 38.4	109.7 / 75.6		161.8 / 108.3
	es-en4	37.9 / 25.0	88.7 / 48.7	165.8 / 89.0	241.5 / 127.4
	es-en3	77.0 / 56.7	139.8 / 82.5	**186.4 / 94.6**	**185.2 / 102.0**
	fr-en	53.5 / 44.3	**110.0 / 69.3**	151.8 / 90.9	**90.8 / 59.0**

Table 2: Arithmetic means with standard deviations of PLM6 and P4IBM1$_{sh}$ scores for four translation outputs: first two rows present decently separated classes, third row illustrates the overlap problem concerning the *bad* and the *edit*$^-$ class, the last row illustrates the overlap problem concerning the *bad* and the *edit*$^+$ class.

mean and *rank*>. The results are shown in Table 3. In can be seen that the best individual features are POS IBM1 scores followed by POS LM score.

The next step was to investigate combinations of the individual features. First, we calculated arithmetic mean of POS based features only, since they are more promising than the morpheme based ones, however we did not yield any improvements over the individual *mean* values. As a next step, we introduced weights to the features according to their mean correlations, i.e. we did not omit the morpheme features but put more weight on the POS based ones. Nevertheless, this also did not result in an improvement. Furthermore, we tried a simple arithmetic mean of all features, and this resulted in a better Spearman correlation coefficients.

Following all these observations, we decided to submit the arithmetic mean of all features to the WMT 2012 quality estimation task. Our submission consisted only of sentence ranking without scores, since we did not convert our scores to the interval [1,5]. Therefore we did not get any MAE or RMSE results, only DeltaAvg and Spearman correlation coefficients which were both 0.46. The highest scores in the shared task were 0.63, the lowest about 0.15, and for the "baseline" system which uses a set of well established features with an SVM classifier about 0.55.

5 Conclusions and outlook

The results presented in this article show that the IBM1 and the LM scores calculated on POS tags and morphemes have the potential to be used for the estimation of translation quality. These results are very preliminary, offering many directions for future work. The most important points are to use a classifier, as well as to combine the proposed features with already established features. Furthermore, the *bad* class overlapping problem described in Section 4.1 should be further investigated and understood.

Acknowledgments

This work has been partly developed within the TARAXÜ project financed by TSB Technologies-

mean		*rank>*	
0.449	P4IBM1$_{sh}$	70.4	P4IBM1$_{sh}$
0.445	P4IBM1$_{hs}$	68.5	P4IBM1$_{hs}$
0.444	PLM6	61.1	PLM6
0.430	MLM6	27.7	MLM6
0.426	MIBM1$_{sh}$	20.3	MIBM1$_{sh}$
0.420	MIBM1$_{hs}$	9.2	MIBM1$_{hs}$
0.450	arithmetic mean	**83.3**	arithmetic mean

Table 3: Features sorted by average correlation (column 1) and *rank>* value (column 2). The most promising score is the arithmetic mean of all individual features. The most promising individual features are POS-4gram IBM1 scores followed by POS-6gram language model score.

tiftung Berlin – Zukunftsfonds Berlin, co-financed by the European Union – European fund for regional development.

References

John Blatz, Erin Fitzgerald, George Foster, Simona Gandrabur, Cyril Goutte, Alex Kulesza, Alberto Sanchis, and Nicola Ueffing. 2003. Confidence estimation for machine translation. Final report, JHU/CLSP Summer Workshop.

Peter F. Brown, Stephen A. Della Pietra, Vincent J. Della Pietra, and Robert L. Mercer. 1993. The mathematics of statistical machine translation: Parameter estimation. *Computational Linguistics*, 19(2):263–311, June.

Chris Callison-Burch, Philipp Koehn, Christof Monz, and Omar Zaidan. 2011. Findings of the 2011 Workshop on Statistical Machine Translation. In *Proceedings of the Sixth Workshop on Statistical Machine Translation (WMT 2011)*, pages 22–64, Edinburgh, Scotland, July.

Mathias Creutz and Krista Lagus. 2005. Unsupervised morpheme segmentation and morphology induction from text corpora using morfessor 1.0. Technical Report Report A81, Computer and Information Science, Helsinki University of Technology, Helsinki, Finland, March.

Franz Josef Och, Daniel Gildea, Sanjeev Khudanpur, Anoop Sarkar, Kenji Yamada, Alex Fraser, Shankar Kumar, Libin Shen, David Smith, Katherine Eng, Viren Jain, Zhen Jin, and Dragomir Radev. 2003. Syntax for statistical machine translation. Technical report, Johns Hopkins University 2003 Summer Workshop on Language Engineering, Center for Language and Speech Processing, Baltimore, MD, USA, August.

Maja Popović, David Vilar Torres, Eleftherios Avramidis, and Aljoscha Burchardt. 2011. Evaluation without references: IBM1 scores as evaluation metrics. In *Proceedings of the Sixth Workshop on Statistical Machine Translation (WMT 2011)*, pages 99–103, Edinburgh, Scotland, July.

Maja Popović. 2011. Morphemes and POS tags for n-gram based evaluation metrics. In *Proceedings of the Sixth Workshop on Statistical Machine Translation (WMT 2011)*, pages 104–107, Edinburgh, Scotland, July.

Lucia Specia, Marco Turchi, Zhuoran Wang, John Shawe-Taylor, and Craig Saunders. 2009. Improving the confidence of machine translation quality estimates. In *Machine Translation Summit XII*, Ottawa, Canada.

Lucia Specia, Nicola Cancedda, and Marc Dymetman. 2010. A Dataset for Assessing Machine Translation Evaluation Metrics. In *Proceedings of the Seventh conference on International Language Resources and Evaluation (LREC'2010)*, pages 3375–3378, Valletta, Malta, May.

Lucia Specia. 2011. Exploiting Objective Annotations for Measuring Translation Post-editing Effort. In *Proceedings of the 15th Annual Conference of the European Association for Machine Translation (EAMT 11)*, pages 73–80, Leuven, Belgium, May.

Drahomíra "Johanka" Spoustová, Jan Hajič, Jan Raab, and Miroslav Spousta. 2009. Semi-Supervised Training for the Averaged Perceptron POS Tagger. In *Proceedings of the 12th Conference of the European Chapter of the ACL (EACL 2009)*, pages 763–771, Athens, Greece, March.

Andreas Stolcke. 2002. SRILM – an extensible language modeling toolkit. In *Proceedings of the 7th International Conference on Spoken Language Processing (ICSLP 02)*, volume 2, pages 901–904, Denver, CO, September.

DCU-Symantec Submission for the WMT 2012 Quality Estimation Task

Raphael Rubino[†‡], Jennifer Foster[†], Joachim Wagner[†],
Johann Roturier[‡], Rasul Samad Zadeh Kaljahi[†‡], Fred Hollowood[‡]
[†]Dublin City University, [‡]Symantec, Ireland
[†]`firstname.lastname@computing.dcu.ie`
[‡]`firstname_lastname@symantec.com`

Abstract

This paper describes the features and the machine learning methods used by Dublin City University (DCU) and SYMANTEC for the WMT 2012 quality estimation task. Two sets of features are proposed: one *constrained*, i.e. respecting the data limitation suggested by the workshop organisers, and one *unconstrained*, i.e. using data or tools trained on data that was not provided by the workshop organisers. In total, more than 300 features were extracted and used to train classifiers in order to predict the translation quality of unseen data. In this paper, we focus on a subset of our feature set that we consider to be relatively novel: features based on a topic model built using the Latent Dirichlet Allocation approach, and features based on source and target language syntax extracted using part-of-speech (POS) taggers and parsers. We evaluate nine feature combinations using four classification-based and four regression-based machine learning techniques.

1 Introduction

For the first time, the WMT organisers this year propose a Quality Estimation (QE) shared task, which is divided into two sub-tasks: scoring and ranking automatic translations. The aim of this workshop is to define useful sets of features and machine learning techniques in order to predict the quality of a machine translation (MT) output T (Spanish) given a source segment S (English). Quality is measured using a 5-point likert scale which is based on post-editing effort, following the scoring scheme:

1. The MT output is incomprehensible
2. About 50-70% of the MT output needs to be edited
3. About 25-50% of the MT output needs to be edited
4. About 10-25% of the MT output needs to be edited
5. The MT output is perfectly clear and intelligible

The final score is a combination of the scores assigned by three evaluators. The use of a 5-point scale makes the scoring task more difficult than a binary classification task where a translation is considered to be either *good* or *bad*. However, if the task is successfully carried out, the score produced is more useful.

Dublin City University and Symantec jointly address the scoring task. For each pair (S, T) of source segment S and machine translation T, we train three classifiers and one classifier combination using the training data provided by the organisers to predict 5-point Likert scores. In this paper, we present the classification results on the test set along with additional results obtained using regression techniques. We evaluate the usefulness of two new sets of features:

1. topic-based features using Latent Dirichlet Allocation (LDA (Blei et al., 2003)),
2. syntax-based features using POS taggers and parsers (Wagner et al., 2009)

The remainder of this paper is organised as follows. In Section 2, we give an overview of all the features employed in our QE system. Then, in Section 3, we describe the topic and syntax-based features in more detail. Section 4 presents the various classification and regression techniques we explored. Our results are presented and discussed in Section 5. Finally, we summarise and outline our plans in Section 6.

2 Features Overview

In this section, we describe the features used in our QE system. In the first subsection, the features included in our constrained system are presented. In the second subsection, we detail the features included in our unconstrained system. Both of these systems include the 17 baseline features provided for the shared task.

2.1 Constrained System

The constrained system is based only on the data provided by the organisers. We extracted 70 features in total (including the baseline features) and we present them here according to the type of information they capture.

Word and Phrase-Level Features

- **Ratio of source and target segment length**: the number of source words divided by the number of target words
- **Ratio of source and target number of punctuation marks**: the number of source punctuation marks divided by the number of target ones
- **Number of phrases comprising the MT output**: given a phrase-table, we assume that a sentence composed of several phrases indicates uncertainty on the part of the MT system.
- **Average length of source and target phrases**: concatenating short phrases may result in lower fluency compared to the use of longer ones.
- **Ratio of source and target averaged phrase length**
- **Number of source prepositions and conjunctions word**: our assumption here is that segments containing a relatively high number of prepositions and conjunctions may be more complex and difficult to translate.
- **Number of source out-of-vocabulary words**

Language Model Features

All the language models (LMs) used in our work are n-gram LMs with Kneser-Ney smoothing built with the SRI Toolkit (Stolcke, 2002).

- **Backward 2-gram and 3-gram source and target log probabilities**: as proposed by Duchateau et al. (2002)
- **Log probability of target segments on 5-gram MT-output-based LM**: using MOSES (Koehn et al., 2007) trained on the provided parallel corpus, we translated the English side of this corpus into Spanish, assuming that the MT output contains mistakes. This MT output is used to build a LM that models the behavior of the MT system. We assume that for a given MT output, a high n-gram probability (or a low perplexity) of the LM indicates that the MT output contains mistakes.

MT-system Features

- **15 scores provided by *Moses***: phrase-table, language model, reordering model and word penalty (weighted and unweighted)
- **Number of n-bests for each source segment**
- **MT output back-translation**: from Spanish to English using MOSES trained on the provided parallel corpus, scored with TER (Snover et al., 2006), BLEU (Papineni et al., 2002) and the Levenshtein distance (Levenshtein, 1966), based on the source segments as a translation reference

Topic Model Features

- **Probability distribution over topics**: Source and target segment probability distribution over topics for a 10-dimension topic model
- **Cosine distance between source and target topic vectors**

More details about these two features are provided in Section 3.1.

2.2 Unconstrained System

In addition to the features used for the constrained system, a further 238 unconstrained features were included in our *unconstrained* system.

MT System Features

As for our *constrained* system, we use MT output back-translation from Spanish to English, but this time using *Bing Translator*[1] in addition to *Moses*. Each back-translated segment is scored with TER, BLEU and the Levenshtein distance, based on the source segments as a translation reference.

Source Syntax Features

Wagner et al. (2007; 2009) propose a series of features to measure sentence grammaticality. These features rely on a part-of-speech tagger, a probabilistic parser and a precision grammar/parser. We have at our disposal these tools for English and so we apply them to the source data. The features themselves are described in more detail in Section 3.2.

Target Syntax Features

We use a part-of-speech tagger trained on Spanish to extract from the target data the subset of grammaticality features proposed by Wagner et al. (2007; 2009) that are based on POS n-grams. In addition we extract features which reflect the prevalence of particular POS tags in each target segment. These are explained in more detail in Section 3.2 below.

Grammar Checker Features

LANGUAGETOOL (based on (Naber, 2003)) is an open-source grammar and style proofreading tool that finds errors based on pre-defined, language-specific rules. The latest version of the tool can be run in server mode, so individual sentences can be checked and assigned a total number of errors (which may or may not be true positives).[2] This number is used as a feature for each source segment and its corresponding MT output.

3 Topic and Syntax-based Features

In this section, we focus on the set of features that aim to capture *adequacy* using topic modelling and *grammaticality* using POS tagging and syntactic parsing.

3.1 Topic-based Features

We extract source and target features based on a topic model built using LDA. The main idea in topic modelling is to produce a set of thematic word clusters from a collection of documents. Using the parallel corpus provided for the task, a bilingual corpus is built where each line is composed of a source segment and its translation separated by a space. Each pair of segments is considered as a bilingual document. This corpus is used to train a bilingual topic model after stopwords removal. The resulting model is one set of bilingual topics z containing words w with a probability $p(w_n|z_n, \beta)$ (with n equal to the vocabulary size in the whole parallel corpus). This model can be used to infer the probability distribution of unseen source and target segments over bilingual topics. During the test step, each source segment and its translation are considered individually, as two monolingual documents. This method allows us to compare the source and target topic distributions. We assume that a source segment and its translation share topic similarities.

We propose two ways of using topic-based features for quality estimation: keeping source and target topic vectors as two sets of k features, or computing a vector distance between these two vectors and using one feature only. To measure the proximity of two vectors, we decided to used the *Cosine* distance, as it leads to the best results in terms of classification accuracy. However, we plan to study different metrics in further experiments, like the *Manhattan* or the *Euclidean* distances. Some parameters related to LDA have to be studied more carefully too, such as the number of topics (dimensions in the topic space), the number of words per topic, the Dirichlet hyperparameter α, etc. In our experiments, we built a topic model composed of 10 dimensions using Gibbs sampling with 1000 iterations. We assume that a higher dimensionality can lead to a better repartitioning of the vocabulary over the topics.

Multilingual LDA has been used before in natural language processing, e.g. polylingual topic models (Mimno et al., 2009) or multilingual topic models for unaligned text (Boyd-Graber and Blei, 2009). In the field of machine translation, Tam et al. (2007) propose to adapt a translation and a lan-

[1] http://www.microsofttranslator.com/

[2] The list of English and Spanish rules is available at: http://languagetool.org/languages.

guage model to a specific topic using Latent Semantic Analysis (LSA, or Latent Semantic Indexing, LSI (Deerwester et al., 1990)). More recently, some studies were conducted on the use of LDA to adapt SMT systems to specific domains (Gong et al., 2010; Gong et al., 2011) or to extract bilingual lexicon from comparable corpora (Rubino and Linarès, 2011). Extracting features from a topic model is, to the best of our knowledge, the first attempt in machine translation quality estimation.

3.2 Syntax-based Features

Syntactic features have previously been used in MT for confidence estimation and for building automatic evaluation measures. Corston-Oliver et al. (2001) build a classifier using 46 parse tree features to predict whether a sentence is a human translation or MT output. Quirk (2004) uses a single parse tree feature in the quality estimation task with a 4-point scale, namely whether a spanning parse can be found, in addition to LM perplexity and sentence length. Liu and Gildea (2005) measure the syntactic similarity between MT output and reference translation. Albrecht and Hwa (2007) measure the syntactic similarity between MT output and reference translation and between MT output and a large monolingual corpus. Gimenez and Marquez (2007) explore lexical, syntactic and shallow semantic features and focus on measuring the similarity of MT output to reference translation. Owczarzak et al. (2007) use labelled dependencies together with WordNet to avoid penalising valid syntactic and lexical variations in MT evaluation. In what follows, we describe how we make use of syntactic information in the QE task, i.e. evaluating MT output without a reference translation.

Wagner et al. (2007; 2009) use three sources of linguistic information in order to extract features which they use to judge the grammaticality of English sentences:

1. For each POS n-gram (with n ranging from 2 to 7), a feature is extracted which represents the frequency of the least frequent n-gram in the sentence according to some reference corpus. TreeTagger (Schmidt, 1994) is used to produce POS tags.
2. Features provided by a hand-crafted, broad-coverage precision grammar of English (Butt et al., 2002) and a Lexical Functional Grammar parser (Maxwell and Kaplan, 1996). These include whether or not a sentence could be parsed without resorting to robustness measures, the number of analyses found and the parsing time.
3. Features extracted from the output of three probabilistic parsers of English (Charniak and Johnson, 2005), one trained on Wall Street Journal trees (Marcus et al., 1993), one trained on a distorted version of the treebank obtained by automatically creating grammatical error and adjusting the parse trees, and the third trained on the union of the original and distorted versions.

These features were originally designed to distinguish grammatical sentences from ungrammatical ones and were tested on sentences from learner corpora by Wagner et al. (2009) and Wagner (2012). In this work we extract all three sets of features from the source side of our data and the POS-based subset from the target side.[3] We use the publicly available pre-trained TreeTagger models for English and Spanish[4]. The reference corpus used to obtain POS n-gram frequences is the MT translation model training data.[5]

In addition to the POS-based features described in Wagner et al. (2007; 2009), we also extract the following features from the Spanish POS-tagged data: for each POS tag P and target segment T, we extract a feature which is the proportion of words in T that are tagged as P. Two additional features are extracted to represent the proportion of words in T that are assigned more than one tag by the tagger,

[3]Unfortunately, due to time constraints, we were unable to source a suitable probabilistic phrase-structure parser and a precision grammar for Spanish and were thus unable to extract parser-based features for Spanish. We expect that these features would be more useful on the target side than the source side.

[4]`http://www.ims.uni-stuttgart.de/projekte/corplex/TreeTagger/`

[5]To aid machine learning methods that linearly combine feature values, we add binarised features derived from the raw XLE and POS n-gram features described above, for example we add a feature indicating whether the frequency of the least frequent POS 5-gram is below 10. We base the choice of binary features on (a) decision rules observed in decision trees trained for a binary scoring task and (b) decision rules of simple classifiers (decision trees with just one decision node and 2 leaf nodes) that form a convex hull of optimal classifiers in ROC space.

and the proportion of words in T that are unknown to the tagger.

4 Machine Learning

In this section, we describe the machine learning methods that we experimented with. Our final systems submitted for the shared task are based on classification methods. However, we also performed some experiments with regression methods.

We evaluate the systems on the test set using the official evaluation script and the reference scores. We report the evaluation results as Mean Average Error (MAE) and Root Mean Squared Error (RMSE).

4.1 Classification

In order to apply classification algorithms to the set of features associated with each source and target segment, we rounded the training data scores to the closest integer. We tested several classifiers and empirically chose three algorithms: Support Vector Machine using sequential minimal optimization and RBF kernel (parameters optimized by grid-search) (Platt, 1999), Naive Bayes (John and Langley, 1995) and Random Forest (Breiman, 2001) (the latter two techniques were applied with default parameters). We use the Weka toolkit (Hall et al., 2009) to train the classifiers and predict the scores on the test set. Each method is evaluated individually and then combined by averaging the predicted scores.

4.2 Regression

We applied three different regression techniques: SVM epsilon-SVR with RBF kernel, Linear Regression and M5P (Quinlan, 1992; Wang and Witten, 1997). The two latter algorithms were used with default parameters, whereas SVM parameters (γ, c and ϵ) were optimized by grid-search. We also performed a combination of the three algorithms by averaging the predicted scores. We apply a linear function on the predicted scores S in order to keep them in the correct range (from 1 to 5) as detailed in (1), where S' is the rescaled sentence score, S_{min} is the lowest predicted score and S_{max} is the highest predicted score.

$$S' = 1 + 4 \times \frac{S - S_{min}}{S_{max} - S_{min}} \qquad (1)$$

5 Evaluation

Table 1 shows the results obtained by our classification approach on various feature subsets. Note that the two submitted systems used the combined classifier approach with the constrained and unconstrained feature sets. Table 2 shows the results for the same feature combinations, this time using regression rather than classification.

The results of quality estimation using classification methods show that the baseline and the syntax-based features with the classifier combination leads to the best results with an MAE of 0.71 and an RMSE of 0.87. However, these scores are substantially lower than the ones obtained using regression, where the unconstrained set of features with SVM leads to an MAE of 0.62 and an RMSE of 0.78.

It seems that the classification methods are not suitable for this task according to the different sets of features studied. Furthermore, the topic-distance feature is not correlated with the quality scores, according to the regression results. On the other hand, the syntax-based features appear to be the most informative and lead to an MAE of 0.70.

6 Conclusion

We presented in this paper our submission for the WMT12 Quality Estimation shared task. We also presented further experiments using different machine learning techniques and we evaluated the impact of two sets of features - one set which is based on linguistic features extracted using POS tagging and parsing, and a second set which is based on topic modelling. The best results are obtained by our unconstrained system containing all features and using an ϵ-SVR regression method with a Radial Basis Function kernel. This setup leads to a Mean Average Error of 0.62 and a Root Mean Squared Error of 0.78. Unfortunately, we did not submit our best configuration for the shared task.

We plan to continue working on the task of machine translation quality estimation. Our immediate next steps are to continue to investigate the contribution of individual features, to explore feature selection in a more detailed fashion and to apply our best system to other types of data including sentences taken from an online discussion forum.

Features	SMO		NAIVE BAYES		RANDOM FOREST		Combination	
	MAE	RMSE	MAE	RMSE	MAE	RMSE	MAE	RMSE
baseline	**0.74**	**0.89**	0.85	1.10	0.84	1.06	0.71	0.88
topic distribution	0.84	1.02	1.09	1.38	0.91	1.15	0.78	0.98
topic distance	0.88	1.11	0.93	1.17	1.04	1.23	0.84	1.04
syntax	0.78	0.97	1.01	1.27	0.83	1.05	0.72	0.90
baseline + topic	0.82	1.01	1.00	1.31	0.84	1.05	0.75	0.95
baseline + syntax	0.76	0.94	1.01	1.25	0.79	0.98	**0.71**	**0.87**
baseline + topic + syntax	0.82	1.04	1.03	1.29	0.79	0.98	0.74	0.93
all constrained	0.99	1.26	1.12	1.46	**0.71**	**0.88**	0.86 ○	1.12 ○
all unconstrained	0.97	1.25	**0.80**	**1.02**	0.79	0.99	0.75 •	0.97 •

Table 1: MAE and RMSE results for different sets of features using three classification methods. The results with ○ and • correspond to the *DCU-SYMC_constrained* and the *DCU-SYMC_unconstrained* systems respectively, submitted for the shared task.

Features	SVM		LINEAR REG.		M5P		Combination	
	MAE	RMSE	MAE	RMSE	MAE	RMSE	MAE	RMSE
baseline	0.78	0.93	0.80	0.99	0.73	0.91	0.72	0.88
topic distribution	0.78	0.95	**0.79**	**0.96**	0.80	0.96	0.79	0.95
topic distance	1.38	1.67	1.31	1.62	1.85	2.09	1.00	1.24
syntax	0.70	0.88	0.97	1.22	1.41	1.65	0.76	0.92
baseline + topic	0.78	0.96	1.06	1.31	1.16	1.42	0.88	1.10
baseline + syntax	0.67	0.82	0.90	1.12	2.17	2.38	0.98	1.22
baseline + topic + syntax	0.68	0.84	0.93	1.16	2.12	2.33	0.97	1.21
all constrained	0.83	1.02	0.94	1.18	0.78	0.99	**0.71**	**0.88**
all unconstrained	**0.62**	**0.78**	1.33	1.60	**0.71**	**0.89**	0.73	0.91

Table 2: MAE and RMSE results for different sets of features using three regression methods.

References

J. Albrecht and R. Hwa. 2007. A re-examination of machine learning approaches for sentence-level MT evaluation. In *Proceedings of the 45th Annual Meeting of the ACL*, pages 880–887.

D.M. Blei, A.Y. Ng, and M.I. Jordan. 2003. Latent Dirichlet Allocation. *The Journal of Machine Learning Research*, 3:993–1022.

Jordan Boyd-Graber and David M. Blei. 2009. Multilingual topic models for unaligned text. In *Proceedings of the 25th Conference on Uncertainty in Artificial Intelligence*, pages 75–82.

L. Breiman. 2001. Random forests. *Machine learning*, 45(1):5–32.

M. Butt, H. Dyvik, T. Holloway King, H. Masuichi, and C. Rohrer. 2002. The parallel grammar project. In *Proceedings of the Coling Workshop on Grammar Engineering and Evaluation*.

E. Charniak and M. Johnson. 2005. Course-to-fine n-best-parsing and maxent discriminative reranking. In *Proceedings of the 43rd Annual Meeting of the ACL*, pages 173–180, Ann Arbor.

S. Corston-Oliver, M. Gamon, and C. Brockett. 2001. A machine learning approach to the automatic evaluation of machine translation. In *Proceedings of 39th Annual Meeting of the Association for Computational Linguistics*, pages 148–155, Toulouse, France, July.

S. Deerwester, S.T. Dumais, G.W. Furnas, T.K. Landauer, and R. Harshman. 1990. Indexing by Latent Semantic Analysis. *Journal of the American Society for Information Science*, 41(6):391–407.

J. Duchateau, K. Demuynck, and P. Wambacq. 2002. Confidence scoring based on backward language models. In *Proceedings IEEE international conference on acoustics, speech, and signal processing, ICASSP'2002*, volume 1, pages 221–224.

J. Giménez and L. Màrquez. 2007. Linguistic features for automatic evaluation of heterogenous MT systems. In *Proceedings of the Second Workshop on Statistical Machine Translation*, pages 256–264, Prague, Czech Republic, June.

Z. Gong, Y. Zhang, and G. Zhou. 2010. Statistical machine translation based on lda. In *Universal Communication Symposium (IUCS), 2010 4th International*, pages 286–290.

Z. Gong, G. Zhou, and L. Li. 2011. Improve smt with source-side "topic-document" distributions. In *MT Summit*, pages 496–501.

M. Hall, E. Frank, G. Holmes, B. Pfahringer, P. Reutemann, and I.H. Witten. 2009. The weka data mining software: an update. *ACM SIGKDD Explorations Newsletter*, 11(1):10–18.

G.H. John and P. Langley. 1995. Estimating continuous distributions in bayesian classifiers. In *Eleventh conference on uncertainty in artificial intelligence*, pages 338–345. Morgan Kaufmann Publishers Inc.

P. Koehn, H. Hoang, A. Birch, C. Callison-Burch, M. Federico, N. Bertoldi, B. Cowan, W. Shen, C. Moran, R. Zens, et al. 2007. Moses: Open source toolkit for statistical machine translation. In *ACL*, pages 177–180.

V.I. Levenshtein. 1966. Binary codes capable of correcting deletions, insertions, and reversals. In *Soviet Physics Doklady*, volume 10-8, pages 707–710.

D. Liu and D. Gildea. 2005. Syntactic features for evaluation of machine translation. In *Proceedings of the ACL Workshop on Intrinsic and Extrinsic Evaluation Measures for Machine Translation and/or Summarization*, pages 25–32, Ann Arbor, Michigan.

M. P. Marcus, B. Santorini, and M. A. Marcinkiewicz. 1993. Building a large annotated corpus of english: the penn treebank. *Computational Linguistics*, 19(2):313–330.

John Maxwell and Ron Kaplan. 1996. An Efficient Parser for LFG. In *Proceedings of LFG-96*, Grenoble.

D. Mimno, H.M. Wallach, J. Naradowsky, D.A. Smith, and A. McCallum. 2009. Polylingual topic models. In *Proceedings of EMNLP: Volume 2-Volume 2*, pages 880–889. Association for Computational Linguistics.

D. Naber. 2003. A rule-based style and grammar checker. Technical report, Bielefeld University Bielefeld, Germany.

K. Owczarzak, J. van Genabith, and A. Way. 2007. Labelled dependencies in machine translation evaluation. In *Proceedings of the Second Workshop on Statistical Machine Translation*, pages 104–111, Prague, Czech Republic, June.

K. Papineni, S. Roukos, T. Ward, and W.J. Zhu. 2002. Bleu: a method for automatic evaluation of machine translation. In *ACL*, pages 311–318.

J.C. Platt. 1999. Fast training of support vector machines using sequential minimal optimization. In *Advances in kernel methods*, pages 185–208. MIT Press.

R. J. Quinlan. 1992. Learning with continuous classes. In *5th Australian Joint Conference on Artificial Intelligence*, pages 343–348, Singapore. World Scientific.

C. Quirk. 2004. Training a sentence-level machine translation confidence measure. In *Proceedings of LREC*, Lisbon, June.

R. Rubino and G. Linarès. 2011. A multi-view approach for term translation spotting. *Computational Linguistics and Intelligent Text Processing*, 6609:29–40.

H. Schmidt. 1994. Probabilistic part-of-speech tagging using decision trees. In *Proceedings of the International Conference on New Methods in Natural Language Processing.*

M. Snover, B. Dorr, R. Schwartz, L. Micciulla, and J. Makhoul. 2006. A study of translation edit rate with targeted human annotation. In *Proceedings of Association for Machine Translation in the Americas*, pages 223–231.

A. Stolcke. 2002. SRILM-an extensible language modeling toolkit. In *InterSpeech*, volume 2, pages 901–904.

Y.C. Tam, I. Lane, and T. Schultz. 2007. Bilingual lsa-based adaptation for statistical machine translation. *Machine Translation*, 21(4):187–207.

J. Wagner, J. Foster, and J. van Genabith. 2007. A comparative evaluation of deep and shallow approaches to the automatic detection of common grammatical errors. In *Proceedings of EMNLP-CoNLL*, pages 112–121, Prague, Czech Republic, June.

J. Wagner, J. Foster, and J. van Genabith. 2009. Judging grammaticality: Experiments in sentence classification. *CALICO Journal*, 26(3):474–490.

J. Wagner. 2012. *Detecting grammatical errors with treebank-induced probabilistic parsers*. Ph.D. thesis, Dublin City University.

Y. Wang and I. H. Witten. 1997. Induction of model trees for predicting continuous classes. In *Poster papers of the 9th European Conference on Machine Learning*. Springer.

The SDL Language Weaver Systems in the WMT12 Quality Estimation Shared Task

Radu Soricut **Nguyen Bach** **Ziyuan Wang**
SDL Language Weaver
6060 Center Drive, Suite 101
Los Angeles, CA, USA
{rsoricut,nbach,zwang}@sdl.com

Abstract

We present in this paper the system submissions of the SDL Language Weaver team in the WMT 2012 Quality Estimation shared-task. Our MT quality-prediction systems use machine learning techniques (M5P regression-tree and SVM-regression models) and a feature-selection algorithm that has been designed to directly optimize towards the official metrics used in this shared-task. The resulting submissions placed 1st (the M5P model) and 2nd (the SVM model), respectively, on both the Ranking task and the Scoring task, out of 11 participating teams.

1 Introduction

The WMT 2012 Quality Estimation shared-task focused on automatic methods for estimating machine translation output quality at run-time (sentence-level estimation). Different from MT evaluation metrics, quality prediction (QP) systems do not rely on reference translations and are generally built using machine learning techniques to estimate quality scores (Specia et al., 2009; Soricut and Echihabi, 2010; Bach et al., 2011; Specia, 2011).

Some interesting uses of sentence-level MT quality prediction are the following: decide whether a given translation is good enough for publishing as-is (Soricut and Echihabi, 2010), or inform monolingual (target-language) readers whether or not they can rely on a translation; filter out sentences that are not good enough for post-editing by professional translators (Specia, 2011); select the best translation among options from multiple MT systems (Soricut and Narsale, 2012), etc.

This shared-task focused on estimating the quality of English to Spanish automatic translations. The training set distributed for the shared task comprised of 1, 832 English sentences taken from the news domain and their Spanish translations. The translations were produced by the Moses SMT system (Koehn et al., 2007) trained on Europarl data. Translations also had a quality score derived from an average of three human judgements of Post-Editing effort using a 1-5 scale (1 for worse-quality/most-effort, and 5 for best-quality/least-effort). Submissions were evaluated using a blind official test set of 422 sentences produced in the same fashion as the training set. Two sub-tasks were considered: (i) scoring translations using the 1-5 quality scores (Scoring), and (ii) ranking translations from best to worse (Ranking). The official metrics used for the Ranking task were DeltaAvg (measuring how valuable a proposed ranking is from the perspective of extrinsic values associated with the test entries, in this case post-editing effort on a 1-5 scale; for instance, a DeltaAvg of 0.5 means that the top-ranked quantiles have +0.5 better quality on average compared to the entire set), as well as the Spearman ranking correlation. For the Scoring task the metrics were Mean-Absolute-Error (MAE) and Root Mean Squared Error (RMSE). The interested reader is referred to (Callison-Burch et al., 2012) for detailed descriptions of both the data and the evaluation metrics used in the shared-task.

The SDL Language Weaver team participated with two submissions based on M5P and SVM regression models in both the Ranking and the Scoring tasks. The models were trained and used to predict Post-Editing–effort scores. These scores were used as-such for the Scoring task, and also used to generate sentence rankings for the Ranking task by simply (reverse) sorting the predicted scores. The submissions of the SDL Language Weaver team placed 1st (the M5P model) and 2nd (the SVM model) on both the Ranking task (out of 17 entries) and the Scoring task (out of 19 entries).

2 The Feature Set

Both SDLLW system submissions were created starting from 3 distinct sets of features: the baseline feature set (here called BFs), the internal features available in the decoder logs of Moses (here called MFs), and an additional set of features that we developed internally (called LFs). We are presenting each of these sets in what follows.

2.1 The Baseline Features

The WMT Quality Estimation shared-task defined a set of 17 features to be used as "baseline" features. In addition to that, all participants had access to software that extracted the corresponding feature values from the inputs and necessary resources (such as the SMT-system's training data, henceforth called SMT_{src} and SMT_{trg}). For completeness, we are providing here a brief description of these 17 baseline features (BFs):

BF1 number of tokens in the source sentence

BF2 number of tokens in the target sentence

BF3 average source token length

BF4 LM probability of source sentence

BF5 LM probability of the target sentence

BF6 average number of occurrences of the target word within the target translation

BF7 average number of translations per source word in the sentence (as given by IBM 1 table thresholded so that $Prob(t|s) > 0.2$)

BF8 average number of translations per source word in the sentence (as given by IBM 1 table thresholded so that $Prob(t|s) > 0.01$) weighted by the inverse frequency of each word in the source corpus

BF9 percentage of unigrams in quartile 1 of frequency (lower frequency words) in SMT_{src}

BF10 percentage of unigrams in quartile 4 of frequency (higher frequency words) in SMT_{src}

BF11 percentage of bigrams in quartile 1 of frequency of source words in SMT_{src}

BF12 percentage of bigrams in quartile 4 of frequency of source words in SMT_{src}

BF13 percentage of trigrams in quartile 1 of frequency of source words in SMT_{src}

BF14 percentage of trigrams in quartile 4 of frequency of source words in SMT_{src}

BF15 percentage of unigrams in the source sentence seen in SMT_{src}

BF16 number of punctuation marks in source sentence

BF17 number of punctuation marks in target sentence

These features, together with the other ones we present here, are entered into a feature-selection component that decides which feature set to use for optimum performance (Section 3.2).

In Table 1, we are presenting the performance on the official test set of M5P and SVM-regression (SVR) models using only the BF features. The M5P model is trained using the Weka package [1] and the default settings for M5P decision-trees (weka.classifiers.trees.M5P). The SVR model is trained using the LIBSVM toolkit [2]. The following options are used: "-s 3" (ϵ-SVR) and "-t 2" (radial basis function). The following parameters were optimized via 5-fold cross-validation on the training data: "-c cost", the parameter C of ϵ-SVR; "-g gamma", the γ parameter of the kernel function; "-p epsilon", the ϵ for the loss-function of ϵ-SVR.

[1] http://www.cs.waikato.ac.nz/ml/weka/

[2] http://www.csie.ntu.edu.tw/~cjlin/libsvm/

Systems	Ranking		Scoring		
	DeltaAvg	Spearman	MAE	RMSE	Predict. Interval
17 BFs with M5P	0.53	0.56	0.69	0.83	[2.3-4.9]
17 BFs with SVR	0.55	0.58	0.69	0.82	[2.0-5.0]
best-system	0.63	0.64	0.61	0.75	[1.7-5.0]

Table 1: Performance of the Baseline Features using M5P and SVR models on the test set.

The results in Table 1 are compared against the "best-system" submission, in order to offer a comparison point. The "17 BFs with SVM" system actually participated as an entry in the shared-task, representing the current state-of-the-art in MT quality-prediction. This system has been ranked 6th (out of 17 entries) in the Ranking task, and 8th (out of 19 entries) in the Scoring task.

2.2 The Decoder Features

The current Quality Estimation task has been defined as a glass-box task. That is, the prediction component has access to everything related to the internal workings of the MT system for which the quality prediction is made. As such, we have chosen to use the internal scores of the Moses [3] decoder (available to all the participants in the shared-task) as a distinct set of features. These features are the following:

MF1 Distortion cost

MF2 Word penalty cost

MF3 Language-model cost

MF4 Cost of the phrase-probability of source given target $\Phi(s|t)$

MF5 Cost of the word-probability of source given target $\Phi_{lex}(s|t)$

MF6 Cost of the phrase-probability of target given source $\Phi(t|s)$

MF7 Cost of the word-probability of target given source $\Phi_{lex}(t|s)$

MF8 Phrase penalty cost

[3] http://www.statmt.org/moses/

These features are then entered into a feature-selection component that decides which feature set to use for achieving optimal performance.

The results in Table 2 present the performance on the test set of the Moses features (with an M5P model), presented against the "best-system" submission. These numbers indicate that the Moses-internal features, by themselves, are fueling a QP system that surpasses the performance of the strong "baseline" system. We note here that the "8 MFs with M5P" system would have been ranked 4th (out of 17 entries) in the Ranking task, and 5th (out of 19 entries) in the Scoring task.

2.3 Language Weaver Features

In addition to the features presented until this point, we have created and tested additional features that helped our systems achieve improved performance. In addition to the SMT training corpus, these features also use the SMT tuning dev set (henceforth called Dev_{src} and Dev_{trg}). These features are the following:

LF1 number of out-of-vocabulary tokens in the source sentence

LF2 LM perplexity for the source sentence

LF3 LM perplexity for the target sentence

LF4 geometric mean (λ-smoothed) of 1-to-4–gram precision scores (i.e., BLEU score without brevity-penalty) of source sentence against the sentences of SMT_{src} used as "references"

LF5 geometric mean (λ-smoothed) of 1-to-4–gram precision scores of target translation against the sentences of SMT_{trg} used as "references"

Systems	Ranking		Scoring		
	DeltaAvg	Spearman-Corr	**MAE**	RMSE	Predict. Interval
8 MFs with M5P	0.58	0.58	0.65	0.81	[1.8-5.0]
best-system	0.63	0.64	0.61	0.75	[1.7-5.0]

Table 2: Performance of the Moses-based Features with an M5P model on the test set.

LF6 geometric mean (λ-smoothed) of 1-to-4–gram precision scores of source sentence against the top BLEU-scoring quartile of Dev_{src}

LF7 geometric mean (λ-smoothed) of 1-to-4–gram precision scores of target translation against the top BLEU-scoring quartile of Dev_{trg}

LF8 geometric mean (λ-smoothed) of 1-to-4–gram precision scores of source sentence against the bottom BLEU-scoring quartile of Dev_{src}

LF9 geometric mean (λ-smoothed) of 1-to-4–gram precision scores of target translation against the bottom BLEU-scoring quartile Dev_{trg}

LF10 geometric mean (λ-smoothed) of 1-to-4–gram precision scores of target translation against a pseudo-reference produced by a second MT Eng-Spa system

LF11 count of one-to-one (O2O) word alignments between source and target translation

LF12 ratio of O2O alignments over source sentence

LF13 ratio of O2O alignments over target translation

LF14 count of O2O alignments with Part-of-Speech–agreement

LF15 ratio of O2O alignments with Part-of-Speech–agreement over O2O alignments

LF16 ratio of O2O alignments with Part-of-Speech–agreement over source

LF17 ratio of O2O alignments with Part-of-Speech–agreement over target

Most of these features have been shown to help Quality Prediction performance, see (Soricut and Echihabi, 2010) and (Bach et al., 2011). Some of them are inspired from word-based confidence estimation, in which the alignment consensus between the source words and target-translation words are informative indicators for gauging the quality of a translation hypothesis. The one-to-one (O2O) word alignments are obtained from the decoding logs of Moses. We use the TreeTagger to obtain Spanish POS tags[4] and a maximum-entropy POS tagger for English. Since Spanish and English POS tag sets are different, we normalize their fine-grained POS tag sets into a coarser tag set by mapping the original POS tags into more general linguistic concepts such as noun, verb, adjective, adverb, preposition, determiner, number, and punctuation.

3 The Models

3.1 The M5P Prediction Model

Regression-trees built using the M5P algorithm (Wang and Witten, 1997) have been previously shown to give good QP performance (Soricut and Echihabi, 2010). For these models, the number of linear equations used can provide a good indication whether the model overfits the training data. In Table 3, we compare the performance of several M5P models: one trained on all 42 features presented in Section 2, and two others trained on only 15 and 14 features, respectively (selected using the method described in Section 3.2). We also present the number of linear equations (L.Eq.) used by each model. Aside from the number of features they employ, these models were trained under identical conditions: default parameters of the Weka implementation, and 1527 training instances (305 instances were held-out for the feature-selection step, from the total 1832 labeled instances available for the shared-task).

As the numbers in Table 3 clearly show, the set of

[4]http://www.ims.uni-stuttgart.de/projekte/corplex/TreeTagger/

Systems	#L.Eq.	Dev Set		Test Set	
		DeltaAvg	MAE	DeltaAvg	MAE
42 FFs with M5P	10	0.60	0.58	0.56	0.64
(best-system) 15 FFs with M5P	**2**	**0.63**	**0.52**	**0.63**	**0.61**
14 FFs with M5P	6	0.62	**0.50**	0.61	0.62

Table 3: M5P-model performance for different feature-function sets (15-FFs $\in$ 42-FFs; 14-FFs $\in$ 42-FFs).

feature-functions that an M5P model is trained with matters considerably. On both our development set and the official test set, the 15-FF M5P model outperforms the 42-FF model (even if 15-FF $\in$ 42-FF). The 42-FF model would have been ranked 5th (out of 17 entries) in the Ranking task, and also 5th (out of 19 entries) in the Scoring task. In comparison, the 15-FF model (feature set optimized for best performance under the DeltaAvg metric) was our official M5P submission (SDLLW_M5PBestDeltaAvg), and ranked 1st in the Ranking task and also 1st in the Scoring task. The 14-FF model (also a subset of the 42-FF set, optimized for best performance under the MAE metric) was not part of our submission, but would have been ranked 2nd on both the Ranking and Scoring tasks.

The number of linear equations used (see #L.Eq. in Table 3) is indicative for our results. When using 42 FFs, the M5P model seems to overfit the training data (10 linear equations). In contrast, the model trained on a subset of 15 features has only 2 linear equations. This latter model is less prone to overfitting, and performs well given unseen test data. The same number for the 14-FF model indicates slight overfit on the training and dev data: with 6 equations, this model has the best MAE numbers on the Dev set, but slightly worse MAE numbers on the Test score compared to the 15-FF model.

3.2 Feature Selection

As we already pointed out, some of the features of the entire 42-FF set are highly overlapping and capture roughly the same amount of information. To achieve maximum performance given this feature-set, we applied a computationally-intensive feature-selection method. We have used the two official metrics, DeltaAvg and MAE, and a development set of 305 instances to perform an extensive feature-selection procedure that directly optimizes the two official metrics using M5P regression-trees.

The overall space that needs to be explored for 42 features is huge, on the order of 2^{42} possible combinations. We performed the search in this space in several steps. In a first step, we eliminated the obviously overlapping features (e.g., BF5 and MF3 are both LM costs of the target translation), and also excluded the POS-based features (LF14-LF17, see Section 2.3). This step reduced the overall number of features to 24, and therefore left us with an order of 2^{24} possible combinations. Next, we exhaustively searched all these combinations by building and evaluating M5P models. This operation is computationally-intensive and takes approximatively 60 hours on a cluster of 800 machines. At the conclusion of this step, we ranked the results and considered the top 64 combinations. The performance of these top combinations was very similar, and a set of 15 features was selected as the superset of active feature-functions present in most of the top 64 combinations.

DeltaAvg optim.	BF1 BF3 BF4 BF6 BF12 BF13 BF14 MF3 MF4 MF6 LF1 LF10 LF14 LF15 LF16
MAE optim.	BF1 BF3 BF4 BF6 BF12 BF14 BF16 MF3 MF4 MF6 LF1 LF10 LF14 LF17

Table 4: Feature selection results.

The second round of feature selection considers these 15 feature-functions plus the 4 POS-based feature-functions, for a total of 19 features and therefore a space of 2^{19} possible combinations (2^{15} of these already covered by the first search pass). A second search procedure was executed exhaustively

SVR Model (C;γ;ϵ)	#S.V.	Dev Set DeltaAvg	Dev Set MAE	Test Set DeltaAvg	Test Set MAE
1.0 ; 0.00781; 0.50	695	0.62	0.52	0.60	0.66
1.74; 0.00258; 0.3299	**952**	**0.63**	**0.51**	**0.61**	**0.64**
8.0 ; 0.00195; 0.0078	1509	0.64	0.50	0.60	0.68
16.0; 0.00138; 0.0884	1359	0.63	0.51	0.59	0.70

Table 5: SVR-model performance for dev and test sets.

over the set of all the new possible combinations. In the end, we selected the winning feature-function combination as our final feature-function sets: 15 features for DeltaAvg optimization and 14 features for MAE optimization. They are given in Table 4, using the feature id-s given in Section 2. The performance of these two feature-function sets using M5P models can be found in Table 3.

3.3 The SVM Prediction Model

The second submission of our team consists of rankings and scores produced by a system using an ϵ-SVM regression model (ϵ-SVR) and a subset of 19 features. This model is trained on 1,527 training examples by the LIBSVM package using radial basis function (RBF) kernel. We have found that the feature-set obtained by the feature-selection optimization for M5P models described in Section 3.2 does not achieve the same performance for SVR models on our development set. Therefore, we have performed our SVR experiments using a hand-selected set of features: 9 features from the BF family (BF1 BF3 BF4 BF6 BF10 BF11 BF12 BF14 BF16); all 8 features from the MF family; and 2 features from the LF family (LF1 LF10).

We optimize the three hyper parameters C, γ, and ϵ of the SVR method using a grid-search method and measure their performance on our development set of 305 instances. The C parameter is a penalty factor: if C is too high, we have a high penalty for non-separable points and may store many support vectors and therefore overfit the training data; if C is too low, we may end up with a model that is poorly fit. The ϵ parameter determines the level of accuracy of the approximated function; however, getting too close to zero may again overfit the training data. The γ parameter relates to the RBF kernel: large γ values give the model steeper and more flexible kernel functions, while small gamma values give the model smoother functions. In general, C, ϵ, and γ are all sensitive parameters and instantiate ϵ-SVR models that may behave very differently.

In order to cope with the overfitting issue given a small amount of training data and grid search optimization, we train our models with 10-fold cross validation and restart the tuning process several times using different starting points and step sizes. We select the best model parameters based on a couple of indicators: the performance on the development set and the number of support vectors of the model. In Table5 we present the performance of different model parameters on both the development set and the official test set. Our second submission (SDLLW_SVM), which placed 2nd in both the Ranking and the Scoring tasks, is the entry in bold font. It was chosen based on good performance on the Dev set and also a setting of the (C, γ, ϵ) parameters that provides a number of support vectors that is neither too high nor too low. As a contrastive point, the model on the row below it uses 1,509 support vectors extracted from 1,527 training vectors, which represents a clear case of overfitting. Indeed, the performance of this model is marginally better on the Dev set, but ends up underperforming on the Test data.

4 Conclusions

The WMT 2012 Quality Estimation shared-task provided the opportunity for the comparing different QP systems using shared datasets and standardized evaluation metrics. Our participation in this shared-task revealed two important aspects of Quality Prediction for MT that we regard as important for the future. First, our experiments indicated that the

Moses-internal features, by themselves, can fuel a QP-system that surpasses the performance of the strong "baseline" system used in this shared task to represent state-of-the-art performance in MT quality prediction. This is a surprising finding, considering that these decoder-internal features have been primarily designed to gauge differences in translation quality when starting from the same source sentence. In contrast, for quality-prediction tasks like ranking one needs to gauge differences in quality of translations of different source sentences.

The second aspect relates to the importance of feature selection. Given the availability and good scalability of Machine Learning toolkits today, it is tempting to throw as much features as possible at this problem and let the built-in mechanisms of these learning algorithms deal with issues relating to feature overlapping, training-data overfitting, etc. However, these learning algorithms have their own limitations in these regards, and, in conjunction with the limited availability of the labeled data, can easily produce models that are underperforming on blind tests. There is a need for careful engineering of the models and evaluation of the resulting performance in order to achieve optimal performance using the current state-of-the-art supervised learning techniques.

References

Nguyen Bach, Fei Huang, and Yaser Al-Onaizan. 2011. Goodness: A method for measuring machine translation confidence. In *Proceedings of the ACL/HLT*, Portland, Oregon, USA.

Chris Callison-Burch, Philipp Koehn, Christof Monz, Matt Post, Radu Soricut, and Lucia Specia. 2012. Findings of the 2012 Workshop on Statistical Machine Translation. In *Proceedings of the Seventh Workshop on Statistical Machine Translation*, Montreal, Canada, June. Association for Computational Linguistics.

Philipp Koehn, Hieu Hoang, Alexandra Birch, Chris Callison-Burch, Marcello Federico, Nicola Bertoldi, Brooke Cowan, Wade Shen, Christine Moran, Richard Zens, Chris Dyer, Ondrej Bojar, Alexandra Constantin, and Evan Herbst. 2007. Moses: Open source toolkit for statistical machine translation. In *Proceedings of the 45th Annual Meeting of the Association for Computational Linguistics Companion Volume Proceedings of the Demo and Poster Sessions*.

Radu Soricut and Abdessamad Echihabi. 2010. Trustrank: Inducing trust in automatic translations via ranking. In *Proceedings of ACL*.

Radu Soricut and Sushant Narsale. 2012. Combining quality prediction and system selection for improved automatic translation output. In *Proceedings of the Seventh Workshop on Statistical Machine Translation*, Montreal, Canada, June. Association for Computational Linguistics.

Lucia Specia, Nicola Cancedda, Marc Dymetman, Marcho Turchi, and Nello Cristianini. 2009. Estimating the sentence-level quality of machine translation. In *Proceedings of EAMT*.

Lucia Specia. 2011. Exploiting objective annotations for measuring translation post-editing effort. In *Proceedings of EAMT*.

Y. Wang and I. H. Witten. 1997. Induction of model trees for predicting continuous classes. In *Proceedings of the 9th European Conference on Machine Learning*.

Regression with Phrase Indicators for Estimating MT Quality*

Chunyang Wu **Hai Zhao**†
Center for Brain-Like Computing and Machine Intelligence,
Department of Computer Science and Engineering, Shanghai Jiao Tong University
chunyang506@sjtu.edu.cn, zhaohai@cs.sjtu.edu.cn

Abstract

We in this paper describe the regression system for our participation in the quality estimation task of WMT12. This paper focuses on exploiting special phrases, or word sequences, to estimate translation quality. Several feature templates on this topic are put forward subsequently. We train a SVM regression model for predicting the scores and numerical results show the effectiveness of our phrase indicators and method in both ranking and scoring tasks.

1 Introduction

The performance of machine translation (MT) systems has been considerable promoted in the past two decades. However, since the quality of the sentence given by MT decoder is not guaranteed, an important issue is to automatically predict or identify its characteristics. Recent studies on quality estimation or confidence estimation have focused on measuring the translating quality at run-time, instead of involving reference corpus. Researches on this topic contribute to offering advices or warnings for users even without knowledge about either side of languages and illuminating some other potential MT applications.

This paper describes the regression system for our participation in the WMT12 quality estimation task. In this shared task, we analyzed the pattern of translating errors and studied on capturing such patterns among the corpus. The basic objective in this paper is to recognize those phrases, or special word sequence combinations which can indicate the quality of a translation instance. By introducing no external NLP toolkits, we exploited several feasible techniques to extract such patterns directly on the corpus. One contribution of this paper is those feature templates on the basis of this topic. Numerical results show their positive effects on both ranking and scoring subtasks.

The rest of this paper is organized as follows: In Section 2, we show the related work. In Section 3, we specify the details of our system architecture. The experimental results are reported in Section 4. Finally, the conclusion is given in Section 5.

2 Related Work

Compared with traditional MT metrics such as BLEU (Papineni et al., 2002), the fundamental goal of quality estimation (QE) is predicting the quality of output sentences without involving reference sentences.

Early works (Quirk, 2004; Gamon et al., 2005) have demonstrated the consistency of the automatic score and human evaluation. Several further works aimed at predicting automatic scores in order to better select MT n-best candidates (Specia and Farzindar, 2010), measure post-editing effort (Specia et

*This work was partially supported by the National Natural Science Foundation of China (Grant No. 60903119 and Grant No. 61170114), the National Research Foundation for the Doctoral Program of Higher Education of China under Grant No. 20110073120022, the National Basic Research Program of China (Grant No. 2009CB320901), the Science and Technology Commission of Shanghai Municipality (Grant No. 09511502400), and the European Union Seventh Framework Program (Grant No. 247619).

†corresponding author

al., 2011) or combine SMT and TM systems (He et al., 2010). Instead of estimating on word or sentence levels, Soricut and Echihabi (2010) proposed a document-level ranking system which grants the user to set quality threshold. Besides, recent studies on the QE topic introduced syntactic and linguistic information for better estimating the quality such as dependency preservation checking (Bach et al., 2011).

3 System Description

We specify the details of our system in this section. Following previous approaches for quality estimation, it is first trained on the corpus with labeled quality scores and then it is able to predict the score for unlabeled instances.

A major challenge for this estimating task is to exploit effective indicators, or features, to identify the quality of the translating results. In this paper, all the features are extracted from the official corpora, involving no external tools such as pre-trained parsers or POS taggers. Most of the feature templates focus on special phrases or word sequences. Some of the phrases could introduce translation errors and others might declare the merit of the MT output. Their weights are automatically given by the regressor.

3.1 Regression Model

For obtaining MT quality predictor, we utilize SVM^{light} (Joachims, 1999)[1] to train this regression model. The radial basis function kernel is chosen as the kernel of this model. The label for each instance is the score annotated manually and the input vector consists of a large amount of indicators described in Section 3.2.

3.2 Features

For training the regression model, we utilize the 17 baseline features: number of source/target tokens, average source token length, source/target LM probability, target-side average of target word occurrences, original/inverse frequency average of translations per source word, source/target percentage of uni-/bi-/tri-grams in quartile 1 or 4, source percentage of unigrams in the training corpus and source/target number of punctuation. Besides, several features and templates are proposed as follows:

- **Inverted Automatic Scores:** For each Spanish system output sentence, we translate it to English and get its scores of BLEU and METEOR (Denkowski and Lavie, 2011). These scores are treated as features named *inverted automatic scores*. In order to obtain these numerals, we train a Spanish-to-English phrase-based Moses[2] (Koehn et al., 2007) decoder with default parameters on the official parallel corpus. The original training corpus is split into a developing set containing the last 3000 sentence pairs at the end of the corpus and a training set with the remained pairs. The word alignment information is generated by GIZA++ (Och and Ney, 2003) and the feature weights are tuned on the developing set by Z-MERT (Zaidan, 2009).

- **Minimal/Maximal link likelihood of general language model:** In the word graph of each decoding instance, denote the minimal and maximal general language model likelihood of links as l_{min} and l_{max}. We treat $\exp(l_{min})$ and $\exp(l_{max})$ as features respectively.

- **Trace Density:** Define the trace density ρ_T as the quotient of decoding trace length and sentence length:

$$\rho_T = \text{TraceLength / SentenceLength}. \quad (1)$$

- **Average of Phrase Length:** This feature is also obtained from the decoding trace information.

- **Number of Name Entity:** This feature cannot be obtained exactly due to the resource constrains. We in this task count the number of the word whose first letter is capitalized, and that is not the first word in the sentence.

We also extract several special phrases or sequences. The total of each phrase/sequence type and each pattern are respectively defined as features. When an instance matches a pattern, the entry representing this pattern in its vector is set to $|1/Z|$. In

[1] http://svmlight.joachims.org/

[2] http://www.statmt.org/moses/

this paper the regressor term Z is the size of the template which the pattern belongs to. The detail description of such templates is presented as follows:

- **Reference 2∼5-grams:** All the 2∼5-grams of the reference sentences provided in the official data are generated as features.

- **Bi-gram Source Splitting:** This template comes from the GIZA alignment document. We scan the parallel corpus: for each bi-gram in the source sentence, if its words' counterparts in the target side are separated, we add it to the *bi-gram source splitting* feature template.

The part-of-speech tags of the words seem to be effective to this task. Since it is not provided, we utilize a trick design for obtaining similar information:

- **Target Functional Word Patterns:** On the target corpus, we scan those words whose length is smaller than or equal to three. Such a word w is denoted as *functional word*. Any bi-gram in the corpus starting or ending with w is added to a dictionary $\mathbb{D}$. For each system-output translation instance, we compare the analogous bi-grams in it with this dictionary, all bi-grams not in $\mathbb{D}$ are extracted as features.

Denote the collection of 2∼5-grams of the system-output sentences scored lower than 1.5 as $\mathbb{B}$; that with scores higher than 4.5 as $\mathbb{G}$. Here the "score" is the manual score provided in the official resource.

- **Target Bad 2∼5-grams:** $\mathbb{B} - \mathbb{G}$

- **Target Good 2∼5-grams:** $\mathbb{G} - \mathbb{B}$

- **Source Bad/Good 2∼5-grams:** Analogous phrases on the source side are also extracted by the same methods as *Target Bad/Good n-grams*.

For each output-postedit sentence pair, we construct a bipartite graph by aligning the same words between these two sentences. By giving a maximal matching, the output sentence can be split to several segments by the unmatched words.

- **Output-Postedit Different 2∼5-grams:** For each unaligned segments, we attach the previous word to the left side and the next word to the right. 2∼5-grams in this refined segment are extracted as features.

- **Output-Postedit Different Anchor:** Denote the refined unaligned segment as

  $$s_r = (\text{prevWord}, s_1, s_2, \ldots, s_n, \text{nextWord}).$$

  A special sequence with two word segments

  $$\underline{\text{prevWord}\ s_1}\ \ldots\ \underline{s_n\ \text{nextWord}}$$

  is given as a feature.

In the source-side scenario with the inverted translations, similar feature templates are extracted as well:

- **Source-Invert Different 2∼5-grams/Anchor**

A significant issue to be considered in this shared task is that the training data set is not a huge one, containing about two thousand instances. Although carefully designed, the feature templates however cannot involve enough cases. In order to overcome this drawback, we adopt the following strategy:

For any template $\mathbb{T}$, we compare its patterns with the items in the phrase table. If the phrase item p is similar enough with the pattern g, p is added to the template $\mathbb{T}$. Two similarity metrics are utilized: Denote the longest common sequence as $LCSQ(p, g)$ and the longest common segment as $LCSG(p, g)$ [3],

$$\frac{LCSQ(p, g)^2}{|p||g|} > 0.6, \tag{2}$$

$$LCSG(p, g) \geq 3. \tag{3}$$

Besides, when training the regression model or testing, the entry representing the similar items in the feature vector are also set to $1/|\text{template size}|$.

4 Experiments

4.1 Data

In order to conduct this experiment, we randomly divide the official training data into two parts: one

[3] To simplify, the sequence allows separation while the segment should be contiguous. For example, $LCSQ(p, g)$ and $LCSG(p, g)$ for "*I am happy*" and "*I am very happy*" are "*I, am, happy*" and "*I, am*", respectively.

Data Set	Score Distribution			
	[1-2)	[2-3)	[3-4)	[4-5)
Original	3.2%	24.1%	38.7%	34.0%
Train	3.2%	24.2%	38.3%	34.4%
Dev	3.3%	24.0%	40.3%	32.4%

Table 1: The comparison of the score distributions among three data sets: Original, Training (Train) and Development (Dev).

	Ranking		Scoring	
	DA	SC	MAE	RMSE
Baseline	0.47	0.49	0.61	0.79
This paper	**0.49**	**0.52**	**0.60**	**0.77**

Table 2: The experiment results on the ranking and scoring tasks. In this table, DA, SC, MAE and RMSE are DeltaAvg, Spearman Correlation, Mean-Average-Error and Root-Mean-Squared-Error respectively.

training set with about 3/4 items and one development set with the other 1/4 items. The comparison of the score distribution among these data sets is listed in Table 1.

4.2 Results

The baseline of this experiment is the regression model trained on the 17 baseline features. The parameters of the classifier are firstly tuned on the baseline features. Then the settings for both the baseline and our model remain unchanged. The numerical results for the ranking and scoring tasks are listed in Table 2. The ranking task is evaluated on the DeltaAvg metric (primary) and Spearman correlation (secondary) and the scoring task is evaluated on Mean-Average-Error and Root-Mean-Squared-Error. For the ranking task, our system outperforms 0.02 on DeltaAvg and 0.03 on Spearman correlation; for the scoring task, 0.01 lower on MAE and 0.02 lower on RMSE.

The official evaluation results are listed in Table 3. The official LibSVM[4] model is a bit better than our submission. Our system was further improved after the official submission. Different combinations of the rates defined in Equation 2$\sim$3 and regressor parameter settings are tested. As a result, the "Refined" model in Table 3 is the results of the refined version. Compared with the official model, it gives similar ranking results and performs better on the scoring task.

[4]http://www.csie.ntu.edu.tw/ cjlin/libsvm/

	Ranking		Scoring	
	DA	SC	MAE	RMSE
SJTU	0.53	0.53	0.69	0.83
Official SVM	0.55	0.58	0.69	0.82
Refined	0.55	0.57	**0.68**	**0.81**
Best Workshop	0.63	0.64	0.61	0.75

Table 3: The official evaluation results.

5 Conclusion

We presented the SJTU regression system for the quality estimation task in WMT 2012. It utilized a support vector machine approach with several features or feature templates extracted from the decoding and corpus documents. Numerical results show the effectiveness of those features as indicators for training the regression model. This work could be extended by involving syntax information for extracting more effective indicators based on phrases in the future.

References

Nguyen Bach, Fei Huang, and Yaser Al-Onaizan. 2011. Goodness: a method for measuring machine translation confidence. In *Proceedings of the 49th Annual Meeting of the Association for Computational Linguistics: Human Language Technologies - Volume 1*, HLT '11, pages 211–219, Stroudsburg, PA, USA. Association for Computational Linguistics.

Michael Denkowski and Alon Lavie. 2011. Meteor 1.3: Automatic Metric for Reliable Optimization and Evaluation of Machine Translation Systems. In *Proceedings of the EMNLP 2011 Workshop on Statistical Machine Translation*.

Michael Gamon, Anthony Aue, and Martine Smets. 2005. Sentence-level mt evaluation without reference translations: Beyond language modeling. In *In European Association for Machine Translation (EAMT)*.

Yifan He, Yanjun Ma, Josef van Genabith, and Andy Way. 2010. Bridging smt and tm with translation recommendation. In *Proceedings of the 48th Annual Meeting of the Association for Computational Linguistics*, pages 622–630, Uppsala, Sweden, July. Association for Computational Linguistics.

Thorsten Joachims. 1999. Advances in kernel methods. chapter Making large-scale support vector machine learning practical, pages 169–184. MIT Press, Cambridge, MA, USA.

Philipp Koehn, Hieu Hoang, Alexandra Birch, Chris Callison-Burch, Marcello Federico, Nicola Bertoldi, Brooke Cowan, Wade Shen, Christine Moran, Richard Zens, Chris Dyer, Ondrej Bojar, Alexandra Constantin, and Evan Herbst. 2007. Moses: Open Source Toolkit for Statistical Machine Translation. In *Proceedings of the Association for Computational Linguistics Companion Demo and Poster Sessions*, pages 177–180, Prague, Czech Republic. Association for Computational Linguistics.

Franz Josef Och and Hermann Ney. 2003. A systematic comparison of various statistical alignment models. *Comput. Linguist.*, 29(1):19–51, March.

Kishore Papineni, Salim Roukos, Todd Ward, and Wei-Jing Zhu. 2002. Bleu: a method for automatic evaluation of machine translation. In *Proceedings of the 40th Annual Meeting on Association for Computational Linguistics*, ACL '02, pages 311–318, Stroudsburg, PA, USA. Association for Computational Linguistics.

Christopher B. Quirk. 2004. Training a sentence-level machine translation confidence metric. *LREC*, 4:2004.

Radu Soricut and Abdessamad Echihabi. 2010. Trustrank: Inducing trust in automatic translations via ranking. In *Proceedings of the 48th Annual Meeting of the Association for Computational Linguistics*, pages 612–621, Uppsala, Sweden, July. Association for Computational Linguistics.

Lucia Specia and Atefeh Farzindar. 2010. Estimating machine translation post-editing effort with hter. In *AMTA 2010- workshop, Bringing MT to the User: MT Research and the Translation Industry*. The Ninth Conference of the Association for Machine Translation in the Americas, nov.

Lucia Specia, Hajlaoui N., Hallett C., and Aziz W. 2011. Predicting machine translation adequacy. In *Machine Translation Summit XIII*.

Omar F. Zaidan. 2009. Z-MERT: A fully configurable open source tool for minimum error rate training of machine translation systems. *The Prague Bulletin of Mathematical Linguistics*, 91:79–88.

Non-Linear Models for Confidence Estimation

Yong Zhuang*
Zhejiang University
866 Yuhangtang Road
Hangzhou, China
yong.zhuang22@gmail.com

Guillaume Wisniewski and **François Yvon**
Univ. Paris Sud and LIMSI–CNRS
rue John von Neumann
91403 Orsay CEDEX, France
{firstname.lastname}@limsi.fr

Abstract

This paper describes our work with the data distributed for the WMT'12 Confidence Estimation shared task. Our contribution is twofold: *i)* we first present an analysis of the data which highlights the difficulty of the task and motivates our approach; *ii)* we show that using non-linear models, namely random forests, with a simple and limited feature set, succeeds in modeling the complex decisions required to assess translation quality and achieves results that are on a par with the second best results of the shared task.

1 Introduction

Confidence estimation is the task of predicting the quality of a system prediction without knowledge of the expected output. It is an important step in many Natural Language Processing applications (Gandrabur et al., 2006). In Machine Translation (MT), this task has recently gained interest (Blatz et al., 2004; Specia et al., 2010b; Soricut and Echihabi, 2010; Bach et al., 2011). Indeed, professional translators are more and more requested to post-edit the outputs of a MT system rather than to produce a translation from scratch. Knowing in advance the segments they should focus on would be very helpful (Specia et al., 2010a). Confidence estimation is also of great interest for developers of MT system, as it provides them with a way to analyze the systems output and to better understand the main causes of errors.

Even if several studies have tackled the problem of confidence estimation in machine translation, until now, very few datasets were publicly available and comparing the proposed methods was difficult, if not impossible. To address this issue, WMT'12 organizers proposed a shared task aiming at predict the quality of a translation and provided the associated datasets, baselines and metrics.

This paper describes our work with the data of the WMT'12 Confidence Estimation shared task. Our contribution is twofold: *i)* we first present an analysis of the provided data that will stress the difficulty of the task and motivate the choice of our approach; *ii)* we show how using non-linear models, namely random forests, with a simple and limited features set succeed in modeling the complex decisions require to assess translation quality and achieve the second best results of the shared task.

The rest of this paper is organized as follows: Section 2 summarizes our analysis of the data; in Section 3, we describe our learning method; our main results are finally reported in Section 4.

2 Data Analysis

In this section, we quickly analyze the data distributed in the context of the WMT'12 Confidence Estimation Shared Task in order to evaluate the difficulty of the task and to find out what predictors shall be used. We will first describe the datasets, then the features usually considered in confidence estimation tasks and finally summarize our analyses.

2.1 Datasets

The datasets used in our experiments were released for the WMT'12 Quality Estimation Task. All the data provided in this shared task are based on the test set of WMT'09 and WMT'10 translation tasks.

The training set is made of 1,832 English sentences and their Spanish translations as computed by a standard Moses system. Each sentence pair is accompanied by an estimate of its translation quality. This score is the average of ordinal grades assigned by three human evaluators. The human grades are in the range 1 to 5, the latter standing for a very good translation that hardly requires post-editing, while the former stands for a bad translation that does

*This work was conducted during an internship at LIMSI–CNRS

not deserve to be edited, meaning that the machine output useless and that translation should better be produced from scratch. The test contains 422 sentence pairs, the quality of which has to be predicted.

The training set also contains additional material, namely two references (the reference originally given by WMT and a human post-edited one), which will allow us to better interpret our results. No references were provided for the test set.

2.2 Features

Several works have studied the problem of confidence estimation (Blatz et al., 2004; Specia et al., 2010b) or related problems such as predicting readability (Kanungo and Orr, 2009) or developing automated essay scoring systems (Burstein et al., 1998). They all use the same basic features:

IBM 1 score measures the quality of the "association" of the source and the target sentence using bag-of-word translation models;

Language model score accounts for the "fluency", "grammaticality" and "plausibility" of a target sentence;

Simple surface features like the sentence length, the number of out-of-vocabulary words or words that are not aligned. These features are used to account for the difficulty of the translation task.

More elaborated features, derived, for instance, from parse trees or dependencies analysis have also been used in past studies. However they are far more expensive to compute and rely on the existence of external resources, which may be problematic for some languages. That is why we only considered a restricted number of basic features in this work[1]. Another reason for considering such a small set of features is the relatively small size of the training set: in our preliminary experiments, considering more features, especially lexicalized features that would be of great interest for failure analysis, always resulted in overfitting.

2.3 Data Analysis

The distribution of the human scores on the training set is displayed in Figure 1. Surprisingly enough, the baseline translation system used to generate the data seems to be pretty good: 73% of the sentences have a score higher than 3 on a 1 to 5 scale. It also appears that most scores are very close: more than half of them are located around the mean. As a consequence, it seems that distinguishing between them will require to model subtle nuances.

[1]The complete list of features is given in Appendix A.

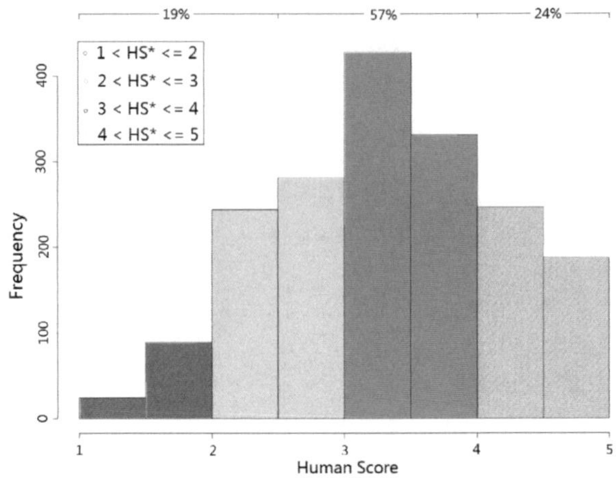

Figure 1: Distribution of the human scores on the train set. (HS* stands for Human Scores)

Figure 2 plots the distribution of quality scores as a function of the Spanish-to-English IBM 1 score and of the probability of the target sentence. These two scores were computed with the same models that were used to train the MT systems that have generated the training data. It appears that even if the examples are clustered by their quality, these clusters overlap and the frontiers between them are fuzzy and complex. Similar observations were made for others features.

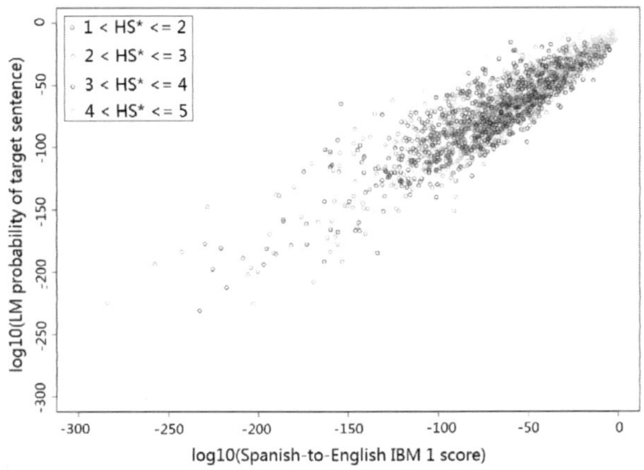

Figure 2: Quality scores as a function of the Spanish-to-English IBM 1 score and of the probability of the target sentence (HS* stands for Human Scores)

These observations prove that a predictor of the translation quality has to capture complex interaction patterns in the training data. Standard results from machine learning show that such structures can be described either by a linear model using a large number of features or by a non-linear model using a (potentially) smaller set of features. As only a small number of training examples is available, we decided to focus on non-linear models in this work.

3 Inferring quality scores

Predicting the quality scores can naturally be cast as a standard regression task, as the reference scores used in the evaluation are numerical (real) values. Regression is the approach adopted in most works on confidence estimation for MT (Albrecht and Hwa, 2007; Specia et al., 2010b). A simpler way to tackle the problem would be to recast it as binary classification task aiming at distinguishing "good" translations from "bad" ones (Blatz et al., 2004; Quirk, 2004). It is also possible, as shown by (Soricut and Echihabi, 2010), to use ranking approaches. However, because the shared task is evaluated by comparing the actual value of the predictions with the human scores, using these last two frameworks is not possible.

In our experiments, following the observations reported in the previous section, we use two well-known non-linear regression methods: polynomial regression and random forests. We also consider linear regression as a baseline. We will now quickly describe these three methods.

Linear regression (Hastie et al., 2003) is a simple model in which the prediction is defined by a linear combination of the feature vector $\mathbf{x}$: $\hat{y} = \beta_0 + x^\top \boldsymbol{\beta}$, where β_0 and $\boldsymbol{\beta}$ are the parameters to estimate. These parameters are usually learned by minimizing the sum of squared deviations on the training set, which is an easy optimization problem with a close-form solution.

Polynomial regression (Hastie et al., 2003) is a straightforward generalization of linear regression in which the relationship between the features and the label is modeled as a n-th order polynomial. By carefully extending the feature vector, the model can be reduced to a linear regression model and trained in the same way.

Random forest regressor (Breiman, 2001) is an ensemble method that learns many regression trees and predicts an aggregation of their result. In contrast with standard decision tree, in which each node is split using the best split among all features, in a random forest the split is chosen randomly. In spite of this simple and counter-intuitive learning strategy, random forests have proven to be very good "out-of-the-box" learners and have achieved state-of-the-art performance in many tasks, demonstrating both their robustness to overfitting and their ability to take into account complex interactions between features.

In our experiments, we use the implementation provided by scikit-learn (Pedregosa et al., 2011). Hyper-parameters of the random forest (the number of trees and the stopping criterion) were chosen by 10-fold cross-validation.

4 Experimental Setting

4.1 Features

In all our experiments, we considered a simple description of the translation hypotheses relying on 31 features. The complete list of features is given in Appendix A. All these features have already been used in works related to ours and are simple features that can be easily computed using only a limited number of external resources.

A key finding in our preliminary experiments is the need to re-scale the features by dividing their value by the length of the corresponding sentence (e.g. the language model score of a source sentence will be divided by its length of the source sentence, and the one of a target sentence will be done by its length of the target sentence). This rescaling makes features that depend on the sentence length (like the LM score) comparable and results in a large improvement of the performance of the associated feature.

4.2 Metrics

The two metrics used to evaluate prediction performance are the standard metrics for regression: *Mean Absolute Error* (MAE) and *Root Mean Squared Error* (RMSE) defined by:

$$\text{MAE} = \frac{1}{n}\sum_{i=1}^{n} |\hat{y}_i - y_i|$$

$$\text{RMSE} = \sqrt{\frac{1}{n}\sum_{i=1}^{n} (\hat{y}_i - y_i)^2}$$

where n is the number of examples, y_i and $\hat{y}_i$ the true label and predicted label of the ith example. MAE can be understood as the averaged error made in predicting the quality of a translation. As it is easy to interpret, we will use it to analyze our results. RMSE scores are reported to facilitate comparison with other submissions to the shared task.

All the reported scores have been computed using the tools provided by the Quality Estimation task organizers[2].

[2] `https://github.com/lspecia/QualityEstimation`

4.3 Results

Table 1 details the results achieved by the different methods introduced in the previous section. All of them achieve similar performances: their MAE is between 0.64 and 0.66, which is a pretty good result as the best reported MAE in the shared task is 0.61. Our best model is the second-best when submissions are ranked according to their MAE.

Even if their results are very close (significance of the score differences will be investigated in the following subsection), all non-linear models outperform a simple linear regression, which corroborates the observations made in Section 2.

For the polynomial regression, we tried different polynomial orders in order to achieve an optimal setting. Even if this method achieves the best results when the model is selected on the *test* set, it is not usable in practice: when we tried to select the polynomial degree by cross-validation, the regressors systematically overfitted due to the reduction of the number of examples. That is why random forests, which do not suffer from overfitting and can learn good predictor even when features outnumber examples, is our method of choice.

4.4 Interpretation

To get a better understanding of the task difficulty and to make interpretation of the error rate easier, we train another regressor using an "oracle" feature: the hTER score. It is clear that this feature can only be computed on the training set and that considering it does not make much sense in a "real-life" scenario. However, this feature is supposed to be highly relevant to the quality prediction task and should therefore result in a "large" reduction of the error rates. Quantifying what "large" means in this context will allow us to analyze the results presented in Table 1.

Training a random forest with this additional feature on 1,400 examples of the train set chosen randomly reduces the MAE evaluated on the 432 remaining examples by 0.10 and the RMSE by 0.12. This small reduction stresses how difficult the task is. Comparatively, the 0.02 reduction achieved by replacing a linear model with a non-linear model should therefore be considered noteworthy. Further investigations are required to find out whether the difficulty of the task results from the way human scores are collected (low inter-annotators agreement, bias in the gathering of the collection, ...) or from the impossibility to solve the task using only surface features.

Another important question in the analysis of our results concerns the usability of our approach: an error of 0.6 seems large on a 1 to 5 scale and may question the interest of our approach. To allow a fine-grained analysis, we report the correlation between the predicted score and the human score (Figure 3) and the distribution of the absolute error (Figure 4). These figures show that the actual error is often quite small: for more than 45% of the examples, the error is smaller than 0.5 and for 23% it is smaller than 0.2. Figure 3 also shows that the correlation between our predictions and the true labels is "substantial" according to the established guidelines of (Landis and Koch, 1977) (the Pearson correlation coefficient is greater than 0.6). The difference between the mean of the two distributions is however quite large. Centering the predictions on the mean of the true label may improves the MAE. This observation also suggests that we should try to design evaluation metrics that do not rely on the actual predicted values.

Figure 3: Correlation between our predictions and the true label (HS* stands for Human Scores)

5 Conclusion

In this work, we have presented, a simple, yet efficient, method to predict the quality of a translation. Using simple features and a non-linear model, our approach has achieved results close to the best submission to the Confidence Estimation shared task, which supports the results of our analysis of the data. In our future work, we aim at considering more features, avoiding overfitting thanks to features selection methods.

Even if a fine-grained analysis of our results shows the interest and usefulness of our approach, more remains to be done to develop reliable confidence estimation methods. Our results also highlight the need to continue gathering high-quality resources to train and investigate confidence estimation systems: even when considering only very few features, our systems

Methods	parameters	Train MAE	Train RMSE	Test MAE	Test RMSE
linear regression	—	0.58	0.71	0.66	0.82
polynomial regression	n=2	0.55	0.68	0.64	0.79
	n=3	0.54	0.67	0.64	0.79
	n=4	0.54	0.67	0.65	0.85
random forest	cross-validated	0.39	0.46	0.64	0.80

Table 1: Prediction performance achieved by different regressors

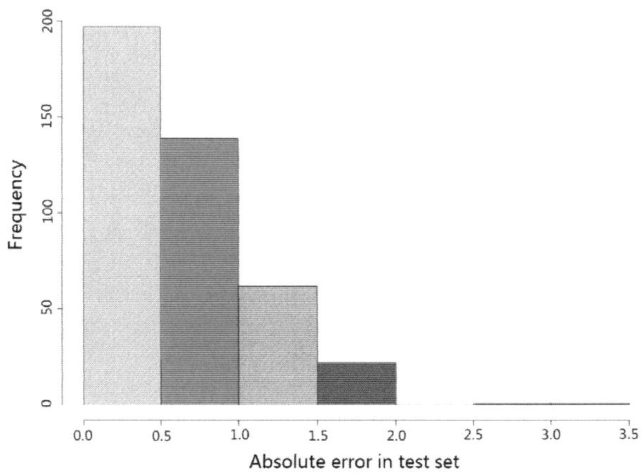

Figure 4: Distribution of the absolute error ($|y_i - \hat{y}_i|$) of our predictions

were prone to overfitting. Developing more elaborated systems will therefore only be possible if more training resource is available.

Acknowledgment

The authors would like to thank Nicolas Usunier for helpful discussions about ranking and regression using random forest. This work was partially funded by the French National Research Agency under project ANR-CONTINT-TRACE.

References

Joshua Albrecht and Rebecca Hwa. 2007. Regression for sentence-level mt evaluation with pseudo references. In *Proceedings of the 45th Annual Meeting of the Association of Computational Linguistics*, pages 296–303, Prague, Czech Republic, June. Association for Computational Linguistics.

Nguyen Bach, Fei Huang, and Yaser Al-Onaizan. 2011. Goodness: a method for measuring machine translation confidence. In *Proceedings of the 49th Annual Meeting of the Association for Computational Linguistics: Human Language Technologies - Volume 1*, HLT '11, pages 211–219, Stroudsburg, PA, USA. Association for Computational Linguistics.

John Blatz, Erin Fitzgerald, George Foster, Simona Gandrabur, Cyril Goutte, Alex Kulesza, Alberto Sanchis, and Nicola Ueffing. 2004. Confidence estimation for machine translation. In *Proceedings of the 20th international conference on Computational Linguistics*, COLING '04, Stroudsburg, PA, USA. Association for Computational Linguistics.

Leo Breiman. 2001. Random forests. *Mach. Learn.*, 45(1):5–32, October.

Jill Burstein, Karen Kukich, Susanne Wolff, Chi Lu, Martin Chodorow, Lisa Braden-Harder, and Mary Dee Harris. 1998. Automated scoring using a hybrid feature identification technique. In *Proceedings of the 17th international conference on Computational linguistics - Volume 1*, COLING '98, pages 206–210, Stroudsburg, PA, USA. Association for Computational Linguistics.

Simona Gandrabur, George Foster, and Guy Lapalme. 2006. Confidence estimation for nlp applications. *ACM Trans. Speech Lang. Process.*, 3(3):1–29, October.

T. Hastie, R. Tibshirani, and J. H. Friedman. 2003. *The Elements of Statistical Learning*. Springer, July.

Tapas Kanungo and David Orr. 2009. Predicting the readability of short web summaries. In *Proceedings of the Second ACM International Conference on Web Search and Data Mining*, WSDM '09, pages 202–211, New York, NY, USA. ACM.

R. J. Landis and G. G. Koch. 1977. The measurement of observer agreement for categorical data. *Biometrics*, 33(1):159–174.

F. Pedregosa, G. Varoquaux, A. Gramfort, V. Michel, B. Thirion, O. Grisel, M. Blondel, P. Prettenhofer, R. Weiss, V. Dubourg, J. Vanderplas, A. Passos, D. Cournapeau, M. Brucher, M. Perrot, and E. Duchesnay. 2011. Scikit-learn: Machine Learning in Python . *Journal of Machine Learning Research*, 12:2825–2830.

Chris Quirk. 2004. Training a sentence-level machine translation confidence metric. In *Proceedings of the 4th International Conference on Language Resources and Evaluation (LREC)*, pages 825–828.

Radu Soricut and Abdessamad Echihabi. 2010. Trustrank: Inducing trust in automatic translations via ranking. In *Proceedings of the 48th Annual Meeting of the Association for Computational Linguistics*, pages 612–621, Uppsala, Sweden, July. Association for Computational Linguistics.

Lucia Specia, Nicola Cancedda, and Marc Dymetman. 2010a. A dataset for assessing machine translation evaluation metrics. In *7th Conference on International Language Resources and Evaluation (LREC-2010)*, pages 3375–3378, Valletta, Malta.

Lucia Specia, Dhwaj Raj, and Marco Turchi. 2010b. Machine translation evaluation versus quality estimation. *Machine Translation*, 24(1):39–50, March.

A Features List

Here is the whole list of the 31 features we used in our experiments († has been used in the baseline of the shared task organizer):

- † Number of tokens in the source sentence
- † Number of tokens in the target sentence
- † Average token length in source sentence
- English-Spanish IBM 1 scores
- Spanish-English IBM 1 scores
- English-Spanish IBM 1 scores divided by the length of source sentence
- English-Spanish IBM 1 scores divided by the length of target sentence
- Spanish-English IBM 1 scores divided by the length of source sentence
- Spanish-English IBM 1 scores divided by the length of target sentence
- Number of out-of-vocabulary in source sentence
- Number of out-of-vocabulary in target sentence
- Out-of-vocabulary rates in source sentence
- Out-of-vocabulary rates in target sentence
- $\log_{10}$(LM probability of source sentence)
- $\log_{10}$(LM probability of target sentence)
- $\log_{10}$(LM probability of source sentence) divided by the length of source sentence
- $\log_{10}$(LM probability of target sentence) divided by the length of target sentence
- Ratio of functions words in source sentence
- Ratio of functions words in target sentence
- † Number of occurrences of the target word within the target hypothesis (averaged for all words in the hypothesis - type/token ratio)
- † Average number of translations per source word in the sentence (as given by IBM 1 table thresholded so that $\text{prob}(t|s) > 0.2$)
- † Average number of translations per source word in the sentence (as given by IBM 1 table thresholded so that $\text{prob}(t|s) > 0.01$) weighted by the inverse frequency of each word in the source corpus
- † Percentage of unigrams in quartile 1 of frequency (lower frequency words) in a corpus of the source language (SMT training corpus)
- † Percentage of unigrams in quartile 4 of frequency (higher frequency words) in a corpus of the source sentence
- † Percentage of bigrams in quartile 1 of frequency of source words in a corpus of the source language
- † Percentage of bigrams in quartile 4 of frequency of source words in a corpus of the source language
- † Percentage of trigrams in quartile 1 of frequency of source words in a corpus of the source language
- † Percentage of trigrams in quartile 4 of frequency of source words in a corpus of the source language
- † Percentage of unigrams in the source sentence seen in a corpus (SMT training corpus)
- † Number of punctuation marks in the source sentence
- † Number of punctuation marks in the target sentence

Combining Quality Prediction and System Selection for Improved Automatic Translation Output

Radu Soricut
SDL Language Weaver
6060 Center Drive, Suite 150
Los Angeles, CA 90045
rsoricut@sdl.com

Sushant Narsale*
Google Inc
1600 Amphitheatre Parkway
Mountain View, CA 94043
snarsale@google.com

Abstract

This paper presents techniques for reference-free, automatic prediction of Machine Translation output quality at both sentence- and document-level. In addition to helping with document-level quality estimation, sentence-level predictions are used for system selection, improving the quality of the output translations. We present three system selection techniques and perform evaluations that quantify the gains across multiple domains and language pairs.

1 Introduction

Aside from improving the performance of core-translation models, there additionally exist two orthogonal approaches via which fully-automatic translations can achieve increased acceptance and better integration in real-world use cases. These two approaches are: improved translation accuracy via system combination (Rosti et al., 2008; Karakos et al., 2008; Hildebrand and Vogel, 2008), and automatic quality-estimation techniques used as an additional layer on top of MT systems, which present the user only with translations that are predicted as being accurate (Soricut and Echihabi, 2010; Specia, 2011).

In this paper, we describe new contributions to both these approaches. First, we present a novel and superior technique for performing quality estimation at document level. We achieve this by changing the granularity of the prediction mechanism from document-level (Soricut and Echihabi, 2010) to sentence-level, and predicting BLEU scores via directly modeling the sufficient statistics for BLEU computation. A document-level score is then recreated based on the predicted sentence-level sufficient statistics. A second contribution is related to system combination (or, to be more precise, system selection). This is an intended side-effect of the granularity change: since the sentence-level statistics allow us to make quality predictions at sentence level, we can use these predictions to perform system combination by selecting among various sentence-level translations produced by different MT systems. That is, instead of presenting the user with a document with sentences translated entirely by a single system, we can present documents for which, say, 60% of the sentences were translated by system A, and 40% were translated by system B. We contribute a novel set of features and several techniques for choosing between competing machine translation outputs. The evaluation results show better output quality, across multiple domains and language pairs.

2 Related Work

Several approaches to reference-free automatic MT quality assessment have been proposed, using classification (Kulesza and Shieber, 2004), regression (Albrecht and Hwa, 2007), and ranking (Ye et al., 2007; Duh, 2008). The focus of these approaches is on system performance evaluation, as they use a constant test set and measure various MT systems against it.

In contrast, we are interested in evaluating the quality of the translations themselves, while treat-

*Research was completed before the author started in his current role at Google Inc. The opinions stated are his own and not of Google Inc.

ing the MT components as constants. In this respect, the goal is more related to the area of confidence estimation for MT (Blatz et al., 2004). Confidence estimation is usually concerned with identifying words/phrases for which one can be confident in the quality of the translation. A sentence-level approach to quality estimation is taken on the classification-based work of Gamon et al. (2005) and regression-based work of Specia et al. (2009).

Our approach to quality estimation focuses on both sentence-level and document-level estimation. We improve on the quality estimation technique that is proposed for document-level estimation in (Soricut and Echihabi, 2010). Furthermore, we exploit the availability of multiple translation hypotheses to perform system combination. Our system combination methods are based on generic Machine Learning techniques, applied on 1-best output strings. In contrast, most of the approaches to MT system combination combine N-best lists from multiple MT systems via confusion network decoding (Karakos et al., 2008; Rosti et al., 2008). The closest system combination approach to our work is (Hildebrand and Vogel, 2008), where an ensemble of hypotheses is generated by combining N-best lists from all the participating systems, and a log-linear model is trained to select the best translation from all the possible candidates.

In our work, we show that it is possible to gain significant translation quality by taking advantage of only two participating systems. This makes the system-combination proposition much more palatable in real production deployment scenarios for Machine Translation, as opposed to pure research scenarios as the ones used in the previous NIST and DARPA/GALE MT efforts (Olive et al., 2011). As our evaluations show, the two participating systems can be at very similar performance levels, and yet a system-selection procedure using Machine Learning techniques can achieve significant translation improvements in quality. In addition, in a scenario where quality estimation needs to happen as a requirement for MT integration in large applications, having two translation systems producing translations for the same inputs is part of the deployment set-up (Soricut and Echihabi, 2010). The improvement in overall translation quality comes in these cases at near-zero cost.

3 Sentence-level Quality Predictions

The requirement for document-level quality estimation comes from the need to present a fully-automated translation solution, in which translated documents are either good enough to be directly published (or otherwise must undergo, say, a human-driven post-processing pipeline). In the proposal of Soricut and Echihabi (2010), regression models predict BLEU-like scores for each document, based on document-level features.

However, even if the predicted value is at document-level, the actual feature computation and model prediction does not necessarily need to happen at document-level. It is one of the goals of this work to determine if the models of prediction work better at a coarser granularity (such as document level) or finer granularity (such as sentence-level).

We describe here a mechanism for predicting BLEU scores at sentence level, and then combining these scores into document-level scores. To make explicit our prediction mechanism, we present here in detail the formula for computing BLEU scores (Papineni et al., 2002). First, n-gram precision scores P_n are computed as follows:

$$P_n = \frac{\sum_{C \in Candidates} \sum_{n\text{-gram} \in C} Count_{clip}(n\text{-gram})}{\sum_{C \in Candidates} \sum_{n\text{-gram} \in C} Count(n\text{-gram})} \quad (1)$$

where $Count_{clip}(n\text{-gram})$ is the maximum number of n-grams co-occurring in a candidate translation and a reference translation, and $Count(n\text{-gram})$ is the number of n-grams in the candidate translation. To prevent very short translations that try to maximize their precision scores, BLEU adds a brevity penalty, BP, to the formula:

$$BP = \begin{cases} 1 & \text{if } |c| > |r| \\ e^{(1-|r|/|c|)} & \text{if } |c| \le |r| \end{cases} \quad (2)$$

where $|c|$ is the length of the candidate translation and $|r|$ is the length of the reference translation. The BLEU formula is then written as follows:

$$BLEU = BP \cdot exp(\sum_{n=1}^{N} w_n \log p_n) \quad (3)$$

where the weighting factors w_n are set to $1/N$, for all $1 \le n \le 4$.

3.1 The learning method

The results we report in this section are obtained using the freely-available Weka engine. [1] For both sentence-level and document-level quality prediction, we report all the results using Weka implementation of M5P regression trees (weka.classifiers.trees.M5P).

We use the components of the BLEU score (Equations 1 and 2) to train fine-granularity M5P models using our set of features (Section 3.2), for a total of five individual regression-tree models (four for the sentence-level precision scores $P_n, 1 \leq n \leq 4$ factors, and one for the BP factor). The numbers produced individually by our models are then combined using the BLEU equation 3 into a sentence-level BLEU score. The sentence-level predicted BLEU scores play an important role in our system combination mechanism (see Section 4).

At the same time, we sum up the sufficient statistics for the sentence-level precision scores P_n (Equation 1) over all the sentences in a document, thus obtaining document-level precision scores. A document-level BP score (Equation 2) is similarly obtained by summing over all sentences. Finally, we plug the predicted document-level P_n and BP scores in the BLEU formula (Equation 3) and arrive at a document-level predicted BLEU score.

3.2 The features

Most of the features we use in this work are not internal features of the MT system, but rather derived starting from input/output strings. Therefore, they can be applied for a large variety of MT approaches, from statistical-based to rule-based approaches. The features we use can be divided into text-based, language-model–based, pseudo-reference–based, example-based, and training-data–based feature types (these latter features assume that the engine is statistical and one has access to the training data). These feature types can be computed both on the source-side (MT input) and on the target-side (MT output).

Text-based features

These features compute the length of the input in terms of (tokenized) number of words. The source-side text feature is computed on the input string, while the target-side text feature is computed to the output translation string. These two features are useful in modeling the relationship between the number of words in the input and output and the expected BLEU score for these sizes.

Language-model–based features

These features are among the ones that were first proposed as possible differentiators between good and bad translations (Gamon et al., 2005). They are a measure of how likely a collection of strings is under a language model trained on monolingual data (either on the source or target side).

The language-model–based feature values we use here are computed as perplexity numbers using a 5-gram language model trained on the MT training set. This can be achieved, for instance, by using the publicly-available SRILM toolkit [2]. These two features are useful in modeling the relationship between the likelihood of a string (or set of strings) under an n-gram language model and the expected BLEU score for that input/output pair.

Pseudo-reference–based features

Previous work has shown that, in the absence of human-produced references, automatically-produced ones are still helpful in differentiating between good and bad translations (Albrecht and Hwa, 2008). When computed on the target side, this type of features requires one (or possibly more) secondary MT system(s), used to generate translations starting from the same input. These pseudo-references are useful in gauging translation convergence, using BLEU scores as feature values. In intuitive terms, their usefulness can be summarized as follows: "if system X produced a translation A and system Y produced a translation B starting from the same input, and A and B are similar, then A is probably a good translation".

An important property here is that systems X and Y need to be as different as possible from each other. This property ensures that a convergence on similar translations is not just an artifact of the systems sharing the same translation model/resources, but a true indication that the translations converge. The secondary systems we use in this work are

[1] Weka software at http://www.cs.waikato.ac.nz/ml/weka/.

[2] Available at www-speech.sri.com/projects/srilm.

still phrase-based, but equipped with linguistically-oriented modules similar with the ones proposed in (Collins et al., 2005; Xu et al., 2009). Our experiments indicate that this single feature is one of the most powerful ones in terms of its predictive power.

Example-based features

For example-based features, we use a development set of parallel sentences, for which we produce translations and compute sentence-level BLEU scores. We set aside the top BLEU scoring sentences and bottom BLEU scoring sentences. These sets are used as positive examples (with better-than-average BLEU) and negative examples (with worse-than-average BLEU), respectively. We define a positive-example–based feature function as a geometric mean of 1-to-4–gram precision scores (i.e., the BLEU equation 3 with the BP term set to 1) between a string (on either source or target side) and the positive examples used as references. That is, we compute precision scores against all the positive examples at the same time, similar with how multiple references are used to increase the precision of the BLEU metric. (The negative-example–based features are defined in an analogous way.) The set of positive and negative examples is a fixed set that is used in the same manner both at training-time (to compute the example-based feature values for the training examples) and at test-time (to compute the example-based feature values for the test examples).

The intuition behind these features can be summarized as follows: "if system X translated A well/poorly, and A and B are similar, then system X probably translates B well/poorly". The total number of features on this type is 4 (2 for positive examples against source/target strings, 2 for negative examples against source/target strings).

Training-data–based features

If the system for which we make the predictions is trained on a parallel corpus, the data in this corpus can be exploited towards assessing translation quality (Specia et al., 2009; Soricut and Echihabi, 2010; Specia, 2011). In our context, the documents that make up this corpus can be used in a fashion similar with the positive examples. One type of training-data–based features operates by computing the number of out-of-vocabulary (OOV) tokens with respect to the training data (on source side).

A more powerful type of training-data–based features operates by computing a geometric mean of 1-to-4–gram precision score between a string (source or target side) and the training-data strings used as references. Intuitively, these features assess the coverage of the candidate strings with respect to the training data: "if the n-grams of input string A are well covered by the source-side of the training data, then the translation of A is probably good" (on the source side); "if the n-grams in the output translation B are well covered by the target-side of the parallel training data, then B is probably a good translation" (on the target side). The total number of features on this type is 3 (1 for the OOV counts, and 2 for the source/target-side n-gram coverage).

Given the described 12 feature functions, the training for our five M5P prediction models is done using the feature-function values at sentence-level, and associating these values with reference labels that are automatically-produced from parallel-text using the sufficient-statistics of the BLEU score (Equations 1 and 2).

3.3 Metrics for Quality Prediction Performance

The metrics we use here are designed to answer the following question: how well can we automatically separate better translations from worse translations (in the absence of human-produced references)?

A first metric we use is Ranking Accuracy (rAcc), see (Gunawardana and Shani, 2009; Soricut and Echihabi, 2010). In the general case, it measures how well N elements are assigned into n quantiles as a result of a ranking procedure. The formula is:

$$\text{rAcc}[n] = \text{Avg}_{i=1}^{n} \frac{\text{TP}_i}{\frac{N}{n}} = \frac{1}{N} \times \sum_{i=1}^{n} \text{TP}_i$$

where TP_i (True-Positive$_i$) is the number of correctly-assigned documents in quantile i. Intuitively, this formula is an average of the ratio of elements correctly assigned in each quantile. For simplicity, we present here results using only 2 quantiles ($n = 2$), which effectively makes the rAcc[2] metric equivalent with binary classification accuracy when the two sets are required to have equal size. That is, we measure the accuracy of placing the 50%

	Training	BLEU		Ranking	rAcc[2]		DeltaAvg[2]	
	Size	Sys1	Sys2	Test Size	Doc	Sent	Doc	Sent
WMT09 Hungarian-English	26 Mw	26.9	26.9	510 Kw	88%	89%	+8.3	+8.4
Travel English-French	30 Mw	32.3	34.6	282 Kw	77%	80%	+9.1	+10.1
Travel English-German	44 Mw	40.6	43.4	186 Kw	74%	79%	+9.8	+11.7
HiTech English-French	0.4 Mw	44.1	44.7	69 Kw	75%	77%	+4.4	+6.0
HiTech English-Korean	16 Mw	37.4	36.1	80 Kw	78%	79%	+9.3	+10.0

Table 1: MT system performance and ranking performance using BLEU prediction at Doc- and Sent-level.

best-translated documents (as measured by BLEU against human reference) in the top 50% of ranked documents. Note that a random assignment gives a performance lower bound of 50% accuracy.

A second metric we use here is the DeltaAvg metric (Callison-Burch et al., 2012). The goal of the DeltaAvg metric is to measure how valuable a proposed ranking (hypothesis) is from the perspective of an extrinsic metric associated with the test entries (in our case, the BLEU scores). The following notations are used: for a given entry sentence s, $V(s)$ represents the function that associates an extrinsic value to that entry; we extend this notation to a set S, with $V(S)$ representing the average of all $V(s), s \in S$. Intuitively, $V(S)$ is a quantitative measure of the "quality" of the set S, as induced by the extrinsic values associated with the entries in S. For a set of ranked entries S and a parameter n, we denote by S_1 the first quantile of set S (the highest-ranked entries), S_2 the second quantile, and so on, for n quantiles of equal sizes.[3] We also use the notation $S_{i,j} = \bigcup_{k=i}^{j} S_k$. Using these notations, the metric is defined as:

$$\text{DeltaAvg}_V[n] = \frac{\sum_{k=1}^{n-1} V(S_{1,k})}{n-1} - V(S) \quad (4)$$

When the valuation function V is clear from the context, we write DeltaAvg$[n]$ for DeltaAvg$_V[n]$. The parameter n represents the number of quantiles we want to split the set S into. For simplicity, we consider there only the case for $n = 2$, which gives DeltaAvg[2] = $V(S_1) - V(S)$. This measures the difference between the quality of the top quantile (top half) S_1 and the overall quality (represented by $V(S)$). For the results presented here, the valuation function V is taken to be the BLEU function (Equation 3).

[3]If the size $|S|$ is not divisible by n, then the last quantile S_n is assumed to contain the rest of the entries.

3.4 Experimental Results

We measure the impact in ranking accuracy using a variety of European and Asian language pairs, using parallel data from various domains. One domain we use is the publicly available WMT09 data (Koehn and Haddow, 2009), a combination of European parliament and news data. Another domain, called Travel, consists of user-generated reviews and descriptions; and a third domain, called HiTech, consists of parallel data from customer support for the high-tech industry. Using these parallel data sets, we train statistical phrase-based MT system similar to (Och and Ney, 2004) as primary systems (Sys1). As secondary systems (Sys2) we use phrase-based systems equipped with linguistically-oriented modules similar with the ones proposed in (Collins et al., 2005; Xu et al., 2009). Table 1 lists the size of the parallel training data on which the MT systems were trained in the first column, and BLEU scores for the primary and secondary systems on held-out 1000-sentence test sets in the next two columns.

The training material for the regression-tree models consists of 1000-document held-out sets. (For parallel data for which we do not have document boundaries, we simply simulate document boundaries after every 10 consecutive sentences.) Similarly, the Ranking test sets we use consist of 1000-document held-out sets (see column 4 in Table 1 for size). In the last four columns of Table 1, we show the results for ranking the translations produced by the primary MT system (Sys1). We measure the ranking performance for the two granularity cases. The one labeled as "Doc" is an implementation of the work described in (Soricut and Echihabi, 2010), where the BLEU prediction is done using document-level feature values and models. The one labeled as "Sent" is the novel one proposed in this paper, where the BLEU prediction is done using sentence-level feature values and models, which are then aggregated into document-level BLEU scores.

Both rAcc[2] and DeltaAvg[2] numbers support the choice of making document-level BLEU prediction at a finer, sentence-based granularity level. For Travel English-French, for instance, the accuracy of the ranking improves from 77% to 80%. To put some intuition behind these numbers, it means that 4 out of every 5 sentences that the ranker places in the top 50% do belong there. At the same time, the DeltaAvg[2] numbers for Travel English-French indicate that the translation quality of the top 50% of the 1000 Ranking Test documents exceeds by 10.1 BLEU points the overall quality of the translations (up from 9.1 BLEU points for the document-level prediction). This large gap in the BLEU score of the top 50% ranked sentences and the overall-corpus BLEU indicates that these top-ranked translations are indeed of much better quality (closer to the human-produced references). The same large numbers are measured on the WMT09 data for Hungarian-English. This is a set for which it is hard to obtain significant improvements via core-model translation improvements. Our quality-estimation method allows one to automatically identify the top 50% of the sentences with 89% accuracy. This set of top 50% sentences also has an overall BLEU score of 35.3, which is better by +8.4 BLEU-points compared to the overall BLEU score of 26.9 (we only show the base overall BLEU score and the BLEU-point gain in Table 2 to avoid displaying redundant information).

4 System Combination at Sentence Level

Since we produce two translations for every input sentence for the purpose of quality estimation, we exploit the availability of these competing hypotheses in order to choose the best one. In this section we describe three system combination schemes that choose between the output of the primary and secondary MT systems.

4.1 System Combination using Regression

This combination scheme makes use of the regression-based sentence-level BLEU prediction mechanism described in Section 3. It requires that we also train and use an additional BLEU prediction mechanism for which the secondary MT system is now considered primary, and vice-versa. As a consequence, we can predict a sentence-level BLEU score for each of the two competing hypotheses. We then simply choose the hypothesis with the highest predicted BLEU score.

4.2 System Combination using Ranking

This approach is based on ranking the candidate translations and then selecting the highest-ranked translation as the final output. To this end we use SVM-rank (Joachims, 1999), a ranking algorithm built on SVM. We use SVM-rank with a linear kernel and the same feature set as the regression-based method (we make the observation here that only the target-based features have discriminative power in this context).

4.3 System Combination using Classification

In this approach, we model the problem of selecting the best output from the two candidate translations into a binary classification problem. We use the same feature set as before for each candidate translation (again, only the target-based features have discriminative power in this context).

The final feature vectors are obtained by subtracting the values of the primary-system feature vector from the values of the secondary-system feature vector. The binary classifier is trained to predict "0" if the primary-system is better, and "1" if the secondary-system is better.

4.4 Experimental Results

In Table 2, we summarize the results for the three system combination techniques discussed before across our domains (WMT09, Travel, and Hi-Tech). To get an upper bound on the performance of these system combination techniques, we also compute an oracle function which selects the translation with highest BLEU score computed against human-produced references.

The results in Table 2 indicate that the BLEU improvements obtained by our system combina-

	BLEU		Oracle	Regression	Rank	Classify
	Sys1	Sys2				
WMT09 Hungarian-English	26.9	26.9	30.7(+3.8)	29.0(**+2.1**)	29.0(**+2.1**)	28.9(**+2.0**)
Travel English-French	32.3	34.6	38.7(+3.9)	36.2(**+1.6**)	36.0(**+1.4**)	35.7(+1.1)
Travel English-German	40.6	43.4	47.2(+3.8)	44.5(+1.1)	44.0(+0.6)	44.9(**+1.5**)
HiTech English-French	44.1	44.7	49.8(+5.1)	46.1(+1.4)	46.3(**+1.7**)	45.3(+0.6)
HiTech English-Korean	37.4	36.1	42.2(+4.8)	39.4(**+2.0**)	39.1(+1.7)	38.8(+1.4)

Table 2: BLEU scores for the proposed system combination techniques across domains and language pairs.

	Travel Eng-Fra			Hi-Tech Eng-Fra		
	Sys1	Sys2	KL	Sys1	Sy2	KL
BLEU score	32.3	34.6	-	44.1	44.7	-
Oracle distr.	34.9%	65.1%	0.00	34.5%	65.5%	0.00
Regression distr.	**31.2%**	**68.9%**	**0.68**	**32.3%**	**67.7%**	**0.11**
Rank distr.	43.4%	56.6%	1.92	47.0%	53.0%	3.31
Classify distr.	47.4%	52.7%	3.78	63.9%	36.1%	17.88

Table 3: Distribution of sentences selected from the participating system for Eng-Fra, across domains (Travel and Hi-Tech).

tion techniques are significant. For instance, both the Regression-based system combination and the Ranking-based system combination achieve a BLEU score of 29.0 on the WMT09 Hungarian-English test set, an increase of +2.1 BLEU points. In the case of Travel English-French, an increase of +1.6 BLEU points is obtained by the Regression-based system combination, in spite of the fact that one of the systems is measured to be 2.3 BLEU points lower in translation accuracy. Increases in the range of +1.5-2.0 BLEU points are obtained across all the experimental conditions that we tried: three different domains, various language pairs (both in and out of English), and various training data sizes (from 0.4Mw to 40Mw).

Since our system-combination methods chose one system translation over another system translation, we can also measure the distribution of choices made between the two participating systems. These bimodal distributions can help us gauge the performance of various methods, when compared against the BLEU Oracle distribution.

In Table 3, we report the percentages of sentences selected from each system in the oracle combination and each of the described system combination methods. We also report the Kullback-Liebler divergence (KL) between the BLEU Oracle distribution and the distribution induced by each of the system combination methods. The results indicate that, for both English-French cases that we considered (in the Travel and HiTech domains), the choice distribution of the Regression-based system combination method is much closer to the oracle distribution (KL of 0.68 and 0.11, respectively), compared to the other two methods. Note that this does not necessarily correlate with the evaluation based on overall BLEU score of the system-combination methods (Table 2). For instance, for HiTech English-French the best BLEU improvement is obtained by the Rank-based method with +1.7 BLEU points, but the KL divergence score of 3.31 is higher than the one for the Regression-based method (KL score of 0.11). Nevertheless, the choice distributions are an important factor in judging the performance of a given system selection method.

5 Conclusions

Document-level quality estimation is an important component for building fully-automated translation solutions where the translated documents are directly published, without the need for human intervention. Such approaches are the only possible solution to mitigate the imperfection of current MT technology and the need to translate large volumes of data on a continuous basis.

We show in this paper that sentence-level predictions, when aggregated to document-level predictions, outperform previously-proposed document-level quality estimation algorithms. In addition to that, these finer-granularity, sentence-level predictions can be used as part of a system selection scheme. The three alternative system selection techniques we describe here are intuitive, computationally cheap, and bring significant BLEU gains across multiple domains and language pairs. The finding that the regression-based system selection technique performs as well (or sometimes better) compared to the discriminative methods fits well with the overall theme of using two systems for both improved quality estimation and improved MT performance.

References

Joshua Albrecht and Rebecca Hwa. 2007. Regression for sentence-level MT evaluation with pseudo references. In *Proceedings of ACL*.

Joshua Albrecht and Rebecca Hwa. 2008. The role of pseudo references in MT evaluation. In *Proceedings of ACL*.

John Blatz, Erin Fitzgerald, George Foster, Simona Gandrabur, Cyril Gouette, Alex Kulesza, Alberto Sanchis, and Nicola Ueffing. 2004. Confidence estimation for machine translation. In *Proceedings of COLING*.

Chris Callison-Burch, Philipp Koehn, Christof Monz, Matt Post, Radu Soricut, and Lucia Specia. 2012. Findings of the 2012 workshop on statistical machine translation. In *Proceedings of the Seventh Workshop on Statistical Machine Translation*, Montreal, Canada, June. Association for Computational Linguistics.

Michael Collins, Philipp Koehn, and Ivona Kucerova. 2005. Clause restructuring for statistical machine translation. In *Proceedings of ACL*.

Kevin Duh. 2008. Ranking vs. regression in machine translation evaluation. In *Proceedings of the ACL Third Workshop on Statistical Machine Translation*.

Michael Gamon, Anthony Aue, and Martine Smets. 2005. Sentence-level MT evaluation without reference translations: Beyond language modeling. In *Proceedings of EAMT*.

Asela Gunawardana and Guy Shani. 2009. A survey of accuracy evaluation metrics of recommendation tasks. *Journal of Machine Learning Research*, 10:2935–2962.

Almut Silja Hildebrand and Stephan Vogel. 2008. Combination of machine translation systems via hypothesis selection. In *Proceedings of AMTA*.

T. Joachims. 1999. *Making large-Scale SVM Learning Practical*. M.I.T. Press.

Damianos Karakos, Jason Eisner, Sanjeev Khudanpur, and Markus Dreyer. 2008. Machine translation system combination using ITG-based alignments. In *Proceedings of ACL*.

Philipp Koehn and Barry Haddow. 2009. Edinburgh's submission to all tracks of the WMT2009 shared task with reordering and speed improvements to Moses. In *Proceedings of EACL Workshop on Statistical Machine Translation*.

Alex Kulesza and Stuart M. Shieber. 2004. A learning approach to improving sentence-level MT evaluation. In *Proceedings of the 10th International Conference on Theoretical and Methodological Issues in Machine Translation*.

Franz Josef Och and Hermann Ney. 2004. The alignment template approach to statistical machine translation. *Computational Linguistics*, 30(4):417–449.

Joseph Olive, Caitlin Christianson, and John McCary, editors. 2011. *Handbook of Natural Language Processing and Machine Translation: DARPA Global Autonomous Language Exploitation*. Springer.

Kishore Papineni, Salim Roukos, Todd Ward, and Wei-Jing Zhu. 2002. BLEU: a method for automatic evaluation of machine translation. In *Proceedings of ACL*.

Antti-Veikko Rosti, Bing Zhang, Spyros Matsoukas, and Richard Schwartz. 2008. Incremental hypothesis alignment for building confusion networks with application to machine translation system combination. In *Proceedings of Third Workshop on Statistical Machine Translation*.

Radu Soricut and Abdessamad Echihabi. 2010. Trustrank: Inducing trust in automatic translations via ranking. In *Proceedings of ACL*.

Lucia Specia, Nicola Cancedda, Marc Dymetman, Marcho Turchi, and Nello Cristianini. 2009. Estimating the sentence-level quality of machine translation. In *Proceedings of EAMT*.

Lucia Specia. 2011. Exploiting objective annotations for measuring translation post-editing effort. In *Proceedings of EAMT*.

Peng Xu, Jaeho Kang, Michael Ringaard, and Franz Och. 2009. Using a dependency parser to improve SMT for Subject-Object-Verb languages. In *Proceedings of ACL*.

Yang Ye, Ming Zhou, and Chin-Yew Lin. 2007. Sentence level machine translation evaluation as a ranking. In *Proceedings of the ACL Second Workshop on Statistical Machine Translation*.

Match without a Referee: Evaluating MT Adequacy without Reference Translations

Yashar Mehdad **Matteo Negri** **Marcello Federico**
Fondazione Bruno Kessler, FBK-irst
Trento , Italy
{mehdad|negri|federico}@fbk.eu

Abstract

We address two challenges for automatic machine translation evaluation: a) avoiding the use of reference translations, and b) focusing on adequacy estimation. From an economic perspective, getting rid of costly hand-crafted reference translations (a) permits to alleviate the main bottleneck in MT evaluation. From a system evaluation perspective, pushing semantics into MT (b) is a necessity in order to complement the shallow methods currently used overcoming their limitations. Casting the problem as a cross-lingual textual entailment application, we experiment with different benchmarks and evaluation settings. Our method shows high correlation with human judgements and good results on all datasets without relying on reference translations.

1 Introduction

While syntactically informed modelling for statistical MT is an active field of research that has recently gained major attention from the MT community, work on integrating semantic models of adequacy into MT is still at preliminary stages. This situation holds not only for system development (most current methods disregard semantic information, in favour of statistical models of words distribution), but also for system evaluation. To realize its full potential, however, MT is now in the need of semantic-aware techniques, capable of complementing frequency counts with meaning representations.

In order to integrate semantics more deeply into MT technology, in this paper we focus on the evaluation dimension. Restricting our investigation to some of the more pressing issues emerging from this area of research, we provide two main contributions.

1. An automatic evaluation method that avoids the use of reference translations. Most current metrics are based on comparisons between automatic translations and human references, and reward lexical similarity at the n-gram level (*e.g.* BLEU (Papineni et al., 2002), NIST (Doddington, 2002), METEOR (Banerjee and Lavie, 2005), TER (Snover et al., 2006)). Due to the variability of natural languages in terms of possible ways to express the same meaning, reliable lexical similarity metrics depend on the availability of multiple hand-crafted (costly) realizations of the same source sentence in the target language. Our approach aims to avoid this bottleneck by adapting cross-lingual semantic inference capabilities and judging a translation only given the source sentence.

2. A method for evaluating translation adequacy. Most current solutions do not consistently reward translation adequacy (semantic equivalence between source sentence and target translation). The scarce integration of semantic information in MT, specifically at the multilingual level, led to MT systems that are "illiterate" in terms of semantics and meaning. Moreover, current metrics are often difficult to interpret. In contrast, our method targets the adequacy dimension, producing easily interpretable results (*e.g.* judgements in a 4-point scale).

Our approach builds on recent advances in cross-lingual textual entailment (CLTE) recognition, which provides a natural framework to address MT adequacy evaluation. In particular, we approach the problem as an application of CLTE where bidirectional entailment between source and target is considered as evidence of translation adequacy. Besides avoiding the use of references, the proposed solution differs from most previous methods which typically rely on surface-level features, often extracted from the source or the target sentence taken in isolation. Although some of these features might correlate well with adequacy, they capture semantic equivalence only indirectly, and at the level of a probabilistic prediction. Focusing on a combination of surface, syntactic and semantic features, extracted from *both* source and target (*e.g.* "source-target length ratio", "dependency relations in common"), our approach leads to informed adequacy judgements derived from the actual observation of a translation given the source sentence.

2 Background

Some recent works proposed metrics able to approximately assess meaning equivalence between candidate and reference translations. Among these, (Giménez and Màrquez, 2007) proposed a heterogeneous set comprising overlapping and matching metrics, compiled from a rich set of variants at five different linguistic levels: lexical, shallow-syntactic, syntactic, shallow-semantic and semantic. More similar to our approach, (Padó et al., 2009) proposed semantic adequacy metrics that exploit feature representations motivated by Textual Entailment (TE). Both metrics, however, highly depend on the availability of multiple reference translations.

Early attempts to avoid reference translations addressed *quality estimation* (QE) by means of large numbers of source, target, and system-dependent features to discriminate between "good" and "bad" translations (Blatz et al., 2004; Quirk, 2004). More recently (Specia et al., 2010b; Specia and Farzindar, 2010; Specia, 2011) conducted a series of experiments using features designed to estimate translation post-editing effort (in terms of volume and time) as an indicator of MT output quality. Good results in QE have been achieved by adding linguistic information such as shallow parsing, POS tags (Xiong et al., 2010), or dependency relations (Bach et al., 2011; Avramidis et al., 2011) as features. However, in general these approaches do not distinguish between fluency (*i.e.* syntactic correctness of the output translation) and adequacy, and mostly rely on fluency-oriented features (*e.g.* "number of punctuation marks"). As a result, a simple surface form variation is given the same importance of a content word variation that changes the meaning of the sentence. To the best of our knowledge, only (Specia et al., 2011) proposed an approach to frame MT evaluation as an adequacy estimation problem. However, their method still includes many features which are not focused on adequacy, and often look either at the source or at the target in isolation (see for instance "source complexity" and "target fluency" features). Moreover, the actual contribution of the adequacy features used is not always evident and, for some testing conditions, marginal.

Our approach to adequacy evaluation builds on and extends the above mentioned works. Similarly to (Padó et al., 2009) we rely on the notion of textual entailment, but we cast it as a cross-lingual problem in order to bypass the need of reference translations. Similarly to (Blatz et al., 2004; Quirk, 2004), we try to discriminate between "good" and "bad" translations, but we focus on adequacy. To this aim, like (Xiong et al., 2010; Bach et al., 2011; Avramidis et al., 2011; Specia et al., 2010b; Specia et al., 2011) we rely on a large number of features, but focusing on source-target dependent ones, aiming at informed adequacy evaluation of a translation given the source instead of a more generic quality assessment based on surface features.

3 CLTE for adequacy evaluation

We address adequacy evaluation by adapting cross-lingual textual entailment recognition as a way to measure to what extent a source sentence and its automatic translation are semantically similar. CLTE has been proposed by (Mehdad et al., 2010) as an extension of textual entailment (Dagan and Glickman, 2004) that consists in deciding, given a text T and a hypothesis H *in different languages*, if the meaning of H can be inferred from the meaning of T.

The main motivation in approaching adequacy evaluation using CLTE is that an adequate translation and the source text should convey the same meaning. In terms of entailment, this means that an adequate MT output and the source sentence should entail each other (bi-directional entailment). Losing or altering part of the meaning conveyed by the source sentence (*i.e.* having more, or different information in one of the two sides) will change the entailment direction and, consequently, the adequacy judgement. Framed in this way, CLTE-based adequacy evaluation methods can be designed to distinguish meaning-preserving variations from true divergence, regardless of reference translations.

Similarly to many monolingual TE approaches, CLTE solutions proposed so far adopt supervised learning methods, with features that measure to what extent the hypotheses can be mapped into the texts. The underlying assumption is that the probability of entailment is proportional to the number of words in H that can be mapped to words in T (Mehdad et al., 2011). Such mapping can be carried out at different word representation levels (*e.g.* tokens, lemmas, stems), possibly with the support of lexical knowledge in order to cross the language barrier between T and H (*e.g.* dictionaries, phrase tables).

Under the same assumption, since in the adequacy evaluation framework the entailment relation should hold in both directions, the mapping is performed both from the source to the target and vice-versa, building on features extracted from both sentences. Moreover, to improve over previous CLTE methods and boost MT adequacy evaluation performance, we explore the joint contribution of a number of lexical, syntactic and semantic features (Mehdad et al., 2012).

Concerning the features used, it's worth observing that the cost of implementing our approach (in terms of required resources and linguistic processors), and the need of reference translations are intrinsically different bottlenecks for MT. While the limited availability of processing tools for some language pairs is a "temporary" bottleneck, the acquisition of multiple references is a "permanent" one. The former cost is reducing over time due to the progress in NLP research; the latter represents a fixed cost that has to be eliminated. Similar considerations hold regarding the need of annotated data to develop our supervised learning approach. Concerning this, the cost of labelling source-target pairs with adequacy judgments is significantly lower compared to the creation of multiple references.

3.1 Features

In order to learn models for classification and regression we used the Support Vector Machine (SVM) algorithms implemented in the LIBSVM package (Chang and Lin, 2011) with a linear kernel and default parameters setting. Aiming at objective adequacy evaluation, our method limits the recourse to MT system-dependent features to reduce the bias of evaluating MT technology with its own core methods. The experiments described in the following sections are carried out on publicly available English-Spanish datasets, exploring the potential of a combination of surface, syntactic and semantic features. Language-dependent ones are extracted by exploiting processing tools for the two languages (part-of-speech taggers, dependency parsers and named entity recognizers), most of which are available for many languages.

Our feature set can be described as follows:

Surface Form (F) features consider the number of words, punctuation marks and non-word markers (*e.g.* quotations and brackets) in source and target, as well as their ratios (source/target and target/source), and the number of out of vocabulary terms encountered.

Shallow Syntactic (SSyn) features consider the number and ratios of common part-of-speech (POS) tags in source and target. Since the list of valid POS tags varies for different languages, we mapped English and Spanish tags into a common list using the FreeLing tagger (Carreras et al., 2004).

Syntactic (Syn) features consider the number and ratios of dependency roles common to source and target. To create a unique list of roles, we used the DepPattern (Otero and Lopez, 2011) package, which provides English and Spanish dependency parsers.

Phrase Table (PT) matching features are calculated as in (Mehdad et al., 2011), with a phrasal matching algorithm that takes advantage of a lexical phrase table extracted from a bilingual parallel corpus. The algorithm determines the number of phrases in the source (1 to 5-grams, at the level of tokens, lemmas and stems) that can be mapped into target word sequences, and vice-versa. To build our English-Spanish phrase table, we used the Europarl, News Commentary and United Nations Spanish-English parallel corpora. After tokenization, the Giza++ (Och and Ney, 2000) and the Moses toolkit (Koehn et al., 2007) were respectively used to align the corpora and extract the phrase table. Although the phrase table was generated using MT technology, its use to compute our features is still compatible with a system-independent approach since the extraction is carried out without tuning the process towards any particular task. Moreover, our phrase matching algorithm integrates matches from overlapping n-grams of different size and nature (tokens, lemmas and stems) which current MT decoding algorithms cannot explore for complexity reasons.

Dependency Relation (DR) matching features target the increase of CLTE precision by adding syntactic constraints to the matching process. These features capture similarities between dependency relations, combining syntactic and lexical levels. We define a dependency relation as a triple that connects pairs of words through a grammatical relation. In a valid match, while the relation has to be the same, the connected words can be either the same, or semantically equivalent terms in the two languages. For example, *"nsubj (loves, John)"* can match *"nsubj (ama, John)"* and *"nsubj (quiere, John)"* but not *"dobj (quiere, John)"*. Term matching is carried out by means of a bilingual dictionary extracted from parallel corpora during PT creation. Given the dependency tree representations of source and target produced with DepPattern, for each grammatical relation r we calculate two DR matching scores as the number of matching occurrences of r in both source and target, respectively normalized by: *i)* the number of occurrences of r in the source, and *ii)* the number of occurrences of r in the target.

Semantic Phrase Table (SPT) matching features represent a novel way to leverage the integration of semantics and MT-derived techniques. Semantically enhanced phrase tables are used as a recall-oriented complement to the lexical PT matching features. SPTs are extracted from the same parallel corpora used to build lexical PTs, augmented with shallow semantic labels. To this aim, we first annotate the corpora with the FreeLing named-entity tagger, replacing named entities with general semantic labels chosen from a coarse-grained taxonomy (person, location, organization, date and numeric expression). Then, we combine the sequences of unique labels into one single token of the same label. Finally, we extract the semantic phrase table from the augmented corpora in the same way mentioned above. The resulting SPTs are used to map phrases between NE-annotated source-target pairs, similar to PT matching. SPTs offer three main advantages: *i)* semantic tags allow to match tokens that do not occur in the original parallel corpora used to extract the phrase table, *ii)* SPT entries are often short generalizations of longer original phrases, so the matching process can benefit from the increased probability of mapping higher order n-grams (*i.e.* those providing more contextual information), and *iii)* their smaller size has positive impact on system's efficiency, due to the considerable search space reduction.

4 Experiments and results

4.1 Datasets

Datasets with manual evaluation of MT output have been made available through a number of shared evaluation tasks. However, most of these datasets are not specifically annotated for adequacy measurement purposes, and the available adequacy judgements are limited to few hundred sentences for some language pairs. Moreover, most datasets are created by comparing reference translations with MT systems' output, disregarding the input sentences. Such judgements are hence biased towards the reference. Furthermore, the inter-annotator agreement is often low (Callison-Burch et al., 2007). In light of these limitations, most of the available datasets are *per se* not fully suitable for adequacy evaluation methods based on supervised learning, nor to provide stable and meaningful results. To partially cope with these problems, our experiments have been carried out over two different datasets:

- **16K:** *16.000* English-Spanish pairs, with Spanish translations produced by multiple MT systems, annotated by professional translators with *quality* scores in a 4-point scale (Specia et al., 2010a).

- **WMT07:** *703* English-Spanish pairs derived from MT systems' output, with explicit *adequacy* judgements on a 5-point scale.

The two datasets present complementary advantages and disadvantages. On the one hand, although it is not annotated to explicitly capture meaning-related aspects of MT output, the quality oriented dataset has the main advantage of being large enough for supervised approaches. Moreover, it should allow to check the effectiveness of our feature set in estimating adequacy as a latent aspect of the more general notion of MT output quality. On the other hand, the smaller dataset is less suitable for supervised learning, but represents an appropriate benchmark for MT adequacy evaluation.

4.2 Adequacy and quality prediction

To experiment with our CLTE-based evaluation method minimizing overfitting, we randomized each dataset 5 times (D1 to D5), and split them into 80% for training and 20% for testing. Using different feature sets, we then trained and tested various regression models over each of the five splits, and computed correlation coefficients between the CLTE model predictions and the human gold standard annotations ([1-4] for quality, and [1-5] for adequacy).

16K quality-based dataset

In Table 1 we compare the Pearson's correlation coefficient of our SVM regression models against the results reported in (Specia et al., 2010b), calculated with the same three common MT evaluation metrics with a single reference: BLEU, TER and Meteor. For the sake of comparison, we also report the average quality correlation (QE) obtained by (Specia et al., 2010b) over the same dataset.[1]

The results show that the integration of syntactic and semantic information allows our adequacy-oriented model to achieve a correlation with human quality judgements that is always significantly higher[2] than the correlation obtained by the MT evaluation metrics used for comparison. As expected a considerable improvement over surface features is achieved by the integration of syntactic information. A further increase, however, is brought by the complementary contribution of SPT (*recall-oriented*, due to the higher coverage of semantics-aware phrase tables with respect to lexical PTs), and DR matching features (*precision-oriented*, due to the syntactic constraints posed to matching text portions). Although they are meant to capture meaning-related aspects of MT output, our features allow to outperform the results obtained by the generic quality-oriented features used by (Specia et al., 2010b), which do not discriminate between adequacy and fluency.[3] When dependency relations and phrase tables (both lexical and semantics-aware) are used in combination, our scores also outperform the average QE score. Finally, looking at the different random splits of the same dataset (D1 to D5), our correlation scores remain substantially stable, proving the robustness of our approach not only for adequacy, but also for quality estimation.

WMT07 adequacy-based dataset

In Table 2 we compare our regression model, obtained in the same way previously described, against three commonly used MT evaluation metrics (Callison-Burch et al., 2007). In this case, the reported results do not show the same consistency over the 5 randomized datasets (D1 to D5). However, it is worth pointing out that: *i)* the small dataset is particularly challenging to train models with higher correlation with humans, *ii)* our aim is checking how far we get using only adequacy-oriented features rather than outperforming BLEU/TER/Meteor at any cost, and *iii)* our results are not far from those achieved by metrics that rely on reference translations. Compared with Meteor, the correlation is even higher proving the effectiveness of the proposed method.

[1] We only show the average results reported in (Specia et al., 2010b), since the distributions of the 16K dataset is different from our randomized distribution.

[2] $p < 0.05$, calculated using the approximate randomization test implemented in (Padó, 2006).

[3] As reported in (Specia et al., 2010b), more than 50% (39 out of 74) of the features used is translation-independent (only source-derived features).

Features	D1	D2	D3	D4	D5	AVG
F	0.2506	0.2578	0.2436	0.2527	0.2443	0.25
SSyn+Syn	0.4387	0.4114	0.3994	0.4114	0.3793	0.41
F+SSyn+Syn	0.4215	0.4398	0.4059	0.4464	0.4255	0.428
F+SSyn+Syn+DR	0.4668	0.4602	0.4386	0.4437	0.4454	**0.451**
F+SSyn+Syn+DR+PT	0.4724	0.4715	0.4852	0.5028	0.4653	**0.48**
F+SSyn+Syn+DR+PT+SPT	0.4967	0.4802	0.4688	0.4894	0.4887	**0.485**
BLEU						0.2268
TER						0.1938
METEOR						0.2713
QE (Specia et al., 2010b)						0.4792

Table 1: Pearson's correlation between SVM regression and human quality annotation over 16K dataset.

Features	D1	D2	D3	D4	D5	AVG
F	0.10	0.03	0.04	0.10	0.14	0.083
SSyn+Syn	0.299	0.351	0.1834	0.2962	0.2417	0.274
F+SSyn+Syn	0.2648	0.2870	0.4061	0.3601	0.1327	0.29
F+SSyn+Syn+DR	0.3196	0.4568	0.2860	0.5057	0.4066	**0.395**
F+SSyn+Syn+DR+PT	0.3254	0.4710	0.3921	0.4599	0.3501	**0.40**
F+SSyn+Syn+DR+PT+SPT	0.3487	0.4032	0.4803	0.4380	0.3929	**0.413**
BLEU						0.466
TER						0.437
METEOR						0.357

Table 2: Pearson's correlation between SVM regression and human adequacy annotation over WMT07.

4.3 Multi-class classification

To further explore the potential of our CLTE-based MT evaluation method, we trained an SVM multi-class classifier to predict the exact adequacy and quality scores assigned by human judges. The evaluation was carried out measuring the accuracy of our models with 10-fold cross validation to minimize overfitting. As a baseline, we calculated the performance of the Majority Class (MjC) classifier proposed in (Specia et al., 2011), which labels all examples with the most frequent class among all classes. The performance improvement over the result obtained by the MjC baseline (Δ) has been calculated to assess the contribution of different feature sets.

16K quality-based dataset

The accuracy results reported in Table 3a show that also in this testing condition, syntactic and semantic features improve over surface form ones. Besides that, we observe a steady improvement over the MjC baseline (from 5% to 12%). This demonstrates the effectiveness of our adequacy-based features to predict exact quality scores in a 4-point scale, although this is a more challenging and difficult task than regression and binary classification. Such improvement is even more interesting considering that (Specia et al., 2010b) reported discouraging results with multi-class classification to predict quality scores. Moreover, while they claimed that removing target-independent features (*i.e.* those only looking at the source text) significantly degrades their QE performance, we achieved good results without using any of these features.

WMT07 adequacy-based dataset

As we can observe in Table 3b, all variations of adequacy estimation models significantly outperform the MjC baseline, with improvements rang-

Features	10-fold acc.	Δ
F	42.16%	5.16
Syn+SSyn	46.61%	9.61
F+Syn+SSyn	47.10%	10.10
F+Syn+SSyn+DR	47.26%	10.26
F+Syn+SSyn+DR+PT	48.15%	11.15
F+Syn+SSyn+DR+PT+SPT	**48.74**%	11.74
MjC	37%	-

(a) 16K dataset.

Features	10-fold acc.	Δ
F	50.07%	14.07
Syn+SSyn	54.19%	18.19
F+Syn+SSyn	54.34%	18.34
F+Syn+SSyn+DR	56.47%	20.47
F+Syn+SSyn+DR+PT	56.61%	20.61
F+Syn+SSyn+DR+PT+SPT	**56.75**%	20.75
MjC	36%	-

(b) WMT07 dataset

Table 3: Multi-class classification accuracy of the quality/adequacy scores.

Features	10-fold acc.	Δ
F	65.85%	11.85
Syn+SSyn	69.59%	15.59
F+Syn+SSyn	70.89%	16.89
F+Syn+SSyn+DR	71.39%	17.39
F+Syn+SSyn+DR+PT	71.92%	17.92
F+Syn+SSyn+DR+PT+SPT	**72.21**%	18.21
MjC	54%	-

(a) 16k dataset.

Features	10-fold acc.	Δ
F	83.24%	12.84
Syn+SSyn	83.67%	13.27
F+Syn+SSyn	84.31%	13.91
F+Syn+SSyn+DR	84.86%	14.46
F+Syn+SSyn+DR+PT	84.96%	14.56
F+Syn+SSyn+DR+PT+SPT	**85.20**%	14.80
MjC	70.4%	-

(b) WMT07 dataset.

Table 4: Accuracy of the binary classification into "good" or "adequate", and "bad" or "inadequate".

ing from 14% to 20%. Interestingly, although the dataset is small and the number of classes is higher (5-point scale), the improvement and overall results are better than those obtained on the 16K dataset. Such result confirms our hypothesis that adequacy-based features extracted from both source and target perform better on a dataset explicitly annotated with adequacy judgements. In addition, the improvement over the MjC baseline (Δ) of our best model is much higher (20%) than the one reported in (Specia et al., 2011) on adequacy estimation (6%). We are aware that their results are calculated over a dataset for a different language pair (*i.e.* English-Arabic) which brings up more challenges. However, our smaller dataset (700 vs 2580 pairs) and the higher number of classes (5 vs 4) compensate to some extent the difficulty of dealing with English-Arabic pairs.

4.4 Recognizing "good" vs "bad" translations

Last but not least, we considered the traditional scenario for quality and confidence estimation, which is a binary classification of translations into "good" and "bad" or, from the meaning point of view, "adequate" and "inadequate". Adequacy-oriented binary classification has many potential applications in the translation industry, ranging from the design of confidence estimation methods that reward meaning-preserving translations, to the optimization of the translation workflow. For instance, an "adequate" translation can be just post-edited in terms of fluency by a target language native speaker, without having any knowledge of the source language. On the other hand, an "inadequate" translation should be sent to a human translator or to another MT system, in order to reach acceptable adequacy. Effective automatic binary classification has an evident positive impact on such workflow.

16K quality-based dataset

We grouped the quality scores in the 4-point scale into two classes, where scores {1,2} are considered as "bad" or "inadequate", while {3,4} are taken as "good" or "adequate". We carried out learning and classification using different sets of features with 10-fold cross validation. We also compared our accuracy with the MjC baseline, and calculated the improvement of each model (Δ) against it.

The results reported in Table 4a demonstrate that the accuracy of our models is always significantly superior to the MjC baseline. Moreover, also in this case there is a steady improvement using syntactic and semantic features over the results obtained by surface form features. Additionally, it is worth mentioning that the best model improvement over the baseline (Δ) is much higher (about 18%) than the improvement reported in (Specia et al., 2010b) over the same dataset (about 8%), considering the average score obtained with their data distribution. This confirms the effectiveness of our CLTE approach also in classifying "good" and "bad" translations.

WMT07 adequacy-based dataset

We mapped the 5-point scale adequacy scores into two classes, with {1,2,3} judgements assigned to the "inadequate" class, and {4,5} judgements assigned to the "adequate" class. The main motivation for this distribution was to separate the examples in a way that adequate translations are substantially acceptable, while inadequate translations present evident meaning discrepancies with the source.

The results reported in Table 4b show that the accuracy of the binary classifiers to distinguish between "adequate" and "inadequate" classes was significantly superior (up to about 15%) to the MjC baseline. We also notice that surface form features have a significant contribution to deal with the adequacy-oriented dataset, while the gain obtained using syntactic and semantic features (2%) is lower than the improvement observed in the 16K dataset. This might be due to the more unbalanced distribution of the classes which: *i)* leads to a high baseline, and *ii)* together with the small size of the WMT07 dataset, makes supervised learning more challenging. Finally, the improvement of all models (Δ) over the MjC baseline is much higher than the gain reported in (Specia et al., 2011) over their adequacy-oriented dataset (around 2%).

5 Conclusions

In the effort of integrating semantics into MT technology, we focused on automatic MT evaluation, investigating the potential of applying cross-lingual textual entailment techniques for adequacy assessment. The underlying assumption is that MT output adequacy can be determined by verifying that an entailment relation holds from the source to the target, and vice-versa. Within such framework, this paper makes two main contributions.

First, in contrast with most current metrics based on the comparison between automatic translations and multiple references, we avoid the bottleneck represented by the manual creation of such references.

Second, beyond current approaches biased towards fluency or general quality judgements, we tried to isolate the adequacy dimension of the problem, exploring the potential of adequacy-oriented features extracted from the observation of source and target.

To achieve our objectives, we successfully extended previous CLTE methods with a variety of linguistically motivated features. Altogether, such features led to reliable judgements that show high correlation with human evaluation. Coherent results on different datasets and classification schemes demonstrate the effectiveness of the approach and its potential for different applications.

Future works will address both the improvement of our adequacy evaluation method and its integration in SMT for optimization purposes. On one hand, we plan to explore new features capturing other semantic dimensions. A possible direction is to consider topic modelling techniques to measure the relatedness of source and target. Another interesting direction is to investigate the use of Wikipedia entity linking tools to support the mapping between source and target terms. On the other hand, we plan to explore the integration of our model as an error criterion in SMT system training.

Acknowledgments

This work has been partially supported by the CoSyne project (FP7-ICT-4-24853) and T4ME network of excellence (FP7-IST-249119), funded by the European Commission under the 7th Framework Programme. The authors would like to thank Hanna Bechara, Antonio Valerio Miceli Barone and Daniele Pighin for their contributions during the MT Marathon 2011.

References

E. Avramidis, M. Popovic, V. Vilar Torres, and A. Burchardt. 2011. Evaluate with Confidence Estimation: Machine Ranking of Translation Outputs using Grammatical Features. In *Proceedings of the Sixth Workshop on Statistical Machine Translation (WMT '11)*.

N. Bach, F. Huang, and Y. Al-Onaizan. 2011. Goodness: A Method for Measuring Machine Translation Confidence. In *Proceedings of the 49th Annual Meeting of the Association for Computational Linguistics (ACL 2011)*.

S. Banerjee and A. Lavie. 2005. METEOR: An Automatic Metric for MT Evaluation with Improved Correlation with Human Judgments. In *Proceedings of the ACL Workshop on Intrinsic and Extrinsic Evaluation Measures for Machine Translation and/or Summarization*.

J. Blatz, E. Fitzgerald, G. Foster, S. Gandrabur, C. Goutte, A. Kulesza, A. Sanchis, and N. Ueffing. 2004. Confidence Estimation for Machine Translation. In *Proceedings of the 20th international conference on Computational Linguistics (COLING '04)*. Association for Computational Linguistics.

C. Callison-Burch, C. Fordyce, P. Koehn, C. Monz, and J. Schroeder. 2007. (Meta-) Evaluation of Machine Translation. In *Proceedings of the Second Workshop on Statistical Machine Translation (WMT '07)*.

X. Carreras, I. Chao, L. Padró, and M. Padró. 2004. FreeLing: An Open-Source Suite of Language Analyzers. In *Proceedings of the 4th International Conference on Language Resources and Evaluation (LREC'04)*.

C.C. Chang and C.J. Lin. 2011. LIBSVM: A Library for Support Vector Machines. *ACM Transactions on Intelligent Systems and Technology (TIST)*, 2(3).

I. Dagan and O. Glickman. 2004. Probabilistic Textual Entailment: Generic Applied Modeling of Language Variability. In *Proceedings of the PASCAL Workshop of Learning Methods for Text Understanding and Mining*.

G. Doddington. 2002. Automatic Evaluation of Machine Translation Quality Using N-gram Co-Occurrence Statistics. In *Proceedings of the second international conference on Human Language Technology Research*, HLT '02.

J. Giménez and L. Màrquez. 2007. Linguistic Features for Automatic Evaluation of Heterogenous MT Systems. In *Proceedings of the Second Workshop on Statistical Machine Translation (StatMT '07)*.

P. Koehn, H. Hoang, A. Birch, C. Callison-Burch, M. Federico, N. Bertoldi, B. Cowan, W. Shen, C. Moran, R. Zens, C. Dyer, O. Bojar, A. Constantin, and E. Herbst. 2007. Moses: Open Source Toolkit for Statistical Machine Translation. In *Proceedings of the 45th Annual Meeting of the ACL on Interactive Poster and Demonstration Sessions (ACL 2007)*.

Y. Mehdad, M. Negri, and M. Federico. 2010. Towards Cross-Lingual Textual Entailment. In *Proceedings of the 11th Annual Conference of the North American Chapter of the Association for Computational Linguistics (NAACL HLT 2010)*.

Y. Mehdad, M. Negri, and M. Federico. 2011. Using Bilingual Parallel Corpora for Cross-Lingual Textual Entailment. In *Proceedings of the 49th Annual Meeting of the Association for Computational Linguistics: Human Language Technologies (ACL HLT 2011)*.

Y. Mehdad, M. Negri, and M. Federico. 2012. Detecting Semantic Equivalence and Information Disparity in Cross-lingual Documents. In *Proceedings of the ACL'12*.

F.J. Och and H. Ney. 2000. Improved Statistical Alignment Models. In *Proceedings of the 38th Annual Meeting of the Association for Computational Linguistics (ACL 2000)*.

P.G. Otero and I.G. Lopez. 2011. A Grammatical Formalism Based on Patterns of Part-of-Speech Tags. *International journal of corpus linguistics*, 16(1).

S. Padó, M. Galley, D. Jurafsky, and C. D. Manning. 2009. Textual Entailment Features for Machine Translation Evaluation. In *Proceedings of the Fourth Workshop on Statistical Machine Translation (StatMT '09)*.

S. Padó, 2006. *User's guide to `sigf`: Significance testing by approximate randomisation*.

K. Papineni, S. Roukos, T. Ward, and W.J. Zhu. 2002. BLEU: a Method for Automatic Evaluation of Machine Translation (ACL 2002. In *Proceedings of the 40th annual meeting on association for computational linguistics*.

C.B. Quirk. 2004. Training a Sentence-Level Machine Translation Confidence Measure. In *Proceedings of LREC 2004*.

M. Snover, B. Dorr, R. Schwartz, L. Micciulla, and J. Makhoul. 2006. A Study of Translation Edit Rate with Targeted Human Annotation. In *Proceedings of Association for Machine Translation in the Americas (AMTA 2006)*.

L. Specia and A. Farzindar. 2010. Estimating Machine Translation Post-Editing Effort with HTER. In *Proceedings of the AMTA-2010 Workshop, Bringing MT to the User: MT Research and the Translation Industry*.

L. Specia, N. Cancedda, and M. Dymetman. 2010a. A Dataset for Assessing Machine Translation Evaluation Metrics. In *Proceedings of the 7th international conference on Language Resources and Evaluation (LREC10)*.

L. Specia, D. Raj, and M. Turchi. 2010b. Machine Translation Evaluation Versus Quality Estimation. *Machine translation*, 24(1).

L. Specia, N. Hajlaoui, C. Hallett, and W. Aziz. 2011. Predicting Machine Translation Adequacy. In *Proceedings of the 13th Machine Translation Summit (MT-Summit 2011)*.

L. Specia. 2011. Exploiting Objective Annotations for Minimising Translation Post-editing Effort. In *Proceedings of the 15th Conference of the European Association for Machine Translation (EAMT 2011)*.

D. Xiong, M. Zhang, and H. Li. 2010. Error Detection for Statistical Machine Translation Using Linguistic Features. In *Proceedings of the 48th Annual Meeting of the Association for Computational Linguistics (ACL 2010)*. Association for Computational Linguistics.

Comparing human perceptions of post-editing effort with post-editing operations

Maarit Koponen
University of Helsinki, Dept of Modern Languages
PO Box 24
00014 University of Helsinki, Finland
maarit.koponen@helsinki.fi

Abstract

Post-editing performed by translators is an increasingly common use of machine translated texts. While high quality MT may increase productivity, post-editing poor translations can be a frustrating task which requires more effort than translating from scratch. For this reason, estimating whether machine translations are of sufficient quality to be used for post-editing and finding means to reduce post-editing effort are an important field of study. Post-editing effort consists of different aspects, of which temporal effort, or the time spent on post-editing, is the most visible and involves not only the technical effort needed to perform the editing, but also the cognitive effort required to detect and plan necessary corrections. Cognitive effort is difficult to examine directly, but ways to reduce the cognitive effort in particular may prove valuable in reducing the frustration associated with post-editing work. In this paper, we describe an experiment aimed at studying the relationship between technical post-editing effort and cognitive post-editing effort by comparing cases where the edit distance and a manual score reflecting perceived effort differ. We present results of an error analysis performed on such sentences and discuss the clues they may provide about edits requiring great cognitive effort compared to the technical effort, on one hand, or little cognitive effort, on the other.

1 Introduction

An increasingly common use for machine translation is producing texts to be post-edited by translators. While sufficiently high-quality MT has been shown to produce benefits for productivity, a well-known problem is that post-editing poor machine translation can require more effort than translating from scratch. Measuring and estimating post-editing effort is therefore a growing concern addressed by Confidence Estimation (CE) (Specia, 2011).

Time spent on post-editing can be seen as the most visible and economically most important aspect of post-editing effort (Krings, 2001); however, post-editing effort can be defined and approached in different ways. Krings (2001) divides post-editing effort into three types: 1. temporal, 2. cognitive and 3. technical. Temporal effort refers to post-editing time. Cognitive effort involves identifying the errors in the MT and the necessary steps to correct the output. Technical effort then consists of the keystrokes and cut-and-paste operations needed to produce the post-edited version after the errors have been detected and corrections planned. These different aspects of effort are not necessarily equal in various situations. In some cases, the errors may be easy to detect but involve several technical operations to be corrected. In other cases, parsing the sentence and detecting the errors may require considerable cognitive effort, although the actual technical operations required are quick and easy. According to Krings (2001), temporal effort is a combination of both cognitive and technical effort, with cognitive effort being the decisive factor. Assessing and reducing the cognitive effort involved in MT post-editing would therefore be important but the task is far from simple. Past experiments have involved cognitive approaches such as think-aloud protocols (Krings, 2001; O'Brien, 2005; Carl et al., 2011) and post-editing effort scores assigned by human evaluators (Specia et al., 2009; Specia, 2011; Specia et al., 2011).

While edit operations reflect the amount of technical effort needed, subjective assessments of perceived post-editing effort needed can serve as a measure of cognitive post-editing effort: in order to give such an estimate, the evaluator needs to cognitively process the segment in order to detect the errors and plan the necessary corrections. Using these two measures, a comparison of technical effort and perceived amount of post-editing effort can serve as a way to evaluate cognitive post-editing effort. We propose that studying cases where the perceived effort necessary is greater or smaller than the number of actual edit operations performed may provide clues to situations where the cognitive and technical effort differ. Cases where the human editor overestimates the need for editing (as compared to number of edit operations performed) could indicate that these segments contain errors requiring considerable cognitive effort. On the other hand, cases where the manual score underestimates the amount of editing needed could indicate errors that require relatively little cognitive effort compared to the number of technical operations.

To examine the question of differences in technical and cognitive post-editing effort, we present an analysis of MT segments that have different levels of post-editing indicated by the manual effort score and actual number of post-edit operations indicated by the edit distance. By analyzing cases where these two measures of post-editing effort differ, it may be possible to isolate cases that require more cognitive effort than technical effort and vice versa. Section 3 describes the material and method used in the experiment, and the results of the analysis are presented in Section 4.

2 Related work

As the temporal aspect of post-editing effort is important for the practice of machine translation post-editing, post-editing time has been a commonly used measure of post-editing effort (Krings, 2001; O'Brien, 2005; Specia et al., 2009; Tatsumi, 2009; Tatsumi and Roturier, 2010; Specia, 2011; Carl et al., 2011). The technical aspect of post-editing effort has been approached by following keystrokes and cut-and-paste operations (Krings, 2001; O'Brien, 2005; Carl et al., 2011) or using automatic metrics for edit distance between the raw MT and post-edited version (Tatsumi, 2009; Temnikova, 2010; Tatsumi and Roturier, 2010; Specia and Farzindar, 2010; Specia, 2011; Blain et al., 2011). Several edit operations may also be incorporated in one "post-edit action (PEA)", introduced by Blain et al. (2011). For example, changing the number of a noun propagates changes to other words, such as the determiners and adjectives modifying it. Tatsumi and Roturier (2010) also explore the relationship between temporal and technical aspects of post-editing effort.

Cognitive aspects of post-editing effort have been approached with the help of keystroke logging (Krings, 2001; O'Brien, 2005; Carl et al., 2011) and gaze data (Carl et al., 2011), attempting to measure cognitive effort in terms of pauses and fixations. O'Brien (2005) also experiments with the use of choice network analysis (CNA) and think-aloud protocols (TAP). Human scores for post-editing effort have involved assessing the amount of post-editing needed (Specia et al., 2009; Specia, 2011) or adequacy of the MT (Specia et al., 2011).

Temnikova (2010) proposes the analysis of the types of changes and comparison to post-editing time as a way to explore cognitive effort. For this purpose, Temnikova (2010) builds upon the MT error classification by Vilar et al. (2006) and their own post-editing experiments using controlled language to draft a classification for the cognitive effort required for correcting different types of MT errors. This classification defines ten types of errors and ranks them from 1 to 10 with 1 indicating the easiest and 10 the hardest error type to correct. The easiest errors are considered to be connected to the morphological level, or correct words with incorrect form, followed by the lexical level, involving incorrect style synonyms, incorrect words, extra words, missing words and erroneously translated idiomatic expressions. The hardest errors in the classification relate to syntactic level and include wrong punctuation, missing punctuation, then word order at word level and finally word order at phrase level. The ranking is based on studies in written language comprehension and error detection. Results reported in Temnikova (2010) suggest that pre-edited machine translations that had previously been found to require less post-editing effort measured by post-edit time and edit distance contain less errors that are cognitively more difficult compared to MT that had not been pre-edited.

In this study, we aim to investigate the relationship between the cognitive effort and the technical effort involved in post-editing. Edit distance between MT segments and their post-edited versions is used as a measure of technical effort and human effort scores as a measure of cognitive effort.

3 Material and method

The data used in this study consists of English to Spanish MT segments from the evaluation task training set provided for the quality estimation task at the NAACL 2012 Seventh Workshop on Statistical Machine Translation WMT12. [1] The training set consists English to Spanish machine translations of news texts, produced by a phrase-based SMT system. The data available for each segment includes the English source segment, Spanish reference translation produced by a human translator, machine translation into Spanish, post-edited version of the machine translation and a manual score indicating how much editing would be required to transform the MT segment into a useful translation. The manual score included is the average of scoring conducted by three professional translators using a 5-point scale where (1) indicates the segment is incomprehensible and needs to be translated from scratch, (2) significant editing is required (50-70% of the output), (3) about 25-50% of the output needs to be edited, (4) about 10-25% needs to be edited, and (5) little to no editing is required.

Additional information includes the SMT alignment tables. The alignments were not part of the original set, and in some cases differed slightly from the segments that had been used for the manual scoring. As we intended to make use of the alignments from source to MT, we included only segments that were identical in the original evaluated set.

To measure the amount of editing performed on the segments, the translation edit rate (TER) (Snover et al., 2006) was calculated using the post-edited versions as reference. TER measures the minimum number of edits that are needed to transform the machine translation into the post-edited segment used as reference. Edits can be insertion, deletion, substitution or reordering and the score is calculated as the number of edits divided by the number of tokens in the reference. The higher the TER score, the more edits have been performed.

As our aim was to focus on cases where the perceived effort score and the amount of editing differed, we looked for two types of sentences at the opposite ends of the manual effort scoring scale: (1) Cases where the manual score indicated more editing was needed than had actually been performed. (2) Cases where the manual score indicated less editing was needed than had actually been performed.

For Case (1), we selected segments with a manual score of 2.5 or lower, meaning that at least 50% of the segment needed editing according to the evaluators. We looked for the ones with the lowest TER scores, trying to find at least 30 sentences. The set selected for analysis consists of 37 sentences with a manual effort score of 2.5 or lower and TER score 0.33 or lower. For comparison, we also selected the same number of sentences with similar TER scores but with manual scores of 4 or above. These sets are referred to as the low TER set.

For Case (2), we selected segments with a manual score of 4 or above, meaning that no more than 25% of the segment needed editing according to the evaluator. Again, we looked for about 30 sentences with the highest TER scores. The set selected consists of 35 sentences with a manual effort score of 4 or higher, and TER score 0.45 or higher. For comparison, we also selected sentences with similar TER scores but low manual scores. These sets are referred to as the high TER set.

The selected MT segments and post-edited versions were then tagged with the FreeLing Spanish tagger (Padró et al., 2010). The tagged versions contain the surface form of the word, lemma and a tag with part-of-speech (POS) and grammatical information. Other tools such as dependency parsing were considered, but within the scope of this study, we decided to experiment what changes can be observed using only the basic lemma, POS and form information.

The tagged versions were aligned manually, first

[1] http://www.statmt.org/wmt12/quality-estimation-task.html

matching identical tokens (words and punctuation) in the sentence, then matching words with the same lemma but different surface form. The alignment table was consulted to match substitutions that involved a different word and even different POS. Each matched pair of words in the MT and post-edited versions was then labeled to indicate whether the match was identical or involved editing the word form, substituting with a different word of the same POS or a word of different POS. Words appearing in the post-edited version but not in the MT were labeled as insertions and words appearing in the MT but not in the post-edited version as deletions. In cases where several MT words were replaced with one in the post-edited version or one MT word was replaced with many in the post-edited, a match was made between words of the same POS and form, if such was found, or the first word in the sequence if none matched. The remaining words were labeled as inserted/deleted.

The positions of the matched words were also compared. For matching the word order, changes caused only by insertion or deletion of other words were ignored, and words that had remained in the same order after post-editing were labeled as same. In cases where the word order did not match, the word was labeled with the distance it had been moved and whether it had been moved alone or as a part of a larger group.

The totals of changes within a sentence were then calculated and the patterns of changes made by editors were examined. In addition to the total number of edit operations, we considered the possibility that editing certain parts-of-speech might require more effort than others. In particular, editing content words such as verbs or nouns might require more effort than editing function words such as determiners, because they are more central to conveying the content of the sentence. Further, as Blain et al. (2011) argue, changes to these words may propagate changes to other words in the sentence. Punctuation was also treated separately to follow Temnikova's (2010) classification of punctuation errors as a class of their own.

The patterns found in the sample sentences were compared to the comparison sets of sentences with similar TER scores. Additionally, Spearman rank correlations between the manual effort score and the various edit categories were calculated for all tokens and specific POS classes. The next section presents the results of these comparisons.

4 Results

This section presents the results from the analysis of post-editing changes. The total number of segments and tokens and the percentages of edited and reordered tokens in each set are shown in Table 1. Comparisons of the edit patterns between segments with similar TER scores but different manual scores are shown in Figures 1 to 4. Figure 1 presents the distributions of edit categories in the low TER sets and Figure 3 in the high TER sets. Figure 2 presents the percentages of changed tokens and reordered tokens by POS class in the low TER set and Figure 4 in the high TER sets. In Figures 2 and 4, nouns, verbs, adjectives and determiners are shown separately, while other parts-of-speech are combined into "Other". Punctuation is also presented separately.

Tables 2 and 3 present Spearman rank correlations between the manual score and different edit categories. Overall correlations regardless of POS are given for all edit categories. For specific POS classes, only the edit categories with strongest correlations are listed in each case.

4.1 Case 1: Low TER set

These sentences represent a case where the human evaluators indicated that significant post-editing would be needed but the low TER score indicated that relatively little editing had been performed. The most noticeable difference between segments with high and low manual scores is the number of tokens: low-scored segments have about twice as many tokens on average than the high-scored ones (see Table 1) and the number of tokens in the post-edited segment has a strong negative correlation (Table 2). Besides segment length, other strong correlations involve different types of reordering. Reorderings involving a distance of one step show weaker correlation than changes involving a longer distance. No correlation was found for any of the word change categories in this case.

Broken down by the POS class, results are similar to the overall result in that reordering categories have the strongest (negative) correlations with the

TER score	Manual score	Number of segments	Number of tokens	Edited tokens	Reordered tokens
Low	Low	37	1480	23%	24%
Low	High	37	695	21%	15%
High	Low	35	943	45%	45%
High	High	35	556	42%	33%

Table 1: Total number of sentences and tokens per set, percentage of tokens edited and percentage of tokens reordered.

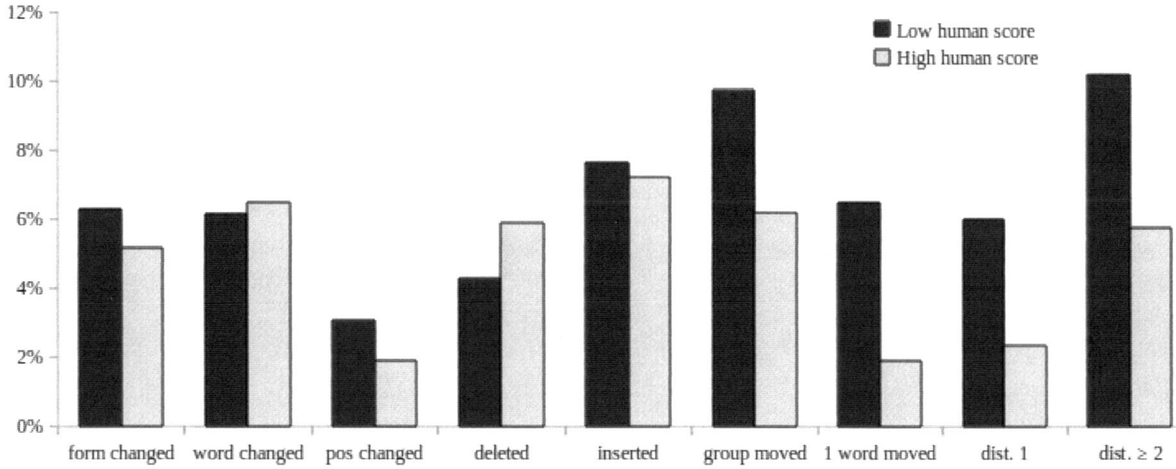

Figure 1: Distribution of edit categories - Low TER.

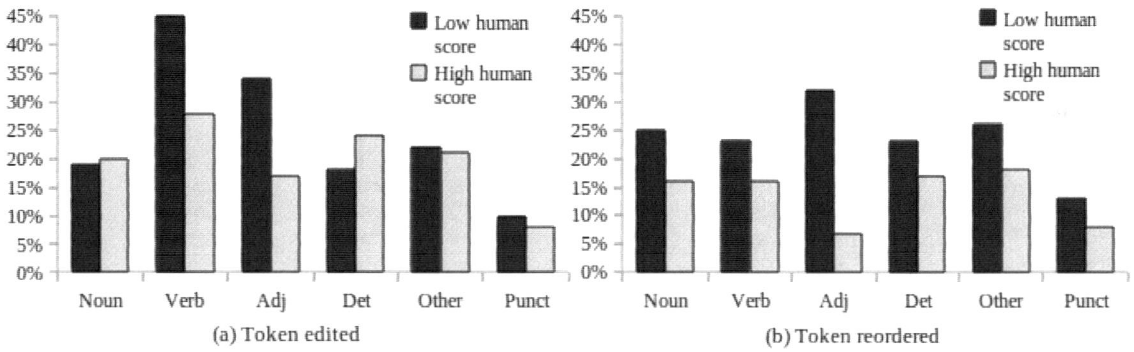

Figure 2: Edited and reordered tokens by POS - Low TER

effort score. Strongest correlations also mostly involve nouns, adjectives or verbs. As shown in Figure 2, the differences in percentage of edited tokens are largest for verbs and adjectives. In high-scored sentences, 72% of verbs were unchanged by the editor compared to 55% in the low-scored ones. In both cases, most edits to verbs involved changing the form of the verb, (23% in low-scored vs 11% in high-scored). Adjectives have a similar pattern with 18% of edited adjective forms in low-scored vs 7% in high-scored sentences.

Sentences with high manual scores actually have more cases of edited determiners and nouns, although for nouns the difference is only 1%. Most edits to determiners involved deletion (15% of determiners) or changed form (11%) in the case of high-scored sentences. In low-scored sentences, insertion was most common (10% of determiners). Within

Overall correlations		
number of tokens	-0.51	***
word match	0.11	
form changed	-0.10	
word changed	-0.15	
pos changed	-0.15	
deleted	0.08	
inserted	-0.15	
order same	0.51	***
group moved	-0.48	***
1 word moved	-0.47	***
dist. 1	-0.37	**
dist ≥ 2	-0.53	***
Strongest correlations by POS		
Noun, order same	0.49	***
Adj, order same	0.47	***
Noun, group moved	-0.46	***
Adj, dist. ≥ 2	-0.46	***
Noun, dist. ≥ 2	-0.45	***
Other, group moved	-0.44	***
Verb, 1 word moved	-0.44	***
Verb, dist. ≥ 2	-0.43	***
Other, order same	0.41	***
Det, group moved	-0.40	***
Verb, word match	0.39	***
Adj, 1 word moved	-0.38	***

*** $p < 0.001$, ** $p < 0.01$, * $p < 0.05$

Table 2: Spearman rank correlations between effort score and edit categories - Low TER.

the class "Other" combining numbers, adverbs, conjunctions, pronouns and prepositions, adverbs were an similar case in that there were more unchanged adverbs in the low-rated sentences (86%) than in the high-rated (72%). However, the total number of adverbs in either set was very small.

4.2 Case 2: High TER set

These sentences represent a case where the human evaluators indicated only a little editing was needed but the high TER score indicated much more editing had been performed. Again one noticeable difference between the sentences with low and high manual scores is the number of tokens (see Table 1), although the negative correlation shown in Table 3 was not as strong as for the low TER set.

For these sentences, word changes have stronger correlations with the manual effort score (Table 3). While the shares of fully matched words are fairly equal between the sentences, differences appear in some of the edit categories. Sentences with high manual scores have more cases where the word form has been edited (Figure 3), and changed form has the strongest (positive) correlation after number of tokens. High-scored segments also appear to have more deletions, but essentially no correlation was found between the manual score and deletions on the segment level. As shown in Figure 3, low-scored segments have more cases of substitution with different word. Reordering is again more common in low-scored segments, but correlations for reordering are weaker than in the low TER set. Cases where one word has been moved alone rather than as a part of a group has the strongest correlation among the reordering categories.

Overall correlations		
number of tokens	-0.43	***
word match	0.14	
form changed	0.36	**
word changed	-0.25	*
pos changed	-0.28	*
deleted	0.14	
inserted	-0.22	
order same	0.21	
group moved	-0.12	
1 word moved	-0.34	**
dist. 1	-0.22	
dist. ≥ 2	-0.25	*
Strongest correlations by POS		
Other, inserted	-0.38	**
Noun, 1 word moved	-0.36	**
Noun, pos changed	-0.35	**
Noun, word changed	-0.30	*
Adj, order same	0.28	*
Det, inserted	-0.27	*
Adj, dist. ≥ 2	-0.25	*
Noun, word match	0.24	*

*** $p < 0.001$, ** $p < 0.01$, * $p < 0.05$

Table 3: Spearman rank correlations between effort score and edit categories - High TER.

For specific POS classes, the strongest correlation

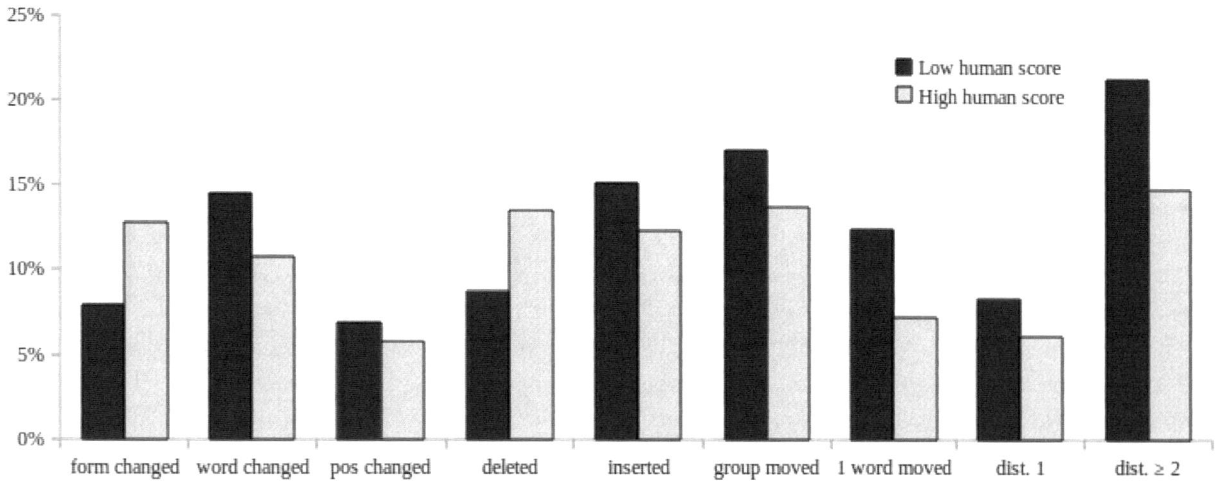

Figure 3: Distribution of edit types - High TER.

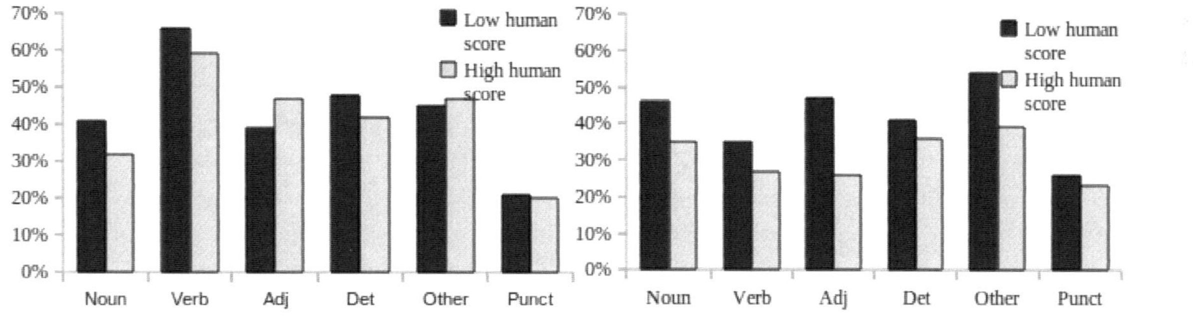

(a) Token edited

(b) Token reordered

Figure 4: Edited and reordered tokens by POS - High TER

in Table 3 involves insertion of words in the combined class "Other" (numbers, adverbs, conjunctions, pronouns and prepositions). Within this class, pronouns actually required most edits: in low-scored segments, 50% of pronouns were inserted by the editor (32% in high-scored segments). The largest difference in the percentage of edited tokens is seen with nouns (41% edited in low-scored segments vs 32% in high-scored, and edits related to nouns are also among the strongest correlations for this set. In the case of adjectives, the segments with low manual score actually have more cases where no editing of the word has been required (61% vs 53%), but high-scored sentences contain a larger share of cases (32% vs 16%) where only the form of the adjective has been edited. However, these correlations remained weak. Reordering involving nouns and adjectives, on the other hand, again appears among the strongest correlations.

5 Discussion

Perhaps the most obvious difference between segments with high and low manual scores is segment length: long segments tend to get low scores even when the amount of editing turns out to be less than estimated. The effect of sentence length has also been observed in other studies, e.g. (Tatsumi, 2009). One simple explanation would be that a high total number of words leads to a high total number of changes to be made and therefore involves considerable technical post-editing effort. However, as the case of segments with low manual scores but low TER show, sometimes these long sentences do not, in fact, require a large number of edit operations.

This suggests also increased cognitive effort, as the sheer length may make it difficult for the evaluator/editor to perceive what needs to be changed and plan the edits.

We also noticed during the analysis that some of the very long segments actually consisted of two sentences. Furthermore, in some these cases, one of the sentences contained few changes while most of the changes were confined to the other. Similarly, long segments consisting of only one sentence sometimes contained long unchanged passages while some other part of the sentence was edited significantly. In these cases, such unchanged passages could be useful to the post-editor in real life situations, but the error-dense passage affects perception of the segment as a whole. Perhaps this suggests that assessing MT for post-editing and post-editing itself could benefit from presenting longer segments in shorter units, allowing the evaluator or editor to choose and discard different units within a longer segment.

Tatsumi (2009) also found that very short sentences increased post-editing time. In this study, all extremely short sentences found had received high scores from the human evaluators. Some are found in the low TER/high manual score set used for comparison purposes, but there are also some in the set of sentences with high TER/high manual score, meaning that there were relatively many edits compared to the length of the segment but the evaluators had indicated that little editing was needed. At least for the segments analyzed here, it appears that the evaluators did not consider short sentences to require much effort regardless of the actual number of edits performed. In Tatsumi's (2009) results, also other aspects, such as source sentence structure and dependency errors in the MT were discovered to have an effect on post-editing time. In this study, sentence structure and dependency errors were not explicitly examined, but these aspects would be of interest in future work.

Edits related to reordering also appear to be connected to low manual scores, as low-scored sentences involved more reordering than high-scored ones in both cases. This reflects Temnikova's (2010) error ranking where errors involving word order, particularly at phrase level, are considered the most difficult to correct. Besides the number of reorderings necessary, the results of this study may suggest some differences in whether reordering involves isolated words or groups of words and distances of one step (word level order) or longer distances.

Examining the results by parts-of-speech may suggest that overall, edits related to nouns, verbs or adjectives take more effort than other POS, because in both sets, strongest correlations mainly involved nouns, verbs and adjectives. In both sets, sentences with low manual scores contained more cases of edited verbs, and verb matches had one of the strongest correlations in the low TER set. On the other hand, edits related to nouns appeared to have particularly strong correlations in the high TER set. In this set, however, the strongest negative correlation was found for insertion of the other POS (mainly pronouns), so at least some of the other POS may also be difficult to edit.

Some cases where relatively little cognitive effort is required may be suggested by the situations where the high-scored sentences in fact contain more edits than the low-scored ones. In the high TER set, sentences with high manual scores contained more cases where only the form of a word has been edited, whereas sentences with low manual scores contained more cases of substitution with a different word or even different POS. This reflects the ranking of such errors in (Temnikova, 2010), where word form errors are considered cognitively easiest. This particularly appears to be the case for adjectives in this set. Although segments with a high manual score actually have a smaller number of fully correct adjectives than low-scored ones, they contain a larger share of instances where only the form of the adjective has been edited. Another example of edits involving less cognitive effort might be determiners in the low TER set, where again sentences with high manual scores contain more edited determiners than those with low scores. In this case, deletion of determiners was common in addition to changing the form.

Overall, deletion and insertion or extra words and missing words appeared to have little effect. While sentences with high manual scores have a slightly higher percentage of deleted words in both sets, the correlation was weak. Most of the deletions of content words seemed to involve auxiliary verbs, but in some instances it is difficult to say whether the editor has, in fact, considered something "extra" information and why, whether there has been a deliberate choice to implicitate certain information or whether the deletion has been at least partly unintentional. During the alignment process of the MT and post-edited version, it appeared that some source elements, in some cases entire clauses and in others certain words, were completely missing in the post-edited version. On the other hand, some of the insertions were also difficult to map onto anything in the source segment and the editor appeared to have brought in something extra. One clear example involved adding a conversion from miles per hour to km per hour that did not appear in the MT or source text. Such deletions and insertions concerned only a few isolated cases which were not examined in detail within the scope of this work. Some error classifications, such as Blain et al. (2011), do also take errors made by post-editors into account, and one interesting aspect of post-editing would be to study the correctness of post-edits. If it would turn out that post-editors are more prone to make errors or to fail to correct errors, (particularly errors related to content as opposed to typographical errors etc.) in certain situations, this might suggest situations that involve particular cognitive effort or mislead the editor.

6 Conclusion and Future Work

We have presented an experiment aimed at exploring the difference between cognitive and technical aspects of MT post-editing effort by comparing human scores of perceived effort necessary to actual edits made by post-editors. We examined cases where considerably more or considerably less post-editing was done than predicted by the evaluators' estimate of post-editing needed. The results show that one of the factors most affecting the perception of post-editing necessary involves segment length: long segments are perceived to involve much effort and therefore receive low scores even when the actual number of edits turns out to be small. This suggests that sentence length affects the cognitive effort required in identifying errors and planning the corrections, and presenting MT for this type of evaluation and post-editing may benefit from displaying segments to the evaluator or editor in smaller units.

The results also suggest other features affecting cognitive effort. Sentences with low manual scores were found to involve more reordering, indicating increased cognitive effort, while sentences with high manual scores were found to involve more cases of correct words with incorrect form, suggesting that these errors are cognitively easier. Examining edit type distributions in different POS classes suggests that edits related to certain parts-of-speech, namely nouns, verbs and adjectives, may also be associated with perception of more effort. On the other hand, sentences with high scores in some cases contained even more editing of some other POS and types, such as editing forms of adjectives or deleting determiners, which may indicate that these errors affect perception of effort to a lesser extent. As the number of sentences used was relatively low, however, such effects would require more study.

In future work, we aim to more explicitly examine combinations of edit operations, (e.g. changing the form and reordering, moving a group and substituting one word within the group) and features such as dependency errors (Tatsumi, 2009). Further experiments with data on other language pairs would also be needed. Another interesting aspect for future work would be trying to distinguish between edits made for reasons of incorrect language and edits for reasons of incorrect content. Further, examining the success of post-editing and exploring whether post-editors themselves are prone to make errors or fail to correct errors in certain situations could be an interesting avenue for discovering situations that involve significant cognitive effort.

Acknowledgments

This work has been supported by LANGNET Finnish Graduate School in Language Studies.

References

Frédéric Blain, Jean Senellart, Holger Schwenk, Mirko Plitt and Johann Roturier 2011. Qualitative analysis of post-editing for high quality machine translation. In *MT Summit XIII: the Thirteenth Machine Translation Summit* [organized by the] Asia-Pacific Association for Machine Translation (AAMT), pages 164-171. 19-23 September 2011, Xiamen, China.

Michael Carl, Barbara Dragsted, Jakob Elming, Daniel Hardt and Arnt Lykke Jakobsen. 2011. The process of post-editing: a pilot study. In *Proceedings of the 8th international NLPSC workshop. Special theme: Human-machine interaction in translation*, pages 131-142. Copenhagen Business School, 20-21 August 2011. (Copenhagen Studies in Language 41), Frederiksberg: Samfundslitteratur.

Hans P. Krings. 2001. *Repairing texts: Empirical investigations of machine translation post-editing process*. The Kent State University Press, Kent, OH.

Sharon O'Brien 2005. Methodologies for Measuring the Correlations between Post-Editing Effort and Machine Translatability. *Machine Translation*, 19(1):37-58.

Lluís Padró, Miquel Collado, Samuel Reese, Marina Lloberes and Irene Castellón. 2010. FreeLing 2.1: Five Years of Open-Source Language Processing Tools. In *LREC 2010: proceedings of the seventh international conference on Language Resources and Evaluation*, pages 3485-3490. 17-23 May 2010, Valletta, Malta.

Matthew Snover, Bonnie Dorr, Richard Schwartz, Linnea Micciulla and John Makhoul. 2006. A Study of Translation Edit Rate with Targeted Human Annotation. In *Proceedings of Association for Machine Translation in the Americas*, pages 223-231. August 8-12, 2006, Cambridge, Massachusetts, USA.

Lucia Specia, Marco Turchi, Nicola Cancedda, Marc Dymetman and Nello Cristianini 2009. Estimating the Sentence-Level Quality of Machine Translation Systems. In *Proceedings of the 13th Annual Conference of the EAMT*, pages 28-35. Barcelona, May 2009.

Lucia Specia and Atefeh Farzindar. 2010. Estimating Machine Translation Post-Editing Effort with HTER. In *Proceedings of the Second Joint EM+/CNGL Workshop Bringing MT to the User: Research on Integrating MT in the Translation Industry (JEC 10)*, pages 33-41. Denver, CO, 4 November 2010.

Lucia Specia. 2011. Exploiting Objective Annotations for Measuring Translation Post-Editing Effort. In *Proceedings of the 15th Conference of the European Association for Machine Translation*, pages 73-80. Leuven, Belgium, May 2011.

Lucia Specia, Najeh Hajlaoui, Catalina Hallett and Wilker Aziz. 2011. Predicting Machine Translation Adequacy. In *MT Summit XIII: the Thirteenth Machine Translation Summit* [organized by the] Asia-Pacific Association for Machine Translation (AAMT), pages 513-520. 19-23 September 2011, Xiamen, China.

Midori Tatsumi. 2009. Correlation between Automatic Evaluation Metric Scores, Post-Editing Speed, and Some Other Factors. In *MT Summit XII: proceedings of the twelfth Machine Translation Summit*, pages 332-339 August 26-30, 2009, Ottawa, Ontario, Canada.

Midori Tatsumi and Johann Roturier. 2010. Source Text Characteristics and Technical and Temporal Post-Editing Effort: What is Their Relationship?. In *Proceedings of the Second Joint EM+/CNGL Workshop Bringing MT to the User: Research on Integrating MT in the Translation Industry (JEC 10)*, pages 43-51. Denver, CO, 4 November 2010.

Irina Temnikova. 2010. Cognitive Evaluation Approach for a Controlled Language Post-Editing Experiment. In *LREC 2010: proceedings of the seventh international conference on Language Resources and Evaluation*, pages 3485-3490. 17-23 May 2010, Valletta, Malta.

David Vilar, Jia Xu, Luis Fernando D'Haro and Hermann Ney. 2006. Error analysis of statistical machine translation output. In *LREC-2006: Fifth International Conference on Language Resources and Evaluation. Proceedings*, pages 697-702. Genoa, Italy, 22-28 May 2006.

Review of Hypothesis Alignment Algorithms for MT System Combination via Confusion Network Decoding

Antti-Veikko I. Rosti[a*], **Xiaodong He**[b], **Damianos Karakos**[c], **Gregor Leusch**[d†], **Yuan Cao**[c], **Markus Freitag**[e], **Spyros Matsoukas**[f], **Hermann Ney**[e], **Jason R. Smith**[c] and **Bing Zhang**[f]

[a]Apple Inc., Cupertino, CA 95014
`arosti@apple.com`
[b]Microsoft Research, Redmond, WA 98052
`xiaohe@microsoft.com`
[c]Johns Hopkins University, Baltimore, MD 21218
`{damianos,yuan.cao,jrsmith}@jhu.edu`
[d]SAIC, Monheimsallee 22, D-52062 Aachen, Germany
`gregor.leusch@saic.com`
[e]RWTH Aachen University, D-52056 Aachen, Germany
`{freitag,ney}@cs.rwth-aachen.de`
[f]Raytheon BBN Technologies, 10 Moulton Street, Cambridge, MA 02138
`{smatsouk,bzhang}@bbn.com`

Abstract

Confusion network decoding has proven to be one of the most successful approaches to machine translation system combination. The hypothesis alignment algorithm is a crucial part of building the confusion networks and many alternatives have been proposed in the literature. This paper describes a systematic comparison of five well known hypothesis alignment algorithms for MT system combination via confusion network decoding. Controlled experiments using identical pre-processing, decoding, and weight tuning methods on standard system combination evaluation sets are presented. Translation quality is assessed using case insensitive BLEU scores and bootstrapping is used to establish statistical significance of the score differences. All aligners yield significant BLEU score gains over the best individual system included in the combination. Incremental indirect hidden Markov model and a novel incremental inversion transduction grammar with flexible matching consistently yield the best translation quality, though keeping all things equal, the differences between aligners are relatively small.

*The work reported in this paper was carried out while the authors were at Raytheon BBN Technologies and

†RWTH Aachen University.

1 Introduction

Current machine translation (MT) systems are based on different paradigms, such as rule-based, phrase-based, hierarchical, and syntax-based. Due to the complexity of the problem, systems make various assumptions at different levels of processing and modeling. Many of these assumptions may be suboptimal and complementary. The complementary information in the outputs from multiple MT systems may be exploited by system combination. Availability of multiple system outputs within the DARPA GALE program as well as NIST Open MT and Workshop on Statistical Machine Translation evaluations has led to extensive research in combining the strengths of diverse MT systems, resulting in significant gains in translation quality.

System combination methods proposed in the literature can be roughly divided into three categories: (i) hypothesis selection (Rosti et al., 2007b; Hildebrand and Vogel, 2008), (ii) re-decoding (Frederking and Nirenburg, 1994; Jayaraman and Lavie, 2005; Rosti et al., 2007b; He and Toutanova, 2009; Devlin et al., 2011), and (iii) confusion network decoding. Confusion network decoding has proven to be the most popular as it does not require deep N-best lists[1] and operates on the surface strings. It has

[1] N-best lists of around $N = 10$ have been used in confusion network decoding yielding small gains over using 1-best

also been shown to be very successful in combining speech recognition outputs (Fiscus, 1997; Mangu et al., 2000). The first application of confusion network decoding in MT system combination appeared in (Bangalore et al., 2001) where a multiple string alignment (MSA), made popular in biological sequence analysis, was applied to the MT system outputs. Matusov et al. (2006) proposed an alignment based on GIZA++ Toolkit which introduced word reordering not present in MSA, and Sim et al. (2007) used the alignments produced by the translation edit rate (TER) (Snover et al., 2006) scoring. Extensions of the last two are included in this study together with alignments based on hidden Markov model (HMM) (Vogel et al., 1996) and inversion transduction grammars (ITG) (Wu, 1997).

System combinations produced via confusion network decoding using different hypothesis alignment algorithms have been entered into open evaluations, most recently in 2011 Workshop on Statistical Machine Translation (Callison-Burch et al., 2011). However, there has not been a comparison of the most popular hypothesis alignment algorithms using the same sets of MT system outputs and otherwise identical combination pipelines. This paper attempts to systematically compare the quality of five hypothesis alignment algorithms. Alignments were produced for the same system outputs from three common test sets used in the 2009 NIST Open MT Evaluation and the 2011 Workshop on Statistical Machine Translation. Identical pre-processing, decoding, and weight tuning algorithms were used to quantitatively evaluate the alignment quality. Case insensitive BLEU score (Papineni et al., 2002) was used as the translation quality metric.

2 Confusion Network Decoding

A confusion network is a linear graph where all paths visit all nodes. Two consecutive nodes may be connected by one or more arcs. Given the arcs represent words in hypotheses, multiple arcs connecting two consecutive nodes can be viewed as alternative words in that position of a set of hypotheses encoded by the network. A special NULL token represents a skipped word and will not appear in the system combination output. For example, three hypotheses "twelve big cars", "twelve cars", and "dozen cars" may be aligned as follows:

twelve	big	blue	cars
twelve	NULL	NULL	cars
dozen	NULL	blue	cars

This alignment may be represented compactly as the confusion network in Figure 1 which encodes a total of eight unique hypotheses.

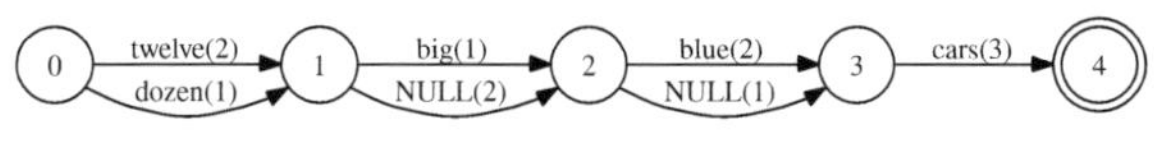

Figure 1: Confusion network from three strings "twelve big blue cars", "twelve cars", and "dozen blue cars" using the first as the skeleton. The numbers in parentheses represent counts of words aligned to the corresponding arc.

Building confusion networks from multiple machine translation system outputs has two main problems. First, one output has to be chosen as the skeleton hypothesis which defines the final word order of the system combination output. Second, MT system outputs may have very different word orders which complicates the alignment process. For skeleton selection, Sim et al. (2007) proposed choosing the output closest to all other hypotheses when using each as the reference string in TER. Alternatively, Matusov et al. (2006) proposed leaving the decision to decoding time by connecting networks built using each output as a skeleton into a large lattice. The subnetworks in the latter approach may be weighted by prior probabilities estimated from the alignment statistics (Rosti et al., 2007a). Since different alignment algorithm produce different statistics and the gain from the weights is relatively small (Rosti et al., 2011), weights for the subnetworks were not used in this work. The hypothesis alignment algorithms used in this work are briefly described in the following section.

The confusion networks in this work were represented in a text lattice format shown in Figure 2. Each line corresponds to an arc, where J is the arc index, S is the start node index, E is the end node index, SC is the score vector, and W is the word label. The score vector has as many elements as there are input systems. The elements correspond to each system and indicate whether a word from a particular

outputs (Rosti et al., 2011).

```
J=0 S=0 E=1 SC=(1,1,0) W=twelve
J=1 S=0 E=1 SC=(0,0,1) W=dozen
J=2 S=1 E=2 SC=(1,0,0) W=big
J=3 S=1 E=2 SC=(0,1,1) W=NULL
J=4 S=2 E=3 SC=(1,0,1) W=blue
J=5 S=2 E=3 SC=(0,1,0) W=NULL
J=6 S=3 E=4 SC=(1,1,1) W=cars
```

Figure 2: A lattice in text format representing the confusion network in Figure 1. J is the arc index, S and E are the start and end node indexes, SC is a vector of arc scores, and W is the word label.

system was aligned to a given link[2]. These may be viewed as system specific word confidences, which are binary when aligning 1-best system outputs. If no word from a hypothesis is aligned to a given link, a NULL word token is generated provided one does not already exist, and the corresponding element in the NULL word token is set to one. The system specific word scores are kept separate in order to exploit system weights in decoding. Given system weights w_n, which sum to one, and system specific word scores s_{nj} for each arc j (the SC elements), the weighted word scores are defined as:

$$s_j = \sum_{n=1}^{N_s} w_n s_{nj} \tag{1}$$

where N_s is the number of input systems. The hypothesis score is defined as the sum of the log-word-scores along the path, which is linearly interpolated with a logarithm of the language model (LM) score and a non-NULL word count:

$$S(E|F) = \sum_{j \in \mathcal{J}(E)} \log s_j + \gamma S_{LM}(E) + \delta N_w(E) \tag{2}$$

where $\mathcal{J}(E)$ is the sequence of arcs generating the hypothesis E for the source sentence F, $S_{LM}(E)$ is the LM score, and $N_w(E)$ is the number of non-NULL words. The set of weights $\theta = \{w_1, \ldots, w_{N_s}, \gamma, \delta\}$ can be tuned so as to optimize an evaluation metric on a development set.

Decoding with an n-gram language model requires expanding the lattice to distinguish paths with unique n-gram contexts before LM scores can be assigned the arcs. Using long n-gram context may require pruning to reduce memory usage. Given uniform initial system weights, pruning may remove desirable paths. In this work, the lattices were expanded to bi-gram context and no pruning was performed. A set of bi-gram decoding weights were tuned directly on the expanded lattices using a distributed optimizer (Rosti et al., 2010). Since the score in Equation 2 is not a simple log-linear interpolation, the standard minimum error rate training (Och, 2003) with exact line search cannot be used. Instead, downhill simplex (Press et al., 2007) was used in the optimizer client. After bi-gram decoding weight optimization, another set of 5-gram rescoring weights were tuned on 300-best lists generated from the bi-gram expanded lattices.

[2]A link is used as a synonym to the set of arcs between two consecutive nodes. The name refers to the confusion network structure's resemblance to a sausage.

3 Hypothesis Alignment Algorithms

Two different methods have been proposed for building confusion networks: pairwise and incremental alignment. In pairwise alignment, each hypothesis corresponding to a source sentence is aligned independently with the skeleton hypothesis. This set of alignments is consolidated using the skeleton words as anchors to form the confusion network (Matusov et al., 2006; Sim et al., 2007). The same word in two hypotheses may be aligned with a different word in the skeleton resulting in repetition in the network. A two-pass alignment algorithm to improve pairwise TER alignments was introduced in (Ayan et al., 2008). In incremental alignment (Rosti et al., 2008), the confusion network is initialized by forming a simple graph with one word per link from the skeleton hypothesis. Each remaining hypothesis is aligned with the partial confusion network, which allows words from all previous hypotheses be considered as matches. The order in which the hypotheses are aligned may influence the alignment quality. Rosti et al. (2009) proposed a sentence specific alignment order by choosing the unaligned hypothesis closest to the partial confusion network according to TER. The following five alignment algorithms were used in this study.

3.1 Pairwise GIZA++ Enhanced Hypothesis Alignment

Matusov et al. (2006) proposed using the GIZA++ Toolkit (Och and Ney, 2003) to align a set of target language translations. A parallel corpus where each system output acting as a skeleton appears as a translation of all system outputs corresponding to the same source sentence. The IBM Model 1 (Brown et al., 1993) and hidden Markov model (HMM) (Vogel et al., 1996) are used to estimate the alignment. Alignments from both "translation" directions are used to obtain symmetrized alignments by interpolating the HMM occupation statistics (Matusov et al., 2004). The algorithm may benefit from the fact that it considers the entire test set when estimating the alignment model parameters; i.e., word alignment links from all output sentences influence the estimation, whereas other alignment algorithms only consider words within a pair of sentences (pairwise alignment) or all outputs corresponding to a single source sentence (incremental alignment). However, it does not naturally extend to incremental alignment. The monotone one-to-one alignments are then transformed into a confusion network. This aligner is referred to as GIZA later in this paper.

3.2 Incremental Indirect Hidden Markov Model Alignment

He et al. (2008) proposed using an indirect hidden Markov model (IHMM) for pairwise alignment of system outputs. The parameters of the IHMM are estimated indirectly from a variety of sources including semantic word similarity, surface word similarity, and a distance-based distortion penalty. The alignment between two target language outputs are treated as the hidden states. A standard Viterbi algorithm is used to infer the alignment. The pairwise IHMM was extended to operate incrementally in (Li et al., 2009). Sentence specific alignment order is not used by this aligner, which is referred to as iIHMM later in this paper.

3.3 Incremental Inversion Transduction Grammar Alignment with Flexible Matching

Karakos et al. (2008) proposed using inversion transduction grammars (ITG) (Wu, 1997) for pairwise alignment of system outputs. ITGs form an edit distance, invWER (Leusch et al., 2003), that permits properly nested block movements of substrings. For well-formed sentences, this may be more natural than allowing arbitrary shifts. The ITG algorithm is very expensive due to its $O(n^6)$ complexity. The search algorithm for the best ITG alignment, a best-first chart parsing (Charniak et al., 1998), was augmented with an A^* search heuristic of quadratic complexity (Klein and Manning, 2003), resulting in significant reduction in computational complexity. The finite state-machine heuristic computes a lower bound to the alignment cost of two strings by allowing arbitrary word re-orderings. The ITG hypothesis alignment algorithm was extended to operate incrementally in (Karakos et al., 2010) and a novel version where the cost function is computed based on the stem/synonym similarity of (Snover et al., 2009) was used in this work. Also, a sentence specific alignment order was used. This aligner is referred to as iITGp later in this paper.

3.4 Incremental Translation Edit Rate Alignment with Flexible Matching

Sim et al. (2007) proposed using translation edit rate scorer[3] to obtain pairwise alignment of system outputs. The TER scorer tries to find shifts of blocks of words that minimize the edit distance between the shifted reference and a hypothesis. Due to the computational complexity, a set of heuristics is used to reduce the run time (Snover et al., 2006). The pairwise TER hypothesis alignment algorithm was extended to operate incrementally in (Rosti et al., 2008) and also extended to consider synonym and stem matches in (Rosti et al., 2009). The shift heuristics were relaxed for flexible matching to allow shifts of blocks of words as long as the edit distance is decreased even if there is no exact match in the new position. A sentence specific alignment order was used by this aligner, which is referred to as iTER later in this paper.

3.5 Incremental Translation Edit Rate Plus Alignment

Snover et al. (2009) extended TER scoring to consider synonyms and paraphrase matches, called

[3] http://www.cs.umd.edu/~snover/tercom/

TER-plus (TERp). The shift heuristics in TERp were also relaxed relative to TER. Shifts are allowed if the words being shifted are: (i) exactly the same, (ii) synonyms, stems or paraphrases of the corresponding reference words, or (iii) any such combination. Xu et al. (2011) proposed using an incremental version of TERp for building consensus networks. A sentence specific alignment order was used by this aligner, which is referred to as iTERp later in this paper.

4 Experimental Evaluation

Combination experiments were performed on (i) Arabic-English, from the informal system combination track of the 2009 NIST Open MT Evaluation[4]; (ii) German-English from the system combination evaluation of the 2011 Workshop on Statistical Machine Translation (Callison-Burch et al., 2011) (WMT11) and (iii) Spanish-English, again from WMT11. Eight top-performing systems (as evaluated using case-insensitive BLEU) were used in each language pair. Case insensitive BLEU scores for the individual system outputs on the tuning and test sets are shown in Table 1. About 300 and 800 sentences with four reference translations were available for Arabic-English tune and test sets, respectively, and about 500 and 2500 sentences with a single reference translation were available for both German-English and Spanish-English tune and test sets. The system outputs were lower-cased and tokenized before building confusion networks using the five hypothesis alignment algorithms described above. Unpruned English bi-gram and 5-gram language models were trained with about 6 billion words available for these evaluations. Multiple component language models were trained after dividing the monolingual corpora by source. Separate sets of interpolation weights were tuned for the NIST and WMT experiments to minimize perplexity on the English reference translations of the previous evaluations, NIST MT08 and WMT10. The system combination weights, both bi-gram lattice decoding and 5-gram 300-best list re-scoring weights, were tuned separately for lattices build with each hypothesis alignment algorithm. The final re-scoring outputs were detokenized before computing case insensitive BLEU scores. Statistical significance was computed for each pairwise comparison using bootstrapping (Koehn, 2004).

[4] http://www.itl.nist.gov/iad/mig/tests/mt/2009/ResultsRelease/indexISC.html

	Decode		Oracle	
Aligner	tune	test	tune	test
GIZA	60.06	57.95	75.06	74.47
iTER	59.74	58.63†	73.84	73.20
iTERp	60.18	59.05†	76.43	75.58
iIHMM	60.51	59.27†‡	76.50	76.17
iITGp	60.65	59.37†‡	76.53	76.05

Table 2: Case insensitive BLEU scores for NIST MT09 Arabic-English system combination outputs. Note, four reference translations were available. Decode corresponds to results after weight tuning and Oracle corresponds to graph TER oracle. Dagger (†) denotes statistically significant difference compared to GIZA and double dagger (‡) compared to iTERp and the aligners above it.

The BLEU scores for Arabic-English system combination outputs are shown in Table 2. The first column (Decode) shows the scores on tune and test sets for the decoding outputs. The second column (Oracle) shows the scores for oracle hypotheses obtained by aligning the reference translations with the confusion networks and choosing the path with lowest graph TER (Rosti et al., 2008). The rows representing different aligners are sorted according to the test set decoding scores. The order of the BLEU scores for the oracle translations do not always follow the order for the decoding outputs. This may be due to differences in the compactness of the confusion networks. A more compact network has fewer paths and is therefore less likely to contain significant parts of the reference translation, whereas a reference translation may be generated from a less compact network. On Arabic-English, all incremental alignment algorithms are significantly better than the pairwise GIZA, incremental IHMM and ITG with flexible matching are significantly better than all other algorithms, but not significantly different from each other. The incremental TER and TERp were statistically indistinguishable. Without flexible matching, iITG yields a BLEU score of 58.85 on test. The absolute BLEU gain over the best individual system was between 6.2 and 7.6 points on the test set.

System	Arabic		German		Spanish	
	tune	test	tune	test	tune	test
A	48.84	48.54	21.96	21.41	27.71	27.13
B	49.15	48.97	22.61	21.80	28.42	27.90
C	49.30	49.50	22.77	21.99	28.57	28.23
D	49.38	49.59	22.90	22.41	29.00	28.41
E	49.42	49.75	22.90	22.65	29.15	28.50
F	50.28	50.69	22.98	22.65	29.53	28.61
G	51.49	50.81	23.41	23.06	29.89	29.82
H	51.72	51.74	24.28	24.16	30.55	30.14

Table 1: Case insensitive BLEU scores for the individual system outputs on the tune and test sets for all three source languages.

Aligner	Decode		Oracle	
	tune	test	tune	test
GIZA	25.93	26.02	37.32	38.22
iTERp	26.46	26.10	38.16	38.76
iTER	26.27	26.39†	37.00	37.66
iIHMM	26.34	26.40†	37.87	38.48
iITGp	26.47	26.50†	37.99	38.60

Table 3: Case insensitive BLEU scores for WMT11 German-English system combination outputs. Note, only a single reference translation per segment was available. Decode corresponds to results after weight tuning and Oracle corresponds to graph TER oracle. Dagger (†) denotes statistically significant difference compared to iTERp and GIZA.

Aligner	Decode		Oracle	
	tune	test	tune	test
iTERp	34.20	33.61	50.45	51.28
GIZA	34.02	33.62	50.23	51.20
iTER	34.44	33.79	50.39	50.39
iITGp	34.41	33.85	50.55	51.33
iIHMM	34.61	34.05†	50.48	51.27

Table 4: Case insensitive BLEU scores for WMT11 Spanish-English system combination outputs. Note, only a single reference translation per segment was available. Decode corresponds to results after weight tuning and Oracle corresponds to graph TER oracle. Dagger (†) denotes statistically significant difference compared to aligners above iIHMM.

The BLEU scores for German-English system combination outputs are shown in Table 3. Again, the graph TER oracle scores do not follow the same order as the decoding scores. The scores for GIZA and iTERp are statistically indistinguishable, and iTER, iIHMM, and iITGp are significantly better than the first two. However, they are not statistically different from each other. Without flexible matching, iITG yields a BLEU score of 26.47 on test. The absolute BLEU gain over the best individual system was between 1.9 and 2.3 points on the test set.

The BLEU scores for Spanish-English system combination outputs are shown in Table 4. All aligners but iIHMM are statistically indistinguishable and iIHMM is significantly better than all other aligners. Without flexible matching, iITG yields a BLEU score of 33.62 on test. The absolute BLEU gain over the best individual system was between 3.5 and 3.9 points on the test set.

5 Error Analysis

Error analysis was performed to better understand the gains from system combination. Specifically, (i) how the different types of translation errors are affected by system combination was investigated; and (ii) an attempt to quantify the correlation between the word agreement that results from the different aligners and the translation error, as measured by TER (Snover et al., 2006), was made.

5.1 Influence on Error Types

For each one of the individual systems, and for each one of the three language pairs, the per-sentence errors that resulted from that system, as well as from each one of the the different aligners studied in this paper, were computed. The errors were broken down into insertions/deletions/substitutions/shifts based on the TER scorer.

The error counts at the document level were aggregated. For each document in each collection, the number of errors of each type that resulted from each individual system as well as each system combination were measured, and their difference was computed. If the differences are mostly positive, then it can be said (with some confidence) that system combination has a significant impact in reducing the error of that type. A paired Wilcoxon test was performed and the p-value that quantifies the probability that the measured error reduction was achieved under the null hypothesis that the system combination performs as well as the best system was computed.

Table 5 shows all conditions under consideration. All cases where the p-value is below 10^{-2} are considered statistically significant. Two observations are in order: (i) all alignment schemes significantly reduce the number of substitution/shift errors; (ii) in the case of insertions/deletions, there is no clear trend; there are cases where the system combination increases the number of insertions/deletions, compared to the individual systems.

5.2 Relationship between Word Agreement and Translation Error

This set of experiments aimed to quantify the relationship between the translation error rate and the amount of agreement that resulted from each alignment scheme. The amount of system agreement at a level x is measured by the number of cases (confusion network arcs) where x system outputs contribute the same word in a confusion network bin. For example, the agreement at level 2 is equal to 2 in Figure 1 because there are exactly 2 arcs (with words "twelve" and "blue") that resulted from the agreement of 2 systems. Similarly, the agreement at level 3 is 1, because there is only 1 arc (with word "cars") that resulted from the agreement of 3 systems. It is hypothesized that a sufficiently high level of agreement should be indicative of the correctness of a word (and thus indicative of lower TER). The agreement statistics were grouped into two values: the "weak" agreement statistic, where at most half of the combined systems contribute a word, and the "strong" agreement statistic, where more than half of the combined systems contribute a word. To signify the fact that real words and "NULL" tokens have different roles and should be treated separately, two sets of agreement statistics were computed.

	non-NULL words		NULL words	
	weak	strong	weak	strong
Arabic	0.087	-0.068	0.192	0.094
German	0.117	-0.067	0.206	0.147
Spanish	0.085	-0.134	0.323	0.102

Table 6: Regression coefficients of the "strong" and "weak" agreement features, as computed with a generalized linear model, using TER as the target variable.

A regression with a generalized linear model (glm) that computed the coefficients of the agreement quantities (as explained above) for each alignment scheme, using TER as the target variable, was performed. Table 6 shows the regression coefficients; they are all significant at p-value < 0.001. As is clear from this table, the negative coefficient of the "strong" agreement quantity for the non-NULL words points to the fact that good aligners tend to result in reductions in translation error. Furthermore, increasing agreements on NULL tokens does not seem to reduce TER.

6 Conclusions

This paper presented a systematic comparison of five different hypothesis alignment algorithms for MT system combination via confusion network decoding. Pre-processing, decoding, and weight tuning were controlled and only the alignment algorithm was varied. Translation quality was compared qualitatively using case insensitive BLEU scores. The results showed that confusion network decoding yields a significant gain over the best individual system irrespective of the alignment algorithm. Differences between the combination output using different alignment algorithms were relatively small, but incremental alignment consistently yielded better translation quality compared to pairwise alignment based on these experiments and previously published literature. Incremental IHMM and a novel incremental ITG with flexible matching consistently yield highest quality combination outputs. Furthermore, an error analysis shows that most of the per-

Language	Aligner	ins	del	sub	shft
Arabic	GIZA	2.2e-16	0.9999	2.2e-16	2.2e-16
	iHMM	2.2e-16	0.433	2.2e-16	2.2e-16
	iITGp	0.8279	2.2e-16	2.2e-16	2.2e-16
	iTER	4.994e-07	3.424e-11	2.2e-16	2.2e-16
	iTERp	2.2e-16	1	2.2e-16	2.2e-16
German	GIZA	7.017e-12	2.588e-06	2.2e-16	2.2e-16
	iHMM	6.858e-07	0.4208	2.2e-16	2.2e-16
	iITGp	0.8551	0.2848	2.2e-16	2.2e-16
	iTER	0.2491	1.233e-07	2.2e-16	2.2e-16
	iTERp	0.9997	0.007489	2.2e-16	2.2e-16
Spanish	GIZA	2.2e-16	0.8804	2.2e-16	2.2e-16
	iHMM	2.2e-16	1	2.2e-16	2.2e-16
	iITGp	2.2e-16	0.9999	2.2e-16	2.2e-16
	iTER	2.2e-16	1	2.2e-16	2.2e-16
	iTERp	3.335e-16	1	2.2e-16	2.2e-16

Table 5: p-values which show which error types are statistically significantly improved for each language and aligner.

formance gains from system combination can be attributed to reductions in substitution errors and word re-ordering errors. Finally, better alignments of system outputs, which tend to cause higher agreement rates on words, correlate with reductions in translation error.

References

Necip Fazil Ayan, Jing Zheng, and Wen Wang. 2008. Improving alignments for better confusion networks for combining machine translation systems. In *Proc. Coling*, pages 33–40.

Srinivas Bangalore, German Bordel, and Giuseppe Riccardi. 2001. Computing consensus translation from multiple machine translation systems. In *Proc. ASRU*, pages 351–354.

Peter F. Brown, Stephen A. Della Pietra, Vincent J. Della Pietra, and Robert L. Mercer. 1993. The mathematics of statistical machine translation: Parameter estimation. *Computational Linguistics*, 19(2):263–311.

Chris Callison-Burch, Philipp Koehn, Christof Monz, and Omar F. Zaidan. 2011. Findings of the 2011 workshop on statistical machine translation. In *Proc. WMT*, pages 22–64.

Eugene Charniak, Sharon Goldwater, and Mark Johnson. 1998. Edge-based best-first chart parsing. In *Proc. Sixth Workshop on Very Large Corpora*, pages 127–133. Morgan Kaufmann.

Jacob Devlin, Antti-Veikko I. Rosti, Shankar Ananthakrishnan, and Spyros Matsoukas. 2011. System combination using discriminative cross-adaptation. In *Proc. IJCNLP*, pages 667–675.

Jonathan G. Fiscus. 1997. A post-processing system to yield reduced word error rates: Recognizer output voting error reduction (ROVER). In *Proc. ASRU*, pages 347–354.

Robert Frederking and Sergei Nirenburg. 1994. Three heads are better than one. In *Proc. ANLP*, pages 95–100.

Xiaodong He and Kristina Toutanova. 2009. Joint optimization for machine translation system combination. In *Proc. EMNLP*, pages 1202–1211.

Xiaodong He, Mei Yang, Jianfeng Gao, Patrick Nguyen, and Robert Moore. 2008. Indirect-hmm-based hypothesis alignment for combining outputs from machine translation systems. In *Proc. EMNLP*, pages 98–107.

Almut S. Hildebrand and Stephan Vogel. 2008. Combination of machine translation systems via hypothesis selection from combined n-best lists. In *AMTA*, pages 254–261.

Shyamsundar Jayaraman and Alon Lavie. 2005. Multi-engine machine translation guided by explicit word matching. In *Proc. EAMT*.

Damianos Karakos, Jason Eisner, Sanjeev Khudanpur, and Markus Dreyer. 2008. Machine translation system combination using ITG-based alignments. In *Proc. ACL*, pages 81–84.

Damianos Karakos, Jason R. Smith, and Sanjeev Khudanpur. 2010. Hypothesis ranking and two-pass approaches for machine translation system combination. In *Proc. ICASSP*.

Dan Klein and Christopher D. Manning. 2003. A* parsing: Fast exact Viterbi parse selection. In *Proc. NAACL*, pages 40–47.

Philipp Koehn. 2004. Statistical significance tests for machine translation evaluation. In *Proc. EMNLP*, pages 388–395.

Gregor Leusch, Nicola Ueffing, and Hermann Ney. 2003. A novel string-to-string distance measure with applications to machine translation evaluation. In *Proc. MT Summit 2003*, pages 240–247, September.

Chi-Ho Li, Xiaodong He, Yupeng Liu, and Ning Xi. 2009. Incremental hmm alignment for mt system combination. In *Proc. ACL/IJCNLP*, pages 949–957.

Lidia Mangu, Eric Brill, and Andreas Stolcke. 2000. Finding consensus in speech recognition: Word error minimization and other applications of confusion networks. *Computer Speech and Language*, 14(4):373–400.

Evgeny Matusov, Richard Zens, and Hermann Ney. 2004. Symmetric word alignments for statistical machine translation. In *Proc. COLING*, pages 219–225.

Evgeny Matusov, Nicola Ueffing, and Hermann Ney. 2006. Computing consensus translation from multiple machine translation systems using enhanced hypotheses alignment. In *Proc. EACL*, pages 33–40.

Franz J. Och and Hermann Ney. 2003. A systematic comparison of various statistical alignment models. *Computational Linguistics*, 29(1):19–51.

Franz J. Och. 2003. Minimum error rate training in statistical machine translation. In *Proc. ACL*, pages 160–167.

Kishore Papineni, Salim Roukos, Todd Ward, and Wei-Jing Zhu. 2002. BLEU: a method for automatic evaluation of machine translation. In *Proc. ACL*, pages 311–318.

William H. Press, Saul A. Teukolsky, William T. Vetterling, and Brian P. Flannery. 2007. *Numerical recipes: the art of scientific computing*. Cambridge University Press, 3rd edition.

Antti-Veikko I. Rosti, Spyros Matsoukas, and Rirchard Schwartz. 2007a. Improved word-level system combination for machine translation. In *Proc. ACL*, pages 312–319.

Antti-Veikko I. Rosti, Bing Xiang, Spyros Matsoukas, Richard Schwartz, Necip Fazil Ayan, and Bonnie J. Dorr. 2007b. Combining outputs from multiple machine translation systems. In *Proc. NAACL-HLT*, pages 228–235.

Antti-Veikko I. Rosti, Bing Zhang, Spyros Matsoukas, and Richard Schwartz. 2008. Incremental hypothesis alignment for building confusion networks with application to machine translation system combination. In *Proceedings of the Third Workshop on Statistical Machine Translation*, pages 183–186.

Antti-Veikko I. Rosti, Bing Zhang, Spyros Matsoukas, and Richard Schwartz. 2009. Incremental hypothesis alignment with flexible matching for building confusion networks: BBN system description for WMT09 system combination task. In *Proc. WMT*, pages 61–65.

Antti-Veikko I. Rosti, Bing Zhang, Spyros Matsoukas, and Richard Schwartz. 2010. BBN system description for WMT10 system combination task. In *Proc. WMT*, pages 321–326.

Antti-Veikko I. Rosti, Evgeny Matusov, Jason Smith, Necip Fazil Ayan, Jason Eisner, Damianos Karakos, Sanjeev Khudanpur, Gregor Leusch, Zhifei Li, Spyros Matsoukas, Hermann Ney, Richard Schwartz, Bing Zhang, and Jing Zheng. 2011. Confusion network decoding for MT system combination. In Joseph Olive, Caitlin Christianson, and John McCary, editors, *Handbook of Natural Language Processing and Machine Translation: DARPA Global Autonomous Language Exploitation*, pages 333–361. Springer.

Khe Chai Sim, William J. Byrne, Mark J.F. Gales, Hichem Sahbi, and Phil C. Woodland. 2007. Consensus network decoding for statistical machine translation system combination. In *Proc. ICASSP*.

Matthew Snover, Bonnie Dorr, Richard Schwartz, Linnea Micciula, and John Makhoul. 2006. A study of translation edit rate with targeted human annotation. In *Proc. AMTA*, pages 223–231.

Matthew Snover, Nitin Madnani, Bonnie Dorr, and Richard Schwartz. 2009. Fluency, adequacy or HTER? exploring different human judgments with a tunable MT metric. In *Proc. WMT*, pages 259–268.

Stephan Vogel, Hermann Ney, and Christoph Tillman. 1996. HMM-based word alignment in statistical translation. In *Proc. ICCL*, pages 836–841.

Dekai Wu. 1997. Stochastic inversion transduction grammars and bilingual parsing of parallel corpora. *Computational Linguistics*, 23(3):377–403, September.

Daguang Xu, Yuan Cao, and Damianos Karakos. 2011. Description of the JHU system combination scheme for WMT 2011. In *Proc. WMT*, pages 171–176.

On Hierarchical Re-ordering and Permutation Parsing for Phrase-based Decoding

Colin Cherry
National Research Council
colin.cherry@nrc-cnrc.gc.ca

Robert C. Moore
Google
bobmoore@google.com

Chris Quirk
Microsoft Research
chrisq@microsoft.com

Abstract

The addition of a deterministic permutation parser can provide valuable hierarchical information to a phrase-based statistical machine translation (PBSMT) system. Permutation parsers have been used to implement hierarchical re-ordering models (Galley and Manning, 2008) and to enforce inversion transduction grammar (ITG) constraints (Feng et al., 2010). We present a number of theoretical results regarding the use of permutation parsers in PBSMT. In particular, we show that an existing ITG constraint (Zens et al., 2004) does not prevent all non-ITG permutations, and we demonstrate that the hierarchical re-ordering model can produce analyses during decoding that are inconsistent with analyses made during training. Experimentally, we verify the utility of hierarchical re-ordering, and compare several theoretically-motivated variants in terms of both translation quality and the syntactic complexity of their output.

1 Introduction

Despite the emergence of a number of syntax-based techniques, phrase-based statistical machine translation remains a competitive and very efficient translation paradigm (Galley and Manning, 2010). However, it lacks the syntactically-informed movement models and constraints that are provided implicitly by working with synchronous grammars. Therefore, re-ordering must be modeled and constrained explicitly. Movement can be modeled with a distortion penalty or lexicalized re-ordering probabilities (Koehn et al., 2003; Koehn et al., 2007), while decoding can be constrained by distortion limits or by mimicking the restrictions of inversion transduction grammars (Wu, 1997; Zens et al., 2004).

Recently, we have begun to see deterministic permutation parsers incorporated into phrase-based decoders. These efficient parsers analyze the sequence of phrases used to produce the target, and assemble them into a hierarchical translation history that can be used to inform re-ordering decisions. Thus far, they have been used to enable a hierarchical re-ordering model, or HRM (Galley and Manning, 2008), as well as an ITG constraint (Feng et al., 2010). We discuss each of these techniques in turn, and then explore the implications of ITG violations on hierarchical re-ordering.

We present one experimental and four theoretical contributions. Examining the HRM alone, we present an improved algorithm for extracting HRM statistics, reducing the complexity of Galley and Manning's solution from $O(n^4)$ to $O(n^2)$. Examining ITG constraints alone, we demonstrate that the three-stack constraint of Feng et al. can be reduced to one augmented stack, and we show that another phrase-based ITG constraint (Zens et al., 2004) actually allows some ITG violations to pass. Finally, we show that in the presence of ITG violations, the original HRM can fail to produce orientations that are consistent with the orientations collected during training. We propose three HRM variants to address this situation, including an approximate HRM that requires no permutation parser, and compare them experimentally. The variants perform similarly to the original in terms of BLEU score, but differently in terms of how they permute the source sentence.

We begin by establishing some notation. We view the phrase-based translation process as producing a sequence of source/target blocks in their target order. For the purposes of this paper, we disregard the lexical content of these blocks, treating blocks spanning the same source segment as equivalent. The block $[s_i, t_i]$ indicates that the source segment $w_{s_i+1}, \ldots, w_{t_i}$ was translated as a unit to produce the ith target phrase. We index between words; therefore, a block's length in tokens is $t - s$, and for a sentence of length n, $0 \leq s \leq t \leq n$. Empty blocks have $s = t$, and are used only in special cases. Two blocks $[s_{i-1}, t_{i-1}]$ and $[s_i, t_i]$ are *adjacent* iff $t_{i-1} = s_i$ or $t_i = s_{i-1}$. Note that we concern ourselves only with adjacency in the source. Adjacency in the target is assumed, as the blocks are in target order. Figure 1 shows an example block sequence, where adjacency corresponds to cases where block corners touch. In the shift-reduce permutation parser we describe below, the parsing state is encoded as a stack of these same blocks.

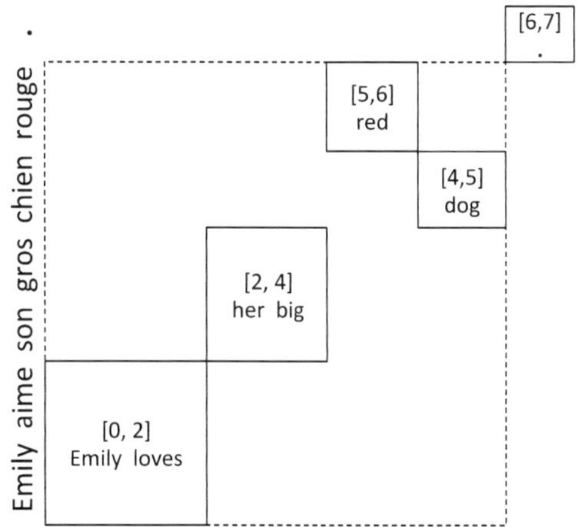

Figure 1: A French-to-English translation with 5 blocks.

2 Hierarchical Re-ordering

Hierarchical re-ordering models (HRMs) for phrase-based SMT are an extension of lexicalized re-ordering models (LRMs), so we begin by briefly reviewing the LRM (Tillmann, 2004; Koehn et al., 2007). The goal of an LRM is to characterize how a phrase-pair tends to be placed with respect to the block that immediately precedes it. Both the LRM and the HRM track orientations traveling through the target from left-to-right as well as right-to-left. For the sake of brevity and clarity, we discuss only the left-to-right direction except when stated otherwise. Re-ordering is typically categorized into three orientations, which are determined by examining two sequential blocks $[s_{i-1}, t_{i-1}]$ and $[s_i, t_i]$:

- Monotone Adjacent (M): $t_{i-1} = s_i$
- Swap Adjacent (S): $t_i = s_{i-1}$
- Disjoint (D): otherwise

Figure 1 shows a simple example, where the first two blocks are placed in monotone orientation, followed by a disjoint "red", a swapped "dog" and a disjoint period. The probability of an orientation $O_i \in \{M, S, D\}$ is determined by a conditional distribution: $Pr(O_i|\textit{source phrase}_i, \textit{target phrase}_i)$. To build this model, orientation counts can be extracted from aligned parallel text using a simple heuristic (Koehn et al., 2007).

The HRM (Galley and Manning, 2008) maintains similar re-ordering statistics, but determines orientation differently. It is designed to address the LRM's dependence on the previous block $[s_{i-1}, t_{i-1}]$. Consider the period [6,7] in Figure 1. If a different segmentation of the source had preceded it, such as one that translates "chien rouge" as a single [4,6] block, the period would have been in monotone orientation. Galley and Manning (2008) introduce a deterministic shift-reduce parser into decoding, so that the decoder always has access to the largest possible previous block, given the current translation history. The parser has two operations: *shift* places a newly translated block on the top of the stack. If the top two blocks are adjacent, then a *reduce* is immediately performed, replacing them with a single block spanning both. Table 1 shows the parser states corresponding to our running example. Whether "chien rouge" is translated using [5,6],[4,5] or [4,6] alone, the shift-reduce parser provides a consolidated previous block of [0,6] at the top of the stack (shown with dotted lines). Therefore, [6,7] is placed in monotone orientation in both cases.

The parser can be easily integrated into a phrase-based decoder's translation state, so each partial hypothesis carries its own shift-reduce stack. Time and memory costs for copying and storing stacks can be kept small by sharing tails across decoder states. The stack subsumes the coverage vector in that it contains strictly more information: every covered

Op	Stack
S	[0,2]
S	[0,2],[2,4]
R	[0,4]
S	[0,4],[5,6]
S	[0,4],[5,6],[4,5]
R	[0,4],[4,6]
R	[0,6]
S	[0,6],[6,7]
R	[0,7]

Table 1: Shift-reduce states corresponding to Figure 1.

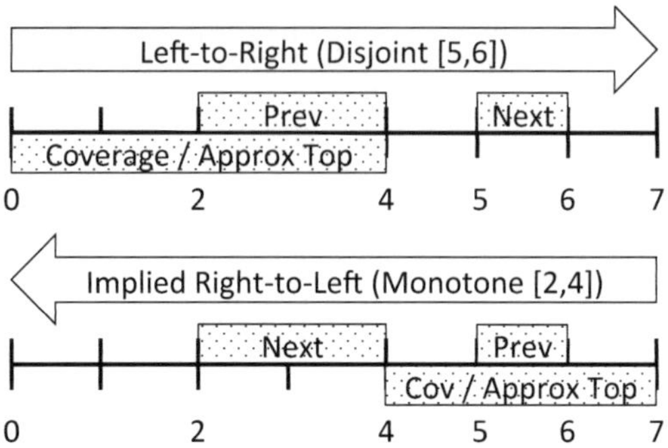

Figure 2: Illustration of the coverage-vector stack approximation, as applied to right-to-left HRM orientation.

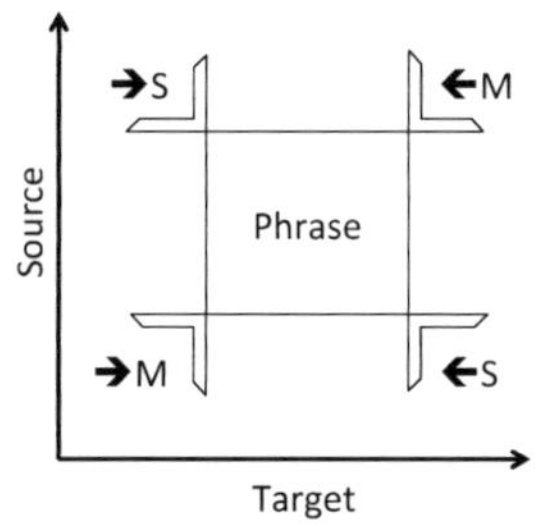

Figure 3: Relevant corners in HRM extraction. → indicates left-to-right orientation, and ← right-to-left.

word will be present in one of the stack's blocks. However, it can be useful to maintain both.

The top item of a parser's stack can be approximated using only the coverage vector. The approximate top is the largest block of covered words that contains the last translated block. This approximation will always be as large or larger than the true top of the stack, and it will often match the true top exactly. For example, in Figure 1, after we have translated [2,4], we can see that the coverage vector contains all of [0,4], making the approximate top [0,4], which is also the true top. In fact, this approximation is correct at every time step shown in Figure 1. Keep this approximation in mind, as we return to it in Sections 3.2 and 4.3.

We do not use a shift-reduce parser that consumes source words from right-to-left;[1] therefore, we apply the above approximation to handle the right-to-left HRM. Before doing so, we re-interpret the decoder state to simulate a right-to-left decoder. The last block becomes $[s_i, t_i]$ and the next block becomes $[s_{i-1}, t_{i-1}]$, and the coverage vector is inverted so that covered words become uncovered and vice versa. Taken all together, the approximate test for right-to-left adjacency checks that any gap between $[s_{i-1}, t_{i-1}]$ and $[s_i, t_i]$ is *uncovered* in the original coverage vector.[2] Figure 2 illustrates how a monotone right-to-left orientation can be (correctly) determined for $[2, 4]$ after placing $[5, 6]$ in Figure 1.

Statistics for the HRM can be extracted from word-aligned training data. Galley and Manning (2008) propose an algorithm that begins by running standard phrase extraction (Och and Ney, 2004) without a phrase-length limit, noting the corners of each phrase found. Next, the left-to-right and right-to-left orientation for each phrase of interest (those within the phrase-length limit) can be determined by checking to see if any corners noted in the previous step are adjacent, as shown in Figure 3.

2.1 Efficient Extraction of HRM statistics

The time complexity of phrase extraction is bounded by the number of phrases to be extracted, which is determined by the sparsity of the input word alignment. Without a limit on phrase length, a sentence pair with n words in each language can have as many as $O(n^4)$ phrase-pairs.[3] Because it relies on unrestricted phrase extraction, the corner collection step for determining HRM orientation is also $O(n^4)$.

By leveraging the fact that the first step collects corners, not phrase-pairs, we can show that HRM extraction can actually be done in $O(n^2)$ time, through a process we call *corner propagation*. Instead of running unrestricted phrase-extraction, corner propagation begins by extracting all minimal

[1] This would require a second, right-to-left decoding pass.

[2] Galley and Manning (2008) present an under-specified approximation that is consistent with what we present here.

[3] Consider a word-alignment with only one link in the center of the grid.

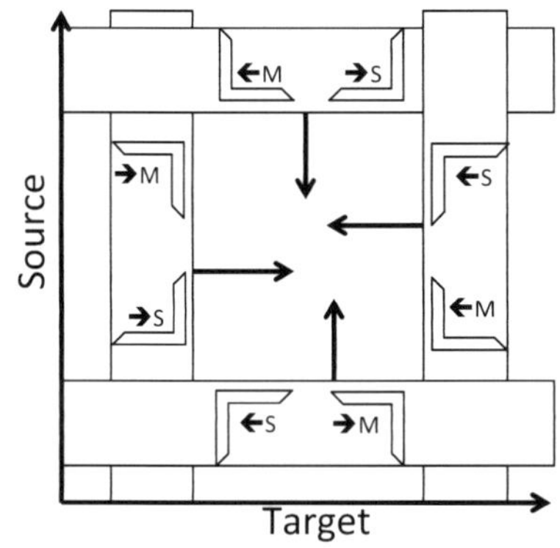

Figure 4: Corner Propagation: Each of the four passes propagates two types of corners along a single dimension.

phrase-pairs; that is, those that do not include unaligned words at their boundaries. The complexity of this step is $O(n^2)$, as the number of minimal phrases is bounded by the minimum of the number of monolingual phrases in either language. We note corners for each minimal pair, as in the original HRM extractor. We then carry out four non-nested propagation steps to handle unaligned words, traversing the source (target) in forward and reverse order, with each unaligned row (column) copying corners from the previous row (column). Each pass takes $O(n^2)$ time, for a total complexity of $O(n^2)$. This process is analogous to the growing step in phrase extraction, but computational complexity is minimized because each corner is considered independently. Pseudo-code is provided in Algorithm 1, and the propagation step is diagrammed in Figure 4. In our implementation, corner propagation is roughly two-times faster than running unrestricted phrase-extraction to collect corners.

Note that the trickiest corners to catch are those that are diagonally separated from their minimal block (they result from unaligned growth in both the source and target). These cases are handled correctly because each corner type is touched by two propagators, one for the source and one for the target (see Figure 4). For example, the top-right-corner array $A^{\urcorner}$ is populated by both propagate-right and propagate-up. Thus, one propagator can copy a corner along one dimension, while the next propagator copies the copies along the other dimension, moving the original corner diagonally.

Algorithm 1 Corner Propagation

Initialize target-source indexed binary arrays $A^{\urcorner}[m][n]$, $A_{\lrcorner}[m][n]$, $A^{\ulcorner}[m][n]$ and $A_{\llcorner}[m][n]$ to record corners found in minimal phrase-pairs.
{Propagate Right}
for i from 2 to m s.t. $target[i]$ is unaligned **do**
  for j from 1 to n **do**
    $A^{\urcorner}[i][j]$ = True if $A^{\urcorner}[i-1][j]$ is True
    $A_{\lrcorner}[i][j]$ = True if $A_{\lrcorner}[i-1][j]$ is True
{Propagate Up}
for j from 2 to n s.t. $source[j]$ is unaligned **do**
  for i from 1 to m **do**
    $A^{\ulcorner}[i][j]$ = True if $A^{\ulcorner}[i][j-1]$ is True
    $A^{\urcorner}[i][j]$ = True if $A^{\urcorner}[i][j-1]$ is True
{Propagate Left and Down are similar}
return $A^{\urcorner}$, $A_{\lrcorner}$, $A^{\ulcorner}$ and $A_{\llcorner}$

3 ITG-Constrained Decoding

Phrase-based decoding places no implicit limits on re-ordering; all $n!$ permutations are theoretically possible. This is undesirable, as it leads to intractability (Knight, 1999). Therefore, re-ordering is limited explicitly, typically using a distortion limit. One particularly well-studied re-ordering constraint is the ITG constraint, which limits source permutations to those achievable by a binary bracketing synchronous context-free grammar (Wu, 1997). ITG constraints are known to stop permutations that generalize 3142 and 2413,[4] and can drastically limit the re-ordering space for long strings (Zens and Ney, 2003). There are two methods to incorporate ITG constraints into a phrase-based decoder, one using the coverage vector (Zens et al., 2004), and the other using a shift-reduce parser (Feng et al., 2010). We begin with the latter, returning to the coverage-vector constraint later in this section.

Feng et al. (2010) describe an ITG constraint that is implemented using the same permutation parser used in the HRM. To understand their method, it is important to note that the set of ITG-compliant permutations is exactly the same as those that can be reduced to a single-item stack using the shift-reduce permutation parser (Zhang and Gildea, 2007). In fact, this manner of parsing was introduced to SMT

[4] 2413 is shorthand notation that denotes the block sequence [1,2],[3,4],[0,1],[2,3] as diagrammed in Figure 5a.

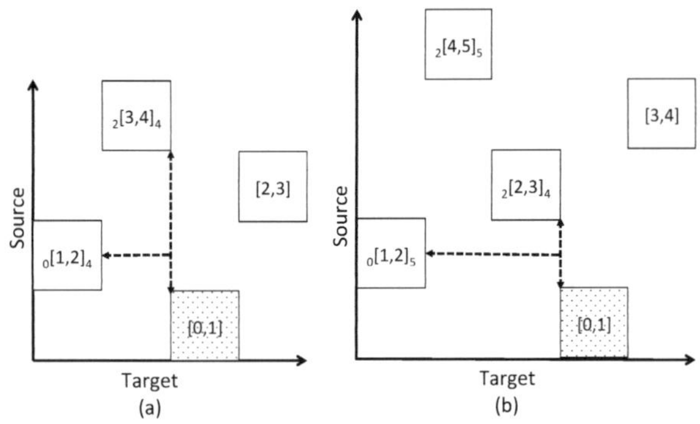

Figure 5: Two non-ITG permutations. Violations of potential adjacency are indicated with dotted spans. Bounds for the one-stack constraint are shown as subscripts.

in order to binarize synchronous grammar productions (Zhang et al., 2006). Therefore, enforcing an ITG constraint in the presence of a shift-reduce parser amounts to ensuring that every shifted item can eventually be reduced. To discuss this constraint, we introduce a notion of *potential adjacency*, where two blocks are potentially adjacent if any words separating them have not yet been covered. Formally, blocks $[s,t]$ and $[s',t']$ are potentially adjacent iff one of the following conditions holds:

· they are adjacent ($t' = s$ or $t = s'$)
· $t' < s$ and $[t', s]$ is uncovered
· $t < s'$ and $[t, s']$ is uncovered

Recall that a reduction occurs when the top two items of the stack are adjacent. To ensure that reductions remain possible, we only shift items onto the stack that are potentially adjacent to the current top. Figure 5 diagrams two non-ITG permutations and highlights where potential adjacency is violated. Note that no reductions occur in either of these examples; therefore, each block $[s_i, t_i]$ is also the top of the stack at time i. Potential adjacency can be confirmed with some overhead using the stack and coverage vector together, but Feng et al. (2010) present an elegant three-stack solution that provides potentially adjacent regions in constant time, without a coverage vector. We improve upon their method later this section. From this point on, we abbreviate potential adjacency as PA.

We briefly sketch a proof that maintaining potential adjacency maintains reducibility, by showing that non-PA shifts produce irreducible stacks, and that PA shifts are reducible. It is easy to see that every non-PA shift leads to an irreducible stack. Let $[s', t']$ be an item to be shifted onto the stack, and $[s, t]$ be the current top. Assume that $t' < s$ and the two items are not PA (the case where $t < s'$ is similar). Because they are not PA, there is some index k in $[t', s]$ that has been previously covered. Since it is covered, k exists somewhere in the stack, buried beneath $[s, t]$. Because k cannot be re-used, no series of additional shift and reduce operations can extend $[s', t']$ so that it becomes adjacent to $[s, t]$. Therefore, $[s, t]$ will never participate in a reduction, and parsing will close with at least two items on the stack. Similarly, one can easily show that every PA shift is reducible, because the uncovered space $[t', s]$ can be filled by extending the new top toward the previous top using strictly adjacent shifts.

3.1 A One-stack ITG Constraint

As mentioned earlier, Feng et al. (2010) provide a method to track potential adjacency that does not require a coverage vector. Instead, they maintain three stacks, the original stack and two others to track potentially adjacent regions to the left and right respectively. These regions become available to the decoder only when the top of the original stack is adjacent to one of the adjacency stacks.

We show that the same goal can be achieved with even less book-keeping by augmenting the items on the original stack to track the regions of potential adjacency around them. The intuition behind this technique is that on a shift, the new top inherits all of the constraints on the old top, and the old top becomes a constraint itself. Each stack item now has four fields, the original block $[s,t]$, plus a left and right adjacency bound, denoted together as ${}_\ell[s,t]_r$, where ℓ and r are indices for the maximal span containing $[s,t]$ that is uncovered except for $[s,t]$. If the top of the stack is ${}_\ell[s,t]_r$, then shifted items must fall inside one of the two PA regions, $[\ell, s]$ or $[t, r]$. The region shifted into determines new item's bounds.

The stack is initialized with a special ${}_0[0,0]_n$ item, and we then shift unannotated blocks onto the stack. As we shift $[s', t']$ onto the stack, rules derive bounds ℓ' and r' for the new top based on the old top ${}_\ell[s,t]_r$:

- Shift-left ($t' \le s$): $\ell' = \ell$, $r' = s$
- Shift-right ($t \le s'$): $\ell' = t$, $r' = r$

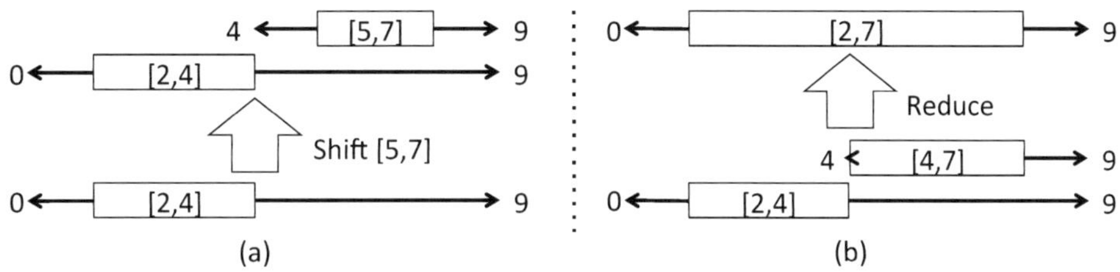

Figure 6: Two examples of boundaries for the one-stack solution for potential adjacency. Stacks are built from bottom to top, blocks indicate [s,t] blocks, while tails are left and right adjacency boundaries.

Meanwhile, when reducing a stack with ${}_{\ell'}[s', t']_{r'}$ at the top and ${}_{\ell}[s, t]_{r}$ below it, the new top simply copies ℓ and r. The merged item is larger than $[s, t]$, but it is PA to the same regions. Figure 6 diagrams a shift-right and a reduce, while Figure 5 annotates bounds for blocks during its ITG violations.

3.2 The Coverage-Vector ITG Constraint is Incomplete

The stack-based solution for ITG constraints is elegant, but there is also a proposed constraint that uses only the coverage vector (Zens et al., 2004). This constraint can be stated with one simple rule: if the previously translated block is $[s_{i-1}, t_{i-1}]$ and the next block to be translated is $[s_i, t_i]$, one must be able to travel along the coverage vector from $[s_{i-1}, t_{i-1}]$ to $[s_i, t_i]$ without transitioning from an uncovered word to a covered word. Feng et al. (2010) compare the two ITG constraints, and show that they perform similarly, but not identically. They attribute the discrepancy to differences in *when* the constraints are applied, which is strange, as the two constraints need not be timed differently.

Let us examine the coverage-vector constraint more carefully, assuming that $t_i < s_{i-1}$ (the case where $t_{i-1} < s_i$ is similar). The constraint consists of two phases: first, starting from s_{i-1}, we travel to the left toward t_i, consuming covered words until we reach the first uncovered word. We then enter into the second phase, and the path must remain uncovered until we reach t_i. The first step over covered positions corresponds to finding the left boundary of the largest covered block containing $[s_{i-1}, t_{i-1}]$, which is an approximation to the top of the stack (Section 2). The second step over uncovered positions corresponds to determining whether $[s_i, t_i]$ is PA to the approximate top. That is, the coverage-vector ITG constraint checks for potential adjacency using the same top-of-stack approximation as the right-to-left HRM.

This implicit approximation implies that there may well be cases where the coverage-vector constraint makes the wrong decision. Indeed this is the case, which we prove by example. Consider the irreducible sequence 25314, illustrated in Figure 5b. This non-ITG permutation is allowed by the coverage-vector approximation, but not by the stack-based constraint. Both constraints allow the placement of the first three blocks $[1, 2]$, $[4, 5]$ and $[2, 3]$. After adding $[0, 1]$, the stack-based solution detects a PA-violation. Meanwhile, the vector-based solution checks the path from 2 to 1 for a transition from uncovered to covered. This short path touches only covered words. Similarly, as we add $[3, 4]$, the path from 1 to 3 is also completely covered. The entire permutation is accepted without complaint. The proof provided by Zens et al. (2004) misses this case, as it accounts for phrasal generalizations of the 2413 ITG-forbidden substructure, but it does not account for generalizations where the substructure is interrupted by a discontiguous item, such as in $25\{3\}14$, where 2413 is revealed not by merging items but by deleting 3.

4 Inconsistencies in HRM parsing

We have shown that the HRM and the ITG constraints for phrase-based decoding use the same deterministic shift-reduce parser. The entirety of the ITG discussion was devoted to preventing the parser from reaching an irreducible state. However, up until now, work on the HRM has not addressed the question of irreducibility (Galley and Manning, 2008; Nguyen et al., 2009).

Irreducible derivations do occur during HRM decoding, and when they do, they can create inconsistencies with respect to HRM extraction from word-

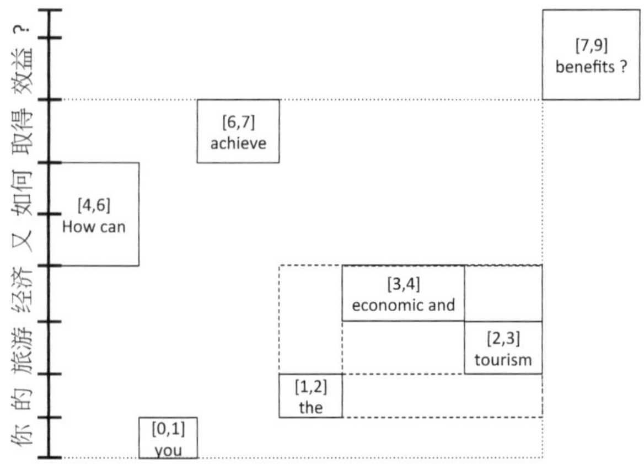

Figure 7: An example irreducible derivation, drawn from our Chinese-to-English decoder's k-best output.

Last translated block		2-red	*-red	approx
How can	$[4, 6]$	[4,6]	[4,6]	[4,6]
you	$[0, 1]$	[0,1]	[0,1]	[0,1]
achieve	$[6, 7]$	[6,7]	[6,7]	**[4,7]**
the	$[1, 2]$	[1,2]	[1,2]	**[0,2]**
economic and	$[3, 4]$	[3,4]	[3,4]	**[3,7]**
tourism	$[2, 3]$	**[1,4]**	[0,7]	[0,7]
benefits?	$[7, 9]$	**[7,9]**	[0,9]	[0,9]

Table 2: Top of stack at each time step in Figure 7, under 2-reduction (as in the original HRM), *-reduction, and the coverage-vector approximation.

aligned training data. In Figure 7, we show an irreducible block sequence, extracted from a Chinese-English decoder. The parser can perform a few small reductions, creating a [1,4] block indicated with a dashed box, but translation closes with 5 items on the stack. One can see that [7,9] is assigned a disjoint orientation by the HRM. However, if the same translation and alignment were seen during training, the unrestricted phrase extractor would find a phrase at [0,7], indicated with a dotted box, and [7,9] would be assigned monotone orientation. This inconsistency penalizes this derivation, as "benefits ?" is forced into an unlikely disjoint orientation. One potential implication is that the decoder will tend to avoid irreducible states, as those states will tend to force unlikely orientations, resulting in a hidden, soft ITG-constraint. Indeed, our decoder does not select this hypothesis, but instead a (worse) translation that is fully reducible. The impact of these inconsistencies on translation quality can only be determined empirically. However, to do so, we require alternatives that address these inconsistencies. We describe three such variants below.

4.1 ITG-constrained decoding

Perhaps the most obvious way to address irreducible states is to activate ITG constraints whenever decoding with an HRM. Irreducible derivations will disappear from the decoder, along with the corresponding inconsistencies in orientation. Since both techniques require the same parser, there is very little overhead. However, we will have also limited our decoder's re-ordering capabilities.

4.2 Unrestricted shift-reduce parsing

The deterministic shift-reduce parser used throughout this paper is actually a special case of a general class of permutation parsers, much in the same way that a binary ITG is a special case of synchronous context-free grammar. Zhang and Gildea (2007) describe a family of k-reducing permutation parsers, which can reduce the top k items of the stack instead of the top 2. For $k \geq 2$ we can generalize the adjacency requirement for reduction to a *permutation* requirement. Let $\{[s_i, t_i]|\text{i=1...k}\}$ be the top k items of a stack; they are a permutation iff:

$$\max_i(t_i) - \min_i(s_i) = \sum_i [t_i - s_i]$$

That is, every number between the max and min is present somewhere in the set. Since two adjacent items always fulfill this property, we know the original parser is 2-reducing. k-reducing parsers reduce by moving progressively deeper in the stack, looking for the smallest $2 \leq i \leq k$ that satisfies the permutation property (see Algorithm 2). As in the original parser, a k-reduction is performed every time the top of the stack changes; that is, after each shift and each successful reduction.

If we set $k = \infty$, the parser will find the smallest possible reduction without restriction; we refer to this as a *-reducing parser. This parser will never reach an irreducible state. In the worst case, it reduces the entire permutation as a single n-reduction after the last shift. This means it will exactly mimic unrestricted phrase-extraction when predicting orientations, eliminating inconsistencies without restricting our re-ordering space. The disadvantage is

Algorithm 2 k-reduce a stack

input stack $\{[s_i, t_i] | i = 1 \ldots l\}$; $i = 1$ is the top
input max reduction size k, $k \geq 2$
set $s' = s_1$; $t' = t_1$; $size = t_1 - s_1$
for i from 2 to $\min(k, l)$ **do**
  set $s' = \min(s', s_i)$; $t' = \max(t', t_i)$
  set $size = size + (t_i - s_i)$
  if $t' - s' == size$ **then**
    pop $\{[s_j, t_j] | j = 1 \ldots i\}$ from the stack
    push $[s', t']$ onto the stack;
    return `true` // *successful reduction*
return `false` // *failed to reduce*

that reduction is no longer a constant-time operation, but is instead $O(n)$ in the worst case (consider Algorithm 2 with $k = \infty$ and $l = n$ items on the stack).[5] As a result, we will carefully track the impact of this parser on decoding speed.

4.3 Coverage vector approximation

One final option is to adopt the top-of-stack approximation for left-to-right orientations, in addition to its current use for right-to-left orientations, eliminating the need for any permutation parser. The next block $[s_i, t_i]$ is adjacent to the approximate top of the stack only if any space between $[s_i, t_i]$ and the previous block $[s_{i-1}, t_{i-1}]$ is covered. But before committing fully to this approximation, we should better understand it. Thus far, we have implied that this approximation can fail to predict correct orientations, but we have not specified when these failures occur. We now show that incorrect orientations can only occur while producing a non-ITG permutation.

Let $[s_{i-1}, t_{i-1}]$ be the last translated block, and $[s_i, t_i]$ be the next block. Recall that the approximation determines the top of the stack using the largest block of covered words that contains $[s_{i-1}, t_{i-1}]$. The approximate top always contains the true top, because they both contain $[s_{i-1}, t_{i-1}]$ and the approximate top is the largest block that does so. Therefore, the approximation errs on the side of adjacency, meaning it can only make mistakes when

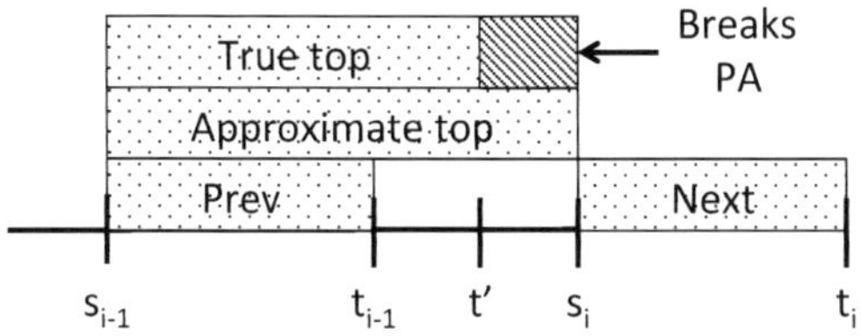

Figure 8: Indices for when the coverage approximation predicts a false M.

assigning an M or S orientation; if it assigns a D, it is always correct. Let us consider the false M case (the false S case is similar). If we assign a false M, then $t_{i-1} < s_i$ and s_i is adjacent to the approximate top; therefore, all positions between t_{i-1} and s_i are covered. However, since the M is false, the true top of the stack must end at some $t' : t_{i-1} \leq t' < s_i$. Since we know that every position between t' and s_i is covered, $[s_i, t_i]$ cannot be PA to the true top of the stack, and we must be in the midst of making a non-ITG permutation. See Figure 8 for an illustration of the various indices involved. As it turns out, both the approximation and the 2-reducing parser assign incorrect orientations only in the presence of ITG violations. However, the approximation may be preferable, as it requires only a coverage vector.

4.4 Qualitative comparison

Each solution manages its stack differently, and we illustrate the differences in terms of the top of the stack at time i in Table 2. The *-reducing parser is the gold standard, so we highlight deviations from its decisions in bold. As one can see, the original 2-reducing parser does fine before and during an ITG violation, but can create false disjoint orientations after the violation is complete, as the top of its stack becomes too small due to missing reductions. Conversely, the coverage-vector approximation makes errors inside the violation: the approximate top becomes too large, potentially creating false monotone or swap orientations. Once the violation is complete, it recovers nicely.

5 Experiments

We compare the LRM, the HRM and the three HRM variants suggested in Section 4 on a Chinese-to-English translation task. We measure the impact on translation quality in terms of BLEU score (Papineni et al., 2002), as well as the impact on permutation

[5]Zhang and Gildea (2007) provide an efficient algorithm for *-reduction that uses additional book-keeping so that the number of permutation checks as one traverses the entire sequence is linear in aggregate; however, we implement the simpler, less efficient version here to simplify decoder integration.

	BLEU			NIST 08 Complexity Counts						Speed
Method	nist04	nist06	nist08	> 2	4	5	6	7	≥ 8	sec/sent
LRM	38.00	33.79	27.12	241	146	40	32	12	11	3.187
HRM 2-red	38.53	34.20	27.57	176	113	31	20	8	4	3.353
HRM apprx	38.58	34.09	27.60	280	198	41	26	13	2	3.231
HRM *-red	38.39	34.22	27.41	328	189	71	34	20	14	3.585
HRM itg	38.70	34.26	27.33	0	0	0	0	0	0	3.274

Table 3: Chinese-to-English translation results, comparing the LRM and 4 HRM variants: the original 2-reducing parser, the coverage vector approximation, the *-reducing parser, and an ITG-constrained decoder.

complexity, as measured by the largest k required to k-reduce the translations.

5.1 Data

The system was trained on data from the NIST 2009 Chinese MT evaluation, consisting of more than 10M sentence pairs. The training corpora were split into two phrase tables, one for Hong Kong and UN data, and one for all other data. The dev set was taken from the NIST 05 evaluation set, augmented with some material reserved from other NIST corpora; it consists of 1.5K sentence pairs. The NIST 04, 06, and 08 evaluation sets were used for testing.

5.2 System

We use a phrase-based translation system similar to Moses (Koehn et al., 2007). In addition to our 8 translation model features (4 for each phrase table), we have a distortion penalty incorporating the minimum possible completion cost described by Moore and Quirk (2007), a length penalty, a 5-gram language model trained on the NIST09 Gigaword corpus, and a 4-gram language model trained on the target half of the parallel corpus. The LRM and HRM are represented with six features, with separate weights for M, S and D in both directions (Koehn et al., 2007). We employ a gap constraint as our only distortion limit (Chang and Collins, 2011). This restricts the maximum distance between the start of a phrase and the earliest uncovered word, and is set to 7 words. Parameters are tuned using a batch-lattice version of hope-fear MIRA (Chiang et al., 2008; Cherry and Foster, 2012). We re-tune parameters for each variant.

5.3 Results

Our results are summarized in Table 3. Speed and complexity are measured on the NIST08 test set, which has 1357 sentences. We measure permutation complexity by parsing the one-best derivations from each system with an external *-reducing parser, and noting the largest k-reduction for each derivation. Therefore, the $>$2 column counts the number of non-ITG derivations produced by each system.

Regarding quality, we have verified the effectiveness of the HRM: each HRM variant outperforms the LRM, with the 2-reducing HRM doing so by 0.4 BLEU points on average. Unlike Feng et al. (2010), we see no consistent benefit from adding hard ITG constraints, perhaps because we are building on an HRM-enabled system. In fact, all HRM variants perform more or less the same, with no clear winner emerging. Interestingly, the approximate HRM is included in this pack, which implies that groups wishing to augment their phrase-based decoder with an HRM need not incorporate a shift-reduce parser.

Regarding complexity, the 2-reducing HRM produces about half as many non-ITG derivations as the *-reducing system, confirming our hypothesis that a 2-reducing HRM acts as a sort of soft ITG constraint. Both the approximate and *-reducing decoders produce more violating derivations than the LRM. This is likely due to their encouragement of more movement overall. The largest reduction we observed was $k = 11$.

Our speed tests show that all of the systems translate at roughly the same speed, with the LRM being fastest and the *-reducing HRM being slowest. The *-reducing system is less than 7% slower than the 2-reducing system, alleviating our concerns regarding the cost of *-reduction.

6 Discussion

We have presented a number of theoretical contributions on the topic of phrase-based decoding with an on-board permutation parser. In particular, we have shown that the coverage-vector ITG constraint is actually incomplete, and that the original HRM can produce inconsistent orientations in the presence of ITG violations. We have presented three HRM variants that address these inconsistencies, and we have compared them in terms of both translation quality and permutation complexity. Though our results indicate that a permutation parser is actually unnecessary to reap the benefits of hierarchical re-ordering, we are excited about the prospects of further exploring the information provided by these on-board parsers. In particular, we are interested in using features borrowed from transition-based parsing while decoding.

References

Yin-Wen Chang and Michael Collins. 2011. Exact decoding of phrase-based translation models through lagrangian relaxation. In *EMNLP*, pages 26–37, Edinburgh, Scotland, UK., July.

Colin Cherry and George Foster. 2012. Batch tuning strategies for statistical machine translation. In *HLT-NAACL*, Montreal, Canada, June.

David Chiang, Yuval Marton, and Philip Resnik. 2008. Online large-margin training of syntactic and structural translation features. In *EMNLP*, pages 224–233.

Yang Feng, Haitao Mi, Yang Liu, and Qun Liu. 2010. An efficient shift-reduce decoding algorithm for phrase-based machine translation. In *COLING*, pages 285–293, Beijing, China, August.

Michel Galley and Christopher D. Manning. 2008. A simple and effective hierarchical phrase reordering model. In *EMNLP*, pages 848–856, Honolulu, Hawaii, October.

Michel Galley and Christopher D. Manning. 2010. Accurate non-hierarchical phrase-based translation. In *HLT-NAACL*, pages 966–974, Los Angeles, California, June.

Kevin Knight. 1999. Squibs and discussions: Decoding complexity in word-replacement translation models. *Computational Linguistics*, 25(4):607–615, December.

Philipp Koehn, Franz J. Och, and Daniel Marcu. 2003. Statistical phrase-based translation. In *HLT-NAACL*, pages 127–133.

Philipp Koehn, Hieu Hoang, Alexandra Birch, Chris Callison-Burch, Marcello Federico, Nicola Bertoldi, Brooke Cowan, Wade Shen, Christine Moran, Richard Zens, Chris Dyer, Ondrej Bojar, Alexandra Constantin, and Evan Herbst. 2007. Moses: Open source toolkit for statistical machine translation. In *ACL*, pages 177–180, Prague, Czech Republic, June.

Robert C. Moore and Chris Quirk. 2007. Faster beam-search decoding for phrasal statistical machine translation. In *MT Summit XI*, September.

Vinh Van Nguyen, Akira Shimazu, Minh Le Nguyen, and Thai Phuong Nguyen. 2009. Improving a lexicalized hierarchical reordering model using maximum entropy. In *MT Summit XII*, Ottawa, Canada, August.

Franz Josef Och and Hermann Ney. 2004. The alignment template approach to statistical machine translation. *Computational Linguistics*, 30(4), December.

Kishore Papineni, Salim Roukos, Todd Ward, and Wei-Jing Zhu. 2002. BLEU: a method for automatic evaluation of machine translation. In *ACL*, pages 311–318.

Christoph Tillmann. 2004. A unigram orientation model for statistical machine translation. In *HLT-NAACL*, pages 101–104, Boston, USA, May.

Dekai Wu. 1997. Stochastic inversion transduction grammars and bilingual parsing of parallel corpora. *Computational Linguistics*, 23(3):377–403.

Richard Zens and Hermann Ney. 2003. A comparative study on reordering constraints in statistical machine translation. In *ACL*, pages 144–151.

Richard Zens, Hermann Ney, Taro Watanabe, and Eiichiro Sumita. 2004. Reordering constraints for phrase-based statistical machine translation. In *COLING*, pages 205–211, Geneva, Switzerland, August.

Hao Zhang and Daniel Gildea. 2007. Factorization of synchronous context-free grammars in linear time. In *Proceedings of SSST, NAACL-HLT 2007 / AMTA Workshop on Syntax and Structure in Statistical Translation*, pages 25–32, Rochester, New York, April.

Hao Zhang, Liang Huang, Daniel Gildea, and Kevin Knight. 2006. Synchronous binarization for machine translation. In *HLT-NAACL*, pages 256–263, New York City, USA, June.

CCG Syntactic Reordering Models for Phrase-based Machine Translation

Dennis N. Mehay
The Ohio State University
Columbus, OH, USA
mehay@ling.ohio-state.edu

Chris Brew
Educational Testing Service
Princeton, NJ, USA
cbrew@ets.org

Abstract

Statistical phrase-based machine translation requires no linguistic information beyond word-aligned parallel corpora (Zens et al., 2002; Koehn et al., 2003). Unfortunately, this linguistic agnosticism often produces ungrammatical translations. *Syntax*, or sentence structure, could provide guidance to phrase-based systems, but the "non-constituent" word strings that phrase-based decoders manipulate complicate the use of most recursive syntactic tools. We address these issues by using Combinatory Categorial Grammar, or CCG, (Steedman, 2000), which has a much more flexible notion of constituency, thereby providing more labels for putative non-constituent multiword translation phrases. Using CCG parse charts, we train a syntactic analogue of a lexicalized reordering model by labelling phrase table entries with multiword labels and demonstrate significant improvements in translating between Urdu and English, two language pairs with divergent sentence structure.

1 Introduction

Statistical phrase-based machine translation (PMT) is attractive, as it requires no linguistic information beyond word-aligned parallel corpora (Zens et al., 2002; Koehn et al., 2003). Unfortunately, this linguistic agnosticism leaves phrase-based systems with no precise characterization of the word order relationships between languages, often leading to ungrammatical translations. Syntax could provide guidance to phrase-based systems, by steering them towards reorderings that reflect the structural relationships between languages, but using syntax to guide a phrase-based system is problematic. Phrase-based systems build the result incrementally from the beginning of the target string to the end, and the intermediate strings need not constitute complete traditional syntactic constituents. It is difficult to reconcile traditional recursive syntactic processing with this regime, because not all intermediate strings considered by the decoder would even have a syntactic category to assess. As a result, most phrase-based decoders control reordering using simple distance-based distortion models, which penalize all reordering equally, and lexicalized reordering models (Tillmann, 2004; Axelrod et al., 2005), which probabilistically score various reordering configurations conditioned on specific lexical translations. While undoubtedly better than nothing, these models perform poorly when languages diverge considerably in sentence structure. Distance-based distortion models are too coarse-grained to distinguish correct from incorrect reordering, while lexical reordering models suffer from data sparsity and fail to capture more general patterns. We argue that finding a way to label translation phrases with syntactic labels will abstract over the observed reordering configurations thereby address both all three deficiencies of granularity, data sparsity and lack of generality.

The present work presents a novel syntactic analogue of the lexicalized reordering model that uses multiword syntactic labels to capture the general reordering patterns between two languages with very different word order. We accomplish this by using Combinatory Categorial Grammar, or CCG (Steedman, 2000), a word-centered syntax that allows a great deal of flexibility in how sentence analyses are formed. Syntactic derivations in CCG are massively *spuriously ambiguous*, i.e., there are many ways to derive the same semantic analysis of a sentence, similar to how a mathematical equation can be reduced by canceling out variables in different orders. Despite its name, spurious ambiguity is a benefit to us, as it provides many different labelled bracketings for the same dependency graph of the same sentence, thereby increasing the chance that any substring of that sentence will have a syntactic label. Our approach exploits this property of CCG to derive multiword CCG syntactic labels for target translation strings in a phrase table, thus providing a firmer basis on which to collect syntactic reordering statistics. In particular:

- We show how CCG can derive constituent labels for target-side phrase-table entries that are often lamented as "non-constituents" or as "crossing a phrase boundary".

- Our CCG categories are not limited to single-word *supertags*. Rather, as these labels are drawn from CCG parse charts, they can span multiple words. Further, the labels are tailored specifically to each translation constituent's boundaries (Section 2.1). As a consequence, $\approx$70% of phrase table entries receive a single syntactic label (Section 5), largely removing the terminological inconsistency of calling lexical translation constituents "phrases". Now, more of them actually are syntactic phrases.

- We use these labels to train a target-language bidirectional reordering model over CCG syntactic sequences (Section 3), which, when added to the baseline system, is found to be superior to systems that use both lexicalized reordering models and supertag reordering models (Section 5).

With only minor modifications, we incorporate these enhancements into a state-of-the-art PMT decoder (Koehn et al., 2007), achieving significant improvements over two competitive baselines in an Urdu-English translation task (Sections 5). This language pair was chosen to highlight the promise of this approach for languages with considerable, but syntactically governed, word-order differences to one another. Finally, in a small discussion we provide qualitative evidence that the improvements in automatic metric scores correspond to real gains in target language fluency.

2 Syntax, Constituency and Phrase-based MT

Consider the following German-English PMT phrase pair that we have extracted from a parallel European parliamentary transcript:[1]

Ich hoffe, daß $\Leftrightarrow$ I hope that

Neither word string is a well-formed constituent in traditional theories of syntax. But tradition is at odds with the intuition that that such "non-constituent" sequences are still well-formed substrings, governed by rules of how they can be combined with other word strings — e.g., declarative sentence translation rules like es möglich sein wird $\Leftrightarrow$ it will be possible can grammatically extend each, but a noun phrase rule cannot.

As Figure 1 illustrates, putative non-constituent word sequences abound in phrase-based MT. Here a translation "phrase" is simply any contiguous word string that is consistent with a word alignment (a relation between source and target words), usually produced by a language-independent alignment procedure (Zens et al., 2002). The figure also highlights the need for linguistic syntax in controlling how translations are assembled; the successful translation is merely one among many possible reorderings, many of which (despite their ungrammaticality) might score well on a word n-gram model. But rather than changing the word alignments or PMT "phrase" boundaries to fit a syntactic theory, we choose to use a flexible syntax which can produce a wider range of bracketings to accommodate the results of alignment-derived translations. To this end, we use Combinatory Categorial Grammar, or CCG, (Steedman, 2000). To understand how CCG allows this, we illustrate its use with some simple examples.

[1]Throughout this paper, the term "PMT phrase" refers to an unbroken sequence of words used by a PMT system, whereas "phrase" (without context) refers to a syntactic constituent.

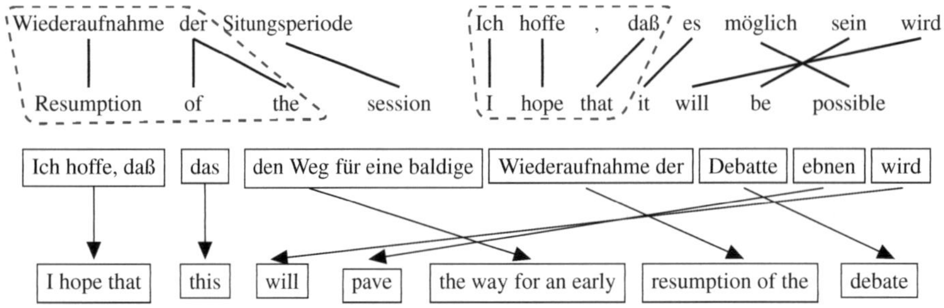

Figure 1: Two phrase-based MT word groups are extracted from aligned words (the dashed outlines) and then used to form a new translation (bottom). [Adapted from parallel sentences in the Europarl German-English corpus, v6.]

2.1 CCG, Spurious Ambiguity and PMT: Turning "Phrases" into Phrases

CCG is a derivational syntax, where words are assigned a *lexical category*[2] and sentence structures are then recursively built using a small set of deductive rule schemata known as *combinators* (Steedman, 2000). Lexical syntactic categories can be richly structured in CCG, indicating how words can combine. A syntactic category of the form $\mathsf{X/Y}$, e.g., states that a category of type X can be formed if combined with a Y to its right — i.e., a function from rightward Ys to X. This can be accomplished with the *forward function application* combinator (>),[3] which is written in derivational form as follows:[4]

$$\dfrac{\mathsf{X/Y} \quad \mathsf{Y}}{\mathsf{X}}>$$

This derivation of the symbol X is known as the *normal-form* derivation (Steedman, 2000), since it uses function application whenever possible. But CCG has the ability to construct the same result by using a different, *non-normal-form* sequence of combinatory inferences. For example, by using the *backward type-raising* combinator ($\mathbf{T}_<$) and then *backward function application* (<), we can arrive at the same result:

$$\dfrac{\dfrac{\mathsf{X/Y}}{} \quad \dfrac{\mathsf{Y}}{\mathsf{X\backslash(X/Y)}}\mathbf{T}_<}{\mathsf{X}}<$$

This derivation shows how the argument Y to the functional type $\mathsf{X/Y}$[5] can "raise" its type to become a function that consumes that functional type, $\mathsf{X\backslash(X/Y)}$, only to produce same result as before, namely X. This property of CCG is often referred to as "spurious ambiguity", because there are many ways of reaching the same result as the canonical, normal-form derivation.

Despite the name, this property is useful for our purposes. Considering the target translation in Figure 1, we then observe in Figure 2 how CCG can derive not only a bracketing similar to a more traditional Penn Treebank-style parse, but also a non-normal-form variant that gives us a single category for the English translation string [I hope that] — namely the category $\mathsf{S[dcl]/S[dcl]}$ (a declarative sentence lacking a declarative sentence complement to its right).

We use this fact about CCG to label a wider range of PMT phrases with genuine syntactic constituent labels. First we parse the English sentences in our training data with the C&C parser, a state-of-the-art, treebank-trained CCG parser (Clark and Curran, 2007), producing normal-form CCG derivations. We then enumerate all non-normal-form derivations that result in the same top-level symbol, packing all derivations (normal-form and non-normal-form) into a parse chart (see Figure 4).

[2]When represented by a strings, lexical categories are called *supertags*.

[3]CCG actually respects the rule-to-rule hypothesis (Bach, 1976), where, for every syntactic term built, there is a corresponding semantic term, but, for simplicity of exposition, we focus only on syntax here.

[4]The reader will notice that CCG derivations are in fact trees, but that they "grow" in the direction opposite to how parse trees are often depicted in NLP.

[5]Also referred to as a *functor*.

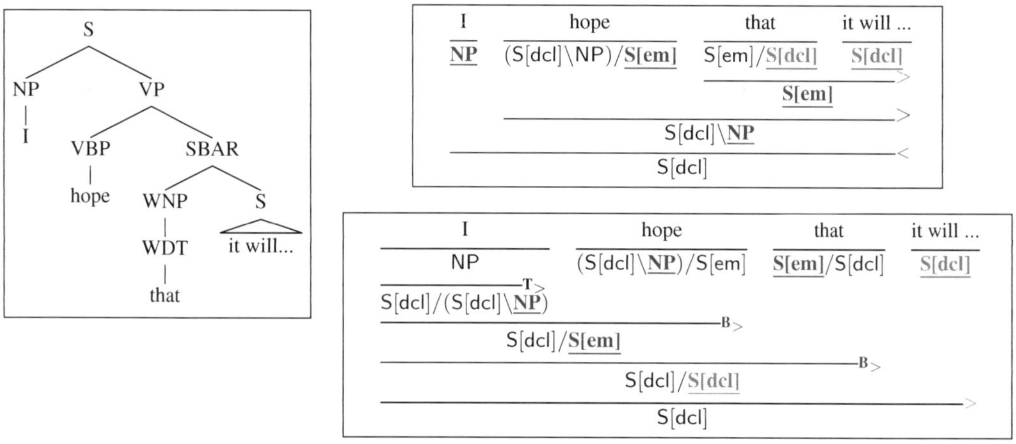

Figure 2: *Left:* a traditional syntactic derivation; *top right:* a normal-form CCG derivation with the same subject+predicate bracketing; *bottom right:* one of many non-normal-form variants. Combinator symbol key: >=forward function application, <=backward function application, $\mathbf{T}_>$=forward type-raising, $\mathbf{B}_>$=forward composition. Note: the CCG dependencies that are discharged in different orders are indicated by color-coding (if available in your medium) and underlining the appropriate categories (type-raising discharges no dependencies). Both CCG derivations lead to the same symbol (S[dcl]), and dependencies.

	UR.-EN.
SINGLE-LABEL COVERAGE	69%
AVE. EN. PHRASE LEN.	2.8 wds
AVE. CCG LABEL SPAN	2.3 wds
AVE. CCG LABS/ENTRY	1.4

Table 1: Training data statistics (top to bottom): (1) % of single CCG labels spanning entire English translation phrases, (2) average length of English translation phrase, (3) average CCG label span and (4) average CCG labels per English translation phrase. (Maximum translation phrase length is 7 words.)

For the English string of each phrase table entry, we inspect the chart for the English-side sentence that it came from and extract a list of labels as in Figure 3. For each span, this procedure either (lines 5–9) finds the topmost single label, only using type-raised categories when no others exist,[6] or (lines 10–19) recursively and greedily finds the longest spanning labels from left to right, if no single label exists. The degenerate case is the single-word level (supertags). In this way we find single labels for 69% of the English-side phrase training instances. Table 1 gives more details.

[6]Type-raisings are almost always possible, and will always be closer to the top-level symbol. Many type-raisings, however, are superfluous – i.e., produce no novel bracketings. Therefore we only use type-raised symbols to derive a label for a span of words when necessary.

```
GETLABELS(C,s)
 1  ▷ C: a packed chart of derivations of E
 2  ▷ s = (e_l, e_r): a span in target sentence E
 3  ▷ RETURN: a list of labels covering all words
 4  ▷              from E in span s
 5  if EXISTSSINGLESPANNINGLABEL(C,S)
 6    then ▷ Get the topmost label
 7         ▷ non-type-raised, if possible
 8         lb ← GETTOPMOSTLABEL(C,s)
 9         return [ lb ]
10    else ▷ Get the longest label starting at e_l
11         for i ← (e_r − 1) to (e_l + 1)
12         do lbs ← GETLABELS(C,(e_l, i))
13            if LENGTH(lbs)=1
14              then e_l' ← i + 1
15                   lb ← HEAD(lbs)
16                   BREAK
17              else CONTINUE
18         return
19           CONS(lb,GETLABELS(C,(e_l', e_r)))
```

Figure 3: Algorithm for labeling English sides of phrase table instances.

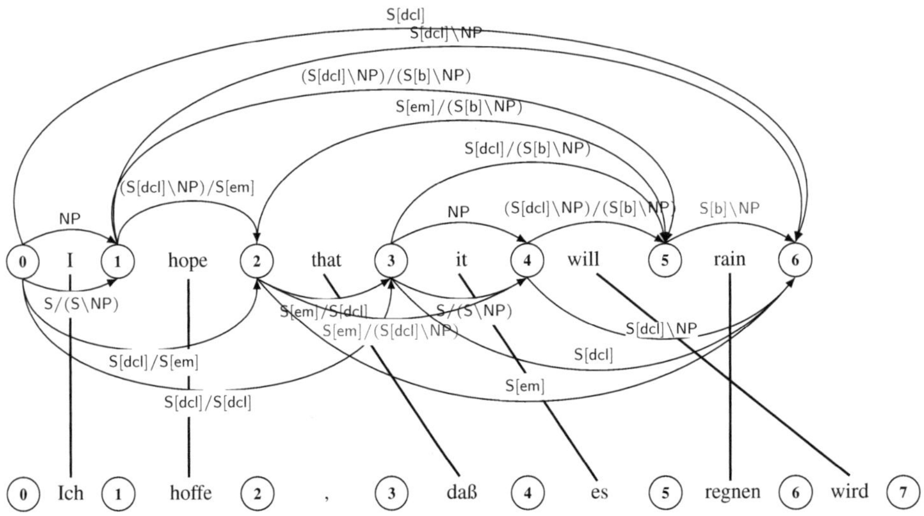

Figure 4: A packed CCG parse chart with multiple semantically equivalent derivations and two word-aligned strings. (Not all derivations are depicted.)

3 Reordering Models: from Words to Supertags to Parses

In phrase-based MT systems, the standard reordering model that controls the order in which the source string is translated is the lexicalized reordering model (Tillmann, 2004; Axelrod et al., 2005). In its simplest form, a lexicalized reordering model estimates, for each translation phrase pair $(\mathbf{f}_{i...j}, \mathbf{e}_{k...l})$ (where the indices sit "in-between" words, as in Figure 4), the probability of $p(\textsc{o} \mid \mathbf{f}_{i...j}, \mathbf{e}_{k...l})$, where $\textsc{o} \in \{\textsc{Mono}, \textsc{Swap}, \textsc{Discontinuous}\}$ (abbreviated M, S and D) is the orientation of the phrase pair $(\mathbf{f}_{i...j}, \mathbf{e}_{k...l})$ w.r.t. the previously translated source phrase $\mathbf{f}_{u...v}$. If $v = i$, then $\textsc{o} = \text{M}$; if $u = j$, then $\textsc{o} = \text{S}$; otherwise $\textsc{o} = \text{D}$. This model, known as a *unidirectional* MSD lexicalized reordering model, can also be enriched with statistics over orientations to the next source phrase translated (i.e., it can be a *bidirectional* model), as well as with more fine-grained distinctions in the third class D (i.e., whether it is D_{LEFT} or D_{RIGHT}). All models in the present work are bidirectional MSD models.

During decoding, orientations are predicted based on previously translated (or following) phrases in the decoder's search state, but, when extracting orientation statistics, there are many different possible phrasal segmentations of both strings. A simple solution, known as *word-based extraction*, is to look for neighboring alignment points that support the various orientations. In Figure 4, e.g., a word-based extraction regime would count the phrase hoffe ⇔ hope as being in orientation D w.r.t. to what follows, because its rightmost index, 2, is discontiguous with the next aligned source point, (3,4). Another approach, known as *phrase-based extraction* aims to remedy this situation by conditioning the extraction of orientations on translation phrases consistent with the alignment. In Figure 4 there is a translation phrase that follows the phrase in question — *viz.*, , daß ⇔ that — and an orientation of M is therefore tallied.

Regardless of the method of extraction, lexicalized reordering model statistics rely on exact word-string pairs, $(\mathbf{f}, \mathbf{e})$, which can lead problems with data sparsity. Moreover, even given ample data, cross-phrasal reordering generalizations will be missed. E.g., the fact that regnen ⇔ rain has orientation S w.r.t. the previous phrase pair does not support the fact that other infinitival German verbs should also behave similarly in relative clausal environments.

To remedy this we might substitute abstract symbols for each word in **e**, and train a syntactic bidirectional MSD reordering model. For this we use CCG supertags (cf. the single-word labels in the parse chart in Figure 4), which are richly structured parts of speech that describe their potential to combine with other words (cf. Section 2.1). Given the same phrase from Figure 4, we can estimate the probability of orientation S, given [regnen] ⇔ [S[b]\NP]. A further level of abstraction is to use CCG parse charts packed with all derivations. The phrase [daß es] ⇔ [that it] can therefore be abstracted to [daß es] ⇔ [S[em]/(S[dcl]\NP)] (a "that" clause lacking a verb phrase to the right).

Except in cases of high ambiguity, the source phrase effectively encodes the target phrase, meaning that these extensions will suffer from data sparsity similarly to the baseline lexicalized model. We therefore omit the source phrase in our syntactic reordering models, estimating probability distributions $p(\text{O}|\text{LAB}(\mathbf{e}))$ where $\text{LAB}(\mathbf{e})$ is the syntactic label sequence derived from the chart (or supertagged string, as the case may be) using the algorithm in Figure 3.[7] Orientations are determined using the phrase-based extraction regime described in (Tillmann, 2004), but statistics are tallied only for the syntactic label sequence of the target string. More precisely, for phrase pair $(\mathbf{f}_{i...j}, \mathbf{e}_{k...l})$, if a phrase $(\mathbf{f}_{a...i}, \mathbf{e}_{b...k})$ exists in the alignment grid, an orientation of M is assigned to $\text{LAB}(\mathbf{e}_{k...l})$. Otherwise, if a phrase $(\mathbf{f}_{j...p}, \mathbf{e}_{l...m})$ exists in the alignment grid, an orientation of S is assigned. In all other cases, an orientation of D is assigned.

Using these statistics, we deploy target-side reordering models, as described below.

4 Related Work

As noted, lexicalized reordering models can be trained and configured in many different ways. In addition to the standard word-based extraction (Axelrod et al., 2005) and phrase-based extraction (Tillmann, 2004) cases, more recent work has explored using dynamic programming to extract and later score orientations based on *hierarchical configurations* of phrases consistent with an alignment (Galley and Manning, 2008). This means that the reordering model can be conditioned on an unbounded amount of context and can capture the fact that many translations are monotonic w.r.t. the previously translated block, but are mistakenly identified as having orientation S or D.

Su and colleagues (2010) observe that the space of phrase pairs consistent with an alignment can be viewed in its entirety, as a *graph* of phrases, thereby collecting reordering statistics w.r.t. the entire space of surrounding phrases. Ling and colleagues (2011) extend this approach by weighting orientation counts with multiple scored alignments. All of these more sophisticated reordering extraction approaches are compatible with the current approach, and could be straightforwardly applied to our labelled target-side word strings.

Syntax-driven reordering approaches in phrase-based MT abound, but, perhaps due to the incompatibility of phrase table entries and traditional syntactic constituency, most research has avoided using recursive target-side syntax during decoding. Tillmann (2008) presents an algorithm that reorders using part-of-speech based permutation patterns during the decoding process. Others have side-stepped the issue by restructuring the source language *before decoding* to resemble the target language using syntactic rules, either automatically extracted (Xia and McCord, 2004), or hand-crafted (Collins et al., 2005; Wang et al., 2007; Xu and Seneff, 2008).

The flexibility of CCG syntax is also gaining recognition as a useful tool for constraining statistical MT decoders. Hassan (2009) describes an incremental CCG parsing language model, although his model does not beat a supertag factored PMT approach. Almaghout and colleagues (2010) also use a CCG chart to improve translation, augmenting SCFG rules by consulting the multiple derivations in the parse chart of Clark and Curran's (2007) CCG parser. We note two key differences to our use of spurious ambiguity. First, they use a chart packed with *multiple* dependency analyses, unlike our spuriously ambiguous reworkings of the parser's *single*-best analysis. Second, the C&C parser restrains type-raising to a small number of possibilities, thereby blocking many non-normal-form derivations that we do not.

Two SCFG approaches that employ categorial syntax that resembles CCG are the *syntax-augmented MT* (SAMT) system described in (Venugopal et al., 2007), and the target dependency lan-

[7] Note that a tagged string can be viewed as a very impoverished parse chart, and so the algorithm defined in Figure 3 can be applied to the supertagging case as well.

guage model of of (Shen et al., 2008). (Venugopal et al., 2007) uses a Penn Treebank-trained CFG parser to label target strings and then reworks the CFG parse trees, if needed,x to account for non-traditional constituents. This on-demand reworking process, however, is bounded by tree depth, and sometimes produces conjoined categories, rather than consistently produce the functional "slash" categories that a full CCG would — e.g., a [subject + transitive verb] string might sometimes be labelled [NP + V] and other times [S/NP]. The approach in (Shen et al., 2010) uses a simple categorial grammar with only a single atomic symbol — i.e., every functional category has the form C\X or C/X, where X is either C or another slash category C\X or C/X. In contrast to these two approaches, the CCG parser we use is trained on a CCG treebank that is the result of a carefully engineered Penn Treebank-to-CCG conversion (Hockenmaier and Steedman, 2007) and we impose no limits on deriving categorial functional categories (X/Y). We view our reworking of CCG charts as a potentially useful extension to such approaches.

5 Experimental Results

We empirically validate our technique by translating from Urdu into English. Urdu has a canonical word order of SOV — subject, object(s), verb — whereas English has SVO, leading to indefinitely long distances between corresponding verbs and objects. This language pair is therefore a strong test case for a reordering model.

For decoding we use Moses (Koehn et al., 2007), a state-of-the-art PMT decoder, with IRST LM (Federico and Cettolo, 2007) for language model inference. For Urdu-English parallel data, we use the OpenMT 2008 training set which consists of 88 thousand sentence-level translations and a translation dictionary of ≈114 thousand word and phrase translations. We use half of the OpenMT 2008 Urdu-English evaluation data for development and perform development testing on the other half. Both halves are ≈900 sentences long and were balanced to contain approximately the same number of tokens. Our blind test set is the entire OpenMT 2009 Urdu-English evaluation set. All evaluation sets had 4 reference translations for each tuning or testing instance. All system component weights were tuned using minimum error-rate training (Och, 2003), with three tuning runs for each condition. The data was normalized, tokenized and the English sentences were lowercased,[8]

As a baseline, we train a standard phrase-based system with a bidirectional MSD lexicalized reordering model using word-based extraction. Our CCG-augmented reordering system has all of the model components of the baseline, as well as a bidirectional orientation reordering model over target-side multiword syntactic labels. To directly test the effect of using CCG parse charts — as opposed to simply using a CCG supertagger — we also added a CCG supertag bidirectional MSD reordering model to the baseline set-up. All systems were tuned and tested with distortion limit of 15 words, and test runs were performed with and without 200-best minimum Bayes' risk (MBR) hypothesis selection (Kumar and Byrne, 2004).

To acquire CCG labels for our English parallel data, we use the C&C CCG toolkit of Clark and Curran (2007). We build CCG parse charts by reworking the normal-form derivations from the C&C parser in all spuriously ambiguous ways, as described in Section 2.1. For supertags, we tag with the C&C supertagger. Rather than training separate phrase tables for our CCG systems, however, we instead decorate the baseline phrase tables with CCG multiword labels or supertags. To smooth over parsing and tagging errors, we only use those labels whose relative frequency (rf) is sufficiently high w.r.t. the most frequent label for that phrase pair $\text{LAB}^*_{[f\Leftrightarrow e]}$. More precisely, for each phrase pair, we use the set of labels:[9]

$$\{\text{LAB}_{[f\Leftrightarrow e]} | \text{rf}(\text{LAB}_{[f\Leftrightarrow e]}) \geq \beta \cdot \text{rf}(\text{LAB}^*_{[f\Leftrightarrow e]})\}$$

This is reminiscent of the β-best tagging approach of (Clark and Curran, 2004), but performed in a batch process when creating the syntactic phrase tables (both supertag and CCG chart-derived). We set

[8] N.B. We use Penn Treebank III-compatible tokenization for English and a specially designed tokenization script for Urdu, cf. (Baker et al., 2010), Appendix C

[9] Recalling that ≈31% of the time, a phrase pair might have a list of labels, rather than a single label, the word 'label' here refers to a single token that can be the concatenation of multiple symbols.

	DEVTEST (NIST-08) (MBR/NON-MBR)				NIST-09 TEST (MBR/NON-MBR)			
	BLEU-4	METEOR	TER	LENGTH	BLEU-4	METEOR	TER	LENGTH
LR	25.3/24.7	28.3/28.2	64.2/64.4	98.2/97.6	29.1/28.8	30.0/28.8	60.0/60.1	**98.2**/97.8
NO-LR	22.5/22.1	27.5/27.3	66.3/66.3	97.6/97.1	26.2/25.8	29.2/29.1	61.9/62.0	97.1/96.6
ST+LR	24.5/24.2	28.4/28.3	64.6/64.5	97.9/97.3	28.5/28.2	30.0/**30.0**	60.3/60.2	97.9/97.3
CCG+LR	**25.6/25.2**	**28.7/28.5**	64.3/64.5	**98.7/98.1**	29.1/**29.2**	30.1/**30.2**	**59.5/59.8**	97.4/**97.9**

Table 2: Case-insensitive BLEU-4, METEOR, TER and hypothesis/reference length ratio (LENGTH) for a lexicalized reordering baseline (LR), a system with only a distance-based distortion model (NO-LR), a system with an additional CCG supertag reordering model (ST+LR) and our system with an additional CCG chart-derived reordering model (CCG+LR). Systems were run with (left of slash) and without (right of slash) 200-best-list MBR hypothesis selection. All boldfaced results were found to be significantly better than the baseline at $\geq$ the 95% confidence level using method described in (Clark et al., 2011) with 3 separate MERT tuning runs for each system. Non-boldfaced numbers are statistically indistinguishable from (or worse than) the baseline.

$\beta = 0.5$ in all of our CCG experiments.

To minimize disruption to the Moses decoder (which only supports single-word labels in phrase-based mode), we project multiword labels across the words they label as single-word factors with bookkeeping characters, similar to the "microtag" annotations of asynchronous factored translation models (Cettolo et al., 2008). We modified to the decoder to reassemble the multiple single-word factors into a single label before querying the reordering model. As an example, we might have the phrase pair [le vélo rouge] ⇔ [the|NP(red|NP+ bike|NP)]. Before querying the reordering model, the factor sequence NP(NP+ NP) is collapsed into the single, multiword label 'NP' by the rule schema `X( ... X+ ... X)` → `X`.

We train a language model using all of the WMT 2011 NEWSCRAWL, NEWSCOMENTARY and EUROPARL monolingual data,[10] tokenized and lowercased as above, but de-duplicated to address the redundancy of the Web-crawled portion of that data set. We also train a separate language model on the English portion of the Urdu-English parallel corpus (minus the dictionary entries), and interpolate the two models by optimizing perplexity on our tuning set.

Table 2 lists our results, where we see significant improvement over both of our baselines, lexicalized reordering (LR) and supertag reordering plus lexicalized reordering (ST+LR). To test the effects of the lexicalized reordering model itself, we also evaluate a system with no lexicalized reordering model (only a distance-based distortion model). This last system (a system which almost always prefers not to reorder) is considerably worse than all other systems, demonstrating the need for non-monotonic reordering configurations when accounting for the Urdu-English data.

[10] `http://www.statmt.org/wmt11/translation-task.html`

6 Analysis and Discussion

Our CCG system (CCG+LR) outperforms both baseline systems (LR and ST+LR) in a majority of metrics in both MBR and non-MBR conditions. We see that, even though MBR decoding closes the performance gap somewhat, our system continues to match or outperform (if sometimes insignificantly) in all areas. Note that the CCG+LR non-MBR configuration outperforms both LR and ST+LR in MBR and non-MBR decoding conditions in its METEOR score on the NIST-09 test set. We note also that, in the NIST-09 test case, the CCG+LR system's poorer performance is perhaps due to a mismatch in hypothesis length, which could be harming its scores, particularly the BLEU brevity penalty.

6.1 Poor Performance of CCG Supertag Model

We have no firm explanation for the poor performance of the CCG supertag model (ST-LR), but it is important to note that the supertag reordering model does not unify statistics across phrases of different lengths, as the CCG chart-derived model does. E.g., the phrase pair [den Weg für eine] ⇔ [the way for an] will query the CCG chart-derived reordering model with the same symbol as the phrase pair [den Weg für eine baldige] ⇔ [the way for an early]

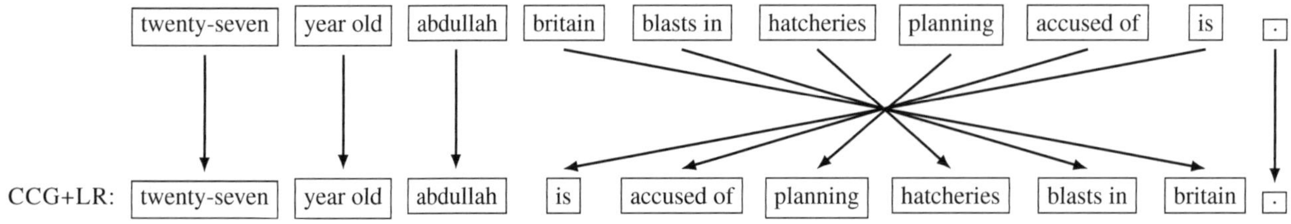

LR: twenty-seven years on charges of planning bombings hatcheries , abdullah in britain .
Reference 1: 27 years old abdullah is accused of planning explosions in britain .
Reference 2: twenty-seven years old abdullah is blamed for planning attacks in britain .
Reference 3: abdullah , 27 , has been blamed for planning the blasts in britain .
Reference 4: abdullah , 27 , has been blamed for planning the blasts in britain .

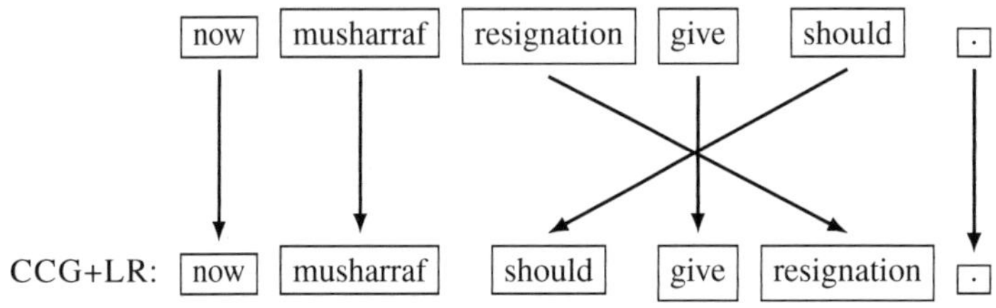

LR: now musharraf resignation should be given .
Reference 1: now musharraf should resign .
Reference 2: now , musharraf should resign .
Reference 3: now , musharraf should resign .
Reference 4: musharraf should resign .

Figure 5: Sample devtest (NIST-08) translations of the median-performing tuned CCG syntactic reordering model (CCG+LR) compared to the median-performing baseline lexicalized reordering model (LR).

— *viz.*, NP/N. The CCG supertag model, however, will have two distinct label sequences for these phrases — *viz.*, NP/N_N_(NP\NP)/NP_NP/N and NP/N_N_(NP\NP)/NP_NP/N_N/N, resp. — both of which could be reduced to the single label, NP/N, using CCG's syntactic combinators. The supertag system does not have the means of relating the reordering patterns of strings of symbols such as this.[11] Such data fragmentation may be leading to decreased performance, which would indicate the use of *recursive* CCG syntax.

6.2 Qualitative Improvements

In addition to improved metric scores, we noted real qualitative improvements in some examples, as Figure 5 shows. These examples demonstrate the ability of the reordering model to navigate the massive, structure-governed reorderings needed to approximate the correct answer with the phrase inventory it is given.

[11] Its reordering table has more than twice as many entries as that of the chart-derived model.

6.3 Comparison to the State of the Art

To our knowledge, the state of the art in Urdu-English translation using the OpenMT data is listed in the NIST OpenMT 2009 evaluation results (`http://www.itl.nist.gov/iad/mig/tests/mt/2009/ResultsRelease/currentUrdu.html`). This evaluation accepted only single system outputs, and used cased references. Therefore we had to choose a single system output and recase its text.

For system selection, we picked the tuned system that performed best on the development test set. For recasing, we trained a lowercased-to-cased monolingual phrase-based "translation model" with no reordering and a cased language model, similar to what is described in (Baker et al., 2010). The training text is simply the non-dictionary portion of the Urdu-English parallel corpus, with its lowercased version as the source and the original cased text as the target, both halves tokenized as above. We tuned on a similar version of the English half of our tuning references. The lowercased output of our system is fed to this model and the first token of each casing "translation" is capitalized (if not already).

The official metric of the NIST 2009 evaluation is BLEU (as implemented in the NIST-distributed `mteval-v13a.pl` script).[12] The best-performing system in the constrained data evaluation scored **0.312** w.r.t. the cased references, with the second and third place systems scoring **0.2395** and **0.2322**, respectively.[13] Our best performing MERT-tuned system (as determined on the devtest data) scores **0.2734** on the test set, putting it between the top two systems. For comparison, our devtest-best baseline LR system scores **0.2683** on the test set.

While is generally not useful to test experimental manipulations based on a single tuning run (Clark et al., 2011) and with different monolingual language modelling data, we note these figures simply to situate our results within the state of the art.

7 Conclusion

We have argued for the use of CCG in phrase-based translation, due to its flexibility in providing a wealth of different bracketings that better accommodate lexical translation strings. We have also presented a novel method for using CCG constituent labels in a syntactic reordering model where the syntactic labels span multiple words, do not cross translation constituent boundaries and are tailored specifically to each translation constituent. The result is a significant improvement in Urdu-English (SOV $\rightarrow$ SVO) translation scores over two baselines: a traditional phrase-based baseline with a lexicalized reordering model and a phrase-based baseline with an additional supertag reordering model. Moreover, we have provided qualitative examples that confirm the improvements in automatic metrics.

In future work we would like explore whether further improvements can be gained by using more sophisticated reordering models, such as reordering graphs (Su et al., 2010) and hierarchical reordering models (Galley and Manning, 2008) both for our word-based and syntactic reordering models. Further, as in prior work (Zollmann et al., 2006; Shen et al., 2010; Almaghout et al., 2010), our categorial labels could also be used to derive CCG-augmented SCFG rules, both lexicalized and unlexicalized, cf. (Zhao and Al-onaizan, 2008) — the latter being the SCFG analogue of our current model.

[12] `ftp://jaguar.ncsl.nist.gov/mt/resources/mteval-v13a-20091001.tar.gz`.

[13] We exclude combination entries that are combinations of multiple systems with different algorithmic approaches.

Acknowledgments

The authors would like to thank Chong Min Lee, Aoife Cahill and Nitin Madnani at ETS for taking the time to read earlier drafts of this (and closely related) work. Their comments and suggestions made this a better paper. We would also like to thank the anonymous reviewers for their very helpful feedback. The views expressed in this paper do not necessarily reflect those of The Ohio State University or of Educational Testing Service.

References

Hala Almaghout, Jie Jiang, and Andy Way. 2010. CCG Augmented Hierarchical Phrase-based Machine Translation. In *Proceedings of the 7th International Workshop on Spoken Language Translation*, Paris, France.

Amittai Axelrod, Ra Birch Mayne, Chris Callison-Burch, Miles Osborne, and David Talbot. 2005. Edinburgh System Description for the 2005 IWSLT Speech Translation Evaluation. In *Proceedings of the International Workshop on Spoken Language Translation (IWSLT-05)*, Pittsburgh, PA, USA.

Emmon Bach. 1976. An Extension of Classical Transformational Grammar. In *Proceedings of the 1976 Conference on Problems of Linguistic Metatheory*, pages 183–224, East Lansing, MI, USA.

Kathy Baker, Steven Bethard, Michael Bloodgood, Ralf Brown, Chris Callison-Burch, Glen Coppersmith, Bonnie Dorr, Wes Filardo, Kendall Giles, Anni Irvine, Mike Kayser, Lori Levin, Justin Martineau, Jim Mayeld, Scott Miller, Aaron Phillips, Andrew Philpot, Christine Piatko, Lane Schwartz, and David Zajic. 2010. Semantically informed machine translation. Technical Report 002, Johns Hopkins University, Baltimore, MD, Human Language Technology Center of Excellence.

Mauro Cettolo, Marcello Federico, Daniele Pighin, and Nicola Bertoldi. 2008. Shallow-syntax Phrase-based Translation: Joint versus Factored String-to-chunk Models. In *Proceedings of AMTA 2008*, Honolulu, HI, USA.

Stephen Clark and James R. Curran. 2004. The Importance of Supertagging for Wide-Coverage CCG Parsing. In *Proceedings of the 20th International Con-*

ference on Computational Linguistics (COLING-04), Geneva, Switzerland.

Stephen Clark and James R. Curran. 2007. Wide-Coverage Efficient Statistical Parsing with CCG and Log-Linear Models. *Computational Linguistics*, 33(4):493–552.

Jonathan H. Clark, Chris Dyer, Alon Lavie, and Noah A. Smith. 2011. Better Hypothesis Testing for Machine Translation: Controlling for Optimizer Instability. In *Proceedings of the Meeting of the Association for Computational Linguistics (ACL-11)*, Portland, OR, USA.

Michael Collins, Philipp Koehn, and Ivona Kucerova. 2005. Clause Restructuring for Statistical Machine Translation. In *Proceedings of the Association for Computational Linguistics (ACL-05)*, Ann Arbor, MI, USA.

Marcello Federico and Mauro Cettolo. 2007. Efficient Handling of n-gram Language Models for Statistical Machine Translation. In *Proceedings of Association for Computational Linguistics*, Prague, The Czech Republic.

Michel Galley and Christopher D. Manning. 2008. A Simple and Effective Hierarchical Phrase Reordering Model. In *Proceedings of EMNLP-08*.

Hany Hassan. 2009. *Lexical Syntax for Statistical Machine Translation*. Ph.D. thesis, Dublin City University, Dublin, Ireland.

Julia Hockenmaier and Mark Steedman. 2007. CCGbank: A Corpus of CCG Derivations and Dependency Structures Extracted from the Penn Treebank. *Computational Linguistics*, 33(3):355–396.

Philipp Koehn, Franz Joseph Och, and Daniel Marcu. 2003. Statistical Phrase-based Translation. In *Proceedings of NAACL-HLT*, pages 48–54, Edmonton, Alberta, CA.

Philipp Koehn, Hieu Hoang, Alexandra Birch, Chris Callison-Burch, Marcello Federico, Nicola Bertoldi, Brooke Cowan, Wade Shen, Christine Moran, Richard Zens, Chris Dyer, Ondrej Bojar, Alexandra Constantin, and Evan Herbst. 2007. Moses: Open Source Toolkit for Statistical Machine Translation. In *Proceedings of the Association for Computational Linguistics, Companion Volume Proceedings of the Demo and Poster Sessions*, Prague, Czech Republic, June.

Shankar Kumar and William Byrne. 2004. Minimum Bayes-Risk Decoding for Statistical Machine Translation. In *Proceedings of HLT-NAACL*.

Wang Ling, Jo ao Graça, David Martins de Matos, Isabel Trancoso, and Alan Black. 2011. Discriminative Phrase-based Lexicalized Reordering Models using Weighted Reordering Graphs. In *Proceedings of the 5th International Joint Conference on Natural Language Processing*.

Franz Joseph Och. 2003. Minimum Error Rate Training in Statistical Machine Translation. In *Proceedings of the 41st Annual Meeting of the Association for Computational Linguistics*, pages 160–167, Sapporo, Japan.

Libin Shen, Jinxi Xu, and Ralph Weischedel. 2008. A New String-to-dependency Machine Translation Algorithm with a Target Dependency Language Model. In *Proceedings of the Joint Meeting of the Association for Computational Linguistics and Human Language Technologies (ACL-08:HLT)*, Columbus, OH, USA.

Libin Shen, Jinxi Xu, and Ralph Weischedel. 2010. String-to-Dependency Statistical Machine Translation. *Computational Linguistics*, 36(4):649–671.

Mark Steedman. 2000. *The Syntactic Process*. MIT Press, Cambridge, MA, USA.

Jinsong Su, Yang Liu, Yajuan Lü, Haitao Mi, and Qun Liu. 2010. Learning Lexicalized Reordering Models from Reordering Graphs. In *Proceedings of the ACL 2010; Short Papers*.

Christoph Tillmann. 2004. A Unigram Orientation Model for Statistical Machine Translation. In *Proceedings of HLT-NAACL 2004: Short Papers*, HLT-NAACL-Short '04.

Christoph Tillmann. 2008. A Rule-Driven Dynamic Programming Decoder for Statistical MT. In *Proceedings of the Second Workshop on Syntax and Structure in Statistical Translation (SSST-08)*.

Ashish Venugopal, Andreas Zollmann, and Stephan Vogel. 2007. An Efficient Two-pass Approach to Synchronous-CFG Driven Statistical MT. In *Proceedings of the Human Language Technology and North American Association for Computational Linguistics Conference (HLT/NAACL-07)*, Rochester, NY.

Chao Wang, Michael Collins, and Philipp Koehn. 2007. Chinese Syntactic Reordering for Statistical Machine Translation. In *Proceedings of EMNLP/CoNLL-07*, Prague, The Czech Republic.

Fei Xia and Michael McCord. 2004. Improving a Statistical MT System with Automatically Learned Rewrite Patterns. In *Proceedings of International Conference on Computational Linguistics (COLING-04)*, Geneva, Switzerland.

Yushi Xu and Stephanie Seneff. 2008. Two-stage Translation: A Combined Linguistic and Statistical Machine Translation Framework. In *Proceedings of the 8th Conference of the Association for Machine Translation in the Americas (AMTA-08)*, Waikiki, Honolulu, HI, USA.

Richard Zens, Franz Josef Och, and Hermann Ney. 2002. Phrase-Based Statistical Machine Translation. In M. Jarke, J. Koehler, and G. Lakemeyer, editors, *KI-2002: Advances in Artificial Intelligence, Proceedings of the 25th Annual German Conference on AI, (KI-2002)*, pages 18–32. Springer Verlag, Aachen, Germany.

Bing Zhao and Yaser Al-onaizan. 2008. Generalizing Local and Non-Local Word-Reordering Patterns for Syntax-Based Machine Translation. In *Proceedings of The Conference on Empirical Methods in Natural Language Processig (EMNLP-08)*.

Andreas Zollmann, Ashish Venugopal, Stephan Vogel, and Alex Waibel. 2006. The CMU-UKA Syntax Augmented Machine Translation System for IWSLT-06. In *Proceedings of International Workshop on Spoken Language Translation (IWSLT-06)*, Kyoto, Japan.

Using Categorial Grammar to Label Translation Rules

Jonathan Weese and **Chris Callison-Burch** and **Adam Lopez**
Human Language Technology Center of Excellence
Johns Hopkins University

Abstract

Adding syntactic labels to synchronous context-free translation rules can improve performance, but labeling with phrase structure constituents, as in GHKM (Galley et al., 2004), excludes potentially useful translation rules. SAMT (Zollmann and Venugopal, 2006) introduces heuristics to create new non-constituent labels, but these heuristics introduce many complex labels and tend to add rarely-applicable rules to the translation grammar. We introduce a labeling scheme based on categorial grammar, which allows syntactic labeling of many rules with a minimal, well-motivated label set. We show that our labeling scheme performs comparably to SAMT on an Urdu–English translation task, yet the label set is an order of magnitude smaller, and translation is twice as fast.

1 Introduction

The Hiero model of Chiang (2007) popularized the usage of synchronous context-free grammars (SCFGs) for machine translation. SCFGs model translation as a process of isomorphic syntactic derivation in the source and target language. But the Hiero model is formally, not linguistically syntactic. Its derivation trees use only a single non-terminal label X, carrying no linguistic information. Consider Rule 1.

$$X \rightarrow \langle \text{ maison ; house } \rangle \quad (1)$$

We can add syntactic information to the SCFG rules by parsing the parallel training data and projecting parse tree labels onto the spans they yield and their translations. For example, if *house* was parsed as a noun, we could rewrite Rule 1 as

$$N \rightarrow \langle \text{ maison ; house } \rangle$$

But we quickly run into trouble: how should we label a rule that translates *pour l'établissement de* into *for the establishment of*? There is no phrase structure constituent that corresponds to this English fragment. This raises a model design question: what label do we assign to spans that are natural translations of each other, but have no natural labeling under a syntactic parse? One possibility would be to discard such translations from our model as implausible. However, such non-compositional translations are important in translation (Fox, 2002), and they have been repeatedly shown to improve translation performance (Koehn et al., 2003; DeNeefe et al., 2007).

Syntax-Augmented Machine Translation (SAMT; Zollmann and Venugopal, 2006) solves this problem with heuristics that create new labels from the phrase structure parse: it labels *for the establishment of* as IN+NP+IN to show that it is the concatenation of a noun phrase with a preposition on either side. While descriptive, this label is unsatisfying as a concise description of linguistic function, fitting uneasily alongside more natural labels in the phrase structure formalism. SAMT introduces many thousands of such labels, most of which are seen very few times. While these heuristics are effective (Zollmann et al., 2008), they inflate grammar size, hamper effective parameter estimation due to feature sparsity, and slow translation speed.

Our objective is to find a syntactic formalism that

enables us to label most translation rules without relying on heuristics. Ideally, the label should be small in order to improve feature estimation and reduce translation time. Furthering an insight that informs SAMT, we show that *combinatory categorial grammar* (CCG) satisfies these requirements.

Under CCG, *for the establishment of* is labeled with ((S\NP)\(S\NP))/NP. This seems complex, but it describes exactly how the fragment should combine with other English words to create a complete sentence in a linguistically meaningful way. We show that CCG is a viable formalism to add syntax to SCFG-based translation.

- We introduce two models for labeling SCFG rules. One uses labels from a 1-best CCG parse tree of training data; the second uses the top labels in each cell of a CCG parse chart.

- We show that using 1-best parses performs as well as a syntactic model using phrase structure derivations.

- We show that using chart cell labels performs almost as well than SAMT, but the nonterminal label set is an order of magnitude smaller and translation is twice as fast.

2 Categorial grammar

Categorial grammar (CG) (Adjukiewicz, 1935; Bar-Hillel et al., 1964) is a grammar formalism in which words are assigned grammatical types, or *categories*. Once categories are assigned to each word of a sentence, a small set of universal combinatory rules uses them to derive a sentence-spanning syntactic structure.

Categories may be either atomic, like N, VP, S, and other familiar types, or they may be complex *function types*. A function type looks like A/B and takes an argument of type B and returns a type A. The categories A and B may themselves be either primitives or functions. A lexical item is assigned a function category when it takes an *argument* — for example, a verb may be function that needs to be combined with its subject and object, or an a adjective may be a function that takes the noun it modifies as an argument.

Lexical item	Category
and	conj
cities	NP
in	(NP\NP)/NP
own	(S\NP)/NP
properties	NP
they	NP
various	NP/NP
villages	NP

Table 1: An example lexicon, mapping words to categories.

We can combine two categories with *function application*. Formally, we write

$$X/Y \quad Y \;\Rightarrow\; X \qquad (2)$$

to show that a function type may be combined with its argument type to produce the result type. *Backward* function application also exists, where the argument occurs to the left of the function.

Combinatory categorial grammar (CCG) is an extension of CG that includes more *combinators* (operations that can combine categories). Steedman and Baldridge (2011) give an excellent overview of CCG.

As an example, suppose we want to analyze the sentence “They own properties in various cities and villages” using the lexicon shown in Table 1. We assign categories according to the lexicon, then combine the categories using function application and other combinators to get an analysis of S for the complete sentence. Figure 1 shows the derivation.

As a practical matter, very efficient CCG parsers are available (Clark and Curran, 2007). As shown by Fowler and Penn (2010), in many cases CCG is context-free, making it an ideal fit for our problem.

2.1 Labels for phrases

Consider the German–English phrase pair *der große Mann – the tall man*. It is easily labeled as an NP and included in the translation table. By contrast, *der große– the tall*, doesn't typically correspond to a complete subtree in a phrase structure parse. Yet translating *the tall* is likely to be more useful than translating *the tall man*, since it is more general—it can be combined with any other noun translation.

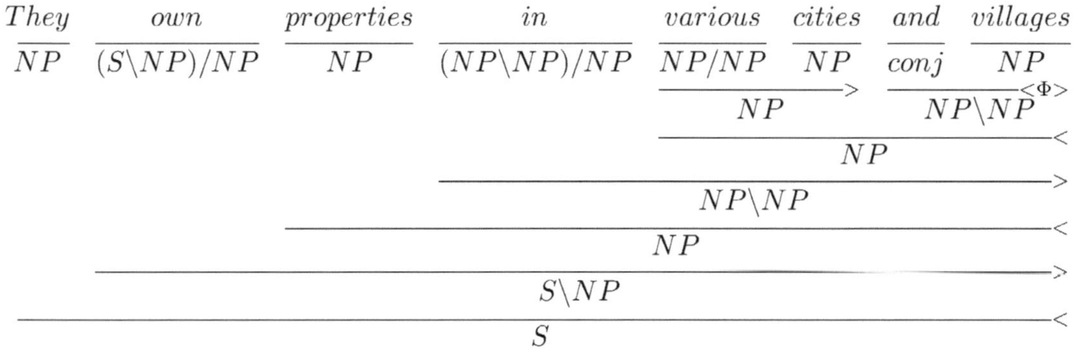

Figure 1: An example CCG derivation for the sentence "They own properties in various cities and villages" using the lexicon from Table 1. Φ indicates a conjunction operation; $>$ and $<$ are forward and backward function application, respectively.

Using CG-style labels with function types, we can assign the type (for example) NP/N to *the tall* to show that it can be combined with a noun on its right to create a complete noun phrase.[1] In general, CG can produce linguistically meaningful labels of most spans in a sentence simply as a matter of course.

2.2 Minimal, well-motivated label set

By allowing slashed categories with CG, we increase the number of labels allowed. Despite the increase in the number of labels, CG is advantageous for two reasons:

1. Our labels are derived from CCG derivations, so phrases with slashed labels represent well-motivated, linguistically-informed derivations, and the categories can be naturally combined.

2. The set of labels is small, relative to SAMT — it's restricted to the labels seen in CCG parses of the training data.

In short, using CG labels allows us to keep more linguistically-informed syntactic rules without making the set of syntactic labels too big.

3 Translation models

3.1 Extraction from parallel text

To extract SCFG rules, we start with a heuristic to extract phrases from a word-aligned sentence pair

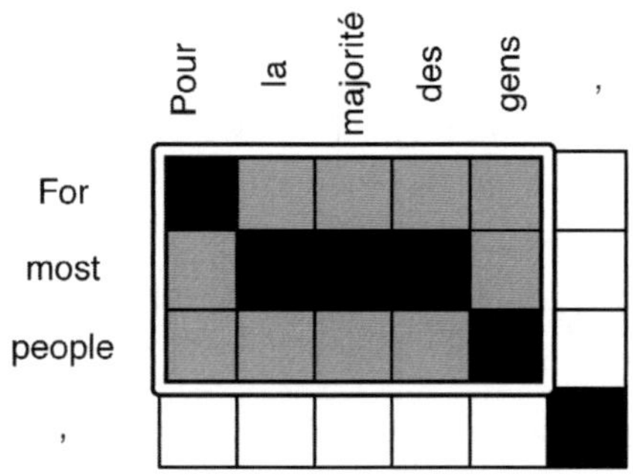

Figure 2: A word-aligned sentence pair fragment, with a box indicating a consistent phrase pair.

(Tillmann, 2003). Figure 2 shows a such a pair, with a *consistent phrase pair* inside the box. A phrase pair (f, e) is said to be consistent with the alignment if none of the words of f are aligned outside the phrase e, and vice versa – that is, there are no alignment points directly above, below, or to the sides of the box defined by f and e.

Given a consistent phrase pair, we can immediately extract the rule

$$X \rightarrow \langle f, e \rangle \tag{3}$$

as we would in a phrase-based MT system. However, whenever we find a consistent phrase pair that is a sub-phrase of another, we may extract a hierarchical rule by treating the inner phrase as a gap in the larger phrase. For example, we may extract the rule

$$X \rightarrow \langle \text{ Pour X ; For X } \rangle \tag{4}$$

from Figure 3.

[1] We could assign NP/N to the determiner *the* and N/N to the adjective *tall*, then combine those two categories using *function composition* to get a category NP/N for the two words together.

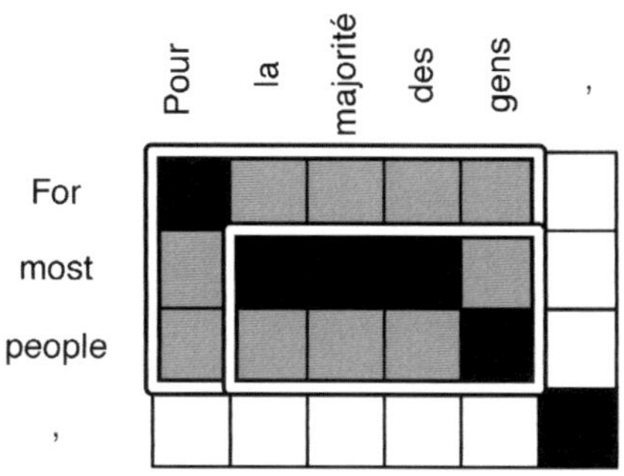

Figure 3: A consistent phrase pair with a sub-phrase that is also consistent. We may extract a hierarchical SCFG rule from this training example.

The focus of this paper is how to assign labels to the left-hand non-terminal X and to the non-terminal gaps on the right-hand side. We discuss five models below, of which two are novel CG-based labeling schemes.

3.2 Baseline: Hiero

Hiero (Chiang, 2007) uses the simplest labeling possible: there is only one non-terminal symbol, X, for all rules. Its advantage over phrase-based translation in its ability to model phrases with gaps in them, enabling phrases to reorder subphrases. However, since there's only one label, there's no way to include syntactic information in its translation rules.

3.3 Phrase structure parse tree labeling

One first step for adding syntactic information is to get syntactic labels from a phrase structure parse tree. For each word-aligned sentence pair in our training data, we also include a parse tree of the target side.

Then we can assign syntactic labels like this: for each consistent phrase pair (representing either the left-hand non-terminal or a gap in the right hand side) we see if the target-language phrase is the exact span of some subtree of the parse tree.

If a subtree exactly spans the phrase pair, we can use the root label of that subtree to label the non-terminal symbol. If there is no such subtree, we throw away any rules derived from the phrase pair.

As an example, suppose the English side of the phrase pair in Figure 3 is analyzed as

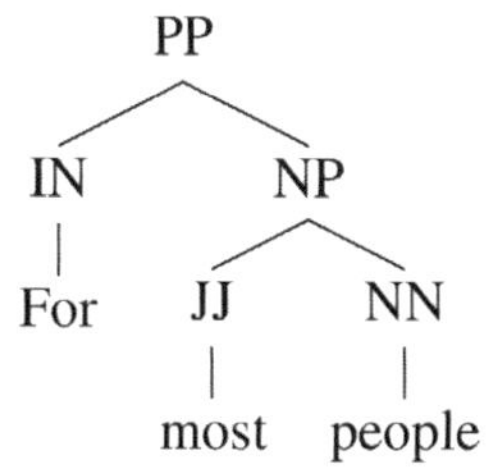

Then we can assign syntactic labels to Rule 4 to produce

$$\text{PP} \rightarrow \langle \text{ Pour NP ; For NP } \rangle \tag{5}$$

The rules extracted by this scheme are very similar to those produced by GHKM (Galley et al., 2004), in particular resulting in the "composed rules" of Galley et al. (2006), though we use simpler heuristics for handling of unaligned words and scoring in order to bring the model in line with both Hiero and SAMT baselines. Under this scheme we throw away a lot of useful translation rules that don't translate exact syntactic constituents. For example, we can't label

$$X \rightarrow \langle \text{ Pour la majorité des ; For most } \rangle \tag{6}$$

because no single node exactly spans *For most*: the PP node includes *people*, and the NP node doesn't include *For*.

We can alleviate this problem by changing the way we get syntactic labels from parse trees.

3.4 SAMT

The Syntax-Augmented Machine Translation (SAMT) model (Zollmann and Venugopal, 2006) extracts more rules than the other syntactic model by allowing different labels for the rules. In SAMT, we try several different ways to get a label for a span, stopping the first time we can assign a label:

- As in simple phrase structure labeling, if a subtree of the parse tree exactly spans a phrase, we assign that phrase the subtree's root label.
- If a phrase can be covered by two adjacent subtrees with labels A and B, we assign their concatenation A+B.
- If a phrase spans part of a subtree labeled A that could be completed with a subtree B to its right, we assign A/B.

- If a phrase spans part of a subtree A but is missing a B to its left, we assign A\B.
- Finally, if a phrase spans three adjacent subtrees with labels A, B, and C, we assign A+B+C.

Only if all of these assignments fail do we throw away the potential translation rule.

Under SAMT, we can now label Rule 6. *For* is spanned by an IN node, and *most* is spanned by a JJ node, so we concatenate the two and label the rule as

$$\text{IN+JJ} \rightarrow \langle \text{ Pour la majorité des ; For most } \rangle \quad (7)$$

3.5 CCG 1-best derivation labeling

Our first CG model is similar to the first phrase structure parse tree model. We start with a word-aligned sentence pair, but we parse the target sentence using a CCG parser instead of a phrase structure parser.

When we extract a rule, we see if the consistent phrase pair is exactly spanned by a category generated in the 1-best CCG derivation of the target sentence. If there is such a category, we assign that category label to the non-terminal. If not, we throw away the rule.

To continue our extended example, suppose the English side of Figure 3 was analyzed by a CCG parser to produce

$$\begin{array}{ccc} For & most & people \\ \hline (S/S)/N & N/N & N \\ & \multicolumn{2}{c}{\overline{\quad N \quad}>} \\ \multicolumn{3}{c}{\overline{\quad S/S \quad}>} \end{array}$$

Then just as in the phrase structure model, we project the syntactic labels down onto the extractable rule yielding

$$\text{S/S} \rightarrow \langle \text{ Pour N ; For N } \rangle \quad (8)$$

This does not take advantage of CCG's ability to label almost any fragment of language: the fragments with labels in any particular sentence depend on the order that categories were combined in the sentence's 1-best derivation. We can't label Rule 6, because no single category spanned *For most* in the derivation. In the next model, we increase the number of spans we can label.

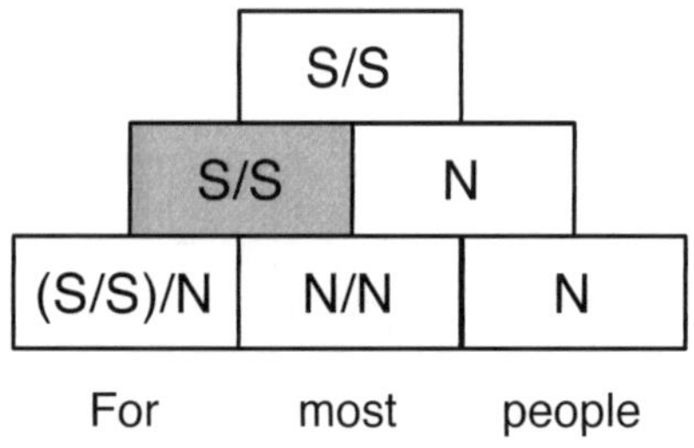

Figure 4: A portion of the parse chart for a sentence starting with "For most people ...." Note that the gray chart cell is not included in the 1-best derivation of this fragment in Section 3.5.

3.6 CCG parse chart labeling

For this model, we do not use the 1-best CCG derivation. Instead, when parsing the target sentence, for each cell in the parse chart, we read the most likely label according to the parsing model. This lets us assign a label for almost any span of the sentence just by reading the label from the parse chart.

For example, Figure 4 represents part of a CCG parse chart for our example fragment of "For most people." Each cell in the chart shows the most probable label for its span. The white cells of the chart are in fact present in the 1-best derivation, which means we could extract Rule 8 just as in the previous model.

But the 1-best derivation model cannot label Rule 6, and this model can. The shaded chart cell in Figure 4 holds the most likely category for the span *For most*. So we assign that label to the X:

$$S/S \rightarrow \langle \text{ Pour la majorité des ; For most } \rangle \quad (9)$$

By including labels from cells that weren't used in the 1-best derivation, we can greatly increase the number of rules we can label.

4 Comparison of resulting grammars

4.1 Effect of grammar size and label set on parsing efficiency

There are sound theoretical reasons for reducing the number of non-terminal labels in a grammar. Translation with a synchronous context-free grammar requires first parsing with the source-language projection of the grammar, followed by intersection of the target-language projection of the resulting grammar with a language model. While there are many possible algorithms for these operations, they all depend on the size of the grammar.

Consider for example the popular cube pruning algorithm of Chiang (2007), which is a simple extension of CKY. It works by first constructing a set of items of the form $\langle A, i, j \rangle$, where each item corresponds to (possibly many) partial analyses by which nonterminal A generates the sequence of words from positions i through j of the source sentence. It then produces an augmented set of items $\langle A, i, j, u, v \rangle$, in which items of the first type are augmented with left and right language model states u and v. In each pass, the number of items is linear in the number of nonterminal symbols of the grammar. This observation has motivated work in grammar transformations that reduce the size of the nonterminal set, often resulting in substantial gains in parsing or translation speed (Song et al., 2008; DeNero et al., 2009; Xiao et al., 2009).

More formally, the upper bound on parsing complexity is always at least linear in the size of the grammar constant G, where G is often loosely defined as a *grammar constant*; Iglesias et al. (2011) give a nice analysis of the most common translation algorithms and their dependence on G. Dunlop et al. (2010) provide a more fine-grained analysis of G, showing that for a variety of implementation choices that it depends on either or both the number of rules in the grammar and the number of nonterminals in the grammar. Though these are worst-case analyses, it should be clear that grammars with fewer rules or nonterminals can generally be processed more efficiently.

4.2 Number of rules and non-terminals

Table 2 shows the number of rules we can extract under various labeling schemes. The rules were extracted from an Urdu–English parallel corpus with 202,019 translations, or almost 2 million words in each language.

As we described before, moving from the phrase-structure syntactic model to the extended SAMT model vastly increases the number of translation rules — from about 7 million to 40 million rules. But the increased rule coverage comes at a cost: the non-terminal set has increased in size from 70 (the size of the set of Penn Treebank tags) to over 18,000.

Model	Rules	NTs
Hiero	4,171,473	1
Syntax	7,034,393	70
SAMT	40,744,439	18,368
CG derivations	8,042,683	505
CG parse chart	28,961,161	517

Table 2: Number of translation rules and non-terminal labels in an Urdu–English grammar under various models.

Comparing the phrase structure syntax model to the 1-best CCG derivation model, we see that the number of extracted rules increases slightly, and the grammar uses a set of about 500 non-terminal labels. This does not seem like a good trade-off; since we are extracting from the 1-best CCG derivation there really aren't many more rules we can label than with a 1-best phrase structure derivation.

But when we move to the full CCG parse chart model, we see a significant difference: when reading labels off of the entire parse chart, instead of the 1-best derivation, we don't see a significant increase in the non-terminal label set. That is, most of the labels we see in parse charts of the training data already show up in the top derivations: the complete chart doesn't contain many new labels that have never been seen before.

But by using the chart cells, we are able to assign syntactic information to many more translation rules: over 28 million rules, for a grammar about $\frac{3}{4}$ the size of SAMT's. The parse chart lets us extract many more rules without significantly increasing the size of the syntactic label set.

4.3 Sparseness of nonterminals

Examining the histograms in Figure 5 gives us a different view of the non-terminal label sets in our models. In each histogram, the horizontal axis measures label frequency in the corpus. The height of each bar shows the number of non-terminals with that frequency.

For the phrase structure syntax model, we see there are maybe 20 labels out of 70 that show up on rules less than 1000 times. All the other labels show up on very many rules.

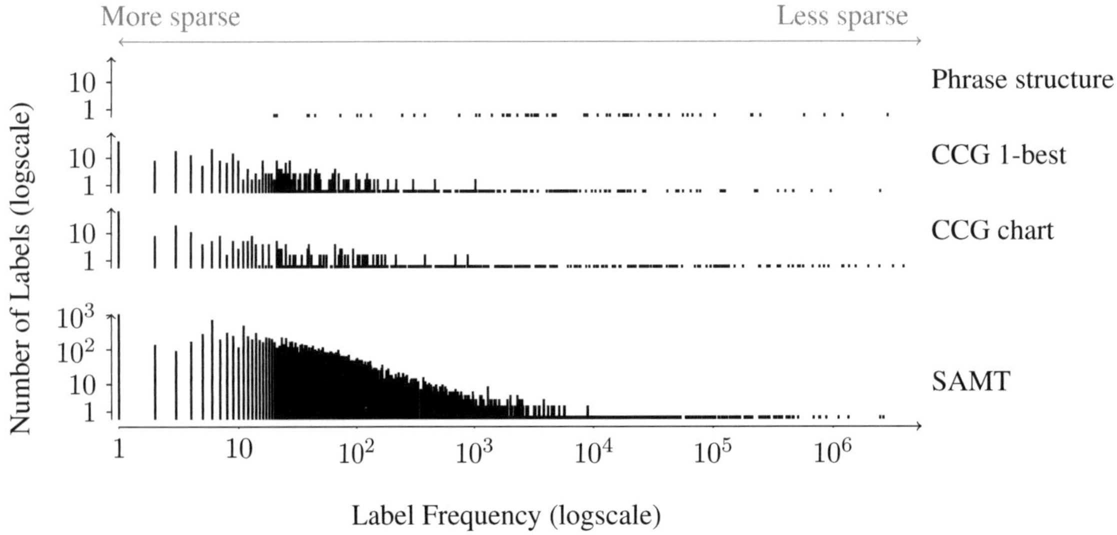

Figure 5: Histograms of label frequency for each model, illustrating the sparsity of each model.

Moving to SAMT, with its heuristically-defined labels, shows a very different story. Not only does the model have over 18,000 non-terminal labels, but thousands of them show up on fewer than 10 rules apiece. If we look at the rare label types, we see that a lot of them are improbable three way concatenations A+B+C.

The two CCG models have similar sparseness profiles. We do see some rare labels occurring only a few times in the grammars, but the number of singleton labels is an order of magnitude smaller than SAMT. Most of the CCG labels show up in the long tail of very common occurrences. Interestingly, when we move to extracting labels from parse charts rather than derivations, the number of labels increases only slightly. However, we also obtain a great deal more evidence for each observed label, making estimates more reliable.

5 Experiments

5.1 Data

We tested our models on an Urdu–English translation task, in which syntax-based systems have been quite effective (Baker et al., 2009; Zollmann et al., 2008). The training corpus was the National Institute of Standards and Technology Open Machine Translation 2009 Evaluation (NIST Open MT09). According to the MT09 Constrained Training Conditions Resources list[2] this data includes NIST Open MT08 Urdu Resources[3] and the NIST Open MT08 Current Test Set Urdu–English[4]. This gives us 202,019 parallel translations, for approximately 2 million words of training data.

5.2 Experimental design

We used the scripts included with the Moses MT toolkit (Koehn et al., 2007) to tokenize and normalize the English data. We used a tokenizer and normalizer developed at the SCALE 2009 workshop (Baker et al., 2009) to preprocess the Urdu data. We used GIZA++ (Och and Ney, 2000) to perform word alignments.

For phrase structure parses of the English data, we used the Berkeley parser (Petrov and Klein, 2007). For CCG parses, and for reading labels out of a parse chart, we used the C&C parser (Clark and Curran, 2007).

After aligning and parsing the training data, we used the Thrax grammar extractor (Weese et al., 2011) to extract all of the translation grammars.

We used the same feature set in all the translation grammars. This includes, for each rule $C \rightarrow \langle f; e \rangle$, relative-frequency estimates of the probabil-

[2] `http://www.itl.nist.gov/iad/mig/tests/mt/2009/MT09_ConstrainedResources.pdf`

[3] LDC2009E12

[4] LDC2009E11

Model	BLEU	sec./sent.
Hiero	25.67 (0.9781)	0.05
Syntax	27.06 (0.9703)	3.04
SAMT	28.06 (0.9714)	63.48
CCG derivations	27.3 (0.9770)	5.24
CCG parse chart	27.64 (0.9673)	33.6

Table 3: Results of translation experiments on Urdu–English. Higher BLEU scores are better. BLEU's brevity penalty is reported in parentheses.

ities $p(f|A)$, $p(f|e)$, $p(f|e, A)$, $p(e|A)$, $p(e|f)$, and $p(e|f, A)$.

The feature set also includes lexical weighting for rules as defined by Koehn et al. (2003) and various binary features as well as counters for the number of unaligned words in each rule.

To train the feature weights we used the Z-MERT implementation (Zaidan, 2009) of the Minimum Error-Rate Training algorithm (Och, 2003).

To decode the test sets, we used the Joshua machine translation decoder (Weese et al., 2011). The language model is a 5-gram LM trained on English GigaWord Fourth Edition.[5]

5.3 Evaluation criteria

We measure machine translation performance using the BLEU metric (Papineni et al., 2002). We also report the translation time for the test set in seconds per sentence. These results are shown in Table 3.

All of the syntactic labeling schemes show an improvement over the Hiero model. Indeed, they all fall in the range of approximately 27–28 BLEU. We can see that the 1-best derivation CCG model performs slightly better than the phrase structure model, and the CCG parse chart model performs a little better than that. SAMT has the highest BLEU score. The models with a larger number of rules perform better; this supports our assertion that we shouldn't throw away too many rules.

When it comes to translation time, the three smaller models (Hiero, phrase structure syntax, and CCG 1-best derivations) are significantly faster than the two larger ones. However, even though the CCG parse chart model is almost $\frac{3}{4}$ the size of SAMT in terms of number of rules, it doesn't take $\frac{3}{4}$ of the time. In fact, it takes only half the time of the SAMT model, thanks to the smaller rule label set.

[5]LDC2009T13

6 Discussion and Future Work

Finding an appropriate mechanism to inform phrase-based translation models and their hierarchical variants with linguistic syntax is a difficult problem that has attracted intense interest, with a variety of promising approaches including unsupervised clustering (Zollmann and Vogel, 2011), merging (Hanneman et al., 2011), and selection (Mylonakis and Sima'an, 2011) of labels derived from phrase-structure parse trees very much like those used by our baseline systems. What we find particularly attractive about CCG is that it naturally assigns linguistically-motivated labels to most spans of a sentence using a reasonably concise label set, possibility obviating the need for further refinement. Indeed, the analytical flexibility of CCG has motivated its increasing use in MT, from applications in language modeling (Birch et al., 2007; Hassan et al., 2007) to more recent proposals to incorporate it into phrase-based (Mehay, 2010) and hierarchical translation systems (Auli, 2009).

Our new model builds on these past efforts, representing a more fully instantiated model of CCG-based translation. We have shown that the label scheme allows us to keep many more translation rules than labels based on phrase structure syntax, extracting almost as many rules as the SAMT model, but keeping the label set an order of magnitude smaller, which leads to more efficient translation. This simply scratches the surface of possible uses of CCG in translation. In future work, we plan to move from a formally context-free to a formally CCG-based model of translation, implementing combinatorial rules such as application, composition, and type-raising.

Acknowledgements

Thank you to Michael Auli for providing code to inspect the full chart from the C&C parser. This research was supported in part by the NSF under grant IIS-0713448 and in part by the EuroMatrix-Plus project funded by the European Commission (7th Framework Programme). Opinions, interpretations, and conclusions are the authors' alone.

References

Kazimierz Adjukiewicz. 1935. Die syntaktische konnexität. In Storrs McCall, editor, *Polish Logic 1920–1939*, pages 207–231. Oxford University Press.

Michael Auli. 2009. CCG-based models for statistical machine translation. Ph.D. Proposal, University of Edinburgh.

Kathy Baker, Steven Bethard, Michael Bloodgood, Ralf Brown, Chris Callison-Burch, Glen Coppersmith, Bonnie Dorr, Wes Filardo, Kendall Giles, Ann Irvine, Mike Kayser, Lori Levin, Justin Marinteau, Jim Mayfield, Scott Miller, Aaron Phillips, Andrew Philpot, Christine Piatko, Lane Schwartz, and David Zajic. 2009. Semantically informed machine translation: Final report of the 2009 summer camp for advanced language exploration (scale). Technical report, Human Language Technology Center of Excellence.

Yehoshua Bar-Hillel, Chaim Gaifman, and Eliyahu Shamir. 1964. On categorial and phrase-structure grammars. In Yehoshua Bar-Hillel, editor, *Language and Information*, pages 99–115. Addison-Wesley.

Alexandra Birch, Miles Osborne, and Philipp Koehn. 2007. CCG supertags in factored statistical machine translation. In *Proc. of WMT*.

David Chiang. 2007. Hierarchical phrase-based translation. *Computational Linguistics*, 33(2):201–228.

Stephen Clark and James R. Curran. 2007. Wide-coverage efficient statistical parsing with CCG and log-linear models. *Computational Linguistics*, 33(4).

Steve DeNeefe, Kevin Knight, Wei Wang, and Daniel Marcu. 2007. What can syntax-based MT learn from phrase-based MT? In *Proc. EMNLP*.

John DeNero, Mohit Bansal, Adam Pauls, and Dan Klein. 2009. Efficient parsing for transducer grammars. In *Proc. NAACL*, pages 227–235.

Aaron Dunlop, Nathan Bodenstab, and Brian Roark. 2010. Reducing the grammar constant: an analysis of CYK parsing efficiency. Technical report CSLU-2010-02, OHSU.

Timothy A. D. Fowler and Gerald Penn. 2010. Accurate context-free parsing with combinatory categorial grammar. In *Proc. ACL*, pages 335–344.

Heidi J. Fox. 2002. Phrasal cohesion and statistical machine translation. In *Proc. of EMNLP*.

Michel Galley, Mark Hopkins, Kevin Knight, and Daniel Marcu. 2004. What's in a translation rule? In *Proc. of HLT-NAACL*.

Michel Galley, Jonathan Graehl, Kevin Knight, Daniel Marcu, Steve Deneefe, Wei Wang, and Ignacio Thayer. 2006. Scalable inference and training of context-rich syntactic translation models. In *In ACL*, pages 961–968.

Greg Hanneman, Michelle Burroughs, and Alon Lavie. 2011. A general-purpose rule extractor for SCFG-based machine translation. In *Proc. of WMT*.

Hany Hassan, Khalil Sima'an, and Andy Way. 2007. Supertagged phrase-based statistical machine translation. In *Proc. of ACL*.

Gonzalo Iglesias, Cyril Allauzen, William Byrne, Adrià de Gispert, and Michael Riley. 2011. Hierarchical phrase-based translation representations. In *Proc. EMNLP*, pages 1373–1383.

Philipp Koehn, Franz Josef Och, and Daniel Marcu. 2003. Statistical phrase-based translation. In *Proc. of HLT-NAACL*.

Philipp Koehn, Hieu Hoang, Alexandra Birch, Chris Callison-Burch, Marcello Frederico, Nicola Bertoldi, Brooke Cowan, Wade Shen, Christine Moran, Richard Zens, Chris Dyer, Ondrej Bojar, Alexandra Constantin, and Evan Herbst. 2007. Moses: Open source toolkit for statistical machine translation. In *Proc. ACL Demonstration Session*.

Dennis Mehay. 2010. Linguistically motivated syntax for machine translation. Ph.D. Proposal, Ohio State University.

Markos Mylonakis and Khalil Sima'an. 2011. Learning hierarchical translation structure with linguistic annotations. In *Proc. of ACL-HLT*.

F. J. Och and H. Ney. 2000. Improved statistical alignment models. In *Proc. of ACL*.

Franz Josef Och. 2003. Minimum error rate training in statistical machine translation. In *Proc. ACL*, pages 160–167.

Kishore Papineni, Salim Roukos, Todd Ward, and Wei-Jing Zhu. 2002. Bleu: a method for automatic evaluation of machine translation. In *Proc. of ACL*.

Slav Petrov and Dan Klein. 2007. Improved inference for unlexicalized parsing. In *Proc. HLT-NAACL*.

Xinying Song, Shilin Ding, and Chin-Yew Lin. 2008. Better binarization for the CKY parsing. In *Proc. EMNLP*, pages 167–176.

Mark Steedman and Jason Baldridge. 2011. Combinatory categorial grammar. In Robert Borsley and Kersti Börjars, editors, *Non-Transformational Syntax*. Wiley-Blackwell.

Christoph Tillmann. 2003. A projection extension algorithm for statistical machine translation. In *Proc. of EMNLP*.

Jonathan Weese, Juri Ganitkevitch, Chris Callison-Burch, Matt Post, and Adam Lopez. 2011. Joshua 3.0: Syntax-based machine translation with the thrax grammar extractor. In *Proc. of WMT*.

Tong Xiao, Mu Li, Dongdong Zhang, Jingbo Zhu, and Ming Zhou. 2009. Better synchronous binarization for machine translation. In *Proc. EMNLP*, pages 362–370.

Omar F. Zaidan. 2009. Z-MERT: A fully configurable open source tool for minimum error rate training of machine translation systems. *The Prague Bulletin of Mathematical Linguistics*, 91(1):79–88.

Andreas Zollmann and Ashish Venugopal. 2006. Syntax augmented machine translation via chart parsing. In *Proceedings on the Workshop on Statistical Machine Translation*.

Andreas Zollmann and Stephan Vogel. 2011. A word-class approach to labeling PSCFG rules for machine translation. In *Proc. of ACL-HLT*.

Andreas Zollmann, Ashish Venugopal, Franz Och, and Jay Ponte. 2008. A systematic comparison of phrase-based, hierarchical and syntax-augmented statistical MT. In *Proc. of COLING*.

Using Syntactic Head Information in Hierarchical Phrase-Based Translation

Junhui Li **Zhaopeng Tu**[†] **Guodong Zhou**[‡] **Josef van Genabith**
Centre for Next Generation Localisation
School of Computing, Dublin City University
[†] Key Lab. of Intelligent Info. Processing
Institute of Computing Technology, Chinese Academy of Sciences
[‡]School of Computer Science and Technology
Soochow University, China
{jli,josef}@computing.dcu.ie
tuzhaopeng@ict.ac.cn gdzhou@suda.edu.cn

Abstract

Chiang's hierarchical phrase-based (HPB) translation model advances the state-of-the-art in statistical machine translation by expanding conventional phrases to hierarchical phrases – phrases that contain sub-phrases. However, the original HPB model is prone to over-generation due to lack of linguistic knowledge: the grammar may suggest more derivations than appropriate, many of which may lead to ungrammatical translations. On the other hand, limitations of glue grammar rules in the original HPB model may actually prevent systems from considering some reasonable derivations. This paper presents a simple but effective translation model, called the Head-Driven HPB (HD-HPB) model, which incorporates head information in translation rules to better capture syntax-driven information in a derivation. In addition, unlike the original glue rules, the HD-HPB model allows improved reordering between any two neighboring non-terminals to explore a larger reordering search space. An extensive set of experiments on Chinese-English translation on four NIST MT test sets, using both a small and a large training set, show that our HD-HPB model consistently and statistically significantly outperforms Chiang's model as well as a source side SAMT-style model.

1 Introduction

Chiang's hierarchical phrase-based (HPB) translation model utilizes synchronous context free grammar (SCFG) for translation derivation (Chiang, 2005; Chiang, 2007) and has been widely adopted in statistical machine translation (SMT). Typically, such models define two types of translation rules: hierarchical (translation) rules which consist of both terminals and non-terminals, and glue (grammar) rules which combine translated phrases in a monotone fashion. However, due to lack of linguistic knowledge, Chiang's HPB model contains only one type of non-terminal symbol X, often making it difficult to select the most appropriate translation rules.[1]

One important research question is therefore how to refine the non-terminal category X using linguistically motivated information: Zollmann and Venugopal (2006) (SAMT) e.g. use (partial) syntactic categories derived from CFG trees while Zollmann and Vogel (2011) use word tags, generated by either POS analysis or unsupervised word class induction. Almaghout et al. (2011) employ CCG-based supertags. Mylonakis and Sima'an (2011) use linguistic information of various granularities such as *Phrase-Pair*, *Constituent*, *Concatenation of Constituents*, and *Partial Constituents*, where applicable.

By contrast, and inspired by previous work in parsing (Charniak, 2000; Collins, 2003), our Head-Driven HPB (HD-HPB) model is based on the intuition that linguistic heads provide important information about a constituent or distributionally defined fragment, as in HPB. We identify heads using linguistically motivated dependency parsing, and use head information to refine X.

Furthermore, Chiang's HPB model suffers from limited phrase reordering by combining translated

[1]Another non-terminal symbol S is used in glue rules.

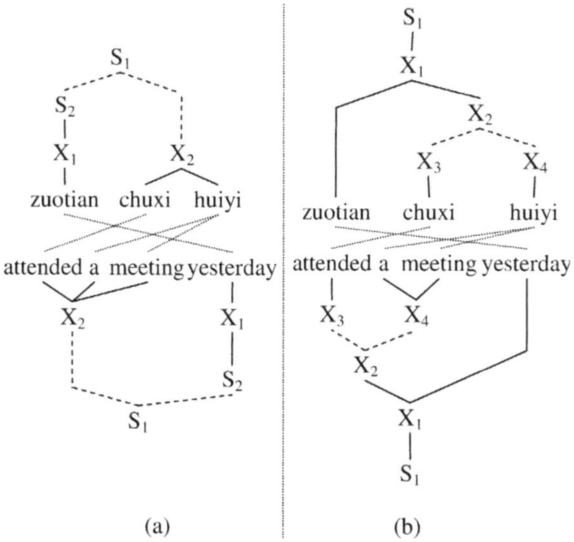

Figure 1: Example of derivations disallowed in Chiang's HPB model. The rules with dotted lines are not covered in Chiang's model.

phrases in a monotonic way with glue rules. In addition, once a glue rule is adopted, it requires all rules above it to be glue rules. For example, given a Chinese-English sentence pair (昨天*/zuotian*$_1$ 出席*/chuxi*$_2$ 会议*/huiyi*$_3$, *Attended*$_2$ *a*$_3$ *meeting*$_3$ *yesterday*$_1$), a correct translation is impossible via HPB derivations in Figure 1. For the derivation in Figure 1(a), swap reordering in the glue rule (i.e., $S_1 \rightarrow \langle S_2X_2,\ X_2S_2\rangle$) is disallowed and, even if such a swap reordering is available, it lacks useful information for rule selection. For the derivation in Figure 1(b), the combination of two non-terminals (i.e., $X_2 \rightarrow \langle X_3X_4,\ X_3X_4\rangle$) is disallowed to form a new non-terminal which in turn is a sub-phrase of a hierarchical rule. These limitations prevent traditional HPB systems from even considering some reasonable derivations.

To tackle the problem of glue rules, He (2010) extended the HPB model by using bracketing transduction grammar (Wu, 1996) instead of the monotone glue rules, and trained an extra classifier for glue rules to predict reorderings of neighboring phrases. By contrast, our HD-HPB model refines the non-terminal symbol X with syntactic head information and provides flexible reordering rules, including swap, which can mix freely with hierarchical translation rules for better interleaving of translation and reordering in translation derivations.

Different from the soft constraint modeling adopted in (Chan et al., 2007; Marton and Resnik, 2008; Shen et al., 2009; He et al., 2010; Huang et al., 2010; Gao et al., 2011), our approach encodes syntactic information in translation rules. However, the two approaches are not mutually exclusive, as we could also include a set of syntax-driven features into our translation model. Our approach maintains the advantages of Chiang's HPB model while at the same time incorporating head information and flexible reordering in a derivation in a natural way. Experiments on Chinese-English translation using four NIST MT test sets show that our HD-HPB model significantly outperforms Chiang's HPB as well as a SAMT-style refined version of HPB.

The paper is structured as follows: Section 2 describes the synchronous context-free grammar (SCFG) in our HD-HPB translation model. Section 3 presents our model and features, followed by the decoding algorithm in Section 4. We report experimental results in Section 5. Finally we conclude in Section 6.

2 Head-Driven HPB Translation Model

Like Chiang (2005) and Chiang (2007), our HD-HPB translation model adopts a synchronous context free grammar, a rewriting system which generates source and target side string pairs simultaneously using a context-free grammar. In particular, each synchronous rule rewrites a non-terminal into a pair of strings, s and t, where s (or t) contains terminals and non-terminals from the source (or target) language and there is a one-to-one correspondence between the non-terminal symbols on both sides.

A good and informative inventory of non-terminal symbols is always important, especially for a successful SCFG-based translation model. Instead of collapsing all non-terminals in the source language into a single symbol X as in Chiang (2007), ideally non-terminals should capture important information of the word sequences they cover to be able to properly discriminate between similar and different word sequences during translation. This motivates our approach to provide syntax-enriched non-terminal symbols. Given a word sequence f_j^i from position i to position j, we refine the non-terminal symbol X to reflect some of the internal syntactic structure of

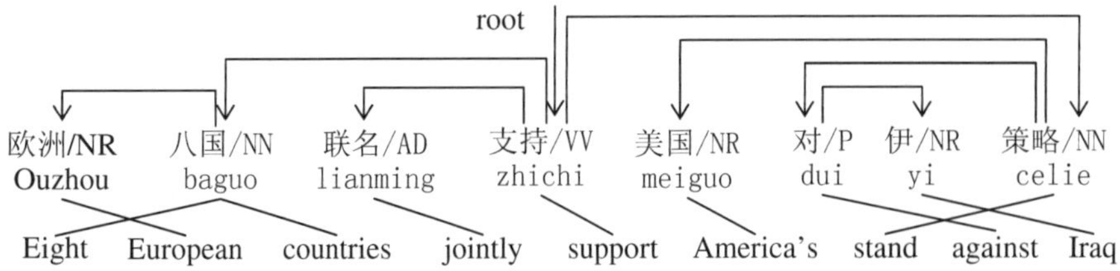

Figure 2: An example word alignment for a Chinese-English sentence pair with the dependency parse tree for the Chinese sentence. Here, each Chinese word is attached with its POS tag and Pinyin.

the word sequence covered by X. A correct translation rule selection therefore not only maps terminals into terminals, but is both constrained and guided by syntactic information in the non-terminals. At the same time, it is not clear whether an "ideal" approach that captures a full syntactic analysis of the string fragment covered by a non-terminal is feasible: the diversity of syntactic structures could make training impossible and lead to serious data sparseness issues. As a compromise, given a word sequence f_j^i, we first find **heads** and then concatenate the POS tags of these heads as f_j^i's non-terminal symbol.[2] Our approach is guided by the intuition that linguistic heads provide important information about a constituent or distributionally defined fragment, as in HPB. Specifically, we adopt dependency structure to derive heads, which are defined as:

Definition 1. *For word sequence f_j^i, word f_k $(i \leq k \leq j)$ is regarded as a **head** if it is dominated by a word outside of this sequence.*

Note that this definition (i) allows for a word sequence to have one or more heads (largely due to the fact that a word sequence is not necessarily linguistically constrained) and (ii) ensures that heads are always the highest heads in the sequence from a dependency structure perspective. For example, the word sequence *ouzhou baguo lianming* in Figure 2 has two heads (i.e., *baguo* and *lianming*, *ouzhou* is not a head of this sequence since its headword *baguo* falls within this sequence) and the non-terminal corresponding to the sequence is thus labeled as *NN-AD*. It is worth noting that in this paper we only refine non-terminal X on the source side to head-informed ones, while still using X on the target side.

[2] Note that instead of POS tags, it is also possible to use other types of syntactic information associated with heads to refine non-terminal symbols (Section 5.5.2).

In our HD-HPB model, the SCFG is defined as a tuple $\langle \Sigma, N, \Delta, \Lambda, \Re \rangle$, where Σ is a set of source language terminals, N is a set of non-terminals categorizing terminals in Σ, Δ is a set of target language terminals, Λ is a set of non-terminals categorizing terminals in Δ, and $\Re$ is a set of translation rules. A rule γ in $\Re$ is in the form of $\langle P_s \rightarrow s, P_t \rightarrow t, \phi \rangle$, where:

- $P_s \in N$ and $P_t \in \Lambda$;
- $s \in (\Sigma \cup N)^+$ and $t \in (\Delta \cup \Lambda)^+$
- ϕ is a bijection between non-terminals in s and t.

According to the occurrence of terminals in s and t, we group the rules in the HD-HPB model into two categories: head-driven hierarchical rules (HD-HRs) and non-terminal reordering rules (NRRs), where the former have at least one terminal on both source and target sides and the later have no terminals. For rule extraction, we first identify *initial phrase pairs* on word-aligned sentence pairs by using the same criterion as most phrase-based translation models (Och and Ney, 2004) and Chiang's HPB model (Chiang, 2005; Chiang, 2007). We extract HD-HRs and NRRs based on initial phrase pairs, respectively.

2.1 HD-HRs: Head-Driven Hierarchical Rules

As mentioned, a HD-HR has at least one terminal on both source and target sides. This is the same as the hierarchical rules defined in Chiang's HPB model (Chiang, 2007), except that we use head POS-informed non-terminal symbols in the source language. We look for initial phrase pairs that contain other phrases and then replace sub-phrases with their corresponding non-terminal symbols. Given the word alignment as shown in Figure 2, Table 1 demonstrates the difference between hierarchical rules in Chiang (2007) and HD-HRs defined here.

phrase pairs	hierarchical rule	head-driven hierarchical rule
celie, stand	X→celie, stand	NN→celie, X→stand
dui yi celie$_1$, stand$_1$ against Iraq	X→dui yi X$_1$, X$_1$ against Iraq	NN→dui yi NN$_1$, X→X$_1$ against Iraq
zhichi meiguo, support America's	X→zhichi meiguo, support America's	VV-NR→zhichi meiguo, X→support America's
zhichi meiguo$_1$ dui yi celie$_2$, support America's$_1$ stand$_2$ against Iraq	X→X$_1$ dui yi X$_2$, X$_1$ X$_2$ against Iraq	VV→VV-NR$_1$ dui yi NN$_2$, X→X$_1$ X$_2$ against Iraq

Table 1: Comparison of hierarchical rules in Chiang (2007) and HD-HRs. Indexed underlines indicate sub-phrases and corresponding non-terminal symbols. The non-terminals in HD-HRs (e.g., NN, VV, VV-NR) capture the head(s) POS tags of the corresponding word sequence in the source language.

Similar to Chiang's HPB model, our HD-HPB model will result in a large number of rules causing problems in decoding. To alleviate these problems, we filter our HD-HRs according to the same constraints as described in Chiang (2007). Moreover, we discard rules that have non-terminals with more than four heads.

2.2 NRRs: Non-terminal Reordering Rules

NRRs are translation rules without terminals. Given an initial phrase pair $\left\langle f_j^i, e_{j^*}^{i^*} \right\rangle$, we check all other initial phrase pairs $\left\langle f_l^k, e_{l^*}^{k^*} \right\rangle$ which satisfy $k = j+1$ (i.e., phrase f_l^k is located immediately to the right of f_j^i in the source language). For their target side translations, there are four possible positional relationships: monotone, discontinuous monotone, swap, and discontinuous swap. In order to differentiate non-terminals from those in the target language (i.e., X), we use Y as a variable for non-terminals in the source language, and obtain four types of NRRs:

- Monotone $\langle Y \rightarrow Y_1 Y_2, X \rightarrow X_1 X_2 \rangle$;
- Discontinuous monotone $\langle Y \rightarrow Y_1 Y_2, X \rightarrow X_1 \ldots X_2 \rangle$;
- Swap $\langle Y \rightarrow Y_1 Y_2, X \rightarrow X_2 X_1 \rangle$;
- Discontinuous swap $\langle Y \rightarrow Y_1 Y_2, X \rightarrow X_2 \ldots X_1 \rangle$.

For example in Figure 2, the NRR for initial phrase pairs $\langle$*zhichi meiguo, support America's*$\rangle$ and $\langle$*dui yi celie, stand against Iraq*$\rangle$ would be $\langle VV \rightarrow VV\text{-}NR_1\, NN_2,\ X \rightarrow X_1\, X_2 \rangle$.

Merging two neighboring non-terminals into a single non-terminal, NRRs enable the translation model to explore a wider search space. During training, we extract four types of NRRs and calculate probabilities for each type. To speed up decoding, we currently (i) only use monotone and swap NRRs and (ii) limit the number of non-terminals in a NRR to 2.

3 Log-linear Model and Features

Following Och and Ney (2002), we depart from the traditional noisy-channel approach and use a general log-linear model. Let *d* be a derivation from sentence *f* in the source language to sentence *e* in the target language. The probability of *d* is defined as:

$$P(d) \propto \prod_i \emptyset_i (d)^{\lambda_i} \qquad (1)$$

where $\emptyset_i$ are features defined on derivations and λ_i are feature weights. In particular, we use a feature set analogous to the default feature set of Chiang (2007), which includes:

- $P_{hd\text{-}hr}(t|s)$ and $P_{hd\text{-}hr}(s|t)$, translation probabilities for HD-HRs;
- $P_{lex}(t|s)$ and $P_{lex}(s|t)$, lexical translation probabilities for HD-HRs;
- $Pty_{hd\text{-}hr} = exp(-1)$, rule penalty for HD-HRs;
- $P_{nrr}(t|s)$, translation probability for NRRs;
- $Pty_{nrr} = exp(-1)$, rule penalty for NRRs;
- $P_{lm}(e)$, language model;
- $Pty_{word}(e) = exp(-|e|)$, word penalty.

Algorithm 1: Decoding Algorithm

Input: Sentence f_n^1 in the source language
Dependency structure of f_n^1
HD-HR rule set *HDHR*
NRR rule set *NRR*
Initial phrase length K
Output: Best derivation d^*
1. set *chart[i, j]=NIL* $(1 \leq i \leq j \leq n)$;
2. **for** l from 1 to n **do**
3. **for** all i, j such that $j - i = l$ **do**
4. **if** $l \leq K$ **do**
5. **for** all derivations d derived from *HDHR* spanning from i to j **do**
6. add d into $chart[i, j]$
7. **for** all derivations d derived from *NRR* spanning from i to j **do**
8. add d into $chart[i, j]$
9. set d^* as the top derivation of $chart[1, n]$
10. **return** d^*

It is worth pointing out that we define translation probabilities for NRRs only for the direction from source language to target language, although translation probabilities for HD-HRs are defined for both directions. This is mostly due to the fact that a NRR excludes terminals and has only two options on the target side (i.e., either $X \rightarrow X_1X_2$ or $X \rightarrow X_2X_1$).

4 Decoding

Our decoder is based on CKY-style chart parsing with beam search. Given an input sentence f, it finds a sentence e in the target language derived from the best derivation d^* among all possible derivations D:

$$d^* = \arg\max_{d \in D} P(D) \tag{2}$$

Algorithm 1 presents the decoding process. Given a source sentence, it searches for the best derivation bottom-up. For a source span $[i, j]$, it applies both types of HD-HRs and NRRs. However, HD-HRs are only applied to generate derivations spanning no more than K words – the initial phrase length limit used in training to extract HD-HRs – while NRRs are applied to derivations spanning any length. Unlike in Chiang (2007), it is possible for a non-terminal generated by a NRR to be included afterwards by a HD-HR or another NRR. Similar to Chiang (2007) in generating k-best derivations from i to j, we make use of cube pruning (Huang and Chiang, 2005) with an integrated language model for each derivation.

5 Experiments

We evaluate the performance of our HD-HPB model and compare it with our implementation of Chiang's HPB model (Chiang, 2007), a source-side SAMT-style refined version of HPB (SAMT-HPB), and the Moses implementation of HPB. For fair comparison, we adopt the same parameter settings for HD-HPB, HPB and SAMT-HPB systems, including initial phrase length (as 10) in training, the maximum number of non-terminals (as 2) in translation rules, maximum number of non-terminals plus terminals (as 5) on the source, prohibition of non-terminals to be adjacent on the source, beam threshold β (as 10^{-5}) (to discard derivations with a score worse than β times the best score in the same chart cell), beam size b (as 200) (i.e. each chart cell contains at most b derivations). For Moses HPB, we use "grow-diag-final-and" to obtain symmetric word alignments, 10 for the maximum phrase length, and the recommended default values for all other parameters.

5.1 Experimental Settings

To examine the efficacy of our approach on training datasets of different scales, we first train translation models on a small-sized corpus, and then scale to a larger one. We use the 2002 NIST MT evaluation test data (878 sentence pairs) as the development data, and the 2003, 2004, 2005, 2006-news NIST MT evaluation test data (919, 1788, 1082, and 616 sentence pairs, respectively) as the test data. To find heads, we parse the source sentences with the Berkeley Parser[3] (Petrov and Klein, 2007) trained on Chinese TreeBank 6.0 and use the Penn2Malt toolkit[4] to obtain dependency structures.

We obtain the word alignments by running GIZA++ (Och and Ney, 2000) on the corpus in both directions, applying "grow-diag-final-and" refinement (Koehn et al., 2003). We use the SRI language modeling toolkit to train a 5-gram language model on the Xinhua portion of the Gigaword corpus and standard MERT (Och, 2003) to tune the feature

[3]http://code.google.com/p/berkeleyparser/
[4]http://w3.msi.vxu.se/~nivre/research/Penn2Malt.html/

weights on the development data.

For evaluation, the NIST BLEU script (version 12) with the default settings is used to calculate the NIST and the BLEU scores, which measures case-insensitive matching of n-grams with n up to 4. To test whether a performance difference is statistically significant, we conduct significance tests following the paired bootstrap approach (Koehn, 2004). In this paper, '**' and '*' denote p-values less than 0.01 and in-between [0.01, 0.05), respectively.

5.2 Results on Small Data

To test the HD-HPB models, we firstly carried out experiments using the FBIS corpus as training data, which contains ~240K sentence pairs. Table 2 lists the rule table sizes. The full rule table size (including HD-HRs and NRRs) of our HD-HPB model is about 1.5 times that of Chiang's, largely due to refining the non-terminal symbol X in Chiang's model into head-informed ones in our model. It is also unsurprising, that the test set-filtered rule table size of our model is only about 0.8 times that of Chiang's: this is due to the fact that some of the refined translation rule patterns required by the test set are unattested in the training data. Furthermore, the rule table size of NRRs is much smaller than that of HD-HRs since a NRR contains only two non-terminals. Table 3 lists the translation performance with NIST and BLEU scores. Note that our re-implementation of Chiang's original HPB model performs on a par with Moses HPB. Table 3 shows that our HD-HPB model significantly outperforms Chiang's HPB model with an average improvement of 1.32 in BLEU and 0.16 in NIST (and similar improvements over Moses HPB).

Although HD-HPB has small size of phrase tables compared to HPB, it still consumes more time in decoding (e.g., 15.1 vs. 11.0), mostly due to the flexible reordering of NRRs.

5.3 Results on Large Data

We also conduct experiments on larger training data with ~1.5M sentence pairs from the LDC dataset.[5] Table 4 lists the rule table sizes and Table 5 presents translation performance with NIST and BLEU scores. It shows that our HD-HPB model consistently outperforms Chiang's HPB model with an average improvement of 1.91 in BLEU and 0.35 in NIST (similar for Moses HPB). Compared to the improvement achieved on the small data, it is encouraging to see that our HD-HPB model benefits more from larger training data with little adverse effect on decoding time which increases only slightly from 15.1 to 16.6 seconds per sentence.

5.4 Comparison with SAMT-HPB

Comparing the performance of SAMT-HPB with regular HPB in Table 3 and Table 5, it is interesting to see that in general the SAMT-style approach leads to a deterioration of translation performance for the small training set (e.g., 30.09 for SAMT-HPB vs. 30.64 for HPB) while it comes into its own for the large training set (e.g., 33.54 for SAMT-HPB vs. 32.95 for HPB), indicating that the SAMT-style approach is more prone to data sparseness than HPB (or, indeed, HD-HPB).

Comparing the performance of SAMT-HPB with HD-HPB, shows that our head-driven non-terminal refining approach consistently outperforms the SAMT-style approach on an extensive set of experiments (for each test set $p < 0.01$), indicating that head information is more effective than (partial) CFG categories. To make the comparison fair, it is important to note that our implementation of source-side SAMT-HPB includes the same sophisticated non-terminal re-ordering NRR rules as HD-HPB (Section 2.2). Thus the performance differences reported here are not due to different reordering capabilities, but to the discriminative impact of the head information in HD-HPB over SAMT-style annotation. Taking *lianming zhichi* in Figure 2 as an example, HD-HPB labels the span *VV*, as *lianming* is dominated by *zhichi*, effecively ignoring *lianming* in the translation rule, while the SAMT label is *ADVP:AD+VV*[6] which is more susceptible to data sparsity (Table 2 and Table 4). In addition, SAMT resorts to *X* if a text span fails to satisify pre-defined categories. Examining initial phrases extracted from the SAMT training data shows that 28% of them are labeled as *X*. Finally, for Chinese syntactic analy-

[5] This dataset includes LDC2002E18, LDC2003E07, LDC2003E14, Hansards portion of LDC2004T07, LDC2004T08 and LDC2005T06

[6] The constituency structure for *lianming zhichi* is *(VP (ADVP (AD lianming)) (VP (VV zhichi) ...))*.

System	Total Rules	MT 03	MT 04	MT 05	MT 06	Avg.
HPB	39.6M	2.8M	4.7M	3.3M	3.0M	3.4M
HD-HPB	59.5/0.6M	1.9/0.1M	3.4/0.2M	2.3/0.2M	2.0/0.1M	2.4/0.2M
SAMT-HPB	70.1/0.4M	2.2/0.2M	4.0/0.2M	2.7/0.2M	2.3/0.2M	2.8/0.2M

Table 2: Rule table sizes of different models trained on small data. Note: 1) SAMT-HPB indicates our HD-HPB model with the non-terminal scheme of Zollmann and Venugopal (2006); 2) For HD-HPB and SAMT-HPB, the rule sizes separated by / indicate HD-HRs and NRRs, respectively; 2) Except for "Total Rules", the figures correspond to rules filtered on the corresponding test set.

System	MT 03		MT 04		MT 05		MT 06		Avg.		Time
	NIST	BLEU	NIST	BLEU	NIST	BLEU	NIST	BLEU	NIST	BLEU	
Moses HPB	7.377	29.67	8.209	33.60	7.571	29.49	6.773	28.90	7.483	30.42	NA
HPB	8.137	29.75	9.050	34.06	8.264	30.09	7.788	28.64	8.310	30.64	11.0
HD-HPB	**8.308**	**31.01****	**9.211**	**35.11****	**8.426**	**31.57****	**7.930**	**30.15****	**8.469**	**31.96**	15.1
SAMT-HPB	7.886	29.14*	8.703	33.32**	7.961	29.49*	7.307	28.41	7.964	30.09	17.3
HD-HR+Glue	7.966	29.51	8.826	33.68	8.116	29.84	7.474	28.51	8.095	30.39	5.4

Table 3: NIST and BLEU (%) scores of different models trained on small data. Note: 1) HD-HR+Glue indicates our HD-HPB model replacing NRRs with glue rules; 2) Significance tests for Moses HPB, HD-HPB, SAMT-HPB and HD-HR+Glue are done against HPB.

System	Total Rules	MT 03	MT 04	MT 05	MT 06	Avg.
HPB	206.8M	11.3M	17.6M	12.9M	10.4M	13.0M
HD-HPB	318.6/2.3M	7.3/0.3M	12.2/0.4M	8.5/0.3M	6.7/0.2M	8.7/0.3M
SAMT-HPB	371.0/1.1M	8.6/0.3M	14.3/0.4M	10.1/0.3M	7.9/0.3M	10.2/0.3M

Table 4: Rule table sizes of different models trained on large data.

System	MT 03		MT 04		MT 05		MT 06		Avg.		Time
	NIST	BLEU	NIST	BLEU	NIST	BLEU	NIST	BLEU	NIST	BLEU	
Moses HPB	7.914	32.94*	8.429	35.16	7.962	32.18	6.483	29.88*	7.697	32.54	NA
HPB	8.583	33.59	9.114	35.39	8.465	32.20	7.532	30.60	8.423	32.95	13.7
HD-HPB	**8.885**	**35.50****	**9.494**	**37.61****	**8.871**	**34.56****	**7.839**	**31.78****	**8.772**	**34.86**	16.6
SAMT-HPB	8.644	34.07	9.245	36.52**	8.618	32.90*	7.543	30.66	8.493	33.54	19.1
HD-HR+Glue	8.831	34.58**	9.435	36.55**	8.821	33.84**	7.863	31.06	8.737	34.01	6.7

Table 5: NIST and BLEU (%) scores of different models trained on large data. Note: System labels and significance testing as in Table 3.

sis, dependency structure is more reliable than constituency structure. Moreover, SAMT-HPB takes more time in decoding than HD-HPB due to larger phrase tables.

5.5 Discussion

5.5.1 Individual Contribution of HD-HRs and NRRs

Examining translation output shows that on average each sentence employs 16.6/5.2 HD-HRs/NRRs in our HD-HPB model, compared to 15.9/3.6 hierarchical rules/glue rules in Chiang's model, providing further indication of the importance of NRRs in translation. In order to separate out the individual contributions of the novel HD-HRs and NRRs, we carry out an additional experiment (HD-HR+Glue) using HD-HRs with monotonic glue rules only (adjusted to refined rule labels, but effectively switching off the extra reordering power of full NRRs) both on the small and the large datasets, with interesting results: Table 3 (HD-HR+Glue) shows that for the small training set most of the improvement of our full HD-HPB model comes from the NRRs, as RR+Glue performs on the same level as Chiang's original and Moses HPB (the differences are not statistically significant), perhaps indicating sparseness for the refined HD-HRs given the small training set. Table 5 shows that for the large training set, HD-HRs come into their own: on average more than half of the improvement over HPB (Chiang and Moses) comes from the refined HD-HRs, the rest from NRRs.

It is not surprising that compared to the others HD-HR+Glue takes much less time in decoding. This is due to the fact that 1) compared to HPB, the refined translation rule patterns on the source side have fewer entries in phrase table; 2) compared to HD-HPB, HD-HR+Glue switches off the extra reordering of NRRs. The decoding time for HD-HPB and HD-HR+Glue suggests that NRRs are more than doubling the time required to decode.

5.5.2 Different Head Label Sets

Examining initial phrases extracted from the large size training data shows that there are 63K types of refined non-terminals with respect to 33 types of POS tags. Considering the sparseness in translation rules caused by this comparatively detained POS tag set, we carry out an experiment with a reduced set of non-terminal types by using a less granular POS tag set (C-HPB). Moreover, due to the fact that concatenation of POS tags of heads mostly captures internal structure of a text span, it is interesting to examine the effect of other syntactic labels, in particular dependency labels, to try to better capture the impact of the external context on the text span. To this end, we replace the POS tag of head with its incoming dependency label (DL-HPB), or the combination of (the original fine-grained) POS tag and its dependency label (POS-DL-HPB). For C-HPB we use the coarse POS tag set obtained by grouping the 33 types of Chinese POS tags into 11 types following Xia (2000). For example, we generalize all verbal tags (e.g., *VA*, *VC*, *VE*, and *VV*) and all nominal tags (e.g., *NR*, *NT*, and *NN*) into *Verb* and *Noun*, respectively. We use the dependency labels in Penn2Malt which defines 9 types of dependency labels for Chinese, including *AMOD*, *DEP*, *NMOD*, *P*, *PMOD*, *ROOT*, *SBAR*, *VC*, and *VMOD*.[7]

Table 6 shows the results trained on large data. Although the number of non-terminal types decreased sharply from 63K to 3K, using the coarse POS tag set in C-HPB surprisingly lowers the performance with 1.1 BLEU scores on average (e.g., 33.75 vs. 34.86), indicating that grouping POS tags using simple linguistic rules is inappropriate for HD-HPB. We still believe that this initial negative finding should be supplemented by future work on groupping POS tags using machine learning techniques considering contextual information.

Table 6 also shows that replacing POS tags of heads with their dependency labels (DL-HPB) substantially lowers the average performance from 34.86 on BLEU score to 32.54, probably due to the very coarse granularity of the dependency labels used. In addition, replacing non-terminal label with more refined tags (e.g., combination of original POS tag and dependency label) also lowers translation performance (POS-DL-HPB). Further experiments with more fine-grained dependency labels are required.

[7]Some other types of dependency labels (e.g., *SUB*, *OBJ*) are generated from function tags which are not available in our automatic parse trees.

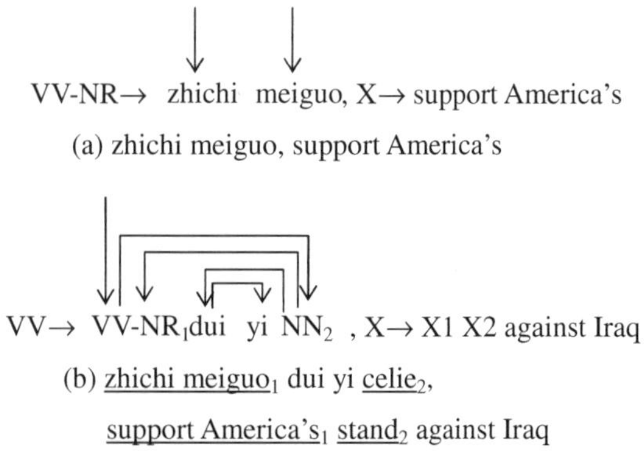

Figure 3: Examples of pharse pairs and their head-driven translation rules with dependency relation, regarding Figure 2

System	MT 03	MT 04	MT 05	MT 06	Avg.
HPB	33.59	35.39	32.20	30.60	32.95
HD-HPB	**35.50**	37.61	34.56	31.78	34.86
C-HPB	34.10	36.43	33.46	31.00	33.75
DL-HPB	32.81	35.19	32.27	29.89	32.54
POS-DL-HPB	34.08	36.78	33.14	30.43	33.61
HD-DEP-HPB	35.48	**38.17**	**34.81**	**32.38**	**35.21**

Table 6: BLEU (%) scores of models trained on large data.

5.5.3 Encoding Full Dependency Relations in Translation Rule

Xie et al. (2011) present a dependency-to-string translation model with a complete dependency structure on the source side and a moderate average improvement of 0.46 BLEU over the HPB baseline. By contrast, in our HD-HPB approach, dependency information is used to identify heads in the strings covered by non-terminals in HD-HR rules, and to refine non-terminal labels accordingly, with an average improvement of 1.91 in BLEU over the HPB baseline (when trained on the large data). This raises the question whether and to what extent complete (unlabeled) dependency information between the string and the heads in head-labeled non-terminal parts of the source side of SCFGs in HD-HPB can further improve results.

Given the source side of a translation rule (either HD-HR or NRR), say $P_s \rightarrow s_1 \ldots s_m$ (where each s_i is either a terminal or a head POS in a refined non-terminal), in a further set of experiments we keep the full unlabeled dependency relations between $s_1 \ldots s_m$ so as to capture contextual syntactic information in translation rules. For example, on the source side of Figure 3 (b) where *VV-NR* maps into words *zhichi* and *meiguo* while *NN* maps into word *celie*, we keep the full unlabeled dependency relations among words $\{$*zhichi, meiguo, dui, yi, celie*$\}$. HD-DEP-HPB (Table 6) augments translation rules in HD-HPB with full dependency relations on the source side. This further boosts the performance by 0.35 BLEU scores on average over HD-HPB and outperforms the HPB baseline by 2.26 BLEU scores on average.

5.5.4 Error Analysis

We carried out a manual error analysis comparing the outputs of our HD-HPB system with those of Chiang's (both trained on the large data). We observe that improved BLEU score often correspond to better topological ordering of phrases in the hierarchical structure of the source side, with a direct impact on which words in a source sentence should be translated first, and which later. As ungrammatical translations are often due to inappropriate topological orderings of phrases in the hierarchical structure, guiding the translation through appropriate topological ordering should improve translation quality. To give an example, consider the following input sentence from the 04 NIST MT test data and its two translation results:

- Input: 中国$_0$ 派团$_1$ 赴$_2$ 美$_3$ 采购$_4$ 二十多亿$_5$ 美元$_6$ 高$_7$ 科技$_8$ 设备$_9$
- HPB: chinese delegation to us dollar purchase of more high technology equipment
- HD-HPB: chinese delegation went to the united states to buy more us high - tech equipment

Figure 4 demonstrates the topological orderings in the two hierarchical structures. In addition to disfluency and some grammar errors (e.g., a main verb is missing), the basic HPB system also makes mistakes in reordering (e.g., 采购$_4$ 二十多亿$_5$ 美元$_6$ translated as *dollar purchase of more*). The poor translation quality, unsurprisingly, is caused by inappropriate topological ordering (Figure 4(a)). By comparison, the topological ordering reflected in the hierarchical structure of our HD-HPB model better respects syntactic structure (Figure 4(b)). Let

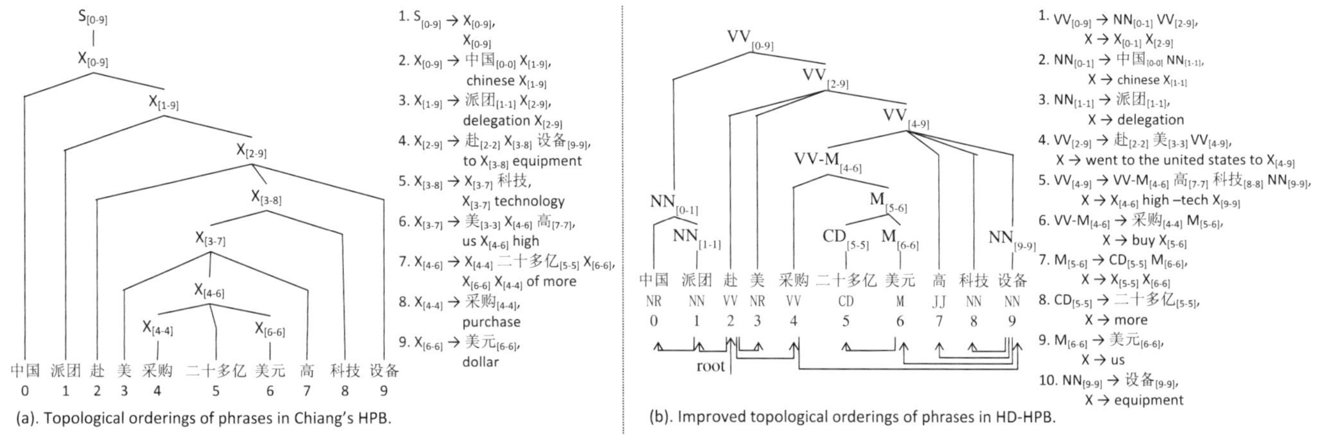

Figure 4: An example Chinese sentence and its two hierarchical structures. Note: subscript $[i\text{-}j]$ represents spanning from word i to word j on the source side.

us refer to the HD-HPB hierarchical structure on the source side as *translation parse tree* and to the treebank-based parser derived tree as *syntactic parse tree* from which we obtain unlabeled dependency structure. Examining the translation parse trees of our HD-HPB model shows that phrases with 1/2/3/4 heads account for 64.9%/23.1%/8.8%/3.2%, respectively. Compared to 37.9% of the phrases in the translation parse trees of the HPB model, 43.2% of the phrases of our HD-HPB model correspond to a linguistically motivated constituent in the syntactic parse tree with exactly the same text span. In sum, therefore, instead of simply enforcing hard linguistic constraints imposed by a full syntactic parse structure, our model opts for a successful mix of linguistically motivated and combinatorial (matching subphrases in HPB) constraints.

6 Conclusion

In this paper, we present a head-driven hierarchical phrase-based translation model, which adopts head information (derived through unlabeled dependency analysis) in the definition of non-terminals to better differentiate among translation rules. In addition, improved and better integrated reordering rules allow better reordering between consecutive non-terminals through exploration of a larger search space in the derivation. Our model maintains the strengths of Chiang's HPB model while at the same time it addresses the over-generation problem caused by using a uniform non-terminal symbol. Experimental results on Chinese-English translation across a wide range of training and test sets demonstrate significant and consistent improvements of our HD-HPB model over Chiang's HPB model as well as over a source side version of the SAMT-style model.

Currently, we only consider head information in a word sequence. In the future work, we will exploit more syntactic and semantic information to systematically and automatically define the inventory of non-terminals (in source and target). For example, for a non-terminal symbol *VV*, we believe it will benefit translation if we use fine-grained dependency labels (subject, object etc.) used to link it to its governing head elsewhere in the translation rule.

Acknowledgments

This work was supported by Science Foundation Ireland (Grant No. 07/CE/I1142) as part of the Centre for Next Generation Localisation (www.cngl.ie) at Dublin City University. It was also partially supported by Project 90920004 under the National Natural Science Foundation of China and Project 2012AA011102 under the "863" National High-Tech Research and Development of China. We thank the reviewers for their insightful comments.

References

Hala Almaghout, Jie Jiang, and Andy Way. 2011. CCG contextual labels in hierarchical phrase-based SMT. In *Proceedings of EAMT 2011*, pages 281–288.

Yee Seng Chan, Hwee Tou Ng, and David Chiang. 2007. Word sense disambiguation improves statistical machine translation. In *Proceedings of ACL 2007*, pages 33–40.

Eugene Charniak. 2000. A maximum-entropy-inspired parser. In *Proceedings of NAACL 2000*, pages 132–139.

David Chiang. 2005. A hierarchical phrase-based model for statistical machine translation. In *Proceedings of ACL 2005*, pages 263–270.

David Chiang. 2007. Hierarchical phrase-based translation. *Computational Linguistics*, 33(2):201–228.

Michael Collins. 2003. Head-driven statistical models for natural language parsing. *Computational Linguistics*, 29(4):589–637.

Yang Gao, Philipp Koehn, and Alexandra Birch. 2011. Soft dependency constraints for reordering in hierarchical phrase-based translation. In *Proceedings of EMNLP 2011*, pages 857–868.

Zhongjun He, Yao Meng, and Hao Yu. 2010. Maximum entropy based phrase reordering for hierarchical phrase-based translation. In *Proceedings of EMNLP 2010*, pages 555–563.

Liang Huang and David Chiang. 2005. Better k-best parsing. In *Proceedings of IWPT 2005*, pages 53–64.

Zhongqiang Huang, Martin Cmejrek, and Bowen Zhou. 2010. Soft syntactic constraints for hierarchical phrase-based translation using latent syntactic distributions. In *Proceedings of EMNLP 2010*, pages 138–147.

Philipp Koehn, Franz Josef Och, and Daniel Marcu. 2003. Statistical phrase-based translation. In *Proceedings of NAACL 2003*, pages 48–54.

Philipp Koehn. 2004. Statistical significance tests for machine translation evaluation. In *Proceedings of EMNLP 2004*, pages 388–395.

Yuval Marton and Philip Resnik. 2008. Soft syntactic constraints for hierarchical phrased-based translation. In *Proceedings of ACL-HLT 2008*, pages 1003–1011.

Markos Mylonakis and Khalil Sima'an. 2011. Learning hierarchical translation structure with linguistic annotations. In *Proceedings of ACL-HLT 2011*, pages 642–652.

Franz Josef Och and Hermann Ney. 2000. Improved statistical alignment models. In *Proceedings of ACL 2000*, pages 440–447.

Franz Josef Och and Hermann Ney. 2002. Discriminative training and maximum entropy models for statistical machine translation. In *Proceedings of ACL 2002*, pages 295–302.

Franz Josef Och and Hermann Ney. 2004. The alignment template approach to statistical machine translation. *Computational Linguistics*, 30(4):417–449.

Franz Josef Och. 2003. Minimum error rate training in statistical machine translation. In *Proceedings of ACL 2003*, pages 160–167.

Slav Petrov and Dan Klein. 2007. Improved inference for unlexicalized parsing. In *Proceedings of NAACL 2007*, pages 404–411.

Libin Shen, Jinxi Xu, Bing Zhang, Spyros Matsoukas, and Ralph Weischedel. 2009. Effective use of linguistic and contextual information for statistical machine translation. In *Proceedings of EMNLP 2009*, pages 72–80.

Dekai Wu. 1996. A polynomial-time algorithm for statistical machine translation. In *Proceedings of ACL 1996*, pages 152–158.

Fei Xia. 2000. The part-of-speech tagging guidelines for the Penn Chinese Treebank (3.0). Technical Report IRCS-00-07, University of Pennsylvania Institute for Research in Cognitive Science Technical.

Jun Xie, Haitao Mi, and Qun Liu. 2011. A novel dependency-to-string model for statistical machine translation. In *Proceedings of EMNLP 2011*, pages 216–226.

Andreas Zollmann and Ashish Venugopal. 2006. Syntax augmented machine translation via chart parsing. In *Proceedings of NAACL 2006 - Workshop on Statistical Machine Translation*, pages 138–141.

Andreas Zollmann and Stephan Vogel. 2011. A word-class approach to labeling PSCFG rules for machine translation. In *Proceedings of ACL-HLT 2011*, pages 1–11.

SOME FORMULAS/TEXT MAY BE MISSING DUE TO FORMATTING ISSUES IN THE ORIGINAL E-MEDIA VERSION

Fully Automatic Semantic MT Evaluation

Chi-kiu Lo, Anand Karthik Tumuluru and **Dekai Wu**
HKUST
Human Language Technology Center
Department of Computer Science and Engineering
Hong Kong University of Science and Technology
{jackielo,aktumuluru,dekai}@cs.ust.hk

Abstract

We introduce the first fully automatic, fully semantic frame based MT evaluation metric, MEANT, that outperforms all other commonly used automatic metrics in correlating with human judgment on translation adequacy. Recent work on HMEANT, which is a human metric, indicates that machine translation can be better evaluated via semantic frames than other evaluation paradigms, requiring only minimal effort from monolingual humans to annotate and align semantic frames in the reference and machine translations. We propose a surprisingly effective Occam's razor automation of HMEANT that combines standard shallow semantic parsing with a simple maximum weighted bipartite matching algorithm for aligning semantic frames. The matching criterion is based on lexical similarity scoring of the semantic role fillers through a simple context vector model which can readily be trained using any publicly available large monolingual corpus. Sentence level correlation analysis, following standard NIST MetricsMATR protocol, shows that this fully automated version of HMEANT achieves significantly higher Kendall correlation with human adequacy judgments than BLEU, NIST, METEOR, PER, CDER, WER, or TER. Furthermore, we demonstrate that performing the semantic frame alignment automatically actually tends to be just as good as performing it manually. Despite its high performance, fully automated MEANT is still able to preserve HMEANT's virtues of simplicity, representational transparency, and inexpensiveness.

1 Introduction

We introduce the first fully automatic semantic-frame-based MT evaluation metric capable of outperforming all other commonly used automatic metrics like BLEU, NIST, METEOR, PER, CDER, WER, and TER for evaluating translation adequacy. This work, MEANT, can be seen as a fully automated version of HMEANT, which is a human metric, introduced by Lo and Wu (2011b). Despite its high performance, MEANT is still able to preserve HMEANT's virtues of Occam's razor simplicity, representational transparency, and inexpensiveness.

For the past decade, MT evaluation has relied heavily on inexpensive automatic metrics such as BLEU (Papineni *et al.*, 2002), NIST (Doddington, 2002), METEOR (Banerjee and Lavie, 2005), PER (Tillmann *et al.*, 1997), CDER (Leusch *et al.*, 2006), WER (Nießen *et al.*, 2000), and TER (Snover *et al.*, 2006). In large part, this is because automatic metrics significantly shorten the evaluation cycle by providing a fast, easy and cheap quantitative evaluation which can be effectively incorporated into modern SMT training methods.

Despite the fact that HMEANT, a human metric recently proposed by Lo and Wu (2011b,c,d), was shown to reflect translation adequacy more accurately than all of these automatic metrics, it is unfortunately infeasible to incorporate the HMEANT metrics directly into SMT training methods, due to the non-automatic processes of (1) semantic parsing and (2) aligning semantic frames. In this paper we introduce an automatic metric in which both the semantic parsing and the alignment of semantic frames are fully automated. Our aim is to show that even with full automation, this new metric still outperforms all the previous automatic metrics mentioned, thus providing a foundation for future incorporation into the training of SMT to drive system improvements in providing more adequate translation output.

N-gram oriented automatic MT evaluation metrics like BLEU perform well at capturing translation fluency, and ranking overall systems with respect to each other when their scores are averaged over entire documents or corpora. However, they do not fare so well in ranking translations of individual sentences. As MT systems improve, the n-gram based evaluation metrics have begun to show their limits. State-of-the-art MT systems are often able to output translations containing roughly the correct words, while failing to convey important aspects of the meaning of the input sentence. Cases where BLEU strongly disagrees with human judgment of translation quality were reported in large scale MT evaluation tasks by Callison-Burch *et al.* (2006) and Koehn and Monz (2006).

Motivated by the goal of addressing the weaknesses of n-gram oriented automatic MT evaluation metrics at evaluating translation adequacy, the HMEANT metric assesses translation utility by matching the basic event structure—"who did what to whom, when, where and why" (Pradhan *et al.*, 2004)—representing the central meaning conveyed by sentences. As mentioned above, however, HMEANT requires humans to manually annotate semantic frames in the reference and machine translations, and then to align the semantic frames—making it difficult to incorporate HMEANT as an objective function in the MT system training, evaluating, and optimizing cycle.

We argue in this paper that both the human semantic parsing and the semantic frame alignment tasks performed within HMEANT can be successfully automated to produce a state-of-the-art automatic metric. Moreover, we show that the spirit of Occam's razor can be preserved even for the semantic frame alignment, by demonstrating the effectiveness of a simple maximum weighted bipartite matching algorithm based on the lexical similarity between semantic frames. In addition, we show empirically that performing this semantic frame alignment automatically tends to be just as good as performing it manually. Our results indicate that MEANT, the fully automatic version of HMEANT, achieves levels of correlation with human adequacy judgment (in our experiments, approximately 0.37) which significantly outperforms the commonly used automatic metrics BLEU, NIST, METEOR, PER, CDER, WER, and TER (in our experiments, ranging between 0.20 and 0.29).

2 Related Work

2.1 Automatic lexical similarity based metrics

BLEU (Papineni *et al.*, 2002) remains the most widely used MT evaluation metric despite the fact that a number of large scale meta-evaluations (Callison-Burch *et al.*, 2006; Koehn and Monz, 2006) report cases where it strongly disagrees with human judgments of translation accuracy. Other lexical similarity based automatic MT evaluation metrics, like NIST (Doddington, 2002), METEOR (Banerjee and Lavie, 2005), PER (Tillmann *et al.*, 1997), CDER (Leusch *et al.*, 2006), WER (Nießen *et al.*, 2000), and TER (Snover *et al.*, 2006), also perform well in capturing translation fluency, but share the same problem that although evaluation with these metrics can be done very quickly at low cost, their underlying assumption—that a "good" translation is one that shares the same lexical choices as the reference translation—is not justified semantically. Lexical similarity does not adequately reflect similarity in meaning.

Generating a translation that contains roughly the correct words may be necessary—but is far from sufficient—to preserve the essence of the meaning. We argue that a translation metric that reflects meaning similarity needs to be based on similarity of semantic structure, and not merely flat lexical similarity.

2.2 HMEANT (human SRL based metric)

As mentioned above, despite the fact that the semi-automatic HMEANT metric recently proposed by Lo and Wu (2011b,c,d) shows a higher correlation with human adequacy judgments than all commonly used automatic MT evaluation metrics, as with other human metrics like HTER (Snover *et al.*, 2006), it is unfortunately infeasible to incorporate the HMEANT metrics directly into SMT training methods. HMEANT requires non-automatic manual steps of (1) semantic parsing and (2) aligning semantic frames. Monolingual (or bilingual) annotators must label the semantic roles in both the reference and machine translations, and then to align the semantic predicates and role fillers in the MT output to the reference translations. These annotations allow HMEANT to then look at the aligned role fillers, and aggregate the translation accuracy for each role. In the spirit of Occam's razor and representational transparency, the HMEANT score is defined simply in terms of a weighted f-score over these aligned predicates and role fillers. More precisely, HMEANT is defined as follows:

1. Human annotators annotate the shallow semantic structures of both the references and MT output.
2. Human judges align the semantic frames between the references and MT output by judging the correctness of the predicates.
3. For each pair of aligned semantic frames,
   (a) Human judges determine the translation correctness of the semantic role fillers.
   (b) Human judges align the semantic role fillers between the reference and MT output according to the correctness of the semantic role fillers.
4. Compute the weighted f-score over the matching role labels of these aligned predicates and role fillers.

$$\equiv \frac{\text{\#tokens filled in aligned frame i of MT}}{\text{total \#tokens in MT}}$$

$$\equiv \frac{\text{\#tokens filled in aligned frame i of REF}}{\text{total \#tokens in REF}}$$

$$, \equiv \text{total \# ARG j of aligned frame i in MT}$$

$$, \equiv \text{total \# ARG j of aligned frame i in REF}$$

$$, \equiv \text{\# correct ARG j of aligned frame i in MT}$$

$$, \equiv \text{\# partially correct ARG j of aligned frame i in MT}$$

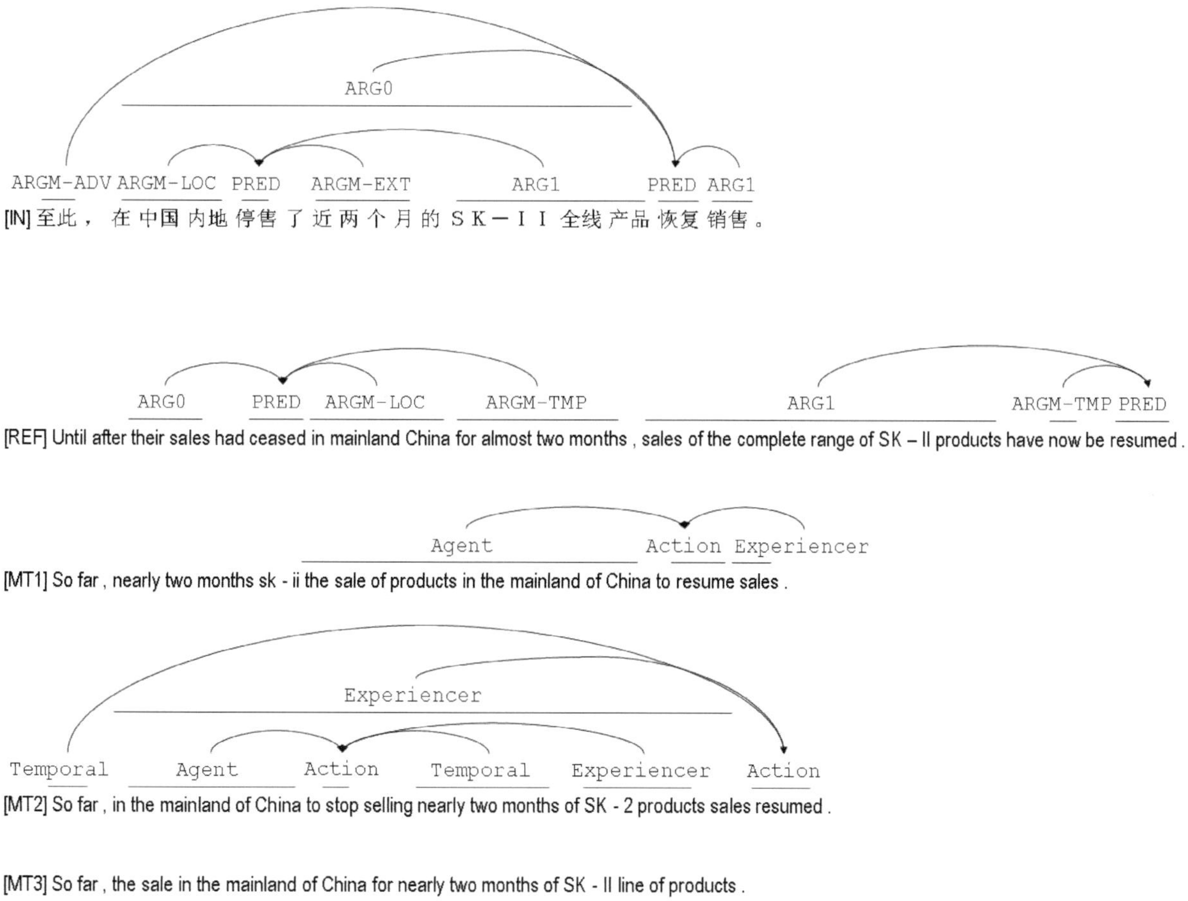

Figure 1: Examples of human semantic frame annotation. Semantic parses of the Chinese input and the English reference translation are from the Propbank gold standard. The MT output is semantically parsed by monolingual lay annotators according to the HMEANT guidelines. There are no semantic frames for MT3 because there is no predicate.

$$\text{precision} = \frac{\sum \frac{+\sum \;(\quad + \quad)}{+\sum}}{\sum}$$

$$\text{recall} = \frac{\sum \frac{+\sum \;(\quad + \quad)}{+\sum}}{\sum}$$

where and are the weights for frame, , in the MT/REF respectively. These weights estimate the degree of contribution of each frame to the overall meaning of the sentence. , and , are the total counts of argument of type in frame in the MT and REF respectively. , and , are the count of the correctly and partial correctly translated argument of type in frame in the MT output. Figure 1 shows examples of human semantic frame annotation on reference and machine translations as used in HMEANT. Table 1 shows examples of human judges' decisions for semantic frame alignment and translation correctness for each semantic roles, for the "MT2" output from Figure 1.

Unlike HMEANT, MEANT is fully automatic; but nevertheless, it adheres to HMEANT's principles of Occam's razor simplicity and representational transparency. These properties crucially facilitate error analysis and credit/blame assignment that are invaluable for MT system modeling.

Furthermore, being fully automatic, MEANT is even less expensive than HMEANT, which was already shown by Lo and Wu (2011b,c,d) to be significantly less expensive than HTER. This makes MEANT a much better candidate than HMEANT for future incorporation into the automatic training of SMT systems to drive improvements in translation adequacy.

2.3 Semantic role labels as features in aggregate metrics

Giménez and Màrquez (2007, 2008) introduced ULC, an automatic MT evaluation metric that aggregates many types of features, including several shallow semantic similarity features. However, unlike Lo and Wu (2011b),

Table 1: Example of SRL annotation for the MT2 output from figure 1 along with the human judgements of translation correctness for each argument. *Notice that although the decision made by the human judge for "in mainland China" in the reference translation and "the mainland of China" in MT2 is "correct", nevertheless the HMEANT computation will not count this as a match since their role labels do not match.

REF roles	REF	MT2 roles	MT2	decision
PRED	ceased	Action	stop	match
ARG0	their sale	—	—	incorrect
ARGM-LOC	in mainland China	Agent	the mainland of China	correct*
ARGM-TMP	for almost two months	Temporal	nearly two months	correct
—	—	Experiencer	SK - 2 products	incorrect
PRED	resumed	Action	resume	match
ARG0	sales of complete range of SK - II products	Experiencer	in the mainland of China to stop selling nearly two months of SK - 2 products sales	incorrect
ARGM-TMP	Until after , their sales had ceased in mainland China for almost two months	Temporal	So far	partial
ARGM-TMP	now	—	—	incorrect

the ULC representation is based on flat semantic role label features that do not capture the structural *relations* in semantic frames, i.e., the predicate-argument relations. Also unlike HMEANT, which weights each semantic role type according to its empirically determined relative importance to the adequate preservation of meaning, ULC uses uniform weights. Although the automatic ULC metric shows an improved correlation with human judgment of translation quality (Callison-Burch *et al.*, 2007; Giménez and Màrquez, 2007; Callison-Burch *et al.*, 2008; Giménez and Màrquez, 2008), it is not commonly used in large-scale MT evaluation campaigns, perhaps due to its high time cost and/or the difficulty of interpreting its score because of its highly complex combination of many heterogeneous types of features.

Like system combination approaches, ULC is a vastly more complex aggregate metric compared to widely used metrics like BLEU. We believe it is important for automatic semantic MT evaluation metrics to provide representational transparency via simple, clear, and transparent scoring schemes that are (a) easily human readable to support error analysis, and (b) potentially directly usable for automatic credit/blame assignment in tuning tree-structured SMT systems.

3 MEANT: A fully automatic semantic MT evaluation metric

Like HMEANT, our guiding principle is that a good translation is one that is useful, in the sense that human readers may successfully understand at least the basic event structure—*who did what to whom, when, where and why* (Pradhan *et al.*, 2004)—representing the central meaning of the source utterances. Whereas HMEANT measures this using a f-score of correctly translated semantic roles in MT output that are annotated and compared by monolingual human annotators, MEANT *automates* HMEANT as follows (the differences from HMEANT are italicized):

1. *Apply an automatic shallow semantic parser* on both the references and MT output.

2. *Apply maximum weighted bipartite matching algorithm to* align the semantic frames between the references and MT output by the *lexical similarity of the predicates.*

3. For each pair of aligned semantic frames,

   (a) *Lexical similarity scores* determine the *similarity* of the semantic role fillers.

   (b) *Apply maximum weighted bipartite matching algorithm to* align the semantic role fillers between the reference and MT output according to their *lexical similarity.*

4. Compute the weighted f-score over the matching role labels of these aligned predicates and role fillers.

3.1 Automatic semantic parsing

To automate the process of human semantic role labeling, we apply an automatic shallow semantic parser on both the reference and MT output that takes the raw translation as input and outputs the corresponding predicate-argument structure. We choose to semantically parse the translation independently, instead of inducing the parses

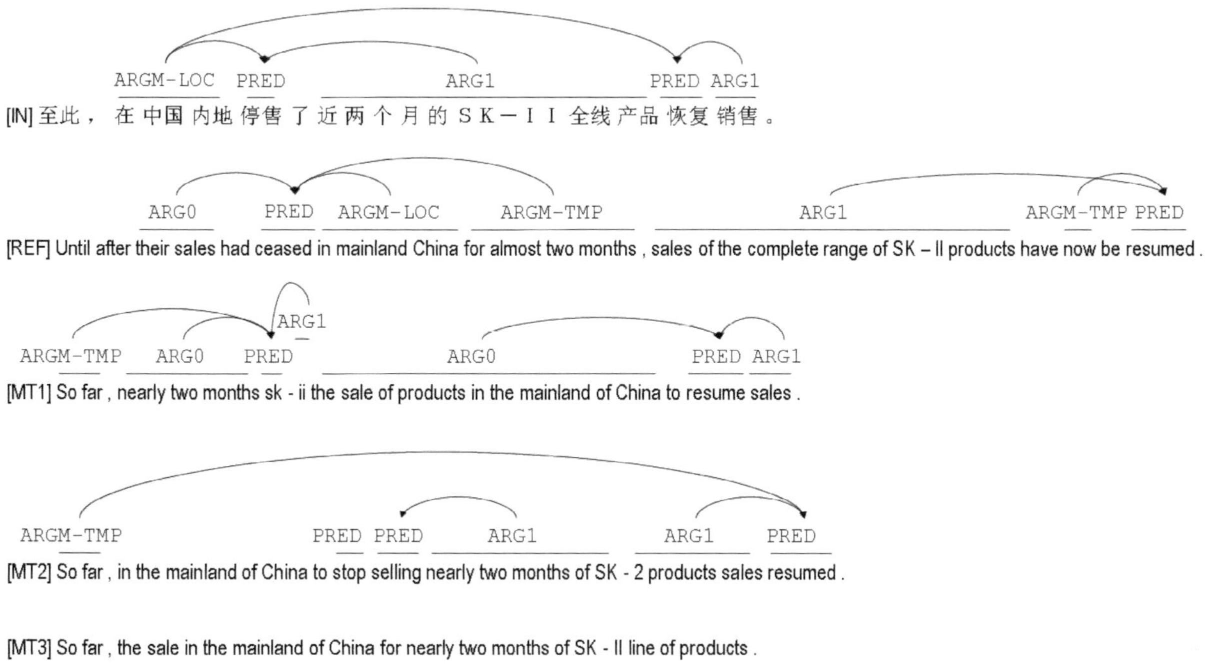

Figure 2: Examples of automatic shallow semantic parses. The Chinese input is parsed by a Chinese automatic shallow semantic parser. The English reference and machine translations are parsed by an English automatic shallow semantic parser. There are no semantic frames for mt3 since there is no predicate.

from the input, because it captures the raw meaning conveyed in the translation rather than predicting the meaning conveyed in the translation from the input. Figure 2 shows examples of automatic shallow semantic parses on both reference and machine translations.

3.2 Automatic semantic frame alignment

After reconstructing the shallow semantic parse, the manual semantic frame alignment process is automated by applying the maximum weighted bipartite matching algorithm where the weights of the edges represent the lexical similarity of the predicates. A wide range of lexical similarity measures are available to us, including for example BLEU, METEOR, cosine similarity based on context vector models (Dagan, 2000), and so forth. In Section 4, we will show the performance of the fully automatic semantic MT evaluation metric, MEANT ,couple with different lexical similarity metrics and other commonly used automatic MT evaluation metrics. In Section 6, we will discuss aligning the semantic frames according to all semantic role fillers, instead of the predicates only.

Then, for each pair of aligned semantic frames, we estimate the similarity of the semantic role fillers by summing all the lexical similarity of all the pairwise combination of tokens between the references and MT output. After obtaining the similarity of the semantic role fillers, we again apply the maximum weighted bipartite matching algorithm to align the semantic role fillers between the references and MT output. Table 2 shows examples of the human judges' decisions on semantic frame alignment and translation correctness for each semantic role in the "MT2" output from Figure 2.

3.3 Scoring the semantic similarity

After aligning the semantic frames automatically, the computation of the MEANT score is largely the same as stated in Lo and Wu (2011d), except that we now replace the counts of correctly and partially correctly translated semantic role fillers by the similarity scores of the predicates and arguments between the references and MT output.

$$\equiv \frac{\text{\#tokens filled in aligned frame i of MT}}{\text{total \#tokens in MT}}$$

$$\equiv \frac{\text{\#tokens filled in aligned frame i of REF}}{\text{total \#tokens in REF}}$$

$$, \equiv \text{total \# ARG j of aligned frame i in MT}$$

$$, \equiv \text{total \# ARG j of aligned frame i in REF}$$

$$_{,\text{pred}} \equiv \text{sim. of pred of REF and MT in aligned frame i}$$

$$, \equiv \text{sim. of ARG j of REF and MT in aligned frame i}$$

$$\text{precision} = \frac{\sum \frac{+\sum}{+\sum}}{\sum}$$

$$\text{recall} = \frac{\sum \frac{+\sum}{+\sum}}{\sum}$$

Table 2: Automatic semantic frame alignment of the MT2 output from figure 2, along with the automatic lexical similarity scoring on translation correctness for each argument.

REF roles	REF	MT2 roles	MT2	similarity
PRED	ceased	PRED	stop	0.0377
ARG0	their sales	—	—	—
ARGM-LOC	in mainland China	—	—	—
ARGM-TMP	for almost two months	—	—	—
—	—	PRED	selling	—
—	—	ARG1	nearly two months of SK	—
PRED	resumed	PRED	resumed	1.0
ARG1	sales of complete range of SK - II products	ARG1	2 products sales	0.0836
ARGM-TMP	now	ARGM-TMP	So far	0.0459

where , , , , are defined the same as in HMEANT, and and are the lexical similarities (BLEU, METEOR, cosine similarity based on a context vector model, and so on, as discussed in the following section) of the predicates and arguments of type between the reference translations and the MT output.

4 MEANT outperforms all automatic metrics

We will first show that the fully automatic semantic MT evaluation metric, MEANT, outperforms all the other commonly used automatic metrics.

4.1 Experimental setup

For assessing lexical similarity, a wide range of lexical similarity scoring models are available. We describe a representative subset of a wide range of experiments we have performed using all the most typical and commonly used measures. On one hand, we report experiments with integrating two commonly used MT evaluation metrics, BLEU and METEOR, as the lexical similarity. On the other hand, we also report experiments on integrating two common similarity measures—cosine similarity measure and min/max with mutual information (Dagan, 2000)—that are based on context vector models, and trained from the Gigaword corpus with window sizes of 3 and 5.

The cosine similarity between two sequences of word tokens, $\vec{}$ and $\vec{}$, is defined as follows:

$$\vec{} = \text{context vector of word token x}$$
$$= \text{attribute i of context vector } \vec{}$$

$$(\, , \,) = \frac{\text{count}(\, , \,)}{\text{count}(\,)}$$

$$\text{cosine}(\, , \,) = \frac{\Sigma (\, , \,) \times (\, , \,)}{\sqrt{\Sigma (\, , \,)^2}\sqrt{\Sigma (\, , \,)^2}}$$

$$\text{cosine}(\vec{}, \vec{}) = \Sigma\Sigma\text{cosine}(\, , \,)$$

Using the same definition of , the min/max with mutual information similarity between two sequences of word tokens, $\vec{}$ and $\vec{}$, is defined as follows:

$$(\,) = \frac{\text{count}(\, , \,)}{\sum \text{count}(\, , \,)}$$

$$(\,) = \frac{\sum \text{count}(\, , \,)}{\sum \sum \text{count}(\, , \,)}$$

$$\text{MI}(\, , \,) = \log\left(\frac{(\,)}{(\,)}\right)$$

$$\text{MinMax-MI}(\, , \,) = \frac{\Sigma \min(\text{MI}(\, , \,), \text{MI}(\, , \,))}{\Sigma \max(\text{MI}(\, , \,), \text{MI}(\, , \,))}$$

$$\text{MinMax-MI}(\vec{}, \vec{}) = \Sigma\Sigma\text{MinMax-MI}(\, , \,)$$

For our benchmark comparison, the evaluation data for our experiments is the same two sets of sentences, GALE-A and GALE-B that were used in Lo and Wu (2011d), where GALE-A is used for estimating the weight parameters of the metric by optimizing the correlation with human adequacy judgment, and then the learned weights are applied to testing on GALE-B.

For the automatic semantic role labeling, we used the publicly available off-the-shelf shallow semantic parser, ASSERT (Pradhan *et al.*, 2004).

The correlation with human adequacy judgments on sentence-level system ranking is assessed by the standard NIST MetricsMaTr procedure (Callison-Burch *et al.*, 2010) using Kendall correlation coefficients.

Table 3: Sentence-level correlation with human adequacy judgment on GALE-A (training) and GALE-B (testing) comparing all commonly used MT evaluation metrics against our proposed new fully automatic semantic frame based MT evaluation metric integrated with various lexical similarity scores between semantic role fillers: (a) BLEU, (b) METEOR, (c) cosine similarity and (d) MinMax with mutual information.

	GALE-A (training)	GALE-B (testing)
Human metrics		
HMEANT	0.49	0.27
HTER	0.43	0.20
Automatic metrics		
MEANT	—	—
- with MinMax-MI on context vector model of window size 3	**0.37**	0.19
- with MinMax-MI on context vector model of window size 5	0.37	0.17
- with Cosine on context vector model of window size 3	0.32	0.13
- with Cosine on context vector model of window size 5	0.30	0.08
- with METEOR	0.17	—
- with BLEU	0.00	—
METEOR	0.20	**0.21**
NIST	0.29	0.09
TER	0.20	0.10
BLEU	0.20	0.12
PER	0.20	0.07
WER	0.10	0.11
CDER	0.12	0.10

4.2 Results

Table 3 shows that MEANT significantly outperforms all the other automatic MT evaluation metrics when integrated with a simple similarity measure based on word context vectors trained from a large monolingual corpus. We can also see that using min/max with mutual information is significantly better than using cosine similarity. Furthermore, context vector models using a window size of 3 appear to be as good or better than those using a window size of 5.

Although the human metrics, HMEANT and HTER, obviously remain superior, MEANT performs far better than almost all other automatic metrics. The only exception is the GALE-B dataset, where METEOR performs marginally better than MEANT and even HTER. Data analysis shows that the marginally higher correlation of METEOR on the GALE-B dataset is a statistical outlier; it is quite rare for a lexically based automatic metric to outperform even the *human-driven* HTER metric.

Interestingly and somewhat surprisingly, using the n-gram based MT evaluation metrics BLEU and METEOR as lexical similarity scores does not work well at all for this purpose, even on the training data (thus obviating the need to obtain results on the testing data). Analysis indicates that the reason for this is that variation between alternative paraphrasing of the role fillers makes the number of matching n-grams quite small, since there are many synonyms and few exact consecutive n-gram matches.

Table 4: Sentence-level correlation with human adequacy judgment on GALE-A (training) and GALE-B (testing) for aligning sematnic frame automatically and manually.

Semantic frame alignment	GALE-A	GALE-B
Automatic	0.37	0.19
Manual	0.35	0.17

In the following sections, we turn to considering several questions that naturally arise following these strong results.

5 Don't align semantic frames manually

One obvious question is whether the automatic alignment of semantic frames degrades MEANT's accuracy, and if so, the extent to which it hurts.

5.1 Experimental setup

To test this question, we compare the best fully automatic results of the previous section against a semi-automatic variant of our proposed metric. In the semi-automatic variant, the semantic parsing is still performed automatically. However, the semantic frame alignment is instead done manually by human annotators.

The rest of the experimental setup is the same as that used in Section 4.

5.2 Results

Table 4 shows that performing the alignment of semantic frames automatically is as good—or even better than—doing the alignment manually. We believe the success of automatic semantic frame alignment reflects the high degree of reliability of our chosen lexical similarity metric, when the candidates for role fillers are restricted to the fairly small set defined by the sentence pairs.

6 Look only at predicates when aligning semantic frames

Given the positive results of the previous sections, it is worth asking a deeper question: would it further improve the correlation with human adequacy judgment of the metric if the semantic frames were aligned not only by matching predicates (as HMEANT did), but in addition by trying to also maximize the match of the semantic role fillers?

The reason to revisit this question is that even though Lo and Wu (2011a) showed that in the case of HMEANT it is effective for *human* annotators to align semantic frames according to the predicates only, this could easily be due to the mental challenge for lay annotators to compare and keep in mind all the semantic role fillers at the same time. But in the case of a fully automatic metric, on the other hand, it is easy for an algorithm to compute the individual similarities between all the semantic role fillers and consider the aggregate similarity when optimizing the alignment of semantic frames.

Surprisingly, however, the results will show that even in the automated case, this still does *not* help improve the correlation with human adequacy judgments.

6.1 Experimental setup

To align semantic frames using all semantic roles, we aggregate the lexical similarity of all the semantic role fillers into a semantic frame similarity score. We experiment on two variations of the aggregation function (1) simple linear average of the lexical similarity over the number of aligned semantic roles in the frames; or (2) the inverse of the sum of the negative log of the role fillers similarity.

The rest of the experimental setup is the same as that used in Section 4.

6.2 Results

Table 5 shows that to align semantic frames, using only the lexical similarity of the predicates between the frames in the reference translations and the MT output (0.37 Kendall in GALE-A and 0.19 Kendall in GALE-B) is more robust than either of the two natural ways of aggregating the lexical similarity of the aligned semantic role fillers. Aggregating by linear average yields a lower 0.35 Kendall in GALE-A and 0.10 Kendall in GALE-B. Aggregating by the inverse of the sum of negative logs yields a lower 0.30 Kendall in GALE-A and 0.17 Kendall in GALE-B.

Table 5: Sentence-level correlation with human adequacy judgments on GALE-A (training set) and GALE-B (testing set) for aligning semantic frames using predicate only vs. using all semantic role fillers aggregated by (1) the linear average of the lexical similarity vs. (2) the inverse of the sum of negative log of the lexical similarity.

Frame alignment	GALE-A	GALE-B
Predicate only	0.37	0.19
Linear average	0.35	0.10
Inverse of sum of neg. log	0.30	0.17

What might explain this perhaps surprising result? Our conjecture is that aggregating the lexical similarities of the semantic role fillers fails to help find better semantic frame alignments because the lexical similarities are aggregated with uniform weight across different types of role fillers. Therefore, the aggregation ignores the fact that different types of role types contribute to a widely varying degree to the meaning of an entire semantic frame—in reality, some role types are much more important than others. However, the complexity of the metric would be greatly increased if we added weights for each semantic roles type for semantic frame alignment process, and this would not be likely to be worthwhile given that automatic alignment is already performing as well as human alignment of semantic frames.

7 Don't word align semantic role fillers

Another question that naturally arises from the positive results above is: when aligning the semantic frames, would word-aligning the tokens within role fillers help? Specifically, if we had word alignments for every candidate pair of role filler strings, we could sum the lexical similarities only between the aligned tokens—instead of what we did above, which was to sum the lexical similarities of *all* pairwise combinations of tokens.

However, experimental results will show that, surprisingly, to judge the similarity of semantic role fillers, summing the lexical similarities over only word-aligned tokens—instead of all pairwise combinations of tokens—does *not* help to improve the correlation of the semantic MT evaluation with human adequacy judgment.

7.1 Experimental setup

To avoid the danger of aligning a token in one segment to excessive numbers of tokens in the other segment, we adopt a variant of competitive linking by Melamed (1996). Competitive linking is a greedy best-first word alignment algorithm.

Table 6: Sentence-level correlation with human adequacy judgments on GALE-A (training set) and GALE-B (testing set) for judging semantic role fillers similarity using pairwise tokens vs. only aligned tokens.

Semantic role filler similarity	GALE-A	GALE-B
All pairwise tokens	0.37	0.19
Only aligned tokens	0.36	0.17

The rest of the experimental setup is the same as that used in Section 4.

7.2 Results

Table 6 shows that, surprisingly, judging semantic role filler similarity using only the aligned tokens (selected by competitive linking word alignment algorithm) does *not* help the correlation with human adequacy judgment. This is surprising as, intuitively, using only the aligned tokens should avoid the introduction of noise in judging the similarity between semantic role fillers because it avoids adding in similarities for words within semantic role fillers whose meanings are not close to each other.

How might this outcome be explained? We conjecture that the word alignments over-constrain the calculation of segment similarities. The individual lexical similarities are already weighted fairly accurately, so the lexical similarities between words that do not correspond do not hurt since they are already close to zero. On the other hand, in cases where the word alignment is ambiguous, it is better to aggregate over different possible pairwise alignments—strictly obeying a hard word alignment undesirably forces dropping of some individual lexical similarity scores that are actually relevant.

8 Conclusion

We have introduced a new fully automatic semantic MT evaluation metric, MEANT, that is fundamentally based on semantic frames, that is the first such metric to outperform all other commonly used automatic MT evaluation metrics. Experimental results following the standard NIST MetricsMATR protocol indicate that our proposed metric achieves levels of correlation with human adequacy judgment (in our experiments, approximately 0.37) that significantly outperform BLEU, NIST, METEOR, PER, CDER, WER, and TER (in our experiments, ranging between 0.20 and 0.29).

We have also shown in this paper that the spirit of Occam's razor of HMEANT can be preserved even under full automation by (1) replacing human semantic role annotation with automatic shallow semantic parsing and (2) replacing human semantic frame alignment with a simple maximum weighted bipartite matching algorithm based on the lexical similarity between semantic frames. Under analysis, we have further shown empirically that performing this semantic frame alignment automatically tends to be just as good as performing it manually. Furthermore, we have shown surprisingly that (1) for aligning semantic frames, using *only* the similarity of predicates is more accurate than also taking into account the similarity of semantic role fillers, and (2) to judge similarity between semantic role fillers, aggregating similarity of *all* pairwise combination of word tokens is more accurate than considering only the similarity of the tokens that obey word alignments.

Papineni et al. (2002) stated in their conclusion that "We believe that BLEU will accelerate the MT R&D cycle by allowing researchers to rapidly home in on effective modeling ideas." since fully automatic metrics allow inexpensive training and tuning of SMT systems. Developments in the past decade have more than borne witness to this statement. However, SMT has progressed to the stage where simple metrics like BLEU are no longer capable of driving progress toward preservation of meaning with respect to proper event structure. We believe that MEANT that rapidly and accurately reflects the translation adequacy of MT output by directly assessing *who did what to whom, when, where and why* is needed to bring MT R&D to a new level of improvement in generating more meaningful MT output.

Acknowledgments

This material is based upon work supported in part by the Defense Advanced Research Projects Agency (DARPA) under BOLT contract no. HR0011-12-C-0016, and GALE contract nos. HR0011-06-C-0022 and HR0011-06-C-0023; by the European Union under the FP7 grant agreement no. 287658; and by the Hong Kong Research Grants Council (RGC) research grants GRF621008, GRF612806, DAG03/04.EG09, RGC6256/00E, and RGC6083/99E. Any opinions, findings and conclusions or recommendations expressed in this material are those of the authors and do not necessarily reflect the views of the RGC, EU, or DARPA.

References

Satanjeev Banerjee and Alon Lavie. METEOR: An Automatic Metric for MT Evaluation with Improved Correlation with Human Judgments. In *Proceedings of the 43th Annual Meeting of the Association of Computational Linguistics (ACL-05)*, pages 65–72, 2005.

Chris Callison-Burch, Miles Osborne, and Philipp Koehn. Re-evaluating the role of BLEU in Machine Translation Research. In *Proceedings of the 13th Conference of the European Chapter of the Association for Computational Linguistics (EACL-06)*, pages 249–256, 2006.

Chris Callison-Burch, Cameron Fordyce, Philipp Koehn, Christof Monz, and Josh Schroeder. (Meta-) evaluation of

Machine Translation. In *Proceedings of the 2nd Workshop on Statistical Machine Translation*, pages 136–158, 2007.

Chris Callison-Burch, Cameron Fordyce, Philipp Koehn, Christof Monz, and Josh Schroeder. Further Meta-evaluation of Machine Translation. In *Proceedings of the 3rd Workshop on Statistical Machine Translation*, pages 70–106, 2008.

Chris Callison-Burch, Philipp Koehn, Christof Monz, Kay Peterson, Mark Pryzbocki, and Omar Zaidan. Findings of the 2010 Joint Workshop on Statistical Machine Translation and Metrics for Machine Translation. In *Proceedings of the Joint 5th Workshop on Statistical Machine Translation and MetricsMATR*, pages 17–53, Uppsala, Sweden, 15-16 July 2010.

Ido Dagan. Contextual word similarity. In Robert Dale, Herman Moisl, and Harold Somers, editors, *Handbook of Natural Language Processing*, pages 459–476. Marcel Dekker, New York, 2000.

G. Doddington. Automatic Evaluation of Machine Translation Quality using N-gram Co-occurrence Statistics. In *Proceedings of the 2nd International Conference on Human Language Technology Research (HLT-02)*, pages 138–145, San Francisco, CA, USA, 2002. Morgan Kaufmann Publishers Inc.

Jesús Giménez and Lluís Màrquez. Linguistic Features for Automatic Evaluation of Heterogenous MT Systems. In *Proceedings of the 2nd Workshop on Statistical Machine Translation*, pages 256–264, Prague, Czech Republic, June 2007. Association for Computational Linguistics.

Jesús Giménez and Lluís Màrquez. A Smorgasbord of Features for Automatic MT Evaluation. In *Proceedings of the 3rd Workshop on Statistical Machine Translation*, pages 195–198, Columbus, OH, June 2008. Association for Computational Linguistics.

Philipp Koehn and Christof Monz. Manual and Automatic Evaluation of Machine Translation between European Languages. In *Proceedings of the Workshop on Statistical Machine Translation*, pages 102–121, 2006.

Gregor Leusch, Nicola Ueffing, and Hermann Ney. CDer: Efficient MT Evaluation Using Block Movements. In *Proceedings of the 13th Conference of the European Chapter of the Association for Computational Linguistics (EACL-06)*, 2006.

Chi-kiu Lo and Dekai Wu. A Radically Simple, Effective Annotation and Alignment Methodology for Semantic Frame Based SMT and MT Evaluation. In *Proceedings of International Workshop on Using Linguistic Information for Hybrid Machine Translation (LiHMT 2011), organized by OpenMT-2.*, 2011.

Chi-kiu Lo and Dekai Wu. MEANT: An Inexpensive, High-Accuracy, Semi-Automatic Metric for Evaluating Translation Utility based on Semantic Roles. In *Proceedings of the Joint conference of the 49th Annual Meeting of the Association for Computational Linguistics : Human Language Technologies (ACL-HLT-11)*, 2011.

Chi-kiu Lo and Dekai Wu. SMT vs. AI redux: How semantic frames evaluate MT more accurately. In *Proceedings of the 22nd International Joint Conference on Artificial Intelligence (IJCAI-11)*, 2011.

Chi-kiu Lo and Dekai Wu. Structured vs. Flat Semantic Role Representations for Machine Translation Evaluation. In *Proceedings of the 5th Workshop on Syntax and Structure in Statistical Translation (SSST-5)*, 2011.

I. Dan Melamed. Automatic construction of clean broad-coverage translation lexicons. In *Proceedings of the 2nd Conference of the Association for Machine Translation in the Americas (AMTA-1996)*, 1996.

Sonja Nießen, Franz Josef Och, Gregor Leusch, and Hermann Ney. A Evaluation Tool for Machine Translation: Fast Evaluation for MT Research. In *Proceedings of the 2nd International Conference on Language Resources and Evaluation (LREC-2000)*, 2000.

Kishore Papineni, Salim Roukos, Todd Ward, and Wei-Jing Zhu. BLEU: A Method for Automatic Evaluation of Machine Translation. In *Proceedings of the 40th Annual Meeting of the Association for Computational Linguistics (ACL-02)*, pages 311–318, 2002.

Sameer Pradhan, Wayne Ward, Kadri Hacioglu, James H. Martin, and Dan Jurafsky. Shallow Semantic Parsing Using Support Vector Machines. In *Proceedings of the 2004 Conference on Human Language Technology and the North American Chapter of the Association for Computational Linguistics (HLT-NAACL-04)*, 2004.

Matthew Snover, Bonnie J. Dorr, Richard Schwartz, Linnea Micciulla, and John Makhoul. A Study of Translation Edit Rate with Targeted Human Annotation. In *Proceedings of the 7th Conference of the Association for Machine Translation in the Americas (AMTA-06)*, pages 223–231, 2006.

Christoph Tillmann, Stephan Vogel, Hermann Ney, Arkaitz Zubiaga, and Hassan Sawaf. Accelerated DP Based Search For Statistical Translation. In *Proceedings of the 5th European Conference on Speech Communication and Technology (EUROSPEECH-97)*, 1997.

Probes in a Taxonomy of Factored Phrase-Based Models *

Ondřej Bojar, Bushra Jawaid, Amir Kamran
Charles University in Prague, Faculty of Mathematics and Physics
Institute of Formal and Applied Linguistics
Malostranské nám. 25, Praha 1, CZ-118 00, Czech Republic
{bojar,jawaid,kamran}@ufal.mff.cuni.cz

Abstract

We introduce a taxonomy of factored phrase-based translation scenarios and conduct a range of experiments in this taxonomy. We point out several common pitfalls when designing factored setups. The paper also describes our WMT12 submissions CU-BOJAR and CU-POOR-COMB.

Number of Translation Steps	Number of Independent Searches	Structure of Searches	Nickname
One	One	–	Direct
Several	One	–	Single-Step
	Several	Serial	Two-Step
		Complex	Complex

Figure 1: A taxonomy of factored phrase-based models.

1 Introduction

Koehn and Hoang (2007) introduced "factors" to phrase-based MT to explicitly capture arbitrary features in the phrase-based model. In essence, input and output tokens are no longer atomic units but rather vectors of atomic values encoding e.g. the lexical and morphological information separately. Factored translation has been successfully applied to many language pairs and with diverse types of information encoded in the additional factors, i.a. (Bojar, 2007; Avramidis and Koehn, 2008; Stymne, 2008; Badr et al., 2008; Ramanathan et al., 2009; Koehn et al., 2010; Yeniterzi and Oflazer, 2010). On the other hand, it happens quite frequently, that the factored setup causes a loss compared to the phrase-based baseline. The underlying reason is the complexity of the search space which gets boosted when the model explicitly includes detailed information, see e.g. Bojar and Kos (2010) or Toutanova et al. (2008).

* This work was supported by the project EuroMatrixPlus (FP7-ICT-2007-3-231720 of the EU and 7E09003+7E11051 of the Czech Republic) and the Czech Science Foundation grants P406/11/1499 and P406/10/P259. We are grateful for reviewers' comments but we have to obey the 6 page limit. Thanks also to Aleš Tamchyna for supplementary material on MERT.

In this paper, we first provide a taxonomy of (phrase-based) translation setups and then we examine a range of sample configurations in this taxonomy. We don't state universal rules, because the applicability of each of the setups depends very much on the particular language pair, text domain and amount of data available, but we hope to draw attention to relevant design decisions.

The paper also serves as the description of our WMT12 submissions CU-BOJAR and CU-POOR-COMB between English and Czech.

2 A Taxonomy of Factored P-B Models

Figure 1 suggests a taxonomy of various Moses setups. Following the definitions of Koehn and Hoang (2007), a *search* consists of several *translation* and *generation* steps: translation steps map source factors to target factors and generation steps produce target factors from other target factors.

The taxonomy is vaguely linked to the types of problems that can be expected with a given configuration. Direct translation is likely to suffer from out-of-vocabulary issues (due to insufficient generalization) on either side. Single-step scenarios have a very high risk of combinatorial explosion of translation options (think cartesian product of all target side factors) and/or of spurious ambiguity (several derivations leading to the same output). Such added ambiguity can lead to n-best lists with way fewer unique items than the given n, which in turn renders MERT unstable, see also Bojar and Tamchyna (2011). Serially connected setups (two as our TwoStep or more) can lose relevant candidates between the searches, unless some ambiguous representation like lattices is passed between the steps.

An independent axis on which Moses setups can be organized consists of the number and function of factors on the source and the target side.

We use a very succint notation for the setups except the "complex" one: *t***X**-**Y** denotes a translation step between the factors **X** in the source language and **Y** in the target language. Generation steps are denoted with *g***Y**-**Z**, where both **Y** and **Z** are target-side factors. Individual mapping steps are combined with a plus, while individual source or target factors are combined with an "*a*".

As a simple example, *tF-F* denotes the direct translation from source form (*F*) to the target form. A linguistically motivated scenario with one search can be written as *tL-L+tT-T+gLaT-F*: translate (1) the lemma (L) to lemma, (2) the morphological tag (T) to tag independently and (3) finally generate the target form from the lemma and the tag.

We use two more operators: ":" delimits alternative decoding paths (Birch et al., 2007) used within one search and "=" delimits two independent searches. A plausible setup is e.g. *tF-LaT=tLaT-F:tL-F* motivated as follows: the source word form is translated to the lemma and tag in the target language. Then a second search (whose translation tables can be trained on larger monolingual data) consists of two alternative decoding paths: either the pair of *L* and *T* is translated into the target form, or as a fallback, the tag is disregarded and the target form is guessed only from the lemma (and the context as scored by the language model). The example also illustrated the priorities of the operators.

3 Common Settings

Throughout the experiments, we use the Moses toolkit (Koehn et al., 2007) and GIZA++ (Och and Ney, 2000). The texts were processed using the Treex platform (Popel and Žabokrtský, 2010)[1], which included lemmatization and tagging by Morce (Spoustová et al., 2007). After the tagging, we tokenized further so words like "23-year" or "Aktualne.cz" became three tokens.

Dataset	Sents (cs/en)	Toks (cs/en)	Source
Small	197k parallel	4.2M/4.8M	CzEng 1.0 news
Large	14.8M parallel	205M/236M	CzEng 1.0 all
Mono	18M/50M	317M/1.265G	WMT12 mono

Table 1: Summary of training data.

Decoding Path	Language Models	BLEU
tF-FaLaT	form + lemma + tag	13.05±0.44
tF-FaT	form + tag	13.01±0.44
tF-FaLaT	form + tag	12.99±0.44
tF-F (baseline)	form	12.42±0.44
tF-FaT	form	12.19±0.44
tF-FaLaT	form	12.08±0.45

Table 2: Direct en→cs translation (a single search with one translation step only).

Our training data is summarized in Table 1.[2]

In most experiments reported here, we use the Small dataset only. The language model (LM) for these experiments is a 5-gram one based on the target-side of Small only.

Our WMT12 submissions are based on the Large and Mono data. The language model for the large experiments uses 6-grams of forms and optionally 8-grams of morphological tags. As in previous years, the language models are interpolated (towards the best cross entropy on WMT08 dataset) from domain-specific LMs, e.g. czeng-news, czeng-techdoc, wmtmono-2011, wmtmono-2012.

Except where stated otherwise, we tune on the official WMT10 test set and report BLEU (Papineni et al., 2002) scores on the WMT11 test set.

4 Direct Setups

Table 2 lists our experiments with direct translation, various factors and language models in our notation.

[1] http://ufal.mff.cuni.cz/treex/

[2] We did not include the parallel en-cs data made available by the WMT12 organizers. This probably explains our loss compared to UEDIN but allows a direct comparison with CU TECTOMT, a deep syntactic MT based on the same data.

Decoding Paths	LMs	Avg. BLEU	Eff. Nbl. Size
tL-L+tT-T+gLaT-F:tF-FaLaT	F + L + T	13.31±0.06	12.24±1.33
tL-L+tT-T+gLaT-F	F + L + T	13.30±0.05	40.33±3.82
tL-L+tT-T+gLaT-F	F + T	13.17±0.01	39.91±2.58
tL-L+tT-T+gLaT-F:tF-FaLaT, 200-best-list	F + L + T	13.15±0.24	20.47±5.63
tF-FaLaT	F + L + T	13.13±0.06	34.28±3.08
tL-L+tT-T+gLaT-F:tF-FaLaT	L + T	13.09±0.06	16.65±1.07
tF-FaT	F + T	13.08±0.05	39.67±2.21
tL-L+tT-T+gLaT-F:tF-FaT	F + T	13.01±0.43	14.87±5.04
tF-F (baseline)	F	12.38±0.03	43.13±0.48
tL-L+tT-T+gLaT-F:tF-F	F	12.30±0.03	17.83±3.27

Table 3: Results of three MERT runs of several single-step configurations.

Explicit modelling of target-side morphology improves translation quality, compare tF-FaLaT with the baseline tF-F. However, two results document that if some detailed information is distinguished in the output, it introduces target ambiguity and leads to a loss in BLEU, unless the detailed information is actually used in the language model: (1) tF-FaLaT with LM on forms is worse than the baseline tF-F but tF-FaLaT with all the three language models is better, (2) tF-FaLaT with two LMs (forms and tags) is negligibly worse than tF-FaT with the same language models.

5 Single-Step Experiments

Single-step scenarios consist of more than one translation steps within a single search. We do not distinguish whether all the translation steps belong to the same decoding path or to alternative decoding paths.

Table 3 lists several single-step configurations (and three direct translations for a comparison). The single-step configurations always include the linguistically-motivated tL-L+tT-T+gLaT-F with varying language models and optionally with an alternative decoding path to serve as the fallback.

Aware of the low stability of MERT (Clark et al., 2011), we run MERT three times and report the average BLEU score including the standard deviation.

The last column in Table 3 lists the average number of *distinct* candidates per sentence in the n-best lists during MERT, dubbed "effective n-best list size". Unless stated otherwise, we used 100-best lists. We see that due to spurious ambiguity, e.g. various segmentations of the input into phrases, the effective size does not reach even a half of the limit.

We make three observations here:

(1) In this small data setting with a very morphologically rich language, the complex setup tL-L+tT-T+gLaT-F does not even need the alternative decoding path tF-F. Ramanathan et al. (2009) report gains in English-to-Hindi translation and also probably do not use alternative decoding paths.

(2) Reducing the range of language models used leads to worse scores, which is in line with the observation made with direct setups. We are surprised by the relative importance of the lemma-based LM.

(3) Alternative decoding paths significantly reduce effective n-best list size to just 12–18 unique candidates per sentence. However, we don't see an obvious relation to the stability of MERT: the standard deviations of BLEU average are very similar except for two outliers: 13.15±0.24 and 13.01±0.43. One of the outliers, 13.15, is actually a repeated run of the 13.31 with n-best-list size set to 200. Here we see a slight increase in the effective size (20 instead of 12) but also a slight loss in BLEU. We repeated the 13.31 experiment also with $n \in \{300, 400, 500, 600\}$, three MERT runs for each n. All the runs reached BLEU of about 13.30 except for one ($n = 600$) where the score dropped to 11.50. The low result was obtained when MERT ended at 25 iterations, the standard limit. On the other hand, several successful runs also exhausted the limit.

Figure 2 plots the BLEU scores in the 25 iterations of the underperforming run with $n = 600$. The MERT implementation in the Moses toolkit reports at each iteration what we call "predicted BLEU", i.e. the BLEU of translations selected by the current

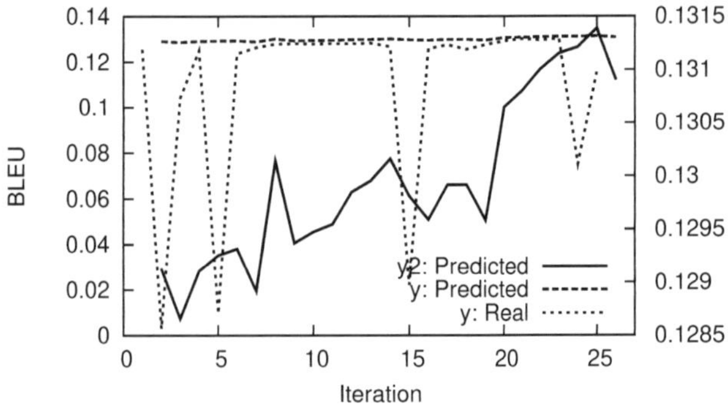

Figure 2: Predicted and real devset BLEU scores.

weight settings *from the (accumulated) n-best list.* We plot this predicted BLEU twice: once on the y2 axis alone and for the second time on the primary y axis together with the real BLEU, i.e. the BLEU of the dev set when Moses is actually run with the weight settings. The real BLEU drops several times, indicating that the prediction was misleading. Similar drops were observed in all runs. With bad luck as here, the iteration limit is reached when the optimization is still recovering from such a drop.

To avoid such a pitfall, one should check the real BLEU and continue or simply rerun the optimization if the iteration limit was reached.

6 Two-Step Experiments

The linguistically motivated setups used in the previous sections are prohibitively expensive for large data, see also Bojar et al. (2009). A number of researchers have thus tried diving the complexity of search into two independent phases: (1) translation and reordering, and (2) conjugation and declination. The most promising results were obtained with the second step predicting individual morphological features using a specialized tool (Toutanova et al., 2008; Fraser et al., 2012). Here, we simply use one more Moses search as Bojar and Kos (2010).

In the first step, source English gets translated to a simplified Czech and in the second step, the simplified Czech gets fully inflected.

6.1 Factors in Two-Step Setups

Two-step setups can use factors in the source, middle or the target language. We experiment with factors only in the middle language (affecting both the first and the second search) and use only the form in both source and target sides.

In the middle language, we experiment with one or two factors. For presentation purposes, we always speak about two factors: "LOF" ("lemma or form", i.e. a representation of the lexical information) and "MOT" ("modified tag", i.e. representing the morphological properties). In the single-factor experiments the LOF and MOT are simply concatenated into a token in the shape LOF+MOT.

Figure 3 illustrates the range of LOFs and MOTs we experimented with. LOF_0 and MOT_0 are identical to the standard Czech lemma and morphological tag as used e.g. in the Prague Dependency Treebank (Hajič et al., 2006).

LOF_1 and MOT_1 together make what Bojar and Kos (2010) call "pluslemma". MOT_1 is less complex than the full tag by disregarding morphological attributes not generally overt in the English source side. For most words, LOF_1 is simply the lemma, but for frequent words, the full form is used. This includes punctuation, pronouns and the verbs "být" (to be) and "mít" (to have).

MOT_2 uses a more coarse grained part of speech (POS) than MOT_1. Depending on the POS, different attributes are included: gender and number for nouns, pronouns, adjectives and verbs; case for nouns, pronouns, adjectives and prepositions; negation for nouns and adjectives; tense and voice for verbs and finally grade for adjectives. The remaining grammatical categories are encoded using POS, number, grade and negation.

6.2 Decoding Paths in Two-Step Setups

Each of the searches in the two-step setup can be as complex as the various single-step configurations. We test just one decoding path for the one or two factors in the middle language.

All experiments with one middle factor (i.e. "+") follow this config: tF-LOF+MOT = tLOF+MOT-F, i.e. two direct translations where the first one produces the concatenated LOF and MOT tokens and the second one consumes them. The first step uses a 5-gram LOF+MOT language model and the second step uses a 5-gram LM based on forms.

This setup has the capacity to improve translation quality by producing forms of words never seen aligned with a given source form. For example the English word *green* would be needed in the parallel

Word Form	LOF_0	LOF_1	MOT_0	MOT_1	MOT_2	Gloss
lidé	člověk	člověk	NNMP1-----A---1	NPA-	NMP1-A	people
by	být	by	Vc-------------	c---	V-----	would
neočekávali	očekávat	očekávat	VpMP---XR-NA---	pPN-	VMP-RA	expect

Figure 3: Examples of LOFs and MOTs used in our experiments.

Middle Factors	1 +	2 |
LOF_0 +/| MOT_0	11.11±0.48	12.42±0.48
LOF_1 +/| MOT_1	12.10±0.48	11.85±0.42
LOF_1 +/| MOT_2	11.87±0.51	12.47±0.51

Table 4: Two-step experiments.

data with all the morphological variants of the Czech word *zelený*. Adding the middle step with appropriately reduced morphological information so that only features overt in the source are represented in the middle tokens (e.g. negation and number but not the case) allows the model to find the necessary form anywhere in the target-side data only:

$$green \longrightarrow zelený{+}NSA\text{-} \longrightarrow \begin{cases} zeleného \text{ (genitive)} \\ zelenému \text{ (dative)} \\ \dots \end{cases}$$

The experiments with two middle factors (i.e. "|") use this path: tF-LOFaMOT = tLOFaMOT-F:LOF-F. The first step is identical, except that now we use two separate LMs, one for LOFs and one for MOTs. The second step has two alternative decoding paths: (1) as before, producing the form from both the LOF and the MOT, and (2) ignoring the morphological features from the source altogether and using just target-side context to choose an appropriate form of the word. This setup is capable of sacrificing adequacy for a more fluent output.

6.3 Experiments with Two-Step Setups

Table 4 reports the BLEU scores when changing the number of factors ("+" vs. "|") in the middle language and the type of the LOF and MOT.

We see an interesting difference between MOT_1 and $MOT_{0 \text{ or } 2}$. The more fine-grained $MOT_{0 \text{ or } 2}$ work better in the two-factor "|" setup that allows to disregard the MOT, while MOT_1 works better in the direct translation "+".

Overall, we see no improvement over the tF-F baseline (BLEU of 12.42) and this is mainly due to to the fact that we used Small data in both steps.

7 A Complex Moses Setup

Obviously, many setups fall under the "complex" category of our taxonomy, including also some system combination approaches. We tried to combine three Moses systems: (1) CU-BOJAR as described below, (2) same setup like CU-BOJAR but optimized towards 1-TER (Snover et al., 2006), and (3) a large-data two-step setup.[3] The system combination is performed using a fourth Moses search that gets a lattice (Dyer et al., 2008) of individual systems' outputs, performs an identity translation and scores the candidates by language models and other features. The lattice is created from the individual system outputs in the ROVER style (Matusov et al., 2008) utilizing the source-to-hypothesis word alignments as produced by the individual systems. We use our simple implementation for constructing the confusion networks and converting them to the lattices. The "combination Moses" was tuned on the WMT11 test set towards BLEU. The resulting system is called CU-POOR-COMB, because we felt it underperformed the individual systems not only in BLEU but also in an informal subjective evaluation.

Surprisingly, CU-POOR-COMB won the WMT12 automatic evaluation in TER. In the retrospect, this is caused by TER overemphasizing word-level precision. CU-POOR-COMB skipped words not confirmed by several systems and its hypotheses are shorter (18.1 toks/sent) than those by CU-BOJAR (20.1 toks/sents) or the reference (21.9 toks/sent). A quick manual inspection of 32 sentences suggests that about one third or quarter of CU-POOR-COMB suffer from some information loss whereas the rest are acceptable or even better paraphrases. Prelim-

[3]The large two-step setup is identical to the one by (Bojar and Kos, 2010), except that we use only the current Large and Mono datasets as described in Section 3.

	Test Set	Our Scoring newstest-2011		newstest-2012		matrix.statmt.org	
	Metric	BLEU	TER*100	BLEU	TER*100	BLEU	TER
→cs	CU-POOR-COMB	–used–for–	–tuning–	14.17±0.53	**64.07±0.53**	14.0	**0.741**
	CU-BOJAR (tFaT-FaT, lex. r.)	**18.10±0.55**	62.84±0.71	**16.07±0.55**	65.52±0.59	**15.9**	0.759
	As ↑ but towards 1-TER	16.10±0.54	**61.64±0.59**	14.13±0.54	64.28±0.55	–	–
	Large Two-Step	17.34±0.57	63.47±0.66	15.37±0.54	65.85±0.57	–	–
	Unused (tFaT-FaT, dist. reord.)	18.07±0.56	62.74±0.70	15.92±0.57	65.50±0.60	–	–
	Unused (tF-FaT, dist. reord.)	17.85±0.58	63.13±0.68	15.73±0.55	65.85±0.58	–	–
	Unused (tF-F, lex. reord.)	17.73±0.58	63.04±0.68	15.61±0.57	65.76±0.58	–	–
	Unused (tFaT-F, dist. reord.)	17.62±0.56	62.97±0.70	15.33±0.58	65.70±0.59	–	–
	Unused (tF-F, dist. reord.)	17.51±0.57	63.32±0.69	15.48±0.56	65.79±0.58	–	–
→en	CU-BOJAR (tF-F:tL-F, dist. reord.)	**24.65±0.60**	**58.54±0.66**	**23.09±0.59**	**61.24±0.68**	**21.5**	**0.726**
	Unused (tF-F, dist. reord.)	24.62±0.59	58.66±0.66	22.90±0.56	61.63±0.67	–	–

Table 5: Summary of large data runs and systems submitted to WMT12 manual evaluation. The upper part lists the two submissions in en→cs translation and two more systems used in CU-POOR-COMB. The lower part of the table shows the scores for CU-BOJAR when translating to English. All systems reported here use the Large and Mono data.

inary results of WMT 12 manual ranking indicate that overall, our system combination performs poor.

8 Overview of Systems Submitted

Table 5 summarizes the scores for our two system submissions. We report the scores in our tokenization on the official test sets of WMT11 and WMT12 and also the scores as measured by `http://matrix.statmt.org`. Note that for the latter, we use the detokenized outputs processed by the recommended normalization script.[4]

8.1 Details of CU-BOJAR for en→cs

We deliberately used only direct setups for the large data and due to time constraints, we ran just a few configurations, see Table 5.

We knew from previous years that including English (source) POS tag improves overall target sentence structure: English words are often ambiguous between noun and verb, so without the POS information, verbs got often translated as nouns, rendering the sentence incomprehensible. Tagging and including the source tag helps, as confirmed by the tFaT-F setup being somewhat better than tF-F.

We also knew that target-side tag LM is helpful (esp. if we can afford up to 8-grams in the LM). This was confirmed by tF-FaT being better than tF-F. Ultimately, we use tags on both sides: tFaT-FaT and get the best scores. This confirms that our parallel data is sufficiently large so that even the added sparsity due to tags does not cause any trouble.

A little gain comes from a lexicalized reordering model (or-bi-fe) based on word forms, see CU-BOJAR reaching 18.10 BLEU on WMT11 test set.

8.2 Details of CU-BOJAR for cs→en

For the translation into English, we tested just two setups: tF-F and tF-F:tL-T. The latter setup falls back to the Czech lemma, if the exact form is not available. The gain is only small, because our parallel data is already quite large.

9 Conclusion

We introduced a simple taxonomy of factored phrase-based setups and conducted several probes for English→Czech translation. We gained small improvements in both small and large data settings.

We also warned about some common pitfalls: (1) all target-side factors should be accompanied with a language model to compensate for the added sparseness, (2) alternative decoding paths significantly reduce the effective n-best list size, and (3) the infamous instability of MERT can be caused by bad luck at exhausted iteration limit.

On a general note, we learnt that a breadth-first search for best configurations should be automated as much as possible so that more human effort can be invested into analysis.

[4] `http://www.statmt.org/wmt11/normalize-punctuation.perl`

References

Eleftherios Avramidis and Philipp Koehn. 2008. Enriching morphologically poor languages for statistical machine translation. In *Proceedings of ACL-08: HLT*, pages 763–770, Columbus, Ohio, June. Association for Computational Linguistics.

Ibrahim Badr, Rabih Zbib, and James Glass. 2008. Segmentation for english-to-arabic statistical machine translation. In *Proceedings of the 46th Annual Meeting of the Association for Computational Linguistics on Human Language Technologies: Short Papers*, HLT-Short '08, pages 153–156, Stroudsburg, PA, USA. Association for Computational Linguistics.

Alexandra Birch, Miles Osborne, and Philipp Koehn. 2007. CCG Supertags in Factored Statistical Machine Translation. In *Proceedings of the Second Workshop on Statistical Machine Translation*, pages 9–16, Prague, Czech Republic, June. Association for Computational Linguistics.

Ondřej Bojar and Kamil Kos. 2010. 2010 Failures in English-Czech Phrase-Based MT. In *Proceedings of the Joint Fifth Workshop on Statistical Machine Translation and MetricsMATR*, pages 60–66, Uppsala, Sweden, July. Association for Computational Linguistics.

Ondřej Bojar and Aleš Tamchyna. 2011. Improving Translation Model by Monolingual Data. In *Proceedings of the Sixth Workshop on Statistical Machine Translation*, pages 330–336, Edinburgh, Scotland, July. Association for Computational Linguistics.

Ondřej Bojar, David Mareček, Václav Novák, Martin Popel, Jan Ptáček, Jan Rouš, and Zdeněk Žabokrtský. 2009. English-Czech MT in 2008. In *Proceedings of the Fourth Workshop on Statistical Machine Translation*, Athens, Greece, March. Association for Computational Linguistics.

Ondřej Bojar. 2007. English-to-Czech Factored Machine Translation. In *Proceedings of the Second Workshop on Statistical Machine Translation*, pages 232–239, Prague, Czech Republic, June. Association for Computational Linguistics.

Jonathan H. Clark, Chris Dyer, Alon Lavie, and Noah A. Smith. 2011. Better hypothesis testing for statistical machine translation: Controlling for optimizer instability. In *ACL (Short Papers)*, pages 176–181. The Association for Computer Linguistics.

Christopher Dyer, Smaranda Muresan, and Philip Resnik. 2008. Generalizing word lattice translation. In *Proceedings of ACL-08: HLT*, pages 1012–1020, Columbus, Ohio, June. Association for Computational Linguistics.

Alexander Fraser, Marion Weller, Aoife Cahill, and Fabienne Cap. 2012. Modeling Inflection and Word-Formation in SMT. In *Proc. of EACL 2012*. Association for Computational Linguistics.

Jan Hajič, Jarmila Panevová, Eva Hajičová, Petr Sgall, Petr Pajas, Jan Štěpánek, Jiří Havelka, Marie Mikulová, Zdeněk Žabokrtský, and Magda Ševčíková Razímová. 2006. Prague Dependency Treebank 2.0. LDC2006T01, ISBN: 1-58563-370-4.

Philipp Koehn and Hieu Hoang. 2007. Factored Translation Models. In *Proc. of EMNLP*.

Philipp Koehn, Hieu Hoang, Alexandra Birch, Chris Callison-Burch, Marcello Federico, Nicola Bertoldi, Brooke Cowan, Wade Shen, Christine Moran, Richard Zens, Chris Dyer, Ondřej Bojar, Alexandra Constantin, and Evan Herbst. 2007. Moses: Open Source Toolkit for Statistical Machine Translation. In *ACL 2007, Proceedings of the 45th Annual Meeting of the Association for Computational Linguistics Companion Volume Proceedings of the Demo and Poster Sessions*, pages 177–180, Prague, Czech Republic, June. Association for Computational Linguistics.

Philipp Koehn, Barry Haddow, Philip Williams, and Hieu Hoang. 2010. More linguistic annotation for statistical machine translation. In *Proceedings of the Joint Fifth Workshop on Statistical Machine Translation and MetricsMATR*, WMT '10, pages 115–120, Stroudsburg, PA, USA. Association for Computational Linguistics.

Evgeny Matusov, Gregor Leusch, Rafael E. Banchs, Nicola Bertoldi, Daniel Dechelotte, Marcello Federico, Muntsin Kolss, Young-Suk Lee, Jose B. Marino, Matthias Paulik, Salim Roukos, Holger Schwenk, and Hermann Ney. 2008. System Combination for Machine Translation of Spoken and Written Language. *IEEE Transactions on Audio, Speech and Language Processing*, 16(7):1222–1237, September.

Franz Josef Och and Hermann Ney. 2000. A Comparison of Alignment Models for Statistical Machine Translation. In *Proceedings of the 17th conference on Computational linguistics*, pages 1086–1090. Association for Computational Linguistics.

Kishore Papineni, Salim Roukos, Todd Ward, and Wei-Jing Zhu. 2002. BLEU: a Method for Automatic Evaluation of Machine Translation. In *ACL 2002, Proceedings of the 40th Annual Meeting of the Association for Computational Linguistics*, pages 311–318, Philadelphia, Pennsylvania.

Martin Popel and Zdeněk Žabokrtský. 2010. TectoMT: Modular NLP Framework. In Hrafn Loftsson, Eirikur Rögnvaldsson, and Sigrun Helgadottir, editors, *Lecture Notes in Artificial Intelligence, Proceedings of the 7th International Conference on Advances in Natural Language Processing (IceTAL 2010)*, volume 6233 of *Lecture Notes in Computer Science*, pages 293–

304, Berlin / Heidelberg. Iceland Centre for Language Technology (ICLT), Springer.

Ananthakrishnan Ramanathan, Hansraj Choudhary, Avishek Ghosh, and Pushpak Bhattacharyya. 2009. Case markers and morphology: addressing the crux of the fluency problem in english-hindi smt. In *Proceedings of the Joint Conference of the 47th Annual Meeting of the ACL and the 4th International Joint Conference on Natural Language Processing of the AFNLP: Volume 2 - Volume 2*, ACL '09, pages 800–808, Stroudsburg, PA, USA. Association for Computational Linguistics.

Matthew Snover, Bonnie Dorr, Richard Schwartz, Linnea Micciulla, and John Makhoul. 2006. A Study of Translation Edit Rate with Targeted Human Annotation. In *Proceedings AMTA*, pages 223–231, August.

Drahomíra Spoustová, Jan Hajič, Jan Votrubec, Pavel Krbec, and Pavel Květoň. 2007. The best of two worlds: Cooperation of statistical and rule-based taggers for czech. In *Proceedings of the Workshop on Balto-Slavonic Natural Language Processing, ACL 2007*, pages 67–74, Praha.

Sara Stymne. 2008. German Compounds in Factored Statistical Machine Translation. In Bengt Nordstrm and Aarne Ranta, editors, *Advances in Natural Language Processing*, volume 5221 of *Lecture Notes in Computer Science*, pages 464–475. Springer Berlin / Heidelberg.

Kristina Toutanova, Hisami Suzuki, and Achim Ruopp. 2008. Applying morphology generation models to machine translation. In *Proceedings of ACL-08: HLT*, pages 514–522, Columbus, Ohio, June. Association for Computational Linguistics.

Reyyan Yeniterzi and Kemal Oflazer. 2010. Syntax-to-morphology mapping in factored phrase-based statistical machine translation from english to turkish. In *Proceedings of the 48th Annual Meeting of the Association for Computational Linguistics*, pages 454–464, Uppsala, Sweden, July. Association for Computational Linguistics.

The CMU-Avenue French-English Translation System

Michael Denkowski **Greg Hanneman** **Alon Lavie**
Language Technologies Institute
Carnegie Mellon University
Pittsburgh, PA, 15213, USA
{mdenkows,ghannema,alavie}@cs.cmu.edu

Abstract

This paper describes the French-English translation system developed by the Avenue research group at Carnegie Mellon University for the Seventh Workshop on Statistical Machine Translation (NAACL WMT12). We present a method for training data selection, a description of our hierarchical phrase-based translation system, and a discussion of the impact of data size on best practice for system building.

1 Introduction

We describe the French-English translation system constructed by the Avenue research group at Carnegie Mellon University for the shared translation task in the Seventh Workshop on Statistical Machine Translation. The core translation system uses the hierarchical phrase-based model described by Chiang (2007) with sentence-level grammars extracted and scored using the methods described by Lopez (2008). Improved techniques for data selection and monolingual text processing significantly improve the performance of the baseline system.

Over half of all parallel data for the French-English track is provided by the Giga-FrEn corpus (Callison-Burch et al., 2009). Assembled from crawls of bilingual websites, this corpus is known to be noisy, containing sentences that are either not parallel or not natural language. Rather than simply including or excluding the resource in its entirety, we use a relatively simple technique inspired by work in machine translation quality estimation to select the best portions of the corpus for inclusion in our training data. Including around 60% of the Giga-FrEn chosen by this technique yields an improvement of 0.7 BLEU.

Prior to model estimation, we process all parallel and monolingual data using in-house tokenization and normalization scripts that detect word boundaries better than the provided WMT12 scripts. After translation, we apply a monolingual rule-based post-processing step to correct obvious errors and make sentences more acceptable to human judges. The post-processing step alone yields an improvement of 0.3 BLEU to the final system.

We conclude with a discussion of the impact of data size on important decisions for system building. Experimental results show that "best practice" decisions for smaller data sizes do not necessarily carry over to systems built with "WMT-scale" data, and provide some explanation for why this is the case.

2 Training Data

Training data provided for the French-English translation task includes parallel corpora taken from European Parliamentary proceedings (Koehn, 2005), news commentary, and United Nations documents. Together, these sets total approximately 13 million sentences. In addition, a large, web-crawled parallel corpus termed the "Giga-FrEn" (Callison-Burch et al., 2009) is made available. While this corpus contains over 22 million parallel sentences, it is inherently noisy. Many parallel sentences crawled from the web are neither parallel nor sentences. To make use of this large data source, we employ data selection techniques discussed in the next subsection.

Corpus	Sentences
Europarl	1,857,436
News commentary	130,193
UN doc	11,684,454
Giga-FrEn 1stdev	7,535,699
Giga-FrEn 2stdev	5,801,759
Total	27,009,541

Table 1: Parallel training data

Parallel data used to build our final system totals 27 million sentences. Precise figures for the number of sentences in each data set, including selections from the Giga-FrEn, are found in Table 1.

2.1 Data Selection as Quality Estimation

Drawing inspiration from the workshop's featured task, we cast the problem of data selection as one of quality estimation. Specia et al. (2009) report several estimators of translation quality, the most effective of which detect difficult-to-translate source sentences, ungrammatical translations, and translations that align poorly to their source sentences. We can easily adapt several of these predictive features to select good sentence pairs from noisy parallel corpora such as the Giga-FrEn.

We first pre-process the Giga-FrEn by removing lines with invalid Unicode characters, control characters, and insufficient concentrations of Latin characters. We then score each sentence pair in the remaining set (roughly 90% of the original corpus) with the following features:

Source language model: a 4-gram modified Kneser-Ney smoothed language model trained on French Europarl, news commentary, UN doc, and news crawl corpora. This model assigns high scores to grammatical source sentences and lower scores to ungrammatical sentences and non-sentences such as site maps, large lists of names, and blog comments. Scores are normalized by number of n-grams scored per sentence (length + 1). The model is built using the SRILM toolkit (Stolke, 2002).

Target language model: a 4-gram modified Kneser-Ney smoothed language model trained on English Europarl, news commentary, UN doc, and news crawl corpora. This model scores grammaticality on the target side.

Word alignment scores: source-target and target-source MGIZA++ (Gao and Vogel, 2008) force-alignment scores using IBM Model 4 (Och and Ney, 2003). Model parameters are estimated on 2 million words of French-English Europarl and news commentary text. Scores are normalized by the number of alignment links. These features measure the extent to which translations are parallel with their source sentences.

Fraction of aligned words: source-target and target-source ratios of aligned words to total words. These features balance the link-normalized alignment scores.

To determine selection criteria, we use this feature set to score the news test sets from 2008 through 2011 (10K parallel sentences) and calculate the mean and standard deviation of each feature score distribution. We then select two subsets of the Giga-FrEn, "1stdev" and "2stdev". The 1stdev set includes sentence pairs for which the score for *each* feature is above a threshold defined as the development set mean minus one standard deviation. The 2stdev set includes sentence pairs not included in 1stdev that meet the per-feature threshold of mean minus two standard deviations. Hard, per-feature thresholding is motivated by the notion that a sentence pair must meet *all* the criteria discussed above to constitute good translation. For example, high source and target language model scores are irrelevant if the sentences are not parallel.

As primarily news data is used for determining thresholds and building language models, this approach has the added advantage of preferring parallel data in the domain we are interested in translating. Our final translation system uses data from both 1stdev and 2stdev, corresponding to roughly 60% of the Giga-FrEn corpus.

2.2 Monolingual Data

Monolingual English data includes European Parliamentary proceedings (Koehn, 2005), news commentary, United Nations documents, news crawl, the English side of the Giga-FrEn, and the English Gigaword Fourth Edition (Parker et al., 2009). We use all available data subject to the following selection decisions. We apply the initial filter to the Giga-FrEn to remove non-text sections, leaving approximately 90% of the corpus. We exclude the known prob-

Corpus	Words
Europarl	59,659,916
News commentary	5,081,368
UN doc	286,300,902
News crawl	1,109,346,008
Giga-FrEn	481,929,410
Gigaword 4th edition	1,960,921,287
Total	3,903,238,891

Table 2: Monolingual language modeling data (uniqued)

lematic New York Times section of the Gigaword. As many data sets include repeated boilerplate text such as copyright information or browser compatibility notifications, we unique sentences from the UN doc, news crawl, Giga-FrEn, and Gigaword sets by source. Final monolingual data totals 4.7 billion words before uniqueing and 3.9 billion after. Word counts for all data sources are shown in Table 2.

2.3 Text Processing

All monolingual and parallel system data is run through a series of pre-processing steps before construction of the language model or translation model. We first run an in-house normalization script over all text in order to convert certain variably encoded characters to a canonical form. For example, thin spaces and non-breaking spaces are normalized to standard ASCII space characters, various types of "curly" and "straight" quotation marks are standardized as ASCII straight quotes, and common French and English ligatures characters (e.g. œ, ﬁ) are replaced with standard equivalents.

English text is tokenized with the Penn Treebank-style tokenizer attached to the Stanford parser (Klein and Manning, 2003), using most of the default options. We set the tokenizer to Americanize variant spellings such as *color* vs. *colour* or *behavior* vs. *behaviour*. Currency-symbol normalization is avoided.

For French text, we use an in-house tokenization script. Aside from the standard tokenization based on punctuation marks, this step includes French-specific rules for handling apostrophes (French *elision*), hyphens in subject-verb inversions (including the French *t euphonique*), and European-style numbers. When compared to the default WMT12-provided tokenization script, our custom French rules more accurately identify word boundaries, particularly in the case of hyphens. Figure 1 highlights the differences in sample phrases. Subject-verb inversions are broken apart, while other hyphenated words are unaffected; French *aujourd'hui* ("today") is retained as a single token to match English.

Parallel data is run through a further filtering step to remove sentence pairs that, by their length characteristics alone, are very unlikely to be true parallel data. Sentence pairs that contain more than 95 tokens on either side are globally discarded, as are sentence pairs where either side contains a token longer than 25 characters. Remaining pairs are checked for length ratio between French and English, and sentences are discarded if their English translations are either too long or too short given the French length. Allowable ratios are determined from the tokenized training data and are set such that approximately the middle 95% of the data, in terms of length ratio, is kept for each French length.

3 Translation System

Our translation system uses `cdec` (Dyer et al., 2010), an implementation of the hierarchical phrase-based translation model (Chiang, 2007) that uses the KenLM library (Heafield, 2011) for language model inference. The system translates from cased French to cased English; at no point do we lowercase data.

The Parallel data is aligned in both directions using the MGIZA++ (Gao and Vogel, 2008) implementation of IBM Model 4 and symmetrized with the `grow-diag-final` heuristic (Och and Ney, 2003). The aligned corpus is then encoded as a suffix array to facilitate sentence-level grammar extraction and scoring (Lopez, 2008). Grammars are extracted using the heuristics described by Chiang (Chiang, 2007) and feature scores are calculated according to Lopez (2008).

Modified Knesser-Ney smoothed (Chen and Goodman, 1996) n-gram language models are built from the monolingual English data using the SRI language modeling toolkit (Stolke, 2002). We experiment with both 4-gram and 5-gram models.

System parameters are optimized using minimum error rate training (Och, 2003) to maximize the corpus-level cased BLEU score (Papineni et al.,

Base:	`Y a-t-il un collègue pour prendre la parole`
Custom:	`Y a -t-il un collègue pour prendre la parole`
Base:	`Peut-être , à ce sujet , puis-je dire à M. Ribeiro i Castro`
Custom:	`Peut-être , à ce sujet , puis -je dire à M. Ribeiro i Castro`
Base:	`le procès-verbal de la séance d' aujourd' hui`
Custom:	`le procès-verbal de la séance d' aujourd'hui`
Base:	`s' établit environ à 1,2 % du PIB`
Custom:	`s' établit environ à 1.2 % du PIB`

Figure 1: Customized French tokenization rules better identify word boundaries.

pré-électoral	→	pre-electoral
mosaîque	→	mosaique
déragulation	→	deragulation

Figure 2: Examples of cognate translation

2002) on news-test 2008 (2051 sentences). This development set is chosen for its known stability and reliability.

Our baseline translation system uses Viterbi decoding while our final system uses segment-level Minimum Bayes-Risk decoding (Kumar and Byrne, 2004) over 500-best lists using 1 - BLEU as the loss function.

3.1 Post-Processing

Our final system includes a monolingual rule-based post-processing step that corrects obvious translation errors. Examples of correctable errors include capitalization, mismatched punctuation, malformed numbers, and incorrectly split compound words. We finally employ a coarse cognate translation system to handle out-of-vocabulary words. We assume that uncapitalized French source words passed through to the English output are cognates of English words and translate them by removing accents. This frequently leads to (in order of desirability) fully correct translations, correct translations with foreign spellings, or correct translations with misspellings. All of the above are generally preferable to untranslated foreign words. Examples of cognate translations for OOV words in newstest 2011 are shown in Figure 2.[1]

[1]Some OOVs are caused by misspellings in the dev-test source sentences. In these cases we can salvage misspelled English words in place of misspelled French words

	BLEU	(cased)	Meteor	TER
base 5-gram	28.4	27.4	33.7	53.2
base 4-gram	29.1	28.1	34.0	52.5
+1stdev GFE	29.3	28.3	34.2	52.1
+2stdev GFE	29.8	28.9	34.5	51.7
+5g/1K/MBR	29.9	29.0	34.5	51.5
+post-process	30.2	29.2	34.7	51.3

Table 3: Newstest 2011 (dev-test) translation results

4 Experiments

Beginning with a baseline translation system, we incrementally evaluate the contribution of additional data and components. System performance is evaluated on newstest 2011 using BLEU (uncased and cased) (Papineni et al., 2002), Meteor (Denkowski and Lavie, 2011), and TER (Snover et al., 2006). For full consistency with WMT11, we use the NIST scoring script, TER-0.7.25, and Meteor-1.3 to evaluate cased, detokenized translations. Results are shown in Table 3, where each evaluation point is the result of a full tune/test run that includes MERT for parameter optimization.

The baseline translation system is built from 14 million parallel sentences (Europarl, news commentary, and UN doc) and all monolingual data. Grammars are extracted using the "tight" heuristic that requires phrase pairs to be bounded by word alignments. Both 4-gram and 5-gram language models are evaluated. Viterbi decoding is conducted with a cube pruning pop limit (Chiang, 2007) of 200. For this data size, the 4-gram model is shown to significantly outperform the 5-gram.

Adding the 1stdev and 2stdev sets from the Giga-FrEn increases the parallel data size to 27 million

	BLEU	(cased)	Meteor	TER
587M tight	29.1	28.1	34.0	52.5
587M loose	29.3	28.3	34.0	52.5
745M tight	29.8	28.9	34.5	51.7
745M loose	29.6	28.6	34.3	52.0

Table 4: Results for extraction heuristics (dev-test)

	BLEU	(cased)	Meteor	TER
587M 4-gram	29.1	28.1	34.0	52.5
587M 5-gram	28.4	27.4	33.7	53.2
745M 4-gram	29.8	28.9	34.5	51.7
745M 5-gram	29.8	28.9	34.4	51.7

Table 5: Results for language model order (dev-test)

sentences and further improves performance. These runs require new grammars to be extracted, but use the same 4-gram language model and decoding method as the baseline system. With large training data, moving to a 5-gram language model, increasing the cube pruning pop limit to 1000, and using Minimum Bayes-Risk decoding (Kumar and Byrne, 2004) over 500-best lists collectively show a slight improvement. Monolingual post-processing yields further improvement. This decoding/processing scheme corresponds to our final translation system.

4.1 Impact of Data Size

The WMT French-English track provides an opportunity to experiment in a space of data size that is generally not well explored. We examine the impact of data sizes of hundreds of millions of words on two significant system building decisions: grammar extraction and language model estimation. Comparative results are reported on the newstest 2011 set.

In the first case, we compare the "tight" extraction heuristic that requires phrases to be bounded by word alignments to the "loose" heuristic that allows unaligned words at phrase edges. Lopez (2008) shows that for a parallel corpus of 107 million words, using the loose heuristic produces much larger grammars and improves performance by a full BLEU point. However, even our baseline system is trained on substantially more data (587 million words on the English side) and the addition of the Giga-FrEn sets increases data size to 745 million words, seven times that used in the cited work. For each data size, we decode with grammars extracted using each heuristic and a 4-gram language model. As shown in Table 4, the differences are much smaller and the tight heuristic actually produces the best result for the full data scenario. We believe this to be directly linked to word alignment quality: smaller training data results in sparser, noisier word alignments while larger data results in denser, more accurate alignments. In the first case, accumulating unaligned words can make up for shortcomings in alignment quality. In the second, better rules are extracted by trusting the stronger alignment model.

We also compare 4-gram and 5-gram language model performance with systems using tight grammars extracted from 587 million and 745 million sentences. As shown in Table 5, the 4-gram significantly outperforms the 5-gram with smaller data while the two are indistinguishable with larger data[2]. With modified Kneser-Ney smoothing, a lower order model will outperform a higher order model if the higher order model constantly backs off to lower orders. With stronger grammars learned from larger parallel data, the system is able to produce output that matches longer n-grams in the language model.

5 Summary

We have presented the French-English translation system built for the NAACL WMT12 shared translation task, including descriptions of our data selection and text processing techniques. Experimental results have shown incremental improvement for each addition to our baseline system. We have finally discussed the impact of the availability of WMT-scale data on system building decisions and provided comparative experimental results.

References

Chris Callison-Burch, Philipp Koehn, Christof Monz, and Josh Schroeder. 2009. Findings of the 2009 Workshop on Statistical Machine Translation. In *Proc. of ACL WMT 2009.*

[2]We find that for the full data system, also increasing the cube pruning pop limit and using MBR decoding yields a very slight improvement with the 5-gram model over the same decoding scheme with the 4-gram.

Stanley F. Chen and Joshua Goodman. 1996. An Empirical Study of Smoothing Techniques for Language Modeling. In *Proc. of ACL 1996.*

David Chiang. 2007. Hierarchical Phrase-Based Translation.

Michael Denkowski and Alon Lavie. 2011. Meteor 1.3: Automatic Metric for Reliable Optimization and Evaluation of Machine Translation Systems. In *Proc. of the EMNLP WMT 2011.*

Chris Dyer, Adam Lopez, Juri Ganitkevitch, Johnathan Weese, Ferhan Ture, Phil Blunsom, Hendra Setiawan, Vladimir Eidelman, and Philip Resnik. 2010. cdec: A Decoder, Alignment, and Learning Framework for Finite-State and Context-Free Translation Models. In *Proc. of ACL 2010.*

Qin Gao and Stephan Vogel. 2008. Parallel Implementations of Word Alignment Tool. In *Proc. of ACL WSETQANLP 2008.*

Kenneth Heafield. 2011. KenLM: Faster and Smaller Language Model Queries. In *Proc. of EMNLP WMT 2011.*

Dan Klein and Christopher D. Manning. 2003. Accurate Unlexicalized Parsing. In *Proc. of ACL 2003.*

Philipp Koehn. 2005. Europarl: A Parallel Corpus for Statistical Machine Translation. In *Proc. of MT Summit 2005.*

Shankar Kumar and William Byrne. 2004. Minimum Bayes-Risk Decoding for Statistical Machine Translation. In *Proc. of NAACL/HLT 2004.*

Adam Lopez. 2008. Tera-Scale Translation Models via Pattern Matching. In *Proc. of COLING 2008.*

Franz Josef Och and Hermann Ney. 2003. A Systematic Comparison of Various Statistical Alignment Models. *Computational Linguistics*, 29.

Franz Josef Och. 2003. Minimum Error Rate Training for Statistical Machine Translation. In *Proc. of ACL 2003.*

Kishore Papineni, Salim Roukos, Todd Ward, and Wei-Jing Zhu. 2002. BLEU: a Method for Automatic Evaluation of Machine Translation. In *Proc. of ACL 2002.*

Robert Parker, David Graff, Junbo Kong, Ke Chen, and Kazuaki Maeda. 2009. English Gigaword Fourth Edition. Linguistic Data Consortium, LDC2009T13.

Matthew Snover, Bonnie Dorr, Richard Schwartz, Linnea Micciulla, and John Makhoul. 2006. A Study of Translation Edit Rate with Targeted Human Annotation. In *Proc. of AMTA 2006.*

Lucia Specia, Craig Saunders, Marco Turchi, Zhuoran Wang, and John Shawe-Taylor. 2009. Improving the Confidence of Machine Translation Quality Estimates. In *Proc. of MT Summit XII.*

Andreas Stolke. 2002. SRILM - an Extensible Language Modeling Toolkit. In *Proc. of ICSLP 2002.*

Formemes in English-Czech Deep Syntactic MT *

Ondřej Dušek, Zdeněk Žabokrtský, Martin Popel,
Martin Majliš, Michal Novák, and **David Mareček**
Charles University in Prague, Faculty of Mathematics and Physics
Institute of Formal and Applied Linguistics
Malostranské náměstí 25, Prague
`{odusek,zabokrtsky,popel,majlis,mnovak,marecek}@ufal.mff.cuni.cz`

Abstract

One of the most notable recent improvements of the TectoMT English-to-Czech translation is a systematic and theoretically supported revision of *formemes*—the annotation of morpho-syntactic features of content words in deep dependency syntactic structures based on the Prague tectogrammatics theory. Our modifications aim at reducing data sparsity, increasing consistency across languages and widening the usage area of this markup. Formemes can be used not only in MT, but in various other NLP tasks.

1 Introduction

The cornerstone of the TectoMT tree-to-tree machine translation system is the deep-syntactic language representation following the Prague tectogrammatics theory (Sgall et al., 1986), and its application in the Prague Dependency Treebank (PDT) 2.0[1] (Hajič et al., 2006), where each sentence is analyzed to a dependency tree whose nodes correspond to content words. Each node has a number of attributes, but the most important (and difficult) for the transfer phase are *lemma*—lexical information, and *formeme*—surface morpho-syntactic information, including selected auxiliary words (Ptáček and Žabokrtský, 2006; Žabokrtský et al., 2008).

This paper focuses on formemes—their definition and recent improvements of the annotation, which has been thoroughly revised in the course of preparation of the CzEng 1.0 parallel corpus (Bojar et al., 2012b), whose utilization in TectoMT along with the new formemes version has brought the greatest benefit to our English-Czech MT system in the recent year. However, the area of possible application of formemes is not limited to MT only or to the language pair used in our system; the underlying ideas are language-independent.

We summarize the development of morpho-syntactic annotations related to formemes (Section 2), provide an overview of the whole TectoMT system (Section 3), then describe the formeme annotation (Section 4) and our recent improvements (Section 5), as well as experimental applications, including English-Czech MT (Section 6). The main asset of the formeme revision is a first systematic reorganization of the existing practical aid, providing it with a solid theoretical base, but still bearing its intended applications in mind.

2 Related Work

Numerous theoretical approaches had been made to morpho-syntactic description, mainly within valency lexicons, starting probably with the work by Helbig and Schenkel (1969). Perhaps the best one for Czech is PDT-VALLEX (Hajič et al., 2003), listing all possible subtrees corresponding to valency arguments (Urešová, 2009). Žabokrtský (2005) gives an overview of works in this field.

* This research has been supported by the grants FP7-ICT-2009-4-247762 (FAUST), FP7-ICT-2009-4-249119 (Metanet), LH12093 (Kontakt II), DF12P01OVV022 (NAKI), 201/09/H057 (Czech Science Foundation), GAUK 116310, and SVV 265 314. This work has been using language resources developed and/or stored and/or distributed by the LINDAT-Clarin project of the Ministry of Education of the Czech Republic (project LM2010013).

[1] `http://ufal.mff.cuni.cz/pdt2.0`

This kind of information has been most exploited in structural MT systems, employing semantic relations (Menezes and Richardson, 2001) or surface tree substructures (Quirk et al., 2005; Marcu et al., 2006). Formemes, originally developed for Natural Language Generation (NLG) (Ptáček and Žabokrtský, 2006), have been successfully applied to MT within the TectoMT system. Our revision of formeme annotation aims to improve the MT performance, keeping other possible applications in mind.

3 The TectoMT English-Czech Machine Translation System

The TectoMT system is a structural machine translation system with deep transfer, first introduced by Žabokrtský et al. (2008). It currently supports English-to-Czech translation. Its analysis stage follows the Prague tectogrammatics theory (Sgall, 1967; Sgall et al., 1986), proceeding over two layers of structural description, from shallow (*analytical*) to deep (*tectogrammatical*) (see Section 3.1).

The transfer phase of the system is based on Maximum Entropy context-sensitive translation models (Mareček et al., 2010) and Hidden Tree Markov Models (Žabokrtský and Popel, 2009). It is factorized into three subtasks: lemma, formeme and grammatemes translation (see Sections 3.2 and 3.3).

The subsequent generation phase consists of rule-based components that gradually change the deep target language representation into a shallow one, which is then converted to text (cf. Section 6.1).

The version of TectoMT submitted to WMT12[2] builds upon the WMT11 version. Several rule-based components were slightly refined. However, most of the effort was devoted to creating a better and bigger parallel treebank—CzEng 1.0[3] (Bojar et al., 2012b), and re-training the statistical components on this resource. Apart from bigger size and improved filtering, one of the main differences between CzEng 0.9 (Bojar and Žabokrtský, 2009) (used in WMT11) and CzEng 1.0 (used in WMT12) is the revised annotation of formemes.

[2] http://www.statmt.org/wmt12

[3] http://ufal.mff.cuni.cz/czeng

3.1 Layers of structural analysis

There are two distinct structural layers used in the TectoMT system:

- *Analytical layer*. A surface syntax layer, which includes all tokens of the sentence, organized into a labeled dependency tree. The labels correspond to surface syntax functions.

- *Tectogrammatical layer*. A deep syntax/semantic layer describing the linguistic meaning of the sentence. Its dependency trees include only content words as nodes, assigning to each of them a deep lemma (*t-lemma*), a semantic role label (*functor*), and other deep linguistic features (*grammatemes*), such as semantic part-of-speech, person, tense or modality.

The analytical layer can be obtained using different dependency parsers (Popel et al., 2011); the tectogrammatical representation is then created by rule-based modules from the analytical trees.

In contrast to the original PDT annotation, the TectoMT tectogrammatical layer also includes *formemes* describing the surface morpho-syntactic realization of the nodes (cf. also Section 3.3).

3.2 Transfer: Translation Factorization and Symmetry

Using the tectogrammatical representation in structural MT allows separating the problem of translating a sentence into relatively independent simpler subtasks: lemma, functors, and grammatemes translation (Bojar et al., 2009; Žabokrtský, 2010). Since topology changes to deep syntax trees are rare in MT transfer, each of these three subtasks allows a virtually symmetric source-target one-to-one mapping, thus simplifying the initial n-to-m mapping of word phrases or surface subtrees.

Žabokrtský et al. (2008) obviated the need for transfer via functors (i.e. semantic role detection) by applying a formeme transfer instead. While formeme values are much simpler to obtain by automatic processing, this approach preserved the advantage of symmetric one-to-one value translation.

Moreover, translations of a given source morpho-syntactic construction usually follow a limited number of patterns in the target language regardless of their semantic functions, e.g. a finite clause will most often be translated as a finite clause.

3.3 Motivation for the Introduction of Formemes

Surface-oriented formemes have been introduced into the semantics-oriented tectogrammatical layer, as it proves beneficial to combine the deep syntax trees, smaller in size and more consistent across languages, with the surface morphology and syntax to provide for a straightforward transition to the surface level (Žabokrtský, 2010).

The three-fold factorization of the transfer phase (see Section 3.2) helps address the data sparsity issue faced by today's MT systems. As the translation of lemmas and their morpho-syntactic forms is separated, combinations unseen in the training data may appear on the output.

To further reduce data sparsity, only minimal information needed to reconstruct the surface form is stored in formemes; morphological categories derivable from elsewhere, i.e. morphological agreement or grammatemes, are discarded.

4 Czech and English Formemes in TectoMT

A *formeme* is a concise description of relevant morpho-syntactic features of a node in a tectogrammatical tree (deep syntactic tree whose nodes usually correspond to content words). The general shape of revised Czech and English formemes, as implemented within the Treex[4] NLP framework (Popel and Žabokrtský, 2010) for the TectoMT system, consists of three main parts:

1. *Syntactic part-of-speech.*[5] The number of syntactic parts-of-speech is very low, as only content words are used on the deep layer and the categories of pronouns and numerals have been divided under nouns and adjectives according to syntactic behavior (Ševčíková-Razímová and Žabokrtský, 2006). The possible values are `v` for verbs, `n` for nouns, `adj` for adjectives, and `adv` for adverbs.

2. *Subordinate conjunction/preposition.* Applies only to formemes of prepositional phrases and subordinate clauses introduced by a conjunction and contains the respective conjunction or preposition; e.g. `if`, `on` or `in_case_of`.

3. *Form.* This part represents the morpho-syntactic form of the node in question and depends on the part-of-speech (see Table 1).

The two or three parts are concatenated into a human-readable string to facilitate usage in hand-written rules as well as statistical systems (Žabokrtský, 2010), producing values such as `v:inf`, `v:if+fin` or `n:into+X`. Formeme values of nodes corresponding to uninflected words are atomic.

Formemes are detected by rule-based modules operating on deep and surface trees. Example deep syntax trees annotated with formemes are shown in Fig. 1. A listing of all possible formeme values is given in Table 1.

Verbal formemes remain quite consistent in both languages, except for the greater range of forms in English (Czech uses adjectives or nouns instead of gerunds and verbal attributes). Nominal formemes differ more significantly: Czech is a free-word order language with rich morphology, where declension is important to syntactic relations—case is therefore included in formemes. As English makes its syntactic relations visible rather with word-order than with morphology, English formemes indicate the syntactic position instead. The same holds for adjectival complements to verbs. Posession is expressed mostly using nouns in English and adjectives in Czech, which is also reflected in formemes.

5 Recent Markup Improvements

Our following markup innovations address several issues found in the previous version and aim to adapt the range of values more accurately to the intended applications.

5.1 General Form Changes

The relevant preposition and subordinate conjunction nodes had been selected based on their dependency labels; we use a simple part-of-speech tag filter instead in order to minimize the influence of parsing errors and capture more complex prepositions,

[4] `http://ufal.mff.cuni.cz/treex/`, `https://metacpan.org/module/Treex`

[5] Cf. Section 5.2 for details.

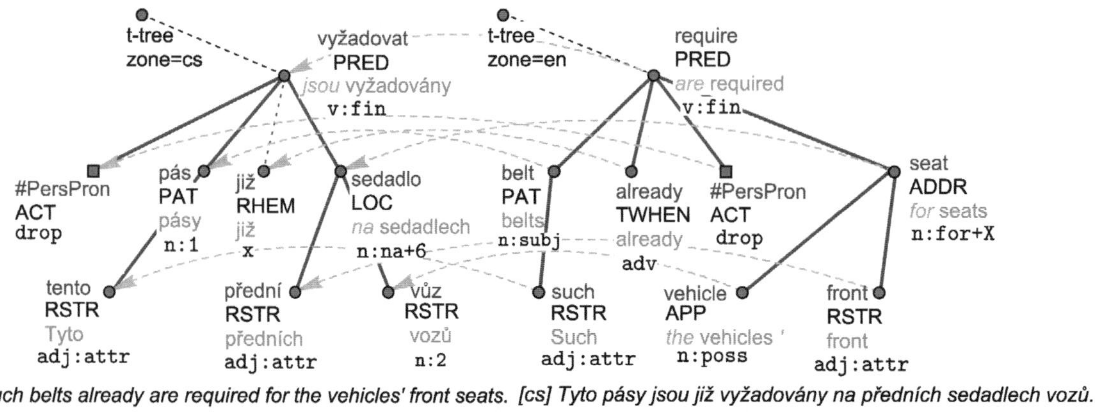

Figure 1: An example English and Czech deep sentence structure annotated with formemes (in typewriter font).

Formeme	Language	Definition
`v:`*(P+)*`fin`	both	Verbs as heads of finite clauses
`v:rc`	both	Verbs as heads of relative clauses
`v:`*(P+)*`inf`	both	Infinitive clauses; typically with the particle *to* in English*
`v:`*(P+)*`ger`	EN	Gerunds, e.g. *I like reading* (`v:ger`), *but I am tired of arguing* (`v:of+ger`).
`v:attr`	EN	Present or past participles (i.e. *-ing* or *-ed* forms) in the attributive syntactic position, e.g. *Striking* (`v:attr`) *teachers hate bored* (`v:attr`) *students.*
`n:[1..7]`	CS	Bare nouns; the numbers indicate morphological case†
`n:X`	CS	Bare nouns that cannot be inflected
`n:subj`	EN	Nouns in the subject position (i.e. in front of the main verb of the clause)
`n:obj`	EN	Nouns in the object position (i.e. following the verb with no preposition)
`n:obj1, n:obj2`	EN	Nouns in the object position; distinguishing the two objects of ditransitive verbs (e.g. *give, consider*)
`n:adv`	EN	Nouns in an adverbial position, e.g. *The sales went up by 1 % last month*
`n:`*P+*`X`	EN	Prepositional phrases
`n:`*P+*`[1..7]`	CS	Prepositional phrases; the preposition surface form is combined with the required case‡
`n:attr`	both	Nominal attributes, e.g. *insurance company* or *president Smith* in English and *prezident Smith* in Czech
`n:poss`	EN	English possessive pronouns and nouns with the *'s* suffix
`adj:attr`	both	Adjectival attributes (Czech inflection forms need not be stored thanks to congruency with the parent noun)
`adj:compl`	EN	Direct adjectival complements to verbs
`adj:[1..7]`	CS	Direct adjectival complements to verbs (morphological case must be stored in Czech, as it is determined by valency)
`adj:poss`	CS	Czech possesive adjectives and pronouns; a counterpart to English `n:poss`
`adv`	both	Adverbs (not inflected, can take no prepositions etc.)
`x`	both	Coordinating conjunctions, other uninflected words
`drop`	both	Deep tree nodes which do not appear on the surface (e.g. pro-drop pronouns)

*I.e. infinitives as head of clauses, not infinitives as parts of compound verb forms with finite auxiliary verbs.
†Numbers are traditionally used to mark morphological case in Czech; `1` stands for nominative, `2` for genitive etc.
‡Since many prepositions may govern multiple cases in Czech, the case number is necessary.

Table 1: A listing of all possible formeme values, indicating their usage in Czech, English or both languages. "*P+*" denotes the (lowercased) surface form of a preposition or a subordinate conjunction. Round brackets denote optional parts, square brackets denote a set of alternatives.

e.g. *in case of*. Our revision also allows combining prepositions with all English gerunds and infinitives, preventing a loss of important data.

We also use the lowercased surface form in the middle formeme part instead of lemmas to allow for a more straightforward surface form generation.

5.2 Introducing Syntactic Part-of-Speech

Formemes originally contained the semantic part-of-speech (sempos) (Razímová and Žabokrtský, 2006) as their first part. We replaced it with a *syntactic* part-of-speech (syntpos), since it proved complicated to assign sempos reliably by a rule-based module and morpho-syntactic behavior is more relevant to formemes than semantics.

The syntpos is assigned in two steps:

1. A preliminary syntpos is selected, using our categorization based on the part-of-speech tag and lemma.

2. The final syntpos is selected according to the syntactic position of the node, addressing nominal usage of adjectives and cardinal numerals (see Sections 5.4 and 5.5).

5.3 Capturing Czech Nominal Attributes

Detecting the attributive usage of nouns is straightforward for English, where any noun depending directly on another noun is considered an attribute. In Czech, one needs to distinguish case-congruent attributes from others that have a fixed case. We aimed at assigning the `n:attr` formeme only in the former case and thus replaced the original method based on word order with a less error-prone one based on congruency and named entity recognition.

5.4 Numerals: Distinguishing Usage and Correcting Czech Case

The new formemes now distinguish adjectival and nominal usage of cardinal numerals (cf. also Section 5.2), e.g. the number in *5 potatoes* is now assigned the `adj:attr` formeme, whereas *Apollo 11* is given `n:attr`. The new situation is analogous in Czech, with nominal usages of numerals having their morphological case marked in formemes.

To reduce data sparsity in the new formemes version, we counter the inconsistent syntactic behavior of Czech cardinal numerals, where 1-4 behave like adjectives but other numerals behave like nouns and shift their semantically governing noun to the position of a genitive attribute. An example of this change is given in Fig. 2.

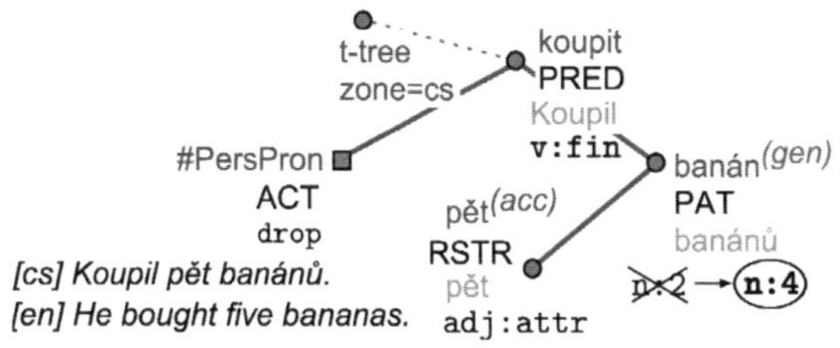

The word *banán* is in genitive (`n:2`), but would have an accusative (`n:4`) form if the numeral behaved like an adjective.

Figure 2: Case correction with numerals in Czech.

5.5 Adjectives: Nominal Usage and Case

The new formemes address the usage of adjectives in the syntactic position of nouns (cf. Section 5.2), which occurs only rarely, thus preventing sparse values, namely in these syntactic positions:

- *The subject.* We replaced the originally assigned `adj:compl` value, which was impossible to tell from adjectival objects, with the formeme a noun would have in the same position, e.g. in the sentence *Many of them were late*, the subject *many* is assigned `n:subj`.
- *Prepositional phrases.* Syntactic behavior of adjectives is identical to nouns here; we thus assign them the formeme values a noun would receive in the same position, e.g. `n:of+X` instead of `adj:of+X` in *He is one of the best at school.*

In Czech, we detect nominal usage of adjectives in verbal direct objects as well, employing large-coverage valency lexicons (Lopatková et al., 2008; Hajič et al., 2003).

Instead of assigning the `compl` value in Czech, our formemes revision includes the case of adjectival complements, which depends on the valency of the respective verb.

5.6 Mutual Information Across Languages

The changes described above have been motivated not only by theoretical linguistic description of the languages in question, but also by the intended usage within the TectoMT translation system. Instead of retraining the translation model after each change, we devised a simpler and faster estimate to measure the asset of our innovations: using Mutual Information (MI) (Manning and Schütze, 1999, p. 66) of formemes in Czech and English trees.

We expect that an inter-language MI increase will lead to lower noise in formeme-to-formeme translation dictionary (Bojar et al., 2009, cf. Section 3.2), thus achieving higher MT output quality.

Using the analysis pipeline from CzEng1.0, we measured the inter-language MI on sentences from the Prague Czech-English Dependency Treebank (PCEDT) 2.0 (Bojar et al., 2012a). The overall results show an MI increase from 1.598 to 1.687 (Bojar et al., 2012b). Several proposed markup changes have been discarded as they led to an inter-language MI drop; e.g. removing the `v:rc` relative clause formeme or merging the `v:attr` and `adj:attr` values in English.

6 Experimental Usage

We list here our experiments with the newly developed annotation: an NLG experiment aimed at assessing the impact of formemes on the synthesis phase of the TectoMT system, and the usage in the English-Czech MT as a whole.

6.1 Czech Synthesis

The synthesis phase of the TectoMT system relies heavily on the information included in formemes, as its rule-based blocks use solely formemes and grammar rules to gradually change a deep tree node into a surface subtree.

To directly measure the suitability of our changes for the synthesis stage of the TectoMT system, we used a Czech-to-Czech round trip—deep analysis of Czech PDT 2.0 development set sentences using the CzEng 1.0 pipeline (Bojar et al., 2012b), followed directly by the synthesis part of the TectoMT system. The results were evaluated using the BLEU metric (Papineni et al., 2002) with the original sentences as reference; they indicate a higher suitability of the new formemes for deep Czech synthesis (see Table 2).

6.2 English-Czech Machine Translation

To measure the influence of the presented formeme revision on the translation quality, we compared two translation scenarios—one using the original formemes and the second using the revised formemes in the formeme-to-formeme translation model. Due to time reasons, we were able to train both translation models only on $1/2$ of the CzEng 1.0 training data.

Version	BLEU
Original formemes	0.6818
Revised formemes	0.7092

Table 2: A comparison of formeme versions in Czech-to-Czech round trip.

Version	BLEU
Original formemes	0.1190
Revised formemes	0.1199

Table 3: A comparison of formeme versions in English-to-Czech TectoMT translation on the WMT12 test set.

The results in Table 3 demonstrate a slight[6] BLEU gain when using the revised formemes version. The gain is expected to be greater if several rule-based modules of the transfer phase are adapted to the revisions.

7 Conclusion and Further Work

We have presented a systematic and theoretically supported revision of a surface morpho-syntactic markup within a deep dependency annotation scenario, designed to facilitate the TectoMT transfer phase. Our first practical experiments proved the merits of our innovations in the tasks of Czech synthesis and deep structural MT as a whole. We have also experimented with formemes in the functor assignment (semantic role labelling) task and gained moderate improvements (ca. 1-1.5% accuracy).

In future, we intend to tune the rule-based parts of our MT transfer for the new version of formemes and examine further possibilities of data sparsity reduction (e.g. by merging synonymous formemes). We are also planning to create formeme annotation modules for further languages to widen the range of language pairs used in the TectoMT system.

[6] Significant at 90% level using pairwise bootstrap resampling test (Koehn, 2004).

References

O. Bojar and Z. Žabokrtský. 2009. CzEng 0.9: Large Parallel Treebank with Rich Annotation. *Prague Bulletin of Mathematical Linguistics*, 92.

O. Bojar, D. Mareček, V. Novák, M. Popel, J. Ptáček, J. Rouš, and Z. Žabokrtský. 2009. English-Czech MT in 2008. In *Proceedings of the Fourth Workshop on Statistical Machine Translation*, pages 125–129. Association for Computational Linguistics.

O. Bojar, J. Hajič, E. Hajičová, J. Panevová, P. Sgall, S. Cinková, E. Fučíková, M. Mikulová, P. Pajas, J. Popelka, J. Semecký, J. Šindlerová, J. Štěpánek, J. Toman, Z. Urešová, and Z. Žabokrtský. 2012a. Announcing Prague Czech-English Dependency Treebank 2.0. In *Proceedings of LREC 2012*, Istanbul, Turkey, May. ELRA, European Language Resources Association. In print.

O. Bojar, Z. Žabokrtský, O. Dušek, P. Galuščáková, M. Majliš, D. Mareček, J. Maršík, M. Novák, M. Popel, and A. Tamchyna. 2012b. The Joy of Parallelism with CzEng 1.0. In *Proceedings of LREC 2012*, Istanbul, Turkey, May. ELRA, European Language Resources Association. In print.

J. Hajič, J. Panevová, Z. Urešová, A. Bémová, V. Kolárová, and P. Pajas. 2003. PDT-VALLEX: Creating a large-coverage valency lexicon for treebank annotation. In *Proceedings of The Second Workshop on Treebanks and Linguistic Theories*, volume 9, pages 57–68.

J. Hajič, J. Panevová, E. Hajičová, P. Sgall, P. Pajas, J. Štěpánek, J. Havelka, M. Mikulová, Z. Žabokrtský, and M. Ševčíková-Razímová. 2006. Prague Dependency Treebank 2.0. *CD-ROM LDC2006T01, LDC, Philadelphia*.

G. Helbig and W. Schenkel. 1969. *Wörterbuch zur Valenz und Distribution deutscher Verben*. VEB Bibliographisches Institut, Leipzig.

P. Koehn. 2004. Statistical Significance Tests for Machine Translation Evaluation. In *Proceedings of EMNLP 2004*, Barcelona, Spain.

M. Lopatková, Z. Žabokrtský, V. Kettnerová, and K. Skwarska. 2008. *Valenční slovník českých sloves*. Karolinum, Prague.

C.D. Manning and H. Schütze. 1999. *Foundations of statistical natural language processing*. MIT Press.

D. Marcu, W. Wang, A. Echihabi, and K. Knight. 2006. SPMT: Statistical machine translation with syntactified target language phrases. In *Proceedings of the 2006 Conference on Empirical Methods in Natural Language Processing*, pages 44–52. Association for Computational Linguistics.

D. Mareček, M. Popel, and Z. Žabokrtský. 2010. Maximum entropy translation model in dependency-based MT framework. In *Proceedings of the Joint Fifth Workshop on Statistical Machine Translation and Metrics (MATR)*, pages 201–206. Association for Computational Linguistics.

A. Menezes and S. D. Richardson. 2001. A best-first alignment algorithm for automatic extraction of transfer mappings from bilingual corpora. In *Proceedings of the workshop on Data-driven methods in machine translation - Volume 14*, DMMT '01, pages 1–8, Stroudsburg, PA. Association for Computational Linguistics.

K. Papineni, S. Roukos, T. Ward, and W.J. Zhu. 2002. BLEU: a method for automatic evaluation of machine translation. In *Proceedings of the 40th annual meeting on association for computational linguistics*, pages 311–318. Association for Computational Linguistics.

M. Popel and Z. Žabokrtský. 2010. TectoMT: modular NLP framework. *Advances in Natural Language Processing*, pages 293–304.

M. Popel, D. Mareček, N. Green, and Z. Žabokrtský. 2011. Influence of parser choice on dependency-based MT. In Chris Callison-Burch, Philipp Koehn, Christof Monz, and Omar Zaidan, editors, *Proceedings of the Sixth Workshop on Statistical Machine Translation*, pages 433–439, Edinburgh, UK. Association for Computational Linguistics.

J. Ptáček and Z. Žabokrtský. 2006. Synthesis of Czech sentences from tectogrammatical trees. In *Text, Speech and Dialogue*, pages 221–228. Springer.

C. Quirk, A. Menezes, and C. Cherry. 2005. Dependency treelet translation: Syntactically informed phrasal SMT. In *Proceedings of the 43rd Annual Meeting on Association for Computational Linguistics*, pages 271–279. Association for Computational Linguistics.

M. Razímová and Z. Žabokrtský. 2006. Annotation of grammatemes in the Prague Dependency Treebank 2.0. In *Proceedings of the LREC 2006 Workshop on Annotation Science*, pages 12–19.

M. Ševčíková-Razímová and Z. Žabokrtský. 2006. Systematic parameterized description of pro-forms in the Prague Dependency Treebank 2.0. In J. Hajič and J. Nivre, editors, *Proceedings of the Fifth Workshop on Treebanks and Linguistic Theories (TLT)*, pages 175–186, Prague.

P. Sgall, E. Hajičová, J. Panevová, and J. Mey. 1986. *The meaning of the sentence in its semantic and pragmatic aspects*. Springer.

P. Sgall. 1967. *Generativní popis jazyka a česká deklinace*. Academia, Prague.

Z. Urešová. 2009. Building the PDT-VALLEX valency lexicon. In *On-line proceedings of the fifth Corpus Linguistics Conference*. University of Liverpool.

Z. Žabokrtský, J. Ptáček, and P. Pajas. 2008. TectoMT: highly modular MT system with tectogrammatics used as transfer layer. In *Proceedings of the Third Workshop on Statistical Machine Translation*, StatMT '08, pages 167–170, Stroudsburg, PA. Association for Computational Linguistics.

Z. Žabokrtský. 2005. *Valency Lexicon of Czech Verbs*. Ph.D. thesis, Charles University in Prague.

Z. Žabokrtský. 2010. *From Treebanking to Machine Translation*. Habilitation thesis, Charles University in Prague.

Z. Žabokrtský and M. Popel. 2009. Hidden Markov Tree Model in Dependency-based Machine Translation. In *Proceedings of the ACL-IJCNLP 2009 Conference Short Papers*, pages 145–148, Suntec, Singapore.

The TALP-UPC phrase-based translation systems for WMT12: Morphology simplification and domain adaptation

Lluís Formiga, Carlos A. Henríquez Q., Adolfo Hernández,
José B. Mariño, Enric Monte and José A. R. Fonollosa
TALP Research Centre
Universitat Politècnica de Catalunya
Barcelona, Spain
{lluis.formiga,carlos.henriquez,adolfo.hernandez
jose.marino,enric.monte,jose.fonollosa}@upc.edu

Abstract

This paper describes the UPC participation in the WMT 12 evaluation campaign. All systems presented are based on standard phrase-based Moses systems. Variations adopted several improvement techniques such as morphology simplification and generation and domain adaptation. The morphology simplification overcomes the data sparsity problem when translating into morphologically-rich languages such as Spanish by translating first to a morphology-simplified language and secondly leave the morphology generation to an independent classification task. The domain adaptation approach improves the SMT system by adding new translation units learned from MT-output and reference alignment. Results depict an improvement on TER, METEOR, NIST and BLEU scores compared to our baseline system, obtaining on the official test set more benefits from the domain adaptation approach than from the morphological generalization method.

1 Introduction

TALP-UPC (Center of Speech and Language Applications and Technology at the Universitat Politècnica de Catalunya) has participated in the WMT12 shared task translating across two directions: English to Spanish and Spanish to English tasks.

For the Spanish to English task we submitted a baseline system that uses all parallel training data and a combination of different target language models (LM) and Part-Of-Speech (POS) language models. A similar configuration was submitted for the English to Spanish task as baseline. Our main approaches enriched the latter baseline in two independent ways: morphology simplification and domain adaptation by deriving new units into the phrase-table. Furthermore, additional specific strategies have been addressed on all systems to deal with well known linguistic phenomena in Spanish such as clitics and contractions.

The paper is presented as follows. Section 2 presents the main rationale for the phrase-based system and the main pipeline of our baseline system. Section 3 presents the approaches taken to improve the baseline system on the English to Spanish task. Section 4 presents the obtained results on internal and official test sets while conclusions and further work are presented in Section 5.

2 Baseline system: Phrase-Based SMT

Classically, a phrase-based translation system implements a log-linear model in which a foreign language sentence $f_1^j = f_1, f_2, \ldots, f_j$ is translated into another language sentence $e_1^I = e_1, e_2, \ldots, e_I$ by searching for the translation hypothesis that maximizes a log-linear combination of feature models (Brown et al., 1990):

$$\hat{e}_1^I = \arg\max_{e_1^I} \left\{ \sum_{m=1}^{M} \lambda_m h_m \left(e_1^I, f_1^J\right) \right\} \quad (1)$$

where the separate feature functions h_m refer to the system models and the set of λ_m refers to the weights corresponding to these models. As feature functions we used the standard models available

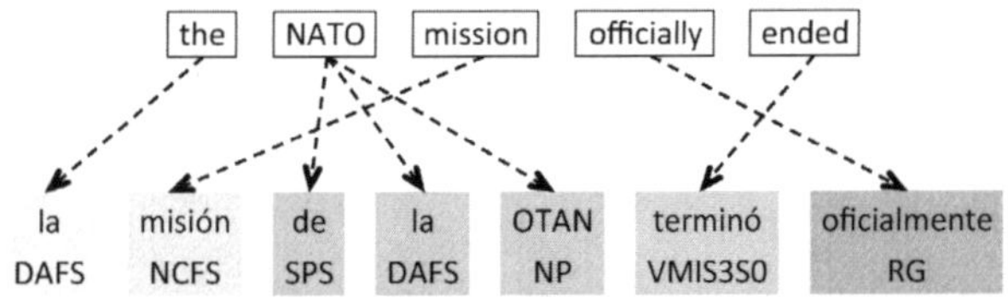

Figure 1: Factored phrase-based MT based on translation from surface to surface and Part-of-Speech

Corpus		Sent.	Words	Vocab.	avg.len.
EPPS	Eng	1.90 M	49.40 M	124.03 k	26.05
	Spa		52.66 M	154.67 k	27.28
News.Com	Eng	0.15 M	3.73 M	62.70 k	24.20
	Spa		4.33 M	73.97 k	28.09
UN	Eng	8.38 M	205.68 M	575.04 k	24.54
	Spa		239.40 M	598.54 k	28.56

Table 1: English-Spanish corpora statistics for NAACL-WMT 2012 after cleaning process

on Moses, i.e., relative frequencies, lexical weights, word and phrase penalty, *wbe-msd-bidirectional-fe* reordering models and two language models, one for surface and one for POS tags. Phrase scoring was computed using Good-Turing discounting (Foster et al., 2006).

The tuning process was done using MERT (Och, 2003) with Minimum Bayes-Risk decoding (MBR) (Kumar and Bryne, 2004) on Moses and focusing on minimizing the BLEU score (Papineni et al., 2002) of the development set. Final translations were also computed using MBR decoding.

Additionally to the settings mentioned before, we worked with a factored version of the corpus. Factored corpora augments surface forms with additional information, such as POS tags or lemmas as shown in Figure 1. In that case, factors other than surface (e.g. POS) are usually less sparse, allowing to build factor-specific language models with higher-order n-grams. These higher-order language models usually help to obtain more syntactically correct output. Concretely we map input source surfaces to target surfaces and POS tags.

2.1 Corpus used

The baseline system was trained using all parallel corpora, i.e. the European Parliament (EPPS) (Koehn, 2005), News Commentary and United Nations. Table 1 shows the statistics of the training data after the cleaning process described later on Subsection 2.2.

Regarding the monolingual data, there was also more News corpora separated by years for Spanish and English and there was the Gigaword monolingual corpus for English. All data can be found on the Translation Task's website[1]. We used all News corpora (and Gigaword for English) to build the language model. Initially, a LM was built for every corpus and then they were combined to produce de final LM. Table 2 presents the statistics of each corpora, again after the cleaning process.

Corpus		Sent.	Words	Vocab.
EPPS	Eng	2.22 M	59.88 M	144.03 k
	Spa	2.12 M	61.97 M	174.92 k
News.Com.	Eng	0.21 M	5.08 M	72.55 k
	Spa	0.18 M	5.24 M	81.56 k
UN	Eng	11.20 M	315.90 M	767.12 k
	Spa	11.20 M	372.21 M	725.73 k
News.07	Eng	3.79 M	90.25 M	711.55 k
	Spa	0.05 M	1.33 M	64.10 k
News.08	Eng	13.01 M	308.82 M	1555.53 k
	Spa	1.71 M	49.97 M	377.56 k
News.09	Eng	14.75 M	348.24 M	1648.05 k
	Spa	1.07 M	30.57 M	287.81 k
News.10	Eng	6.81 M	158.15 M	915.14 k
	Spa	0.69 M	19.58 M	226.76 k
News.11	Eng	13.46 M	312.50 M	1345.79 k
	Spa	5.11 M	151.06 M	668.63 k
Giga	Eng	22.52 M	657.88 M	3860.67 k

Table 2: Details of monolingual corpora used for building language-models.

For internal testing we used the News 2011's data and concatenated the remaining three years of News data as a single parallel corpus for development. Table 3 shows the statistics for these two sets and includes in the last rows the statistics of the official test set for this year's translation task.

2.2 Corpus processing

All corpora were processed in order to remove or normalize ambiguous or special characters such as quotes and spaces. Among other TALP-UPC specific scripts, we used a modified version of the normalized-punctuation script provided by the organizers in order to skip the reordering rules which involved quotes and stop punctuation signs.

[1]http://www.statmt.org/wmt12/translation-task.html

Corpus		Sent.	Words	Vocab.	avg.len.
dev	Eng	7.57 k	189.01 k	18.61 k	24.98
	Spa		202.80 k	21.75 k	26.80
test11	Eng	3.00 k	74.73 k	10.82 k	24.88
	Spa		81.01 k	12.16 k	26.98
test12	Eng	3.00 k	72.91 k	10.24 k	24.28
	Spa		80.38 k	12.02 k	26.77

Table 3: Detail of development and test corpora used to tune and test the system.

POS-Tagging and tokenization for both Spanish and English data sets were obtained using FreeLing (Padró et al., 2010). Freeling tokenization is able to deal with contractions ("del" → "de el") and clitics separation ("cómpramelo" → "compra me lo") in Spanish and English. Stemming was performed using Snowball (Porter, 2001).

Surface text was lowercased conditionally based on the POS tagging: proper nouns and adjectives were separated from other POS categories to determine if a string should be fully lowercased (no special property), partially lowercased (proper noun or adjective) or not lowercased at all (acronym).

Bilingual corpora were cleaned with *clean-corpus-n* script of Moses (Koehn et al., 2007) removing all sentence pair with more than 70 words in any language, considering the already tokenized data. That script also ensures a maximum length ratio below of nine (9) words between source and target sentences.

Postprocessing in both languages consisted of a recasing step using Moses recaser script. Furthermore we built an additional script in order to check the casing of output names with respect to source sentence names and case them accordingly, with exception of names placed at beginning of the sentence. After recasing, a final detokenization step was performed using standard Moses tools. Spanish postprocessing also included two special scripts to recover contractions and clitics.

2.3 Language Model and alignment configuration

Word alignment was performed at stem level with GIZA++ toolkit (Och and Ney, 2003) and *grow-diag-final-and* joint alignment.

Language models were built from the monolingual data provided covering different domains: Europarl, News and UN. We built them using Kneser-Ney algorithm (Chen and Goodman, 1999), interpolation in order to avoid over-fitting and considering unknown words. First we built a 5-gram language model for each corpus; then, the final LM was obtained interpolating them all towards the development set. We used SRI Language Model (Stolcke, 2002) toolkit, which provides *compute-best-mix* script for the interpolation.

The POS language model was built analogously to the surface language with some variants: it was a 7-gram LM, without discounting nor interpolation.

3 Improvement strategies

3.1 Motivations

In order to improve the baseline system we present two different strategies. First we present an improvement strategy based on morphology simplification plus generation to deal with the problems raised by morphological rich languages such as Spanish. Second we present a domain adaptation strategy that consists in deriving new units into the phrase-table.

3.2 Morphology simplification

The first improvement strategy is based on morphology simplification when translating from English to Spanish.

The problems raised when translating from a language such as English into richer morphology languages are well known and are a research line of interest nowadays (Popovic and Ney, 2004; Koehn and Hoang, 2007; de Gispert and Mariño, 2008; Toutanova et al., 2008; Clifton and Sarkar, 2011). In that direction, inflection causes a very large target-language lexicon with a significant data sparsity problem. In addition, system output is limited only to the inflected phrases available in the parallel training corpus. Hence, SMT systems cannot generate proper inflections unless they have learned them from the appropriate phrases. That would require to have a parallel corpus containing all possible word inflections for all phrases available, which it is an unfeasible task.

The morphology related problems in MT have been addressed from different approaches and may

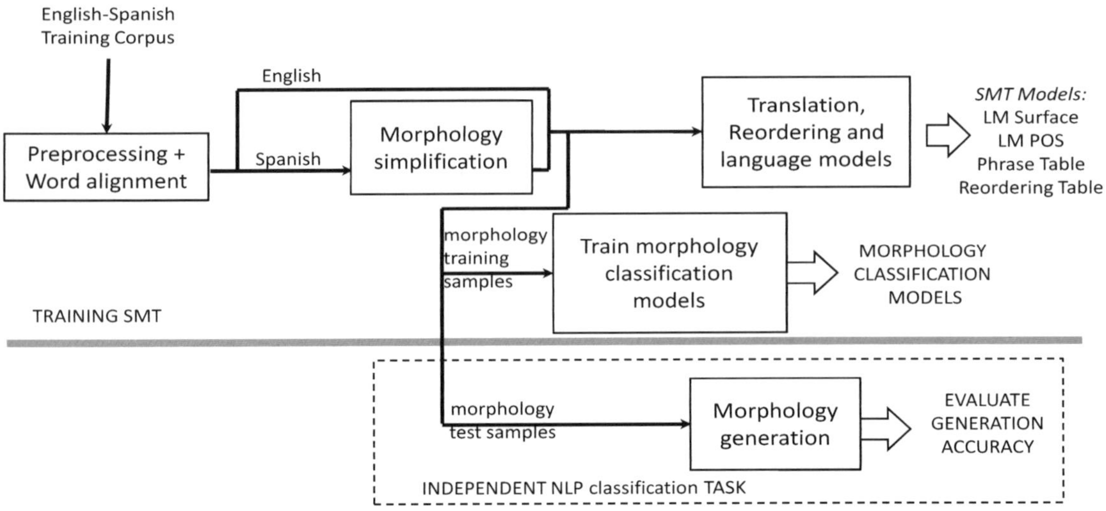

Figure 2: Above, flow diagram of the training of simplified morphology translation models. Below, Spanish morphology generation as an independent classification task.

Type	Text
PLAIN TARGET:	la Comisión **puede** llegar a paralizar el programa
TARGET+PoS (Gen. Sur.):	la Comisión **VMIP3S0[poder]** llegar a paralizar el programa
TARGET+PoS (Simpl. PoS):	la Comisión **VMIPpn0[poder]** llegar a paralizar el programa

Table 4: Example of morphology simplification steps taken for Spanish verbs.

be summarized in four categories: *i*) factored models (Koehn and Hoang, 2007), enriched input models (Avramidis and Koehn, 2008; Ueffing and Ney, 2003), segmented translation (Virpioja et al., 2007) and morphology generation (Toutanova et al., 2008; de Gispert and Mariño, 2008).

Our strategy for dealing with morphology generation is based in the latter approach (de Gispert and Mariño, 2008) (Figure 2). We center our strategy in simplifying only verb forms as previous studies indicate that they contribute to the main improvement (Ueffing and Ney, 2003; de Gispert and Mariño, 2008). That strategy makes clear the real impact of morphology simplification by providing an upper bound oracle for the studied scenarios.

The approach is as follows: First, target verbs are simplified substituting them with their simplified forms (Table 4). In this example, the verb form 'puede' (he can) is transformed into 'VMIPpn0[poder]', indicating simplified POS and base form (lemma); where 'p' and 'n' represent any person and number once simplified (from 3rd person singular). Secondly, standard MT models are obtained from English into simplified morphology Spanish. Morphology prediction acts as a black box, with its models estimated over a simplified morphology parallel texts (including target language model and lexicon models).

Generation is implemented by Decision Directed Acyclic Graphs (DDAG) (Platt et al., 2000) compound of binary SVM classifiers. In detail, a DDAG combines many two-class classifiers to a multiclassification task (Hernández et al., 2010).

3.3 Domain adaptation

Depending on the available resources, different domain adaptation techniques are possible. Usually, the baseline system is built with a large out-of-domain corpus (in our case the European Parliament) and we aim to adapt to another domain that has limited data, either only monolingual or hopefully bilingual as well. The WMT Translation Task focuses on adapting the system to a news domain, offering an in-domain parallel corpus to work with.

In case of additional target monolingual data, previous works have focused on language model interpolations (Bulyko et al., 2007; Mohit et al., 2009; Wu et al., 2008). When parallel in-domain data is available, the latest researches have focused on mixture model adaptation of the translation model (Civera and Juan, 2007; Foster and Kuhn, 2007; Foster et al., 2010). Our work is closer to the latest approaches. We used the in-domain parallel data to adapt the translation model, but focusing on the decoding errors that the out-of-domain baseline system made while translating the in-domain corpus. The idea is to detect where the system made its mistakes and use the in-domain data to teach it how to correct them.

Our approach began with a baseline system built with the Parliament and the United Nations parallel corpora but without the News parallel corpus. The rest of the configuration remained the same for the baseline. With this alternative baseline system, we translated the source side of the News parallel corpus to obtain a revised corpus of it, as defined in (Henríquez Q. et al., 2011). The revised corpus consists of the source side, the output translation and the target side, also called the target correction. The output translation and its reference are then compare to detect possible mistakes that the system caused during decoding.

The translation was used as a pivot to find a word-to-word alignment between the source side and the target correction. The word-to-word alignment between source side and translation was provided by Moses during decoding. The word-to-word alignment between the output translation and target correction was obtained following these steps:

1. Translation Edit Rate (Snover et al., 2006) between each output translation and target correction sentence pair was computed to obtain its edit path and detect which words do not change between sentences. Words that did not change were directly linked

2. Going from left to right, for each unaligned word w_{out} on the output translation sentence and each word w_{trg} on the target correction sentence, a similarity function was computed between them and w_{out} got aligned with the word w_{trg} that maximized this similarity.

The similarity function was defined as a linear combination of features that considered if the words w_{out} and w_{trg} were identical, if the previous or following word of any of them were aligned with each other and a lexical weight between them using the bilingual lexical features from the baseline as references.

With both word-to-word alignments computed for a sentence pair, we linked source word w_{src} with target word w_{trg} is and only if exists a output translation word w_{out} such that there is a link between w_{src} and w_{out} and a link between w_{out} and w_{trg}.

After aligning the corpus, we built the translation and reordering model of it, using the baseline settings. We called these translation and reordering models, revised models. They include phrases found in the baseline that were correctly chosen during decoding and also new phrases that came from the differences between the output translation and its correction.

Finally, the revised translation model features were linearly combined with their corresponding baseline features to build the final translation model, called the derived translation model. The combination was computed in the following way:

$$h_d^i(s,t) = \alpha h_b^i(s,t) + (1-\alpha) h_r^i(s,t) \qquad (2)$$

where $h_d^i(s,t)$ is the derived feature function i for the bilingual phrase (s,t), $h_b^i(s,t)$ is the baseline feature function of and $h_r^i(s,t)$ the revised feature function. A value of $\alpha = 0.60$ was chosen after determining it was the one that maximized the BLEU score of the development set during tuning. Different values for α were considered, between 0.50 and 0.95 with increments of 0.05 between them.

Regarding the reordering model, we added the unseen phrases from the revised reordering model into the baseline reordering model, leaving the remaining baseline phrase reordering weights intact.

4 Results

4.1 Language Model perplexities

LM	Perplexity	
	Surface	POS
Baseline	205.36	13.23
Simplified	193.66	12.66

Table 6: Perplexities obtained across baseline and morphology simplification.

Before evaluating translation performance, we studied to what extent the morphology simplifica-

EN→ES		BLEU		NIST		TER	METEOR
		CS	CI	CS	CI	CS	CI
test11	Baseline	30.7	32.53	7.820	8.120	57.19	55.05
	Morph. Oracle	31.56	33.35	7.949	8.233	56.44	–
	Morph. Gen.	31.03	32.85	7.866	8.163	56.95	55.39
	Adaptation	31.16	32.93	7.857	8.155	56.88	55.19
test12	Baseline	31.21	32.74	7.981	8.244	55.76	55.48
	Morph. Oracle	32	33.41	8.090	8.339	55.15	–
	Morph. Gen.	31.46	32.98	8.010	8.274	55.62	55.66
	Adaptation	31.73	33.24	8.037	8.294	55.37	55.82

(a) English→Spanish

ES→EN		BLEU		NIST		TER	METEOR
		CS	CI	CS	CI	CS	CI
test11	Baseline	28.81	30.29	7.670	7.933	59.01	51.09
test12		32.27	33.81	8.014	8.282	56.26	53.96

(b) Spanish→English

Table 5: Automatic scores for English↔Spanish translations. CS and CI indicate Case-Sensitive or Case-Insensitive evaluations.

tion strategy may help decreasing the language models perplexity.

In table 6 we can see the effects of simplification. Perplexity is computed from the corresponding internal test sets to the baseline or simplified language models.

In general terms, the simplification process is slightly effective, yielding an averaged improvement of -5.02%.

4.2 Translation performance

Evaluations were performed with different translation quality measures: BLEU, NIST, TER and METEOR (Denkowski and Lavie, 2011) which evaluate distinct aspects of the quality of the translations. First we evaluated the WMT11 test (test11) as an internal indicator of our systems. Later we did the same analysis with the WMT12 official test files.

Table 5 presents the obtained results. Experiments began building the baseline system, which included the special treatment for clitics, contractions and casing as described in Section 2.2. Once the baseline was set, we proceeded with two parallel lines, one for morphology simplification and the other for domain adaptation.

For morphology generation approach (Table 5) oracles (Morph. Oracle) represent how much gain we could expect with a perfect generation module and generation (Morph. Gen.) represent the actual performance combining simplification and the generation strategies. Oracles achieve a promising averaged improvement of +1.79% (depending on the metric or the test set) with respect to the baseline. However, generation only improves the baseline by a +0.61%, encouraging us to keep working on that strategy.

Regarding the domain adaptation approach, we evaluated the internal test set (test11). As we can see again on Table 5a the adaptation strategy outperforms the baseline on all quality measures starting with an averaged gain of $+0.94\%$.

Comparing the two approaches, we can see that the domain adaptation method was better in terms of BLEU score and TER than the morphology generation but the latter was better on NIST and METEOR on our internal test set. This made us decided for the latter as the primary system submitted, leaving the domain adaptation approach system as a contrastive submission. Additionally to the automatic quality measures, we are particularly interested in the manual evaluation results, as we believe the morphology generation will be more sensitive to this type of evaluation than to automatic metrics.

Official results (test12) can be found on Table 5b. Surprisingly, this time the domain adaptation approach performed better than the morphology simplification on all metrics: BLEU, NIST, TER and METEOR, with an averaged gain of $+1.04\%$ over the baseline system, which ranks our submissions second and third in terms of BLEU scores (contrastive and primary respectively) when compared with all other submissions for the WMT12 translation task.

5 Conclusions and further work

This papers describes the UPC participation during the 2012 WMT's Translation Task. We have participated with a baseline system for Spanish-to-English, a baseline system for English-to-Spanish and two independent enhancements to the baseline system for English-to-Spanish as well.

Our primary submission applied morphology simplification and generation with the objective of ease the translation process when dealing with rich morphology languages like Spanish, deferring the morphology generation as an external post-process classification task.

The second approach focused on domain adaptation. Instead of concatenating the training News parallel data together with the European Parliament and United Nations, a preliminary system was built with the latter two and separated translation and reordering models were computed using the News parallel data. These models were then added to the preliminary models in order to build the adapted system.

Results showed that both approaches performed better than the baseline system, being the domain adaptation configuration the one that performed better for 2012 test in terms of all automatic quality indicators: BLEU, NIST, TER and METEOR. We look forward the the manual evaluation results as we believe our primary system may be more sensitive to this type of human evaluation.

Future work should focus on combining the two approaches, applying first morphological generalization to the training data and then using the domain adaptation technique on the resulting corpora in order to determine the joined benefits of both strategies.

Acknowledgments

This work has been partially funded by the Spanish Government (Buceador, TEC2009-14094-C04-01) and the European Community's FP7 program under grant agreement number 247762 (FAUST, FP7-ICT-2009-4-247762).

References

E. Avramidis and P. Koehn. 2008. Enriching morphologically poor languages for statistical machine translation. *Proceedings of ACL-08: HLT*, pages 763–770.

P.F. Brown, J. Cocke, S.A.D. Pietra, V.J.D. Pietra, F. Jelinek, J.D. Lafferty, R.L. Mercer, and P.S. Roossin. 1990. A statistical approach to machine translation. *Computational linguistics*, 16(2):79–85.

Ivan Bulyko, Spyros Matsoukas, Richard Schwartz, Long Nguyen, and John Makhoul. 2007. Language model adaptation in machine translation from speech. *Test*, 4:117–120.

S.F. Chen and J. Goodman. 1999. An empirical study of smoothing techniques for language modeling. *Computer Speech & Language*, 13(4):359–393.

Jorge Civera and Alfons Juan. 2007. Domain adaptation in statistical machine translation with mixture modelling. In *Proceedings of the Second Workshop on Statistical Machine Translation*, StatMT '07, pages 177–180, Stroudsburg, PA, USA. Association for Computational Linguistics.

A. Clifton and A. Sarkar. 2011. Combining morpheme-based machine translation with post-processing morpheme prediction. In *Proceedings of the 49th Annual Meeting of the Association for Computational Linguistics: Human Language Technologies. Portland, OR, USA*.

Adrià de de Gispert and José B. Mariño. 2008. On the impact of morphology in English to Spanish statistical MT. *Speech Communication*, 50(11-12):1034–1046.

Michael Denkowski and Alon Lavie. 2011. Meteor 1.3: Automatic Metric for Reliable Optimization and Evaluation of Machine Translation Systems. In *Proceedings of the EMNLP 2011 Workshop on Statistical Machine Translation*.

George Foster and Roland Kuhn. 2007. Mixture-Model Adaptation For SMT. In *Proceedings of the Second Workshop on Statistical Machine Translation*, StatMT '07, pages 128–135, Stroudsburg, PA, USA. Association for Computational Linguistics.

George Foster, Roland Kuhn, and Howard Johnson. 2006. Phrasetable smoothing for statistical machine translation. In *Proceedings of the 2006 Conference on Empirical Methods in Natural Language Processing*,

EMNLP '06, pages 53–61, Stroudsburg, PA, USA. Association for Computational Linguistics.

George Foster, Cyril Goutte, and Roland Kuhn. 2010. Discriminative instance weighting for domain adaptation in statistical machine translation. In *Proceedings of the 2010 Conference on Empirical Methods in Natural Language Processing*, pages 451–459, Cambridge, MA, October. Association for Computational Linguistics.

Carlos A. Henríquez Q., José B. Mariño, and Rafael E. Banchs. 2011. Deriving translation units using small additional corpora. In *Proceedings of the 15th Conference of the European Association for Machine Translation.*

Adolfo Hernández, Enric Monte, and José B. Mariño. 2010. Multiclass classification for Morphology generation in statistical machine translation. In *Proceedings of the VI Jornadas en Tecnología del Habla" and II Iberian SLTech Workshop*, pages 179–182, November. http://fala2010.uvigo.es.

Philipp Koehn and Hieu Hoang. 2007. Factored translation models. In *Proceedings of the 2007 Joint Conference on Empirical Methods in Natural Language Processing and Computational Natural Language Learning (EMNLP-CoNLL)*, pages 868–876, Prague, Czech Republic, June. Association for Computational Linguistics.

P. Koehn, H. Hoang, A. Birch, C. Callison-Burch, M. Federico, N. Bertoldi, B. Cowan, W. Shen, C. Moran, R. Zens, et al. 2007. Moses: Open source toolkit for statistical machine translation. In *Proceedings of the 45th Annual Meeting of the ACL on Interactive Poster and Demonstration Sessions*, pages 177–180. Association for Computational Linguistics.

Philipp Koehn. 2005. Europarl: A Parallel Corpus for Statistical Machine Translation. In *Machine Translation Summit.*

Shankar Kumar and William Bryne. 2004. Minimum bayes-risk decoding for statistical machine translation. In *Proceedings of the Human Language Technology and North American Association for Computational Linguistics Conference (HLT/NAACL)*, Boston,MA, May 27-June 1.

Behrang Mohit, Frank Liberato, and Rebecca Hwa. 2009. Language Model Adaptation for Difficult to Translate Phrases. In *Proceedings of the 13th Annual Conference of the EAMT.*

Franz Josef Och and Hermann Ney. 2003. A systematic comparison of various statistical alignment models. *Computational Linguistics*, 29(1):19–51.

Franz J. Och. 2003. Minimum error rate training in statistical machine translation. In *Proceedings of the Annual Meeting of the Association for Computational Linguistics (ACL).*

Lluís Padró, Miquel Collado, Samuel Reese, Marina Lloberes, and Irene Castellón. 2010. Freeling 2.1: Five years of open-source language processing tools. In *Proceedings of 7th Language Resources and Evaluation Conference (LREC 2010)*, La Valletta, MALTA, May. ELRA.

Kishore Papineni, Salim Roukos, Todd Ward, and Wei-Jing Zhu. 2002. BLEU: a method for automatic evaluation of machine translation. In *Proceedings of the Annual Meeting of the Association for Computational Linguistics (ACL).*

John C. Platt, Nello Cristianini, and John Shawe-taylor. 2000. Large margin DAGs for multiclass classification. In *Advances in Neural Information Processing Systems*, pages 547–553. MIT Press.

Maja Popovic and Hermann Ney. 2004. Towards the use of word stems and suffixes for statistical machine translation. In *Proceedings of the 4th International Conference on Language Resources and Evaluation, LREC'04*, pages 1585–1588, May.

M. Porter. 2001. Snowball: A language for stemming algorithms.

Matthew Snover, Bonnie Dorr, Richard Schwartz, Linnea Micciulla, and John Makhoul. 2006. A Study of Translation Edit Rate with Targeted Human Annotation. In *Proceedings of Association for Machine Translation in the Americas.*

A. Stolcke. 2002. Srilm-an extensible language modeling toolkit. In *Seventh International Conference on Spoken Language Processing.*

Kristina Toutanova, Hisami Suzuki, and Achim Ruopp. 2008. Applying morphology generation models to machine translation. In *Proceedings of ACL-08: HLT*, pages 514–522, Columbus, Ohio, June. Association for Computational Linguistics.

Nicola Ueffing and Hermann Ney. 2003. Using pos information for statistical machine translation into morphologically rich languages. In *Proceedings of the tenth conference on European chapter of the Association for Computational Linguistics - Volume 1*, EACL '03, pages 347–354, Stroudsburg, PA, USA. Association for Computational Linguistics.

S. Virpioja, J.J. Väyrynen, M. Creutz, and M. Sadeniemi. 2007. Morphology-aware statistical machine translation based on morphs induced in an unsupervised manner. *Machine Translation Summit XI*, 2007:491–498.

Hua Wu, Haifeng Wang, and Chengqing Zong. 2008. Domain adaptation for statistical machine translation with domain dictionary and monolingual corpora. In *Proceedings of the 22nd International Conference on Computational Linguistics - Volume 1*, COLING '08, pages 993–1000, Stroudsburg, PA, USA. Association for Computational Linguistics.

Joshua 4.0: Packing, PRO, and Paraphrases

Juri Ganitkevitch[1], Yuan Cao[1], Jonathan Weese[1], Matt Post[2], and Chris Callison-Burch[1]
[1]Center for Language and Speech Processing
[2]Human Language Technology Center of Excellence
Johns Hopkins University

Abstract

We present Joshua 4.0, the newest version of our open-source decoder for parsing-based statistical machine translation. The main contributions in this release are the introduction of a compact grammar representation based on packed tries, and the integration of our implementation of pairwise ranking optimization, J-PRO. We further present the extension of the Thrax SCFG grammar extractor to pivot-based extraction of syntactically informed sentential paraphrases.

1 Introduction

Joshua is an open-source toolkit[1] for parsing-based statistical machine translation of human languages. The original version of Joshua (Li et al., 2009) was a reimplementation of the Python-based Hiero machine translation system (Chiang, 2007). It was later extended to support grammars with rich syntactic labels (Li et al., 2010a). More recent efforts introduced the Thrax module, an extensible Hadoop-based extraction toolkit for synchronous context-free grammars (Weese et al., 2011).

In this paper we describe a set of recent extensions to the Joshua system. We present a new compact grammar representation format that leverages sparse features, quantization, and data redundancies to store grammars in a dense binary format. This allows for both near-instantaneous start-up times and decoding with extremely large grammars. In Section 2 we outline our packed grammar format and present experimental results regarding its impact on decoding speed, memory use and translation quality.

Additionally, we present Joshua's implementation of the pairwise ranking optimization (Hopkins and May, 2011) approach to translation model tuning. J-PRO, like Z-MERT, makes it easy to implement new metrics and comes with both a built-in perceptron classifier and out-of-the-box support for widely used binary classifiers such as MegaM and MaxEnt (Daumé III and Marcu, 2006; Manning and Klein, 2003). We describe our implementation in Section 3, presenting experimental results on performance, classifier convergence, and tuning speed.

Finally, we introduce the inclusion of bilingual pivoting-based paraphrase extraction into Thrax, Joshua's grammar extractor. Thrax's paraphrase extraction mode is simple to use, and yields state-of-the-art syntactically informed sentential paraphrases (Ganitkevitch et al., 2011). The full feature set of Thrax (Weese et al., 2011) is supported for paraphrase grammars. An easily configured feature-level pruning mechanism allows to keep the paraphrase grammar size manageable. Section 4 presents details on our paraphrase extraction module.

2 Compact Grammar Representation

Statistical machine translation systems tend to perform better when trained on larger amounts of bilingual parallel data. Using tools such as Thrax, translation models and their parameters are extracted and estimated from the data. In Joshua, translation models are represented as synchronous context-free grammars (SCFGs). An SCFG is a collection of

[1] `joshua-decoder.org`

rules $\{\mathbf{r}_i\}$ that take the form:

$$\mathbf{r}_i = C_i \rightarrow \langle \alpha_i, \gamma_i, \sim_i, \vec{\varphi}_i \rangle, \quad (1)$$

where *left-hand side* C_i is a nonterminal symbol, the *source side* α_i and the *target side* γ_i are sequences of both nonterminal and terminal symbols. Further, $\sim_i$ is a one-to-one correspondence between the nonterminal symbols of α_i and γ_i, and $\vec{\varphi}_i$ is a vector of features quantifying the probability of α_i translating to γ_i, as well as other characteristics of the rule (Weese et al., 2011). At decoding time, Joshua loads the grammar rules into memory in their entirety, and stores them in a trie data structure indexed by the rules' source side. This allows the decoder to efficiently look up rules that are applicable to a particular span of the (partially translated) input.

As the size of the training corpus grows, so does the resulting translation grammar. Using more diverse sets of nonterminal labels – which can significantly improve translation performance – further aggravates this problem. As a consequence, the space requirements for storing the grammar in memory during decoding quickly grow impractical. In some cases grammars may become too large to fit into the memory on a single machine.

As an alternative to the commonly used trie structures based on hash maps, we propose a packed trie representation for SCFGs. The approach we take is similar to work on efficiently storing large phrase tables by Zens and Ney (2007) and language models by Heafield (2011) and Pauls and Klein (2011) – both language model implementations are now integrated with Joshua.

2.1 Packed Synchronous Tries

For our grammar representation, we break the SCFG up into three distinct structures. As Figure 1 indicates, we store the grammar rules' source sides $\{\alpha_i\}$, target sides $\{\gamma_i\}$, and feature data $\{\vec{\varphi}_i\}$ in separate formats of their own. Each of the structures is packed into a flat array, and can thus be quickly read into memory. All terminal and nonterminal symbols in the grammar are mapped to integer symbol id's using a globally accessible vocabulary map. We will now describe the implementation details for each representation and their interactions in turn.

2.1.1 Source-Side Trie

The source-side trie (or source trie) is designed to facilitate efficient lookup of grammar rules by source side, and to allow us to completely specify a matching set of rule with a single integer index into the trie. We store the source sides $\{\alpha_i\}$ of a grammar in a downward-linking trie, i.e. each trie node maintains a record of its children. The trie is packed into an array of 32-bit integers. Figure 1 illustrates the composition of a node in the source-side trie. All information regarding the node is stored in a contiguous block of integers, and decomposes into two parts: a *linking block* and a *rule block*.

The linking block stores the links to the child trie nodes. It consists of an integer n, the number of children, and n blocks of two integers each, containing the symbol id a_j leading to the child and the child node's address s_j (as an index into the source-side array). The children in the link block are sorted by symbol id, allowing for a lookup via binary or interpolation search.

The rule block stores all information necessary to reconstruct the rules that share the source side that led to the current source trie node. It stores the number of rules, m, and then a tuple of three integers for each of the m rules: we store the symbol id of the left-hand side, an index into the target-side trie and a *data block id*. The rules in the data block are initially in an arbitrary order, but are sorted by application cost upon loading.

2.1.2 Target-Side Trie

The target-side trie (or target trie) is designed to enable us to uniquely identify a target side γ_i with a single pointer into the trie, as well as to exploit redundancies in the target side string. Like the source trie, it is stored as an array of integers. However, the target trie is a *reversed*, or upward-linking trie: a trie node retains a link to its parent, as well as the symbol id labeling said link.

As illustrated in Figure 1, the target trie is accessed by reading an array index from the source trie, pointing to a trie node at depth d. We then follow the parent links to the trie root, accumulating target side symbols g_j into a target side string g_1^d as we go along. In order to match this traversal, the target strings are entered into the trie in reverse order, i.e. last word first. In order to determine d from a

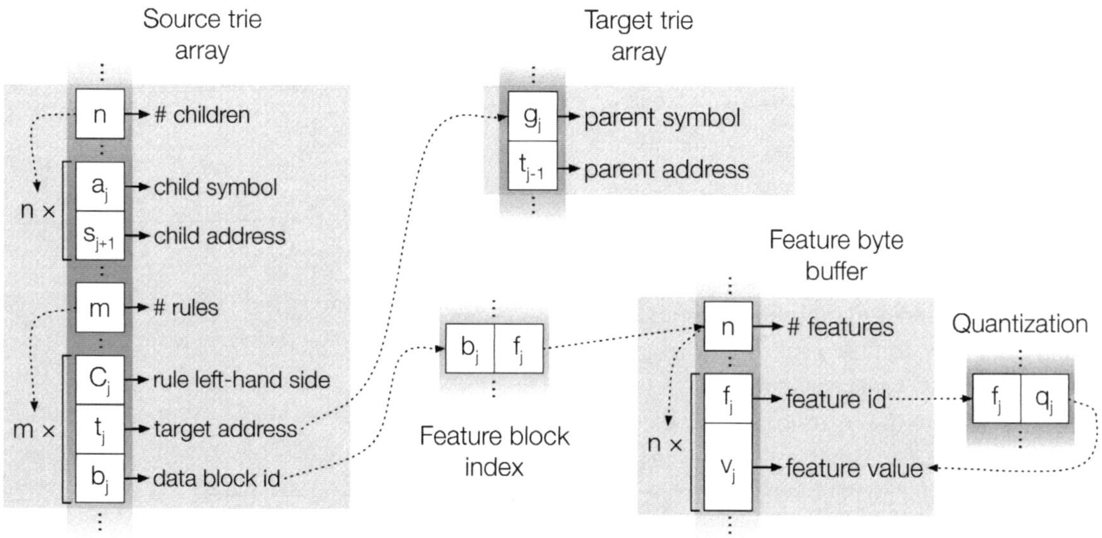

Figure 1: An illustration of our packed grammar data structures. The source sides of the grammar rules are stored in a packed trie. Each node may contain n children and the symbols linking to them, and m entries for rules that share the same source side. Each rule entry links to a node in the target-side trie, where the full target string can be retrieved by walking up the trie until the root is reached. The rule entries also contain a data block id, which identifies feature data attached to the rule. The features are encoded according to a type/quantization specification and stored as variable-length blocks of data in a byte buffer.

pointer into the target trie, we maintain an offset table in which we keep track of where each new trie level begins in the array. By first searching the offset table, we can determine d, and thus know how much space to allocate for the complete target side string.

To further benefit from the overlap there may be among the target sides in the grammar, we drop the nonterminal labels from the target string prior to inserting them into the trie. For richly labeled grammars, this collapses all lexically identical target sides that share the same nonterminal reordering behavior, but vary in nonterminal labels into a single path in the trie. Since the nonterminal labels are retained in the rules' source sides, we do not lose any information by doing this.

2.1.3 Features and Other Data

We designed the data format for the grammar rules' feature values to be easily extended to include other information that we may want to attach to a rule, such as word alignments, or locations of occurrences in the training data. In order to that, each rule $\mathbf{r}_i$ has a unique block id b_i associated with it. This block id identifies the information associated with the rule in every attached data store. All data stores are implemented as memory-mapped byte buffers that are only loaded into memory when actually requested by the decoder. The format for the feature data is detailed in the following.

The rules' feature values are stored as sparse features in contiguous blocks of variable length in a byte buffer. As shown in Figure 1, a lookup table is used to map the b_i to the index of the block in the buffer. Each block is structured as follows: a single integer, n, for the number of features, followed by n feature entries. Each feature entry is led by an integer for the feature id f_j, and followed by a field of variable length for the feature value v_j. The size of the value is determined by the type of the feature. Joshua maintains a quantization configuration which maps each feature id to a type handler or *quantizer*. After reading a feature id from the byte buffer, we retrieve the responsible quantizer and use it to read the value from the byte buffer.

Joshua's packed grammar format supports Java's standard primitive types, as well as an 8-bit quantizer. We chose 8 bit as a compromise between compression, value decoding speed and transla-

Grammar	Format	Memory
Hiero (43M rules)	Baseline	13.6G
	Packed	1.8G
Syntax (200M rules)	Baseline	99.5G
	Packed	9.8G
	Packed 8-bit	5.8G

Table 1: Decoding-time memory use for the packed grammar versus the standard grammar format. Even without lossy quantization the packed grammar representation yields significant savings in memory consumption. Adding 8-bit quantization for the real-valued features in the grammar reduces even large syntactic grammars to a manageable size.

tion performance (Federico and Bertoldi, 2006). Our quantization approach follows Federico and Bertoldi (2006) and Heafield (2011) in partitioning the value histogram into 256 equal-sized buckets. We quantize by mapping each feature value onto the weighted average of its bucket. Joshua allows for an easily per-feature specification of type. Quantizers can be share statistics across multiple features with similar value distributions.

2.2 Experiments

We assess the packed grammar representation's memory efficiency and impact on the decoding speed on the WMT12 French-English task. Table 1 shows a comparison of the memory needed to store our WMT12 French-English grammars at runtime. We can observe a substantial decrease in memory consumption for both Hiero-style grammars and the much larger syntactically annotated grammars. Even without any feature value quantization, the packed format achieves an 80% reduction in space requirements. Adding 8-bit quantization for the log-probability features yields even smaller grammar sizes, in this case a reduction of over 94%.

In order to avoid costly repeated retrievals of individual feature values of rules, we compute and cache the stateless application cost for each grammar rule at grammar loading time. This, alongside with a lazy approach to rule lookup allows us to largely avoid losses in decoding speed.

Figure shows a translation progress graph for the WMT12 French-English development set. Both sys-

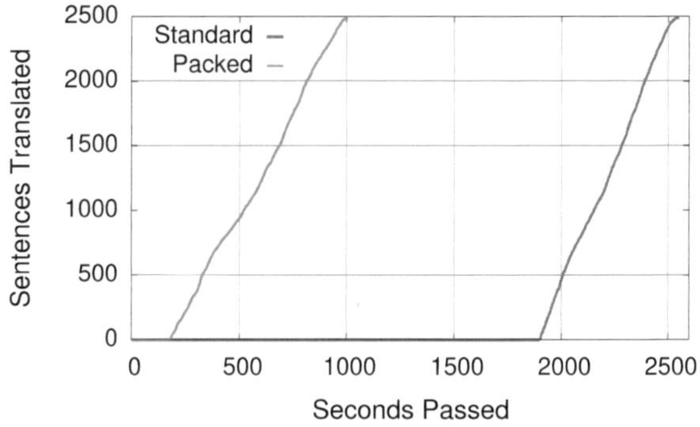

Figure 2: A visualization of the loading and decoding speed on the WMT12 French-English development set contrasting the packed grammar representation with the standard format. Grammar loading for the packed grammar representation is substantially faster than that for the baseline setup. Even with a slightly slower decoding speed (note the difference in the slopes) the packed grammar finishes in less than half the time, compared to the standard format.

tems load a Hiero-style grammar with 43 million rules, and use 16 threads for parallel decoding. The initial loading time for the packed grammar representation is dramatically shorter than that for the baseline setup (a total of 176 seconds for loading and sorting the grammar, versus 1897 for the standard format). Even though decoding speed is slightly slower with the packed grammars (an average of 5.3 seconds per sentence versus 4.2 for the baseline), the effective translation speed is more than twice that of the baseline (1004 seconds to complete decoding the 2489 sentences, versus 2551 seconds with the standard setup).

3 J-PRO: Pairwise Ranking Optimization in Joshua

Pairwise ranking optimization (PRO) proposed by (Hopkins and May, 2011) is a new method for discriminative parameter tuning in statistical machine translation. It is reported to be more stable than the popular MERT algorithm (Och, 2003) and is more scalable with regard to the number of features. PRO treats parameter tuning as an n-best list reranking problem, and the idea is similar to other pairwise ranking techniques like ranking SVM and IR SVMs

(Li, 2011). The algorithm can be described thusly:

Let $h(c) = \langle \mathbf{w}, \mathbf{\Phi}(c) \rangle$ be the linear model score of a candidate translation c, in which $\mathbf{\Phi}(c)$ is the feature vector of c and $\mathbf{w}$ is the parameter vector. Also let $g(c)$ be the metric score of c (without loss of generality, we assume a higher score indicates a better translation). We aim to find a parameter vector $\mathbf{w}$ such that for a pair of candidates $\{c_i, c_j\}$ in an n-best list,

$$(h(c_i) - h(c_j))(g(c_i) - g(c_j)) = \\ \langle \mathbf{w}, \mathbf{\Phi}(c_i) - \mathbf{\Phi}(c_j) \rangle (g(c_i) - g(c_j)) > 0,$$

namely the order of the model score is consistent with that of the metric score. This can be turned into a binary classification problem, by adding instance

$$\Delta\mathbf{\Phi}_{ij} = \mathbf{\Phi}(c_i) - \mathbf{\Phi}(c_j)$$

with class label $sign(g(c_i) - g(c_j))$ to the training data (and symmetrically add instance

$$\Delta\mathbf{\Phi}_{ji} = \mathbf{\Phi}(c_j) - \mathbf{\Phi}(c_i)$$

with class label $sign(g(c_j) - g(c_i))$ at the same time), then using any binary classifier to find the $\mathbf{w}$ which determines a hyperplane separating the two classes (therefore the performance of PRO depends on the choice of classifier to a large extent). Given a training set with T sentences, there are $O(Tn^2)$ pairs of candidates that can be added to the training set, this number is usually much too large for efficient training. To make the task more tractable, PRO samples a subset of the candidate pairs so that only those pairs whose metric score difference is large enough are qualified as training instances. This follows the intuition that high score differential makes it easier to separate good translations from bad ones.

3.1 Implementation

PRO is implemented in Joshua 4.0 named J-PRO. In order to ensure compatibility with the decoder and the parameter tuning module Z-MERT (Zaidan, 2009) included in all versions of Joshua, J-PRO is built upon the architecture of Z-MERT with similar usage and configuration files(with a few extra lines specifying PRO-related parameters). J-PRO inherits Z-MERT's ability to easily plug in new metrics. Since PRO allows using any off-the-shelf binary classifiers, J-PRO provides a Java interface that enables easy plug-in of any classifier. Currently, J-PRO supports three classifiers:

- *Perceptron* (Rosenblatt, 1958): the perceptron is self-contained in J-PRO, no external resources required.
- *MegaM* (Daumé III and Marcu, 2006): the classifier used by Hopkins and May (2011).[2]
- *Maximum entropy classifier* (Manning and Klein, 2003): the Stanford toolkit for maximum entropy classification.[3]

The user may specify which classifier he wants to use and the classifier-specific parameters in the J-PRO configuration file.

The PRO approach is capable of handling a large number of features, allowing the use of sparse discriminative features for machine translation. However, Hollingshead and Roark (2008) demonstrated that naively tuning weights for a heterogeneous feature set composed of both dense and sparse features can yield subpar results. Thus, to better handle the relation between dense and sparse features and provide a flexible selection of training schemes, J-PRO supports the following four training modes. We assume M dense features and N sparse features are used:

1. Tune the dense feature parameters only, just like Z-MERT (M parameters to tune).
2. Tune the dense + sparse feature parameters together ($M + N$ parameters to tune).
3. Tune the sparse feature parameters only with the dense feature parameters fixed, and sparse feature parameters scaled by a manually specified constant (N parameters to tune).
4. Tune the dense feature parameters and the scaling factor for sparse features, with the sparse feature parameters fixed (M+1 parameters to tune).

J-PRO supports n-best list input with a sparse feature format which enumerates only the firing features together with their values. This enables a more compact feature representation when numerous features are involved in training.

[2] `hal3.name/megam`

[3] `nlp.stanford.edu/software`

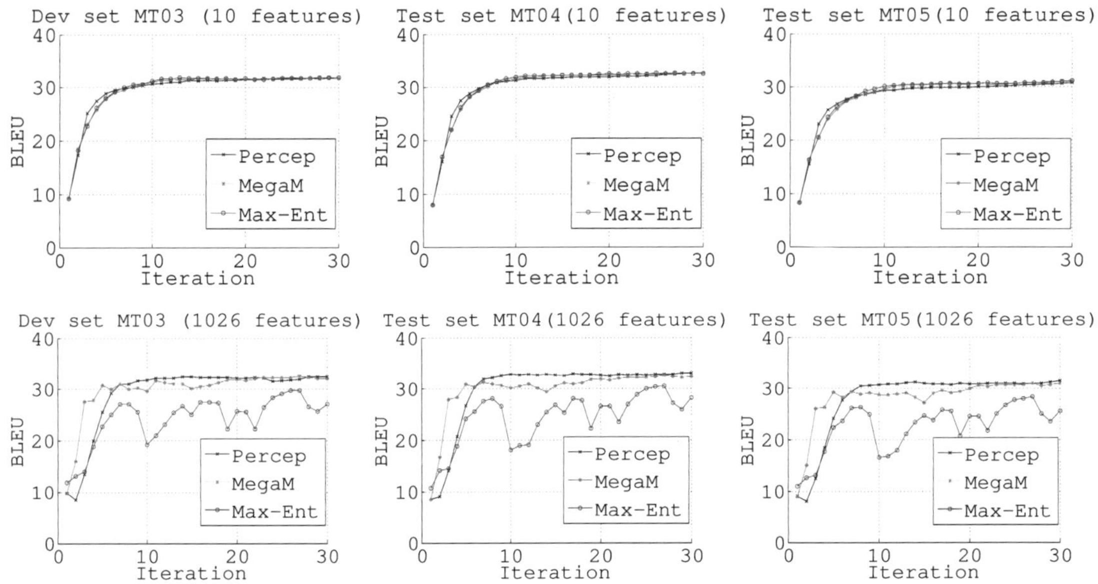

Figure 3: Experimental results on the development and test sets. The x-axis is the number of iterations (up to 30) and the y-axis is the BLEU score. The three curves in each figure correspond to three classifiers. Upper row: results trained using only dense features (10 features); Lower row: results trained using dense+sparse features (1026 features). Left column: development set (MT03); Middle column: test set (MT04); Right column: test set (MT05).

Datasets	Z-MERT	J-PRO		
		Percep	MegaM	Max-Ent
Dev (MT03)	32.2	31.9	32.0	32.0
Test (MT04)	32.6	32.7	32.7	32.6
Test (MT05)	30.7	30.9	31.0	30.9

Table 2: Comparison between the results given by Z-MERT and J-PRO (trained with 10 features).

3.2 Experiments

We did our experiments using J-PRO on the NIST Chinese-English data, and BLEU score was used as the quality metric for experiments reported in this section.[4] The experimental settings are as the following:

Datasets: MT03 dataset (998 sentences) as development set for parameter tuning, MT04 (1788 sentences) and MT05 (1082 sentences) as test sets.

Features: Dense feature set include the 10 regular features used in the Hiero system; Sparse feature set includes 1016 target-side rule POS bi-gram features as used in (Li et al., 2010b).

Classifiers: Perceptron, MegaM and Maximum entropy.

PRO parameters: $\Gamma = 8000$ (number of candidate pairs sampled uniformly from the n-best list), $\alpha = 1$ (sample acceptance probability), $\Xi = 50$ (number of top candidates to be added to the training set).

Figure 3 shows the BLEU score curves on the development and test sets as a function of iterations. The upper and lower rows correspond to the results trained with 10 dense features and 1026 dense+sparse features respectively. We intentionally selected very bad initial parameter vectors to verify the robustness of the algorithm. It can be seen that

[4]We also experimented with other metrics including TER, METEOR and TER-BLEU. Similar trends as reported in this section were observed. These results are omitted here due to limited space.

with each iteration, the BLEU score increases monotonically on both development and test sets, and begins to converge after a few iterations. When only 10 features are involved, all classifiers give almost the same performance. However, when scaled to over a thousand features, the maximum entropy classifier becomes unstable and the curve fluctuates significantly. In this situation MegaM behaves well, but the J-PRO built-in perceptron gives the most robust performance.

Table 2 compares the results of running Z-MERT and J-PRO. Since MERT is not able to handle numerous sparse features, we only report results for the 10-feature setup. The scores for both setups are quite close to each other, with Z-MERT doing slightly better on the development set but J-PRO yielding slightly better performance on the test set.

4 Thrax: Grammar Extraction at Scale

4.1 Translation Grammars

In previous years, our grammar extraction methods were limited by either memory-bounded extractors. Moving towards a parallelized grammar extraction process, we switched from Joshua's formerly built-in extraction module to Thrax for WMT11. However, we were limited to a simple pseudo-distributed Hadoop setup. In a pseudo-distributed cluster, all tasks run on separate cores on the same machine and access the local file system simultaneously, instead of being distributed over different physical machines and harddrives. This setup proved unreliable for larger extractions, and we were forced to reduce the amount of data that we used to train our translation models.

For this year, however, we had a permanent cluster at our disposal, which made it easy to extract grammars from all of the available WMT12 data. We found that on a properly distributed Hadoop setup Thrax was able to extract both Hiero grammars and the much larger SAMT grammars on the complete WMT12 training data for all tested language pairs. The runtimes and resulting (unfiltered) grammar sizes for each language pair are shown in Table 3 (for Hiero) and Table 4 (for SAMT).

Language Pair	Time	Rules
Cs – En	4h41m	133M
De – En	5h20m	219M
Fr – En	16h47m	374M
Es – En	16h22m	413M

Table 3: Extraction times and grammar sizes for Hiero grammars using the Europarl and News Commentary training data for each listed language pair.

Language Pair	Time	Rules
Cs – En	7h59m	223M
De – En	9h18m	328M
Fr – En	25h46m	654M
Es – En	28h10m	716M

Table 4: Extraction times and grammar sizes for the SAMT grammars using the Europarl and News Commentary training data for each listed language pair.

4.2 Paraphrase Extraction

Recently English-to-English text generation tasks have seen renewed interest in the NLP community. Paraphrases are a key component in large-scale state-of-the-art text-to-text generation systems. We present an extended version of Thrax that implements distributed, Hadoop-based paraphrase extraction via the pivoting approach (Bannard and Callison-Burch, 2005). Our toolkit is capable of extracting syntactically informed paraphrase grammars at scale. The paraphrase grammars obtained with Thrax have been shown to achieve state-of-the-art results on text-to-text generation tasks (Ganitkevitch et al., 2011).

For every supported translation feature, Thrax implements a corresponding *pivoted feature* for paraphrases. The pivoted features are set up to be aware of the prerequisite translation features they are derived from. This allows Thrax to automatically detect the needed translation features and spawn the corresponding map-reduce passes before the pivoting stage takes place. In addition to features useful for translation, Thrax also offers a number of features geared towards text-to-text generation tasks such as sentence compression or text simplification.

Due to the long tail of translations in unpruned

Source Bitext	Sentences	Words	Pruning	Rules
Fr – En	1.6M	45M	$p(e_1\|e_2), p(e_2\|e_1) > 0.001$	49M
{Da + Sv + Cs + De + Es + Fr} – En	9.5M	100M	$p(e_1\|e_2), p(e_2\|e_1) > 0.02$	31M
			$p(e_1\|e_2), p(e_2\|e_1) > 0.001$	91M

Table 5: Large paraphrase grammars extracted from EuroParl data using Thrax. The sentence and word counts refer to the English side of the bitexts used.

translation grammars and the combinatorial effect of pivoting, paraphrase grammars can easily grow very large. We implement a simple feature-level pruning approach that allows the user to specify upper or lower bounds for any pivoted feature. If a paraphrase rule is not within these bounds, it is discarded. Additionally, pivoted features are aware of the bounding relationship between their value and the value of their prerequisite translation features (i.e. whether the pivoted feature's value can be guaranteed to never be larger than the value of the translation feature). Thrax uses this knowledge to discard overly weak translation rules before the pivoting stage, leading to a substantial speedup in the extraction process.

Table 5 gives a few examples of large paraphrase grammars extracted from WMT training data. With appropriate pruning settings, we are able to obtain paraphrase grammars estimated over bitexts with more than 100 million words.

5 Additional New Features

- With the help of the respective original authors, the language model implementations by Heafield (2011) and Pauls and Klein (2011) have been integrated with Joshua, dropping support for the slower and more difficult to compile SRILM toolkit (Stolcke, 2002).

- We modified Joshua so that it can be used as a parser to analyze pairs of sentences using a synchronous context-free grammar. We implemented the two-pass parsing algorithm of Dyer (2010).

6 Conclusion

We present a new iteration of the Joshua machine translation toolkit. Our system has been extended towards efficiently supporting large-scale experiments in parsing-based machine translation and text-to-text generation: Joshua 4.0 supports compactly represented large grammars with its packed grammars, as well as large language models via KenLM and BerkeleyLM.We include an implementation of PRO, allowing for stable and fast tuning of large feature sets, and extend our toolkit beyond pure translation applications by extending Thrax with a large-scale paraphrase extraction module.

Acknowledgements This research was supported by in part by the EuroMatrixPlus project funded by the European Commission (7th Framework Programme), and by the NSF under grant IIS-0713448. Opinions, interpretations, and conclusions are the authors' alone.

References

Colin Bannard and Chris Callison-Burch. 2005. Paraphrasing with bilingual parallel corpora. In *Proceedings of ACL*.

David Chiang. 2007. Hierarchical phrase-based translation. *Computational Linguistics*, 33(2):201–228.

Hal Daumé III and Daniel Marcu. 2006. Domain adaptation for statistical classifiers. *Journal of Artificial Intelligence Research*, 26(1):101–126.

Chris Dyer. 2010. Two monolingual parses are better than one (synchronous parse). In *Proceedings of HLT/NAACL*, pages 263–266. Association for Computational Linguistics.

Marcello Federico and Nicola Bertoldi. 2006. How many bits are needed to store probabilities for phrase-based translation? In *Proceedings of WMT06*, pages 94–101. Association for Computational Linguistics.

Juri Ganitkevitch, Chris Callison-Burch, Courtney Napoles, and Benjamin Van Durme. 2011. Learning sentential paraphrases from bilingual parallel corpora for text-to-text generation. In *Proceedings of EMNLP*.

Kenneth Heafield. 2011. Kenlm: Faster and smaller language model queries. In *Proceedings of the Sixth Workshop on Statistical Machine Translation*, pages 187–197. Association for Computational Linguistics.

Kristy Hollingshead and Brian Roark. 2008. Reranking with baseline system scores and ranks as features. Technical report, Center for Spoken Language Understanding, Oregon Health & Science University.

Mark Hopkins and Jonathan May. 2011. Tuning as ranking. In *Proceedings of EMNLP*.

Zhifei Li, Chris Callison-Burch, Chris Dyer, Juri Ganitkevitch, Sanjeev Khudanpur, Lane Schwartz, Wren Thornton, Jonathan Weese, and Omar Zaidan. 2009. Joshua: An open source toolkit for parsing-based machine translation. In *Proc. WMT*, Athens, Greece, March.

Zhifei Li, Chris Callison-Burch, Chris Dyer, Juri Ganitkevitch, Ann Irvine, Sanjeev Khudanpur, Lane Schwartz, Wren N.G. Thornton, Ziyuan Wang, Jonathan Weese, and Omar F. Zaidan. 2010a. Joshua 2.0: a toolkit for parsing-based machine translation with syntax, semirings, discriminative training and other goodies. In *Proc. WMT*.

Zhifei Li, Ziyuan Wang, and Sanjeev Khudanpur. 2010b. Unsupervised discriminative language model training for machine translation using simulated confusion sets. In *Proceedings of COLING*, Beijing, China, August.

Hang Li. 2011. *Learning to Rank for Information Retrieval and Natural Language Processing*. Morgan & Claypool Publishers.

Chris Manning and Dan Klein. 2003. Optimization, maxent models, and conditional estimation without magic. In *Proceedings of HLT/NAACL*, pages 8–8. Association for Computational Linguistics.

Franz Och. 2003. Minimum error rate training in statistical machine translation. In *Proceedings of the 41rd Annual Meeting of the Association for Computational Linguistics (ACL-2003)*, Sapporo, Japan.

Adam Pauls and Dan Klein. 2011. Faster and smaller n-gram language models. In *Proceedings of ACL*, pages 258–267, Portland, Oregon, USA, June. Association for Computational Linguistics.

Frank Rosenblatt. 1958. The perceptron: A probabilistic model for information storage and organization in the brain. *Psychological Review*, 65(6):386–408.

Andreas Stolcke. 2002. Srilm - an extensible language modeling toolkit. In *Seventh International Conference on Spoken Language Processing*.

Jonathan Weese, Juri Ganitkevitch, Chris Callison-Burch, Matt Post, and Adam Lopez. 2011. Joshua 3.0: Syntax-based machine translation with the Thrax grammar extractor. In *Proceedings of WMT11*.

Omar F. Zaidan. 2009. Z-MERT: A fully configurable open source tool for minimum error rate training of machine translation systems. *The Prague Bulletin of Mathematical Linguistics*, 91:79–88.

Richard Zens and Hermann Ney. 2007. Efficient phrase-table representation for machine translation with applications to online MT and speech translation. In *Proceedings of HLT/NAACL*, pages 492–499, Rochester, New York, April. Association for Computational Linguistics.

Syntax-aware Phrase-based Statistical Machine Translation: System Description

Ulrich Germann
University of Toronto
Toronto, Ontario, Canada
germann@cs.toronto.edu

Abstract

We present a variant of phrase-based SMT that uses source-side parsing and a constituent reordering model based on word alignments in the word-aligned training corpus to predict hierarchical block-wise reordering of the input. Multiple possible translation orders are represented compactly in a source order lattice. This source order lattice is then annotated with phrase-level translations to form a lattice of tokens in the target language. Various feature functions are combined in a log-linear fashion to evaluate paths through that lattice.

1 Introduction

Dealing with word order differences is one of the major challenges in automatic translation between human languages. With its moderate context sensitivity and reliance on n-gram language models, *phrase-based statistical machine translation* (PB-SMT) (Koehn *et al.*, 2003) is usually quite good at performing small word order changes — for instance, the inversion of adjective and noun in English-to-French translation and vice versa. However, it regularly fails to execute word order changes over long distances, as they are required, for example, to accommodate the substantial differences in the word order in subordinate clauses between German and English, or to cope with the phenomenon of the "sentence bracket" (*Satzklammer*) in German main clauses, in which the finite part of the verb complex and additional elements (separable prefixes, participles, infinitives, etc.) form a bracket that encloses most of the arguments and other adverbial constituents, as shown in Fig. 1. In order to keep decoding complexity in check, phrase-based decoders such as the *Moses* system (Koehn *et al.*, 2007) routinely limit the maximum distance for word order changes to six or seven word positions, thus ruling out, a priori, word order changes necessary to achieve good and fluent translations.

As is generally acknowledged, word order differences are not entirely arbitrary. By and large they follow syntactic structure. An analysis of word-aligned French-English data by Fox (2002) showed that word alignment links rarely cross syntactic boundaries. Wu's (1997) *Inversion Transaction Grammar* (ITG), assumes that word order differences can be accounted for by hierarchical inversion of adjacent blocks of text. Yamada and Knight (2001) present a stochastic model for transforming English parse trees into Japanese word sequences within a source-channel framework for Japanese-to-English translation. Collins *et al.* (2005) perform heuristic word re-ordering from German into English word order based on German parse trees with a particular focus on the aforementioned drastic word order differences between German and English clause structure.

Building on Chiang (2007), several systems under active development (e.g., Weese *et al.*, 2011; Dyer *et al.*, 2010) rely on synchronous context-free grammars to deal with word order differences. In essence, these systems parse the input while synchronously building a parse tree in the translation target language, using probabilities of the source and target trees as well as correspondence probabilities to evaluate translation hypotheses.

"Dieser$_1$ Vorschlag$_2$ [wird$_3$] sicherlich$_4$ im$_5$ Ausschuß$_6$ gründlich$_7$ [diskutiert$_8$ werden$_9$ müssen$_{10}$]."

"This$_1$ proposal$_2$ will$_3$ certainly$_4$ have$_{10}$ to$_{10}$ be$_9$ discussed$_8$ toroughly$_7$ in$_5$ the$_5$ commission$_6$."

Figure 1: The sentence bracket (*Satzklammer*) in German.

The system presented in this paper takes a slightly different route and is closer to the approach taken by Collins *et al.* (2005): we parse only monolingually on the source side, re-order, and then translate. However, unlike Collins *et al.* we do not use a series of rules to perform the transformations (nor do we re-order the training data on the source side), but try to learn reordering rules from the word-aligned corpus with the original word order on both sides. Moreover, we do not commit to a single parse and a single re-ordering of the source at translation time but consider multiple parse alternatives to create a lattice of possible translation orders. Each vertex in the lattice corresponds to a specific subset of source words translated up to that point.

Individual edges and sequences of edges in this lattice are annotated with word- and phrase[1]-level translations extracted from the word-aligned training corpus, in the same way as phrase tables for PBSMT are constructed[2]. An optimal path through the lattice is determined by dynamic programming, considering a variety of feature functions combined in a log-linear fashion.

In the following, we first describe the individual processing steps in more detail and then try to shed some light on the system's performance in this year's shared task. Due to space limitations, many details will have to be skipped.

2 System Description

2.1 Grammatical framework

The central idea underlying this work is that grammar constrains word reordering: we are allowed to permute siblings in a CFG tree, or the governor and its dependents in a dependency structure, but we are not allowed to break phrase coherence by moving words out of their respective sub-tree. Obviously, we need to be careful in the precise formulation of our grammar, so as not to over-constrain word order options. For example, the German parse tree for the phrase *ein*$_1$ [*zu hoher*]$_2$ *Preis*$_3$ in Fig. 2 below rules out the proper word order of its English translation [*too high*]$_2$ *a*$_1$ *price*$_3$.

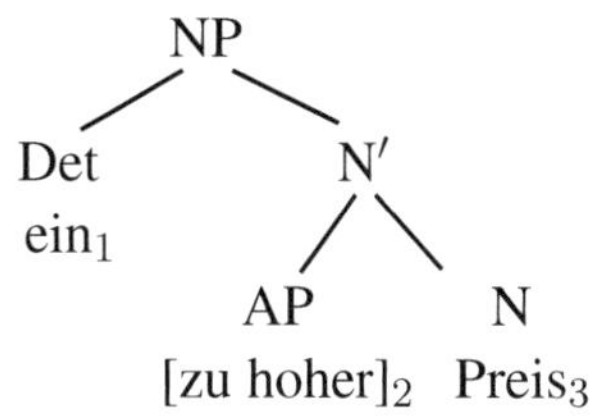

Figure 2: X-bar syntax can be too restrictive. This tree does not allow the word order of the English translation [*too high*]$_2$ *a*$_1$ *price*$_3$.

In her analysis of phrasal cohesion in translation, Fox (2002) pointed out that phrasal cohesion is greater with respect to dependency structure than with respect to constituent structure. We therefore decided to rely on the segmentation granularity inherent in dependency parses.

2.2 Parsing

For parsing, we developed our own hybrid left-corner dependency parser for German. In many respects, it is inspired by the work on dependency parsing by Eisner (1996) (edge factorization) and McDonald *et al.* (2005) (choice of features for edge scores). From the generative point of view, we can imagine the following generative process: We start with the root word of the sentence. A Markov process then generates this word's immediate dependents from left to right, at some point placing the head word itself. The dependents (but not the head word) are then expanded recursively in the same fashion. At parse time we process the input left to right, deciding for each word what its governors are, or whether it governs some items to its left or right.

[1]"Phrase" being any contiguous sequence of words in this context, as in PBSMT.

[2]Except that we do not pre-compute phrase tables but construct them dynamically on the fly using suffix arrays, as suggested by Callison-Burch *et al.* (2005).

Since each word has exactly one governor (bar the root word), we renormalize edge scores by marginalizing over the potential governors. If the word is potentially the left corner of a sub-tree, we establish a new rule (akin to a dotted rule in an Earley parser) and add it to the parse chart. For potential governors to the left, we scan the parse chart for partial productions that end immediately before the word in question and extend them by the word in question. Whenever we add an item to a partial production that is "past or reaching its head" (i.e., the span covered by the rule includes the sub-tree's root or the newly added item is the root), we treat the sub-tree as a new item in a bottom-up fashion, i.e., determine potential governors outside of the span covered, add a new rule if the sub-tree could be the left corner of a larger sub-tree, etc. In addition to the joint probability of all individual edges, we also consider the cost of adding an item to a partial production. To reduce parse complexity, we use a beam to limit the number of potential governors that are considered for each item. Unlike conventional CFGs, the set of "rules" in this grammar is not finite; rules are generated on the fly by a Markov process. This adds robustness; we can always attach an item (token or sub-tree) to one of its immediate neighbors.

2.3 Construction of a source order lattice (SOL)

Rows and columns in the parse chart correspond to the start and end positions of parse spans in the sentence. Each cell contains zero or more production rules that correspond to different segmentations of the respective span into sub-spans that may be reordered during translation. Based on the underlying part-of-speech tags, we retrieve similar syntactic configurations from the word-aligned, source-side-parsed training corpus.

For each example retrieved from the training corpus, we determine, from the word alignment information in the training corpus, the order in which the dependents and the head word are translated. To reduce noise from alignment errors, each example is weighted by the joint lexical translation probability of the words immediately involved in the production (i.e., the head and its dependents, but not grandchildren). Thus, examples with unlikely word alignments count less than examples that have highly probable word alignments. If exact matches for the production rule in question cannot be found in the corpus (which happens frequently), we fall back on a factorized model that maps from source to target positions based on the part-of-speech of the dependent in question and its governor. Words that are part of the verb complex (auxiliaries, separable prefixes, the 'lexical head', etc.) are grouped together and receive special treatment. (This is currently work in progress; at this point, we translate only the lexical head, but ignore negation and auxiliaries.)

For each of the top N segmentations suggested by the parser, translation order probabilities are computed on the basis of the weighted occurrence counts, and used to set the edge weights in a lattice of possible translation orders, which we call the Source Order Lattice (SOL). Each vertex in this lattice corresponds to a specific set of source words translated so far. (In principle, the number of vertices in this lattice is exponential in the length of the input sentence; in practice, since we consider only a small number of possibilities, their number is quite manageable.) For each chunk of text in the suggested order of translation, we increase the weight of the edge between the vertex representing the set of words translated so far and the vertex representing the set of words translated after this chunk has been translated by the probability of translating the chunk in question at this particular point in the translation process. Edges representing two or more consecutive words (with the exception of those representing a verb complex) are recursively replaced by local SOLs, until each edge corresponds to a single word in the source sentence.

2.4 Constructing a target word lattice

The global SOL thus constructed is then transformed into a Target Word Lattice (TWL), while maintaining underlying alignment information. Each individual edge or sequence of adjacent edges corresponding to a contiguous sequence of words in the source sentence is replaced by a lattice that encodes the range of possible translations for the respective word or phrase. Translations are extracted from the word-aligned bilingual training corpus with the phrase-extraction method that is commonly used in phrase-based SMT. As it is done in the *Joshua* system (Weese *et al.*, 2011), we extract phrase translations on the fly from the word-aligned bilingual corpus using suffix arrays instead of using pre-computed phrase tables.

2.5 Search

Once constructed, the TWL is searched with dynamic programming with a beam search. Hypotheses are scored by a log-linear combination of the following feature functions. Feature values are normalized by hypothesis length unless noted otherwise, to safeguard against growth of cumulative feature values at different rates as the length of a hypothesis increases, and to keep hypotheses of different lengths mutually comparable.

- **Distortion probabilities** from the SOL as described above.
- **Relative phrase translation frequencies** based on counts in the training corpus.
- **Lexical translation probabilities**: forward ($\mathrm{p}\,(\textit{target} \mid \textit{source})$; normalized by target length) and backward ($\mathrm{p}\,(\textit{source} \mid \textit{target})$; normalized by source length). Lexical translation probabilities are based on alignment link counts in the word-aligned corpus.
- ***N*-gram language model probability** as estimated with the SRILM toolkit.
- **Fluency**. Simple length-based normalization of joint n-gram probabilities is problematic. It entices the decoder to "throw in" additional, highly frequent words to increase the language model score. Inversely, lack of normalization provides an incentive to keep translation hypotheses as short as possible, even at the expense of fluency. This fluency feature function computes the ratio of the language model probability of each proposed target word in context and its unigram probability. Rewards ($\mathrm{p}\,(w_i \mid w_{i-k+1} \ldots w_{i-1}) > \mathrm{p}\,(w_i)$) and penalties ($\mathrm{p}\,(w_i \mid w_{i-k+1} \ldots w_{i-1}) < \mathrm{p}\,(w_i)$) receive different weights in the log-linear combination. Rewards are normalized by target length; penalties by the number of source words translated. The rationale between the different forms of normalization is this: if we don't normalize rewards by hypothesis length, we have an incentive to pad the translation with highly frequent tokens (commas, 'the') wherever their probability in context is higher than their simple unigram probability. Awkwardly placed tokens, on the other hand, should always trigger a penalty, and the system should not be allowed to soften the blow by adding more poorly, but not quite as poorly placed tokens. Normalization of penalties by covered source length is an acknowledgement of the fact that in longer sentences, the probability of having points of disfluency increases. We use two reward/penalty pairs sets of fluency feature functions. One operates on surface forms, the other one on part-of-speech tag sequences.
- **Cumulative probability density of observed n-gram counts.** This feature function penalizes n-grams that do not occur as often as they should (even if observed), based on prior observation, and rewards those that do. Consider the following sequence of words in English:

  can you are

  The sequence *can you* is fairly frequent, and so is *you are*. However, *can you are* is not. With standard n-gram back-off models, the model, upon not finding the full context *can you* for *are*, will back off to the context *you* and thus assign an inappropriately high probability to $\mathrm{p}\,(\textit{are} \mid \textit{can you})$.

  The n-gram cdf feature models the event as a Bernoulli experiment. Suppose, for example, that $p\,(\textit{are} \mid \textit{you}) = .01$, and we have observed *can you* 1000 times, but have never seen *can you are*. Then the expected count of observations is 10 and

  $$\mathrm{cdf}\,(0 \mid 1000; .01) = (1 - .01)^{1000} \approx .000043$$

3 Training and tuning

The system was trained on the German-English part of Europarl corpus (v.5). The language model for English was trained on all monolingual data available for WMT-2010. We true-cased, but did not lower-case the data. Word alignment was performed with multi-threaded Giza++ (Gao and Vogel, 2008).

In order to bootstrap training data for our parser, we parsed the German side of the Europarl corpus with the Berkeley Parser (Petrov *et al.*, 2006; Petrov and Klein, 2007) and converted the CFG structures to dependency structures using simple hand-written heuristics to identify the head in each phrase, similar to those used by Magerman (1995) and Collins (1996). This head was then selected as the governor of the respective phrase. Part-of-speech tagging and lemmatization on the English side as well as the German development and test data was performed with the tool TreeTagger (Schmid, 1995).

For tuning the model parameters, we tried to apply pairwise rank optimization (PRO) (Hopkins and May, 2011), but we were not able to achieve results that beat our hand-tuned parameter settings.

4 Evaluation

Unfortunately, with a BLEU score of .121, (.150 after several bug fixes in the program code), our system performed extremely poorly in the shared task. We have since tried to track down the reasons for the poor performance, but have not been able to find a compelling explanation for it.

A partial explanation may lie in the fact that we used only the Europarl data for training.[3] However, our system also lags far behind a baseline Moses system trained on the same subset of data used for our system, which achieves a BLEU score of .184.

Since our feature functions are very similar to those used in MOSES, we suspect that better tuning of the feature weights might close the gap. We are currently in the process of implementing and testing other parameter tuning methods (in addition to manual tuning and PRO), specifically lattice-based minimum error rate training (Macherey *et al.*, 2008) and batch MIRA (Cherry and Foster, 2012).

5 Conclusion

We have presented a variant of PBSMT that uses syntactic information from source-side parses in order to account better for word-order differences in German-to-English machine translation, while preserving the advantages of PBSMT. Several components were developed from scratch, such as a dependency parser for German and a reordering model for parse constituents, as well as several novel variants of n-gram based fluency measures. While our results for this year's shared task are certainly disappointing, we nevertheless believe that we are on the right track. We are not ready to give up quite yet.

[3]Participation in the shared task was a short term decision, and we did not have the time to re-train our system.

References

Callison-Burch, Chris, Colin Bannard, and Josh Schroeder. 2005. "Scaling phrase-based statistical machine translation to larger corpora and longer phrases." *43rd Annual Meeting of the Association for Computational Linguistics (ACL '05)*, 255–262. Ann Arbor, Michigan.

Cherry, Colin and George Foster. 2012. "Batch tuning strategies for statistical machine translation." *2012 Meeting of the North American Chapter of the Association for Computational Linguistics: Human Language Technologies*. Montréal, Quebéc, Canada.

Chiang, David. 2007. "Hierarchical phrase-based translation." *Computational Linguistics*, 33(2):1–28.

Collins, Michael, Philipp Koehn, and Kučerová Ivona. 2005. "Clause restructuring for statistical machine translation." *43rd Annual Meeting of the Association for Computational Linguistics (ACL '05)*. Ann Arbor, MI, USA.

Collins, Michael John. 1996. "A new statistical parser based on bigram lexical dependencies." *Proceedings of the 34th Annual Meeting of the Association for Computational Linguistics*, 184–191. Santa Cruz, California, USA.

Dyer, Chris, Adam Lopez, Juri Ganitkevitch, Jonathan Weese, Ferhan Ture, Phil Blunsom, Hendra Setiawan, Vladimir Eidelman, and Philip Resnik. 2010. "cdec: A decoder, alignment, and learning framework for finite-state and context-free translation models." *Proceedings of the ACL 2010 System Demonstrations*, 7–12. Uppsala, Sweden.

Eisner, Jason M. 1996. "Three new probabilistic models for dependency parsing: An exploration." *The 16th International Conference on Computational Linguistics (COLING '96)*, 340–345. Copenhagen, Denmark.

Fox, Heidi J. 2002. "Phrasal cohesion and statistical machine translation." *Conference on Em-*

pirical Methods in Natural Language Processing (EMNLP '02), 304–311. Philadelphia, PA.

Gao, Qin and Stephan Vogel. 2008. "Parallel implementations of word alignment tool." *Workshop on Software Engineering, Testing, and Quality Assurance for Natural Language Processing*, 49–57. Columbus, Ohio.

Hopkins, Mark and Jonathan May. 2011. "Tuning as ranking." *Conference on Empirical Methods in Natural Language Processing (EMNLP '11)*. Edinburgh, UK.

Koehn, Philipp, Hieu Hoang, Alexandra Birch, Chris Callison-Burch, Marcello Federico, Nicola Bertoldi, Brooke Cowan, Wade Shen, Christine Moran, Richard Zens, Chris Dyer, Ondrej Bojar, Alexandra Constantin, and Evan Herbst. 2007. "Moses: Open source toolkit for statistical machine translation." *45th Annual Meeting of the Association for Computational Linguistics (ACL '07): Demonstration Session*. Prague, Czech Republic.

Koehn, Philipp, Franz Josef Och, and Daniel Marcu. 2003. "Statistical phrase-based translation." *Human Language Technology Conference of the North American Chapter of the Association for Computational Linguistics (HLT-NAACL '03)*, 48–54. Edmonton, AB, Canada.

Macherey, Wolfgang, Franz Och, Ignacio Thayer, and Jakob Uszkoreit. 2008. "Lattice-based minimum error rate training for statistical machine translation." *Conference on Empirical Methods in Natural Language Processing (EMNLP '08)*, 725–734. Honolulu, Hawaii.

Magerman, David M. 1995. "Statistical decision-tree models for parsing." *Proceedings of the Annual Meeting of the ACL*, 276–283.

McDonald, Ryan, Koby Crammer, and Fernando Pereira. 2005. "Online large-margin training of dependency parsers." *Proceedings of the 43rd Annual Meeting of the Association for Computational Linguistics (ACL'05)*, 91–98. Ann Arbor, Michigan.

Petrov, Slav, Leon Barrett, Romain Thibaux, and Dan Klein. 2006. "Learning accurate, compact, and interpretable tree annotation." *Proceedings of the 21st International Conference on Computational Linguistics and 44th Annual Meeting of the Association for Computational Linguistics*, 433–440. Sydney, Australia.

Petrov, Slav and Dan Klein. 2007. "Improved inference for unlexicalized parsing." *Human Language Technologies 2007: The Conference of the North American Chapter of the Association for Computational Linguistics; Proceedings of the Main Conference*, 404–411. Rochester, New York.

Schmid, Helmut. 1995. "Improvements in part-of-speech tagging with an application to German." *In Proceedings of the ACL SIGDAT-Workshop*, 47–50. Dublin, Ireland.

Weese, Jonathan, Juri Ganitkevitch, Chris Callison-Burch, Matt Post, and Adam Lopez. 2011. "Joshua 3.0: Syntax-based machine translation with the Thrax grammar extractor." *Proceedings of the Sixth Workshop on Statistical Machine Translation*, 478–484. Edinburgh, Scotland.

Wu, Dekai. 1997. "Stochastic inversion transduction grammars and bilingual parsing of parallel corpora." *Computational Linguistics*, 23(3):377–403.

Yamada, Kenji and Kevin Knight. 2001. "A syntax-based statistical translation model." *39th Annual Meeting of the Association for Computational Linguistics (ACL '01)*. Toulouse, France.

QCRI at WMT12: Experiments in Spanish-English and German-English Machine Translation of News Text

Francisco Guzmán, Preslav Nakov, Ahmed Thabet, Stephan Vogel
Qatar Computing Research Institute
Qatar Foundation
Tornado Tower, floor 10, PO box 5825
Doha, Qatar
{fguzman,pnakov,ahawad,svogel}@qf.org.qa

Abstract

We describe the systems developed by the team of the Qatar Computing Research Institute for the WMT12 Shared Translation Task. We used a phrase-based statistical machine translation model with several non-standard settings, most notably tuning data selection and phrase table combination. The evaluation results show that we rank second in BLEU and TER for Spanish-English, and in the top tier for German-English.

1 Introduction

The team of the Qatar Computing Research Institute (QCRI) participated in the Shared Translation Task of WMT12 for two language pairs:[1] Spanish-English and German-English. We used the state-of-the-art phrase-based model (Koehn et al., 2003) for statistical machine translation (SMT) with several non-standard settings, e.g., data selection and phrase table combination. The evaluation results show that we rank second in BLEU (Papineni et al., 2002) and TER (Snover et al., 2006) for Spanish-English, and in the top tier for German-English.

In Section 2, we describe the parameters of our baseline system and the non-standard settings we experimented with. In Section 3, we discuss our primary and secondary submissions for the two language pairs. Finally, in Section 4, we provide a short summary.

[1]The WMT12 organizers invited systems translating between English and four other European languages, in both directions: French, Spanish, German, and Czech. However, we only participated in Spanish→English and German→English.

2 System Description

Below, in Section 2.1, we first describe our initial configuration; then, we discuss our incremental improvements. We explored several non-standard settings and extensions and we evaluated their impact with respect to different baselines. These baselines are denoted in the tables below by a #number that corresponds to systems in Figures 1 for Spanish-English and in Figure 2 for German-English.

We report case insensitive BLEU calculated on the news2011 testing data using the NIST scoring tool v.11b.

2.1 Initial Configuration

Our baseline system can be summarized as follows:

- Training: News Commentary + Europarl training bi-texts;
- Tuning: news2010;
- Testing: news2011;
- Tokenization: splitting words containing a dash, e.g., *first-order* becomes *first @-@ order*;
- Maximum sentence length: 100 tokens;
- Truecasing: convert sentence-initial words to their most frequent case in the training dataset;
- Word alignments: directed IBM model 4 (Brown et al., 1993) alignments in both directions, then *grow-diag-final-and* heuristics;
- Maximum phrase length: 7 tokens;
- Phrase table scores: forward & reverse phrase translation probabilities, forward & reverse lexical translation probabilities, phrase penalty;

- Language model: 5-gram, trained on the target side of the two training bi-texts;
- Reordering: lexicalized, *msd-bidirectional-fe*;
- Detokenization: reconnecting words that were split around dashes;
- Model parameter optimization: minimum error rate training (MERT), optimizing BLEU.

2.2 Phrase Tables

We experimented with two non-standard settings:

Smoothing. The four standard scores associated with each phrase pair in the phrase table (forward & reverse phrase translation probabilities, forward & reverse lexical translation probabilities) are normally used unsmoothed. We also experimented with Good-Turing and Kneser-Ney smoothing (Chen and Goodman, 1999). As Table 1 shows, the latter works a bit better for both Spanish-English and German-English.

	es-en	de-en
Baseline (es:#3,de:#4)	29.98	22.03
Good Turing	29.98	22.07
Kneser-Ney	**30.16**	**22.30**

Table 1: **Phrase table smoothing.**

Phrase table combination. We built two phrase tables, one for News Commentary + Europarl and an additional one for the UN bi-text. We then merged them,[2] adding additional features to each entry in the merged phrase table: F_1, F_2, and F_3. The value of F_1/F_2 is 1 if the phrase pair came from the first/second phrase table, and 0.5 otherwise, while F_3 is 1 if the phrase pair was in both tables, and 0.5 otherwise. We optimized the weights for all features, including the additional ones, using MERT.[3] Table 2 shows that this improves by +0.42 BLEU points.

[2]In theory, we should also re-normalize the conditional probabilities (forward/reverse phrase translation probability, and forward/reverse lexicalized phrase translation probability) since they may not sum to one anymore. In practice, this is not that important since the log-linear phrase-based SMT model does not require that the phrase table features be probabilities (e.g., F_1, F_2, F_3, and the phrase penalty are not probabilities); moreover, we have extra features whose impact is bigger.

[3]This is similar but different from (Nakov, 2008): when a phrase pair appeared in both tables, they only kept the entry from the first table, while we keep the entries from both tables.

	es-en
Baseline (es:#7)	30.94
Merging (1) News+EP with (2) UN	**31.36**

Table 2: **Phrase table merging.**

2.3 Language Models

We built the language models (LM) for our systems using a probabilistic 5-gram model with Kneser-Ney (KN) smoothing. We experimented with LMs trained on different training datasets. We used the SRILM toolkit (Stolcke, 2002) for training the language models, and the KenLM toolkit (Heafield and Lavie, 2010) for binarizing the resulting ARPA models for faster loading with the Moses decoder (Koehn et al., 2007).

2.3.1 Using WMT12 Corpora Only

We trained 5-gram LMs on datasets provided by the task organizers. The results are presented in Table 3. The first line reports the baseline BLEU scores using a language model trained on the target side of the News Commentary + Europarl training bi-texts. The second line shows the results when using an interpolation (minimizing the perplexity on the news2010 tuning dataset) of different language models, trained on the following corpora:

- the monolingual News Commentary corpus plus the English sides of all training News Commentary v.7 bi-texts (for French-English, Spanish-English, German-English, and Czech-English), with duplicate sentences removed (5.5M word tokens; one LM);
- the News Crawl 2007-2011 corpora, (1213M word tokens; separate LM for each of these five years);
- the Europarl v.7 monolingual corpus (60M word tokens; one LM);
- the English side of the Spanish-English UN bi-text (360M word tokens; one LM).

The last line in Table 3 shows the results when using an additional 5-gram LM in the interpolation, one trained on the English side of the 10^9 French-English bi-text (662M word tokens).

We can see that using these interpolations yields very sizable improvements of 1.7-2.5 BLEU points over the baseline. However, while the impact of adding the 10^9 bi-text to the interpolation is clearly visible for Spanish-English (+0.47 BLEU), it is almost negligible for German-English (+0.06 BLEU).

Corpora	es-en	de-en
Baseline (es:#1, de:#2)	27.34	20.01
News + EP + UN (interp.)	29.36	21.66
News + EP + UN + 10^9 (interp.)	**29.83**	**21.72**

Table 3: **LMs using the provided corpora only.**

2.3.2 Using Gigaword

In addition to the WMT12 data, we used the LDC Gigaword v.5 corpus. We divided the corpus into reasonably-sized chunks of text of about 2GB per chunk, and we built a separate intermediate language model for each chunk. Then, we interpolated these language models, minimizing the perplexity on the news2010 development set as with the previous LMs. We experimented with two different strategies for creating the chunks by segmenting the corpus according to (a) data source, e.g., AFP, Xinhua, etc., and (b) year of release. We thus compared the advantages of interpolating epoch-consistent LMs vs. source-coherent LMs. We trained individual LMs for each of the segments and we added them to a pool. Finally, we selected the ten most relevant ones from this pool based on their perplexity on the news2010 devset, and we interpolated them.

The results are shown in Table 4. The first line shows the baseline, which uses an interpolation of the nine LMs from the previous subsection. The following two lines show the results when using an LM trained on Gigaword only. We can see that for Spanish-English, interpolation by year performs better, while for German-English, it is better to use the by-source chunks. However, the following two lines show that when we translate with two LMs, one built from the WMT12 data only and one built using Gigaword data only, interpolation by year is preferable for Gigaword for both language pairs. For our submitted systems, we used the LMs shown in bold in Table 4: we used a single LM for Spanish-English and two LMs for German-English.

Language Models	es-en	de-en
Baseline (es:#5, de:#6)	30.31	22.48
GW by year	**30.68**	22.32
GW by source	30.52	22.56
News-etc + GW by year	30.60	**22.71**
News-etc + GW by source	30.55	22.54

Table 4: **LMs using Gigaword.**

2.4 Parameter Tuning and Data Selection

Parameter tuning is a very important step in SMT. The standard procedure consists of performing a series of iterations of MERT to choose the model parameters that maximize the translation quality on a development set, e.g., as measured by BLEU. While the procedure is widely adopted, it is also recognized that the selection of an appropriate development set is important since it biases the parameters towards specific types of translations. This is illustrated in Table 5, which shows BLEU on the news2011 testset when using different development sets for MERT.

Devset	es-en
news2008	29.47
news2009	29.14
news2010	**29.61**

Table 5: **Using different tuning sets for MERT.**

To address this problem, we performed a selection of development data using an n-gram-based similarity ranking. The selection was performed over a pool of candidate sentences drawn from the news2008, news2009, and news2010 tuning datasets. The similarity metric was defined as follows:

$$\texttt{sim}(f,g) = \texttt{2match}(f,g) * \texttt{lenpen}(f,g) \quad (1)$$

where `2match` represents the number of bi-gram matches between sentences f and g, and `lenpen` is a length penalty to discourage unbalanced matches.

We penalized the length difference using an inverted-squared sigmoid function:

$$\texttt{lenpen}(f,g) = 3 - 4 * \texttt{sig}\left(\left[\frac{|f| - |g|}{\alpha}\right]^2\right) \quad (2)$$

where $|.|$ denotes the length of a sentence in number of words, α controls the maximal tolerance to differences, and sig is the sigmoid function.

To generate a suitable development set, we averaged the similarity scores of candidate sentences w.r.t. to the target testset. For instance:

$$s_f = \frac{1}{|G|} \sum_{g \in G} \mathtt{sim}(f, g) \quad (3)$$

where G is the set of the test sentences.

Finally, we selected a pool of candidates f from news2008, news2009 and news2011 to generate a 2000-best tuning set. The results when using each of the above penalty functions are presented on Table 6.

devset	es-en
baseline (es:#6)	30.68
selection ($\alpha = 5$)	**30.94**
selection ($\alpha = 10$)	30.90

Table 6: **Selecting sentences for MERT.**

The average length of the source-side sentences in our selected sentence pairs was smaller than in our baseline, the news2011 development dataset. This means that our selected source-side sentences tended to be shorter than in the baseline. Moreover, the standard deviation of the sentence lengths was smaller for our samples as well, which means that there were fewer long sentences; this is good since long sentences can take very long to translate. As a result, we observed sizable speedup in parameter tuning when running MERT on our selected tuning datasets.

2.5 Decoding and Hypothesis Reranking

We experimented with two decoding settings: (1) monotone at punctuation reordering (Tillmann and Ney, 2003), and (2) minimum Bayes risk decoding (Kumar and Byrne, 2004). The results are shown in Table 7. We can see that both yield improvements in BLEU, even if small.

2.6 System Combination

As the final step in our translation system, we performed hypothesis re-combination of the output of several of our systems using the Multi-Engine MT system (MEMT) (Heafield and Lavie, 2010).

	es-en	de-en
Baseline (es:#2,de:#3)	29.83	21.72
+MP	**29.98**	**22.03**
Baseline (es:#4,de:#5)	30.16	22.30
+MBR	**30.31**	**22.48**

Table 7: **Decoding parameters.** Experiments with monotone at punctuation (MP) reordering, and minimum Bayes risk (MBR) decoding.

The results for the actual news2012 testset are shown in Table 8: the system combination results are our primary submission. We can see that system combination yielded 0.4 BLEU points of improvement for Spanish-English and 0.2-0.3 BLEU points for German-English.

3 Our Submissions

Here we briefly describe the cumulative improvements when applying the above modifications to our baseline system, leading to our official submissions for the WMT12 Shared Translation Task.

3.1 Spanish-English

The development of our final Spanish-English system involved several incremental improvements, which have been described above and which are summarized in Figure 1. We started with a baseline system (see Section 2.1), which scored 27.34 BLEU points. From there, using a large interpolated language model trained on the provided data (see Section 2.3.1) yielded +2.49 BLEU points of improvement. Monotone-at-punctuation decoding contributed an additional improvement of +0.15, smoothing the phrase table using Kneser-Ney boosted the score by +0.18, and using minimum Bayes risk decoding added another +0.15 BLEU points. Changing the language model to one trained on Gigaword v.5 and interpolated by year yielded +0.37 additional points of improvement. Another +0.26 points came from tuning data selection. Finally, using the UN data in a merged phrase table (see Section 2.2) yielded another +0.42 BLEU points. Overall, we achieve a total improvement over our initial baseline of about 4 BLEU points.

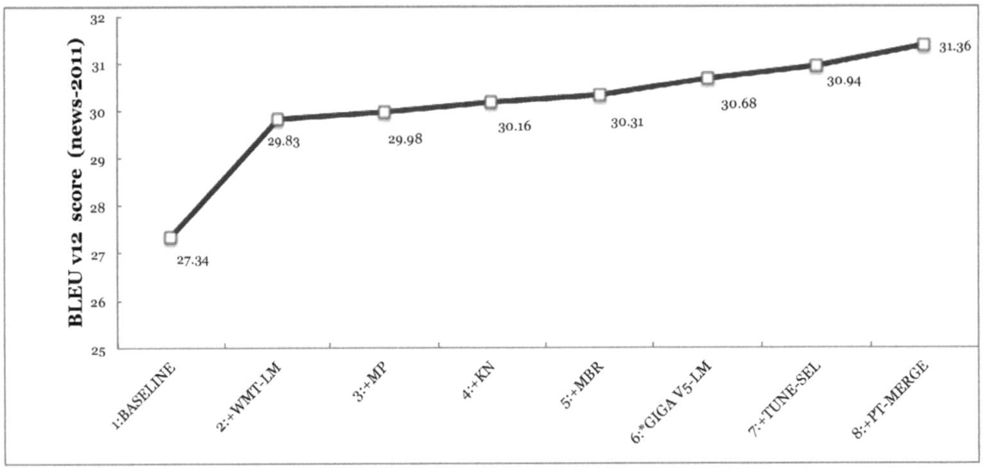

Figure 1: **Incremental improvements for the Spanish-English system.**

3.2 German-English

Figure 2 shows a similar sequence of improvements for our German-English system. We started with a baseline (see Section 2.1) that scored 19.79 BLEU points. Next, we performed compound splitting for the German side of the training, the development and the testing bi-texts, which yielded +0.22 BLEU points of improvement. Using a large interpolated language model trained on the provided corpora (see Section 2.3.1) added another +1.71. Monotone-at-punctuation decoding contributed +0.31, smoothing the phrase table using Kneser-Ney boosted the score by +0.27, and using minimum Bayes risk decoding added another +0.18 BLEU points. Finally, adding a second language model trained on the Gigaword v.5 corpus interpolated by year yielded +0.23 additional BLEU points. Overall, we achieved about 3 BLEU points of total improvement over our initial baseline.

3.3 Final Submissions

For both language pairs, our primary submission was a combination of the output of several of our best systems shown in Figures 1 and 2, which use different experimental settings; our secondary submission was our best individual system, i.e., the right-most one in Figures 1 and 2.

The official BLEU scores, both cased and lower-cased, for our primary and secondary submissions, as evaluated on the news2012 dataset, are shown in Table 8. For Spanish-English, we achieved the second highest BLEU and TER scores, while for German-English we were ranked in the top tier.

	news2012	
	lower	cased
Spanish-English		
Primary	34.0	32.9
Secondary	33.6	32.5
German-English		
Primary	23.9	22.6
Secondary	23.6	22.4

Table 8: **The official BLEU scores for our submissions to the WMT12 Shared Translation Task.**

4 Conclusion

We have described the primary and the secondary systems developed by the team of the Qatar Computing Research Institute for Spanish-English and German-English machine translation of news text for the WMT12 Shared Translation Task.

We experimented with phrase-based SMT, exploring a number of non-standard settings, most notably tuning data selection and phrase table combination, which we described and evaluated in a cumulative fashion. The automatic evaluation metrics,[4] have ranked our system second for Spanish-English and in the top tier for German-English.

We plan to continue our work on data selection for phrase table and the language model training, in addition to data selection for tuning.

[4]The evaluation scores for WMT12 are available online: `http://matrix.statmt.org/`

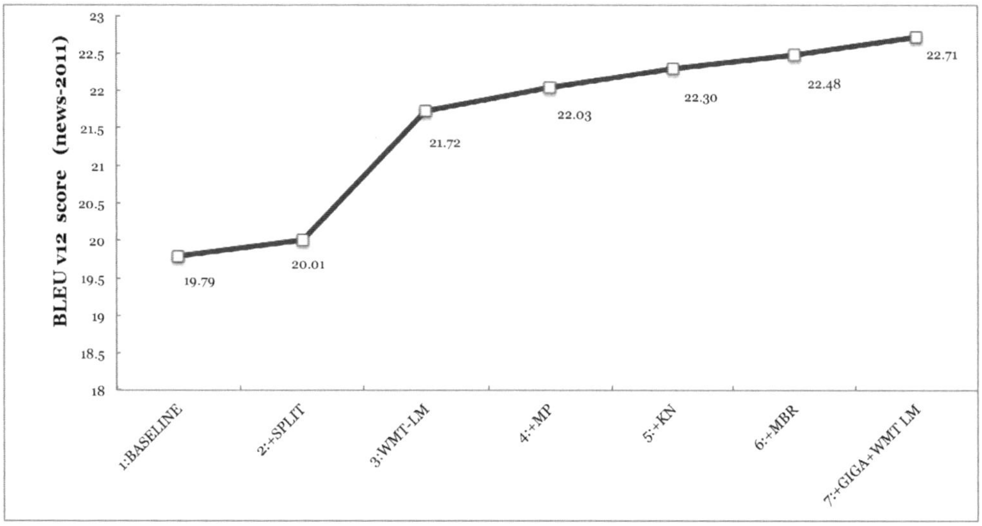

Figure 2: **Incremental improvements for the German-English system.**

Acknowledgments

We would like to thank the anonymous reviewers for their useful comments, which have helped us improve the text of this paper.

References

Peter Brown, Vincent Della Pietra, Stephen Della Pietra, and Robert Mercer. 1993. The mathematics of statistical machine translation: parameter estimation. *Computational Linguistics*, 19(2):263–311.

Stanley Chen and Joshua Goodman. 1999. An empirical study of smoothing techniques for language modeling. *Computer Speech & Language*, 13(4):359–393.

Kenneth Heafield and Alon Lavie. 2010. Combining machine translation output with open source: The Carnegie Mellon multi-engine machine translation scheme. *The Prague Bulletin of Mathematical Linguistics*, 93(1):27–36.

Philipp Koehn, Franz Josef Och, and Daniel Marcu. 2003. Statistical phrase-based translation. In *Proceedings of the 2003 Conference of the North American Chapter of the Association for Computational Linguistics on Human Language Technology - Volume 1*, NAACL '03, pages 48–54, Edmonton, Canada.

Philipp Koehn, Hieu Hoang, Alexandra Birch, Chris Callison-Burch, Marcello Federico, Nicola Bertoldi, Brooke Cowan, Wade Shen, Christine Moran, Richard Zens, Chris Dyer, Ondrej Bojar, Alexandra Constantin, and Evan Herbst. 2007. Moses: Open source toolkit for statistical machine translation. In *Proceedings of ACL. Demonstration session*, ACL '07, pages 177–180, Prague, Czech Republic.

Shankar Kumar and William Byrne. 2004. Minimum Bayes-risk decoding for statistical machine translation. In Susan Dumais, Daniel Marcu, and Salim Roukos, editors, *Proceedings of the Annual Meeting of the North American chapter of the Association for Computational Linguistics*, HLT-NAACL '04, pages 169–176, Boston, MA.

Preslav Nakov. 2008. Improving English-Spanish statistical machine translation: Experiments in domain adaptation, sentence paraphrasing, tokenization, and recasing. In *Proceedings of the Third Workshop on Statistical Machine Translation*, WMT '07, pages 147–150, Prague, Czech Republic.

Kishore Papineni, Salim Roukos, Todd Ward, and Wei-Jing Zhu. 2002. BLEU: a method for automatic evaluation of machine translation. In *Proceedings of the Annual Meeting of the Association for Computational Linguistics*, ACL '02, pages 311–318, Philadelphia, PA.

Matthew Snover, Bonnie Dorr, Richard Schwartz, Linnea Micciulla, and John Makhoul. 2006. A study of translation edit rate with targeted human annotation. In *Proceedings of the Annual Meetig of the Association for Machine Translation in the Americas*, AMTA '06, pages 223–231.

Andreas Stolcke. 2002. SRILM – an extensible language modeling toolkit. In *Proceedings of Intl. Conf. on Spoken Language Processing*, volume 2 of *ICSLP '02*, pages 901–904, Denver, CO.

Christoph Tillmann and Hermann Ney. 2003. Word reordering and a dynamic programming beam search algorithm for statistical machine translation. *Computational Linguistics*, 29(1):97–133.

The RWTH Aachen Machine Translation System for WMT 2012

Matthias Huck, Stephan Peitz, Markus Freitag, Malte Nuhn and Hermann Ney
Human Language Technology and Pattern Recognition Group
Computer Science Department
RWTH Aachen University
D-52056 Aachen, Germany
`<surname>@cs.rwth-aachen.de`

Abstract

This paper describes the statistical machine translation (SMT) systems developed at RWTH Aachen University for the translation task of the *NAACL 2012 Seventh Workshop on Statistical Machine Translation* (WMT 2012). We participated in the evaluation campaign for the French-English and German-English language pairs in both translation directions. Both hierarchical and phrase-based SMT systems are applied. A number of different techniques are evaluated, including an insertion model, different lexical smoothing methods, a discriminative reordering extension for the hierarchical system, reverse translation, and system combination. By application of these methods we achieve considerable improvements over the respective baseline systems.

1 Introduction

For the WMT 2012 shared translation task[1] RWTH utilized state-of-the-art phrase-based and hierarchical translation systems as well as an in-house system combination framework. We give a survey of these systems and the basic methods they implement in Section 2. For both the French-English (Section 3) and the German-English (Section 4) language pair, we investigate several different advanced techniques. We concentrate on specific research directions for each of the translation tasks and present the respective techniques along with the empirical results they yield: For the French→English task (Section 3.1), we apply a standard phrase-based system. For the English→French task (Section 3.2), we augment a hierarchical phrase-based setup with a number of enhancements like an insertion model, different lexical smoothing methods, and a discriminative reordering extension. For the German→English (Section 4.3) and English→German (Section 4.4) tasks, we utilize morpho-syntactic analysis to preprocess the data (Section 4.1) and employ system combination to produce a consensus hypothesis from normal and reverse translations (Section 4.2) of phrase-based and hierarchical phrase-based setups.

[1] `http://www.statmt.org/wmt12/translation-task.html`

2 Translation Systems

2.1 Phrase-Based System

The phrase-based translation (PBT) system used in this work is an in-house implementation of the state-of-the-art decoder described in (Zens and Ney, 2008). We use the standard set of models with phrase translation probabilities and lexical smoothing in both directions, word and phrase penalty, distance-based distortion model, an n-gram target language model and three binary count features. The parameter weights are optimized with minimum error rate training (MERT) (Och, 2003).

2.2 Hierarchical Phrase-Based System

For our hierarchical phrase-based translation (HPBT) setups, we employ the open source translation toolkit Jane (Vilar et al., 2010; Stein et al., 2011; Vilar et al., 2012), which has been developed at RWTH and is freely available for non-commercial use. In hierarchical phrase-based translation (Chiang, 2007), a weighted synchronous context-free grammar is induced from parallel text.

In addition to contiguous *lexical* phrases, *hierarchical* phrases with up to two gaps are extracted. The search is carried out with a parsing-based procedure. The standard models integrated into our Jane systems are: phrase translation probabilities and lexical smoothing probabilities in both translation directions, word and phrase penalty, binary features marking hierarchical phrases, glue rule, and rules with non-terminals at the boundaries, four binary count features, and an n-gram language model. Optional additional models comprise IBM model 1 (Brown et al., 1993), discriminative word lexicon (DWL) models and triplet lexicon models (Mauser et al., 2009), discriminative reordering extensions (Huck et al., 2011a), insertion and deletion models (Huck and Ney, 2012), and several syntactic enhancements like preference grammars (Stein et al., 2010) and string-to-dependency features (Peter et al., 2011). We utilize the cube pruning algorithm (Huang and Chiang, 2007) for decoding and optimize the model weights with MERT.

2.3 System Combination

System combination is used to produce consensus translations from multiple hypotheses generated with different translation engines. The basic concept of RWTH's approach to machine translation system combination is described in (Matusov et al., 2006; Matusov et al., 2008). This approach includes an enhanced alignment and reordering framework. A lattice is built from the input hypotheses. The translation with the best score within the lattice according to a couple of statistical models is selected as consensus translation.

2.4 Other Tools and Techniques

We employ GIZA++ (Och and Ney, 2003) to train word alignments. The two trained alignments are heuristically merged to obtain a symmetrized word alignment for phrase extraction. All language models (LMs) are created with the SRILM toolkit (Stolcke, 2002) and are standard 4-gram LMs with interpolated modified Kneser-Ney smoothing (Kneser and Ney, 1995; Chen and Goodman, 1998). We evaluate in truecase, using the BLEU (Papineni et al., 2002) and TER (Snover et al., 2006) measures.

		French	English
EP + NC	Sentences	2.1M	
	Running Words	63.3M	57.6M
	Vocabulary	147.8K	128.5K
	Singletons	5.4K	5.1K
+ 10^9	Sentences	22.9M	
	Running Words	728.6M	624.0M
	Vocabulary	1.7M	1.7M
	Singletons	0.8M	0.8M
+ UN	Sentences	35.4M	
	Running Words	1 113.5M	956.4M
	Vocabulary	1.9M	2.0M
	Singletons	0.9M	1.0M

Table 1: Corpus statistics of the preprocessed French-English parallel training data. *EP* denotes Europarl, *NC* denotes News Commentary. In the data, numerical quantities have been replaced by a single category symbol.

3 French-English Setups

We trained phrase-based translation systems for French→English and hierarchical phrase-based translation systems for English→French. Corpus statistics for the French-English parallel data are given in Table 1. The LMs are 4-grams trained on the provided resources for the respective language (Europarl, News Commentary, UN, 10^9, and monolingual News Crawl language model training data).[2] For French→English we also investigate a smaller English LM on Europarl and News Commentary data only. For English→French we experiment with additional target-side data from the LDC French Gigaword Second Edition (LDC2009T28), which is an archive of newswire text data that has been acquired over several years by the LDC.[3] The LDC French Gigaword v2 is permitted for constrained submissions in the WMT shared translation task. As a development set for MERT, we use newstest2009 in all setups.

3.1 Experimental Results French→English

For the French→English task, the phrase-based SMT system (PBT) is set up using the standard models listed in Section 2.1. We vary the training data we use to train the system and compare the results.

[2]The parallel 10^9 corpus is often also referred to as *WMT Giga French-English release 2*.

[3]`http://www.ldc.upenn.edu`

French→English	newstest2008		newstest2009		newstest2010		newstest2011	
	BLEU	TER	BLEU	TER	BLEU	TER	BLEU	TER
PBT baseline	20.3	63.8	23.0	60.0	23.2	59.1	24.7	57.3
+ LM: +10^9+UN	22.5	61.4	26.2	57.3	26.6	56.1	27.7	54.5
+ TM: +10^9	23.3	60.8	27.6	56.2	27.6	55.4	29.1	53.4

Table 2: Results for the French→English task (truecase). newstest2009 is used as development set. BLEU and TER are given in percentage.

English→French	newstest2008		newstest2009		newstest2010		newstest2011	
	BLEU	TER	BLEU	TER	BLEU	TER	BLEU	TER
HPBT	20.9	66.0	23.6	62.5	25.1	60.2	27.4	57.6
+ 10^9 and UN	22.5	63.2	25.4	59.8	27.0	57.1	29.9	53.9
+ LDC Gigaword v2	23.0	63.0	25.9	59.4	27.3	56.9	29.6	54.1
+ insertion model	23.0	62.9	26.1	59.2	27.2	56.8	30.0	53.7
+ noisy-or lexical scores	23.2	62.5	26.1	59.0	27.6	56.4	30.2	53.4
+ DWL	23.3	62.5	26.2	58.9	27.9	55.9	30.4	53.2
+ IBM-1	23.4	62.3	26.2	58.8	28.0	55.7	30.4	53.1
+ discrim. RO	23.5	62.2	26.7	58.5	28.1	55.9	30.8	52.8

Table 3: Results for the English→French task (truecase). newstest2009 is used as development set. BLEU and TER are given in percentage.

It should be noted that these setups do not use any English LDC Gigaword data for LM training at all.

Our baseline system uses the Europarl and News Commentary data for training LM and phrase table. Corpus statistics are shown in the "EP+NC" section of Table 1. This results in a performance of 24.7 points BLEU on newstest2011. Then we add the 10^9 as well as UN data and more monolingual English data from the News Crawl corpus to the data used for training the language model. This system obtains a score of 27.7 points BLEU on newstest2011. Our final system uses Europarl, News Commentary, 10^9 and UN data and News Crawl monolingual data for LM training and the Europarl, News Commentary and 10^9 data (Table 1) for phrase table training. Using these data sets the system reaches 29.1 points BLEU.

The experimental results are summarized in Table 2.

3.2 Experimental Results English→French

For the English→French task, the baseline system is a hierarchical phrase-based setup including the standard models as listed in Section 2.2, apart from the binary count features. We limit the recursion depth for hierarchical rules with a shallow-1 grammar (de Gispert et al., 2010).

In a shallow-1 grammar, the generic non-terminal X of the standard hierarchical approach is replaced by two distinct non-terminals XH and XP. By changing the left-hand sides of the rules, lexical phrases are allowed to be derived from XP only, hierarchical phrases from XH only. On all right-hand sides of hierarchical rules, the X is replaced by XP. Gaps within hierarchical phrases can thus solely be filled with purely lexicalized phrases, but not a second time with hierarchical phrases. The initial rule is substituted with

$$\begin{aligned} S &\rightarrow \langle XP^{\sim 0}, XP^{\sim 0} \rangle \\ S &\rightarrow \langle XH^{\sim 0}, XH^{\sim 0} \rangle , \end{aligned} \tag{1}$$

and the glue rule is substituted with

$$\begin{aligned} S &\rightarrow \langle S^{\sim 0} XP^{\sim 1}, S^{\sim 0} XP^{\sim 1} \rangle \\ S &\rightarrow \langle S^{\sim 0} XH^{\sim 1}, S^{\sim 0} XH^{\sim 1} \rangle . \end{aligned} \tag{2}$$

The main benefit of a restriction of the recursion depth is a gain in decoding efficiency, thus allowing us to set up systems more rapidly and to explore more model combinations and more system configurations.

The experimental results for English→French are given in Table 3. Starting from the shallow hierarchical baseline setup on Europarl and News Commentary parallel data only (but Europarl, News Commentary, 10^9, UN, and News Crawl data for LM training), we are able to improve translation quality considerably by first adopting more parallel (10^9 and UN) and monolingual (French LDC Gigaword v2) training resources and then employing several different models that are not included in the baseline already. We proceed with individual descriptions of the methods we use and report their respective effect in BLEU on the test sets.

10^9 and UN (up to +2.5 points BLEU) While the amount of provided parallel data from Europarl and News Commentary sources is rather limited (around 2M sentence pairs in total), the UN and the 10^9 corpus each provide a substantial collection of further training material. By appending both corpora, we end up at roughly 35M parallel sentences (cf. Table 1). We utilize this full amount of data in our system, but extract a phrase table with only lexical (i.e. non-hierarchical) phrases from the full parallel data. We add it as a second phrase table to the baseline system, with a binary feature that enables the system to reward or penalize the application of phrases from this table.

LDC Gigaword v2 (up to +0.5 points BLEU) The LDC French Gigaword Second Edition (LDC2009T28) provides some more monolingual French resources. We include a total of 28.2M sentences from both the AFP and APW collections in our LM training data.

insertion model (up to +0.4 points BLEU) We add an insertion model to the log-linear model combination. This model is designed as a means to avoid the omission of content words in the hypotheses. It is implemented as a phrase-level feature function which counts the number of inserted words. We apply the model in source-to-target and target-to-source direction. A target-side word is considered inserted based on lexical probabilities with the words on the foreign language side of the phrase, and vice versa for a source-side word. As thresholds, we compute individual arithmetic averages for each word from the vocabulary (Huck and Ney, 2012).

noisy-or lexical scores (up to +0.4 points BLEU) In our baseline system, the $t_{\text{Norm}}(\cdot)$ lexical scoring variant as described in (Huck et al., 2011a) is employed with a relative frequency (RF) lexicon model for phrase table smoothing. The single-word based translation probabilities of the RF lexicon model are extracted from word-aligned parallel training data, in the fashion of (Koehn et al., 2003). We exchange the baseline lexical scoring with a noisy-or (Zens and Ney, 2004) lexical scoring variant $t_{\text{NoisyOr}}(\cdot)$.

DWL (up to +0.3 points BLEU) We augment our system with phrase-level lexical scores from discriminative word lexicon (DWL) models (Mauser et al., 2009; Huck et al., 2011a) in both source-to-target and target-to-source direction. The DWLs are trained on News Commentary data only.

IBM-1 (up to +0.1 points BLEU) On News Commentary and Europarl data, we train IBM model-1 (Brown et al., 1993) lexicons in both translation directions and also use them to compute phrase-level scores.

discrim. RO (up to +0.4 points BLEU) The modification of the grammar to a shallow-1 version restricts the search space of the decoder and is convenient to prevent overgeneration. In order not to be too restrictive, we reintroduce more flexibility into the search process by extending the grammar with specific reordering rules

$$\begin{aligned} XP &\rightarrow \langle XP^{\sim 0} XP^{\sim 1}, XP^{\sim 1} XP^{\sim 0} \rangle \\ XP &\rightarrow \langle XP^{\sim 0} XP^{\sim 1}, XP^{\sim 0} XP^{\sim 1} \rangle . \end{aligned} \tag{3}$$

The upper rule in Equation (3) is a swap rule that allows adjacent lexical phrases to be transposed, the lower rule is added for symmetry reasons, in particular because sequences assembled with these rules are allowed to fill gaps within hierarchical phrases. Note that we apply a length constraint of 10 to the number of terminals spanned by an XP. We introduce two binary indicator features, one for each of the two rules in Equation (3). In addition to adding

	German	English
Sentences	2.0M	
Running Words	55.3M	55.7M
Vocabulary	191.6K	129.0K
Singletons	75.5K	51.8K

Table 4: Corpus statistics of the preprocessed German-English parallel training data (Europarl and News Commentary). In the data, numerical quantities have been replaced by a single category symbol.

these rules, a discriminatively trained lexicalized reordering model is applied (Huck et al., 2012).

4 German-English Setups

We trained phrase-based and hierarchical translation systems for both translation directions of the German-English language pair. Corpus statistics for German-English can be found in Table 4. The language models are 4-grams trained on the respective target side of the bilingual data as well as on the provided News Crawl corpus. For the English language model the 10^9 French-English, UN and LDC Gigaword Fourth Edition corpora are used additionally. For the 10^9 French-English, UN and LDC Gigaword corpora we apply the data selection technique described in (Moore and Lewis, 2010). We examine two different language models, one with LDC data and one without. All German→English systems are optimized on newstest2010. For English→German, we use newstest2009 as development set. The newstest2011 set is used as test set and the scores for newstest2008 are included for completeness.

4.1 Morpho-Syntactic Analysis

In order to reduce the source vocabulary size for the German→English translation, the German text is preprocessed by splitting German compound words with the frequency-based method described in (Koehn and Knight, 2003). To further reduce translation complexity of PBT, we employ the long-range part-of-speech based reordering rules proposed by Popović and Ney (2006).

4.2 Reverse Translation

For reverse translations we need to change the word order of the bilingual corpus. For example, if we reverse both source and target language, the original training example "der Hund mag die Katze . → the dog likes the cat ." is converted into a new training example ". Katze die mag Hund der → . cat the likes dog the". We call this type of modification of source or target language *reversion*. A system trained of this data is called *reverse*. This modification changes the corpora and hence the language model and alignment training produce different results.

4.3 Experimental Results German→English

Our results for the German→English task are shown in Table 5. For this task, we apply the idea of reverse translation for both the phrase-based and the hierarchical approach. It seems that the reversed systems perform slightly worse. However, when we employ system combination using both reverse translation setups (*PBT reverse* and *HPBT reverse*) and both baseline setups (*PBT baseline* and *HPBT baseline*), the translation quality is improved by up to 0.4 points in BLEU and 1.0 points TER compared to the best single system.

The addition of LDC Gigaword corpora (+GW) to the language model training data of the baseline setups shows improvements in both BLEU and TER. Furthermore, with the system combination including these setups, we are able to report an improvement of up to 0.7 points BLEU and 1.0 points TER over the best single setup. Compared to the system combination based on systems which are not using the LDC Gigaword corpora, we gain 0.3 points in BLEU and 0.4 points in TER.

4.4 Experimental Results English→German

Our results for the English→German task are shown in Table 6. For this task, we first compare systems using one, two or three language models of different parts of the data. The language model for systems with only one language model is created with all monolingual and parallel data. A language model with all monolingual data and a language model with all parallel data is created for the systems with two language models. For the systems with three language models, we also split the parallel data in two parts consisting of either only Europarl data or only News Commentary data. For PBT the system with two language models performs best for all test sets. Further, we apply the idea of reverse

German→English	newstest2008		newstest2009		newstest2010		newstest2011	
	BLEU	TER	BLEU	TER	BLEU	TER	BLEU	TER
PBT baseline	21.1	62.3	20.8	61.4	23.7	59.3	21.3	61.3
PBT reverse	20.8	62.4	20.6	61.5	23.6	59.2	21.2	61.2
HPBT baseline	21.3	62.5	20.9	61.7	23.9	59.4	21.3	61.6
HPBT reverse	21.2	63.5	20.9	62.0	23.6	59.2	21.4	61.9
system combination (secondary)	21.5	61.6	21.2	60.6	24.3	58.3	21.7	60.3
PBT baseline +GW	21.5	61.9	21.2	61.1	24.0	59.0	21.3	61.4
PBT reverse	20.8	62.4	20.6	61.5	23.6	59.2	21.2	61.2
HPBT baseline +GW	21.6	62.3	21.3	61.3	24.0	59.4	21.6	61.5
HPBT reverse	21.2	63.5	20.9	62.0	23.6	59.2	21.4	61.9
system combination (primary)	21.9	61.2	21.4	60.5	24.7	58.0	21.9	60.2

Table 5: Results for the German→English task (truecase). *+GW* denotes the usage of LDC Gigaword data for the language model, newstest2010 serves as development set. BLEU and TER are given in percentage.

English→German	newstest2008		newstest2009		newstest2010		newstest2011	
	BLEU	TER	BLEU	TER	BLEU	TER	BLEU	TER
PBT baseline 1 LM	14.6	71.7	14.8	70.8	15.8	66.9	15.3	70.0
PBT baseline 2 LM (*)	14.9	70.9	14.9	70.4	16.0	66.3	15.4	69.5
PBT baseline 3 LM	14.8	71.5	14.9	70.5	16.0	66.7	15.1	70.1
PBT reverse 2 LM (*)	14.9	71.4	15.1	70.2	15.9	66.5	15.0	69.7
HPBT baseline 2 LM (*)	15.1	71.8	15.3	71.1	16.2	67.4	15.4	70.3
HPBT baseline 2 LM opt on 4bleu-ter	15.2	68.4	15.0	67.7	15.9	64.6	15.1	67.1
HPBT reverse 2 LM (*)	15.4	71.3	15.3	70.7	16.7	66.9	15.5	70.1
syscombi of (*)	15.6	69.2	15.4	68.9	16.5	65.0	15.6	68.0

Table 6: Results for the English→German task (truecase). newstest2009 is used as development set. BLEU and TER are given in percentage.

translation for both the phrase-based and the hierarchical approach. The *PBT reverse 2 LM* systems perform slightly worse compared to *PBT baseline 2 LM*. The *HPBT reverse 2 LM* performs better compared to *HPBT baseline 2 LM*. When we employ system combination using both reverse translation setups (*PBT reverse 2 LM* and *HPBT reverse 2 LM*) and both baseline setups (*PBT baseline 2 LM* and *HPBT baseline 2 LM*), the translation quality is improved by up to 0.2 points in BLEU and 2.1 points in TER compared to the best single system.

5 Conclusion

For the participation in the WMT 2012 shared translation task, RWTH experimented with both phrase-based and hierarchical translation systems. Several different techniques were evaluated and yielded considerable improvements over the respective baseline systems as well as over our last year's setups (Huck et al., 2011b). Among these techniques are an insertion model, the noisy-or lexical scoring variant, additional phrase-level lexical scores from IBM model 1 and discriminative word lexicon models, a discriminative reordering extension for hierarchical translation, reverse translation, and system combination.

Acknowledgments

This work was achieved as part of the Quaero Programme, funded by OSEO, French State agency for innovation.

References

Peter F. Brown, Stephen A. Della Pietra, Vincent J. Della Pietra, and Robert L. Mercer. 1993. The Mathematics of Statistical Machine Translation: Parameter Estimation. *Computational Linguistics*, 19(2):263–311, June.

Stanley F. Chen and Joshua Goodman. 1998. An Empirical Study of Smoothing Techniques for Language Modeling. Technical Report TR-10-98, Computer Science Group, Harvard University, Cambridge, Massachusetts, USA, August.

David Chiang. 2007. Hierarchical Phrase-Based Translation. *Computational Linguistics*, 33(2):201–228.

Adrià de Gispert, Gonzalo Iglesias, Graeme Blackwood, Eduardo R. Banga, and William Byrne. 2010. Hierarchical Phrase-Based Translation with Weighted Finite-State Transducers and Shallow-n Grammars. *Computational Linguistics*, 36(3):505–533.

Liang Huang and David Chiang. 2007. Forest Rescoring: Faster Decoding with Integrated Language Models. In *Proceedings of the 45th Annual Meeting of the Association for Computational Linguistics*, pages 144–151, Prague, Czech Republic, June.

Matthias Huck and Hermann Ney. 2012. Insertion and Deletion Models for Statistical Machine Translation. In *Proceedings of the North American Chapter of the Association for Computational Linguistics - Human Language Technologies conference*, Montreal, Canada, June.

Matthias Huck, Saab Mansour, Simon Wiesler, and Hermann Ney. 2011a. Lexicon Models for Hierarchical Phrase-Based Machine Translation. In *International Workshop on Spoken Language Translation*, pages 191–198, San Francisco, California, USA, December.

Matthias Huck, Joern Wuebker, Christoph Schmidt, Markus Freitag, Stephan Peitz, Daniel Stein, Arnaud Dagnelies, Saab Mansour, Gregor Leusch, and Hermann Ney. 2011b. The RWTH Aachen Machine Translation System for WMT 2011. In *EMNLP 2011 Sixth Workshop on Statistical Machine Translation*, pages 405–412, Edinburgh, UK, July.

Matthias Huck, Stephan Peitz, Markus Freitag, and Hermann Ney. 2012. Discriminative Reordering Extensions for Hierarchical Phrase-Based Machine Translation. In *16th Annual Conference of the European Association for Machine Translation*, Trento, Italy, May.

Reinhard Kneser and Hermann Ney. 1995. Improved Backing-Off for M-gram Language Modeling. In *Proceedings of the International Conference on Acoustics, Speech, and Signal Processing*, volume 1, pages 181–184, May.

Philipp Koehn and Kevin Knight. 2003. Empirical Methods for Compound Splitting. In *Proceedings of European Chapter of the ACL (EACL 2009)*, pages 187–194.

Philipp Koehn, Franz Joseph Och, and Daniel Marcu. 2003. Statistical Phrase-Based Translation. In *Proc. of the Human Language Technology Conf. (HLT-NAACL)*, pages 127–133, Edmonton, Canada, May/June.

Evgeny Matusov, Nicola Ueffing, and Hermann Ney. 2006. Computing Consensus Translation from Multiple Machine Translation Systems Using Enhanced Hypotheses Alignment. In *Conference of the European Chapter of the Association for Computational Linguistics (EACL)*, pages 33–40, Trento, Italy, April.

E. Matusov, G. Leusch, R.E. Banchs, N. Bertoldi, D. Dechelotte, M. Federico, M. Kolss, Y.-S. Lee, J.B. Marino, M. Paulik, S. Roukos, H. Schwenk, and H. Ney. 2008. System Combination for Machine Translation of Spoken and Written Language. *IEEE Transactions on Audio, Speech and Language Processing*, 16(7):1222–1237.

Arne Mauser, Saša Hasan, and Hermann Ney. 2009. Extending Statistical Machine Translation with Discriminative and Trigger-Based Lexicon Models. In *Proc. of the Conf. on Empirical Methods for Natural Language Processing (EMNLP)*, pages 210–218, Singapore, August.

Robert C. Moore and William Lewis. 2010. Intelligent Selection of Language Model Training Data. In *ACL (Short Papers)*, pages 220–224, Uppsala, Sweden, July.

Franz Josef Och and Hermann Ney. 2003. A Systematic Comparison of Various Statistical Alignment Models. *Computational Linguistics*, 29(1):19–51, March.

Franz Josef Och. 2003. Minimum Error Rate Training in Statistical Machine Translation. In *Proc. of the 41th Annual Meeting of the Association for Computational Linguistics (ACL)*, pages 160–167, Sapporo, Japan, July.

Kishore Papineni, Salim Roukos, Todd Ward, and Wei-Jing Zhu. 2002. Bleu: a Method for Automatic Evaluation of Machine Translation. In *Proceedings of the 41st Annual Meeting of the Association for Computational Linguistics*, pages 311–318, Philadelphia, Pennsylvania, USA, July.

Jan-Thorsten Peter, Matthias Huck, Hermann Ney, and Daniel Stein. 2011. Soft String-to-Dependency Hierarchical Machine Translation. In *International Workshop on Spoken Language Translation*, pages 246–253, San Francisco, California, USA, December.

Maja Popović and Hermann Ney. 2006. POS-based Word Reorderings for Statistical Machine Translation. In *International Conference on Language Resources and Evaluation*, pages 1278–1283, Genoa, Italy, May.

Matthew Snover, Bonnie Dorr, Richard Schwartz, Linnea Micciulla, and John Makhoul. 2006. A Study of Translation Edit Rate with Targeted Human Annotation. In *Proceedings of the 7th Conference of the*

Association for Machine Translation in the Americas, pages 223–231, Cambridge, Massachusetts, USA, August.

Daniel Stein, Stephan Peitz, David Vilar, and Hermann Ney. 2010. A Cocktail of Deep Syntactic Features for Hierarchical Machine Translation. In *Conf. of the Association for Machine Translation in the Americas (AMTA)*, Denver, Colorado, USA, October/November.

Daniel Stein, David Vilar, Stephan Peitz, Markus Freitag, Matthias Huck, and Hermann Ney. 2011. A Guide to Jane, an Open Source Hierarchical Translation Toolkit. *The Prague Bulletin of Mathematical Linguistics*, (95):5–18, April.

Andreas Stolcke. 2002. SRILM – An Extensible Language Modeling Toolkit. In *Proc. of the Int. Conf. on Speech and Language Processing (ICSLP)*, volume 2, pages 901–904, Denver, Colorado, USA, September.

David Vilar, Daniel Stein, Matthias Huck, and Hermann Ney. 2010. Jane: Open source hierarchical translation, extended with reordering and lexicon models. In *ACL 2010 Joint Fifth Workshop on Statistical Machine Translation and Metrics MATR*, pages 262–270, Uppsala, Sweden, July.

David Vilar, Daniel Stein, Matthias Huck, and Hermann Ney. 2012. Jane: an advanced freely available hierarchical machine translation toolkit. *Machine Translation*, pages 1–20. http://dx.doi.org/10.1007/s10590-011-9120-y.

Richard Zens and Hermann Ney. 2004. Improvements in Phrase-Based Statistical Machine Translation. In *Proc. Human Language Technology Conf. / North American Chapter of the Association for Computational Linguistics Annual Meeting (HLT-NAACL)*, pages 257–264, Boston, Massachusetts, USA, May.

Richard Zens and Hermann Ney. 2008. Improvements in Dynamic Programming Beam Search for Phrase-based Statistical Machine Translation. In *International Workshop on Spoken Language Translation*, pages 195–205, Honolulu, Hawaii, USA, October.

Machine Learning for Hybrid Machine Translation

Sabine Hunsicker
DFKI GmbH
Language Technology Lab
Saarbrücken, Germany
sabine.hunsicker@dfki.de

Chen Yu
DFKI GmbH
Language Technology Lab
Saarbrücken, Germany
yu.chen@dfki.de

Christian Federmann
DFKI GmbH
Language Technology Lab
Saarbrücken, Germany
cfedermann@dfki.de

Abstract

We describe a substitution-based system for hybrid machine translation (MT) that has been extended with machine learning components controlling its phrase selection. The approach is based on a rule-based MT (RBMT) system which creates template translations. Based on the rule-based generation parse tree and target-to-target alignments, we identify the set of "interesting" translation candidates from one or more translation engines which could be substituted into our translation templates. The substitution process is either controlled by the output from a binary classifier trained on feature vectors from the different MT engines, or it is depending on weights for the decision factors, which have been tuned using MERT. We are able to observe improvements in terms of BLEU scores over a baseline version of the hybrid system.

1 Introduction

In recent years, machine translation (MT) systems have achieved increasingly better translation quality. Still each paradigm has its own challenges: while statistical MT (SMT) systems suffer from a lack of grammatical structure, resulting in ungrammatical sentences, RBMT systems have to deal with a lack of lexical coverage. Hybrid architectures intend to combine the advantages of the individual paradigms to achieve an overall better translation.

Federmann et al. (2010) and Federmann and Hunsicker (2011) have shown that using a substitution-based approach can improve the translation quality of a baseline RBMT system. Our submission to WMT12 is a new, improved version following these approaches. The output of an RBMT engine serves as our translation backbone, and we substitute noun phrases by translations mined from other systems.

2 System Architecture

Our hybrid MT system combines translation output from:

a) the Lucy RBMT system, described in more detail in (Alonso and Thurmair, 2003);

b) the Linguatec RBMT system (Aleksic and Thurmair, 2011);

c) Moses (Koehn et al., 2007);

d) Joshua (Li et al., 2009).

Lucy provides us with the translation skeleton, which is described in more detail in Section 2.2 while systems *b)–d)* are aligned to this translation template and mined for substitution candidates. We give more detailed information on these systems in Section 2.3.

2.1 Basic Approach

We first identify "interesting" phrases inside the rule-based translation and then compute the most probable correspondences in the translation output from the other systems. For the resulting phrases, we apply a factored substitution method that decides whether the original RBMT phrase should be kept or rather be replaced by one of the candidate phrases. A schematic overview of our hybrid system and its main components is given in Figure 1.

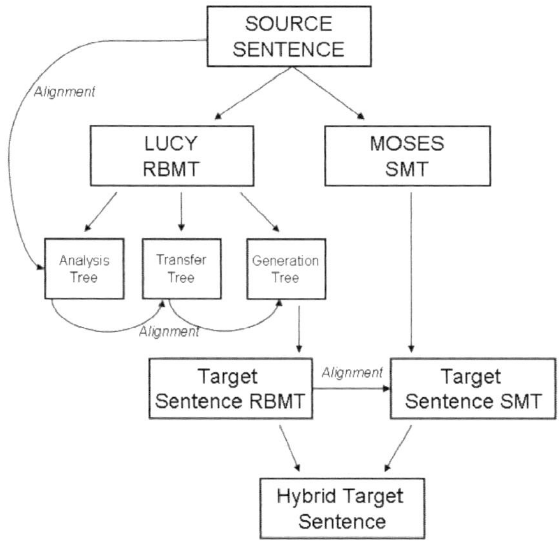

Figure 1: Schematic overview of the architecture of our substitution-based, hybrid MT system.

In previous years, it turned out that the alignment of the candidate translations to the source contained too many errors. In this version of our system, we thus changed the alignment method that connects the other translations. Only the rule-based template is aligned to the source. As we make use of the Lucy RBMT analysis parse trees, this alignment is very good. The other translations are now connected to the rule-based template using a confusion network approach. This also reduces computational efforts, as we now can compute the substitution candidates directly from the template without detouring over the source. During system training and tuning, this new approach has resulted in a reduced number of erroneous alignment links.

Additionally, we also changed our set of decision factors, increasing their total number. Whereas an older version of this system only used four factors, we now consider the following twelve factors:

1. **frequency:** frequency of a given candidate phrase compared to total number of candidates for the current phrase;
2. **LM(phrase):** language model (LM) score of the phrase;
3. **LM(phrase+1):** phrase with right-context;
4. **LM(phrase-1):** phrase with left-context;
5. **Part-of-speech match?:** checks if the part-of-speech tags of the left/right context match the current candidate phrase's context;
6. **LM(pos)** LM score for part-of-speech (PoS);
7. **LM(pos+1)** PoS with right-context;
8. **LM(pos-1)** PoS with left-context;
9. **Lemma** checks if the lemma of the candidate phrase fits the reference;
10. **LM(lemma)** LM score for the lemma;
11. **LM(lemma+1)** lemma with right-context;
12. **LM(lemma-1)** lemma with left-context.

The language model was trained using the SRILM toolkit (Stolcke, 2002), on the EuroParl (Koehn, 2005) corpus, and lemmatised or part-of-speech tagged versions, respectively. We used the Tree-Tagger (Schmid, 1994) for lemmatisation as well as part-of-speech tagging.

The substitution algorithm itself was also adapted. We investigated two machine learning approaches. In the previous version, the system used a hand-written decision tree to perform the substitution:

1. the first of the two new approaches consisted of machine learning this decision tree from annotated data;
2. the second approach was to assign a weight to each factor and using MERT tuning of these weights on a development set.

Both approaches are described in more detail later in Section 2.4.

2.2 Rule-Based Translation Templates

The Lucy RBMT system provides us with parse tree structures for each of the three phases of its transfer-based translation approach: *analysis*, *transfer* and *generation*. Out of these structures, we can extract linguistic phrases which later represent the "slots" for substitution. Previous work has shown that these structures are of a good grammatical quality due to the grammar Lucy uses.

2.3 Substitution Candidate Translations

Whereas in our previous work, we solely relied on candidates retrieved from SMT systems, this time we also included an additional RBMT system into the architecture. Knowing that statistical systems make similar errors, we hope to balance out this fact by exploiting also a system of a different paradigm, namely RBMT.

To create the statistical translations, we used state-of-the-art SMT systems. Both our Moses and Joshua systems were trained on the EuroParl corpus and News Commentary[1] training data. We performed tuning on the "newstest2011" data set using MERT.

We compile alignments between translations with the alignment module of MANY (Barrault, 2010). This module uses a modified version of TERp (Snover et al., 2009) and a set of different costs to create the best alignment between any two given sentences. In our case, each single candidate translation is aligned to the translation template that has been produced by the Lucy RBMT system. As we do not use the source in this alignment technique, we can use any translation system, regardless of whether this system provides us with a source-to-target alignment.

In earlier versions of this system, we compiled the source-to-target alignments for the candidate translations using GIZA++ (Och and Ney, 2003), but these alignments contained many errors. By using target-to-target alignments, we are able to reduce the amount of those errors which is, of course, preferred.

2.4 Substitution Approaches

Using the parse tree structures provided by Lucy, we extract "interesting" phrases for substitution. This includes noun phrases of various complexity, then simple verb phrases consisting of only the main verb, and finally adjective phrases. Through the target-to-target alignments we identify and collect the set of potential substitution candidates. Phrase substitution can be performed using two methods.

2.4.1 Machine-Learned Decision Tree

Previous work used hand-crafted rules. These are now replaced by a classifier which was trained on annotated data. Our training set D can formally be represented as

$$D = \{(x_i, y_i) | x_i \in \mathbb{R}^p, y_i \in \{-1, 1\}\}_{i=1}^{n} \quad (1)$$

where each x_i represents the *feature vector* for some sentence i while the y_i value contains the annotated class information. We use a binary classification scheme, simply defining 1 as "good" and -1 as "bad" translations.

In order to make use of machine (ML) learning methods such as decision trees (Breiman et al., 1984), Support Vector Machines (Vapnik, 1995), or the Perceptron (Rosenblatt, 1958) algorithm, we have to prepare our training set with a sufficiently large amount of annotated training instances.

To create the training data set, we computed the feature vectors and all possible substitution candidates for the WMT12 "newstest2011" development set. Human annotators were then given the task to assign to each candidate whether it was a "good" or a "bad" substitution. We used Appraise (Federmann, 2010) for the annotation, and collected a set of 24,996 labeled training instances with the help of six human annotators. Table 1 gives an overview of the data sets characteristics. The decision tree learned from this data replaces the hand-crafted rules.

2.4.2 Weights Tuned with MERT

Another approach we followed was to assign weights to the chosen decision factors and to use Minimal Error Rate Training to get the best weights. Using the twelve factors described in Section 2.1, we assign uniformly distributed weights and create n-best lists. Each n-best lists contains a total of $n+2$ hypotheses, with n being the number of candidate systems. It contains the Lucy template translations, the hybrid translation using the best candidates as well as a hypothesis for each candidate system. In the latter translation, each potential candidate for substitution is selected and replaces the original sub phrase in the baseline. The n-best list is

	Translation Candidates		
	Total	"good"	"bad"
Count	24,996	10,666	14,330

Table 1: Training data set characteristics

[1] Available at http://www.statmt.org/wmt12/

	Hybrid Systems			Baseline Systems			
	Baseline	+Decision Tree	+MERT	Lucy	Linguatec	Joshua	Moses
BLEU	13.9	14.2	**14.3**	14.0	14.7	14.6	**15.9**
BLEU-cased	13.5	13.8	**13.9**	13.7	14.2	13.5	**14.9**
TER	0.776	0.773	**0.768**	0.774	0.775	**0.772**	0.774

Table 2: Experimental results for all component and hybrid systems applied to the WMT12 "newstest2012" test set data for language pair English→German.

sorted by the final score of the feature vectors making up each hypothesis. We used Z-MERT (Zaidan, 2009) to optimise the set of feature weights on the "newstest2011" development set.

3 Evaluation

Using the "newstest2012" test set, we created baseline translations for the four MT systems used in our hybrid system. Then we performed three runs of our hybrid system:

a) a baseline run, using the factors and uniformly distributed weights;

b) a run using the weights trained on the development set;

c) a run using the decision tree learned from annotated data.

Table 2 shows the results for automatic metrics' scores. Besides BLEU (Papineni et al., 2001), we also report its case-sensitive variant, BLEU-cased, and TER (Snover et al., 2006) scores.

Comparing the scores, we see that both advanced hybrid methods perform better than the original, baseline hybrid as well as the Lucy baseline system. The MERT approach performs slightly better than the decision tree. This proves that using machine-learning to adapt the substitution approach results in better translation quality.

Other baseline systems, however, still outperform the hybrid systems. In part this is due to the fact that we are preserving the basic structure of the RBMT translation and do not reorder the new hybrid translation. To improve the hybrid approach further, there is more research required.

4 Conclusion and Outlook

In this paper, we have described how machine-learning approaches can be used to improve the phrase substitution component of a hybrid machine translation system.

We reported on two different approaches, the first using a binary classifier learned from annotated data, and the second using feature weights tuned with MERT. Both systems achieved improved automatic metrics' scores on the WMT12 "newstest2012" test set for the language pair English→German.

Future work will have to investigate ways how to achieve a closer integration of the individual baseline translations. This might be done by also taking into account reordering of the linguistic phrases as shown in the tree structures. We will also need to examine the differences between the classifier and MERT approach, to see whether we can integrate them to improve the selection process even further.

Also, we have to further evaluate the machine learning performance via, e.g., cross-validation-based tuning, to improve the prediction rate of the classifier model. We intend to explore other machine learning techniques such as SVMs as well.

Acknowledgments

This work has been funded under the Seventh Framework Programme for Research and Technological Development of the European Commission through the T4ME contract (grant agreement no.: 249119). It was also supported by the EuroMatrix-Plus project (IST-231720). We are grateful to the anonymous reviewers for their valuable feedback. Special thanks go to Hervé Saint-Amand for help with fixing the automated metrics scores.

References

Vera Aleksic and Gregor Thurmair. 2011. Personal Translator at WMT 2011. In *Proceedings of the Sixth Workshop on Statistical Machine Translation*, pages 303–308, Edinburgh, Scotland, July. Association for Computational Linguistics.

Juan A. Alonso and Gregor Thurmair. 2003. The Comprendium Translator System. In *Proceedings of the Ninth Machine Translation Summit*.

Loïc Barrault. 2010. MANY : Open Source Machine Translation System Combination. *Prague Bulletin of Mathematical Linguistics, Special Issue on Open Source Tools for Machine Translation*, 93:147–155, January.

L. Breiman, J. Friedman, R. Olshen, and C. Stone. 1984. *Classification and Regression Trees*. Wadsworth and Brooks, Monterey, CA.

Christian Federmann and Sabine Hunsicker. 2011. Stochastic parse tree selection for an existing rbmt system. In *Proceedings of the Sixth Workshop on Statistical Machine Translation*, pages 351–357, Edinburgh, Scotland, July. Association for Computational Linguistics.

Christian Federmann, Andreas Eisele, Yu Chen, Sabine Hunsicker, Jia Xu, and Hans Uszkoreit. 2010. Further experiments with shallow hybrid mt systems. In *Proceedings of the Joint Fifth Workshop on Statistical Machine Translation and MetricsMATR*, pages 77–81, Uppsala, Sweden, July. Association for Computational Linguistics.

Christian Federmann. 2010. Appraise: An Open-Source Toolkit for Manual Phrase-Based Evaluation of Translations. In Nicoletta Calzolari (Conference Chair), Khalid Choukri, Bente Maegaard, Joseph Mariani, Jan Odijk, Stelios Piperidis, Mike Rosner, and Daniel Tapias, editors, *Proceedings of the Seventh International Conference on Language Resources and Evaluation (LREC'10)*, Valletta, Malta, May. European Language Resources Association (ELRA).

Philipp Koehn, Hieu Hoang, Alexandra Birch, Chris Callison-Burch, Marcello Federico, Nicola Bertoldi, Brooke Cowan, Wade Shen, Christine Moran, Richard Zens, Chris Dyer, Ondrej Bojar, Alexandra Constantin, and Evan Herbst. 2007. Moses: Open Source Toolkit for Statistical Machine Translation. In *Proceedings of ACL Demo and Poster Sessions*, pages 177–180. Association for Computational Linguistics, June.

Philipp Koehn. 2005. Europarl: A Parallel Corpus for Statistical Machine Translation. In *Proceedings of the MT Summit 2005*.

Zhifei Li, Chris Callison-Burch, Chris Dyer, Sanjeev Khudanpur, Lane Schwartz, Wren Thornton, Jonathan Weese, and Omar Zaidan. 2009. Joshua: An Open Source Toolkit for Parsing-Based Machine Translation. In *Proceedings of the Fourth Workshop on Statistical Machine Translation*, pages 135–139, Athens, Greece, March. Association for Computational Linguistics.

Evgeny Matusov, Nicola Ueffing, and Hermann Ney. 2006. Computing Consensus Translation from Multiple Machine Translation Systems Using Enhanced Hypotheses Alignment. In *Conference of the European Chapter of the Association for Computational Linguistics*, pages 33–40, Stroudsburg, PA, USA, April. Association for Computational Linguistics.

Franz Josef Och and Hermann Ney. 2003. A Systematic Comparison of Various Statistical Alignment Models. *Computational Linguistics*, 29(1):19–51, March.

Kishore Papineni, Salim Roukos, Todd Ward, and Wei-Jing Zhu. 2001. Bleu: a Method for Automatic Evaluation of Machine Translation. IBM Research Report RC22176(W0109-022), IBM.

F. Rosenblatt. 1958. The Perceptron: A Probabilistic Model for Information Storage and Organization in the Brain. *Psychological Review*, 65:386–408.

Helmut Schmid. 1994. Probabilistic Part-of-Speech Tagging Using Decision Trees. In *Proceedings of the International Conference on New Methods in Language Processing*, Manchester, UK.

Toby Segaran. 2007. *Programming Collective Intelligence: Building Smart Web 2.0 Applications*. O'Reilly, Beijing.

Matthew Snover, Bonnie Dorr, Richard Schwartz, Linnea Micciulla, and John Makhoul. 2006. A Study of Translation Edit Rate with Targeted Human Annotation. In *Proceedings of the Conference of the Association for Machine Translation in the Americas*, pages 223–231.

Matthew Snover, Nitin Madnani, Bonnie Dorr, and Richard Schwartz. 2009. Fluency, Adequacy, or HTER? Exploring Different Human Judgments with a Tunable MT Metric. In *Proceedings of the Fourth Workshop on Statistical Machine Translation at the 12th Meeting of the European Chapter of the Association for Computational Linguistics (EACL-2009)*, Athens, Greece, March.

Andreas Stolcke. 2002. SRILM - An Extensible Language Modeling Toolkit. In *Proceedings of the International Conference on Spoken Language Processing*, pages 257–286, November.

V. N. Vapnik. 1995. *The Nature of Statistical Learning Theory*. Springer, New York.

Omar F. Zaidan. 2009. Z-MERT: A fully configurable open source tool for minimum error rate training of machine translation systems. *The Prague Bulletin of Mathematical Linguistics*, 91:79–88, January.

Towards Effective Use of Training Data in Statistical Machine Translation

Philipp Koehn and Barry Haddow
University of Edinburgh
Edinburgh, United Kingdom
{pkoehn,bhaddow}@inf.ed.ac.uk

Abstract

We report on findings of exploiting large data sets for translation modeling, language modeling and tuning for the development of competitive machine translation systems for eight language pairs.

1 Introduction

We report on experiments carried out for the development of competitive systems on the datasets of the 2012 Workshop on Statistical Machine Translation. Our main focus was directed on the effective use of all the available training data during training of translation and language models and tuning.

We use the open source machine translation system Moses (Koehn et al., 2007) and other standard open source tools, hence all our experiments are straightforwardly replicable[1].

Compared to all single system submissions by participants of the workshop we achieved the best BLEU scores for four language pairs (es-en, en-es, cs-en, en-cs), the 2nd best results for two language pairs (fr-en, de-en), as well as a 3rd place (en-de) and a 5th place (en-fr) for the remaining pairs. We improved upon this in the post-evaluation period for some of the language pairs by more systematically applying our methods.

During the development of our system, we saw most gains from using large corpora for translation model training, especially when using subsampling techniques for out-of-domain sets, using large corpora for language model training, and larger tuning sets. We also observed mixed results with alternative tuning methods. We also experimented with hierarchical models and semi-supervised training, but did not achieve any improvements.

[1]Configuration files and instructions are available at http://www.statmt.org/wmt12/uedin/.

LP	Baseline	+UN
fr-en	28.2	28.4 (+.2)
es-en	29.1	28.9 (–.2)
en-fr	28.8	28.7 (–.1)
en-es	31.0	30.9 (–.1)
LP	**Baseline**	**+GigaFrEn**
fr-en	28.7	29.1 (+.4)
en-fr	29.3	30.3 (+1.0)

Table 1: Gains from larger translation models: UN (about 300 million English words), GigaFrEn (about 550 million English words).

We report all results in case-sensitive BLEU (mteval13a) on the newstest2011 test set (Callison-Burch et al., 2011). Please also note that baseline scores vary throughout the paper, since different methods were investigated at different time points.

2 Better Translation Models

2.1 Using Large Training Sets

The WMT evaluation campaign works with the largest training sets in the field. Our French-English systems are trained on a parallel corpus with 1,072 million French and 934 million English words. Training a system on this amount of data takes about two weeks.

The basic data sets for the language pairs are the Europarl and NewsCommentary corpora consist of about 50 million words and 3 million words, respectively. These corpora are quite close to the target domain of news reports, and give quite good results. Table 1 shows the gains from using the much larger UN (about 300 million words) and GigaFrEn corpora (about 550 million words).

From these results, it is not clear if the UN is helpful, but the GigaFrEn corpus gives large gains (+0.4 BLEU and +1.0 BLEU).

LP	Base-line	Model 1				Moore-Lewis			
		Before		After		Before		After	
		10%	50%	10%	50%	10%	50%	10%	50%
fr-en	29.3	28.5(–.8)	29.1(–.2)	28.6(–.7)	28.9(–.4)	29.1(–.2)	**29.6(+.3)**	29.1(–.2)	29.4(+.1)
en-fr	30.1	29.1(–1.0)	30.1(±.0)	29.3(–.8)	29.8(–.3)	29.9(–.2)	**30.2(+.1)**	29.9(–.2)	30.1(±.0)
es-en	29.0	28.9(–.1)	29.0(±.0)	29.0(±.0)	29.0(±.0)	29.0(±.0)	29.1(+.1)	**29.4(+.4)**	29.2(+.2)
en-es	30.9	30.9(±.0)	31.0(+.1)	30.8(–.1)	30.7(–.2)	31.4(+.5)	**31.5(+.6)**	**31.5(+.6)**	31.3(+.4)

Table 2: Subsampling UN and GigaFrEn corpora using Model 1 and Moore-Lewis filtering, before and after word alignment

2.2 Subsampling

We experimented with two different types of subsampling techniques – Model 1, similar to that used by Schwenk et al. (2011), and modified Moore-Lewis (Axelrod et al., 2011) – for the language pairs es-en, en-es, fr-en and en-fr. In each case the idea was to include the NewsCommentary and Europarl corpora in their entirety, and to score the sentences in the remaining corpora (the selection corpus) using one of the two measures, adding either the top 10% or top 50% of the selection corpus to the training data.

For Model 1 filtering, we trained IBM Model 1 on Europarl and NewsCommentary concatenated, in both directions, and scored the sentences in the selection corpus using the length-normalised sum of the IBM Model scores. For the modified Moore-Lewis filtering, we trained two 5-gram language models for source and target, the first on 5M sentences from the news2011 monolingual data, and the second on 5M words from the selection corpus, using the same vocabulary. The modified Moore-Lewis score for a sentence is the sum of the source and target's perplexity difference for the two language models.

For the Spanish experiments, the selection corpus was the UN data, whilst for the French experiments it was the UN data and the GigaFrEn data, concatenated and with duplicates removed.

The results of the subsampling are shown in Table 2, where the BLEU scores are averaged over 2 tuning runs. The conclusion was that modified Moore-Lewis subsampling was effective (and was used in our final submissions), but Model 1 sampling made no difference for the Spanish systems, and was harmful for the French systems.

3 Better Language Models

In previous years, we were not able to make use of the monolingual LDC Gigaword corpora due to lack of sufficiently powerful computing resources. These corpora exist for English (4.3 billion words), Spanish (1.1 billion words), and French (0.8 billion words). With the acquisition of large memory machines[2], we were now able to train language models on this data. Use of these large language models during decoding is aided by more efficient storage and inference (Heafield, 2011).

Still, even with that much RAM it is not possible to train a language model with SRILM (Stolke, 2002) in one pass. Hence, we broke up the training corpus by source (*New York Times*, *Washington Post*, ...) and trained separate language model for each. The largest individual corpus was the English *New York Times* portion which consists of 1.5 billion words and took close to 100GB of RAM. We also trained individual language models for each year of WMT12's monolingual corpus.

We interpolated the language models using the SRILM toolkit. The toolkit has a limit of 10 language models to be merged at once, so we had to interpolate sub-groups of some of the language models (the WMT12 monolingual news models) first. It is not clear if this is harmful, but building separate language model for each source and year and interpolate those many more models did hurt significantly.

Table 3 shows that we gain around half a BLEU point into Spanish and French, as well as German–English, and around one and a half BLEU points for the other language pairs into English.

[2]Dell Poweredge R710, equipped with two 6-core Intel Xeon X5660 CPUs running at 2.8GHz, with each core able to run two threads (24 threads total), six 3TB disks and 144GB RAM, and cost £6000.

LP	Baseline	+LDC Giga
de-en	21.9	22.4 (+.5)
cs-en	24.2	25.6 (+1.4)
fr-en	29.1	31.0 (+1.9)
es-en	29.1	30.7 (+1.6)
en-es	31.5	31.8 (+.3)
en-fr	30.3	30.8 (+.5)

Table 3: Using the LDC Gigaword corpora to train larger language models.

LP	Baseline	Big-Tune
de-en	21.4	21.6 (+.2)
fr-en	28.4	28.7 (+.3)
es-en	28.9	29.0 (+.1)
cs-en	23.9	24.1 (+.2)
en-de	15.8	15.9 (+.1)
en-fr	28.7	29.2 (+.5)
en-es	30.9	31.2 (+.2)
en-cs	17.2	17.4 (+.2)

Table 4: Using a larger tuning set (7567 sentences) by combining newstest 2008 to 2010.

4 Better Tuning

4.1 Bigger Tuning Sets

In recent experiments, mainly geared towards using much larger feature sets, we learned that larger tuning sets may give better and more stable results. We tested this hypothesis here as well.

By concatenating the sets from three years (2008-2010), we constructed a tuning set of 7567 sentences per language. Table 4 shows that we gain on average about +0.2 BLEU points.

4.2 Pairwise Ranked Optimization

We recently added an implementation of the pairwise ranked optimization (PRO) tuning method (Hopkins and May, 2011) to Moses as an alternative to Och's (2003) minimum error rate training (MERT). We checked if this method gives us better results. Table 5 shows a mixed picture. PRO gives slightly shorter translations, probably because it optimises sentence rather than corpus BLEU, which has a noticeable effect on the BLEU score. For 2 language pairs we see better results, for 4 worse, and for 1 there is no difference. On other data and language conditions we have observed better and more stable results with PRO.

LP	MERT	PRO	PRO-MERT
de-en	21.7 (1.01)	21.9 (1.00) +.2	21.7 (1.01) ±.0
es-en	29.1 (1.02)	29.1 (1.01) ±.0	29.1 (1.02) ±.0
cs-en	24.2 (1.03)	24.5 (1.00) +.3	24.2 (1.03) ±.0
en-de	16.0 (1.00)	15.7 (0.96) –.3	16.0 (1.00) ±.0
en-fr	29.3 (0.98)	28.9 (0.96) –.4	29.3 (0.98) ±.0
en-es	31.5 (0.98)	31.3 (0.97) –.2	31.4 (0.98) –.1
en-cs	17.4 (0.97)	16.9 (0.92) –.5	17.3 (0.97) –.1

Table 5: Replacing the line search method of MERT with pairwise ranked optimization (PRO).

We tried to use PRO to generate starting points for MERT optimization. Theoretically this will lead to better optimization on the tuning set, since MERT optimization steps on PRO weights will never lead to worse results on the sampled n-best lists. This method (PRO-MERT in the table) applied here, however, did not lead to significantly different results than plain MERT.

5 What did not Work

Not everything we tried worked out. Notably, two promising directions — hierarchical models and semi-supervised learning — did not yield any improvements. It is not clear if we failed or if the methods failed, but we will investigate this further in future work.

5.1 Hierarchical Models

Hierarchical models (Chiang, 2007) have been supported already for a few years by Moses, and they give significantly better performance for Chinese–English over phrase-based models. While we have not yet seen benefits for many other language pairs, the eight language pairs of WMT12 allowed us to compare these two models more extensively, also in view of recent enhancements resulting in better search accuracy.

Since hierarchical models are much larger (roughly 10 times bigger), we trained hierarchical models on downsized training data for most language pairs. For Spanish and French, this excludes UN and GigaFrEn; for Czech some parts of the CzEng corpus were excluded based on their lower language model interpolation weights relative

LP	Phrase	Downsized	Hierarchical
de-en	21.6	same	21.4 (–.2)
fr-en	28.7	27.9	27.6 (–.3)
es-en	29.0	28.9	28.4 (–.5)
cs-en	24.1	22.4	22.0 (–.4)
en-de	15.9	same	15.5 (–.4)
en-fr	29.2	28.8	28.0 (–.8)
en-es	31.2	30.8	30.4 (–.4)
en-cs	17.4	16.2	15.6 (–.6)

Table 6: Hierarchical phrase models vs. baseline phrase-based models.

Setup	Baseline	+synthetic	+syn-half
fr-en ep+nc	28.0	28.1 (+.1)	28.0 (±.0)
+un	28.7	28.6 (–.1)	28.5 (–.2)
en-fr ep+nc	28.8	28.2 (–.6)	28.1 (–.7)
+un	29.3	28.9 (–.4)	28.9 (–.4)

Table 7: Using semi-supervised methods to add synthetic parallel data to a baseline system trained on Europarl (ep)m News Commentary (nc) and United Nations (un). We added all generated data (synthetic) or filtered out half based on model scores (syn-half).

to their size.

Table 6 shows inferior performance for all language pairs (by about half a BLEU point), although results for German–English are close (–0.2 BLEU).

5.2 Semi-Supervised Learning

Other research groups have reported improvements using semi-supervised learning methods to create synthetic parallel data from monolingual data (Schwenk et al., 2008; Abdul-Rauf and Schwenk, 2009; Bertoldi and Federico, 2009; Lambert et al., 2011). The idea is to translate in-domain monolingual data with a baseline system and filter the result for use as an additional parallel corpus.

Table 7 shows out results when trying to emulate the approach of Lambert et al. (2011). We translate the some of the 2011 monolingual news data (139 million words for French and 100 million words for English) from the target language into the source language with a baseline system trained on Europarl and News Commentary. Adding all the obtained data hurts (except for minimal improvements over a small French-English system). When we filtered out half of the sentences based on translation scores, results were even worse.

Acknowledgments

This work was supported by the EuroMatrixPlus project funded by the European Commission (7th Framework Programme).

References

Abdul-Rauf, S. and Schwenk, H. (2009). On the use of comparable corpora to improve SMT performance. In *Proceedings of the 12th Conference of the European Chapter of the ACL (EACL 2009)*, pages 16–23, Athens, Greece. Association for Computational Linguistics.

Axelrod, A., He, X., and Gao, J. (2011). Domain adaptation via pseudo in-domain data selection. In *Proceedings of the 2011 Conference on Empirical Methods in Natural Language Processing*, pages 355–362, Edinburgh, Scotland, UK. Association for Computational Linguistics.

Bertoldi, N. and Federico, M. (2009). Domain adaptation for statistical machine translation with monolingual resources. In *Proceedings of the Fourth Workshop on Statistical Machine Translation*, pages 182–189, Athens, Greece. Association for Computational Linguistics.

Callison-Burch, C., Koehn, P., Monz, C., and Zaidan, O. (2011). Findings of the 2011 workshop on statistical machine translation. In *Proceedings of the Sixth Workshop on Statistical Machine Translation*, pages 22–64, Edinburgh, Scotland. Association for Computational Linguistics.

Chiang, D. (2007). Hierarchical phrase-based translation. *Computational Linguistics*, 33(2).

Heafield, K. (2011). Kenlm: Faster and smaller language model queries. In *Proceedings of the Sixth Workshop on Statistical Machine Translation*, pages 187–197, Edinburgh, Scotland. Association for Computational Linguistics.

Hopkins, M. and May, J. (2011). Tuning as ranking. In *Proceedings of the 2011 Conference on Empirical Methods in Natural Language Processing*, pages 1352–1362, Edinburgh, Scotland, UK. Association for Computational Linguistics.

Koehn, P., Hoang, H., Birch, A., Callison-Burch, C., Federico, M., Bertoldi, N., Cowan, B., Shen, W., Moran, C., Zens, R., Dyer, C. J., Bojar, O., Constantin, A., and Herbst, E. (2007). Moses: Open source toolkit for statistical machine translation. In *Proceedings of the 45th Annual Meeting of the Association for Computational Linguistics Companion Volume Proceedings of the Demo and Poster Sessions*, pages 177–180, Prague, Czech Republic. Association for Computational Linguistics.

Lambert, P., Schwenk, H., Servan, C., and Abdul-Rauf, S. (2011). Investigations on translation model adaptation using monolingual data. In *Proceedings of the Sixth Workshop on Statistical Machine Translation*, pages 284–293, Edinburgh, Scotland. Association for Computational Linguistics.

Och, F. J. (2003). Minimum error rate training for statistical machine translation. In *Proceedings of the 41st Annual Meeting of the Association of Computational Linguistics (ACL).*

Schwenk, H., Estève, Y., and Rauf, S. A. (2008). The LIUM Arabic/English statistical machine translation system for IWSLT 2008. In *Proceedings of the International Workshop on Spoken Language Translation (IWSLT)*, pages 63–68.

Schwenk, H., Lambert, P., Barrault, L., Servan, C., Abdul-Rauf, S., Afli, H., and Shah, K. (2011). Lium's smt machine translation systems for wmt 2011. In *Proceedings of the Sixth Workshop on Statistical Machine Translation*, pages 464–469, Edinburgh, Scotland. Association for Computational Linguistics.

Stolke, A. (2002). SRILM - an extensible language modeling toolkit. In *Proceedings of the International Conference on Spoken Language Processing*.

Joint WMT 2012 Submission of the QUAERO Project

*Markus Freitag, *Stephan Peitz, *Matthias Huck, *Hermann Ney,
†Jan Niehues, †Teresa Herrmann, †Alex Waibel,
‡Le Hai-son, ‡Thomas Lavergne, ‡Alexandre Allauzen,
§Bianka Buschbeck, §Josep Maria Crego, §Jean Senellart
*RWTH Aachen University, Aachen, Germany
†Karlsruhe Institute of Technology, Karlsruhe, Germany
‡LIMSI-CNRS, Orsay, France
§SYSTRAN Software, Inc.
*surname@cs.rwth-aachen.de
†firstname.surname@kit.edu
‡firstname.lastname@limsi.fr §surname@systran.fr

Abstract

This paper describes the joint QUAERO submission to the WMT 2012 machine translation evaluation. Four groups (RWTH Aachen University, Karlsruhe Institute of Technology, LIMSI-CNRS, and SYSTRAN) of the QUAERO project submitted a joint translation for the WMT German→English task. Each group translated the data sets with their own systems and finally the RWTH system combination combined these translations in our final submission. Experimental results show improvements of up to 1.7 points in BLEU and 3.4 points in TER compared to the best single system.

1 Introduction

QUAERO is a European research and development program with the goal of developing multimedia and multilingual indexing and management tools for professional and general public applications (http://www.quaero.org). Research in machine translation is mainly assigned to the four groups participating in this joint submission. The aim of this WMT submission was to show the quality of a joint translation by combining the knowledge of the four project partners. Each group develop and maintain their own different machine translation system. These single systems differ not only in their general approach, but also in the preprocessing of training and test data. To take the advantage of these differences of each translation system, we combined all hypotheses of the different systems, using the RWTH system combination approach.

This paper is structured as follows. In Section 2, the different engines of all four groups are introduced. In Section 3, the RWTH Aachen system combination approach is presented. Experiments with different system selections for system combination are described in Section 4. Finally in Section 5, we discuss the results.

2 Translation Systems

For WMT 2012 each QUAERO partner trained their systems on the parallel Europarl and News Commentary corpora. All single systems were tuned on the newstest2009 or newstest2010 development set. The newstest2011 dev set was used to train the system combination parameters. Finally, the newstest2008-newstest2010 dev sets were used to compare the results of the different system combination settings. In this Section all four different system engines are presented.

2.1 RWTH Aachen Single Systems

For the WMT 2012 evaluation the RWTH utilized RWTH's state-of-the-art phrase-based and hierarchical translation systems. GIZA++ (Och and Ney, 2003) was employed to train word alignments, language models have been created with the SRILM toolkit (Stolcke, 2002).

2.1.1 Phrase-Based System

The phrase-based translation (PBT) system is similar to the one described in Zens and Ney (2008). After phrase pair extraction from the word-aligned parallel corpus, the translation probabilities are estimated by relative frequencies. The standard feature set also includes an n-gram language model, phrase-level IBM-1 and word-, phrase- and distortion-penalties, which are combined in log-linear fashion. The model weights are optimized with standard Mert (Och, 2003) on 200-best lists. The optimization criterium is BLEU.

2.1.2 Hierarchical System

For the hierarchical setups (HPBT) described in this paper, the open source Jane toolkit (Vilar et al., 2010) is employed. Jane has been developed at RWTH and implements the hierarchical approach as introduced by Chiang (2007) with some state-of-the-art extensions. In hierarchical phrase-based translation, a weighted synchronous context-free grammar is induced from parallel text. In addition to contiguous *lexical* phrases, *hierarchical* phrases with up to two gaps are extracted. The search is typically carried out using the cube pruning algorithm (Huang and Chiang, 2007). The model weights are optimized with standard Mert (Och, 2003) on 100-best lists. The optimization criterium is 4BLEU −TER.

2.1.3 Preprocessing

In order to reduce the source vocabulary size translation, the German text was preprocessed by splitting German compound words with the frequency-based method described in (Koehn and Knight, 2003a). To further reduce translation complexity for the phrase-based approach, we performed the long-range part-of-speech based reordering rules proposed by (Popović et al., 2006).

2.1.4 Language Model

For both decoders a 4-gram language model is applied. The language model is trained on the parallel data as well as the provided News crawl, the 10^9 French-English, UN and LDC Gigaword Fourth Edition corpora. For the 10^9 French-English, UN and LDC Gigaword corpora RWTH applied the data selection technique described in (Moore and Lewis, 2010).

2.2 Karlsruhe Institute of Technology Single System

2.2.1 Preprocessing

We preprocess the training data prior to training the system, first by normalizing symbols such as quotes, dashes and apostrophes. Then smart-casing of the first words of each sentence is performed. For the German part of the training corpus we use the hunspell[1] lexicon to learn a mapping from old German spelling to new German spelling to obtain a corpus with homogenous spelling. In addition, we perform compound splitting as described in (Koehn and Knight, 2003b). Finally, we remove very long sentences, empty lines, and sentences that probably are not parallel due to length mismatch.

2.2.2 System Overview

The KIT system uses an in-house phrase-based decoder (Vogel, 2003) to perform translation and optimization with regard to the BLEU score is done using Minimum Error Rate Training as described in Venugopal et al. (2005).

2.2.3 Translation Models

The translation model is trained on the Europarl and News Commentary Corpus and the phrase table is based on a discriminative word alignment (Niehues and Vogel, 2008).

In addition, the system applies a bilingual language model (Niehues et al., 2011) to extend the context of source language words available for translation.

Furthermore, we use a discriminative word lexicon as introduced in (Mauser et al., 2009). The lexicon was trained and integrated into our system as described in (Mediani et al., 2011).

At last, we tried to find translations for out-of-vocabulary (OOV) words by using quasi-morphological operations as described in Niehues and Waibel (2011). For each OOV word, we try to find a related word that we can translate. We modify the ending letters of the OOV word and learn quasi-morphological operations to be performed on the known translation of the related word to synthesize a translation for the OOV word. By this approach we were for example able to translate *Kaminen* into *chimneys* using the known translation *Kamin # chimney*.

2.2.4 Language Models

We use two 4-gram SRI language models, one trained on the News Shuffle corpus and one trained

[1] `http://hunspell.sourceforge.net/`

on the Gigaword corpus. Furthermore, we use a 5-gram cluster-based language model trained on the News Shuffle corpus. The word clusters were created using the MKCLS algorithm. We used 100 word clusters.

2.2.5 Reordering Model

Reordering is performed based on part-of-speech tags obtained using the TreeTagger (Schmid, 1994). Based on these tags we learn probabilistic continuous (Rottmann and Vogel, 2007) and discontinuous (Niehues and Kolss, 2009) rules to cover short and long-range reorderings. The rules are learned from the training corpus and the alignment. In addition, we learned tree-based reordering rules. Therefore, the training corpus was parsed by the Stanford parser (Rafferty and Manning, 2008). The tree-based rules consist of the head node of a subtree and all its children as well as the new order and a probability. These rules were applied recursively. The reordering rules are applied to the source sentences and the reordered sentence variants as well as the original sequence are encoded in a word lattice which is used as input to the decoder. For the test sentences, the reordering based on parts-of-speech and trees allows us to change the word order in the source sentence so that the sentence can be translated more easily. In addition, we build reordering lattices for all training sentences and then extract phrase pairs from the monotone source path as well as from the reordered paths.

2.3 LIMSI-CNRS Single System

LIMSI's system is built with *n*-code (Crego et al., 2011), an open source statistical machine translation system based on bilingual *n*-gram[2]. In this approach, the translation model relies on a specific decomposition of the joint probability of a sentence pair $P(\mathbf{s},\mathbf{t})$ using the *n*-gram assumption: a sentence pair is decomposed into a sequence of bilingual units called *tuples*, defining a joint segmentation of the source and target. In the approach of (Mariño et al., 2006), this segmentation is a by-product of source reordering which ultimately derives from initial word and phrase alignments.

[2] `http://ncode.limsi.fr/`

2.3.1 An Overview of *n*-code

The baseline translation model is implemented as a stochastic finite-state transducer trained using a *n*-gram model of (source,target) pairs (Casacuberta and Vidal, 2004). Training this model requires to reorder source sentences so as to match the target word order. This is performed by a stochastic finite-state reordering model, which uses part-of-speech information[3] to generalize reordering patterns beyond lexical regularities.

In addition to the translation model, *eleven* feature functions are combined: a *target-language model*; four *lexicon models*; two *lexicalized reordering models* (Tillmann, 2004) aiming at predicting the orientation of the next translation unit; a 'weak' distance-based *distortion model*; and finally a *word-bonus model* and a *tuple-bonus model* which compensate for the system preference for short translations. The four *lexicon models* are similar to the ones used in a standard phrase based system: two scores correspond to the relative frequencies of the tuples and two lexical weights estimated from the automatically generated word alignments. The weights associated to feature functions are optimally combined using a discriminative training framework (Och, 2003), using the *newstest2009* development set.

The overall search is based on a beam-search strategy on top of a dynamic programming algorithm. Reordering hypotheses are computed in a preprocessing step, making use of reordering rules built from the word reorderings introduced in the tuple extraction process. The resulting reordering hypotheses are passed to the decoder in the form of word lattices (Crego and Mariño, 2007).

2.3.2 Continuous Space Translation Models

One critical issue with standard *n*-gram translation models is that the elementary units are bilingual pairs, which means that the underlying vocabulary can be quite large. Unfortunately, the parallel data available to train these models are typically smaller than the corresponding monolingual corpora used to train target language models. It is very likely then, that such models should face severe estimation problems. In such setting, using neural network language

[3] Part-of-speech labels for English and German are computed using the TreeTagger (Schmid, 1995).

model techniques seem all the more appropriate. For this study, we follow the recommendations of Le et al. (2012), who propose to factor the joint probability of a sentence pair by decomposing tuples in two (source and target) parts, and further each part in words. This yields a *word factored translation model* that can be estimated in a continuous space using the SOUL architecture (Le et al., 2011).

The design and integration of a SOUL model for large SMT tasks is far from easy, given the computational cost of computing n-gram probabilities. The solution used here was to resort to a two pass approach: the first pass uses a conventional back-off n-gram model to produce a k-best list; in the second pass, the k-best list is reordered using the probabilities of m-gram SOUL translation models. In the following experiments, we used a fixed context size for SOUL of $m = 10$, and used $k = 300$.

2.3.3 Corpora and Data Preprocessing

The parallel data is word-aligned using MGIZA++[4] with default settings. For the English monolingual training data, we used the same setup as last year[5] and thus the same target language model as detailed in (Allauzen et al., 2011).

For English, we took advantage of our in-house text processing tools for tokenization and detokenization steps (Déchelotte et al., 2008) and our system was built in "true-case". As German is morphologically more complex than English, the default policy which consists in treating each word form independently is plagued with data sparsity, which is detrimental both at training and decoding time. Thus, the German side was normalized using a specific pre-processing scheme (Allauzen et al., 2010; Durgar El-Kahlout and Yvon, 2010), which notably aims at reducing the lexical redundancy by (i) normalizing the orthography, (ii) neutralizing most inflections and (iii) splitting complex compounds.

2.4 SYSTRAN Software, Inc. Single System

The data submitted by SYSTRAN were obtained by a system composed of the standard SYSTRAN MT engine in combination with a *statistical post editing* (SPE) component.

[4]`http://geek.kyloo.net/software`

[5]The fifth edition of the English Gigaword (LDC2011T07) was not used.

The SYSTRAN system is traditionally classified as a rule-based system. However, over the decades, its development has always been driven by pragmatic considerations, progressively integrating many of the most efficient MT approaches and techniques. Nowadays, the baseline engine can be considered as a linguistic-oriented system making use of dependency analysis, general transfer rules as well as of large manually encoded dictionaries (100k - 800k entries per language pair).

The SYSTRAN phrase-based SPE component views the output of the rule-based system as the source language, and the (human) reference translation as the target language, see (L. Dugast and Koehn, 2007). It performs corrections and adaptions learned from the 5-gram language model trained on the parallel target-to-target corpus. Moreover, the following measures - limiting unwanted statistical effects - were applied:

- Named entities, time and numeric expressions are replaced by special tokens on both sides. This usually improves word alignment, since the vocabulary size is significantly reduced. In addition, entity translation is handled more reliably by the rule-based engine.
- The intersection of both vocabularies (i.e. vocabularies of the rule-based output and the reference translation) is used to produce an additional parallel corpus to help to improve word alignment.
- Singleton phrase pairs are deleted from the phrase table to avoid overfitting.
- Phrase pairs not containing the same number of entities on the source and the target side are also discarded.

The SPE language model was trained on 2M bilingual phrases from the news/Europarl corpora, provided as training data for *WMT 2012*. An additional language model built from 15M phrases of the English LDC Gigaword corpus using Kneser-Ney (Kneser and Ney, 1995) smoothing was added. Weights for these separate models were tuned by the Mert algorithm provided in the Moses toolkit (P. Koehn et al., 2007), using the provided news development set.

3 RWTH Aachen System Combination

System combination is used to produce consensus translations from multiple hypotheses produced with different translation engines that are better in terms of translation quality than any of the individual hypotheses. The basic concept of RWTH's approach to machine translation system combination has been described by Matusov et al. (2006; 2008). This approach includes an enhanced alignment and reordering framework. A lattice is built from the input hypotheses. The translation with the best score within the lattice according to a couple of statistical models is selected as consensus translation.

4 Experiments

This year, we tried different sets of single systems for system combination. As RWTH has two different translation systems, we put the output of both systems into system combination. Although both systems have the same preprocessing and language model, their hypotheses differ because of their different decoding approach. Compared to the other systems, the system by SYSTRAN has a completely different approach (see section 2.4). It is mainly based on a rule-based system. For the German→English pair, SYSTRAN achieves a lower BLEU score in each test set compared to the other groups. However, since the SYSTRAN system is very different to the others, we still obtain an improvement when we add it also to system combination.

We did experiments with different optimization criteria for the system combination optimization. All results are listed in Table 1 (unoptimized), Table 2 (optimized on BLEU) and Table 3 (optimized on TER-BLEU). Further, we investigated, whether we will loose performance, if a single system is dropped from the system combination. The results show that for each optimization criteria we need all systems to achieve the best results.

For the BLEU optimized system combination, we obtain an improvement compared to the best single systems for all dev sets. For newstest2008, we get an improvement of 1.5 points in BLEU and 1.5 points in TER compared to the best single system of Karlsruhe Institute of Technology. For newstest2009 we get an improvement of 1.9 points in BLEU and 1.5 points in TER compared to the best single system. The system combination of all systems outperforms the best single system with 1.9 points in BLEU and 1.9 points in TER for newstest2010. For newstest2011 the improvement is 1.3 points in BLEU and 2.9 points in TER.

For the TER-BLEU optimized system combination, we achieved more improvement in TER compared to the BLEU optimized system combination. For newstest2008, we get an improvement of 0.8 points in BLEU and 3.0 points in TER compared to the best single system of Karlsruhe Institute of Technology. The system combinations performs better on newstest2009 with 1.3 points in BLEU and 2.7 points in TER. For newstest2010, we get an improvement of 1.7 points in BLEU and 3.4 points in TER and for newstest2011 we get an improvement of 0.7 points in BLEU and 2.5 points in TER.

5 Conclusion

The four statistical machine translation systems of Karlsruhe Institute of Technology, RWTH Aachen and LIMSI and the very structural approach of SYSTRAN produce hypotheses with a huge variability compared to the others. Finally, the RWTH Aachen system combination combined all single system hypotheses to one hypothesis with a higher BLEU and a lower TER score compared to each single system. For each optimization criteria the system combinations using all single systems outperforms the system combinations using one less single system. Although the single system of SYSTRAN has the worst error scores and the RWTH single systems are similar, we achieved the best result in using all single systems. For the WMT 12 evaluation, we submitted the system combination of all systems optimized on BLEU.

Acknowledgments

This work was achieved as part of the Quaero Programme, funded by OSEO, French State agency for innovation.

References

Alexandre Allauzen, Josep M. Crego, İlknur Durgar El-Kahlout, and Francois Yvon. 2010. LIMSI's statistical translation systems for WMT'10. In *Proc. of the*

Table 1: All systems for the WMT 2012 German→English translation task (truecase). BLEU and TER results are in percentage. sc denotes system combination. All system combinations are **unoptimized**.

system	newstest2008		newstest2009		newstest2010		newstest2011		
	BLEU	TER	BLEU	TER	BLEU	TER	BLEU	TER	TER-BLEU
KIT	22.2	61.8	21.3	61.0	24.1	59.0	22.4	60.2	37.9
RWTH.PBT	21.4	62.0	21.3	61.1	23.9	59.1	21.4	61.2	39.7
Limsi	22.2	63.0	22.0	61.8	23.9	59.9	21.8	62.0	40.2
RWTH.HPBT	21.5	62.6	21.5	61.6	23.6	60.2	21.5	61.8	40.4
SYSTRAN	18.3	64.6	17.9	63.4	21.1	60.5	18.3	63.1	44.8
sc-withAllSystems	23.4	59.7	22.9	59.0	26.2	56.5	23.3	58.8	35.5
sc-without-RWTH.PBT	23.2	59.8	22.8	59.0	25.9	56.6	23.1	58.7	35.6
sc-without-RWTH.HPBT	23.2	59.6	22.7	58.9	26.1	56.2	23.1	58.7	35.6
sc-without-Limsi	22.7	60.1	22.4	59.2	25.5	56.7	22.8	58.8	36.0
sc-without-SYSTRAN	23.0	60.3	22.5	59.5	25.7	57.2	23.1	59.2	36.1
sc-without-KIT	23.0	59.9	22.5	59.1	25.9	56.6	22.9	59.1	36.3

Table 2: All systems for the WMT 2012 German→English translation task (truecase). BLEU and TER results are in percentage. sc denotes system combination. All system combinations are **optimized on BLEU** .

system	newstest2008		newstest2009		newstest2010		newstest2011		
	BLEU	TER	BLEU	TER	BLEU	TER	BLEU	TER	TER-BLEU
sc-withAllSystems	23.7	60.3	23.2	59.5	26.0	57.1	23.7	59.2	35.6
sc-without-RWTH.PBT	23.4	61.1	23.1	59.8	25.5	57.6	23.5	59.5	36.1
sc-without-SYSTRAN	23.3	61.1	22.6	60.5	25.3	58.1	23.5	60.0	36.5
sc-without-Limsi	23.1	60.7	22.6	59.7	25.4	57.5	23.3	59.4	36.2
sc-without-KIT	23.4	60.7	23.0	59.7	25.6	57.7	23.3	59.8	36.5
sc-without-RWTH.HPBT	23.3	59.4	22.8	58.6	26.1	56.0	23.1	58.4	35.2

Table 3: All systems for the WMT 2012 German→English translation task (truecase). BLEU and TER results are in percentage. sc denotes system combination. All system combinations are **optimized on TER-BLEU** .

system	newstest2008		newstest2009		newstest2010		newstest2011		
	BLEU	TER	BLEU	TER	BLEU	TER	BLEU	TER	TER-BLEU
sc-withAllSystems	23.0	58.8	22.4	58.3	25.8	55.6	23.1	57.7	34.6
sc-without-RWTH.PBT	23.0	59.3	22.5	58.5	25.6	56.0	23.1	58.0	34.9
sc-without-RWTH.HPBT	23.1	59.0	22.6	58.3	25.8	55.6	23.0	58.0	35.0
sc-without-SYSTRAN	22.9	59.7	22.4	59.1	25.6	56.7	23.2	58.5	35.3
sc-without-Limsi	22.7	59.4	22.2	58.7	25.3	56.1	22.7	58.1	35.5
sc-without-KIT	22.9	59.3	22.4	58.5	25.7	55.8	22.7	58.1	35.4

Joint Workshop on Statistical Machine Translation and MetricsMATR, pages 54–59, Uppsala, Sweden.

Alexandre Allauzen, Gilles Adda, Hélène Bonneau-Maynard, Josep M. Crego, Hai-Son Le, Aurélien Max, Adrien Lardilleux, Thomas Lavergne, Artem Sokolov, Guillaume Wisniewski, and François Yvon. 2011. LIMSI @ WMT11. In *Proceedings of the Sixth Workshop on Statistical Machine Translation*, pages 309–315, Edinburgh, Scotland, July. Association for Computational Linguistics.

F. Casacuberta and E. Vidal. 2004. Machine translation with inferred stochastic finite-state transducers. *Computational Linguistics*, 30(3):205–225.

D. Chiang. 2007. Hierarchical Phrase-Based Translation. *Computational Linguistics*, 33(2):201–228.

J.M. Crego and J.B. Mariño. 2007. Improving statistical MT by coupling reordering and decoding. *Machine Translation*, 20(3):199–215.

Josep M. Crego, Franois Yvon, and Jos B. Mario. 2011. N-code: an open-source Bilingual N-gram SMT Toolkit. *Prague Bulletin of Mathematical Linguistics*, 96:49–58.

D. Déchelotte, O. Galibert G. Adda, A. Allauzen, J. Gauvain, H. Meynard, and F. Yvon. 2008. LIMSI's statistical translation systems for WMT'08. In *Proc. of the NAACL-HTL Statistical Machine Translation Workshop*, Columbus, Ohio.

Ilknur Durgar El-Kahlout and Franois Yvon. 2010. The pay-offs of preprocessing for German-English Statistical Machine Translation. In Marcello Federico, Ian Lane, Michael Paul, and Franois Yvon, editors, *Proceedings of the seventh International Workshop on Spoken Language Translation (IWSLT)*, pages 251–258.

L. Huang and D. Chiang. 2007. Forest Rescoring: Faster Decoding with Integrated Language Models. In *Proc. Annual Meeting of the Association for Computational Linguistics*, pages 144–151, Prague, Czech Republic, June.

R. Kneser and H. Ney. 1995. Improved backing-off for m-gram language modeling. In *Proceedings of the International Conference on Acoustics, Speech, and Signal Processing, ICASSP'95*, pages 181–184, Detroit, MI.

P. Koehn and K. Knight. 2003a. Empirical Methods for Compound Splitting. In *EACL*, Budapest, Hungary.

P. Koehn and K. Knight. 2003b. Empirical Methods for Compound Splitting. In *Proceedings of European Chapter of the ACL (EACL 2009)*, pages 187–194.

J. Senellart L. Dugast and P. Koehn. 2007. Statistical post-editing on systran's rule-based translation system. In *Proceedings of the Second Workshop on Statistical Machine Translation*, StatMT '07, pages 220–223, Stroudsburg, PA, USA. Association for Computational Linguistics.

Hai-Son Le, Ilya Oparin, Alexandre Allauzen, Jean-Luc Gauvain, and François Yvon. 2011. Structured output layer neural network language model. In *Proceedings of ICASSP'11*, pages 5524–5527.

Hai-Son Le, Alexandre Allauzen, and François Yvon. 2012. Continuous space translation models with neural networks. In *NAACL '12: Proceedings of the 2012 Conference of the North American Chapter of the Association for Computational Linguistics on Human Language Technology*.

José B. Mariño, R. Banchs, J.M. Crego, A. de Gispert, P. Lambert, J.A.R. Fonollosa, and M.R. Costa-jussà. 2006. N-gram-based machine translation. *Computational Linguistics*, 32(4).

E. Matusov, N. Ueffing, and H. Ney. 2006. Computing Consensus Translation from Multiple Machine Translation Systems Using Enhanced Hypotheses Alignment. In *Conference of the European Chapter of the Association for Computational Linguistics (EACL)*, pages 33–40.

E. Matusov, G. Leusch, R.E. Banchs, N. Bertoldi, D. Dechelotte, M. Federico, M. Kolss, Y.-S. Lee, J.B. Mari no, M. Paulik, S. Roukos, H. Schwenk, and H. Ney. 2008. System Combination for Machine Translation of Spoken and Written Language. *IEEE Transactions on Audio, Speech and Language Processing*, 16(7):1222–1237.

Arne Mauser, Saša Hasan, and Hermann Ney. 2009. Extending Statistical Machine Translation with Discriminative and Trigger-based Lexicon Models. In *Proceedings of the 2009 Conference on Empirical Methods in Natural Language Processing: Volume 1 - Volume 1*, EMNLP '09, Singapore.

Mohammed Mediani, Eunah Cho, Jan Niehues, Teresa Herrmann, and Alex Waibel. 2011. The KIT English-French Translation Systems for IWSLT 2011. In *Proceedings of the Eighth International Workshop on Spoken Language Translation (IWSLT)*.

R.C. Moore and W. Lewis. 2010. Intelligent Selection of Language Model Training Data. In *ACL (Short Papers)*, pages 220–224, Uppsala, Sweden, July.

J. Niehues and M. Kolss. 2009. A POS-Based Model for Long-Range Reorderings in SMT. In *Fourth Workshop on Statistical Machine Translation (WMT 2009)*, Athens, Greece.

J. Niehues and S. Vogel. 2008. Discriminative Word Alignment via Alignment Matrix Modeling. In *Proc. of Third ACL Workshop on Statistical Machine Translation*, Columbus, USA.

Jan Niehues and Alex Waibel. 2011. Using Wikipedia to Translate Domain-specific Terms in SMT. In *Pro-*

ceedings of the Eighth International Workshop on Spoken Language Translation (IWSLT), San Francisco, CA.

Jan Niehues, Teresa Herrmann, Stephan Vogel, and Alex Waibel. 2011. Wider Context by Using Bilingual Language Models in Machine Translation. In *Sixth Workshop on Statistical Machine Translation (WMT 2011)*, Edinburgh, UK.

F.J. Och and H. Ney. 2003. A Systematic Comparison of Various Statistical Alignment Models. *Computational Linguistics*, 29(1):19–51.

F.J. Och. 2003. Minimum Error Rate Training for Statistical Machine Translation. In *Proc. Annual Meeting of the Association for Computational Linguistics*, pages 160–167, Sapporo, Japan, July.

A. Birch P. Koehn, H. Hoang, C. Callison-Burch, M. Federico, N. Bertoldi, B. Cowan, W. Shen, C. Moran, R. Zens, C. Dyer, O. Bojar, A. Constantin, and E. Herbst. 2007. Moses: open source toolkit for statistical machine translation. In *Proceedings of the 45th Annual Meeting of the ACL on Interactive Poster and Demonstration Sessions*, ACL '07, pages 177–180, Stroudsburg, PA, USA. Association for Computational Linguistics.

M. Popović, D. Stein, and H. Ney. 2006. Statistical Machine Translation of German Compound Words. In *FinTAL - 5th International Conference on Natural Language Processing, Springer Verlag, LNCS*, pages 616–624.

Anna N. Rafferty and Christopher D. Manning. 2008. Parsing three German treebanks: lexicalized and unlexicalized baselines. In *Proceedings of the Workshop on Parsing German.*

K. Rottmann and S. Vogel. 2007. Word Reordering in Statistical Machine Translation with a POS-Based Distortion Model. In *TMI*, Skövde, Sweden.

H. Schmid. 1994. Probabilistic Part-of-Speech Tagging Using Decision Trees. In *International Conference on New Methods in Language Processing*, Manchester, UK.

Helmut Schmid. 1995. Improvements in part-of-speech tagging with an application to German. In Evelyne Tzoukermann and SusanEditors Armstrong, editors, *Proceedings of the ACL SIGDATWorkshop*, pages 47–50. Kluwer Academic Publishers.

A. Stolcke. 2002. SRILM - an extensible language modeling toolkit. In *Proc. Int. Conf. on Spoken Language Processing*, volume 2, pages 901–904, Denver, Colorado, USA, September.

C. Tillmann. 2004. A unigram orientation model for statistical machine translation. In *Proceedings of HLT-NAACL 2004*, pages 101–104. Association for Computational Linguistics.

A. Venugopal, A. Zollman, and A. Waibel. 2005. Training and Evaluation Error Minimization Rules for Statistical Machine Translation. In *Workshop on Data-drive Machine Translation and Beyond (WPT-05)*, Ann Arbor, MI.

D. Vilar, S. Stein, M. Huck, and H. Ney. 2010. Jane: Open Source Hierarchical Translation, Extended with Reordering and Lexicon Models. In *ACL 2010 Joint Fifth Workshop on Statistical Machine Translation and Metrics MATR*, pages 262–270, Uppsala, Sweden, July.

S. Vogel. 2003. SMT Decoder Dissected: Word Reordering. In *Int. Conf. on Natural Language Processing and Knowledge Engineering*, Beijing, China.

R. Zens and H. Ney. 2008. Improvements in Dynamic Programming Beam Search for Phrase-based Statistical Machine Translation. In *Proc. of the Int. Workshop on Spoken Language Translation (IWSLT)*, Honolulu, Hawaii, October.

LIMSI @ WMT'12

Hai-Son Le[1,2], Thomas Lavergne[2], Alexandre Allauzen[1,2],
Marianna Apidianaki[2], Li Gong[1,2], Aurélien Max[1,2],
Artem Sokolov[2], Guillaume Wisniewski[1,2], François Yvon[1,2]
Univ. Paris-Sud[1] and LIMSI-CNRS[2]
rue John von Neumann, 91403 Orsay cedex, France
{firstname.lastname}@limsi.fr

Abstract

This paper describes LIMSI's submissions to the shared translation task. We report results for French-English and German-English in both directions. Our submissions use n-code, an open source system based on bilingual n-grams. In this approach, both the translation and target language models are estimated as conventional smoothed n-gram models; an approach we extend here by estimating the translation probabilities in a continuous space using neural networks. Experimental results show a significant and consistent BLEU improvement of approximately 1 point for all conditions. We also report preliminary experiments using an "on-the-fly" translation model.

1 Introduction

This paper describes LIMSI's submissions to the shared translation task of the Seventh Workshop on Statistical Machine Translation. LIMSI participated in the French-English and German-English tasks in both directions. For this evaluation, we used n-code, an open source in-house Statistical Machine Translation (SMT) system based on bilingual n-grams[1]. The main novelty of this year's participation is the use, in a large scale system, of the continuous space translation models described in (Hai-Son et al., 2012). These models estimate the n-gram probabilities of bilingual translation units using neural networks. We also investigate an alternative approach where the translation probabilities of a phrase based system are estimated "on-the-fly" by sampling relevant examples, instead of considering the entire training set. Finally we also describe the use in a rescoring step of several additional features based on IBM1 models and word sense disambiguation information.

The rest of this paper is organized as follows. Section 2 provides an overview of the baseline systems built with n-code, including the standard translation model (TM). The continuous space translation models are then described in Section 3. As in our previous participations, several steps of data preprocessing, cleaning and filtering are applied, and their improvement took a non-negligible part of our work. These steps are summarized in Section 5. The last two sections report experimental results obtained with the "on-the-fly" system in Section 6 and with n-code in Section 7.

[1] `http://ncode.limsi.fr/`

2 System overview

n-code implements the bilingual n-gram approach to SMT (Casacuberta and Vidal, 2004; Mariño et al., 2006; Crego and Mariño, 2006). In this framework, translation is divided in two steps: a source reordering step and a (monotonic) translation step. Source reordering is based on a set of learned rewrite rules that non-deterministically reorder the input words. Applying these rules result in a finite-state graph of possible source reorderings, which is then searched for the best possible candidate translation.

2.1 Features

Given a source sentence $\mathbf{s}$ of I words, the best translation hypothesis $\hat{\mathbf{t}}$ is defined as the sequence of J words that maximizes a linear combination of feature functions:

$$\hat{\mathbf{t}} = \arg\max_{\mathbf{t},\mathbf{a}} \left\{ \sum_{m=1}^{M} \lambda_m h_m(\mathbf{a}, \mathbf{s}, \mathbf{t}) \right\} \quad (1)$$

where λ_m is the weight associated with feature function h_m and $\mathbf{a}$ denotes an alignment between source and target phrases. Among the feature functions, the peculiar form of the translation model constitute one of the main difference between the n-gram approach and standard phrase-based systems. This will be further detailled in section 2.2 and 3.

In addition to the translation model, *fourteen* feature functions are combined: a *target-language model* (Section 5.3); four *lexicon models*; six *lexicalized reordering models* (Tillmann, 2004; Crego et al., 2011) aiming at predicting the orientation of the next translation unit; a "weak" distance-based *distortion model*; and finally a *word-bonus model* and a *tuple-bonus model* which compensate for the system preference for short translations. The four *lexicon models* are similar to the ones used in standard phrase-based systems: two scores correspond to the relative frequencies of the tuples and two lexical weights are estimated from the automatic word alignments. The weights vector λ is learned using a discriminative training framework (Och, 2003) (Minimum Error Rate Training (MERT)) using the *newstest2009* as development set and BLEU (Papineni et al., 2002) as the optimization criteria.

2.2 Standard n-gram translation models

n-gram translation models rely on a specific decomposition of the joint probability of a sentence pair $P(\mathbf{s}, \mathbf{t})$: a sentence pair is assumed to be decomposed into a sequence of L bilingual units called *tuples* defining a joint segmentation: $(\mathbf{s}, \mathbf{t}) = u_1, ..., u_L$[2]. In the approach of (Mariño et al., 2006), this segmentation is a by-product of source reordering obtained by "unfolding" initial word alignments.

In this framework, the basic translation units are *tuples*, which are the analogous of phrase pairs and represent a matching $u = (\bar{s}, \bar{t})$ between a source $\bar{s}$ and a target $\bar{t}$ phrase (see Figure 1). Using the n-gram assumption, the joint probability of a segmented sentence pair decomposes as:

$$P(\mathbf{s}, \mathbf{t}) = \prod_{i=1}^{L} P(u_i | u_{i-1}, ..., u_{i-n+1}) \quad (2)$$

During the training phase (Mariño et al., 2006), tuples are extracted from a word-aligned corpus (using MGIZA++[3] with default settings) in such a way that a unique segmentation of the bilingual corpus is achieved. A baseline n-gram translation model is then estimated over a training corpus composed of tuple sequences using modified Knesser-Ney Smoothing (Chen and Goodman, 1998).

2.3 Inference

During decoding, source sentences are represented in the form of word lattices containing the most promising reordering hypotheses, so as to reproduce the word order modifications introduced during the tuple extraction process. Hence, only those reordering hypotheses are translated and they are introduced using a set of reordering rules automatically learned from the word alignments.

In the example in Figure 1, the rule [*prix nobel de la paix* ⇝ *nobel de la paix prix*] reproduces the invertion of the French words that is observed when translating from French into English. Typically, part-of-speech (POS) information is used to increase the generalization power of these rules. Hence, rewrite rules are built using POS rather than surface word forms (Crego and Mariño, 2006).

3 SOUL translation models

A first issue with the model described by equation (2) is that the elementary units are bilingual pairs. As a consequence, the underlying vocabulary, hence the number of parameters, can be quite large, even for small translation tasks. Due to data sparsity issues, such model are bound to face severe estimation problems. Another problem with (2) is that the source and target sides play symmetric roles: yet, in decoding, the source side is known and only the target side must be predicted.

3.1 A word factored translation model

To overcome these issues, the n-gram probability in equation (2) can be factored by decomposing tuples

[2] From now on, $(\mathbf{s}, \mathbf{t})$ thus denotes an *aligned* sentence pair, and we omit the alignment variable $\mathbf{a}$ in further developments.

[3] `http://www.kyloo.net/software/doku.php`

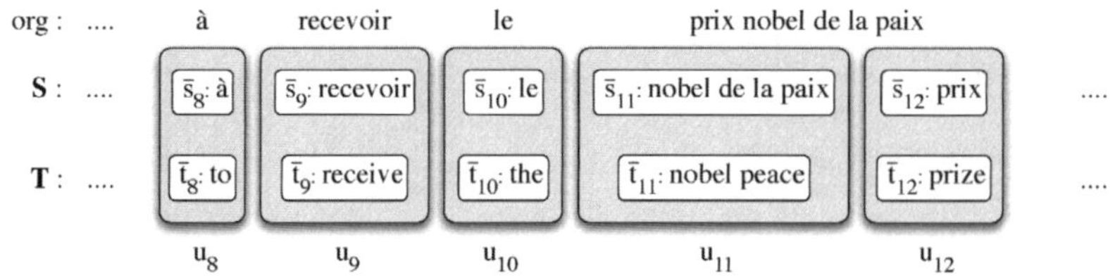

Figure 1: Extract of a French-English sentence pair segmented into bilingual units. The original (*org*) French sentence appears at the top of the figure, just above the reordered source $\mathbf{s}$ and target $\mathbf{t}$. The pair $(\mathbf{s}, \mathbf{t})$ decomposes into a sequence of L bilingual units (*tuples*) $u_1, ..., u_L$. Each tuple u_i contains a source and a target phrase: $\bar{s}_i$ and $\bar{t}_i$.

in two parts (source and target), and by taking words as the basic units of the n-gram TM. This may seem to be a regression with respect to current state-of-the-art SMT systems, as the shift from the word-based model of (Brown et al., 1993) to the phrase-based models of (Zens et al., 2002) is usually considered as a major breakthrough of the recent years. Indeed, one important motivation for considering phrases was to capture local context in translation and reordering. It should however be emphasized that the decomposition of phrases into words is only re-introduced here as a way to mitigate the parameter estimation problems. Translation units are still pairs of *phrases*, derived from a bilingual segmentation in tuples synchronizing the source and target n-gram streams. In fact, the estimation policy described in section 4 will actually allow us to take into account *larger contexts* than is possible with conventional n-gram models.

Let s_i^k denote the kth word of source tuple $\bar{s}_i$. Considering the example of Figure 1, s_{11}^1 denotes the source word *nobel*, s_{11}^4 the source word *paix*. We finally denote $h^{n-1}(t_i^k)$ the sequence made of the $n-1$ words preceding t_i^k in the target sentence: in Figure 1, $h^3(t_{11}^2)$ thus refers to the three words context *receive the nobel* associated with t_{11}^2 *peace*. Using these notations, equation (2) is rewritten as:

$$P(\mathbf{a}, \mathbf{s}, \mathbf{t}) = \prod_{i=1}^{L} \Big[\prod_{k=1}^{|\bar{t}_i|} P\big(t_i^k | h^{n-1}(t_i^k), h^{n-1}(s_{i+1}^1)\big) \times \prod_{k=1}^{|\bar{s}_i|} P\big(s_i^k | h^{n-1}(t_i^1), h^{n-1}(s_i^k)\big) \Big] \quad (3)$$

This decomposition relies on the n-gram assumption, this time at the word level. Therefore, this model estimates the joint probability of a sentence pair using two sliding windows of length n, one for each language; however, the moves of these windows remain synchronized by the tuple segmentation. Moreover, the context is not limited to the current phrase, and continues to include words from adjacent phrases. Using the example of Figure 1, the contribution of the target phrase $\bar{t}_{11} =$ *nobel, peace* to $P(\mathbf{s}, \mathbf{t})$ using a 3- gram model is:

$$P\big(\text{nobel} | [\text{receive, the}], [\text{la, paix}]\big) \times P\big(\text{peace} | [\text{the, nobel}], [\text{la, paix}]\big).$$

A benefit of this new formulation is that the vocabularies involved only contain words, and are thus much smaller that tuple vocabularies. These models are thus less at risk to be plagued by data sparsity issues. Moreover, the decomposition (3) now involves two models: the first term represents a TM, the second term is best viewed as a reordering model. In this formulation, the TM only predicts the target phrase, given its source and target contexts.

$$P(\mathbf{s}, \mathbf{t}) = \prod_{i=1}^{L} \Big[\prod_{k=1}^{|\bar{s}_i|} P\big(s_i^k | h^{n-1}(s_i^k), h^{n-1}(t_{i+1}^1)\big) \times \prod_{k=1}^{|\bar{t}_i|} P\big(t_i^k | h^{n-1}(s_i^1), h^{n-1}(t_i^k)\big) \Big] \quad (4)$$

4 The principles of SOUL

In section 3.1, we defined a n-gram translation model based on equations (3) and (4). A major difficulty with such models is to reliably estimate their parameters, the numbers of which grow exponentially with the order of the model. This problem is aggravated in natural language processing due to the well-known data sparsity issue. In this work, we take advantage of the recent proposal of (Le et al., 2011). Using a specific neural network architecture (the *Structured OUtput Layer* or SOUL model), it becomes possible to handle large vocabulary language modeling tasks. This approach was experimented last year for target language models only and is now extended to translation models. More details about the SOUL architecture can be found in (Le et al., 2011), while its extension to translation models is more precisely described in (Hai-Son et al., 2012).

The integration of SOUL models for large SMT tasks is carried out using a two-pass approach: the first pass uses conventional back-off n-gram translation and language models to produce a k-best list (the k most likely translations); in the second pass, the probability of a m-gram SOUL model is computed for each hypothesis and the k-best list is accordingly reordered. In all the following experiments, we used a context size for SOUL of $m = 10$, and used $k = 300$. The two decompositions of equations (3) and (4) are used by introducing 4 scores during the rescoring step.

5 Corpora and data pre-processing

Concerning data pre-processing, we started from our submissions from last year (Allauzen et al., 2011) and mainly upgraded the corpora and the associated language-dependent pre-processing routines.

5.1 Pre-processing

We used in-house text processing tools for the tokenization and detokenization steps (Déchelotte et al., 2008). Previous experiments have demonstrated that better normalization tools provide better BLEU scores: all systems are thus built in "true-case". Compared to last year, the pre-processing of utf-8 characters was significantly improved.

As German is morphologically more complex than English, the default policy which consists in treating each word form independently is plagued with data sparsity, which severely impacts both training (alignment) and decoding (due to unknown forms). When translating from German into English, the German side is thus normalized using a specific pre-processing scheme (described in (Allauzen et al., 2010; Durgar El-Kahlout and Yvon, 2010)), which aims at reducing the lexical redundancy by (i) normalizing the orthography, (ii) neutralizing most inflections and (iii) splitting complex compounds. All parallel corpora were POS-tagged with the TreeTagger (Schmid, 1994); in addition, for German, fine-grained POS labels were also needed for pre-processing and were obtained using the RF-Tagger (Schmid and Laws, 2008).

5.2 Bilingual corpora

As for last year's evaluation, we used all the available parallel data for the German-English language pair, while only a subpart of the French-English parallel data was selected. Word alignment models were trained using all the data, whereas the translation models were estimated on a subpart of the parallel data: the UN corpus was discarded for this step and about half of the French-English Giga corpus was filtered based on a perplexity criterion as in (Allauzen et al., 2011)).

For French-English, we mainly upgraded the training material from last year by extracting the new parts from the common data. The word alignment models trained last year were then updated by running a forced alignment [4] of the new data. These new word-aligned data was added to last year's parallel corpus and constitute the training material for the translation models and feature functions described in Section 2. Given the large amount of available data, three different bilingual n-gram models are estimated, one for each source of data: News-Commentary, Europarl, and the French-English Giga corpus. These models are then added to the weighted mixture defined by equation (1). For German-English, we simply used all the available parallel data to train one single translation models.

5.3 Monolingual corpora and language models

For the monolingual training data, we also used the same setup as last year. For German, all the training data allowed in the constrained task were divided into several sets based on dates or genres: News-Commentary, the news crawled from the Web grouped by year, and Europarl. For each subset, a standard 4-gram LM was estimated using interpolated Kneser-Ney smoothing (Kneser and Ney,

[4]The forced alignment step consists in an additional EM iteration.

1995; Chen and Goodman, 1998). The resulting LMs are then linearly combined using interpolation coefficients chosen so as to minimize the perplexity of the development set. The German vocabulary is created using all the words contained in the parallel data and expanded to reach a total of 500k words by including the most frequent words observed in the monolingual News data for 2011.

For French and English, the same monolingual corpora as last year were used[5]. We did not observe any perplexity decrease in our attempts to include the new data specifically provided for this year's evaluation. We therefore used the same language models as in (Allauzen et al., 2011).

6 "On-the-fly" system

We also developped an alternative approach implementing "on-the-fly" estimation of the parameter of a standard phase-based model, using Moses (Koehn et al., 2007) as the decoder. Implementing on-the-fly estimation for n-code, while possible in theory, is less appealing due to the computational cost of estimating a smoothed language model. Given an input source file, it is possible to compute only those statistics which are required to translate the phrases it contains. As in previous works on *on-the-fly* model estimation for SMT (Callison-Burch et al., 2005; Lopez, 2008), we compute a suffix array for the source corpus. This further enables to consider only a subset of translation examples, which we select by deterministic random sampling, meaning that the sample is chosen randomly with respect to the full corpus but that the same sample is always returned for a given value of sample size, hereafter denoted N. In our experiments, we used $N = 1,000$ and computed from the sample and the word alignments (we used the same tokenization and word alignments as in all other submitted systems) the same translation[6] and lexical reordering models as the standard training scripts of the Moses system.

Experiments were run on the data sets used for WMT English-French machine translation evaluation tasks, using the same corpora and optimization procedure as in our other experiments. The only notable difference is our use of the Moses decoder instead of the n-gram-based system. As shown in Table 1, our on-the-fly system achieves a result (31.7 BLEU point) that is slightly worst than the n-code baseline (32.0) and slightly better than the equivalent Moses baseline (31.5), but does it much faster. Model estimation for the test file is reduced to 2 hours and 50 minutes, with an additional overhead for loading and writing files of one and a half hours, compared to roughly 210 hours for our baseline systems under comparable hardware conditions.

7 Experimental results

7.1 n-code with SOUL

Table 1 summarizes the experimental results submitted to the shared translation for French-English and German-English in both directions. The performances are measured in terms of BLEU on *newstest2011*, last year's test set, and this year's test set *newstest2012*. For the former, BLEU scores are computed with the NIST script *mteva-v13.pl*, while we provide for *newstest2012* the results computed by the organizers [7]. The *Baseline* results are obtained with standard n-gram models estimated with back-off, both for the bilingual and monolingual target models. With standard n-gram estimates, the order is limited to $n = 4$. For instance, the n-code French-English baseline achieves a 0.5 BLEU point improvement over a Moses system trained with the same data setup in both directions.

From Table 1, it can be observed that adding the SOUL models (translation models and target language model) consistently improves the baseline, with an increase of 1 BLEU point. Contrastive experiments show that the SOUL target LM does not bring significant gain when added to the SOUL translation models. For instance, a gain of 0.3 BLEU point is observed when translating from French to English with the addition of the SOUL target LM. In the other translation directions, the differences are negligible.

[5]The fifth edition of the English Gigaword (LDC2011T07) was *not* used.

[6]An approximation is used for $p(f|e)$, and *coherent* translation estimation is used; see (Lopez, 2008).

[7]All results come from the official website: `http://matrix.statmt.org/matrix/`.

Direction	*System*	BLEU	
		test2011	*test2012**
en2fr	Baseline	32.0	28.9
	+ SOUL TM	33.4	29.9
	on-the-fly	31.7	28.6
fr2en	Baseline	30.2	30.4
	+ SOUL TM	31.1	31.5
en2de	Baseline	15.4	16.0
	+ SOUL TM	16.6	17.0
de2en	Baseline	21.8	22.9
	+ SOUL TM	22.8	23.9

Table 1: Experimental results in terms of BLEU scores measured on the newstest2011 and newstest2012. For newstest2012, the scores are provided by the organizers.

7.2 Experiments with additional features

For this year's evaluation, we also investigated several additional features based on IBM1 models and word sense disambiguation (WSD) information in rescoring. As for the SOUL models, these features are added after the n-best list generation step.

In previous work (Och et al., 2004; Hasan, 2011), the IBM1 features (Brown et al., 1993) are found helpful. As the IBM1 model is asymmetric, two models are estimated, one in both directions. Contrary to the reported results, these additional features do not yield significant improvements over the baseline system. We assume that the difficulty is to add information to an already extensively optimized system. Moreover, the IBM1 models are estimated on the same training corpora as the translation system, a fact that may explain the redundancy of these additional features.

In a separate series of experiments, we also add WSD features calculated according to a variation of the method proposed in (Apidianaki, 2009). For each word of a subset of the input (source language) vocabulary, a simple WSD classifier produces a probability distribution over a set of translations[8]. During reranking, each translation hypothesis is scanned and the word translations that match one of the proposed variant are rewarded using an additional score. While this method had given some small gains on a smaller dataset (IWSLT'11), we did not observe here any improvement over the baseline system. Additional analysis hints that (i) most of the proposed variants are already covered by the translation model with high probabilities and (ii) that these variants are seldom found in the reference sentences. This means that, in the situation in which only one reference is provided, the hypotheses with a high score for the WSD feature are not adequately rewarded with the actual references.

8 Conclusion

In this paper, we described our submissions to WMT'12 in the French-English and German-English shared translation tasks, in both directions. As for our last year's participation, our main systems are built with n-code, the open source Statistical Machine Translation system based on bilingual n-grams. Our contributions are threefold. First, we have experimented a new kind of translation models, where the bilingual n-gram distribution are estimated in a continuous space with neural networks. As shown in past evaluations with target language model, there is a significant reward for using this kind of models in a rescoring step. We observed that, in general, the continuous space translation model yields a slightly larger improvement than the target translation model. However, their combination does not result in an additional gain.

We also reported preliminary results with a system "on-the-fly", where the training data are sampled according to the data to be translated in order to train contextually adapted system. While this system achieves comparable performance to our baseline system, it is worth noticing that its total training time is much smaller than a comparable Moses system. Finally, we investigated several additional features based on IBM1 models and word sense disambiguation information in rescoring. While these methods have sometimes been reported to help improve the results, we did not observe any improvement here over the baseline system.

Acknowledgment

This work was partially funded by the French State agency for innovation (OSEO) in the Quaero Programme.

[8] The difference with the method described in (Apidianaki, 2009) is that no sense clustering is performed, and each translation is represented by a separate weighted source feature vector which is used for disambiguation

References

Alexandre Allauzen, Josep M. Crego, İlknur Durgar El-Kahlout, and François Yvon. 2010. LIMSI's statistical translation systems for WMT'10. In *Proc. of the Joint Workshop on Statistical Machine Translation and MetricsMATR*, pages 54–59, Uppsala, Sweden.

Alexandre Allauzen, Gilles Adda, Hélène Bonneau-Maynard, Josep M. Crego, Hai-Son Le, Aurélien Max, Adrien Lardilleux, Thomas Lavergne, Artem Sokolov, Guillaume Wisniewski, and François Yvon. 2011. LIMSI @ WMT11. In *Proceedings of the Sixth Workshop on Statistical Machine Translation*, pages 309–315, Edinburgh, Scotland, July. Association for Computational Linguistics.

Marianna Apidianaki. 2009. Data-driven semantic analysis for multilingual WSD and lexical selection in translation. In *Proceedings of the 12th Conference of the European Chapter of the ACL (EACL 2009)*, pages 77–85, Athens, Greece, March. Association for Computational Linguistics.

Peter F. Brown, Vincent J. Della Pietra, Stephen A. Della Pietra, and Robert L. Mercer. 1993. The mathematics of statistical machine translation: parameter estimation. *Comput. Linguist.*, 19(2):263–311.

Chris Callison-Burch, Colin Bannard, and Josh Schroeder. 2005. Scaling phrase-based statistical machine translation to larger corpora and longer phrases. In *Proceedings of the 43rd Annual Meeting of the Association for Computational Linguistics (ACL'05)*, pages 255–262, Ann Arbor, Michigan, June. Association for Computational Linguistics.

Francesco Casacuberta and Enrique Vidal. 2004. Machine translation with inferred stochastic finite-state transducers. *Computational Linguistics*, 30(3):205–225.

Stanley F. Chen and Joshua T. Goodman. 1998. An empirical study of smoothing techniques for language modeling. Technical Report TR-10-98, Computer Science Group, Harvard Un iversity.

Josep M. Crego and José B. Mariño. 2006. Improving statistical MT by coupling reordering and decoding. *Machine Translation*, 20(3):199–215.

Josep M. Crego, François Yvon, and José B. Mariño. 2011. N-code: an open-source Bilingual N-gram SMT Toolkit. *Prague Bulletin of Mathematical Linguistics*, 96:49–58.

Ilknur Durgar El-Kahlout and François Yvon. 2010. The pay-offs of preprocessing for German-English Statistical Machine Translation. In Marcello Federico, Ian Lane, Michael Paul, and François Yvon, editors, *Proceedings of the seventh International Workshop on Spoken Language Translation (IWSLT)*, pages 251–258.

Daniel Déchelotte, Gilles Adda, Alexandre Allauzen, Olivier Galibert, Jean-Luc Gauvain, Hélène Maynard, and François Yvon. 2008. LIMSI's statistical translation systems for WMT'08. In *Proc. of the NAACL-HTL Statistical Machine Translation Workshop*, Columbus, Ohio.

Hai-Son, Alexandre Allauzen, and François Yvon. 2012. Continuous space translation models with neural networks. In *NAACL '12: Proceedings of the 2012 Conference of the North American Chapter of the Association for Computational Linguistics on Human Language Technology*.

Saša Hasan. 2011. *Triplet Lexicon Models for Statistical Machine Translation*. Ph.D. thesis, RWTH Aachen University.

Reinhard Kneser and Herman Ney. 1995. Improved backing-off for m-gram language modeling. In *Proceedings of the International Conference on Acoustics, Speech, and Signal Processing, ICASSP'95*, pages 181–184, Detroit, MI.

Philipp Koehn, Hieu Hoang, Alexandra Birch, Chris Callison-Burch, Marcello Federico, Nicola Bertoldi, Brooke Cowan, Wade Shen, Christine Moran, Richard Zens, Chris Dyer, Ondrej Bojar, Alexandra Constantin, and Evan Herbst. 2007. Moses: Open source toolkit for statistical machine translation. In *Proceedings of the 45th Annual Meeting of the Association for Computational Linguistics Companion Volume Proceedings of the Demo and Poster Sessions*, pages 177–180, Prague, Czech Republic, June. Association for Computational Linguistics.

Hai-Son Le, Ilya Oparin, Alexandre Allauzen, Jean-Luc Gauvain, and François Yvon. 2011. Structured output layer neural network language model. In *Proceedings of ICASSP'11*, pages 5524–5527.

Adam Lopez. 2008. Tera-scale translation models via pattern matching. In *Proceedings of the 22nd International Conference on Computational Linguistics (Coling 2008)*, pages 505–512, Manchester, UK, August. Coling 2008 Organizing Committee.

José B. Mariño, Rafael E. Banchs, Josep M. Crego, Adrià de Gispert, Patrick Lambert, José A.R. Fonollosa, and Marta R. Costa-Jussà. 2006. N-gram-based machine translation. *Computational Linguistics*, 32(4):527–549.

Franz Josef Och, Daniel Gildea, Sanjeev Khudanpur, Anoop Sarkar, Kenji Yamada, Alex Fraser, Shankar Kumar, Libin Shen, David Smith, Katherine Eng, Viren Jain, Zhen Jin, and Dragomir Radev. 2004. A smorgasbord of features for statistical machine translation. In Daniel Marcu Susan Dumais and Salim Roukos, editors, *HLT-NAACL 2004: Main Proceedings*, pages 161–168, Boston, Massachusetts, USA,

May 2 - May 7. Association for Computational Linguistics.

Franz Josef Och. 2003. Minimum error rate training in statistical machine translation. In *ACL '03: Proc. of the 41st Annual Meeting on Association for Computational Linguistics*, pages 160–167.

Kishore Papineni, Salim Roukos, Todd Ward, and Wei-Jing Zhu. 2002. BLEU: a method for automatic evaluation of machine translation. In *ACL '02: Proc. of the 40th Annual Meeting on Association for Computational Linguistics*, pages 311–318. Association for Computational Linguistics.

Helmut Schmid and Florian Laws. 2008. Estimation of conditional probabilities with decision trees and an application to fine-grained POS tagging. In *Proceedings of the 22nd International Conference on Computational Linguistics (Coling 2008)*, pages 777–784, Manchester, UK, August.

Helmut Schmid. 1994. Probabilistic part-of-speech tagging using decision trees. In *Proc. of International Conference on New Methods in Language Processing*, pages 44–49, Manchester, UK.

Christoph Tillmann. 2004. A unigram orientation model for statistical machine translation. In *Proceedings of HLT-NAACL 2004*, pages 101–104. Association for Computational Linguistics.

Richard Zens, Franz Josef Och, and Hermann Ney. 2002. Phrase-based statistical machine translation. In *KI '02: Proceedings of the 25th Annual German Conference on AI*, pages 18–32, London, UK. Springer-Verlag.

UPM system for WMT 2012

Verónica López-Ludeña, Rubén San-Segundo and Juan M. Montero
GTH-IEL-ETSI Telecomunicación
Universidad Politécnica de Madrid
{veronicalopez, lapiz, juancho}@die.upm.es

Abstract

This paper describes the UPM system for the Spanish-English translation task at the NAACL 2012 workshop on statistical machine translation. This system is based on Moses. We have used all available free corpora, cleaning and deleting some repetitions. In this paper, we also propose a technique for selecting the sentences for tuning the system. This technique is based on the similarity with the sentences to translate. With our approach, we improve the BLEU score from 28.37% to 28.57%. And as a result of the WMT12 challenge we have obtained a 31.80% BLEU with the 2012 test set. Finally, we explain different experiments that we have carried out after the competition.

1 Introduction

The Speech Technology Group at the Technical University of Madrid has participated in the seventh workshop on statistical machine translation in the Spanish-English translation task.

Our submission is based on the state-of-the-art SMT toolkit Moses (Koehn et al., 2007). Firstly, we have proved different corpora for training the system: cleaning the whole corpus and deleting some repetitions in order to have a better performance of the translation model.

There are several related works on filtering the training corpus by removing noisy data that use a similarity measure based on the alignment score or based on sentences length (Khadivi and Ney, 2005).

In this paper, we also propose a technique for selecting the most appropriate sentences for tuning the system, based on the similarity with the Spanish sentences to translate. This technique is an update of the technique proposed by our group in the last WMT11 challenge (López-Ludeña and San-Segundo, 2011). There are other works related to select the development set (Hui et al., 2010) that combine different development sets in order to find the more similar one with test set.

There are also works related to select sentences, but for training instead of tuning, based on the similarity with the source test sentences. Some of them are based on transductive learning: semi-supervised methods for the effective use of monolingual data from the source language in order to improve translation quality (Ueffing, 2007); methods using instance selection with feature decay algorithms (Bicici and Yuret, 2011); or using TF-IDF algorithm (Lü et al., 2007). There are also works based on selecting training material with active learning: using language model adaptation (Shinozaki et al., 2011); or perplexity-based methods (Mandal et al., 2008).

In this work, we have used the proposed selection method only for tuning.

The rest of the paper is organized as follows. Next section overviews the system. Section 3 describes the used corpora. Section 4 explains the experiments carried out before the competition. Section 5 describes the sentences selection technique for tuning. Section 6 summarizes the results: before the WMT12 challenge, the corresponding to the competition and the last experiments. Finally, section 7 shows the conclusions.

2 Overall description of the system

The translation system used is based on Moses, the software released to support the translation task (http://www.statmt.org/wmt12/) at the NAACL 2012 workshop on statistical machine translation.

The Moses decoder is used for the translation process (Koehn et al., 2007). This program is a beam search decoder for phrase-based statistical machine translation models.

We have used GIZA++ (Och and Ney, 2003) for the word alignment computation. In order to generate the translation model, the parameter "alignment" was fixed to "grow-diag-final" (default value), and the parameter "reordering" was fixed to "msd-bidirectional-fe" as the best option, based on experiments on the development set.

In order to extract phrases (Koehn et al 2003), the considered alignment was grow-diag-final. And the parameter "max-phrase-length" was fixed to "7" (default value), based on experiments on the development set.

Finally, we have built a 5-gram language model, using the IRSTLM language modeling toolkit (Federico and Cettolo, 2007).

Additionally, we have used the following tools for pre-processing the training corpus: tokenizer.perl, lowercase.perl, clean-corpus-n.perl. And the following ones for recasing, detokenizer and normalizing punctuation in the translation output: train-recaser.perl, recase.perl, detokenizer.perl and normalize-punctuation.perl.

In addition, we have used Freeling (Padró et al., 2010) in some experiments, an open source library of natural language analyzers, but we did not improve our experiments by using Freeling. We used this tool in order to extract factors for Spanish words in order to train factored translation models.

3 Corpora used in these experiments

For the system development, only the free corpora distributed in the NAACL 2012 translation task has been used, so any researcher can validate these experiments easily.

In order to train the translation model, we used the union of the Europarl corpus, the United Nations Organization (UNO) corpus and the News Commentary corpus.

A 5-gram language model was built joining the following monolingual corpora: Europarl, News commentary, United Nations and News Crawl. We have not used the Gigaword corpus.

In order to tune the model weights, the 2010 and 2011 test set were used for development. We did not use the complete set, but a sentences selection in order to improve the tuning process. This selection will be explained in section 5.

The main characteristics of the corpora are shown in Table 1. All the parallel corpora has been cleaned with clean-corpus-n.perl, lowercased with lowercase.perl and tokenized with tokenizer.perl.

All these tools can be also free downloaded from http://www.statmt.org/wmt12/.

We observed that the parallel corpora, specially the UNO corpus, have many repeated sentences. We noted that these repetitions can cause a bad training. So, after cleaning the parallel corpora with the clean-corpus-n.perl tool, we eliminated all repetitions that appear more than 3 times in the parallel corpus.

		Original sentences
Translation Model (TM)	Europarl (EU)	1,965,734
	UNO	11,196,913
	News commentary (NC)	157,302
	Total	13,319,949
	Total clean	9,530,335
	Total without repetitions	**4,907,778**
Language Model (LM)	Europarl	2,218,201
	UNO	11,196,913
	News commentary (NC)	212,517
	News Crawl (NCR)	51,827,710
	Total	**65,455,341**
Tuning	news-test2010	2,489
	news-test2011	3,003
	Total	5,492
	Total selected	**4,500**
Test	news-test2012	3,003

Table 1: Size of the corpora used in our experiments

4 Previous experiments

Several experiments were carried out by using different number of sentences, as it is shown in Table 2.

In these experiments, we used the 2010 test set for tuning (news-test2010) and the 2011 test set for test (news-test2011). And a 5-gram language model was built with the IRSTLM tool. For evaluating the performance of the translation system, the BLEU (BiLingual Evaluation Understudy) metric has been computed using the NIST tool (mteval.pl) (Papipeni et al., 2002).

Firstly, we checked the contribution of UNO corpus in the final result. As it is shown in Table 2, the results improve when we add the UNO corpus, although this difference is small compared to the increasing of number of sentences: with 1,643,597 sentences we have a 28.24% BLEU and if we add around other 8 million sentences more, the BLEU score only increase 0.13 points (28.37%).

Training	Deleting repetitions	Number of sentences	BLEU (%)
EU+NC	NO	1,643,597	28.24
EU+NC+ UNO	NO	9,530,335	28.37
EU+NC+ UNO	YES (> 1)	2,112,968	28.12
EU+NC +UNO	**YES (> 3)**	**4,907,778**	**28.47**
EU+NC+ UNO	YES (> 5)	6,270,441	28.28

Table 2: Previous experiments using news-test2010 for tuning and news-test2011 as test set

We observed that UNO corpus have a lot of repeated sentences. So, we decided to remove repetitions in the whole corpus. With this action, we aimed to keep the UNO sentences that let us to improve the BLEU score and, on the other hand, to delete the sentences that do not contribute in any way, reducing the training time.

We did some experiments deleting repetitions: allowing 5 repetitions, 3 repetitions and, finally, 1 repetition (no repetitions). Table 2 shows how the results improve deleting more than 3 repetitions. So, finally, we improved the BLEU score from 23.24% without UNO corpus to 28.37% adding the UNO and to 28.47% deleting all sentences repeated more than 3 times.

5 Selecting the development corpus

When the system is trained, different model weights must be tuned corresponding to the main four features of the system: translation model, language model, reordering model and word penalty. Initially, these weights are equal, but it is necessary to optimize their values in order to get a better performance. Development corpus is used to adapt the different weights used in the translation process for combining the different sources of information. The weight selection is performed by using the minimum error rate training (MERT) for log-linear model parameter estimation (Och, 2003).

It is not demonstrated that the weights with better performance on the development set provide better results on the unseen test set. Because of this, this paper proposes a sentence selection technique that allows selecting the sentences of the development set that have more similarity with the sentences to translate (source test set): if the weights are tuned with sentences more similar to the sentence in the test set, the tuned weights will allow obtaining better translation results.

We have considered two alternatives for computing the similarity between a sentence and the test set. As it will be shown, with these methods the results improve.

The first alternative consists of the similarity method proposed in (López-Ludeña and San-Segundo, 2011), that computed a 3-gram language model considering the source language sentences from the test set. After that, the system computes the similarity of each source sentence in the validation corpus considering the language model obtained in the first step and, finally, a threshold is defined for selecting a subset with the higher similarity.

The second method that we propose now is a modification of the first one. With the formula of the first method, it was observed that, in some cases, the unigram probabilities had a relevant significance in the similarity, compared to 2-gram or 3-grams. The system was selecting sentences that have more unigrams that coincide with the source test sentences. However, these unigrams sometimes were not part of "good" bigrams or trigrams. Moreover, it was detected that the previous strategy was selecting short sentences, leaving the long ones out.

Considering the previous aspects, a second method was proposed and evaluated, trying to correct these effects. The proposal was to remove the unigram effect by normalizing the similarity measure with the unigram probabilities of the word sequence. So, the similarity measure is computed now using the following equation:

$$sim = \frac{1}{n}\sum_{i=1}^{n}\log(P_n) - \frac{1}{n}\sum_{i=1}^{n}\log(P_{unig,n})$$

Where Pn is the probability of the word 'n' in the sentence considering the language model trained with the source language sentences of the test set.

For example, if one sentence is "A B C D" (where each letter is a word of the validation sentence):

$$sim\_norm = \frac{1}{4}(\log(P_A) + \log(P_{AB}) + \log(P_{ABC}) + \log(P_{BCD})) - \frac{1}{4}(\log(P_A) + \log(P_B) + \log(P_C) + \log(P_D))$$

Each probability is extracted from the language model calculated in the first step. This similarity is the negative of the source sentence perplexity given the language model.

With all the similarities organized in a sorted list, it is possible to define a threshold selecting a subset with the higher similarity. For example, calculating the similarity of all sentences in our development corpus (around 2,500 sentences) a similarity histogram is obtained (Figure 1).

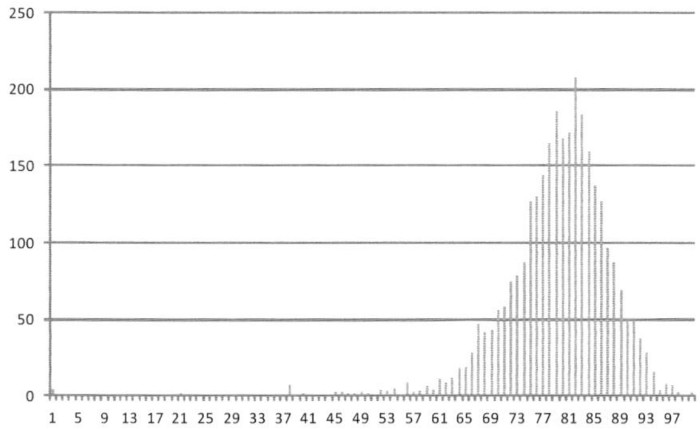

Figure 1: Similarity histogram of the source development sentences respect to the language model trained with the source language sentence of the test set

This histogram indicates the number of sentences inside each interval. There are 100 different intervals: the minimum similarity is mapped into 0 and the maximum one into 100. As it is shown, the similarity distribution is very similar to a Gaussian distribution.

Finally, source development sentences with a similarity lower than the threshold are eliminated from the development set (the corresponding target sentences are also removed).

All the experiments have been carried out in the Spanish into English translation system, using the corpora described in section 3 to generate the translation and language models.

In order to evaluate the system, the test set of the EMNLP 2011 workshop on statistical machine translation (news-test2011) was considered.

In order to adapt the different weights used in the translation process, the test set of the ACL 2010 workshop on statistical machine translation (news-test2010) has been used for weight tuning. The previous selection strategies allow filtering this validation set, selecting the most similar sentences to the test set.

Figure 2 and Table 3 show the different results with each number of selected sentences.

Sentences selected for development	BLEU results (%)	
	Normalized similarity	Similarity (López-Ludeña and San-Segundo, 2011)
500	28.01	28.36
1,000	28.11	28.47
1,500	**28.57**	**28.51**
2,000	28.57	28.36
2,489 (Baseline)	28.47	28.47
ORACLE	28.91	28.91

Table 3: Results with different number of development sentences

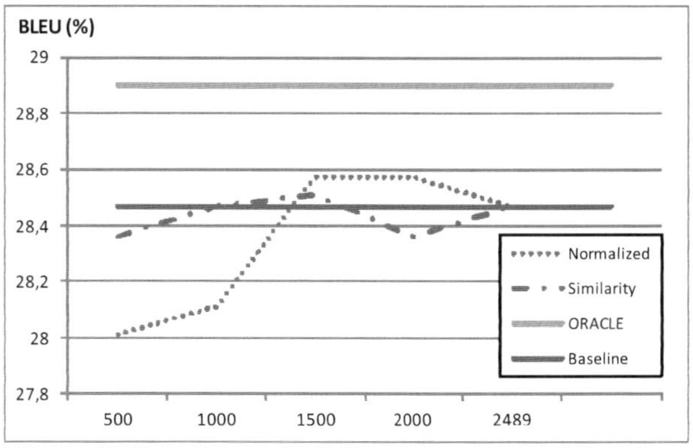

Figure 2: Results with different number of development sentences

Figure 2 shows that the BLEU score improves when the number of sentences of the development corpus increases from 0 to around 1,500 sentences with both methods. However, with more than 1,500 sentences (selected with the first similarity computation method) and more than 2,000 (selected with the normalized similarity method), the BLEU score starts to decrease. This decrement reveals that there is a subset of sentences that are quite different from the test sentences and they are not appropriate for tuning the model weights.

The best obtained result has been 28.57% BLEU with 1,500 sentences of the development corpus, selected with the normalized similarity method. The improvement reached is 30% of the possible improvement (considering the ORACLE experiment). This result is better than using the complete development corpus (28.47% BLEU).

When comparing both alternatives to compute the similarity between a sentence (from the validation set) and a set of sentences (source sentences from the test set), we can see that the normalized similarity method allows a higher improvement. The main reason is that the similarity method selects sentences including information about similar unigrams, but sometimes, these unigrams are not part of "good" bigrams or trigrams. Moreover, this strategy selects short sentences, leaving the long ones out. When using the normalized similarity method, these two problems are reduced.

6 Results

	Test set	BLEU (%)	BLEU cased (%)	TER (%)
Baseline	news-test2011	28.37	25.76	59.9
Best result	news-test2011	28.57	25.98	59.8
WMT12 result	**news-test2012**	**31.80**	**28.90**	**57.9**

Table 4: Final results of the translation system

Table 4 shows the results with the 2011 test set: we have a 28.37% BLEU as baseline using the whole corpora and finally we obtain a 28.57% BLEU with the deletion of repetitions and the sentences selection for tuning.

With this configuration, we have obtained a 31.8% BLEU with the 2012 test set as a result of the competition of this year.

6.1 Other experiments

We have carried out other experiments with the 2012 test set: factored models, Minimum Bayes Risk Decoding (MBR) and other sets for tuning. However, they did not finish before the competition deadline.

- **Factored models using Freeling**

Firstly, we have trained factored models in Spanish with Moses (Koehn and Hoang, 2007). We have only factored the source language (Spanish) and, in order to obtain the factors for each Spanish word, we have used Freeling (http://nlp.lsi.upc.edu/freeling/).

When running the Freeling analyzer with a Spanish sentence and the output option "tagged", we obtain, for each word, an associated lemma, a coded tag with morphological and syntactic information, and a probability. For instance, with the sentence "*la inflación europea se deslizó en los alimentos*", we obtain:

word	*lemma*	*tag*	*probability*
la	**el**	DA0FS0	0.972
inflación	**inflación**	NCFS000	1.000
europea	**europeo**	AQ0FS0	0.900
se	**se**	P00CN000	0.465
deslizó	**deslizar**	VMIS3S0	1.000
en	**en**	SPS00	1.000
los	**el**	DA0MP0	0.976
alimentos	**alimento**	NCMP000	1.000

Table 5: Freeling analyzer output

We take advantage of the lemma (second column) associated to each word and we use it as factor. So, the previous sentence is factorized as "*la|el inflación|inflación europea|europeo se|se deslizó|deslizar en|en los|el alimentos|alimento*"

This way, two models are generated in the translation process. For the GIZA++ alignment we used the second factor (lemma) instead of the word.

Results show that there is not improvement by using Freeling. BLEU score is a bit lower (30.95% in contrast to the 31.80% obtained without Freeling). However, we want to continue doing experiments with Freeling with other different GIZA++ alignment options different to the default value "grow-diag-final".

On the other hand, we want to prove different sets for tuning. When using factored models, there are more weights to be adjusted and it is possible that 4,500 sentences are insufficient.

- **MBR**

The use of Minumum Bayes Risk (MBR) (Kumar and Byrne, 2004) consists of, instead of selecting the translation with the highest probability, minimum Bayes risk decoding selects the translation that is most similar to the highest scoring translations. The idea is to choose hypotheses that minimize Bayes Risk as oppose to those that maximize posterior probability.

If we set up this option for decoding, the results improve from 31.80% to 31.99%.

- **Tuning with a 2008-2011 test set sentences selection**

We have also changed the set for tuning, including the 2008 and 2009 test set in addition to the 2009 and 2010 sets. With the four sets we have around 10,000 sentences. For tuning, we have selected 8,000 of these sentences with the normalized similarity method explained in section 5.

Table 6 shows that the results are worse. However, we have established the threshold based on previous experiments with the 2010 and 2011 sets. Now, we should test different threshold with the four sets in order to determine the best one.

	BLEU (%)	BLEU cased (%)	TER (%)
WMT result	31.80	28.90	53.5
Freeling	30.95	28.03	54.9
MBR	**31.99**	**29.06**	**53.4**
Tuning sets (2008-2011)	31.55	28.62	53.8

Table 6: Results of the experiments after competition

7 Conclusions

This paper has described the UPM statistical machine translation system for the Spanish-English translation task at the WMT12. This system is based on Moses. We have checked that deleting repetitions of the corpus, we can improve lightly the results: we increase the BLEU score from 28.37% with the whole corpora to 28.47% allowing only 3 repetitions of each sentence. Although this improvement is not significant (we have a confidence interval of ±0.35), we can say that we obtain a similar result by reducing very much the training time.

We have also proposed a method for selecting the sentences used for tuning the system. This selection is based on the normalized similarity with the source language test set. With this technique we improve the BLEU score from 28.47% to 28.57%. Although this result is not significant, we can appreciate an improving tendency by selecting the training sentences.

As a result of WMT12 challenge, we have obtained a 31.8% BLEU in Spanish-English translation with the 2012 test set. Our system takes around 40 hours for training, 16 hours for tuning (with 5 minutes for the sentences selection) and 3 hours to translate and to recase the test sentences in an 3.33 GHz Intel PC with 24 cores.

Finally, we have presented other additional experiments after the competition. We can improve a bit more the results to 32% BLEU by using the MBR decoding option.

Acknowledgments

The work leading to these results has received funding from the European Union under grant agreement n° 287678. It has also been supported by TIMPANO (TIN2011-28169-C05-03), ITALIHA (CAM-UPM), INAPRA (MICINN, DPI2010-21247-C02-02), and MA2VICMR (Comunidad Autónoma de Madrid, S2009/TIC-1542), Plan Avanza Consignos Exp Nº: TSI-020100-2010-489 and the European FEDER fund projects.

References

E. Bicici, D. Yuret, 2011. *Instance Selection for Machine Translation using Feature Decay Algorithms*. In Proceedings of the 6th Workshop on Statistical Machine Translation, pages 272–283.

M. Federico, M. Cettolo, 2007 *Efficient Handling of N-gram Language Models for Statistical Machine Translation*. Proceedings of the Second Workshop on Statistical Machine Translation, pages 88–95.

C. Hui, H. Zhao, Y. Song, B. Lu, 2010. *An Empirical Study on Development Set Selection Strategy for Machine Translation Learning*. On Fifth Workshop on Statistical Machine Translation.

S. Khadivi, H. Ney, 2005. *Automatic filtering of bilingual corpora for statistical machine translation*. In Natural Language Processing and Information Systems, 10th Int. Conf. on Applications of Natural Language to Information Systems, volume 3513 of Lecture Notes in Computer Science, pages 263–274, Alicante, Spain, June. Springer.

P. Koehn and H. Hoang, 2007 *Factored Translation Models*, Conference on Empirical Methods in Natural Language Processing (EMNLP), Prague, Czech Republic.

P. Koehn, H. Hoang, A. Birch, C. Callison-Burch, M. Federico, N. Bertoldi, B. Cowan, W. Shen, C. Moran, R. Zens, C. Dyer, O. Bojar, A. Constantin, E. Herbst, 2007. *Moses: Open Source Toolkit for Statistical Machine Translation*, Annual Meeting of the Association for Computational Linguistics (ACL), demonstration session, Prague, Czech Republic.

P. Koehn, F.J. Och, D. Marcu, 2003. *Statistical Phrase-based translation*. Human Language Technology Conference 2003 (HLT-NAACL 2003), Edmonton, Canada, pp. 127-133, May 2003.

S. Kumar and W. J. Byrne. 2004. *Minimum bayes-risk decoding for statistical machine translation*. In HLT-NAACL, pages 169–176.

V. López-Ludeña and R. San-Segundo. 2011. *UPM system for the translation task*. In Proceedings of the Sixth Workshop on Statistical Machine Translation.

Y. Lü, J. Huang, Q. Liu. 2007. *Improving statistical machine translation performance by training data selection and optimization*. In Proceedings of the 2007 Joint Conference on Empirical Methods in Natural Language Processing and Computational Natural Language Learning (EMNLP-CoNLL), pages 343–350.

A. Mandal, D. Vergyri, W. Wang, J. Zheng, A. Stolcke, G. Tur, D. Hakkani-Tur and N.F. Ayan. 2008. *Efficient data selection for machine translation*. In Spoken Language Technology Workshop. SLT 2008. IEEE, pages 261 –264.

F. J. Och, 2003. *Minimum error rate training in statistical machine translation*. In Proceedings of the 41st Annual Meeting of the Association for Computational Linguistics, pages 160–167, Sapporo, Japan, July. Association for Computational Linguistics.

F. J. Och, H. Ney, 2003. *A systematic comparison of various alignment models*. Computational Linguistics, Vol. 29, No. 1 pp. 19-51, 2003.

L. Padró, M. Collado, S. Reese, M. Lloberes, I. Castellón, 2010. *FreeLing 2.1: Five Years of Open-Source Language Processing Tools* Proceedings of 7th Language Resources and Evaluation Conference (LREC 2010), ELRA La Valletta, Malta. May.

K. Papineni, S. Roukos, T. Ward, W.J. Zhu. 2002. *BLEU: a method for automatic evaluation of machine translation*. 40th Annual Meeting of the Association for Computational Linguistics (ACL), Philadelphia, PA, pp. 311-318.

N. Ueffing, G. Haffari, A. Sarkar, 2007. *Transductive learning for statistical machine translation*. On ACL Second Workshop on Statistical Machine Translation.

PROMT DeepHybrid system for WMT12 shared translation task

Alexander Molchanov
PROMT LLC
16A, Dobrolubova av.
197198, St. Petersburg, Russia
Alexander.Molchanov@promt.ru

Abstract

This paper describes the PROMT submission for the WMT12 shared translation task. We participated in two language pairs: English-French and English-Spanish. The translations were made using the PROMT DeepHybrid engine, which is the first hybrid version of the PROMT system. We report on improvements over our baseline RBMT output both in terms of automatic evaluation metrics and linguistic analysis.

1 Introduction

In this paper we present the PROMT DeepHybrid submission for WMT12 shared translation task for two language pairs: English-French and English-Spanish.

A common approach to create hybrid machine translation (MT) systems on the basis of rule-based machine translation (RBMT) systems is to build a statistical phrase-based post-editing (SPE) system using state-of-the-art SMT technologies (see Simard et al. 2007). An SPE system views the output of the RBMT system as the source language, and reference human translations as the target language. SPE systems are used to correct typical mistakes of the RBMT output and to adapt RBMT systems to specific domains. (Dugast et al. 2007) report on good results both in terms of automatic evaluation metrics and human evaluation for the SPE systems based on PORTAGE (Sadat et al. 2005) and Moses (Koehn et al. 2007). However, an SMT model in fact makes translation output less predictable in comparison with RBMT output. We propose a different approach to hybrid MT technology. We developed and incorporated the SPE component into our translation system (the statistical post-editing data is controlled by the PROMT hybrid translation engine). Besides, we have an internal language model (LM) component that scores the generated translation candidates.

The remainder of the paper is organized as follows: in section 2 we provide the detailed description of our hybrid MT technology. In section 3 we evaluate the performance of the technology on two language pairs: English-French and English-Spanish. We gain improvements over the baseline RBMT system in terms of BLEU score on test sets. We also introduce the results of linguistic evaluation performed by our experts. Section 4 summarizes the key findings and outlines open issues for future work.

2 System description

The PROMT DeepHybrid system is based on our RBMT engine. The baseline system has been augmented with several modules for hybrid training and translation. The training technology is fully automated, but each step can be fulfilled and tuned separately.

2.1 Rule-based component

PROMT covers 51 language pairs for 13 different source languages. Our system is traditionally classified as a 'rule-based' system. PROMT uses morphosyntactic analyzers to analyze the source sentence and transfer rules to translate the sentence into the target language. The crucial component of our system is the PROMT bilingual dictionaries which contain up to 250K entries for each language pair. Each entry is supplied with various linguistic (lexical and grammatical, morphological, semantic) features. Besides the 'baseline' dictionaries the PROMT system has a large number of domain-specific dictionaries.

2.2 Parallel corpus processing

We have a specific component for processing parallel corpora before training the hybrid system. This component can process data in plain text and XML formats. We also perform substantial data filtering. All punctuation and special symbols (ligatures etc.) are normalized. The length of the words in a sentence and the length of sentences are taken into account (sentences having length above a set threshold are discarded). All duplicated sentences are discarded as well. On top of that, we remove parallel segments with different number of sentences because such segments corrupt phrase alignment. Strings containing few alphabetic symbols and untranslated sentences are filtered out from the parallel corpus.

2.3 Automated dictionary extraction

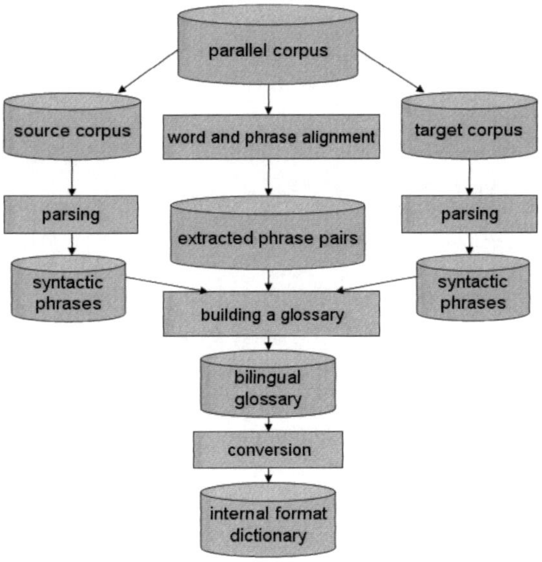

Figure 1. Dictionary extraction pipeline.

The extraction technology is shown in figure 1. The whole process can be subdivided into two separate tasks: 1) statistical alignment of a parallel corpus 2) extraction of syntactic phrases from the source and target sides of the parallel corpus. We then combine the results of these tasks to extract bilingual terminology. We use GIZA++ to perform the word alignment (Och and Ney, 2003). Then we use the common heuristics to extract parallel phrase pairs (Koehn et al. 2007). We use the PROMT parsers to extract grammatically correct phrases from source and target sides of the parallel corpora. PROMT parsers are rule-based multi-level morphosyntactic analyzers. Parsers extract noun phrases, verb phrases and adverbial phrases. The extraction is done as follows: each sentence of the corpus is parsed, a parse tree is created, the extracted syntactic phrases are stored in memory; after the whole corpus is processed, all extracted phrases are lemmatized and presented in a list. Each phrase is supplied with a set of linguistic features (part of speech, lemma, lemma frequency etc.). The next step is building a bilingual glossary using two sets of syntactic phrases extracted from the source and the target sides of the parallel corpus on the one hand and a statistically aligned set of phrase pairs on the other hand. We do not add geographic names, proper names and named entities (dates etc.) to the glossary because they are well processed by the RBMT engine.

2.4 Statistical phrase-based post-editing

The technology of obtaining data for statistical post-editing is standard. We translate the source corpus using the RBMT engine. Then we align the MT corpus and the target corpus using GIZA++ and extract parallel phrase pairs to obtain a phrase-table. Then the phrase-table is filtered. The phrase length and translation probability are taken into account. Only pairs having length of the source phrase from three to seven words are selected. This specific length range was chosen according to the detailed analysis of the resulting hybrid MT quality performed by our linguists. The selected phrase pairs are stored in the special SPE component of the hybrid engine and are used to apply post-editing to the translation candidates generated by the RBMT engine during the translation process.

2.5 Language model component

The language model (LM) component is used to score the translation candidates generated by the engine. The RBMT engine can generate several translation candidates depending on the number of homonymic words and phrases and transfer rules variants. Statistical phrase-based post-editing is applied separately to each of the generated candidates. All of the candidates (with and without post-edition) are scored by the LM component and the candidate with the lowest perplexity one is selected.

3 Experimental setting

We used the total Europarliament (EP) and NewsCommentary (NC) corpora provided by the organizers for the English-Spanish submission. We translated both (EP and NC) corpora using the RBMT engine and then built a single phrase-table for both corpora. Then we filtered the phrase-table according to the source phrase length and translation probabilities as described in section 2.4. Only 10% of the initial phrase-table were used as statistical post-editing data. The target 5-gram language model was trained on all provided monolingual data except the LDC corpora. We did not extract the dictionary for this language pair.

As for the English-French submission, we performed bilingual training data selection from EP and United Nations (UN) corpora. We trained the source and target language models on English and French monolingual News corpora respectively. These models were used to score each sentence pair of EP and UN corpora. Then we selected sentence pairs from EP and UN corpora via the geometric mean of perplexities of the source and target sentences. About 85% of EP (35M words of the source corpus) and 35% of UN (68M words of the source corpus) were selected. Then we translated the selected EP and UN subcorpora and the whole NC corpus with the RBMT engine. A single phrase-table was built for all three corpora. The phrase-table was fitered with the same parameters as for the English-Spanish submission. Approximately 8% of the initial phrase-table were used as statistical post-editing data. The target 5-gram language model was trained on all provided monolingual data except the LDC corpora.

We also performed automated dictionary extraction for the English-French pair. Examples of the extracted entries can be found in Table 1. The details about the extracted dictionary can be found in Table 2. We only extracted verbs, nouns and noun phrases for this shared task. The translations for extracted verbs and nouns are automatically added into the existing PROMT dictionary entries using our multifunctional dictionary component. Thus we increase the number of lexical variants and generated translation candidates. The extracted noun phrases are added to the PROMT dictionary as new entries. We only extract 'informative' entries, i.e. the noun phrases which are absent in the baseline PROMT dictionary or have an incorrect or infrequent translation. It should also be mentioned that the initial size of the noun phrases glossary was over 25K entries, but we decided to raise the source phrase frequency threshold a bit. Our hypothesis was that non-frequent phrases from out-of-domain corpora (EP and UN) would not fit for translation of news texts. 20K entries are selected.

KEY	KEY_FRQ	TRANSLATION	PROB	POS
comprehensive peace agreement	2427	accord de paix global	0,803049	n
automaker	7	constructeur automobile	0,428571	n
contemplate	452	envisager	0,400443	v

Table 1. Examples of extracted dictionary entries.

Part of speech	nouns	noun phrases	verbs
Number of entries	1187	19780	215

Table 2. Number of entries in the extracted English-French dictionary.

4 Experimental results and linguistic evaluation

In this section we present the results of our experiments on *newstest2012*. BLEU scores for different system configurations are presented in Table 3. The percentage of sentences changed by statistical post-editing compared to baseline RBMT output is presented in Table 4. We also provide details of linguistic evaluation performed for the English-French submission.

System configuration	BLEU (English-French)	BLEU (English-Spanish)
RBMT (baseline)	24.00	27.26
Hybrid (+LM)	24.09	27.26
Hybrid (+LM +dictionary)	24.25	-
Hybrid (+LM +SPE)	-	28.60
Hybrid (+LM +dictionary +SPE)	24.80	-

Table 3. Translation results in terms of BLEU score for *newstest2012*.

Language pair	Impact
English-French	43%
English-Spanish	48%

Table 4. Impact of statistical post-editing on *newstest2012* (percentage of sentences changed by statistical post-editing).

Language pair	Improv	Degrad	Equiv
English-French	54	16	30
English-Spanish	48	20	32

Table 5. Statistics on improvements, degradations and equivalents for the DeepHybrid translation compared to baseline RBMT output (*newstest2012*).

Our linguists compared 100 random RBMT and DeepHybrid (with extracted dictionary and statistical post-editing) translations for both language pairs in terms of improvements and degradations. The results presented in Table 5 show that the DeepHybrid engine outperforms the RBMT engine according to human evaluation. Most of the degradations are minor grammatical issues (wrong number, disagreement etc.).

5 Conclusions and future work

We presented the PROMT DeepHybrid system submissions for WMT12 shared translation task. We showed improvements both in terms of BLEU scores and human evaluation compared to baseline PROMT RBMT engine.

We extracted a dictionary from a corpus of over 200M words. The size of the dictionary (~20K entries) is relatively small due to our robust linguistic and statistical data filtering. However, such filtering minimizes the number of possible mistranslations and guarantees that the extracted entries are universal. We are planning to add the extracted data to our baseline English-French dictionary after manual check and perform the same experiments for other language pairs.

As for statistical post-editing, the impact on the RBMT output is quite moderate (less than 50%). This is also due to our approach which includes filtering out infrequent phrase pairs from statistical post-editing data. We assume that the RBMT output is already good enough and therefore does not require much statistical post-editing to be applied. It should be mentioned that for the present we only use perplexity to score translation candidates. Several other features will be implemented in the next version of the hybrid engine. To avoid grammatical inconsistency in the hybrid MT output, we are planning to apply linguistic filters to statistical post-editing data.

References

L. Dugast, J. Senellart, and P. Koehn. 2007. *Statistical Post-Edition on SYSTRAN Rule-Based Translation System.* In Proceedings of the Second Workshop On Statistical Machine Translation, Prague, Czech Republic.

Koehn Philipp, Hieu Hoang, Alexandra Birch, Chris Callison-Burch, Marcello Federico, Nicola Bertoldi, Brooke Cowan, Wade Shen, Christine Moran, Richard Zens, Chris Dyer, Ondrej Bojar, Alexandra Constantin, and Evan Herbst. 2007. *Moses: Open source toolkit for statistical machine translation.* ACL 2007, demonstration session. Prague, Czech Republic.

Och, Franz Josef and Hermann Ney. 2003. *A Systematic Comparison of Various Statistical Alignment Models.* Computational Linguistics, Vol. 29(1). 19-51.

F. Sadat, H. Johnson, A. Agbago, G. Foster, R. Kuhn, J. Martin, and A. Tikuisis. 2005. *PORTAGE: A Phrase-Based Machine Translation System.* In Proceedings of the ACL Workshop on Building and Using Parallel Texts, pages 129-132, Ann Arbor, USA.

M. Simard, C. Goutte, and P. Isabelle. 2007. *Statistical Phrase-Based Post-Editing.* In Human Language Technologies 2007: The Conference of the North American Chapter of the Association for Computational Linguistics; Proceedings of the Main Conference, pages 08.515, Rochester, USA.

The Karlsruhe Institute of Technology Translation Systems for the WMT 2012

Jan Niehues, Yuqi Zhang, Mohammed Mediani, Teresa Herrmann, Eunah Cho and Alex Waibel
Karlsruhe Institute of Technology
Karlsruhe, Germany
firstname.lastname@kit.edu

Abstract

This paper describes the phrase-based SMT systems developed for our participation in the WMT12 Shared Translation Task. Translations for English↔German and English↔French were generated using a phrase-based translation system which is extended by additional models such as bilingual, fine-grained part-of-speech (POS) and automatic cluster language models and discriminative word lexica. In addition, we explicitly handle out-of-vocabulary (OOV) words in German, if we have translations for other morphological forms of the same stem. Furthermore, we extended the POS-based reordering approach to also use information from syntactic trees.

1 Introduction

In this paper, we describe our systems for the NAACL 2012 Seventh Workshop on Statistical Machine Translation. We participated in the Shared Translation Task and submitted translations for English↔German and English↔French. We use a phrase-based decoder that can use lattices as input and developed several models that extend the standard log-linear model combination of phrase-based MT. In addition to the POS-based reordering model used in past years, for German-English we extended it to also use rules learned using syntax trees.

The translation model was extended by the bilingual language model and a discriminative word lexicon using a maximum entropy classifier. For the French-English and English-French translation systems, we also used phrase table adaptation to avoid overestimation of the probabilities of the huge, but noisy Giga corpus. In the German-English system, we tried to learn translations for OOV words by exploring different morphological forms of the OOVs with the same lemma.

Furthermore, we combined different language models in the log-linear model. We used word-based language models trained on different parts of the training corpus as well as POS-based language models using fine-grained POS information and language models trained on automatic word clusters.

The paper is organized as follows: The next section gives a detailed description of our systems including all the models. The translation results for all directions are presented afterwards and we close with a conclusion.

2 System Description

For the French↔English systems the phrase table is based on a GIZA++ word alignment, while the systems for German↔English use a discriminative word alignment as described in Niehues and Vogel (2008). The language models are 4-gram SRI language models using Kneser-Ney smoothing trained by the SRILM Toolkit (Stolcke, 2002).

The problem of word reordering is addressed with POS-based and tree-based reordering models as described in Section 2.3. The POS tags used in the reordering model are obtained using the TreeTagger (Schmid, 1994). The syntactic parse trees are generated using the Stanford Parser (Rafferty and Manning, 2008).

An in-house phrase-based decoder (Vogel, 2003) is used to perform translation. Optimization with regard to the BLEU score is done using Minimum Error Rate Training as described in Venugopal et al. (2005). During decoding only the top 10 translation options for every source phrase are considered.

2.1 Data

Our translation models were trained on the EPPS and News Commentary (NC) corpora. Furthermore, the additional available data for French and English (i.e. UN and Giga corpora) were exploited in the corresponding systems.

The systems were tuned with the news-test2011 data, while news-test2011 was used for testing in all our systems. We trained language models for each language on the monolingual part of the training corpora as well as the News Shuffle and the Gigaword (version 4) corpora. The discriminative word alignment model was trained on 500 hand-aligned sentences selected from the EPPS corpus.

2.2 Preprocessing

The training data is preprocessed prior to training the system. This includes normalizing special symbols, smart-casing the first word of each sentence and removing long sentences and sentences with length mismatch.

For the German parts of the training corpus, in order to obtain a homogenous spelling, we use the hunspell[1] lexicon to map words written according to old German spelling rules to new German spelling rules.

In order to reduce the OOV problem of German compound words, Compound splitting as described in Koehn and Knight (2003) is applied to the German part of the corpus for the German-to-English system.

The Giga corpus received a special preprocessing by removing noisy pairs using an SVM classifier as described in Mediani et al. (2011). The SVM classifier training and test sets consist of randomly selected sentence pairs from the corpora of EPPS, NC, tuning, and test sets. Giving at the end around 16 million sentence pairs.

2.3 Word Reordering

In contrast to modeling the reordering by a distance-based reordering model and/or a lexicalized distortion model, we use a different approach that relies on POS sequences. By abstracting from surface words to POS, we expect to model the reordering more accurately. For German-to-English, we additionally apply reordering rules learned from syntactic parse trees.

2.3.1 POS-based Reordering Model

In order to build the POS-based reordering model, we first learn probabilistic rules from the POS tags of the training corpus and the alignment. Continuous reordering rules are extracted as described in Rottmann and Vogel (2007) to model short-range reorderings. When translating between German and English, we apply a modified reordering model with non-continuous rules to cover also long-range reorderings (Niehues and Kolss, 2009).

2.3.2 Tree-based Reordering Model

Word order is quite different between German and English. And during translation especially verbs or verb particles need to be shifted over a long distance in a sentence. Using discontinuous POS rules already improves the translation tremendously. In addition, we apply a tree-based reordering model for the German-English translation. Syntactic parse trees provide information about the words in a sentence that form constituents and should therefore be treated as inseparable units by the reordering model. For the tree-based reordering model, syntactic parse trees are generated for the whole training corpus. Then the word alignment between the source and target language part of the corpus is used to learn rules on how to reorder the constituents in a German source sentence to make it matches the English target sentence word order better. In order to apply the rules to the source text, POS tags and a parse tree are generated for each sentence. Then the POS-based and tree-based reordering rules are applied. The original order of words as well as the reordered sentence variants generated by the rules are encoded in a word lattice. The lattice is then used as input to the decoder.

For the test sentences, the reordering based on POS and trees allows us to change the word order in the source sentence so that the sentence can be translated more easily. In addition, we build reordering lattices for all training sentences and then extract

[1] `http://hunspell.sourceforge.net/`

phrase pairs from the monotone source path as well as from the reordered paths.

2.4 Translation Models

In addition to the models used in the baseline system described above, we conducted experiments including additional models that enhance translation quality by introducing alternative or additional information into the translation modeling process.

2.4.1 Phrase table adaptation

Since the Giga corpus is huge, but noisy, it is advantageous to also use the translation probabilities of the phrase pair extracted only from the more reliable EPPS and News commentary corpus. Therefore, we build two phrase tables for the French↔English system. One trained on all data and the other only trained on the EPPS and News commentary corpus. The two models are then combined using a log-linear combination to achieve the adaptation towards the cleaner corpora as described in (Niehues et al., 2010). The newly created translation model uses the four scores from the general model as well as the two smoothed relative frequencies of both directions from the smaller, but cleaner model. If a phrase pair does not occur in the in-domain part, a default score is used instead of a relative frequency. In our case, we used the lowest probability.

2.4.2 Bilingual Language Model

In phrase-based systems the source sentence is segmented by the decoder according to the best combination of phrases that maximize the translation and language model scores. This segmentation into phrases leads to the loss of context information at the phrase boundaries. Although more target side context is available to the language model, source side context would also be valuable for the decoder when searching for the best translation hypothesis. To make also source language context available we use a bilingual language model, in which each token consists of a target word and all source words it is aligned to. The bilingual tokens enter the translation process as an additional target factor and the bilingual language model is applied to the additional factor like a normal language model. For more details see Niehues et al. (2011).

2.4.3 Discriminative Word Lexica

Mauser et al. (2009) have shown that the use of discriminative word lexica (DWL) can improve the translation quality. For every target word, they trained a maximum entropy model to determine whether this target word should be in the translated sentence or not using one feature per one source word.

When applying DWL in our experiments, we would like to have the same conditions for the training and test case. For this we would need to change the score of the feature only if a new word is added to the hypothesis. If a word is added the second time, we do not want to change the feature value. In order to keep track of this, additional bookkeeping would be required. Also the other models in our translation system will prevent us from using a word too often.

Therefore, we ignore this problem and can calculate the score for every phrase pair before starting with the translation. This leads to the following definition of the model:

$$p(e|f) = \prod_{j=1}^{J} p(e_j|f) \tag{1}$$

In this definition, $p(e_j|f)$ is calculated using a maximum likelihood classifier.

Each classifier is trained independently on the parallel training data. All sentences pairs where the target word e occurs in the target sentence are used as positive examples. We could now use all other sentences as negative examples. But in many of these sentences, we would anyway not generate the target word, since there is no phrase pair that translates any of the source words into the target word.

Therefore, we build a target vocabulary for every training sentence. This vocabulary consists of all target side words of phrase pairs matching a source phrase in the source part of the training sentence. Then we use all sentence pairs where e is in the target vocabulary but not in the target sentences as negative examples. This has shown to have a postive influence on the translation quality (Mediani et al., 2011) and also reduces training time.

2.4.4 Quasi-Morphological Operations for OOV words

Since German is a highly inflected language, there will be always some word forms of a given Ger-

Figure 1: Quasi-morphological operations

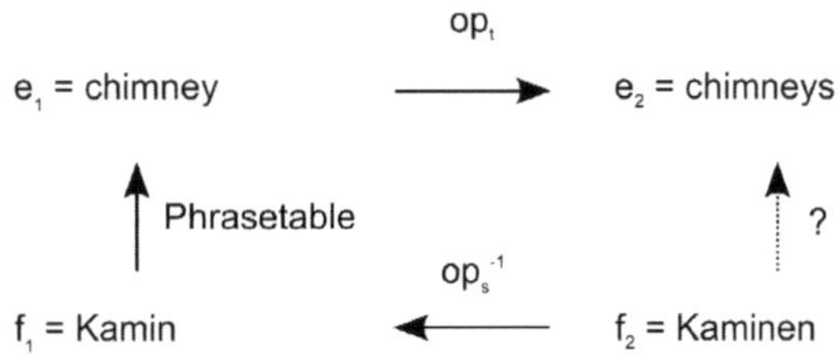

man lemma that did not occur in the training data. In order to be able to also translate unseen word forms, we try to learn quasi-morphological operations that change the lexical entry of a known word form to the unknown word form. These have shown to be beneficial in Niehues and Waibel (2011) using Wikipedia[2] titles. The idea is illustrated in Figure 1.

If we look at the data, our system is able to translate a German word *Kamin* (engl. *chimney*), but not the dative plural form *Kaminen*. To address this problem, we try to automatically learn rules how words can be modified. If we look at the example, we would like the system to learn the following rule. If an *"en"* is appended to a German word, as it is done when creating the dative plural form of *Kaminen*, we need to add an *"s"* to the end of the English word in order to perform the same morphological word transformation. We use only rules where the ending of the word has at most 3 letters.

Depending on the POS, number, gender or case of the involved words, the same operation on the source side does not necessarily correspond to the same operation on the target side.

To account for this ambiguity, we rank the different target operation using the following four features and use the best ranked one. Firstly, we should not generate target words that do not exist. Here, we have an advantage that we can use monolingual data to determine whether the word exists. In addition, a target operation that often coincides with a given source operation should be better than one that is rarely used together with the source operation. We therefore look at pairs of entries in the lexicon and count in how many of them the source operation can be applied to the source side and the target operation can be applied to the target side. We then use only operations that occur at least ten times. Furthermore, we use the ending of the source and target word to determine which pair of operations should be used.

Integration We only use the proposed method for OOVs and do not try to improve translations of words that the baseline system already covers. We look for phrase pairs, for which a source operation op_s exists that changes one of the source words f_1 into the OOV word f_2. Since we need to apply a target operation to one word on the target side of the phrase pair, we only consider phrase pairs where f_1 is aligned to one of the target words of the phrase containing e_1. If a target operation exists given f_1 and op_s, we select the one with the highest rank. Then we generate a new phrase pair by applying op_s to f_1 and op_t to e_1 keeping the original scores from the phrase pairs, since the original and synthesized phrase pair are not directly competing anyway. We do not add several phrase pairs generated by different operations, since we would then need to add the features used for ranking the operations into the MERT. This is problematic, since the operations were only used for very few words and therefore a good estimation of the weights is not possible.

2.5 Language Models

The 4-gram language models generated by the SRILM toolkit are used as the main language models for all of our systems. For English-French and French-English systems, we use a good quality corpus as in-domain data to train in-domain language models. Additionally, we apply the POS and cluster language models in different systems. All language models are integrated into the translation system by a log-linear combination and received optimal weights during tuning by the MERT.

2.5.1 POS Language Models

The POS language model is trained on the POS sequences of the target language. In this evaluation, the POS language model is applied for the English-German system. We expect that having additional information in form of probabilities of POS sequences should help especially in case of the rich morphology of German. The POS tags are generated with the RFTagger (Schmid and Laws, 2008) for German, which produces fine-grained tags that include person, gender and case information. We

[2] `http://www.wikipedia.org/`

use a 9-gram language model on the News Shuffle corpus and the German side of all parallel corpora. More details and discussions about the POS language model can be found in Herrmann et al. (2011).

2.5.2 Cluster Language Models

The cluster language model follows a similar idea as the POS language model. Since there is a data sparsity problem when we substitute words with the word classes, it is possible to make use of larger context information. In the POS language model, POS tags are the word classes. Here, we generated word classes in a different way. First, we cluster the words in the corpus using the MKCLS algorithm (Och, 1999) given a number of classes. Second, we replace the words in the corpus by their cluster IDs. Finally, we train an n-gram language model on this corpus consisting of cluster IDs. Generally, all cluster language models used in our systems are 5-gram.

3 Results

Using the models described above we performed several experiments leading finally to the systems used for generating the translations submitted to the workshop. The following sections describe the experiments for the individual language pairs and show the translation results. The results are reported as case-sensitive BLEU scores (Papineni et al., 2002) on one reference translation.

3.1 German-English

The experiments for the German-English translation system are summarized in Table 1. The Baseline system uses POS-based reordering, discriminative word alignment and a language model trained on the News Shuffle corpus. By adding lattice phrase extraction small improvements of the translation quality could be gained.

Further improvements could be gained by adding a language model trained on the Gigaword corpus and adding a bilingual and cluster-based language model. We used 50 word classes and trained a 5-gram language model. Afterwards, the translation quality was improved by also using a discriminative word lexicon. Finally, the best system was achieved by using Tree-based reordering and using special treatment for the OOVs. This system generates a BLEU score of 22.31 on the test data. For the last two systems, we did not perform new optimization runs.

System	Dev	Test
Baseline	23.64	21.32
+ Lattice Phrase Extraction	23.76	21.36
+ Gigaward Language Model	24.01	21.73
+ Bilingual LM	24.19	21.91
+ Cluster LM	24.16	22.09
+ DWL	24.19	22.19
+ Tree-based Reordering	-	22.26
+ OOV	-	**22.31**

Table 1: Translation results for German-English

3.2 English-German

The English-German baseline system uses also POS-based reordering, discriminative word alignment and a language model based on EPPS, NC and News Shuffle. A small gain could be achieved by the POS-based language model and the bilingual language model. Further gain was achieved by using also a cluster-based language model. For this language model, we use 100 word classes and trained a 5-gram language model. Finally, the best system uses the discriminative word lexicon.

System	Dev	Test
Baseline	17.06	15.57
+ POSLM	17.27	15.63
+ Bilingual LM	17.40	15.78
+ Cluster LM	17.77	16.06
+ DWL	**17.75**	**16.28**

Table 2: Translation results for English-German

3.3 English-French

Table 3 summarizes how our English-French system evolved. The baseline system here was trained on the EPPS, NC, and UN corpora, while the language model was trained on all the French part of the parallel corpora (including the Giga corpus). It also uses short-range reordering trained on EPPS and NC. This system had a BLEU score of around 26.7. The Giga parallel data turned out to be quite beneficial for this task. It improves the scores by more than 1 BLEU point. More importantly, additional language models boosted the system quality: around 1.8 points. In fact, three language models were log-linearly combined: In addition to the aforementioned, two additional language models were trained on the monolingual sets (one for News and one for Gigaword). We could get an improvement of around 0.2 by retraining the reordering rules on EPPS and NC only, but using Giza alignment from the whole data. Adapting the translation model by using EPPS and NC as in-domain data improves the BLEU score by only 0.1. This small improvement might be due to the fact that the news domain is very broad and that the Giga corpus has already been carefully cleaned and filtered. Furthermore, using a bilingual language model enhances the BLEU score by almost 0.3. Finally, incorporating a cluster language model adds an additional 0.1 to the score. This leads to a system with 30.58.

System	Dev	Test
Baseline	24.96	26.67
+ GigParData	26.12	28.16
+ Big LMs	29.22	29.92
+ All Reo	29.14	30.10
+ PT Adaptation	29.15	30.22
+ Bilingual LM	29.17	30.49
+ Cluster LM	**29.08**	**30.58**

Table 3: Translation results for English-French

3.4 French-English

The development of our system for the French-English direction is summarized in Table 4. The baseline system for this direction was trained on the EPPS, NC, UN and Giga parallel corpora, while the language model was trained on the French part of the parallel training corpora. The baseline system includes the POS-based reordering model with short-range rules. The largest improvement of 1.7 BLEU score was achieved by the integration of the bigger language models which are trained on the English version of News Shuffle and the Gigaword corpus (v4). We did not add the language models from the monolingual English version of EPPS and NC data, since the experiments have shown that they did not provide improvement in our system. The second largest improvement came from the domain adaptation that includes an in-domain language model and adaptations to the phrase extraction. The BLEU score has improved about 1 BLEU in total. The in-domain data we used here are parallel EPPS and NC corpus. Further gains were obtained by augmenting the system with a bilingual language model adding around 0.2 BLEU to the previous score. The submitted system was obtained by adding the cluster 5-gram language model trained on the News Shuffle corpus with 100 clusters and thus giving 30.25 as the final score.

System	Dev	Test
Baseline	25.81	27.15
+ Indomain LM	26.17	27.91
+ PT Adaptation	26.33	28.11
+ Big LMs	28.90	29.82
+ Bilingual LM	29.14	30.09
+ Cluster LM	**29.31**	**30.25**

Table 4: Translation results for French-English

4 Conclusions

We have presented the systems for our participation in the WMT 2012 Evaluation for English↔German and English↔French. In all systems we could improve by using a class-based language model. Furthermore, the translation quality could be improved by using a discriminative word lexicon. Therefore, we trained a maximum entropy classifier for every target word. For English↔French, adapting the phrase table helps to avoid using wrong parts of the noisy Giga corpus. For the German-to-English system, we could improve the translation quality additionally by using a tree-based reordering model and by special handling of OOV words. For the inverse direction we could improve the translation quality by using a 9-gram language model trained on the fine-grained POS tags.

Acknowledgments

This work was realized as part of the Quaero Programme, funded by OSEO, French State agency for innovation.

References

Teresa Herrmann, Mohammed Mediani, Jan Niehues, and Alex Waibel. 2011. The karlsruhe institute of technology translation systems for the wmt 2011. In *Proceedings of the Sixth Workshop on Statistical Machine Translation*, pages 379–385, Edinburgh, Scotland, July. Association for Computational Linguistics.

Philipp Koehn and Kevin Knight. 2003. Empirical Methods for Compound Splitting. In *EACL*, Budapest, Hungary.

Arne Mauser, Saša Hasan, and Hermann Ney. 2009. Extending Statistical Machine Translation with Discriminative and Trigger-based Lexicon Models. In *Proceedings of the 2009 Conference on Empirical Methods in Natural Language Processing: Volume 1 - Volume 1*, EMNLP '09, Singapore.

Mohammed Mediani, Eunah Cho, Jan Niehues, Teresa Herrmann, and Alex Waibel. 2011. The kit english-french translation systems for iwslt 2011. In *Proceedings of the eight International Workshop on Spoken Language Translation (IWSLT)*.

Jan Niehues and Muntsin Kolss. 2009. A POS-Based Model for Long-Range Reorderings in SMT. In *Fourth Workshop on Statistical Machine Translation (WMT 2009)*, Athens, Greece.

Jan Niehues and Stephan Vogel. 2008. Discriminative Word Alignment via Alignment Matrix Modeling. In *Proc. of Third ACL Workshop on Statistical Machine Translation*, Columbus, USA.

Jan Niehues and Alex Waibel. 2011. Using wikipedia to translate domain-specific terms in smt. In *Proceedings of the eight International Workshop on Spoken Language Translation (IWSLT)*.

Jan Niehues, Mohammed Mediani, Teresa Herrmann, Michael Heck, Christian Herff, and Alex Waibel. 2010. The KIT Translation system for IWSLT 2010. In Marcello Federico, Ian Lane, Michael Paul, and François Yvon, editors, *Proceedings of the seventh International Workshop on Spoken Language Translation (IWSLT)*, pages 93–98.

Jan Niehues, Teresa Herrmann, Stephan Vogel, and Alex Waibel. 2011. Wider Context by Using Bilingual Language Models in Machine Translation. In *Sixth Workshop on Statistical Machine Translation (WMT 2011)*, Edinburgh, UK.

Franz Josef Och. 1999. An efficient method for determining bilingual word classes. In *Proceedings of the ninth conference on European chapter of the Association for Computational Linguistics*, EACL '99, pages 71–76, Stroudsburg, PA, USA. Association for Computational Linguistics.

Kishore Papineni, Salim Roukos, Todd Ward, and Wei-Jing Zhu. 2002. Bleu: a Method for Automatic Evaluation of Machine Translation. Technical Report RC22176 (W0109-022), IBM Research Division, T. J. Watson Research Center.

Anna N. Rafferty and Christopher D. Manning. 2008. Parsing three german treebanks: lexicalized and unlexicalized baselines. In *Proceedings of the Workshop on Parsing German*.

Kay Rottmann and Stephan Vogel. 2007. Word Reordering in Statistical Machine Translation with a POS-Based Distortion Model. In *TMI*, Skövde, Sweden.

Helmut Schmid and Florian Laws. 2008. Estimation of Conditional Probabilities with Decision Trees and an Application to Fine-Grained POS Tagging. In *COLING 2008*, Manchester, Great Britain.

Helmut Schmid. 1994. Probabilistic Part-of-Speech Tagging Using Decision Trees. In *International Conference on New Methods in Language Processing*, Manchester, UK.

Andreas Stolcke. 2002. SRILM – An Extensible Language Modeling Toolkit. In *Proc. of ICSLP*, Denver, Colorado, USA.

Ashish Venugopal, Andreas Zollman, and Alex Waibel. 2005. Training and Evaluation Error Minimization Rules for Statistical Machine Translation. In *Workshop on Data-drive Machine Translation and Beyond (WPT-05)*, Ann Arbor, MI.

Stephan Vogel. 2003. SMT Decoder Dissected: Word Reordering. In *Int. Conf. on Natural Language Processing and Knowledge Engineering*, Beijing, China.

Kriya - The SFU System for Translation Task at WMT-12

Majid Razmara and Baskaran Sankaran and Ann Clifton and Anoop Sarkar
School of Computing Science
Simon Fraser University
8888 University Drive
Burnaby BC. V5A 1S6. Canada
{razmara, baskaran, aca69, anoop}@cs.sfu.ca

Abstract

This paper describes our submissions for the WMT-12 translation task using *Kriya* - our hierarchical phrase-based system. We submitted systems in French-English and English-Czech language pairs. In addition to the baseline system following the standard MT pipeline, we tried *ensemble* decoding for French-English. The ensemble decoding method improved the BLEU score by 0.4 points over the baseline in newstest-2011. For English-Czech, we segmented the Czech side of the corpora and trained two different segmented models in addition to our baseline system.

1 Baseline Systems

Our shared task submissions are trained in the hierarchical phrase-based model (Chiang, 2007) framework. Specifically, we use *Kriya* (Sankaran et al., 2012) - our in-house Hiero-style system for training and decoding. We now briefly explain the baseline systems in French-English and English-Czech language pairs.

We use GIZA++ for word alignments and the Moses (Koehn et al., 2007) phrase-extractor for extracting the initial phrases. The translation models are trained using the rule extraction module in Kriya. In both cases, we pre-processed the training data by running it through the usual pre-processing pipeline of tokenization and lowercasing.

For French-English baseline system, we trained a simplified hierarchical phrase-based model where the right-hand side can have at most one non-terminal (denoted as 1NT) instead of the usual two non-terminal (2NT) model. In our earlier experiments we found the 1NT model to perform comparably to the 2NT model for close language pairs such as French-English (Sankaran et al., 2012) at the same time resulting in a smaller model. We used the shared-task training data consisting of Europarl (v7), News commentary and UN documents for training the translation models having a total of 15 M sentence pairs (we did not use the Fr-En Giga parallel corpus for the training). We trained a 5-gram language model for English using the English Gigaword (v4).

For English-Czech, we trained a standard Hiero model that has up to two non-terminals on the right-hand side. We used the Europarl (v7), news commentary and CzEng (v0.9) corpora having 7.95M sentence pairs for training translation models. We trained a 5-gram language model using the Czech side of the parallel corpora and did not use the Czech monolingual corpus.

The baseline systems use the following 8 standard Hiero features: rule probabilities $p(e|f)$ and $p(f|e)$; lexical weights $p_l(e|f)$ and $p_l(f|e)$; word penalty, phrase penalty, language model and glue rule penalty.

1.1 LM Integration in Kriya

The kriya decoder is based on a modified CYK algorithm similar to that of Chiang (2007). We use a novel approach in computing the language model (LM) scores in Kriya, which deserves a mention here.

The CKY decoder in Hiero-style systems can freely combine target hypotheses generated in intermediate cells with hierarchical rules in the higher cells. Thus the generation of the target hypotheses are fragmented and out of order in Hiero, compared to the left to right order preferred by n-gram language models.

This leads to challenges in estimating LM scores for partial target hypotheses and this is typically addressed by adding a sentence initial marker (<s>) to the beginning of each derivation path.[1] Thus the language model scores for the hypothesis in the intermediate cell are approximated, with the true language model score (taking into account sentence boundaries) being computed in the last cell that spans the entire source sentence.

Kriya uses a novel idea for computing LM scores: for each of the target hypothesis fragment, it finds the best position for the fragment in the final sentence and uses the corresponding score. Specifically, we compute three different scores corresponding to the three states where the fragment can end up in the final sentence, viz. sentence initial, middle and final and choose the best score. Thus given a fragment t_f consisting of a sequence of target tokens, we compute LM scores for (i) <s> t_f, (ii) t_f and (iii) t_f </s> and use the best score (*only*) for pruning.[2] While this increases the number of LM queries, we exploit the language model state information in KenLM (Heafield, 2011) to optimize the queries by saving the scores for the unchanged states. Our earlier experiments showed significant reduction in search errors due to this approach, in addition to a small but consistent increase in BLEU score (Sankaran et al., 2012).

2 French-English System

In addition to the baseline system, we also trained separate systems for *News* and *Non-News* genres for applying *ensemble* decoding (Razmara et al., 2012). The news genre system was trained only using the news-commentary corpus (about 137K sentence pairs) and the non-news genre system was trained on the Europarl and UN documents data (14.8M sentence pairs). The ensemble decoding framework combines the models of these two systems dynamically when decoding the testset. The idea is to effectively use the small amount of news genre data in order to maximize the performance on the news-based testsets. In the following sections, we explain in broader detail how this system combination technique works as well as the details of this experiment and the evaluation results.

2.1 Ensemble Decoding

In the ensemble decoding framework we view translation task as a domain mixing problem involving news and non-news genres. The official training data is from two major sources: news-commentary data and Europarl/UN data and we hope to exploit the distinctive nature of the two genres. Given that the news data is smaller comparing to parliamentary proceedings data, we could tune the ensemble decoding to appropriately boost the weight for the news genre mode during decoding. The ensemble decoding approach (Razmara et al., 2012) takes advantage of multiple translation models with the goal of constructing a system that outperforms all the component models. The key strength of this system combination method is that the systems are combined dynamically at decode time. This enables the decoder to pick the best hypotheses for each span of the input.

In ensemble decoding, given a number of translation systems which are already trained and tuned, all of the hypotheses from component models are used in order to translate a sentence. The scores of such rules are combined in the decoder (i.e. CKY) using various mixture operations to assign a single score to them. Depending on the mixture operation used for combining the scores, we would get different mixture scores.

Ensemble decoding extends the log-linear framework which is found in state-of-the-art machine translation systems. Specifically, the probability of a phrase-pair $(\bar{e}, \bar{f})$ in the ensemble model is:

$$p(\bar{e} \mid \bar{f}) \propto \exp\left(\underbrace{\mathbf{w_1} \cdot \boldsymbol{\phi_1}}_{1^{st}\text{ model}} \oplus \underbrace{\mathbf{w_2} \cdot \boldsymbol{\phi_2}}_{2^{nd}\text{ model}} \oplus \cdots \right)$$

[1] Alternately systems add sentence boundary markers (<s> and </s>) to the training data so that they are explicitly present in the translation and language models. While this can speed up the decoding as the cube pruning is more aggressive, it also limits the applicability of rules having the boundary contexts.

[2] This ensures the the LM score estimates are never underestimated for pruning. We retain the LM score for fragment (case ii) for estimating the score for the full candidate sentence later.

where $\oplus$ denotes the mixture operation between two or more model scores.

Mixture operations receive two or more scores (probabilities) and return the mixture score (probability). In this section, we explore different options for this mixture operation.

Weighted Sum (wsum): in *wsum* the ensemble probability is proportional to the weighted sum of all individual model probabilities.

$$p(\bar{e} \mid \bar{f}) \;\propto\; \sum_{m}^{M} \lambda_m \exp\left(\mathbf{w}_m \cdot \boldsymbol{\phi}_m\right)$$

where m denotes the index of component models, M is the total number of them and λ_i is the weight for component i.

Weighted Max (wmax): where the ensemble score is the weighted max of all model scores.

$$p(\bar{e} \mid \bar{f}) \;\propto\; \max_{m}\left(\lambda_m \exp\left(\mathbf{w}_m \cdot \boldsymbol{\phi}_m\right)\right)$$

Product (prod): in *prod*, the probability of the ensemble model or a rule is computed as the product of the probabilities of all components (or equally the sum of log-probabilities). When using this mixture operation, ensemble decoding would be a generalization of the log-linear framework over multiple models. Product models can also make use of weights to control the contribution of each component. These models are generally known as *Logarithmic Opinion Pools (LOPs)* where:

$$p(\bar{e} \mid \bar{f}) \;\propto\; \exp\left(\sum_{m}^{M} \lambda_m \, \mathbf{w}_m \cdot \boldsymbol{\phi}_m\right)$$

Model Switching: in model switching, each cell in the CKY chart gets populated only by rules from one of the models and the other models' rules are discarded. This is based on the hypothesis that each component model is an expert on different parts of sentence. In this method, we need to define a binary indicator function $\delta(\bar{f}, m)$ for each span and component model.

$$\delta(\bar{f}, m) = \begin{cases} 1, & m = \underset{n \in M}{\text{argmax}}\ \psi(\bar{f}, n) \\ 0, & \text{otherwise} \end{cases}$$

The criteria for choosing a model for each cell, $\psi(\bar{f}, n)$, could be based on:

Max: for each cell, the model that has the highest weighted top-rule score wins:

$$\psi(\bar{f}, n) = \lambda_n \max_{\bar{e}}(\mathbf{w}_n \cdot \boldsymbol{\phi}_n(\bar{\mathbf{e}}, \bar{\mathbf{f}}))$$

Sum: Instead of comparing only the score of the top rules, the model with the highest weighted sum of the probability of the rules wins (taking into account the *ttl*(translation table limit) limit on the number of rules suggested by each model for each cell):

$$\psi(\bar{f}, n) = \lambda_n \sum_{\bar{e}} \exp\left(\mathbf{w}_n \cdot \boldsymbol{\phi}_n(\bar{\mathbf{e}}, \bar{\mathbf{f}})\right)$$

The probability of each phrase-pair $(\bar{e}, \bar{f})$ is computed as:

$$p(\bar{e} \mid \bar{f}) = \sum_{m} \delta(\bar{f}, m)\, p_m(\bar{e} \mid \bar{f})$$

Since log-linear models usually look for the best derivation, they do not need to normalize the scores to form probabilities. Therefore, the scores that different models assign to each phrase-pair may not be in the same scale. Therefore, mixing their scores might wash out the information in one (or some) of the models. We applied a heuristic to deal with this problem where the scores are normalized over a shorter list. So the list of rules coming from each model for a certain cell in the CKY chart is normalized before getting mixed with other phrase-table rules. However, experiments showed using normalized scores hurts the BLEU score radically. So we use the normalized scores only for pruning and for mixing the actual scores are used.

As a more principled way, we used a toolkit, CONDOR (Vanden Berghen and Bersini, 2005), to optimize the weights of our component models on a dev-set. CONDOR, which is publicly available, is a direct optimizer based on Powell's algorithm that does not require explicit gradient information for the objective function.

2.2 Experiments and Results

As mentioned earlier all the experiments reported for French-English use a simpler Hiero translation

Method	Devset	Test-11	Test-12
Baseline Hiero	26.03	27.63	**28.15**
News data	24.02	26.47	26.27
Non-news data	26.09	27.87	28.15
Ensemble PROD	25.66	**28.25**	28.09

Table 1: French-English BLEU scores. Best performing setting is shown in **Boldface**.

model having at most one non-terminal (1NT) on the right-hand side. We use 7567 sentence pairs from news-tests 2008 through 2010 for tuning and use news-test 2011 for testing in addition to the 2012 test data. The feature weights were tuned using MERT (Och, 2003) and we report the devset (IBM) BLEU scores and the testset BLEU scores computed using the official evaluation script (mteval-v11b.pl).

The results for the French-English experiments are reported in Table 1. We note that both baseline Hiero model and the model trained from the non-news genre get comparable BLEU scores. The news genre model however gets a lesser BLEU score and this is to be expected due to the very small training data available for this genre.

Table 2 shows the results of applying various mixture operations on the devset and testset, both in normalized (denoted by Norm.) and un-normalized settings (denoted by Base). We present results for these mixture operations using uniform weights (i.e. untuned weights) and for PROD we also present the results using the weights optimized by CONDOR. Most of the mixture operations outperform the Test-11 BLEU of the baseline models (shown in Table 1) even with uniform (untuned) weights. We took the best performing operation (i.e. PROD) and tuned its component weights using our optimizer which lead to 0.26 points improvement over its uniform-weight version.

The last row in Table 1 reports the BLEU score for this mixture operation with the tuned weights on the Test-12 dataset and it is marginally less than the baseline model. While this is disappointing, this also runs counter to our empirical results from other datasets. We are currently investigating this aspect as we hope to improve the robustness and applicability of our ensemble approach for different datasets and language pairs.

Mix. Operation	Weights	Base	Norm.
WMAX	uniform	27.67	27.94
WSUM	uniform	27.72	27.95
SWITCHMAX	uniform	27.96	26.21
SWITCHSUM	uniform	27.98	27.98
PROD	uniform	**27.99**	**28.09**
PROD	optimized	**28.25**	28.11

Table 2: Applying ensemble decoding with different mixture operations on the Test-11 dataset. Best performing setting is shown in **Boldface**.

3 English-Czech System

3.1 Morpheme Segmented Model

For English-Czech, we additionally experimented using morphologically segmented versions of the Czech side of the parallel data, since previous work (Clifton and Sarkar, 2011) has shown that segmentation of morphologically rich languages can aid translation. To derive the segmentation, we built an unsupervised morphological segmentation model using the Morfessor toolkit (Creutz and Lagus, 2007).

Morfessor uses minimum description length criteria to train a HMM-based segmentation model. Varying the perplexity threshold in Morfessor does not segment more word types, but rather oversegments the same word types. We hand tuned the model parameters over training data size and perplexity; these control the granularity and coverage of the segmentations. Specifically, we trained different segmenter models on varying sets of most frequent words and different perplexities and identified two sets that performed best based on a separate held-out set. These two sets correspond to 500k most frequent words and a perplexity of 50 (denoted SM1) and 10k most frequent words and a perplexity of 20 (denoted SM2). We then used these two models to segment the entire data set and generate two different segmented training sets. These models had the best combination of segmentation coverage of the training data and largest segments, since we found empirically that smaller segments were less meaningful in the translation model. The SM2 segmentation segmented more words than SM1, but more frequently segmented words into single-character units.

For example, the Czech word 'dlaební' is broken into the useful components 'dlaeb + ní' by SM1, but is oversegmented into 'dl + a + e + b + ní' by SM2. However, SM1 fails to find a segmentation at all for the related word 'dlaebními', while SM2 breaks it up similiarly with an additional suffix: 'dl + a + e + b + ní + mi'.

With these segmentation models, we segmented the target side of the training and dev data before training the translation model. Similarly, we also train segmented language models corresponding to the two sets SM1 and SM2. The MERT tuning step uses the segmented dev-set reference to evaluate the segmented hypotheses generated by the decoder for optimizing the weights for the BLEU score. However for evaluating the test-set, we stitched the segments in the decoder output back into unsegmented forms in a post-processing step, before performing evaluation against the original unsegmented references. The hypotheses generated by the decoder can have incomplete dangling segments where one or more prefixes and/or suffixes are missing. While these dangling segments could be handled in a different way, we use a simple heuristic of ignoring the segment marker '+' by just removing the segment marker. In next section, we report the results of using the unsegmented model as well as its segmented counterparts.

3.2 Experiments and Results

In the English-Czech experiments, we used the same datasets for the dev and test sets as in French-English experiments (dev: news-tests 2008, 2009, 2010 with 7567 sentence pairs and test: news-test2011 with 3003 sentence pairs). Similarly, MERT (Och, 2003) has been used to tune the feature weights and we report the BLEU scores of two test-sets computed using the official evaluation script (mteval-v11b.pl).

Table 3.2 shows the results of different segmentation schemes on the WMT-11 and WMT-12 test-sets. SM1 slightly outperformed the other two models in Test-11, however the unsegmented model performed best in Test-12, though marginally. We are currently investigating this and are also considering the possibility employing the idea of morpheme prediction in the post-decoding step in combination with this morpheme-based translation as suggested by Clifton and Sarkar (2011).

Segmentation	Test-11	Test-12
Baseline Hiero	14.65	**12.40**
SM1 : 500k-ppl50	**14.75**	12.34
SM2 : 10k-ppl20	14.57	12.34

Table 3: The English-Czech results for different segmentation settings. Best performing setting is shown in **Boldface**.

4 Conclusion

We submitted systems in two language pairs French-English and English-Czech for WMT-12 shared task. In French-English, we experimented the ensemble decoding framework that effectively utilizes the small amount of *news* genre data to improve the performance in the testset belonging to the same genre. We obtained a moderate gain of 0.4 BLEU points with the ensemble decoding over the baseline system in newstest-2011. For newstest-2012, it performs comparably to that of the baseline and we are presently investigating the lack of improvement in newstest-2012. For Cz-En, We found that the BLEU scores do not substantially differ from each other and also the minor differences are not consistent for Test-11 and Test-12.

References

David Chiang. 2007. Hierarchical phrase-based translation. *Computational Linguistics*, 33.

Ann Clifton and Anoop Sarkar. 2011. Combining morpheme-based machine translation with post-processing morpheme prediction. In *Proceedings of the 49th Annual Meeting of the Association for Computational Linguistics: Human Language Technologies - Volume 1*, pages 32–42.

Mathias Creutz and Krista Lagus. 2007. Unsupervised models for morpheme segmentation and morphology learning. *ACM Transactions on Speech and Language Processing*, 4(1):3:1–3:34, February.

Kenneth Heafield. 2011. KenLM: Faster and smaller language model queries. In *Proceedings of the Sixth Workshop on Statistical Machine Translation*, pages 187–197.

Philipp Koehn, Hieu Hoang, Alexandra Birch, Chris Callison-Burch, Marcello Federico, Nicola Bertoldi, Brooke Cowan, Wade Shen, Christine Moran, Richard

Zens, Chris Dyer, Ondřej Bojar, Alexandra Constantin, and Evan Herbst. 2007. Moses: open source toolkit for statistical machine translation. In *Proceedings of the 45th Annual Meeting of the ACL on Interactive Poster and Demonstration Sessions*, pages 177–180. Association for Computational Linguistics.

Franz Josef Och. 2003. Minimum error rate training in statistical machine translation. In *Proceedings of the Annual Meeting of Association of Computational Linguistics*, pages 160–167.

Majid Razmara, George Foster, Baskaran Sankaran, and Anoop Sarkar. 2012. Mixing multiple translation models in statistical machine translation. In *Proceedings of the 50th Annual Meeting of the Association for Computational Linguistics*, Jeju, Republic of Korea, July. Association for Computational Linguistics. *To appear*.

Baskaran Sankaran, Majid Razmara, and Anoop Sarkar. 2012. Kriya an end-to-end hierarchical phrase-based mt system. *The Prague Bulletin of Mathematical Linguistics*, 97(97):83–98, April.

Frank Vanden Berghen and Hugues Bersini. 2005. CONDOR, a new parallel, constrained extension of powell's UOBYQA algorithm: Experimental results and comparison with the DFO algorithm. *Journal of Computational and Applied Mathematics*, 181:157–175, September.

DEPFIX: A System for Automatic Correction of Czech MT Outputs*

Rudolf Rosa, David Mareček and Ondřej Dušek
Charles University in Prague, Faculty of Mathematics and Physics
Institute of Formal and Applied Linguistics
Malostranské náměstí 25, Prague
{rosa,marecek,odusek}@ufal.mff.cuni.cz

Abstract

We present an improved version of DEPFIX (Mareček et al., 2011), a system for automatic rule-based post-processing of English-to-Czech MT outputs designed to increase their fluency. We enhanced the rule set used by the original DEPFIX system and measured the performance of the individual rules.

We also modified the dependency parser of McDonald et al. (2005) in two ways to adjust it for the parsing of MT outputs. We show that our system is able to improve the quality of the state-of-the-art MT systems.

1 Introduction

The today's outputs of Machine Translation (MT) often contain serious grammatical errors. This is particularly apparent in statistical MT systems (SMT), which do not employ structural linguistic rules. These systems have been dominating the area in the recent years (Callison-Burch et al., 2011). Such errors make the translated text less fluent and may even lead to unintelligibility or misleading statements. The problem is more evident in languages with rich morphology, such as Czech, where morphological agreement is of a relatively high importance for the interpretation of syntactic relations.

The DEPFIX system (Mareček et al., 2011) attempts to correct some of the frequent SMT systems' errors in English-to-Czech translations.[1] It analyzes the *target* sentence (the SMT output in Czech language) using a morphological tagger and a dependency parser and attempts to correct it by applying several rules which enforce consistency with the Czech grammar. Most of the rules use the *source* sentence (the SMT input in English language) as a source of information about the sentence structure. The *source* sentence is also tagged and parsed, and word-to-word alignment with the *target* sentence is determined.

In this paper, we present DEPFIX 2012, an improved version of the original DEPFIX 2011 system. It makes use of a new parser, described briefly in Section 3, which is adapted to handle the generally ungrammatical *target* sentences better. We have also enhanced the set of grammar correction rules, for which we give a detailed description in Section 4. Section 5 gives an account of the experiments performed to evaluate the DEPFIX 2012 system and compare it to DEPFIX 2011. Section 6 then concludes the paper.

2 Related Work

Our approach can be regarded as converse to the more common way of using an SMT system to automatically post-edit the output of a rule-based translation system, as described e.g. in (Simard et al., 2007) or (Lagarda et al., 2009).

The DEPFIX system is implemented in the

*This research has been supported by the European Union Seventh Framework Programme (FP7) under grant agreement n° 247762 (Faust), and by the grants GAUK116310, GA201/09/H057 (Res-Informatica), and LH12093.

[1] Although we apply the DEPFIX system just to SMT systems in this paper as it mainly targets the errors induced by this type of MT systems, it can be applied to virtually any MT system (Mareček et al., 2011).

TectoMT/Treex NLP framework (Popel and Žabokrtský, 2010),[2] using the Morče tagger (Spoustová et al., 2007) and the MST parser (McDonald et al., 2005) trained on the CoNLL 2007 Shared Task English data (Nivre et al., 2007) to analyze the *source* sentences. The *source* and *target* sentences are aligned using GIZA++ (Och and Ney, 2003).

3 Parsing

The DEPFIX 2011 system used the MST parser (McDonald et al., 2005) with an improved feature set for Czech (Novák and Žabokrtský, 2007) trained on the Prague Dependency Treebank (PDT) 2.0 (Hajič and others, 2006) to analyze the *target* sentences. DEPFIX 2012 uses a reimplementation of the MST parser capable of utilizing parallel features from the *source* side in the parsing of the *target* sentence.

The *source* text is usually grammatical and therefore is likely to be analyzed more reliably. The *source* structure obtained in this way can then provide hints for the *target* parser. We use local features projected through the GIZA++ word alignment – i.e. for each *target* word, we add features computed over its aligned *source* word, if there is one.

To address the differences between the gold standard training data and SMT outputs, we "worsen" the treebank used to train the parser, i.e. introduce errors similar to those found in *target* sentences: The trees retain their correct structure, only the word forms are modified to resemble SMT output.

We have computed a "part-of-speech tag error model" on parallel sentences from the Prague Czech-English Dependency Treebank (PCEDT) 2.0 (Bojar et al., 2012), comparing the gold standard Czech translations to the output of an SMT system (Koehn et al., 2007) and estimating the Maximum Likelihood probabilities of errors for each part-of-speech tag. We then applied this error model to the Czech PCEDT 2.0 sentences and used the resulting "worsened" treebank to train the parser.

4 Rules

DEPFIX 2012 uses 20 hand-written rules, addressing various frequent errors in MT output. Each rule takes an analyzed *target* sentence as its input, often together with its analyzed *source* sentence, and attempts to correct any errors found – usually by changing morphosyntactic categories of a word (such as number, gender, case, person and dependency label) and regenerating the corresponding word form if necessary, more rarely by deleting superfluous particles or auxiliary words or changing the *target* dependency tree structure. However, neither word order problems nor bad lexical choices are corrected.

Many rules were already present in DEPFIX 2011. However, most were modified in DEPFIX 2012 to achieve better performance (denoted as ***modified***), and new rules were added (***new***). Rules not modified since DEPFIX 2011 are denoted as ***reused***.

The order of rule application is important as there are dependencies among the rules, e.g. FixPrepositionNounAgreement (enforcing noun-preposition congruency) depends on FixPrepositionalCase (fixing incorrectly tagged prepositional case). The rules are applied in the order listed in Table 2.

4.1 Analysis Fixing Rules

Analysis fixing rules try to detect and rectify tagger and parser errors. They do not change word forms and are therefore invisible on the output as such; however, rules of other types benefit from their corrections.

FixPrepositionalCase *(new)*

This rule corrects part-of-speech-tag errors in prepositional phrases. It looks for all words that depend on a preposition and do not match its part-of-speech tag case. It tries to find and assign a common morphological case fitting for both the word form and the preposition. Infrequent preposition-case combinations are not considered.

FixReflexiveTantum *(new)*

If the word form 'se' or 'si' is classified as reflexive tantum particle by the parser, but does not belong to an actual reflexive tantum verb (or a deverbative noun or an adjective), its dependency label is changed to a different value, based on the context.

FixNounNumber *(reused)*

If a noun is tagged as singular in *target* but as plural in *source*, the tag is likely to be incorrect. This rule tries to find a tag that would match both the

[2] `http://ufal.mff.cuni.cz/treex`

source number and the *target* word form, changing the *target* case if necessary.

FixPrepositionWithoutChildren ***(reused)***

A *target* preposition with no child nodes is clearly an analysis error. This rule tries to find children for childless prepositions by projecting the children of the aligned *source* preposition to the *target* side.

FixAuxVChildren ***(new)***

Since auxiliary verbs must not have child nodes, we rehang all their children to the governing full verb.

4.2 Agreement Fixing Rules

These rules relate to morphological agreement required by Czech grammar, which they try to enforce in case it is violated. Czech grammar requires agreement in morphological gender, number, case and person where applicable.

These rules typically use the *source* sentence only for confirmation.

FixRelativePronoun ***(new)***

The Czech word relative pronoun 'který' is assigned gender and number identical to the closest preceding noun or pronoun, if the *source* analysis confirms that it depends on this noun/pronoun.

FixSubject ***(modified)***

The subject (if the subject dependency label is confirmed by the *source* analysis) will have its case set to nominative; the number is changed if this leads to the word form staying unchanged.

FixVerbAuxBeAgreement ***(modified)***

If an auxiliary verb is a child of an infinitive, the auxiliary verb receives the gender and number of the subject, which is a child of the infinitive (see also FixAuxVChildren).

FixSubjectPredicateAgreement ***(modified)***

An active verb form receives the number and person from its subject (whose relation to the verb must be confirmed by the *source*).

FixSubjectPastParticipleAgreement ***(modified)***

A past participle verb form receives the number and gender from its subject (confirmed by the *source* analysis).

FixPassiveAuxBeAgreement ***(modified)***

An auxiliary verb 'být' ('to be') depending on a passive verb form receives its gender and number.

FixPrepositionNounAgreement ***(modified)***

A noun or adjective depending on a preposition receives its case. The dependency must be confirmed in the *source*.

FixNounAdjectiveAgreement ***(modified)***

An adjective (or an adjective-like pronoun or numeral) preceding its governing noun receives its gender, number and case.

4.3 Translation Fixing Rules

The following rules detect and correct structures often mistranslated by SMT systems. They usually depend heavily on the *source* sentence.

FixBy ***(new)***

English preposition 'by' is translated to Czech using the instrumental case (if modifying a verb, e.g. 'built by David': 'postaveno Davidem') or using the genitive case (if modifying a noun, e.g. 'songs by David': 'písně Davida').

FixPresentContinuous ***(modified)***

If the *source* sentence is in a continuous tense (e.g. 'Ondřej isn't experimenting.'), the auxiliary verb 'to be' must not appear on the output, which is often the case (e.g. *'Ondřej není experimentovat.'). This rule deletes the auxiliary verb in *target* and transfers its morphological categories to the main verb (e.g. 'Ondřej neexperimentuje.').

FixVerbByEnSubject ***(new)***

If the subject of the *source* sentence is a personal pronoun, its following morphological categeries are propagated to the *target* predicate:

- person
- number (except for 'you', which does not exhibit number)
- gender (only in case of 'he' or 'she', which exhibit the natural gender)

FixOf ***(new)***

English preposition 'of' modifying a noun is translated to Czech using the genitive case (e.g. 'pictures of Rudolf': 'obrázky Rudolfa').

FixAuxT ***(reused)***

Reflexive tantum particles ‘se’ or ‘si’ not belonging to any verb or adjective are deleted. This situation usually occurs when the meaning of the *source* verb/adjective is lost in translation and only the particle is produced.

4.4 Other Rules

VocalizePrepos ***(reused)***

Prepositions ‘k’, ‘s’, ‘v’, ‘z’ are *vocalized* (i.e. changed to ‘ke’, ‘se’, ‘ve’, ‘ze’) where necessary. The vocalization rules in Czech are similar to ‘a’/‘an’ distinction in English.

FixFirstWordCapitalization ***(new)***

If the first word of *source* is capitalized and the first word of *target* is not, this rule capitalizes it.

5 Experiments and Results

For parameter tuning, we used datasets from the WMT10 translation task and translations by ONLINEB and CU-BOJAR systems.

5.1 Manual Evaluation

Manual evaluation of both DEPFIX 2011 and DEPFIX 2012 was performed on the WMT11[3] test set translated by ONLINEB. 500 sentences were randomly selected and blind-evaluated by two independent annotators, who were presented with outputs of ONLINEB, DEPFIX 2011 and DEPFIX 2012. (For 246 sentences, at least one of the DEPFIX setups modified the ONLINEB translation.) They provided us with a pairwise comparison of the three setups, with the possibility to mark the sentence as “indefinite” if translations were of equal quality. The results are given in Table 1.

In Table 2, we use the manual evaluation to measure the performance of the individual rules in DEPFIX 2012. For each rule, we ran DEPFIX 2012 with this rule disabled and compared the output to the output of the full DEPFIX 2012. The number of affected sentences on the whole WMT11 test set, given as “changed”, represents the impact of the rule. The number of affected sentences selected for manual evaluation is listed as “evaluated”. Finally, the annotators’ ratings of the “evaluated” sentences

[3]http://www.statmt.org/wmt11

A / B	Setup 1 better	Setup 2 better	Indefinite
Setup 1 better	55%	1%	11%
Setup 2 better	1%	8%	4%
Indefinite	3%	2%	15%

Table 3: Inter-annotator agreement matrix for ONLINEB + DEPFIX 2012 as Setup 1 and ONLINEB as Setup 2.

(suggesting whether the rule improved or worsened the translation, or whether the result was indefinite) were counted and divided by the number of annotators to get the average performance of each rule. Please note that the lower the “evaluated” number, the lower the confidence of the results.

The inter-annotator agreement matrix for comparison of ONLINEB + DEPFIX 2012 (denoted as Setup 1) with ONLINEB (Setup 2) is given in Table 3. The results for the other two setup pairs were similar, with the average inter-annotator agreement being 77%.

5.2 Automatic Evaluation

We also performed several experiments with automatic evaluation using the standard BLEU metric (Papineni et al., 2002). As the effect of DEPFIX in terms of BLEU is rather small, the results are not as confident as the results of manual evaluation.[4]

In Table 4, we compare the DEPFIX 2011 and DEPFIX 2012 systems and measure the contribution of parser adaptation (Section 3) and rule improvements (Section 4). It can be seen that the combined effect of applying both system modifications is greater than when they are applied alone. The improvement of DEPFIX 2012 over ONLINEB without DEPFIX is statistically significant at 95% confidence level.

The effect of DEPFIX 2012 on the outputs of some of the best-scoring SMT systems in the WMT12 Translation Task[5] is shown in Table 5. Although DEPFIX 2012 was tuned only on ONLINEB and CU-BOJAR system outputs, it improves the BLEU score of all the best-scoring systems, which suggests that

[4]As already noted by Mareček et al. (2011), BLEU seems not to be very suitable for evaluation of DEPFIX. See (Kos and Bojar, 2009) for a detailed study of BLEU performance when applied to evaluation of MT systems with Czech as the target language.

[5]http://www.statmt.org/wmt12

Setup 1	Setup 2	Differing sentences	Annotator	Setup 1 better	Setup 2 better	Indefinite
ONLINEB + DEPFIX 2011	ONLINEB	169	A	58%	13%	29%
			B	47%	11%	42%
ONLINEB + DEPFIX 2012	ONLINEB	234	A	65%	14%	21%
			B	59%	11%	30%
ONLINEB + DEPFIX 2012	ONLINEB + DEPFIX 2011	148	A	54%	24%	22%
			B	56%	22%	22%

Table 1: Manual pairwise comparison on 500 sentences from WMT11 test set processed by ONLINEB, ONLINEB + DEPFIX 2011 and ONLINEB + DEPFIX 2012. Evaluated by two independent annotators.

	Sentences							
Rule	changed	evaluated	impr.	%	wors.	%	indef.	%
FixPrepositionalCase	34	5	3	60	2	40	0	0
FixReflexiveTantum	1	0	–	–	–	–	–	–
FixNounNumber	80	11	5	45	5	45	1	9
FixPrepositionWithoutChildren	16	6	3	50	3	50	0	0
FixBy	75	13	10.5	81	1	8	1.5	12
FixAuxVChildren	26	6	4.5	75	0	0	1.5	25
FixRelativePronoun	56	8	6	75	2	25	0	0
FixSubject	142	18	13.5	75	3	17	1.5	8
FixVerbAuxBeAgreement	8	2	1	50	1	50	0	0
FixPresentContinuous	30	7	5.5	79	1	14	0.5	7
FixSubjectPredicateAgreement	87	10	5.5	55	1	10	3.5	35
FixSubjectPastParticipleAgreement	396	63	46.5	74	9.5	15	7	11
FixVerbByEnSubject	25	6	5	83	0	0	1	17
FixPassiveAuxBeAgreement	43	8	6	75	0.5	6	1.5	19
FixPrepositionNounAgreement	388	62	40	65	13	21	9	15
FixOf	84	13	11.5	88	0	0	1.5	12
FixNounAdjectiveAgreement	575	108	69.5	64	20	19	18.5	17
FixAuxT	38	7	4	57	1	14	2	29
VocalizePrepos	53	12	6	50	2.5	21	3.5	29
FixFirstWordCapitalization	0	0	–	–	–	–	–	–

Table 2: Impact and accuracy of individual DEPFIX 2012 rules using manual evaluation on 500 sentences from WMT11 test set translated by ONLINEB. The number of changed sentences is counted on the whole WMT11 test set, i.e. 3003 sentences. The numbers of improved, worsened and indefinite translations are averaged over the annotators.

DEPFIX setup	BLEU
without DEPFIX	19.37
DEPFIX 2011	19.41
DEPFIX 2011 + new parser	19.42
DEPFIX 2011 + new rules	19.48
DEPFIX 2012	19.56

Table 4: Performance of ONLINEB and various DEPFIX setups on the WMT11 test set.

System	BLEU
ONLINEB	16.25
ONLINEB + DEPFIX 2012	16.31
UEDIN	15.54
UEDIN + DEPFIX 2012	15.75
CU-BOJAR	15.41
CU-BOJAR + DEPFIX 2012	15.45
CU-TAMCH-BOJ	15.35
CU-TAMCH-BOJ + DEPFIX 2012	15.39

Table 5: Comparison of BLEU of baseline system output and corrected system output on WMT12 test set.

it is able to improve the quality of various SMT systems when applied to their outputs. (The improvement on UEDIN is statistically significant at 95% confidence level.) We submitted the ONLINEB + DEPFIX 2012 system to the WMT12 Translation Task as CU-DEPFIX.

6 Conclusion

We have presented two improvements to DEPFIX, a system of rule-based post-editing of English-to-Czech Machine Translation outputs proven by manual and automatic evaluation to improve the quality of the translations produced by state-of-the-art SMT systems. First, improvements in the existing rules and implementation of new ones, which can be regarded as an additive, evolutionary change. Second, a modified dependency parser, adjusted to parsing of SMT outputs by training it on a parallel treebank with worsened word forms on the Czech side. We showed that both changes led to a better performance of the new DEPFIX 2012, both individually and combined.

In future, we are planning to incorporate deeper analysis, devising rules that would operate on the deep-syntactic, or *tectogrammatical*, layer. The Czech and English tectogrammatical trees are more similar to each other, which should enable us to exploit more information from the *source* sentences. We also hope to be able to perform more complex corrections, such as changing the part of speech of a word when necessary.

Following the success of our modified parser, we would also like to modify the tagger in a similar way, since incorrect analyses produced by the tagger often hinder the correct function of our rules, sometimes leading to a rule worsening the translation instead of improving it.

As observed e.g. by Groves and Schmidtke (2009) for English-to-German and English-to-French translations, SMT systems for other language pairs also tend to produce reoccurring grammatical errors. We believe that these could be easily detected and corrected in a rule-based way, using an approach similar to ours.

References

Ondřej Bojar, Jan Hajič, Eva Hajičová, Jarmila Panevová, Petr Sgall, Silvie Cinková, Eva Fučíková, Marie Mikulová, Petr Pajas, Jan Popelka, Jiří Semecký, Jana Šindlerová, Jan Štěpánek, Josef Toman, Zdeňka Urešová, and Zdeněk Žabokrtský. 2012. Announcing Prague Czech-English Dependency Treebank 2.0. In *Proceedings of LREC 2012*, Istanbul, Turkey, May. ELRA, European Language Resources Association. In print.

Chris Callison-Burch, Philipp Koehn, Christof Monz, and Omar Zaidan. 2011. Findings of the 2011 workshop on statistical machine translation. In *Proceedings of the Sixth Workshop on Statistical Machine Translation*, pages 22–64, Edinburgh, Scotland, July. Association for Computational Linguistics.

Declan Groves and Dag Schmidtke. 2009. Identification and analysis of post-editing patterns for MT. *Proceedings of MT Summit XII*, pages 429–436.

Jan Hajič et al. 2006. Prague Dependency Treebank 2.0. CD-ROM, Linguistic Data Consortium, LDC Catalog No.: LDC2006T0 1, Philadelphia.

Philipp Koehn, Hieu Hoang, Alexandra Birch, Chris Callison-Burch, Marcello Federico, Nicola Bertoldi, Brooke Cowan, Wade Shen, Christine Moran, Richard Zens, Chris Dyer, Ondřej Bojar, Alexandra Constantin, and Evan Herbst. 2007. Moses: Open Source Toolkit for Statistical Machine Translation. In *ACL 2007, Proceedings of the 45th Annual Meeting of the*

Association for Computational Linguistics Companion Volume Proceedings of the Demo and Poster Sessions, pages 177–180, Prague, Czech Republic, June. Association for Computational Linguistics.

Kamil Kos and Ondřej Bojar. 2009. Evaluation of machine translation metrics for czech as the target language. *The Prague Bulletin of Mathematical Linguistics*, 92(-1):135–148.

Antonio L. Lagarda, Vicent Alabau, Francisco Casacuberta, Roberto Silva, and Enrique Diaz-de Liano. 2009. Statistical post-editing of a rule-based machine translation system. In *Proceedings of Human Language Technologies: The 2009 Annual Conference of the North American Chapter of the Association for Computational Linguistics, Companion Volume: Short Papers*, pages 217–220. Association for Computational Linguistics.

David Mareček, Rudolf Rosa, Petra Galuščáková, and Ondřej Bojar. 2011. Two-step translation with grammatical post-processing. In *Proceedings of the Sixth Workshop on Statistical Machine Translation*, pages 426–432. Association for Computational Linguistics.

Ryan McDonald, Fernando Pereira, Kiril Ribarov, and Jan Hajič. 2005. Non-projective dependency parsing using spanning tree algorithms. In *HLT '05: Proceedings of the conference on Human Language Technology and Empirical Methods in Natural Language Processing*, pages 523–530, Vancouver, British Columbia, Canada.

Joakim Nivre, Johan Hall, Sandra Kübler, Ryan McDonald, Jens Nilsson, Sebastian Riedel, and Deniz Yuret. 2007. The CoNLL 2007 shared task on dependency parsing. In *Proceedings of the CoNLL 2007 Shared Task. Joint Conf. on Empirical Methods in Natural Language Processing and Computational Natural Language Learning (EMNLP-CoNLL)*, June.

Václav Novák and Zdeněk Žabokrtský. 2007. Feature engineering in maximum spanning tree dependency parser. In Václav Matoušek and Pavel Mautner, editors, *Lecture Notes in Artificial Intelligence, Proceedings of the 10th I nternational Conference on Text, Speech and Dialogue*, Lecture Notes in Computer Science, pages 92–98, Pilsen, Czech Republic. Springer Science+Business Media Deutschland GmbH.

Franz Josef Och and Hermann Ney. 2003. A Systematic Comparison of Various Statistical Alignment Models. *Computational Linguistics*, 29(1):19–51.

Kishore Papineni, Salim Roukos, Todd Ward, and Wei-Jing Zhu. 2002. BLEU: a Method for Automatic Evaluation of Machine Translation. In *ACL 2002, Proceedings of the 40th Annual Meeting of the Association for Computational Linguistics*, pages 311–318, Philadelphia, Pennsylvania.

Martin Popel and Zdeněk Žabokrtský. 2010. TectoMT: modular NLP framework. In *Proceedings of the 7th international conference on Advances in natural language processing*, IceTAL'10, pages 293–304, Berlin, Heidelberg. Springer-Verlag.

Michel Simard, Cyril Goutte, and Pierre Isabelle. 2007. Statistical phrase-based post-editing. In *Human Language Technologies 2007: The Conference of the North American Chapter of the Association for Computational Linguistics; Proceedings of the Main Conference*, pages 508–515, Rochester, New York, April. Association for Computational Linguistics.

Drahomíra Spoustová, Jan Hajič, Jan Votrubec, Pavel Krbec, and Pavel Květoň. 2007. The best of two worlds: Cooperation of statistical and rule-based taggers for czech. In *Proceedings of the Workshop on Balto-Slavonic Natural Language Processing, ACL 2007*, pages 67–74, Praha.

LIUM's SMT Machine Translation Systems for WMT 2012

**Christophe Servan, Patrik Lambert, Anthony Rousseau,
Holger Schwenk and Loïc Barrault**
LIUM, University of Le Mans
72085 Le Mans cedex 9, FRANCE
FirstName.LastName@lium.univ-lemans.fr

Abstract

This paper describes the development of French–English and English–French statistical machine translation systems for the 2012 WMT shared task evaluation. We developed phrase-based systems based on the Moses decoder, trained on the provided data only. Additionally, new features this year included improved language and translation model adaptation using the cross-entropy score for the corpus selection.

1 Introduction

This paper describes the statistical machine translation systems developed by the Computer Science laboratory at the University of Le Mans (LIUM) for the 2012 WMT shared task evaluation. We only considered the translation between French and English (in both directions). The main differences with respect to previous year's system (Schwenk et al., 2011) are as follows: (i) use of more training data as provided by the organizers and (ii) better selection of the monolingual and parallel data according to the domain, using the cross-entropy difference with respect to in-domain and out-of-domain language models (Moore and Lewis, 2010). We kept some previous features: the improvement of the translation model adaptation by unsupervised training, a parallel corpus retrieved by Information Retrieval (IR) techniques and finally, the rescoring with a continuous space target language model for the translation into French. These different points are described in the rest of the paper, together with a summary of the experimental results showing the impact of each component.

2 Resources Used

The following sections describe how the resources provided or allowed in the shared task were used to train the translation and language models of the system.

2.1 Bilingual data

The latest version of the News-Commentary (NC) corpus and of the Europarl (Eparl) corpus (version 7) were used. We also took as training data a subset of the French–English Gigaword (10^9) corpus. This year we changed the filters applied to select this subset (see Sect. 2.4). We also included in the training data the test sets from previous shared tasks, that we called the ntsXX corpus and which was composed of newstest2008, newstest2009, newssyscomb2009.

2.2 Development data

Development was initially done on *newstest2010*, and *newstest2011* was used as internal test set (Section 3.1). The development and internal test sets were then (Section 4) switched (tuning was done on *newstest2011* and internal evaluation on *newstest2010*). The default Moses tokenization was used. However, we added abbreviations for the French tokenizer. All our models are case sensitive and include punctuation. The BLEU scores reported in this paper were calculated with the mteval-v13 tool and are case insensitive.

2.3 Use of Automatic Translations

Available human translated bitexts such as the Europarl or 10^9 corpus seem to be out-of domain for this task. We used two types of automatically extracted resources to adapt our system to the domain.

First, we generated automatic translations of the provided monolingual News corpus in French and English, for years 2009, 2010 and 2011, and selected the sentences with a normalised translation cost (returned by the decoder) inferior to a threshold. The resulting bitexts contain no new translations, since all words of the translation output come from the translation model, but they contain new combinations (phrases) of known words, and reinforce the probability of some phrase pairs (Schwenk, 2008). Like last year, we directly used the word-to-word alignments produced by the decoder at the output instead of GIZA's alignments. This speeds-up the procedure and yields the same results in our experiments. A detailed comparison is given in (Lambert et al., 2011).

Second, as in last year's evaluation, we automatically extracted and aligned parallel sentences from comparable in-domain corpora. We used the AFP (Agence France Presse) and APW (Associated Press Worldstream Service) news texts since there are available in the French and English LDC Gigaword corpora. The general architecture of our parallel sentence extraction system is described in detail by Abdul-Rauf and Schwenk (2009). We first translated 91M words from French into English using our first stage SMT system. These English sentences were then used to search for translations in the English AFP and APW texts of the Gigaword corpus using information retrieval techniques. The Lemur toolkit (Ogilvie and Callan, 2001) was used for this purpose. Search was limited to a window of ± 5 days of the date of the French news text. The retrieved candidate sentences were then filtered using the Translation Error Rate (TER) with respect to the automatic translations. In this study, sentences with a TER below 75% were kept. Sentences containing a large fraction of numbers were discarded. By these means, about 27M words of additional bitexts were obtained.

2.4 Domain-based Data selection

Before training the target language models, a text selection has been made using the cross-entropy difference method (Moore and Lewis, 2010). This technique works by computing the difference between two cross-entropy values.

We first score an out-of-domain corpus against a language model trained on a set of in-domain data and compute the cross-entropy for each sentence. Then, we score the same out-of-domain corpus against a language model trained on a random sample of itself, with a size roughly equal to the in-domain corpus. From this point, the difference between in-domain cross-entropy and out-of-domain cross-entropy is computed for each sentence, and these sentences are sorted regarding this score.

By estimating and minimizing on a development set the perplexity of several percentages of the sorted out-of-domain corpus, we can then estimate the theoretical best point of data size for this specific corpus. According the original paper and given our results, this leads to better selection than the simple perplexity sorting (Gao et al., 2002). This way, we can be assured to discard the vast majority of noise in the corpora and to select data well-related to the task.

In this task, the French and English target language models were trained on data selected from all provided monolingual corpora. In addition, LDC's Gigaword collection was used for both languages. Data corresponding to the development and test periods were removed from the Gigaword collections. We had time to apply the domain-based data selection only for French. Thus all data were used for English.

We used this method to filter the French–English 10^9 parallel corpus as well, based on the difference between in-domain cross-entropy and out-of-domain cross-entropy calculated for each sentence of the English side of the corpus. We kept 49 million words (in the English side) to train our models, called 10^9_f.

3 Architecture of the SMT system

The goal of statistical machine translation (SMT) is to produce a target sentence e from a source sentence f. We have build phrase-based systems (Koehn et al., 2003; Och and Ney, 2003), using the standard log linear framework in order to introduce several models explaining the translation process:

$$\begin{aligned} e^* &= \arg\max p(e|f) \\ &= \arg\max_e \{exp(\sum_i \lambda_i h_i(e,f))\} \end{aligned} \quad (1)$$

The feature functions h_i are the system models and the λ_i weights are typically optimized to maximize a scoring function on a development set (Och, 2003). The phrase-based system uses fourteen features functions, namely phrase and lexical translation probabilities in both directions, seven features for the lexicalized distortion model, a word and a phrase penalty and a target language model (LM).

The system is based on the Moses SMT toolkit (Koehn et al., 2007) and is constructed as follows. First, word alignments in both directions are calculated. We used a multi-threaded version of the GIZA++ tool (Gao and Vogel, 2008).[1] This speeds up the process and corrects an error of GIZA++ that can appear with rare words.

Phrases and lexical reorderings are extracted using the default settings of the Moses toolkit. The parameters of Moses were tuned using the MERT tool. We repeated the training process three times, each with a different seed value for the optimisation algorithm. In this way we have a rough idea of the error introduced by the tuning process.

4-gram back-off LMs were used. The word list contains all the words of the bitext used to train the translation model and all words that appear at least ten times in the monolingual corpora. Words of the monolingual corpora containing special characters or sequences of uppercase characters were not included in the word list. Separate LMs were build on each data source with the SRI LM toolkit (Stolcke, 2002) and then linearly interpolated, optimizing the coefficients with an EM procedure. The perplexities of these LMs on newstest2011 were 119.1 for French and 174.8 for English. In addition, we build a 5-gram continuous space language model for French (Schwenk, 2007). These models were trained on all the available texts using a resampling technique. The continuous space language model is interpolated with the 4-gram back-off model and used to rescore n-best lists. This reduces the perplexity by about 13% relative.

3.1 Number translation

We have also performed some experiments with number translation. English and French do not use the same conventions for integer and decimal numbers. For example, the English decimal number 0.99 is translated in French by 0,99. In the same way, the English integer 32,000 is translated in French by 32 000. It should be possible to perform these modifications by rules.

In this study, we first replaced the numbers by a tag `@@NUM` for integer and `@@DEC` for decimal numbers. Integers in the range 1 to 31 were not replaced since they appear in dates. Then, we created the target language model using the tagged corpora. Table 1 shows results of experiments performed with and without rule-based number translation.

Corpus	NT	BLEU	TER
NC	no	26.57 (0.07)	58.13 (0.06)
NC	yes	**26.84 (0.15)**	**57.71 (0.34)**
Eparl+NC	no	29.28 (0.11)	55.28 (0.13)
Eparl+NC	yes	29.26 (0.10)	55.44 (0.29)

Table 1: Results of the study on number translation (NT) from English to French

We did observe small gains in the translation quality when only the news-commentary bitexts are used, but there were no differences when more training data is available. Due to time constraints, this procedure was not used in the submitted system.

4 Results and Discussion

The results of our SMT systems are summarized in Table 2. The MT metric scores for the development set are the average of three optimisations performed with different seeds (see Section 3). For the test set, they are the average of four values: the three values corresponding to these different optimisations, plus a fourth value obtained by taking as weight for each model, the average of the weights obtained in the three optimisations (Cettolo et al., 2011). The numbers in parentheses are the standard deviation of these three or four values. The standard deviation gives a lower bound of the significance of the difference between two systems. If the difference between two average scores is less than the sum of the standard deviations, we can say that this difference is not significant. The reverse is not true.

The results of Table 2 show that adding several adapted corpora (the filtered 10^9 corpus, the syn-

[1]The source is available at `http://www.cs.cmu.edu/~qing/`

Bitext	#Source Words (M)	newstest2011 BLEU	newstest2011 TER	newstest2010 BLEU	newstest2010 TER
Translation : En→Fr					
Eparl+NC	57	30.91 (0.05)	53.61 (0.12)	28.45 (0.08)	56.29 (0.20)
Eparl+NC+ntsXX	58	31.12 (0.08)	53.67 (0.08)	28.49 (0.04)	56.45 (0.12)
Eparl+NC+ntsXX+10^9_f	107	31.67 (0.06)	53.29 (0.03)	29.38 (0.12)	55.45 (0.15)
Eparl+NC+ntsXX+10^9_f+IR	133	32.41 (0.02)	52.20 (0.02)	29.48 (0.11)	55.33 (0.20)
Eparl+NC+ntsXX+10^9_f+news+IR	162	32.26 (0.04)	52.24 (0.12)	29.79 (0.12)	55.04 (0.20)
Translation : Fr→En					
Eparl+NC	64	29.59 (0.12)	51.86 (0.06)	28.12 (0.05)	53.19 (0.06)
Eparl+NC+ntsXX	64	29.59 (0.04)	51.89 (0.14)	28.32 (0.08)	53.22 (0.08)
Eparl+NC+ntsXX+10^9_f	120	30.69 (0.06)	50.77 (0.04)	28.95 (0.14)	52.62 (0.14)
Eparl+NC+ntsXX+10^9_f+IR	149	30.56 (0.02)	50.94 (0.15)	28.67 (0.11)	52.78 (0.06)
Eparl+NC+ntsXX+10^9_f+news+IR	179	30.85 (0.07)	50.72 (0.03)	28.94 (0.05)	52.57 (0.02)

Table 2: English–French and French–English results: number of source words (in million) and scores on the development (newstest2011) and internal test (newstest2010) sets for the different systems developed. The BLEU scores and the number in parentheses are the average and standard deviation over 3 or 4 values when available (see Section 4.)

thetic corpus and the corpus retrieved via IR methods) to the Eparl+NC+ntsXX baseline, a gain of 1.1 BLEU points and 1.4 TER points was achieved for the English–French system.

On the other hand, adding the bitexts extracted from the comparable corpus (`IR`) does actually hurt the performance of the French–English system: the BLEU score decreases from 28.95 to 28.67 on our internal test set. During the evaluation period, we added all the corpora at once and we observed this only in our analysis after the evaluation.

In both translation directions our best system was the one trained on Eparl+NC+ntsXX+10^9_f+News+IR. Finally, we applied a continuous space language model for the system translating into French.

Acknowledgments

This work has been partially funded by the European Union under the EuroMatrixPlus project ICT-2007.2.2-FP7-231720 and the French government under the ANR project COSMAT ANR-09-CORD-004.

References

Sadaf Abdul-Rauf and Holger Schwenk. 2009. On the use of comparable corpora to improve SMT performance. In *Proceedings of the 12th Conference of the European Chapter of the ACL (EACL 2009)*, pages 16–23, Athens, Greece.

Mauro Cettolo, Nicola Bertoldi, and Marcello Federico. 2011. Methods for smoothing the optimizer instability in SMT. In *Proc. of Machine Translation Summit XIII*, Xiamen, China.

Qin Gao and Stephan Vogel. 2008. Parallel implementations of word alignment tool. In *Software Engineering, Testing, and Quality Assurance for Natural Language Processing*, pages 49–57, Columbus, Ohio, June. Association for Computational Linguistics.

Jianfeng Gao, Joshua Goodman, Mingjing Li, and Kai-Fu Lee. 2002. Toward a unified approach to statistical language modeling for chinese. In *ACM Transactions on Asian Language Information Processing*.

Philipp Koehn, Franz Josef Och, and Daniel Marcu. 2003. Statistical phrased-based machine translation. In *HLT/NACL*, pages 127–133.

Philipp Koehn, Hieu Hoang, Alexandra Birch, Chris Callison-Burch, Marcello Federico, Nicola Bertoldi, Brooke Cowan, Wade Shen, Christine Moran, Richard Zens, Chris Dyer, Ondrej Bojar, Alexandra Constantin, and Evan Herbst. 2007. Moses: Open source toolkit for statistical machine translation. In *ACL, demonstration session*.

Patrik Lambert, Holger Schwenk, Christophe Servan, and Sadaf Abdul-Rauf. 2011. Investigations on translation model adaptation using monolingual data. In *Sixth Workshop on SMT*, pages 284–293.

Robert C. Moore and William Lewis. 2010. Intelligent selection of language model training data. In *Proceedings of the ACL 2010 Conference Short Papers*.

Franz Josef Och and Hermann Ney. 2003. A systematic comparison of various statistical alignement models. *Computational Linguistics*, 29(1):19–51.

Franz Josef Och. 2003. Minimum error rate training in statistical machine translation. In *Proc. of the Annual Meeting of the Association for Computational Linguistics*, pages 160–167.

Paul Ogilvie and Jamie Callan. 2001. Experiments using the Lemur toolkit. In *In Proceedings of the Tenth Text Retrieval Conference (TREC-10)*, pages 103–108.

Holger Schwenk, Patrik Lambert, Loïc Barrault, Christophe Servan, Sadaf Abdul-Rauf, Haithem Afli, and Kashif Shah. 2011. Lium's smt machine translation systems for WMT 2011. In *Proceedings of the Sixth Workshop on Statistical Machine Translation*, pages 464–469, Edinburgh, Scotland, July. Association for Computational Linguistics.

Holger Schwenk. 2007. Continuous space language models. *Computer Speech and Language*, 21:492–518.

Holger Schwenk. 2008. Investigations on large-scale lightly-supervised training for statistical machine translation. In *IWSLT*, pages 182–189.

A. Stolcke. 2002. SRILM: an extensible language modeling toolkit. In *Proc. of the Int. Conf. on Spoken Language Processing*, pages 901–904, Denver, CO.

Selecting Data for English-to-Czech Machine Translation *

Aleš Tamchyna, Petra Galuščáková, Amir Kamran, Miloš Stanojević, Ondřej Bojar
Charles University in Prague, Faculty of Mathematics and Physics
Institute of Formal and Applied Linguistics
Malostranské nám. 25, Praha 1, CZ-118 00, Czech Republic
{tamchyna,galuscakova,kamran,bojar}@ufal.mff.cuni.cz,
milosh.stanojevic@gmail.com

Abstract

We provide a few insights on data selection for machine translation. We evaluate the quality of the new CzEng 1.0, a parallel data source used in WMT12. We describe a simple technique for reducing out-of-vocabulary rate after phrase extraction. We discuss the benefits of tuning towards multiple reference translations for English-Czech language pair. We introduce a novel approach to data selection by full-text indexing and search: we select sentences similar to the test set from a large monolingual corpus and explore several options of incorporating them in a machine translation system. We show that this method can improve translation quality. Finally, we describe our submitted system CU-TAMCH-BOJ.

1 Introduction

Selecting suitable data is important in all stages of creating an SMT system. For training, the data size plays an essential role, but the data should also be as clean as possible. The new CzEng 1.0 was prepared with the emphasis on data quality and we evaluate it against the previous version to show whether the effect for MT is positive.

Out-of-vocabulary rate is another problem related to data selection. We present a simple technique to reduce it by including words that became spurious OOVs during phrase extraction.

Another topic we explore is to use multiple references for tuning to make the procedure more robust as suggested by Dyer et al. (2011). We evaluate this approach for translating from English into Czech.

The main focus of our paper however lies in presenting a method for data selection using full-text search. We index a large monolingual corpus and then extract sentences from it that are similar to the input sentences. We use these sentences in several ways: to create a new language model, a new phrase table and a tuning set. The method can be seen as a kind of domain adaptation. We show that it contributes positively to translation quality and we provide a thorough evaluation.

2 Data and Tools

2.1 Comparison of CzEng 1.0 and 0.9

As this year's WMT is the first to include the new version of CzEng (Bojar et al., 2012b), we carried out a few experiments to compare its suitability for MT with its predecessor, CzEng 0.9. Apart from size (which has almost doubled), there are important differences between the two versions. In CzEng 0.9, the largest portion by far came from movie subtitles (a data source of varying quality), followed by EU legislation and technical manuals. On the other hand, CzEng 1.0 has over 4 million sentence pairs from fiction and nearly the same amount of data from EU legislation. Roughly 3 million sentence pairs come from movie subtitles. This proportion of domains suggests a higher quality of data. Moreover, sentences in CzEng 1.0 were automatically filtered using a maximum entropy classifier that uti-

* This work was supported by the project EuroMatrixPlus (FP7-ICT-2007-3-231720 of the EU and 7E09003+7E11051 of the Czech Republic) and the Czech Science Foundation grants P406/11/1499 and P406/10/P259.

Corpus and Domain		Sents	BLEU	Vocab. [k] En	Vocab. [k] Cs
CzEng 0.9	all	1M	14.77±0.12	187	360
CzEng 1.0			**15.23±0.18**	221	396
CzEng 0.9	news	100k	**14.34±0.05**	53	125
CzEng 1.0			14.01±0.13	47	113

Table 1: Comparison of CzEng 0.9 and 1.0.

lized a variety of features.

We trained contrastive phrase-based Moses SMT systems—the first one on 1 million randomly selected sentence pairs from CzEng 0.9, the other on the same amount of data from CzEng 1.0. Another contrastive pair of MT systems was based on small in-domain data only: 100k sentences from the *news* sections of CzEng 0.9 and 1.0. For each experiment, the random selection was done 5 times. In both experiments, identical data were used for the LM (News Crawl corpus from 2011), tuning (WMT10 test set) and evaluation (WMT11 test set).

Table 1 shows the results. The ± sign in this case denotes the standard deviation over the 5 experiments (each with a different random sample of training data). The results indicate that overall, CzEng 1.0 is a more suitable source of parallel data—most likely thanks to the more favorable distribution of domains. However in the small in-domain setting, using CzEng 0.9 data resulted in significantly higher BLEU scores.

The vocabulary size of the news section seems to have dropped since 0.9. We attribute this to the filtering: sentences with obscure words are hard to align so they are likely to be filtered out (the word alignment score as output by Giza++ received a large weight in the classifier training). These unusual words then do not appear in the vocabulary.

2.2 Lucene

Apache Lucene[1] is a high performance open-source search engine library written in Java. We use Lucene to take advantage of the information retrieval (IR) technique for domain adaptation. Each sentence of a large corpus is indexed as a separate document; a document is the unit of indexing and searching in Lucene. The sentences (documents) can then be retrieved based on Lucene similarity formula[2], given a "query corpus". Lucene uses Boolean model for initial filtering of documents. Vector Space Model with a refined version of Tf-idf statistic is then used to score the remaining candidates.

In the normal IR scenario, the query is usually small. However, for domain adaptation a query can be a whole corpus. Lucene does not allow such big queries. This problem is resolved by taking the query corpus sentence by sentence and searching many times. The final score of a sentence in the index is calculated as the average of the scores from the sentence-level queries. Methods that make use of this functionality are discussed in Section 5.

3 Reducing OOV by Relaxing Alignments

Out-of-vocabulary (OOV) rate has been shown to increase during phrase extraction (Bojar and Kos, 2010). This is due to unfortunate alignment of some words—no consistent phrase pair that includes them can be extracted. This issue can be partially overcome by adding translations of these "lost" words (according to Giza++ word alignment) to the extracted phrase table. This is not our original technique, it was suggested by Mermer and Saraclar (2011), though it is not included in the published abstract.

The extraction of phrases in the (hierarchical) decoder Jane (Stein et al., 2011) offers a range of similar heuristics. Tinsley et al. (2009) also observes gains when extending the set of phrases consistent with the word alignment by phrases consistent with aligned parses.

We evaluated this technique on two sets of training data—the news section of CzEng 1.0 and the whole CzEng 1.0. The OOV rate of the phrase table was reduced nearly to the corpus OOV rate in both cases, however the improvement was negligible—only a handful of the newly added words occurred in the test set. Table 2 shows the results. Translation performance using the improved phrase table was identical to the baseline.

[1] `http://lucene.apache.org`

[2] `http://tiny.cc/ca2ccw`

CzEng Sections	Test Set OOV % Baseline	Test Set OOV % Reduced	New Phrases
news (197k sents)	3.69	3.66	12034
all (14.8M sents)	1.09	1.09	154204

Table 2: Source-side phrase table OOV.

Sections	1 reference	3 references
news	11.37±0.47	**11.62±0.50**
all	**16.07±0.55**	15.90±0.57

Table 3: BLEU scores on WMT12 test set when tuning on WMT11 test set towards one or more references.

4 Tuning to Multiple Reference Translations

Tuning towards multiple reference translations has been shown to help translation quality, see Dyer et al. (2011) and the cited works. Thanks to the other references, more possible translations of each word are considered correct, as well as various orderings of words.

We tried two approaches: tuning to one true reference and one pseudo-reference, and tuning to multiple human-translated references.

For the first method, which resembles computer-generated references via paraphrasing as used in (Dyer et al., 2011), we created the pseudo-reference by translating the development set using TectoMT, a deep syntactic MT with rich linguistic processing implemented in the Treex platform[3]. We hoped that the very different output of this decoder would be beneficial for tuning, however we achieved no improvement at all.

For the second experiment we used 3 translations of WMT11 test set. One is the true reference distributed for the shared task and two were translated manually from the German version of the data into Czech. We achieved a small improvement in final BLEU score when training on a small data set. On the complete constrained training data for WMT12, there was no improvement—in fact, the BLEU score as evaluated on the WMT12 test set was negligibly lower. Table 3 summarizes our results. The ± sign denotes the confidence bounds estimated via bootstrap resampling (Koehn, 2004).

[3] `http://ufal.ms.mff.cuni.cz/treex/`

Used Models	Selected per Trans.	Sel. Sents Total	Avg BLEU±std
None	—	0	12.39±0.06
LM	—	16k – rand. sel.	12.18±0.06
LM	3	16k	12.73±0.04
LM	100	502k	14.21±0.11
LM	1000	3.8M	15.12±0.08
LM	All Sents	18.3M	**15.55±0.11**

Table 4: Results of experiments with Lucene, language model adapted.

5 Experiments with Domain Adaptation

Domain adaptation is widely recognized as a technique which can significantly improve translation quality (Wu et al., 2008; Bertoldi and Federico, 2009; Daumé and Jagarlamudi, 2011). In our experiments we tried to select sentences close to the source side of the test set and use them to improve the final translation.

The parallel data used in this section are only small: the news section of CzEng 1.0 (197k sentence pairs, 4.2M Czech words, 4.8M English words). We tuned the models on WMT09 test set and evaluated on WMT11 test set. The techniques examined here rely on a large monolingual corpus to select data from. We used all the monolingual data provided by the organizers of WMT11 (18.3M sentences, 316M words).

5.1 Tailoring the Language Model

Our first attempt was to tailor the language model to the test set. Our approach is similar to Zhao et al. (2004). In Moore and Lewis (2010), the authors compare several approaches to selecting data for LM and Axelrod et al. (2011) extend their ideas and apply them to MT.

Naturally, we only used the source side of the test set. First we translated the test set using a baseline translation system. Lucene indexer was then used to select sentences similar to the translated ones in the large target-side monolingual corpus. Finally, a new language model was created from the selected sentences.

The weight of the new LM has to reflect the importance of the language model during both MERT tuning as well as final application on (a different) test set. If the new LM were based only on the final test set, MERT would underestimate its value and vice versa. Therefore, we actually translated both our development (WMT09) as well as final test set (WMT11) using the baseline model and created a LM relevant to their union.

The results of performed experiments with domain adaptation are in Table 4. To compensate for low stability of MERT, we ran the optimization five times and report the average BLEU achieved. The $\pm$ value indicates the standard deviation of the five runs.

The first row provides the scores for the baseline experiment with no tailored language model. We have run the experiment for three values of selected sentences per one sentence of the test corpus: 3, 100 and 1000 closest-matching sentences were extracted. With more and more data in the LM, the scores increase. The second line in Table 4 confirms the usefulness of the sentence selection. Picking the same amount of 16k sentences randomly performs worse. As the last row indicates, taking all available data leads to the best score.

Note that when selecting the sentences, we used lemmas instead of word forms to reduce data sparseness. So Lucene was actually indexing the lemmatized version of the monolingual data and the baseline translation translated English lemmas to Czech lemmas when creating the "query corpus". The final models were created from the original sentences, not their lemmatized versions.

5.2 Tailoring the Translation Model

Reverse self-training is a trick that allows to improve the translation model using (target-side) monolingual data and can lead to a performance improvement (Bojar and Tamchyna, 2011; Lambert et al., 2011).

In our scenario, we translated the selected sentences (in the opposite direction, i.e. from the target into the source language). Then we created a new translation model (in the original direction) based on the alignment of selected sentences and their reverse translation. This new model is finally combined with the baseline model and weighted by MERT. The whole scenario is shown in Figure 1.

The results of our experiments are in Table 5. We ran the experiment with translation model adaptation for 100 most similar sentences selected by Lucene. Each experiment was again performed five times. Due to the low stability of tuning, we also tried increasing the size of n-best lists used by MERT.

Experiments with tailored translation model are significantly better than the baseline but the improvement against the experiment with only the language model adapted (with the corresponding 100 sentences selected) is very small.

5.3 Discussion of Domain Adaptation Experiments

According to the results, using Lucene improves translation performance already in the case when only three sentences are selected for each translated sentence. Our results are further supported by the contrastive setup that used a language model created from a random selection of the same number of sentences—the translation quality even slightly degraded.

On the other hand, adding more sentences to language model further improves results and the best result is achieved when the language model is created using the whole monolingual corpus. This could have two reasons:

Too good domain match. The domain of the whole monolingual corpus is too close to the test corpus. Adding the whole monolingual corpus is thus the best option. For more diverse monolingual data, some domain-aware subsampling like our approach is likely to actually help.

Our style of retrieval. Our queries to Lucene represent sentences as simple bags of words. Lucene prefers less frequent words and the structure of the sentence is therefore often ignored. For example it prefers to retrieve sentences with the same proper name rather than sentences with similar phrases or longer expressions. This may not be the best option for language modelling.

Our method can thus be useful mainly in the case when the data available are too large to be processed as a whole. It can also highly reduce the computation power and time necessary to achieve good translation quality: the result achieved using the language model created via Lucene for 1000 selected sentences is not significantly worse than the result achieved using the whole monolingual corpus but the required data are 5 times smaller.

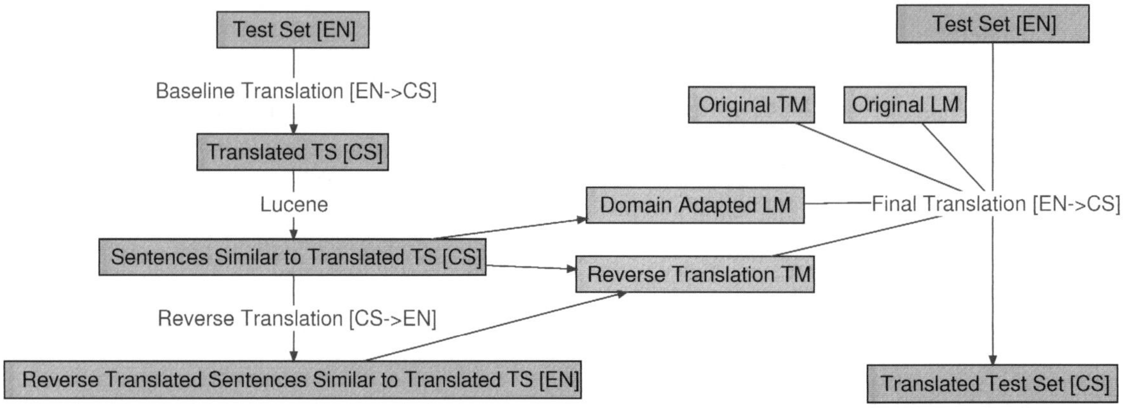

Figure 1: Scenario of reverse self-training.

Used Models	N-Best	Sel. Sents per Trans. Sent.	Sel. Sents Total	Avg BLEU±std
None	100	—	0	12.39±0.06
None	200	—	0	12.4±0.03
LM + TM	100	100	502k	14.32±0.13
LM + TM	200	100	502k	**14.36±0.07**

Table 5: Results of experiments with Lucene, translation model applied.

5.4 Tuning Towards Selected Data

Domain adaptation can also be done by selecting a suitable development corpus (Zheng et al., 2010; Li et al., 2004). The final model parameters depend on the domain of the development corpus. By choosing a development corpus that is close to our test set we might tune in the right direction. We implemented this adaptation by querying the source side of our large parallel corpus using the source side of the test corpus. After that, the development corpus is constructed from the selected sentences and their corresponding reference translations.

This experiment uses a fixed model based on the news section of CzEng 1.0. We only use different tuning sets and run the MERT optimization. All the resulting systems are tested on the WMT11 test set:

Baseline system is tuned on 2489 sentence pairs selected randomly from whole CzEng 1.0 parallel corpus. **Lucene** system uses 2489 sentence pairs selected from CzEng 1.0 using Lucene. The selection is done by choosing the most similar sentences to the source side of the final test set. **WMT10** system is tuned on 2489 sentence pairs of WMT10 test set. To identify an upper bound, we also include a **Perfect selection** system which is tuned on the final WMT11 test set. Naturally, this is not a fair competitor.

System	avg BLEU±std
Baseline	11.41±0.25
Lucene	12.31±0.01
WMT10	**12.37±0.02**
Perfect selection	12.64±0.02
Bad selection	6.37±0.64

Table 6: Results of tuning with different corpora

In order to make the results more reliable, it is necessary to repeat the experiment several times (Clark et al., 2011). Lucene and the WMT10 system were tuned 3 times while baseline system was tuned 9 times because of randomness in selection of tuning corpora (3 different tuning corpora each tuned 3 times). The results are shown in Table 6.

Even though the variance of the baseline system is high (because we randomly selected corpora 3 times), the difference in scores between baseline and Lucene system is high enough to conclude that tuning on Lucene-selected corpus helps translation quality. Still it does not give better BLEU score than system tuned on WMT10 corpus. One possible reason is that the whole CzEng 1.0 is of somewhat lower quality than the news section. Given that our final test set (WMT11) is also from the news domain, tuning towards WMT10 corpus probably leads to a better domain adaptation that tuning towards all the domains in CzEng.

The tuning set must not overlap with the training set. To illustrate the problem, we did a small experiment with the same settings as above and randomly selected 2489 sentences from training corpora. We again ran the random selection 3 times and tuned 3 times with each of the extracted tuning sets, see the "Bad selection" in Table 6.

In all the experiments with badly selected sentences, the distortion and language model get an extremely low weight compared to the weights of translation model. This is because they are not useful in translation of tuning data which was already seen during training. Instead of reordering two short phrases A and B, system already knows the translation of the phrase A B so no distortion is needed. On unseen sentences, such weights lead to poor results.

This amplifies a drawback of our approach: source texts have to be known prior to system tuning or even before phrase extraction.

There are methods available that could tackle this problem. Wuebker et al. (2010) store phrase pair counts per sentence when extracting phrases and thus they can reestimate the probabilities when a sentence has to be excluded from the phrase tables. For large parallel corpora, suffix arrays (Callison-Burch et al., 2005) have been used. Suffix arrays allow for a quick retrieval of relevant sentence pairs, the phrase extraction is postponed and performed on the fly for each input sentence. It is trivial to filter out sentences belonging to the tuning set during this delayed extraction. With dynamic suffix arrays (Levenberg et al., 2010), one could even simply remove the tuning sentences from the suffix array.

6 Submitted Systems

This paper covers the submissions CU-TAMCH-BOJ. We translated from English into Czech. Our setup was very similar to CU-BOJAR (Bojar et al., 2012a), but our primary submission is tuned on multiple reference translations as described in Section 4.

Apart from the additional references, this is a constrained setup. CzEng 1.0 were the only parallel data used in training. We used a factored model to translate the combination of English surface form and part-of-speech tag into Czech form+POS. We used separate 6-gram language models trained on CzEng 1.0 (interpolated by domain) and all News Crawl corpora (18.3M setences, interpolated by years). Additionaly, we created an 8-gram language model on target POS tags. For reordering, we employed a lexicalized model trained on CzEng 1.0.

Table 7 summarizes the official result of the primary submission and a contrastive baseline (tuned to just one reference translation). There is a slight decrease in BLEU, but the translation error rate (TER) is slightly better when more references were used. The differences are however very small, suggesting that tuning to more references did not have any significant effect.

System	BLEU	TER
multiple references	14.5	**0.765**
contrastive baseline	**14.6**	0.774

Table 7: Scores of the submitted systems.

7 Conclusion

We showed that CzEng 1.0 is of better overall quality than its predecessor. We described a technique for reducing phrase-table OOV rate, but achieved no improvement for WMT12. Similarly, tuning to multiple references did not prove very beneficial.

We introduced a couple of techniques that exploit full-text search in large corpora. We showed that adding selected sentences as an additional LM improves translations. Adding a new phrase table acquired via reverse self-training resulted only in small gains. Tuning to selected sentences resulted in a better system than tuning to a random set. However the Lucene-selected corpus fails to outperform good-quality in-domain tuning data.

References

Amittai Axelrod, Xiaodong He, and Jianfeng Gao. 2011. Domain adaptation via pseudo in-domain data selection. In *Proceedings of the Conference on Empirical Methods in Natural Language Processing*, EMNLP '11, pages 355–362, Stroudsburg, PA, USA. Association for Computational Linguistics.

Nicola Bertoldi and Marcello Federico. 2009. Domain adaptation for statistical machine translation with monolingual resources. In *Proceedings of the Fourth Workshop on Statistical Machine Translation*, StatMT '09, pages 182–189, Stroudsburg, PA, USA. Association for Computational Linguistics.

Ondřej Bojar and Kamil Kos. 2010. 2010 Failures in English-Czech Phrase-Based MT. In *Proceedings of the Joint Fifth Workshop on Statistical Machine Translation and MetricsMATR*, pages 60–66, Uppsala, Sweden, July. Association for Computational Linguistics.

Ondřej Bojar and Aleš Tamchyna. 2011. Forms Wanted: Training SMT on Monolingual Data. Abstract at Machine Translation and Morphologically-Rich Languages. Research Workshop of the Israel Science Foundation University of Haifa, Israel, January.

Ondřej Bojar, Bushra Jawaid, and Amir Kamran. 2012a. Probes in a Taxonomy of Factored Phrase-Based Models. In *Proceedings of the Seventh Workshop on Statistical Machine Translation*, Montreal, Canada, June. Association for Computational Linguistics. Submitted.

Ondřej Bojar, Zdeněk Žabokrtský, Ondřej Dušek, Petra Galuščáková, Martin Majliš, David Mareček, Jiří Maršík, Michal Novák, Martin Popel, and Aleš Tamchyna. 2012b. The Joy of Parallelism with CzEng 1.0. In *Proceedings of LREC2012*, Istanbul, Turkey, May. ELRA, European Language Resources Association. In print.

Chris Callison-Burch, Colin Bannard, and Josh Schroeder. 2005. Scaling phrase-based statistical machine translation to larger corpora and longer phrases. In *Proceedings of the 43rd Annual Meeting of the ACL*, pages 255–262.

Jonathan Clark, Chris Dyer, Alon Lavie, and Noah Smith. 2011. Better Hypothesis Testing for Statistical Machine Translation: Controlling for Optimizer Instability. In *Proceedings of the Association for Computational Lingustics*. Association for Computational Linguistics.

Hal Daumé, III and Jagadeesh Jagarlamudi. 2011. Domain adaptation for machine translation by mining unseen words. In *Proceedings of the 49th Annual Meeting of the Association for Computational Linguistics: Human Language Technologies: short papers - Volume 2*, HLT '11, pages 407–412, Stroudsburg, PA, USA. Association for Computational Linguistics.

Chris Dyer, Kevin Gimpel, Jonathan H. Clark, and Noah A. Smith. 2011. The CMU-ARK German-English Translation System. In *Proceedings of the Sixth Workshop on Statistical Machine Translation*, pages 337–343, Edinburgh, Scotland, July. Association for Computational Linguistics.

Philipp Koehn. 2004. Statistical Significance Tests for Machine Translation Evaluation. In *Proceedings of EMNLP 2004*, Barcelona, Spain.

Patrik Lambert, Holger Schwenk, Christophe Servan, and Sadaf Abdul-Rauf. 2011. Investigations on translation model adaptation using monolingual data. In *Proceedings of the Sixth Workshop on Statistical Machine Translation*, pages 284–293, Edinburgh, Scotland, July. Association for Computational Linguistics.

Abby Levenberg, Chris Callison-Burch, and Miles Osborne. 2010. Stream-based translation models for statistical machine translation. In *Human Language Technologies: The 2010 Annual Conference of the North American Chapter of the ACL*, pages 394–402.

Mu Li, Yinggong Zhao, Dongdong Zhang, and Ming Zhou. 2004. Adaptive development data selection for log-linear model in statistical machine translation. In *In Proceedings of COLING 2004*.

Coskun Mermer and Murat Saraclar. 2011. Unsupervised Turkish Morphological Segmentation for Statistical Machine Translation. Abstract at Machine Translation and Morphologically-Rich Languages. Research Workshop of the Israel Science Foundation University of Haifa, Israel, January.

Robert C. Moore and William Lewis. 2010. Intelligent selection of language model training data. In *Proceedings of the ACL 2010 Conference Short Papers*, ACLShort '10, pages 220–224, Stroudsburg, PA, USA. Association for Computational Linguistics.

Daniel Stein, David Vilar, Stephan Peitz, Markus Freitag, Matthias Huck, and Hermann Ney. 2011. A Guide to Jane, an Open Source Hierarchical Translation Toolkit. *Prague Bulletin of Mathematical Linguistics*, 95:5–18, March.

John Tinsley, Mary Hearne, and Andy Way. 2009. Exploiting parallel treebanks to improve phrase-based statistical machine translation. In Alexander F. Gelbukh, editor, *CICLing*, volume 5449 of *Lecture Notes in Computer Science*, pages 318–331. Springer.

Hua Wu, Haifeng Wang, and Chengqing Zong. 2008. Domain adaptation for statistical machine translation with domain dictionary and monolingual corpora. In *Proceedings of the 22nd International Conference on Computational Linguistics - Volume 1*, COLING '08, pages 993–1000, Stroudsburg, PA, USA. Association for Computational Linguistics.

Joern Wuebker, Arne Mauser, and Hermann Ney. 2010. Training phrase translation models with leaving-one-out. In *Proceedings of the 48th Annual Meeting of the Association for Computational Linguistics*, pages 475–484.

Bing Zhao, Matthias Eck, and Stephan Vogel. 2004. Language model adaptation for statistical machine translation with structured query models. In *Proceedings of the 20th international conference on Computational Linguistics*, COLING '04, Stroudsburg, PA, USA. Association for Computational Linguistics.

Zhongguang Zheng, Zhongjun He, Yao Meng, and Hao Yu. 2010. Domain adaptation for statistical machine translation in development corpus selection. In *Universal Communication Symposium (IUCS), 2010 4th International*, pages 2 –7, oct.

DFKI's SMT System for WMT 2012

David Vilar
German Research Center for Artificial Intelligence (DFKI GmbH)
Language Technology Lab
Berlin, Germany
david.vilar@dfki.de

Abstract

We describe DFKI's statistical based submission to the 2012 WMT evaluation. The submission is based on the freely available machine translation toolkit Jane, which supports phrase-based and hierarchical phrase-based translation models. Different setups have been tested and combined using a sentence selection method.

1 Introduction

In this paper we present DFKI's submission for the 2012 MT shared task based on statistical approaches. We use a variety of phrase-based and hierarchical phrase-based translation systems with different configurations and enhancements and compare their performance. The output of the systems are later combined using a sentence selection mechanism. Somewhat disappointingly the sentence selection hardly improves over the best single system.

DFKI participated in the German to English and English to German translation tasks. Technical problems however hindered a more complete system for this last translation direction.

This paper is organized as follows: Section 2 reports on the different single systems that we built for this shared task. Section 3 describes the sentence selection mechanism used for combining the output of the different systems. Section 4 concludes the paper.

2 Single Systems

For all our setups we used the Jane toolkit (Vilar et al., 2010a), which in its current version supports both phrase-based and hierarchical phrase-based translation models. In this Section we present the different settings that we used for the task.

The bilingual training data used for training all systems was the combination of the provided Europarl and News data. We also used two baseline 4-gram language models trained on the same Europarl training data and on the enhanced News Commentary monolingual training data. The newstest2010 dataset was used for optimization of the systems.

2.1 Phrase-based System

The first system is a baseline phrase-based system trained on the available bilingual training data. Word alignments is trained using GIZA++ (Och and Ney, 2003), phrase extraction is performed with Jane using standard settings, i.e. maximum source phrase length 6, maximum target phrase length 12, count features, etc. Consult the Jane documentation for more details. For reordering the standard distance-based reordering model is computed. Scaling factors are trained using MERT on n-best lists.

2.1.1 Verb reorderings

Following (Popović and Ney, 2006), for German to English translation, we perform verb reordering by first POS-tagging the source sentence and afterwards applying hand-defined rules. This includes rules for reordering verbs in subordinate clauses and participles.

2.1.2 Moore LM

Moore and Lewis (2010) propose a method for filtering large quantities of out-of-domain language-model training data by comparing the cross-entropy of an in-domain language model and an out-of-domain language model trained on a random sampling of the data. We followed this approach to filter the news-crawl corpora provided the organizers. By experimenting on the development set we decided to use a 4-gram language model trained on 15M filtered sentences (the original data comprising over 30M sentences).

2.2 Hierarchical System

We also trained a hierarchical system on the same data as the phrase-based system, and also tried the additional language model trained according to Section 2.1.2, as well as the verb reorderings described in Section 2.1.1.

2.2.1 Poor Man's Syntax

Vilar et al. (2010b) propose a "syntax-based" approach similar to (Venugopal et al., 2009), but using automatic clustering methods instead of linguistic parsing for defining the non-terminals used in the resulting grammar. The main idea of the method is to cluster the words (mimicking the concept of Part-of-Speech tagging), performing a phrase extraction pass using the word classes instead of the actual words and performing another clustering on the phrase level (corresponding to the linguistic classes in a parse tree).

2.2.2 Lightly-Supervised Training

Huck et al. (2011) propose to augment the monolingual training data by translating available additional monolingual data with an existing translation system. We adapt this approach by translating the data selected according to Section 2.1.2 with the phrase-based translation system described in Section 2.1, and use this additional data to expand the bilingual data available for training the hierarchical phrase-based system.[1]

2.3 Experimental Results

Table 1 shows the results obtained for the German to English translation direction on the newstest2011 dataset. The baseline phrase-based system obtains a BLEU score of 18.2%. The verb reorderings achieve an improvement of 0.6% BLEU, and adding the additional language model obtains an additional 1.6% BLEU improvement.

The hierarchical system baseline achieves a better BLEU score than the baseline PBT system, and is comparable to the PBT system with additional reorderings. In fact, adding the verb reorderings to the hierarchical system slightly degrades its performance. This indicates that the hierarchical model is able to reflect the verb reorderings necessary for this translation direction. Adding the bigger language model of Section 2.1.2 also obtains a nice improvement of 1.4% BLEU for this system. On the other hand and somewhat disappointingly, the lightly supervised training and the poor man's syntax approach are not able to improve translation quality.

For the English to German translation direction we encountered some technical problems, and we were not able to perform as many experiments as for the opposite direction. The results are shown in Table 2 and show similar trends as for the German to English direction, except that the hierarchical system in this case does not outperform the PBT baseline.

3 Sentence Selection

In this section we will describe the system combination method based on sentence selection that we used for combining the output of the systems described in Section 2. This approach was tried successfully in (Vilar et al., 2011).

We use a log-linear model for computing the scores of the different translation hypotheses, generated by all the systems described in Section 2, i.e. those listed in Tables 1 and 2. The model scaling factors are computed using a standard MERT run on the newstest2011 dataset, optimizing for BLEU. This is comparable to the usual approach used for rescoring n-best lists generated by a single system, and has been used previously for sentence selection purposes (see (Hildebrand and Vogel, 2008) which uses a very similar approach to our own). Note that no system dependent features like translation probabilities were computed, as we wanted to keep the system general.

We will list the features we compute for each of

[1] The decision of which system to use to produce the additional training material follows mainly a practical reason. As the hierarchical model is more costly to train and at decoding time, we chose the phrase-based system as the generating system.

System	BLEU[%]
PBT Baseline	18.2
PBT + Reordering	18.8
PBT + Reordering + Moore LM	20.4
Hierarchical Baseline	18.7
Hierarchical + Moore LM	20.1
Hierarchical + Moore LM + Lightly Supervised	19.8
Poor Man's Syntax	18.6
Hierarchical + Reordering	18.5

Table 1: Translation results for the different single systems, German to English.

System	BLEU[%]
PBT Baseline	12.4
Hierarchical Baseline	11.6
Hierarchical + Moore LM	13.1
Poor Man's Syntax	11.6

Table 2: Translation results for the different single systems, English to German

the systems. We have used features that try to focus on characteristics that humans may use to evaluate a system.

3.1 Cross System BLEU

BLEU was introduced in (Papineni et al., 2002) and it has been shown to have a high correlation with human judgement. In spite of its shortcomings (Callison-Burch et al., 2006), it has been considered the standard automatic measure in the development of SMT systems (with new measures being added to it, but not substituting it, see for e.g. (Cer et al., 2010)).

Of course, the main problem of using the BLEU score as a feature for sentence selection in a real-life scenario is that we do not have the references available. We overcame this issue by generating a custom set of references for each system, using the other systems as gold translations. This is of course inexact, but n-grams that appear on the output of different systems can be expected to be more probable to be correct, and BLEU calculated this way gives us a measure of this agreement. This approach can be considered related to n-gram posteriors (Zens and Ney, 2006) or minimum Bayes risk decoding (e.g. (Ehling et al., 2007)) in the context of n-best rescoring, but applied without prior weighting (unavailable directly) and more focused on the evaluation interpretation.

We generated two features based on this idea. The first one is computed at the system level, i.e. it is the same for each sentence produced by a system and serves as a kind of prior weight similar to the one used in other system combination methods (e.g. (Matusov et al., 2008)). The other feature was computed at the sentence level. For this we used the smoothed version of BLEU proposed in (Lin and Och, 2004), again using the output of the rest of the systems as pseudo-reference. As optimization on BLEU often tends to generate short translations, we also include a word penalty feature.

3.2 Error Analysis Features

It is safe to assume that a human judge will try to choose those translations which contain the least amount of errors, both in terms of content and grammaticality. A classification of errors for machine translation systems has been proposed in (Vilar et al., 2006), and (Popović and Ney, 2011) presents how to compute a subset of these error categories automatically. The basic idea is to extend the familiar Word Error Rate (WER) and Position independent word Error Rate (PER) measures on word and base-form[2] levels to identify the different kind of errors. For our system we included following features:

Extra Word Errors (EXTer) Extra words in the hypothesis not present in the references.

Inflection Errors (hINFer) Words with wrong inflection. Computed comparing word-level errors and base-form-level errors.

Lexical Errors (hLEXer) Wrong lexical choices in the hypothesis with respect to the references.

Reordering Errors (hRer) Wrong word order in the hypothesis.

Missing Words (MISer) Words present in the reference that are missing in the hypothesis.

All these features are computed using the open source Hjerson[3] tool (Popović, 2011), which also outputs the standard WER metric, which we added as an additional feature.

As was the case in Section 3.1, for computing these measures we do not have a reference available, and thus we use the rest of the systems as pseudo-references. This has the interesting effect that some "errors" are actually beneficial for the performance of the system. For example, it is known that systems optimised on the BLEU metric tend to produce short hypotheses. In this sense, the extra words considered as errors by the EXTer measure may be actually beneficial for the overall performance of the system.

3.3 IBM1 Scores

IBM1-like scores on the sentence level are known to perform well for the rescoring of n-best lists from a single system (see e.g. (Hasan et al., 2007)). Additionally, they have been shown in (Popovic et al., 2011) to correlate well with human judgement for evaluation purposes. We thus include them as additional features.

[2]Computed using the TreeTagger tool (http://www.ims.uni-stuttgart.de/projekte/corplex/TreeTagger/)

[3]The abbreviations for the features are taken over directly from the output of the tool.

	De-En	En-De
Best System	20.4	13.1
Worst System	18.2	11.6
Sentence Selection	20.9	13.3

Table 3: Sentence selection results

3.4 Additional Language Model

We used a 5-gram language model trained on the whole news-crawl corpus as an additional model for rescoring. We used a different language model as the one described in Section 2.1.2 as not to favor those systems that already included it at decoding time.

3.5 Experimental Results

The sentence selection improved a little bit over the best single system for German to English translation, but hardly so for English to German, as shown in Table 3. For English to German this can be due to the small amount of systems that were available for the sentence selection system. Note also that these results are measured on the same corpus the system was trained on, so we expect the improvement on unseen test data to be even smaller. Nevertheless the sentence selection system constituted our final submission for the MT task.

4 Conclusions

For this year's evaluation DFKI used a statistical system based around the Jane machine translation toolkit (Vilar et al., 2010a), working in its two modalities: phrase-based and hierarchical phrase-based models. Different enhancements were tried in addition to the baseline configuration: POS-based verb reordering, monolingual data selection, poor man's syntax and lightly supervised training, with mixed results.

A sentence selection mechanism has later been applied in order to combine the output of the different configurations. Although encouraging results had been obtained in (Vilar et al., 2011), for this task we found only a small improvement. This may be due to the strong similarity of the systems, as they are basically trained on the same data. In (Vilar et al., 2011) the training data was varied across the systems, which may have produced a bigger variety in the translation outputs that can be of advantage for the selection mechanism. This is an issue that should be explored in more detail for further work.

We also plan to do a comparison with system combination approaches where new hypotheses can be generated (instead of selecting one from a predefined set), and study under which conditions each approach is more suited than the other.

5 Acknowledgements

This work was done with the support of the TaraXŰ Project[4], financed by TSB Technologiestiftung Berlin-Zukunftsfonds Berlin, co-financed by the European Union-European fund for regional development.

References

Chris Callison-Burch, Miles Osborne, and Philipp Koehn. 2006. Re-evaluating the Role of Bleu in Machine Translation Research. In *Proc. of the 11th Conference of the European Chapter of the Association for Computational Linguistics*, pages 249–256, Trento, Italy, April.

Daniel Cer, Christopher D. Manning, and Daniel Jurafsky. 2010. The best lexical metric for phrase-based statistical mt system optimization. In *Human Language Technologies: The 2010 Annual Conference of the North American Chapter of the Association for Computational Linguistics*, HLT '10, pages 555–563, Los Angeles, CA, USA.

Nicola Ehling, Richard Zens, and Hermann Ney. 2007. Minimum Bayes risk decoding for BLEU. In *Annual Meeting of the Assoc. for Computational Linguistics*, pages 101–104, Prague, Czech Republic, June.

Saša Hasan, Richard Zens, and Hermann Ney. 2007. Are very large N-best lists useful for SMT? In *Human Language Technology Conf. / North American Chapter of the Assoc. for Computational Linguistics Annual Meeting*, pages 57–60, Rochester, NY, April. Association for Computational Linguistics.

A.S. Hildebrand and S. Vogel. 2008. Combination of machine translation systems via hypothesis selection from combined n-best lists. In *MT at work: Proc. of the Eighth Conference of the Association for Machine Translation in the Americas*, pages 254–261.

Matthias Huck, David Vilar, Daniel Stein, and Hermann Ney. 2011. Lightly-Supervised Training for Hierarchical Phrase-Based Machine Translation. In *The EMNLP 2011 Workshop on Unsupervised Learning in NLP*, Edinburgh, UK, July.

Chin-Yew Lin and Franz Josef Och. 2004. ORANGE: a Method for Evaluating Automatic Evaluation Metrics for Machine Translation. In *Proc. of the 20th international conference on Computational Linguistics*, COLING '04, Geneva, Switzerland.

Evgeny Matusov, Gregor Leusch, Rafael E. Banchs, Nicola Bertoldi, Daniel Dechelotte, Marcello Federico, Muntsin Kolss, Young-Suk Lee, Jose B. Marino, Matthias Paulik, Salim Roukos, Holger Schwenk, and Hermann Ney. 2008. System combination for machine translation of spoken and written language. *IEEE Transactions on Audio, Speech and Language Processing*, 16(7):1222–1237, September.

R.C. Moore and W. Lewis. 2010. Intelligent selection of language model training data. In *Proceedings of the ACL 2010 Conference Short Papers*, pages 220–224. Association for Computational Linguistics.

Franz Josef Och and Hermann Ney. 2003. A Systematic Comparison of Various Statistical Alignment Models. *Computational Linguistics*, 29(1):19–51, March.

Kishore Papineni, Salim Roukos, Todd Ward, and Wei-Jing Zhu. 2002. Bleu: a Method for Automatic Evaluation of Machine Translation. In *Proc. of the 41st Annual Meeting of the Association for Computational Linguistics*, pages 311–318, Philadelphia, Pennsylvania, USA, July.

Maja Popović and Hermann Ney. 2006. POS-based word reorderings for statistical machine translation. In *International Conference on Language Resources and Evaluation*, pages 1278–1283, Genoa, Italy, May.

Maja Popović and Hermann Ney. 2011. Towards Automatic Error Analysis of Machine Translation Output. *Computational Linguistics*, 37(4):657–688, December.

Maja Popovic, David Vilar, Eleftherios Avramidis, and Aljoscha Burchardt. 2011. Evaluation without references: Ibm1 scores as evaluation metrics. In *Proc. of the Sixth Workshop on Statistical Machine Translation*, pages 99–103. Association for Computational Linguistics, July.

Maja Popović. 2011. Hjerson: An Open Source Tool for Automatic Error Classification of Machine Translation Output. *The Prague Bulletin of Mathematical Linguistics*, pages 59–68.

Ashish Venugopal, Andreas Zollmann, Noah A. Smith, and Stephan Vogel. 2009. Preference Grammars: Softening Syntactic Constraints to Improve Statistical Machine Translation. In *Proceedings of Human Language Technologies: The 2009 Annual Conference of the North American Chapter of the Association for Computational Linguistics*, pages 236–244, Boulder, Colorado, USA, June.

[4]http://taraxu.dfki.de

David Vilar, Jia Xu, Luis Fernando D'Haro, and Hermann Ney. 2006. Error Analysis of Machine Translation Output. In *International Conference on Language Resources and Evaluation*, pages 697–702, Genoa, Italy, May.

David Vilar, Daniel Stein, Matthias Huck, and Hermann Ney. 2010a. Jane: Open Source Hierarchical Translation, Extended with Reordering and Lexicon Models. In *Proc. of the Joint Fifth Workshop on Statistical Machine Translation and MetricsMATR*, pages 262–270, Uppsala, Sweden, July.

David Vilar, Daniel Stein, Stephan Peitz, and Hermann Ney. 2010b. If I Only Had a Parser: Poor Man's Syntax for Hierarchical Machine Translation. In *International Workshop on Spoken Language Translation*, pages 345–352, Paris, France, December.

David Vilar, Eleftherios Avramidis, Maja Popović, and Sabine Hunsicker. 2011. Dfki's sc and mt submissions to iwslt 2011. In *International Workshop on Spoken Language Translation*, San Francisco, CA, USA, December.

R. Zens and H. Ney. 2006. N-gram Posterior Probabilities for Statistical Machine Translation. In *Human Language Technology Conf. / North American Chapter of the Assoc. for Computational Linguistics Annual Meeting (HLT-NAACL), Workshop on Statistical Machine Translation*, pages 72–77, New York City, June.

GHKM Rule Extraction and Scope-3 Parsing in Moses

Philip Williams and **Philipp Koehn**
School of Informatics
University of Edinburgh
10 Crichton Street
EH8 9AB, UK
p.j.williams-2@sms.ed.ac.uk
pkoehn@inf.ed.ac.uk

Abstract

We developed a string-to-tree system for English–German, achieving competitive results against a hierarchical model baseline. We provide details of our implementation of GHKM rule extraction and scope-3 parsing in the Moses toolkit. We compare systems trained on the same data using different grammar extraction methods.

1 Introduction

Over the last few years, syntax-based rule extraction has largely developed along two lines, one originating in hierarchical phrase-based translation (Chiang, 2005; Chiang, 2007) and the other in GHKM (Galley et al., 2004; Galley et al., 2006).

Hierarchical rule extraction generalizes the established phrase-based extraction method to produce formally-syntactic synchronous context-free grammar rules without any requirement for linguistic annotation of the training data. In subsequent work, the approach has been extended to incorporate linguistic annotation on the target side (as in SAMT (Zollmann and Venugopal, 2006)) or on both sides (Chiang, 2010).

In contrast, GHKM places target-side syntactic structure at the heart of the rule extraction process, producing extended tree transducer rules that map between strings and tree fragments.

Ultimately, both methods define rules according to a sentence pair's word-alignments. Without any restriction on rule size they will produce an exponentially large set of rules and so in practice only a subgrammar can be extracted. It is the differing rule selection heuristics that distinguish these two approaches, with hierarchical approaches being motivated by phrasal coverage and GHKM by target-side tree coverage.

The Moses toolkit (Koehn et al., 2007) has included support for hierarchical phrase-based rule extraction since the decoder was first extended to support syntax-based translation (Hoang et al., 2009). In this paper we provide some implementation details for the recently-added GHKM rule extractor and for the related scope-3 decoding algorithm. We then describe the University of Edinburgh's GHKM-based English-German submission to the WMT translation task and present comparisons with hierarchical systems trained on the same data. To our knowledge, these are the first GHKM results presented for English-German, a language pair with a high degree of reordering and rich target-side morphology.

2 GHKM Rule Extraction in Moses

A basic GHKM rule extractor was first developed for Moses during the fourth Machine Translation Marathon[1] in 2010. We have recently extended it to support several key features that are described in the literature, namely: composition of rules (Galley et al., 2006), attachment of unaligned source words (Galley et al., 2004), and elimination of fully non-lexical unary rules (Chung et al., 2011).

We provide some basic implementation details in the remainder of this section. In section 4 we present

[1] http://www.mtmarathon2010.info

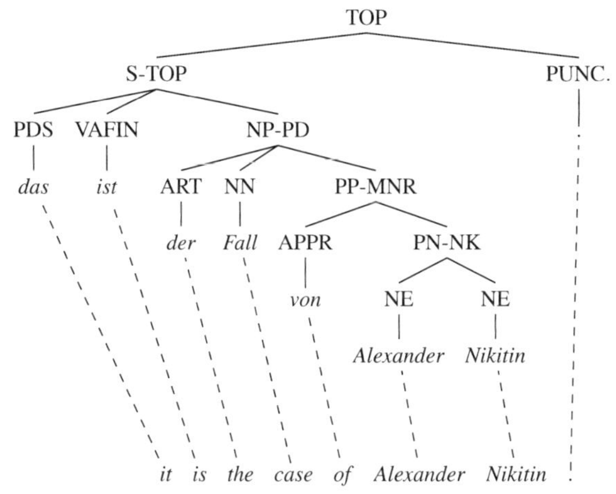

Figure 1: Sentence pair from training data.

experimental results comparing performance against Moses' alternative rule extraction methods.

2.1 Composed Rules

Composition of minimal GHKM rules into larger, contextually-richer rules has been found to significantly improve translation quality (Galley et al., 2006). Allowing any combination of adjacent minimal rules without restriction is unfeasible and so in practice various constraints are imposed on composition. Our implementation includes three configurable parameters for this purpose, which we describe with reference to the example alignment graph shown in Figure 1. All three are defined in terms of the target tree fragment.

Rule depth is defined as the maximum distance from the composed rule's root node to any other node within the fragment, not counting preterminal expansions (such as NE → *Nikitin*). By default, the rule depth is limited to three. If we consider the composition of rules rooted at the S-TOP node in Figure 1 then, among many other possibilities, this setting permits the formation of a rule with the target side:

S-TOP → *das ist der Fall von* PN-NK

since the maximum distance from the rule's root node to another node is three (to APPR or to PN-NK). However, a rule with the target side:

S-TOP → *das ist der Fall von* NE *Nikitin*

is not permitted since it has a rule depth of four (from S-TOP to either of the NE nodes).

Node count is defined as the number of target tree nodes in the composed rule, excluding target words. The default limit is 15, which for the example is large enough to permit any possible composed rule (the full tree has a node count of 13).

Rule size is the measure defined in DeNeefe et al. (2007): the number of non-part-of-speech, non-leaf constituent labels in the target tree. The default rule size limit is three.

2.2 Unaligned Source Words

Unaligned source words are attached to the tree using the following heuristic: if there are aligned source words to both the left and the right of an unaligned source word then it is attached to the lowest common ancestor of its nearest such left and right neighbours. Otherwise, it is attached to the root of the parse tree.

2.3 Unary Rule Elimination

Moses' chart decoder does not currently support the use of grammars containing fully non-lexical unary rules (such as NP → X_1 | NN_1). Unless the `--AllowUnary` option is given, the rule extractor eliminates these rules using the method described in Chung et al. (2011).

2.4 Scope Pruning

Unlike hierarchical phrase-based rule extraction, GHKM places no restriction on the rank of the resulting rules. In order that the grammar can be parsed efficiently, one of two approaches is usually taken: (i) *synchronous binarization* (Zhang et al., 2006), which transforms the original grammar to a weakly equivalent form in which no rule has rank greater than two. This makes the grammar amenable to decoding with a standard chart-parsing algorithm such as CYK, and (ii) *scope pruning* (Hopkins and Langmead, 2010), which eliminates rules in order to produce a subgrammar that can be parsed in cubic time.

Of these two approaches, Moses currently supports only the latter. Both rule extractors prune the extracted grammar to remove rules with scope greater than three. The next section describes the parsing algorithm that is used for scope-3 grammars.

3 Scope-3 Parsing in Moses

Hopkins and Langmead (2010) show that a sentence of length n can be parsed using a scope-k grammar in $O(n^k)$ chart updates. In this section, we describe some details of Moses' implementation of their chart parsing method.

3.1 The Grammar Trie

The grammar is stored in a trie-based data structure. Each edge is labelled with either a symbol from the source terminal vocabulary or a generic gap symbol, and the trie is constructed such that for any path originating at the root vertex, the sequence of edge labels represents the prefix of a rule's source right-hand-side (RHS_s, also referred to as a rule pattern). Wherever a path corresponds to a complete RHS_s, the vertex stores an associative array holding the set of grammar rules that share that RHS_s. The associative array maps a rule's sequence of target non-terminal symbols to the subset of grammar rules that share those symbols.

Figure 2 shows a sample of the grammar rules that can be extracted from the example alignment graph of Figure 1, and Figure 3 shows the corresponding grammar trie.

3.2 Initialization

The first step is to construct a secondary trie that records all possible applications of rule patterns from the grammar to the sentence under consideration. This trie is built during a single depth-first traversal of the grammar trie in which the terminal edge labels are searched for in the input sentence. If a matching input word is found then the secondary trie is extended by one vertex for each sentence position at which the word occurs and trie traversal continues along that path. A search for a gap label always results in a match. Edges in the secondary trie are labelled with the matching symbol and the position of the word in the input sentence (or a null position for gap labels). Each vertex in the secondary trie stores a pointer to the corresponding grammar trie vertex.

Once the secondary trie has been built, it is easy to determine the set of subspans to which each rule pattern applies. A set of pairs is recorded against each subspan, each pair holding a pointer to a grammar trie vertex and a record of the sentence positions covered by the symbols (which will be ambiguous if the pattern contains a sequence of $k > 1$ adjacent gap symbols covering more than k sentence positions).

After this initialization step, the secondary trie is discarded.

3.3 Subspan Processing

The parsing algorithm proceeds by processing chart cells in order of increasing span width (i.e. bottom-up). At each cell, a *stack lattice* is constructed for each rule pattern that was found during initialization. The stack lattice compactly represents all possible applications of that pattern over the span, together with pointers to the underlying hypothesis stacks for every gap. A full path through the lattice corresponds to a single application context. By selecting a derivation class (i.e. target-side non-terminal label) at each arc, the path can be bound to a set of grammar rules that differ only in the choice of target words or LHS label.

Recall that for every rule pattern found during initialization, the corresponding grammar trie vertex was recorded and that the vertex holds an associative array in which the keys are sequences of target-side non-terminal labels and the mapped values are grammar rules (together with associated feature model scores). The algorithm now loops over the associated array's key sequences, searching the lattice for matching paths. Where found, the grammar rule is bound with a sequence of underlying stack pointers. The cell's stacks are then populated by applying cube pruning (Chiang, 2007) to the set of bound grammar rules.

4 Experiments

This section describes the GHKM-based English-German system submitted by the University of Edinburgh. Subsequent to submission, a further set of comparative experiments were run using a hierarchical phrase-based system and a hierarchical system with target side syntactic annotation.

4.1 Data

We made use of all available English-German European and News Commentary data. For the hierarchical phrase-based experiments, this totalled

1. NP-PD → *the case of Alexander Nikitin* | *der Fall von Alexander Nikitin*
2. NP-PD → *the case* X_1 | *der Fall* PP-MNR$_1$
3. NP-PD → X_1 *case* X_2 | ART$_1$ *Fall* PP-MNR$_2$
4. PP-MNR → *of* X_1 | *von* PN-NK$_1$
5. PP-MNR → *of* X_1 X_2 | *von* NE$_1$ NE$_2$

Figure 2: A sample of the rules extractable from the alignment graph in Figure 1. Rules are written in the form LHS → RHS$_s$ | RHS$_t$.

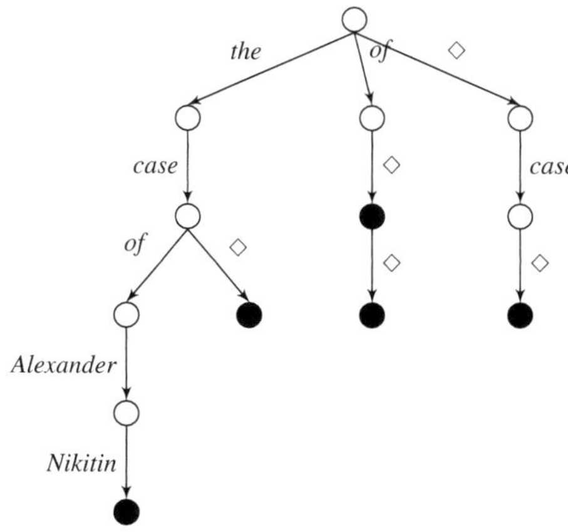

Figure 3: Example grammar trie. The filled vertices hold associative array values.

2,043,914 sentence pairs. For the target syntax experiments, the German-side of the parallel corpus was parsed using the BitPar[2] parser. If a parse failed then the sentence pair was discarded, leaving a total of 2,028,556 pairs. The parallel corpus was then word-aligned using MGIZA++ (Gao and Vogel, 2008), a multi-threaded implementation of GIZA++ (Och and Ney, 2003).

We used all available monolingual German data to train seven 5-gram language models (one each for Europarl, News Commentary, and the five News data sets). These were interpolated using weights optimised against the development set and the resulting language model was used in experiments. We used the SRILM toolkit (Stolcke, 2002) with Kneser-Ney smoothing (Chen and Goodman, 1998).

The baseline system's feature weights were tuned on the *news-test2008* dev set (2,051 sentence pairs) using Moses' implementation of minimum error rate training (Och, 2003).

[2]`http://www.ims.uni-stuttgart.de/tcl/SOFTWARE/BitPar.html`

4.2 Rule Extraction

For the hierarchical phrase-based model we used the default Moses rule extraction settings, which are taken from Chiang (2007). For target-annotated models, the syntactic constraints imposed by the parse trees reduce the grammar size significantly. This allows us to relax the rule extraction settings, which we have previously found to benefit translation quality, without producing an unusably large grammar. We use identical settings to those used in WMT's 2010 translation task (Koehn et al., 2010). Specifically, we relax the hierarchical phrase-based extraction settings in the following ways:

- Up to seven source-side symbols are allowed.
- Consecutive source non-terminals are permitted.
- Single-word lexical phrases are allowed for hierarchical subphrase subtraction.
- Initial phrases are limited to 15 source words (instead of 10).

By using the scope-3 parser we can also relax the restriction on grammar rank. For comparison, we extract two target-annotated grammars, one with a maximum rank of two, and one with an unlimited rank but subject to scope-3 pruning.

GHKM rule extraction uses the default settings[3] as described in section 2.

Table 1 shows the sizes of the extracted grammars after filtering for the `newstest2011` test set. Filtering removes any rule in which the source right-hand-side contains a sequence of terminals and gaps that does not appear in any test set sentence.

[3]GHKM rule extraction is now fully integrated into Moses' Experiment Management System (EMS) and can be enabled for string-to-tree pipelines using the `TRAINING:use-ghkm` parameter.

Experiment	Grammar Size
Hierarchical	118,649,771
Target Syntax	12,748,259
Target Syntax (scope-3)	40,661,639
GHKM	27,002,733

Table 1: Grammar sizes (distinct rule counts) after filtering for the `newstest-2011` test set

4.3 Features

Our feature functions include the n-gram language model probability of the derivation's target yield, its word count, and various scores for the synchronous derivation. We score grammar rules according to the following functions:

- $p(\mathrm{RHS}_s|\mathrm{RHS}_t, \mathrm{LHS})$, the noisy-channel translation probability.
- $p(\mathrm{LHS}, \mathrm{RHS}_t|\mathrm{RHS}_s)$, the direct translation probability.
- $p_{lex}(\mathrm{RHS}_t|\mathrm{RHS}_s)$ and $p_{lex}(\mathrm{RHS}_s|\mathrm{RHS}_t)$, the direct and indirect lexical weights (Koehn et al., 2003).
- $p_{pcfg}(\mathrm{FRAG}_t)$, the monolingual PCFG probability of the tree fragment from which the rule was extracted (GHKM and target-annotated systems only). This is defined as $\prod_{i=1}^{n} p(r_i)$, where $r_1 \ldots r_n$ are the constituent CFG rules of the fragment. The PCFG parameters are estimated from the parse of the target-side training data. All lexical CFG rules are given the probability 1. This is similar to the p_{cfg} feature used in Marcu et al. (2006) and is intended to encourage the production of syntactically well-formed derivations.
- $exp(-1/count(r))$, a rule rareness penalty.
- $exp(1)$, a rule penalty. The main grammar and glue grammars have distinct penalty features.

4.4 Decoder Settings

For the submitted GHKM system we used a maximum chart span setting of 25. For the other systems we used settings that matched the rule extraction spans: 10 for hierarchical phrase-based, 15 for target syntax, and unlimited for GHKM.

We used the scope-3 parsing algorithm (enabled using the option `-parsing-algorithm 1`) for all systems except the hierarchical system, which used the CYK+ algorithm (Chappelier and Rajman, 1998).

For all systems we set the `ttable-limit` parameter to 50 (increased from the default value of 20). This setting controls the level of grammar pruning that is performed after loading: only the top scoring translations are retained for a given source RHS.

4.5 Results

Following the recommendation of Clark et al. (2011), we ran the optimization three times and repeated evaluation with each set of feature weights. Table 2 presents the averaged single-reference BLEU scores. To give a rough indication of how much use the systems make of syntactic information for reordering, we also report glue rule statistics taken from the 1-best derivations.

There is a huge variation in decoding time between the systems, much of which can be attributed to the differing chart span limits. To give a comparison of system performance we selected an 80-sentence subset of `newstest2011`, randomly choosing ten sentences of length 1-10, ten of length 11-20, and so on. We decoded the test set four times for each system, discarding the first set of results (to allow for filesystem cache priming) and then averaging the remaining three. Table 3 shows the total decoding times for each system and the peak virtual memory usage[4]. Figure 4 shows a plot of sentence length against decoding time for the two GHKM systems.

5 Conclusion

We developed a GHKM-based string-to-tree system for English to German, achieving competitive results compared to a hierarchical model baseline. We extended the Moses toolkit to include a GHKM rule extractor and scope-3 parsing algorithm and provided details of our implementation. We intend to further improve this system in future work.

[4]The server has 142GB physical memory. The decoder was run single-threaded in performance tests. For the hierarchical system we used an on-disk rule table, which reduces memory requirements at the cost of increased rule lookup time. For all other systems we used in-memory rule tables.

Experiment	newstest2009 BLEU	s.d.	newstest2010 BLEU	s.d.	newstest2011 BLEU	s.d.	Glue Rule Apps Mean	s.d.
GHKM (max span 25)	**15.2**	0.1	**16.7**	0.1	15.4	0.1	3.1	0.3
Hierarchical	**15.2**	0.0	16.4	0.1	**15.5**	0.0	13.9	0.5
Target	14.6	0.1	16.0	0.1	14.9	0.1	8.4	5.0
Target (scope-3)	14.7	0.0	16.4	0.2	15.0	0.0	9.7	1.2
GHKM (no span limit)	15.0	0.3	16.6	0.1	15.2	0.2	1.9	1.3

Table 2: Average BLEU scores and standard deviations over three optimization runs. GHKM (max span 25) is the submitted system. Also shown is the average number of rule applications per sentence for the 1-best output of the three test sets, averaged over the three optimization runs.

System	Max span	Time (s)	VM (MB)
Hierarchical	10	122	5,345
Target	15	367	8,688
Target (scope-3)	15	1,539	19,761
GHKM	25	3,529	17,424
GHKM	None	11,196	18,060

Table 3: Total decoding time and peak virtual memory usage for the 80-sentence subset of `newstest2011`.

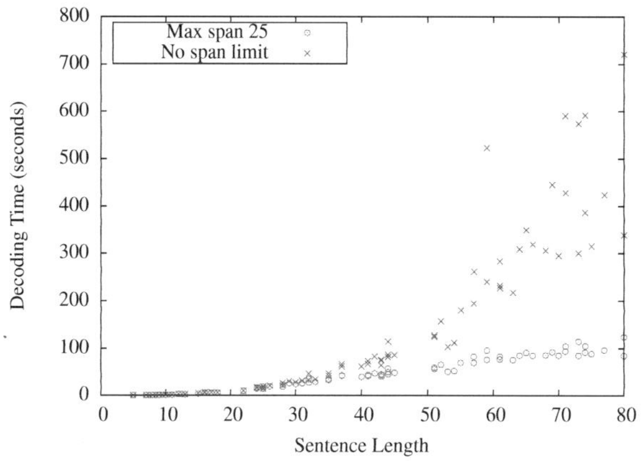

Figure 4: Sentence length vs decoding time for the GHKM (max span 25) and GHKM (no limit) systems

Acknowledgments

We would like to thank the anonymous reviewers for their helpful feedback and suggestions. This work was supported by the EuroMatrixPlus project funded by the European Commission (7th Framework Programme) and made use of the resources provided by the Edinburgh Compute and Data Facility.[5] The ECDF is partially supported by the eDIKT initiative.[6] This work was also supported in part under the GALE program of the Defense Advanced Research Projects Agency, Contract No. HR0011-06-C-0022. The first author was supported by an EPSRC Studentship.

References

J.-C. Chappelier and M. Rajman. 1998. A generalized CYK algorithm for parsing stochastic CFG. In *Proceedings of the First Workshop on Tabulation in Parsing and Deduction*, pages 133–137.

Stanley F. Chen and Joshua Goodman. 1998. An empirical study of smoothing techniques for language modeling. Technical report, Harvard University.

David Chiang. 2005. A hierarchical phrase-based model for statistical machine translation. In *ACL '05: Proceedings of the 43rd Annual Meeting on Association for Computational Linguistics*, pages 263–270, Morristown, NJ, USA. Association for Computational Linguistics.

David Chiang. 2007. Hierarchical phrase-based translation. *Comput. Linguist.*, 33(2):201–228.

David Chiang. 2010. Learning to translate with source and target syntax. In *Proceedings of the 48th Annual Meeting of the Association for Computational Linguis-*

[5] `http://www.ecdf.ed.ac.uk`
[6] `http://www.edikt.org.uk`

tics, pages 1443–1452, Uppsala, Sweden, July. Association for Computational Linguistics.

Tagyoung Chung, Licheng Fang, and Daniel Gildea. 2011. Issues concerning decoding with synchronous context-free grammar. In *Proceedings of the 49th Annual Meeting of the Association for Computational Linguistics: Human Language Technologies*, pages 413–417, Portland, Oregon, USA, June. Association for Computational Linguistics.

Jonathan H. Clark, Chris Dyer, Alon Lavie, and Noah A. Smith. 2011. Better hypothesis testing for statistical machine translation: Controlling for optimizer instability. In *Proceedings of the 49th Annual Meeting of the Association for Computational Linguistics: Human Language Technologies*, pages 176–181, Portland, Oregon, USA, June. Association for Computational Linguistics.

Steve DeNeefe, Kevin Knight, Wei Wang, and Daniel Marcu. 2007. What can syntax-based MT learn from phrase-based MT? In *Proceedings of the 2007 Joint Conference on Empirical Methods in Natural Language Processing and Computational Natural Language Learning (EMNLP-CoNLL 2007). June 28-30, 2007. Prague, Czech Republic.*

Michel Galley, Mark Hopkins, Kevin Knight, and Daniel Marcu. 2004. What's in a translation rule? In *HLT-NAACL '04.*

Michel Galley, Jonathan Graehl, Kevin Knight, Daniel Marcu, Steve DeNeefe, Wei Wang, and Ignacio Thayer. 2006. Scalable inference and training of context-rich syntactic translation models. In *ACL-44: Proceedings of the 21st International Conference on Computational Linguistics and the 44th annual meeting of the Association for Computational Linguistics*, pages 961–968, Morristown, NJ, USA. Association for Computational Linguistics.

Qin Gao and Stephan Vogel. 2008. Parallel implementations of word alignment tool. In *Software Engineering, Testing, and Quality Assurance for Natural Language Processing*, SETQA-NLP '08, pages 49–57, Stroudsburg, PA, USA. Association for Computational Linguistics.

Hieu Hoang, Philipp Koehn, and Adam Lopez. 2009. A unified framework for phrase-based, hierarchical, and syntax-based statistical machine translation. In *In Proceedings of IWSLT, December 2009.*

Mark Hopkins and Greg Langmead. 2010. SCFG decoding without binarization. In *Proceedings of the 2010 Conference on Empirical Methods in Natural Language Processing*, pages 646–655, Cambridge, MA, October. Association for Computational Linguistics.

Philipp Koehn, Franz Josef Och, and Daniel Marcu. 2003. Statistical phrase-based translation. In *NAACL '03: Proceedings of the 2003 Conference of the North American Chapter of the Association for Computational Linguistics on Human Language Technology*, pages 48–54, Morristown, NJ, USA. Association for Computational Linguistics.

Philipp Koehn, Hieu Hoang, Alexandra Birch, Chris Callison-Burch, Marcello Federico, Nicola Bertoldi, Brooke Cowan, Wade Shen, Christine Moran, Richard Zens, Chris Dyer, Ondřej Bojar, Alexandra Constantin, and Evan Herbst. 2007. Moses: open source toolkit for statistical machine translation. In *Proceedings of the 45th Annual Meeting of the ACL on Interactive Poster and Demonstration Sessions*, ACL '07, pages 177–180, Morristown, NJ, USA. Association for Computational Linguistics.

Philipp Koehn, Barry Haddow, Philip Williams, and Hieu Hoang. 2010. More linguistic annotation for statistical machine translation. In *Proceedings of the Joint Fifth Workshop on Statistical Machine Translation and MetricsMATR*, pages 115–120, Uppsala, Sweden, July. Association for Computational Linguistics.

Daniel Marcu, Wei Wang, Abdessamad Echihabi, and Kevin Knight. 2006. SPMT: statistical machine translation with syntactified target language phrases. In *EMNLP '06: Proceedings of the 2006 Conference on Empirical Methods in Natural Language Processing*, pages 44–52, Morristown, NJ, USA. Association for Computational Linguistics.

Franz Josef Och and Hermann Ney. 2003. A systematic comparison of various statistical alignment models. *Comput. Linguist.*, 29(1):19–51, March.

Franz Josef Och. 2003. Minimum error rate training in statistical machine translation. In *Proceedings of the 41st Annual Meeting on Association for Computational Linguistics - Volume 1*, ACL '03, pages 160–167, Morristown, NJ, USA. Association for Computational Linguistics.

Andreas Stolcke. 2002. SRILM - an extensible language modeling toolkit. In *Intl. Conf. Spoken Language Processing, Denver, Colorado, September 2002.*

Hao Zhang, Liang Huang, Daniel Gildea, and Kevin Knight. 2006. Synchronous binarization for machine translation. In *Proceedings of the main conference on Human Language Technology Conference of the North American Chapter of the Association of Computational Linguistics*, pages 256–263, Morristown, NJ, USA. Association for Computational Linguistics.

Andreas Zollmann and Ashish Venugopal. 2006. Syntax augmented machine translation via chart parsing. In *StatMT '06: Proceedings of the Workshop on Statistical Machine Translation*, pages 138–141, Morristown, NJ, USA. Association for Computational Linguistics.

Data Issues of the Multilingual Translation Matrix

Daniel Zeman
Charles University in Prague, Faculty of Mathematics and Physics,
Institute of Formal and Applied Linguistics
Malostranské náměstí 25, CZ-11800 Praha, Czechia
zeman@ufal.mff.cuni.cz

Abstract

We describe our experiments with phrase-based machine translation for the WMT 2012 Shared Task. We trained one system for 14 translation directions between English or Czech on one side and English, Czech, German, Spanish or French on the other side. We describe a set of results with different training data sizes and subsets.

1 Introduction

With so many official languages, Europe is a paradise for machine translation research. One of the largest bodies of electronically available parallel texts is being nowadays generated by the European Union and its institutions. At the same time, the EU also provides motivation and boosts potential market for machine translation outcomes.

Most of the major European languages belong to one of three branches of the Indo-European language family: Germanic, Romance or Slavic. Such relatedness is responsible for many structural similarities in European languages, although significant differences still exist. Within the language portfolio selected for the WMT shared task, English, French and Spanish seem to be closer to each other than to the rest.

German, despite being genetically related to English, differs in many properties. Its word order rules, shifting verbs from one end of the sentence to the other, easily create long-distance dependencies. Long German compound words are notorious for increasing out-of-vocabulary rate, which has led many researchers to devising unsupervised compound-splitting techniques. Also, uppercase/lowercase distinction is more important because all German nouns start with an uppercase letter by the rule.

Czech is a language with rich morphology (both inflectional and derivational) and relatively free word order. In fact, the predicate-argument structure, often encoded by fixed word order in English, is usually captured by inflection (especially the system of 7 grammatical cases) in Czech. While the free word order of Czech is a problem when translating to English (the text should be parsed first in order to determine the syntactic functions and the English word order), generating correct inflectional affixes is indeed a challenge for English-to-Czech systems. Furthermore, the multitude of possible Czech word forms (at least order of magnitude higher than in English) makes the data sparseness problem really severe, hindering both directions.

Our goal is to run one system under as similar conditions as possible to all fourteen translation directions, to compare their translation accuracies and see why some directions are easier than others. Future work will benefit from knowing what are the special processing needs for a given language pair. The current version of the system does not include really language-specific techniques: we neither split German compounds, nor do we address the peculiarities of Czech mentioned above.

2 The Translation System

Our translation system is built around Moses[1] (Koehn et al., 2007). Two-way word alignment was computed using GIZA++[2] (Och and Ney, 2003), and alignment symmetrization using the *grow-diag-final-and* heuristic (Koehn et al., 2003). Weights of the system were optimized using MERT (Och, 2003). No lexical reordering model was trained.

For language modeling we use the SRILM toolkit[3] (Stolcke, 2002) with modified Kneser-Ney smoothing (Kneser and Ney, 1995; Chen and Goodman, 1998).

3 Data and Pre-processing Pipeline

We applied our system to all the eight official language pairs. In addition, we also experimented with translation between Czech on one side and German, Spanish or French on the other side. Training data for these additional language pairs were obtained by combining parallel corpora of the officially supported pairs. For instance, to create the Czech-German parallel corpus, we identified the intersection of the English sides of Czech-English and English-German corpora, respectively; then we combined the corresponding Czech and German sentences.

We took part in the constrained task. Unless explicitly stated otherwise, the translation model in our experiments was trained on the combined News-Commentary v7 and Europarl v7 corpora.[4] Table 1 shows the sizes of the training data.

The News Test 2010 data set[5] (2489 sentences in each language) was used as development data for MERT. BLEU scores reported in this paper were computed on the News Test 2012 set (3003 sentences each language). We do not use the News Tests 2008, 2009 and 2011.

[1] `http://www.statmt.org/moses/`

[2] `http://code.google.com/p/giza-pp/`

[3] `http://www-speech.sri.com/projects/srilm/`

[4] `http://www.statmt.org/wmt12/translation-task.html\#download`

[5] `http://www.statmt.org/wmt12/translation-task.html`

Corpus	SentPairs	Tokens lng1	Tokens lng2
cs-en	782,756	17,997,673	20,964,639
de-en	2,079,049	55,143,719	57,741,141
es-en	2,123,036	61,784,972	59,217,471
fr-en	2,144,820	69,568,241	59,939,548
de-cs	652,193	17,422,620	15,383,601
es-cs	692,118	20,189,811	16,324,910
fr-cs	686,300	22,220,780	16,190,365

Table 1: Number of sentence pairs and tokens for every language pair in the parallel training corpus. Languages are identified by their ISO 639 codes: cs = Czech, de = German, en = English, es = Spanish, fr = French. Every line corresponds to the respective version of EuroParl + News Commentary.

All parallel and monolingual corpora underwent the same preprocessing. They were tokenized and some characters normalized or cleaned. A set of language-dependent heuristics was applied in an attempt to restore and normalize the directed (opening/closing) quotation marks (i.e. `"quoted"` → “quoted”). The motivation is twofold here: First, we hope that paired quotation marks could occasionally work as brackets and better denote parallel phrases for Moses; second, if Moses learns to output directed quotation marks, subsequent detokenization will be easier.

The data are then tagged and lemmatized. We used the Morče tagger for Czech and English lemmatization and TreeTagger for German, Spanish and French lemmatization. All these tools are embedded in the Treex analysis framework (Žabokrtský et al., 2008).

The lemmas are used later to compute word alignment. Besides, they are needed to apply “supervised truecasing” to the data: we cast the case of the lemma to the form, relying on our morphological analyzers and taggers to identify proper names, all other words are lowercased. Note that guessing of the true case is only needed for the sentence-initial token. Other words can typically be left in their original form, unless they are uppercased as a form of HIGHLIGHTING.

3.1 Quotation Marks

A broad range of characters is used to represent quotation marks in the training data: straight ASCII quotation mark; Unicode directed quotation marks (U+2018 to U+201F); acute and grave accents; math symbols such as prime and double prime (U+2032 to U+2037) etc. Spaces around quotes in the original untokenized text ought to provide hints as to the direction of the quotes (no space between the opening quote and the next word, and no space between the closing quote and the previous word) but unfortunately there are numerous cases where superfluous spaces are inserted or required spaces are missing.

Nested quoting is also possible, such as in

As the Wise Men ' s Report also says , and I quote : ' It is elementary ' common sense ' that the Commission should have supported the Parliament ' s decision - making process . '

We want all possible quotation marks converted to one pair of characters. We do not mind the distinction between single and double quotes but we want to keep (or restore) the distinction between opening and closing quotes. In addition, we want to identify the apostrophe acting as grapheme in some languages, and keep it (or normalize it, as it could also be mis-typed as acute accent or something else):

As the Wise Men ' s Report also says , and I quote : “ It is elementary “ common sense ” that the Commission should have supported the Parliament ' s decision - making process . ”

We attempt at solving the problem by a set of rules that consider mutual positions of quotation marks, spaces and other punctuation, and also some language-dependent rules (especially on the lexical apostrophe, e.g. in French *d', l'*).

Our rules applied to 1.84 % of Spanish sentences, 2.47 % Czech, 2.77 % German, 4.33 % English and 16.9 % French (measured on Europarl data).

Our approach is different from the normalization script provided and applied by the organizers of the shared task, which merely converts all quotes to the undirected ASCII characters. We believe that such MT output is incorrect, so we submitted two versions of each system run: the *primary* version is intended for human evaluation and does not apply the “official” normalization of punctuation. In contrast, the *secondary* version is normalized, which naturally leads to higher scores in the automatic evaluation.

4 Experiments

In the following section we describe several different settings and corpora combinations we experimented with. BLEU scores have been computed by our system, comparing truecased tokenized hypothesis with truecased tokenized reference translation.

Such scores must differ from the official evaluation—see Section 4.4 for discussion of the final results.

The confidence interval for most of the scores lies between ±0.5 and ±0.6 BLEU % points.

4.1 Baseline Experiments

The set of baseline experiments were trained on the supervised truecased combination of News Commentary and Europarl. As we had lemmatizers for the languages, word alignment was computed on lemmas. (But our previous experiments showed that there was little difference between using lemmas and lowercased 4-character “stems”.) A hexagram language model was trained on the monolingual version of the News Commentary + Europarl corpus (typically a slightly larger superset of the target side of the parallel corpus).

4.2 Larger Monolingual Data

Besides the monolingual halves of the parallel corpora, additional monolingual data were provided / permitted:

- The Crawled News corpus from the years 2007 to 2011, various sizes for each language and year.
- The Gigaword corpora published by the Linguistic Data Consortium, available only for English (4th edition), Spanish (3rd) and French (3rd).

Due to bugs in the lemmatizers, we were not able to process certain parts of the large corpora in time. Table 2 gives the sizes of the subsets available for our experiments and Table 3 compares BLEU scores with large language models against the baseline.

Corpus	Segments	Tokens
newsc+euro.cs	819,434	18,491,692
newsc+euro.de	2,360,811	58,683,607
newsc+euro.en	2,430,718	65,934,441
newsc+euro.es	2,307,429	66,072,443
newsc+euro.fr	2,361,764	74,083,166
news.all.cs	14,552,899	244,728,011
news.all.de	24,446,319	462,924,303
news.all.en	42,161,804	1,039,806,242
news.all.es	8,627,438	249,022,213
news.all.fr	16,708,622	438,489,352
gigaword.en	70,592,779	2,546,581,646
gigaword.es	31,304,148	1,064,660,498
gigaword.fr	21,674,453	963,571,174

Table 2: Number of segments (paragraphs in Gigaword, sentences elsewhere) and tokens of additional monolingual training corpora. "newsc+euro" are the monolingual versions of the News Commentary and Europarl parallel corpora. "news.all" denotes all years of the Crawled News corpus for the given language.

The Crawled News corpora, in-domain and larger than the parallel corpora by an order of magnitude, turned out to help significantly improve the scores of all language pairs. On the other hand, and to our surprise, we were not able to achieve any further improvement by using the Gigaword corpora. Taking into account the extra requirements on memory when building such big language models, this makes the usefulness of Gigaword questionable. We have no plausible explanation at the moment.

4.3 Larger Parallel Data

Even stranger behavior was observed when adding the large UN parallel corpus (over 10 million sentence pairs). When used separately (even for language model) it decreased BLEU significantly, which could be explained by different domain. When used together with News Commentary and Europarl, and with a language model trained on the Crawled News corpus, it barely outperformed the same setting without the UN corpus.[6] However, the es-en direction is a notable exception where the UN corpus alone gave by far the best score. See Table 4 for details.

Direction	Baseline	news.all	gigaword
en-cs	0.1196	0.1434	
en-de	0.1426	0.1629	
en-es	0.2778	0.3136	0.3136
en-fr	0.2599	0.2897	0.2874
cs-en	0.1796	0.2031	0.2013
de-en	0.1877	0.2136	0.2144
es-en	0.2219	0.2428	0.2390
fr-en	0.2459	0.2764	0.2756
cs-de	0.1365	0.1550	
cs-es	0.1952	0.2211	0.2184
cs-fr	0.1953	0.2167	0.2147
de-cs	0.1212	0.1400	
es-cs	0.1281	0.1489	
fr-cs	0.1253	0.1442	

Table 3: BLEU scores of the baseline experiments (left column) on News Test 2012 data, computed by the system on tokenized data, versus similar setup with large monolingual corpus (news.all, middle column). Gigaword never brought significant improvement.

We failed to lemmatize the giga French-English corpus in time, so we do not present any results with that corpus.

4.4 Final Results

Table 5 compares our BLEU scores with those computed at `matrix.statmt.org`.

BLEU (without flag) denotes BLEU score computed by our system, comparing truecased tokenized hypothesis with truecased tokenized reference translation.

The official evaluation by `matrix.statmt.org` gives typically lower numbers, reflecting the loss caused by detokenization and new (different) tokenization.

[6]One of the anonymous reviewers mentioned that the quality of the UN corpus is relatively low. That could explain our observations.

Direction	Parallel	Mono	*BLEU*
en-es	news-euro-un	news.all	0.3194
en-es	news-euro	news.all	0.3136
en-es	un	un	0.2694
en-fr	news-euro	news.all	0.2897
en-fr	un	un	0.2541
es-en	un	un	**0.2688**
es-en	news-euro	news.all	0.2428
fr-en	news-euro	news.all	0.2764
fr-en	un	un	0.2392

Table 4: BLEU scores with different parallel corpora.

4.5 Efficiency

The baseline experiments were conducted mostly on 64bit AMD Opteron quad-core 2.8 GHz CPUs with 32 GB RAM (decoding run on 15 machines in parallel) and the whole pipeline typically required between a half and a whole day.

However, we used machines with up to 500 GB RAM to train the large language models and translation models. Aligning the UN corpora with Giza++ took around 5 days.

5 Conclusion

We have described the Moses-based SMT system we used for the WMT 2012 shared task. We discussed experiments with large data for many language pairs from the point of view of both the translation accuracy and efficiency. We were unable to process all data that was available; even the experiments where we did use larger data did not outperform the smaller experiments significantly. Nevertheless, using the Crawled News monolingual corpus proved essential.

Direction	*BLEU*	$BLEU_l$	$BLEU_t$
en-cs	0.1434	0.144	0.136
en-de	0.1629	0.159	0.154
en-es	0.3136	0.316	0.297
en-fr	0.2897	0.263	0.251
cs-en	0.2031	0.207	0.192
de-en	0.2136	0.214	0.200
es-en	0.2428	0.253	0.240
fr-en	0.2764	0.280	0.266
cs-de	0.1550	0.153	0.147
cs-es	0.2211	0.224	0.207
cs-fr	0.2167	0.197	0.186
de-cs	0.1400	0.141	0.134
es-cs	0.1489	0.150	0.143
fr-cs	0.1442	0.145	0.138

Table 5: BLEU scores with the large language models. *BLEU* is computed by the system, $BLEU_l$ is the official lowercased evaluation by `matrix.statmt.org`. $BLEU_t$ is official truecased evaluation. Although lower official scores are expected, notice the larger gap in en-fr and cs-fr translation. There seems to be a problem in our French detokenization procedure.

Acknowledgements

The work on this project was supported by the grant P406/11/1499 of the Czech Science Foundation (GAČR).

References

Stanley F. Chen and Joshua Goodman. 1998. An empirical study of smoothing techniques for language modeling. In *Technical report TR-10-98, Computer Science Group*, Harvard, MA, USA, August. Harvard University.

Reinhard Kneser and Hermann Ney. 1995. Improved backing-off for m-gram language modeling. In *Proceedings of the IEEE International Conference on Acoustics, Speech and Signal Processing*, pages 181–184, Los Alamitos, California, USA. IEEE Computer Society Press.

Philipp Koehn, Franz Josef Och, and Daniel Marcu. 2003. Statistical phrase-based translation. In *NAACL '03: Proceedings of the 2003 Conference of the North American Chapter of the Association for Computational Linguistics on Human Language Technology*, pages 48–54, Morristown, NJ, USA. Association for Computational Linguistics.

Philipp Koehn, Hieu Hoang, Alexandra Birch, Chris Callison-Burch, Marcello Federico, Nicola Bertoldi, Brooke Cowan, Wade Shen, Christine Moran, Richard Zens, Chris Dyer, Ondřej Bojar, Alexandra Constantin, and Evan Herbst. 2007. Moses: Open Source Toolkit for Statistical Machine Translation. In *Proceedings of the 45th Annual Meeting of the Association for Computational Linguistics Companion Volume Proceedings of the Demo and Poster Sessions*, pages 177–180, Praha,

Czechia, June. Association for Computational Linguistics.

Franz Josef Och and Hermann Ney. 2003. A systematic comparison of various statistical alignment models. *Computational Linguistics*, 29(1):19–51.

Franz Josef Och. 2003. Minimum error rate training in statistical machine translation. In *ACL '03: Proceedings of the 41st Annual Meeting on Association for Computational Linguistics*, pages 160–167, Morristown, NJ, USA. Association for Computational Linguistics.

Andreas Stolcke. 2002. Srilm – an extensible language modeling toolkit. In *Proceedings of International Conference on Spoken Language Processing*, Denver, Colorado, USA.

Zdeněk Žabokrtský, Jan Ptáček, and Petr Pajas. 2008. TectoMT: Highly modular MT system with tectogrammatics used as transfer layer. In *ACL 2008 WMT: Proceedings of the Third Workshop on Statistical Machine Translation*, pages 167–170, Columbus, OH, USA. Association for Computational Linguistics.

Constructing Parallel Corpora for Six Indian Languages via Crowdsourcing

Matt Post⋆ and **Chris Callison-Burch**⋆† and **Miles Osborne**‡
⋆Human Langage Technology Center of Excellence, Johns Hopkins University
†Center for Language and Speech Processing, Johns Hopkins University
‡School of Informatics, University of Edinburgh

Abstract

Recent work has established the efficacy of Amazon's Mechanical Turk for constructing parallel corpora for machine translation research. We apply this to building a collection of parallel corpora between English and six languages from the Indian subcontinent: Bengali, Hindi, Malayalam, Tamil, Telugu, and Urdu. These languages are low-resource, under-studied, and exhibit linguistic phenomena that are difficult for machine translation. We conduct a variety of baseline experiments and analysis, and release the data to the community.

1 Introduction

The quality of statistical machine translation (MT) systems is strongly related to the amount of parallel text available for the language pairs. However, most language pairs have little or no readily available bilingual training data available. As a result, most contemporary MT research tends to opportunistically focus on language pairs with large amounts of parallel data.

A consequence of this bias is that language exhibiting certain linguistic phenomena are underrepresented, including languages with complex morphology and languages with divergent word orderings. In this paper, we describe our work gathering and refining document-level parallel corpora between English and each of six verb-final languages spoken on the Indian subcontinent: Bengali, Hindi, Malayalam, Tamil, Telugu, and Urdu. This paper's contributions are as follows:

- We apply an established protocol for using Amazon's Mechanical Turk (MTurk) to collect parallel data to train and evaluate translation systems for six Indian languages.
- We investigate the relative performance of syntactic translation models over hierarchical ones, showing that syntax results in higher BLEU scores in most cases.
- We explore the impact of training data quality on the quality of the resulting model.
- We release the corpora to the research community under the Creative Commons Attribution-Sharealike 3.0 Unported License (CC BY-SA 3.0).[1]

2 Why Indian languages?

Indian languages are important objects of study for a number of reasons. These languages are low-resource languages in terms of the availability of MT systems[2] (and NLP tools in general) yet together they represent nearly half a billion native speakers (Table 1). Their speakers are well-educated, with many of them speaking English either natively or as a second language. Together with the degree of Internet penetration in India, it is reasonably straightforward to find and hire non-expert translators through crowdsourcing services like Amazon's Mechanical Turk.

[1] `joshua-decoder.org/indian-parallel-corpora`

[2] See `sampark.iiit.ac.in/sampark/web/index.php/content` for a notable growing effort.

ெனட்டர்	அவளை	கருத்துக்கள்	தயார்
senator	*her*	*remarks*	*prepared*

Figure 1: An example of SOV word ordering in Tamil. Translation: *The senator prepared her remarks.*

হাত	কি	ল	আম
walk	*CONT*	*PAST*	*1p*

Figure 2: An example of the morphology of the Bengali word হাত্সলিাম, meaning *[I] was walking*. CONT denotes the continuous aspect, while PAST denotes past tense.

In addition to a general desire to collect suitable training corpora for low-resource languages, Indian languages demonstrate a variety of linguistic phenomena that are divergent from English and understudied. One example is head-finalness, exhibited most obviously in a subject-object-verb (SOV) pattern of sentence structure, in contrast to the general SVO ordering of English sentences. One of the motivations underlying linguistically-motivated syntactic translation systems like GHKM (Galley et al., 2004; Galley et al., 2006) or SAMT (Zollmann and Venugopal, 2006) is to describe such transformations. This difference in word order has the potential to serve as a better test bed for syntax-based MT[3] compared to translating between English and European languages, most of which largely share its word order. Figure 1 contains an example of SOV reordering in Tamil.

A second important phenomenon present in these languages is a high degree of morphological complexity relative to English (Figure 2). Indian languages can be highly agglutinative, which means that words are formed by concatenating morphological affixes that convey information such as tense, person, number, gender, mood, and voice. Morphological complexity is a considerable hindrance at all stages of the MT pipeline, but particularly alignment, where inflectional variations mask patterns from alignment tools that treat words as atoms.

[3]We use *hierarchical* to denote translation grammars that use only a single nonterminal (Chiang, 2007), in contrast to *syntactic* systems, which make use of linguistic annotations (Zollmann and Venugopal, 2006; Galley et al., 2006).

language	script	family	L1
Bengali	বাংলা	Indo-Aryan	181M
Hindi	मानक हिन्दी	Indo-Aryan	180M
Malayalam	മലയാളം	Dravidian	35M
Tamil	தமிழ்	Dravidian	65M
Telugu	తెలుగు	Dravidian	69M
Urdu	اردو	Indo-Aryan	60M

Table 1: Languages. L1 is the worldwide number of native speakers according to Lewis (2009).

3 Data collection

The source of the documents for our translation task for each of the languages in Table 1 was the set of the top-100 most-viewed documents from each language's Wikipedia. These lists were obtained using page view statistics compiled from `dammit.lt/wikistats` over a one year period. We did not apply any filtering for topic or content. Table 2 contains a manually categorized list of documents for Hindi, with some minimal annotations indicating how the documents relate to those in the other languages. These documents constitute a diverse set of topics, including culture, the internet, and sex.

We collected the parallel corpora using a three-step process designed to ensure the integrity of the non-professional translations. The first step was to build a bilingual dictionary (§3.1). These dictionaries were used to bootstrap the experimental controls in the collection of four translations of each source sentence (§3.2). Finally, as a measure of data quality, we independently collect votes on the which of the four redundant translations is the best (§3.3).

3.1 Dictionaries

A key component of managing MTurk workers is to ensure that they are competently and conscientiously undertaking the tasks. As non-speakers of all of the Indian languages, we had no simple and scalable way to judge the quality of the workers' translations. Our solution was to bootstrap the process by first building bilingual dictionaries for each of the datasets. The dictionaries were then used to produce glosses of the complete source sentences, which we compared to the translations produced by the workers as a rough means of manually gauging trust (§3.2).

The dictionaries were built in a separate MTurk

PLACES	PEOPLE	PEOPLE	TECHNOLOGY	LANGUAGE AND CULTURE	RELIGION
Agra	A. P. J. Abdul Kalam	Premchand	Blog	Ayurveda	Bhagavad Gita
Bihar	Aishwarya Rai	Rabindranath Tagore	**Google**	Constitution of India	Diwali
China	Akbar	Rani Lakshmibai	Hindi Web Resources	Cricket	Hanuman
Delhi	Amitabh Bachchan	Sachin Tendulkar	**Internet**	**English language**	Hinduism
Himalayas	**Barack Obama**	Sarojini Naidu	Mobile phone	Hindi Cable News	Hinduism
India	Bhagat Singh	Subhas Chandra Bose	News aggregator	Hindi literature	Holi
Mumbai	Dainik Jagran	Surdas	RSS	Hindi-Urdu grammar	**Islam**
Nepal	Gautama Buddha	Swami Vivekananda	**Wikipedia**	Horoscope	Mahabharata
Pakistan	Harivansh Rai Bachchan	Tulsidas	YouTube	Indian cuisine	Puranas
Rajasthan	Indira Gandhi			Sanskrit	Quran
Red Fort	Jaishankar Prasad	THINGS	SEX	Standard Hindi	Ramayana
Taj Mahal	Jawaharlal Nehru	Air pollution	Anal sex		Shiva
United States	Kabir	**Earth**	**Kama Sutra**	EVENTS	Shiva
Uttar Pradesh	Kalpana Chawla	Essay	**Masturbation**	History of India	Taj Majal: Shiva Temple?
	Mahadevi Varma	Ganges	**Penis**	**World War II**	Vedas
	Meera	General knowledge	Sex positions		**Vishnu**
	Mohammed Rafi	**Global warming**	**Sexual intercourse**		
	Mohandas Karamchand Gandhi	Pollution	**Vagina**		
	Mother Teresa	Solar energy			
	Navbharat Times	Terrorism			

Table 2: The 100 most viewed Hindi Wikipedia articles (titles translated to English using inter-language links and Google translate and manually categorized). Entries in **bold** were present in the top 100 lists of at least four of the Indian top 100 lists. *Earth*, *India*, *World War II*, and *Wikipedia* were in the top 100 lists of all six languages.

language	**entries**	**translations**
Bengali	4,075	6,011
Hindi	-	-
Malayalam	41,502	144,505
Tamil	11,592	69,128
Telugu	12,193	38,532
Urdu	26,363	113,911

Table 3: Dictionary statistics. *Entries* is the number of source-language types, while *translations* lists the number of words or phrases they translated to (i.e., the number of pairs in the dictionary). Controls for Hindi were obtained using Google translate, the only one of these languages that were available at the outset of this project.

task, in which workers were asked to translate single words and short phrases from the complete set of Wikipedia documents. For each word, MTurk workers were presented with three sentences containing that word, which provided context. The control for this task was obtained from the Wikipedia article titles which are linked across languages, and can thus be assumed to be translations of each other. Workers who performed too poorly on these known translations had their work rejected.

Table 3 lists the size of the dictionaries we constructed.

3.2 Translations

With the dictionaries in hand, we moved on to translate the entire Wikipedia documents. Each human intelligence task (HIT) posted on MTurk contained ten sequential source-language sentences from a document, and asked the worker to enter a free-form translation for each. We collected four translations from different translators for each source sentence. To discourage cheating through cutting-and-pasting into automatic translation systems, sentences were presented as images. Workers were paid \$0.70 per HIT. We then manually determined whether to accept or reject a worker's HITs based on a review of each worker's submissions, which included a comparison of the translations to a monotonic gloss (produced with the dictionary), the percentage of empty translations, the amount of time the worker took to complete the HIT, geographic location (self-reported and geolocated by way of the worker's IP address), and by comparing different translations of the same source segments against one another.

We obtained translations of the source-language documents in a relatively short amount of time. Figure 3 depicts the number of translations collected as a function of the amount of time from the posting of the task. Malayalam provided the highest throughput, generating half a million words in just under a

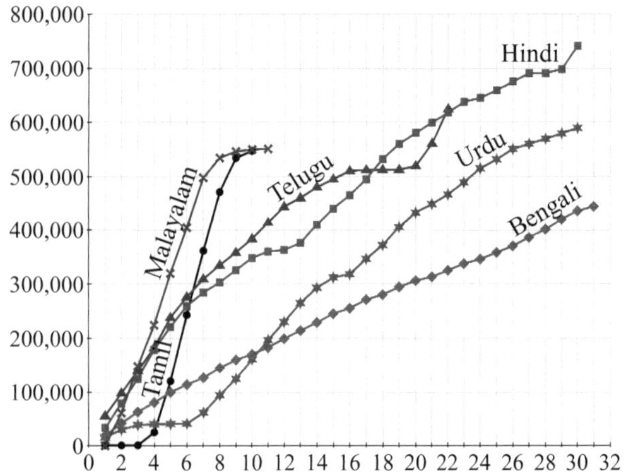

Figure 3: The total volume of translations (measured in English words) as a function of elapsed days. For Malayalam, we collected half a million words of translations in just under a week.

week. For comparison, the Europarl corpus (Koehn, 2005) has about 50 million words of English for each of the Spanish and French parallel corpora.

As has been previously reported (Zbib et al., 2012), cost is another advantage of building training data on Mechanical Turk. Germann (2001) puts the cost of professionally translated English at about \$0.30 per word for translation from Tamil. Our translations were obtained for less than \$0.01 per word. The rate of collection could likely be increased by raising these payments, but it is unclear whether quality would be affected by raising the base pay (although it could be improved by paying for subsequent quality control HITs, like editing).

The tradeoff for low-cost translations is increased variance in translation quality when compared to the more consistently-good professional translations. Figure 4 contains some hand-picked examples of the sorts of translations we obtained. Later, in the Experiments section (§4), we will investigate the effects this variance in translation quality has on the quality of the models that can be constructed. For now, the variance motivated the collection of an additional dataset, described in the next section.

3.3 Votes

A prevailing issue with translations collected on MTurk is the prevalence of low-quality translations. Quality suffers for a variety of reasons: Turkers lack formal training, often translate into a nonnative tongue, may give insufficient attention to the task, and likely desire to maximize their throughput (and thus their wage). Unlike Zaidan and Callison-Burch (2011), who embed controls containing source language sentences with known professional translations, we had no professionally translated data. Therefore, we could not measure the BLEU score of the Turkers.

Motivated by desire to have some measure of the relative quality and variance of the translations, we designed another task in which we presented an independent set of Turkers with an original sentence and its four translations, and asked them to vote on which was best.[4] Five independent workers voted on the translations of each source sentence. Tallying the resulting votes, we found that roughly 65% of the sentences had five votes cast on just one or two of the translations, and about 95% of the sentences had all the votes cast on one, two, or three sentences. This suggests both (1) that there was a difference in the quality of the translations, and (2) the voters were able to discern these differences, and took their task seriously enough to report them.

3.4 Data sets

For each parallel corpus, we created a standardized test set in the following manner. We first manually assigned each of the Wikipedia documents for each language into one of the following nine categories: EVENTS, LANGUAGE AND CULTURE, PEOPLE, PLACES, RELIGION, SEX, TECHNOLOGY, THINGS, or MISC. We then assigned documents to training, development, development test, and test sets in round-robin fashion using a ratio of roughly 7:1:1:1. For training data, each source sentence was repeated four times in order to allow it to be paired with each of its translations. For the development and test sets, the multiple translations served as alternate references. Table 4 lists sentence- and word-level statistics for the datasets for each language pair (these counts are prior to any tokenization).

[4] We did not collect votes for Malayalam.

மார்ச் 15,2007இல் ஆக்ஸ்ஃபோர்டு ஆங்கில அகராதி யில் விக்கி இடம்பெற்றது.

In March 15,2007 Wiki got a place in Oxford English dictionary.
On March 15, 2007 wiki was included in the Oxford English dictionary. (5)
ON MARCH 15, 2007, WIKI FOUND A PLACE IN THE OXFORD ENGLISH DICTIONARY
March 15, 2007 oxford english index of wiki's place.

Figure 4: An example of the variance in translation quality for the human translations of a Tamil sentence; the formatting of the translations has been preserved exactly. The parenthesized number indicates the number of votes received in the voting task (§3.3).

language	dict	train	dev	devtest	test
Bengali	16k	539k	63k	61k	69k
	6k	20k	914	907	1k
Hindi	0	1,249k	67k	98k	74k
	0	37k	1k	993	1k
Malayalam	410k	664k	61k	68k	70k
	144k	29k	1k	1k	1k
Tamil	189k	747k	62k	53k	54k
	69k	35k	1k	1k	1k
Telugu	106k	951k	52k	45k	49k
	38k	43k	1k	916	1k
Urdu	253k	1,198k	67k	49k	42k
	113k	33k	736	777	605

Table 4: Data set sizes for each language pair: words in the first row, parallel sentences in the second. (The dictionaries contains short phrases in addition to words, which accounts for the difference in dictionary word and line counts.)

4 Experiments

In this section, we present experiments on the collected data sets in order to quantify their performance. The experiments aim to address the following questions:

1. How well can we translate the test sets?
2. Do linguistically motivated translation models improve translation results?
3. What is the effect of data quality on model quality?

4.1 Setup

A principal point of comparison in this paper is between Hiero grammars (Chiang, 2007) and SAMT grammars (Zollmann and Venugopal, 2006), the latter of which make use of linguistic annotations to improve nonterminal reordering. These grammars were trained with the Thrax grammar extractor using its default settings, and translated using Joshua (Weese et al., 2011). We tuned with minimum error-rate training (Och, 2003) using Z-MERT (Zaidan, 2009) and present the mean BLEU score on test data over three separate runs (Clark et al., 2011). MBR reranking (Kumar and Byrne, 2004) was applied to Joshua's 300-best (unique) output, and evaluation was conducted with case-insensitive BLEU with four references.

The training data was produced by pairing a source sentence with each of its four translations. We also added the dictionaries to the training data. We built five-gram language models from the target side of the training data using interpolated Kneser-Ney smoothing. We also experimented with a larger-scale language model built from English Gigaword, but, notably, found a drop of over a point in BLEU score. This points forward to some of the difficulties encountered with the lack of text normalization, discussed in §5.

4.2 Baseline translations

We begin by presenting BLEU scores for Hiero and SAMT translations of each of the six Indian language test sets (Table 5). For comparison purposes, we also present BLEU scores from Google translations of these languages (where available).

We observe that systems built with SAMT grammars improve measurably above the Hiero models, with the exception of Tamil and Telugu. As an external reference point, the Google baseline translation scores far surpass the results of any of our systems, but were likely constructed from much larger datasets.

Table 6 lists some manually-selected examples of

language	Hiero	SAMT	diff	Google
Bengali	12.72	13.53	+0.81	20.01
Hindi	15.53	17.29	+1.76	25.21
Malayalam	13.72	14.28	+0.56	-
Tamil	9.81	9.85	+0.04	13.51
Telugu	12.46	12.61	+0.15	16.03
Urdu	19.53	20.99	+1.46	23.09

Table 5: BLEU scores translating into English (four references). BLEU scores are the mean of three MERT runs.

the sorts of translations we obtained from our systems. While anecdotal and not characteristic of overall quality, together with the generally good BLEU scores, these examples provide a measure of the ability to obtain good translations from this dataset.

4.3 Voted training data

We noted above the high variance in the quality of the translations obtained on MTurk. For data collection efforts, there is a question of how much time and effort to invest in quality control, since it comes at the expense of simply collecting more data. We can either collect additional redundant translations (to increase quality) or translate more foreign sentences (to increase coverage).

To test this, we constructed two smaller datasets, each making use of only one of the four translations of each source sentence:

- Selected randomly
- Selected by choosing the translation that received a plurality of the votes (§3.3), breaking ties randomly (*best*)

We again included the dictionaries in the training data (where available). Table 7 contains results on the same test sets as before. These results do not clearly indicate that quality control through redundant translations are worth the extra expense. Novotney and Callison-Burch (2010) had a similar finding for crowdsourced transcriptions.

5 Further Analysis

The previous section has shown that reasonable BLEU scores can be obtained from baseline translation systems built from these corpora. While translation quality is an issue (for example, very literal translations, etc), the previous section's voted dataset experiments suggest this is not one of the most important issues to address.

இலங்கையில் சோழர் ஆட்சி
in srilanka ***solar government***
chola *rule in sri lanka*
in srilanka ***chozhas*** *ruled*
chola *reign in sri lanka*

Figure 5: An example of inconsistent orthography. Words in bold are translations of the second Tamil word.

In this section, we undertake a manual analysis of the collected datasets to inform future work. There are a number of issues that arise due to non-Roman scripts, high-variance translation quality, and the relatively small amount of training data.

5.1 Orthographic issues

Manual analysis demonstrates that inconsistencies with orthography are a serious problem. An example of this can be found in Figure 5, which contains a set of translations of a Tamil sentence. In particular, the spelling of the Tamil word சோழர் has three different realizations among the sentence's translations. The discrepancy between *zha* and *la* is due to phonetic variants (phonetic similarity may also account for the word *solar*). This discrepancy is present throughout the training and test data, where the *-la* variant is preferred to *-zha* by about 6:1 (the counts are 848 and 142, respectively).

In addition to mistakes potentially caused by foreign scripts, there are many mistakes that are simply spelling errors. Table 8 contains examples of misspellings (along with their counts) in the training portion of the Urdu-English dataset. As a point of comparison, there are no misspellings of the word in Europarl.

Such errors are present in many collections, of course, but they are particularly harmful in small datasets, and they appear to be especially prevalent in datasets like these, translated as they were by non-native speakers. Whether caused by Turker carelessness or difficulty in translation from non-Roman scripts, these are common issues, solutions for which could yield significant improvement in translation performance.

Bengali	এই সময়ই ১৯২১ সালে ঢাকা বিশ্ববিদ্যালয় স্থাপিত হয়।
Hiero	in this time dhaka university was established on the year 1921 .
SAMT	in this time dhaka university was established in 1921 .
Malayalam	സൂര്യന്റെ ദൃശ്യമാകുന്ന ഉപരിതലത്തി ൽ താപനില 5 , 700 °k ലേക്ക് താഴ്ന്നിരിക്കും .
Hiero	the surface temperature of sun 5 , 700 degree k to down to .
SAMT	temperature in the surface of the sun 5 , 700 degree k to down to .

Table 6: Some example translations.

	Hiero		SAMT	
language	random	best	random	best
Bengali	**9.43**	9.29	**9.65**	9.50
Hindi	11.74	**12.18**	12.61	**12.69**
Tamil	**7.73**	7.48	**7.88**	7.76
Telugu	10.49	**10.61**	**10.75**	10.72
Urdu	13.51	**14.26**	14.63	**16.03**

Table 7: BLEU scores translating into English on a quarter of the training data (plus dictionary), selected in two ways: best (result of vote), and random. There is little difference, suggesting quality control may not be terribly important. We did not collect votes for Malayalam.

misspelling	**count**
japenese	91
japans	40
japenes	9
japenies	3
japeneses	3
japeneese	1
japense	1

Table 8: Misspellings of *japanese* (947) in the training portion of the Urdu-English data, along with their counts.

5.2 Alignments

Inconsistent orthography fragments the training data, exacerbating problems already present due to morpohological richness. One place this is manifested is during alignment, where different spellings mask patterns from the standard alignment techniques. We observe a large number of poor alignments, due to interactions among these problems, as well as the small size of the training data, well-documented alignment mistakes (such as garbage collecting), and the divergent sentence structures. In particular, it seems that the defacto alignment heuristics may be particularly ill-suited to these language pairs and data conditions. Figure 6 (top) contains an example of a particularly poor alignment produced by the default alignment heuristic, the *grow-diag-and* method described in Koehn et al. (2003).

As a means of testing this, we varied the alignment combination heuristics using five alternatives described in Koehn et al. (2003) and available in the `symal` program distributed with Moses (Koehn et al., 2007). Experiments on Tamil produce a range of BLEU scores between 7.45 and 10.19 (each result is the average of three MERT runs). If we plot grammar size versus BLEU score, we observe a general trend that larger grammars seem to positively correlate with BLEU score. We tested this more generally across languages using the Berkeley aligner[5] (Liang et al., 2006) instead of GIZA alignments, and found a consistent increase in BLEU score for the Hiero grammars, often putting them on par with the original SAMT results (Table 9). Manual analysis suggests that the Berkeley aligner produces fewer, more reasonable-looking alignments than the Moses heuristics (Figure 6). This suggest a fruitful approaches in revisiting assumptions underlying alignment heuristics.

6 Related Work

Crowdsourcing datasets has been found to be helpful for many tasks in natural language processing. Germann (2001) showed that humans could perform surprisingly well with very poor translations obtained from non-expert translators, in part likely because coarse-level translational adequacy is sufficient for the tasks they evaluated. That work was also pitched as a rapid resource acquisition task, meant to test our ability to quickly build systems in emergency settings. This work further demonstrates the ability to quickly acquire training data for MT systems with

[5] `code.google.com/p/berkeleyaligner/`

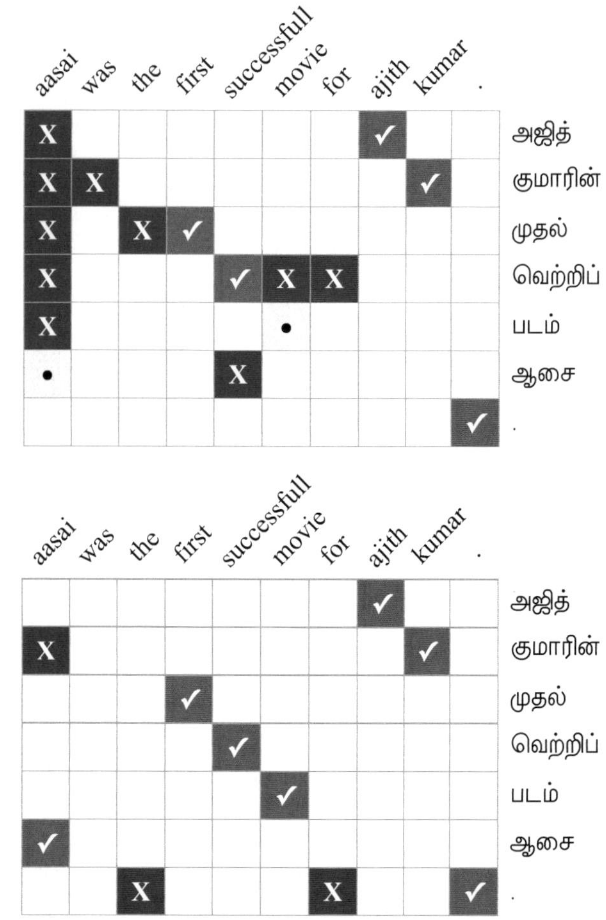

Figure 6: A bad Tamil alignment produced with the *grow-diag-and* alignment combination heuristic (top); the Berkeley aligner is better (bottom). A ✓ is a correct guess, an X marks a false positive, and a • denotes a false negative. Hiero's extraction heuristics yield 4 rules for the top alignment and 16 for the bottom.

reasonable translation accuracy.

Closely related to our work here is that of Novotney and Callison-Burch (2010), who showed that transcriptions for training speech recognition systems could be obtained from Mechanical Turk with near baseline recognition performance and at a significantly lower cost. They also showed that redundant annotation was not worthwhile, and suggested that money was better spent obtaining more data. Separately, Ambati and Vogel (2010) probed the MTurk worker pool for workers capable of translating a number of low-resource languages, including Hindi, Telugu, and Urdu, demonstrating that such workers could be found and quantifying acceptable wages and collection rates.

pair	grammar size GIZA++	Berkeley	BLEU	gain
Bengali	15m	27m	13.54	**+0.82**
Hindi	34m	60m	16.47	+0.94
Malayalam	12m	27m	12.70	-1.02
Tamil	19m	30m	10.10	**+0.29**
Telugu	28m	46m	13.36	**+0.90**
Urdu	38m	58m	20.41	**+0.88**

Table 9: Hiero translation results using Berkeley alignments instead of GIZA++ heuristics. The *gain* columns denotes improvements relative to the Hiero systems in Table 5. In many cases (**bold** gains), the BLEU scores are at or above even the SAMT models from that table.

The techniques described here are similar to those described in Zaidan and Callison-Burch (2011), who showed that crowdsourcing with appropriate quality controls could be used to produce professional-level translations for Urdu-English translation. This paper extends that work by applying their techniques to a larger set of Indian languages and scaling it to training-data-set sizes.

7 Summary

We have described the collection of six parallel corpora containing four-way redundant translations of the source-language text. The Indian languages of these corpora are low-resource and understudied, and exhibit markedly different linguistic properties compared to English. We performed baseline experiments quantifying the translation performance of a number of systems, investigated the effect of data quality on model quality, and suggested a number of approaches that could improve the quality of models constructed from the datasets. The parallel corpora provide a suite of SOV languages for translation research and experiments.

Acknowledgments We thank Lexi Birch for discussions about strategies for selecting and assembling the data sets. This research was supported in part by gifts from Google and Microsoft, the EuroMatrixPlus project funded by the European Commission (7th Framework Programme), and a DARPA grant entitled "Crowdsourcing Translation". The views in this paper are the authors' alone.

References

Vamshi Ambati and Stephan Vogel. 2010. Can crowds build parallel corpora for machine translation systems? In *Proceedings of the NAACL HLT 2010 Workshop on Creating Speech and Language Data with Amazon's Mechanical Turk*, Los Angeles, California.

David Chiang. 2007. Hierarchical phrase-based translation. *Computational Linguistics*, 33(2):201–228.

Jonathan H. Clark, Chris Dyer, Alon Lavie, and Noah A. Smith. 2011. Better hypothesis testing for statistical machine translation: Controlling for optimizer instability. In *ACL*, pages 176–181. Association for Computational Linguistics.

Michel Galley, Mark Hopkins, Kevin Knight, and Daniel Marcu. 2004. What's in a translation rule? In *Proc. NAACL*, Boston, Massachusetts, USA, May.

Michel Galley, Jonathan Graehl, Kevin Knight, Daniel Marcu, Steve DeNeefe, Wei Wang, and Ignacio Thayer. 2006. Scalable inference and training of context-rich syntactic translation models. In *Proc. ACL*, Sydney, Australia, July.

Ulrich Germann. 2001. Building a statistical machine translation system from scratch: how much bang for the buck can we expect? In *ACL workshop on Data-driven methods in machine translation*, Toulouse, France, July. Association for Computational Linguistics.

Philipp Koehn, Franz Josef Och, and Daniel Marcu. 2003. Statistical phrase-based translation. In *Proc. NAACL*, Edmonton, Alberta, Canada, May–June.

Philipp Koehn, Hieu Hoang, Alexandra Birch, Chris Callison-Burch, Marcello Federico, Nicola Bertoldi, Brooke Cowan, Wade Shen, Christine Moran, Richard Zens, Chris Dyer, Ondřej Bojar, Alexandra Constantin, and Evan Herbst. 2007. Moses: Open source toolkit for statistical machine translation. In *Proceedings of the Annual Meeting of the ACL on Interactive Poster and Demonstration Sessions*, Prague, Czech Republic, June.

Philipp Koehn. 2005. Europarl: A parallel corpus for statistical machine translation. In *Machine translation summit*.

Shankar Kumar and William Byrne. 2004. Minimum bayes-risk decoding for statistical machine translation. In *Proc. NAACL*, Boston, Massachusetts, USA, May.

M. Paul Lewis, editor. 2009. *Ethnologue: Languages of the World*. SIL International, Dallas, TX, USA, sixteenth edition.

Percy Liang, Ben Taskar, and Dan Klein. 2006. Alignment by agreement. In *HLT-NAACL*, pages 104–111. Association for Computational Linguistics.

Scott Novotney and Chris Callison-Burch. 2010. Cheap, fast and good enough: Automatic speech recognition with non-expert transcription. In *Proc. NAACL*, Los Angeles, California, June.

Franz Josef Och. 2003. Minimum error rate training in statistical machine translation. In *Proc. ACL*, Sapporo, Japan, July.

Jonathan Weese, Juri Ganitkevitch, Chris Callison-Burch, Matt Post, and Adam Lopez. 2011. Joshua 3.0: Syntax-based machine translation with the thrax grammar extractor. In *Proceedings of the Sixth Workshop on Statistical Machine Translation*.

Omar F. Zaidan and Chris Callison-Burch. 2011. Crowdsourcing translation: professional quality from non-professionals. In *Proc. ACL*, Portland, Oregon, USA, June.

Omar F. Zaidan. 2009. Z-MERT: A fully configurable open source tool for minimum error rate training of machine translation systems. *The Prague Bulletin of Mathematical Linguistics*, 91:79–88.

Rabih Zbib, Erika Malchiodi, Jacob Devlin, David Stallard, Spyros Matsoukas, Richard Schwartz, John Makhoul, Omar F. Zaidan, and Chris Callison-Burch. 2012. Machine translation of arabic dialects. In *Proc. NAACL*, Montreal, June.

Andreas Zollmann and Ashish Venugopal. 2006. Syntax augmented machine translation via chart parsing. In *Proceedings of the Workshop on Statistical Machine Translation*, New York, New York, USA, June.

Twitter Translation using Translation-Based Cross-Lingual Retrieval

Laura Jehl and **Felix Hieber** and **Stefan Riezler**
Department of Computational Linguistics
Heidelberg University
69120 Heidelberg, Germany
{jehl,hieber,riezler}@cl.uni-heidelberg.de

Abstract

Microblogging services such as Twitter have become popular media for real-time user-created news reporting. Such communication often happens in parallel in different languages, e.g., microblog posts related to the same events of the Arab spring were written in Arabic and in English. The goal of this paper is to exploit this parallelism in order to eliminate the main bottleneck in automatic Twitter translation, namely the lack of bilingual sentence pairs for training SMT systems. We show that translation-based cross-lingual information retrieval can retrieve microblog messages across languages that are similar enough to be used to train a standard phrase-based SMT pipeline. Our method outperforms other approaches to domain adaptation for SMT such as language model adaptation, meta-parameter tuning, or self-translation.

1 Introduction

Among the various social media platforms, microblogging services such as Twitter[1] have become popular communication tools. This is due to the easy accessibility of microblogging platforms via internet or mobile phones, and due to the need for a fast mode of communication that microblogging satisfies: Twitter messages are short (limited to 140 characters) and simultaneous (due to frequent updates by prolific microbloggers). Twitter users form a social network by "following" the updates of other users, either reciprocal or one-way. The topics discussed in Twitter messages range from private chatter to important real-time witness reports.

Events such as the Arab spring have shown the power and also the shortcomings of this new mode of communication. Microblogging services played a crucial role in quickly spreading the news about important events, furthermore they were useful in helping organizers plan their protest. The fact that news on microblogging platforms is sometimes ahead of newswire is one of the most interesting facets of this new medium. However, while Twitter messaging is happening in multiple languages, most networks of "friends" and "followers" are monolingual and only about 40% of all messages are in English[2]. One solution to sharing news quickly and internationally was crowdsourcing manual translations, for example at Meedan[3], a nonprofit organization built to share news and opinion between the Arabic and English speaking world, by translating articles and blogs, using machine translation and human expert corrections.

The goal of our research is to automate this translation process, with a further aim of providing rapid crosslingual data access for downstream applications. The automated translation of microblogging messages is facing two main problems. First, there are no bilingual sentence pair data from microblogging domains available. Second, the colloquial, non-standard language of many microblogging messages makes it very difficult to adapt a machine translation system trained on any of the available bilingual resources such as transcriptions from political organizations or news text.

The approach presented in this paper aims to exploit the fact that microblogging often happens in

[1] http://twitter.com/

[2] http://semiocast.com/publications/2011_11_24_Arabic_highest_growth_on_Twitter

[3] http://news.meedan.net

parallel in different languages, e.g., microblog posts related to the same events of the Arab spring were published in parallel in Arabic and in English. The central idea is to crawl a large set of topically related Arabic and English microblogging messages, and use Arabic microblog messages as search queries in a cross-lingual information retrieval (CLIR) setup. We use the probabilistic translation-based retrieval technique of Xu et al. (2001) that naturally integrates translation tables for cross-lingual retrieval. The retrieval results are then used as input to a standard SMT pipeline to train translation models, starting from unsupervised induction of word alignments (Och and Ney, 2000) to phrase-extraction (Och and Ney, 2004) and phrase-based decoding (Koehn et al., 2007). We investigate several filtering techniques for retrieval and phrase extraction (Munteanu and Marcu, 2006; Snover et al., 2008) and find a straightforward application of phrase extraction from symmetrized alignments to be optimal. Furthermore, we compare our approach to related domain adaptation techniques for SMT and find our approach to yield large improvements over all related techniques.

Finally, a side-product of our research is a corpus of around 1,000 Arabic Twitter messages with 3 manual English translations each, which were created using crowdsourcing techniques. This corpus is used for development and testing in our experiments.

2 Related Work

SMT for user-generated noisy data has been pioneered at the 2011 Workshop on Statistical Machine Translation that featured a translation task of Haitian Creole emergency SMS messages[4]. This task is very similar to the problem of Twitter translation since SMS contain noisy, abbreviated language. The research papers related to the featured translation task deploy several approaches to domain adaptation, including crowdsourcing (Hu et al., 2011) or extraction of parallel sentences from comparable data (Hewavitharana et al., 2011).

The use of crowdsourcing to evaluate machine translation and to build development sets was pioneered by Callison-Burch (2009) and Zaidan and Callison-Burch (2009). Crowdsourcing has its limits when it comes to generating parallel training data on the scale of millions of parallel sentences. In our work, we use crowdsourcing via Amazon Mechanical Turk[5] to create a development and test corpus that includes 3 English translations for each of around 1,000 Arabic microblog messages.

There is a substantial amount of previous work on extracting parallel sentences from comparable data such as newswire text (Fung and Cheung, 2004; Munteanu and Marcu, 2005; Tillmann and ming Xu, 2009) and on finding parallel phrases in non-parallel sentences (Munteanu and Marcu, 2006; Quirk et al., 2007; Cettolo et al., 2010; Vogel and Hewavitharana, 2011). The approach that is closest to our work is that of Munteanu and Marcu (2006): They use standard information retrieval together with simple word-based translation for CLIR, and extract phrases from the retrieval results using a clean bilingual lexicon and an averaging filter. In this approach, filtering and cleaning techniques in alignment and phrase extraction have to compensate for low-quality retrieval results. In our approach, the focus is on high-quality retrieval.

As our experimental results show, the main improvement of our technique is a decrease in out-of-vocabulary (OOV) rate at an increase of the percentage of correctly translated unigrams and bigrams. Similar work on solving domain adaptation for SMT by mining unseen words has been presented by Snover et al. (2008) and Daumé and Jagarlamudi (2011). Both approaches show improvements by adding new phrase tables; however, both approaches rely on techniques that require larger comparable texts for mining unseen words. Since in our case documents are very short (they consist of 140 character sequences), these techniques are not applicable. However, the advantage of the fact that microblog messages resemble sentences is that we can apply standard word- and phrase-alignment techniques directly to the retrieval results.

Further approaches to domain adaptation for SMT include adaptation using in-domain language models (Bertoldi and Federico, 2009), meta-parameter tuning on in-domain development sets (Koehn and Schroeder, 2007), or translation model adaptation

[4] `http://www.statmt.org/wmt11/featured-translation-task.html`

[5] `http://www.turk.com`

using self-translations of in-domain source language texts (Ueffing et al., 2007). In our experiments we compare our approach to these domain adaptation techniques.

3 Cross-Lingual Retrieval via Statistical Translation

3.1 Retrieval Model

In our approach, comparable candidates for domain adaptation are selected via cross-lingual retrieval. In a probabilistic retrieval framework, we estimate the probability of a relevant document microblog message D given a query microblog message Q, $P(D|Q)$. Following Bayes rule, this can be simplified to ranking documents according to the likelihood $P(Q|D)$ if we assume a uniform prior over documents.

$$score(Q, D) = P(D|Q) = \frac{P(D)P(Q|D)}{P(Q)} \quad (1)$$

Our model is defined as follows:

$$score(Q, D) = P(Q|D) = \prod_{q \in Q} P(q|D) \quad (2)$$

$$P(q|D) = \lambda \underbrace{P_{mix}(q|D)}_{\text{mixture model}} + (1 - \lambda) \underbrace{P_{ML}(q|C)}_{\text{query collection backoff}} \quad (3)$$

$$P_{mix}(q|D) = \underbrace{\beta \sum_{d \in D} T(q|d) P_{ML}(d|D)}_{\text{translation model}} + (1 - \beta) \underbrace{P_{ML}(q|D)}_{\text{self-translation}} \quad (4)$$

Our retrieval model is related to monolingual retrieval models such as the language-modeling approach of Ponte and Croft (1998) and the monolingual statistical translation approach of Berger and Lafferty (1999). Xu et al. (2001) extend the former approaches to the cross-lingual setting by adding a term translation table. They describe their model in terms of a Hidden Markov Model with two states that generate query terms: First, a *document state* generates terms d in the document language and then translates them into a query term q. Second, a *backoff state* generates query terms q directly in the query language. In the *document state* the probability of emitting q depends on all d that translate to q, according to a translation distribution T. This is estimated by marginalizing out d as $\sum_d T(q|d)P(d|D)$. In the *backoff state* the probability $P_{ML}(q|C)$ of emitting a query term is estimated as the relative frequency of this term within a corpus in the query language. The probability of transitioning into the document state or the backoff state is given by λ and $1 - \lambda$.

We view this model from a smoothing perspective where the backoff state is linearly interpolated with the translation probability using a mixture weight λ to control the weighting between both terms. Furthermore, we expand Xu et al. (2001)'s generative model to incorporate the concept of "self-translation", introduced by Xue et al. (2008) in a monolingual question-answering context: Twitter messages across languages usually share relevant terms such as hashtags, named entities or user mentions. Therefore, we model the event of a query term literally occurring in the document in a separate model that is itself linearly interpolated with a parameter β with the translation model.

We implemented the model based on a Lucene[6] index, which allows efficient storage of term-document and document-term vectors. To minimize retrieval time, we consider only those documents as retrieval candidates where at least one term translates to a query term, according to the translation table T. Stopwords were removed for both queries and documents. Compared to common inverted index retrieval implementations, our model is quite slow since the document-term vectors have to be loaded. However, multi-threading support and batch retrieval on a Hadoop cluster made the model tractable. On the upside, the translation-based model allows greater precision in finding the candidates for comparable microblog messages than simpler approaches that use a combination of *tfidf* matching and n-best query term expansion: The translation-based retrieval exploits all possible alignments between query and document terms which is particularly important for short documents such as microblog messages.

3.2 In-Domain Phrase Extraction

To prepare the extraction of phrases from retrieval results, we conducted cross-lingual retrieval in both directions: retrieving Arabic documents using English microblog messages as queries and vice versa.

[6] http://lucene.apache.org/core/

For each run we kept the top N retrieved documents. Each document was then paired with its query to generate pseudo-parallel data.

We tried two approaches for using this data to improve our translations. The first, more restrictive method makes use of the word alignments we obtained from 5.8 million clean parallel training data from the NIST evaluation campaign. The retrieval step generates word-alignments in the direction $D \rightarrow Q$. After retrieval, the reverse alignment for each query-document pair is also generated by using a translation table in the direction $Q \rightarrow D$. An alignment point between a query term q and a document term d is created, iff $T(q|d)$ or $T(d|q)$ exist in the translation tables $D \rightarrow Q$ or $Q \rightarrow D$. Based on these word-alignments, we extract phrases by applying the *grow-diag-final-and* heuristic and using Och and Ney (2004)'s phrase extraction algorithm as implemented in Moses[7] (Koehn et al., 2007). We conducted experiments using different constraints on the number of alignment points required for a pair to be considered as well as the value of N. Our first technique resembles the technique of Munteanu and Marcu (2006) who also perform phrase extraction by combining clean alignment lexica for initial signals with heuristics to smooth alignments for final fragment extraction.

While we obtained some gains using our heuristics, we are aware that our method is severely restricted in that it only learns new words which are in the vicinity of known words. We therefore also tried the bolder approach of treating our data as parallel and running unsupervised word alignment[8] (Och and Ney, 2000) directly on the query-document pairs to obtain new world alignments and build a phrase table. In contrast to previous work (Snover et al., 2008; Daumé and Jagarlamudi, 2011), we can take advantage of the sentence-like character of microblog messages and treat queries and retrieval results similar to sentence aligned data.

For both extraction methods, the standard five translation features from the new phrase table (phrase translation probability and lexical weighting in both directions, phrase penalty) were added to the translation features in Moses. We tried different modes of combining new and original phrase table, namely using either one or using the new phrase table as backoff in case no phrase translation is found in the original phrase table.

[7]http://statmt.org/moses/

[8]http://code.google.com/p/giza-pp/

al-Gaddafi, al-Qaddhafi, assad, babrain, bahrain, egypt, gadaffi, gaddaffi, gaddafi, Gheddafi, homs, human rights, human-rights, humanrights, libia, libian, libya, libyan, lybia, lybian, lybya, lybyan, manama, Misrata, nabeelrajab, nato, oman, PositiveLibyaTweets, Qaddhafi, sirte, syria, tripoli, tripolis, yemen;

Table 1: Keywords used for Twitter crawl.

4 Data

4.1 Twitter Crawl

We crawled Twitter messages from September 20, 2011 until January 23, 2012 via the Streaming API[9] in keyword-tracking mode, obtaining 25.5M Twitter messages (*tweets*) in various languages. Table 1 shows the list of keywords that were chosen to retrieve microblog messages related to the events of the Arab spring.[10]

In order to separate the microblog message corpus by languages, we applied a Naive Bayes language identifier[11]. This yielded a distribution with the six most common languages (of 52) being Arabic (57%), English (33%), Somali (2%), Spanish (2%), Indonesian (1.5%), German (0.7%). We kept only microblog messages classified as English or Arabic with confidence greater 0.9. Keyword-based crawling creates a strong bias towards the domain of the keywords and it does not guarantee that all microblog messages regarding a certain topic or region are retrieved or that all retrieved messages are related to the Arab Spring and human righs in the middle east. Additionally, retweets artificially in-

[9]https://dev.twitter.com/docs/streaming-api/

[10]The Twitter Streaming API allows up to 400 tracking keywords that are matched to uppercase, lowercase and quoted variations of the keywords. Partial matching such as "tripolis" matching "tripoli" as well as Arabic Unicode characters are not supported. We extended our keywords over time by analyzing the crawl, e.g., by introducing spelling variants and hashtags.

[11]Language Detection Library for Java, by Shuyo Nakatani (http://code.google.com/p/language-detection/).

	Arabic	English
tweets + retweets	14,565,513	8,501,788
tweets	6,614,126	5,129,829
avg. retweet/tweet	11.62	7.27
unique users	180,271	865,202
avg. tweets/user	36.6	5.9

Table 2: Twitter corpus statistics

flate the size of the data, although there are no new terms added. Therefore, we removed all duplicate retweets that did not introduce additional terms to the original tweet. Table 2 explains the shrinkage of the dataset after removing retweets - compared to English users, a smaller number of Arabic users produced a much larger number of retweets. Interestingly, 56,087 users tweet a substantial amount in both languages. This suggests that users spread messages simultaneously in Arabic and English.

4.2 Creating a Small Parallel Twitter Corpus using Crowdsourcing

For the evaluation of our method, a small amount of parallel in-domain data was required. Since there are no corpora of translated microblog messages, we decided to use Amazon Mechanical Turk[12] to create our own evaluation set, following the exploratory work of Zaidan and Callison-Burch (2011b). We randomly selected 2,000 Arabic microblog messages. Hashtags, user mentions and URLs were removed from each microblog message beforehand, because they do not need to be translated and would just artificially inflate scores at test time. The microblog messages were then manually cleaned and pruned. We discarded messages which contained almost no text or large portions of other languages and removed remaining Twitter markup. In the end, 1,022 microblog messages were used in the Mechanical Turk task. We split the data into batches of ten sentences which comprised one HIT (human intelligence task). Each HIT had to be completed by three workers. In order to have some control over translation quality, we inserted one control sentence per HIT, taken from the LDC-GALE Phase 1 Arabic Blog Parallel Text. Turkers were rewarded 10 cents per translation. Following Zaidan and Callison-Burch (2011b), all Arabic sentences were converted into images in order to prevent turkers from pasting them into online machine translation engines. Our final corpus consists of 1,022 translated microblog messages with three translations each. An example containing translations for one of the sentences which we inserted for quality checking purposes, along with the reference translation, is given in table 3. It can be seen that translators sometimes made grammar mistakes or odd word choices. They also tended to omit punctuation marks. However, translations also contained reasonable translation alternatives (such as "gathered" or "collected"). We also asked translators to insert an "unknown" token whenever they were unable to translate a word. Our HIT setup did not allow workers to skip a sentence, forcing them to complete an entire batch. In order to account for translation variants we decided to use all three translations obtained via Mechanical Turk as multiple references instead of just keeping the top translation. We randomly split our small parallel corpus, using half of the microblog messages for development and half for testing.

4.3 Preprocessing

Besides removal of Twitter markup, several additional preprocessing steps such as digit normalization were applied to the data. We also decided to apply the Buckwalter Arabic transliteration scheme[13] to avoid encoding difficulties. Habash and Sadat (2006) have shown that tokenization is helpful for translating Arabic. We therefore decided to apply a more involved tokenization scheme than simple whitespace splitting to our data. As the retrieval relies on translation tables, all data need to be tokenized the same way. We are aware of the MADA+TOKAN Arabic morphological analyzer and tokenizer (Habash and Rambow, 2005), however, this toolkit produces very in-depth analyses of the data and thus led to difficulties when we tried to scale it to millions of sentences/microblog messages. That is why we only used MADA for transliteration and chose to implement the simpler approach by Lee et al. (2003) for tokenization. This approach only requires a small set of annotated data to obtain a list of prefixes and suffixes and uses n-

[12]http://www.turk.com

[13]http://www.qamus.org/transliteration.htm

REFERENCE	breaking the silence, a campaign group made up of israeli soldiers, gathered anonymous accounts from 26 soldiers.
TRANSLATION1	and breaking silence is a group of israeli soldiers that had unknown statistics from 26 soldiers israeli
TRANSLATION2	breaking the silence by a group of israeli soldiers who gathered unidentified statistics from 26 israeli soldier.
TRANSLATION3	breaking the silence is a group of israeli soldiers that collected unknown statistics of 26 israeli soldiers

Table 3: Example turker translations.

gram-models to determine the most likely *prefix*-stem-suffix** split of a word.[14]

5 Twitter Translation Experiments

We conducted a series of experiments to evaluate our strategy of using CLIR and phrase-extraction to extract comparable data in the Twitter domain. We also explored more standard ways of domain adaptation such as using English microblog messages to build an in-domain language model, or generating synthetic bilingual corpora from monolingual data.

All experiments were conducted using the Moses machine translation system[15] (Koehn et al., 2007) with standard settings. Language models were built using the SRILM toolkit[16] (Stolcke, 2002). For all experiments, we report lowercased BLEU-4 scores (Papineni et al., 2001) as calculated by Moses' `multi-bleu` script. For assessing significance, we apply the approximate randomization test (Noreen, 1989; Riezler and Maxwell, 2005). We consider pairwise differing results scoring a p-value < 0.05 as significant.

Our baseline model was trained using 5,823,363 million parallel sentences in Modern Standard Arabic (MSA) (198,500,436 tokens) and English (193,671,201 tokens) from the NIST evaluation campaign. This data contains parallel text from different domains, including UN reports, newsgroups, newswire, broadcast news and weblogs.

5.1 Domain Adaption using Monolingual Resources

As a first step, we used the available in-domain data for a combination of domain adaptation techniques similar to Bertoldi and Federico (2009). There were three different adaptation measures: First, the turker-generated development set was used for optimizing the weights of the decoding meta-parameters, as introduced by Koehn and Schroeder (2007). Second, the English microblog messages in our crawl were used to build an in-domain language model. This adaptation technique was first proposed by Zhao et al. (2004). Third, the Arabic portion of our crawl was used to synthetically generate additional parallel training data. This was accomplished by machine-translating the Arabic microblog messages with the best system after performing the first two adaptation steps. Since decoding is very time-intensive, only 1 million randomly selected Arabic microblog messages were used to generate synthetic parallel data. This new data was then used to train another phrase table. Such self-translation techniques have been introduced by Ueffing et al. (2007). All results were evaluated against a baseline of using only NIST data for translation model, language model and weight optimization.

Our results are shown in table 4. Using an in-domain development set while leaving everything else untouched led to an improvement of approximately 1 BLEU point. Three experiments involving the Twitter language model confirm Bertoldi and Federico (2009)'s findings that the language model was most helpful. The BLEU-score could be improved by 1.5 to 2 points in all experiments. When using an in-domain language model, there was no significant difference between deploying an in-domain or out-of-domain development set. We also compared the effect of using only the in-domain language model to that of adding the in-domain language model as an extra feature while keeping the NIST language model.[17] There was no signif-

[14]The n-gram-model required for tokenization was trained on 5.8 million Modern Standard Arabic sentences from the NIST evaluation campaign. This data had previously been tokenized with the same method, trained to match the Penn Arabic Treebank, v3.

[15]`http://statmt.org/moses/`

[16]`http://www.speech.sri.com/projects/srilm/`

[17]The weights for both language models were optimized along with all other translation feature weights, rather than running an extra optimization step to interpolate between both language models, since Koehn and Schroeder (2007) showed that

Run	Translation Model	Language Model	Dev Set	BLEU %
1	NIST	NIST	NIST	13.90
2	NIST	NIST	Twitter	14.83*
3	NIST	Twitter	NIST	15.98*
4	NIST	Twitter	Twitter	15.68*
5	NIST	Twitter & NIST	Twitter	16.04*
6	self-train	Twitter & NIST	Twitter	15.79*
7	self-train & NIST	Twitter & NIST	Twitter	15.94*

Table 4: Domain adaptation experiments. Asterisks indicate significant improvements over baseline (1).

Run	Twitter Phrases	extraction method	# sentence pairs	# extracted phrases	BLEU %
8	top 3 retrieval results	heuristics	14,855,985	6,508,141	17.04*
9	top 1 retrieval results	GIZA++	5,141,065	54,260,537	18.73**
10	retrieval intersection	GIZA++	3,452,566	29,091,009	18.85**
11	retrieval intersection as backoff	GIZA++	3,452,566	29,091,009	18.93**

Table 5: CLIR domain adaptation experiments. All weights were optimized on the Twitter dev set and used the Twitter and NIST language models. One Asterisk indicates a significant improvement over baseline run (5) from table 4. Two Asterisks indicate a significant improvement over run (8).

icant difference between both runs. However, for further adaptation experiments we used the system with the highest absolute BLEU score. In our case, using synthetically generated data was not helpful, yielding similar results as the language model experiments above. As has been observed before by Bertoldi and Federico (2009), it did not matter whether the synthetic data were used on their own or in addition to the original training data.

5.2 Domain Adaptation using Translation-based CLIR

Meta-parameters $\lambda, \beta \in [0, 1]$ of the retrieval model were tuned in a mate-finding experiment: Mate-finding refers to the task of retrieving the single relevant document for a query. In our case, each source tweet in the crowdsourced development set had exactly one "mate", namely the crowdsourced translation that was ranked best in a further crowdsourced ranking task. Using the retrieval model described in section 3 we achieved precision@1 scores above 95% in finding the translations of a tweet when λ and β were set to 0.9. We fixed these parameter settings for all following experiments. The translation table was taken from the baseline experiments in table 4. During retrieval, we kept up to 10 highest scoring documents per query.

both strategies yielded the same results.

We first employed heuristic phrase extraction based on the word alignments generated from the NIST data as described above. To avoid learning too much noise, maximum phrase length was restricted to 3 (the default is 7). To evaluate the effects of choosing more restrictive or more lax settings, we ran experiments varying the following configurations:

1. Constraints on alignment points:
   - no constraints,
   - 3+ alignment points in each direction,
   - 3+ alignment points in both directions,
   - 5+ alignment points in both directions.
2. Constraints on retrieval ranking:
   - top 10 results,
   - top 3 results,
   - top 1 results,
   - retrieval intersection (results found in both retrieval directions)

We obtained improvements for all combinations of these configurations. However, we observed that requiring 5 common alignment points was too strict, since few pairs met this constraint. We also noticed that using only the top 3 retrieval results was beneficial to performance, suggesting that more comparable microblog messages were indeed ranked higher.

Using extraction heuristics we gained maximally 1.0 BLEU using the top 3 retrieval results and requiring at least 3 alignment points in both alignment directions (see first line in table 5). However, other configurations produced very similar results.

While heuristics led to small incremental improvements, we achieved a much larger improvement by training a new phrase table from scratch using GIZA++. Again, we restricted maximum phrase length to 3 words. In order to keep phrase table size manageable, we had to restrict retrieval to top-1 results or only use retrieval results in the intersection of retrieval directions. Best results are obtained when combining phrase tables extracted from GIZA++ alignments in the intersection of retrieval results with NIST phrase tables in backoff mode (see last line in table 5).

6 Error Analysis

Our cross-lingual retrieval approach succeeded in finding nearly parallel tweets, confirming our hypothesis that such data actually exists. Examples are given in table 6.

Table 7 shows a more detailed breakdown of our translation scores. First, standard adaptation methods increased n-gram precision, suggesting that using in-domain adaptation data caused the system to choose more suitable words. As expected, there was no reduction in OOVs, since using an in-domain language model and development set does not introduce new vocabulary. Heuristic phrase extraction again produced small improvements in n-gram precision while reducing the number of unknown words. Learning a new phrase table with GIZA++ produced substantial improvements both in OOV-rate and in n-gram precision.

Nevertheless, even the scores of the adapted system are still fairly low and translation quality as judged by inspection of the output can be very poor. This suggests that the language used on Twitter still poses a great challenge, due to its variety of styles as well as the users' tendency to use non-standard spelling and colloquial or dialectal expressions. Our development set contained many different genres, from Qu'ran verses over news headlines to personal chatter. Another difficulty was posed by dialectal Arabic content. To gain an impression of the amount of dialectal content in our data, we used the Arabic Online Commentary Dataset created by Zaidan and Callison-Burch (2011a) to classify our test set. Table 8 shows the distribution of dialects in our test data according to language model probability. This distribution should be viewed with a grain of salt, since the shortness of tweets might cause unreliable results when using a model based on word frequencies for classification. Still, the results suggest that there is a high proportion of dialectal content and spelling variation in our data, causing a large number of OOVs. For example, the preposition في, meaning "in" is often written as فى. Our phrase table trained only on standard Arabic data as well as our extraction heuristic failed to translate this frequently occurring word. Only when retraining a phrase table with GIZA++ did we translate it correctly.

Dialect	# Sentences
Egyptian	141
Levantine	147
Gulf	78
Modern Standard Arabic	145

Table 8: Dialectal content in our test set as classified by the AOC dataset.

Table 9 gives examples of translations generated using different adaptation methods in comparison to the references and the Google translation service to illustrate strengths and weaknesses of our approach. *Example 1* shows a case where unknown words were learned through translation model adaptation. Note that even the Google translator did not recognize the word مسيلات which was transliterated as "Msellat". Zaidan and Callison-Burch (2011a) point out that dialectal variants are often transliterated by Google. Note also, that the unadapted translation erroneously translated the place name "sitra" as "jacket", a mistake which was also made in two of the references and by Google. The same happened to the place name "wadyan", which could also be taken as meaning "and religions". This error was enforced by our preprocessing step incorrectly splitting off the prefix "w" which often carries the meaning "and". In addition to that, the two runs which used translation model adaptation each dropped a part of the input sentence ("in sitra", "firing"). We

ARABIC TWEET	ا ف ب الرئيس الفرنسي يؤكد ان القذافي سيحاكم ويدعوا الليبيين الى الصفح
GOOGLE TRANSLATION	*AFP confirms that the French President Gaddafi Libyans tried to call and forgiveness*
ENGLISH TWEET	french president assures that will be taken to court and tells the libyans to forgive each other
ARABIC TWEET	جهاز تنظيم الاتصالات يقرر زيادة رقم جميع شركات المحمول فى مصر دء ا من الخميس
GOOGLE TRANSLATION	*NTRA decide to increase the number of all mobile operators in Egypt a commencement from Thursday*
ENGLISH TWEET	ntra decide to increase the number of all mobile operators in starting from thursday
ARABIC TWEET	الشهيد امين على احمد يوم يناير عن طريق طلق ناري
GOOGLE TRANSLATION	*Shahid Amin AA Day January through gunshot*
ENGLISH TWEET	martyr amin ali ahmed on jan by gunshot

Table 6: Examples of nearly parallel tweets found by our retrieval method.

Adaptation method	OOV-rate %/absolute	unigram precision %/absolute	bigram precision %/absolute	output length (words)
None	22.56/2216	51.1/5020	20.2/1882	9832
LM and Dev	20.05/2220	51.4/5442	22.1/2227	10595
Retrieval (heuristic)	17.47/1790	53.5/5484	23.6/2299	10246
Retrieval (GIZA++)	4.22/439	56.1/5834	26.1/2575	10395

Table 7: OOV-rate and precision for different adaptation methods.

attribute this to that fact that the phrase table extraction often produced one-to-many alignments when only one alignment point was known. In *Example 2* GIZA++ extraction clearly outperformed heuristic phrase extraction. This example also shows that our method is good at learning proper names. While the first two examples resemble news text, *Example 3* is a more informal message. It is particularly interesting to note that with GIZA++ extraction the term "shabiha" is learned, which is commonly used in Syria to mean "thugs" and specifically refers to armed civilians who assault protesters against Bashir Al-Assad's regime. *Example 4* also shows substantial OOV reduction. However, the term بسنترال الأوبرا ("in Opera Central", the location of Telecom Egypt) is incorrectly translated as "really opera".

7 Conclusion

We presented an approach to translation of microblog messages from the Twitter domain. The main obstacle to state-of-the-art SMT of such data is the complete lack of sentence-parallel training data. We presented a technique that uses translation-based CLIR to find relevant Arabic Twitter messages given English Twitter queries, and applies a standard pipeline for unsupervised training of phrase-based SMT to retrieval results. We found this straightforward technique to outperform more conservative techniques to extract phrases from comparable data and also to outperform techniques using monolingual resources for language model adaptation, meta-parameter tuning, or self-translation.

The greatest benefit of our approach is a significant reduction of OOV terms at a simultaneous improvement of correct unigram and bigram translations. Despite this positive net effect, we still find a considerable amount of noise in the automatically extracted phrase tables. Noise reduction by improved pre-processing and by more sophisticated training will be subject to future work. Furthermore, we would like to investigate a tighter integration of CLIR and SMT training by using forced decoding techniques for CLIR and by a integrating a feedback loop into retrieval and training.

Acknowledgments

We would like to thank Julia Ostertag for several iterations of manual error analysis of Arabic translation output.

	EXAMPLE 1
SRC	سترة قوات الشغب تقتحم واديان مترجلة وتطلق مسيلات الدموع
GOOGLE	*Riot troops stormed the jacket and religions foot and launches Msellat tears*
NO ADAPTATION	jacket riot forces storm and religions foot وتطلق مسيلات tears
LM AND DEV	sitra and religions of the foot of the riot forces storm وتطلق مسيلات tears
RETRIEVAL (HEURISTIC)	in sitra riot police storming and religions of tear gas on foot
RETRIEVAL (GIZA++)	the riot police stormed and religions of the foot firing tear gas
REF0	vest riot forces break into wadyan by foot and trough gas tear
REF1	sotra the riot forces enter on foot and shoot tear bombs
REF2	the cover for riot police enters wadian walking and shoot tear bombs
	EXAMPLE 2
SRC	أوباما سيتحدث اليوم عن مقتل العولقى
GOOGLE	*Obama will speak today the death of al-Awlaki*
NO ADAPTATION	أوباما سيتحدث today killed العولقى
LM AND DEV	أوباما سيتحدث friday for the killing of العولقى
RETRIEVAL (HEURISTIC)	أوباما today on the killing of
RETRIEVAL (GIZA++)	obama today on the al awlaki killing
REF0	obama will talk today about the killing of al - awlaki
REF1	obama is talking today about el awlaqi death
REF2	obama will speak today about the killing of al - awlaqi
	EXAMPLE 3
SRC	الشبيحة في حماة يستغيثون :)
GOOGLE	Cbihh in Hama are crying :)
NO ADAPTATION	الشبيحة mired in calling for help :)
LM AND DEV	الشبيحة in hama calling for help :)
RETRIEVAL (HEURISTIC)	inside the protectors of the calling for help :)
RETRIEVAL (GIZA++)	shabiha in hama calling for help :)
REF0	the gangsters in hama are asking for help
REF1	the gangs in hamah are peading :)
REF2	the thugs in hama are calling for help :)
	EXAMPLE 4
SRC	حـريـه :: عاملون بالمصرية للاتصالات يحتجزون رئيس الشركة فى غرفة بسنترال الأوبرا
GOOGLE	*Freedom :: Telecom Egypt workers holding company's president in a room Psontral Opera*
NO ADAPTATION	: : free workers بالمصرية للاتصالات holding company chairman فى بسنترال الأوبرا chamber
LM AND DEV	: : workers free بالمصرية للاتصالات holding company chairman بسنترال الأوبرافى room
RETRIEVAL (HEURISTIC)	free : : afcd بالمصرية hold ceo hostage ppl is the president of the chamber of بسنترال الأوبرا
RETRIEVAL (GIZA++)	egypt : : workers telecom workers are holding the head of the company in the chamber of really opera
REF0	freedom :: workers in the egyptian for communication are holding the company president in a room in the opera central
REF1	freedom , workers in egypt for calls detain the head of the company in a room in opera central
REF2	hurriya :: workers in telecom egypt detaining the president of the company in a room in the opera central

Table 9: Example output using different adaptation methods.

References

Adam Berger and John Lafferty. 1999. Information retrieval as statistical translation. In *Proceedings of the 22nd ACM SIGIR Conference on Research and Development in Information Retrieval (SIGIR'99)*, Berkeley, CA.

Nicola Bertoldi and Marcello Federico. 2009. Domain adaptation for statistical machine translation with monolingual resources. In *Proceedings of the 4th EACL Workshop on Statistical Machine Translation*, Athens, Greece.

Chris Callison-Burch. 2009. Fast, cheap, and creative: Evaluating translation quality using amazon's mechanical turk. In *Proceedings of the Conference on Empirical Methods in Natural Language Processing (EMNLP'09)*, Singapore.

M. Cettolo, M. Federico, and N. Bertoldi. 2010. Mining parallel fragments from comparable texts. In *Proceedings of the 7th International Workshop on Spoken*

Language Translation, Paris, France.

Hal Daumé and Jagadeesh Jagarlamudi. 2011. Domain adaptation for machine translation by mining unseen words. In *Proceedings of the 49th Annual Meeting of the Association for Computational Linguistics: Human Language Technologies (ACL-HLT'11)*, Portland, OR.

Pascale Fung and Percy Cheung. 2004. Mining very-non-parallel corpora: Parallel sentence and lexicon extraction via bootstrapping and EM. In *Proceedings of the 2004 Conference on Empirical Methods in Natural Language Processing (EMNLP'04)*, Barcelona, Spain.

Nizar Habash and Owen Rambow. 2005. Arabic tokenization, part-of-speech tagging and morphological disambiguation in one fell swoop. In *Proceedings of the 43rd Annual Meeting on Association for Computational Linguistics (ACL'05)*, Ann Arbor, MI.

Nizar Habash and Fatiha Sadat. 2006. Arabic preprocessing schemes for statistical machine translation. In *Proceedings of the Human Language Technology Conference - North American Chapter of the Association for Computational Linguistics annual meeting (HLT-NAACL'06)*, New York, NY.

Sanjika Hewavitharana, Nguyen Bach, Qin Gao, Vamshi Ambati, and Stephan Vogel. 2011. CMU haitian creole-english translation system for WMT 2011. In *Proceedings of the 6th Workshop on Statistical Machine Translation*, Edinburgh, Scotland, UK.

Chang Hu, Philip Resnik, Yakov Kronrod, Vladimir Eidelman, Olivia Buzek, and Benjamin B. Bederson. 2011. The value of monolingual crowdsourcing in a real-world translation scenario: Simulation using haitian creole emergency SMS messages. In *Proceedings of the 6th Workshop on Statistical Machine Translation*, Edinburgh, Scotland, UK.

Philipp Koehn and Josh Schroeder. 2007. Experiments in domain adaptation for statistical machine translation. In *Proceedings of the Second Workshop on Statistical Machine Translation*, Prague, Czech Republic.

Philipp Koehn, Hieu Hoang, Alexandra Birch, Chris Callison-Birch, Marcello Federico, Nicola Bertoldi, Brooke Cowan, Wade Shen, Christine Moran, Richard Zens, Chris Dyer, Ondrej Bojar, Alexandra Constantin, and Evan Herbst. 2007. Moses: Open source toolkit for statistical machine translation. In *Proceedings of the ACL 2007 Demo and Poster Sessions*, Prague, Czech Republic.

Young-Suk Lee, Kishore Papineni, Salim Roukos, Ossama Emam, and Hany Hassan. 2003. Language model based arabic word segmentation. In *Proceedings of the 41st Annual Meeting on Association for Computational Linguistics (ACL'03)*, Sapporo, Japan.

Dragos Stefan Munteanu and Daniel Marcu. 2005. Improving machine translation performance by exploiting non-parallel corpora. *Computational Linguistics*, 31(4):477–504.

Dragos Stefan Munteanu and Daniel Marcu. 2006. Extracting parallel sub-sentential fragments from non-parallel corpora. In *Proceedings of the 21st International Conference on Computational Linguistics and the 44th annual meeting of the Association for Computational Linguistics (COLING-ACL'06)*, Sydney, Australia.

Eric W. Noreen. 1989. *Computer Intensive Methods for Testing Hypotheses. An Introduction*. Wiley, New York.

Franz Josef Och and Hermann Ney. 2000. Improved statistical alignment models. In *Proceedings of the 38th Annual Meeting of the Association for Computational Linguistics (ACL'00)*, Hongkong, China.

Franz Josef Och and Hermann Ney. 2004. The alignment template approach to statistical machine translation. *Computational Linguistics*, 30(4):417–449.

Kishore Papineni, Salim Roukos, Todd Ward, and Wei-Jing Zhu. 2001. Bleu: a method for automatic evaluation of machine translation. Technical Report IBM Research Division Technical Report, RC22176 (W0190-022), Yorktown Heights, N.Y.

Jay M. Ponte and Bruce W. Croft. 1998. A language modeling approach to information retrieval. *Proceedings of the 21st annual international ACM SIGIR conference on Research and development in information retrieval (SIGIR'98)*.

Chris Quirk, Raghavendra Udupa U, and Arul Menezes. 2007. Generative models of noisy translations with applications to parallel fragment extraction. In *Proceedings of MT Summit XI*, Copenhagen , Denmark.

Stefan Riezler and John Maxwell. 2005. On some pitfalls in automatic evaluation and significance testing for MT. In *Proceedings of the ACL-05 Workshop on Intrinsic and Extrinsic Evaluation Measures for MT and/or Summarization*, Ann Arbor, MI.

Matthew Snover, Bonnie Dorr, and Richard Schwartz. 2008. Language and translation model adaptation using comparable corpora. In *Proceedings of the Conference on Empirical Methods in Natural Language Processing (EMNLP'08)*, Honolulu, Hawaii.

Andreas Stolcke. 2002. SRILM - an extensible language modeling toolkit. In *Proceedings of the International Conference on Spoken Language Processing*, Denver, CO.

Christoph Tillmann and Jian ming Xu. 2009. A simple sentence-level extraction algorithm for comparable data. In *Proceedings of Human Language Technologies: The 2009 Annual Conference of the North Ameri-*

can Chapter of the Association for Computational Linguistic (NAACL-HLT'09), Boulder, CO.

Nicola Ueffing, Gholamreza Haffari, and Anoop Sarkar. 2007. Transductive learning for statistical machine translation. In *Proceedings of the 45th Annual Meeting of the Association of Computational Linguistics (ACL'07)*, Prague, Czech Republic.

Stephan Vogel and Sanjika Hewavitharana. 2011. Extracting parallel phrases from comparable data. In *Proceedings of the 4th Workshop on Building and Using Comparable Corpora: Comparable Corpora and the Web*, Portland, OR.

Jinxi Xu, Ralph Weischedel, and Chanh Nguyen. 2001. Evaluating a probabilistic model for cross-lingual information retrieval. In *Proceedings of the 24th Annual International ACM SIGIR Conference on Research and Development in Information Retrieval (SIGIR'01)*, New York, NY.

Xiaobing Xue, Jiwoon Jeon, and Bruce Croft. 2008. Retrieval models for question and answer archives. In *Proceedings of the 31st Annual International ACM SIGIR Conference on Research and Development in Information Retrieval (SIGIR'08)*, Singapore.

Omar F. Zaidan and Chris Callison-Burch. 2009. Feasibility of human-in-the-loop minimum error rate training. In *Proceedings of the Conference on Empirical Methods in Natural Language Processing (EMNLP'09)*, Singapore.

Omar F. Zaidan and Chris Callison-Burch. 2011a. The arabic online commentary dataset: an annotated dataset of informal arabic with high dialectal content. In *Proceedings of the 49th Annual Meeting of the Association for Computational Linguistics (ACL'11)*, Portland, OR.

Omar F. Zaidan and Chris Callison-Burch. 2011b. Crowdsourcing translation: Professional quality from non-professionals. In *Proceedings of the 49th Annual Meeting of the Association for Computational Linguistics (ACL'11)*, Portland, OR.

Bing Zhao, Matthias Eck, and Stephan Vogel. 2004. Language model adaptation for statistical machine translation with structured query models. In *Proceedings of the 20th International Conference on Computational Linguistics (COLING'04)*, Geneva, Switzerland.

Analysing the Effect of Out-of-Domain Data on SMT Systems

Barry Haddow and Philipp Koehn
School of Informatics
University of Edinburgh
Edinburgh, EH8 9AB, Scotland
{bhaddow,pkoehn}@inf.ed.ac.uk

Abstract

In statistical machine translation (SMT), it is known that performance declines when the training data is in a different domain from the test data. Nevertheless, it is frequently necessary to supplement scarce in-domain training data with out-of-domain data. In this paper, we first try to relate the effect of the out-of-domain data on translation performance to measures of corpus similarity, then we separately analyse the effect of adding the out-of-domain data at different parts of the training pipeline (alignment, phrase extraction, and phrase scoring). Through experiments in 2 domains and 8 language pairs it is shown that the out-of-domain data improves coverage and translation of rare words, but may degrade the translation quality for more common words.

1 Introduction

In statistical machine translation (SMT), domain adaptation can be thought of as the problem of training a system on data mainly drawn from one domain (e.g. parliamentary proceedings) and trying to maximise its performance on a different domain (e.g. news). There is likely to be some parallel data similar to the test data, but as such data is expensive to create, it tends to be scarce. The concept of "domain" is rarely given a precise definition, but it is normally understood that data from the same domain is in some sense similar (for example in the words and grammatical constructions used) and data from different domains shows less similarities. Data from the same domain as the test set is usually referred to as *in-domain* and data from a different domain is referred to as *out-of-domain*.

The aim of this paper is to shed some light on what domain actually is, and why it matters. The fact that a mismatch between training and test data domains reduces translation performance has been observed in previous studies, and will be confirmed here for multiple data sets and languages, but the question of why domain matters for performance has not been fully addressed in the literature. Experiments in this paper will be conducted on phrase-based machine translation (PBMT) systems, but similar conclusions are likely to apply to other types of SMT systems. Furthermore, we will mainly be concerned with the effect of domain on the translation model, since it depends on parallel data which is more likely to be in short supply than monolingual data, and domain adaptation for language modelling has been more thoroughly studied.

The effect of a shift of domain in the parallel data is complicated by the fact that training a translation model is a multi-stage process. First the parallel data is word-aligned, normally using the IBM models (Brown et al., 1994), then phrases are extracted using some heuristics (Och et al., 1999) and scored using a maximum likelihood estimate. Since the effect of domain may be felt at the alignment stage, the extraction stage, or the scoring stage, we have designed experiments to try to tease these apart. Experiments comparing the effect of domain at the alignment stage with the extraction and scoring stages have already been presented by (Duh et al., 2010), so we focus more on the differences between extraction and scoring. In other words, we examine whether adding more data (in or out-of domain) helps improve coverage of the phrase table, or helps improve the scoring of phrases.

A further question that we wish to address is

whether adding out-of-domain parallel data affects words with different frequencies to different degrees. For example, a large out-of-domain data set may improve the translation of rare words by providing better coverage, but degrade translation of more common words by providing erroneous out-of-domain translations. In fact, the evidence presented in Section 3.5 will show a much clearer effect on low frequency words than on medium or high frequency words, but the total token count of these low frequency words is still small, so they don't necessarily have much effect on overall measures of translation quality.

In summary, the main contributions of this paper are:

- It presents experiments on 8 language pairs and 2 domains showing the effect on BLEU of adding out-of-domain data.
- It provides evidence that the difference between in and out-of domain translation performance is correlated with differences in word distribution and out-of-vocabulary rates.
- It develops a method for separating the effects of phrase extraction and scoring, showing that good coverage is nearly always more important than good scoring, and that out-of-domain data can adversely affect phrase scores.
- It shows that adding out-of-domain data clearly improves translation of rare words, but may have a small negative effect on more common words.

2 Related Work

The most closely related work to the current one is that of (Duh et al., 2010). In this paper they consider the domain adaptation problem for PBMT, and investigate whether the out-of-domain data helps more at the word alignment stage, or at the phrase extraction and scoring stages. Extensive experiments on 4 different data sets, and 10 different language pairs show mixed results, with the overall conclusion being that it is difficult to predict how best to include out-of-domain data in the PBMT training pipeline. Unlike in the current work, Duh et al. do not separate phrase extraction and scoring in order to analyse the effect of domain on them separately. They make the point that adding extra out-of-domain data may degrade translation by introducing unwanted lexical ambiguity, showing anecdotal evidence for this. Similar arguments were presented in (Sennrich, 2012).

A recent paper which does attempt to tease apart phrase extraction and scoring is (Bisazza et al., 2011). In this work, the authors try to improve a system trained on in-domain data by including extra entries (termed "fill-up") from out-of-domain data – this is similar to the `nc+epE` and `st+epE` systems in Section 3.4. It is shown by Bisazza et al. that this fill-up technique has a similar effect to using MERT to weight the in and out-of domain phrase tables. In the experiments in Section 3.4 we confirm that fill-up techniques mostly provide better results than using a concatenation of in and out-of domain data.

There has been quite a lot of work on finding ways of weighting in and out-of domain data for SMT (as opposed to simply concatenating the data sets), both for language and translation modelling. Interpolating language models using perplexity is fairly well-established (e.g. Koehn and Schroeder (2007)), but for phrase-tables it is unclear whether perplexity minimisation (Foster et al., 2010; Sennrich, 2012) or linear or log-linear interpolation (Foster and Kuhn, 2007; Civera and Juan, 2007; Koehn and Schroeder, 2007) is the best approach. Also, other authors (Foster et al., 2010; Niehues and Waibel, 2010; Shah et al., 2010) have tried to weight the input sentences or extracted phrases before the phrase tables are built. In this type of approach, the main problem is how to train the weights of the sentences or phrases, and each of the papers has followed a different approach.

Instead of weighting the out-of-domain data, some authors have investigated data selection methods for domain adaptation (Yasuda et al., 2008; Mansour et al., 2011; Schwenk et al., 2011; Axelrod et al., 2011). This is effectively the same as using a 1-0 weighting for input sentences, but has the advantage that it is usually easier to tune a threshold than it is to train weights for all input sentences or phrases. The other advantage of doing data selection is that it can potentially remove noisy (e.g. incorrectly aligned) data. However it will be seen later in this paper that out-of-domain data can usually contribute something useful to the translation system, so the 1-0 weighting of data-selection may be somewhat heavy-handed.

3 Experiments

3.1 Corpora and Baselines

The experiments in this paper used data from the WMT09 and WMT11 shared tasks (Callison-Burch et al., 2009; Callison-Burch et al., 2011), as well as OpenSubtitles data[1] released by the OPUS project (Tiedemann, 2009).

From the WMT data, both news-commentary-v6 (`nc`) and europarl-v6 (`ep`) were used for training translation models and language models, with `nc-devtest2007` used for tuning and `nc-test2007` for testing. The experiments were run on all language pairs used in the WMT shared tasks, i.e. English (en) into and out of Spanish (es), German (de), French (fr) and Czech (cs).

From the OpenSubtitles (`st`) data, we chose 8 language pairs – English to and from Spanish, French, Czech and Dutch (nl) – selected because they have at least 200k sentences of parallel data available. 2000 sentence tuning and test sets (`st-dev` and `st-devtest`) were selected from the parallel data by extracting every nth sentence, and a 200k sentence training corpus was selected from the remaining data.

Using test sets from both news-commentary and OpenSubtitles gives two domain adaptation tasks, where in both cases the out-of-domain data is europarl, a significantly larger training set than the in-domain data. The three data sets in use in this paper are summarised in Table 1.

The translation systems consisted of phrase tables and lexicalised reordering tables estimated using the standard Moses (Koehn et al., 2007) training pipeline, and 5-gram Kneser-Ney smoothed language models estimated using the SRILM toolkit (Stolcke, 2002), with KenLM (Heafield, 2011) used at runtime. Separate language models were built on the target side of the in-domain and out-of-domain training data, then linearly interpolated using SRILM to minimise perplexity on the tuning set (e.g. Koehn and Schroeder (2007)). Tuning of models used minimum error rate training (Och, 2003), repeated 3 times and averaged (Clark et al., 2011). Performance is evaluated using case-insensitive BLEU (Papineni et al., 2002), as implemented using the Moses `multi-bleu.pl` script.

[1]`www.opensubtitles.org`

Name	Language pairs	train	tune	test
Europarl (`ep`)	en↔fr	1.8M	n/a	n/a
	en↔es	1.8M	n/a	n/a
	en↔de	1.7M	n/a	n/a
	en↔cs	460k	n/a	n/a
	en↔nl	1.8M	n/a	n/a
News Commentary (`nc`)	en↔fr	114k	1000	2000
	en↔es	130k	1000	2000
	en↔de	135k	1000	2000
	en↔cs	122k	1000	2000
Subtitles (`st`)	en↔fr	200k	2000	2000
	en↔es	200k	2000	2000
	en↔nl	200k	2000	2000
	en↔cs	200k	2000	2000

Table 1: Summary of the data sets used, with approximate sentence counts

3.2 Comparing In-domain and Out-of-domain Data

The aim of this section is to provide both a qualitative and quantitative comparison of the three data sets used in this paper.

Firstly, consider the extracts from the English sections of the three training sets shown in Figure 1. The first extract, from the Europarl corpus, shows a formal style with long sentences. However this is still spoken text so contains a preponderance of first and second person forms. In terms of subject matter, the corpus covers a broad range of topics, but all from the angle of European legislation, institutions and policies. Where languages (e.g. English, French and Spanish) have new world and old world variants, Europarl sticks to the old world variants.

The extract from the News Commentary corpus again shows a formal tone, but because this is news analysis, it tends to favour the third person. It is written text, and covers a wider range of subjects than Europarl, and also encompasses both new and old world versions of the European languages.

The Subtitles text shown in the last example appears qualitatively more different from the other two. It is spoken text, like Europarl, but consists of short, informal sentences with many colloquialisms, as well as possible optical character recognition er-

Although, as you will have seen, the dreaded 'millennium bug' failed to materialise, still the people in a number of countries suffered a series of natural disasters that truly were dreadful.
You have requested a debate on this subject in the course of the next few days, during this part-session.
In the meantime, I should like to observe a minute' s silence, as a number of Members have requested, on behalf of all the victims concerned, particularly those of the terrible storms, in the various countries of the European Union.

(a) Europarl

Desperate to hold onto power, Pervez Musharraf has discarded Pakistan's constitutional framework and declared a state of emergency.
His goal?
To stifle the independent judiciary and free media.
Artfully, though shamelessly, he has tried to sell this action as an effort to bring about stability and help fight the war on terror more effectively.

(b) News commentary

I'il call in 30 minutes to check
Is your mother here, too?
Why are you outside?
It's no fun listening to women's talk
Well, why don't we go in together

(c) OpenSubtitles

Figure 1: Extracts from the English portion of the training corpora

rors. It is likely to contain a mixture of regional variations of the languages, reflecting the diversity of the film sources.

In order to obtain a quantitative measure of domain differences, we used both language model (LM) perplexity, and out-of-vocabulary (OOV) rate, in the two test domains. For the `nc` domain, perplexity was compared by training trigram LMs (with SRILM and Kneser-Ney smoothing) on each of the `ep`, `nc` and `ep+nc` training sets, taking the intersection of the `ep` and `nc` vocabularies as the LM vocabulary. The perplexities of the `nc` test set wer calculated using each of the LMs. A corresponding set of LMs was trained to compare perplexities on the `st` test set, and all perplexity comparisons were performed on all five languages. The SRILM toolkit was also used to calculate OOV rates on the test set, by training language models with an open vocabulary, and using no unknown word probability estimation.

The perplexities and OOV rates on each test corpora are shown in Figure 2. The pattern of perplexities is quite distinct across the two test domains, with the perplexity from out-of-domain data relatively much higher for the `st` test set. The in-domain data LM also shows the lowest perplexity consistently on this test set, whilst for `nc`, the in-domain LM has a similar perplexity to the `ep+nc` LM. In fact for 3/5 languages (fr,cs and de) the `ep+nc` LM has the lowest perplexity.

With regard to the OOV rates, it is notable that for `nc` the rate is actually higher for the in-domain LM than the out-of-domain LM in three of the languages: French, German and Spanish. The most likely reason for this is that these languages have a relatively rich morphology, so the larger out-of-domain corpus (Table 1) gives greater coverage of the different grammatical suffixes. Czech shows a different pattern because in this case the out-of-domain corpus is not much bigger than the in-domain corpus, and English is morphologically much simpler so the increase in corpus size does not help the OOV rate so much.

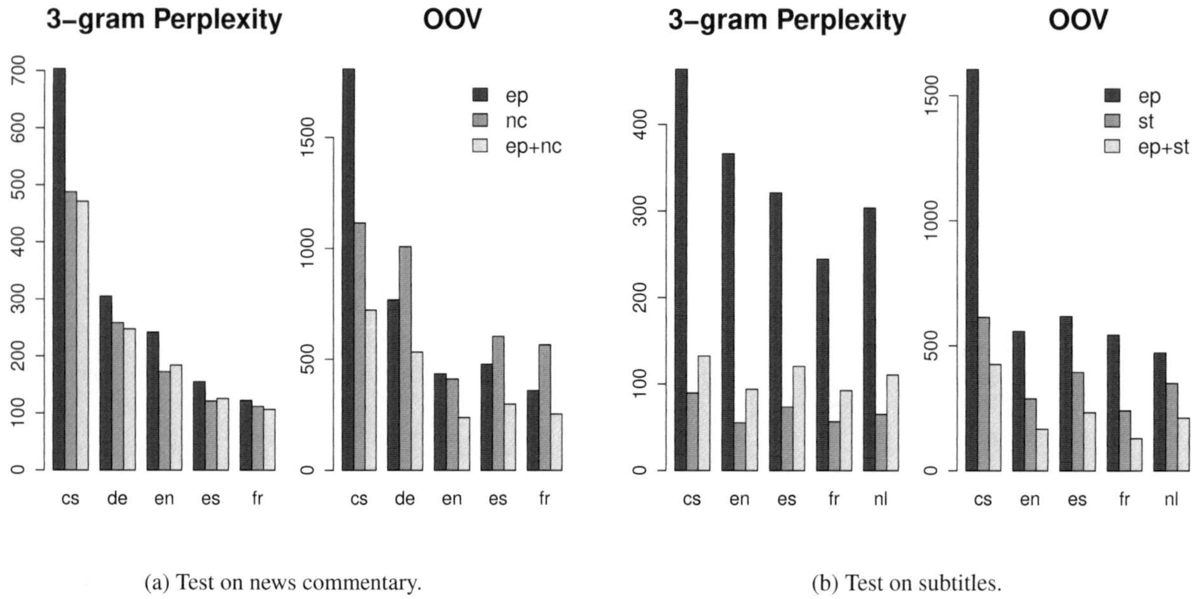

Figure 2: Comparison of perplexities and OOV rates on in-domain test data

3.3 Comparing Translation Performance of In and Out-of-domain Systems

Translation performance was measured on each of the test sets (nc and st) using systems built from just the in-domain parallel data, from just the out-of-domain parallel data, and on a concatenation of the in and out-of domain data. In other words, systems built from the ep, nc and ep+nc parallel texts were evaluated on the nc test data, and systems built from ep, st and ep+st were evaluated on the st test data. In all cases, the parallel training set was used to build both the phrase table and the lexicalised reordering models, the language model was the interpolated one described in Section 3.1, and the system was tuned on data from the same domain as the test set.

From Figure 3 it is clear that the difference between the in and out-of domain training sets is much bigger for st than for nc. The BLEU scores on nc for the nc trained systems are on average 1.3 BLEU points higher than those for the ep trained systems, whilst the scores on st gain an average of 6.0 BLEU points when the training data is switched from ep to st. The patterns are quite consistent across languages for the st tested systems, with the gains varying just from 5.2 to 7.2. However for the nc tested systems there are some language pairs which show a gain of more than 2 BLEU points when moving from out-of to in-domain training data (cs-en, en-es and es-en), whereas en-fr shows no change. The main link between the perplexity and OOV results in Figure 2 and the BLEU score variations in Figure 3 is that the larger in/out differences between the two domains is reflected in larger BLEU differences. However it is also notable that the two languages which display a rise in perplexity between nc and ep+nc are es and en, and for both es-en and en-es the ep+nc translation system performs worse than the nc trained system.

The BLEU gain from concatenating the in and out-of domain data, over just using the in-domain data can be quite small. For the nc domain this averages at 0.5 BLEU (with 3/8 language pairs showing a decrease), whilst for the st domain the average gain is only 0.2 BLEU (with again 3/8 language pairs showing a decrease). So even though adding the out-of-domain data increases the training set size by a factor of 10 in most cases, its effect on BLEU score is small.

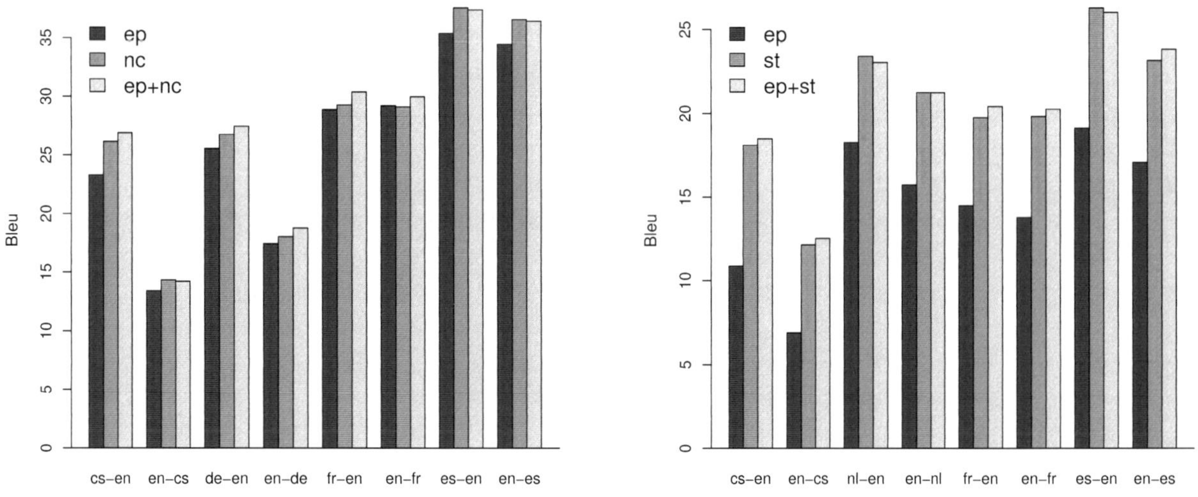

(a) Test on news commentary

(b) Test on subtitles

Figure 3: Comparison of translation performance using models from in-domain, out-of-domain and joint data.

3.4 Why Does Adding Parallel Data Help?

In the previous section it was found that, across all language pairs and both data sets, adding in-domain data to an out-of-domain training set nearly always has a positive impact on performance, whilst adding out-of-domain data to an in-domain training set can sometimes have a small positive effect. In this section several experiments are performed with "intermediate" phrase tables (built from a single parallel corpus, augmented with some elements of the other parallel corpus) in order to determine how different aspects of the extra data affect performance. In particular, the experiments are designed to show the effect of the extra data on the alignments, the phrase scoring and the phrase coverage, whether adding in-domain data to an existing out-of-domain trained system, or vice-versa.

For each of the language pairs used in this paper, and each of the two domains, two series of experiments were run comparing systems built from a single parallel training set, intermediate systems, and systems built from a concatenation of the in and out-of-domain parallel data sets. Only the parallel data was varied, the language models were as described in Section 3.1, and the lexicalised reordering models were built from both training sets in all cases, except for the systems built from a single parallel data set[2]. This gives a total of four series of experiments, where the ordered pair of data sets (`x`,`y`) was set to one of (`ep`,`nc`), (`nc`,`ep`), (`ep`,`st`), (`st`,`ep`). In each of these series, the following translation systems were trained:

- `x` The translation table and lexicalised reordering model were estimated from the `x` corpus alone.
- `x+y` The translation system built from the `x` and `y` parallel corpora concatenated.
- `x+yA` As `x` but using the additional `y` corpus to create the alignments. This means that GIZA++ was run across the entire `x+y` corpus, but only the `x` section of it was used to extract and score phrases.
- `x+yW` As `x+yA` but using the phrase scores from the `x+y` phrase table. This is effectively the `x+y` system, with any entries in the phrase table that are just found in the `y` corpus removed.

[2]Further experiments were run using the parallel data from a single data set to build the translation model, and both data sets to build the lexicalised reordering model, but the difference in score compared to the `x` system was small ($<$ 0.1 BLEU)

x+yE As x+yA but adding the extra entries from the x+y phrase table. This is effectively the x+y system, but with the scores on all phrases that are found in x phrase table set to their values from that table.

All systems were tuned and tested on the appropriate in-domain data set (either nc or st). Note that in the intermediate systems, the phrase table scores may no longer correspond to valid probability distributions, but this is not important as the probabilistic interpretation is never used in decoding anyway.

The graphs in Figure 4 show the performance comparison between the single corpus systems, the intermediate systems, and the concatenated corpus systems, averaged across all 8 language pairs. Table 2 shows the full results broken down by language pair, for completeness, but the patterns are reasonably consistent across language pair.

Firstly, compare the x+yW and x+yE systems, i.e. the systems where we add just the weights from the second parallel data set versus those where we add just the entries. When x is the out-of-domain (ep) data, then it is clearly more profitable to update the phrase-table entries than the weights from the in-domain data. In fact for the systems tested on st, the difference is quite striking with a +5.7 BLEU gain for the ep+stE system over the baseline ep system, but only a +1.5 gain for the ep+stW system. For the systems tested on the nc, adding the entries from nc gives a larger gain in BLEU than adding the weights (+1.3 versus +0.8), but both improve the BLEU scores over the ep+ncA system. The conclusion is that the extra entries from the in-domain data (the "fill-up" of Bisazza et al. (2011)) are more important than the improvements in phrase scoring that in-domain data may provide.

Looking at the other two sets of x+yW and x+yE systems, i.e. those where x is the in-domain data, tells another story. In this case, the results on both the nc and st test sets (Figure 4(b)) suggest that it is generally more useful to use the out-of-domain data as only a source of extra phrase-table entries. This is because the x+epE systems are the highest scoring in both cases, scoring higher than systems built from all the data concatenated by margins of 0.5 (for nc) and 0.4 (for st). This pattern is consistent across all the language pairs for nc, and across 5 of the 8 language pairs for st. Using the out-of-domain data set to update only the weights (the x+epW systems) generally degrades performance when compared to the systems that only use the ep data at alignment time (the x+epA systems).

The size of the effect of adding extra data to the alignment stage only is mixed (as observed by (Duh et al., 2010)), but in general all the x+yA systems show an improvement over the x systems. In fact, for the st domain, adding ep at the alignment stage is the only consistent way to improve BLEU. Adding the weights, entries, or the complete out-of-domain data set does not always help.

3.5 Word Precision Versus Frequency

The final set of experiments addresses the question of whether the change of translation quality when adding out-of-domain has a different effect depending on word frequency. To do this, the systems trained on in-domain only are compared with the systems trained on all data concatenated, using a technique for measuring the precision of the translation for each word type.

To calculate the precision of a word type, it is necessary to examine each translated sentence to see which source words were translated correctly. This is done by recording the word alignment in the phrase mappings and tracking it through the translation process. If a word is produced multiple times in the translation, but occurs a fewer number of times in the reference, then it is assigned partial credit. Many-to-many word alignments are treated similarly. Precision for each word type is then calculated in the usual way, as the number of times that word appears correctly in the output, divided by the total number of appearances. The word types are then binned according to the log2 of their frequency in the in-domain corpus and the average precision for each bin calculated, then these are in turn averaged across language pairs.

The graphs in Figure 5 compare the in-domain source frequency versus precision relationship for systems built using just the in-domain data, and systems built using both in and out-of domain data. There is a consistent increase in precision for lower frequency words (occurring less than 30 times in training), but the total number of occurrences of these words is low, so they contribute less to over-

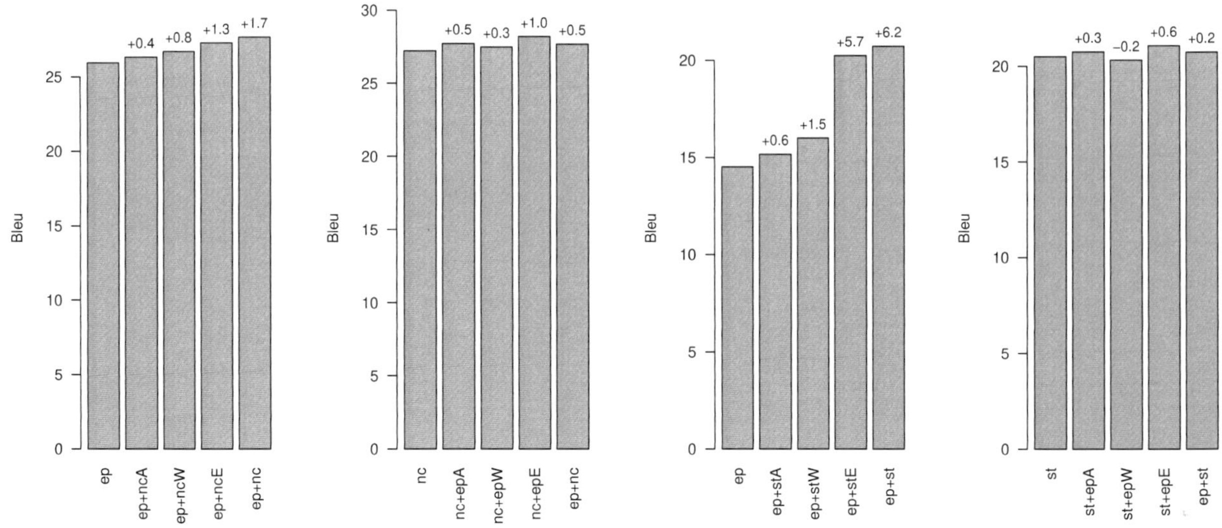

(a) Start with ep, test on nc. (b) Start with nc, test on nc. (c) Start with ep, test on st. (d) Start with st, test on st

Figure 4: Showing the performance change when starting with either in or out-of domain data, and adding elements of the other data set. The "A" indicates that the second data set is only used for alignments, the "W" indicates that it contributes alignments and phrase scores, and the "E" indicates that it contributes alignments and phrase entries. The figures above each bar shows the performance change relative to the single corpus system.

System	cs-en	en-cs	de-en	en-de	fr-en	en-fr	es-en	en-es
ep	23.3	13.4	25.5	17.5	28.9	29.2	35.4	34.5
ep+ncA	23.5 (+0.2)	13.8 (+0.4)	25.9 (+0.4)	17.9 (+0.4)	29.3 (+0.4)	29.6 (+0.4)	35.7 (+0.3)	34.9 (+0.5)
ep+ncW	24.0 (+0.7)	14.2 (+0.8)	26.3 (+0.8)	18.2 (+0.7)	29.4 (+0.5)	29.8 (+0.6)	36.3 (+0.9)	35.6 (+1.1)
ep+ncE	26.2 (+2.9)	14.0 (+0.6)	27.0 (+1.5)	18.5 (+1.0)	29.7 (+0.9)	30.0 (+0.8)	37.0 (+1.7)	35.7 (+1.3)
nc	26.1 (+2.9)	14.3 (+0.9)	26.7 (+1.2)	18.0 (+0.6)	29.3 (+0.4)	29.1 (-0.1)	37.6 (+2.2)	36.5 (+2.1)
nc+epA	26.8 (+3.5)	14.6 (+1.2)	27.5 (+2.0)	18.5 (+1.0)	30.4 (+1.5)	29.9 (+0.7)	37.7 (+2.3)	36.4 (+2.0)
nc+epW	26.6 (+3.3)	14.4 (+1.0)	27.4 (+1.9)	18.4 (+1.0)	29.5 (+0.6)	29.8 (+0.6)	37.2 (+1.8)	36.5 (+2.0)
nc+epE	**27.4 (+4.1)**	**14.7 (+1.3)**	**28.1 (+2.6)**	**19.0 (+1.5)**	**30.9 (+2.0)**	**30.2 (+1.0)**	**38.4 (+3.0)**	**36.9 (+2.4)**
ep+nc	26.9 (+3.6)	14.2 (+0.8)	27.4 (+1.9)	18.8 (+1.3)	30.4 (+1.5)	30.0 (+0.8)	37.4 (+2.0)	36.4 (+2.0)

System	cs-en	en-cs	nl-en	en-nl	fr-en	en-fr	es-en	en-es
ep	10.9	6.9	18.2	15.7	14.5	13.8	19.1	17.1
ep+stA	11.9 (+1.0)	7.5 (+0.6)	19.0 (+0.8)	16.3 (+0.5)	15.0 (+0.5)	14.1 (+0.3)	19.8 (+0.7)	17.8 (+0.7)
ep+stW	12.2 (+1.3)	8.1 (+1.2)	20.0 (+1.7)	17.4 (+1.7)	15.8 (+1.3)	14.9 (+1.1)	20.8 (+1.7)	18.8 (+1.8)
ep+stE	18.0 (+7.1)	12.4 (+5.5)	22.5 (+4.2)	20.6 (+4.9)	19.6 (+5.1)	19.9 (+6.1)	25.6 (+6.5)	23.3 (+6.3)
st	18.0 (+7.2)	12.2 (+5.3)	23.4 (+5.1)	21.3 (+5.6)	19.7 (+5.2)	19.8 (+6.0)	26.3 (+7.2)	23.2 (+6.1)
st+epA	18.4 (+7.6)	12.4 (+5.5)	23.6 (+5.4)	21.3 (+5.6)	20.2 (+5.7)	20.1 (+6.3)	**26.4 (+7.3)**	23.5 (+6.5)
st+epW	18.2 (+7.3)	12.2 (+5.3)	22.4 (+4.2)	21.0 (+5.3)	19.9 (+5.4)	19.8 (+6.0)	25.8 (+6.7)	23.2 (+6.1)
st+epE	**19.1 (+8.3)**	12.5 (+5.6)	**24.0 (+5.8)**	**21.7 (+6.0)**	**20.6 (+6.1)**	**20.9 (+7.1)**	26.0 (+6.9)	23.7 (+6.6)
ep+st	18.5 (+7.6)	**12.5 (+5.6)**	23.0 (+4.8)	21.2 (+5.5)	20.4 (+5.9)	20.2 (+6.5)	26.0 (+6.9)	**23.8 (+6.8)**

Table 2: Complete scores for the experiments described in Section 3.4 and summarised in Figure 4. Naming of the systems is explained in the text, and in the caption for Figure 4

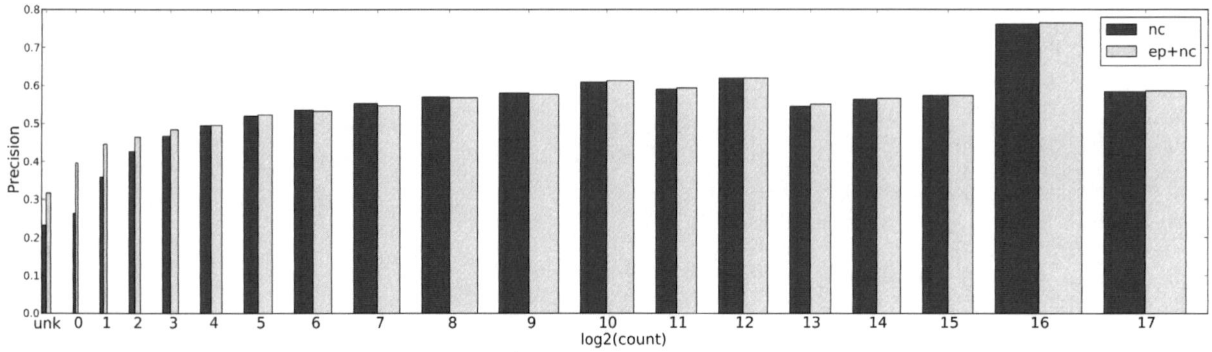

(a) News commentary

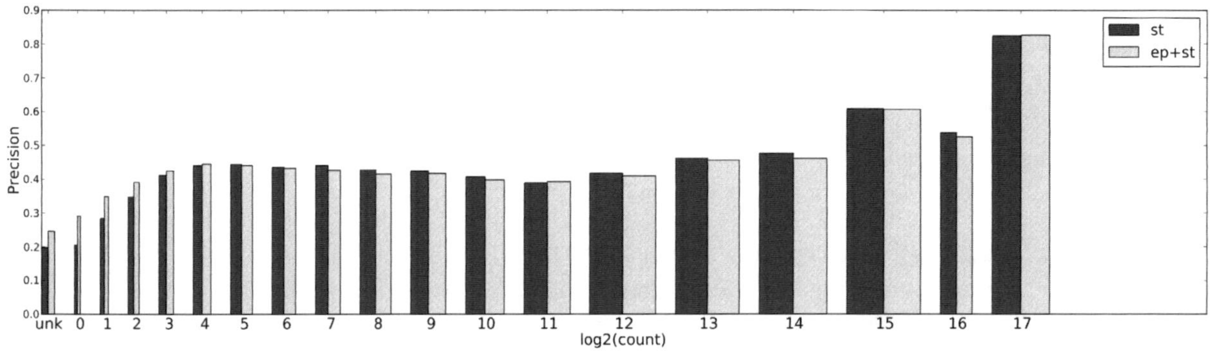

(b) Subtitles

Figure 5: Performance comparison of in-domain systems versus systems built from in and out-of domain data concatenated. Precision is plotted against log2 of in-domain training frequency, and averaged across all 8 language pairs. The width of the bars indicates the average total number of occurrences in the test set.

all measures of translation quality. For the words with moderate training set frequencies, the precision is actually slightly higher for the systems built with just in-domain data, an effect that is more marked for the `st` domain.

4 Conclusions

In this paper we have attempted to give an in-depth analysis of the domain adaptation problem for two different domain adaptation problems in phrase-based MT. The differences between the two problems are clearly illustrated by the results in Figures 2 and 3, where we see that the difference between the in-domain and out-of-domain data are larger for the OpenSubtitles domain than for the News-Commentary domain. This can be detected by the differences in word distribution and out-of-vocabulary rates observed in Figure 2, and is reflected by the differing translation results in Figure 3.

However, the experiments of Sections 3.4 and 3.5 show some common themes emerging in the two domains. In both cases, the out-of-domain data helps most when it is just allowed to add entries (i.e. "fill in") the phrase-table, and using the scores provided by out-of-domain data has a tendency to be harmful to translation quality. The precision results of Section 3.5 show out-of-domain data (when it is simply added to the training set) mainly helping with the low frequency words, and having a neutral or harmful effect for higher frequency words. This explains why approaches which try to weight the out-of-domain data in some way (e.g. corpus weighting or instance weighting) can be more successful than simply concatenating data sets. It also suggests that the way forward is to look for methods that use the out-of-domain data mainly for rarer words, and not to change translations which have a lot of evidence in the in-domain data.

5 Acknowledgments

This work was supported by the EuroMatrixPlus[3] and Accept[4] projects funded by the European Commission (7th Framework Programme).

References

Amittai Axelrod, Xiaodong He, and Jianfeng Gao. 2011. Domain Adaptation via Pseudo In-Domain Data Selection. In *Proceedings of the 2011 Conference on Empirical Methods in Natural Language Processing*, pages 355–362, Edinburgh, Scotland, UK., July. Association for Computational Linguistics.

Arianna Bisazza, Nick Ruiz, and Marcello Federico. 2011. Fill-up versus Interpolation Methods for Phrase-based SMT Adaptation. In *Proceedings of IWSLT*.

Peter F. Brown, Stephen Della Pietra, Vincent J. Della Pietra, and Robert L. Mercer. 1994. The Mathematics of Statistical Machine Translation: Parameter Estimation. *Computational Linguistics*, 19(2):263–311.

Chris Callison-Burch, Philipp Koehn, Christof Monz, and Josh Schroeder. 2009. Findings of the 2009 Workshop on Statistical Machine Translation. In *Proceedings of the Fourth Workshop on Statistical Machine Translation*, pages 1–28, Athens, Greece, March. Association for Computational Linguistics.

Chris Callison-Burch, Philipp Koehn, Christof Monz, and Omar Zaidan. 2011. Findings of the 2011 Workshop on Statistical Machine Translation. In *Proceedings of the Sixth Workshop on Statistical Machine Translation*, pages 22–64, Edinburgh, Scotland, July. Association for Computational Linguistics.

Jorge Civera and Alfons Juan. 2007. Domain Adaptation in Statistical Machine Translation with Mixture Modelling. In *Proceedings of the Second Workshop on Statistical Machine Translation*, pages 177–180, Prague, Czech Republic, June. Association for Computational Linguistics.

Jonathan Clark, Chris Dyer, Alon Lavie, and Noah Smith. 2011. Better hypothesis testing for statistical machine translation: Controlling for optimizer instability. In *Proceedings of ACL*.

[3]www.euromatrixplus.net

[4]www.accept.unige.ch

Kevin Duh, Katsuhito Sudoh, and Hajime Tsukada. 2010. Analysis of translation model adaptation in statistical machine translation. In *Proceedings of IWSLT*.

George Foster and Roland Kuhn. 2007. Mixture-model adaptation for SMT. In *Proceedings of the Second Workshop on Statistical Machine Translation*, pages 128–135, Prague, Czech Republic, June. Association for Computational Linguistics.

George Foster, Cyril Goutte, and Roland Kuhn. 2010. Discriminative Instance Weighting for Domain Adaptation in Statistical Machine Translation. In *Proceedings of the 2010 Conference on Empirical Methods in Natural Language Processing*, pages 451–459, Cambridge, MA, October. Association for Computational Linguistics.

Kenneth Heafield. 2011. KenLM: Faster and Smaller Language Model Queries. In *Proceedings of the Sixth Workshop on Statistical Machine Translation*, pages 187–197, Edinburgh, Scotland, July. Association for Computational Linguistics.

Philipp Koehn and Josh Schroeder. 2007. Experiments in Domain Adaptation for Statistical Machine Translation. In *Proceedings of the Second Workshop on Statistical Machine Translation*, pages 224–227, Prague, Czech Republic, June. Association for Computational Linguistics.

Philipp Koehn, Hieu Hoang, Alexandra Birch, Chris Callison-Burch, Marcello Federico, Nicola Bertoldi, Brooke Cowan, Wade Shen, Christine Moran, Richard Zens, Chris Dyer, Ondrej Bojar, Alexandra Constantin, and Evan Herbst. 2007. Moses: Open Source Toolkit for Statistical Machine Translation. In *Proceedings of the ACL Demo Sessions*, pages 177–180, Prague, Czech Republic, June. Association for Computational Linguistics.

Saab Mansour, Joern Wuebker, and Hermann Ney. 2011. Combining Translation and Language Model Scoring for Domain-Specific Data Filtering. In *Proceedings of IWSLT*.

Jan Niehues and Alex Waibel. 2010. Domain Adaptation in Statistical Machine Translation using Factored Translation Models. In *Proceedings of EAMT*.

Franz J. Och, Christoph Tillman, and Hermann Ney. 1999. Improved Alignment Models for Statistical Machine Translation. In *Joint SIGDAT Conference on Empirical Methods in Natural Language Processing and Very Large Corpora*.

Franz J. Och. 2003. Minimum Error Rate Training in Statistical Machine Translation. In *Proceedings of ACL*.

Kishore Papineni, Salim Roukos, Todd Ward, and Wei-Jing Zhu. 2002. Bleu: a Method for Automatic Evaluation of Machine Translation. In *Proceedings of 40th*

Annual Meeting of the Association for Computational Linguistics, pages 311–318, Philadelphia, Pennsylvania, USA, July. Association for Computational Linguistics.

Holger Schwenk, Patrik Lambert, Loïc Barrault, Christophe Servan, Sadaf Abdul-Rauf, Haithem Afli, and Kashif Shah. 2011. LIUM's SMT Machine Translation Systems for WMT 2011. In *Proceedings of the Sixth Workshop on Statistical Machine Translation*, pages 464–469, Edinburgh, Scotland, July. Association for Computational Linguistics.

Rico Sennrich. 2012. Perplexity Minimization for Translation Model Domain Adaptation in Statistical Machine Translation. In *Proceedings of EACL*.

Kashif Shah, Loïc Barrault, and Holger Schwenk. 2010. Translation Model Adaptation by Resampling. In *Proceedings of the Joint Fifth Workshop on Statistical Machine Translation and MetricsMATR*, pages 392–399, Uppsala, Sweden, July. Association for Computational Linguistics.

Andreas Stolcke. 2002. SRILM – An Extensible Language Modeling Toolkit. In *Proc. Intl. Conf. on Spoken Language Processing, vol. 2*, pages 901–904.

Jörg Tiedemann. 2009. News from OPUS - A Collection of Multilingual Parallel Corpora with Tools and Interfaces. In N. Nicolov, K. Bontcheva, G. Angelova, and R. Mitkov, editors, *Recent Advances in Natural Language Processing (vol V)*, pages 237–248. John Benjamins, Amsterdam/Philadelphia.

Keiji Yasuda, Ruiqiang Zhang, Hirofumi Yamamoto, and Eiichiro Sumita. 2008. Method of Selecting Training Data to Build a Compact and Efficient Translation Model. In *Proceedings of IJCNLP*.

Evaluating the Learning Curve of Domain Adaptive Statistical Machine Translation Systems

Nicola Bertoldi Mauro Cettolo Marcello Federico
Fondazione Bruno Kessler
via Sommarive 18
38123 Trento, Italy
<surename>@fbk.eu

Christian Buck
University of Edinburgh
10 Crichton Street
EH8 9AB Edinburgh, UK
christian.buck@ed.ac.uk

Abstract

The new frontier of computer assisted translation technology is the effective integration of statistical MT within the translation workflow. In this respect, the SMT ability of incrementally learning from the translations produced by users plays a central role. A still open problem is the evaluation of SMT systems that evolve over time. In this paper, we propose a new metric for assessing the quality of an adaptive MT component that is derived from the theory of learning curves: the percentage slope.

1 Introduction

Translation memories and computer assisted translation (CAT) tools are currently the dominant technologies in the translation and localization market, but recent achievements in statistical MT have raised new expectations in the translation industry. So far, statistical MT has focused on providing ready-to-use translations, rather than outputs that minimize the effort of a human translator. The MateCAT project[1] aims at pushing what can be considered the new frontier of CAT technology: how to effectively integrate statistical MT within the translation workflow.

One pursued research direction is developing *domain adaptive* SMT models, i.e. models that dynamically adapt to the translations that are continuously added to the translation memory by the user during her/his work. The ideal goal is to progressively reduce the mismatch between training and testing data, in such a way that the adapted SMT engine will be able to provide the user with *useful suggestions* – i.e. perfect or worth being post-edited – when the translation memory fails to retrieve perfect or almost perfect matches. Among the well known machine learning paradigms that fit with this scenario are *online learning* and *incremental learning*, which basically differ in the amount of data that is employed to dynamically adapt the system: a single piece of data in the first case and a batch of data in the latter. Notice that in both cases one assumes that domain adaptation is performed efficiently, i.e. by only processing the newly received data. Moreover, although the quantity of acquired in-domain data is generally limited, their high quality and relevance to the translation task justify their exploitation by all means possible.

Domain adaptive SMT embeds two challenges: (1) the design of effective adaptation algorithms, and (2) the evaluation of MT systems evolving over time. Since the ultimate goal of our efforts is to increase the productivity of human translators, the most accurate assessment methodology would be of course to run a field test. This way, we could compare productivity of human translators receiving suggestions from an MT engine featuring dynamic domain adaptation against the productivity of human translators working with a static MT engine. As this evaluation is infeasible during daily MT development, we can resort to the several automatic MT metrics, which however, as we will see later, are unsuitable to track the dynamic behaviors we are interested to investigate. Metrics for measuring performance in the case of interactive MT, see for example (Khadivi,

[1] http://www.matecat.com/

2008), like Key-Stroke Ratio (KSR), Mouse-Action Ratio (MAR), Key-Stroke and Mouse-Action Ratio (KSMR) are known to correlate well with the productivity of human translators, but their computation requires the actual use of an interactive MT system, i.e. a field test.

In the SMART project,[2] the evaluation of adaptive interactive MT is explored (Cesa-Bianchi et al., 2008). While no specific metric is proposed, the analysis is based on a plot of cumulative differences of BLEU scores between a baseline and an adaptive system. These differences are computed sentence by sentence and present an interesting view of the dynamic change of the MT system. We are going to further elaborate on this idea.

Other metrics like Character Error Rate (CER) and Translation Edit Rate (TER) would accurately predict the translators' productivity if references were generated by using the CAT system; on the contrary, references are usually, as in this paper, generated from scratch based only on the source text and can thus be quite far from CAT-based translations, both lexically and syntactically. The Human-targeted variant of TER, HTER (Snover et al., 2006), needs human intervention and is therefore unfit to meet our requirements.

The main goal of this paper is to design an objective automatic evaluation methodology for an MT system adapting over time. We propose to use the *percentage slope* from the theory on learning curves to measure the learning ability of adaptive MT systems.

To assess the proposed metric, we have implemented a simple but effective adaptation strategy suitable for an MT system integrated in a CAT tool. We show that the percentage slope is able to expose different dynamic behaviors, such as learning, no learning, and forgetting.

2 Dynamic Adaptation Framework

In the MateCAT project scenario, the MT system, which is embedded in the CAT tool to increase the translators' productivity, adapts over time by exploiting translations generated by the user. The adapted system is then used to provide the user with translation suggestions for the next sentences. We refer to this process as *dynamic* (or *incremental*) *adaptation* to emphasize that adaptation happens continuously based on a stream of data.

2.1 Abstract View of the Adaptation Process

From an abstract point of view, the framework of incremental adaptation can be summarized as follows:

i) before the process starts, an initial system is built on available data including a parallel corpus;

ii) a stream of parallel data becomes available that is split into blocks of (not necessarily) similar size;

iii) the first/next block is considered, but only the source is available yet;

iv) the latest instance of the adapting system translates the source text of the current block;

v) the target part of the current block becomes available for use;[3]

vi) the system is adapted using the current parallel block and possibly all the previous ones;

vii) the loop continues from step iii) until all blocks are processed.

In each adaptation step, all of the data available so far can be used, but no look ahead is possible. Note that, in principle, each block is translated with a different instance of the adapting system; hence, the same text occurring in two different blocks can be translated differently.

2.2 Evaluation Goals and Requirements

Although dynamic adaptation is closely related to static domain adaptation (Foster and Kuhn, 2007), in this scenario we are not interested in the quality of the final model. In fact, this model is only available once the stream is depleted and therefore is not used anymore.

What we are interested in, and what we want to compare among different approaches, is the systems evolvement over time.

Consider a translator who uses such an incrementally adapting system and performs post-editing on its suggested translations. The highest productivity

[2] http://www.smart-project.eu

[3] In the CAT framework, the target part of a block is the translation post-edited by the user.

gain is achieved when the adaptation is quick and persistent.

Even though in this paper we are concerned with an automatic metric, it is important to keep the use case of CAT in mind, in particular the presence of a human translator. The TransType2 project[4] has found that repeated correction of the same error is strongly disliked by editors (Macklovitch, 2006) and may lead to rejection of the entire system. Similarly, segments that were translated correctly by previous, less adapted systems, should not be negatively affected by updates. We will refer to these particular aspects of adaptation as *backward reliability*.

Automatic measures, which are aimed at static MT modules, can not take the evolution of the system into account and are therefore unable to pinpoint such problems. Thus, they are not suitable for the dynamic adaptation scenario.

A new evaluation methodology should satisfy the following requirements:

- ability to compare different strategies
- show behavior over time and reward early improvements and consistent adaptation
- expose possible overfitting, i.e. check whether generalization is lost due to overly aggressive adaptation
- strong correlation to human productivity
- estimate benefit over a static baseline model without adaptation
- check backward reliability.

2.3 Evaluation Protocol

The performance of adaptive systems as sketched in Section 2.1 is evaluated on different parts of the stream as opposed to the global evaluation used for static systems. We distinguish between two protocols which differ in their use of historic data.

For *block-wise evaluation* only the translations of the most recent block are evaluated with respect to the correct translations once these become available. Any static automatic MT score, e.g. TER (Snover et al., 2006), BLEU (Papineni et al., 2001), can be used, provided that it is reliable on a block of usually relatively small size.

In contrast, in *incremental evaluation* the scores are computed on all blocks available so far. The translations of previous blocks are kept fixed, i.e. blocks are *not* translated again once a newly adapted system becomes available as this new system has already seen this data.

Both the block-wise and incremental protocols yield a sequence of scores that reflects the adaptation behavior over time. The former is useful to expose potential weaknesses as discussed above: we expect to see improvement at first and after a while, when enough adaptation data is available, a level curve. If this is not the case, this indicates a problem:

i) should the scores deteriorate over time we might be facing overfitting, possibly due to unexpected heterogeneity in our corpus;
ii) if the scores continue to improve, then the adaptation method is not aggressive enough and the system underfits.

The incremental evaluation on the other hand allows for easy comparison of different adaptation strategies. While the performance on the most recent block becomes less important over time, the performance on all the blocks processed so far nicely reflects the utility of the system in the application setting.

The metric we are going to propose in the next section processes such sequences of partial scores. It accumulates the trend into a single number and offers an interpretation that relates adaptive behavior to productivity gains.

3 The Percentage Slope

Learning curves (see (Stump P.E., 2002) for a detailed introduction) are mathematical models used to estimate the efficiency gain when an activity is repeated. The *learning effect* was noted in industrial environment: the underlying notion is that when people repeat an activity, there tends to be a gain in efficiency. That is exactly the expected behavior of our dynamically adapting MT system: it should improve its performance on texts including terms and expressions whose proper translation has been previously provided. Thus we decided to exploit elements from learning theory to measure the evolution of translation capability.

Several learning curve models have been proposed, but only two are in widespread use, the *unit*

[4] http://tt2.atosorigin.es

(U) model due to Crawford and the *cumulative average* (CA) model due to Wright. Both models are based on a common mathematical form:

$$y = ax^b \quad (1)$$

where:

- a represents the theoretical labor hours required to build the first unit produced (a positive number)
- b represents the rate of learning (negative value, except for "forgetting")
- x represents the number of an item in the production sequence (unit $\#1, \#2, \#3, \ldots$)

The models differ in the interpretation of y:

U: y is the labor hours required to build unit $\#x$

CA: y is the average labor hours per unit required to build the first x units

Since b is a mathematically appropriate but counter-intuitive number for describing the slope, the *percentage slope* S is typically used:

$$S = 10^{b \log_{10}(2)+2} \quad (2)$$

S provides the rate of learning on a scale of 0 to 100, as a percentage. A 100% slope represents no learning at all, zero percentage reflects a theoretically infinite rate of learning. In practice, human operations hardly ever achieve a rate of learning faster than 70% as measured on this scale.

The correspondence between our block-wise evaluation (Section 2.3) with the U model, and the incremental evaluation with the CA model is straightforward. In the first case, y is the number of errors done in the translation of the block $\#x$; in the second case, y is the average number of errors (that is the TER score or the 100-BLEU score) made on the first x blocks.

From a practical point of view, the sequence of scores can be provided while the adapting system is being used; the learning curve which best matches the sequence is then found[5] and eventually the percentage slope S is computed.

[5]Notice that the best fitting learning curve can be estimated in the log scale with a simple linear regression analysis.

set	#sent.	#src words	#tgt words
train	1.2M	18.9M	19.4M
test	3.4k	57.0k	61.4k

Table 1: Overall statistics on parallel data of the IT domain used for training and testing the SMT system. Counts of (English) source words and (Italian) target words refer to tokenized texts.

4 Experiments

In order to test-drive the evaluation metric introduced in Section 3, several SMT systems showing effective, weak, poor or absent adaptation capability have been developed. Moreover, a preliminary investigation on backward reliability has been carried out. The next paragraphs detail and discuss the experiments performed.

4.1 Data

The task considered in this work involves the translation from English into Italian of documents in the Information Technology (IT) domain.

The training set consists of a large Translation Memory in the IT domain and several OPUS[6] sub-corpora, namely KDE4, KDEdoc and PHP. The test set includes the human generated translation of 6 documents, disjoint from the training set. Although in the same domain, the test set is quite different from the training data as shown by comparing values of perplexity (650 vs. 40) and OOV rate (2.4% vs. 0.4%) computed on the source side.[7] Furthermore, the 6 documents significantly differ among each other: perplexity and OOV rate range from 465 to 880 and from 0.8 to 3.3, respectively. Table 1 collects overall statistics on training and test sets.

To simulate the stream of fresh data, the IT test set has been split into blocks of about a thousand[8] words each. Before splitting, sentences have been scrambled, with the rationale of generating a large number of homogeneous blocks, simulating a test set consisting of a single document.

[6]`http://opus.lingfil.uu.se`

[7]Figures for the training data were measured through a cross-validation technique.

[8]Different sizes have been also considered (three and five thousands) to test different adaptation rates, but results were qualitatively similar to those on shorter blocks and then are not reported.

4.2 Baseline System

The SMT baseline system is built upon the open-source MT toolkit Moses[9] (Koehn et al., 2007). The translation and the lexicalized reordering models are estimated on parallel training data with the default setting; a 5-gram LM smoothed through the improved Kneser-Ney technique (Chen and Goodman, 1999) is estimated on monolingual texts via the IRSTLM toolkit (Federico et al., 2008). Hereinafter, these models are referred to as background (BG) models. The log-linear interpolation weights are optimized by means of the standard MERT procedure provided within the Moses toolkit.

4.3 Adaptive System

The adapting SMT system is built on Moses as well. Besides the BG models of the baseline system, translation, reordering and language models estimated on the stream of fresh data are employed as additional features. Hereinafter, these models are referred to as foreground (FG) models. Unless differently specified, the FG models employed to translate a given block are trained on all preceding blocks. Note that the first instance of the adapting system (i.e. that translating the first block) is exactly the baseline system, because no adaptation data is available to train FG models yet. FG translation and reordering models are trained in the same way as the BG models. Due to the limited amount of adaptation data, the FG LM is a 3-gram LM smoothed through the more robust Witten-Bell technique (Witten and Bell, 1991).

The interpolation weights are inherited from a companion system trained and tuned on a different domain – official documents of the European Union organization – and are kept fixed.

4.4 Experiments on Adaptive SMT

First of all, the baseline and adapting systems were run on the scrambled test set and compared at both block-wise and incremental mode (see Section 2.3).

Figure 1 plots block-wise TER and BLEU scores of the baseline and adapting systems as functions of the amount (number of words) of adaptation data. On one hand, it can be guessed that the adapting system performs gradually better and better than the baseline; on the other hand, it is evident that such plots are not the most effective way to show the evolution of the adapting system. In fact, the translation difficulty of contiguous blocks can differ a lot. Hence, scores computed on them are not comparable and the corresponding curves are jagged.

The block-wise differences of TER and BLEU scores between the adapting and the baseline systems are plotted in Figure 2: the plots are now cleaner and more readable and vaguely suggest a positive trend, but still remain too jagged and do not provide any information about the absolute performance of the systems.

Figure 3 plots the incremental TER and BLEU scores of the baseline and adapting systems as functions of the amount of adaptation data. First of all, it is worth noting that the right-most values are the scores computed on the whole test set. In standard evaluation, those would be the only scores provided to show how the adapting system outperforms the baseline system; in particular, the relative improvement is larger for TER (9.3%) than for BLEU (3.9%) supposedly because tuning was performed to optimize BLEU score which thus is harder to improve. However, the overall scores obscure the way they are reached, that is the evolution over time of the systems, which is especially important for adaptive systems.

Secondly, the incremental evaluation yields much smoother plots clearly showing that after initial fluctuations: (i) performance of the baseline stabilizes around an average which does not change over time; (ii) scores of the adapting system tend to get increasingly better as more adaptation data is available for updating FG models.

The evaluation metric we are proposing, the percentage slope introduced in Section 3, is indeed able to spot such kind of paradigmatic behaviors as we will see in the next section. But before going on with the assessment of the metric, some further comments on Figure 3:

- in early stages, the adaptation is not effective, likely because of the scarcity of data. This raises two issues: design of more effective adaptation strategies and, in the CAT framework, identifying the appropriate time to replace the baseline with the adapting system;
- the adaptive system outperforms the baseline in

[9] http://www.statmt.org/moses

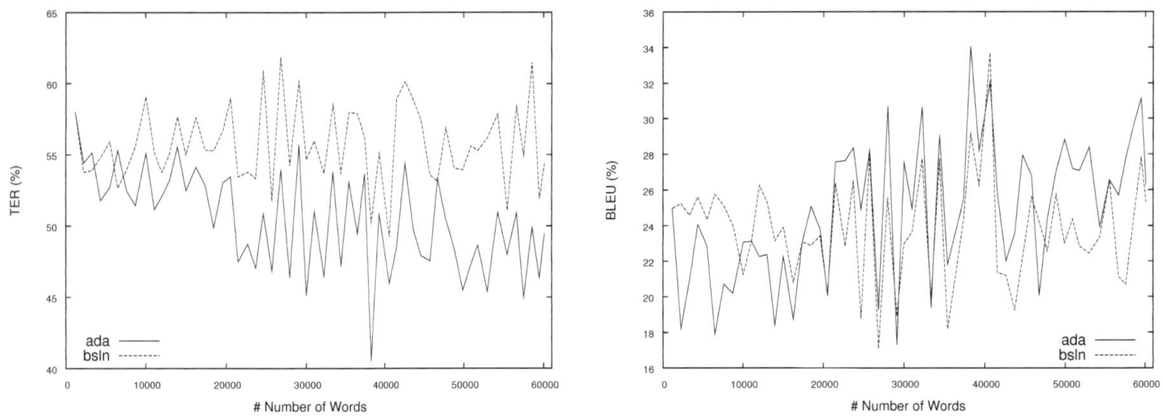

Figure 1: Block-wise TER (on the left) and BLEU (right) scores of the baseline and the dynamically adapting systems.

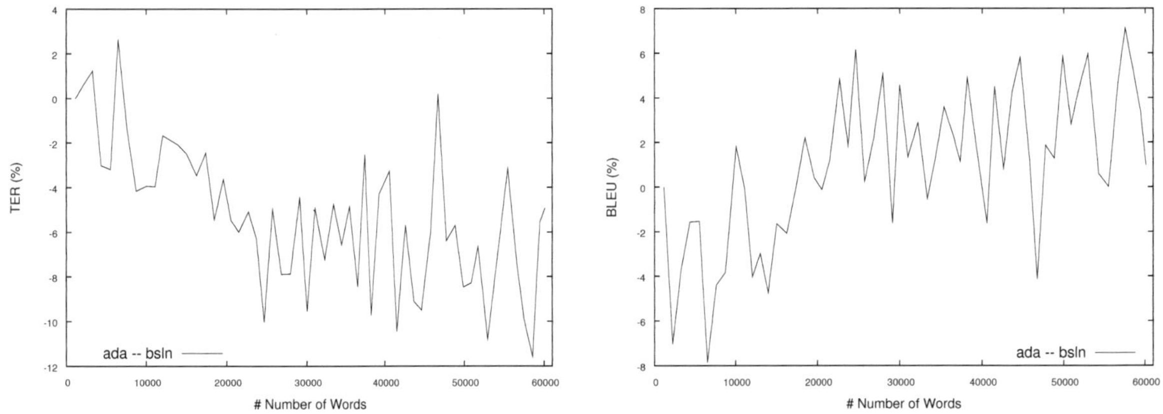

Figure 2: Block-wise TER (left) and BLEU (right) differences between the baseline and the dynamically adapting systems.

terms of TER very soon, while the overtaking with regard to BLEU is observed much later. This is because the baseline SMT system was tuned with respect to the BLEU score on in-domain data, differently to the adapting system.

Both these issues are out of the scope of this paper and will be subject of future investigations.

4.5 Assessment of the Percentage Slope

To assess its effectiveness, the percentage slope has been computed on errors committed by the baseline system, the adapting system and an adapting system featuring only FG models (that is without BG models). The FG-only system was used to translate each block either fairly and unfairly: the former mode fits the adaptation process sketched in Section 2.1; in the latter mode, the FG model is adapted on the block *before* its translation starts.

Figure 4 shows the TER and BLEU scores of such systems in the incremental evaluation. The four different behaviors are expected to correspond to different percentage slopes. In fact, the S values collected in Table 2 confirm the expectations:

- the baseline, completely unable to learn, has in fact an S of 100%
- the adapting system, that learns through a dynamic adaptation of FG models and generalizes thanks to BG models, has an S of 96-98%
- the FG-only adapting system tested in unfair mode worsens its performance as the models become larger, i.e. less focused on the block to be translated: this is evidenced by an S greater than 100%

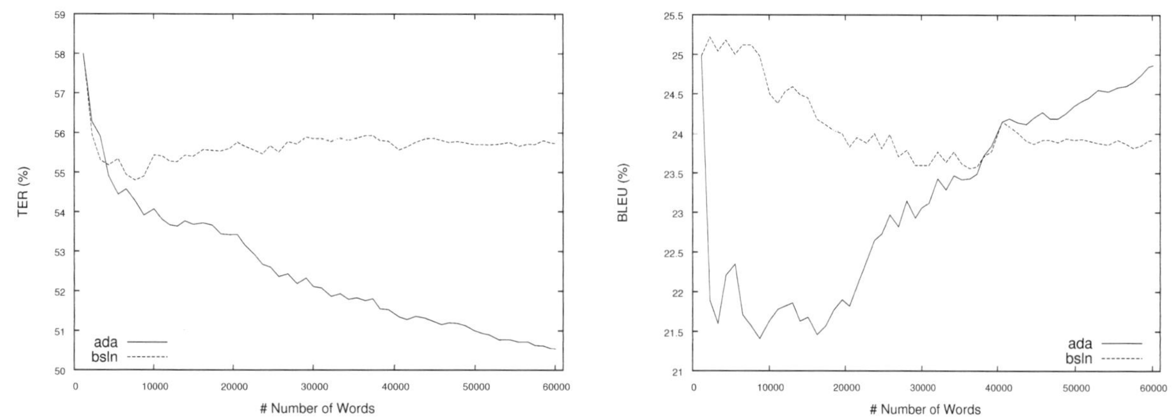

Figure 3: Incremental TER (left) and BLEU (right) scores of the baseline and the dynamically adapting systems.

model	system			
	baseline	adapting	FG-only adapting fair	FG-only adapting unfair
U	100.4	96.9	96.2	107.2
CA	100.3	97.7	96.5	107.4

Table 2: S values of 4 SMT systems (see text) for the block-wise TER evaluation, corresponding to the U model, and the incremental evaluation, corresponding to the CA model.

- the FG-only adapting system tested in fair mode increases its performance as the models become larger, i.e. more general, as evidenced by an S similar to that of our original adapting system (96%).

Therefore, we can state that S exposes common behaviors of evolving SMT systems; however, standard metrics like TER and BLEU are still in charge of providing absolute performance measures.

In order to give a hint for properly interpreting the values reported, we summarize the discussion in (Stump P.E., 2002) about "typical learning slopes". Operations that are fully automated tend to have slopes of 100%, 70% if entirely manual, an intermediate value if mixed. In real industrial environments, the average slope depends on the type of manufacturing activity: for example, in aircraft industry it is about 85%, it ranges in 90-95% in electronics and in machining. Hence, a 96-98% slope as we measured in our experiments must be considered a significant learning ability of a fully automated system.

4.6 Experiments on Backward Reliability

A proper assessment of the backward reliability of an evolving system as defined in Section 2.2 would require the identification of patterns translated differently by the system during its life. We will investigate this issue in the future. For the moment, we try to attack the problem from a global point of view: we simply check that the adaptive system does "remember" its previous translation capabilities "on average", while it learns to better translate novel texts.

To this end, a cross-validation policy was followed: the first two thirds of each test set document are used for dynamically training the FG models, while the remaining portions are used as held-out test sets.

Figure 5 reports the TER and BLEU scores on the 6 test sets of three systems: the baseline system (`bsln`), the adapting system (`ada`) fed by incrementally merging the available reduced adaptation sets, and the system adapted on all adaptation data sets (`final`).

The `final` system achieves performance close to `ada` system on each held-out set; this reveals that our adaptation process is effective both in learning and in remembering.

We think that the monitoring of the backward reliability of adapting systems is a good practice. A cross validation scheme like ours allows not only to reveal the backward reliability as shown before, but also to discover the forgetting trend of, for example, an MT system featuring an overly aggressive learn-

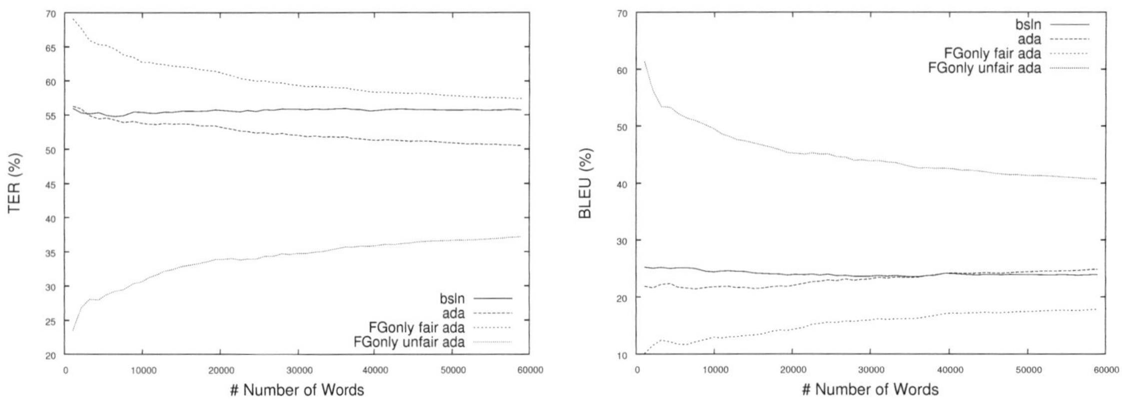

Figure 4: Incremental TER (left) and BLEU (right) of 4 systems showing different learning slopes.

ing method. On the other hand, it only provides cues about the average behavior and it is not as quickly informative as a single score could be. Hence, the design of a proper metric for measuring the backward reliability of MT systems is a challenging task that should be faced by the research community.

5 Summary and Future Work

The evaluation of a dynamically adapting system is an open issue. Metrics used in interactive MT such as HTER or field tests, are infeasible in the daily development as they involve human translators/judges. On the other hand, standard MT evaluation metrics either do not expose changes over time (BLEU, TER) or cannot be applied (CER).

The main contribution of this paper is to propose the use of the percentage slope for the evaluation of adapting MT systems, a metric borrowed from the theory on learning curves. For assessing its effectiveness, we have developed a simple but effective adapting SMT system suitable to work in the context of a CAT tool supported by MT. We have compared several ways to plot the change in error rate over time for different systems and identified the most suitable for computing the percentage slope. Finally, we have shown that the percentage slope well exposes the paradigmatic behaviors of evolving SMT systems.

The MateCAT project has scheduled field tests for the near future which will allow for inclusion of human productivity in the assessment of the percentage slope. Moreover, efforts will be devoted to the design of adaptation techniques which are more sophisticated than the simple approach used in this work.

We have also identified the issue of backward reliability of an adapting system, that is the ability to learn without forgetting the past, and the importance of monitoring it. A best practice based on a cross validation scheme has been proposed. Future investigations will concern finding an effective metric to measure backward reliability.

Acknowledgments

This work was supported by the MateCAT project, which is funded by the EC under the 7th Framework Programme.

References

N. Cesa-Bianchi, G. Reverberi, and S. Szedmak. 2008. Online learning algorithms for computer-assisted translation. Deliverable 4.2, SMART project (FP6). `http://www.smart-project.eu/files/D42.pdf`.

S. F. Chen and J. Goodman. 1999. An empirical study of smoothing techniques for language modeling. *Computer Speech and Language*, 4(13):359–393.

M. Federico, N. Bertoldi, and M. Cettolo. 2008. IRSTLM: an Open Source Toolkit for Handling Large Scale Language Models. In *Proc. of Interspeech*, pp. 1618–1621, Melbourne, Australia.

G. Foster and R. Kuhn. 2007. Mixture-Model Adaptation for SMT. In *Proc. of WMT*, pp. 128–135, Prague, Czech Republic.

S. Khadivi. 2008. *Statistical Computer-Assisted Translation*. Ph.D. thesis, RWTH Aachen University,

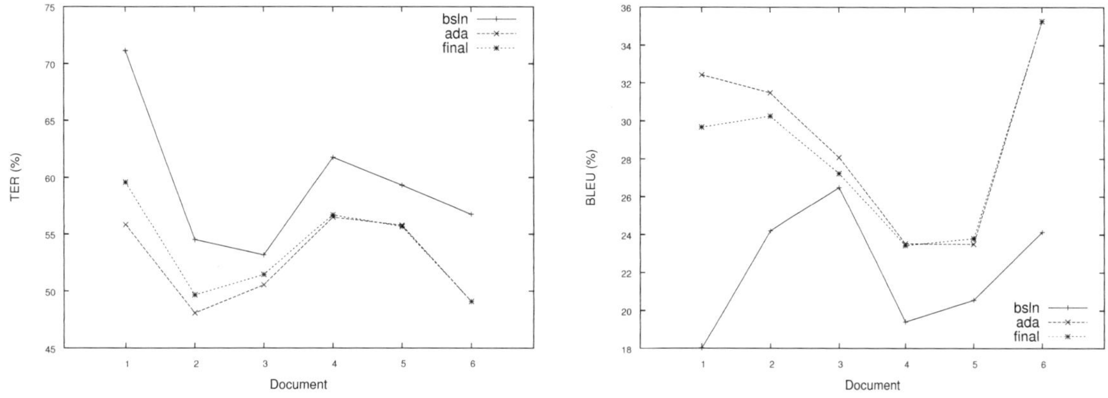

Figure 5: TER (left) and BLEU (right) scores of the baseline system, the evolving system and the final adapted system on the document-specific held-out test sets.

Aachen, Germany. Advisors: Hermann Ney and Enrique Vidal.

P. Koehn, H. Hoang, A. Birch, C. Callison-Burch, M. Federico, N. Bertoldi, B. Cowan, W. Shen, C. Moran, R. Zens, C. Dyer, O. Bojar, A. Constantin, and E. Herbst. 2007. Moses: Open Source Toolkit for Statistical Machine Translation. In *Proc. of ACL: Demo and Poster Sessions*, pp. 177–180, Prague, Czech Republic.

E. Macklovitch. 2006. Transtype2: The last word. In *Proc. of LREC 2006*, Genoa, Italy.

K. Papineni, S. Roukos, T. Ward, and W.-J. Zhu. 2001. Bleu: a method for automatic evaluation of machine translation. Research Report RC22176, IBM Research Division, Thomas J. Watson Research Center.

M. Snover, B. Dorr, R. Schwartz, L. Micciulla, and J. Makhoul. 2006. A study of translation edit rate with targeted human annotation. In *Proc. of AMTA*, Boston, US-MA.

E. Stump P.E. 2002. All about learning curves. In *Proc. of SCEA*. `http://www.galorath.com/images/uploads/LearningCurves1.pdf`.

I. H. Witten and T. C. Bell. 1991. The zero-frequency problem: Estimating the probabilities of novel events in adaptive text compression. *IEEE Trans. Inform. Theory*, IT-37(4):1085–1094.

The Trouble with SMT Consistency

Marine Carpuat and **Michel Simard**
National Research Council Canada
283 Alexandre-Taché Boulevard
Building CRTL, Room F-2007
Gatineau (Québec) J8X 3X7
Firstname.Lastname@nrc.ca

Abstract

SMT typically models translation at the sentence level, ignoring wider document context. Does this hurt the consistency of translated documents? Using a phrase-based SMT system in various data conditions, we show that SMT translates documents remarkably consistently, even without document knowledge. Nevertheless, translation inconsistencies often indicate translation errors. However, unlike in human translation, these errors are rarely due to terminology inconsistency. They are more often symptoms of deeper issues with SMT models instead.

1 Introduction

While Statistical Machine Translation (SMT) models translation at the sentence level (Brown et al., 1993), human translators work on larger translation units. This is partly motivated by the importance of producing consistent translations at the document level. Consistency checking is part of the quality assurance process, and complying with the terminology requirements of each task or client is crucial. In fact, many automatic tools have been proposed to assist humans in this important task (Itagaki et al., 2007; Dagan and Church, 1994, among others).

This suggests that wider document-level context information might benefit SMT models. However, we do not have a clear picture of the impact of sentence-based SMT on the translation of full documents. From a quality standpoint, it seems safe to assume that translation consistency is as desirable for SMT as for human translations. However, consistency needs to be balanced with other quality requirements. For instance, strict consistency might result in awkward repetitions that make translations less fluent. From a translation modeling standpoint, while typical SMT systems do not explicitly enforce translation consistency, they can learn lexical choice preferences from training data in the right domain.

In this paper, we attempt to get a better understanding of SMT consistency. We conduct an empirical analysis using a phrase-based SMT system in a variety of experimental settings, focusing on two simple, yet understudied, questions. Is SMT output consistent at the document level? Do inconsistencies indicate translation errors?

We will see that SMT consistency issues are quite different from consistency issues in human translations. In fact, while inconsistency errors in SMT output might be particularly obvious to the human eye, SMT is globally about as consistent as human translations. Furthermore, high translation consistency does not guarantee quality: weaker SMT systems trained on less data translate more consistently than stronger larger systems. Yet, inconsistent translations often indicate translation errors, possibly because words and phrases that translate inconsistently are the hardest to translate.

After discussing related work on consistency and document modeling for SMT (Section 2), we describe our corpora in Section 3 and our general methodology in Section 4. In Section 5, we discuss the results of an automatic analysis of translation consistency, before turning to manual analysis in Section 6.

2 Related work

While most SMT systems operate at the sentence level, there is increased interest in modeling document context and consistency in translation.

In earlier work (Carpuat, 2009), we investigate whether the "one sense per discourse" heuristic commonly used in word sense disambiguation (Gale et al., 1992) can be useful in translation. We show that "one translation per discourse" largely holds in automatically word-aligned French-English news stories, and that enforcing translation consistency as a simple post-processing constraint can fix some of the translation errors in a phrase-based SMT system. Ture et al. (2012) provide further empirical support by studying the consistency of translation rules used by a hierarchical phrase-based system to force-decode Arabic-English news documents from the NIST evaluation.

Several recent contributions integrate translation consistency models in SMT using a two-pass decoding approach. In phrase-based SMT, Xiao et al. (2011) show that enforcing translation consistency using post-processing and redecoding techniques similar to those introduced in Carpuat (2009) can improve the BLEU score of a Chinese-English system. Ture et al. (2012) also show significant BLEU improvements on Arabic-English and Chinese-English hierarchical SMT systems. During the second decoding pass, Xiao et al. (2011) use only translation frequencies from the first pass to encourage consistency, while Ture et al. (2012) also model word rareness by adapting term weighting techniques from information retrieval.

Another line of work focuses on cache-based adaptive models (Tiedemann, 2010a; Gong et al., 2011), which lets lexical choice in a sentence be informed by translations of previous sentences. However, cache-based models are sensitive to error propagation and can have a negative impact on some data sets (Tiedemann, 2010b). Moreover, this approach blurs the line between consistency and domain modeling. In fact, Gong et al. (2011) reports statistically significant improvements in BLEU only when combining pure consistency caches with topic and similarity caches, which do not enforce consistency but essentially perform domain or topic adaptation.

There is also work that indirectly addresses consistency, by encouraging the re-use of translation memory matches (Ma et al., 2011), or by using a graph-based representation of the test set to promote similar translations for similar sentences (Alexandrescu and Kirchhoff, 2009).

All these results suggest that consistency can be a useful learning bias to improve overall translation quality, as measured by BLEU score. However, they do not yet give a clear picture of the translation consistency issues faced by SMT systems. In this paper, we directly check assumptions on SMT consistency in a systematic analysis of a strong phrase-based system in several large data conditions.

3 Translation Tasks

We use PORTAGE, the NRC's state-of-the-art phrase-based SMT system (Foster et al., 2009), in a number of settings. We consider different language pairs, translation directions, training sets of different nature, domain and sizes. Dataset statistics are summarized in Table 1, and a description follows.

Parliament condition These conditions are designed to illustrate an ideal situation: a SMT system trained on large high-quality in-domain data.

The training set consists of Canadian parliamentary text, approximately 160 million words in each language (Foster et al., 2010). The test set also consists of documents from the Canadian parliament: 807 English and 476 French documents. Each document contains transcript of speech by a single person, typically focusing on a single topic. The source-language documents are relatively short: the largest has 1079 words, the average being 116 words for English documents, 124 for French. For each document, we have two translations in the other language: the first is our SMT output; the second is a postedited version of that output, produced by translators of the Canadian Parliamentary Translation and Interpretation services.

Web condition This condition illustrates a perhaps more realistic situation: a "generic" SMT system, trained on large quantities of heterogeneous data, used to translate slightly out-of-domain text.

The SMT system is trained on a massive corpus of documents harvested from the Canadian federal government's Web domain "gc.ca": close to 40M

lang	train data	# tgt words	test data	#tgt words	#docs	BLEU	WER
en-fr	parl	167M	parl	104k	807	45.2	47.1
fr-en	parl	149M	parl	51k	446	58.0	31.9
en-fr	gov web	641M	gov doc	336k	3419	29.4	60.4
zh-en	small (fbis)	10.5M	nist08	41k	109	23.6	68.9
zh-en	large (nist09)	62.6M	nist08	41k	109	27.2	66.1

Table 1: Experimental data

unique English-French sentence pairs. The test set comes from a different source to guarantee that there is no overlap with the training data. It consists of more than 3000 English documents from a Canadian provincial government organization, totalling 336k words. Reference translations into French were produced by professional translators (not postedited). Documents are quite small, each typically focusing on a specific topic over a varied range of domains: agriculture, environment, finance, human resources, public services, education, social development, health, tourism, etc.

NIST conditions These conditions illustrate the situation with a very different language pair, Chinese-to-English, under two different scenarios: a system built using small in-domain data and one using large more heterogeneous data.

Following Chen et al. (2012), in the *Small* data condition, the SMT system is trained using the FBIS Chinese-English corpus (10.5M target words); the *Large* data condition uses all the allowed bilingual corpora from NIST Open Machine Translation Evaluation 2009 (MT09), except the *UN*, *Hong Kong Laws* and *Hong Kong Hansard* datasets, for a total of 62.6M target words. Each system is then used to translate 109 Chinese documents from the 2008 NIST evaluations (MT08) test set. For this dataset, we have access to four different reference translations. The documents are longer on average than for the previous conditions, with approximately 470 words per document.

4 Consistency Analysis Method

We study *repeated phrases*, which we define as a pair $\langle p, d \rangle$ where d is a document and p a phrase type that occurs more than once in d.

Since this study focuses on SMT lexical choice consistency, we base our analysis on the actual translation lexicon used by our phrase-based translation system (i.e., its phrase-table.) For each document d in a given collection of documents, we identify all source phrases p from the SMT phrase-table that occur more than once. We only consider source phrases that contain at least one content word.

We then collect the set of translations T for each occurrence of the repeated phrase in d. Using the word-alignment between source and translation, for each occurrence of p in d, we check whether p is aligned to one of its translation candidates in the phrase-table. A repeated phrase is translated consistently if all the strings in T are identical — ignoring differences due to punctuation and stopwords.

The word-alignment is given by the SMT decoder in SMT output, and is automatically infered from standard IBM models for the reference[1].

Note that, by design, this approach introduces a bias toward components of the SMT system. A human annotator asked to identify translation inconsistencies in the same data would not tag the exact same set of instances. Our approach might detect translation inconsistencies that a human would not annotate, because of alignment noise or negligible variation in translations for instance. We address these limitations in Section 6. Conversely, a human annotator would be able to identify inconsistencies for phrases that are not in the phrase-table vocabulary. Our approach is not designed to detect these inconsistencies, since we focus on understanding lexical choice inconsistencies based on the knowledge available to our SMT system at translation time.

[1]We considered using forced decoding to align the reference to the source, but lack of coverage led us to use IBM-style word alignment instead.

lang	train	test	translator	# repeated phrases	consistent (%)	avg within doc freq (inconsistent)	avg within doc freq (all)	#docs with repeated phrases	% consistent that match reference	% inconsistent that match reference	% easy fixes
en-fr	parl	parl	SMT	4186	73.03	2.627	2.414	529	70.82	34.37	10.12
en-fr	parl	parl	reference	3250	75.94	2.542	2.427	468			
fr-en	parl	parl	SMT	2048	85.35	2.453	2.351	303	82.72	52.67	3.52
fr-en	parl	parl	reference	1373	82.08	2.455	2.315	283			
en-fr	gov web	gov doc	SMT	79248	88.92	6.262	3.226	2982	60.71	13.05	15.53
en-fr	gov web	gov doc	reference	25300	82.73	4.071	2.889	2166			
zh-en	small	nist08	SMT	2300	63.61	2.983	2.725	109	56.25	18.40	9.81
zh-en	small	nist08	reference	1431	71.49	2.904	2.695	109			
zh-en	large	nist08	SMT	2417	60.20	3.055	2.717	109	60.00	17.88	10.89
zh-en	large	nist08	reference	1919	68.94	2.851	2.675	109			

Table 2: Statistics on the translation consistency of repeated phrases for SMT and references in five translation tasks. See Section 5 for details

5 Automatic Analysis

Table 2 reports various statistics for the translations of repeated phrases in SMT and human references, for all tasks described in Section 3.

5.1 Global SMT consistency

First, we observe that SMT is remarkably consistent. This suggests that consistency in the source-side local context is sufficient to constrain the SMT phrase-table and language model to produce consistent translations for most of the phrases considered in our experiments.

The column "*consistent (%)*" in Table 2 shows that the majority of repeated phrases are translated consistently for all translation tasks considered. For French-English tasks, the percentage of repeated phrases ranges from 73 to 89% . The consistency percentages are lower for Chinese-English, a more distant language pair. The *Parliament* task shows that translating into the morphologically richer language yields slightly lower consistency, all other dimensions being identical. However, morphological variations only explain part of the difference: translating into French under the *Web* condition yields the highest consistency percentage of all tasks, which might be explained by the very short and repetitive nature of the documents. As can be expected, inconsistently translated phrases are repeated in a document more often than average for all tasks (columns "*avg within doc freq*").

Interestingly, the smaller and weaker Chinese-English translation system (23.6 BLEU) is more consistent than its stronger counterpart (27.2 BLEU) according to the consistency percentages.The smaller training condition yields a smaller phrase-table with a lower coverage of the *nist08* source, fewer translation alternatives and therefore more consistent translations. Clearly consistency does not correlate with translation quality, and global consistency rates are not indicators of the translation quality of particular system.

5.2 Consistency of reference translations

Surprisingly, the percentage of consistently translated phrases are very close in SMT output and human references, and even higher in SMT for 2 out of 5 tasks (Table 2).

Note that there are fewer instances of repeated phrases for human references than for SMT, because the phrase-table used as a translation lexicon naturally covers SMT output better than independently produced human translations. Word alignment is also noisier between source and reference.

lang	train	test	translator	# repeated phrases	consistent (%)	avg within doc freq (inconsistent)	avg within doc freq (all)	#docs with repeated phrases	% consistent that match reference	% inconsistent that match reference	% easy fixes
zh-en	small	nist08	human1	1496	71.59	2.974	2.725	109	68.91	34.59	9.71
			human2	1356	69.40	2.913	2.687	109	73.22	36.63	7.60
			human2	1296	71.60	2.870	2.671	109	71.88	36.68	8.15
zh-en	large	nist08	human1	2017	70.25	2.943	2.692	109	66.13	30.83	9.64
			human2	1855	67.17	2.854	2.667	109	69.42	31.86	9.16
			human3	1739	69.70	2.854	2.660	109	68.23	33.78	8.31

Table 3: Statistics on the translation consistency of repeated phrases in the multiple human references available on the Chinese-English NIST08 test set. See Section 5 for details

There is a much wider gap in coherence percentages between references and SMT for Chinese-English than French-English tasks, as can be expected for the harder language pair. In addition, the same *nist08* reference translations are more consistent according to the phrase-table learned in the small training condition than according to the larger phrase-table. This confirms that consistency can signal a lack of coverage for new contexts.

5.3 Consistency and correctness

While translation consistency is generally assumed to be desirable, it does not guarantee correctness: SMT translations of repeated phrases can be consistent and incorrect, or inconsistent and correct. In order to evaluate correctness automatically, we check whether translations of repeated phrases are found in the corresponding reference sentences. This is an approximation since the translation of a source phrase can be correct even if it is not found in the reference, and a target phrase found in the reference sentence is not necessarily a correct translation of the source phrase considered. Post-edited references alleviate some approximation errors for the *Parliament* tasks: if the translated phrase matches the references, it means that it was considered correct by the human post-editor who left it in. However, phrases modified during post-edition are not necessarily incorrect. We will address this approximation in Section 6.

The columns "% consistent that match reference" and "% inconsistent that match reference" in Table 2 show that consistently translated phrases match the references more often than the inconsistent ones. With the post-edited references in the *Parliament* condition, a non-negligible percentage of consistently translated phrases are wrong: 17% when translating into English, and 30% when translating into French. In contrast, inconsistently translated phrases are more likely to be incorrect: more than 65% into French and 47% into English. For all other tasks, fewer translations match the references since the references are not produced by post-edition, but we still observe the same trend as in the *Parliament* condition: inconsistent translations are more likely to be incorrect than consistent translations overall.

Four reference translations are available for the Chinese-English *nist08* test set. We only use the first one as a reference translation (in order to minimize setting variations with French-English conditions.) The three remaining human translations are used differently. We compare them against the reference, exactly as we do for SMT output. The resulting statistics are given in Table 3. Since we know that the human translations are correct, this shows that many correct translations are not identified when using our simple match technique to check correctness. However, it is interesting to note that (1) consistent human translations tend to match the human references more often than the inconsistent ones, and (2) inconsistent MT translations match references much less often than inconsistent human references.

Language	Examples $\langle p, d\rangle$	False Inconsistencies Same lemma		Misaligned	
en→fr	79	15	(19%)	8	(10%)
fr→en	92	12	(13%)	24	(26%)
Total	171	27	(16%)	32	(19%)

Table 4: False positives in the automatic identification of translation inconsistencies.

What goes wrong when inconsistent translations are incorrect? This question is hard to answer with automatic analysis only. As a first approximation, we check whether we could correct translations by replacing them with machine translations produced elsewhere in the document. In Table 2, we refer to this as "easy fixes" and show that only very few inconsistency errors can be corrected this way. These errors are therefore unlikely to be fixed by post-processing approaches that enforce hard consistency constraints (Carpuat, 2009).

6 Manual Analysis

In order to better understand what goes wrong with inconsistent translations, we conduct a manual analysis of these errors in the *Parliament* test condition (see Table 1). We randomly sample inconsistently translated phrases, and examine a total of 174 repeated phrases ($\langle p, d\rangle$ pairs, as defined in Section 4.)

6.1 Methodological Issues

We first try to quantify the limitations of our approach, and verify whether the inconsistencies detected automatically are indeed real inconsistencies. The results of this analysis are presented in Table 4. Given the set of translations for a repeated phrase, we ask questions relating to morphology and automatic word-level alignment:

Morphology Are some of the alternate translations for phrase p only different inflections of the same lemma? Assuming that inflectional morphology is governed by language-internal considerations more often than translational constraints, it is probably inaccurate to label morphological variations of the same word as inconsistencies. The annotations reveal that this only happens for 16% of our sample (column "*Same lemma*" in Table 4). Work is under way to build an accurate French lemmatizer to automatically abstract away from morphological variations.

Alignment Are some of the alternate translations only a by-product of word alignment errors? This happens for instance when the French word *partis* is identified as being translated in English sometimes as *parties* and sometimes as *political* in the same document: the apparent inconsistency is actually due to an incorrect alignment within the frequent phrase *political parties*. We identify 19% of word alignment issues in our manually annotated sample (column "*Misaligned*" in Table 4). While it is clear that alignment errors should be avoided, it is worth noting that such errors are sometimes indicative of translation problems: this happens, for instance, when a key content word is left untranslated by the SMT system.

Overall, this analysis confirms that, despite the approximations used, a majority of the examples detected by our method are real inconsistencies.

6.2 Analysis of Translation Errors

We then directly evaluate translation accuracy in our sample by checking whether the system translation match the post-edited references. Here we focus our attention on those 112 examples from our sample of inconsistently translated phrases that do not suffer from lemmatization or misalignment problems. For comparison, we also analyze 200 randomly sampled examples of consistently translated phrases. Note that the identification of consistent phrases is not subject to alignment and lemmatization problems, which we therefore ignore in this case. Details of this analysis can be found in Table 5.

We first note that 40% of all inconsistently translated phrase types were not postedited at all: their translation can therefore be considered correct. In the case of consistently translated phrases, the rate of unedited translations rises to 75%.

Focusing now on those phrases whose translation was postedited, we classify each in one of three broad categories of MT errors: *meaning*, *terminology*, and *style/syntax* errors (columns labeled "*Type of Correction*" in Table 5).

Terminology Errors Surprisingly, among the inconsistently translated phrases, we find only 13% of true terminological consistency errors, where

	Language	Examples $\langle p, d\rangle$	Unedited	(%)	Type of Correction (% of edited examples) Meaning		Terminology		Style/Syntax	
Inconsistent	en→fr	56	20	(36%)	8	(22%)	4	(11%)	27	(75%)
Translations	fr→en	56	25	(45%)	10	(32%)	5	(16%)	20	(65%)
	Total	112	45	(40%)	16	(24%)	9	(13%)	47	(70%)
Consistent	en→fr	100	70	(70%)	3	(10%)	0	(0%)	27	(90%)
Translations	fr→en	100	79	(79%)	5	(24%)	0	(0%)	16	(76%)
	Total	200	149	(75%)	8	(16%)	0	(0%)	43	(84%)

Table 5: Manual Classification of Posteditor Corrections on the *Parliament* Task

the SMT output is acceptable but different from standard terminology in the test domain. For instance, the French term *personnes handicapées* can be translated as either *persons with disabilities* or *people with disabilities*, but the former is prefered in the Parliament domain. In the case of consistently translated phrases, no such errors were detected. This contrasts with human translation, where enforcing term consistency is a major concern. In the large-data in-domain condition considered here, SMT mostly translates terminology consistently and correctly. It remains to be seen whether this still holds when translating out-of-domain, or for different genres of documents.

Meaning Errors *Meaning* errors occur when the SMT output fails to convey the meaning of the source phrase. For example, in a medical context, our MT system sometimes translates the French word *examen* into English as *review* instead of the correct *test* or *investigation*. Such errors make up 24% of all corrections on inconsistently translated phrases, 16% in the case of consistent translations.

Style/Syntax Errors By far the most frequent category turns out to be *style/syntax errors* (70% of corrections on inconsistently translated phrases, 84% on consistently translated phrases): these are situations where the SMT output preserves the meaning of the source phrase, but is still post-edited for syntactic or stylistic preference. This category actually covers a wide range of corrections. The more benign cases are more cosmetic in nature, for example when the posteditor changes the MT output "*In terms of the cost associated with...*" into "*With regard to spending related to...*". In the more severe cases, the posteditor completely rewrites a seriously disfluent machine translation. However, errors to which we have assigned this label have a common denominator: the inconsistent phrase that is the focus of our attention is not the source of the error, but rather "collateral damage" in the war against mediocre translations.

Taken together, these results show that translation inconsistencies in SMT tend to be symptoms of generic SMT problems such as meaning and fluency or syntax errors. Only a minority of observed inconsistencies turn out to be the type of terminology inconsistencies that are a concern in human translations.

7 Conclusion

We have presented an in-depth study of machine translation consistency, using state-of-the-art SMT systems trained and evaluated under various realistic conditions. Our analysis highlights a number of important, and perhaps overlooked, issues regarding SMT consistency.

First, SMT systems translate documents remarkably consistently, even without explicit knowledge of extra-sentential context. They even exhibit global consistency levels comparable to that of professional human translators.

Second, high translation consistency does not correlate with better quality: as can be expected in phrase-based SMT, weaker systems trained on less data produce translations that are more consistent than higher-quality systems trained on larger more heterogeneous data sets.

However, this does not imply that inconsistencies are good either: inconsistently translated phrases coincide with translation errors much more often than consistent ones. In practice, translation inconsistency could therefore be used to detect words and phrases that are hard to translate for a given system.

Finally, manual inspection of inconsistent translations shows that only a small minority of errors are the kind of terminology problems that are the main concern in human translations. Instead, the majority of errors highlighted by inconsistent translations are symptoms of other problems, notably incorrect meaning translation, and syntactic or stylistic issues. These problems are just as prevalent with consistent as with inconsistent translations.

While directly enforcing translation consistency in MT may prove useful in some situations, our analysis suggests that the phrase-based SMT systems considered here would benefit more from directly tackling the underlying —- and admittedly more complex — problems of meaning and syntactic errors.

In future work, we plan to improve our analysis by extending our diagnosis methods, and consider additional data conditions and genres. We also plan to explore the potential of consistency for confidence estimation and error detection.

Acknowledgments

We would like to thank the Canadian Translation Bureau and the Portage team at the National Research Council for providing the post-edited and machine translations used in this study.

References

Andrei Alexandrescu and Katrin Kirchhoff. 2009. Graph-based learning for statistical machine translation. In *Proceedings of Human Language Technologies: The 2009 Annual Conference of the North American Chapter of the Association for Computational Linguistics*, pages 119–127, Boulder, CO, June.

Peter E. Brown, Vincent J. Della Pietra, Stephen A. Della Pietra, and Robert L. Mercer. 1993. The Mathematics of Statistical Machine Translation: Parameter Estimation. *Computational Linguistics*, 19(2):263–312.

Marine Carpuat. 2009. One translation per discourse. In *Proceedings of the Workshop on Semantic Evaluations: Recent Achievements and Future Directions (SEW-2009)*, pages 19–27, Boulder, CO, June.

Boxing Chen, Roland Kuhn, and Samuel Larkin. 2012. PORT: a Precision-Order-Recall MT evaluation metric for Tuning. In *Proceedings of the 50th Annual Meeting of the Association for Computational Linguistics (ACL-2012)*.

Ido Dagan and Ken Church. 1994. Termight: Identifying and translating technical terminology. In *Proceedings of the Fourth Conference on Applied Natural Language Processing*, pages 34–40, Stuttgart, Germany, October.

George Foster, Boxing Chen, Eric Joanis, Howard Johnson, Roland Kuhn, and Samuel Larkin. 2009. PORTAGE in the NIST 2009 MT Evaluation. Technical report, NRC-CNRC.

George Foster, Pierre Isabelle, and Roland Kuhn. 2010. Translating structured documents. In *Proceedings of the Ninth Conference of the Association for Machine Translation in the Americas (AMTA 2010)*, Denver, Colorado, November.

William A. Gale, Kenneth W. Church, and David Yarowsky. 1992. One Sense Per Discourse. In *Proceedings of the workshop on Speech and Natural Language*, Harriman, NY, February.

Zhengxian Gong, Min Zhang, and Guodong Zhou. 2011. Cache-based document-level statistical machine translation. In *Proceedings of the 2011 Conference on Empirical Methods in Natural Language Processing*, pages 909–919, July.

Masaki Itagaki, Takako Aikawa, and Xiaodong He. 2007. Automatic validation of terminology translation consistency with statistical method. In *Proceedings of Machine Translation Summit XI*, pages 269–274, September.

Yanjun Ma, Yifan He, Andy Way, and Josef van Genabith. 2011. Consistent translation using discriminative learning - a translation memory-inspired approach. In *Proceedings of the 49th Annual Meeting of the Association for Computational Linguistics: Human Language Technologies*, pages 1239–1248, Portland, Oregon, USA, June.

Jörg Tiedemann. 2010a. Context adaptation in statistical machine translation using models with exponentially decaying cache. In *Proceedings of the 2010 Workshop on Domain Adaptation for Natural Language Processing*, pages 8–15, Uppsala, Sweden, July.

Jörg Tiedemann. 2010b. To Cache or Not To Cache? Experiments with Adaptive Models in Statistical Machine Translation. In *Joint Fifth Workshop on Statistical Machine Translation and MetricsMATR*, pages 195–200, Uppsala, Sweden, July.

Ferhan Ture, Douglas W. Oard, and Philip Resnik. 2012. Encouraging consistent translation choices. In *Proceedings of the 2012 Conference of the North American Chapter of the Association for Computational Linguistics: Human Language Technologies (NAACL HLT 2012)*, Montreal, Canada, June.

Tong Xiao, Jingbo Zhu, Shujie Yao, and Hao Zhang. 2011. Document-level Consistency Verification in Machine Translation. In *Machine Translation Summit XIII*, pages 131–138, Xiamen, China, September.

Phrase Model Training for Statistical Machine Translation with Word Lattices of Preprocessing Alternatives

Joern Wuebker and Hermann Ney
Human Language Technology and Pattern Recognition Group
RWTH Aachen University
Aachen, Germany
{wuebker,ney}@cs.rwth-aachen.de

Abstract

In statistical machine translation, word lattices are used to represent the ambiguities in the preprocessing of the source sentence, such as word segmentation for Chinese or morphological analysis for German. Several approaches have been proposed to define the probability of different paths through the lattice with external tools like word segmenters, or by applying indicator features. We introduce a novel lattice design, which explicitly distinguishes between different preprocessing alternatives for the source sentence. It allows us to make use of specific features for each preprocessing type and to lexicalize the choice of lattice path directly in the phrase translation model. We argue that forced alignment training can be used to learn lattice path and phrase translation model simultaneously. On the news-commentary portion of the German→English WMT 2011 task we can show moderate improvements of up to 0.6% BLEU over a state-of-the-art baseline system.

1 Introduction

The application of statistical machine translation (SMT) to word lattice input was first introduced for the translation of speech recognition output. Rather than translating the single-best transcription, the speech recognition system encodes all possible transcriptions and their probabilities within a word lattice, which is then used as input for the machine translation system (Ney, 1999; Matusov et al., 2005; Bertoldi et al., 2007).

Since then, several groups have adapted this approach to model ambiguities in representing the source language with lattices and were able to report improvements over their respective baselines. The probabilities for different paths through the lattice are usually modeled by assigning probabilities to arcs as a byproduct of the lattice generation or by defining binary indicator features. Applying the first method only makes sense if the lattice construction is based on a single, comprehensive probabilistic method, like a Chinese word segmentation model as is used by Xu et al. (2005). In applications like the one described by Dyer et al. (2008), where several different segmenters for Chinese are combined to create the lattice, this is not possible. Also, our intuition suggests that simply defining indicator features for each of the segmenters may not be ideal, if we assume that there is not a single best segmenter, but rather that for different data instances a different one works best.

In this paper, we propose to model the lattice path implicitly within the phrase translation model. We introduce a novel lattice design, which explicitly distinguishes between different ways of preprocessing the source sentence. It enables us to define specific binary features for each preprocessing type and to learn lexicalized lattice path probabilities and the phrase translation model simultaneously with a forced alignment training procedure.

To train the phrase translation model, most state-of-the-art SMT systems rely on heuristic phrase extraction from a word-aligned training corpus. Using a modified version of the translation decoder to force-align the training data provides a more consistent way of training. Wuebker et al. (2010) introduce a leave-one-out method which can overcome the over-fitting effects inherent to this training procedure (DeNero et al., 2006). The authors report this to yield both a significantly smaller phrase table and higher translation quality than the heuristic phrase extraction.

We argue that applying forced alignment training helps to exploit the full potential of word lattice translation. The effects of the training on lattice input are analyzed on the news-commentary portion of the German→English WMT 2011 task. Our results show moderate improvements of up to 0.6% BLEU over the baseline.

This paper is organized as follows: We will review related work in Section 2, describe the decoder in Section 3 and present our novel lattice design in Section 4. The phrase training algorithm is introduced in Section 5, and Section 6 gives a detailed account of the experimental setup and discusses the results. Finally, our findings are summarized in Section 7.

2 Related work

Word lattices have been used for machine translation of text in a variety of ways. Dyer et al. (2008) use it to encode different Chinese word segmentations or Arabic morphological analyses. For the phrase-based model, they report improvements of up to 0.9% BLEU for Chinese→English and 1.6% BLEU for Arabic→English over the respective single best word segmented and morphologically analyzed source. These results are achieved without an explicit way of modeling probabilities for different paths within the lattice. The training of the phrase model is done by generating one version of the training data for each segmentation method or morphological analysis. The word alignments are trained separately, and are then concatenated for phrase extraction. Our work differs from (Dyer et al., 2008) in that we explicitly distinguish the various preprocessing types in the lattice so that we can define specific path features and lexicalize the lattice path probabilities within the phrase model.

In (Xu et al., 2005) the probability of a segmentation, as given by the Chinese word segmentation model, and the translation model are combined into a global decision rule. This is done by weighting the lattice edges with a source language model. The authors report an improvement of 1.5% BLEU over translation of the single best segmentation with a phrase-based SMT system.

Dyer (2009) introduces a maximum entropy model for compound word splitting, which he uses to create word lattices for translation input. He shows improvements in German-English, Hungarian-English and Turkish-English over state-of-the-art baselines.

For the German→English WMT 2010 task, Hardmeier et al. (2010) encode the morphological reduction and decompounding of the German surface form as alternative paths in a word lattice. They show improvements of roughly 0.5% BLEU over the baseline. A binary indicator feature is added to the log-linear framework for the alternative edges. Additionally, they integrate long-range reorderings of the source sentence into the lattice, in order to match the word order of the English language, which yields another improvement of up to 0.5% BLEU.

Niehues and Kolss (2009) also use lattices to encode different alternative reorderings of the source sentence which results in an improvement of 2.0% BLEU over the baseline on the WMT 2008 German→English task.

Onishi et al. (2010) propose a method of modeling paraphrases in a lattice. They perform experiments on the English→Japanese and English→Chinese IWSLT 2007 tasks, and report improvements of 1.1% and 0.9% BLEU over a paraphrase-augmented baseline.

Schroeder et al. (2009) generalize usage of lattices to combine input from multiple source languages.

Factored translation models (Koehn and Hoang, 2007) approach the idea of integrating annotation into translation from the opposite direction. Where lattices allow the decoder to choose a single level of annotation as translation source, factored models are designed to jointly translate several annotation levels (factors). Thus, they are more suited to integrate low-level annotation that by itself does not provide sufficient information for accurate translation, like part-of-speech tags, gender, etc. On the other hand, they require a one-to-one correspondence between the factors, which makes them unsuitable to model word segmentation or decompounding.

The problem of performing real training for the phrase translation model has been approached in a number of different ways in the past. The first one, to the best of our knowledge, was the joint probability phrase model presented by Marcu and Wong (2002). It is shown to perform slightly inferior to the standard heuristic phrase extraction from word alignments by Koehn et al. (2003).

A detailed analysis of the inherent over-fitting problems when training a generative phrase model with the EM algorithm is given in (DeNero et al., 2006). These findings are in principle confirmed by Moore and Quirk (2007) who, however, can show that their model is less sensitive to reducing computational resources than the state-of-the-art heuristic.

Birch et al. (2006) and DeNero et al. (2008) present alternative training procedures for the joint model introduced by Marcu and Wong (2002), which are shown to improve its performance.

In (Mylonakis and Sima'an, 2008) a phrase model is described, whose training procedure is designed to counteract the inherent over-fitting problem by including prior probabilities based on Inversion Transduction Grammar and smoothing as learning objective. It yields a small improvement over a standard phrase-based baseline.

Ferrer and Juan (2009) present an approach, where the phrase model is trained by a semi-hidden Markov model.

In this work we apply the phrase training method introduced by Wuebker et al. (2010), where the phrase translation model of a fully competitive SMT system is trained in a generative way. The key to avoiding the over-fitting effects described by DeNero et al. (2006) is their novel leave-one-out procedure.

3 Decoding

3.1 Phrase-based translation

We use a standard phrase-based decoder which searches for the best translation $\hat{e}_1^{\hat{I}}$ for a given input sentence f_1^J by maximizing the posterior probability

$$\hat{e}_1^{\hat{I}} = \operatorname*{arg\,max}_{I,e_1^I} Pr(e_1^I|f_1^J). \tag{1}$$

Generalizing the noisy channel approach (Brown et al., 1990) and making use of the maximum approximation (Viterbi), the decoder directly models the posterior probability by a log-linear combination of several feature functions $h_m(e_1^I, s_1^K, f_1^J)$ weighted with scaling factors λ_m, which results in the decision rule (Och and Ney, 2004)

$$\hat{e}_1^{\hat{I}} = \operatorname*{arg\,max}_{I,e_1^I,K,s_1^K} \left\{ \sum_{m=1}^{M} \lambda_m h_m(e_1^I, s_1^K, f_1^J) \right\}. \tag{2}$$

Here, s_1^K denotes the segmentation of e_1^I and f_1^J into K phrase-pairs and their alignment. The features used are the language model, phrase translation and lexical smoothing models in both directions, word and phrase penalty and a simple distance-based reordering penalty.

3.2 Lattice translation

For lattice input we generalize Equation 2 to also maximize over the set of sentences $\mathcal{F}(\mathcal{L})$ encoded by a given source word lattice $\mathcal{L}$:

$$\hat{e}_1^{\hat{I}} = \operatorname*{arg\,max}_{I,e_1^I,K,s_1^K,f_1^J \in \mathcal{F}(\mathcal{L})} \left\{ \sum_{m=1}^{M} \lambda_m h_m(e_1^I, s_1^K, f_1^J) \right\} \tag{3}$$

Note that in this formulation there are no probabilities assigned to the arcs of $\mathcal{L}$. We define additional binary indicator features h_m and lexicalize path probabilities by encoding the path into the word identities. To translate lattice input, we adapt the standard phrase-based decoding algorithm as described in (Matusov et al., 2008). The decoder keeps track of the covered *slots*, which represent the topological order of the nodes, rather than the covered words. When expanding a hypothesis, it has to be verified that there is no overlap between the covered nodes and that a path exists from start to goal node,

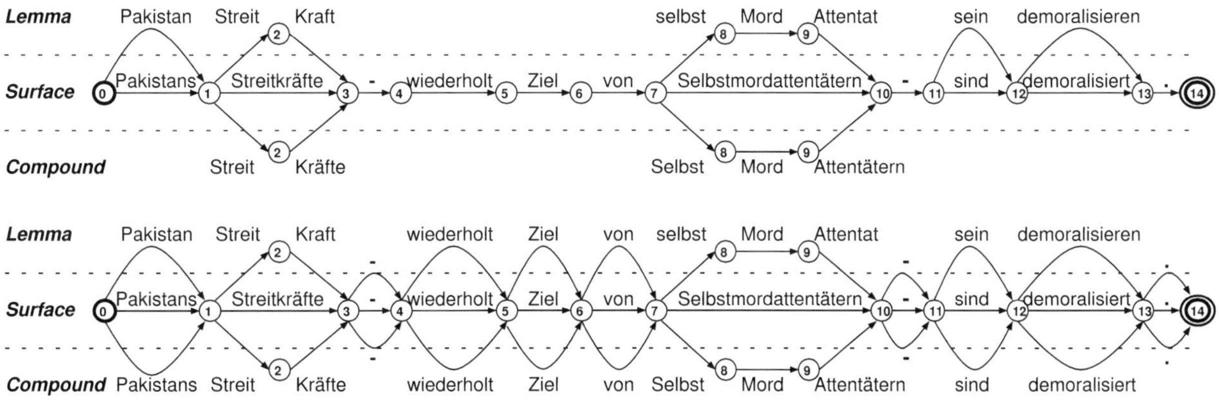

Figure 1: Top: Slim lattice. Bottom: Full lattice. The sentence is taken from the training data. The three layers *Surface*, *Compound* and *Lemma* are separated with dashed lines. Nodes are labeled with slot information. Slots are ordered horizontally, layers vertically.

which passes through all covered nodes. In practice, when considering a possible expansion covering slots $j', ..., j''$ with start and end states n' and n'', we make sure that the following two conditions hold:

- n' is reachable from the lattice node that corresponds to the nearest already covered slot to the left of j'.
- The node that corresponds to the nearest already covered slot to the right of j'' is reachable from n''.

It was noted by Dyer et al. (2008) that the standard distance-based reordering model needs to be redefined for lattice input. We define the distortion penalty as the difference in slot number. Using the shortest path within the lattice is reported to have better performance in (Dyer et al., 2008), however we did not implement it due to time constraints.

4 Lattice design

We construct lattices from three different preprocessing variants of the German source side of the data. The surface form is the standard tokenization of the source sentence. The word compounds are produced by the frequency-based compound splitting method described in (Koehn and Knight, 2003), applied to the tokenized sentence. From the compound split sentence we produce the lemma of the German words by applying the TreeTagger toolkit (Schmid, 1995). Each of the different preprocessing variants is assigned a separate *layer* within the lattice. For the phrase model, word identities are defined by both the word and its layer. In this way, the phrase model can assign different scores to phrases in different layers, allowing it to guide the search towards a specific layer for each word. In practice, this is done by annotating words with a unique identifier for each layer. For example, the word *sein* from the lemmatized layer will be written as *LEM.sein* within both the data and the phrase table. If *sein* appears in the surface form layer, it will be written as *SUR.sein* and is treated as a different word. *SUR* is the identifier for the compound layer.

We experiment with two different lattice designs. In the *full* lattice, all three layers are included for each source word in surface form. The *slim* lattice only includes arcs for the lemma layer if it differs from the surface form, and only includes arcs for the compound layer if it differs from both surface form and lemma. Figure 1 shows a slim and a full lattice for the same training data sentence.

For each layer, we add two indicator features to the phrase table: One binary feature which is set to 1 if the phrase is taken from this layer, and one feature which is equal to the number of words from this layer. This results in six additional feature functions, whose weights are optimized jointly with the standard features described in Section 3.1. We will denote them as *layer features*.

5 Phrase translation model training

To train the phrase model, we use a modified version of the translation decoder to force-align the training data. We apply the method described in (Wuebker et al., 2010), but with word lattices on the source side. To avoid over-fitting, we use their cross-validation technique, which is described as a low-cost alternative to leave-one-out. For cross-validation we segment the training data into batches containing 5000 sentences. For each batch, the phrase table is updated by reducing the phrase counts by the local counts produced by the current batch in the previous training iteration. For the first iteration, we perform the standard phrase extraction separately for each batch to produce the local counts. Singleton phrases are assigned the probability $\beta^{(|\tilde{f}|+|\tilde{e}|)}$ with the source and target phrase lengths $|\tilde{f}|$ and $|\tilde{e}|$ and fixed $\beta = e^{-5}$ (length-based leave-one-out). Sentences for which the decoder is not able to find an alignment are discarded (about 4% for our experiments). To estimate the probabilities of the phrase model, we count all phrase pairs used in training within an n-best list (equally weighted). The translation probability for a phrase pair $(\tilde{f}, \tilde{e})$ is estimated as

$$p_{FA}(\tilde{e}|\tilde{f}) = \frac{C_{FA}(\tilde{f}, \tilde{e})}{C_{mon}(\tilde{f})}, \quad (4)$$

where $C_{FA}(\tilde{f}, \tilde{e})$ is the count of the phrase pair $(\tilde{f}, \tilde{e})$ in the force-aligned training data. In order to learn the lattice path along with the phrase translation probabilities, we make the following modification to the original formulation in (Wuebker et al., 2010). The denominator $C_{mon}(\tilde{f})$ is the count of $\tilde{f}$ in the target side of the training data, rather than using the real marginal counts. This means that it is independent of the training procedure, and can be computed by ignoring one side of the training data and performing a simple n-gram count on the other. In this way the model learns to prefer lattice paths which are taken more often in training. For example, if the phrase *(LEM.Streit LEM.Kraft)* is used to align the sentence from Figure 1, $C_{mon}(\tilde{f})$ will be increased for $\tilde{f}$ = *(SUR.Streitkräfte)* and $\tilde{f}$ = *(SPL.Streit SPL.Kräfte)* without affecting their joint counts. This leads to a lower probability for these phrases, which is not the case if marginal counts are used. Note that on the source side we have one training corpus for each lattice layer, which are concatenated to compute $C_{mon}(\tilde{f})$. The size of the n-best lists used in this work is fixed to 20000. Using smaller n-best lists was tested, but seems to have disadvantages for the application to lattices. After re-estimation of the phrase model, the feature weights are optimized again.

In order to achieve a good coverage of the training data, we allow the decoder to generate *backoff phrases*. If a source phrase consisting of a single word does not have any translation candidates left after the bilingual phrase matching, one phrase pair is added to the translation candidates for each word in the target sentence. The backoff phrases are assigned a fixed probability $\gamma = e^{-12}$. Note that this is smaller than the probability the phrase would be assigned according to the length-based leave-one-out heuristic, leading to a preference of singleton phrases over backoff phrases. The lexical smoothing models are applied in the usual way to both singleton and backoff phrases. After each sentence, the backoff phrases are discarded. However, in the experiments for this work, introducing backoff phrases only increases the coverage from 95.8% to 96.2% of the sentences.

6 Experimental evaluation

6.1 Experimental setup

Our experiments are carried out on the news-commentary portion of the German→English data provided for the *EMNLP 2011 Sixth Workshop on Statistical Machine Translation* (WMT 2011).* We use `newstest2008` as development set and `newstest2009` and `newstest2010` as unseen test sets. The word alignments are produced with GIZA++ (Och and Ney, 2003). To optimize the log-linear parameters, the Downhill-Simplex algorithm (Nelder and Mead, 1965) is applied with BLEU (Papineni et al., 2002) as optimization criterion. The

*`http://www.statmt.org/wmt11`

		German			English
		Surface	Compound	Lemma	
Train	Sentences	136K			
	Running Words	3.4M	3.5M		3.3M
	Vocabulary Size	118K	81K	52K	57K
newstest2008	Sentences	2051			
	Running Words	48K	50K		50K
	Vocabulary Size	10.3K	9.7K	7.3K	8.1K
	OOVs (Running Words)	3041	2092	1742	2070
newstest2009	Sentences	2525			
	Running Words	63K	66K		66K
	Vocabulary Size	12.2K	11.4K	8.4K	9.4K
	OOVs (Running Words)	4058	2885	2400	2729
newstest2010	Sentences	2489			
	Running Words	62K	65K		62K
	Vocabulary Size	12.3K	11.4K	8.5K	9.2K
	OOVs (Running Words)	4357	2952	2565	2742

Table 1: Corpus Statistics for the WMT 2011 news-commentary data, the development set (`newstest2008`) and the two test sets (`newstest2009`, `newstest2010`). For the source side, three different preprocessing alternatives are included: Surface, Compound and Lemma.

language model is a standard 4-gram LM with modified Kneser-Ney smoothing (Chen and Goodman, 1998) produced with the SRILM toolkit (Stolcke, 2002). It is trained on the full bilingual data and parts of the monolingual News crawl corpus provided for WMT 2011. Numbers are replaced with a single category symbol in a separate preprocessing step and we apply the long-range part-of-speech based reordering rules proposed by (Popović and Ney, 2006).

Table 1 shows statistics for the bilingual training data and the development and test corpora for the three different German preprocessing alternatives. It can be seen that both compound splitting and lemmatization reduce the vocabulary size and number of out-of-vocabulary (OOV) words. Results are measured in BLEU and TER (Snover et al., 2006), which are computed case-insensitively with a single reference.

6.2 Baseline experiments

To get an overview over the effects of the different preprocessing alternatives for the German source, we built three baseline systems, one for each preprocessing type. The phrase tables are extracted heuristically in the standard way from the word-aligned training data. Additionally, we performed phrase training for the compound split version of the data. The results are shown in Table 2. When moving from the Surface to the Compound layer, we observe improvements of up to 1.0% in BLEU and 1.1% in TER. Reducing the morphological richness further (Lemma) leads to a clear performance drop. Application of phrase training on the compound split data yields a small degradation in TER on all data sets and in BLEU on `newstest2010`. We assume that this is due to the small size of the training data and its heterogeneity, which makes it hard for the decoder to find good phrase alignments.

6.3 Lattice experiments: Heuristic extraction

We generated both slim and full lattices for all data sets. Similar to (Dyer et al., 2008), we concatenate the three training data sets and their word alignments to extract the phrases. Note that this only produces single-layer phrases. It can be seen in Table 2 that without the application of layer features the slim lattice slightly outperforms the full lattice. In-

		newstest2008		newstest2009		newstest2010	
		BLEU [%]	TER [%]	BLEU [%]	TER [%]	BLEU [%]	TER [%]
Baseline	Surface	19.5	64.6	18.6	64.4	20.6	62.8
	Compounds	20.5	**63.5**	19.1	63.5	21.1	61.9
	FA Compounds	20.5	63.9	19.1	63.8	20.9	62.3
	Lemma	19.2	65.4	18.2	65.2	19.9	63.9
Slim Lattice (heuristic)	without layer feat.	19.9	64.4	18.9	64.1	20.8	62.6
	with layer feat.	20.5	63.8	19.4	63.9	21.0	62.4
Full Lattice (heuristic)	without layer feat.	19.8	64.6	18.7	64.2	20.6	62.8
	with layer feat.	20.4	64.0	19.5	63.8	21.3	62.3
Full Lattice (FA w/o layer feat.)	without layer feat.	20.0	64.3	19.3	64.1	20.8	62.6
	with layer feat.	20.2	64.3	19.1	64.2	20.7	62.8
Full Lattice (FA w/ layer feat.)	without layer feat.	20.5	63.7	19.5	63.6	21.3	62.1
	with layer feat.	**20.7**	63.6	**19.7**	**63.4**	**21.4**	**61.8**

Table 2: Results on the German-English WMT 2011 data. Scores are computed case-insensitively for BLEU [%] and TER [%]. We evaluate performance of the baseline systems, one for each of the three different encodings, with both slim and full lattices using heuristic phrase extraction and with full lattices using forced alignment phrase model training (*FA*). All lattice systems are evaluated with and without layer features. The best scores in each column are in boldface, statistically significant improvement over the *Compounds* baseline is marked with blue color.

troducing layer features boosts the performance for both lattice types. However, the performance increase is considerably larger for the full lattice systems, which now outperform the slim lattice systems on `newstest2009` and `newstest2010`. Compared to the *Compounds* baseline, the full lattice system with layer features shows a small improvement of up to 0.4% BLEU on `newstest2009` and `newstest2010`, but a degradation in TER.

6.4 Lattice experiments: Phrase training

The experiments on phrase training are setup as follows. The phrase table is initialized with the standard extraction and is identical to the one used for the experiments in Section 6.3. The log-linear scaling factors used in training are the optimized parameters on the corresponding lattice, also taken from the experiments described in Section 6.3. The forced alignment procedure was run for one iteration. Further iterations were tested, but did not give any improvements.

The phrase training was performed on the full lattice design. The reason for this is that we want the system to learn all possible phrases. Even if there is no difference in wording between the layers in training, the additional phrases could be useful for unseen test data. The training was performed both with and without layer features. The resulting systems were also optimized with and without layer features, resulting in four different setups.

From the results in Table 2 it is clear that phrase training without layer features does not have the desired effect. Even if we apply layer features to the system trained without them, we do not reach the performance of the best standard lattice system. We conclude that, without these indicator features, the standard lattice system does not produce good phrase alignments.

When the layer features are applied for both training and translation, we observe improvements of up to 0.2% in BLEU and 0.5% in TER over the corresponding standard lattice system. The gap between the systems with and without layer features is much smaller than for the heuristically trained lattices. This indicates that our goal of encoding the best lattice path directly in the phrase model was at least partially achieved. However, in order to exceed the performance of our state-of-the-art baseline on both measures, the layer features are still needed within the phrase training procedure and for translation. Al-

source	Das Warten hat gedauert mehr als NUM Minuten, was im Fall einer Straße, wo werden erwartet NUM Menschen, **ist unverständlich.**
reference	The wait lasted more than NUM minutes, something incomprehensible for a race where you expect more than NUM people.
lattice (heuristic)	The wait has taken more than NUM minutes, which in the case of a street, where NUM people are expected to be, **can't understand it.**
lattice (FA)	The wait has taken more than NUM minutes, which in the case of a street, where expected NUM people, **is incomprehensible.**

Figure 2: Example sentence from the `newstest2009` data set. The faulty phrase in the heuristic lattice translation is marked in boldface.

together, our phrase trained lattice approach outperforms the state-of-the-art baseline on all three data sets by up to 0.6% BLEU. On `newstest2009`, this result is statistically significant with 95% confidence according to the bootstrap resampling method described by Koehn (2004).

For a direct comparison between the heuristic and phrase-trained full lattice systems, we manually inspected the optimized log-linear parameter values for the layer features. We observe that for the standard lattices, paths through the lemmatized layer are heavily penalized. In the phrase trained lattice setup, the penalty is much smaller. As a result, the number of words from the Lemma layer used for translation of the `newstest2009` data set is increased by 49% from 1828 to 2715 words. However, a manual inspection of the translations reveals that the main improvement seems to come from a better choice of phrases from the Compound layer. More specifically, the used phrases tend to be shorter – the average phrase length of Compound layer phrases is 1.5 words for both the baseline and the heuristic lattice system. In the phrase trained lattice system, it is 1.3 words. An example is given in Figure 2. We focus on the end of the sentence, where the heuristic system uses the rather disfluent phrase (ist unverständlich. # can't understand it.), whereas the forced alignment trained system applies the three phrases (ist # is), (unverständlich # incomprehensible) and (. # .).

This effect can be explained by the leave-one-out procedure. As lemmatized phrases usually map to several phrases in the other layers, their count is generally higher. Application of leave-one-out, which reduces the counts of all phrases extracted from the current sentence by a fixed value, therefore has a stronger penalizing effect on Surface and Compound layer phrases. In the extreme case, phrases which are singletons in the Compound layer are unlikely to be used at all in training, if the corresponding phrase in the Lemma layer has a higher count. While this rarely leads to the competing lemmatized phrases being used in free translation, it allows for shorter, more general phrases from the more expressive layers to be applied. Indeed, the 'bad' phrase (ist unverständlich. # can't understand it.) from the example in Figure 2 is a singleton.

7 Conclusion and future work

In this work we apply a forced alignment phrase training technique to input word lattices in SMT for the first time. The goal of encoding better lattice path probabilities directly into the phrase model was at least partially successful. The proposed method outperforms our baseline by up to 0.6% BLEU. To achieve this, we presented a novel lattice design, which distinguishes between different *layers*, for which we can define separate indicator features. Although these layer features are still necessary for the final system to improve over state-of-the-art performance, they are less important than in the heuristically trained setup.

One advantage of our approach is its adaptability to a variety of scenarios. In future work, we plan to apply it to additional language pairs. Arabic and Chinese on the source side, where the layers could represent different word segmentations, seem a natural choice. We also hope to be able to leverage larger training data sets. As a natural extension we plan to allow learning of cross-layer phrases. Further, applying this framework to lattices modeling different reorderings could be an interesting direction.

Acknowledgments

This work was partially realized as part of the Quaero Programme, funded by OSEO, French State agency for innovation, and also partially funded by the European Union under the FP7 project T4ME Net, Contract No. 249119.

References

N. Bertoldi, R. Zens, and M. Federico. 2007. Speech translation by confusion network decoding. In *Proceedings of ICASSP 2007*, pages 1297–1300, Honolulu, Hawaii, April.

Alexandra Birch, Chris Callison-Burch, Miles Osborne, and Philipp Koehn. 2006. Constraining the phrase-based, joint probability statistical translation model. In *Proceedings of the Workshop on Statistical Machine Translation*, pages 154–157, Jun.

Peter F. Brown, John Cocke, Stephen A. Della Pietra, Vincent J. Della Pietra, Fredrick Jelinek, John D. Lafferty, Robert L. Mercer, and Paul S. Roossin. 1990. A statistical approach to machine translation. *Computational Linguistics*, 16:79–85, June.

Stanley F. Chen and Joshua Goodman. 1998. An empirical study of smoothing techniques for language modeling. Technical Report TR-10-98, Computer Science Group, Harvard University, Aug.

John DeNero, Dan Gillick, James Zhang, and Dan Klein. 2006. Why Generative Phrase Models Underperform Surface Heuristics. In *Proceedings of the Workshop on Statistical Machine Translation*, pages 31–38, New York City, June.

John DeNero, Alexandre Buchard-Côté, and Dan Klein. 2008. Sampling Alignment Structure under a Bayesian Translation Model. In *Proceedings of the 2008 Conference on Empirical Methods in Natural Language Processing*, pages 314–323, Honolulu, October.

C. Dyer, S. Muresan, and P. Resnik. 2008. Generalizing word lattice translation. In *Proceedings of Annual Meeting of the Association for Computational Linguistics*, pages 1012–1020, Columbus, Ohio, June.

Chris Dyer. 2009. Using a maximum entropy model to build segmentation lattices for mt. In *Proceedings of the 2009 Annual Conference of the North American Chapter of the ACL*, pages 406–414, Boulder, Colorado, June.

Jesús-Andrés Ferrer and Alfons Juan. 2009. A phrase-based hidden semi-markov approach to machine translation. In *Proceedings of European Association for Machine Translation (EAMT)*, Barcelona, Spain, May. European Association for Machine Translation.

C. Hardmeier, A. Bisazza, and M. Federico. 2010. FBK at WMT 2010: Word Lattices for Morphological Reduction and Chunk-based Reordering. In *Proceedings of the Joint 5th Workshop on Statistical Machine Translation and MetricsMATR*, pages 88–92, Uppsala, Sweden, July.

Philipp Koehn and Hieu Hoang. 2007. Factored translation models. In *In Proceedings of the 2007 Joint Conference on Empirical Methods in Natural Language Processing and Computational Natural Language Learning (EMNLP-CoNLL)*, pages 868–876.

P. Koehn and K. Knight. 2003. Empirical Methods for Compound Splitting. In *Proceedings of European Chapter of the ACL (EACL 2009)*, pages 187–194.

Philipp Koehn, Franz Josef Och, and Daniel Marcu. 2003. Statistical phrase-based translation. In *Proceedings of the 2003 Conference of the North American Chapter of the Association for Computational Linguistics on Human Language Technology - Volume 1*, pages 48–54, Morristown, NJ, USA. Association for Computational Linguistics.

Philipp Koehn. 2004. Statistical Significance Tests for Machine Translation Evaluation. pages 388–395, Barcelona, Spain, July.

Daniel Marcu and William Wong. 2002. A phrase-based, joint probability model for statistical machine translation. In *Proceedings of the Conference on Empirical Methods in Natural Language Processing (EMNLP-2002)*, July.

E. Matusov, H. Ney, and R. Schlüter. 2005. Phrase-based translation of speech recognizer word lattices using loglinear model combination. In *Proceedings of the IEEE Automatic Speech Recognition and Understanding Workshop (ASRU)*, pages 110–115, San Juan, Puerto Rico.

Evgeny Matusov, Björn Hoffmeister, and Hermann Ney. 2008. ASR Word Lattice Translation with Exhaustive Reordering is Possible. In *Interspeech*, pages 2342–2345, Brisbane, Australia, September.

Robert C. Moore and Chris Quirk. 2007. An iteratively-trained segmentation-free phrase translation model for statistical machine translation. In *Proceedings of the Second Workshop on Statistical Machine Translation*, pages 112–119, Prague, June.

Markos Mylonakis and Khalil Sima'an. 2008. Phrase Translation Probabilities with ITG Priors and Smoothing as Learning Objective. In *Proceedings of the 2008 Conference on Empirical Methods in Natural Language Processing*, pages 630–639, Honolulu, October.

J.A. Nelder and R. Mead. 1965. The Downhill Simplex Method. *Computer Journal*, 7:308.

H. Ney. 1999. Speech translation: Coupling of recognition and translation. In *Proceedings of IEEE International Conference on Acoustics, Speech, and Signal Processing (ICASSP)*, pages 517–520, Phoenix, Arizona, USA, March.

Jan Niehues and Muntsin Kolss. 2009. A POS-Based Model for Long-Range Reorderings in SMT. In *Proceedings of the Fourth Workshop on Statistical Machine Translation*, pages 206–214, Athens, Greece, March.

F.J. Och and H. Ney. 2003. A Systematic Comparison of Various Statistical Alignment Models. *Computational Linguistics*, 29(1):19–51.

Franz Josef Och and Hermann Ney. 2004. The alignment template approach to statistical machine translation. *Computational Linguistics*, 30(4):417–449, December.

T. Onishi, M. Utiyama, and E. Sumita. 2010. Paraphrase lattice for statistical machine translation. In *Proceedings of the ACL 2010 Conference Short Papers*, pages 1–5, Uppsala, Sweden, July.

Kishore Papineni, Salim Roukos, Todd Ward, and Wei-Jing Zhu. 2002. Bleu: a method for automatic evaluation of machine translation. In *Proceedings of the 40th Annual Meeting on Association for Computational Linguistics*, pages 311–318, Morristown, NJ, USA. Association for Computational Linguistics.

M. Popović and H. Ney. 2006. POS-based Word Reorderings for Statistical Machine Translation. In *International Conference on Language Resources and Evaluation*, pages 1278–1283.

H. Schmid. 1995. Improvements in Part-of-Speech Tagging with an Application to German. In *Proceedings of the ACL SIGDAT-Workshop*, pages 47–50, Dublin, Ireland, March.

Josh Schroeder, Trevor Cohn, and Philipp Koehn. 2009. Word lattices for multi-source translation. In *Proceedings of the 12th Conference of the European Chapter of the ACL*, pages 719–727, Athens, Greece.

Matthew Snover, Bonnie Dorr, Rich Schwartz, Linnea Micciulla, and John Makhoul. 2006. A study of translation edit rate with targeted human annotation. In *Proc. of AMTA*, pages 223–231, Aug.

A. Stolcke. 2002. SRILM - an extensible language modeling toolkit. In *Proc. Int. Conf. on Spoken Language Processing*, volume 2, pages 901 – 904, Denver, Colorado, USA, September.

Joern Wuebker, Arne Mauser, and Hermann Ney. 2010. Training phrase translation models with leaving-one-out. In *Proceedings of the 48th Annual Meeting of the Assoc. for Computational Linguistics*, pages 475–484, Uppsala, Sweden, July.

Jia Xu, Evgeny Matusov, Richard Zens, and Hermann Ney. 2005. Integrated chinese word segmentation in statistical machine translation. In *International Workshop on Spoken Language Translation*, pages 141–147, Pittsburgh, PA, USA, October.

Leave-One-Out Phrase Model Training for Large-Scale Deployment

Joern Wuebker
Human Language Technology
and Pattern Recognition Group
RWTH Aachen University, Germany
wuebker@cs.rwth-aachen.de

Mei-Yuh Hwang, Chris Quirk
Microsoft Corporation
Redmond, WA, USA
{mehwang,chrisq}@microsoft.com

Abstract

Training the phrase table by force-aligning (FA) the training data with the reference translation has been shown to improve the phrasal translation quality while significantly reducing the phrase table size on medium sized tasks. We apply this procedure to several large-scale tasks, with the primary goal of reducing model sizes without sacrificing translation quality. To deal with the noise in the automatically crawled parallel training data, we introduce on-demand word deletions, insertions, and backoffs to achieve over 99% successful alignment rate. We also add heuristics to avoid any increase in OOV rates. We are able to reduce already heavily pruned baseline phrase tables by more than 50% with little to no degradation in quality and occasionally slight improvement, without any increase in OOVs. We further introduce two global scaling factors for re-estimation of the phrase table via posterior phrase alignment probabilities and a modified absolute discounting method that can be applied to fractional counts.

Index Terms: phrasal machine translation, phrase training, phrase table pruning

1 Introduction

Extracting phrases from large amounts of noisy word-aligned training data for statistical machine translation (SMT) generally has the disadvantage of producing many unnecessary phrases (Johnson et al., 2007). These can include poor quality phrases, composite phrases that are concatenations of shorter ones, or phrases that are assigned very low probabilities, so that they have no realistic chance when competing against higher scoring phrase pairs. The goal of this work is two-fold: (i) investigating forced alignment training as a phrase table pruning method for large-scale commercial SMT systems and (ii) proposing several extensions to the training procedure to deal with practical issues and stimulate further research.

Generative phrase translation models have the inherent problem of over-fitting to the training data (Koehn et al., 2003; DeNero et al., 2006). (Wuebker et al., 2010) introduce a leave-one-out procedure which is shown to counteract over-fitting effects. The authors report significant improvements on the German-English Europarl data with the additional benefit of a severely reduced phrase table size. This paper investigates its impact on a number of commercial large-scale systems and presents several extensions.

The first extension is to deal with the highly noisy training data, which is automatically crawled and sentence aligned. The noise and the baseline pruning of the phrase table lead to low success rates when aligning the source sentence with the target sentence. We introduce on-demand word deletions, insertions, and backoff phrases to increase the success rate so that we can cover essentially the entire training data. Secondly, phrase table pruning makes out-of-vocabulary (OOV) issues even more pronounced. To avoid an increased OOV rate, we retrieve single-word translations from the baseline phrase table. Lastly, we propose two global scaling factors to allow fine-tuning of the phrase counts in an attempt to re-estimate the translation probabilities and a modification of absolute discounting that can be applied to fractional counts.

Our main contribution is applying forced-alignment on the training data to prune the phrase table. The rationale behind this is that by decoding the training data, we can identify the phrases that are actually used by the decoder. Further, we present preliminary experiments on re-estimating the channel models in the phrase table based on counts extracted from the force-aligned data.

This work is organized as follows. We discuss related work in Section 2, describe our decoder and training procedure in Section 3 and the experiments in Section 4. A conclusion and discussion of future work is given in Section 5.

2 Related Work

Force-aligning bilingual data has been explored as a means of model training in previous work. Liang et al. (2006) use it for their *bold updating* strategy to update discriminative feature weights. Utilizing force-aligned data to train a unigram phrase segmentation model is proposed by Shen et al. (2008). Wuebker et al. (2010) apply forced alignment to train the phrase table in an EM-like fashion. They report a significant reduction in phrase table size.

In this work we apply forced alignment training as a pure phrase table pruning technique. Johnson et al. (2007) successfully investigate a number of pruning methods for the phrase inventory based on significance testing. While their approach is more straightforward and less elaborate, we argue that our method is directly tailored to the decoding process and works on top of an already heavily pruned baseline phrase table.

We further experiment with applying the (scaled) phrase alignment posteriors to train the phrase table. A similar idea has been addressed in previous work, e.g. (Venugopal et al., 2003; de Gispert et al., 2010), where word alignment posterior probabilities are leveraged for grammar extraction.

Finally, a number of papers describe extending real phrase training to the hierarchical machine translation paradigm (Blunsom et al., 2008; Cmejrek et al., 2009; Mylonakis and Sima'an, 2010).

3 Phrase Training

3.1 Decoder

Our translation decoder is similar to the open-source toolkit Moses (Koehn et al., 2007). It models translation as a log-linear combination of two phrasal and two lexical channel models, an n-gram language model (LM), phrase, word and distortion penalties and a lexicalized reordering model. The decoding can be summarized as finding the best scoring target sentence T^* given a source sentence S:

$$T^* = \operatorname*{argmax}_T \sum_i \lambda_i \log\, g_i(S,T) \qquad (1)$$

where each g_i represents one feature (the channel models, n-gram, phrase count, etc.). The model weights λ_i are usually discriminatively learned on a development data set via minimum error rate training (MERT) (Och, 2003).

Constraining the decoder to a fixed target sentence is straightforward. Each partial hypothesis is compared to the reference and discarded if it does not match. The language model feature can be dropped since all hypotheses lead to the same target sentence. The training data is divided into subsets for parallel alignment. A bilingual phrase matching is applied to the phrase table to extract only the subset of entries that are pertinent to each subset of training data, for memory efficiency. For forced alignment training, we set the distortion limit Δ to be larger than in regular translation decoding. As unlimited distortion leads to very long training times, we compromise on the following heuristic. The distortion limit is set to be the maximum of 10, twice that of the baseline setting, and 1.5 times the maximum phrase length:

$$\begin{aligned} \Delta \;=\;& \max\{10, \\ & 2*(\text{baseline distortion}), \\ & 1.5*(\text{max phrase length})\} \end{aligned} \qquad (2)$$

To avoid over-fitting, we employ the same leave-one-out procedure as (Wuebker et al., 2010) for training. Here, it is applied on top of the Good-Turing (GT) smoothed phrase table (Foster et al.,

2006). Our phrase table stores the channel probabilites and marginal counts for each phrase pair, but not the discounts applied. Therefore, for each sentence, if the phrase pair (s,t) has a joint count $c(s,t)$ computed from the entire training data, and occurs $c_1(s,t)$ times in the current sentence, the leave-one-out probability $p'(t|s)$ for the current sentence will be:

$$\begin{aligned} p'(t|s) &= \frac{c'(s,t)-d}{c'(s)} \\ &= \frac{c(s,t)-c_1(s,t)-d}{c(s)-c_1(s)} \\ &= \frac{p(t|s)c(s)-c_1(s,t)}{c(s)-c_1(s)} \end{aligned} \quad (3)$$

since $p(t|s)c(s) = c(s,t) - d$, where d is the GT discount value. In the case where $c(s,t) = c_1(s,t)$ (i.e. (s,t) occurs exclusively in one sentence pair), we use a very low probability as the floor value. We apply leave-one-out discounting to the forward and backward translation models only, not to the lexical channel models.

Our baseline phrase extraction applies some heuristic-based pruning strategies. For example, it prunes offensive translations and many-words to many-words singletons (i.e. a joint count of 1 and both source phrase and target phrase contain multiple words)*. Finally the forward and backward translation probabilities are smoothed with Good-Turing discounting.

3.2 Weak Lambda Training with High Distortion

Our leave-one-out training flowchart can be illustrated in Figure 1. To force-align the training data with good quality, we need a set of trained lambda weights, as shown in Equation 1. We can use the lambda weights learned from the baseline system for that purpose. However, ideally we want the lambda values to be learned under a similar configuration as the forced alignment. Therefore, for this purpose we run MERT with the larger distortion limit given in Equation 2.

*The pruned entries are nevertheless used in computing joint counts and marginal counts.

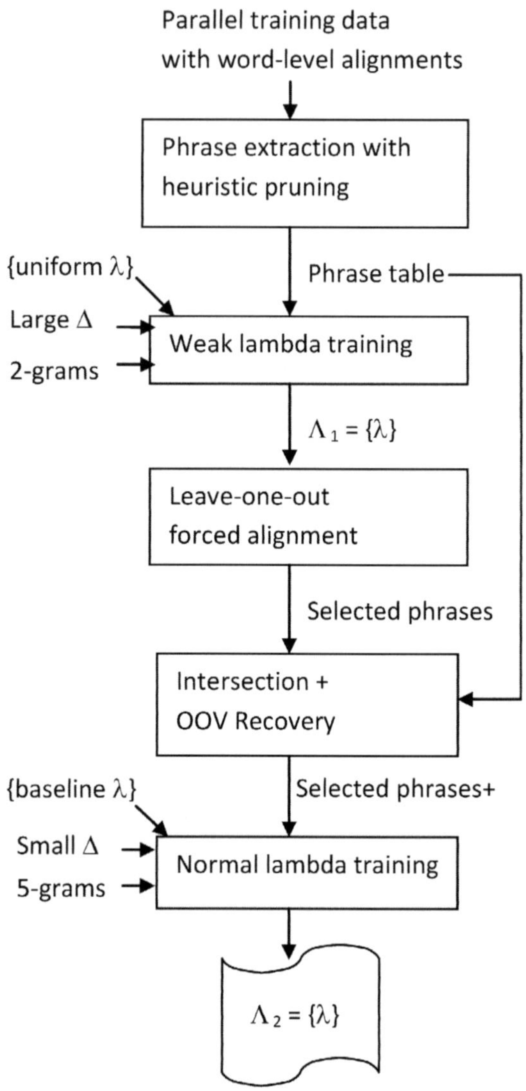

Figure 1: Flowchart of forced-alignment phrase training.

Additionally, since forced alignment does not use the language model, we propose to use a weaker language model for training the lambdas (Λ_1) to be used in the forced alignment decoding.

Using a weaker language model also speeds up the lambda training process, especially when we are using a distortion limit Δ at least twice as high as in the baseline system. In our experiments, the baseline system uses an English 5-gram language model trained on a large amount of monolingual data. The lambda values used for forced alignment are learned using the bigram LM trained on the target side of the parallel corpus for each system.

We compared a number of systems using different degrees of weak models and found out the impact on the final system was minimal. However, using a small bigram LM with large distortion yielded a stable performance in terms of BLEU, and was 25% faster than using a large 5-gram with the baseline distortion. Because of the speed improvement and its stability, this paper adopts the weak bigram lambda training.

3.3 On-demand Word Insertions and Deletions

For many training sentences the translation decoder is not able to find a phrasal alignment. We identified the following main reasons for failed alignments:

- Incorrect sentence alignment or sentence segmentation by the data crawler,
- OOVs due to initial pruning in the phrase extraction phase,
- Faulty word alignments,
- Strongly reordered sentence structure. That is, the distortion limit during forced alignment is too restrictive.

For some of these cases, discarding the sentence pairs can be seen as implicit data cleaning. For others, there do exist valid sub-sentences that are aligned properly. We would like to be able to leverage those sub-sentences, effectively allowing us to do partial sentence removal. Therefore, we introduce on-demand word insertions and deletions. Whenever a partial hypothesis can not be expanded to the next target word t_j, with the given phrase table, we allow the decoder to artificially introduce a phrase pair $(null, t_j)$ to insert the target word into the hypothesis without consuming any source word. These artificial phrase pairs are introduced with a high penalty and are ignored when creating the output phrase table. We can also introduce *backoff* phrase pairs (s_i, t_j) for all source words s_i that are not covered so far, also with a fixed penalty.

After we reach the end of the target sentence, if there are any uncovered source words s_i, we artificially add the deletion phrase pairs $(s_i, null)$ with a high penalty. Introducing on-demand word insertions and deletions increases the data coverage to at least 99% of the training sentences on all tasks we have worked on. Due to the success of insertion/deletion phrases, we have not conducted experiments using backoff phrases within the scope of this work, but leave this to future work.

3.4 Phrase Training as Pruning

This work concentrates on practical issues with large and noisy training data. Our main goal is to apply phrase training to reduce phrase table size without sacrificing quality. We do this by dumping n-best alignments of the training data, where n ranges from 100-200. We prune the baseline phrase table to only contain phrases that appear in any of the n-best phrase alignments, leaving the channel probabilities unchanged. That is, the model scores are still estimated from the original counts. We can control the size of the final phrase table by adjusting the size of the n-best list. Based on the amount of memory we can afford, we can thus keep the most important entries in the phrase table.

3.5 OOV retrieval

When performing phrase table pruning as described in Section 3.4, OOV rates tend to increase. This effect is even more pronounced when deletion/insertion phrases are not used, due to the low alignment success rate. For commercial applications, untranslated words are a major concern for end users, although it rarely has any impact on BLEU scores. Therefore, for the final phrase table after forced alignment training, we check the translations for single words in the baseline phrase table. If any single word has no translation in the new table, we recover the top x translations from the baseline table. In practice, we set $x = 3$.

3.6 Fractional Counts and Model Re-estimation

As mentioned in Section 3.4, for each training sentence pair we produce the n-best phrasal alignments. If we interpret the model score of an alignment as its log likelihood, we can weight the count for each phrase by its posterior probability. However, as the log-linear model weights are trained in a discriminative fashion, they do not directly correspond to probabilities. In order to leverage the model scores, we introduce two scaling factors ϑ and ρ that allow us to shape the count distribution according to our needs. For one sentence pair, the count for the phrase pair (s,t) is defined as

$$c(s,t) = \left(\sum_{i=1}^{n} c(s,t|h_i) \cdot \frac{exp(\vartheta \cdot \phi(h_i))}{\sum_{j=1}^{n} exp(\vartheta \cdot \phi(h_j))} \right)^{\rho}, \quad (4)$$

where h_i is the i-th hypothesis of the n-best list, $\phi(h_i)$ the log-linear model score of the alignment hypothesis h_i and $c(s,t|h_i)$ the count of (s,t) within h_i. If $\vartheta = 0$, all alignments within the n-best list are weighted equally. Setting $\rho = 0$ means that all phrases that are used anywhere in the n-best list receive a count of 1.

Absolute discounting is a popular smoothing method for relative frequencies (Foster et al., 2006). Its application, however, is somewhat difficult, if counts are not required to be integer numbers and can in fact reach arbitrarily small values. We propose a minor modification, where the discount parameter d is added to the denominator, rather than subtracting it from the numerator. The discounted relative frequency for a phrase pair (s,t) is computed as

$$p(s|t) = \frac{c(s,t)}{d + \sum_{s'} c(s',t)} \quad (5)$$

3.7 Round-Two Lambda Training

After the phrase table is pruned with forced alignment (either re-estimating the channel probabilities or not), we recommend a few more iterations of lambda training to ensure our lambda values are robust with respect to the new phrase table. In our experiments, we start from the baseline lambdas and train at most 5 more iterations using the baseline distortion and the 5-gram English language model. The settings have to be consistent with the final decoding; therefore we are not using weak lambda training here.

system	parallel corpus (sent. pairs)	Dev	Test1	WMT
it-en	13.0M	2000	5000	3027
pt-en	16.9M	2448	5000	1000
nl-en	15.0M	499	4996	1000
et-en	3.5M	1317	1500	995

Table 1: Data sizes of the four systems Italian, Portuguese, Dutch and Estonian to English. All numbers refer to sentence pairs.

Empirically we found the final lambdas (Λ_2) made a very small improvement over the baseline lambdas. However, we decided to keep this second round of lambda training to guarantee its stability across all language pairs.

4 Experiments

In this section, we describe our experiments on large-scale training data. First, we prune the original phrase table without re-estimation of the models. We conducted experiments on many language pairs. But due to the limited space here, we chose to present two high traffic systems and the two worst systems so that readers can set the correct expectation with the worst-case scenario. The four systems are: Italian (it), Portuguese (pt), Dutch (nl) and Estonian (et), all translating to English (en).

4.1 Corpora

The amount of data for the four systems is shown in Table 1. There are two test sets: Test1 and WMT. Test1 is our internal data set, containing web page translations among others. WMT is sampled from the English side of the benchmark test sets of the *Workshop on Statistical Machine Translation*†. The sampled English sentences are then manually translated into other languages, as the input to test X-to-English translation. WMT tends to contain news-like and longer sentences. The development set (for learning lambdas) is from our internal data set. We make sure that there is no overlap among the development set, test sets, and the training set.

†www.statmt.org/wmt09

	baseline	FA w/ del.	FA w/o del.
it-en			
suc.rate	–	99.5%	61.2%
Test1	42.27	42.05	42.31
WMT	30.16	30.19	30.19
pt-en			
suc.rate	–	99.5%	66.9%
Test1	47.55	47.47	47.24
WMT	40.74	41.36	41.01
nl-en			
suc.rate	–	99.6%	79.9%
Test1	32.39	31.87	31.18
WMT	43.37	43.06	43.38
et-en			
suc.rate	–	99.1%	73.1%
Test1	46.14	46.35	45.77
WMT	20.08	19.60	19.83

Table 2: BLEU scores of forced-alignment-based phrase-table pruning using weak lambda training. n-best size is 100 except for nl-en, where it is 160. We contrast forced alignment with and without on-demand insertion/deletion phrases. With the on-demand artificial phrases, FA success rate is over 99%.

4.2 Insertion/Deletion Phrases

Unless explicitly stated, all experiments here used the weak bigram LMs to obtain the lambdas used for forced alignment, and on-demand insertion/deletion phrases are applied. For the size of n-best, we use $n = 100$. The only exception is the nl-en language pair, for which we set $n = 160$ because its phrase distortion setting is higher than the others and for its higher number of morphological variations. Table 2 shows the BLEU performance of the four systems, in the baseline setting and in the forced-alignment setting with insertion/deletion phrases and without insertion/deletion phrases. Whether partial sentences should be kept or not (via insertion/deletion phrases) depends on the quality of the training data. One would have to run both settings to decide which is better for each system. In all cases, there is little or no degradation in quality after the table is sufficiently pruned.

Table 3 shows that our main goal of reducing the phrase table size is achieved. On all four language pairs, we are able to prune over 50% of the phrase table. Without on-demand insertions/deletions, the size reduction is even stronger. Notice the size reduction here is relative to the already heavily pruned baseline phrase table.

	PT size reduction	
	w/o del.	w/ del.
it-en	65.4%	54.0%
pt-en	68.5%	61.3%
nl-en	64.1%	56.9%
et-en	63.6%	58.5%

Table 3: % Phrase table size reduction compared with the baseline phrase table

With such a successful size cut, we expected a significant increase in decoding speed in the final system. In practice we experienced 3% to 12% of speedup across all the systems we tested. Both our baseline and the reduced systems use a tight beam width of 20 hypotheses per stack. We assume that with a wider beam, the speed improvement would be more pronounced.

We also did human evaluation on all 8 system outputs (four language pairs, with two test sets per language pair) and all came back positive (more improvements than regressions), even on those that had minor BLEU degradation. We conclude that the size cut in the phrase table is indeed harmless, and therefore we declare our initial goal of phrase table pruning without sacrificing quality is achieved.

In (Wuebker et al., 2010) it was observed, that phrase training reduces the average phrase length. The longer phrases, which are unlikely to generalize, are dropped. We can confirm this obersvation for the it-en and pt-en language pairs in Table 4. However, for nl-en and et-en the average source phrase length is not significantly affected by phrase training, especially with the insertion/deletion phrases. When these artificial phrases are added during forced alignment, they tend to encourage long target phrases as uncovered single target words can be consumed by the insertion phrases. However, these insertion phrases are not dumped into the final phrase table and hence cannot help in reducing the average phrase length of the final phrase table.

	avg. src phrase length		
	baseline	w/o del.	w/ del.
it-en	3.1	2.4	2.4
pt-en	3.7	3.0	3.0
nl-en	3.1	3.0	3.0
et-en	2.9	2.8	3.0

Table 4: Comparison of average source phrase length in the phrase table.

nl-en	Test1	WMT	PT size reduction
baseline	32.29	43.37	–
n=100	31.45	42.90	66.0%
n=160	31.87	43.06	64.1%

et-en	Test1	WMT	PT size reduction
baseline	46.14	20.08	–
n=100	46.35	19.60	63.6%
n=200	46.34	19.88	58.4%

Table 5: BLEU scores of different n-best sizes for the highly inflected Dutch system and the noisy Estonian system.

Table 5 illustrates how the n-best size affects BLEU scores and model sizes for the nl-en and et-en systems.

4.3 Phrase Model Re-estimation

This section conducts a preliminary evaluation of the techniques introduced in Section 3.6. For fast turnaround, these experiments were conducted on approximately $1/3$ of the Italian-English training data. Training is performed with and without insertion/deletion phrases and both with (*FaTrain*) and without (*FaPrune*) re-training of the forward and backward phrase translation probabilities. Table 6 shows the BLEU scores with different settings of the global scaling factor ρ and the inverse discount d. The second global scaling factor is fixed to $\vartheta = 0$. The preliminary results seem to be invariant of the settings. We conclude that using forced alignment posteriors as a feature training method seems to be less effective than using competing hypotheses from free decoding as in (He and Deng, 2012).

	ins/del	ρ	d	BLEU Test1	BLEU WMT
baseline	-	-	-	40.6	28.9
FaPrune	no	-	-	40.7	29.1
FaTrain	no	0	0	40.4	28.9
		0.5	0	40.2	28.9
FaPrune	yes	-	-	40.6	28.9
FaTrain	yes	0	0	40.1	28.6
		0.5	0	40.5	29.1
		0.5	0.2	40.5	29.0
		0.5	0.4	40.5	29.0

Table 6: Phrase pruning (*FaPrune*) vs. further model re-estimation after pruning (*FaTrain*) on 1/3 it-en training data, both with and without on-demand insertions/deletions.

5 Conclusion and Outlook

We applied forced alignment on parallel training data with leave-one-out on four large-scale commercial systems. In this way, we were able to reduce the size of our already heavily pruned phrase tables by at least 54%, with almost no loss in translation quality, and with a small improvement in speed performance. We show that for language pairs with strong reordering, the n-best list size needs to be increased to account for the larger search space.

We introduced several extensions to the training procedure. On-demand word insertions and deletions can increase the data coverage to nearly 100%. We plan to extend our work to use backoff translations (the target word that can not be extended given the input phrase table will be aligned to any uncovered single source word) to provide more alignment varieties, and hence hopefully to be able to keep more good phrase pairs. To avoid higher OOV rates after pruning, we retrieved single-word translations from the baseline phrase table.

We would like to emphasize that this leave-one-out pruning technique is not restricted to phrasal translators, even though all experiments presented in this paper are on phrasal translators. It is possible to extend the principle of forced alignment guided pruning to hierarchical decoders, treelet decoders, or syntax-based decoders, to prune redundant or useless phrase mappings or translation rules.

Re-estimating phrase translation probabilities using forced alignment posterior scores did not yield any noticable BLEU improvement so far. Instead, we propose to apply discriminative training similar to (He and Deng, 2012) after forced-alignment-based pruning as future work.

References

[Blunsom et al.2008] Phil Blunsom, Trevor Cohn, and Miles Osborne. 2008. A discriminative latent variable model for statistical machine translation. In *Proceedings of the 46th Annual Conference of the Association for Computational Linguistics: Human Language Technologies (ACL-08:HLT)*, pages 200–208, Columbus, Ohio, June. Association for Computational Linguistics.

[Cmejrek et al.2009] Martin Cmejrek, Bowen Zhou, and Bing Xiang. 2009. Enriching SCFG Rules Directly From Efficient Bilingual Chart Parsing. In *Proc. of the International Workshop on Spoken Language Translation*, pages 136–143, Tokyo, Japan.

[de Gispert et al.2010] Adriá de Gispert, Juan Pino, and William Byrne. 2010. Hierarchical Phrase-based Translation Grammars Extracted from Alignment Posterior Probabilities. In *Proceedings of the 2010 Conference on Empirical Methods in Natural Language Processing*, pages 545–554, MIT, Massachusetts, U.S.A., October.

[DeNero et al.2006] John DeNero, Dan Gillick, James Zhang, and Dan Klein. 2006. Why Generative Phrase Models Underperform Surface Heuristics. In *Proceedings of the Workshop on Statistical Machine Translation*, pages 31–38, New York City, June.

[Foster et al.2006] George Foster, Roland Kuhn, and Howard Johnson. 2006. Phrasetable Smoothing for Statistical Machine Translation. In *Proc. of the Conf. on Empirical Methods for Natural Language Processing (EMNLP)*, pages 53–61, Sydney, Australia, July.

[He and Deng2012] Xiaodong He and Li Deng. 2012. Maximum Expected BLEU Training of Phrase and Lexicon Translation Models. In *Proceedings of the 50th Annual Meeting of the Association for Computational Linguistics (ACL)*, page to appear, Jeju, Republic of Korea, Jul.

[Johnson et al.2007] J Howard Johnson, Joel Martin, George Foster, and Roland Kuhn. 2007. Improving Translation Quality by Discarding Most of the Phrasetable. In *Proceedings of 2007 Joint Conference on Empirical Methods in Natural Language Processing and Computational Natural Language Learning*, pages 967–975, Prague, June.

[Koehn et al.2003] P. Koehn, F. J. Och, and D. Marcu. 2003. Statistical Phrase-Based Translation. In *Proceedings of the 2003 Meeting of the North American chapter of the Association for Computational Linguistics (NAACL-03)*, pages 127–133, Edmonton, Alberta.

[Koehn et al.2007] Philipp Koehn, Hieu Hoang, Alexandra Birch, Chris Callison-Burch, Marcello Federico, Nicola Bertoldi, Brooke Cowan, Wade Shen, Christine Moran, Richard Zens, Chris Dyer, Ondřej Bojar, Alexandra Constantine, and Evan Herbst. 2007. Moses: Open Source Toolkit for Statistical Machine Translation. In *Annual Meeting of the Association for Computational Linguistics (ACL), demonstration session*, pages 177–180, Prague, Czech Republic, June.

[Liang et al.2006] Percy Liang, Alexandre Buchard-Côté, Dan Klein, and Ben Taskar. 2006. An End-to-End Discriminative Approach to Machine Translation. In *Proceedings of the 21st International Conference on Computational Linguistics and the 44th annual meeting of the Association for Computational Linguistics*, pages 761–768, Sydney, Australia.

[Mylonakis and Sima'an2010] Markos Mylonakis and Khalil Sima'an. 2010. Learning Probabilistic Synchronous CFGs for Phrase-based Translation. In *Proceedings of the Fourteenth Conference on Computational Natural Language Learning*, pages 117–, Uppsala,Sweden, July.

[Och2003] Franz Josef Och. 2003. Minimum Error Rate Training in Statistical Machine Translation. In *Proc. of the 41th Annual Meeting of the Association for Computational Linguistics (ACL)*, pages 160–167, Sapporo, Japan, July.

[Shen et al.2008] Wade Shen, Brian Delaney, Tim Anderson, and Ray Slyh. 2008. The MIT-LL/AFRL IWSLT-2008 MT System. In *Proceedings of IWSLT 2008*, pages 69–76, Hawaii, U.S.A., October.

[Venugopal et al.2003] Ashish Venugopal, Stephan Vogel, and Alex Waibel. 2003. Effective Phrase Translation Extraction from Alignment Models. In *Proceedings of the 41st Annual Meeting on Association for Computational Linguistics*, pages 319–326, Sapporo, Japan, July.

[Wuebker et al.2010] Joern Wuebker, Arne Mauser, and Hermann Ney. 2010. Training phrase translation models with leaving-one-out. In *Proceedings of the 48th Annual Meeting of the Assoc. for Computational Linguistics*, pages 475–484, Uppsala, Sweden, July.

Direct Error Rate Minimization for Statistical Machine Translation

Tagyoung Chung*
University of Rochester
Rochester, NY 14627, USA
chung@cs.rochester.edu

Michel Galley
Microsoft Research
Redmond, WA 98052, USA
mgalley@microsoft.com

Abstract

Minimum error rate training is often the preferred method for optimizing parameters of statistical machine translation systems. MERT minimizes error rate by using a surrogate representation of the search space, such as N-best lists or hypergraphs, which only offer an incomplete view of the search space. In our work, we instead minimize error rate directly by integrating the decoder into the minimizer. This approach yields two benefits. First, the function being optimized is the true error rate. Second, it lets us optimize parameters of translations systems other than standard linear model features, such as distortion limit. Since integrating the decoder into the minimizer is often too slow to be practical, we also exploit statistical significance tests to accelerate the search by quickly discarding unpromising models. Experiments with a phrase-based system show that our approach is scalable, and that optimizing the parameters that MERT cannot handle brings improvements to translation results.

1 Introduction

Minimum error rate training (Och, 2003) is a common method for optimizing linear model parameters, which is an important part of building good machine translation systems. MERT minimizes an arbitrary loss function, usually an evaluation metric such as BLEU (Papineni et al., 2002) or TER (Snover et al., 2006) from a surrogate representation of the search space, such as the N-best candidate translations of a development set. Much of the recent work on minimum error rate training focused on improving the method by Och (2003). Recent efforts extended MERT to work on lattices (Macherey et al., 2008) and hypergraphs (Kumar et al., 2009). Random restarts and random walks (Moore and Quirk, 2008) are commonly used to combat the fact the search space is highly non-convex, often with multiple minima.

Several problems still remain with MERT, three of which are addressed by this work. First, the N-best error surface explored by MERT is generally not the same as the true error surface, which means that the error rate at an optimum[1] of the N-best error surface is not guaranteed to be any close to an optimum of the true error surface. Second, most SMT decoders make search errors, yet MERT ignores the fact that the error surface of an error-prone decoder differs from the one of an exact decoder (Chang and Collins, 2011). MERT calculates an envelope from candidate translations and assumes all translations on the envelope are reachable by the decoder, but these translations may become unreachable due to search errors. Third, MERT is only used to tune linear model parameters, yet SMT systems have many free decoder parameters—such as distortion limit and beam size—that are not handled by MERT. MERT does not provide a principled way to set these parameters.

In order to overcome these issues, we explore the application of direct search methods (Wright, 1995) to SMT. To do this, we integrate the decoder and the evaluation metric inside the objective function,

* This research was conducted during the author's internship at Microsoft Research.

[1]The optimum found by MERT (Och, 2003) is generally not globally optimal. An alternative that optimizes N-best lists exactly is presented by Galley and Quirk (2011), and we do not discuss it further here.

which takes source sentences and a set of weights as inputs, and outputs the evaluation score (e.g., BLEU score) computed on the decoded sentences. Since it is impractical to calculate derivatives of this function, we use derivative-free optimization methods such as the downhill simplex method (Nelder and Mead, 1965) and Powell's method (Powell, 1964), which generally handle such difficult search conditions relatively well. This approach confers several benefits over MERT. First, the function being optimized is the true error rate. Second, integrating the decoder inside the objective function forces the optimizer to account for possible search errors. Third, contrary to MERT, our approach does not require input parameters to be those of a linear model, so our approach can tune a broader range of features, including non-linear and hidden-state parameters (e.g., distortion limit, beam size, and weight vector applied to future cost estimates).

In this paper, we make direct search reasonably fast thanks to two speedup techniques. First, we use a model selection acceleration technique called *racing* (Moore and Lee, 1994) in conjunction with randomization tests (Riezler and Maxwell, 2005) to avoid decoding the entire development set at each function evaluation. This approach discards the current model whenever performance on the translated subset of the development data is deemed significantly worse in comparison to the current best model. Second, we store and re-use search graphs across function evaluations, which eliminates some of the redundancy of regenerating the same translations in different optimization steps.

Our experiments with a strong phrase-based translation system show that the direct search approach is an effective alternative to MERT. The speed of direct search is generally comparable to MERT, and translation accuracy is generally superior. The non-linear and hidden-state features tuned in this work bring gains on three language pairs, with improvements ranging between 0.27 and 0.35 BLEU points.

2 Direct error rate minimization

Most current machine translation systems use a log-linear model:

$$p(e|f) \propto \exp\Big(\sum_i \lambda_i h_i(e,f)\Big)$$

where f is a source sentence, e is a target sentence, h_i is a feature function, and λ_i is the weight of this feature. Given a source sentence f, finding the best target sentence $\hat{e}$ according to the model is a search problem, which is called decoding:

$$\hat{e} = \operatorname*{argmax}_e \exp\Big(\sum_i \lambda_i h_i(e,f)\Big)$$

The target sentence $\hat{e}$ is automatically evaluated against a reference translation r using any metric that is known to be relatively well correlated with human judgment, such as BLEU or TER. Let us refer to such error function as $\mathrm{E}(\cdot)$. Then, the process of finding the best set of weights $\hat{\boldsymbol{\lambda}}$ according to an error function E is another search:

$$\hat{\boldsymbol{\lambda}} = \operatorname*{argmin}_{\boldsymbol{\lambda}} \mathrm{E}\Big(r; \operatorname*{argmax}_e \exp\Big(\sum_i \lambda_i h_i(e,f)\Big)\Big)$$

The typical MERT process solves the problem in an iterative fashion. At each step i, it produces N-best lists by decoding with $\hat{\boldsymbol{\lambda}}_i$, then uses these lists to find $\hat{\boldsymbol{\lambda}}_{i+1}$. Och (2003) presents an efficient multi-directional line search algorithm, which is based on the fact that the error count along each line is piecewise constant and thus easy to optimize exactly. The process is repeated until a certain convergence criterion is met, or until no new candidate sentences are added to the pool. The left side of Figure 1 summarizes this process.

Though simple and effective, there are several limitations to this approach. The primary reason is that it can only tune parameters that are part of the log-linear model. Aside from having parameters from the log-linear model, decoders generally have free parameters $\boldsymbol{\theta}$ that needs to be set manually, such as beam size and distortion limit. These decoder-related parameters have complex interactions with linear model parameters, thus, ideally, we would want to tune them jointly with decoder parameters such as distortion limit.

Direct search addresses these problems by including all feature parameters and all decoder-related parameters within the optimization framework. Figure 1 contrasts MERT with direct search. Rather than optimizing candidate pools of translations, direct search treats the decoder and the evaluation tool

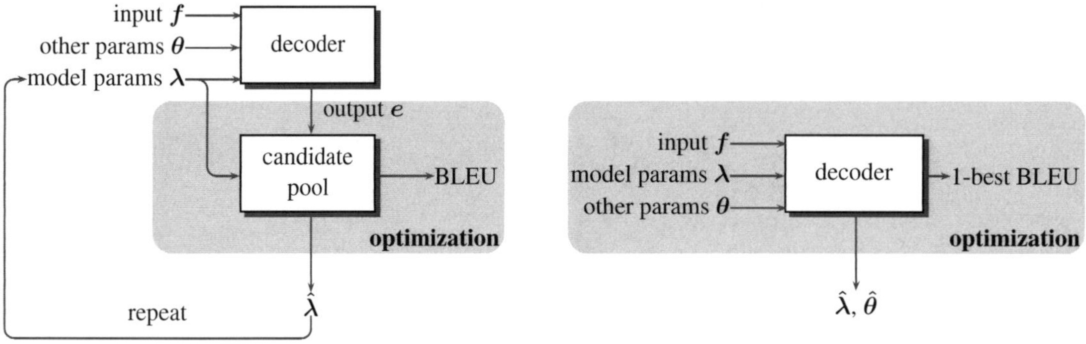

Figure 1: Comparison of MERT (left) and direct search (right).

as a single function:

$$\Phi(f, r; \boldsymbol{\lambda}, \boldsymbol{\theta}) = \mathrm{E}\Big(r; \underset{e}{\operatorname{argmax}} \ \exp\big(\sum_i \lambda_i h_i(e, f)\big)\Big)$$

Then, it uses an optimization method to minimize the function:

$$\underset{\boldsymbol{\lambda},\boldsymbol{\theta}}{\operatorname{argmin}} \ \Phi(f, r; \boldsymbol{\lambda}, \boldsymbol{\theta})$$

This formulation solves the problem mentioned previously, since we jointly optimize $\boldsymbol{\lambda}$ and $\boldsymbol{\theta}$, thus accounting for the dependencies between the two. However, there are two problems to address with direct error minimization. First, this approach requires the entire development set to be re-decoded every time the function is evaluated, which can be prohibitively expensive. To address this problem, we present several methods to speed up the search process in Section 5. Second, since the gradient of standard evaluation metrics such as BLEU is not known and since methods for estimating the gradient numerically require too many function evaluations, we cannot use common search methods that use derivatives of a function. Therefore, we need robust derivative-free optimization methods. We discuss such optimization methods in Section 3.

3 Derivative-free optimization

As discussed in the previous sections, we need to rely on derivative-free optimization methods for direct search. We consider two such optimization methods:

Powell's method For each iteration, Powell's method tries to find a good direction along which the function can be minimized. This direction is determined by searching along each standard base vector. Then, a line search is performed along the direction by using line search methods such as golden section search or Fibonacci search. The process is repeated until convergence. We implement the golden section search as presented by Press et al. (1992) in our experiments. Although the golden section search is only exact when the function is unimodal, we found that it works quite well in practice. More details are presented by Powell (1964).

Nelder-Mead method This approach sets up a simplex on the search space, which is a polytope with $D + 1$ vertices when there are D dimensions, and successively moves the simplex to a lower point to find a minimum of the function. The simplex is moved using different actions, which are taken when certain conditions are met. The basic idea behind these actions is to replace the worst point in the simplex with a new and better point, thereby moving the simplex towards a minimum. This method has the advantage of being able to deal with "bumpy" functions and depending on the configuration of the simplex at the time, it is possible to escape some local minima. This is often refer to as downhill simplex method and more details are presented by Nelder and Mead (1965).

4 Parameters

In this section, we discuss the parameters that we optimize with direct search, in addition to standard linear model parameters:

4.1 Distortion limit

Distortion limit is one of decoder parameters that sets a limit on the number of words the decoder is allowed to skip when deciding which source phrase to translate in order to allow reordering. Figure 2 shows a translation example from English to Japanese. Every word jumped over incurs a distortion cost, which is usually one of the translation model parameters, which thereby discourages reordering of words unless language model supports the reordering.

Since having a large distortion limit leads to slower decoding, having the smallest possible distortion limit that still facilitates correct reordering would be ideal. Not only this speeds up translation, but this also leads to better translation quality by minimizing search errors. Since a larger distortion limit means there are more possible re-orderings of translations, it is prone to more search errors. In fact, there are evidences that tuning the distortion limit is beneficial in improving quality of translation by limiting search errors. Galley and Manning (2008) conduct a line search along increments of distortion limit and separately tune the translation model parameters for each increment of distortion limit. The result shows significant difference in translation quality when distortion limit is tuned along with the model parameters. Separately tuning model parameters for different distortion limit is necessary because model parameters are coupled with distortion limit. A representative example: when distortion limit is zero, the distortion penalty feature can have any weight and not affect BLEU scores, but this is not the case when distortion limit is larger than zero. Tuning distortion limit in direct search in conjunction with related features such linear distortion eliminates the need for a line search for distortion limit.

4.2 Polynomial features

Most phrase-based decoders typically use a distortion penalty feature to discourage (or maybe sometimes encourage) reordering. Whereas distortion limit is a hard constraint—since the decoder never considers jumps larger than the given limit—distortion penalty is a soft constraint, since it penalizes reordering proportionally to the length of the

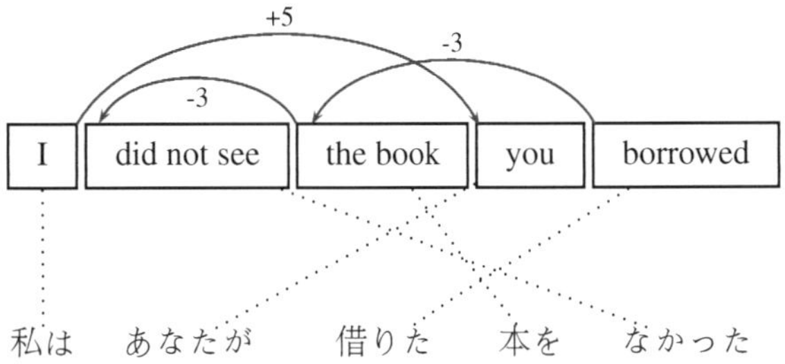

Figure 2: Reordering in phrase-based translation. A minimum distortion limit of five is needed to correctly translate this example. The source sentence is relatively simple but a relatively large distortion limit is needed to accommodate the correct reordering due to typological difference between two languages.

jump. The total distortion penalty is calculated as follows:

$$D(e, f) = \lambda_d \sum_j |d_j|^{p_d}$$

where λ_d is the weight for distortion penalty feature, and d_j is the size of the jump needed to translate the j-th phrase pair. For example, in Figure 2, the total distortion penalty feature value is 11, which is multiplied with λ_d to get the total distortion cost of translating the example sentence. Although p_d is typically set to one (linear), one may consider polynomial distortion penalty (Green et al., 2010). Green et al. (2010) show that setting p_d to a higher value than one improves the translation quality, but uses a predetermined value for p_d. Instead of manually setting the value of p_d, it can be given a value tuned with direct search. Although we only discussed distortion penalty here, it is straightforward to tune p_i for each feature $h_i(e, f)^{p_i}$ using direct error rate minimization, where $h_i(e, f)$ is any linear model feature of the decoder.

4.3 Future cost estimates

Since beam search involves pruning, it is crucial to have good future cost estimation in order to minimize the number of search errors (Koehn et al., 2003). The concept of future cost estimation is related to heuristic functions in the A* search algorithm. The total cost $f(x)$ of a partial translation hypothesis is estimated by combining $g(x)$, which is the actual current cost from the beginning of a sentence to point x and $h(x)$, which is the future cost estimate from point x to the end of the sentence:

$$f(x) = g(x) + h(x)$$

In SMT decoding, the same feature weight vector is generally used when computing $g(x)$ and $h(x)$. However, this may not be ideal since future cost estimators use different heuristics depending on the features. For example, the future cost estimator (Green et al., 2010) for linear distortion always underestimates completion cost, which is generally deemed a good property. Unfortunately, some features have estimators that tend to overestimate completion cost, as it is the case with the language model. This problem is illustrated in Figure 3. The Figure shows that the ratio between the estimated total cost and the actual total cost converges to 1.0. However, in earlier stages of translations, the estimated future cost for language model is larger than it should be, which leads to higher total estimated cost. In the A* search parlance, we are using an inadmissible heuristic since the future cost is overestimated, which leads to suboptimal search. This suggests that separately tuning parameters that are involved in the future cost estimation will lead to better pruning decisions. This essentially doubles the number of linear model parameters, since for every feature used in future cost estimation, we create a counterpart and tune its weight independently.

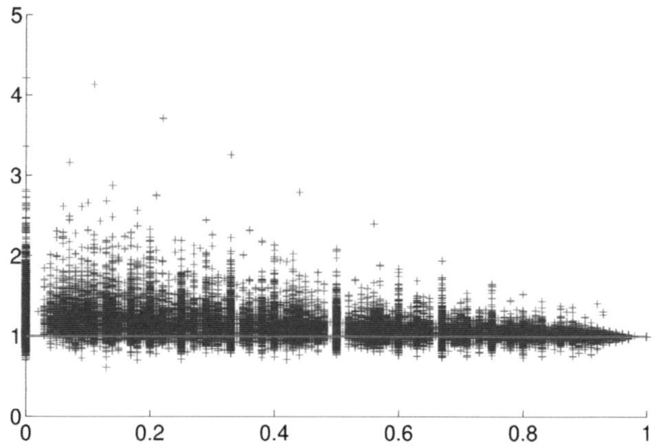

Figure 3: y axis is ratio between estimated total cost vs. actual total cost of language model for thousands of translations. 1.0 means the estimated total cost and the actual total cost are exactly the same, and anything higher than 1.0 means the future cost has been overestimated thereby inflating the estimated total cost. The x-axis represents how much translation has been completed. 0.1 means 10% of a sentence has been translated.

4.4 Search parameters

In addition to the parameters listed above, we also tune general decoder parameters that affect the search quality: beam size and parameters controlling histogram pruning and threshold pruning. While it makes sense to set these parameters automatically instead of manually, the methods we have presented thus far are not particularly fit for this type of parameters. Indeed, if the sole goal is to maximize translation quality (e.g., as measured by standard BLEU), a larger beam size and less pruning is usually preferable. To address this problem, we optimize these three parameters using a slightly different objective function. When tuning any of these three features, the goal of translation is to get the most accurate translation given a pre-defined time limit, so we change the objective to be a time-sensitive objective function. Much akin to brevity penalty in BLEU, we define time penalty as:

$$\mathbf{TP}(\,\cdot\,) = \begin{cases} 1.0 & t_i \leq t_d \\ \exp\left(1 - \frac{t_i}{t_d}\right) & t_i > t_d \end{cases}$$

where $\mathbf{TP}(\,\cdot\,)$ is a time penalty that is multiplied to BLEU, t_i is the time it takes to translate development set under current parameters, and t_d is the desired time limit for translating the development set. With this error metric, we still optimize for the translation quality as long as the translation happens within desired time t_d. With the modified time-sensitive BLEU score as error metric, direct search may tune the parameters that have the speed and accuracy trade-off that we want.[2]

5 Speeding up direct search

Optimizing the true error surface is generally more computationally expensive than with any surrogate error surface, since each function evaluation usually requires decoding or re-decoding the entire development set. Since SMT tuning sets used for error

[2]A disadvantage of using time in the definition of $\mathbf{TP}(\,\cdot\,)$ is that it adds non-determinism that can make optimization unstable. Our solution is to replace time with pseudo-time, a deterministic substitute expressed as a linear combination of the number of n-gram lookups and hypothesis expansions (these two quantities correlate quite well with decoding time).

rate minimization often comprise one thousand sentences or more, each function evaluation can take minutes or more. However, this problem is somewhat mitigated by the fact that translating in batches is highly parallelizable. Since MERT (Och, 2003) is also easily parallelizable, we need to resort to other speedup techniques to make direct search a practical alternative to MERT. We now present two techniques that make optimization of the true error surface more efficient.

5.1 A racing algorithm for speeding up SMT model selection

Error rate minimization as presented in this paper can be seen as a form of model selection, which has been the focus of a lot of work in the learning literature. The most popular approaches to model selection—such as minimizing cross validation error—tend to be very slow in practice; therefore, researchers have addressed the problem of accelerating model selection using statistical tests.

Prior to considering the SMT case, we review one of these methods in the case of leave-one-out cross validation (LOOCV). *Racing* for model selection (Maron and Moore, 1994; Moore and Lee, 1994) works as follows: we are given a collection of N_m models and N_d data points, and we must find the model that minimizes the mean $e_j^* = \frac{1}{N_d}\sum_i e_j(i)$, where $e_j(i)$ is the classification error of model M_j on the ith datapoint when trained on all datapoints except the ith point. The models are evaluated concurrently, and at any given step $k \in [1, N_d]$, each model M_j is associated with two pieces of information: the current estimate of its mean error rate, and the estimate of its variance. As evaluations progress, we eliminate any model that is significantly worse than any other model.[3] We also note that the Racing technique first randomizes the order of the data points to ensure that prefixes of the dataset are generally representative of the entire set.

In this work, we use Racing to speed up direct search for SMT, but this requires two main adjustments compared to the LOOCV case. First, our models have real-valued parameters, so we cannot exhaustively evaluate the set of all models since it is infinite. Instead, we use direct search to select which models compete against each other during Racing. In the case of Powell's method, all points of a grid along the current search direction are evaluated in parallel using Racing, before we turn to the next line search. In the case of the downhill simplex optimizer and in the case of line searches other than grid search (e.g., golden section search), the use of Racing is more difficult because the function evaluations requested by these optimizers have dependencies that generally prevent concurrent function evaluations. Since functions in downhill simplex are evaluated in sequence and not in parallel, our solution is to race the current model against our current best model.[4] When the evaluation of a model M is interrupted because it is deemed significantly worse than the current best model $\hat{M}$, the error rate of M on the entire development set is extrapolated from its relative performance on the decoded subset.[5]

The second main difference with the LOOCV case is that we do not use confidence intervals to determine which of two or models are best. In SMT, it is common to use either bootstrap resampling (Efron and Tibshirani, 1993; Och, 2003) or randomization tests (Noreen, 1989). In this paper, we use the randomization test for discarding unpromising models, since this statistical test was shown to be less likely to cause type-I errors[6] than bootstrap methods (Riezler and Maxwell, 2005). Since both kinds of statistical tests involve a time-consuming sampling step, it

[3]The details of these statistical tests are not so important here since we use different ones in the case of SMT, but we briefly summarize them as follows: Maron and Moore (1994) use a non-parametric method (Hoeffding bounds (Hoeffding, 1963)) for confidence estimation, and places confidence intervals on the mean value of the random variable representing $e_j(i)$. A model is discarded if its confidence interval no longer overlaps with the confidence interval of the current best model. Moore and Lee (1994) use a similar technique, but relies on Bayesian statistics instead of Hoeffding bounds.

[4]Since Racing only discards suboptimal models, the current best model M^* is one for which we have decoded the entire development set. Once a new model M is evaluated, we perform at step j a significance test to determine whether M's translation of sentences $1 \dots j$ is better or worse than M^* translation for the same range of sentences. If M is significantly worse, we discard it. If M^* is worse, we continue evaluating the performance of M, since we need M's output for the full development set if M eventually becomes the new best model.

[5]For example, if error rates of $\hat{M}$ and M are respectively 10% and 11% on the subset decoded by both models and $\hat{M}$'s error on the entire set is 20%, M's extrapolated error is 22%.

[6]A type I error rejects a null hypothesis that is true.

is somewhat wasteful to perform a new test after the decoding of each sentence, so we translate sentences in small batches of K sentences before performing each randomization test.[7]

We finally note that Racing no longer guarantees that the error function observed by the optimizer is the true error function. Racing causes some approximations of the error function, but the degree of approximation is designed to be small in regions with low error rates, and Racing ensures that the most promising function evaluations in our progression towards an optimum are unaffected. In contrast, the approximation of the error function computed from N-best lists or lattice does not share this property.[8]

To further speed up function evaluations in direct search, we employ a method meant to deal with models that are nearly identical, a situation in which Racing usually does not help much. Indeed, when two models produce very similar outputs, we often need to run the race through every sentence of the development set since none of the two models end up being significantly better. A solution to this problem consists of discarding models that are nearly identical to other models, where similarity between models is solely measured from their outputs.[9] To do this, we resort again to a randomization test: Given two models M_a and M_b, this test performs random permutations between outputs of M_a and M_b, that is, it determines for each sentence of index i whether or not to permute the two model outputs, with probability $p = 0.5$. When M_a and M_b are very similar, these permutations have little effect, even when we repeat this sampling process many times. To cope with this problem, we slightly modify the randomization test to discard one of the two nearly identical models. Specifically, we compute the gap—measured in error rate—between the best randomized output and the worst randomized output. If this gap is lower than a pre-defined threshold, we only keep the best model.[10] This adjustment to the significance test makes direct search reasonably fast, since Racing is effective during the initial steps of search (when steps tend to be relatively big, and when differences in error rate are pretty significant), and our modification to randomization tests helps while search converges towards an optimum using increasingly smaller steps.

5.2 Lattice-based decoding

We use another technique to speed up direct search by storing and re-using search graphs, which consist of lattices in the case of phrase-based decoding (Och et al., 1999) and hypergraphs in the case of hierarchical decoding (Chiang, 2005). The successive expansion of translation options in order to construct the search graph is generally done from scratch, but this can be wasteful when the same sentences are translated multiple times, as it is the case with direct search. Even when the parameters of the decoder change across function evaluations, some partial translation are likely to be constructed multiple times, and this is more likely to happen when changes in parameters are relatively small. To overcome this inefficiency, we memoize hypotheses expansions made in all function evaluations, which then allows us to reuse some edges (or hyperedges) from previous iterations to construct the current graph (or hypergraph). Since feature values—including expensive features like language model score—are stored into each edge, the speedup is roughly proportional to the percentage of edges we can reuse.

A more radical way of exploiting search graphs of previous iterations is to use them as constraints in a forced decoding approach. In this framework, the decoder takes as input not only an input sentence, but also a constraining search graph. During decoding, it is forced to discard any translation hypothe-

[7] In our experiments, we set $K = 50$. Some other practical considerations: the significance level used for discarding unpromising models is $p \leq .05$. The randomization test is a sampling-based technique, for which we must specify a sample size R. In this paper, we use $R = 5000$.

[8] In the case of N-best MERT, it is not even guaranteed that we find the true error rate of our current best model M while searching the N-best error surface. In fact, if we take the parameters of our best model M and re-decode the development set, we may get an error rate that is different from what was predicted from the N-best list. With direct search and Racing, no such approximation affects our current best model.

[9] Measuring model similarity only based on parameter values is less effective, since features and other parameters are sometimes redundant, and two models may behave similarly while having fairly distinct parameter values.

[10] In the case where we compare our current best model and a model that is currently being evaluated, we discard the latter. In our experiments with BLEU, we discard if the gap is smaller than 0.1 BLEU point.

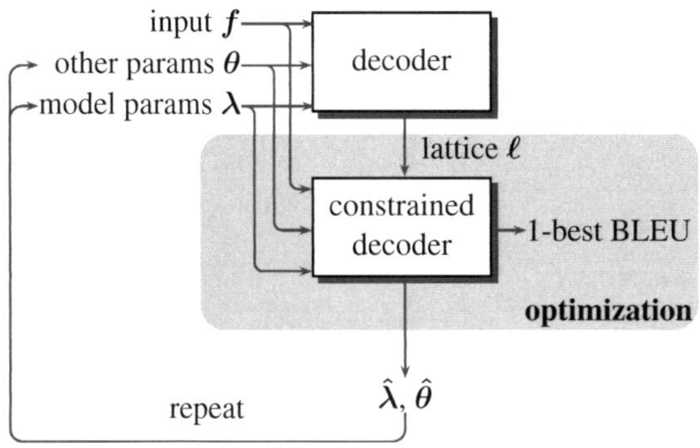

Figure 4: Lattice-constrained decoding for direct search.

ses that violate the constraining search graph. This makes the memoization method presented in the previous paragraph maximally efficient, since lattice-constrained decoding has all linear model feature values already pre-computed. While this approach is similar in spirit to lattice-based MERT (Macherey et al., 2008), there is a crucial difference. The optimization steps in lattice MERT bypass the decoder, but the lattice-based approach presented here does not. The distinction is important when it comes to tuning non-linear and hidden state parameters of the decoder. For instance, the initial lattice may have been constructed with a distortion limit of 4, while the current model specifies a distortion limit of 2. At that stage, optimization via lattice-constrained decoding instead of lattice-based MERT ensures that we will never select a path of the input lattice that corresponds to a distortion limit of more than 2. This is important since the error rate must reflect the fact that jumps of two or more words are not allowed.

Figure 4 shows how direct search with lattice-constrained decoding is structured. Similarly to MERT and as opposed to straight direct search, optimization is repeated multiple times. Since each optimization in the lattice-constrained case does not require recomputing any features, it usually turns into very significant gains in terms of translation speed, though it also causes a small loss of translation accuracy in general. The overall approach depicted in Figure 4 works as follows: a first set of lattices is generated using an initial $\boldsymbol{\lambda}_0$ and $\boldsymbol{\theta}_0$. We then run direct search with a decoder constrained on this set of lattices. After optimization has converged, the optimal $\hat{\boldsymbol{\lambda}}$ and $\hat{\boldsymbol{\theta}}$ are provided as input $\boldsymbol{\lambda}_1$ and $\boldsymbol{\theta}_1$ to start a new iteration of this process. Note that the constraining lattices built at each iteration are always merged with those of the previous ones, so constraining lattices grow over time. The two stopping criteria are similar to MERT: if the norm of the difference between the previous parameter vector—including $\boldsymbol{\lambda}$ and $\boldsymbol{\theta}$—and the current vector falls below a predefined tolerance value, we do not continue to the next iteration. Alternatively, if a new pass of unconstrained decoding generates lattices that are subsumed by lattices constructed at previous iteration, we stop and do not run the next optimization step.

	Train	MERT dev.	Test
Korean-English	7.9M	1000	6000
Arabic-English	11.1M	1000	6000
Farsi-English	739K	1000	2000

Table 1: Size of bitexts in number of sentence pairs.

6 Experiments

6.1 Setup

For our experiments, we use a phrase-based translation system similar to Moses (Koehn et al., 2007). Our decoder uses many of the same features as Moses, including four phrasal and lexicalized translation scores, phrase penalty, word penalty, a language model score, linear distortion, and six lexicalized reordering scores. Unless specified otherwise, the decoder's stack size is 50, and the number of translation options per input phrase is 25.

Table 1 summarizes the amount of training data used to train translation systems from Korean, Arabic, and Farsi into English. These data sets are drawn from various sources, which include news, web, and technical data, as well as United Nations data in the case of Arabic. In order to get the sense of how presented techniques generalize, we evaluate our systems on a fairly broad domain. We use development and test sets are a mix of news, web, and technical data. All systems translate into English, for which we built a 5-gram language model with cutoff counts 1, 1, 1, 2, 3 for unigrams to 5-grams, using a corpus of roughly seven billion English words. This includes the target side of the parallel training data, plus a significant amount of data gathered from the web.

#	Minimizer	Optimized parameters	Arabic		Korean		Farsi	
1	MERT with grid search	lin, DL	29.12	(14.6)	23.30	(20.8)	32.16	(11.7)
2	Direct search (simplex)	lin, DL	29.07	(1.2)	23.42	(4.4)	32.22	(1.3)
3	Direct search (Powell)	lin, DL	29.20	(2.3)	23.39	(5.6)	32.28	(2.1)
4	Direct search (Powell)	lin, extended, DL	29.39	(4.4)	23.61	(8.9)	32.51	(4.9)
5	Lattice-constrained (Powell)	lin, extended, DL	29.27	(0.7)	23.43	(1.3)	32.42	(1.1)
6	Direct search (Powell)	lin, extended, DL, search	29.31	(6.5)	23.46	(9.7)	32.62	(6.2)

Table 2: BLEU-4 scores (%) with one reference, translating into English; the numbers in parentheses are times in hours to run parameter optimization end-to-end. 'Lin' refers to Moses linear model features; 'extended' refers to non-linear and hidden state features (polynomial features, future cost); 'DL' refers to distortion limit; 'search' is the set of parameters controlling search quality (parameters controlling beam size, histogram pruning, and threshold pruning).

Our baseline system is trained for each language pair by running minimum error rate training (Och, 2003) on 1000 sentences. Each iteration of MERT utilizes 19 random starting points, plus the points of convergence at all previous iterations of MERT, and a uniform weight vector. That is, the first iteration of MERT uses 20 starting points, the second uses 21 points, etc. Since MERT is not able to directly optimize search parameters such as distortion limit and beam size, our baseline system uses grid search to optimize them. To make this search more tractable, we only perform the grid search for a single parameter: the distortion limit. For each language pair, the grid search consists of repeating MERT for eight distinct distortion limits ranging from 3 to 10. The optimal distortion limits found for Korean, Arabic, and Farsi, are 8, 5, and 6, respectively.[11] To ensure that the comparison with our approach is consistent, this grid search is made on the MERT dev set itself.

The next subsection contrasts the different direct search methods presented in this paper. Note that all these experiments use the speedup techniques based on statistical significance test presented in Section 5. Indeed, we found that using these techniques resulted in faster speeds without affecting the search in any significant way. Models tuned with or without significance tests often ended up identical.

6.2 Results

The main results are shown in Table 2, and are computed using standard BLEU-4 (Papineni et al., 2002) using one reference translation, and ignoring case. Row 1 displays results of the MERT baseline, with a distortion limit that was found optimal using a grid search on the development set. Rows 2 and 3 show results of direct error rate minimization with downhill simplex and Powell's method, where direct search optimizes both linear model parameters and the distortion limit. We see here that the performance of direct search is comparable and sometimes better than MERT, but the benefit of direct search here is that it does not require an external grid search to find an effective distortion limit (each direct search is initialized with a distortion limit of 10). Row 4 shows the performance of Powell's method using the extended parameter set (Section 4), which includes model weights for future costs and polynomial features. We lack space to present an extensive analysis of the relative impact of the different non-linear features and parameters discussed in this paper, but we generally find that the following parameters work best: distortion limit, polynomial distortion penalty, and weight of future cost estimate of the language model. The fact that Moses-style future cost estimation for language models often overestimates probably explains why the latter feature helps.

In the last row of Table 2, optimization is done using the time-sensitive variant of BLEU presented in Section 4.4, and the set of parameters tuned here includes all the previous ones, in addition to beam size, and the two parameters controlling histogram and threshold pruning in beam search. Clearly, running direct search to directly optimize BLEU would yield a very large beam size and would set pruning parameters that are so permissive that they would almost completely disable pruning. The benefit of using the time-sensitive variant of BLEU is that direct

[11] We rerun MERT for each different distortion limit because of the dependencies between this parameter and linear model features, particularly linear distortion and lexicalized reordering scores. A linear model that is effective with a distortion limit of 4 can be suboptimal for a limit of 8.

search is forced to find parameter weights that offer a good balance between accuracy and speed. To make our results in row 6 as comparable as possible to row 4, we use the running time (on the development set) of row 4 as a time constraint for the model of row 6, which is to decode the entire development set at least as fast. In other words, the system of row 6 is optimized to be no slower than the system of row 4, and is otherwise penalized due to the time penalty. The effect of this is that translation speed at tuning time is almost the same, and speed of systems 4 and 6 is roughly the same at test time. A comparison between rows 4 and 6 suggests that tuning search parameters such as beam size and without affecting time does not provide much gain in terms of translation quality, but the method nevertheless has one advantage: one can target a specific translation speed without having to manually tune any parameter such as beam size, and without even having to decide which parameter to manually tune.

Times to run optimizations end-to-end are reported in parentheses in Table 2 and they take into account the time to run the grid search in the case of MERT. Times to decode test sets are not reported here since they are roughly the same across all models. While translation accuracy with MERT and direct search is roughly the same when the underlying parameter set is the same, direct search wins in running time when it comes to optimizing search parameters like distortion limit. Since each grid search runs MERT eight times, MERT is generally faster than direct search, but the difference of speed remains reasonable if the number of tuned parameters is the same, and direct search is rarely twice as slow.

We finally discuss the case of lattice-constrained decoding, which is shown in row 5 of Table 2. This method is not applicable when tuning parameters that affect search thoroughness (row 6), such as beam size. The reason is that lattice-constrained decoding is a form of forced decoding that considerably narrows the search space. Under a constrained decoding setting, it appears that a large beam size seldom affects translation speed, but this is misleading and largely due to constraints created by the lattice. We thus evaluate the lattice-constrained case without tuning 'search' features, and find that direct search is significantly faster using lattice-constrained, with only a slight degradation of translation quality. Lattice constraints are augmented 2-5 times before it converges.

7 Related work

The use of derivative-free optimization methods to tune machine translation parameters has been tried before. Bender et al. (2004) used the Nelder-Mead method to tune model parameters for a phrase-based translation system. However, their way of making direct search fast and practical is to set distortion limit to zero, which results in poor translation quality for many language pairs. Zens et al. (2007) also use the Nelder-Mead method to tune parameters in a log-linear model to maximize expected BLEU. Zhao and Chen (2009) proposes changes to Nelder-Mead method to better fit parameter tuning in their machine translation setting. They show the modification brings better search of parameters over the regular Nelder-Mead method. Our work is related to the search-based structured prediction (SEARN) model of Daumé (2006), in the sense that direct search also accounts for what happens during search (including search errors) to try to find parameters that are not only good for prediction, but for search as well.

8 Conclusion

This paper addressed the problem of minimizing error rate at a corpus level. We show that a technique to directly minimize the true error rate, rather than one estimated from a surrogate representation such as an N-best list, is in fact feasible. We present two techniques that make this minimization significantly faster, to the point where this technique is a viable alternative to MERT. In the case where free parameters of the decoder (such as distortion limit) also need to be optimized, our technique is in fact much faster. We also optimize non-linear and hidden state features that cannot be tuned using MERT, which yield improvements in translation accuracy. Experiments on large test sets yield gains on three language pairs, and our best configuration outperforms MERT by 0.27 to 0.35 BLEU points using a baseline system trained on large amounts of data.

Acknowledgments

We thank anonymous reviewers, Chris Quirk, Kristina Toutanova, and Anthony Aue for valuable suggestions.

References

Oliver Bender, Richard Zens, Evgeny Matusov, and Hermann Ney. 2004. Alignment templates: the RWTH SMT system. In *Proc. of the International Workshop on Spoken Language Translation*, pages 79–84, Kyoto, Japan.

Yin-Wen Chang and Michael Collins. 2011. Exact decoding of phrase-based translation models through Lagrangian relaxation. In *Proceedings of the 2011 Conference on Empirical Methods in Natural Language Processing*, pages 26–37, Edinburgh, Scotland, UK., July. Association for Computational Linguistics.

David Chiang. 2005. A hierarchical phrase-based model for statistical machine translation. In *Proceedings of the 43rd Annual Conference of the Association for Computational Linguistics (ACL-05)*, pages 263–270, Ann Arbor, MI.

Hal Daumé, III. 2006. *Practical Structured Learning Techniques for Natural Language Processing*. Ph.D. thesis, University of Southern California, Los Angeles, CA, USA.

B. Efron and R. J. Tibshirani. 1993. *An Introduction to the Bootstrap*. Chapman & Hall, New York.

Michel Galley and Christopher D. Manning. 2008. A simple and effective hierarchical phrase reordering model. In *Proceedings of the 2008 Conference on Empirical Methods in Natural Language Processing*, pages 848–856, Honolulu, Hawaii, October. Association for Computational Linguistics.

Michel Galley and Chris Quirk. 2011. Optimal search for minimum error rate training. In *Proceedings of the 2011 Conference on Empirical Methods in Natural Language Processing*, pages 38–49, Edinburgh, Scotland, UK., July. Association for Computational Linguistics.

Spence Green, Michel Galley, and Christopher D. Manning. 2010. Improved models of distortion cost for statistical machine translation. In *Human Language Technologies: The 2010 Annual Conference of the North American Chapter of the Association for Computational Linguistics*, pages 867–875, Los Angeles, California, June. Association for Computational Linguistics.

Wassily Hoeffding. 1963. Probability inequalities for sums of bounded random variables. *Journal of the American Statistical Association*, 58(301):13–30.

Philipp Koehn, Franz Josef Och, and Daniel Marcu. 2003. Statistical phrase-based translation. In *Proceedings of the 2003 Meeting of the North American chapter of the Association for Computational Linguistics (NAACL-03)*, Edmonton, Alberta.

Philipp Koehn, Hieu Hoang, Alexandra Birch, Chris Callison-Burch, Marcello Federico, Nicola Bertoldi, Brooke Cowan, Wade Shen, Christine Moran, Richard Zens, Chris Dyer, Ondrej Bojar, Alexandra Constantin, and Evan Herbst. 2007. Moses: Open source toolkit for statistical machine translation. In *Proceedings of ACL, Demonstration Session*, pages 177–180.

Shankar Kumar, Wolfgang Macherey, Chris Dyer, and Franz Och. 2009. Efficient minimum error rate training and minimum Bayes-risk decoding for translation hypergraphs and lattices. In *Proceedings of the Joint Conference of the 47th Annual Meeting of the ACL and the 4th International Joint Conference on Natural Language Processing of the AFNLP*, pages 163–171, Suntec, Singapore, August. Association for Computational Linguistics.

Wolfgang Macherey, Franz Och, Ignacio Thayer, and Jakob Uszkoreit. 2008. Lattice-based minimum error rate training for statistical machine translation. In *Proceedings of the 2008 Conference on Empirical Methods in Natural Language Processing*, pages 725–734, Honolulu, Hawaii, October. Association for Computational Linguistics.

Oded Maron and Andrew W. Moore. 1994. Hoeffding races: Accelerating model selection search for classification and function approximation. In *Advances in neural information processing systems 6*, pages 59–66. Morgan Kaufmann.

Andrew Moore and Mary Soon Lee. 1994. Efficient algorithms for minimizing cross validation error. In W. W. Cohen and H. Hirsh, editors, *Proceedings of the 11th International Confonference on Machine Learning*, pages 190–198. Morgan Kaufmann.

Robert C. Moore and Chris Quirk. 2008. Random restarts in minimum error rate training for statistical machine translation. In *Proceedings of the 22nd International Conference on Computational Linguistics (Coling 2008)*, pages 585–592, Manchester, UK, August. Coling 2008 Organizing Committee.

J. A. Nelder and R. Mead. 1965. A simplex method for function minimization. *Computer Journal*, 7:308–313.

Eric W. Noreen. 1989. *Computer-Intensive Methods for Testing Hypotheses : An Introduction*. Wiley-Interscience.

Franz Josef Och, Christoph Tillmann, Hermann Ney, and Lehrstuhl Fiir Informatik. 1999. Improved alignment models for statistical machine translation. In *Proceedings of the Conference on Empirical Methods in Natural Language Processing and Very Large Corpora*, pages 20–28.

Franz Josef Och. 2003. Minimum error rate training for statistical machine translation. In *Proceedings of the 41th Annual Conference of the Association for Computational Linguistics (ACL-03)*.

Kishore Papineni, Salim Roukos, Todd Ward, and Wei-Jing Zhu. 2002. BLEU: A method for automatic evaluation of machine translation. In *Proceedings of the 40th Annual Conference of the Association for Computational Linguistics (ACL-02)*.

M. J. D. Powell. 1964. An efficient method for finding the minimum of a function of several variables without calculating derivatives. *The Computer Journal*, 7:155–162.

William H. Press, Saul A. Teukolsky, William T. Vetterling, and Brian P. Flannery. 1992. *Numerical recipes in C (2nd ed.): the art of scientific computing*. Cambridge University Press, New York, NY, USA.

Stefan Riezler and John T. Maxwell. 2005. On some pitfalls in automatic evaluation and significance testing for MT. In *Proceedings of the ACL Workshop on Intrinsic and Extrinsic Evaluation Measures for Machine Translation and/or Summarization*, pages 57–64, June.

Matthew Snover, Bonnie Dorr, Richard Schwartz, Linnea Micciulla, and John Makhoul. 2006. A study of translation edit rate with targeted human annotation. In *Proceedings of Association for Machine Translation in the Americas*, pages 223–231.

M H Wright. 1995. Direct search methods: Once scorned, now respectable. *Numerical Analysis*, 344:191–208.

Richard Zens, Sasa Hasan, and Hermann Ney. 2007. A systematic comparison of training criteria for statistical machine translation. In *Proceedings of the 2007 Joint Conference on Empirical Methods in Natural Language Processing and Computational Natural Language Learning (EMNLP-CoNLL)*, pages 524–532.

Bing Zhao and Shengyuan Chen. 2009. A simplex Armijo downhill algorithm for optimizing statistical machine translation decoding parameters. In *Proceedings of Human Language Technologies: The 2009 Annual Conference of the North American Chapter of the Association for Computational Linguistics, Companion Volume: Short Papers*, pages 21–24, Boulder, Colorado, June. Association for Computational Linguistics.

Optimization Strategies for Online Large-Margin Learning in Machine Translation

Vladimir Eidelman
UMIACS Laboratory for Computational Linguistics and Information Processing
Department of Computer Science
University of Maryland, College Park, MD
vlad@umiacs.umd.edu

Abstract

The introduction of large-margin based discriminative methods for optimizing statistical machine translation systems in recent years has allowed exploration into many new types of features for the translation process. By removing the limitation on the number of parameters which can be optimized, these methods have allowed integrating millions of sparse features. However, these methods have not yet met with wide-spread adoption. This may be partly due to the perceived complexity of implementation, and partly due to the lack of standard methodology for applying these methods to MT. This papers aims to shed light on large-margin learning for MT, explicitly presenting the simple passive-aggressive algorithm which underlies many previous approaches, with direct application to MT, and empirically comparing several widespread optimization strategies.

1 Introduction

Statistical machine translation (SMT) systems represent knowledge sources in the form of features, and rely on parameters, or weights, on each feature, to score alternative translations. As in all statistical models, these parameters need to be learned from the data. In recent years, there has been a growing trend of moving away from discriminative training using batch log-linear optimization, with Minimum-Error Rate Training (MERT) (Och, 2003) being the principle method, to online linear optimization (Chiang et al., 2008; Watanabe et al., 2007; Arun and Koehn, 2007). The major motivation for this has been that while MERT is able to efficiently optimize a small number of parameters directly toward an external evaluation metric, such as BLEU (Papineni et al., 2002), it has been shown that its performance can be erratic, and it is unable to scale to a large set of features (Foster and Kuhn, 2009; Hopkins and May, 2011). Furthermore, it is designed for batch learning, which may be prohibitive or undesirable in certain scenarios, for instance if we have a large tuning set. One or both of these limitations have led to recent introduction of alternative optimization strategies, such as minimum-risk (Smith and Eisner, 2006), PRO (Hopkins and May, 2011), Structured SVM (Cherry and Foster, 2012), and RAMPION (Gimpel and Smith, 2012), which are batch learners, and online large-margin structured learning (Chiang et al., 2009; Watanabe et al., 2007; Watanabe, 2012).

A popular method of large-margin optimization is the margin-infused relaxed algorithm (MIRA) (Crammer et al., 2006), which has been shown to perform well for machine translation, as well as other structured prediction tasks, such as parsing. (McDonald et al., 2005). This is an attractive method because we have a simple analytical solution for the optimization problem at each step, which reduces to dual coordinate descent when using 1-best MIRA. It is also quite easy to implement, as will be shown below.

Despite the proven success of MIRA-based large-margin optimization for both small and large numbers of features, these methods have not yielded wide adoption in the community. Part of the reason for this is a perception that these methods are complicated to implement, which has been cited as motivation for other work (Hopkins and May, 2011; Gimpel and Smith, 2012). Furthermore, there is a divergence between the standard application of these methods in machine learning, and our application in machine translation (Gimpel and Smith, 2012), where in machine learning there are usually clear correct outputs and no latent structures. As a consequence of the above, there is a lack of standard practices for large-margin learning for MT, which has resulted in numerous different implementations of MIRA-based optimizers, which further add to the confusion.

This paper aims to shed light on practical concerns with online large margin training. Specifically, our contribution is first, to present the MIRA passive-aggressive update, which underlies all MIRA-based training, with an eye to application in MT. Then, we empirically compare several widespread as well as novel optimization strategies for large-margin training on Czech-to-English (cs-en) and French-to-English (fr-en) translation. Analyzing the findings, we recommend an optimization strategy which should ensure convergence and stability.

2 Large-Margin Learning

2.1 Description

MIRA is an online large-margin learner, and belongs to a class of passive-aggressive (PA) algorithms (Crammer et al., 2006). Although the exact procedure it employs is different from other subgradient optimizers, in essence it is performing a subgradient descent step, where the step size is adjusted based on each example. The underlying objective of MIRA is the same as that of the margin rescaled Structural SVM (Tsochantaridis et al., 2004; Martins et al., 2010), where we want to predict the correct output over the incorrect one by a margin at least as large as the cost incurred by predicting the incorrect output. However, the norm constraint from SVM is replaced with a proximity constraint, indicating we want to update our parameters, but keep them as close as possible to the previous parameter estimates. In the original formulation for separable classification (Crammer and Singer, 2003), if no constraints are violated, no update occurs. However, when there is a loss, the algorithm updates the parameters to satisfy the constraints. To allow for noise in the data, i.e. nonseparable instances, a slack variable ξ_i is introduced for each example, and we optimize a soft-margin. The usual presentation of MIRA is then given as:

$$\begin{aligned} \mathbf{w_{t+1}} &= \arg\min_{\mathbf{w}} \frac{1}{2}||\mathbf{w} - \mathbf{w_t}||^2 + C\xi_i \\ \text{s.t. } & \mathbf{w}^\top \boldsymbol{f}(x_i, y_i) - \mathbf{w}^\top \boldsymbol{f}(x_i, y') \geq \text{cost}(y_i, y') - \xi_i \end{aligned} \tag{1}$$

where $\boldsymbol{f}(x_i, y_i)$ is a vector of feature functions[1], $\mathbf{w}$ is a vector of corresponding parameters, $y' \in \mathcal{Y}(x_i)$, where $\mathcal{Y}(x_i)$ is the space of possible translations we are able to produce from x,[2] and $\text{cost}(y_i, \cdot)$ is computed using an external measure of quality, such as BLEU.

The underlying structured hinge loss objective function can be rewritten as:

$$\begin{aligned} \ell_h = &-\mathbf{w}^\top \boldsymbol{f}(x_i, y_i) + \\ &\max_{y' \in \mathcal{Y}(x_i)} \left(\mathbf{w}^\top \boldsymbol{f}(x_i, y') + \text{cost}(y_i, y') \right) \end{aligned} \tag{2}$$

2.2 Hypothesis Selection

Our training corpus $\mathcal{T} = (x_i, y_i)_{i=1}^T$ for selecting the parameters $\mathbf{w}$ that optimize this objective consists of input sentences x_i in the source language paired with reference translations y_i in the target language. Notice that ℓ_h depends on computing the margin between $y' \in \mathcal{Y}(x_i)$ and the *correct* output, y_i. However, there is no guarantee that $y_i \in \mathcal{Y}(x_i)$ since our decoder is often incapable of producing the reference translation y_i. Since we need to have some notion of the correct output in order to compute its feature vector for the margin, in practice we revert to using surrogate references in place of y_i. These are often referred to as oracles, y^+, which are selected from the hypothesis space $\mathcal{Y}(x_i)$ of the decoder.

We are also faced with the problem of how best to select the most appropriate y' to shy away from, which we will refer to as y^-. Since optimization will proceed by setting parameters to increase the score of y^+, and decrease the score of y^-, the selection of these two hypotheses is crucial to success. The range of possibilities is presented in Eq. 3 below.

[1] More appropriately, since we only observe translations y_i, which may have many possible derivations d_j, we model the derivations as a latent variable, and our feature functions are actually computed over derivation and translation pairs $\boldsymbol{f}(x_i, y_i, d_j)$. We omit d_j for clarity.

[2] The entire hypergraph in hierarchical translation or lattice in phrase based translation.

$$\ell_r = - \max_{y^+ \in \mathcal{Y}(x_i)} \left(\gamma^+ \mathbf{w}^\top \boldsymbol{f}(x_i, y^+) - \beta^+ \text{cost}(y_i, y^+) \right) + \max_{y^- \in \mathcal{Y}(x_i)} \left(\gamma^- \mathbf{w}^\top \boldsymbol{f}(x_i, y^-) + \beta^- \text{cost}(y_i, y^-) \right) \quad (3)$$

Although this formulation has commonly been referred to as the hinge loss in previous literature, Gimpel and Smith (2012) have recently pointed out that we are in fact optimizing losses that are closer to different variants of the structured ramp loss. The difference in definition between the two is subtle, in that for the ramp loss, y_i is replaced with y^+. Each setting of $\gamma^\pm$ and $\beta^\pm$ corresponds to optimizing a different loss function. Several definitions of ℓ_r have been explored in the literature, and we discuss them below with corresponding settings of $\gamma^\pm$ and $\beta^\pm$.

In selecting y^+, we vary the settings of γ^+ and β^+. Assuming our cost function is based on BLEU, in setting $\beta^+ \rightarrow 1$ and $\gamma^+ \rightarrow 0$, if $\mathcal{Y}(x_i)$ is taken to be the entire space of possible translations, we are selecting the hypothesis with the highest BLEU overall. This is referred to in past work as max-BLEU (Tillmann and Zhang, 2006) (MB). If we approximate the search space by restricting $\mathcal{Y}(x_i)$ to a k-best list, we have the local-update (Liang et al., 2006), where we select the highest BLEU candidate from those hypotheses that the model considers good (LU). With increasing k-best size, the max-BLEU and local-update strategies begin to converge.

Setting both $\beta^+ \rightarrow 1$ and $\gamma^+ \rightarrow 1$, we obtain the cost-diminished hypothesis, which considers both the model and the cost, and corresponds to the "hope" hypothesis in Chiang et al. (2008) (M-C). This can be computed over the entire space of hypotheses or a k-best list. In a sense, this is the intuition that local-updating is after, but expressed more directly.

The alternatives for selecting y^- are quite similar. Setting $\beta^- \rightarrow 1$ and $\gamma^- \rightarrow 0$, we select the hypothesis with the highest cost (MC). Setting $\beta^- \rightarrow 0$ and $\gamma^- \rightarrow 1$, we have the highest scoring hypothesis according to the model, which corresponds to prediction-based selection (Crammer et al., 2006) (PB). Setting both to 1, we have the cost-augmented hypothesis, which is referred to as the "fear" (Chiang et al., 2008), and max-loss (Crammer et al., 2006) (M+C). This hypothesis is considered the most dangerous because it has a high model score along with a high cost.

Considering the settings for both parts of Eq. 3, γ^+, β^+ and γ^-, β^-, assigning all $\gamma^\pm$ and $\beta^\pm$ to 1 corresponds to the most commonly used loss function in MT (Gimpel and Smith, 2012; Chiang et al., 2009). This is the "hope"/"fear" pairing, where we use the cost-diminished hypothesis y^+ and cost-augmented hypothesis y^-. Other loss functions have also been explored, such as $\gamma^\pm \rightarrow 1$, $\beta^+ \rightarrow 1$, $\beta^- \rightarrow 0$ (Liang et al., 2006), and something approximating $\gamma^\pm \rightarrow 1$, $\beta^+ \rightarrow 0$, $\beta^- \rightarrow 1$ (Cherry and Foster, 2012), which is closer to the usual loss used for max-margin in machine learing. To our best knowledge, other loss functions explored below are novel to this work.

Since our external metric, BLEU, is a gain, we can think of the first term in Eq. 3 as the model score plus the BLEU score, and the second term as the model minus the BLEU score. That is, with all $\gamma^\pm$ and $\beta^\pm$ set to 1, we want y^+ to be the hypothesis with a high model score, as well as being close to the reference translation, as indicated by a high BLEU score. While for y^-, we want a high model score, but it should be far away from the reference, as indicated by a low BLEU score. The motivation for choosing y^- in this fashion is grounded in the fact that since we are penalized by this term in the ramp loss objective, we should try to optimize on it directly. In practice, we can compute the cost for both terms as (1-BLEU(y,y_i)), or use that as the cost of the first term, and after selecting y^+, compute the cost of y^- by taking the difference between BLEU(y^+,y_i) and BLEU(y,y_i).

The ramp loss objectives are non-convex, and by separately computing the max for both y^+ and y^-, we are theoretically prohibited from online learning since we are no longer guaranteed to be optimizing the desired loss. This is one motivation for the batch learner, RAMPION (Gimpel and Smith, 2012). However, as with many non-convex optimization problems in NLP, such as those involving latent variables, in practice online learning in this setting behaves quite well.

2.3 Parameter Update

The major practical concern with these methods for SMT is that oftentimes the implementation aspect is unclear, a problem which is further exacerbated by the apparent difficulty of implementation. This is further compounded with a lack of standard practices; both theoretical, such as the objective to optimize, and practical, such as efficient parallelization. The former is a result of the disconnect between the standard machine learning setting, which posits reachable references and lack of latent variables, and our own application. The latter is an active engineering problem. Both of these aspects have been receiving recent attention (McAllester et al., 2010; Mcallester and Keshet, 2011; Gimpel and Smith, 2012; McDonald et al., 2010), and although certain questions remain as to the exact loss being optimized, we now have a better understanding of the theoretical underpinnings of this method of optimization.

The first adaptations of MIRA-based learning for structured prediction in NLP utilized a set of k constraints, either for y^+, y^-, or both. This complicated the optimization by creating a QP problem with a set of linear constraints which needed to be solved with either Hildreth's algorithm or SMO style optimization, thereby precluding the possibility of a simple analytical solution. Later, Chiang (2012) introduced a cutting-plane algorithm, like that of Structural SVM's (Tsochantaridis et al., 2004), which optimizes on a small set of active constraints.

While these methods of dealing with structured prediction may perform better empirically, they come with a higher computational cost. Crammer et al. (2006) shows that satisfying the single most violated margin constraint, commonly referred to as 1-best MIRA, is amenable to a simple analytical solution for the optimization problem at each step. Furthermore, the 1-best MIRA update is conceptually and practically much simpler, while retaining most of the optimization power of the more advanced methods. Thus, this is the method we present below.

Since the MIRA optimization problem is an instance of a general structured problem with an ℓ_2 norm, the update at each step reduces to dual coordinate descent (Smith, 2011). In our soft-margin

Algorithm 1 MIRA Training

Require: : Training set $T = (x_i, y_i)_{i=1}^T$, **w**, C

1: **for** $j \leftarrow$ 1 to N **do**
2:   **for** $i \leftarrow$ 1 to T **do**
3:     $\mathcal{Y}(x_i) \leftarrow$Decode($x_i$,w)
4:     $y^+ \leftarrow$ FindOracle($\mathcal{Y}(x_i)$)
5:     $y^- \leftarrow$ FindPrediction($\mathcal{Y}(x_i)$)
6:     margin $\leftarrow \mathbf{w}^\top \boldsymbol{f}(x_i, y^-) - \mathbf{w}^\top \boldsymbol{f}(x_i, y^+)$
7:     cost $\leftarrow \text{BLEU}(y_i, y^+) - \text{BLEU}(y_i, y^-)$
8:     loss = margin + cost
9:     **if** loss > 0 **then**
10:       $\delta \leftarrow \min\left(C, \frac{\text{loss}}{\|\boldsymbol{f}(x_i,y^+)-\boldsymbol{f}(x_i,y^-)\|^2}\right)$
11:       $\mathbf{w} \leftarrow \mathbf{w} + \delta\left(\boldsymbol{f}(x_i, y^+) - \boldsymbol{f}(x_i, y^-)\right)$
12:     **end if**
13:   **end for**
14: **end for**
15: **return w**

Algorithm 2 FindOracle

Require: : $\mathcal{Y}(x_i)$

if γ^+=0 and β^+=1 **then**
  $y^+ \leftarrow \arg\max_{y \in \mathcal{Y}(x_i)} -\text{cost}(y_i, y)$
else if $\gamma^+ = \beta^+ = 1$ **then**
  $y^+ \leftarrow \arg\max_{y \in \mathcal{Y}(x_i)} \mathbf{w}^\top \boldsymbol{f}(x_i, y) - \text{cost}(y_i, y)$
end if
return y^+

setting, this is analogous to the PA-I update of Crammer et al. (2006). In fact, this update remains largely intact as the inner core within k-best constraint or cutting plane optimization. Algorithm 1 presents the entire training regime necessary for 1-best MIRA training of a machine translation system. As can be seen, the parameter update at step 11 depends on the difference between the features of y^+ and y^-, where δ is the step size, which is controlled by the regularization parameter C; indicating how far we are willing to move at each step. $\mathcal{Y}(x_i)$ may be a k-best list or the entire space of hypotheses.[3]

[3]For a more in depth examination and derivation of large-margin learning in MT, see (Chiang, 2012).

Algorithm 3 FindPrediction

Require: : $\mathcal{Y}(x_i)$

if γ^-=0 and β^-=1 **then**
  $y^- \leftarrow \arg\max_{y \in \mathcal{Y}(x_i)} \text{cost}(y_i, y)$
else if γ^-=1 and β^-=0 **then**
  $y^- \leftarrow \arg\max_{y \in \mathcal{Y}(x_i)} \mathbf{w}^\top \boldsymbol{f}(x_i, y)$
else if $\gamma^- = \beta^- = 1$ **then**
  $y^- \leftarrow \arg\max_{y \in \mathcal{Y}(x_i)} \mathbf{w}^\top \boldsymbol{f}(x_i, y) + \text{cost}(y_i, y)$
end if
return y^-

3 Experiments

3.1 Setup

To empirically analyze which loss, and thereby which strategy, for selecting y^+ and y^- is most appropriate for machine translation, we conducted a series of experiments on Czech-to-English and French-to-English translation. The parallel corpora are taken from the WMT2012 shared translation task, and consist of Europarl data along with the News Commentary corpus. All data were tokenized and lowercased, then filtered for length and aligned using the GIZA++ implementation of IBM Model 4 (Och and Ney, 2003) to obtain bidirectional alignments, which were symmetrized using the grow-diag-final-and method (Koehn et al., 2003). Grammars were extracted from the resulting parallel text and used in our hierarchical phrase-based system using cdec (Dyer et al., 2010) as the decoder. We constructed a 5-gram language model from the provided English News monolingual training data as well as the English side of the parallel corpus using the SRI language modeling toolkit with modified Kneser-Ney smoothing (Chen and Goodman, 1996). This was used to create a KenLM (Heafield, 2011).

As the tuning set for both language pairs, we used the 2051 sentences in news-test2008 (NT08), and report results on the 2525 sentences of news-test2009 (NT09) and 2489 of news-test2010 (NT10).

Corpus	Sentences	Tokens	
		en	*
cs-en	764K	20.5M	17.5M
fr-en	2M	57M	63M

Table 1: Corpus statistics

pair	1	500	50k	100k
cs-en	17.9	24.9	29.4	29.7
fr-en	20.25	29.9	33.8	34.1

Table 2: Oracle score for model 1-best (baseline) and for k-best of size 500, 50k, and 100k on NT08

We approximate cost-augmented decoding by obtaining a k-best list with k=500 unique best from our decoder at each iteration, and selecting the respective hypotheses for optimization from it. To approximate max-BLEU decoding using a k-best list, we set k=50k unique best hypotheses.[4] As can be seen in Table 2, we found this size was sufficient for our purposes as increasing size led to small improvements in oracle BLEU score. C is set to 0.01.

For comparison with MERT, we create a baseline model which uses a small standard set of features found in translation systems: language model probability, phrase translation probabilities, lexical weighting probabilities, and source word, pass-through, and word penalties.

While BLEU is usually calculated at the corpus level, we need to approximate the metric at the sentence level. In this, we mostly follow previous approaches, where in the first iteration through the corpus we use a smoothed sentence level BLEU approximation, similar to Lin and Och (2004), and in subsequently iterations, the BLEU score is calculated in the context of the previous set of 1-best translations of the entire tuning set.

To make parameter estimation more efficient, some form of parallelization is preferred. While earlier versions of MIRA training had complex parallelization procedures which necessitated passing information between learners, performing iterative parameter mixing (McDonald et al., 2010) has been shown to be just as effective (Chiang, 2012). We use a simple implementation of this regime, where we divide the tuning set into n shards and distribute them amongst n learners, along with the parameter vector $\mathbf{w}$. Each learner decodes and updates parame-

[4] We are able to theoretically extract more constraints from a large list, in the spirit of k-constraints or a cutting plane, but Chiang (2012) showed that cutting plane performance is approximately 0.2-0.4 BLEU better than a single constraint, so although there is a trade off between the simplicity of a single constraint and performance, it is not substantial.

cs-en	NT09		NT10	
	LU	M-C	LU	M-C
PB	16.4	18.3	17	19.3
MC	**18.5**	16	**19.1**	17.5
M+C	17.8	**18.7**	18.4	**19.6**

Table 3: Results with different strategies on cs-en translation. MERT baseline is 18.4 for NT09 and 19.7 for NT10

fr-en	NT09		NT10	
	LU	M-C	LU	M-C
PB	20.5	23.1	22.2	25
MC	**23.9**	23	**25.8**	24.8
M+C	22.2	**23.6**	24	**25.4**

Table 4: Results with different strategies on fr-en translation. MERT baseline is 24.2 for NT09 and 26 for NT10

ters on its shard of the tuning set, and once all learners are finished, these n parameter vectors are averaged to form the initial parameter vector for the next iteration. In our experiments, n=20.

3.2 Results

The results of using different optimization strategies for cs-en and fr-en are presented in Tables 3 and 4 below. For all experiments, all settings are kept exactly the same, with the only variation being the selection of the oracle y^+ and prediction y^-. The first column in each table indicates the method for selecting the prediction, y^-. PB indicates prediction-based, MC is the hypothesis with the highest cost, and M+C is cost-augmented selection. Analogously, the headings across the table indicate oracle selection strategies, with LU indicating local updating, and M-C being cost-diminished selection.

From the cs-en results in Table 3, we can see that two settings fair the best: LU oracle selection paired with MC prediction selection (LU/MC), and M-C oracle selection paired with M+C prediction selection (M±C). On both sets, (M±C) performs better, but the results are comparable. Pairing M-C with PB is also a viable strategy, while no other pairing is successful for LU.

When comparing with MERT, note that we use a hypergraph based MERT (Kumar et al., 2009), while the MIRA updates are computed from a k-best list. For max-BLEU oracle selection paired with MC, the performance decreases substantially, to 15.4 and 16.6 BLEU on NT09 and NT10, respectively. Using the augmented k-best list did not significantly affect performance for M-C oracle selection.

For fr-en, we see much the same behavior as in cs-en. However, here LU/MC slightly outperforms M±C. From both tasks, we can see that LU is more sensitive to prediction selection, and can only optimize effectively when paired with MC. M-C on the other hand, is more forgiving, and can make progress with PB and MC, albeit not as effectively as with M+C.

3.3 Large Feature Set

Since one of the primary motivations for large-margin learning is the ability to effectively handle large quantities of features, we further evaluate the ability of the strategies by introducing a large number of sparse features into our model. We introduce sparse binary indicator features of the form commonly found in MT research (Chiang et al., 2009; Watanabe et al., 2007). Specifically, we introduce two types of features based on word alignment from hierarchical phrase pairs and a target bigram feature. The first type, a word pair feature, fires for every word pair (e_i, f_j) observed in the phrase pair. The second, insertion features, account for spurious words on the target side of a phrase pair by firing for unaligned target words, associating them with every source word, i.e. $(e_i, f_j), (e_i, f_{j+1}), etc.$. The target bigram feature fires for every pair of consecutive words on the target side (e_i, e_{i+1}). In all, we introduce 650k features for cs-en, and 1.1M for fr-en. Taking the two best performing strategies from the baseline model, LU/MC and M±C, we compare their performance with the larger feature set in Table 5.

Although integrating these features does not significantly alter the performance on either task, our purpose was to establish once again that the large-margin learning framework is capable of effectively optimizing parameters for a large number of sparse features in the MT setting.

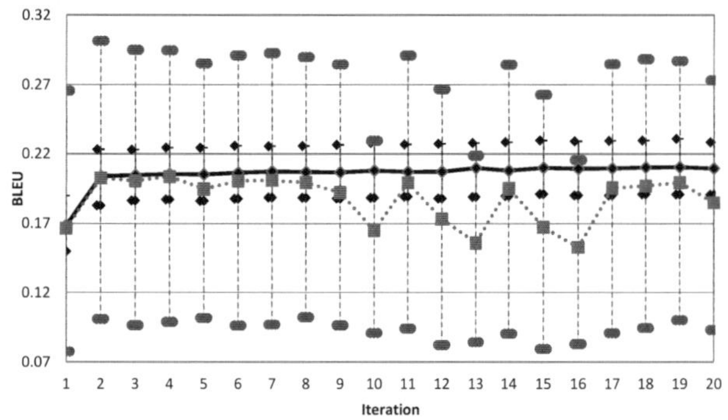

Figure 1: Comparison of performance on development set for cs-en when using LU/MC and M±C selection.

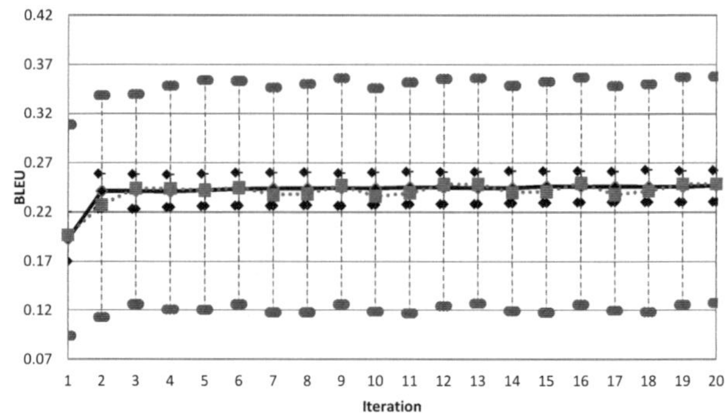

Figure 2: Comparison of performance on development set for fr-en when using LU/MC and M±C selection.

	fr-en		cs-en	
	NT09	NT10	NT09	NT10
LU/MC	23.9	25.7	18.5	19.6
M±C	23.8	25.4	18.6	19.6

Table 5: Results on cs-en and fr-en with extended feature set.

4 Discussion

Although the performance of the two strategies is competitive on the evaluation sets, this does not relay the entire story. For a more complete view of the differences between optimization strategies, we turn to Figures 1-6. Figure 1 and 2 present the comparison of performance on the NT08 development set for cs-en and fr-en, respectively, when using LU/MC to select the oracle and prediction versus M±C selection. M±C is indicated with a solid black line, while LU/MC is a dotted red line. The corpus-level oracle and prediction BLEU scores at each iteration are indicated with error bars around each point, using solid lines for M±C and dotted lines for LU/MC. As can be seen in Figure 1, while optimizing with M±C is stable and smooth, where we converge on our optimum after several iterations, optimizing with LU/MC is highly unstable. This is at least in part due to the wide range in BLEU scores for the oracle and prediction, which are in the range of 10 BLEU points higher or lower than the current model best. On the contrary, the range of BLEU scores for the M±C optimizer is on the order of 2 BLEU points, leading to more gradual changes.

We see a similar, albeit slightly less pronounced behavior on fr-en in Figure 2. M±C optimization is once again smooth, and converges quickly, with a small range for the oracle and prediction scores around the model best. LU/MC remains unstable, oscillating up to 2 BLEU points between iterations.

Figures 3-6 compare the different optimization strategies further. In Figures 3 and 5, we use M-C as the oracle, and show performance on the development set while using the three prediction selection strategies, M+C with a solid blue line, PB with a dotted green line, and MC with a dashed red line. Error bars indicate the oracle and prediction BLEU scores for each pairing as before. In all three cases, the oracle BLEU score is in about the same range, as expected, since all are using the same oracle selection strategy. We can immediately observe that PB has no error bars going down, indicating that the PB method for selecting the prediction keeps pace with the model best at each iteration. On the other hand, MC selection also stands out, since it is the only one with a large drop in prediction BLEU score. Crucially, all learners are stable, and move toward convergence smoothly, which serves to validate our earlier observation that M-C oracle selection can be paired with any prediction selection strategy and optimize effectively. In both cs-en and fr-en, we can observe that M±C performs the best.

In Figures 4 and 6, we use LU as the oracle, and show performance using the three prediction selection strategies, with each line representing the same strategy as described above. The major difference, which is immediately evident, is that the optimizers are highly unstable. The only pairing which shows some stability is LU/MC, with both the other predic-

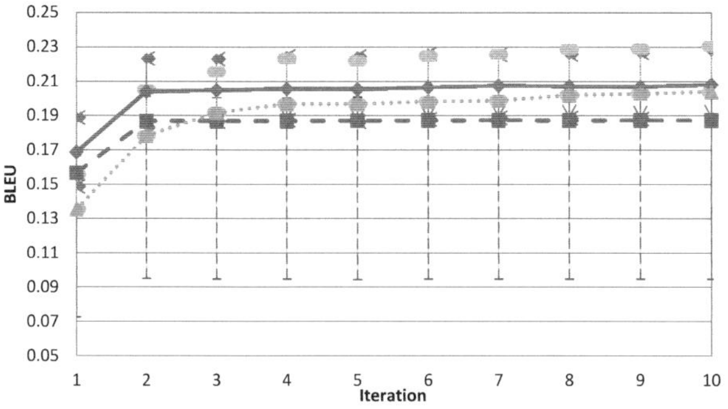

Figure 3: Comparison of performance on development set for cs-en of the three prediction selection strategies when using M-C selection as oracle.

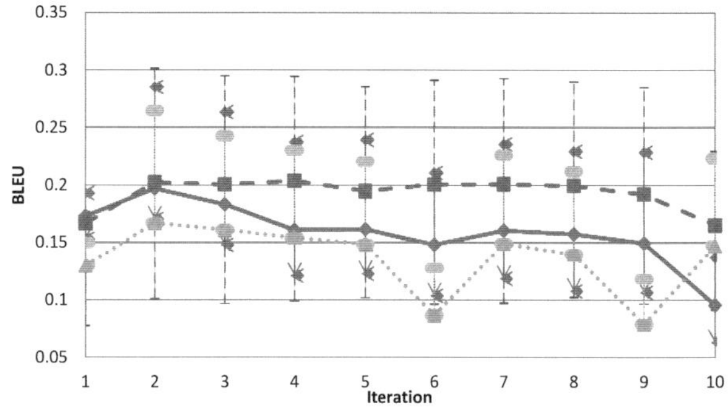

Figure 4: Comparison of performance on development set for cs-en of the three prediction selection strategies when using LU selection as oracle.

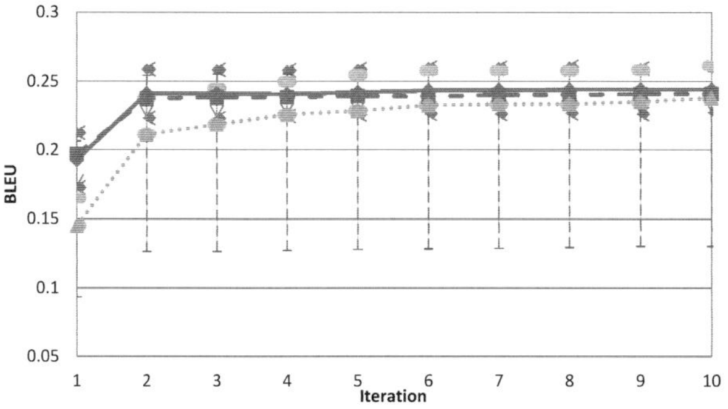

Figure 5: Comparison of performance on development set for fr-en of the three prediction selection strategies when using M-C selection as oracle.

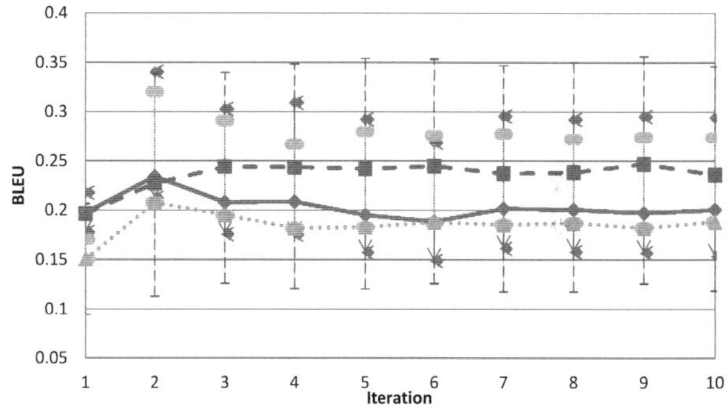

Figure 6: Comparison of performance on development set for fr-en of the three prediction selection strategies when using LU selection as oracle.

tion selection methods, PB and M+C significantly underperforming it.

Given that the translation performance of optimizing the loss functions represented by LU/MC and M$\pm$C selection is comparable on the evaluation sets for fr-en and cs-en, it may be premature to make a general recommendation for one over the other. However, taking the unstable nature of LU/MC into account, the extent of which may depend on the tuning set, as well as other factors which need to be further examined, the current more prudent alternative is selecting the oracle and prediction pair based on M$\pm$C.

5 Conclusion

In this paper, we strove to elucidate aspects of large-margin structured learning with concrete application to the MT setting. Towards this goal, we presented the MIRA passive-aggressive algorithm, which can be used directly to effectively tune a statistical MT system with millions of parameters, in the hope that some confusion surrounding MIRA-based methods may be cleared, and more MT researchers can adopt it for their own use. We then used the presented algorithm to empirically compare several widespread loss functions and strategies for selecting hypotheses for optimization. We showed that although there are two competing strategies with comparable performance, one is an unstable learner, and before we understand more regarding the nature of the instability, the preferred alternative is to use M$\pm$C as the hypothesis pair in optimization.

Acknowledgments

We would like to thank the anonymous reviewers for their comments. The author is supported by the Department of Defense through the National Defense Science and Engineering Graduate Fellowship. Any opinions, findings, conclusions, or recommendations expressed are the author's and do not necessarily reflect those of the sponsors.

References

Abishek Arun and Philipp Koehn. 2007. Online learning methods for discriminative training of phrase based statistical machine translation. In *MT Summit XI*.

Stanley F. Chen and Joshua Goodman. 1996. An empirical study of smoothing techniques for language modeling. In *Proceedings of the 34th Annual Meeting of the Association for Computational Linguistics*, pages 310–318.

Colin Cherry and George Foster. 2012. Batch tuning strategies for statistical machine translation. In *Proceedings of NAACL*.

David Chiang, Yuval Marton, and Philip Resnik. 2008. Online large-margin training of syntactic and structural translation features. In *Proceedings of the 2008 Conference on Empirical Methods in Natural Language Processing*, Honolulu, Hawaii, October.

David Chiang, Kevin Knight, and Wei Wang. 2009. 11,001 new features for statistical machine translation. In *Proceedings of Human Language Technologies: The 2009 Annual Conference of the North American Chapter of the Association for Computational Linguistics*, NAACL '09, pages 218–226.

David Chiang. 2012. Hope and fear for discriminative training of statistical translation models. *To appear in J. Machine Learning Research*.

Koby Crammer and Yoram Singer. 2003. Ultraconservative online algorithms for multiclass problems. *J. Mach. Learn. Res.*, 3:951–991, March.

Koby Crammer, Ofer Dekel, Joseph Keshet, Shai Shalev-Shwartz, and Yoram Singer. 2006. Online passive-aggressive algorithms. *J. Mach. Learn. Res.*, 7:551–585.

Chris Dyer, Adam Lopez, Juri Ganitkevitch, Jonathan Weese, Ferhan Ture, Phil Blunsom, Hendra Setiawan, Vladimir Eidelman, and Philip Resnik. 2010. cdec: A decoder, alignment, and learning framework for finite-state and context-free translation models. In *Proceedings of ACL System Demonstrations*.

George Foster and Roland Kuhn. 2009. Stabilizing minimum error rate training. In *Proceedings of the Fourth Workshop on Statistical Machine Translation*, pages 242–249, Athens, Greece, March. Association for Computational Linguistics.

Kevin Gimpel and Noah A. Smith. 2012. Structured ramp loss minimization for machine translation. In *Proceedings of NAACL*.

Kenneth Heafield. 2011. Kenlm: faster and smaller language model queries. In *Proceedings of the Sixth Workshop on Statistical Machine Translation*, WMT '11, pages 187–197.

Mark Hopkins and Jonathan May. 2011. Tuning as ranking. In *Proceedings of the 2011 Conference on Empirical Methods in Natural Language Processing*, pages 1352–1362, Edinburgh, Scotland, UK., July. Association for Computational Linguistics.

Philipp Koehn, Franz Josef Och, and Daniel Marcu. 2003. Statistical phrase-based translation. In *Proceedings of the 2003 Conference of the North American Chapter of the Association for Computational Linguistics on Human Language Technology - Volume 1*, NAACL '03, Stroudsburg, PA, USA.

Shankar Kumar, Wolfgang Macherey, Chris Dyer, and Franz Och. 2009. Efficient minimum error rate training and minimum bayes-risk decoding for translation hypergraphs and lattices. In *Proceedings of the Joint Conference of the 47th Annual Meeting of the ACL and the 4th International Joint Conference on Natural Language Processing of the AFNLP*, pages 163–171.

Percy Liang, Alexandre Bouchard-Côté, Dan Klein, and Ben Taskar. 2006. An end-to-end discriminative approach to machine translation. In *Proceedings of the 21st International Conference on Computational Linguistics and the 44th annual meeting of the Association for Computational Linguistics*, ACL-44, pages 761–768.

Chin-Yew Lin and Franz Josef Och. 2004. Orange: a method for evaluating automatic evaluation metrics for machine translation. In *Proceedings of the 20th international conference on Computational Linguistics*.

A. F. T. Martins, K. Gimpel, N. A. Smith, E. P. Xing, P. M. Q. Aguiar, and M. A. T. Figueiredo. 2010. Learning structured classifiers with dual coordinate descent. Technical Report CMU-ML-10-109, Carnegie Mellon University.

David Mcallester and Joseph Keshet. 2011. Generalization bounds and consistency for latent structural probit and ramp loss. In J. Shawe-Taylor, R.S. Zemel, P. Bartlett, F.C.N. Pereira, and K.Q. Weinberger, editors, *Advances in Neural Information Processing Systems 24*, pages 2205–2212.

David McAllester, Tamir Hazan, and Joseph Keshet. 2010. Direct loss minimization for structured prediction. In J. Lafferty, C. K. I. Williams, J. Shawe-Taylor, R.S. Zemel, and A. Culotta, editors, *Advances in Neural Information Processing Systems 23*, pages 1594–1602.

Ryan McDonald, Koby Crammer, and Fernando Pereira. 2005. Online large-margin training of dependency parsers. In *Proceedings of the 43rd Annual Meeting on*

Association for Computational Linguistics, ACL '05. Association for Computational Linguistics.

Ryan McDonald, Keith Hall, and Gideon Mann. 2010. Distributed training strategies for the structured perceptron. In *Human Language Technologies: The 2010 Annual Conference of the North American Chapter of the Association for Computational Linguistics*, pages 456–464, Los Angeles, California.

Franz Och and Hermann Ney. 2003. A systematic comparison of various statistical alignment models. In *Computational Linguistics*, volume 29(21), pages 19–51.

Franz Josef Och. 2003. Minimum error rate training in statistical machine translation. In *Proceedings of the 41st Annual Meeting of the Association for Computational Linguistics*, pages 160–167.

Kishore Papineni, Salim Roukos, Todd Ward, and Wei-Jing Zhu. 2002. BLEU: a method for automatic evaluation of machine translation. In *Proceedings of 40th Annual Meeting of the Association for Computational Linguistics*, pages 311–318.

David A. Smith and Jason Eisner. 2006. Minimum risk annealing for training log-linear models. In *Proceedings of the COLING/ACL 2006 Main Conference Poster Sessions*, Sydney, Australia, July. Association for Computational Linguistics.

Noah A. Smith. 2011. *Linguistic Structure Prediction*. Synthesis Lectures on Human Language Technologies. Morgan and Claypool, May.

Christoph Tillmann and Tong Zhang. 2006. A discriminative global training algorithm for statistical mt. In *Proceedings of the 21st International Conference on Computational Linguistics and the 44th annual meeting of the Association for Computational Linguistics*, ACL-44, pages 721–728.

Ioannis Tsochantaridis, Thomas Hofmann, Thorsten Joachims, and Yasemin Altun. 2004. Support vector machine learning for interdependent and structured output spaces. In *Proceedings of the twenty-first international conference on Machine learning*, ICML '04.

Taro Watanabe, Jun Suzuki, Hajime Tsukada, and Hideki Isozaki. 2007. Online large-margin training for statistical machine translation. In *Proceedings of the 2007 Joint Conference on Empirical Methods in Natural Language Processing and Computational Natural Language Learning (EMNLP-CoNLL)*, Prague, Czech Republic, June. Association for Computational Linguistics.

Taro Watanabe. 2012. Optimized online rank learning for machine translation. In *Proceedings of NAACL*.

Author Index